CITIES OF THE UNITED STATES

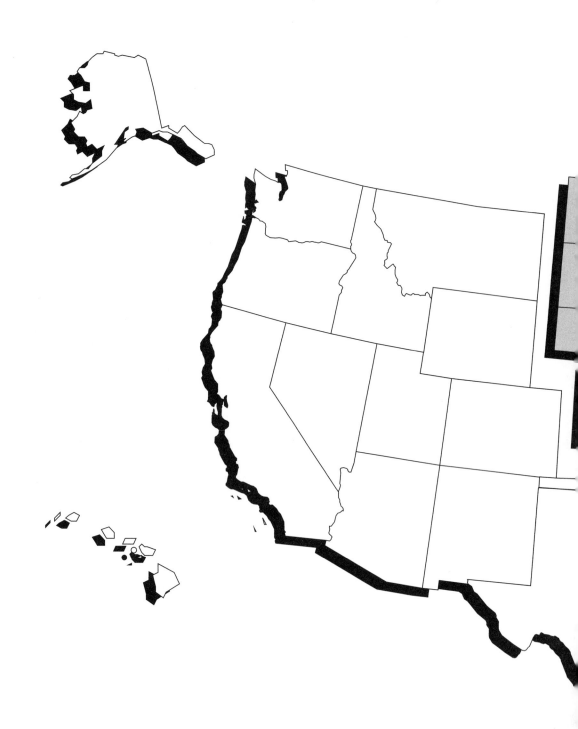

ISSN 0899-6075

CITIES OF THE UNITED STATES

FIFTH EDITION

A Compilation of Current Information on
Economic, Cultural, Geographic, and Social Conditions

In Four Volumes
Volume 3:
The Midwest

Illinois
Indiana
Iowa
Kansas
Michigan
Minnesota
Missouri
Nebraska
North Dakota
Ohio
South Dakota
Wisconsin

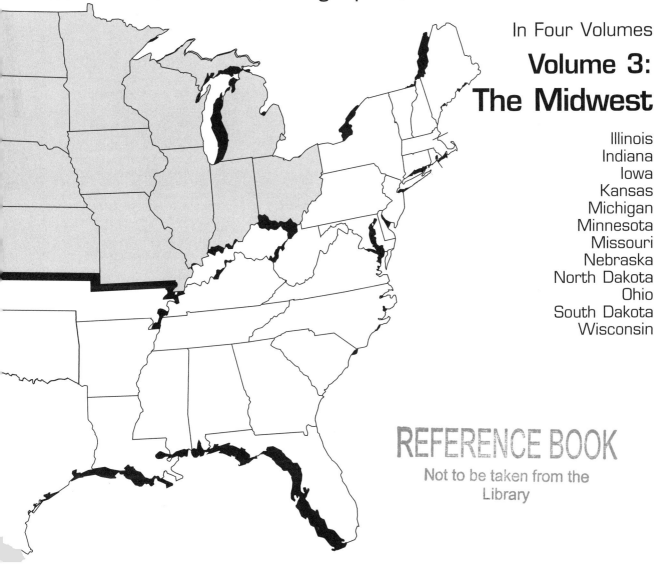

THOMSON
✳
™
GALE

Detroit • New York • San Francisco • San Diego • New Haven, Conn. • Waterville, Maine • London • Munich

Cities of the United States, Fifth Edition

Project Editors
Lisa C. DeShantz-Cook, Jacqueline K. Mueckenheim, Kristy Swartout

Editorial Support Services
Luann Brennan, Grant Eldridge, Wayne D. Fong

Imaging and Multimedia
Leitha Etheridge-Sims, Lezlie Light, Jillean McCommons, Dan Newell, Christine O'Bryan

Rights and Acquisitions
Edna M. Hedblad, Shalice Shah-Caldwell, Kim Smilay

Product Design
Jennifer Wahi

Composition and Electronic Prepress
Evi Seoud

Manufacturing
Rita Wimberley

LIBRARY OF CONGRESS CATALOGING-IN-PUBLICATION DATA

ISBN 0-7876-7369-2 (set)
ISBN 0-7876-7370-6 (v.1)
ISBN 0-7876-7371-4 (v.2)
ISBN 0-7876-7372-2 (v.3)
ISBN 0-7876-7373-0 (v.4)
ISSN 0899-6075

This title is also available as an e-book.
ISBN 1-4144-0600-2 (set)
Contact your Thomson Gale sales representative for ordering information.

Printed in the United States of America
10 9 8 7 6 5 4 3 2 1

Volume 3—The Midwest

Contents

Volume 1—The South

Contents

Volume 2—The West

Contents

Volume 4—The Northeast

Contents

INTRODUCTION

Cities of the United States (CUS) provides a one-stop source for all the vital information you need on 189 of America's top cities—those fastest-growing, as well as those with a particular historical, political, industrial, and/or commercial significance. Spanning the entire country, from Anaheim to Virginia Beach, each geographically-arranged volume of *CUS* brings together a wide range of comprehensive data. The volumes include: *The South; The West; The Midwest;* and *The Northeast.*

Within each volume, the city-specific profiles organize pertinent facts, data, and figures related to demographic, economic, cultural, geographic, social, and recreational conditions. Assembling a myriad of sources, *CUS* offers researchers, travelers, students, and media professionals a convenient resource for discovering each city's past, present, and future.

For this completely updated fifth edition, eleven new cities have been added, providing even greater access to the country's growing urban centers. The new city profiles include:

- Akron, OH
- Aurora, IL
- Casper, WY
- El Paso, TX
- Fort Smith, AR
- Henderson, NV
- Huntington, WV
- Mesa, AZ
- Nampa, ID
- Overland Park, KS
- Warwick, RI

Key Features Unlock Vital Information

Cities of the United States offers a range of key features, allowing easy access to targeted information. Features include:

- Section headings—Comprehensive categories, which include **History, Geography and Climate, Population Profile, Municipal Government, Economy, Education, Research, Health Care, Recreation, Convention Facilities, Transportation,** and **Communications** (including city web sites), make it easy for you to locate answers to your specific questions.

- Combined facts and analysis—Fact-packed charts and detailed descriptions bring you the statistics and the rest of the story.

- "In Brief" fact sheets—One-page "at a glance" overviews provide the essential facts for each state and each city profiled.

- Economic information—Detailed updates about such topics as incentive programs, development projects, and largest employers help you rate the business climate using criteria that matter to you.

- Directory information—Contact information at the end of many entry sections provides addresses, phone numbers, and email addresses for organizations, agencies, and institutions you may need to contact.

- Detailed maps—City landmarks, mileage scales, and regional insets allow you to locate many of the points of interest described in main city entries, as well as provide a greater perspective on the city in which you are interested.

- Selected bibliography listings—Historical accounts, biographical works, and other print resources suggest titles to read if you wish to learn more about a particular city.

- Web sites for vital city resources—Access points to URLs for information-rich sources, such as city government, visitors and convention bureaus, economic development agencies, libraries, schools, and newspapers provide researchers an opportunity to explore cities in more detail.

- Enlightening illustrations—Numerous photographs highlight points of interest to you.

- Handy indexing—A referencing guide not only to main city entries, but also to the hundreds of people and place names that fall within those main entries, leading you directly to the information you seek.

Designed For a Variety of Users

Whether you are a researcher, traveler, or executive on the move, *CUS* serves your needs. This is the reference long sought by a variety of users:

- Business people, market researchers, and other decision-makers will find the current data that helps them stay informed.

- People vacationing, conventioneering, or relocating will consult this source for questions they have about what's new, unique, or significant about where they are going.

- Students, media professionals, and researchers will discover their background work already completed.

Hurricanes of 2005 and Their Impact on the United States

The powerful hurricanes of 2005—Hurricane Katrina on August 29 followed by Hurricane Rita on September 24—devastated the Gulf Coast region of the United States. From Alabama to the shores of Texas, these two hurricanes had profound impact—from the loss of lives to the loss of infrastructure (utilities, roads, commerce), industry, and manufacturing. Cities directly hit by these hurricanes, such as New Orleans, Louisiana and Biloxi, Mississippi, will undergo recovery efforts for years to come, and it is unknown at the time of publication of *Cities of the United States,* 5th edition just how long and how far-reaching that recovery will be.

It is also important to note that not only are the cities hit directly by these hurricanes affected; cities that have offered refuge to evacuees and contributed greatly to the relief efforts will continue to be affected as they work to aid the recovery efforts, putting their own development initiatives on hold. Cities such as Mobile, Alabama; Baton Rouge, Louisiana; and Jackson, Mississippi will also continue to experience the effects of these unprecedented natural disasters.

The essays profiled herein for the states of Alabama, Louisiana, Mississippi, and Texas were updated prior to August 2005 and reflect information that was then current.

Definitions of Key Statistical Resources

Following are explanations of key resources used for statistical data:

ACCRA (The Council for Community Economic Research; formerly the American Chamber of Commerce Researchers Association): The Cost of Living Index, produced quarterly, provides a useful and reasonably accurate measure of living cost differences among urban areas. Items on which the Index is based have been carefully chosen to reflect the different categories of consumer expenditures, such as groceries, housing, utilities, transportation, health care, and miscellaneous goods and services; taxes are excluded. Weights assigned to relative costs are based on government survey data on expenditure patterns for midmanagement households (typically the average professional worker's home, new construction with 2,400 square feet of living space). All items are priced in each place at a specified time and according to standardized specifications. Information regarding ACCRA and the Cost of Living Index can be found at www.accra.org. Please note that the ACCRA Cost of Living Index and ACCRA housing price information are reprinted by permission of ACCRA.

Metropolitan Statistical Area (MSA): The U.S. Office of Management and Budget (OMB) provides that each Metropolitan Statistical Area must include (a) at least one city with 50,000 or more inhabitants, or (b) a U.S. Census Bureau-defined urbanized area (of at least 50,000 inhabitants) and a total metropolitan population of at least 100,000 (75,000 in New England). The term was adopted in 1983. The term "metropolitan area" (MA) became effective in 1990. During the 2000 Census, the MSA standards were revised, establishing Core Based Statistical Areas (CBSAs). CBSAs may be either Metropolitan Statistical Areas or Micropolitan Statistical Areas. It is important to note that standards, and therefore content of 1990 Census MSAs, are not identical to 2000 Census MSA standards. Additional information regarding MSAs can be found at http://census.state.nc.us/glossary/msa.html.

FBI Crime Index Total: The total number of index offenses reported to the FBI during the year through its Uniform Crime Reporting Program. The FBI receives monthly and annual reports from law enforcement agencies throughout the country. City police, sheriffs, and state police file reports on the number of index offenses that become known to them. The FBI Crime Index offenses are: murder and non-negligent manslaughter; forcible rape; robbery; aggravated assault; burglary; larceny; motor vehicle theft; and arson.

Estimates of population: Between decennial censuses, the U.S. Bureau of the Census publishes estimates of the population using the decennial census data as benchmarks and data available from various agencies, both state and federal, including births and deaths, and school statistics, among other data.

Method of Compilation

The editors of *Cities of the United States* consulted numerous sources to secure the kinds of data most valuable to you. Each entry gathers together economic information culled in part from the U.S. Department of Labor/Bureau of Labor Statistics and state departments of labor and commerce, population figures derived from the U.S. Department of Commerce/Bureau of the Census and from city and state agencies, educational and municipal government data supplied by local authorities and historical narrative based on a variety of accounts. Along with material supplied by chambers of commerce, convention and visitors bureaus, and other local sources, background information was drawn from periodicals and books chosen for their timeliness and accuracy. Through print resources, web sites, email contact, and/or phone calls with agency representatives, the information reflects current conditions.

Acknowledgments

The editors are grateful for the assistance provided by dozens of helpful chambers of commerce and convention and visitors bureau professionals, as well as municipal, library, and school employees for their invaluable generosity and expertise.

Comments and Suggestions Welcome

If you have questions, concerns, or comments about *Cities of the United States*, please contact the Project Editors:

> *Cities of the United States*
> Thomson Gale
> 27500 Drake Road
> Farmington Hills, MI 48331
> Phone: (248)699-4253
> Toll-free: (800)347-GALE
> Fax: (248)699-8075
> URL: http://www.gale.com

Map Credits

Regional and city maps for *Cities of the United States,* 5th edition, were created by Teresa San Clementi and XNR Productions Inc.

✳ ✳ ✳ ✳

Photo Credits—Volume 3

Photographs appearing in *Cities of the United States,* 5th edition, Volume 3—*The Midwest* were received from the following sources:

ILLINOIS:
Aurora—showing Phillips Park Sunken Garden, photograph. Courtesy of the Aurora Area Convention and Visitors Bureau. Reproduced by permission: p. 5
Chicago—photograph by James Blank. © James Blank. Reproduced by permission: p. 15; showing Chicago Art Institute, photograph by James Blank. © James Blank. Reproduced by permission: p. 24
Peoria—photograph by James Blank. © James Blank. Reproduced by permission: p. 31; photograph by James Blank. © James Blank. Reproduced by permission: p. 38
Springfield—showing Illinois State Capitol Complex, photograph. Courtesy of the Springfield Convention & Visitors Bureau. Reproduced by permission: p. 41; showing tomb of Abraham Lincoln, photograph. Springfield Illinois Convention & Visitors Bureau. Reproduced by permission: p. 48

INDIANA:
Evansville—photograph. Evansville Convention & Visitors Bureau. Reproduced by permission: p. 55; showing John Augustus Reitz House, photograph. Evansville Convention & Visitors Bureau. Reproduced by permission: p. 62
Fort Wayne—photograph. Fort Wayne Convention & Visitors Bureau. Reproduced by permission: p. 67; showing interior of Lincoln Museum, photograph. Fort Wayne Convention & Visitors Bureau. Reproduced by permission: p. 75
Gary—photograph by Robert A. Victor/LCCVB. Reproduced by permission: p. 79; showing shore of Lake Michigan, photograph. © Dewitt Jones/Corbis: p. 87
Indianapolis—photograph. The Indianapolis Project. Reproduced by permission of Banayote Photography Inc: p. 91
South Bend—showing Hesburgh Library, University of Notre Dame, photograph. South Bend/Mishawaka Convention and Visitors Bureau. Reproduced by permission: p. 105; showing College Football Hall of Fame, photograph. South Bend/Mishawaka Indiana Convention and Visitors Bureau. Reproduced by permission: p. 112

IOWA:
Cedar Rapids—photograph. Cedar Rapids Area Convention & Visitors Bureau. Reproduced by permission: p. 119; showing Cedar Rapids Museum of Art, an old Carnegie Library with post-modern addition by Charles W. Moore & Centerbrook Associates, photograph. Reproduced by permission: p. 127
Davenport—photograph by James Blank. © James Blank. Reproduced by permission: p. 131
Des Moines—photograph by James Blank. © James Blank. Reproduced by permission: p. 141; showing State Capitol, photograph by James Blank. © James Blank. Reproduced by permission: p. 149

KANSAS:
Kansas City—photograph. Kansas City Area Convention & Visitors Bureau, Inc. Reproduced by permission: p. 157
Overland Park—photograph. Courtesy of the Overland Park Convention and Visitors Bureau. Reproduced by permission: p. 167
Topeka—photograph by James Blank. © James Blank. Reproduced by permission: p. 179; showing State Capitol, photograph by James Blank. © James Blank. Reproduced by permission: p. 187
Wichita—photograph. Wichita Convention & Visitors Bureau. Reproduced by permission: p. 191; showing "Keeper of the Plains" statue, photograph by James Blank. © James Blank. Reproduced by permission: p. 199

MICHIGAN:

Ann Arbor—photograph by Dan Newell. Reproduced by permission: p. 207

Detroit—showing skyline from Windsor, Canada, photograph by James Blank. © James Blank. Reproduced by permission: p. 219; showing Fox Theater, photograph. © David G. Houser/Corbis: p. 229

Grand Rapids—photograph by Brian Kelly. Courtesy of Grand Rapids/Kent County Convention & Visitors Bureau. Reproduced by permission: p. 235; showing exhibit in Gerald Ford Museum, photograph. © Layne Kennedy/Corbis: p. 243

Kalamazoo—photograph. Courtesy of Downtown Kalamazoo Inc. Reproduced by permission: p. 247

Lansing—photograph. Greater Lansing Convention and Visitors Bureau. Reproduced by permission: p. 259; showing State Capitol, photograph. © Joseph Sohm/Corbis: p. 267

MINNESOTA:

Duluth—photograph. Visit Duluth/Seaquest Photography. Reproduced by permission: p. 275; showing Beargrease Sled Dog Marathon, photograph. Visit Duluth/Linda Nervick. Reproduced by permission: p. 282

Minneapolis—photograph by James Blank. © James Blank. Reproduced by permission: p. 285

Rochester—photograph by Dean Riggott. Rochester Convention & Visitors Bureau. Reproduced by permission: p. 295; showing historic Plummer House, photograph by Dean Riggott. Rochester Convention & Visitors Bureau. Reproduced by permission: p. 302

St. Paul—photograph by James Blank. © James Blank. Reproduced by permission: p. 305; showing Ice Palace, photograph. © Layne Kennedy/Corbis: p. 312

MISSOURI:

Columbia—showing Bear Creek Trail, photograph. Columbia P and R. Reproduced by permission: p. 319; showing University of Missouri campus, photograph by James Blank. © James Blank. Reproduced by permission: p. 327

Jefferson City—photograph. Courtesy of Jefferson City Convention and Visitors Bureau and Priceless Photography and Graphic Design. Reproduced by permission: p. 331; showing State Capitol, photograph by James Blank. © James Blank. Reproduced by permission: p. 338

Kansas City—showing skyline along Missouri River, photograph by James Blank. © James Blank. Reproduced by permission: p. 343; showing Negro Leagues Baseball Museum, photograph. Kansas City Convention & Visitors Association. Reproduced by permission: p. 351

St. Louis—photograph by James Blank. © James Blank. Reproduced by permission: p. 357; showing Climatron Geodesic Dome in the Missouri Botanical Gardens, photograph. © Buddy Mays/Corbis: p. 366

Springfield—photograph by Dan Samples (Springfield, MO 417-882-4558). Reproduced by permission: p. 371; showing Wilsons Creek National Battlefield, photograph by Ryan Hassler. Springfield Convention and Visitors Bureau. Reproduced by permission: p. 378

NEBRASKA:

Lincoln—photograph by Tom Tidball. Reproduced by permission: p. 385; showing State Capitol, photograph. Lincoln Convention & Visitors Bureau. Reproduced by permission: p. 393

Omaha—showing Central Park, photograph. © Royalty: p. 397; showing Old Market area, photograph by James Blank. © James Blank. Reproduced by permission: p. 405

NORTH DAKOTA:

Bismarck—showing State Capitol, photograph by James Blank. © James Blank. Reproduced by permission: p. 413; showing Port of Bismarck, photograph by Clayton Wolt. Bismarck: p. 421

Fargo—photograph by Lowell Wolff. Reproduced by permission: p. 425; showing Plains Art Museum, photograph. Courtesy of Fargo-Moorhead Convention adn Visitors Bureau. Reproduced by permission: p. 432

Grand Forks—photograph by the University of North Dakota. Courtesy of the Greater Grand Forks Convention and Visitors Bureau. Reproduced by permission: p. 437

OHIO:

Akron—April 29, 1999, photograph by Mark Duncan. AP/Wide World Photos. Reproduced by permission: p. 451; showing Stan Hywet Hall and Gardens, photograph by James Blank. © James Blank. Reproduced by permission: p. 461

Cincinnati—photograph by James Blank. © James Blank. Reproduced by permission: p. 467; showing William Howard Taft National Historic Site, photograph by Kathleen Marcaccio. Reproduced by permission: p. 476

Cleveland—photograph by James Blank. © James Blank. Reproduced by permission: p. 481; showing Rock and Roll Hall of Fame and Museum, photograph by James Blank. © James Blank. Reproduced by permission: p. 490

Columbus—photograph. City of Columbus Department of Trade and Development. Reproduced by permission: p. 495; showing Columbus Museum of Art, photograph by James Blank. © James Blank. Reproduced by permission: p. 503

Dayton—photograph. © W. Cody/Corbis: p. 507

Toledo—showing Maumee River skyline, photograph by James Blank. © James Blank. Reproduced by permission: p. 519

SOUTH DAKOTA:

Pierre—showing State Capitol, photograph by James Blank. © James Blank. Reproduced by permission: p. 533; photograph. © David Muench/Corbis: p. 540

Rapid City—photograph. Rapid City Convention & Visitors Bureau. Reproduced by permission: p. 543; showing Crazy Horse Memorial, photograph. © Craig Lovell/Corbis: p. 550

Sioux Falls—photograph by Dick Kelly. Sioux Falls Convention & Visitors Bureau. Reproduced by permission: p. 555; showing Old Courthouse Museum, photograph by James Blank. © James Blank. Reproduced by permission: p. 563

WISCONSIN:

Appleton—showing skyline from Oneida Street, 1997, photograph. Fox Cities of Wisconsin Convention & Visitors Bureau. Reproduced by permission: p. 571; showing Hearthstone, first residence in U.S. to be powered by centrally located hydroelectric plant, photograph. Fox Cities of Wisconsin Convention & Visitors Bureau. Reproduced by permission: p. 578

Green Bay—showing industrial area, photograph. Green Bay Area Visitor and Convention Bureau. Reproduced by permission: p. 583; showing "The Receiver" statue, photograph. Green Bay Area Visitor and Convention Bureau. Reproduced by permission: p. 590

Madison—photograph. © Skot Weidemann. Courtesy of Greater Madison Convention and Visitors Bureau. Reproduced by permission of Skot Weidemann Photography: p. 595

Milwaukee—photograph by James Blank. © James Blank. Reproduced by permission: p. 607; showing Pabst mansion, photograph by James Blank. © James Blank. Reproduced by permission: p. 616

Racine—showing marina, photograph. Racine County Convention & Visitors Bureau. Reproduced by permission: p. 621; photograph. Racine County Convention & Visitors Bureau. Reproduced by permission: p. 629

CITIES OF THE UNITED STATES

ILLINOIS

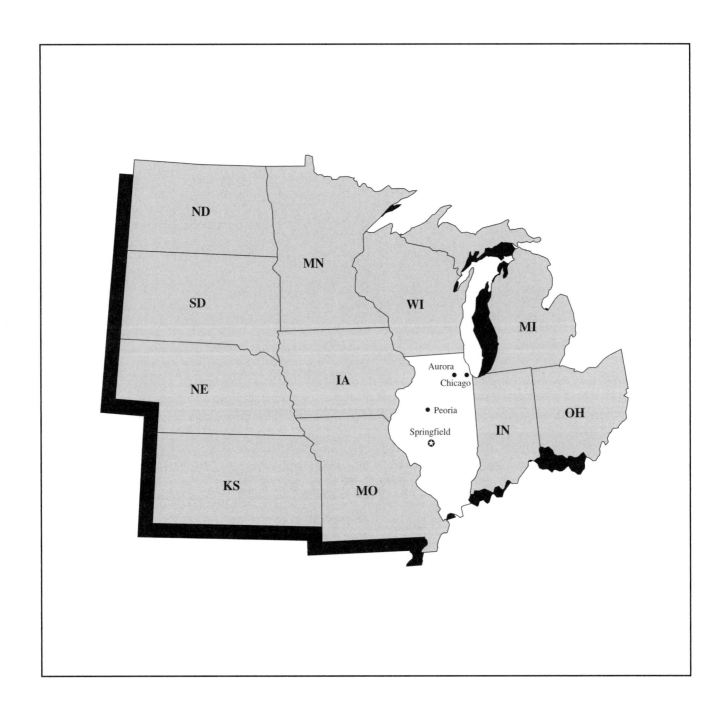

The State in Brief

Nickname: Prairie State
Motto: State sovereignty—national union

Flower: Native violet
Bird: Cardinal

Area: 57,914 square miles (2000; U.S. rank: 25th)
Elevation: Ranges from 279 feet to 1,235 feet above sea level
Climate: Temperate, with hot summers and cold, snowy winters

Admitted to Union: December 3, 1818
Capital: Springfield
Head Official: Governor Rod R. Blagojevich (D) (until 2007)

Population
  1980: 11,427,000
  1990: 11,543,000
  2000: 12,419,647
  2004 estimate: 12,713,634
  Percent change, 1990–2000: 8.6%
  U.S. rank in 2004: 5th
  Percent of residents born in state: 67.1% (2000)
  Density: 223 people per square mile (2000)
  2002 FBI Crime Index Total: 506,086

Racial and Ethnic Characteristics (2000)
  White: 9,125,471
  Black or African American: 1,876,875
  American Indian and Alaska Native: 31,006
  Asian: 423,603
  Native Hawaiian and Pacific Islander: 4,610
  Hispanic or Latino (may be of any race): 1,530,262
  Other: 722,712

Age Characteristics (2000)
  Population under 5 years old: 876,549
  Population 5 to 19 years old: 2,728,957
  Percent of population 65 years and over: 12.1%
  Median age: 34.7 years (2000)

Vital Statistics
  Total number of births (2003): 181,753
  Total number of deaths (2003): 105,575 (infant deaths, 1,361)
  AIDS cases reported through 2003: 14,321

Economy
  Major industries: Manufacturing; mining; agriculture; oil; trade; finance, insurance, and real estate; services
  Unemployment rate: 5.6% (March 2005)
  Per capita income: $33,205 (2003; U.S. rank: 15th)
  Median household income: $45,607 (3-year average, 2001-2003)
  Percentage of persons below poverty level: 11.8% (3-year average, 2001-2003)
  Income tax rate: 3.0%
  Sales tax rate: 6.25%

Aurora

The City in Brief

Founded: 1834 (incorporated 1845)

Head Official: Mayor Tom Wesiner (D) (since 2005)

City Population
  1980: 81,293
  1990: 100,279
  2000: 142,990
  2003 estimate: 162,184
  Percent change, 1990–2000: 42.6%
  U.S. rank in 1990: 201st (State rank: 3rd)
  U.S. rank in 2000: 147th (State rank: 3rd)

Metropolitan Area Population
  1980: 7,937,000
  1990: 8,066,000

  2000: 9,157,540
  Percent change, 1990–2000: 11.1%
  U.S. rank in 1990: 3rd
  U.S. rank in 2000: 3rd

Area: 38.5 square miles (2000)
Elevation: Average 676 feet above sea level
Average Annual Temperature: 47.9° F
Average Annual Precipitation: 38.4 inches

Major Economic Sectors: manufacturing, retail, entertainment
Unemployment Rate: 6.3% (February 2005)
Per Capita Income: $22,131 (1999)

2002 FBI Crime Index Total: Not reported

Major Colleges and Universities: Aurora University, Waubonsee Community College

Daily Newspaper: *The Beacon News*

Introduction

Thirty-five miles west of Chicago, Aurora is the largest city in the Fox River Valley. Aurora developed as an independent city and still sees itself as such, but suburban sprawl has reached westwards from Chicago, and Aurora is now considered part of the broader "Chicagoland" area. While residents escape the rush and the housing prices of nearby Chicago, they're also finding Aurora has much to offer in terms of economical advantages, education, recreation, and overall quality of life—all the while still being close enough to a major city for a day trip or workday commute.

Geography and Climate

Aurora is located in northeastern Illinois, straddling both the east and west sides of the Fox River. The Fox River Valley runs fairly north-south around the river. The area is part of the Great Lakes Plains, which is mainly flat except for some small hills in the west near the start of the Till Plains, the flat fertile area covering most of the state. Aurora is situated far enough away from Lake Michigan to not receive any lake effect snow, but still averages about 38 inches of snow a year, with January being the snowiest month. Temperatures in the summer months average in the low 80s, with about 4 inches of rainfall per month.

Area: 38.5 square miles (2000)

Elevation: Averages 676 feet above sea level

Average Temperatures: January, 20.0° F; July, 72.4° F; annual average, 47.9° F

Average Annual Precipitation: 38.4 inches

History

Originally, Aurora was home to a village of 500 Potawatomi Native Americans, who traded peacefully with white settlers in the area. In 1834, Joseph and Samuel McCarty came west from New York to look for a site to build a sawmill, and they found the Fox River. An island at a bend in the river provided a great location to establish mills and factories where water power could be harnessed. At first, there were two separate settlements on either side of the river, but they merged in 1857 to form the town of Aurora. Aurora quickly developed into a manufacturing town, first known for textiles and later for heavy machinery, foundries, and machine shops. The Chicago, Burlington & Quincy Railroad extended its line to Aurora in

1849. Soon after, the railroad became the area's largest employer, locating its repair and railcar construction shops there. The repair shop necessitated the building of a roundhouse, the largest stone roundhouse constructed in the country. The railroad was the largest employer until the 1960s.

Socially, the town was very progressive from the start. The first free public school district in Illinois was started in Aurora in 1851. The town experienced an influx of European immigrants in the latter half of the nineteenth century, drawn by its industrial jobs. Abolitionist organizations appeared in Aurora before the start of the Civil War, and out of 20 congregations in 1887, two African American churches thrived. By 1870, the city had more than 10,000 residents, and by 1890 there were approximately 20,000 residents—a testament to the city's industrial development.

In 1881, Aurora was the first town in Illinois to light its streets with electric lights, which gave the city its nickname, "The City of Lights." On May 26, 1909, one of the strongest earthquakes to hit Illinois knocked over chimneys in Aurora and was felt over 500,000 square miles. In the 1910s, Aurora was home for a time to six different automobile companies, all of which were eventually unsuccessful.

Aurora continued to be a manufacturing powerhouse through both World Wars and the Great Depression. The railroad shops, which once employed 2,500 and covered 70 acres, closed in 1974, and all but three of the buildings were demolished. In the 1980s, many factories started to close, and unemployment jumped to more than 15 percent. Aurora responded to this by welcoming a riverboat casino to its downtown, developing the area around the casino, developing nearby residential communities and, most importantly, creating multiple business parks on the outer edges of the city.

Today, Aurora is enjoying a population resurgence, having increased more than 40 percent between 1990 and 2000. Businesses continue to move and expand into the area. As real estate prices go up in Chicagoland, the Fox Valley is being seen as a market waiting to be tapped.

Historical Information: Aurora Historical Society, PO Box 905, Aurora, IL 60507; telephone (630)906-0650. Aurora Preservation Commission, 1 South Broadway, Aurora, IL 60507; telephone (630)844-3648; fax (630)906-7430

Population Profile

Metropolitan Area Residents
1980: 7,937,000
1990: 8,066,000

2000: 9,157,540
Percent change, 1990–2000: 11.1%
U.S. rank in 1990: 3rd
U.S. rank in 2000: 3rd

City Residents

1980: 81,293
1990: 100,279
2000: 142,990
2003 estimate: 162,184
Percent change, 1990–2000: 42.6%
U.S. rank in 1990: 201st (State rank: 3rd)
U.S. rank in 2000: 147th (State rank: 3rd)

Density: 3,711.5 people per square mile (2000)

Racial and ethnic characteristics (2000)
   White: 97,340
   Black or African American: 15,817
   American Indian and Alaska Native: 511
   Asian: 4,370
   Native Hawaiian and Pacific Islander: 47
   Hispanic or Latino (may be of any race): 46,557
   Other: 20,762

Percent of residents born in state: 56.0% (2000)

Age characteristics (2000)
   Population under 5 years old: 15,095
   Population 5 to 9 years old: 13,256
   Population 10 to 14 years old: 10,873
   Population 15 to 19 years old: 10,042
   Population 20 to 24 years old: 10,625
   Population 25 to 34 years old: 27,746
   Population 35 to 44 years old: 23,635
   Population 45 to 54 years old: 15,111
   Population 55 to 59 years old: 4,498
   Population 60 to 64 years old: 3,179
   Population 65 to 74 years old: 4,488
   Population 75 to 84 years old: 3,133
   Population 85 years and older: 1,319
   Median age: 29.3 years

Births (2002, Kane County)
   Total number: 8,299

Deaths (2002, Kane County)
   Total number: 2,571 (of which, 45 were infants under
      the age of 1 year)

Money income (1999)
   Per capita income: $22,131
   Median household income: $54,861
   Total households: 46,649

Number of households with income of . . .
   less than $10,000: 2,336
   $10,000 to $14,999: 1,651

$15,000 to $24,999: 4,209
$25,000 to $34,999: 4,779
$35,000 to $49,999: 7,925
$50,000 to $74,999: 10,738
$75,000 to $99,999: 6,838
$100,000 to $149,999: 5,585
$150,000 to $199,999: 1,397
$200,000 or more: 1,191

Percent of families below poverty level: 6.2% (24.7% of
   which were female householder families with related
   children under 5 years)

2002 FBI Crime Index Total: Not reported

Municipal Government

Aurora has a mayor-council form of government. The mayor
is elected at large every four years and is a full-time position.
Of the 12 aldermen composing the council, 10 are elected
from each of the 10 wards, with 2 elected city-wide as
aldermen-at-large. Aldermen are elected for four-year terms,
with half the council running for office on odd-numbered
years. The position of alderman is part-time. The council
has four standing committees: planning and development;
finance; government operations; and buildings, grounds, and
infrastructure.

Head Official: Mayor Tom Wesiner (D) (since 2005; current term expires 2009)

Total Number of City Employees: 2,000 (2005)

City Information: City Hall, 44 East Downer Place, Aurora,
IL 60507; telephone (630)892-8811

Economy

Major Industries and Commercial Activity

Heavy industry helped build Aurora, with the Fox River
being used for power to run saw and textile mills. As the
Industrial Revolution progressed and the railroad came to
town, Aurora became a manufacturer of railroad cars, including some of the first dining cars built in the United
States. Some heavy industry remains in Aurora today with
the Caterpillar plant, which produces construction machinery; in total, the Fox Valley Industrial Association lists
more than 150 manufacturers in the area.

Warehouse and distribution centers are another major part of the economy; with the surge of office and industrial park construction during the 1980s and 1990s, Aurora has become a major distribution channel for auto parts, dry goods, construction equipment, and industrial gases.

Items and goods produced: construction machinery, steel products, tools, office and retail shelving, protective coatings, electronics

Incentive Programs—New and Existing Companies

The Aurora Economic Development Commission (AEDC) was created in 1981 to attract and keep companies in Aurora and the Fox River Valley. It offers a number of services to businesses such as training and education, permit reviews, planning, financing, utilities and infrastructure. Aurora Downtown is an organization created to facilitate projects in the Special Service Tax Area in order to improve and develop the historic downtown area. Tax Increment Financing Zones are also a feature.

Local programs—The City of Aurora, through Aurora Downtown, provides grants for exterior restoration to renew original architectural features, and interior rehabilitation for HVAC, plumbing, structural and electrical work in the historic downtown area. The AEDC, with Waubonsee Community College, has a Small Business Center to help companies with business financing and preparation of business plans. AEDC helps businesses secure financing with tax exempt Industrial Revenue Bonds for qualified applicants.

State programs—The Illinois Development Finance Authority's mission is to issue taxable and tax-exempt bonds and make loans for businesses and non-profit groups in Illinois. They have bond and loan programs for industry and small businesses, as well as for agriculture, health care, education and local governments. The Illinois State Treasurer's Office has many economic programs for businesses, such as below-rate business loans under the Economic Recovery program, low cost financing for development of tourist and historic building restoration through the Experience Illinois Program, and the State Treasurer's Economic Program (STEP). STEP and STEP Small Business provide loans to bring in or expand businesses, and create and retain jobs.

Job training programs—The Aurora Economic Development Commission brings together prospective employers and job training providers through Waubonsee Community College and the College of Du Page. Grants are available for assistance with employee training through AEDC. Waubonsee has many programs in manufacturing and technical skills, computer skills, management training, and health and safety issues. The college also works with the Department of Labor's Bureau of Apprenticeship Training (BAT) to create apprenticeship programs with companies

and organizations around the area. The Illinois Department of Employment Security and the Bureau of Workforce Development combine federal and state money to help with job seekers' training, job search and placement services, and development of core job skills.

Development Projects

With Aurora's population expanding, it's no wonder that business, retail and residential projects have been growing at a steady pace. In 2002, Aurora saw: a 127-room Hampton Inn & Suites and a 148-suite Staybridge Suites open in response to growing business and tourism in the Fox River Valley; Keson Industries, a manufacturer of marking and measuring devices, moved to Aurora and opened a 78,000 square foot facility at the Meridian Business Campus; Luse Companies, an insulation and asbestos and lead abatement contractor, opened a 50,000 square foot headquarters; and more than 1,000 new housing starts were recorded. In 2003 Kraft Foods opened an 850,000 square foot dry foods distribution center at the Prime Aurora Business Park, and Nissan North America expanded by 57,000 square feet at its distribution warehouse at the Meridian Business Park.

More than 3.2 million square feet of commercial and industrial space was developed, and $290 million spent in new investment in 2004. In that year, Chicago Premium Outlets opened, a shopping center with 120 outlet stores that added approximately 1,000 jobs to the community. Aurora University began a 5-year, $50 million plan of new construction and renovation on its campus. Hyundai Motor America expanded its operations in Aurora by opening a $17 million office and parts distribution center. A multiple-year project during the mid-2000s is a plan to upgrade Aurora Airport by building 120 new hangars, spending $7.2 million on refurbishing its runway, and building a new $3.2 million taxiway for the secondary runway.

Economic Development Information: Aurora Economic Development Council, 40 West Downer Place Aurora, IL 60507; phone (630)897-5500; fax (630)897-0469; email aedc@aurora-il.org. Aurora Downtown, Karen Christensen, 1 South Broadway Aurora, IL 60507; telephone (630)844-3670; fax (630)906-7430; email kchristensen@aurora-il .org. Illinois State Treasury Office, 100 West Randolph, Suite 15-600, Chicago, IL 60601; telephone (312)814-1700; fax (312)814-5930

Commercial Shipping

Created as a railroad town, the Burlington Northern, Santa Fe, and the Elgin, Joliet & Eastern railroads still run through town and connect to the nation's largest train gateway, Chicago. For air freight, Chicago's O'Hare and Midway airports are major cargo hubs, with national and international routes. There is one motor freight terminal in Aurora, and seven carriers provide daily service, with one specializing in heavy machinery transport. I-88 runs close by, and other easily accessible Interstates are I-55, 40, I-80, I-90, I-94, and I-355.

Labor Force and Employment Outlook

As Chicagoland expands its influence westward, the commuter rail link makes Aurora a viable destination for workers in Chicago to afford new and vintage homes and condominiums. As the population of the Fox Valley increases, Aurora's long history of development and fairly stable economy serves as an anchor for this growth, along with Naperville to the east. As Aurora's population is now one-third Hispanic and is likely to continue to increase, Aurora Downtown predicts that ''Aurora is poised to be the major Hispanic retail center for the Chicagoland area.''

The following is a summary of data regarding the Chicago-Naperville-Joliet Metropolitan Division labor force, 2004 annual averages.

Size of nonagricultural labor force: 3,748,500

Number of workers employed in . . .
   natural resources and mining: 1,600
   construction: 173,700
   manufacturing: 402,300
   trade, transportation and utilities: 763,400
   information: 87,000
   financial activities: 292,400
   professional and business services: 601,100
   educational and health services: 466,600
   leisure and hospitality: 319,600
   other services: 171,200
   government: 469,600

Average hourly earnings of production workers employed in manufacturing: $15.44

Unemployment rate: 6.3% (February 2005)

Largest city employers	*Number of employees*
Aurora School District #204	3,000
Caterpillar Inc.	3,000
Aurora School District #129	1,300
Aurora School District #131	1,300
Fox Valley Park District	1,300
Waubonsee Community college	1,300
City of Aurora	1,280
Rush-Copley Medical Center	1,265
LTD Commodities	1,200
Provena Mercy Center	1,200
Hollywood Casino Aurora	1,000

Cost of Living

Aurora's cost of living, as well as its housing prices, are slightly below the national average.

The following is a summary of data regarding several key cost of living factors for the Aurora area.

2004 (3rd Quarter) ACCRA Average House Price: $427,451 (Chicago metro)

2004 (3rd Quarter) ACCRA Cost of Living Index: 130.4 (Chicago metro) (U.S. Average = 100.0)

State income tax rate: 3% of federal adjusted gross income with modification

State sales tax rate: 6.25%

Local income tax rate: none

Local sales tax rate: 0.75%

Property tax rate: $7.94 per $100 assessed valuation (2002)

Economic Information: Illinois Department of Commerce and Economic Opportunity, 620 East Adams, Springfield, IL 62701; toll-free (800)252-2923

Education and Research

Elementary and Secondary Schools

Three school districts operate in the city of Aurora: West Aurora District #129, East Aurora District #131, and Indian Prairie District #204. Aurora is also home to the Illinois Mathematics and Science Academy, a public residential high school for grades 10-12. It is internationally known as a school whose students reach the highest levels of achievement in the sciences, technology, and mathematics, by partnering with scientists at state research facilities.

The following is a summary of data regarding the three Aurora public school districts as of the 2002–2003 school year.

Total enrollment: 48,477

Number of facilities
   elementary schools: 55
   junior high/middle schools: 14
   senior high schools: 5
   other: 6

Student/teacher ratio: 17.8:1 (2003)

   Teacher salaries (2004-2005)
      minimum: $32,528
      maximum: $79,193

Funding per pupil: $7,174

There are also 20 religious and Montessori private schools in the city.

Colleges and Universities

Two centers of higher learning are found in Aurora. Aurora University, with 4,300 students, has many undergraduate and graduate programs, including business, fine arts, education, nursing, and social work. Its Spartan athletics is a Division III program, with men's and women's teams in basketball, soccer, tennis, track and field, and men's baseball and football. The University has an additional campus in Williams Bay, Wisconsin. Waubonsee Community College has two-year degree programs in areas such as communications, humanities, fine arts, health and life sciences, science and technology, social sciences, and business, intended for easy transfer to four-year schools. The college has certificate programs, continuing professional education classes, distance learning, and online courses available.

Libraries and Research Centers

The Aurora Public Library has been in existence since 1881 and moved into its current residence in 1904. It was refurbished and expanded in 1969 and again in 1980. Besides the main branch, there is the Eola Road Branch on the east side of the city, and the West Branch, both built in the 1990s. A bookmobile also serves the city. In 2002 a computer training facility was installed at the library.

The Charles B. Phillips Library at Aurora University has more than 99,000 books, 518 periodical subscriptions, a multitude of research materials (including full-text online journals) and access to dozens of databases. Aurora University is home to the Schingoethe Center for Native American Cultures, a museum and research center for studies into Native American cultural artifacts. Waubonsee Community College has the Todd Library to help with its students' research needs.

There are two major national research centers in the area. The Argonne National Laboratory is run by the University of Chicago for the U.S. Department of Energy. Their focus is on energy resources, high energy physics, materials sciences and nanotechnology, environmental management, and national security. The Fermi National Accelerator Laboratory is home to the country's largest particle accelerator, and conducts research on the very basics of energy and matter.

Public Library Information: Aurora Public Library, Main Library, 1 E. Benton Street, Aurora, IL 60505 (630)264-4100

Health Care

Aurora is home to two hospitals: Provena Mercy Medical Center and Rush-Copley Medical Center. Provena, a 356-bed facility, has a family birthing center, an emergency

medicine center, behavioral treatment, and orthopedic services. The Sister Rita Heart Center has a clinic, surgical suites, rehabilitation services, and a pediatric cardiology unit. Rush-Copley offers 150 private rooms on a 98-acre campus. Among Rush-Copley's special services are centers for cancer care, women's health, and neuroscience. Emergency services are provided in a Level II trauma center, with a special designation for pediatric emergency care. The hospital's Vision 2010 plan for expansion is underway with a new emergency department that doubles the current department's size, scheduled for completion in 2005. Dreyer Medical Clinics, owned by Advocate Health Care, provide doctors to communities throughout the Fox River Valley, including three stand-alone clinics in Aurora.

Recreation

Sightseeing

Aurora is home to many historic buildings and residences. A self-guided walking tour of the architecture of the downtown area is available, with historic facts sent to your cell phone, at the Aurora Area Visitor and Convention Bureau. The Stolp Island National Register Historic District in the middle of the Fox River has buildings dating from the 1850s, and has many fine examples of architectural terra cotta. The William Tanner House, an Italianate mansion, is open for tours May through December and is part of the Aurora History Center. The Sri Venkateswara Swami Temple of Greater Chicago is a beautiful Hindu Temple blending ancient design and modern architectural technology. The oldest limestone railroad roundhouse in the country has been restored and converted into Walter Payton's Roundhouse, a brew pub, museum, and live entertainment venue.

The Red Oak Nature Center, on the banks of the Fox River, is in North Aurora. It has many trails to explore, a cave (a rarity in Illinois), and a natural history museum, with an observation deck and picnic areas. The Phillips Park Zoo is free of charge and features animals from the Americas. The African American Heritage Museum and Black Veterans Archives is an amazing display of sculpture created by a self-taught artist, Dr. Charles Smith. Memorials and hundreds of figures from African American history are displayed outdoors in the yard of Dr. Smith's former home.

The riverboat Hollywood Casino Aurora has a 53,000 square foot casino with more than a thousand slot machines and table games, three restaurants, and a theater with live entertainment.

Arts and Culture

The Art Deco Paramount Theater originally opened in 1931 and was the first air-conditioned theater outside of Chicago.

Magnificently restored in 1978, it now presents touring musicians, theatrical performances, improvisation, comedians, and a free film series in the summer. The Riverfront Playhouse has been producing plays since 1978, and also provides a theater series for children. The Borealis Theater Company is the professional theater in residence at Aurora University.

Music venues include Fermilab, which plays host to an eclectic range of concerts, and Walter Payton's Roundhouse, host to music and comedy performers. The Fox Valley Concert Band performs free in Aurora and surrounding communities year round. Aurora University has its Music by the Lake concert series in the summer months at the Allyn Pavilion for the Performing Arts.

The David L. Pierce Art and History Center has rotating art exhibits, as well as displays of military memorabilia from the Grand Army of the Republic. At Aurora University, the Downstairs Dunham Gallery features shows by students and local artists. Gallery 44 is a gallery for local artists showcasing many different media.

The museums and attractions of the Aurora area show great diversity in subject matter, ranging from cutting-edge science to appreciation for its prairie and frontier roots. Blackberry Farms Pioneer Village, run by the Fox Valley Park District, is a living history museum featuring the Farm Museum and its collection of nineteenth century farm implements, a Streets Museum with 11 turn-of-the-century stores, a Discovery Barn, a carousel, pony rides, and a miniature train. Pioneer craft demonstrations, a one-room schoolhouse, and buildings from the 1840s delight school groups and families May through October. The Aurora Historical Society has a collection of artifacts from Aurora's past, including three mastodon skulls unearthed in the 1930s. The Aurora Regional Fire Museum has fire fighting vehicles dating back to 1850, along with thousands of photos and artifacts. The Schingoethe Center for Native American Cultures at Aurora University contains archaeological exhibits, examples of historical and contemporary Native American art, and a research library.

Sci-Tech Hands-On Museum has dozens of exhibits exploring electricity, magnetism, chemistry, life sciences, light, and physics, which make scientific concepts understandable and fun for visitors. Traveling exhibits and an outdoor science park make the museum a destination for families, schools, and scouting groups. In nearby Batavia is the Fermi National Accelerator Laboratory (Fermilab), a high energy physics lab conducting research into the mysteries of matter and energy. Visitors are welcome for tours of the facility and to enjoy the recreational and nature activities on its restored prairie land, including visiting the lab's own herd of bison. The Air Classics Museum of Aviation located at Aurora Municipal Airport has a collection of military jets, prop aircraft, and helicopters from World War II through the

1990s. Visitors are able to sit in some of the aircraft's cockpits, and view aviation uniforms and memorabilia.

Festivals and Holidays

Aurora celebrates the cold winters every February during the Phillips Park Winterfest, with dog sled rides, ice carving, skating, sledding, snowshoeing, nature hikes, and a snowman building contest. Spring brings not only flowers, but myriad events to the Fox River Valley. The Fox River Valley Park District holds an Easter Egg Hunt in April at the Prisco Community Center. In May comes the Taste of Downtown Aurora, featuring booths from area restaurants; the North Aurora Pet Parade; the Memorial Day Parade, and the Aurora Pow-Wow, with dancing, crafts and food from many different Native American tribes. In summer time, Downtown Alive! events include themed dance parties and lunchtime concerts. Blues on the Fox in June is a festival that brings national blues acts to Aurora's downtown. Fourth of July celebrations include a parade, a concert, and fireworks. Also in July is Chase the Moon, a midnight bike ride looping from Aurora to Batavia, the Puerto Rican Cultural Festival, and the Kane County Fair. In August, Soul Fest, featuring home cooked food, games, music, and the Black Business Expo, comes to May Street Park. The Midwest Literary Festival is in September, as is the Fall Harvest Festival at Blackberry Farm's Pioneer Village, and the Downtown Arts Festival. A Veterans Day parade and ceremony runs through downtown Aurora in November. Holiday Magic at the end of November welcomes Santa and Mrs. Claus with the Parade of Lights, fireworks, and a tree lighting ceremony. Through December, the paths at Phillips Park Zoo are lit with holiday lights for strolling at night.

Sports for the Spectator

Since 1991, The Kane County Cougars baseball team plays in Philip B. Elfstrom Field in nearby Geneva, Illinois. Currently a single A affiliate of the Oakland Athletics, the Cougars are part of the Midwest League. Extremely popular in the area, they routinely have more than 500,000 attendees each season. Aurora's sports fans also root for teams in Chicago, like baseball's Cubs and White Sox, football's Bears, basketball's Bulls, hockey's Blackhawks and Wolves, and soccer's Fire.

Sports for the Participant

Aurora's parks are run by the Fox Valley Park District, which has 110 parks in all the communities it serves. The Eola Community Center and Fitness Club has gymnasiums, a track, dance studios, an indoor playground, baseball fields and two sand volleyball courts. The Prisco Community Center is in Aurora's McCullough Park, and was renovated in 2003. The Vaughn Athletic Center features a huge field house for team sports, a 10,000 square foot fitness center, nine tennis courts and two swimming pools. For bicyclists and runners, there are more than 30 miles on four paved trails, two of which run through Aurora. The Aurora Tennis Club is an indoor facility with year-round court times and lessons for kids and adults. The district runs two 18-hole golf courses, Fox Bend and Orchard Valley, which was rated four-stars by Golf Digest magazine. The Aurora City Golf Course, the Aurora Country Club, and six other courses are in the immediate vicinity. The Fox Valley Trail runs along the Fox River from Aurora north to Crystal Lake. The district runs Splash Country Water Park, containing a zero-depth pool, water slides, a kid's water play area, and a 1,100 foot long lazy river. The Phillips Park Aquatic Center also offers several water slides, a zero-depth pool, and kid-friendly areas.

The Sport Zone Park is a multi-sport center for the whole family. Outdoors, it features mini-golf, batting cages, and a go-cart track. The main feature is its 72,000 square foot dome, which is a driving range during the day and is converted to soccer, baseball, or softball fields in the evening. The Aurora Archery Range hosts the annual National Field Archery Association Tournament.

Shopping and Dining

Three large shopping centers are big draws to Aurora. The recently completed Chicago Premium Outlet center has 120 stores, including Ann Taylor, Brooks Brothers, Giorgio Armani, and Kate Spade, and offers discount shopping every day. Westfield Shoppingtown Fox Valley is anchored by four large department stores and has 180 other shops. Northgate Shopping Center has several big-box retailers and other smaller stores. The Route 59 Corridor and the Randall/Orchard Road corridor are main shopping districts for Aurora, North Aurora, and Batavia. The Aurora Farmer's Market is held on Saturday mornings June through October, and is one of several in surrounding communities.

Aurora has a wide variety of family, ethnic and fine dining choices. Steak houses, Italian, Mexican, and Chinese restaurants abound. Notable is Savannah's, at the Fox Valley Mall, featuring Southern Cuisine and afternoon teas.

Visitor Information: Aurora Area Convention and Visitors Bureau, 44 W. Downer Place, Aurora, IL 60506; telephone (630)897-5581; toll-free (800)477-4369; fax (630)897-5589. City of Aurora, 44 East Downer Place, Aurora, IL 60507; telephone (630)264-4636; fax (630)892-0741

Convention Facilities

In nearby St. Charles, Illinois, the Pheasant Run Resort & Spa is the area's largest conference facility. With a 320-seat auditorium, 100,000 square feet of meeting space, four ballrooms, and a 38,000 square foot Exposition Center, it can handle most types of functions. Accommodations and amenities include 473 rooms, an 18-hole golf course, a day spa, and live entertainment. The DuPage County Expo Center, also in St. Charles, has 25,000 square feet of column-free trade show space. The Hilton Garden Inn in St. Charles has 120 rooms and 26,000 square feet of meeting and conference space. The Kane County Fairgrounds are rentable for concerts, exhibitions, auctions, and trade shows.

Aurora has 10 hotels and motels for visitors staying in the city. The Comfort Suites City Center has 82 suites and 3 meeting rooms, and the adjacent Walter Payton's Roundhouse has banquet and catering facilities for up to 600. The Hampton Inn and Suites has a 5,000 square-foot conference and meeting center, and has a 6,000 square foot indoor water park. The Fox Valley Park District also rents out their facilities and community centers.

Convention Information: Aurora Area Convention and Visitors Bureau, 44 W. Downer Place, Aurora, IL 60506; telephone (630)897-5581; toll-free (800)477-4369; fax (630)897-5589

Transportation

Approaching the City

Aurora Municipal Airport is for private and corporate aircraft, with 6,500 and 5,500 feet runways. Helicopter services are also supported. Chicago's Midway and O'Hare International Airports are the major commercial airports of the area. Two interstate highways bring motorists into the Aurora area: I-88 runs east-west, and I-55 runs south and east. METRA, a commuter rail system, connects Aurora with Chicago and its suburbs. Greyhound provides long-distance bus service from a stop at the Aurora Transportation Center.

Traveling in the City

Aurora straddles the Fox River in a mainly north-south direction, with several bridges crossing it at intervals. Public transportation is handled by the PACE bus system, which has 15 routes in Aurora alone, and many others in surrounding communities.

Communications

Newspapers and Magazines

The Beacon News is Aurora's daily newspaper, with a daily circulation of over 27,000. It is published by the Suburban

Chicago Newspaper group of papers, owned by *The Chicago Sun-Times.*

Television and Radio

Aurora is home to Telefuture, a Spanish language UHF television station. Broadcasts from all major commercial networks and several independent and PBS stations in the Chicagoland area are received in Aurora. Four radio stations broadcast talk, rock and Spanish language programming from the city, and are supplemented by broadcasts from Chicago and closer Kane and DuPage county stations.

Media Information: The Beacon News, 101 South River Street, Aurora, Illinois 60506; telephone (630)844-5844

Aurora Online

Aurora Area Convention and Visitors Bureau. Available www.enjoyaurora.com

Aurora Downtown. Available www.auroradowntown.org

Aurora Economic Development Commission. Available www.aurora-il.org/aedc

Aurora Hispanic Chamber of Commerce. Available www.ahcc-il.com

Aurora Historical Preservation Commission. Available www.aurora-il.org/HistoricPreservation/index.html

Aurora Public Library. Available www.aurora.lib.il.us

Aurora University. Available www.aurora.edu

The Beacon News. Available www.suburbanchicagonews.com/beaconnews

City of Aurora Home Page. Available www.aurora-il.org

East Aurora School District. Available www.d131.kane.k12.il.us

Fox Valley Park District. Available www.foxvalleyparkdistrict.org

Greater Aurora Chamber of Commerce. Available www.aurorachamber.com

Indian Prairie School Disrict 204. Available www.ipsd.org

West Aurora School District. Available www.sd129.org

Selected Bibliography

Edwards, Jim and Wynette, *Aurora: A Diverse People Build Their City* (Charleston, SC: Arcadia Publishers, 1998)

Encyclopedia of Illinois (New York, Somerset Publishers, 1994)

Grossman, James R.; Keating, Ann Durkin; Reiff, Janice L. *The Encyclopedia of Chicago* (Chicago: University of Chicago Press, 2004)

Keiser, John H. *Building for the Centuries: Illinois, 1865 to 1898* (Chicago: University of Illinois Press, 1997)

Chicago

The City in Brief

Founded: 1830 (incorporated 1837)

Head Official: Mayor Richard M. Daley (D) (since 1989)

City Population
   1980: 3,005,000
   1990: 2,783,726
   2000: 2,896,016
   2003 estimate: 2,869,121
   Percent change, 1990–2000: 4%
   U.S. rank in 1980: 2nd
   U.S. rank in 1990: 3rd (State rank: 1st)
   U.S. rank in 2000: 3rd (State rank: 1st)

Metropolitan Area Population (PMSA)
   1980: 7,937,290
   1990: 7,410,858
   2000: 9,157,450

   Percent change, 1990–2000: 23.6%
   U.S. rank in 1980: 3rd
   U.S. rank in 1990: 3rd
   U.S. rank in 2000: 3rd

Area: 228.4 square miles (2000)
Elevation: 578.5 feet above sea level
Average Annual Temperature: 49.8° F
Average Annual Precipitation: 35.82 inches

Major Economic Sectors: Services, wholesale and retail trade, manufacturing, government
Unemployment Rate: 6.4% (February 2005)
Per Capita Income: $20,175 (1999)

2002 FBI Crime Index Total: Not Reported

Major Colleges and Universities: University of Chicago; University of Illinois at Chicago; DePaul University; Loyola University of Chicago

Daily Newspapers: *Chicago Tribune; Chicago Sun-Times*

TO SECOND CITY (N. WELLS)   TO ACADEMY OF SCIENCES (N. CLARK)

LINCOLN PARKZOO
NORTH   HISTORICAL SOCIETY

LAKE MICHIGAN

CANADA
WISCONSIN
MICHIGAN
MINNESOTA
NY
IOWA
Chicago
ILLINOIS   INDIANA   OHIO   PA
KS
MISSOURI   KENTUCKY   WEST VIRGINIA
VIRGINIA

0   KILOMETERS   0.5   1

N

MILES   0.25   0.5

CLARK
DEARBORN
STATE
DIVISION
ELM
CEDAR
MAPLE
BELLVUE
OAK
WALTON
DELAWARE
CHESTNUT
PEARSON
CHICAGO
SUPERIOR
STATE
WABASH
RUSH
SUPERIOR
HURON
ERIE
ONTARIO
OHIO
GRAND
ILLINOIS
STATE
WABASH
RUSH
HUBBARD
KINZIE
S WATER
WACKER

JOHN HANCOCK CTR
WATER TOWER PLACE

MICHIGAN - MAGNIFICENT MILE

LAKE SHORE

M.C.A.
FAIRBANKS
NORTH PIER
N WATER
MCLURG
NAVY PIER
ST. CLAIR

TO WRIGLEY FIELD
CLARK
DEARBORN

GRAND   KINGSBURY
PEORIA
GREEN
HALSTED
MILWAUKEE
FRANKLIN
ORLEANS
WELLS
LASALLE
GRAND
HUBBARD
KINZIE
CARROLL
KINZIE
FULTON
CARROLL
LAKE
FULTON
MERCHANDISE MART
CLARK
DEARBORN
WACKER
WACKER

GRAND
HUBBARD
KINZIE   94
CARROLL
FULTON
LAKE
CARPENTER
MORGAN
RANDOLPH
WASHINGTON
DESPLAINES
JEFFERSON
CLINTON
CANAL
WACKER
FRANKLIN

CHICAGO OPERA THEATRE
CITY HALL
DALEY CTR / PICASSO   MALL
SHUBERT THEATRE
MIRO'S CHICAGO
CALDER SCULPTURE
BOARD OF TRADE

BEAUBIEN
STETSON
RANDOLPH

LIBRARY CULTURAL CENTER

THE LOOP

LAKE SHORE

MADISON   CHICAGO STADIUM
MONROE
SAGAMON
PEORIA
GREEN
HALSTED
MONROE
MERCANTILE EXCHANGE
ADAMS
JACKSON
VAN BUREN
290

ADAMS
JACKSON
VAN BUREN
290

ART INSTITUTE
ORCHESTRA HALL

MONROE
PETRILLO MUSIC SHELL
JACKSON
GRANT PARK

SEARS TWR
AUDITORIUM THEATRE
CONGRESS   LIBRARY
CONGRESS PLAZA
BUCKINGHAM FOUNTAIN

HARRISON
90
94
HARRISON
FRANKLIN
WELLS
BLACKSTONE THEATRE
BALBO

POLK
UNIVERSITY OF ILLINOIS
POLK
LASALLE
CLARK
STATE
WABASH
8TH
MICHIGAN
9TH
11TH
COLUMBUS
LAKE SHORE
SHEDD AQUARIUM

TAYLOR
CHICAGO RIVER
TAYLOR

ROOSEVELT
MORGAN
SAGAMON
PEORIA
HALSTED
DESPLAINES
JEFFERSON
CLINTON
CANAL
ROOSEVELT
13TH
14TH
FIELD MUSEUM
SOLDIER FIELD
ADLER PLANETARIUM

14TH
16TH
18TH
CLARK
DEARBORN
STATE
WABASH
MICHIGAN
INDIANA
16TH
18TH
PRAIRIE
CALUMET
MEIGS FIELD

ARCHER
CULLERTON
TO MEXICAN FINE ARTS CENTER

TO COMISKEY PARK   TO MIDWAY AIRPORT   TO DUSABLE MUSEUM   TO MUSEUM OF SCIENCE & INDUSTRY

Introduction

Chicago, the seat of Illinois's Cook County and the third largest city in the country, is the focus of a consolidated metropolitan statistical area that covers the primary metropolitan statistical areas of Gary, Indiana; Kankakee, Illinois; and Kenosha, Wisconsin. "Brawling" was the word Carl Sandburg applied to Chicago in his poem about the city. No longer the "Hog Butcher for the World," at the dawn of the twenty-first century, Chicago is still an enthusiastically combative city with a lively political life. A railroad hub in the latter half of the nineteenth century, when its population had already reached 300,000 people, Chicago became a major force in the nation's development. Today, it is a national transportation, industrial, telecommunications, and financial leader as well as a city of great architectural significance, ethnic diversity, and cultural wealth. The only inland urban area to rank with major East and West Coast metropolises, Chicago has achieved international status through the quality of its cultural institutions and its position as a world financial center.

Geography and Climate

Chicago extends westward on a plain along the southwest shore of Lake Michigan. The climate is continental, with frequently changing weather bringing temperatures that range from relatively warm in the summer to relatively cold in the winter. Temperatures of 96 degrees or higher occur during summers; winters can register a minimum low of minus 15 degrees. Snowfall near the lakeshore is usually heavy because of cold air movement off Lake Michigan. Summer thunderstorms are frequently heavy but variable, as parts of the city may receive substantial rainfall while other sectors will have none. Strong wind gusts in the central business district are caused by the channeling of winds between tall buildings; the nickname "windy city," often applied to Chicago, does not, however, refer to the average wind speed, which is no greater than in many other parts of the country. Chicagoans instead attribute the nickname to their reputed penchant for talking proudly about their city.

Area: 228.4 square miles (2000)

Elevation: 578.5 feet above sea level

Average Temperatures: January, 21.3° F; July, 73.4° F; annual average, 49.8° F

Average Annual Precipitation: 35.82 inches

History

Lakeshore Site Begins With Trading Post, Fort

The earliest known inhabitants of the area they called "Chicaugou" were Native Americans of the Illinois tribe. The meaning of the word "Chicaugou" is variously interpreted to mean great, powerful, or strong, depending on the dialect. In the Chippewa dialect the word "shegahg" meant "wild onion"; it is said that an abundance of wild onions grew in the region.

The first people of European descent to reach Chicago were the explorers Father Jacques Marquette and Louis Joliet, who encamped on the Lake Michigan shore at the mouth of the Chicago River in 1673. A century later, in 1783, Jean-Baptiste Du Sable, the son of a French merchant from Quebec and a Haitian slave, left New Orleans and established a fur-trading post in the same area. The site was advantageous for transportation, because it afforded a short portage between the Chicago River, part of the Great Lakes waterway, and the Des Plaines River, connected to the Mississippi waterway via the Illinois River. Sable mysteriously vanished in 1800, and John Kinzie, the region's first English civilian settler, took over the trading post. Soon a United States garrison, Fort Dearborn, was built to defend the post. In 1812 angry Potawatomi killed most of the traders, except for the Kinzie family, and destroyed Fort Dearborn, which was rebuilt in 1816.

A survey and plat of the growing settlement were filed in 1830, at which time the area numbered 350 inhabitants. Chicago was chartered as a town in 1833 and rechartered as a city in 1837. The completion of the Illinois-Michigan Canal in 1848 turned the city into a marketing center for grain and food products. The first railroad arrived the same year the canal was opened, and within a decade Chicago was the focal point for 3,000 miles of track. The productive grain industry fed cattle and hogs, and Chicago emerged as the site of a major livestock market and meatpacking industry, surpassing Cincinnati as the nation's pork packer. Cattle merchants formed the Union Stock Yards and Transit Company.

Cyrus McCormick opened a factory in the city in 1847 to manufacture his reaper, leading the way for Chicago to become a farm implements hub. The city also became a leader in the processing of lumber for furniture, buildings, and fencing. Chicago industries outfitted Union troops during the Civil War, when the grain and farm machinery industries also experienced wartime growth. George Pullman began to produce railroad sleeping cars in Chicago in 1867. The next year the city's first blast furnace was built. At this time merchants Potter Palmer, Marshall Field, and Levi Leter began shipping consumer goods to general stores in the Midwest.

Growth Creates Challenges, Opportunities

Chicago's rapid growth resulted in congested residential sectors where the poor were relegated to shabby housing without proper sanitation. Chicago was radically changed, however, on October 8, 1871, by a cataclysmic fire that burned for 27 hours. At that time two-thirds of the city's buildings were made of wood and the summer had been especially dry; high winds spread the fire quickly. Although the stockyards, freight yards, and factory district were spared, Chicago's commercial area was completely destroyed; 8,000 buildings and property valued at just under $200 million were lost. More than 90,000 people were left homeless and 300 people lost their lives.

Since the city's industrial infrastructure was unscathed by the fire, rebuilding progressed rapidly, and Chicago was essentially rebuilt within a year. When the economic panic of 1873 swept the rest of the nation, Chicago was relatively protected from the ensuing depression. The city's prosperity in the post-fire era was founded on an expansion of its industrial and marketing base. Assembly-line techniques were introduced in the meat packing industry, and technological improvements benefitted the steel and farm machinery makers. The United States Steel South Works, based in Chicago, became one of the largest such operations in the world. At that time George Pullman established his Palace Car Company in a nearby town he owned and named after himself, which was later annexed to Chicago.

Chicago celebrated its two decades of growth by sponsoring the World's Columbian Exposition of 1893, which also marked the 400th anniversary of Christopher Columbus's discovery of America, and which attracted more than 21 million visitors to the city. Chicago at this time was in the forefront of architectural innovation and became known as the birthplace of the skyscraper. Of particular architectural importance is the Chicago Board of Trade, where commodities futures are bought and sold. A politically active city, Chicago underwent a period of reform in the late 1890s. A civil service was inaugurated in 1895, and numerous reform organizations attempted to influence public opinion.

Political Trends Shape City's Future

Five-term Mayor Carter H. Harrison Jr. brought the reform spirit to a high point, but weak law enforcement and other factors allowed gangsters such as Alphonse "Scarface" Capone and John Dillinger to rise to power in the 1920s and 1930s. Chicago was characterized the world over as a gangster headquarters long after Democratic reform Mayor Anton J. Cermak initiated cleanup efforts. He also introduced a style of ward and district politics copied after the New York City Tammany Hall political machine. Cermak was killed by an assassin's bullet intended for President-elect Franklin

D. Roosevelt, but Cermak's political organization continued under Mayor Edward J. Kelly.

In 1933 Chicago gained world attention once again when it hosted A Century of Progress, a world exposition that celebrated the city's incorporation as a municipality; Chicago's industrial and financial advances and prosperity were on display despite the era's economic depression. In 1942 scientists working in Chicago produced the first nuclear chain reaction and thus advanced the creation of atomic weaponry and energy. During its history, Chicago has frequently been the site of national political meetings, including the Republican Party gathering to nominate Abraham Lincoln in 1860 and the Democratic Party convention that nominated Hubert H. Humphrey in 1968. The latter brought protestors against the Vietnam War to Chicago's streets and drew national attention to Mayor Richard J. Daley's handling of the demonstrators.

The Mayors Daley

The most powerful symbol of Chicago politics, Richard J. Daley served as mayor from 1955 until his death in 1976. Daley was a major force in the national Democratic Party and was considered the last "big city boss." His son, Richard M. Daley, ran for Chicago's mayoral office in 1989 in an election that *Time* magazine characterized as "an ethnic power struggle" that divided the city along racial lines. Chicago's first African American mayor, Harold Washington, had been elected in 1983 and reelected in 1987, but after his death the coalition of African Americans and white liberals that had elected him broke down; African American voter participation was down from previous elections while, according to *Time,* Daley's "richly financed campaign produced a large turnout among whites. Result: Daley, by 55% to 41%." Daley won 58 percent of the vote in 1995. As mayor of a city known for its widely diverse neighborhoods of Germans, Scandinavians, Irish, Jews, Italians, Poles, Eastern Europeans, Asians, Hispanics, and African Americans, Daley has faced the challenge of uniting the spirit of a divided city entering the twenty-first century as an internationally important urban center. With a national reputation as a skilled and astute negotiator, with powerful political supporters at the national level, Mayor Daley received another vote of confidence when the Democratic Party selected Chicago as the site of the 1996 National Convention. Mayor Daley has privatized a number of city government operations and by 1996 had passed balanced budgets seven years in a row; this and other successes accounted for his selection as national spokesperson for the U.S. Conference of Mayors in 1996. In 2005 Mayor Daley outlined his goals for the city in his annual City of Chicago address. These goals included a city in which every family could afford housing in a safe neighborhood, a city in which every child receives a quality education, and a city where good jobs are available to those who want to work.

Today's Chicago exists as a cultural mecca, with world-class museums, restaurants, theater, and arts. Still, the "other side" of Chicago is not as shiny, in terms of blighted housing projects and crime—a stigma hard for any large city to overcome, yet continually addressed by the mayor and city leaders.

Historical Information: Chicago Historical Society, 1629 North Clark Street at North Avenue, Chicago, IL 60614; telephone (312)642-4600

Population Profile

Metropolitan Area Residents (CMSA)
1980: 7,937,290
1990: 7,410,858 (PMSA)
2000: 9,157,450
Percent change, 1990–2000: 23.6%
U.S. rank in 1980: 3rd
U.S. rank in 1990: 3rd
U.S. rank in 2000: 3rd

City Residents
1980: 3,005,000
1990: 2,783,726
2000: 2,896,016
2003 estimate: 2,869,121
Percent change, 1990–2000: 4%
U.S. rank in 1980: 2nd
U.S. rank in 1990: 3rd
U.S. rank in 2000: 3rd

Density: 12,750.3 people per square mile (2000)

Racial and ethnic characteristics (2000)
White: 1,215,315
Black or African American: 1,065,009
American Indian and Alaska Native: 10,290
Asian: 125,974
Native Hawaiian and Pacific Islander: 1,788
Hispanic or Latino (may be of any race): 753,644
Other: 393,203

Percent of residents born in state: 57.7% (2000)

Age characteristics (2000)
Population under 5 years old: 216,868
Population 5 to 9 years old: 224,012
Population 10 to 14 years old: 200,802
Population 15 to 19 years old: 200,962
Population 20 to 24 years old: 239,252
Population 25 to 34 years old: 533,199
Population 35 to 44 years old: 433,268
Population 45 to 54 years old: 330,507
Population 55 to 59 years old: 116,932
Population 60 to 64 years old: 99,757
Population 65 to 74 years old: 159,915
Population 75 to 84 years old: 103,720
Population 85 years and over: 35,168
Median age: 31.5 years

Births (2003)
Total number: 48,044

Deaths (2002)
Total number: 22,298 (of which, 412 were infants under the age of 1 year)

Money income (1999)
Per capita income: $20,175
Median household income: $38,625
Total households: 1,061,964

Number of households with income of . . .
less than $10,000: 146,192
$10,000 to $14,999: 71,103
$15,000 to $24,999: 132,339
$25,000 to $34,999: 133,670
$35,000 to $49,999: 171,140
$50,000 to $74,999: 188,700
$75,000 to $99,999: 95,162
$100,000 to $149,999: 75,743
$150,000 to $199,999: 21,884
$200,000 or more: 26,031

Percent of families below poverty level: 16.6% (48.6% of which were female householder families with related children under 5 years)

2002 FBI Crime Index Total: Not reported

Municipal Government

The Chicago city government is headed by a strong mayor and a nonpartisan, 50-member council; the mayor and council members are elected to four-year terms. Mayor Daley has indicated that creating a good climate for business is an essential goal of his administration. He is committed to being the education mayor by improving Chicago's public schools.

Head Official: Mayor Richard M. Daley (D) (since 1989; current term expires 2007)

Total Number of City Employees: more than 35,978 (2004); excluding employees of Chicago Public Schools, Park District, Water Reclamation District, Transit Authority, Housing Authority, and City Colleges

City Information: Mayor's Office, City of Chicago, 121 N. Lasalle Street, Room 507, Chicago, IL 60602; telephone (312)744-8045

Economy

Major Industries and Commercial Activity

Chicago's diversified economy is based on manufacturing, printing and publishing, finance and insurance, and food processing (the city is still considered the nation's "candy capital") as primary sectors. A substantial industrial base and a major inland port contribute to the city's position as a national transportation and distribution center. The source of nationally distributed magazines, catalogs, educational materials, encyclopedias, and specialized publications, Chicago ranks second only to New York in the publishing industry. The city is home to the Federal Reserve Bank, the Chicago Board of Trade, and the Chicago Mercantile Exchange.

Items and goods produced: telephone equipment, musical instruments, surgical appliances, machinery, earth-moving and agricultural equipment, steel, metal products, diesel engines, printing presses, office machines, radios and television sets, auto accessories, chemicals, soap, paint, food products and confections

Incentive Programs—New and Existing Companies

Local programs—The City of Chicago Department of Planning and Development (DPD) actively promotes growth and development in Chicago's diverse neighborhoods with a focus on the continued economic development of the city. The department works with the existing business community and also works to attract new business to Chicago. All of this is done in the context of holistic, community-based planning, closely coordinating activities with residents and community organizations. The department's Technology Development Division works with the Chicago Partnership for Economic Development to strengthen the city's information technology sector.

DPD promotes effective neighborhood planning by coordinating the strategic allocation of public funds to maximize private investment—and the attraction of new companies—by providing a menu of financial resources, neighborhood improvements, site location assistance, and the expediting of permits and licenses. DPD also has the primary responsibility for preserving city landmarks and protecting the Chicago River and the Lake Michigan shoreline.

State programs—In 1977 the Illinois legislature adopted the Tax Increment Allocation Redevelopment Act to provide municipalities with a unique tool to finance and stimulate urban redevelopment. Through the use of Tax Increment Financing (TIF), cities can stimulate private investment by offering incentives to attract and retain businesses, improve their community areas, and maintain a well-educated and highly trained labor force. TIF is by far the most popular incentive program in Chicago; by the end of 2003, Chicago had invested $870 million in TIF funds and benefitted from $5.4 billion in private investment

Job training programs—The Mayor's Office of Workforce Development (MOWD) assists job seekers—including those who have been laid off—in finding and keeping jobs. The five Chicago Workforce Centers located throughout the city, as well as 30 community-based affiliate organizations, offer services such as basic job skills courses, access to job listings, seminars in resume writing and interviewing, and veterans services. Mayor Daley's WorkNet Chicago assists ex-offenders in reentering the workforce.

Development Projects

In the summer of 2004, the long-anticipated Millennium Park opened. Conceived in the late 1990s with the goal of creating more usable space in Grant Park, the $475 million park is a state-of-the-art example of modern city green space. The Jay Pritzker Pavilion, designed by world-renowned architect Frank Gehry, is an outdoor concert venue that seats 4,000 people. The Cloud Gate, sculpted by Anish Kapoor, is a 110-ton elliptical sculpture made of stainless steel. Visitors can walk under and around the sculpture, which resembles a giant bean and reflects Chicago's skyline. Another popular attraction is the Jarume Plensa-designed Crown Fountain, two 50-foot high towers made of glass blocks and situated in a reflecting pool. The towers feature changing video images of the faces of Chicagoans, from which jets of water appear to descend.

In 2001 The Art Institute of Chicago unveiled plans to construct a new museum wing on the museum's northeast corner. Expected to be completed in 2007, the new wing, designed by architect Renzo Piano, will add approximately 220,000 square feet of space to the museum. The $198 million addition will add a contemporary appeal to the museum's 19th century building.

The O'Hare Modernization Program is Chicago's O'Hare International Airport's plan to add a new western terminal facility and reconfigure existing runways. The $6.6 billion project, to be funded through passenger facility charges, general airport revenue bonds, and federal Airport Improvement Program funds, will require a total of 433 acres in Chicago and surrounding suburbs. Plans for the proposed improvements were submitted to the Federal Aviation Administration for review in October of 2003.

McCormick Place, North America's largest exhibition hall, broke ground in 2004 for McCormick Place West. The $850 million expansion will add approximately 470,000 square feet of exhibition space and 250,000 square feet of meeting space, which will include more than 60 meeting rooms and a 100,000 square foot ballroom. The five-story facility will connect to the existing McCormick Place campus. McCormick Place West is expected to open in 2008.

Economic Development Information: Chicago Department of Planning and Development, 121 N. LaSalle Street, #1003, Chicago, IL 60602; telephone (312)744-4190

Commercial Shipping

Since its founding, Chicago has been an important transportation and distribution point; at one time it was a crucial link between the Great Lakes and Mississippi River waterways and today the city ranks among the world's busiest shipping hubs. The city became a world port in 1959 with the opening of the St. Lawrence Seaway, which provides a direct link from the Great Lakes to the Atlantic Ocean. The Port of Chicago handles marine, rail, and overland freight. The state of Illinois maintains the third-highest combined mileage of railroads and paved highways in the country. Approximately 750 motor freight carriers serve the metropolitan area, and trucking companies ship more than 50 million tons of freight each year; railroads average more than 40 million tons. Chicago's airports handle more than one million metric tons of cargo annually.

Labor Force and Employment Outlook

Chicago's unemployment rate exceeds the national average. The loss of jobs for both unskilled and college-educated workers can be attributed to the Internet bust, an ailing economy, plant closings, and the relocation of companies once headquartered in Chicago. However, the unemployment rate seems to be on a decline; March of 2005 showed the largest gains in employment since 2000. Like many large cities, Chicago has a large immigrant population. The immigrants come from all over the world, including Poland, Mexico, India, the former Soviet Union, the Philippines, and China. Despite fears that low-skilled immigrants would not be assimilated into an increasingly high-tech economy, local analysts say the newcomers are following the success track of earlier groups, working their way into the middle class after performing service and laboring jobs.

The following is a summary of data regarding the Chicago metropolitan area civilian labor force, 2004 annual average:

Size of civilian labor force: 4,231,500

Number of workers employed in . . .
   construction and mining: 175,300
   manufacturing: 402,300

trade, transportation and utilities: 763,400
information: 87,000
financial activities: 292,400
professional and business services: 601,100
educational and health services: 466,600
leisure and hospitality: 319,600
other services: 171,200
government: 469,600

Average hourly earnings of production workers employed in manufacturing: $15.44 (Chicago-Naperville-Joliet metropolitan area, 2004 average)

Unemployment rate: 6.4% (February 2005)

Largest employers	Number of employees
U.S. Government	88,000
Chicago Public Schools	39,402
Jewel-Osco	36,749
City of Chicago	35,978
Cook County	26,505

Cost of Living

The cost of living in Chicago is higher than the national average. The following is a summary of data regarding several key cost of living factors in the Chicago area.

2004 (3rd Quarter) ACCRA Average House Price: $427,451

2004 (3rd Quarter) ACCRA Cost of Living Index: 130.4 (U.S. average = 100.0)

State income tax rate: 3.0%

State sales tax rate: 6.25% (1% on food and drugs) (2005)

Local income tax rate: None

Local sales tax rate: 9%

Property tax rate: 7.247 mills (2002)

Education and Research

Elementary and Secondary Schools

With 613 elementary and high schools, the Chicago Public Schools (CPS) system is the largest public elementary and secondary educational system in Illinois. Several initiatives, such as the Chicago Reading Initiative and the Chicago Math and Science Initiative are programs that have been implemented district-wide to ensure students meet minimum achievement standards in basic subjects. The After School Matters program is a partnership between CPS, the Chicago Park District, the Chicago Public Library, and the City of Chicago. Apprenticeships and club activities offer teens exposure to and on-the-job training in the arts, sports technology, and communications.

Because of the city's large foreign-born population, the school system employs bilingual teachers in 20 languages. Special schools include Chicago High School for Agricultural Sciences, situated on the last farm in the city of Chicago, which prepares students for jobs in "anything to do with food and fiber," and Curie Metropolitan High School, with magnet programs in the performing and creative arts and electronic repair and maintenance. Construction is expected to begin in 2006 on two new high schools, a selective enrollment college prep school and a vocational magnet high school, to be housed in one building on Chicago's west side. When opened in 2008, the schools will replace the existing Westinghouse High School.

The following is a summary of data regarding the Chicago public schools as of the 2004–2005 school year (middle schools are included in the elementary school count).

Total enrollment: 426,812

Number of facilities
  elementary schools: 486
  high schools: 107

Student teacher ratio: elementary, 22.7:1; high school, 19.6 (2003)

Teacher salaries
  average: $62,985 (2003)

Funding per pupil: $8,786 (2003)

The Archdiocese of Chicago operates 235 elementary and 41 high schools in Cook and Lake counties, with an enrollment in excess of 107,000 students. There are also approximately 52 state-recognized public schools in Chicago.

Public Schools Information: Chicago Public Schools, 125 South Clark Street, Chicago, IL 60603; telephone (773)553-1000

Colleges and Universities

Chicago-area institutions of higher education include private, state, and religious universities of national note. The University of Chicago, founded with an endowment by John D. Rockefeller in 1891, enjoys an international reputation for pioneering science research and the "Chicago plan" in undergraduate education. The university claims more than 70 Nobel laureates—far more than any other university in the country. The university, with research funding of $236 million in 2003, administers advanced scholarship and research centers, including the Enrico Fermi Institute, the Enrico Fermi National Accelerator Laboratory, and the Argonne National Laboratory, among others. The University of Illinois at Chicago enrolls approximately 25,000 students

earning bachelor's, master's, and doctoral degrees and first professional degrees in dentistry, medicine, and pharmacy.

The city's three leading Catholic institutions are DePaul University, offering undergraduate, master's and doctorate and law programs to more than 23,000 students; Loyola University of Chicago, which awards bachelor's, master's, and doctoral degrees, first-professional degrees in dentistry, law, and medicine, and a master's degree in divinity to its more than 13,000 students; and Saint Xavier College, where popular recent majors among its 5,700 students were business, nursing, and education. The Illinois Institute of Technology enrolls more than 6,000 students and offers professional programs in the sciences, engineering, law, art, and architecture. The School of the Art Institute of Chicago, with more than 2,700 students, holds national stature in art instruction.

Among the city's many other institutions of higher learning are Chicago City-Wide College, Roosevelt University, Chicago State University, Columbia College, Dr. William M. Scholl College of Podiatric Medicine, Illinois College of Optometry, Rush University, and Vandercook College of Music. Northwestern University is located in nearby Evanston.

Libraries and Research Centers

The Chicago Public Library encompasses 75 branches, two regional libraries, and the central Harold Washington Library Center, which opened in 1991 and is one of the foremost educational and cultural resources in the city of Chicago. At 756,000 square feet, the library center is the largest municipal building in the world. The library's collection consists of about 6.5 million books, 14,500 periodicals and serials, 90,000 audiovisual titles, and 3 million microfiche. A special collection of books and materials in 90 foreign languages is maintained, and the library center is the repository for the Chicago Theater Collection, the Civil War Collection, and the Chicago Blues Archives. The library center also boasts an 18,000-square-foot children's library, a bustling business/science/technology division, and a Teacher Resource Center offering print and online resources to assist educators. On display throughout the building is an extensive public art collection.

Staff members in each library of the public library system build their own collections and tailor services to meet the needs of their local community. Since 1989, the city has built or renovated more than 40 branch libraries. Currently, new construction projects, renovations, expansions, and consolidation projects are underway. All of Chicago's public libraries offer free Internet access and free access to research databases.

The approximately 275 other libraries located in Chicago are affiliated with such entities as government agencies, colleges and universities, cultural and historical societies, professional organizations, research institutes, religious organizations, hospitals and medical associations, private corporations, and law firms.

The University of Chicago, internationally recognized for excellence in education and research, maintains a central library facility with more than 7 million printed works and 30 million manuscripts and archival pieces. Special collections are maintained in American and British literature, American history, theology and biblical criticism, American and British drama, and Continental literature. The University of Chicago operates seven separate facilities, including the D'Angelo Law Library and the Social Service Administration Library.

The Newberry Library, an independent research library, was founded in 1887. Free to the public, the library's non-circulating research materials number more than 1.4 million volumes; among the special collections are materials pertaining to Americana and American Indians.

One of the largest research libraries in Chicago is the Center for Research Libraries, an international not-for-profit consortium of colleges, universities, and libraries that makes available scholarly research resources to users everywhere. It houses more than 5 million books and periodicals; fields of study include Africa, South Asia, South East Asia, Latin America, and war crime trials. The Chicago Academy of Sciences' International Center for the Advancement of Scientific Literacy (ICASL) is the leading research organization in the world studying and measuring the impact of science and technology on public awareness. The National Opinion Research Center collects current opinion poll reports conducted for commercial television networks, newspapers, state governments, professional pollsters such as Gallup and Harris. The Chicago Historical Society maintains research collections on Chicago, the Civil War, Abraham Lincoln, Illinois, and United States history.

The Robert H. Lurie Comprehensive Cancer Center at Northwestern University is the only cancer center in Illinois. The center is dedicated to cancer care, research, prevention, and education. Other research centers in the Chicago area include those maintained by Bell Labs, Nalco Chemical, the ITT Research Institute, the Institute of Gas Technology, the Illinois State Psychiatric Institute, the Institute for Psychoanalysis, and the Institute on the Church in Urban-Industrial Society.

Public Library Information: Chicago Public Library, 400 South State Street, Chicago, IL 60605. Information Center, telephone (312)747-4300

Health Care

Chicago ranks among the country's leading centers for health care and referral as well as for medical training and research, generally due to the university hospitals, teaching centers, and medical facilities. Hospital facilities in Chicago have undergone major changes in the past 25 years, however. Between 1980 and 2004, the number of hospitals in Chicago has shrunk by nearly 35 percent, from 64 hospitals in 1980 to 42 in 2004, representing a decrease in hospital beds by nearly 50 percent.

The University of Chicago Hospitals, nationally recognized for training and research, are associated with the University of Chicago colleges of medicine, dentistry, nursing, and pharmacy; individual facilities are Bernard Mitchell Hospital, Wyler Children's Hospital, the Duchossois Center for Advanced Medicine, and Chicago Lying-in Hospital. A full range of general and specialized services are available as well as a chemical dependence program, corporate health services, an eating disorders program, geriatric and health evaluation services, and centers for treatment of kidney stones and sexually transmitted diseases.

One of Chicago's major privately-run health care facilities is Rush University Medical Center, which is affiliated with Rush Medical College and Rush School of Nursing. The 830-bed hospital operates centers for treatment of cancer, multiple sclerosis, cardiac ailments, sleep disorders, alcohol and substance abuse, Alzheimer's disease, epilepsy, and arthritis. The complex also houses organ and bone marrow transplant units as well as the Chicago and Northeastern Regional Poison Control Center. According to a 2004 report in *U.S. News & World Report's* "America's Best Hospitals" issue, Rush has earned more specialty rankings than any other hospital in Illinois.

Medical Information: Rush University Medical Center physician referral, (888)352-RUSH. University of Chicago Hospitals physician referral, (888)UCH-0200.

Recreation

Sightseeing

Chicago is an ethnically diverse, architecturally important, and culturally rich city. It can be appreciated from the observation floor of the Sears Tower, at 110 stories the third-tallest manmade structure in the world. In fact, three of the world's 10 tallest buildings are located in Chicago, along with the tallest apartment building, the largest hotel, the largest commercial structure, and the largest post office. Guided sightseeing tours are available for viewing the city's architecture, finance and business districts, ethnic neighborhoods, cultural institutions, and even gangland sites from the Prohibition Era.

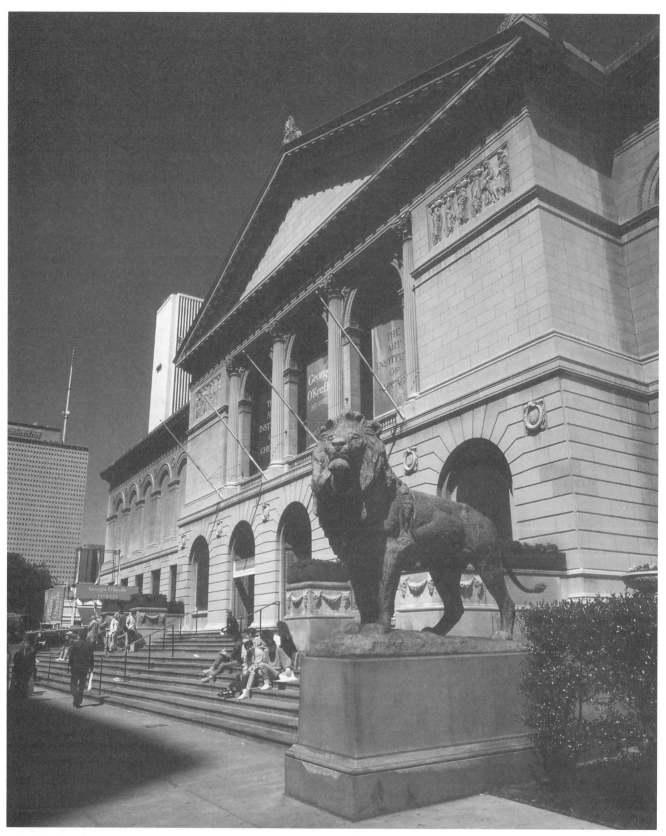

The Art Institute of Chicago has an international reputation for its collections of French Impressionist and Post-Impressionist paintings, as well as American art and photographs.

The distinctive Chicago School of Architecture, with its aesthetic credo, "form follows function," was shaped by such masters as Louis Sullivan, Frank Lloyd Wright, and a later functionalist architect, Ludwig Mies van der Rohe—all of whom designed buildings in the city and produced in Chicago a veritable living architectural museum. Also important are the city's outdoor sculpture and art works. Pablo Picasso's gift to Chicago, a 50-foot-tall sculpture of rusted steel at the Civic Center Plaza, has become a symbol of the city's modernity. Other works include Claes Oldenburg's *Batcolumn,* Alexander Calder's 53-foot-high red Flamingo stabile, Marc Chagall's *Four Seasons* mosaic, Louise Nevelson's *Dawn Shadow,* Joan Miro's *Chicago,* and Jean Dubuffet's *Monument with Standing Beast.*

The Shedd Aquarium, the world's largest indoor aquarium, cares for more than 21,000 aquatic mammals, reptiles, amphibians, invertebrates, and fishes. A major attraction is the Oceanarium, the world's largest indoor marine mammal pavilion, featuring beluga whales, dolphins, Alaskan sea otters, seals, and penguins. In 2003 the aquarium unveiled its Wild Reef shark exhibit. Next to the Shedd Aquarium, the Adler Planetarium and Astronomy Museum sits on a peninsula that juts a half-mile into Lake Michigan. The Museum of Science and Industry, founded in 1933, houses thousands of exhibits, including the Idea Factory and Omnimax Theatre; a full-scale, working coal mine, a WWII captured German submarine, a Boeing 727 airplane that visitors can walk through, and a walk-though model of a human heart. It was the first museum in North America to feature the concept of hands-on exhibits. The Chicago area's two zoos are the Brookfield Zoo and the Lincoln Park Zoo. Just north of the city, the Chicago Botanic Garden features an international collection of flora on 385 acres.

Arts and Culture

Chicago's major cultural institutions rank with the best in the world. The Chicago Symphony Orchestra plays a season of more than 100 concerts at Orchestra Hall from September to June and performs summer concerts at Ravinia Park in Highland Park. Equally prestigious is the Lyric Opera of Chicago, which stages classical and innovative operas at the recently renovated Civic Opera House.

Other musical offerings range from Dixieland jazz imported by the late Louis Armstrong to the electrified urban blues sound pioneered by Muddy Waters, frequently referred to as Chicago Blues. All-night jazz and blues clubs are a Chicago tradition. The Ravinia Festival is a summer season of outstanding classical, popular, and jazz concerts performed by well-known artists.

More than 50 producing theaters delight Chicago audiences with fare ranging from serious to satirical. The Goodman Theatre, Chicago's oldest and largest non-profit profes-

sional theater, presents a season of classical and modern dramatic productions. Chicago theater is perhaps best represented by Steppenwolf Theatre Company, a Tony Award-winning repertory company that focuses on new plays, neglected works, and re-interpretations of masterpieces. Since 1959, The Second City, a resident comedy company that produces biting satires, has had a direct influence on American comedy as its members have gone on to star on the "Saturday Night Live" and "SCTV" television programs and in Hollywood movies. Chicago's historic and architecturally significant theater houses include the restored 1920's Chicago Theatre, Shubert Theatre, and Auditorium Theatre, built by Dankmar Adler and Louis Sullivan in 1889. Chicago's active theater scene includes young companies such as the Lookingglass Theatre Company and dinner theater groups. There are also several dance companies in the city, including the Joffrey Ballet of Chicago.

The Art Institute of Chicago is another local institution with an international reputation. Its collection is recognized for French Impressionist and Post-Impressionist paintings and for comprehensive holdings of American arts and photographs. The Mexican Fine Arts Center Museum is the first Mexican museum in the United States and the only Latino museum accredited by the American Association of Museums; galleries of Polish, Swedish, Chinese, Japanese, and Korean art have opened in the city as well. The National Vietnam Veterans Art Museum houses a permanent collection of more than 500 pieces focusing on war from the soldiers' perspective. Chicago's love of art is even evidenced in the Loop's parking garage, where famous paintings are reproduced.

The Field Museum of Natural History, founded in 1893, is rated among the top museums in the world; its holdings number more than 16 million artifacts and specimens from the fields of anthropology, botany, geology, and zoology. A scientific research institution, the Field Museum examines life and culture from pre-history to the present time.

The Chicago Academy of Sciences, founded in 1857, was Chicago's first museum and features natural science exhibits as well as timely scientific displays. Among the special attractions are life-size dioramas on natural areas of the Great Lakes and the children's gallery with its lifelike animated dinosaurs and prehistoric creatures. The Academy's Peggy Notebaert Nature Museum features 73,000 square feet of interactive, environmental education. The city's oldest cultural institution is the Chicago Historical Society; its galleries are filled with folk art, furniture, costumes, and manuscripts and a unique audiovisual presentation of the Great Chicago Fire. The DuSable Museum is the nation's first museum dedicated to preserving, displaying, and interpreting the culture, history, and achievements of African Americans. The Museum of Contemporary Art, one of the largest of its kind in the country at 151,000 square feet, focuses on contemporary works that are often risk-taking and controversial. Its permanent collection includes works by Christo, Rene Magritte, and Andy Warhol, and at the Chicago Cultural Center, where admission is free, visitors can see the world's largest Tiffany stained-glass dome; the center houses the Museum of Broadcast Communications and hosts free daily concerts, films, lectures, and dance performances. The Chicago Public Library Cultural Center presents hundreds of free programs, concerts, and exhibitions annually.

Arts and Culture Information: Chicago Fine Arts Exchange, telephone (312)850-2787. Chicago Dance and Music Alliance, telephone (312)987-9296

Festivals and Holidays

The Mayor's Office of Special Events, The Chicago Park District, and the city's major cultural institutions sponsor events throughout the year, but special summer programming is designed to tap into Chicago's heritage and to attract tourists. The Chicago Blues Festival takes place the second weekend in June at the Petrillo Music Shell and brings the best blues musicians to one of the world's blues capitals for concerts, food, and exchange of memorabilia. The Printers Row Book Fair, in June, is the largest free literary event in the Midwest. Taste of Chicago, held over two weeks in late June and early July, features food sampling from Chicago restaurants as well as entertainment in Grant Park. Viva Chicago, held in August-September, is a festival celebrating Latino music, food, and arts and crafts at the Petrillo Music Shell. Other music festivals held annually in Chicago include Chicago Gospel Festival (June), Chicago Country Music Festival (June-July), Chicago Jazz Festival (August-September), Celtic Festival Chicago (September), and World Music Fest Chicago (September-October). Mayor Daley's Holiday Sports Festival is held in December. October's Chicago International Film Festival is one of the largest in the country.

Chicago's city parks offer a wealth of free activities in the summer, such as the Grant Park Symphony Orchestra's four weekly concerts at the nation's largest free symphonic music festival.

Festivals Information: Mayor's Office of Special Events, 121 North LaSalle Street, Room 703, Chicago, IL 60602; telephone (312)744-3315

Sports for the Spectator

Chicago fields at least one team in each of the major professional sports and is one of the only cities in the United States with two professional baseball teams in the Major League Baseball Association. The Chicago Cubs compete in the central division of the National League and play their home games at Wrigley Field, a turn-of-the-century steel and concrete structure where seats are close to the field. The Chicago White Sox of the American League's central division play their home games at U.S. Cellular Field on the city's South Side. The teams—and their fans—enjoy a fierce rivalry. The Chicago Bears of the National Football League's National Conference compete in central division home games at the recently renovated Soldier Field. The Chicago Fire, Chicago's Major League Soccer franchise, also play at Soldier Field. The Chicago Blackhawks of the National Hockey League and the Chicago Bulls of the National Basketball Association play their home schedules at the United Center.

Auto racing fans can view competition at Chicago Motor Speedway in Cicero, while horse racing action takes place from July to November at Hawthorne Race Course in Stickney/Cicero.

Sports for the Participant

The Chicago Park District maintains some 552 parks spread out over 7,300 acres, including Lincoln Park, Grant Park, Jackson Park, and Washington Park. Chicago's paved lakefront pathway stretches along the shore from the south side of the city to the north side; thousands of Chicago residents and visitors use the path daily for cycling, strolling, running, in-line skating, and even commuting from one end of the city to the other. Located in the metropolitan area are forest preserves, six golf courses, tennis courts, swimming pools and lagoons, 29 beaches, and more than 1,000 athletic fields. In the summertime Chicago becomes the country's largest beach town as sun fanciers flock to 29 miles of lakefront beaches and yacht clubs to enjoy watersports. Lake Michigan, once one of the most industrially abused regions of the Great Lakes, has experienced a remarkable environmental recovery. The fishing season on Lake Michigan runs year round, while the lake's boating season generally extends from May 15 to October 15; the Park District maintains jurisdiction over the city's nine harbors.

A major attraction is the annual Chicago to Mackinac Island (Michigan) sailboat race, during which participants sail the length of Lake Michigan. Chicago boasts two golf courses built atop a former solid-waste dump. The prize-winning environmental engineering project, called Harborside International Golf Center, is only 16 minutes from downtown Chicago.

The LaSalle Bank Chicago Marathon, started in 1977 as the Mayor Daley Marathon, has become one of the most prestigious—and largest— marathon events in the world. Held each October, nearly 40,000 elite and recreational runners complete the 26.2 mile race that begins and ends at Grant Park. Hundreds of thousands of spectators line the course, which passes through the downtown Loop and many of the city's ethnic neighborhoods. Due to its fast, flat course, several world records have been set at the Chicago Marathon.

Shopping and Dining

Chicago's commercial district, formerly confined to the area known as The Loop, which was defined by a circuit of elevated trains, now pushes north of the Chicago River to Oak Street. Known as the "Magnificent Mile," the shopping area is considered the Rodeo Drive of the Midwest. Here, in and around buildings of architectural interest, are located some of the world's finest specialty stores. Water Tower Place on North Michigan is a seven-level modern shopping emporium with Chicago-based Marshall Field's and Lord & Taylor. A block away, Chicago Place, an eight-level mall, is anchored by Saks Fifth Avenue and houses Talbots, Ann Taylor, and Chiaroscuro. American Girl Place is a popular destination for young girls and their parents, where they can purchase American Girl dolls and accessories, have tea in the café, or view a show in the American Girl Theater. At 900 North Michigan Shops are Bloomingdale's, Coach, Gucci, and teuscher Chocolates of Switzerland. On nearby Oak Street one can find designs from Paris, Milan, and New York. North of the bustling Michigan Avenue shopping area is the Armitage-Halsted-Webster shopping area, with upscale restaurants and shops. Newly refurbished State Street, located downtown, offers a seven-block shopping experience at such landmarks as Carson Pirie Scott & Company and the flagship Marshall Field's.

Downtown Chicago features a remarkable diversity of bookstores, ranging from the Afrocentric Bookstore to The Savvy Traveler. Book lovers might like to pick up a copy of the Greater Loop Book District's pamphlet, showing the location of more than 20 bookstores in the Loop. It is available at airports, bookstores, and all visitor information centers.

On the waterfront, Navy Pier offers more than 50 acres of parks, promenades, gardens, shops, restaurants, and entertainment in a renovated warehouse. On North Orleans Street are the Merchandise Mart, the world's largest wholesale center, and the Chicago Apparel Center.

Chicago is served by some of the nation's finest restaurants. Every type of cuisine, from ethnic to traditional American fare, is available at restaurants in metropolitan Chicago. The city's eateries, housed in elegant turn-of-the-century hotels, modern chrome and glass structures, and neighborhood cafes, are recognized for consistently high quality. Among Chicago's most renowned restaurants are Ambria, Benkay, Charlie Trotter's, The Dining Room (Ritz-Carlton Hotel), Entre Nous (Fairmont Hotel), Frontera Grill, Gordon, Jackie's, La Tour (Park Hyatt), Nick's Fish Market, Restaurant Suntory, Seasons (Four Seasons Hotel), and Yoshi's Cafe. Once known as the city of steak houses by the dozens, Chicago's superior steak restaurants now include Morton's of Chicago, Gibsons Steakhouse, the Palm Restaurant, Eli's The Place for Steak, Chicago Chop House, and The Saloon. The deep-dish style of pizza originated in Chicago.

Visitor Information: Chicago Convention and Tourism Bureau, 2301 South Lake Shore Drive Chicago, IL 60616; telephone (312)567-8500. Chicago Office of Tourism, telephone (312)744-2400. Visitor Information Centers are located at the Chicago Cultural Center and Chicago Water Works.

Convention Facilities

Chicago, one of the most popular convention cities in the United States, is home to McCormick Place, the largest exhibition center in North America. Set on the edge of Lake Michigan, McCormick Place contains more than 2.2 million square feet of exhibit space. The complex also features the 4,249-seat Arie Crown Theater, three 345-seat theaters, 112 meeting rooms, assembly seating for 10,000 people, and 8,000 parking spaces. The addition of the adjoining McCormick Place West, expected to be completed in 2008, will add approximately 470,000 square feet of exhibition space and 250,000 square feet of meeting room space to the facility. Chicago is known for its mix of gracious dowager hotels and modern glass towers with spectacular views of Lake Michigan.

Navy Pier offers space for mid-size events with 170,000 square feet of exhibit space and 36 meeting rooms. Special meeting facilities are available at museums, theaters, stadiums, corporations, and colleges and universities in the Chicago area.

Convention Information: Chicago Convention and Tourism Bureau, 2301 South Lake Shore Drive, Chicago, IL 60616; telephone (312)567-8500

Transportation

Approaching the City

The destination of the majority of air traffic into Chicago is O'Hare International Airport, located 17 miles northwest of downtown, where most major domestic and international commercial carriers schedule more than 880,000 flights annually. One of the busiest air facilities in the world,

O'Hare accommodates more than 190,000 passengers who pass through the gates of the architecturally impressive terminal each day. Continental Airport Express provides van service between O'Hare and all downtown hotels, the North Shore, and Oak Brook suburbs; Chicago Transit Authority (CTA) provides rapid transit train service between O'Hare and downtown. Taxis are available at the lower level curbfront of all terminals.

Several other commuter and general aviation airports are located throughout the Chicago metropolitan area; among them are Midway Airport, ten miles from downtown, which is known as the "premier point-to-point airport in the nation".

Passenger rail service into Chicago is provided by Amtrak from cities in all regions of the United States; the Chicago South Shore and South Bend is an intercity commuter rail line. The Regional Transit Authority (RTA) operates bus and rapid-transit service into the city from the distant suburbs. Regional rail transportation is available through Metropolitan Rail (Metra).

A somewhat complex network of interstate highways facilitates access into the metropolitan area as well as the Loop district. Approaching from the northwest is I-94, which merges with the John F. Kennedy Expressway leading downtown. I-294 (the Tri-State Tollway), an outerbelt on the west side, joins I-80 to the south. Other westerly approaches are: State Road 5, the East-West Tollway, which becomes I-290; I-90, the North-West Tollway, which intersects I-290; and I-55, the Adlai Stevenson Expressway. Approaches from the south include I-94, the Calumet Expressway; I-57; and I-90, the Chicago Skyway; all of these merge with the Dan Ryan Expressway leading into the city. Running south of Chicago is I-80, which connects with I-55, I-57, I-90, and I-94; near the Indiana border I-80 joins I-90 to become the Northern Indiana Toll Road.

Traveling in the City

Chicago streets conform to a consistent grid pattern; major thoroughfares include east-west State Street and north-south Madison Street, which intersect downtown and provide the numerical orientation for all addresses. Lake Shore Drive, affording a scenic view of Lake Michigan and the skyline, extends along the lake from the northern to the southern city limits.

Metra runs commuter trains and buses between the city and suburbs. The Chicago Transit Authority (CTA) operates bus, subway, and elevated train (the "El") routes between the Loop and the nearby suburbs. Cabs are readily available in the downtown area. Parking in Chicago can be problematic; for this reason several city-run parking garages are available.

Communications

Newspapers and Magazines

Chicago's major daily newspapers are the *Chicago Tribune* and the *Chicago Sun-Times,* both of which are distributed in morning and Sunday editions and maintain an Internet presence. A number of African American and ethnic newspapers circulate regularly. More than a hundred community and foreign-language newspapers are published in the city, serving Lithuanian, Polish, Ukrainian, and Hispanic-speaking residents, among others. *The Chicago Reader,* an alternative weekly, covers entertainment, social, and cultural issues.

Chicago is a national leader in publishing and printing; more than 600 newspapers and periodicals originate in the city, including *American Libraries, Ebony, Jet, Poetry* and *Your Money.* Specialized trade magazines cover a comprehensive range of subjects such as health care, international trade, consumer issues, industry and trade, agriculture, politics, business, and professional information. The University of Chicago is the source of several scholarly journals; among the areas covered are philology, literature, the sciences, ethics, business, labor, history, library science, medicine, and law.

Television and Radio

Chicago is a broadcast media center for a wide region of the Midwest. Television viewers receive programming from 12 commercial, public, and independent stations based in the Chicago metropolitan area. Television programs filmed in Chicago for a national audience include *The Oprah Winfrey Show* and the movie review program *Ebert and Roeper.* Nearly 60 AM and 11 FM radio stations broadcast a complete selection of formats, including all major types of music, news, talk shows, public interest features, and market reports.

Media Information: Chicago Tribune, Tribune Publishing, 435 North Michigan, Chicago, IL 60611; telephone (312)222-3232. *Chicago Sun-Times,* 350 North Orleans, Chicago, IL 60654; telephone (312)321-3000. *Chicago Reader,* 11 East Illinois, Chicago, IL 60611; telephone (312)828-0350

Chicago Online

Chicago Convention and Visitors Bureau. Available www .chicago.il.org

Chicago Historical Society. Available www.chicagohs.org

Chicago Public Library. Available www.chipublib.org/cpl .html

Chicago Public Schools. Available www.cps.k12.il.us

Chicago Tribune. Available www.chicago.tribune.com

City of Chicago Home Page. Available www.egov.cityof chicago.org/city/webportal/home.do

Illinois Department of Commerce and Community Affairs. Available www.illinois.gov

McCormick Place Complex. Available www.mccormick place.com

Selected Bibliography

Bellow, Saul, *The Adventures of Augie March* (New York: Avon, 1977, 1953)

Chicago Sun Times, Adrienne Drell, eds. *20th Century Chicago: 100 Years 100 Voices.* (Chicago: Sports Publishing, 1999)

Miller, Donald L., *City of the Century: The Epic of Chicago and the Making of America* (New York: Simon & Schuster, 1996)

Samuelson, Tim, Cheryl Kent et al. *Above Chicago: A New Collection of Historical and Original Aerial Photographs of Chicago.* (Cameron & Company, 1992)

Sinclair, Upton, *The Jungle* (Urbana: University of Illinois Press, 1988)

Peoria

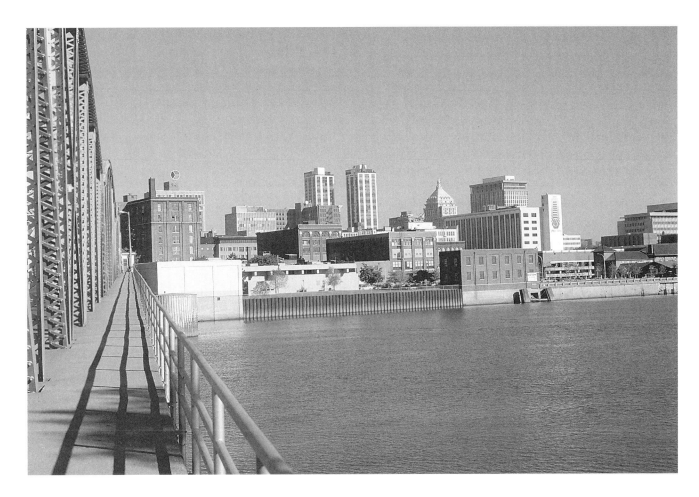

The City in Brief

Founded: 1819 (incorporated, 1835)

Head Official: Mayor David P. Ransburg (since 2001)

City Population
  1980: 124,600
  1990: 113,508
  2000: 112,936
  2003 estimate: 112,907
  Percent change, 1990–2000: −0.5%
  U.S. rank in 1980: 126th
  U.S. rank in 1990: 157th (State rank: 3rd)
  U.S. rank in 2000: 223rd

Metropolitan Area Population
  1980: 366,000
  1990: 339,172
  2000: 347,387

Percent change, 1990–2000: 2.4%
U.S. rank in 1980: 90th
U.S. rank in 1990: Not reported
U.S. rank in 2000: 116th

Area: 40.9 square miles (2000)
Elevation: 652 feet above sea level
Average Annual Temperature: 50.7° F
Average Annual Precipitation: 36.25 inches of rain, 25.10 inches of snow

Major Economic Sectors: Agriculture, manufacturing, information technologies
Unemployment Rate: 6.2% (February 2005)
Per Capita Income: $20,512 (1999)

2002 FBI Crime Index Total: Not reported

Major Colleges and Universities: Bradley University; Eureka College; Illinois Central College

Daily Newspaper: *Journal Star*

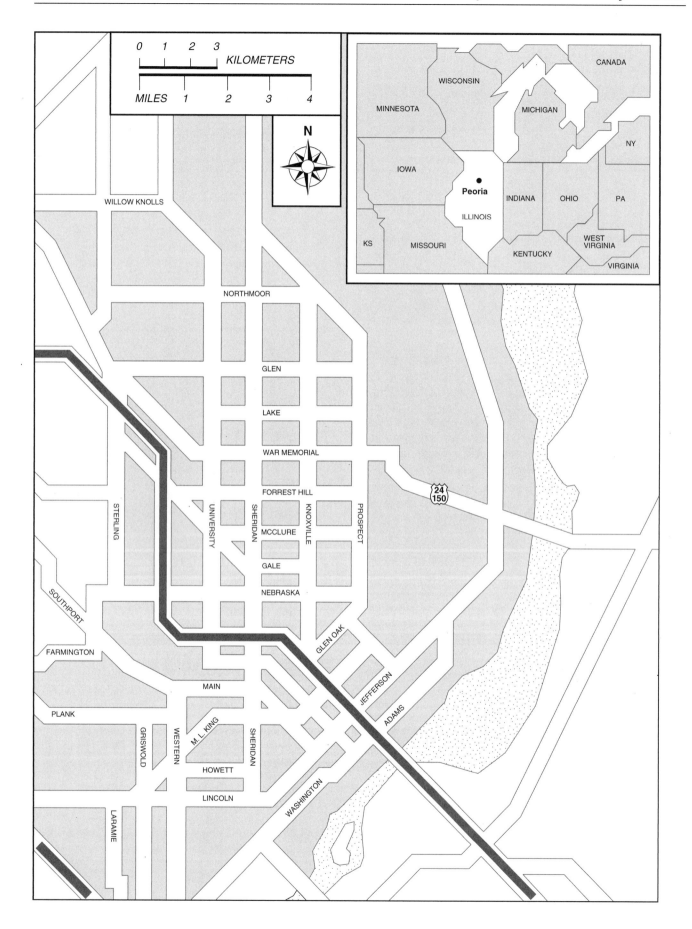

Introduction

Peoria is the seat of Peoria County and the center of an urban complex consisting of Peoria Heights, West Peoria, Bartonville, Bellevue, East Peoria, Creve Coeur, and Pekin. The city is considered the oldest continuously inhabited American community west of the Allegheny Mountains. Another of Peoria's distinctions is its typicality: in terms of such demographic characteristics as median age and purchasing patterns, the city's general makeup is almost identical to that of the United States as a whole, thus making it an ideal test market for consumer researchers.

Geography and Climate

Peoria is set in a level tableland surrounded by gently rolling terrain on the Illinois River. The continental climate produces changeable weather and a wide range of temperature extremes. June and September are generally the most pleasant months; an extended period of warm, dry weather occurs during Indian Summer in late October and early November. Precipitation is heaviest during the growing season and lowest in midwinter.

Area: 40.9 square miles (2000)

Elevation: 652 feet above sea level

Average Temperatures: January, 22° F; July, 76° F; annual average, 50.7° F

Average Annual Precipitation: 36.25 inches of rain, 25.10 inches of snow

History

French Explore Peoria Tribe Territory

Native Americans lived in the area surrounding present-day Peoria for 12,000 years before the coming of Europeans. They took fish from the fresh waters of Peoria Lake and hunted for game in the surrounding valley. They called the river valley *Pimiteoui* (pronounced Pee-Mee-Twee), meaning "land of great abundance" or "fat lake." The valley was known far and wide among Native Americans as a great winter hunting ground.

Peoria was the first European settlement in Illinois and one of the earliest in the middle of America. French explorers Louis Joliet and Pere Marquette canoed into the river valley in 1673 during their exploration of the Mississippi River. Six years later another French explorer, Robert Cavelier, sieur de La Salle, ventured down the Illinois River with a party of 30 men to establish forts and trading posts in order to strengthen France's hold on the middle of America. Because it was winter and the weather inclement, the party was forced to land; LaSalle built a small fort on the east bluff of the Peoria river valley and called it Fort Crevecoeur ("broken heart"). The fort was the first European building to be built in the middle of America. It was mysteriously abandoned after four months and these words were found burned into the side of an unfinished boat found on the site: "Nous sommes tous sauvages" (We are all savages).

With the help of the tribes of the Illini nation, in 1691 the French military, under the charge of Henri de Tonti, built a massive fortification, called Fort Pimiteoui, on Peoria's shores, near the site of present-day Detweiller Marina on the popular Pimiteoui Trail that winds along the riverfront. Outside the walls of the fort, a French settlement grew among the Illini villages, becoming the first European settlement in the state of Illinois.

By 1763 the British flag was being flown over Illinois, but the French Peorians persevered and enjoyed life much as they would have done in the rural countryside of France. One of the villagers, Jean Baptiste Maillet, moved the core of the French village to the site of present-day Downtown Riverfront Park in 1778. Another villager, Jean-Baptiste Du Sable, left in 1784 and became the founder of Chicago.

Following the American Revolution, a number of Peorians received land grants from the U.S. Congress in gratitude for their support during the war. In October 1812, the area felt the pressure of thousands of American settlers heading west; Native American Potawatomi villages in the region were destroyed by troops under the command of the Illinois Territory Governor Ninian Edwards. A month later, American soldiers overran the French village and deported its inhabitants to a wilderness around Alton, Illinois. After 120 years, French Peoria was gone forever.

American soldiers built Fort Clark in 1813; today the fort is commemorated in the riverfront Liberty Park Pavilion. The first American settlers began farming there in 1819. Soon the small village experienced a great economic and population boom.

Economic Growth Paired with Historic Events

With its abundance of natural resources, Peoria industries grew up. They included meat-packing, casting foundries, pottery makers, wholesale warehousing, distilleries, and earth-moving and farm machinery manufacturers. Ancient Indian trails were turned into solid roads, and steamboats and ferries replaced canoes. The city became a massive railroad hub. The area's fresh, clear water, abundance of corn, and ease of transportation contributed to make the city the "Whiskey Capital of the World" by 1900. Distilleries and their related industries brought tremendous wealth, and Peoria became one of the largest tax-paying districts in the country. Prosperity enabled city leaders to strive to develop a model city.

State-of-the-art municipal buildings were erected, such as the red sandstone City Hall (1889). Models of Peoria's innovative schools like the Grail School (1892) were exhibited across the nation. Massive churches such as St. Mary's Cathedral (1889) were built. Beautiful parks such as Glen Oak Park (1896) and Laura Bradley Park (1897) were laid out. Present-day historic districts such as High Street-Moss Avenue, Roanoke-Randolph Street, and Glen Oak Avenue evoke an era that Peoria endeavors to preserve.

The city of Peoria has been the site of historic events and the home of famous Americans. In 1854 Abraham Lincoln, rebutting a speech by Stephen Douglas, for the first time publicly denounced slavery as incompatible with American institutions; this clash predated the famous Lincoln-Douglas debates by four years. The original mold strain for penicillin was discovered by scientists in Peoria. The first African American person to vote in the United States did so in Peoria on April 4, 1870. Peorian Herb Jamison was a medalist in the first modern Olympics in Greece in 1896. A short list of native Peorians include the late Senator Everett Dirksen; Betty Friedan, author of *The Feminine Mystique*; and comedian and actor Richard Pryor.

In the second half of the twentieth century Peoria was awarded an All-America City designation three times; it exists today as the quintessential Midwestern American city. In 2004 *Forbes* ranked Peoria the "#1 most affordable U.S. metropolitan area in which to live." A vaudeville-era phrase "to play in Peoria" is still used to characterize the thoughts and habits of a "typical" American.

Historical Information: Peoria Historical Society, 611 SW Washington Street, Peoria, IL 61602; telephone (309)674-1921

Population Profile

Metropolitan Area Residents
1980: 366,000
1990: 339,172
2000: 347,387
Percent change, 1990–2000: 2.4%
U.S. rank in 1980: 90th
U.S. rank in 1990: Not reported
U.S. rank in 2000: 116th

City Residents
1980: 124,600
1990: 113,508
2000: 112,936
2003 estimate: 112,907
Percent change, 1990–2000: −0.5%
U.S. rank in 1980: 126th
U.S. rank in 1990: 157th
U.S. rank in 2000: 223rd

Density: 2,543.4 people per square mile (2000)

Racial and ethnic characteristics (2000)
  White: 78,254
  Black or African American: 27,992
  American Indian and Alaska Native: 229
  Asian: 2,629
  Native Hawaiian and Pacific Islander: 42
  Hispanic or Latino (may be of any race): 2,839
  Other: 1,355

Percent of residents born in state: 72.3% (2000)

Age characteristics (2000)
  Population under 5 years old: 8,366
  Population 5 to 9 years old: 8,408
  Population 10 to 14 years old: 7,777
  Population 15 to 19 years old: 8,573
  Population 20 to 24 years old: 9,481
  Population 25 to 34 years old: 15,578
  Population 35 to 44 years old: 15,184
  Population 45 to 54 years old: 14,362
  Population 55 to 59 years old: 5,090
  Population 60 to 64 years old: 4,084
  Population 65 to 74 years old: 7,688
  Population 75 to 84 years old: 6,052
  Population 85 years and over: 2,293
  Median age: 33.8 years

Births (2003, Peoria County)
  Total number: 2,602

Deaths (2002)
  Total number: 1,801 (of which, 21 were infants under the age of 1 year)

Money income (1999)
  Per capita income: $20,512
  Median household income: $36,397
  Total households: 45,094

Number of households with income of . . .
  less than $10,000: 5,804
  $10,000 to $14,999: 3,565
  $15,000 to $24,999: 6,567
  $25,000 to $34,999: 5,814
  $35,000 to $49,999: 6,947

$50,000 to $74,999: 8,038
$75,000 to $99,999: 3,937
$100,000 to $149,999: 2,855
$150,000 to $199,999: 677
$200,000 or more: 890

Percent of families below poverty level: 14.1% (62.8% of which were female householder families with related children under 5 years)

2002 FBI Crime Index Total: Not reported

Municipal Government

The city of Peoria operates under a council-manager form of government. One council member is elected from each of five districts and five members are elected at large. The mayor is the official head of the city; he heads the council and is elected by the total electorate.

Head Official: Mayor David P. Ransburg (since 2001)

Total Number of City Employees: 860 (2005)

City Information: City of Peoria, 419 Fulton, Peoria, IL 61602; telephone (309)494-8524

Economy

Major Industries and Commercial Activity

Located at the center of a fertile agricultural region, with corn and soybeans as principal crops, Peoria is an important livestock and grain exporting market. Farm production and livestock sales in the three-county area are among the highest in the nation. Peoria is surrounded by rich bituminous coal fields that hold reserves estimated to last for 150 years and slated for worldwide distribution.

Manufacturing is a major industry; more than 200 diversified firms make nearly 1,000 different products. Peoria is the headquarters of two of the largest U.S. earth-moving equipment makers, which record an average of $2 billion in shipments annually. Local companies produce more than 14 percent of the country's internal-combustion engines and about 8 percent of all construction machinery in North America. The city is also the base for several distilleries and breweries.

The National Center for Agriculture Research is operated in Peoria by the United States Department of Agriculture; there, soil testing and chemical development are important areas of research. Peoria has formed the Biotechnical Research and Development Consortium to allow private devel-

opment and marketing of the products developed at the center's Agricultural Research Lab and to expand the use of patents into the private sector.

Peoria is a main test market for several national consumer research firms such as Nielsen Data Markets, Inc., which has established one of its six facilities in the city. Health care, education, insurance, finance, and government are the other primary non-manufacturing sectors.

Items and goods produced: tractors, beverages, alcohol and solvents, brick, tile, caskets, castings, cordage, cotton goods, fencing and wire products, nails, animal feeds, food and dairy products, pharmaceuticals, steel, paper, household products, storage batteries, electric motor rails and bases, air-conditioning equipment, furnaces, oil burners, road machinery, heavy graders, strawboard, tools, dies, labels, grease and hides, millworking

Incentive Programs—New and Existing Companies

Local programs—Business is encouraged in Peoria through a variety of local programs. Among economic incentives are sales and property tax credits and exemptions, and industrial revenue bonds. Six Urban Enterprise Zones have been established in the Peoria metropolitan area; benefits include state tax exemptions and credits, building permit waivers, and property tax abatement. The Economic Development Council for Central Illinois (EDC) assists Peoria-area businesses in start-up, growth, or expansion.

State programs—In 1977 the Illinois legislature adopted the Tax Increment Allocation Redevelopment Act to provide municipalities with a unique tool to finance and stimulate urban redevelopment. Through the use of Tax Increment Financing (TIF), cities can stimulate private investment by offering incentives to attract and retain businesses, improve their community areas, and maintain a well-educated and highly trained labor force.

Illinois Governor Rod Blagojevich has implemented the Opportunity Returns regional economic development plan throughout the state of Illinois. The state has been divided into ten regions that have common economic strengths and needs; specific economic development plans are created for each region. Opportunity Returns is considered the most aggressive and comprehensive plan for job creation in Illinois history.

Job training programs—Job training is available through state agencies and educational institutions. The Workforce Network is a partnership between local and state workforce organizations that enables them to coordinate their services and offer them through a one-stop system. Their Career Resource Center offers job search, education, and career-training information in a user-friendly environment.

Development Projects

In 2005 Governor Blagojevich announced the Turner Center for Entrepreneurship at Bradley University would receive $250,000 in funding from the Illinois Department of Commerce and Economic Opportunity to further expand its programs. Such programs will include a financial award program of up to $5,000 designed to help small business owners and entrepreneurs obtain professional services for business plan assistance, evaluation of startup and expansion plans, and other approved support services.

Work began in 2002 on a $400 million interstate project that will result in the reconstruction of Interstate 74, which intersects Peoria. When completed the expanded roadway—one of the heaviest traveled sections of I-74—will provide easier access and have improved lighting and landscaping.

Economic Development Information: The Economic Development Council for Central Illinois, 124 SW Adams Street, Suite 300, Peoria, IL 61602-1388; telephone (309)676-7500; Illinois Department of Commerce and Community Affairs, 100 West Randolph Street, Suite 3-400, Chicago, IL 60601; telephone (312)814-7179

Commercial Shipping

With access to three interstate and four federal highways, metropolitan Peoria is linked to markets nationwide by 137 motor freight carriers, 99 of which maintain local terminals, and 13 railroads. Air cargo transfer facilities are available at Greater Peoria Regional Airport and two private airfields. Four barge lines transport more than 48 million tons during a year-round navigation season through the Peoria Lock and Dam, a major link from the Gulf of Mexico to the St. Lawrence Seaway. Peoria is a Foreign Trade Zone.

Labor Force and Employment Outlook

Peoria workers are recognized for their high productivity, which exceeds the state and national averages. More than half the work force is engaged in white-collar occupations in retail trade, professional services, and government; manufacturing accounts for a large portion of the work force. Nearly 70 percent of workers have at least a high school degree. Manufacturers and agribusinesses are said to have been successful in retraining and modernizing the work force through the strong training networks between the private and education sectors.

Chemical distillation of grain and corn, paper products and printed material, coal production, and automotive parts are gaining rapidly as major manufacturing areas. Peoria's has always been a strong retail market; further retail development in the downtown area and more strip malls are expected.

The following is a summary of data regarding the Peoria metropolitan area labor force, 2004 annual average.

Size of non-agricultural labor force: 174,700

Number of workers employed in ...
  construction and mining: 8,400
  manufacturing: 28,200
  trade, transportation and utilities: 33,100
  information: 3,000
  financial activities: 8,500
  professional and business services: 17,200
  educational and health services: 30,400
  leisure and hospitality: 17,500
  other services: 7,400
  government: 21,000

Average hourly earnings of production workers employed in manufacturing: $17.88

Unemployment rate: 6.2% (February 2005)

Largest employers	Number of employees
Caterpillar, Inc.	17,847
St. Francis Medical Center	4,250
School District 150	2,847
Methodist Medical Center	2,600
Keystone Steel and Wire Company	1,675
AES Great Plains-CILCO	1,600
Bradley University	1,200
Komatsu America International	1,100

Cost of Living

The following is a summary of data regarding several key cost of living factors in the Peoria area.

2004 (3rd Quarter) ACCRA Average House Price: $280,500

2004 (3rd Quarter) ACCRA Cost of Living Index: 98.2 (U.S. average = 100.0)

State income tax rate: 3.0%

State sales tax rate: 6.25% (1% on food and drugs)

Local income tax rate: None

Local sales tax rate: 1.5% (2005)

Property tax rate: 7.9419% per $100 assessed valuation (2002)

Education and Research

Elementary and Secondary Schools

The Peoria Public Schools District #150 is the fifth-largest public elementary and secondary school system in the state of Illinois. A seven-member, nonpartisan board of education appoints a superintendent by majority vote.

The following is a summary of data regarding the Peoria public schools as of the 2003–2004 school year.

Total enrollment: 15,001

Number of facilities
    elementary schools: 14
    middle schools: 14
    senior high schools: 5

Student/teacher ratio: elementary, 18.7:1; middle and secondary, 20.3:1

Teacher salaries
    average: $52,741.00

Funding per pupil (2002-2003): $5,379.00

Offering private educations are the Peoria Catholic Diocese, Concordia Lutheran, the Hebrew Day School, Peoria Academy, and Peoria Christian.

Public Schools Information: Peoria Public Schools, 3202 N. Wisconsin Avenue, Peoria, IL 61603

Colleges and Universities

Bradley University, founded in 1897, enrolls more than 6,000 undergraduates and offers 90 undergraduate and 32 graduate programs in such fields as business and accounting, all major engineering specialties, music, nursing, and teacher education. Eureka College, located in Eureka, is a four-year liberal arts college and is the alma mater of former President Ronald Reagan. The University of Illinois College of Medicine at Peoria, the Bradley University School of Nursing, and nursing schools at OSF Saint Francis Medical Center and Methodist Medical Center grant degrees in medical sciences and provide continuing education for health care professionals throughout the Midwest.

Illinois Central College is a two-year institution that schedules courses for more than 12,000 students in university transfer curricula and vocational and continuing education programs. Degrees are offered in 105 fields of study; certificates are offered in more than 60 subjects. Among colleges and universities within commuting distance of Peoria are Illinois State University in Normal, Western Illinois University in Macomb, and Carl Sandburg College and Knox College in Galesburg.

Libraries and Research Centers

The Peoria Public Library maintains a central facility with more than 800,000 volumes and more than 1,300 periodi-

cal titles as well as music recordings, videos, and DVDs; subject interests include business, census materials, early government documents, genealogy, and local history. The library's comprehensive Internet website allows patrons to access the card catalog and research databases. In addition to the main library facility, the library operates five branches. The city's other major library is the Cullom-Davis Library on the Bradley University campus. Holdings total more than 536,000 volumes, and special collections include federal and state documents as well as material pertaining to industrial arts history, Abraham Lincoln, and oral history; the library also houses the Harry L. Spooner Library of the Peoria Historical Society. Among the more than 60 libraries in Peoria are those associated with colleges, hospitals, churches, corporations, and government agencies.

Bradley University supports the Institute for Urban Affairs and Business Research plus research centers in computers and technology. Work done at Peoria's National Center for Agricultural Utilization Research, one of four USDA Agricultural Research Service Labs made possible the mass production of penicillin and the early and economical production of dextran as a blood-volume expander.

Public Library Information: Peoria Public Library, 107 NE Monroe Street, Peoria, IL 61602-1070; (309)497-2000

Health Care

The Peoria metropolitan area is served by seven hospitals supplying nearly 2,600 beds. Among health care professionals affiliated with hospitals, clinics, and other facilities are 836 physicians, 190 dentists, and more than 2,000 nurses. Major hospitals and medical centers include OSF Saint Francis Medical Center (home to the only Level I trauma center in Central Illinois), Methodist Medical Center of Illinois, and Proctor Community Hospital. A full range of services are available at Peoria's hospitals, including cardiovascular services, cancer care, maternity care, bariatric medicine, and children's services. Specialized treatment is available at St. Jude Children's Research Hospital, the Midwest affiliate of St. Jude Children's Research Hospital in Tennessee; the Institute for Physical Medicine and Rehabilitation; and the Allied Agencies Center, which provides research, therapy, and education and training for handicapped patients. Also located in the city are the American Red Cross Peoria Regional Blood Center and Marvin Hult Health Education Center.

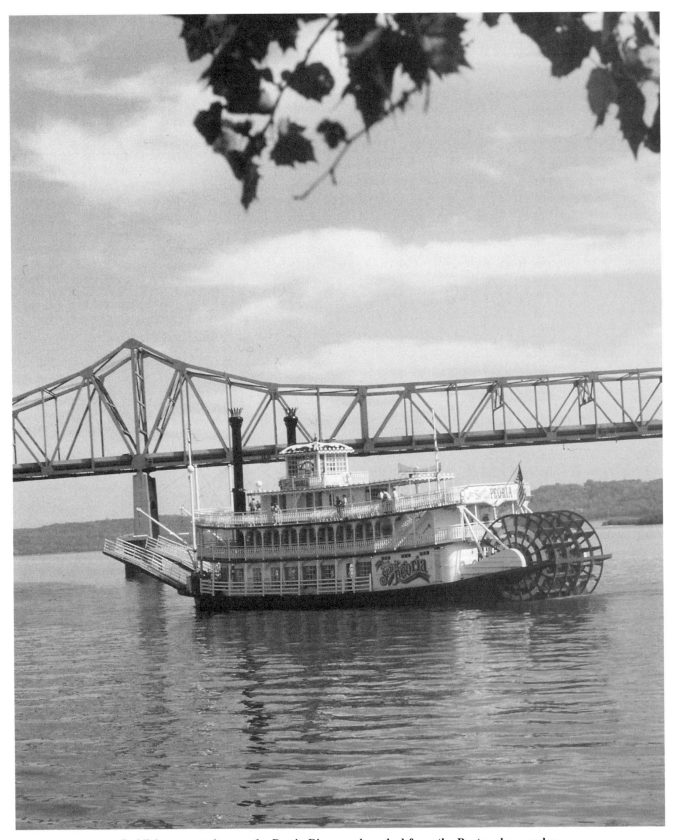

Paddleboat excursions on the Peoria River are launched from the Boatworks complex.

Recreation

Sightseeing

Visitors can get the best experience of the city during the months of May through October, when CityLink provides a two-hour historic trolley tour with narration provided by the Peoria Historical Society.

Glen Oak Park is a 100-acre park with a zoo, conservatory, and gardens; zoo animals range from large cats and marsupials to reptiles and amphibians. The Wildlife Prairie State Park is a 2,000 acre zoological park that provides a habitat for animals native to Illinois, including bison, elk, wolves, cougars, bears, waterfowl, and American bald eagles. The park also contains a country store, pioneer farmstead, walking trails, and a miniature railroad that runs through the grounds. Parks along the riverfront host concerts, festivals, and outdoor sports activities.

Aspects of Peoria's agricultural heritage are the focus of tours of the National Center for Agricultural Utilization Research, Linden Hills Farms, Tanners Orchard, Caterpillar Inc., McGlothlin Farm Park, and Wildlife Prairie Park.

Arts and Culture

The Lakeview Museum of Arts and Sciences houses permanent collections of Illinois folk art and African art, a planetarium, and a children's Discovery Center. The African American Hall of Fame is devoted to the collection, study, and exhibition of African American life and culture.

Peoria performing arts organizations include the Peoria Symphony, Peoria Ballet Company, Opera Illinois, Peoria Area Civic Chorale, and a chapter of the Sweet Adelines. Theater in Peoria is represented by such organizations as Corn Stock Theatre, Peoria Players, Eastlight Theatre, One World Theatre Company, and Zellmer's Dinner Theater.

Festivals and Holidays

Peoria's largest annual event is the Heart of Illinois Fair, which attracts nearly 250,000 people. The celebration of Independence Day is capped by the Fourth of July fireworks display on the riverfront. Oktoberfest, held in September, is a festival that celebrates German culture and food. The century-old Santa Claus Parade, the country's longest running event of its kind, takes place each year on Thanksgiving Day.

Sports for the Spectator

The Peoria Chiefs, a Class A affiliate of the St. Louis Cardinals, are league leaders each year in home game attendance. David Lamb, author of *Stolen Season,* numbers the Chiefs' stadium among his ten favorite places to watch a ball game. The Peoria Rivermen compete in the East Coast Hockey League and play their home games in the modern indoor facility, the Peoria Civic Center. Both Bradley University and Illinois Central College field competitive basketball teams. The annual Steamboat Classic attracts world-class, international middle-distance runners. Racing fans enjoy the Grand National TT Motorcycle Race in August.

Sports for the Participant

The Peoria Pleasure Driveway and Park District consists of nearly 9,000 acres providing facilities for outdoor and indoor sports. Included are 7 golf courses, indoor and outdoor swimming pools, and 39 public tennis courts. Also available are two artificial ice-skating rinks, an archery range, a BMX bicycle racing course, horseshoe pits, shuffleboard courts, and a shooting range. Peoria Lake offers fishing and boating. The Par-A-Dice Riverboat Casino, docked in East Peoria, offers high-stakes gambling on the scenic Illinois River.

Shopping and Dining

Peoria shoppers choose from 60 shopping centers and malls located throughout the greater metropolitan area. The Shops at Grand Prairie is an open air mall with retail tenants such as Bergner's, Banana Republic, Borders, Dick's Sporting Goods, and Old Navy. Shops at The Metro Centre include C.R. Cook's Furs and Fashions, Naturally Yours Grocery, and Rocky Mountain Chocolate Factory. Northwoods Mall is anchored by department stores Famous Barr, JC Penney, and Sears. Unique, one-of-a-kind shops can be found along the Peoria RiverFront. Peoria is also home to the Illinois Antique Center, with more than 100 both spaces.

The dining choices in Peoria feature ethnic food as well as gourmet cuisine and a variety of well known fast food chains and family-style restaurants. Sushi Popo, the only sushi bar in the Peoria area, serves fine-dining Chinese and Japanese cuisine. Irish Fare can be had at Kelleher's Irish Pub and Eatery. Italian choices include Old Chicago Restaurant, Ponte Vecchio, and Rizzi's Italian Ristorante. German American food and European beers are enjoyed at the Peoria Hofbrau. Regional specialties include barbecued ribs and pork tenderloin sandwiches.

Visitor Information: Peoria Area Convention and Visitors Bureau, 456 Fulton Street, Suite 300, Peoria, IL 61602; telephone (800)747-0302

Convention Facilities

Peoria's principal meeting site is the Peoria Civic Center, located in the revitalized downtown district. It features a

12,145-seat arena, 63,668 square feet of exhibit space, and a theater with seating for 2,244 people. Concerts, sporting events, rodeos, ice shows, and operas are among the events held at the Civic Center. Peoria area hotels and motels offer more than 3,000 lodging rooms and also have convention and meeting room facilities.

Convention Information: Peoria Area Convention and Visitors Bureau, 465 Fulton Street, Suite 300, Peoria, IL 61602; telephone (800)747-0302

Transportation

Approaching the City

The Greater Peoria Regional Airport schedules 30 daily flights on 6 airlines to 5 major hubs throughout the country. All parking at the airport is free. Passenger rail transportation into Peoria is available through Amtrak.

Interstate highways 74, 474, 80, and 55 afford easy access into Greater Peoria; the area is also served by four federal highways.

Traveling in the City

Peoria is compact but not crowded. The average commute is 10 minutes. CityLink offers mass public transportation.

Communications

Newspapers and Magazines

The major newspaper in Peoria is the *Journal Star,* which is published every morning. Content and archives of past stories are available on the paper's website. Other neighborhood and suburban newspapers circulate weekly, including the *Morton Times News* and the *Peoria Times Observer.* Central Illinois Business publishers, based in Peoria, publish the monthly community-interest magazines *InterBusiness Issues, The Peoria Woman, ArtsAlive,* and *Peoria Progress.*

A number of special-interest magazines are published in Peoria on such subjects as religion, crafts, cats, guns, helicopters, sewing, and graphic arts.

Television and Radio

Six television stations are based in Peoria; cable service is available. Eight radio stations furnish diversified programming.

Media Information: Peoria Journal Star, 1 News Plaza, Peoria, IL 61643; telephone (309)686-3000

Peoria Online

City of Peoria home page. Available www.ci.peoria.il.us

Economic Development Council for Central Illinois. Available www.edc.centralillinois.org

Illinois Department of Commerce and Community Affairs. Available www.commerce.state.il.us

Peoria Area Chamber of Commerce. Available www.peoriachamber.org

Peoria Area Convention and Visitors Bureau home page. Available www.peoria.org/

Peoria Historical Society. Available www.peoriahistorical society.org

Peoria Journal Star. Available www.pjstar.com

Peoria Park District. Available www.peoriaparks.org

Peoria Public Library. Available www.peoria.lib.il.us

Selected Bibliography

Farmer, Philip Jose. *Nothing Burns in Hell.* (New York: Forge, 1998)

Springfield

The City in Brief

Founded: 1820 (incorporated, 1832)

Head Official: Mayor Timothy J. Davlin (since 2003)

City Population
  1980: 99,637
  1990: 105,227
  2000: 111,454
  2003 estimate: 113,586
  Percent change, 1990–2000: 3.9%
  U.S. rank in 1980: 171st
  U.S. rank in 1990: 183rd (State rank: 4th)
  U.S. rank in 2000: 225th (State rank: 6th)

Metropolitan Area Population
  1980: 187,770
  1990: 189,550
  2000: 188,951

Percent change, 1990–2000: 5.9%
U.S. rank in 1990: Not reported
U.S. rank in 2000: 165th

Area: 54 square miles (2000)
Elevation: 588 feet above sea level
Average Annual Temperature: 53° F
Average Annual Precipitation: 35 inches

Major Economic Sectors: Government, services, whole-sale and retail trade
Unemployment Rate: 5.1% (March 2005)
Per Capita Income: $23,324 (1999)

2002 FBI Crime Index Total: Not reported

Major Colleges and Universities: University of Illinois at Springfield; Southern Illinois University School of Medicine; Lincoln Land Community College; Springfield College in Illinois

Daily Newspaper: *State Journal-Register*

Introduction

Springfield is the capital of Illinois and the seat of Sangamon County, which is included in the Springfield metropolitan area. The city is the commercial, health care, financial, and cultural center for a wide agricultural region. Springfield bills itself as "The City Lincoln Loved," since it served as the home, workplace, and political base of Abraham Lincoln for nearly twenty-four years prior to his election as President of the United States. Springfield is also a popular tourist destination.

Geography and Climate

Springfield is located south of the Sangamon River on level to gently sloping terrain in a fertile agricultural region in central Illinois. The city is 190 miles southwest of Chicago, 95 miles northeast of St. Louis, and 193 miles west of Indianapolis. Springfield's climate consists of four seasons, with warm summers and cold winters; snowfall and ice average twenty-two inches a year. Relative humidity measures 61 percent annually.

Area: 54 square miles (2000)

Elevation: 588 feet above sea level

Average Temperatures: 16.3° F to 87.1° F; annual average, 53° F

Average Annual Precipitation: 35 inches

History

Sangamon River Valley Attracts Settlers

At the time Illinois was admitted to the Union in 1818, the city of Springfield did not exist. In that same year Elisha Kelly of North Carolina, attracted to the fertile Sangamon River valley, built the first homestead at a location that is now the northwest corner of Springfield's Second and Jefferson streets. Other settlers soon arrived and a small settlement began to take shape around the Kelly cabin. When Sangamon County was created in 1821, the Kelly colony was the only one large enough to house county officials. The town was named Springfield in April 1821, the name being derived from Spring Creek and one of the Kelly family's fields. Springfield became the county seat in 1825 and received its incorporation in 1832.

Through the leadership of young Abraham Lincoln, one of the "Long Nine"—seven representatives and two senators whose total height measured 54 feet—the state capital of Illinois was transferred from Vandalia to Springfield. Lincoln, who lived in the village of New Salem, 20 miles northwest of the city, moved to the new capital on April 15, 1837; he remained there until he left for Washington, D.C., on February 11, 1861, as the sixteenth president-elect of the United States on the eve of the American Civil War. During Lincoln's twenty-five years in Springfield as a lawyer and politician, the city experienced prosperity and growth, becoming a city in 1840 and recording a population of 9,400 people by 1860.

Monuments Memorialize Lincoln in Springfield

The city of Springfield is a tribute to Lincoln, rivaling Washington, D.C., in the grandeur and significance of its public monuments, shrines, and historic buildings. The Old State Capitol, a Greek Revival style building constructed in 1837, is one of the most historically significant structures west of the Alleghenies. Lincoln delivered his "House Divided" speech on June 16, 1858, and maintained an office as president-elect there. His body lay in state in the Capitol's House of Representatives on May 5, 1865. The Lincoln Tomb and memorial in Oak Ridge Cemetery was dedicated in 1874. The marble burial chamber holds the bodies of Lincoln, his wife Mary, and sons Edward Baker, William Wallace, and Thomas ("Tad"). The Lincoln Memorial Garden and Nature Center, designed by Jens Jensen, reflects the Illinois landscape of Lincoln's time. The Lincoln Home National Historic Site, the Lincoln-Herndon Law Offices, the Lincoln Depot (formerly Great Western depot, where he gave his farewell speech to Springfield), and the Lincoln Family Pew at the First Presbyterian Church complete the sites memorializing Lincoln's life in Springfield.

At the center of Springfield's history and daily life is state politics. After the Civil War, to prevent the removal of the capital to Peoria, Springfield citizens bought the old capitol building for $200,000, which was then used to finance a new structure. Begun in 1868 and finished 20 years later at a cost of $4.5 million, the capitol rises 461 feet above the city and is in the form of a Latin cross with a vast dome in the center, capped with stained glass. The building was renovated in 1958.

Springfield Emerges as Regional Center

In 1914 the Russell Sage Foundation picked Springfield for one of its sociological surveys to aid social welfare organizations. The creation of man-made Lake Springfield, the largest civic project in the city's history, was approved in 1930 and financed by a bond issue and federal funds. The city became a wholesale and retail center for the thriving agricultural region.

Today, Springfield continues to serve as a center of government, culture, and business for central Illinois. With the addition of the multi-million-dollar Abraham Lincoln Presidential Library and Museum, the city also continues to be an attraction for national and international visitors interested in presidential and American history.

Historical Information: Sangamon County Historical Society, 308 E. Adams St., Springfield, IL 62701; telephone (217)753-4900. Illinois State Historical Society, 210 1/2 S. 6th St., Springfield, IL 62701; telephone (217)525-2781

Population Profile

Metropolitan Area Residents
1980: 187,770
1990: 189,550
2000: 188,951
Percent change, 1990–2000: 5.9%
U.S. rank in 1990: Not reported
U.S. rank in 2000: 165th

City Residents
1980: 99,637
1990: 105,227
2000: 111,454
2003 estimate: 113,586
Percent change, 1990–2000: 3.9%
U.S. rank in 1980: 171st
U.S. rank in 1990: 183rd (State rank: 4th)
U.S. rank in 2000: 225th (State rank: 6th)

Density: 2,063.9 people per square mile (2000)

Racial and ethnic characteristics (2000)
White: 90,287
Black or African American: 17,096
American Indian and Alaska Native: 231
Asian: 1,620
Native Hawaiian and Pacific Islander: 34
Hispanic or Latino (may be of any race): 1,337
Other: 525

Percent of residents born in state: 78.2% (2000)

Age characteristics (2000)
Population under 5 years old: 7,341
Population 5 to 9 years old: 7,631
Population 10 to 14 years old: 7,251
Population 15 to 19 years old: 7,099
Population 20 to 24 years old: 7,152
Population 25 to 34 years old: 15,942
Population 35 to 44 years old: 17,316
Population 45 to 54 years old: 16,011
Population 55 to 59 years old: 5,270
Population 60 to 64 years old: 4,345
Population 65 to 74 years old: 7,821
Population 75 to 84 years old: 5,896
Population 85 years and older: 2,379
Median age: 36.9 years

Births (2003)
Total number: 2,571

Deaths (2002)
Total number: 1,793

Money income (1999)
Per capita income: $23,324
Median household income: $39,388
Total households: 48,753

Number of households with income of . . .
less than $10,000: 4,304
$10,000 to $14,999: 3,399
$15,000 to $24,999: 6,982
$25,000 to $34,999: 6,938
$35,000 to $49,999: 8,467
$50,000 to $74,999: 9,091
$75,000 to $99,999: 4,696
$100,000 to $149,999: 3,179
$150,000 to $199,999: 704
$200,000 or more: 993

Percent of families below poverty level: 8.4% (46.6% of which were female householder families with related children under 5 years)

2002 FBI Crime Index Total: Not reported

Municipal Government

Springfield operates under an aldermanic form of municipal government. The 10 aldermen and the mayor, who is the head official and a member of council, serve four-year terms.

Head Official: Mayor Timothy J. Davlin (since April 2003; current term expires 2007)

Total Number of City Employees: 1,650 (2005)

City Information: City of Springfield, 800 E. Monroe, Springfield, IL 62701; telephone (217)789-2000

Economy

Major Industries and Commercial Activity

Springfield's diversified economic base is balanced between the public and private sectors; government, services, and retail trade are the principal industries. A central location and a highly developed transportation and communications network contribute to the city's position as a center of business and professional activity, particularly health care and finance. Springfield is also the headquarters of 12 national insurance companies and more than 165 state, regional, and national associations. Manufacturing firms in Sangamon County produce goods for national distribution and international export.

Items and goods produced: tractors, electric meters, radio parts, flour, cereal products, automatic coffee makers, mattresses, plastic pipe, farm implements, livestock and poultry feeds, yeast, power plant boiler installations, printed circuits, steel storage tanks

Incentive Programs—New and Existing Companies

Local programs—The city of Springfield runs two loan programs to aid financing for the small business community. For businesses with less than five persons, the Microenterprise Loan Program offers loans between $1,000 and $10,000 for equipment, furniture, fixtures, and working capital, with interest below the market rate. Accounting assistance is also provided. The Business Loan Program provides funding up to $50,000 for non-manufacturing businesses and up to $100,000 for manufacturing businesses. The loans are granted based on job creation and gap financing.

The Springfield Enterprise Zone encourages job creation and capital investment in areas of economic distress and promotes neighborhood revitalization in targeted areas. Companies can take advantage of property tax abatements and a sales tax exemption on all building materials purchased within the state of Illinois.

State programs—In 1977 the Illinois legislature adopted the Tax Increment Allocation Redevelopment Act to provide municipalities with a unique tool to finance and stimulate urban redevelopment. Through the use of Tax Increment Financing (TIF), cities can stimulate private investment by offering incentives to attract and retain businesses, improve their community areas, and maintain a well-educated and highly trained labor force. Currently, Springfield has four TIF districts. The Illinois Department of Commerce and Economic Opportunity offers financial and technical assistance to qualified businesses wishing to locate or expand in Illinois.

Job training programs—The Capital City Center, a partnership between Lincoln Land Community College, Central Management Services, and the University of Illinois at Springfield, provides technology training to interested businesses through scheduled courses and customized training programs.

Development Projects

Springfield has recently undergone a spurt of intense economic development, with many companies and organizations building in or relocating to the area. In 2004 Wells Fargo Home Mortgage opened a new, $41 million, 185,000-square-foot facility, giving the company the capacity to accommodate 750 employees. Later that year a new, 43,000 square foot Illinois Supreme Court Building opened. In 2005 the Illinois Air National Guard received $10 million in federal funding for the construction of a new facility to be located at Springfield Capital Airport. The new facility will have more than 45,000 square feet of space to be used as a dining area, medical clinic, and administrative offices.

In 2005 Springfield opened the Abraham Lincoln Presidential Library and Museum, an event that drew local and national media attention. The 160,000-square-foot, $115 million library and museum serve as the center for research and study of the life and times of Abraham Lincoln and the American Civil War. It is the nation's largest presidential library.

Economic Development Information: City of Springfield Office of Planning and Economic Development, 231 S. 6th St., Springfield, IL 62701; telephone (217)789-2377. Illinois Department of Commerce and Economic Opportunity, 620 E. Adams, Springfield, IL 62701; telephone (217)782-7500

Commercial Shipping

A transportation hub for markets throughout the United States, the Springfield metropolitan area is served by 35 intrastate and 75 interstate motor freight carriers. Forty-one truck terminals are located in the community. Springfield/Sangamon County is linked with major national rail networks via five railroads, two of which operate facilities in the city, and a local rail company that maintains a switch-yard. Capital Airport provides daily commercial flights, as well as complete charter, aircraft repair and maintenance, and fuel services.

Labor Force and Employment Outlook

The Springfield-Sangamon County labor force is one of the largest in central Illinois, with the highest commuting-in rate of any central Illinois community. The labor pool in the Springfield area is extensive and includes unemployed, under-employed, and re-entering retirees, representing a potential available workforce of 228,057 individuals in the Springfield area. Of that number, 31 percent have experience in computers and/or electronics, 37.4 percent in health care or medical devices, 21.5 percent in manufacturing, and 20 percent in agriculture and agribusiness. Sixty-eight percent of the city's underemployed have attended college, and 52 percent are between the ages of 20 and 39. Seventy percent have indicated interest in additional training.

In an audit conducted by The Center for Governmental Studies at Northern Illinois University, researchers found that the overall labor quality in Springfield is considered among the best in the nation by local employers. Employers rated employees good or very good on job performance as it relates to trainability, basic skills, productivity, and attitudes. Employees also showed low rates of turnover and absenteeism.

The following is a summary of data regarding the Springfield metropolitan area labor force, 2004 annual averages.

Size of nonagricultural labor force: 110,200

Number of workers employed in . . .
 construction and mining: 5,100
 manufacturing: 3,400
 trade, transportation and utilities: 17,900
 information: 3,100
 financial activities: 7,500
 professional and business services: 10,500
 educational and health services: 16,200
 leisure and hospitality: 10,200
 other services: 6,400
 government: 29,900

Average hourly earnings of production workers in manufacturing: $15.61 (statewide average)

Unemployment rate: 5.1% (March 2005)

Largest employers (2004)	Number of employees
State of Illinois	17,000
Memorial Health System	3,400
St. John's Hospital	2,839
Illinois National Guard	2,700
Springfield School District #186	2,019
City of Springfield	1,707
Horace Mann Insurance Company	1,280
SIU School of Medicine	1,200
Springfield Clinic, LLP	900
SBC Communications Inc.	900
U.S. Postal Service	900

Cost of Living

With a cost of living level below the national average, Springfield residents are reported to have higher disposable income for recreation, savings, and other discretionary expenditures.

The following is a summary of data regarding several key cost of living factors in the Springfield area.

2004 (3rd Quarter) ACCRA Cost of Living Index: 91.0 (U.S. average = 100.0)

2004 (3rd Quarter) ACCRA Average House Price: $227,414

State income tax rate: 3.0%

State sales tax rate: 5.0%

Local income tax rate: None

Local sales tax rate: 2.5% (plus a county tax of 0.25%)

Property tax rate: 7.87% (valuation is 33.3% of real property)

Economic Information: Greater Springfield Chamber of Commerce, 3 S. Old State Capitol Plaza, Springfield, IL 62701; telephone (217)525-1173

Education and Research

Elementary and Secondary Schools

Springfield Public School District #186, the ninth-largest in the state of Illinois, is administered by a seven-member, nonpartisan board of education that appoints a superintendent. Almost 54 percent of the district's teachers have bachelor's degrees, and 46 percent hold master's degrees or above. The district's average ACT scores recently fell slightly below the state average, and the graduation rate is 89.7 percent.

The following is a summary of data regarding the Springfield public schools as of the 2003–2004 school year.

Total enrollment: 14,807

Number of facilities
 elementary schools: 24
 middle schools: 5
 high schools: 3

Student-teacher ratio: elementary, 17:1; high school, 23:1

Teacher salaries
 average: $48,509

Funding per pupil: $8,212

Springfield is also served by a large number of private and parochial elementary and secondary schools.

Public Schools Information: Springfield Public School District #186, 1900 W. Monroe St., Springfield, IL 62704; telephone (217)525-3000

Colleges and Universities

The University of Illinois at Springfield, Lincoln Land Community College, Springfield College in Illinois, and Southern Illinois University School of Medicine are located in Springfield. Among the technical and vocational schools in Springfield are Capital Area Vocational Center, Brown's Business College, and Robert Morris College.

The University of Illinois at Springfield (UIS), one of three University of Illinois campuses, is a four-year institution with an enrollment of about 4,500 students. The school offers degrees in 39 concentrations including business administration, psychology, and criminal justice. In addition to 20 bachelor's degree programs, UIS administers 18 master's degree programs and a doctorate program in public administration. The school celebrated its 30th anniversary in 2000.

The Southern Illinois University School of Medicine is a state-assisted school established in 1970 to train physicians and develop new models for providing health care in rural areas. Its 174 faculty physicians offer primary care and specialized services. The school also enrolls 288 medical students, 252 residents, 40 doctoral students, and 50 master's degree students.

Founded in 1967, Lincoln Land Community College is a community-based institution with an enrollment of about 12,000 students. The school offers vocational education, programs for returning students, and a transfer curriculum. Springfield College in Illinois is a four-year, faith-based institution offering both associate's and bachelor's degrees. The school was founded in 1929 by Catholic Ursuline Sisters, and was the city's first institution of higher learning.

Libraries and Research Centers

The Lincoln Library, Springfield's public library, holds more than 400,000 books, about 1,000 periodical titles, plus microfilm, films, audio and videotapes, compact discs, maps, charts, and art reproductions. The library operates three branches. Springfield is also home to the Illinois State Library, which houses five million volumes.

Opened in 2004, the Abraham Lincoln Presidential Library and Museum (formerly the Illinois State Historical Library) is a 200,000 square foot complex located in downtown Springfield. The facility was created to foster Abraham Lincoln scholarship and promote a greater appreciation of Illinois history. The library's archives contain more than 12 million documents, books, and artifacts relating to all areas of Illinois history. It also holds more than 5,000 newspaper titles on 89,000 microfilm reels; many date from the early nineteenth century.

Campus library facilities are maintained by Lincoln Land Community College, University of Illinois at Springfield, and Southern Illinois University School of Medicine. The Illinois State Museum disseminates knowledge of natural history, anthropology, and art to the general public and

scientists. Other libraries in the city are affiliated principally with hospitals and with government agencies such as the Illinois State Department of Energy and Natural Resources, the Illinois Environmental Protection Agency, and the Illinois Supreme Court.

Public Library Information: Lincoln Library, 326 S. 7th St., Springfield, IL 62701; telephone (217)753-4900

Health Care

Springfield is a primary health care center for the central Illinois region. Two major hospitals, a world-renowned heart surgery institute, a medical school, more than 40 clinics, and 30 nursing homes provide diagnostic, treatment, and care services. St. John's Hospital has more than 700 beds, making it the largest hospital in downstate Illinois. It has been in operation for more than 125 years, and is one of the largest Catholic hospitals in the United States. The Prairie Heart Institute, a part of St. John's Hospital, has the largest heart program in Illinois. It performs more diagnostic catheterization angioplasties and heart surgeries than any single hospital in the state. Memorial Health System maintains burn and rehabilitative medicine units.

Another valuable resource to the Springfield medical community is Southern Illinois University School of Medicine. The medical school has 174 full-time health care providers covering seven disciplines, including internal medicine, neurology, obstetrics/gynecology, and pediatrics. Additionally, the Springfield Clinic is the second-largest clinic in Illinois.

Health Care Information: St. John's Hospital, 800 E. Carpenter St., Springfield, IL 62769; telephone (217)544-6464. Memorial Health System, 701 N. 1st St., Springfield, IL 62781; telephone (217)788-3000

Recreation

Sightseeing

Historic sites associated with Abraham Lincoln memorialize his presidency and his life in Springfield. The Old State Capitol Hall of Representatives, where Lincoln tried several hundred cases prior to the Civil War, has been reconstructed and completely furnished to re-create Lincoln's Illinois legislative years. The Lincoln Home, the only house Lincoln ever owned, is located in a four-block national historic area administered by the National Park Service. The Quaker-brown residence was home to the Lincoln family for 17

Lincoln's Tomb is where the president, his wife, and their three sons are buried.

years, from 1944 to 1961. It now contains many authentic household furnishings and has been restored as closely as possible to its original condition. Neighboring 1850s-era residences have been similarly restored.

The Lincoln Depot marks the spot where Lincoln bade farewell to the city, and contains restored waiting rooms, exhibits, and a video presentation recreating the 12-day journey to his inauguration. The Lincoln-Herndon Law Offices are in the only surviving structure where Lincoln maintained working law offices. At nearby Oak Ridge Cemetery, the Lincoln Tomb is marked with a sculpture honoring the 16th President. It is the final resting place of Abraham, Mary Todd, Tad, Eddie, and Willie Lincoln. And in nearby New Salem, 23 buildings have been restored to depict Lincoln's life here from 1831 to 1837. Costumed interpreters can be heard throughout the community's timber houses, shops, and stores.

The newest addition to Springfield's Lincoln sites is the Abraham Lincoln Presidential Library and Museum, which opened in 2004. The 200,000-square-foot complex houses the world's largest collection of documentary material on Lincoln and features high-tech exhibits, interactive displays, multimedia programs, and a reproduction of the 1861 White House. Visitors can also witness the 1860 presidential election as if it were happening today, with news coverage and campaign commercials.

There are other popular tourist attractions in the Springfield area. Designed by Frank Lloyd Wright in 1902 for socialite Susan Lawrence Dana, the Dana-Thomas House is an example of one of the architect's best-preserved prairie-style homes, with original furniture, art glass doors, windows, and light fixtures. The Washington Park Botanical Gardens and the Thomas Rees Memorial Carillon in Washington Park are other popular sights in Springfield; the carillon is the third-largest in the world and one of the few open to the public. Animal lovers will enjoy a day spent at the Henson Robinson Zoo, which houses more than 300 animals from five continents.

Visitors to Springfield might consider a trip to nearby Dickson Mounds Museum, a branch of the Illinois State Museum and one of the major on-site archaeological museums in the U.S. It contains more than 15,000 square feet of exhibits focusing on Native Americans, including art and artifact displays, hands-on activities, and multimedia presentations.

Arts and Culture

Sponsoring a season of plays, the Springfield Theatre Centre is a community theater group performing musicals, comedies, and drama from September until June. The Springfield Muni Opera presents four Broadway musicals during the summer season at the 750-seat open-air theater near Lake Springfield. Each performance is accompanied by a full orchestra. The Springfield Symphony Orchestra and the Ballet Company

perform at Sangamon Auditorium and other sites throughout the city and state. During the summer months, Theatre in the Park presents a variety of entertainment in a natural outdoor amphitheater at New Salem State Historic Site; the productions include a play about Lincoln's life at New Salem.

The Illinois State Museum preserves natural, anthropological, and art histories of Illinois with changing and permanent exhibits. The new natural history hall, ''Changes: Dynamic Illinois Environments,'' demonstrates the changes in Illinois environments over the last 500 million years. The Vachel Lindsay Home is a museum and cultural center that pays tribute to one of the state's most famous artist-poets, who was known as ''the prairie troubadour.'' The home was Lindsay's birthplace and remained his only home until his death there in 1931. The Edwards Place, built in 1833 for Benjamin and Helen Edwards, is an Italianate mansion that has been converted into an art gallery, school of art, and art library.

Festivals and Holidays

The Springfield Old Capitol Art Fair is considered one of the best art events in the United States, attracting more than 200 artists who display their work downtown near the Old State Capitol Building on the third weekend in May. The two-day event has been held for more than 40 years, and also features food vendors and live entertainment. A Children's Art Fair accompanies the main attraction. The International Carillon Festival, held seven evenings in June, is one of only a few of its kind in the country; international performers play carillon music on the bronze bells in the Thomas Rees Memorial Carillon, and fireworks cap off the festival.

The Illinois State Fair, held each August over a 10-day period, draws hundreds of thousands of people each year. It hosts one of the nation's largest livestock shows, as well as farm contests and one-mile harness racing on a recognized fast track. For more than 20 years, the springtime Springfield Air Rendezvous has attracted a mix of airshow acts, from internationally known aerobatics entertainment to warbirds and ultralights. In June the city's Taste of Downtown offers visitors a variety of regional and ethnic foods from many Springfield restaurants; festivities include live music, children's activities, and a pitching booth. A Festival of Trees in late November and a Christmas Parade in December inaugurate the winter holiday season, which culminates with First Night Springfield on New Year's Eve, featuring varied musical entertainment, arts events, and a midnight fireworks display.

Sports for the Spectator

Springfield is home to the national champion Springfield Junior Blues hockey team, a member of the North American Hockey League. Sports fans also follow several collegiate teams, including the nationally ranked University of Illinois at Springfield Prairie Stars soccer team. The annual Ladies

Professional Golf Association/State Farm Golf Classic attracts more than 100 professional golfers to compete for $500,000 in prizes.

Sports for the Participant

The Springfield Recreation Department and the Springfield Park District maintain more than 30 parks in the city offering facilities for fishing, hiking, jogging, picnicking, tennis, ice skating, swimming, and softball. Springfield's wildlife sanctuaries provide year-round opportunities to enjoy the countryside of Sangamon County, and golfers will enjoy the city's nine public golf courses. Lake Springfield, a 4,240-acre, artificially constructed reservoir, is surrounded by 57 miles of shoreline. The area supports eight parks and recreational outlets, including boat launches for canoes, motorboats, pontoons, rowboats, and sailboats, and a marina offering boat, water ski, and jet ski rentals.

Recreation Information: Springfield Park District, 2500 S. 11th St., Springfield, IL 62703; telephone (217)544-1751

Shopping and Dining

Springfield is the commercial center for central Illinois, with a thriving downtown area full of shops in restored historic buildings offering unique gifts and clothing. Simon White Oaks Mall has the largest selection of merchandise in the region, with 115 stores, restaurants, and movie theaters. Illinois Artisans Shop at the Illinois State Museum features works by state artists. The Old Capitol Farmers' Market occupies two city blocks of downtown, and offers fresh produce, flowers, and food from more than 60 vendors.

Restaurants in the city offer a selection of American, Continental, Mediterranean, Chinese, Thai, and Korean menus. The ''horseshoe sandwich,'' a local staple created in Springfield in 1928, consists of a ham slice topped with an English cheddar cheese sauce, and crowned with french fries representing the nails of a horseshoe. Another regional favorite is a special ''chilli'' recipe served by a local parlor that has spelled chili with an extra ''l'' since 1909.

Visitor Information: Springfield Convention and Visitors Bureau, 109 N. 7th St., Springfield, IL 62701; telephone (217)789-2360; toll-free 800-545-7300. Downtown Springfield, Inc., 3 W. Old State Capitol Plaza, Ste. 15, Springfield, IL 62704; telephone (217)544-1723

Convention Facilities

The Prairie Capital Convention Center, conveniently located in downtown Springfield, is the city's principal meeting and convention facility. It contains 66,000 square feet of space,

and includes 44,000 square feet of column-free exhibit space. Springfield's many hotels, motels, and inns offer more than 4,000 rooms. Major hotels, such as the Hilton, Renaissance, and Crowne Plaza also operate meeting and conference facilities. The Illinois State Fairgrounds has a 366-acre facility with 29 major buildings available for large events. And for those looking for a unique setting, the Old State Capitol, Dana-Thomas House, and New Salem have facilities available.

Convention Information: Springfield Convention and Visitors Bureau, 109 N. 7th St., Springfield, IL 62701; telephone (217)789-2360; toll-free 800-545-7300

Transportation

Approaching the City

The Abraham Lincoln Capital Airport is the major air transportation facility in the Springfield metropolitan area. The airport is served by the commercial carriers United and American, which make 23 daily commercial flights to and from airports in St. Louis and Chicago. Charter service is also available.

The highway system in Springfield/Sangamon County includes three interstate freeways, a limited-access highway, and several state routes. Intersecting Sangamon County, I-55 runs north to south along the eastern boundary of Springfield; I-72 links the city with Champaign-Urbana, Illinois, to the east. U.S. 36 connects with I-55 south of Springfield and continues west to Jacksonville, Illinois. State routes include 4 (north-south), 29 (east-west), 54 (east-west), and 97 (east-west).

Amtrak schedules six trains daily that provide service from Springfield to Chicago, Illinois, and to St. Louis, Missouri. Greyhound Bus Lines also serve the city.

Traveling in the City

Streets in Springfield are laid out on a grid pattern. Washington Street, bisecting the city from east to west, and Fifth Street and Sixth Street, running parallel north to south, intersect in the center of downtown. The Springfield Mass Transit District operates public bus transportation on regularly scheduled routes Monday through Saturday.

Communications

Newspapers and Magazines

The *State Journal-Register* is Springfield's major daily (morning) newspaper, and Illinois' oldest newspaper. The

Illinois Times appears weekly and is available for free at hundreds of locations in the area. Other journals and magazines published in Springfield are directed toward readers with special interests in such subjects as beef production, anthropology, aviation, engineering, Illinois history, health care, education, building trades, and electrical cooperatives.

Television and Radio

Five television stations are based in Springfield, through the ABC, CBS, NBC, FOX, and PBS networks. Cable television is also available. Radio programming is provided in Springfield by three AM and 12 FM stations, broadcasting rock, contemporary, country, and classical music as well as sports, news, and talk radio.

Media Information: State Journal-Register, PO Box 219, Springfield, IL 62705-0219; telephone (217)788-1300

Springfield Online

Abraham Lincoln Presidential Library and Museum. Available www.alplm.org

City of Springfield home page. Available www.springfield.il.us

Downtown Springfield Inc. Available www.downtownspringfield.org

Economic Development Council of Springfield. Available www.gscc.org/EDC

Greater Springfield Chamber of Commerce. Available www.gscc.org

Illinois State Museum. Available www.museum.state.il.us

Lincoln Home National Historic Site. Available www.nps.gov/liho

Springfield Convention and Visitors Bureau. Available www.visit-springfieldillinois.com

State of Illinois home page. Available www.state.il.us

State Journal-Register. Available www.sj-r.com

Selected Bibliography

Hoffmann, Donald. *Frank Lloyd Wright's Dana House.* (Dover, 1996)

Lindsay, Vachel. *The Golden Book of Springfield* (Lost Utopias Series). (Charles H. Kerr, 2000)

Portwood, Shirley Motley. *Tell Us a Story: An African American Family in the Heartland.* (Southern Illinois University Press, 2000)

INDIANA

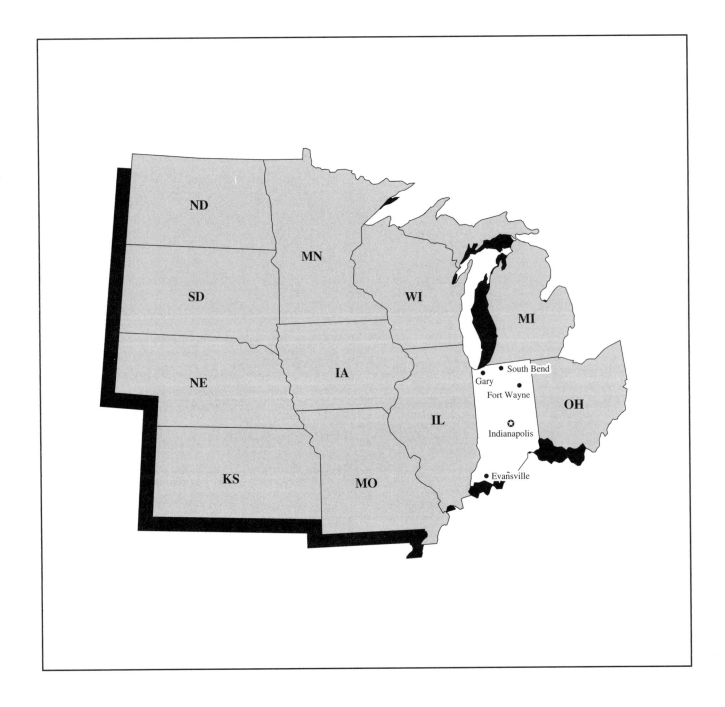

The State in Brief

Nickname: Hoosier State
Motto: Crossroads of America

Flower: Peony
Bird: Cardinal

Area: 36,417 square miles (2000; U.S. rank: 38th)
Elevation: Ranges from 320 feet to 1,257 feet above sea level
Climate: Temperate, with four distinct seasons

Admitted to Union: December 11, 1816
Capital: Indianapolis
Head Official: Governor Mitchell Daniels (R) (until 2009)

Population
1980: 5,490,000
1990: 5,610,000
2000: 6,080,517
2004 estimate: 6,237,569
Percent change, 1990–2000: 9.7%
U.S. rank in 2004: 14th
Percent of residents born in state: 69.3% (2000)
Density: 169.5 people per square mile (2000)
2002 FBI Crime Index Total: 230,966

Racial and Ethnic Characteristics (2000)
White: 5,320,022
Black or African American: 510,034
American Indian and Alaska Native: 15,815
Asian: 59,126
Native Hawaiian and Pacific Islander: 2,005
Hispanic or Latino (may be of any race): 214,536
Other: 97,811

Age Characteristics (2000)
Population under 5 years old: 423,215
Population 5 to 19 years old: 1,340,171
Percent of population 65 years and over: 12.4%
Median age: 35.2 years (2000)

Vital Statistics
Total number of births (2003): 86,865
Total number of deaths (2003): 56,017 (infant deaths, 672)
AIDS cases reported through 2003: 3,686

Economy
Major industries: Manufacturing, agriculture, mining
Unemployment rate: 5.6% (March 2005)
Per capita income: $28,797 (2003; U.S. rank: 33rd)
Median household income: $42,124 (3-year average, 2001-2003)
Percentage of persons below poverty level: 9.2% (3-year average, 2001-2003)
Income tax rate: 3.4%
Sales tax rate: 6.0%

Evansville

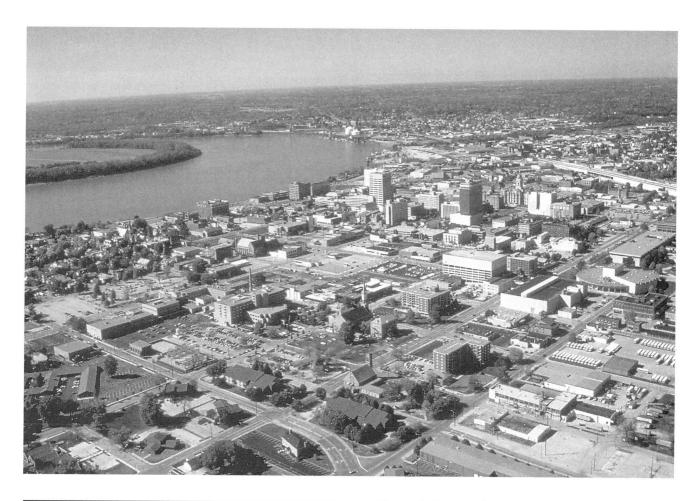

The City in Brief

Founded: 1812 (incorporated, 1847)

Head Official: Mayor Jonathan Weinzapfel (since January 2004)

City Population
   1980: 130,496
   1990: 126,272
   2000: 121,582
   2003 estimate: 117,881
   Percent change, 1990–2000: −3.6%
   U.S. rank in 1980: 121st
   U.S. rank in 1990: Not reported
   U.S. rank in 2000: 199th (State rank: 4th)

Metropolitan Area Population
   1980: 276,000
   1990: 278,990
   2000: 296,195

Percent change, 1990–2000: 6.2%
U.S. rank in 1980: 114th
U.S. rank in 1990: Not reported
U.S. rank in 2000: 133rd

Area: 41 square miles (2000)
Elevation: 385.5 feet above sea level
Average Annual Temperature: 55° F
Average Annual Precipitation: 42 inches of rain, 13 inches of snow

Major Economic Sectors: Services, wholesale and retail trade, manufacturing
Unemployment Rate: 5.5% (March 2005)
Per Capita Income: $18,388 (1999)

2002 FBI Crime Index Total: 6,154

Major Colleges and Universities: University of Evansville; University of Southern Indiana; Ivy Tech State College

Daily Newspapers: *The Evansville Courier & Press*

Introduction

The seat of Vanderburgh County, Evansville is the center of a metropolitan area that includes Warrick, Gibson, and Posey counties in Indiana and Henderson County in Kentucky. Well-positioned in the days of the steamboat, the city occupies a unique prospect on a U-bend of the Ohio River. Today modern architecture mixes with historic structures to make Evansville an effective blend of the present with the past.

Geography and Climate

Evansville lies along the north bank of the Ohio River in a shallow valley at the southwestern tip of Indiana. Low hills surround flat, rolling land to the north, east, and west; the valley opens onto the river to the south. The city's climate is determined by moisture-bearing low pressure formations that move across the area from the western Gulf of Mexico region northeastward over the Mississippi and Ohio valleys to the Great Lakes and northern Atlantic Coast. These storm systems, which produce considerable variation in seasonal temperatures and precipitation, are especially prevalent during the winter and spring months. The growing season lasts approximately 199 days.

Area: 41 square miles

Elevation: 385.5 feet above sea level

Average Temperatures: January, 31.0° F; July, 78.0° F; annual average, 55° F

Average Annual Precipitation: 42 inches of rain, 13 inches of snow

History

River Location Draws Flatboat Commerce

The identity of the city of Evansville evolved from its location on the Ohio River at the spot where the river makes a dramatic U-bend. Evansville's founder was Colonel Hugh McGary, who purchased 200 acres from the federal government and built a cabin at the foot of present-day Main Street, where he started a ferry boat service. Hoping the site would become the county seat, McGary sought the advice of General Robert Evans, a member of the territorial legislature. In 1818 McGary sold a section of land above Main Street to

General Evans, who replanted the town, which was made the seat of Vanderburgh County and named in honor of Evans.

Evansville prospered from the commerce of Ohio River flatboats that were piloted by colorful frontiersmen who served as both guides and navigators. Theatrical troupes, wandering on the rivers in Ohio, played engagements in Evansville even during its early history, establishing a local theatrical tradition that continues today. But it was the age of the steamboat that brought Evansville economic prosperity.

During the first few decades of the nineteenth century, Evansville experienced a difficult period that jeopardized the physical health of the citizens and the economic stability of the town. First the depression of 1824–1829 hit the city hard and then an epidemic of milk sickness swept through, further weakening an already vulnerable populace. Dr. William Trafton, an Evansville physician, found a cure for the ailment that brought the struggling community national recognition. In the winter of 1831–1832 additional hardship came with the freezing of the Ohio River, which paralyzed river trade, followed by floods that covered the town during the spring thaw. In the summer almost 400 people died of cholera. Then Colonel McGary was charged with horse stealing, and although he explained he had traded horses with a relative, rumors forced him to leave town in disgrace.

Business Growth Brings New Residents

In 1836 Evansville was made the southern terminus of the Wabash & Erie Canal, which was completed in 1853 at the same time the first railroad train arrived in town. Although the canal proved not to be a financial success, it stimulated population growth and business development. European craftsmen immigrated to Evansville to work in the local factories and foundries. By 1890 more than 50,000 people lived in Evansville, which had a population of only 4,000 people when it was incorporated as a city in 1847. Serious floods in 1884, 1913, and 1937 finally led to the construction of a giant levee to protect the city, which is now known as ''Plastics Valley'' for the many plastics-related companies there.

Today, Evansville continues to grow and thrive, cultivating a community rich in business opportunities, cultural events, educational outlets, and recreational activities. In 2004 the city was named an ''All-America City'' by the National Civic League. The award, the nation's most respected civic recognition award, was given to Evansville because of the city's progressive economic, educational, and community development initiatives.

Historical Information: Willard Library, 21 First Avenue, Evansville, IN 47710; telephone (812)425-4309. Southwestern Indiana Historical Society, 2205 Lincoln Avenue, Evansville, IN 47714. Vanderburgh County Historical Society, PO Box 2626, Evansville, IN 47728

Population Profile

Metropolitan Area Residents

1980: 276,000
1990: 278,990
2000: 296,195
Percent change, 1990–2000: 6.2%
U.S. rank in 1980: 114th
U.S. rank in 1990: Not reported
U.S. rank in 2000: 133rd

City Residents

1980: 130,496
1990: 126,272
2000: 121,582
2003 estimate: 117,881
Percent change, 1990–2000: − 3.6%
U.S. rank in 1980: 121st
U.S. rank in 1990: Not reported
U.S. rank in 2000: 199th (State rank: 4th)

Density: 2,987 people per square mile (2000)

Racial and ethnic characteristics (2000)
  White: 106,366
  Black or African American: 14,192
  American Indian and Alaska Native: 736
  Asian: 1,131
  Native Hawaiian and Pacific Islander: 111
  Hispanic or Latino (may be of any race): 1,392
  Other: 858

Percent of residents born in state: 69.7% (2000)

Age characteristics (2000)
  Population under 5 years old: 7,835
  Population 5 to 9 years old: 7,735
  Population 10 to 14 years old: 7,533
  Population 15 to 19 years old: 8,186
  Population 20 to 24 years old: 10,314
  Population 25 to 34 years old: 16,665
  Population 35 to 44 years old: 18,089
  Population 45 to 54 years old: 15,234
  Population 55 to 59 years old: 5,519
  Population 60 to 64 years old: 4,726
  Population 65 to 74 years old: 9,386
  Population 75 to 84 years old: 7,578
  Population 85 years and older: 2,782
  Median age: 36.5 years

Births (2002, Vanderburgh County)
  Total number: 2,298

Deaths (2002, Vanderburgh County)
  Total number: 1,912

Money Income (1999)
  Per capita income: $18,388
  Median household income: $31,963
  Total households: 52,373

Number of households with income of . . .
  less than $10,000: 6,166
  $10,000 to $14,999: 4,733
  $15,000 to $24,999: 9,217
  $25,000 to $34,999: 8,249
  $35,000 to $49,999: 9,549
  $50,000 to $74,999: 8,932
  $75,000 to $99,999: 2,982
  $100,000 to $149,999: 1,553
  $150,000 to $199,999: 364
  $200,000 or more: 628

Percent of families below poverty level: 10.1% (53.8% of which were female householder families with related children under 5 years)

2002 FBI Crime Index Total: 6,154

Municipal Government

The city of Evansville is governed by a mayor and nine-member common council, all of whom are elected to a four-year term. The mayor, who is not a member of the council, and appointive boards oversee all municipal operations; the council approves city appropriations.

Head Official: Mayor Jonathan Weinzapfel (since January 2004; current term expires December 31, 2008)

Total Number of City Employees: 1,980 (2005)

Municipal Information: City of Evansville, Office of the Mayor, Civic Center Complex, Room 302, 1 N.W. Martin Luther King, Jr. Boulevard, Evansville, IN 47708; telephone (812)436-4962

Economy

Major Industries and Commercial Activity

Evansville is the industrial, agricultural, retail, and transportation center for the Tri-State region of Indiana, Illinois, and Kentucky. The city is situated in the heart of rich coal fields. Major corporations have established regional operations and corporate headquarters in Evansville, primarily because of the area's rich natural resources, diverse transportation routes, and productive workforce. Industries in the area produce appliances, pharmaceuticals, aluminum, equipment and machinery, food products, furniture, pottery, textiles, plastics, metals, and chemicals.

A fertile farming region, part of the Midwest agricultural belt, surrounds Evansville. Regional farms yield corn, soybeans, wheat, oats, barley, melons, apples, peaches, pears, small fruits, potatoes, and various other vegetables. Meat, fruit, and vegetable packing plants operate in the city.

Evansville retail and wholesale trade areas rank second in size in the state of Indiana. The city's financial community also serves the region with a number of major banks, brokerage firms, credit unions, consumer finance companies, and the loan production offices of national and international banks.

Items and goods produced: appliances, nutritional products, pharmaceuticals, aluminum sheet, automobiles, auto glass, coal, oil, plastics, corn, soybeans, wheat

Incentive Programs—New and Existing Companies

Vision-E, the Evansville Regional Economic Development Corporation, works with the Evansville Chamber of Commerce for the economic well-being of the community and is the regional coordinator for economic development. The nonprofit organization assists companies with location studies, building and site searches, and feasibility studies, working closely with state and local economic development groups. One of these programs, the Strategic Development Fund, teams up two or more state businesses in similar markets, offering grants or loans to spur cooperation and creativity between industrial sectors or regions of the state.

Local programs—Two square miles in Evansville are a designated Urban Enterprise Zone, offering inventory tax credits and other tax credits to eligible businesses. More than 400 companies operate within the zone. The nonprofit Evansville Industrial Foundation develops industrial sites to stimulate economic growth in the area, using a revolving fund to purchase land and develop infrastructure. Through the Tax Incremental Financing program, local municipalities are able to fund infrastructure improvements and new construction in areas needing growth or rehabilitation. The increased tax revenues from the valuator increase are used for repayment of the bond issue.

State programs—The State of Indiana provides many programs to help Evansville area businesses. Grants and loans are available for community infrastructure improvements that would add value to company grounds, including funding for roads, rail spurs, water lines, and sewer lines. EDGE, a state tax credit based on payroll, allows Indiana individual income tax withholdings from company employees to be credited against the company's state corporate income tax liability. Excess withholdings would be refunded to the company.

Job training programs—The Indiana Department of Commerce provides grants to support skills training programs for local businesses. The funds can be used in a variety of ways, including customized training programs in specific skills areas for new employees and skills development training for existing employees. The Indiana Department of Workforce Development also provides labor force recruitment services, including help with the application process, testing, and the assessment and screening of qualified applicants.

Development Projects

Recent development in Evansville has revolved around the creation and improvement of industrial parks and districts, a move that has attracted many new companies to the area. Illinois-based Tenneco Automotive is in the process of building a new 28,000 square foot plant in the Vanderburgh Industrial Park, where the company will manufacture exhaust systems for vehicles. Federal Express is also planning to build a 57,000 square foot ground distribution center in Vanderburgh Industrial Park, employing 72 people. And recently, Evansville received a $280,000 state grant to develop a Downtown Certified Technology Park. Plans include fiberoptic wiring for higher-speed Internet access and the creation of a business incubator to help develop high-tech businesses.

Economic Development Information: Metropolitan Evansville Chamber of Commerce, 100 N.W. 2nd Street, Suite 100, Evansville, IN 47706; telephone (812)425-8147

Commercial Shipping

Three public and several private port facilities receive year-round service from five major barge lines operating on the Ohio River. The river connects Evansville with all river markets in the central United States and on the Great Lakes and with international markets through the port of New Orleans. Evansville has been a U.S. Customs Port of Entry for more than 125 years. Because of this, it is possible to have international cargo shipped to Evansville in bond. The international cargo can then clear Customs in Evansville rather than a coastal port. Linking Evansville's ports to ground and air transportation networks are express and air freight carriers, three major railroads, and more than 40 motor freight companies that maintain terminals in Evansville. There are also six major highway systems providing access to and from the Evansville area.

A location near the geographic center of the nation and access to inland water transportation contribute to Evansville's position as the second largest warehousing hub in Indiana. Services include modern public warehouses, rail-barge-truck-storage facilities, and storage-in-transit privileges with rail carriers.

Labor Force and Employment Outlook

Evansville boasts a highly productive labor force with a Midwestern work ethic and low absentee rates. Indiana's workers' compensation insurance rates and unemployment compensation costs are among the lowest in the country. The city has one of the highest percentages of skilled and semiskilled production workers relative to the total workforce, compared to surrounding states. In addition, the employee turnover rate is less than five percent per year. Because of the close proximity to surrounding counties, and ease of access to the Evansville area, companies regularly draw from a labor force that lies within a 30-mile radius of their work site.

The following is a summary of data regarding the Evansville metropolitan area labor force, 2004 annual averages.

Size of non-agricultural labor force: 177,800

Number of workers employed in . . .
  construction and mining: 12,500
  manufacturing: 35,300
  trade, transportation, and utilities: 36,800
  information: 2,900
  financial activities: 6,400
  professional and business services: 16,700
  educational and health services: 25,200
  leisure and hospitality: 16,500
  other services: 7,500
  government: 18,000

Average hourly earnings of production workers employed in manufacturing: $18.95

Unemployment rate: 5.5% (March 2005)

Largest employers	Number of employees
Toyota Motor Manufacturing	5,000
Shoe Carnival, Inc.	4,250
St. Mary's Medical Center	3,500
Deaconess Hospital	3,000
Bristol Myers Squibb	2,500
Whirlpool Corporation	2,400
ALCOA Warrick Operations	2,294
Vectren	1,769
GE Plastics	1,700
T.J. Maxx	1,500

Cost of Living

The following is a summary of data regarding several key cost of living factors for the Evansville area.

2004 (3rd Quarter) ACCRA Average House Price: $236,020

2004 (3rd Quarter) ACCRA Cost of Living Index: 101.1 (U.S. average = 100.0)

State income tax rate: 3.4%

State sales tax rate: 6.0%

County optional income tax rate: up to 1.0%

Local sales tax rate: None

Property tax rate: up to 10.4% of assessed value

Economic Information: Metropolitan Evansville Chamber of Commerce, 100 N.W. Second Street, Suite 100, Evansville, IN 47706; telephone (812)425-8147. Vision-E, PO Box 20127, Evansville, IN 47708; telephone (812)423-2020

Education and Research

Elementary and Secondary Schools

Education is taken seriously in the Evansville area, and the Evansville Vanderburgh School Corporation works to make sure the school system runs at or above state standards. On the State Comprehensive Test of Basic Skills and the Indiana Test of Educational Proficiencies, local students typically score above the national average in basic skills and above all Indiana urban school corporations on the proficiency tests. Eighty-three percent of the teaching staff have a master's degree or higher. The graduation rate is 89 percent, with 65 percent of these students going on to pursue higher education. In 1997, the Southern Indiana Japanese School opened at the request of Japanese companies locating in southwestern Indiana. The school enables the school-age children of Japanese employees to keep up with their peers in Japan and to help these children integrate smoothly into Japanese school life when they return to Japan.

The following is a summary of data regarding Evansville public schools as of the 2004–2005 school year.

Total enrollment: 22,139

Number of facilities
  elementary schools: 20
  middle schools: 12
  senior high schools: 6
  other: 3

Student/teacher ratio: 16.6:1

Teacher salaries
  minimum: $30,294
  maximum: $56,811

Funding per pupil: $8,700 (average 2003-2004)

The area also offers a system of private, parochial, and charter school opportunities. Evansville Day School is a privately-operated school on the east side of Evansville offering classes from pre-kindergarten through grade 12 to its more than 300 students. Parochial and other church-affiliated schools and a Montessori Academy offer complete educational programs for students in kindergarten through 12th grade.

Public Schools Information: Evansville Vanderburgh School Corporation, 1 S.E. Ninth Street, Evansville, IN 47708; telephone (812)435-8453

Colleges and Universities

Evansville is home to two universities and a technical college. The University of Evansville, founded in 1854, is a private institution granting master's, baccalaureate, and two-year associate degrees on its 80-acre campus. With five colleges and schools, including a campus at Harlexton College in England, the university provides educational opportunities for 3,300 students in 80 academic areas. For the past 11 years in a row, the school has been named one of the top 10 ''best buys'' by *US News and World Report.*

The University of Southern Indiana, founded in 1965, awards baccalaureate and associate degrees in more than 80 fields, including engineering technology, business, nursing, liberal arts, and education. The school's 300-acre campus is utilized by 8,415 full and part-time students from all over the world.

Ivy Tech State College is a public, community-based technical college that schedules courses in programs leading to associate degrees in science and applied science as well as technical certificates. Its 3,900 students study five academic areas: business, health and human services, technology, visual technologies, and general education.

Libraries and Research Centers

The Evansville Vanderburgh Public Library, founded in 1911, holds about 800,000 books, periodicals, CD-ROMs, CDs, audiovisual and audiotapes, films, slides, maps, and federal and state documents. The library operates seven branches in addition to the main library, with special interests including agriculture, business and management, economics, education, and religious studies; the Marcus and Mina Ravdin Memorial Collection is devoted to Judaica. The library also participates in the One Book/One Community program, which encourages residents throughout Southwestern Indiana to read the same book and participate in events and discussions.

The Willard Library of Evansville, founded in 1885, is the oldest operating library in the state of Indiana. It specializes in local history and genealogy as well as nineteenth-century periodical literature. Native Americans and Mississippi Indians are the focus at Angel Mounds State Historic Site Library. Fourteen other libraries in the city are operated by colleges and universities, corporations, the Evansville Museum of Arts and Science, churches, hospitals, and government agencies.

Public Library Information: Evansville Vanderburgh Public Library, 200 S.E. Martin Luther King Jr. Blvd., Evansville, IN 47713; telephone (812)428-8200

Health Care

The Evansville medical community provides health care for the metropolitan region with three general hospitals, diagnostic and rehabilitation clinics, and 16 nursing and convalescent homes. Mental health care is a primary specialty offered by several public and private facilities. More than 500 physicians and specialists and more than 100 dentists practice in Evansville.

Deaconess Hospital offers a broad range of inpatient and outpatient medical, surgical and diagnostic services in its 360-bed tertiary care center. It is one of the largest hospitals in the region, serving a 26-county area of southwestern Indiana, southeastern Illinois, and northwestern Kentucky. St. Mary's Medical Center maintains 520 acute-care patient beds, 32 extended care patient beds, and a special care nursery. Services include a laser center, a chemical dependence center, women's health services, a long-term care program for senior citizens, and a heliport for air transportation. In 1998, St. Mary's Medical Center acquired Welborn Baptist Hospital, a 407 bed facility general hospital providing medical, surgical, and mental health services.

Recreation

Sightseeing

A visit to Evansville might begin at the Old Vanderburgh County Courthouse, a fine example of Beaux-Arts architecture. Completed in 1891, the courthouse exterior features statuary groups, bas-relief limestone carvings, and a giant clock housed in a bell tower; interior touches include marble floors, wainscoting, oak woodwork, brass handrails, and silverplated hardware. Another building of historic interest is the John Augustus Reitz house and museum, a 17-room French Second Empire style home built in 1871. It gives visitors an intimate look into how one of Indiana's wealthi-

The John Augustus Reitz house, a French Second Empire style home built in 1871.

est families lived. Also in downtown Evansville, the Old Post Office and Customs House, built in 1869, is a classic example of the Richardsonian Romanesque architectural style, featuring round arches over window and door openings and extensive use of stone masonry and towers.

Locals can test their luck at Casino Aztar, the state's first gaming riverboat. Named the *City of Evansville,* the riverboat is a 310-foot-long replica of the racing side wheel steamboat *Robert E. Lee,* and can accommodate 2,700 passengers. It offers three levels of casino action, including 1,250 slot machines and more than 70 gaming tables, including blackjack, craps, roulette, Caribbean stud, and a big six wheel. The boat is also home to five restaurants and two sports lounges. Adjacent to the boat is the Aztar hotel, with 250 guest rooms, suites, and meeting and convention facilities.

Angel Mounds State Historic Site, one of the best preserved prehistoric Native American towns in the eastern United States, dates from a period as early as 1200 A.D. when the Mississippians—as the inhabitants have been named by archaeologists—lived on the Ohio River. The site features reconstructed houses, a temple, and partial reconstruction of the original stockade wall that surrounded the settlement. An interpretive center has videos and exhibits on Indian culture and excavation at the site. Angel Mounds also features a burial mound, one of the largest prehistoric structures in the eastern United States.

New Harmony, west of Evansville, was founded by the Harmony Society in 1814 as a utopian religious community and sold in 1824 to Robert Owen, who attracted scholars, scientists, and educators to participate in communal living. The 30,000-acre community still has a population of 850 people, and visitors can take self-guided tours through the tree-lined streets of modest clapboard houses and quaint Victorian-style shops. The Atheneum, the visitors' center designed by architect Richard Meier in 1979, is the starting point in learning about the importance of New Harmony. Nearby, the Workingmen's Institute, established by William Maclure in 1838, stands today as Indiana's oldest continuously open public lending library. The town also houses two labyrinths. A traditional shrubbery maze, based on Harmonist design, was reconstructed by the Indiana Department of Conservation in the late 1930s. And the Cathedral Labyrinth is a recreation of the floor labyrinth at Chartres Cathedral located outside of Paris, France.

Mesker Park Zoo and Botanical Garden, a 67-acre zoological park containing lakes, ponds, and wooded hills, houses more than 500 exotic and domestic animals from 200 species. Many animals are free to roam in open areas surrounded by moats. The zoo also features a petting zoo, the Children's Enchanted Forest, paddle boats, bumper boats, a tram, and the Discovery Center, which focuses on the

world's vanishing rainforests and animals. The Wesselman Woods Nature Preserve is comprised of 200 acres of virgin hardwood forest within the city limits, offering a wide variety of trees, shrubs, and wildflower species. Many trees reach 100 feet tall, and some are estimated to be nearly 300 years old. A Nature Center offers hands-on educational exhibits, a wildlife observation area, gift shop, and special events throughout the year.

Arts and Culture

The Repertory People of Evansville, a local theater group, stages five productions per year, ranging from classical works to one-act shows. Established in 1925, the Evansville Civic Theatre specializes in musicals and comedy, and features local performers in all of its productions. Recent productions have included *Come Blow Your Horn* and *Some Enchanted Evening.* Among other local arts organizations are the Philharmonic Chorus, Symphonic Band, Master Chorale, Dance Theatre, and Children's Theatre. The Evansville Philharmonic Orchestra is recognized as one of the finest orchestras in the Midwest. Its two programs per year feature world-renowned guest musicians and an active supporting guild. The orchestra recently moved into the restored and renovated Victory Theatre, a 1921 movie house reopened as a performing arts center.

The Evansville Museum of Arts and Science, located on the Ohio riverfront, offers more than 30 changing artwork exhibits dating from the sixteenth to the twentieth centuries. Its Main Street exhibit is a re-creation of a 1900 American community. The Koch Planetarium and Science Center, located within the museum, presents changing and permanent exhibits on science and technology; a steam locomotive, tavern car, and caboose are displayed on the grounds. The planetarium offers regular sky shows in its domed theater. At the Lincoln Boyhood National Memorial and State Park, visitors can see the Young Abe Lincoln Outdoor Drama, a living pioneer farm, and the grave of Lincoln's mother. The site is where Abraham Lincoln lived from age 7 to 21.

Festivals and Holidays

The Evansville Freedom Festival, lasting from mid-June to the Fourth of July, is Evansville's biggest celebration. It features a variety of activities for the family, including hydroplane racing, concerts, parades, carnival rides, food, and a fireworks display. Evansville's week-long Fall Festival, sponsored by the West Side Nut Club, is one of the largest street festivals in the country. It features free entertainment, carnival attractions, unique foods, selling booths, amateur talent competitions, and a parade. The annual Ohio River Arts Festival combines art appreciation, food, and family entertainment during the summer, and the First Night Celebration throughout downtown Evansville welcomes in the New Year alcohol-free.

Sports for the Spectator

One of the premier hydroplane races in the Midwest is Thunder on the Ohio, which attracts the fastest unlimited hydroplanes for the main event of Evansville's Freedom Festival celebration. Ellis Park Horse Track, in operation for more than 75 years, sponsors weekly thoroughbred horse racing July through Labor Day. The park offers both dirt and turf racing, and several top training stables base part of their summer season there. The Evansville Otters, a Frontier League baseball team, plays its home games at Evansville's Bosse Field.

The University of Evansville and the University of Southern Indiana field several sports teams, including the University of Evansville Aces, a Division I basketball team, and the University of Southern Indiana Eagles, a NCAA Division II basketball team.

Sports for the Participant

Evansville offers a wealth of recreational activities for active residents and visitors. Activities include camping, fishing, boating, water skiing, hiking, swimming, tennis, and youth and adult sports programs. There are also more than 40 golf courses within an hour's drive of Evansville. Burdette Park features 145 acres of land dedicated to picnic areas, camping facilities, sports facilities, and vacation cottages. It is also home to an aquatic center with water slides, three pools, and a snack bar.

Shopping and Dining

Evansville's shopping options range from unique specialty stores to malls filled with national chains. The city's downtown area, or Main Street, has more than 36 shops and restaurants. Antique and gift shops are especially popular, as are the restaurants featuring Italian, Mediterranean, Korean, Chinese, and local cuisine. The area also houses a number of bars and pubs. Shoppers looking for locally grown and fresh produce head to the Evansville Municipal Market. Built in 1918, the open-air market still offers flowers, local produce, and handmade crafts.

Evansville's dining scene is equally as diverse. Options include everything from fine dining to fast food, and restaurants offer ethnic dishes as well as regional cuisine. Locally-owned favorites, Italian bistros, authentic Mexican, Chinese and Japanese fare, homemade Amish cooking, tasty Indian selections, traditional German restaurants, all-American delis, corner pubs, and terrific barbeque are all available options.

Visitor Information: Evansville Convention and Visitors Bureau, 410 S.E. Riverside Drive, Evansville, IN 47713; telephone (812)421-2200; toll-free (800)433-3025

Convention Facilities

The convention and tourism industry, which brings in millions of dollars annually, is an integral part of the Evansville economy. The Casino Aztar Executive Conference Center offers more than 11,000 square feet of meeting space, with many high-tech amenities. For those looking for larger facilities, the Executive Inn Evansville Hotel and Convention Center provides 33,000 square feet of meeting and banquet space in the heart of Evansville. It also houses 470 guest rooms and suites, and offers full-service catering.

Unique and unusual facilities are also available. The Mesker Amphitheatre offers outdoor seating for 8,500 people, with lush grounds and ample parking. Roberts Stadium, with 12,500 seats, regularly hosts intimate concerts, family shows, sporting events, and trade show exhibits. And the Victory Theatre, in downtown Evansville, recently underwent $20 million in renovations; with nearly 2,000 seats, it is ideal for concerts, shows, and children's programs. It also offers three meeting rooms and a banquet room. More than 3,800 rooms are available as lodging throughout metropolitan Evansville at 40 hotels and motels.

Convention Information: Evansville Convention and Visitors Bureau, 401 S.E. Riverside Dr., Evansville, IN 47713; telephone (812)421-2200; toll-free (800)433-3025

Transportation

Approaching the City

The Evansville Regional Airport is served by major airlines American, Delta, and Northwest, providing nonstop service to international hubs like Chicago, Detroit, St. Louis, Memphis, Dallas, Cincinnati, and Atlanta. The airport handles 30 daily flights and has the capabilities for further expansion and advancement. General aviation facilities are maintained at Evansville Regional Airport and at two smaller area airports.

A system of interstate, federal, state, and local highways provides easy access into the city within the Evansville vicinity and from points throughout the nation. Interstate 64 provides east-west access to Louisville and St. Louis; US 41 provides north-south access to Chicago and Miami; Interstate 69, the planned new NAFTA interstate highway, will extend from Indianapolis to Evansville and connect with several gateways to Mexico. Interstate passenger service is provided by Greyhound Bus Lines.

Traveling in the City

The Metropolitan Evansville Transit System (METS) schedules regular city and suburban bus routes. A motorized trolley also provides transportation along the Downtown Walkway and in the downtown district.

Communications

Newspapers and Magazines

Evansville's major daily newspaper is the *Evansville Courier & Press. Evansville Living* is a bi-monthly city magazine showcasing the people, businesses, and community of Evansville.

Television and Radio

Television programming is available from four stations based in Evansville. Radio listeners tune into 12 AM and FM stations that schedule, among other formats, classical, jazz, rock, and contemporary music, religious programs, and news and special interest features.

Media Information: *Evansville Courier & Press,* 300 E. Walnut St., PO Box 268, Evansville, IN 47702; telephone (812)464-7459

Evansville Online

City of Evansville home page. Available www.evansville gov.org

Evansville Chamber of Commerce. Available www.evans villechamber.com

Evansville Convention and Visitors Bureau. Available www .evansvillecvb.org

Evansville Courier & Press. Available www.courierpress .com

Vision-E, Evansville Regional Economic Development Corporation. Available www.vision2000.org

Selected Bibliography

Bigham, Darrel E., *We Ask Only a Fair Trial: A History of the Black Community of Evansville, Indiana* (Bloomington: Indiana University Press, 1987)

Patry, Robert P., *City of the Four Freedoms: A History of Evansville, Indiana* (Evansville: Friends of Willard Library, 1996)

Fort Wayne

The City in Brief

Founded: 1794 (incorporated, 1829)

Head Official: Mayor Graham Richard (D) (since 2000)

City Population
   1980: 172,196
   1990: 195,680
   2000: 205,727
   2003 estimate: 219,495
   Percent change, 1990–2000: 1.3%
   U.S. rank in 1980: 80th
   U.S. rank in 1990: 99th
   U.S. rank in 2000: 97th

Metropolitan Area Population
   1980: 354,000
   1990: 456,281
   2000: 502,141
   Percent change, 1990–2000: 10.1%
   U.S. rank in 1980: 93rd
   U.S. rank in 1990: Not reported
   U.S. rank in 2000: 81st

Area: 78.95 square miles (2000)
Elevation: 790 feet above sea level
Average Annual Temperature: 49.7° F
Average Annual Precipitation: 34.40 inches

Major Economic Sectors: Trade, manufacturing, services
Unemployment Rate: 6.2% (February 2005)
Per Capita Income: $18,517 (1999)

2002 FBI Crime Index Total: 12,152

Major Colleges and Universities: Indiana-Purdue University at Fort Wayne; Ivy Tech; Indiana Institute of Technology

Daily Newspaper: *The Journal-Gazette; The News-Sentinel*

Introduction

Because of its location at the confluence of three rivers and near the geographic center of the United States, Fort Wayne has from its earliest days been an important marketplace—first as a fur-trading post and now as the headquarters of major corporations. The outpost for ''Mad'' Anthony Wayne during the Indian struggles after the Revolutionary War and later the resting place of John Chapman, known also as Johnny Appleseed, the city figures prominently in the history of the settling of the western frontier. Fort Wayne, three times honored as an All-American City, is Indiana's second-largest city and the seat of Allen County.

Geography and Climate

Fort Wayne, located at the junction of the St. Mary's, St. Joseph, and Maumee rivers in northeastern Indiana, is set in level to rolling terrain. The climate is representative of the Midwestern region, with daily high and low temperature differences averaging about twenty degrees. Annual precipitation is well distributed, and the freeze-free period is usually 173 days. Hailstorms occur about once a year; flooding also occurs. Snow covers the ground for about thirty days each winter, but heavy snowstorms are infrequent.

Area: 78.95 square miles (2000)

Elevation: 790 feet above sea level

Average Temperatures: January, 23.3° F; July, 73.3° F; annual average, 49.7° F

Average Annual Precipitation: 34.40 inches

History

Miami Territory Opened as Frontier

In ancient times, North American Indians hunted the mastodon and other wildlife in a hostile environment after the retreat of the glaciers in the area where Fort Wayne now stands. Later, the Moundbuilders constructed an advanced civilization before mysteriously dying out around the time of the European Middle Ages. The Miami Native Americans ruled the lower peninsula region, fighting against the Iroquois who were armed by English colonists. In time, the Miami reestablished themselves in the Wabash Valley and built their principal village at the Lakeside district in Fort Wayne, which they named Kekionga, meaning ''blackberry patch.'' Kekionga evolved into Miamitown, a large settlement of Native Americans who sided with the British during the American Revolution.

Auguste Mottin de LaBalme, a French soldier fighting for the colonists, captured Miamitown in 1780, only to be defeated by Chief Little Turtle, one of the most feared and respected Miami leaders, in his first major victory. After the revolution, the British encouraged the Miami to attack the new nation, and war parties were sent eastward from Miamitown, prompting President Washington to order armies into the center of Miami territory. Little Turtle defeated the army of General Arthur St. Clair, and President Washington turned to General ''Mad'' Anthony Wayne, the Revolutionary War hero, to quell the rebellious tribes. General Wayne defeated the Miami at Fort Recovery in Ohio and at Fallen Timbers. Wayne marched on Miamitown and built the first American fort there. Wayne turned the fort over to Colonel John Hamtramck on October 21, 1794, and Hamtramck named it Fort Wayne the next day, which is considered the city's founding date.

Two key figures in Fort Wayne's early history were Chief Little Turtle and Williams Wells, who was benefited as a child from his Kentucky family and raised by Little Turtle's family. Wells and Little Turtle signed the Treaty of Greenville, opening up the frontier, and Wells was appointed Indian agent. The two men provided leadership and stability until their deaths in 1812. Potawatomi and Miami factions then invaded Fort Wayne, and General William Henry Harrison's army was sent in to regain control of the city. At the conclusion of the War of 1812 British influence on Native Americans came to a close.

County Seat Becomes Industrial Center

Fort Wayne entered a new stage in its history with the arrival of Judge Samuel Hanna in 1819. Hanna built a trading post and a grist mill, earning himself the name ''builder of the city.'' He was instrumental in realizing the Wabash & Erie Canal and securing Fort Wayne's first railroad. Hanna participated in organizing Allen County in 1824 and helped designate Fort Wayne as the county seat. In 1829 Fort Wayne was incorporated as a town.

Fort Wayne's growth as a Midwestern industrial center was helped along by the number of inventions conceived and developed there. In 1871 Dr. Theodore Horton introduced a hand-operated washing machine and later manufactured the first electrically powered domestic washing machine. Joseph and Cornelius Hoagland and Thomas Biddle developed a baking powder formula that proved successful. The Foster Shirtwaist Factory, capitalizing on the popularity of a boy's size-fourteen shirt among women, made the famous Gibson Girl shirtwaist. Other prominent inventions originating in

Fort Wayne were the self-measuring pump designed by Silvanus Freelove Bowser and the ''arc light'' developed by James Jenney.

Electronics and Lincolniana

The first nighttime professional baseball game took place in Fort Wayne in 1883 under Jenney Arc Lights. George Jacobs' discovery of an economical means of coating electrical wiring, which gave rise to the magnet wire industry, made possible modern electrical-powered products such as radios, telephones, automobiles, computers, and appliances. Homer Capehart's company of engineers invented the jukebox, which was sold to the Wurlitzer Company. Philo T. Farnsworth, a pioneer in the invention of television, bought the Capehart Company in 1938, and in time began the mass production of televisions.

Fort Wayne gained a reputation as a city receptive to innovative companies. The Magnavox Company relocated in Fort Wayne in 1930, and became a world leader in acoustical engineering. During the 1920s the Lincoln National Life Insurance Company emerged as an innovative insurance company. The company established and endowed the Lincoln Library and Museum, which houses the largest collection of materials on one man other than a biblical personage.

In subsequent decades the city's economy continued to diversify. Fort Wayne has seen major growth in the service sector, especially in the health care field. Through its hospitals, Fort Wayne has become a medical center for the tri-state area. Tourism has grown, as visitors are drawn to the city's attractions, historical sites, festivals, and renowned dining options. Fort Wayne prides itself as a community with big city amenities and small town charm.

Historical Information: Allen County-Fort Wayne Historical Society, 302 East Berry Street, Fort Wayne, IN 46802; Indiana Jewish Historical Society, 2743 Wilkie Drive, No. 1, Fort Wayne, IN 46804; telephone (260)459-6862

Population Profile

Metropolitan Area Residents
1980: 354,000
1990: 456,281
2000: 502,141
Percent change, 1990–2000: 10.1%
U.S. rank in 1980: 93rd
U.S. rank in 1990: Not reported
U.S. rank in 2000: 81st

City Residents
1980: 172,196
1990: 195,680
2000: 205,727
2003 estimate: 219,495
Percent change, 1990–2000: 1.3%
U.S. rank in 1980: 80th
U.S. rank in 1990: 99th
U.S. rank in 2000: 97th

Density: 2,605.7 people per square mile

Racial and ethnic characteristics (2000)
   White: 155,231
   Black or African American: 35,752
   American Indian and Alaska Native: 806
   Asian: 3,205
   Native Hawaiian and Pacific Islander: 86
   Hispanic or Latino (may be of any race): 11,884
   Other: 5,993

Percent of residents born in state: 66.5% (2000)

Age characteristics (2000)
   Population under 5 years old: 16,084
   Population 5 to 9 years old: 15,888
   Population 10 to 14 years old: 14,900
   Population 15 to 19 years old: 14,903
   Population 20 to 24 years old: 15,864
   Population 25 to 34 years old: 31,355
   Population 35 to 44 years old: 30,672
   Population 45 to 54 years old: 25,462
   Population 55 to 59 years old: 8,423
   Population 60 to 64 years old: 6,561
   Population 65 to 74 years old: 12,418
   Population 75 to 84 years old: 9,415
   Population 85 years and older: 3,782
   Median age: 32.8 years

Births (2002)
   Total number: 3,826

Deaths (2002)
   Total number: 2,207 (of which, in Allen County, 34 were infants under the age of 1 year)

Money income (1999)
   Per capita income: $18,517
   Median household income: $36,518
   Total households: 83,416

Number of households with income of . . .
   less than $10,000: 7,943
   $10,000 to $14,999: 5,613
   $15,000 to $24,999: 13,334
   $25,000 to $34,999: 12,774
   $35,000 to $49,999: 16,131

$50,000 to $74,999: 16,283
$75,000 to $99,999: 6,285
$100,000 to $149,999: 3,699
$150,000 to $199,999: 610
$200,000 or more: 744

Percent of families below poverty level: 9.6% (35.9% of which were female householder families with related children under 5 years)

2002 FBI Crime Index Total: 12,152

Municipal Government

The head official of the city of Fort Wayne is a strong mayor who administers the government with a nine-member council. The mayor and council members—six elected by district and three elected at large—all serve four-year terms; the mayor is not a member of the council.

Head Official: Mayor Graham Richard (D) (since 2000; current term expires December 31, 2007)

Total Number of City Employees: 1,671 (2003)

City Information: City of Fort Wayne, 1 Main St., Fort Wayne, IN 46802; telephone (219)427-1111

Economy

Major Industries and Commercial Activity

Health care, manufacturing, and insurance have traditionally been the primary industries in Fort Wayne. The city's hospitals form a regional medical center that serves the tri-state area. Demand for health care services has continued to increase alongside the area's population, particularly that of older citizens. The city's two health care networks—Parkview Health System and Lutheran Health Network—are among the city's five top employers.

Dozens of manufacturing companies in the Fort Wayne area employ 100 people or more. Notable among these is General Motors's Fort Wayne Assembly plant, which has approximately 3,000 employees and is one of the top employers in the city. The 2.5 million square-foot plant, which built its first pickup truck in 1986, produced 247,000 pickups in 2004 and is home of the world's first full-size hybrid pickup truck. The home offices of several insurance companies are located in Fort Wayne, including Lincoln Financial Group, which opened for business in 1905—in a small rented space

above a telegraph office in Fort Wayne—as Lincoln National Life Insurance Company. The company grew to become one of the largest insurance companies in the country.

Leading-edge communication service will soon arrive in the Fort Wayne area by Verizon, another of the city's largest employers. In January 2005, the company announced plans for a $65-75 million fiber optic network throughout most of Fort Wayne and nearby New Haven. The network, which will serve approximately 65,000 homes and businesses, will be the first of its kind in the state. Nearly 900 new jobs—approximately 600 contract workers, 200 full-time Verizon jobs, and 80 temporary positions—are expected as a result of this project.

Tourism in Fort Wayne has grown in recent years, following the expansion or the building of new museums, hotels, festival parks, and meeting facilities. In 2003, 5.3 million visitors came to the city, spending $370 million.

Items and goods produced: electric motors and supplies, trucks, tires, clothing, public speaking systems, televisions and electronic equipment, radios, valves, radio parts, copper wire, diamond wire dies, tools, trailers, aluminum pistons, gasoline pumps, liquid metering equipment, tanks and compressors, automotive axles, plastics, boats, feed, beer, paint, cranes and dredges, paper boxes, precision gears and counters, mobile homes

Incentive Programs—New and Existing Companies

Local programs—The Alliance—founded by the City of Fort Wayne, Allen County, and the Greater Fort Wayne Chamber of Commerce—supports business location, expansion, and retention in Allen County. The Alliance is a one-stop-shop for business development, serving as a coordinator of information and resources. It assists companies in many areas, including the development of long-term labor supply strategies, tax abatement on personal and real property, tax incremental financing, employee relocation assistance, site or building options and selection, and community participation.

State programs—The state of Indiana extends various grants and loans to local governments and companies. The state offers a variety of incentives to new and expanding businesses, such as tax credits for investment and training, and through its Community Assistance, Energy Efficiency, Infrastructure, Renewable Energy, Technology, Trade Show, and Training programs. The International Trade Division of the Indiana Department of Commerce encourages foreign investment locally.

Job training programs—The Indiana Department of Workforce Development offers an array of job training programs through its network of nearly 90 WorkOne centers, including one in Fort Wayne. Since 1997, nearly 58,000 workers have been trained through the Advance Indiana program. The Incumbent Worker Training Fund provides grants to employers seeking to improve the skill level of their employees. Career and technical education is also provided by local community and technical colleges.

Development Projects

Numerous major development projects are underway or recently completed in Fort Wayne. Among them is a plan, announced in January 2005, to create a fiber optic communications network—the only one of its kind in the Great Lakes region—that will bring leading edge communication service and nearly 900 new jobs to the Fort Wayne area. In 2001 county taxpayers approved bond financing of an $84 million library expansion project; a massive renovation of the main library is scheduled for completion in 2006. In January 2005 General Motors confirmed a plan to invest approximately $175 million to upgrade its Fort Wayne Assembly plant. A $42 million expansion of the Grand Wayne Convention Center is scheduled for completion in 2005. Area hospitals are also seeing major growth, with a $38 million expansion of Dupont Hospital, to be completed in 2007; a $25 million expansion of Lutheran Hospital, to be completed in 2006; and a $500 million, ten-year strategic plan to expand Parkview Hospital.

Economic Development Information: City of Fort Wayne, Indiana, Economic Development/Redevelopment Commission, City-County Building, Fort Wayne, IN 46802; telephone (219)427-1127

Commercial Shipping

Fort Wayne International Airport is the national and international air transportation center for northeastern Indiana. CSX Railway and Norfolk Southern Railway connect the city with major markets throughout the United States; the carriers maintain local reciprocal switching agreements. An excellent highway system is used by nearly 40 common and contract motor carriers that maintain local terminals that provide overnight delivery to most of the Midwest, Midsouth, and Canada. Triple Crown Services Co., a door-to-door truckload carrier, is headquartered in Fort Wayne.

Labor Force and Employment Outlook

Service employment, which grew steadily in Fort Wayne during the early 2000s, is expected to continue its climb in upcoming years. Manufacturing, in contrast, has experienced some decline, but still remains an essential part of the Fort Wayne economy, comprising a large percentage of Fort Wayne employment—approximately twice that of the national average.

The following is a summary of data regarding the Fort Wayne metropolitan area labor force, 2004 annual averages.

Size of non-agricultural labor force: 211,900

Number of workers employed in . . .
  construction and mining: 11,600
  manufacturing: 36,200
  trade, transportation and utilities: 45,700
  information: 3,500
  financial activities: 13,100
  professional and business services: 19,700
  educational and health services: 32,100
  leisure and hospitality: 19,700
  other services: 8,300
  government: 22,000

Average hourly earnings of production workers employed in manufacturing: $15.79

Unemployment rate: 6.2% (February 2005)

Largest employers	*Number of employees*
Parkview Health System	3,648
Fort Wayne Community Schools	3,445
General Motors Truck and Bus Group	3,050
Lutheran Health Network	2,889
Verizon Communications	2,214
Lincoln Financial Group	2,108
City of Fort Wayne	1,671
Allen County Government	1,585

Cost of Living

The following is a summary of data regarding several key cost of living factors for the Fort Wayne area.

2004 (3rd Quarter) ACCRA Average House Price: $220,384

2004 (3rd Quarter) ACCRA Cost of Living Index: 89.4 (U.S. average = 100.0)

State income tax rate: 3.4% of taxable income

State sales tax rate: 5.0% (food, prescription drugs, and items consumed or used in manufacturing are exempt)

Local income tax rate: 0.8% (county tax)

Local sales tax rate: 1.0% on food and beverages

Property tax rate: 0.8353 per $100 assessed valuation (2000)

Economic Information: City of Fort Wayne, Indiana, Economic Development/Redevelopment Commission, City-County Building, Fort Wayne, IN 46802; telephone (219)427-1127

Education and Research

Elementary and Secondary Schools

Fort Wayne Community Schools is the second-largest district in the state of Indiana. The superintendent is selected by a seven-member, nonpartisan board of education.

The following is a summary of data regarding the Fort Wayne Community Schools as of the 2004–2005 school year.

Total enrollment: nearly 32,000

Number of facilities
  elementary schools: 34
  middle schools: 11
  senior high schools: 6
  other: 2

Student/teacher ratio: 17.5:1 (2002-2003)

Teacher salaries
  average: $46,189

Funding per pupil: $8,892 (2002-2003)

Additionally, Fort Wayne's 39 parochial and private schools offer elementary, high school, and special education opportunities.

Public Schools Information: Fort Wayne Community Schools, 1200 S. Clinton St., Fort Wayne, IN; telephone (260)467-1000

Colleges and Universities

Enrolling nearly 12,000 students, Indiana University-Purdue University at Fort Wayne (IPFW) offers a complete range of undergraduate and graduate programs. The largest university in northeast Indiana, IPFW is a joint campus of two Big Ten schools, and grants both Indiana University and Purdue University degrees. The main campus of Purdue is in West Lafayette, IN, and that of Indiana University is in Bloomington. Long a commuter college, IPFW opened its first student housing in 2004.

Church-affiliated colleges include the University of Saint Francis, a Catholic liberal arts university; Taylor University-Fort Wayne, an interdenominational liberal arts college with campuses in Fort Wayne and Upland, IN; and Concordia Theological Seminary, dedicated to the preparation of Lutheran pastors. Fort Wayne is also home to Indiana Tech, a four-year college providing degree programs in business, engineering, computer science, and human services; International Business College, offering business, health care, and

technology programs; and ITT Technical Institute, offering technology, drafting and design, and business programs. Post-secondary education and technical training are provided by two-year Ivy Tech State College. Other two-year colleges include Michiana College and Indiana Business College-Fort Wayne.

Libraries and Research Centers

The main facility of the Allen County Public Library houses extensive holdings—about 2.3 million books in addition to 10,100 periodical titles, records, tapes, films, slides, art reproductions, and compact discs—and special collections in such fields as local history, genealogy, heraldry, fine arts, business and technology, and federal and state documents. Its Genealogy Research Department, with more than 300,000 printed volumes and 314,000 items of microfilm and microfiche, is considered the most extensive public genealogy research library in the country. The library operates 13 branches. The main library is the 11th busiest library in the country, as measured by circulation. In 2001 county taxpayers approved bond financing of an $84 million library expansion project. Within four years two new branches opened and another was renovated. A massive renovation of the main library is scheduled for completion in 2006.

Area colleges maintain campus libraries. Specialized libraries include the Lincoln Museum Library, specializing in Lincolniana, as well as libraries affiliated with hospitals, corporations, and government agencies. The Community Research Institute is among the nine Centers of Excellence supported by Indiana University-Purdue University Fort Wayne.

Public Library Information: Allen County Public Library, PO Box 2270, 200 E. Berry St., Fort Wayne, IN 46801-2270; telephone (260)421-1200

Health Care

As the largest single industry in Fort Wayne, the health care community serves a three-state region. Approximately half of the admissions to Allen County hospitals are from outside the county. Fort Wayne has six hospitals: Parkview Hospital, 573 beds; Lutheran Hospital, 343 beds; St. Joseph Hospital, 191 beds; Dupont Hospital, 86 beds; Rehabilitation Hospital Fort Wayne, 60 beds; and Parkview North Hospital, 38 beds. The city's two health care networks—Parkview Health System and Lutheran Health Network—are among the city's five top employers. Parkview Hospital, Parkview Health System's flagship hospital, is the fourth-largest hospital in the state and the largest outside Indianapolis. A Level II Trauma Center, Parkview is the only trauma center to be verified by the American College of Surgeons in northern Indiana. The trauma center is comprised of 18 components, including a full-service emergency department, a surgical-trauma intensive care unit, a surgical care center, and a flight program with two medical helicopters. The hospital also houses a cardiac-medical intensive care unit; a continuing care skilled nursing facility; a new life center and neonatal intensive care unit; a children's center; cancer, heart, stroke, and rehabilitation centers; and a sleep disorders lab.

Lutheran Hospital, the flagship hospital of Lutheran Health Network, is the region's only heart transplant facility. Other key services of the hospital include emergency services, inpatient and outpatient surgery, cardiac services, obstetrics, pediatrics, a diabetes treatment center, orthopedics, occupational medicine, and a sleep lab.

Recreation

Sightseeing

American history, exotic animals, and beautiful botanical gardens highlight sightseeing in Fort Wayne. Eleven museums and historical sites are within walking distance in the downtown area. A historic old fort from the War of 1812 is preserved in a park downtown where the St. Mary's and St. Joseph rivers merge to become the Maumee. The Allen County Courthouse, listed on the National Historic Register, was constructed between 1897 and 1902. It combines Greek and Roman architectural themes and is capped with a rotunda, and its ornately designed interior features Italian marble, granite columns, bright tiles, and murals.

The Fort Wayne Children's Zoo is home to more than 1,500 animals from around the world. The central area of the zoo features penguins, macaws, capuchin monkeys, sea lions, giant turtles, and the Indiana Family Farm, where visitors can pet farm animals. At the 22-acre African Veldt area, Jeep safari rides provide views of antelope, giraffes, wildebeest, zebras, and exotic birds. At the zoo's Australian Adventure, visitors can go on walkabouts or take canoe rides to view kangaroos, echidnas, lorikeets, parakeets, and dingoes. The Indonesian Rainforest area features a rare Komodo Dragon, orangutans, and Sumatran tigers. The zoo also contains a 20,000-gallon marine aquarium.

The Foellinger-Freimann Botanical Conservatory preserves rare and exotic tropical plants from around the world in its three gardens under glass: the Floral Showcase has lush, colorful seasonal displays; in the Tropical Garden, orchids, palms, and other exotic plants surround a waterfall; and the Desert House has cacti and other desert plants from the Sonoran Desert of southern Arizona and northern Mexico.

Lakeside Rose Garden in northeast Fort Wayne, with 2,500 labeled plants, is recognized as one of the largest rose gardens in the country.

Science Central offers more than 30 hands-on exhibits to make learning fun. Visitors can dance on giant piano keys, create earthquakes, experience weightlessness over a moonscape, bend rainbows, and ride a high-rail bicycle.

Arts and Culture

At the center of the performing arts in Fort Wayne is the restored Embassy Theater. Built in 1928, it is considered one of the country's most lavish architectural masterpieces. The Embassy is home to the Fort Wayne Philharmonic, which performs a nine-month season of symphony, pops, and chamber music concerts; the theater also hosts touring Broadway shows. The Fort Wayne Civic Theatre, regarded by many as one of the outstanding regional civic theaters in the country, coordinates more than 600 volunteers a year to produce Broadway-style shows. The Fort Wayne Ballet presents two major productions in addition to the annual *Nutcracker* ballet in December. The Fort Wayne Dance Collective, based at the Hall Community Arts Center, is northeast Indiana's only modern dance organization.

The Lincoln Museum, endowed by the Lincoln National Life Insurance Company, is the world's largest private museum and research library for Lincolniana. Housed in a 30,000 square foot, state-of-the-art facility, the museum has interactive, hands-on exhibits for all age groups. The museum's highlights include a collection of personal possessions of Lincoln and his family; original photographs and paintings; and a rare edition of The Emancipation Proclamation, signed by Lincoln in 1864 (one of eight in the world in public collections and the only one on permanent public display); and the inkwell Lincoln used to sign the proclamation.

The Fort Wayne Museum of Art is devoted to American and European artwork from the 19th century to the present. The museum houses more than 1,300 pieces in permanent collections of paintings, prints, and sculpture in three self-contained modern buildings. The History Center, operated by the Allen County-Fort Wayne Historical Society, is located in the Old City Hall, a local architectural landmark; the museum displays artifacts from the Stone Age to the Space Age. Highlights include law enforcement exhibits within the dank cells of the old city jail, a fully-equipped blacksmith shop, a detailed model of an American Indian village, antebellum women's dresses, and a dollhouse from 1886. At the Diehm Museum of Natural History, displays of mounted animals, birds, and fish from North America are featured in reproductions of natural habitats. The museum also has a collection of gems and minerals, as well as Far East artifacts. The Fort Wayne Firefighters Museum exhibits antique firefighting equipment and vehicles. In nearby Auburn the

The Lincoln Museum, the world's largest private museum and research library on the former president and his time.

Auburn-Cord-Duesenberg Museum houses more than 100 examples of the world's grandest automobiles, in a 1930 Art Deco factory showroom.

Festivals and Holidays

June brings three ethnic events to Fort Wayne: the Indiana Highland Games honors Scottish heritage with athletic competitions, bagpipes and dancing, and food; Germanfest recognizes Fort Wayne's largest ethnic group with music, dance, sports, art, and German food; and the Greek Festival brings Greek food, beverages, music, dancing, jewelry, art, clothing, and literature. Three Rivers Festival, held in mid-July for nine days, features more than 200 events that include a Festival of the Arts, Children's Fest, senior's events, a parade, races, and fireworks displays. At the Auburn Cord Deusenberg festival on Labor Day weekend in nearby Auburn, the world's largest classic automobiles are auctioned in a festive atmosphere; the festival also includes a quilt show and an antique sale. The Johnny Appleseed Festival, held in September, brings the early 1800s to life by honoring John Chapman, who introduced apple trees to the Midwest; the festival features re-enactments of pioneer life, period entertainers, and crafts. Holiday festivals from late November through December celebrate the Christmas season with a Festival of Trees, Festival of Gingerbread, a Wonderland of Wreaths at the Botanical Conservatory, and downtown lighting displays.

Sports for the Spectator

The Fort Wayne Komets, a United Hockey League team, plays a home schedule at Memorial Coliseum. The Komets captured the UHL Colonial Cup in the 2002-2003 season. The Wizards, a Class A baseball team, plays at Memorial Stadium. The Fever, a semi-pro soccer team, plays a May-to-July season at Hefner Field. The Fort Wayne Freedom, affiliated with United Indoor Football, is Fort Wayne's newest professional sports franchise; they played their first season in 2003. Indiana-Purdue Fort Wayne Athletics is home to 16 Division I sports; the Mastodons host more than 100 athletic competitions each year.

Sports for the Participant

Fort Wayne's public recreational facilities include 68 tennis courts, 20 soccer fields, 32 softball diamonds, 11 regulation baseball diamonds, four swimming pools, and three golf courses. The city has 56 square miles of parks. The Rivergreenway Trail, a 15-mile-long trail along the banks of the city's three rivers, is ideal for bicycling, hiking, jogging, or rollerblading.

Shopping and Dining

Fort Wayne supports one of the Midwest's largest enclosed malls—Glenbrook Square—that contains four anchor de-partment stores and more than 160 specialty shops and stores. Fort Wayne's new Jefferson Pointe Shopping Center offers 50 shops and restaurants and an 18-screen movie theater in an open-air setting with Mediterranean-style architecture and tree-lined courtyards.

Fort Wayne has long billed itself as "The City of Restaurants," and the 600 eating and drinking establishments in and around the city bolster that claim. Don Hall's and Casa are two local families of restaurants, and are scattered around town. Some Fort Wayne restaurants offer such regional favorites as hearty farm-style meals and desserts.

Visitor Information: Fort Wayne/Allen County Convention and Visitors Bureau, 1021 S. Calhoun St., Fort Wayne, IN 46802; telephone (800)767-7752; fax (260)424-3914; email visitorinfo@visitfortwayne.com

Convention Facilities

Fort Wayne offers meeting planners high-quality site choices. A major facility is the Grand Wayne Center, which is undergoing a $39 million renovation and expansion that is scheduled for completion in mid-2005. This two-year construction project has more than doubled the total size of the center, doubled the amount of ballrooms, doubled the size of the main hall, and tripled the number of meeting rooms. The new 225,000 square-foot facility features a 48,480 square-foot Convention Hall and a 9,955 square-foot Anthony Wayne Ballroom to accommodate conventions, expos, trade shows, banquets, performances, and large corporate meetings and events; and a 6,000 square-foot Calhoun Ballroom, a 1,680 square foot Gallery, and meeting room space totaling 7,684 square feet, for meetings, banquets, luncheons, and seminars.

The Allen County War Memorial Coliseum and Exposition Center, a city landmark, provides versatile facilities for trade shows, concerts, sporting events, stage shows, ice shows, the circus, meetings, and conventions. The facility is a memorial to the armed forces who died in World Wars I and II, and the Korean War. The arena, which recently raised its roof, increasing its seating capacity from 10,000 to 12,500, is ideal for spectator events; the Expo Center provides 108,000 square feet of display area, and has meeting rooms accommodating 250 individuals, plus the Appleseed Room—designed to hold banquets, receptions, and meetings—accommodating up to 540. With more than 4,500 hotel rooms, Fort Wayne has accommodations to suit both large and small group needs.

Convention Information: Fort Wayne/Allen County Convention and Visitors Bureau, 1021 S. Calhoun St., Fort

Wayne, IN 46802; telephone (800)767-7752; fax (260)424-3914; email visitorinfo@visitfortwayne.com

Transportation

Approaching the City

Fort Wayne International Airport is the destination for most air traffic into Fort Wayne. It is one of only a handful of airports in the Midwest with a 12,000-foot runway. Five commercial carriers provide direct flights from major cities throughout the United States; connecting flights for international travel are also available. One of the top three revenue sources for the city of Fort Wayne, the Fort Wayne International Airport accommodates more than one million passengers annually. Smith Field, located north of the city, is a secondary airport for private air traffic.

Highway travel into Fort Wayne is via Interstate 69, which runs north from Indianapolis into Michigan, and Interstate 469, which encircles the city. U.S. Highways 30, 33, 27, and 24 converge in Allen County. Interstate 80, which runs east/west, is located 45 miles north of Fort Wayne via Interstate 69.

Traveling in the City

The Fort Wayne Citilink provides intracity bus service to downtown, urban shopping centers, and area employment locations.

Communications

Newspapers and Magazines

The principal daily newspapers in Fort Wayne are the *Journal-Gazette,* published mornings and Sundays, and the Pulitzer Prize-winning *News-Sentinel,* published Monday through Saturday evenings. An African American community newspaper, *Frost Illustrated,* and the *Macedonian Tri-bune,* are also published in Fort Wayne. *Fort Wayne Magazine* is a bi-monthly publication focusing on the city. Special-interest magazines and journals published in Fort Wayne include *Business People Magazine; CLIO: A Journal of Literature, History, and the Philosophy of History; Concordia Theological Quarterly; The Family Digest; Hunter & Sport Horse;* and *Today's Catholic.*

Television and Radio

Six television stations, including four network affiliates, a PBS station, and an independent station, broadcast from Fort Wayne; cable service is available through six cable companies. Diverse radio programming, covering easy listening, top 40, rock, and country and western music as well as religious features and news and information, is provided by 17 stations (five AM and 12 FM) in the city.

Media Information: Fort Wayne Newspapers, 600 W. Main St., Fort Wayne, IN 46802; telephone (800)324-0505

Fort Wayne Online

Allen County Public Library home page. Available www.acpl.lib.in.us

City of Fort Wayne, Indiana. Available www.cityoffortwayne.org

Fort Wayne Convention and Visitors Bureau. Available www.fwcvb.org or www.visitfortwayne.com

Greater Fort Wayne Chamber of Commerce. Available www.fwchamber.org

The Journal-Gazette. Available www.journalgazette.com

The News-Sentinel. Available www.news-sentinel.com

Selected Bibliography

Kavanaugh, Karen B. *A Genealogist's Guide to the Allen County Public Library, Fort Wayne, Indiana.* (Fort Wayne, IN: The Author, 1981)

Martone, Michael. *Fort Wayne is Seventh on Hitler's List* (Indiana University Press, 1993)

Gary

The City In Brief

Founded: 1906. Designated a city in 1909

Head Official: Mayor Scott L. King (D) (since 1996)

City Population
1980: 151,968
1990: 116,646
2000: 102,746
2003 estimate: 99,961
Percent change, 1990–2000: −11.9%
U.S. rank in 1980: 104th
U.S. rank in 1990: 163rd
U.S. rank in 2000: 251st

Metropolitan Area Population
1980: 643,000
1990: 604,526
2000: 484,564

Percent change, 1990–2000: −19.8
U.S. rank in 1990: 3rd (CMSA)
U.S. rank in 2000: 3rd (CMSA)

Area: 50 square miles (2000)
Elevation: 590 feet above sea level
Average Annual Temperature: 48.9° F
Average Annual Precipitation: 34.66 inches of rain, 39.2 inches of snowfall

Major Economic Sectors: Trade, services, manufacturing, and tourism
Unemployment Rate: 6.6% (March 2005)
Per Capita Income: $14,383 (1999)
2004 ACCRA Average House Price: Not reported
2004 ACCRA Cost of Living Index: Not reported

2002 FBI Crime Index Total: 5,812

Major Colleges and Universities: Indiana University Northwest, Indiana Vocational Technical College

Daily Newspaper: *Post-Tribune*

Introduction

The fourth-largest city in the state, Gary is also the largest U.S. city founded in the twentieth century. Once a leading steel producing center that was often called "Steel City," Gary's beautiful Lake Michigan beaches now host a growing tourist industry drawn to the new multi-million dollar redevelopment project featuring casino boats and marinas. Water and air pollution have been vastly improved in order to help implement this economic shift. The geographical placement of Gary in the Calumet region provides visitors with a huge variety of natural attractions, from the lakeshore to protected inland prairies, nature preserves, numerous parks, and rare wildlife. Gary exists as a port of entry with enough resources to guarantee energy for industrial expansion.

Geography and Climate

The city of Gary is located at the southern tip of Lake Michigan approximately 28 miles southeast of Chicago in an area known as the Calumet region, which includes the northern portions of Lake and Porter counties. Toledo is 210 miles east, Indianapolis is 153 miles southeast, Detroit is 237 miles northeast, and St. Louis is 287 miles southwest of Gary. Gary is in a region of frequently changing weather. The climate is predominantly temperate, ranging from relatively warm in the summer to relatively cold in the winter. However, this is partly modified by Lake Michigan, mostly in the winter. Very low temperatures usually develop in air that flows southward to the west of Lake Superior before reaching Gary. In summer the higher temperatures result from a south or southwest flow and therefore are not modified by the lake.

Area: 50 square miles (2000)

Elevation: 590 feet above sea level

Average Temperatures: January, 20.1° F; July, 72.9° F; annual average, 48.9° F

Average Annual Precipitation: 34.66 inches of rain, 39.2 inches of snowfall

History

Early History

Prehistoric studies indicate that the swamps and sand dunes of the Calumet region presented hostile conditions which discouraged any permanent settlers. Migrant tribes of Mi-

ami, Ottawa, Wea, and Potawatomi hunted, fished, trapped, and sometimes farmed the area. Even these indigenous people didn't build permanent villages until the 1600's. (There were perhaps 50 Potawatomi villages left in northwest Indiana by the early 1800s, most of whom were moved to reservations by the 1850s.) Father Jacques Marquette, great French explorer of the Mississippi River Valley, led a group of fur traders and missionaries through the area using the Calumet River. The story goes that Marquette camped near the mouth of the Grand Calumet, the present site of Gary's Marquette Park. Joseph Bailly, in 1822, was the first European to settle in these Indiana Dunes, which would later become southeastern Illinois and northwestern Indiana.

Creation of City as Major Steel Center

Still, there were not many settlers until the 1900s, although post-Civil War homesteaders flocked to the more fertile farmlands in the southern part of the state. However, as the country's industrial economy grew, land once deemed inhospitable for farming was eyed for factory use. In the late 1880s large amounts of sand were removed from the dunes and shipped to Chicago for building and industrial uses. Swamps, woodlands, and dunes were leveled in order to support enormous factory structures. Gary finally became Gary when, in 1906, work was begun on a site envisioned by its namesake, Elbert H. Gary. Gary had been a judge from 1882 to 1890 and became chairman of U.S. Steel. Realizing that economic growth was moving to the Midwest, he chose the spot for its proximity to Chicago, Great Lakes shipping, and railroad access to bring in ore from Minnesota and coal from the south and east. The enormity of this undertaking necessitated U.S. Steel's forming of two new companies, the Gary Land Company to build housing, and the Indiana Steel Company to construct the plant, which would contain 12 blast furnaces and 47 steel furnaces. In addition, the harbor had to be excavated to accommodate the largest steam ships of the day, and an enormous breakwater and lighthouse were built as well. Three and a half years later a mill opened. Immigrants attracted by thousands of new jobs poured in, both from eastern and southern Europe and from other parts of the United States, filling Gary with more than 16,000 inhabitants for its official designation as a city in 1909.

In one of the few historical footnotes about Gary that isn't directly involved with steel, Octave Chanute first took flight in a glider in 1896, off the windswept dunes that in a decade would become Gary. It was the world's first sustained flight in a heavier than air structure. The Wright brothers later credited Chanute's design with helping them build their first plane.

City Attracts Workers; Growth Continues

In the next 10 years Gary more than tripled its population, with more than 55,000 residents by 1920. The city became a great ethnic melting pot as jobs in the mills continued to attract immigrants from various foreign countries, especially from eastern Europe. Prior to World War I, organized labor failed to gain a foothold among the area's steel workers. Although Judge Gary held the same anti-labor sentiments as his contemporary and rival, Andrew Carnegie, he was somewhat less heavy handed in his approach, seeking to avoid strikes through employee relations programs and an emphasis on job safety. U.S. Steel actually pioneered job safety programs and originated the phrase ''Safety First.'' The corporation adopted a sort of old fashioned, paternalistic relationship with its laborers similar to that of coal or textile mill ''company towns.'' Social events and much of life outside the workplace revolved around the company, while on the downside this meant blacklists kept track of any employee with the wrong political affiliations.

The post WWI period was one of growth for Gary, which had almost instantly become the largest city in the Calumet region. Construction included many apartment buildings and houses, three 10-story buildings, the Hotel Gary, The Gary State Bank, the imposing Knights of Columbus hall, and the massive City Methodist Church. Public structures included Gary City Hall, the courthouse, a 10 acre esplanade (Gateway Park), as well as Marquette Park and Gleason Park. Gary became known as ''Magic City'' and ''City of the Century'' because of its rapid growth. Although large numbers of African Americans were drawn to the city in search of unskilled labor jobs, a quota system kept their work force at no more than 15 percent. Most of the region had segregated public facilities, and housing was racially segregated as well. African Americans were relegated to live in ''the Patch'', the most undesirable housing in the city. Later, Mexican workers, who ironically were brought in as strike breakers, were also forced to reside in the Patch.

City Becomes Model for Public Education

Gary was the center of pivotal early twentieth century development in public education when William A. Wirth established a work/study/play school, popularly known as the ''platoon school.'' It was designed to attract underprivileged children, many of whom were from non-English speaking immigrant families. The curriculum focused on preparing them to function in American society. By 1913 the school had enrolled 4,000 children.

The Great Depression, World War II, and Beyond

Until only very recently, the history of Gary remained intertwined with the fortune or folly of the steel industry. The Great Depression of the 1930s had a devastating effect on Gary's economy, with U.S. Steel dropping from 100 percent capacity in 1929 to 15 percent in 1932. The depression also brought unionization of Gary's industries, with U. S. Steel recognizing the Steelworkers Organizing Committee as the bargaining agent for its workers in 1937. Between 1935 and

1939 the steel worker's wages rose nationally 27 percent, benefitting Gary's workers as well.

During World War II, steel production soared and the tide of prosperity continued for the next two decades. U.S. Steel production peaked in 1953 at more than 35 million tons. The Steelworkers Union held a series of long strikes in 1946 and 1952. These strikes were mostly nonviolent conflicts over wages and benefits rather than the bloody struggles over union recognition that happened elsewhere, but a 116-day long strike in 1959 had the world-changing effect of shutting down 90 percent of production of not only U.S. Steel, but also its competitors. This opened the door to competition from foreign steel, which had had negligible effect before. The long decline of American steel thus began.

Manufacturing in general declined in the region and in the whole country. Between 1979 and 1986 northwest Indiana's loss in manufacturing totaled 42.5 percent, largely in the areas of oil and steel. The world market changed again and the American steel industry rebounded a bit from the late 1980s to the early 1990s. The steel industry is still important to the local economy in Gary, although it is not the world leader it once was.

Changing Demographics Brings African American Majority

Beginning in the 1960s, Gary's population decreased through ''white flight'' to the suburbs. By 1990 the population was made up of 80 percent African Americans. Voters elected Gary's first African American mayor, Richard G. Hatcher, in 1967 and for four subsequent terms. Hatcher's administration improved housing conditions in the city and helped obtain federal job training programs. In 1982 the Genesis Convention Center was built in the heart of Gary's downtown to help in the revitalization of the business district.

Gary made great progress during the 1960s and 1970s in reducing its air pollution caused by smoke from factories and steel mills. The amount of impurities in the air dropped nearly 60 percent from 1966 to 1976. The city issued nearly $180 million in revenue bonds to help U.S. Steel reduce its pollution at local facilities.

The loss of population in Gary during the 1980s, almost 25 percent, was larger than that of any other U.S. city. By 1995, the city's population was 85 percent African American. That year, Scott L. King, who is white, confounded observers when he won an upset victory in the mayoral election. Apparently King's energy and vision for Gary has transcended racial bounds, as he is still at its helm as the city reaches its Centennial.

Still battling poverty, unemployment, a shrinking population, and a less-than-stellar reputation, in the dawn of the twenty-first century the focus of community leaders and businesses in Gary has been to revitalize Gary's downtown and make the city attractive to visitors.

Historical Information: Indiana University Northwest Library, Calumet Regional Archives, 3400 Broadway, Gary, IN 46408; telephone (219)980-6628

Population Profile

Metropolitan Area Residents (PMSA)
1980: 643,000
1990: 604,526
2000: 484,564
Percent change, 1990–2000: −19.8%
U.S. rank in 1990: 3rd (CMSA)
U.S. rank in 2000: 3rd (CMSA)

City Residents
1980: 151,968
1990: 116,646
2000: 102,746
2003 estimate: 99,961
Percent change, 1990–2000: −11.9
U.S. rank in 1980: 104th
U.S. rank in 1990: 163rd
U.S. rank in 2000: 251st

Density: 1,795 people per square mile (2000)

Racial and ethnic characteristics (2000)
   White: 12,245
   Black or African American; 86,340
   American Indian and Alaska Native: 213
   Asian: 140
   Native Hawaiian and Pacific Islander: 24
   Hispanic or Latino (may be of any race): 5,065
   Other: 2,023

Percent of residents born in state: 63.0% (2000)

Age characteristics (2000)
   Population under 5 years old: 8,620
   Population 5 to 9 years old: 8,792
   Population 10 to 14 years old: 8,297
   Population 15 to 19 years old: 8,211
   Population 20 to 24 years old: 7,151
   Population 25 to 34 years old: 11,851
   Population 35 to 44 years old: 13,887
   Population 45 to 54 years old: 13,503
   Population 54 to 59 years old: 5,080
   Population 60 to 64 years old: 4,211
   Population 65 to 74 years old: 7,716
   Population 75 to 84 years old: 4,177

   Population 85 years and older: 1,250
   Median age: 33.6

Births: (2002)
   Total number: 8,621

Deaths: (2002)
   Total number: 5,890 (of which, 72 were infants under the age of 1 year)

Money income (1999)
   Per capita income: $14,383
   Median household income: $27,195
   Total households: 38,244

Number of households with income of . . .
   less than $10,000: 7,899
   $10,000 to $14,999: 3,574
   $15,000 to $24,999: 6,223
   $25,000 to $34,999: 5,153
   $35,000 to $49,999: 5,433
   $50,000 to $74,999: 5,407
   $75,000 to $99,999: 2,547
   $100,000 to $149,999: 1,501
   $150,000 to $199,999: 225
   $200,000 or more: 319

Percent of families below poverty level: 22.2% (38.2% of which were female householder families with children under 5 years)

2002 FBI Crime Index Total: 5,812

Municipal Government

Gary's city government consists of a mayor and nine council members, six of whom are elected by district, the other three at large. Terms for all are four years.

Head Official: Mayor Scott L. King (D) (since 1996; current term expires 2007)

Total Number of City Employees: 2,319 (2005)

City Information: City of Gary, City Hall, 401 Broadway, Gary, IN 46402; telephone (219)881-1301

Economy

Major Industries and Commercial Activity

Manufacturing, especially of steel, has been the heart of Gary and northwest Indiana. Although hard hit by decline of employment in the steel mills, part of that decline was due to automation, and the steel industry is still an integral part of Gary's economy. The factory scene has expanded to more light manufacturing, such as paper products, plastics, chemicals, rubber, and even food processing. The newest industry to jolt the local economy is tourism, with casino boats, restaurants, and entertainment venues available at the newly renovated Buffington Harbor at the lakefront. Gary and Lake County are becoming increasingly popular for people from Chicago and other urban centers who seek weekend recreational getaways. A 20 percent gaming tax is levied on the casino boats.

Items and goods produced: steel and steel finished products including sheet metal, tin plate, tubing, and bridges; hardware, springs, windshield wipers, light fixtures, apparel and bed linens, processed foods.

Incentive Programs—New and Existing Companies

Local programs—The Gary Department of Planning and Development assists businesses in several ways: through commercial development and redevelopment; infrastructure planning and development; job training initiatives' image promotion and public relations; land, buildings, and community tours; liaison between businesses and individuals; information on available sites; tax abatement; and research.

State Programs—Business incentive programs in Gary revolve around the Gary Urban Enterprise Association (GUEA) which manages Gary's Urban Enterprise Zone program. Urban Enterprise Zones are low income neighborhoods which are designated for special state tax credits to businesses who employ people in the zones. Businesses in the Zones are encouraged in several ways: companies may receive full forgiveness of personal property taxes paid for raw materials or finished products; employers can get up to $1,500 per employee for "employment expense credit" when they live in the zone; a loan interest credit lowers the taxes that lending institutions pay on interest earned on loans to businesses in the zone; and an equity investment credit for individual investors who pay into job training programs.

Another state business incentive program is EDGE— Economic Development for a Growing Economy. Intended for larger businesses that create 100 or more jobs and have a payroll equaling at least the county average, EDGE has many smaller programs under its huge umbrella, including credits for state tax liability; and Job Service Matching System, wherein employers can use the state employment system's service to find ideal applicants for specific needs. There is also an Infrastructure Assistance Grants and Loans program, which helps new and expanding companies to finance infrastructure needs such as new roads, water and sewer lines, railroad access, and utilities. Indiana boasts very low costs for Worker's Compensation and Unemployment.

Indiana Strategic Development Fund encourages cooperative projects of two or more Indiana businesses.

Job Training Programs—Jobs 2020 job training program exists under the Urban Enterprise Zone program. Lakeshore Employment Training Partnership (LETP) works with Urban Enterprise Zone programs. Services available to area businesses all focus on providing a well trained work force, including pre-screening of potential new hires, occupational and educational testing, writing training manuals for companies to use on job sites or at various local educational facilities, and analyzing job skills in order to improve performance and productivity on specific tasks. The state of Indiana also offers a program calls Skills 2016, which was initiated in 2001. Skills has five components: the Skills Enhancement Fund helps with costs of training workers of Indiana companies undertaking large capital investment projects; Advance Indiana encompasses many smaller programs which specialize in various types and sizes of businesses that wish to train people in what are termed "transferable skills"; Community Development Block Grants provide federal funding to train people from lower and middle income families; Technology Enhancement for Hoosiers provides $1 million a year for thousands of workers to get technology certification; Training for the Individual Student gives financial aid to students in Indiana universities, colleges, and technological training centers.

More than 16,000 Hoosiers made use of the federal Workforce Investment Act, whose purpose is to improve the quality of the American work force, reduce welfare dependency, and improve the nation's productivity and competitiveness in the world markets. Trade Adjustment Assistance programs focus on workers who have been displaced by increased imports. Building Trades and Indiana Plan programs train people for careers in construction.

Development Projects

The major redevelopment project in Gary since its beginning in 1906 is the Buffington Harbor Lakeshore Redevelopment. The marinas for the casino boats are there, and much of the surrounding 25 square miles needed to be revamped to make it more attractive to the new tourist trade. Neighborhood housing and public services and facilities are being renewed, but natural open spaces, restored brownfields (former industrial sites common in America's Rust Belt) improved marinas and waterways are also underway. Other plans include a health spa, resort, and commercial shopping centers and restaurants, a theater complex, amusement park/water park, museums, golf courses and a golf academy, and new parks and playgrounds. A new arena is being considered for sports, concerts, and conventions. Street improvements and railroad track realignment will be needed to fit in with the new image as well. Downtown redevelopment has three major ongoing projects: street improvements, such as sidewalk resurfacing and lighting; a planned Media Center at 5th and Broadway; and a $45 million baseball park which will be home to the minor league Gary Southshore Railcats. Gary's Housing Authority has several projects underway, most notably the Horace Mann Home ownership project in the heart of downtown Gary, and Duneland. Both are part of the Housing Authority's HOPE VI program. Duneland is a mixed income, mixed finance rental development in the Miller community, which is next to State and Federal Dunes' parks.

Economic Development Information: Department of Planning and Economic Development, 504 Broadway, Suite 625, Gary, IN 46402; telephone (219)881-5235; fax (219)881-1092

Commercial Shipping

Gary Regional Airport, part of the Chicago/Gary Regional Airport Authority, is expanding to become a more major midwest cargo carrier, taking some of the congestion out of Chicago Midway. In addition to the airport, Gary has six truck terminals serving more than 100 trucking firms, most of which can provide overnight shipping within a 300-mile radius. Eight railways have service into Gary. Greyhound Trailways, Vancom, Indiana, and Tri-State provide intercity bus service, and Gary Public Transportation corporation runs buses within the city.

Four major interstate highways offer easy connections to both coasts, the Gulf of Mexico, and Canada.

Labor Force and Employment Outlook

The following is a summary of the Gary metropolitan area labor force, 2004 annual average.

Size of nonagricultural labor force: 323,633

Number of workers employed in . . .
  construction and mining: 18,700
  manufacturing: 38,100
  trade, transportation and utilities: 59,100
  information: 2,500
  financial activities: 10,000
  professional and business services: 22,800
  educational and health services: 39,600
  leisure and hospitality: 30,800
  other services: 12,300
  government: 40,200

Average hourly wage of production workers employed in manufacturing: $16.40

Unemployment rate: 6.6% (March 2005)

Largest county employers	Number of employees
U.S. Steel/Gary Works	6,800
Gary Public School System	3,163
Methodist Hospital Northlake	3,081
City of Gary	2,319
Trump Indiana	1,300
Majestic Star Casino	1,050
NIPSCO	808
U.S. Postal Service	730
Indiana University Northwest	400
Post-Tribune	300
Northwest Indiana Water Company	182
Gary Steel Products	150
Industrial Steel Construction	150
Indiana Vocational Tech College	140

Cost of Living

The cost of housing in northwest Indiana tends to be lower than many other parts of the country, with property taxes as much as 25 percent lower.

The following is a summary of data regarding several key cost of living factors for the Gary area.

2004 ACCRA Cost of Living Index: Not reported

2004 ACCRA Average House Price: Not reported

State income tax rate: 3.4%

State sales tax rate: 6.0% (food, prescription drugs, and items used in manufacturing exempt)

Local income tax rate: none

Local sales tax rate: none

Property tax rate: $23.42 per $100 of assessed value, assessment ratio = 33.33% for residential (2005)

Economic Information: Gary Chamber of Commerce, 504 Broadway, Suite 328, Gary, IN 46402; telephone (219)885-7407

Education and Research

Elementary and Secondary Schools

Indiana's public school standards were retooled in 2000 after an education group criticized the state for not challenging its youth. The standards are applied in Gary by the Gary Community School Corporation, which offers two special education facilities: Norton Park Academy and Lincoln Achievement Center; one career center, Martin Luther King,

Jr. Academy; Emerson Visual and Performing Arts Center; and Chase Alternative Middle School. The Benjamin Banneker Elementary School has been repeatedly singled out by the state Department of Education for meeting high standards of attendance and aptitude scores.

The following is a summary of data regarding the Gary Community School Corporation as of the 2003–2004 school year.

Total enrollment: 17,381

Number of facilities
    elementary schools: 20 (plus one preschool)
    middle schools: 3
    high schools: 7

Student teacher ratio: 18:1

Teacher salaries
    minimum: $34,738
    maximum: $56,982

Funding per pupil: $10,800

Public Schools Information: Gary Community School Corporation, Public Information, 620 East 10th Place, Gary, IN 46402

Colleges and Universities

Indiana University (IU) Northwest, one of eight IU campuses in the state, had 5,138 students enrolled for the fall of 2004. Students can choose from more than 90 programs of study to earn certificates, associate degrees, bachelor's and master's degrees; popular majors are business administration and accounting. The university houses a nursing school and a medical research center. Faculty consists of 160 full-time and 160 part-time staff, 83 percent of whom have a doctorate or the highest degree available in their fields, and their expertise is concentrated into small class sizes with a student-teacher ratio of 14 to one. Full-time and part-time students are roughly half and half, and off campus sites ''bring the college to you.'' Financial assistance is almost equally flexible. Career support programs help the alumni succeed beyond the classroom.

Ivy Tech State College's Gary campus focuses on business education, health and human services, and technical training. Nearby Hammond is home to prestigious Purdue University Calumet. Purdue Calumet has more than 9,000 students enrolled and over 100 fields of study in which one can earn a variety of degrees from quick certifications to master's. Ivy Tech is a large commuter campus with over 165 acres, is three miles from downtown Gary, three miles from the Illinois border, and 25 miles from Chicago.

Libraries and Research Centers

The Gary Public Library has about 570,000 volumes plus CDs, nearly 15,000 items of graphic materials, more than 3,600 films and audiovisuals, and is a U.S. government depository. The library has five branches and one bookmobile. Its special collections focus on city and state history. The system also features free internet access, programs for children and seniors, and an African American history month program. Lake County has its own library system with seven branches, one in the heart of downtown Gary. It provides home service, programs for children and adults, special service to businesses, the Carol A. Derner Art Gallery, and literacy programs, among other services.

Indiana University Northwest Library contains a collection of more than 200,000 books and periodicals and as many government publications. Special purpose areas include the Calumet Regional Archives, the Northwest Indiana Center for Data and Analysis, Lake County Central Law Library, the Educational Resources Room, and services for the visually impaired. The library is backed by 7 million bound volumes and 26 million other materials in the systemwide Indiana University Libraries. Special Collections include an acclaimed series of photographs of U.S. Steel. At the University's Laboratories for Environmental Research, focus is on recycling of byproduct materials for basic industries.

Public Library Information: Gary Public Library, 220 West Fifth Avenue, Gary, IN 46402-1270; telephone (219)886-2484; fax (219)886-6829

Health Care

The major health care organization serving Gary is The Methodist Hospitals, Inc., with more than 700 beds total between its Gary facility (Northlake campus) and its Merrillville facility (Southlake campus); the organization also operates Midlake, an outpatient medical center. A full range of services is provided; special facilities include a Rehabilitation Institute, Center for Interventional Cardiology, Child and Adolescent Program, Women's Health Resource Center, Healthy Start prenatal program, and a sleep disorder center. Other specialties are extracorporeal shock wave lithotripsy (an alternative to surgery which breaks up kidney stone with sound waves), an alcoholism institute, neuroscience institute, gerontology center, and a regional cancer treatment center.

Recreation

Sightseeing

For those interested in architecture, there is plenty to see in Gary, including two Frank Lloyd Wright houses. The Gene-

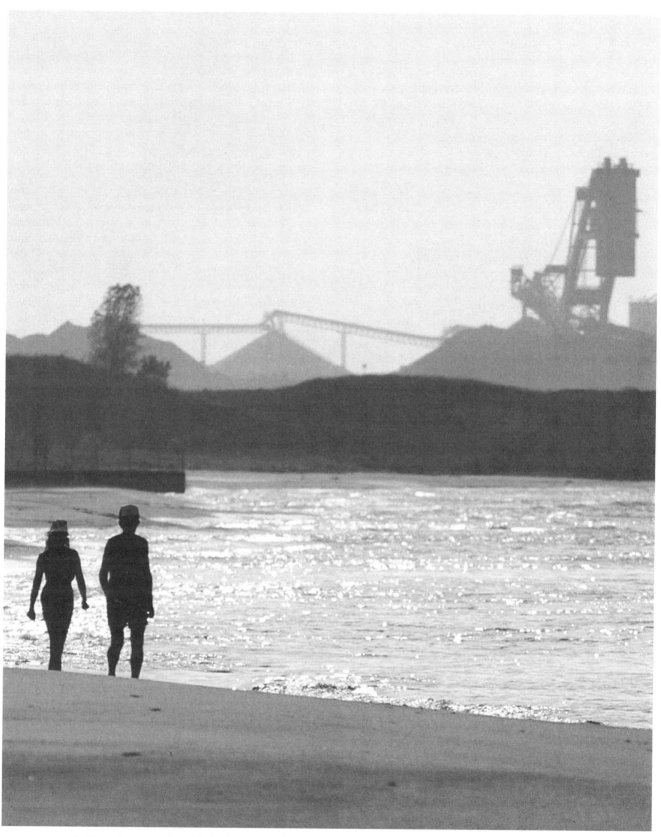

Indiana Dunes National Lakeshore runs for approximately 25 miles along southern Lake Michigan.

sis Convention Center, a modern structure featuring rounded corners and an imposing glass wall across the front, is well worth a viewing. Built in 1921, the Gary Bathing Beach Aquatorium, one of the first examples of modular block construction in the world, underwent restoration in the early 1990s. Other notable buildings include the City Methodist Church, a massive Gothic structure of limestone completed in 1926, and the old west side historic district neighborhood, part of the original company town built by U. S. Steel in 1906, which reflects a variety of architectural styles.

Tours of the Gary Works, one of the largest steel plants in the world, are available by appointment. The Chanute Glider, which made the first sustained flight off the Indiana dunes in 1896, is on display at Gary Regional Airport. Orville Wright credited Octave Chanute with building the prototype of the plane that the Wright Brothers flew four years later, under power for the first time at Kitty Hawk, NC.

The Indiana Dunes pop up intermittently along the shore of Lake Michigan from Gary to Michigan City, IN. Poet Carl Sandbergdescribed the dunes as being ''to the Midwest what the Grand Canyon is to Arizona and Yosemite is to California. They constitute a signature of time and eternity.'' The dunes, refuge for woodland hikers with miles of trails believed to be left from indigenous peoples before the white pioneers, have been recognized as a national treasure by the U.S. Congress. The Paul H. Douglas Environmental Center at the Indiana Dunes National Lakeshore educates people in the fields of ecology and environmental science. Also at the Dunes are the Bailly Homestead, which offers a look at pioneer and Native American life, and the Chellberg Farm, where visitors may catch a glimpse into early 1900's farming. The Brunswick Park Savanna, a 49-acre park on Gary's west side, features rare plants such as black oak, bluejoint grass, and prairie sunflowers that have been safeguarded in the preserve. Brunswick Park also has tennis courts and picnic areas.

Festivals and Holidays

In June the U.S. Steelyard Stadium hosts a gospel festival with plenty of food, activities for children, and top gospel singers and groups. The Fourth of July is one of the biggest festivities of the year in Gary, with an Independence Day parade, fireworks in most parks, and a two day Independence Day Music Festival which always features a nationally known recording artist. In mid-July everyone is treated to the Gary Air Show. The free show is held in Marquette Park, where about 20 acts including every branch of the military plus civilians perform acrobatics in the air. In August there's a Jazz Festival and in September the Labor Day Blues Festival is held.

Sports for the Spectator

Minor league/semi-pro teams have recently come to Gary. The Continental Basketball Association includes a team in

Gary as of 2000, named the Gary Steelheads, who play in the revamped Genesis Center. The Gary Southshore Railcats are a Northern League of Professional Baseball expansion team who began playing in 2002. The following year the Railcats' home stadium was completed, dubbed the U.S. Steel Yard. The Steel Yard seats about 6,000 and is used for concerts and conventions in the off season.

Sports for the Participant

There are 57 parks in Gary, plus Lake Etta, which is a Lake County park whose waters are stocked with a variety of fish. Opportunities abound for swimming, hiking, biking, tennis, hayrides, basketball, horseback riding, running, cross country skiing, softball, and golf. Lake County also offers 20 public golf courses. For those who wish to enjoy 12,000 acres of carefully preserved nature, there is the Indiana Dunes National Lakeshore Park, which stretches across both Lake and Porter counties.

Shopping and Dining

Gary and Lake County offer a wide variety of shopping venues, from quaint antique shops and specialty stores particular to the Miller beach neighborhood, to strip malls with national chain stores.

Restaurants abound, from casual ''soul food'' places and fast food chains to new upscale establishments popping up all around the gaming and marina spots at Buffington Harbor.

Visitor Information: Lake County Convention and Visitors Bureau, 5800 Broadway, Suite S, Merrillville, IN 46410; telephone (219)980-1617; toll-free (800)ALL-LAKE

Convention Facilities

The strikingly designed Genesis Convention Center is the largest such facility in Northwest Indiana and can accommodate up to 7,000 people, with 11 separate meeting rooms for 40 to 400 participants. Besides being home to the Steelheads basketball team, Genesis Center is a multi-function venue for weddings, seminars, conferences and the like. The luxurious new Trump Hotel Casino at Buffington harbor features conference facilities and many amenities such as in-room fax machines, a modern exercise facility, and gaming, entertainment, and dining.

Convention Information: Lake County Convention and Visitors Bureau, 5800 Broadway, Merrillville, IN 46410; telephone (219)980-1617; toll-free (800)ALL-LAKE

Transportation

Approaching the City

Located about 28 miles southeast of Chicago, Gary is accessible from Interstate 65 which runs north and south, and I-94/80, which runs east and west. The Indiana Toll Road I-90 connects to the Chicago Skyway to the west and the Ohio Turnpike to the east. Greyhound Trailways, Indiana, TriState, and Vancom bus lines go into Gary. The South Shore Line is a 90 mile electric railway that can speed commuters to and from Gary and Chicago.

Gary Regional Airport, four miles east of the city on U.S. Route 12, houses Direct Air, which provides passenger service to Pittsburgh, Cleveland, Detroit, and Fort Wayne. Gary Regional Airport advertises itself as an alternative to the congestion of Chicago's Midway and O'Hare airports; it is only 30 minutes from downtown Chicago.

Traveling in the City

Local bus transportation is provided by Gary Public Transit Corporation.

Communications

Newspapers and Magazines

Published in Gary are the general daily paper the *Post-Tribune* and the community newspapers *Gary American* and *Gary Crusader.*

Television and Radio

There are four TV stations in and near Gary. With six AM and three FM radio stations in the area, plus proximity to Chicago, listeners can enjoy virtually any style of music or talk radio.

Media Information: Post-Tribune, 1065 Broadway, Gary, IN 46402; telephone (800)753-5533

Gary Online

Calumet Regional Archives. Available www.lib.iun.indiana .edu/crahome.htm

City of Gary home page. Available www.gary.in.us

Empowerment Zone home page. Available www.hud.gov/cpd/ezec/ezeclist.html

Indiana University Northwest Library. Available www.lib .iun.indiana.edu

Lake County Convention and Visitors Bureau. Available www.alllake.org

Post-Tribune. Available www.post-trib.com

Selected Bibliography

Catlin, Robert A., *Racial Politics and Urban Planning: Gary Indiana 1981-1989* (University of Kentucky, 1993)

Indianapolis

The City in Brief

Founded: 1821 (incorporated, 1847)

Head Official: Mayor Bart Peterson (D) (since January 2000)

City Population
　1980: 701,000
　1990: 731,278
　2000: 781,870
　2003 estimate: 783,438
　Percent change, 1990–2000: 6.9%
　U.S. rank in 1980: 12th
　U.S. rank in 1990: 13th
　U.S. rank in 2000: 17th (State rank: 1st)

Metropolitan Area Population
　1980: 1,167,000
　1990: 1,380,491
　2000: 1,607,486
　Percent change, 1990–2000: 16.4%
　U.S. rank in 1980: 30th
　U.S. rank in 1990: Not reported
　U.S. rank in 2000: 29th

Area: 361 square miles (2000)
Elevation: Ranges from 645 to 910 feet above sea level
Average Annual Temperature: 52.1° F
Average Annual Precipitation: 40 inches of rain, 23 inches of snow

Major Economic Sectors: Trade, services, manufacturing
Unemployment Rate: 5.7% (March 2005)
Per Capita Income: $21,640 (1999)

2002 FBI Crime Index Total: Not reported

Major Colleges and Universities: Indiana University-Purdue University at Indianapolis; Butler University; University of Indianapolis; Ivy-Tech; Marian College

Daily Newspaper: *The Indianapolis Star*

Introduction

Indianapolis is the capital of Indiana and the seat of Marion County; the Indianapolis metropolitan statistical area includes Boone, Hamilton, Hancock, Hendricks, Johnson, Madison, Marion, Morgan, and Shelby counties. Decreed by proclamation in the nineteenth century as the state capital and carved out of the wilderness where only a settlers' camp had previously stood, Indianapolis redefined itself by the end of the twentieth century. The city is undergoing a renaissance of far-ranging proportions through development and improvement projects that are transforming both the image and the character of the downtown area. Building on the fame of the annual Indianapolis 500 automobile race, the city has become a national center for amateur sports and athletics; it is also a major financial, industrial, commercial, and transportation center for the Midwest. Education and the arts flourish in Indianapolis, and Circle Centre, an entertainment and shopping complex, has sparked renewed commercial and economic development in the city center.

Geography and Climate

Situated on level or slightly rolling terrain in central Indiana east of the White River, Indianapolis has a temperate climate; because of even distribution of precipitation throughout the year, there are no pronounced wet or dry seasons. Summers are very warm, and the invasion of polar air from the north often produces frigid winter temperatures with low humidity. Two to three times each winter, snowfalls average three inches or more.

Area: 361 square miles (2000)

Elevation: 645 feet to 910 feet above sea level

Average Temperatures: January, 26.0° F; July, 75.0° F; annual average, 52.1° F

Average Annual Precipitation: 40 inches of rain, 23 inches of snow

History

Site Chosen for Central Location

The city of Indianapolis was established not by settlers but by proclamation when Indiana was granted statehood in 1816. The United States Congress set aside four sections of public land for the site of the capital of the Union's nineteenth state. In January 1820, the Indiana legislature picked 10 commissioners and charged them with the mandate to locate the new capital as near as possible to the center of the state, the purpose being to take advantage of western migration. The following February, George Pogue and John McCormick settled with their families on land that was to become the site of Indianapolis. Other settlers soon arrived and by the summer of 1820 a dozen families had built cabins along the riverbank in a settlement named Fall Creek. In June 1820, the commissioners selected for the capital a location that was close to the exact center of the state; on that spot was the cabin of John McCormick.

After the legislature approved the site in 1821, the name Indianapolis, a combination of Indiana plus the Greek word *polis* for city, was chosen. Four square miles were allotted for the city, but the chief surveyor, E. P. Fordham, plotted an area of only one square mile because it seemed inconceivable that the capital would ever be any larger. Alexander Ralston, who previously had helped plot the District of Columbia, was hired to design the future city. He decided to model it on the nation's capital, with four broad avenues branching out diagonally to the north, south, east and west from a central circle.

In 1821 Indianapolis became the county seat of the newly configured Marion County, and four years later, when the state legislature met for the first time, Indianapolis boasted one street and a population of 600 people. By the time the town was incorporated in 1832 the population had reached only 1,000 people. Growth was slow because Indianapolis—which now holds the distinction of being one of the world's most populous cities not situated near navigable waters—lay on the banks of the White River, which was too shallow for commerce.

Road/Rail Transport Create a Regional Center

The construction of the Central Canal from Broad Ripple to Indianapolis seemed to solve the problem temporarily, but the canal turned out to be useless when water volume decreased. The routing of the national highway through the center of Indianapolis in 1831 provided a more permanent solution, fulfilling the original purpose of the city's location. In 1847, the year Indianapolis was incorporated as a city, the Madison & Indianapolis Railroad arrived, soon to be followed by seven additional major rail lines, which gave the city access to the Ohio River.

On the eve of the Civil War the population, aided by an influx of German immigrants, had increased to 18,611 people; the city now provided modern services and supported a stable, manufacturing-based economy. With 24 army camps and a large ammunition plant, Indianapolis became a major wartime center for Union campaigns on the western front.

Progress continued into the postwar period only to be set back by the inflationary recession of 1873. During the last two decades of the nineteenth century, Indianapolis experienced a period of growth known as the "golden age." It became, in 1881, one of the first American cities to install electric street lighting. Many downtown landmarks were erected in an explosion of public architecture that helped establish the city's identity. A new market, a new statehouse, and Union Station were completed in the late 1880s. The neglected Circle Park had deteriorated and was revived when the Soldiers' and Sailors' Monument was constructed in honor of the people who served in the Civil War. During this period, wealthy citizens built palatial Victorian homes on North Meridian Street, and as the result of the growth of new neighborhoods and suburbs along tree-lined avenues, Indianapolis became known as the "city of homes."

At the turn of the century, Indianapolis was a leader in the burgeoning automobile industry. Local inventor Charles H. Black is credited with building in 1891 the first internal combustion gasoline engine automobile, which eventually proved to be impractical because its ignition required a kerosene torch. Sixty-five different kinds of automobiles were in production before World War I, including Stutz, Coasts, Duesenberg, and Cole. Other Indianapolis industrialists originated many innovations and improvements in automotive manufacturing, including four-wheel brakes and the six-cylinder engine.

Sporting Events Attract International Attention

The most significant development was the Indianapolis Motor Speedway, a 2.5-mile oval track, which was inaugurated in 1911 when an Indianapolis-made car named the Marmon won the first race. The Indianapolis 500, held on Memorial Day weekend each year, has since become one of the premier international sporting events, drawing world-wide attention. Indianapolis was a major industrial center by 1920, with a population of more than 300,000 people, yet retained much of its small-town ambience.

A pivotal event in the total transformation of Indianapolis from a manufacturing to a sporting town occurred in 1969, when a change in federal tax laws required charitable foundations to spend more money. The Lilly Endowment, a local foundation based on the Eli Lilly drug fortune decided to concentrate on Indianapolis. The result was a massive capital infusion promoting sport business in the city and leading to the conversion of the city's convention center into a 61,000-seat football stadium.

In 1970 the creation of UniGov combined city government with Marion County government, immediately making Indianapolis the eleventh largest city in the nation. The city made dramatic strides in its national reputation through initiatives implemented by the UniGov structure. Indianapolis renovated its core historical structures, built new sports facilities, and invested in the arts and entertainment. The city positioned itself as an international amateur sports capital when, in 1987, it invested in athletic facilities and hosted both the World Indoor Track and Field Championships and the Pan American Games, second in importance only to the summer Olympics.

Indianapolis 2000 . . .

In January 2000 Bart Peterson, a Democrat, took office as mayor of Indianapolis. During his 1999 campaign for mayor, Peterson introduced "The Peterson Plan," a bold and detailed vision for Indianapolis in the new millennium. He focused on fighting crime more aggressively, improving public education in Marion County, and delivering better services to neighborhoods. In his first month as mayor, Mayor Peterson convened the nation's first citywide summit on race relations, bringing people together to discuss ways to bridge the gaps that sometimes exist between people of different races, religions and backgrounds. He also appointed the most diverse administration in the city's 180-year history.

. . . and Today

Indianapolis today is a cosmopolitan blend of arts, education, culture, and sports; a city with plenty of vision for its future. Building on momentum gained in the last decade of the twentieth century, the city is in the midst of a cultural and quality-of-life resurgence. World-class sports, a diverse economy, and the presence of healthy and successful businesses round out the story of Indianapolis in the twenty-first century.

Historical Information: Indiana State Library, 140 N. Senate Ave., Indianapolis, IN 46204-2296; telephone (317)232-3675. Indiana Historical Society, Willard Henry Smith Memorial Library, 315 W. Ohio St. Indianapolis, IN 46202-3299; telephone (317)232-1879; fax (317)233-3109

Population Profile

Metropolitan Area Residents
   1980: 1,167,000
   1990: 1,380,491
   2000: 1,607,486
   Percent change, 1990–2000: 16.4%
   U.S. rank in 1980: 30th
   U.S. rank in 1990: Not reported
   U.S. rank in 2000: 29th

City Residents
1980: 701,000
1990: 731,278
2000: 781,870
2003 estimate: 783,438
Percent change, 1990–2000: 6.9%
U.S. rank in 1980: 12th
U.S. rank in 1990: 13th
U.S. rank in 2000: 17th (State rank: 1st)

Density: 2,163 people per square mile (2000)

Racial and ethnic characteristics (2000)
  White: 540,212
  Black or African American: 199,412
  American Indian and Alaska Native: 1,985
  Asian: 11,161
  Native Hawaiian and Pacific Islander: 322
  Hispanic or Latino (may be of any race): 30,636
  Other: 15,921

Percent of residents born in state: 67.5% (2000)

Age characteristics (2000)
  Population under 5 years old: 57,523
  Population 5 to 9 years old: 57,020
  Population 10 to 14 years old: 54,675
  Population 15 to 19 years old: 52,446
  Population 20 to 24 years old: 58,365
  Population 25 to 34 years old: 129,409
  Population 35 to 44 years old: 127,782
  Population 45 to 54 years old: 99,336
  Population 55 to 59 years old: 32,613
  Population 60 to 64 years old: 26,843
  Population 65 to 74 years old: 45,358
  Population 75 to 84 years old: 30,168
  Population 85 years and older: 10,332
  Median age: 33.5 years

Births (2002, Marion County)
  Total number: 14,540

Deaths (2002, Marion County)
  Total number: 7,487

Money income (1999)
  Per capita income: $21,640
  Median household income: $40,051
  Total households: 320,518

Number of households with income of . . .
  less than $10,000: 28,240
  $10,000 to $14,999: 20,046
  $15,000 to $24,999: 44,902
  $25,000 to $34,999: 45,676
  $35,000 to $49,999: 56,718
  $50,000 to $74,999: 63,369
  $75,000 to $99,999: 30,508
  $100,000 to $149,999: 20,506
  $150,000 to $199,999: 5,034
  $200,000 or more: 5,519

Percent of families below poverty level: 9.1% (40.6% of which were female householder families with related children under 5 years)

2002 FBI Crime Index Total: Not reported

Municipal Government

Indianapolis and Marion County operate as a consolidated governmental functions to form Unigov, with jurisdiction including all of Marion County except the town of Speedway and the cities of Beech Grove, Lawrence, and Southport. The mayor, who serves a four-year term, holds executive powers; the 29 members of City-County Council are elected to four-year terms by district and at large. A six-department city government administers Unigov programs.

Head Official: Mayor Bart Peterson (D) (since 2000; current term expires December 2007)

Total Number of City-County Employees: 3,800 (2005)

City Information: City of Indianapolis/Marion County, 200 East Washington Street, City-County Building, Indianapolis, IN 46204; telephone (317)327-3601

Economy

Major Industries and Commercial Activity

Indianapolis is a primary industrial, commercial, and transportation center for the Midwest. Situated in proximity to the vast agricultural region known as the corn belt and to the industrialized cities of the upper Midwest and the East, Indianapolis is supported by a diversified economic base. Prior to the 1980s, the city's principal industry was manufacturing, which has been displaced by retailing and services. Having made a conscious decision to achieve prosperity through sports, Indianapolis quadrupled its tourism trade and doubled its hotel space during the period 1984–1991, largely by hosting amateur sporting events. Since that period, Indianapolis' role in the sports arena has magnified. Each major sporting event pumps tens of millions of dollars into the economy and leads to expanded business opportunities, more jobs, and increasing tax payments to the city. Tourism and conventions, including the hotel industry, are major economic factors.

Top-performing companies based in Indianapolis include Anthem Inc., Conseco Inc., Eli Lilly and Company, Guidant Corp., Duke Realty Corp., Hunt Construction Group, National Wine & Spirits, and Simon Property Group. Major employers include Clarian Health, Dow AgroSciences, Roche Diagnostics, and more than 20 others.

The insurance industry has long been established in Indianapolis; several insurance companies have located their headquarters and regional offices in the city. With the largest stockyards east of Chicago, Indianapolis is also an important meatpacking center.

Items and goods produced: food and allied products, furniture and woodworking, paper and allied products, printing and publishing, chemicals, petroleum and allied products, rubber and plastic products, primary metals, fabricated metal products, machinery, electrical and electronics equipment, transportation equipment, instruments, medical and optical goods, knitted garments, bricks

Incentive Programs—New and Existing Companies

Principal goals of Unigov are stimulation of business growth through a broader distribution of the tax base, streamlined business access to government services, and expansion of city boundaries. The Greater Indianapolis Progress Committee, an independent adjunct of the mayor's office, and the Corporate Community Council facilitate public and private business cooperation.

Local programs—The City of Indianapolis offers a maximum $20,000 grant for remediation of brownfields in its Brownfields Grant Program. The Facade Grant Program offers rebates of up to 50 percent of total cost (or a maximum of $10,000) for facade improvements. Other programs include the Neighborhood Action Grant, tax abatements for Economic Revitalization Area designation, procurement opportunities, and Community Development Block Grants.

State programs—The State of Indiana offers tax credits for businesses expanding in Indiana or newly-operating in Indiana through its Economic Development for a Growing Economy (EDGE) program. Tax Credits are also available through the Enterprise Zone Program. The Skills Enhancement Fund reimburses eligible employee training costs, as does the TECH Fund, GET program, WIN program, and several others. The state grants loans and administers such programs as the Small Business Administration 7A Program, the Indiana Business Modernization and Technology Corporation, the Corporation for Innovation Development, and the Indiana Corporation for Science and Technology (research and development grants).

Job training programs—Indianapolis Private Industry Council Inc. provides job services through seven WorkOne centers throughout the city; it also contracts out federal Workforce Investment Act youth programs and assists businesses with hiring and training programs. IMPACT, Indiana's Welfare-to-Work program, assists in training and skills. JobWorks provides assistance to area businesses and job-seekers throughout Northeastern Indiana.

Development Projects

Indianapolis is in the midst of a cultural and quality-of-life resurgence that shows no signs of slowing. In 1999 White River Gardens, a $15 million ''sister institution'' to the Indianapolis Zoo, opened its 3.3 acres of botanical and water gardens and a five story conservatory. Also that year the $35.7 million Indiana Historical Society headquarters opened downtown, as did the Conseco Fieldhouse, a 750,000 square foot stadium seating 18,500.

In 2000 the Adam's Mark Hotel & Suites opened in a converted building near the state capitol, with 332 luxury suites and guest rooms at a price tag of $50 million. The Indiana Convention Center and RCA Dome added 100,000 square feet of exhibit space, placing the center among the top 25 in the country. At $45 million, the expansion was completed in 2001 and also added new meeting space, a new entrance, pre-function space, and a skywalk linking the center to the new Indianapolis Marriott Downtown (opened the same year).

In 2002 the Indiana State Museum opened a new 270,000 square foot, $105 million building constructed entirely of materials found in Indiana, including sandstone, limestone, steel, brick, and glass. New facilities at the White River State Park were completed in 2003 with a new park entrance, visitor center, and children's play area. That same year ground was broken for a new terminal at the Indianapolis International Airport, slated for completion in 2008. The Children's Museum of Indianapolis opened its new $25 million permanent exhibit, Dinosphere, in 2004; it is the largest exhibit of dinosaur fossils in the nation. Also in 2004 the Indianapolis Museum of Contemporary Art (iMOCA) opened downtown. The Conrad Hotel, the city's first five-star hotel, is under construction and expected to be completed in 2006.

In April 2005 a $900 million financing bill was passed for the creation of a new, multi-purpose stadium and expanded convention center; groundbreaking was expected to begin in the summer of 2005, with a completion date slated for September of 2010. The new facility would more than double the current convention center's space; while the current center just underwent its third expansion since its opening, feasibility studies concluded that still more space is needed. When complete, the project will provide the city with 733,700 square feet of exhibit space, including 583,700 square feet of exhibit space in the convention center, plus 150,000 in the connected multi-purpose stadium.

Economic Development Information: Division of Planning, City of Indianapolis, 200 East Washington St., Suite 1802, Indianapolis, IN 46204; telephone (317)327-5112

Commercial Shipping

Indianapolis is a major transportation and distribution hub for the Midwest. As the most centrally located of the largest 100 cities in the United States, Indianapolis is within 650 miles of 55 percent of all Americans, or more than 50 million households. The city is served by four interstate highways, six railroads, an international airport, and a foreign trade zone. Three ports serve the entire state and are all within a three hour drive of Indianapolis.

The hub of an extensive rail network, Indianapolis has a total of 26 rail corridors in operation, and five key freight facilities. CSX and Norfolk Southern are the two Class 1 operations, and the four shortlines consist of Indiana Railroad Co., Indiana Southern, Louisville & Indiana Rail, and Central Railroad of Indiana.

Labor Force and Employment Outlook

Indianapolis employers draw from a workforce of about one million skilled and educated regional workers; the region boasts a higher than national average worker productivity rate. The economic diversity of the region contributes to its success, as does its attractiveness to companies due to the transportation infrastructure, skilled workforce, business incentives, and quality of life.

With central Indiana becoming less dependent on the automobile industry, manufacturing continues to be the strongest economic sector in Indianapolis. In the third quarter of 2004, Indianapolis manufacturing firms employed just over 13 percent of the labor force. Health care industries supported just over 12 percent of the area's jobs, with retail and accommodation and food service following, with 11.5 percent and 9 percent of the area's jobs, respectively.

The developers of the new convention center project (PricewaterhouseCoopers) estimate that the city could benefit by an additional 18-23 major conventions and trade shows annually as well as 4-5 additional consumer shows annually, generating an additional $165 million as well as creating about 2,700 new jobs.

The multitude of downtown development projects added, and continue to add, jobs in the area as well as to generate billions of dollars to the local economy. Indianapolis continues to attract high-profile companies, who headquarter or set up shop in the city.

The following is a summary of data regarding the Indianapolis metropolitan area labor force, 2004 annual average:

Size of non-agricultural labor force: 878,700

Number of workers employed in . . .
　construction and mining: 51,900
　manufacturing: 101,300
　trade, transportation and utilities: 188,700
　information: 16,500
　financial activities: 63,500
　professional and business services: 118,100
　educational and health services: 106,100
　leisure and hospitality: 84,800
　other services: 34,400
　government: 113,600

Average hourly earnings of production workers employed in manufacturing: $21.48

Unemployment rate: 5.7% (March 2005)

Largest corporate employers	*Number of employees*
Eli Lilly and Company	14,089
Purdue University	13,831
Indiana University-Purdue University at Indiana	7,066
Indiana University	6,987
Marsh Supermarkets	5,800
Rolls-Royce	4,400
FedEx	4,200
Allison Transmission/Division of GMC	4,000
SBC Indiana	3,850
WellPoint Inc.	3,600

Cost of Living

State taxes are consistently rated among the lowest in the country in terms of total state and local tax collections per capita. Utility costs are also relatively low. Overall cost of living consistently ranks at or below the national average.

The following is a summary of data regarding several key cost of living factors in the Indianapolis area.

2004 ACCRA (3rd Quarter) Cost of Living Index: 100.4 (U.S. average = 100.0)

2004 ACCRA (3rd Quarter) Average House Price: $241,667 (Hamilton County)

State income tax rate: 3.4% of adjusted gross income

State sales tax rate: 6.0%

Local income tax rate: 0.7%

Local sales tax rate: 1.0%

Property tax rate: 1.53 per $100 assessed valuation

Economic Information: Greater Indianapolis Chamber of Commerce, 111 Monument Circle, Suite 1950, Indianapolis, IN 46204; telephone (317)464-2200; fax (317)464-2217

Education and Research

Elementary and Secondary Schools

Indiana's public school standards were retooled in 2000 after an education group criticized the state for not challenging its youth. The standards are applied in Indianapolis by the Indianapolis Public Schools (IPS) system, the largest district in the state. A nonpartisan, seven-member school board appoints a superintendent. IPS offers vocational education and alternative school programs; magnet/option programs include athletic careers, business and finance, communications arts, performing and visual arts, foreign language, and 12 others.

The following is a summary of data regarding the Indianapolis public schools as of the 2004–2005 school year.

Total enrollment: 39,115

Number of facilities
   elementary schools: 49
   junior high schools: 13
   senior high schools: 5
   other: 12 (including 8 mixed-grade schools and 4 alternative schools)

Student/teacher ratio: K-5, 20:1; 6-8, 22:1, 9-12, 23:1

Teacher salaries
   average: $49,740

Funding per pupil: $11,913 (2003-2004)

More than 120 other schools, including preschools, alternative centers, religious schools, academies, Montessori-based schools, academies, and others operate within Indianapolis.

Public Schools Information: Indianapolis Public Schools, 120 East Walnut Street, Indianapolis, IN 46204; telephone (317)226-4000

Colleges and Universities

Several public and private institutions of higher learning are located in Indianapolis. Affiliated with the two major state universities is Indiana University-Purdue University at Indianapolis; more than 29,000 students are enrolled in associate, baccalaureate, master's, and doctorate programs. Of the 18 programs and 185 majors offered, areas of specialization include art, engineering technologies, dentistry, law, medical technology, nursing, occupational therapy, and social work. Butler University and the University of Indianapolis, both private institutions, award undergraduate and graduate degrees in such fields as music, pharmacy, nursing, education, and physical therapy.

Among the colleges and technical schools in the Indianapolis metropolitan region are Marian College, offering a liberal arts curriculum, and Indiana Vocational Technical College (Ivy Tech), one of a network of 23 state training and education centers.

Libraries and Research Centers

In addition to its main branch downtown, the Indianapolis-Marion County Public Library operates 22 branches throughout the city. The library, with holdings of more than 1.9 million volumes, has an annual circulation of more than seven million items and maintains special collections of first editions of Indiana authors, early textbooks, and the poetry of James Whitcomb Riley, and is a U.S. document depository. In 2005 the central library existed in an interim home while undergoing expansion and renovation to the original library to bring it to 293,000 square feet of total space. The new central library, once completed in 2006, will include a 350-seat auditorium, a four-story glass atrium, a 400-space underground parking facility, and an Indianapolis Special Collections Room, among other features.

The Indiana State Library, also located downtown, houses more than 2 million printed items plus millions of manuscripts, photographs, microfilms, and federal and state documents. Special collections include the Indiana Academy of Science Library; an Indiana Collection; a large assortment of books on tape, Braille and large print books;. and a Manuscript Section housing almost three million items including war letters and eighteenth century fur traders' papers. The Indiana Historical Society Library specializes in the Civil War, early North American travel accounts, and the history of Indiana and the Northwest Territory.

The University Library at Indiana University-Purdue University at Indianapolis (IUPUI) houses more than 650,000 volumes and more than 4,000 periodical subscriptions; other libraries within the IUPUI system include the Herron School of Art Library, the Ruth Lilly Medical Library, the School of Dentistry Library, and the Ruth Lilly Law Library. Holdings in all the IUPUI libraries combined total more than 2.5 million items. Butler University's holdings include a music and fine arts collection.

Indianapolis is home to a variety of special libraries and research centers, many of them related to the universities. Among them is the Hudson Institute, the internationally renowned policy research organization. State agencies, such as the Indiana Department of Commerce, the Indiana Department of Education, and the Indiana Department of Environmental Management also operate libraries. Other specialized libraries are affiliated with law firms, hospitals, newspapers, publishing houses, museums, and churches and synagogues. Of unique interest are the Indianapolis Zoo Library and the Children's Museum of Indianapolis Library.

Research is conducted at centers administered by or affiliated with Indiana University-Purdue University at Indianapolis, researching topics such as aging, the environment, biology, medicine, law, economics, and many others. Butler University research programs are conducted on a wide variety of topics.

Public Library Information: Indianapolis-Marion County Public Library, PO Box 211, Indianapolis, IN 46206; telephone (317)269-1700

Health Care

Indianapolis is a Midwestern health care hub and home to the state's only medical school. Indianapolis's four major health care systems are Community Health Network, with five hospitals and several outpatient facilities; Clarian Health, with three hospitals including the Riley Hospital for Children and the Indiana University Hospital; St. Francis Hospital and Health Centers, and St. Vincent Hospitals and Health Services. Clarian is the city's largest system, with three hospitals in the city containing a total of 1,322 beds. The city of Indianapolis is divided into four quadrants, each one dominated by one of the city's four main health care systems.

A significant force in the regional medical community is the Indiana University Medical Center, affiliated with the second-largest medical school in the nation. With a faculty of more than 1,100, research is conducted in a variety of areas, including cancer, diabetes, Alzheimer's disease, genetics, and others.

Based in Indianapolis is the national headquarters of a major physical fitness organization, the American College of Sports Medicine, which conducts studies on and aims to increase awareness about physical activity. Local hospitals and private groups offer a diversity of health and fitness programs, ranging from stress management to nutrition and biofeedback therapy.

Recreation

Sightseeing

Easily within driving distance for more than half of the country's population, Indianapolis has set out to make itself an attractive tourist destination by combining diverse cultural opportunities with first-class hotels and fine shopping and dining. Revitalization of the downtown core, where modernized nineteenth-century buildings stand adjacent to

futuristic structures, has made Indianapolis an architecturally interesting city.

The street grid, modeled after Washington, D.C., makes the center-city Mile Square a compact and convenient area for walking tours. In Monument Circle the Soldiers' and Sailors' Monument observation platform offers a panoramic view of the city and the surrounding countryside. The Indiana War Memorial Plaza, a five-block downtown mall providing urban green space, contains a 100-foot granite monolith, flags from all 50 states, and a fountain at University Square. The plaza houses the national headquarters of the American Legion; a museum of martial history is located in the Memorial Shrine building.

Indianapolis has turned its attention back toward the city's most prominent natural feature—the White River. Ignored for generations, the river is now the centerpiece of White River State Park, a 250-acre urban greenspace just blocks from the city's commercial heart. The park is home to the Indianapolis Zoo, the White River Gardens, the NCAA Headquarters and Hall of Fame, the Congressional Medal of Honor Memorial, Victory Field, the Eiteljorg Museum of American Indian and Western Art, the new Indiana State Museum (opened in 2002), and Indiana's only IMAX movie theater. Common spaces in the park attract personal events, such as weddings, family reunions, and picnics, to large festivals, concerts, and even conferences. The Lawn, opened in 2003, features a waterfront bandstand and space for 5,000 people.

The Indianapolis Zoo, the first urban zoo to be built in several decades, houses more than 2,000 animals. The zoo is located on 64 acres in the urban White River State Park. The whale and dolphin pavilion presents shows with bottlenose dolphins, beluga whales, and false killer whales. Piranha and giant snakes live in a simulated Amazon forest; the desert conservatory, covered by an acrylic dome, features plant and animal life from the world's arid regions.

Capitol Commons contains the Indiana Statehouse, which houses the governor's office and the General Assembly. Garfield Park, home of Garfield Park Conservatory, features more than 500 examples of tropical flora, rare carnivorous plants, and tropical birds; the park contains formal gardens, fountains and limestone bridges. The Scottish Rite Cathedral, built of Indiana limestone, is the largest Masonic temple in the world; its 54-bell carillon can be heard city wide.

Victorian architecture enthusiasts can visit the well-preserved James Whitcomb Riley Home; built in 1872, it was the residence—during the last 23 years of his life—of the Hoosier dialect poet who created Little Orphan Annie. The President Benjamin Harrison Home is a 16-room Italianate mansion, completed in 1875, where much of the original Harrison family furniture is displayed. The Massachusetts

Avenue Historic Fire Station was restored in 1988 as a museum equipped with a children's fire safety laboratory.

Arts and Culture

The Indianapolis Art Center is a not-for-profit community arts organization whose mission is to make art accessible to all residents of Indianapolis. The center consists of the Marilyn K. Glick School of Art, designed by architect Michael Graves and comprising 13 art studios, a 224-seat auditorium, a library, and a gift shop; the Cultural Complex, which features a Fiber Studio and individual artist's studios, as well as the Writers' Center of Indiana; and ARTSPARK, opening in 2005. The 12-acre campus sits on the edge of White River and features a riverfront deck, outdoor stage, and sculpture gardens.

The Indianapolis renaissance is most evident in the city's dedication to the renewal of its cultural life. Artsgarden features an eight-story, 12,500-square-foot glass dome suspended over a downtown intersection. The $12 million Artsgarden is linked by skywalks to the RCA Dome, convention center, hotels, and Circle Centre. The Artsgarden serves as a performance, exhibition, and marketing space for the Indianapolis arts community, hosting 350 events annually. A number of historically significant nineteenth-century buildings have also been refurbished in order to present local arts organizations in the best possible environment.

The Indianapolis Symphony Orchestra, founded in 1930, performs year-round in the restored historic Hilbert Circle Theatre and at parks and elsewhere throughout the city and state. Indianapolis Opera presents four full-scale operas per season. The Indianapolis Children's Choir has received international acclaim and has been performing since 1986. The Madame Walker Theatre Center, honoring the country's first female self-made millionaire, houses the Walker Theatre, where "Jazz on the Avenue" concerts are held on Fridays.

Ballet Internationale is a professional resident troupe that performs at Murat Center. Clowes Memorial Hall on the campus of Butler University is home to the Indianapolis Opera and the Indianapolis Chamber Orchestra. Dance Kaleidoscope is the city's contemporary dance troupe.

An active theater community contributes to the city's cultural life. The Indianapolis Civic Theatre, the nation's oldest continuously active civic theater group, performs at Marian Hall Auditorium at Marian College—the groups' interim home while plans are being made to build a new, multipurpose community theatre facility. The Indiana Repertory Theatre, the state's largest equity theater, presents more than 300 performances annually and is housed in the restored Indiana Theatre. European-style performances are the specialty of American Cabaret Theatre, formerly of New York City. Beef and Boards Dinner Theatre presents Broadway shows, concerts, and dinner. Off-Broadway plays are staged by Phoenix Theatre, presenting 16 shows annually in a restored church in the Chatham Arch Historic District.

The Indianapolis Museum of Art (IMA) is located in a wooded cultural park. The Museum of Art holds the largest American collection of works by the nineteenth-century British landscape artist J. M. W. Turner. The J. W. Holliday Collection of Neo-Impressionist art, an extensive collection of Japanese Edo-period paintings, and the Robert Indiana *Love* painting, with a matching outdoor sculpture in large rusted letters, round out one of the most impressive collections in the Midwest. In 2003 and 2004, various parts of the museum were closed as part of a $74 million construction project, adding 164,000 square feet to the museum and renovating 90,000 square feet of existing space. A new entry pavilion, as well as new galleries and the new Deer-Zink Events Pavilion, two new restaurants, and an expanded museum shop were part of the expansion. Parts of the new IMA were opened to the public in May 2005 during a grand reopening celebration; remaining galleries will reopen in phases through 2006.

On the grounds of the IMA is the Oldfields-Lilly House & Gardens, featuring an eighteenth-century French-style chateau, formerly the residence of J. K. Lilly Jr. and now open for tours. The Virginia B. Fairbanks Art & Nature Park offers 100 acres of natural, wooded landscape, with paths, waterways, and opportunities for visitors to experience "interaction of art and nature."

The Children's Museum is the world's largest museum of its type and one of the 20 most-visited museums in the country. The 400,000 square foot facility features a variety of hands-on exhibits and touchable scientific experiments as well as a planetarium. Favorite exhibits include an Egyptian mummy, a Victorian carousel, and the largest public collection of toy trains. In "Passport to the World," children learn about foreign cultures through toys from around the world. Each year more than 1.1 million people visit the Children's Museum. The Eli Lilly Center for Exploration at the museum allows children to explore and experiment with current issues. A $50 million renovation was completed in 2004, opening the new Dinosphere exhibit, an immersive dinosaur experience that allows visitors a close-up look at how dinosaurs may have lived.

The award-winning Conner Prairie Pioneer Settlement, a living history museum, presents an authentic recreation of Hoosier life in the 1800s. The Indiana State Museum chronicles the history and culture of the state and features a collection of more than 400,000 artifacts and an IMAX theater. The National Art Museum of Sports is housed in the Indiana University-Purdue University at Indianapolis campus' University Place and contains ancient and modern art depicting sports motifs; 40 sports are represented in 800 paintings, sculptures, and paper works. Other museums in the city are Indiana Medical History Museum, Hook's Discovery & Learning Center, and Indianapolis Motor Speedway and Hall of Fame Museum.

Festivals and Holidays

Each year Indianapolis presents a host of festivals and fairs that celebrate the city's history, traditions, and ethnic heritage. The most elaborate is the month-long annual 500 Festival in May, which combines events associated with the Indianapolis 500 race as well as other activities, like the Mini Marathon and 5K races, a parade, Mayor's Breakfast, a Kids' Day, and others. The St. Benno Fest in March celebrates the city's German heritage. April holds the Indiana International Film Festival, one of two film festivals in the city. Midwestern artists present their crafts and art work in June at the Talbot Street Art Fair. The Indiana Black Expo Summer Celebration celebrates African American heritage over 10 days in July at the Indiana Convention Center.

Oktoberfest takes place in early September, followed by Penrod Arts Fair, a commemorative celebration of Indianapolis author Booth Tarkington's most famous character, with art exhibits and entertainment at the Indianapolis Museum of Art. A three-day International Festival is held in late October; the Heartland Film Festival in October celebrates independent and theatrically-released films. The Madrigal Dinners ring in the year-end holiday season on the campus of Indiana University-Purdue University at Indianapolis with a grand banquet that recreates the customs, dress, and songs of medieval England. Other festivals and events are hosted throughout the year as part of the universities and museums events schedules; others are held throughout the warmer months as part of the park district's event schedule.

Sports for the Spectator

Best known for the Indianapolis 500 and the Allstate 400 at the Brickyard (formerly the Brickyard 400), Indianapolis made a conscious and successful effort in the 1980s to become an amateur sports capital and a major league city, a distinction that is undisputed today.

Motor sports abound at the Indianapolis Motor Speedway, with three major events and a multitude of smaller ones. The Formula One U.S. Grand Prix began there in 2000; the celebrated event happens annually in mid-July. Since 1911, the Indianapolis 500 has fielded international racecar drivers testing their mettle at speeds above 200 miles per hour for 200 laps around the track; the "Indy 500" attracts more than 350,000 spectators and is held each Memorial Day weekend. The Allstate 400 at the Brickyard features NASCAR racing in August.

The 57,890-seat RCA Dome is home to the Indianapolis Colts of the National Football League (NFL). In early 2005,

plans were finalized for a new stadium for the Colts, with groundbreaking on construction slated for August. The RCA Dome hosts many athletic events, and will be the site of the National Collegiate Athletic Association's Division I Women's Basketball Championship (Final Four) in 2005 and the Men's Final Four in 2006 and 2010. The RCA Dome also houses the National Track & Field Hall of Fame.

The Indiana Pacers of the National Basketball Association (NBA) moved to the 15-story, $183 million arena, Conseco Fieldhouse, in 1999; the structure blends old-style grace with modern conveniences. The Women's National Basketball Association expansion team, the Indiana Fever, also call Conseco Fieldhouse home. The Indianapolis Ice, a minor-league affiliate of the Chicago Blackhawks, play hockey at the Pepsi Coliseum. Kuntz Stadium, a soccer-only stadium, hosts the Indiana Blast soccer team. Professional tennis takes place at the Indianapolis Tennis Center.

The Triple-A Indianapolis Indians play baseball at Victory Field in White River State Park, an open-air, 13,500-seat stadium.

Sports for the Participant

Indianapolis's commitment to sponsor world-class amateur athletic competition has made available excellent facilities to the public. The Major Taylor Velodrome—named for the first African American to win a world championship in any sport—is a state-of-the-art oval bicycle track with a 28-degree banked concrete surface; it is open to the public from March to October. Joggers can try out the track at the Indiana University Track & Soccer Stadium; the university's natatorium offers public facilities, including swimming pools, weight rooms, and a gymnasium. The Indianapolis Tennis Center makes 24 tennis courts available for public use.

The Indy Parks and Recreation Department maintains more than 10,600 acres of land comprising 173 parks; among them is the 4,395-acre Eagle Creek Park, the country's largest municipally owned and operated park, which features a competition-quality rowing course. The park system includes 26 recreation, family, and nature centers; basketball, tennis, and sand volleyball courts; 13 golf courses; softball and baseball diamonds; football and soccer fields; and 22 swimming pools/aquatic centers. Indy Greenways is a series of paved pathways throughout the city; residents walk, run, bike, and skate on the paths.

Shopping and Dining

Circle Centre Mall, covering two city blocks in the heart of downtown Indianapolis, provides tourists and residents with many shopping, dining, and entertainment options. In addition to anchor stores Nordstrom and Parisian, Circle Centre has more than 100 specialty shops, restaurants, and nightclubs, plus a nine-screen cinema, a virtual-reality theme park, and the Indianapolis Artsgarden. Skywalks link Circle Center to seven hotels, the Indiana Convention Center, the RCA Dome, the Indiana Government Center, and offices, shops, and restaurants. Circle Centre has spurred a development boom in adjacent blocks, including the addition of a Hard Rock Cafe and several upscale restaurants.

The Indianapolis City Market, housed in an imposing nineteenth-century building, opened in 1886. Known for its fresh vegetables and meats, the year-round farmer's market is a favorite spot for downtown workers who lunch at small specialty shops. Broad Ripple Village, known as the ''Greenwich Village of Indianapolis,'' is a renovated neighborhood of antique and other shops, art galleries, and nightclubs; a canal and paved walking trail run through it. Recent years have seen a revitalization of Massachusetts Avenue, a Soholike downtown area of art galleries, dining establishments, and coffee houses. The Fountain Square neighborhood, which boasts both classic and trendy eateries, 1950s-style diners, dance and jazz clubs, antique shops, and bookstores, also attracts regular patrons and visitors.

Indianapolis enjoys its share of good restaurants serving a variety of ethnic and traditional food, ranging from Nouvelle American cuisine with a Hoosier touch to authentic German and French specialties. Health food restaurants are popular, as are Japanese, Middle Eastern, coffeehouses, Italian, and Mexican. Mystery Cafe gives patrons a chance to dine and solve a ''Who Dunnit.''

Visitor Information: Indianapolis Convention & Visitors Association, One RCA Dome, Suite 100, Indianapolis, IN 46225; telephone (800)311- INDY

Convention Facilities

Indianapolis is gaining in prominence as a convention destination. The number of convention delegates is well over 1 million annually. The principal meeting facility is the Indiana Convention Center & RCA Dome. The complex, consisting of five exhibit halls and the multiuse RCA Dome, is the site of trade shows, banquets, sporting events, and concerts. Skywalks connect the convention center with the RCA Dome, Circle Centre Mall, and seven major hotels. In 2000 the Indiana Convention Center and RCA Dome underwent its third expansion/renovation. An additional 100,000 square feet of exhibit space was added, to make a total amount of exhibit space of 403,700 square feet. The RCA Dome features 95,000 square feet of floor space. Still, a feasibility study concluded that the city needed more space; construc-

tion on a new, multi-purpose stadium and expanded convention center is expected to begin in the summer of 2005.

More than 120 hotels in Indianapolis offer 28,000 rooms throughout the city. Most of the downtown hotels feature meeting space and ample facilities. University Place Conference Center & Hotel, on the campus of Indiana University-Purdue University at Indianapolis, offers 28 meeting rooms (among them several banquet rooms), a 340-seat auditorium, and 278 guest rooms. The new, five-star Conrad Hilton hotel, with 10,000 square feet of meeting space, is slated to open in 2006 in downtown Indianapolis.

Unique facilities for meetings and special events include the Indianapolis Artsgarden, linked to Circle Centre Mall, Union Station (a Romanesque Revival-style train station built in 1887), and the historic Murat Centre. Following an $11 million renovation, the Murat Centre features a 2,700-seat theater and the Egyptian Room, modeled after King Tut's tomb. The Indianapolis Museum of Art's new Deer-Zink Pavillion offers seating for 500 people in the main dining room and can accommodate 300 in its reception lobby. Other unique meeting spaces include the Indianapolis Zoo, the Indianapolis Motor Speedway, and the NCAA Hall of Champions.

Convention Information: The Indianapolis Convention & Visitors Association, One RCA Dome, Suite 100, Indianapolis, IN 46225; telephone (800)311- INDY

Transportation

Approaching the City

The Indianapolis International Airport is located 8 miles southwest of downtown and is accessible to the city via the Airport Expressway and I-70. Eighteen airlines schedule 280 daily departures to 38 non-stop destinations; more than 7 million passengers were served by the airport in 2003. Five other airports for smaller aircraft also operate in the metropolitan area.

Indianapolis is linked with points throughout the nation by a network of interstate highways. Intersecting the city from east to west is I-70; I-65 passes through the downtown area from the northwest to the southeast. I-69 approaches from the northeast. All of these routes connect with I-465, which encircles the metropolitan area. Amtrak offers both bus and rail service.

Traveling in the City

Streets in Indianapolis are laid out on a grid pattern. The main north-south thoroughfare is Meridian Street, which is intersected in the center of downtown by Washington Street.

Public transportation is provided by Indiana Public Transportation Corp. (IndyGo), with 28 fixed routes and special services like Dial-A-Ride, Open Door Paratransit Service, and Late Night Service.

Communications

Newspapers and Magazines

The major daily newspaper in Indianapolis is the morning *The Indianapolis Star*. The *Indianapolis Business Journal*, the *Indianapolis Recorder*, a newspaper with an African American focus, and several neighborhood and suburban newspapers are published weekly. *Indianapolis Monthly* is a magazine featuring articles on local and state topics.

A number of magazines and special-interest journals are published in the city. Among the nationally-known magazines are *The Saturday Evening Post, Jack and Jill,* and *Humpty Dumpty's Magazine. Quill,* a magazine for journalists and journalism students, is published nine times per year. Topics covered by other Indianapolis-based publications include art, religion, medicine, nursing, law, education, pets, and gymnastics.

Television and Radio

Ten television and four cable stations broadcast from Indianapolis. The city is served by 6 AM and 12 FM radio stations providing a variety of formats such as classical, jazz, public radio, adult contemporary, country, and talk.

Media Information: *The Indianapolis Star,* 307 North Pennsylvania Street, Indianapolis, IN 46204; telephone (317)444-4000; toll-free (800)669-7827

Indianapolis Online

City of Indianapolis and Marion County home page. Available www.indygov.org/home.htm

Greater Indianapolis Chamber of Commerce. Available www.indychamber.com

Indiana Historical Society. Available www.indianahistory.org

Indiana State Library. Available www.statelib.lib.in.us

Indianapolis Downtown. Available www.indydt.com

The Indianapolis Star. Available www.indystar.com

Indy Partnership Regional Economic Development Corporation. Available www.iedc.com

IndyGov Visitors Center home page. Available www.indygov.org/Visiting/home.htm

Selected Bibliography

Berry, S.L. *Indianapolis.* (Minneapolis, MN: Dillon Press, 1990)

Nye, Charlie, and Joe Young, eds. *Hoosier Century: 100 Years of Photography from the Indianapolis Star and News.* (Sports Publishing, Inc., 1999)

South Bend

The City in Brief

Founded: 1820 (incorporated, 1835)

Head Official: Mayor Stephen J. Luecke (D) (since 1997)

City Population
  1980: 109,727
  1990: 105,511
  2000: 107,789
  2003 estimate: 105,540
  Percent change, 1990–2000: 1.6%
  U.S. rank in 1980: 143rd
  U.S. rank in 1990: 182nd (State rank: 5th)
  U.S. rank in 2000: 236th (State rank: 5th)

Metropolitan Area Population
  1980: 241,617
  1990: 247,052

  2000: 265,559
  Percent change, 1990–2000: 7.5%
  U.S. rank in 1990: Not reported
  U.S. rank in 2000: 137th

Area: 38.7 square miles (2000)
Elevation: 773 feet above sea level
Average Annual Temperature: 49.5° F
Average Annual Precipitation: 36.52 inches of rain, 72.9 inches of snow

Major Economic Sectors: Services, wholesale and retail trade, manufacturing
Unemployment Rate: 5.9% (February 2005)
Per Capita Income: $17,121 (1999)

2002 FBI Crime Index Total: 8,203

Major Colleges and Universities: University of Notre Dame; Indiana University-South Bend

Daily Newspaper: *South Bend Tribune*

Introduction

South Bend is the seat of St. Joseph County and the focus of a region known as "Michiana" that extends over six counties in Indiana and two counties in Michigan. Mishawaka lies to the east of South Bend; the two cities comprise a metropolitan statistical area and are in the heart of the nation's industrial belt. With a location on the beautiful St. Joseph River, South Bend is home to the University of Notre Dame, which is nationally recognized for its academic excellence and for "The Fighting Irish," its winning football team.

Geography and Climate

South Bend is located on the Saint Joseph River on mostly level to gently rolling terrain and some former marshlands. The proximity of Lake Michigan—the city is within twenty miles of the nearest shore—produces a moderating effect on South Bend's climate. Temperatures of 100 degrees or higher are rare and cold waves are less severe than at other locations at the same latitude. Distribution of precipitation is relatively even throughout the year; the greatest amounts occur during the growing season, May to October. Winter is characterized by cloudiness and high humidity, with frequent periods of snow. Heavier snowfalls are often borne into the area by a cold northwest wind passing over Lake Michigan.

Area: 38.7 square miles (2000)

Elevation: 773 feet above sea level

Average Temperatures: January, 24.4° F; July, 73.3° F; annual average, 49.5° F

Average Annual Precipitation: 36.52 inches of rain, 72.9 inches of snow

History

French Exploration Establishes South Bend

The first European explorer to reach the region surrounding present-day South Bend was Robert Cavelier, sieur de La Salle, who in 1679 passed near the spot where today the University of Notre Dame's administration building is located. Two years later, La Salle met with Miami and Illinois chiefs under a tree named Council Oak in what was then the heart of the Miami nation; they signed a peace treaty that involved a pledge from the Miami and the Illinois to fight the Iroquois. LaSalle, protected by the treaty, was free to explore the Mississippi River region in which present-day South Bend is included; he then claimed the territory for France, naming it Louisiana.

Pierre Freischutz Navarre, a Frenchman married to a Potawatomi woman, established the first trading post for the American Fur Company in 1820 near South Bend's future site. But Alexis Coquillard is credited with founding South Bend; the town's name was derived from his trading post, which was called "The Bend," and noted its southerly location on the St. Joseph River. Coquillard's business rival and friend, Colonel Lathrop M. Taylor, renamed the settlement St. Joseph in 1827 and then Southold. The U.S. Post Office officially named it South Bend. Coquillard and Taylor worked together to develop the settlement and encouraged settlers with gifts of land and money. The city was platted and named the county seat in 1831, incorporated in 1835, and chartered in 1865.

Industry and Scholarship Enhance the City

In 1852 Henry and Clement Studebaker arrived in South Bend and opened a blacksmith and wagon shop. They built farm wagons, carriages, prairie schooners, and then a gasoline engine automobile in 1904, transforming the company into an automobile plant that remained in business until 1966. James Oliver came to South Bend in 1855, founding the Oliver Chilled Plow Works, which manufactured a superior farm plow that revolutionized farming and introduced a manufacturing process that replaced iron with chilled and hardened steel. The Singer Cabinet Works began production in 1868 in South Bend to take advantage of the proximity of Indiana hardwood forests, emerging as the world's largest cabinet factory by 1901.

The most significant event in the city's history was the arrival of Father Edward Sorin, the founder of the University of Notre Dame, who reached the future site of the university on November 26, 1842, with seven Brothers of the Congregation of the Holy Cross. Bishop Hailandiere of the diocese of Vincennes had given Father Sorin 600 acres to found a college for seminary and secular students as well as to start a mission for the Potawatomi Native Americans. The college's first student was Alexis Coquillard. Enrollment picked up with the arrival of the Lake Shore Railroad in 1851. A fire destroyed the campus in 1879, and the Neo-Gothic Administration Building, with its golden dome topped by a figure of the Virgin Mary, was opened later that year. The golden dome, a tradition of academic excellence, and winning football teams have become familiar symbols of this famous university, which remains a significant part of life in South Bend in the twenty-first century.

Historical Information: Northern Indiana Historical Society, Northern Indiana Center for History, 808 W. Washington Street, South Bend, IN 46601; telephone (574)235-9664

Population Profile

Metropolitan Area Residents
1980: 241,617
1990: 247,052
2000: 265,559
Percent change, 1990-2000: 7.5%
U.S. rank in 1990: Not reported
U.S. rank in 2000: 137th

City Residents
1980: 109,727
1990: 105,511
2000: 107,789
2003 estimate: 105,540
Percent change, 1990–2000: 1.6%
U.S. rank in 1980: 143rd
U.S. rank in 1990: 182nd (State rank: 5th)
U.S. rank in 2000: 236th (State rank: 5th)

Density: 2,786.4 people per square mile

Racial and ethnic characteristics (2000)
White: 71,195
Black or African American: 26,522
American Indian and Alaska Native: 440
Asian: 1,292
Native Hawaiian and Pacific Islander: 69
Hispanic or Latino (may be of any race): 9,110
Other: 8,271

Percent of residents born in state: 63.9%

Age characteristics (2000)
Population under 5 years old: 8,895
Population 5 to 9 years old: 8,471
Population 10 to 14 years old: 7,677
Population 15 to 19 years old: 7,081
Population 20 to 24 years old: 8,518
Population 25 to 34 years old: 16,718
Population 35 to 44 years old: 14,891
Population 45 to 54 years old: 12,371
Population 55 to 59 years old: 4,048
Population 60 to 64 years old: 3,179
Population 65 to 74 years old: 7,312
Population 75 to 84 years old: 6,188
Population 85 years and older: 2,440
Median age: 32.7 years

Births (2002)
Total number: 1,972

Deaths (2002)
Total number: 1,327 (of which, 23 were infants under the age of 1 year)

Money income (1999)
Per capita income: $17,121
Median household income: $32,439
Total households: 42,627

Number of households with income of . . .
less than $10,000: 4,755
$10,000 to $14,999: 3,707
$15,000 to $24,999: 7,404
$25,000 to $34,999: 6,902
$35,000 to $49,999: 8,053
$50,000 to $74,999: 6,714
$75,000 to $99,999: 2,899
$100,000 to $149,999: 1,505
$150,000 to $199,999: 224
$200,000 or more: 464

Percent of families below poverty level: 13.6% (36.9% of which were female householder families with related children under 5 years)

2002 FBI Crime Index Total: 8,203

Municipal Government

The city of South Bend operates under a mayor-council form of government. The mayor and nine council members are elected to four-year terms; the mayor is not a member of council.

Head Official: Mayor Stephen J. Luecke (since 1997; current term expires December 31, 2007)

Total Number of City Employees: 1,400 (2004)

City Information: Office of the Mayor, 1400 East County-City Building, South Bend, IN 46601; telephone (219)235-9261

Economy

Major Industries and Commercial Activity

South Bend's diversified economic base consists principally of educational and health services, wholesale and retail trade, manufacturing, and government. In 2004 *Expansion Management* magazine ranked South Bend—for the first time—among the 40 hottest real estate markets for business. South Bend made the list based on available land, office and industrial space inventory, along with redevelopment opportunities for new and expanding companies.

The city benefits greatly from being a college town; in particular, Notre Dame University has a considerable impact on the economy of South Bend. The area's largest employer, Notre Dame experienced a 21 percent increase in full-time faculty and staff between 1993 and 2002. The university further contributes to the area economy by partnering with area businesses for research and development projects, and providing strong job market candidates.

Health services have also boomed in South Bend in recent years. Memorial Health System has grown to become the area's second-largest employer. From the mid-1990s through 2005, Memorial made approximately $300 million in capital investments to its hospital, located downtown. Memorial's success has been linked to its central location, medical research conducted through Notre Dame, and a recent proliferation of medical-related business startups in the area.

St. Joseph County is the second-largest retail market area in the state next to Indianapolis, with nationally recognized retailers including Old Navy, Marshall Fields, Barnes & Noble, and Ethan Allen, to name a few. Manufacturing industries in the area include non-electrical machinery, transportation equipment, and rubber and various plastic products. AM General, producer of HMMWV (a.k.a. HUMMER) military and special purpose vehicles, is headquartered in South Bend and is one of the city's largest employers. The company's corporate offices are in South Bend, and its production facilities are in nearby Mishawaka.

Another important industry in the county is tourism, which generates a significant number of jobs and revenues. Aside from the Indianapolis Motor Speedway, Notre Dame University attracts the most visitors in Indiana—nearly 700,000 visitors annually—and the county gains nearly $40 million in visitor expenditures through the university's football games alone.

Items and goods produced: airplanes and auto parts, aluminum castings, fixtures, conveyor components, electronic controls, machine tools, dies, drills, fabricated steel products, military vehicles, office furniture, pet food, plastic coated fabrics, corrugated boxes and cartons, windows and doors, printing rollers and inks, paints, food, condiments, metal stampings, wire and cable processing

Incentive Programs—New and Existing Companies

Local programs—The city's Division of Economic Development actively promotes the retention and expansion of existing businesses and the development of new business in the city. Their offerings include financing programs, relocation incentives, land/building availability assistance, industrial revenue bonds for manufacturing facilities, tax abatement, and technical assistance through local partnerships.

State programs—The state of Indiana extends various grants and loans to local governments and companies. The state offers a variety of incentives to new and expanding businesses, such as tax credits for investment and training, and through its Community Assistance, Energy Efficiency, Infrastructure, Renewable Energy, Technology, Trade Show, and Training programs. The International Trade Division of the Indiana Department of Commerce encourages foreign investment locally.

Job training programs—Customized training and consultants are available from a number of state and local providers. Funding to cover training costs is available in some cases.

Development Projects

In 2004 construction started on 147 new homes, a 5 percent increase from the previous year. A new retail project, known as Erskine Village, is being created on the city's east side; it is destined to become a 510,000-square-foot, $35 million retail center. South Bend is redeveloping the old Studebaker Brothers Manufacturing Co. and Oliver Chilled Plow Works industrial corridors for warehousing and distribution, which will become the home of light industrial, warehouse, and distribution facilities. St. Joseph Valley MetroNet, a local not-for-profit corporation, is working to install fiber optic cable in existing city conduit; this state-of-the-art communication system will allow businesses to share large amounts of data quickly and securely. Additionally, South Bend is promoting the creation of a Certified Technology Park.

Economic Development Information: Chamber of Commerce of St. Joseph County, 401 E. Colfax Ave., Ste. 310, South Bend, IN 46617; telephone (574)234-0051

Commercial Shipping

Designated a Foreign Trade Zone, South Bend is a center for manufacturers, suppliers, and vendors throughout the United States and abroad. About six air freight carriers ship goods through South Bend Regional Airport. A network of interstate highways, including I-80/90, the nation's major east-west axis route, provides access to more than 70 motor freight carriers. Rail freight service is provided by Canadian National, Norfolk and Southern, CSX, and Chicago Southshore South Bend Railroad.

Labor Force and Employment Outlook

South Bend and its environs boast one of the highest concentrations of educational institutions per capita in the Midwest. Employment opportunities are on the upswing, as indicated at the University of Notre Dame—business interviews of students in the fall of 2004 were up roughly 30 percent from the previous year. South Bend has a large pool of skilled and semi-skilled laborers that are reported to be available, affordable, and reliable. The wage structure is competitive with other industrial communities.

The following is a summary of data regarding the South Bend-Mishawaka metropolitan area labor force, 2004 annual average:

Size of nonagricultural labor force: 144,100

Number of workers employed in . . .
 construction and mining: 6,700
 manufacturing: 21,700
 trade, transportation and utilities: 28,500
 information: 2,400
 financial activities: 7,100
 professional and business services: 12,200
 educational and health services: 30,800
 leisure and hospitality: 12,100
 other services: 5,600
 government: 16,800

Average hourly earnings of production workers employed in manufacturing: $12.41

Unemployment rate: 5.9% (February 2005)

Largest employers	Number of employees
University of Notre Dame	4,802
Memorial Health System	3,493
South Bend Community School Corp.	3,303
St. Joseph Regional Medical Center	2,935
The Diocese of Fort Wayne/South Bend	2,500
AM General	2,151
St. Joseph County	1,750
Martin's Supermarkets	1,484
City of South Bend	1,400
Indiana University South Bend	1,300

Cost of Living

The following is a summary of data regarding several key cost of living factors in the South Bend area.

2004 (3rd Quarter) ACCRA Average House Price: $241,885

2004 (3rd Quarter) ACCRA Cost of Living Index: 95.5 (U.S. average = 100.0)

State income tax rate: 3.4% of adjusted gross income

State sales tax rate: 6.0% (food, prescription drugs, and items consumed or used in manufacturing are exempt)

Local income tax rate: 0.0075 (county)

Local sales tax rate: None

Property tax rate: Averages 1.2 percent annually (2003)

Economic Information: Chamber of Commerce of St. Joseph County, 401 E. Colfax Ave., Ste. 310, South Bend, IN 46617; telephone (574)234-0051

Education and Research

Elementary and Secondary Schools

The South Bend Community School Corporation is one of the largest school districts in the state. The district has a strong technology program with computers available to every student. Nearly 70 percent of high school seniors continue on to attend college. About 70 percent of the district's teachers hold advanced degrees.

The following is a summary of data regarding South Bend public schools as of the 2002–2003 school year.

Total enrollment: 21,662

Number of facilities
 elementary schools: 19
 middle schools: 10
 high schools: 4
 other: 4

Student/teacher ratio: 16.5:1

Teacher salaries (2003-2004)
 average: $46,700

Funding per pupil: $8,819

Twenty-seven private and parochial schools offer educational alternatives to South Bend area students. Among them are a Roman Catholic elementary and high school system with an enrollment of nearly 5,000 students, as well as Hebrew schools and the Stanley Clark School, a private institution with a limited enrollment.

Public Schools Information: South Bend Community School Corporation, 635 S. Main St., South Bend, IN 46601; telephone (574)283-8000

Colleges and Universities

The University of Notre Dame, a top university affiliated with the Roman Catholic Church, is located in Notre Dame, IN, adjacent to South Bend. Founded in 1842 as a college for men, it became coeducational in 1972, and currently has an enrollment of more than 11,000 students. The university offers graduate and undergraduate degrees in arts and sciences, engineering, business administration, architecture, and law. A unique feature of the curriculum is the ''Executive M.B.A.'' program for working professionals. Notre Dame's graduation rate—95 percent—is exceeded only by Harvard, Yale, and Princeton. Community involvement is highly valued at Notre Dame; approximately 80 percent of its students engage in volunteer work while attending the university.

Saint Mary's College, sister school of Notre Dame, was founded in 1844 and is a women's college with an enrollment of approximately 1,500. Saint Mary's offers undergraduate degrees in 30 major areas of study, and has a cooperative engineering degree program with Notre Dame. In 2005 *U.S. News and World Report* ranked Saint Mary's the number one comprehensive college for bachelor's degrees in the Midwest.

Holy Cross College, formerly Holy Cross Junior College, is adjacent to Notre Dame. Holy Cross opened in 1966 as a two-year college; its baccalaureate program debuted in 2003. The college offers two degree programs: Associate of Arts and Bachelor of Arts in Liberal Studies.

Indiana University-South Bend (IUSB), the third largest in the state's eight-university system, enrolls more than 7,500 students and grants associate through master's degrees in more than 90 fields. IUSB operates a continuing education division that provides evening, weekend, and off-campus instruction.

Bethel College, in nearby Mishawaka, is a liberal arts college affiliated with the United Missionary Church; Bethel grants undergraduate and graduate degrees in a range of programs.

Purdue University Statewide Technology Program at IUSB offers associate degrees in engineering technology and computer technology as well as associate and bachelor degrees in organizational leadership and supervision. Technical and vocational training is also available at a number of other colleges and specialized schools, including Ivy Tech State College and Michiana College.

Libraries and Research Centers

The St. Joseph County Public Library consists of a main library and eight branches housing nearly 640,000 items, including books, periodical subscriptions, computer software, microfiche, audio- and videotapes, CDs, and art reproductions. Special collections include large type books, genealogical materials, and state documents. A renovation of the main library's first floor, adding two meeting rooms and a computer training room, was completed in 2003; an expansion of the second floor is scheduled for completion in 2007. Local colleges and universities maintain campus libraries. Other specialized libraries in the city are associated with hospitals, government agencies, and the Studebaker National Museum.

The University of Notre Dame supports dozens of centers conducting research in a wide variety of areas, such as peace studies, the environment, radiation chemistry, biology, the philosophy of religion, American Catholicism, and international studies. Indiana University-South Bend maintains a bureau of business and economic research, and an institute for applied community research.

Public Library Information: St. Joseph County Public Library, 304 S. Main St., South Bend, IN 46601

Health Care

Hospitals in the South Bend area offer a total of more than 1,500 beds. The three major hospitals are Memorial Hospital, St. Joseph Regional Medical Center-South Bend, and St. Joseph Regional Medical Center-Mishawaka. South Bend's first hospital, established by the Sisters of the Holy Cross in 1882, is now known as St. Joseph Regional Medical Center. Some of the features of the South Bend campus are a complete labor and delivery, postpartum and nursery service; nationally recognized cancer treatments through its Cancer Institute; accredited pain and rehabilitation programs; and a Mind/Body Medical Institute offering an innovative mind-body approach to medical treatment. The Mishawaka campus has been providing health care since 1910; its features include complete labor, delivery, and postpartum care; a cardiac catheterization lab which was the first in the area to implement all-digital technology; an in-house laboratory; and a state-of-the-art radiology department with a new CT scanner and one of only three high-tech X-Ray machines in the United States and the only one in the Midwest. The Mishawaka campus is one of only 20 or so hospitals in the county to follow the Planetree philosophy, a holistic medical approach focusing on patients' mental, emotional, spiritual, as well as physical, well-being.

Memorial Hospital is the region's largest hospital and primary referral center, serving as a 526-bed regional referral center for cardiac, cancer, childbirth, emergency medicine, and rehabilitation services. Features of the hospital's clinical services include a new weight loss and bariatric surgery center; the innovative Memorial Lighthouse Medical Imaging Center; and the new Leighton Heart and Vascular Center, scheduled to open in 2005. Memorial's parent company, Memorial Health System, consisting of four affiliates—Memorial Hospital, Memorial Health Foundation, Memorial Home Care, and Memorial Medical Group—offers care and service at all levels, including inpatient and home care, medical equipment and supplies, pharmacy services, and occupational health services, as well as primary care physicians and specialists. South Bend's Madison Center provides behavioral and mental health care.

South Bend is home to the College Football Hall of Fame.

Recreation

Sightseeing

South Bend is noted for the University of Notre Dame, for its industrial heritage, and for its municipal parks. A good place to begin a campus tour is at Notre Dame's Eck Visitors' Center, which has historical displays and a 20-minute movie about the university. Notre Dame's golden-domed Main Building is the campus's central symbol; inside, the walls are lined with murals depicting the life of Christopher Columbus by Vatican artist Luigi Gregori. The five-story Victorian building recently received a $58 million renovation, restoring its woodwork, lighting fixtures, and walls. Also on the campus are a reproduction of France's Grotto of Lourdes; the ornate Basilica of the Sacred Heart; the Log Chapel, hand-built by Father Stephen Badin—the first Catholic priest ordained in the U.S.—in 1830; the Snite Museum of Art; and an 11-story library.

Young sports fans will enjoy passing and kicking a football at the College Football Hall of Fame, a 58,000 square-foot museum devoted to every aspect of football—its players, fans, cheerleaders, and bands. The museum features interactive exhibits as well as artifacts, mementos, and photographs. Studebaker Museum traces the history of the Studebaker Company from its days as a maker of horse-drawn carriages to its innovations in the manufacture of automobiles. Among the exhibits is the carriage in which President Lincoln rode to Ford's Theater on the night he was assassinated. The Northern Indiana Center for History includes Copshaholm (The Oliver Mansion), a 38-room stone mansion built in 1895; Worker House, a cottage reflecting working-class homes of the 1930s; History Center, which charts local history through industry, individuals, clothing, and even toys; and *kidsfirst* Children's Museum. The Potawatomi Park Zoo, founded in 1902, is the oldest zoo in the state. The 23-acre zoo is home to 400 animals, including several rare and endangered species such as tigers, red pandas, cotton-top tamarins, snow leopards, and lemurs. Visitors to the South Bend Chocolate Company can tour its factory and explore its chocolate museum. Amish Acres, in nearby Nappanee, IN, is an 80-acre, 19th-century farm that showcases the customs, beliefs, and work habits of the Amish people; featured are 18 restored buildings, craft demonstrations, farm animals, musical theatre, restaurants, and quaint shops.

Arts and Culture

The South Bend Symphony, the Broadway Theater League, Southold Dance, and other community arts groups perform at the Morris Performing Arts Center, Indiana's oldest historic theater, built in 1922. The Symphony's concert season includes six Masterworks, three pops, two family, three chamber, and a holiday concert. Broadway Theatre League presents nationally-touring Broadway shows in a season that runs between June and September. Southold Dance offers performances ranging from classic ballet to modern dance; the Nutcracker is a yearly favorite. The South Bend Civic Theatre is the largest community theatre in the state, as measured by operating budget, yearly productions, and membership; it presents a 16-play season, primarily at The Firehouse, a historic landmark.

The Snite Museum of Art, on the Notre Dame campus, holds more than 21,000 pieces in its permanent collection, featuring Rembrandt etchings, 19th-century French art, Old Master and 19th-century drawings, 19th-century European photographs, Mestrovic sculpture and drawings, Olmec and Preclassic Mesoamerican art, 20th-century art, Northern Native American art, and decorative and design arts. The South Bend Regional Art Center features a permanent collection focusing on American—especially Indiana—art, from the 19th century through the present. The Hannah Lindahl Children's museum gives young people a close-up, hands-on look at how life was lived long ago.

Festivals and Holidays

South Bend's parks are the location for many of the city's festivals and special events. A major event at Leeper Park is an art fair the last weekend in June. Rum Village Park hosts Old Fashioned Summer, featuring an antique car show, entertainment, a Native American program and activities, square dancing, trail activities, and more. South Bend's Summer in the City Festival, formerly known as the Ethnic Festival, features entertainment, food, rides, and a parade. Also in June, Merrifield Park, in nearby Mishawaka, hosts Summerfest, which features food, music, craft booths, and a free evening concert. St. Patrick's Park presents a number of events, including the Firefly Festival, an outdoor music, theater, and dance program on weekends from mid-June through early August; the Blues and Ribs Fest in August; and Kee-Boon-Mein-Kaa, a traditional Indian pow wow featuring food, dancing, demonstrations, and crafts, in September.

Sports for the Spectator

The University of Notre Dame Fighting Irish football team is among the most famous college teams in the world. Legendary coach Knute Rockne began the school's success in the 1920s with the ''Four Horsemen'' and ''Seven Mules.'' Throughout Notre Dame's history, the Fighting Irish have been known for great players, outstanding coaches, and a schedule of games against the nation's best football teams. The home schedule is played on Saturday afternoons in the fall in Notre Dame Stadium. The Fighting Irish also field competitive teams in basketball and other sports.

The Stanley Coveleski Regional Stadium is the home field of South Bend's Class A minor league franchise baseball team, the Silver Hawks, who compete in the Midwest League in a season that runs from April to September. The East Race, the first artificial whitewater course in North America and one of six in the world, hosts world-class whitewater slaloms and United States Olympic Trials; this course is capable of matching the Colorado River in its power.

Sports for the Participant

St. Joseph County offers numerous parks and a nature preserve for year-round outdoor fun. Rum Village Park features a nature center and hiking and nature trails, while George Wilson Park offers a disc golf course considered among the best in the country. St. Patrick's Park and Bendix Woods offer cross-country skiing. The South Bend-Mishawaka area boasts ten highly regarded golf courses, such as Blackthorn, which has been highly ranked by *Golf Digest*. South Bend's biggest recreational attraction is East Race Waterway, which offers kayaking and whitewater rafting in the heart of downtown. An exercise trail borders the waterway and is part of a five-mile trail that runs through the city's downtown parks and along the St. Joseph River.

Shopping and Dining

South Bend-Mishawaka offers shopping opportunities ranging from enclosed malls to many small independent specialty shops. A popular stop is the Farmer's Market in South Bend, which features wares ranging from fresh produce and baked goods to flowers, pottery, hand-crafted jewelry, and antiques. Town and Country Shopping Plaza offers eclectic shops. Nearby Mishawaka boasts the second-largest retail area in the state, with its large University Park Mall, as well as numerous shops and strip malls along the Grape Road/Main Street corridor.

Northern Indiana is known for such regional food specialties as frog legs, pan-fried perch, and relishes that include bean salad, cabbage salad, and pickled beets. Other popular dining options include sushi, barbeque, pasta, prime rib, and deli sandwiches. South Bend features unique fine dining options in atmospheric settings, including Tippecanoe Place, in the restored 1888 Studebaker Mansion, resembling a feudal castle; and the Carriage House, in a converted 1850s church. Amish Acres in nearby Nappanee and Das Dutchman Essenhaus in Middlebury offer home-style Amish cooking.

Visitor Information: Convention and Visitors Bureau of South Bend/Mishawaka, Commerce Center, 401 E. Colfax Ave., Ste. 310, South Bend, IN 46634; telephone (800)519-0577

Convention Facilities

South Bend/Mishawaka offers excellent meeting facilities, totaling more than 300,000 square feet of combined meeting space, and the community has nearly 4,000 hotel rooms. The principal meeting site in South Bend is the Century Center, situated on an 11-acre downtown riverfront park with direct access to major hotels and five miles from South Bend Regional Airport. Integrated with theaters, parks, art galleries, and a museum, the Century Center complex consists of three convention and exhibition halls, a great hall, a ballroom, a thrust-stage theater, a recital hall, and suites. Its convention and exhibition halls offer a total of 37,000 square feet of unobstructed meeting and exhibit space. The great hall, a multipurpose courtyard overlooking Island Park and White Water Rapids, is suitable for banquets, receptions, dinner dances, and exhibitions. The ballroom offers nearly 6,600 square feet of space suitable for meetings and banquets. Bendix Theatre has seating for 718 and is suitable for meetings, shows, and performances. The recital hall, with seating for 166, is suitable for breakout sessions and performances. The suites consist of up to 11 variable-sized rooms.

The Morris Performing Arts Center, the oldest theater in Indiana, features an auditorium, restored and renovated in 2000, that can accommodate more than 2,500 attendees for lectures, meetings, and conferences. Morris also houses the lavish Palais Royale ballroom which, restored to its 1923 grandeur in 2002, is considered the city's premier banquet facility. Additional convention facilities can be found on the University of Notre Dame campus at the Athletic and Convocation Center and the Center for Continuing Education.

Convention Information: Convention and Visitors Bureau of South Bend/Mishawaka, Commerce Center, 401 E. Colfax Ave., Ste. 310, South Bend, IN 46634; telephone (800)519-0577

Transportation

Approaching the City

Six commercial airlines schedule direct and connecting flights into South Bend at the South Bend Regional Airport from all major United States cities and points abroad. The airport, which is the second-busiest in Indiana, is the only one in the nation to have developed a multimodal transportation center offering air, intercity rail, and interstate bus service at one convenient location. In 1999 the airport created a Master Plan to further develop the airport; the first phase of the plan, adding 1,300 feet of pavement to its main runway and also lengthening two adjacent taxi runways, was completed in 2002. The closest major airport is O'Hare in Chicago, about 120 miles away.

Passenger rail transportation is available by Amtrak from Boston, New York, and Chicago. The South Shore Line, the nation's only remaining interurban rail service, connects the Chicago Loop with South Bend and Mishawaka, making seven daily trips on weekdays and nine on weekends.

An efficient highway system—including Interstate 80/90 (the Indiana Toll Road,) running east/west; U.S. 6, 20, and 31; and State Routes 2, 4, 23, 104, 331, and 933—affords access into the South Bend metropolitan area.

Traveling in the City

South Bend is laid out on a grid system, the main thoroughfares within the city being north-south Main Street and Michigan Street (U.S. 31) and east-west Colfax Avenue (U.S. 20).

Transpo, the municipal bus service, schedules regular routes in both South Bend and Mishawaka. Transpo Access is available for the elderly and handicapped.

Communications

Newspapers

The major South Bend daily newspaper is the *South Bend Tribune,* which has a circulation of more than 63,000. Other South Bend publications include the weekly *Tri-County News,* and the monthly magazine *Culture Wars,* which explores issues from the point of view of the Catholic Church.

Television and Radio

South Bend, Mishawaka, and neighboring communities receive broadcasts from nine area-based television stations and have access to several Chicago and Elkhart stations, as well as cable. South Bend's 29 radio stations—21 FM and eight AM—serve listeners with music, news and information, and religious programming.

Media Information: South Bend Tribune, 225 W. Colfax Ave., South Bend, IN 46626; telephone (574)235-6474

South Bend Online

Chamber of Commerce of St. Joseph County. Available www.sjchamber.org

South Bend Government web site. Available www.ci.south-bend.in.us

South Bend Tribune. Available www.southbendtribune.com

St. Joseph County Public Library. Available http://sjcpl.lib.in.us

Selected Bibliography

Danielson, Kay Marnon. *South Bend Indiana.* Arcadia Publishing, 2001

Huckfeldt, John, et al. *Citizens, Politics, and Social Communication: Information and Influence in an Election Campaign (Cambridge Studies in Political Psychology).* Cambridge University Press, 1995

Szymarek, Gene. *Cedar Grove Cemetery Inscriptions So. Bend Indiana.* Heritage Books, 1987

IOWA

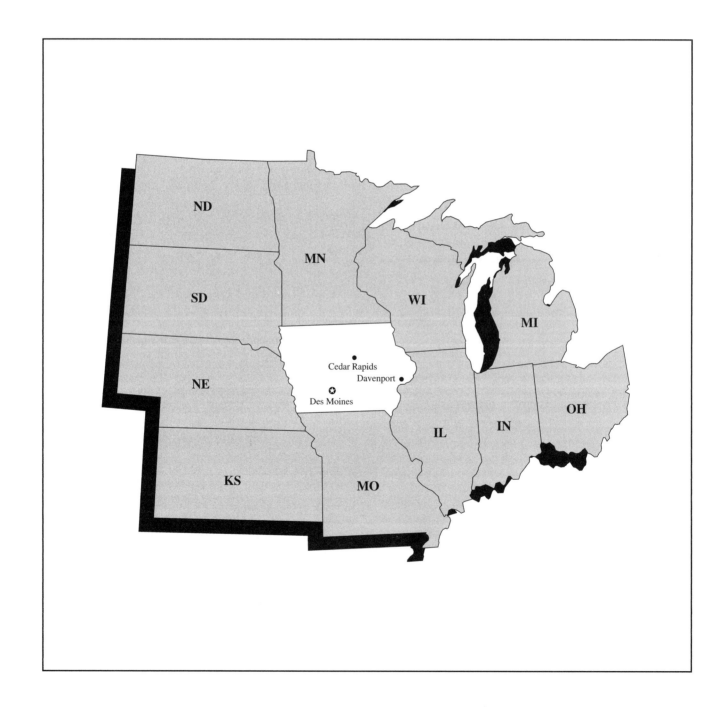

The State in Brief

Nickname: Hawkeye State
Motto: Our liberties we prize and our rights we will maintain

Flower: Wild rose
Bird: Eastern goldfinch

Area: 56,271 square miles (2000; U.S. rank: 26th)
Elevation: Ranges from 480 feet to 1,670 feet above sea level
Climate: Continental, with extremes in temperature (30 degrees in winter, 100 degrees in summer)

Admitted to Union: December 28, 1846
Capital: Des Moines
Head Official: Governor Tom Vilsack (D) (until 2007)

Population
   1980: 2,914,000
   1990: 2,795,000
   2000: 2,926,382
   2004 estimate: 2,954,451
   Percent change, 1990–2000: 5.4%
   U.S. rank in 2004: 30th
   Percent of residents born in state: 74.8% (2000)
   Density: 52.4 people per square mile (2000)
   2002 FBI Crime Index Total: 101,265

Racial and Ethnic Characteristics (2000)
   White: 2,748,640
   Black or African American: 61,853
   American Indian and Alaska Native: 8,989
   Asian: 36,635
   Native Hawaiian and Pacific Islander: 1,009
   Hispanic or Latino (may be of any race): 82,473
   Other: 37,420

Age Characteristics (2000)
   Population under 5 years old: 188,413
   Population 5 to 19 years old: 639,570
   Percent of population 65 years and over: 14.9%
   Median age: 36.6 years (2000)

Vital Statistics
   Total number of births (2003): 38,243
   Total number of deaths (2003): 28,138 (infant deaths, 207)
   AIDS cases reported through 2003: 728

Economy
   Major industries: Manufacturing; agriculture; finance, insurance, and real estate; trade; services
   Unemployment rate: 5.1% (March 2005)
   Per capita income: $28,398 (2003; U.S. rank: 36th)
   Median household income: $41,985 (3-year average, 2001-2003)
   Percentage of persons below poverty level: 8.5% (3-year average, 2001-2003)
   Income tax rate: Ranges from 0.36% to 8.98%
   Sales tax rate: 5.0%

Cedar Rapids

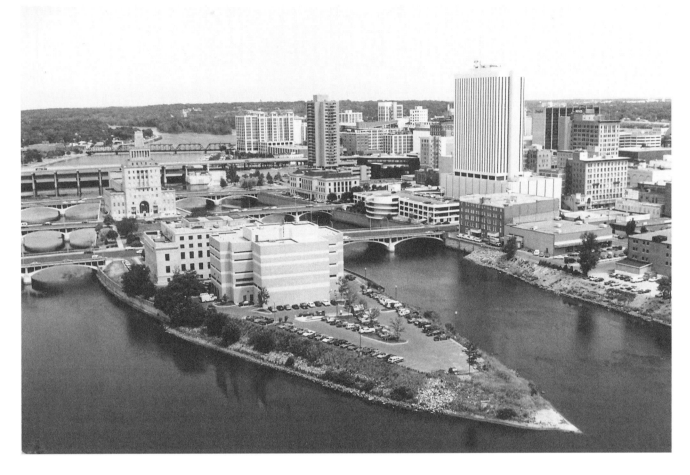

The City in Brief

Founded: 1841 (incorporated, 1849)

Head Official: Mayor Paul D. Pate (since 2002)

City Population
  1980: 110,243
  1990: 108,772
  2000: 120,758
  2003 estimate: 122,542
  Percent change, 1990–2000: 10.9%
  U.S. rank in 1980: 141st
  U.S. rank in 1990: 174th
  U.S. rank in 2000: 181st (State rank: 2nd)

Metropolitan Area Population
  1980: 169,775
  1990: 168,767

  2000: 191,701
  2003 estimate: 196,006
  Percent change, 1990–2000: 13.6%
  U.S. rank in 1990: Not reported
  U.S. rank in 2000: 173rd

Area: 63 square miles (2000)
Elevation: 733 feet above sea level
Average Annual Temperature: 49.6° F
Average Annual Precipitation: 36.39 inches of rain, 34.4 inches of snow

Major Economic Sectors: Services, trade, manufacturing
Unemployment Rate: 5.9% (February 2005)
Per Capita Income: $22,589 (1999)

2002 FBI Crime Index Total: 7,233

Major Colleges and Universities: Coe College; Mount Mercy College

Daily Newspaper: *Cedar Rapids Gazette*

DOWNTOWN (inset)

VISITOR INFO. CENTER
THEATRE CEDAR RAPIDS
FIRST AVE.
FIRST ST. S.E.
SECOND ST. S.E.
THIRD ST. S.E.
FOURTH ST. S.E.
MUSEUM OF ART
THIRD AVE. S.E.
TOWN CENTRE
FOURTH AVE. S.E.
PARAMOUNT THEATRE
SCIENCE STATION/ IMAX
LIBRARY
FIFTH AVE. S.E.
DOWNTOWN

CANADA
WISCONSIN
MINNESOTA
MICHIGAN
NY
Cedar Rapids
IOWA
INDIANA
OHIO
PA
ILLINOIS
KS
MISSOURI
KENTUCKY
WEST VIRGINIA
VIRGINIA

CEDAR RIVER
BOYSON
CEDAR VALLEY NATURE TRAIL
BLAIRS FERRY
BLAIRS FERRY
GRANGER HOUSE
ALBURNETT
151B
TO MARION AIRPORT
CENTER POINT
COUNCIL
C AVE
NE
1ST AVE
Marion
11TH ST
42ND ST
COLLINS
OLD
MARION
EAST POST
WENIG
380
USHERS FERRY HISTORIC VILLAGE
GLASS
32ND ST
SEMINOLE VALLEY PARK & FARM
29TH ST
1ST AVE
380
CENTER POINT
OAKLAND
17TH ST
COTTAGE GROVE
SHAVER
16TH ST
19TH ST
BRUCEMORE
SE
12TH ST
34TH ST
EDGEWOOD
ELLIS
ELLIS PARK
NW
8TH ST
DOWNTOWN
7TH ST
1ST AVE
BEVER
MASONIC LIBRARY
WASHINGTON
F AVE
FIVE SEASONS
CONVENTION & VISITORS BUREAU
3RD AVE
10TH ST
MT VERNON
CITY HALL
MUSEUM OF ART
INDIAN CREEK NATURE CENTER
PARAMOUNT THEATRE
GROUND TRANSPORTATION CTR
LIBRARY
THE HISTORY CENTER
VETERANS MEMORIAL PARK & STADIUM
1ST AVE
SCIENCE STATION
1ST ST
12TH AVE
FARMERS MARKET
CZECH VILLAGE
TO GARRISON
16TH AVE
6TH ST
16TH AVE
C ST
NATIONAL CZECH AND SLOVAK MUSEUM AND LIBRARY
WILLIAMS
SW
WILSON
151B
151
HAWKEYE DOWNS
30 218 151
30 151
TO MT VERNON
TO AMANA COLONIES
218
CEDAR RAPIDS AIRPORT
380
TO IOWA CITY

N

0 1 2 3 KILOMETERS
MILES 1 2 3 4

Introduction

Cedar Rapids preserves a small-town atmosphere in a metropolitan setting. The industrial and cultural center of eastern Iowa, the city has undergone growth and development as it gains prominence in high-technology industries and in export trade. Expansion has been carefully monitored by civic leaders, however, so that international business may be conducted at an unhurried pace and residents may maintain their midwestern traditions. Cedar Rapids is the seat of Linn County and adjoins the city of Marion.

Geography and Climate

Cedar Rapids is situated on the Cedar River, which flows through the city, on rolling terrain in eastern Iowa. The surrounding area is laced with rivers and lakes and dotted with limestone bluffs. The climate consists of four distinct seasons, with warm days and cool nights in spring and autumn.

Area: 63 square miles (2000)

Elevation: 733 feet above sea level

Average Temperatures: January, 19.1° F; July, 74.6° F

Average Annual Precipitation: 36.39 inches of rain, 34.4 inches of snow

History

Cedar River Supports Settlement

The Sac and the Fox, Native American tribes, hunted and trapped along the Cedar River before the arrival of Osgood Shepherd, the area's first permanent settler of European descent. Shepherd lived in a cabin on the river's east side in 1838 at what is now the location of First Avenue and First Street. A survey was made in 1841 and the newly formed town was named Rapids City after the rapids on the Cedar River; the name was changed to Cedar Rapids in 1848. In the early 1840s a dam was built across the river to provide power for the grist and lumber industries. Cedar Rapids was incorporated as a city in 1849; the town of Kingston, located on the west side of the river, was annexed to Cedar Rapids in 1870.

The early history of Cedar Rapids was highlighted by colorful characters and events. An island—now named Municipal Island—in the channel of the Cedar River was until 1851 the headquarters of the Shepherd gang, notorious horse thieves. Local residents built the steamer *The Cedar Rapids* in 1858 and used it for round trips to St. Louis; however, a collision on the Mississippi River and the arrival of the railroad ended river transportation.

Czechoslovakians, known as Bohemians, have made lasting contributions to the Cedar Rapids community. Czechs began arriving in 1852 to work in local packing plants, and soon a "Little Bohemia" was established in the southwest sector of the city (it is now known as "Czech Village"). Josef Sosel, the first Czech lawyer in the United States, was smuggled out of his native country in a barrel after he was accused of revolutionary activities; Sosel settled in Cedar Rapids, where he played a prominent role in the Czech community. In 1869 Czechs established The Reading Society, which evolved into a Little Theater movement, as well as the Light Guard Band. The Czech-language *Cedar Rapids Listy* began publication in 1906.

Industry and Arts Flourish

The economic growth of Cedar Rapids was spurred in 1871 with the arrival, from Ireland, of T. M. Sinclair, who established one of the nation's largest meatpacking companies, T. M. Sinclair Company. Some other major local industries that date from the same era are Cherry-Burrell and the world's largest cereal mill, Quaker Oats. Cultural development was simultaneous with economic expansion, as many Cedar Rapids arts and educational institutions were formed during this period. Greene's Opera House was dedicated in 1880, the same year the Cedar Rapids Business College opened its doors. Among the school's first faculty members was Austin Palmer, the inventor of the Palmer Method of Penmanship.

For more than 60 years, city fathers challenged nearby Marion for designation as the county seat; in 1919, voters endorsed a move to Cedar Rapids. The county courthouse and the Memorial Building, dedicated in 1928 to Americans who have fought in the nation's wars, were built on Municipal Island. Grant Wood, the Iowa artist, designed the 20-foot by 24-foot stained glass window in the Memorial Building and supervised its construction in Munich, Germany.

The artistry of Wood, one of the leading practitioners of Midwestern regionalism, is felt throughout the city. Wood grew up in Cedar Rapids and taught in the community junior high school; after studying in France he returned to the city and, supported by a local patron, set up a studio. Wood's "American Gothic" caused a sensation in the art world for its uncompromising realism when it was unveiled in 1930. Wood's daring work led to success and he was hired in 1934 to teach art at the University of Iowa.

Telecommunications Help Shape City's Future

Private enterprise, a principal force in the city's economic history, continued to be important during the first half of the twentieth century. Another Cedar Rapids native, Arthur Collins, started Collins Radio Company with eight employees during the Great Depression; the small electronics firm soon established a reputation as a leader in the industrial radio business. The company supplied electronic equipment to all branches of the armed services during World War II. Collins Radio, a major employer in the Cedar Rapids area, became a part of Rockwell Collins in 1973. Today the Cedar Rapids metropolitan area is a telecommunications and transportation center, performing an important role in the nation's economy. The Cedar Rapids ''Technology Corridor'' is one of the leading centers in the country for the defense electronics industry. The city has also developed a reputation as a cultural and artistic hub, with a thriving theater community and a wealth of sports and recreational activities for all. Known as the ''City of Five Seasons,'' Cedar Rapids residents profess to have a quality of life that allows for the addition of a fifth season, one to enjoy the community and the other four seasons.

Historical Information: The Carl and Mary Koehler History Center, 615 1st Avenue SE, Cedar Rapids, IA 52401; telephone (319)362-1501

Population Profile

Metropolitan Area Residents
 1980: 169,775
 1990: 168,767
 2000: 191,701
 2003 estimate: 196,006
 Percent change, 1990–2000: 13.6%
 U.S. rank in 1990: Not reported
 U.S. rank in 2000: 173rd

City Residents
 1980: 110,243
 1990: 108,772
 2000: 120,758
 2003 estimate: 122,542
 Percent change, 1990–2000: 10.9%
 U.S. rank in 1980: 141st
 U.S. rank in 1990: 174th
 U.S. rank in 2000: 181st (State rank: 2nd)

Density: 1,912.6 people per square mile (2000)

Racial and ethnic characteristics (2000)
 White: 112,874
 Black or African American: 5,614
 American Indian and Alaska Native: 792
 Asian: 2,564
 Native Hawaiian and Pacific Islander: 116
 Hispanic or Latino (may be of any race): 2,065
 Other: 1,112

Percent of residents born in state: 73.7% (2000)

Age characteristics (2000)
 Population under 5 years old: 8,625
 Population 5 to 9 years old: 8,649
 Population 10 to 14 years old: 7,765
 Population 15 to 19 years old: 8,544
 Population 20 to 24 years old: 9,039
 Population 25 to 34 years old: 18,338
 Population 35 to 44 years old: 18,708
 Population 45 to 54 years old: 15,670
 Population 55 to 59 years old: 5,266
 Population 60 to 64 years old: 4,360
 Population 65 to 74 years old: 7,728
 Population 75 to 84 years old: 5,853
 Population 85 years and older: 2,213
 Median age: 34.7 years

Births (2002)
 Total number: 1,807

Deaths (2002)
 Total number: 1,007

Money income (1999)
 Per capita income: $22,589
 Median household income: $43,704
 Total households: 49,879

Number of households with income of . . .
 less than $10,000: 3,207
 $10,000 to $14,999: 3,001
 $15,000 to $24,999: 6,163
 $25,000 to $34,999: 6,852
 $35,000 to $49,999: 9,272
 $50,000 to $74,999: 11,619
 $75,000 to $99,999: 5,342
 $100,000 to $149,999: 3,039
 $150,000 to $199,999: 614
 $200,000 or more: 770

Percent of families below poverty level: 4.9% (41.6% of which were female householder families with related children under 5 years)

2002 FBI Crime Index Total: 7,233

Municipal Government

Cedar Rapids is administered by a commission-mayor form of government. The City Council has executive, legislative and administrative authority. The five council members and the mayor, who is a member of the council, are elected to two-year, non-partisan terms.

Head Official: Mayor Paul D. Pate (since January 2002; current term expires January 2006)

Total Number of City Employees: 1,700 (2004)

City Information: City of Cedar Rapids, 51 First Avenue Bridge, Cedar Rapids, IA 52401; telephone (319)286-5000

Economy

Major Industries and Commercial Activity

The economy of Cedar Rapids has traditionally been based on the manufacture and processing of agricultural and food products, steel fabricating, tool and die making, and radios and electronics. Manufacturing, which continues to be an important economic sector, has been augmented by high-technology industries and transportation. The Cedar Rapids-Iowa City "Technology Corridor" is one of the leading centers in the country for the defense electronics industry; the fastest-growing segment of the metropolitan area economy is telecommunications and telemarketing. Advanced research and development laboratories, an educated and productive labor force, and a mid-continent location are increasingly attracting new business and industry to Cedar Rapids.

The city's association with high technology dates to the early years of Collins Radio Company. Today, Collins is part of Rockwell Collins, ranked as the largest employer in the Cedar Rapids-Iowa City region. The company provides aviation electronic and communication technology for government, aircraft manufacturers, and hundreds of airline customers. In fact, the company's aircraft electronics are used in almost every airline in the world. Additionally, Rockwell Collins' communication systems transmit almost 70 percent of all U.S. and allied military airborne communication.

In recent years, a number of local public and private organizations joined together to help develop the "Technology Corridor." This hub for technology companies is located throughout 12 communities in Johnson and Linn Counties. Its location near a number of colleges and universities enables Corridor companies to easily access education, training, research, and development. Local firms provide a variety of services such as electronic design and consultation, systems planning, equipment manufacturing, and telemarketing.

While Cedar Rapids has seen tremendous growth in technology, the city continues to succeed in attracting agricultural and food processing manufacturers. It is home to more than 275 different manufacturing plants, including Quaker Food and Beverages, which runs the world's largest cereal milling plant. Other top manufacturing employers include Amana Refrigeration Products, General Mills, Inc., and H.J. Heinz Company.

Items and goods produced: cereal, syrup, sugar, dairy, mining, and road machinery, boxboard and containers, automotive tools and machinery, radio electronics and avionics equipment, oil burners, furniture, pumps, gravel crushers, cranes, snow plows, electric-powered shovels, trailer parts, candy, office and drainage equipment, rubber goods, plastic bags, recycled corrugated cardboard, copper alloy and plastic molding, medical and chemical products, plumbing supplies, auto parts and toys, furnaces, livestock feed, structural steel, compressed gas, pharmaceuticals, avionics and earth-moving equipment, telecommunications equipment, home appliances

Incentive Programs—New and Existing Companies

Local programs—The Cedar Rapids Area Chamber of Commerce and its divisions are active in implementing growth plans, helping existing businesses, and recruiting companies from throughout the world. Its economic development division, Priority One, provides businesses with demographics and trade figures, site location assistance, and workforce development.

State programs—Part of the private-public partnership Cedar Rapids fosters is evident in such state programs as certain property tax exemptions, job training, low-interest loans and forgivable loans for business development, tax abatements on new research and manufacturing facilities, and state tax credits for new job creation. In addition, no sales or use taxes are assessed on equipment or computers and open port warehousing is available.

Job training programs—Cedar Rapids area businesses can take advantage of the Iowa Industrial New Jobs Training Program administered by Kirkwood Community College, which provides education and training for new employees of new and expanding companies at little or no cost.

Development Projects

Many companies have recently been relocating to or expanding current operations in the Cedar Rapids area. Nordstrom is expanding its existing fulfillment center by adding 39,000 square feet of space and creating 275 full-time positions. U.S. Cellular is expanding its engineering and customer call center, adding 15,000 square feet and 100 new jobs. Iowa Glass

Co. is in the process of building a new $10 million corporate headquarters and distribution center, and German fiber manufacturer J. Rettenmaier & Söhne recently announced plans to build a dietary fiber production facility in the city.

Economic Development Information: Priority One, Economic Development Division, Cedar Rapids Area Chamber of Commerce, 424 First Avenue NE, Cedar Rapids, IA 52401; telephone (319)398-5317; email infodesk@priority1.com

Commercial Shipping

A central location, efficient access, and low supply and distribution costs have contributed to the development of Cedar Rapids as a primary transportation hub in the Midwest. The city is at the center of the NAFTA corridor, and international connections are readily accessible. Additionally, Eastern Iowa Airport is a designated Foreign Trade Zone. The 3,200-square-acre airport served one million passengers in 2000, a milestone in its history. A leader in exporting goods, Cedar Rapids works closely with top importers in Canada, Japan, Mexico, Germany and France. Iowa is the only state bordered by two navigable rivers, and many area exports leave via water.

Cedar Rapids' rail system also provides transportation services to many businesses. The Union Pacific East-West mainline travels through the city, as well as the Canadian Pacific Railway and the Cedar Rapids and Iowa City Railway. The lines interchange with a number of major national airlines serving all of North America. In addition, Cedar Rapids is the only area able to serve Minneapolis, Chicago, St. Louis, and Omaha by freight carrier within a one-day round trip. More than 34 motor freight carriers with terminals located in the area provide interstate, intrastate and local freight services.

Labor Force and Employment Outlook

With an educated, available, and skilled workforce, Cedar Rapids maintains a productivity rate that is substantially above the national average. Absenteeism is less than 1 percent and industrial turnover is less than 1.5 percent. Area workers produce 20 percent more than the average American worker and score high in rankings of annual value added per production worker. With 69 percent of the workforce having education beyond high school, and 48 percent having an undergraduate degree or higher, local businesses have a large pool of educated workers to choose from. And in order to further train those workers, Cedar Rapids area businesses can take advantage of the Iowa Industrial New Jobs Training Program, which provides education and training for new employees of new and expanding companies at little or no cost. The program is administered by Kirkwood Community College.

The following is a summary of data regarding the Cedar Rapids metropolitan area labor force, 2004 annual averages.

Size of nonagricultural labor force: 129,500

Number of workers employed in . . .
  construction and mining: 7,100
  manufacturing: 19,300
  trade, transportation, and utilities: 28,100
  information: 5,700
  financial activities: 9,700
  professional and business services: 12,300
  education and health services: 16,000
  leisure and hospitality: 10,600
  other services: 5,300
  government: 15,300

Average hourly earnings of production workers employed in manufacturing: $16.08 (statewide average)

Unemployment rate: 5.9% (February 2005)

Largest employers	Number of employees
Rockwell Collins	7,162
Mercy Medical Center	2,862
Cedar Rapids Community Schools	2,860
AEGON Insurance Group	2,632
St. Luke's Hospital	2,400
Amana Refrigeration Products	2,300
MCI	1,880
City of Cedar Rapids	1,700
Hy-Vee Food Stores	1,691
Alliant Energy	1,650
McLeodUSA Incorporated	1,645

Cost of Living

Cedar Rapids's property taxes are the second-lowest of the state's eight largest cities with more than 50,000 people.

The following is a summary of data regarding several key cost of living factors in the Cedar Rapids area.

2004 (3rd Quarter) ACCRA Average House Price: $221,000

2004 (3rd Quarter) ACCRA Cost of Living Index: 94.2 (U.S. average = 100.0)

State income tax rate: Ranges from 0.36% to 8.98%

State sales tax rate: 5.0%

Local income tax rate: None

Local sales tax rate: None

Property tax rate: $34.50 per $1,000 of assessed valuation for properties within the Cedar Rapids Community School District; 51.6676% of the assessed value is subject to the property tax rate; therefore, a $100,000 house would be taxed as if it were valued at $51,667

Economic Information: Cedar Rapids Area Chamber of Commerce, 424 First Avenue NE, Cedar Rapids, IA 52401; telephone (319)398-5317.

Education and Research

Elementary and Secondary Schools

The Cedar Rapids Community School District is the second-largest of Iowa's 397 public school systems. The average composite ACT score for Iowa high school students is 22.0, ranking Iowa second in the nation; Cedar Rapids' average score is 23.5. The average daily attendance rate in 2003/2004 was 96 percent. As a result of the .38 percent dropout rate for high school students, the district was highlighted in the *Wall Street Journal.* Forty-nine percent of teachers have master's degrees. The district is working through a multi-year, $52 million facilities improvement plan. Additionally, $4.1 million was spent on new curriculum, teaching tools, and technology in 2003.

The following is a summary of data regarding the Cedar Rapids public schools as of the 2003–2004 school year.

Total enrollment: 17,729 (including home-schooled children)

Number of facilities
  elementary schools: 21
  middle schools: 5
  senior high schools: 4 (including one alternative high school)

Student/teacher ratio: 16:1

Teacher salaries (statewide)
  average: $39,432

Funding per pupil: $7,236

Catholic schools in the metropolitan area enroll nearly 3,000 students.

Public Schools Information: Cedar Rapids Community Schools, Community Relations, 346 Second Avenue SW, Cedar Rapids, IA 52404; telephone (319)558-2124

Colleges and Universities

Six institutions of higher learning are located in the Cedar Rapids area. Coe College, Mount Mercy College, and Cornell College are all four-year, private, liberal arts colleges. Coe College, founded in 1851, offers 40 degree choices and small class size, with an enrollment of 1,300 students. Mount Mercy College was founded by the Sisters of Mercy and offers 35 majors, with 1,400 students. Cornell College, founded in 1853, has an enrollment of just over 1,100 students, and is ranked in the top 7 percent of the nation's colleges and universities.

In nearby Iowa City, the University of Iowa offers 100 undergraduate degree programs, 110 graduate degree programs and 74 doctorate degree programs. Its medical, dental, law, pharmacy, and business colleges are nationally recognized. The University of Iowa Education and Conference Center is located in downtown Cedar Rapids.

Kirkwood Community College provides vocational/technical, arts and sciences, and adult continuing education programs. Current full-time enrollment is nearly 14,000 students. Hamilton Business College is the oldest business college in Iowa, offering one year diplomas and two year associate degree programs.

Libraries and Research Centers

The Cedar Rapids Public Library operates an architecturally impressive main facility as well as another branch on the west side of the city. It houses an up-to-date collection and a diverse array of services in comfortable surroundings. The library computer system, CD-ROM and Internet stations make information retrieval easy and convenient. The library offers programs for all ages, including story times, crafts, puppet and magic shows, author lectures, readings, demonstrations, and discussions.

Cedar Rapids is also served by the Coe College and Kirkwood Community College libraries. Among special libraries are the National Czech and Slovak Museum and Library, which collects published and unpublished resources by and about the Czech and Slovak peoples, and the Iowa Masonic Library, which contains 100,000 volumes of reference materials and a collection of colonial, Native American, and foreign exhibits.

The University of Iowa Libraries house more than 4 million volumes and more than 40,000 serials, making it one of the largest research collections in the country. The university's law library was recently ranked as one of the top five law libraries in the nation.

Public Library Information: Cedar Rapids Public Library, 500 First Street SE, Cedar Rapids, IA 52401; telephone (319)398-5123

Health Care

Two major medical centers serve Cedar Rapids: Mercy Medical Center and St. Luke's Hospital, both of which have been recognized to be among the 100 top orthopedic hospitals in the United States. St. Luke's Hospital specializes in cardiac care, behavioral health, obstetrics, rehabilitation, pediatrics, and surgery. In 2000, St. Luke's opened the area's largest ambulatory surgery unit in an effort to make outpatient procedures more convenient for patients and medical staff. Mercy Medical Center's facilities include the Mercy Cancer Center, which participates in National Cancer Institute clinical research programs. In 2002 Mercy built the J. Edward Lundy Pavilion, a 170,000 square foot facility which houses the Katz Cardiovascular Center, Mercy Surgical Services, Women's Center, and Birthplace obstetrical unit. The medical community includes nearly 300 practicing physicians covering every area of specialty. The health care needs of area residents are also attended to at the University of Iowa Hospital and Clinics, the nation's largest teaching hospital, located a 25 minutes away.

Health Care Information: St. Luke's Hospital, 1026 A Avenue NE, Cedar Rapids, IA 52406; telephone (319)369-7211. Mercy Medical Center, 710 Tenth Street SE, Cedar Rapids, IA 52403; telephone (319)398-6011

Recreation

Sightseeing

A trip to Cedar Rapids might include a visit to Brucemore Mansion and Gardens, which is a National Trust Historic Site. A 21-room Queen Anne-style mansion on a 26-acre estate, Brucemore is the ancestral home of three prominent families who used it as a center for culture and arts. Built in 1884, it is now used for a variety of cultural events, including dance and drama performance, historical tours, garden walks, lectures, workshops, and educational programs.

The National Czech & Slovak Museum & Library preserve the city's ethnic heritage; they offer two exhibit galleries that focus on Czech and Slovak history and culture. In the area downtown along the Cedar River known as The Czech Village, shops, bakeries, and stores feature authentic crafts and foods. The Science Station, housed in a refurbished brick 1917 fire station, offers hands-on science and technology exhibits for children and adults. In 2001 the McLeod/Busse IMAX Dome Theatre was added to the property, offering science and nature themed movies on a six-story wraparound screen. The Iowa Equestrian Center at Kirkwood Community College is one of Cedar Rapids' newest attractions, and the state's most comprehensive facilities for horse shows, workshops, programs, and equestrian events. It has indoor and outdoor arenas and facilities for 266 horses.

Several points of interest are within driving distance of Cedar Rapids. The Amana Colonies, 20 minutes south of the city, is Iowa's primary tourist attraction. It is composed of seven villages first settled in 1855 by German immigrants searching for religious freedom. Today, the Colonies are home to furniture stores, wineries, bakeries, and German restaurants run by the settlers' descendents. The Herbert Hoover Presidential Library and National Historic Site is in West Branch, 25 miles from Cedar Rapids. Attractions there include the presidential library and museum, a Quaker meeting house, a blacksmith shop, Hoover's birthplace, and Hoover's grave site.

Arts and Culture

An important part of cultural life in Cedar Rapids is the Museum of Art, with 5,000 works of art under its roof. The museum houses the world's largest collection of works by Grant Wood, Marvin Cone, and Mauricio Lasansky. They also have strong collections of early twentieth century paintings, Malvina Hoffman sculptures, and Regionalist art from the 1930s and 1940s. In 2003 Cedar Rapids also became home to the African American Historical Museum and Cultural Center of Iowa. This building features exhibits on Africa, the nation, and Iowa, and holds community and educational programs.

The city's cultural community presents a variety of concerts and shows and hosts visiting international performance groups. The renovated Paramount Theatre for the Performing Arts, with a hall of mirrors and Broadway-style marquee, is the home of the Cedar Rapids Symphony Orchestra. The symphony performs four concert series: Classics, Pops, Chamber, and Discovery Family. In 1998, the Cedar Rapids Opera Theatre began performing two to three operas per season. Past performances have included *Pirates of Penzance* and *La Traviata*. Its Young Artists Program allows pre-professional singers the opportunity to perform in mainstage productions.

Theatre Cedar Rapids presents eight mainstage shows in a repertoire ranging from musicals to drama, and is one of the 20 largest community theatres in the country. It is housed in the Iowa Theatre Building, first opened in 1928 and extensively renovated in 1980. Off-season the building is busy hosting a variety of other performances, including comedy shows and concerts. The Old Creamery Theatre Company performs an April-to-December season at the Amana Colonies. Area colleges sponsor a host of cultural programs. Among them is the Summer Rep series at the University of Iowa University Theatres, which features works each season by a single modern playwright. The university's Hancher Auditorium hosts more than 40 major international cultural events each year in its 2,500-seat auditorium.

For a taste of small-town Iowa during the turn of the century, visitors can walk through the Ushers Ferry Historic Village. Composed of more than 30 authentic buildings and homes

The Cedar Rapids Museum of Art, opened in 1989, encompasses a restored Beaux Arts building and a newly constructed gallery.

over 10 acres of land, the facility gives tours, workshops, and historical reenactments. Turn-of-the-century farm life can be relived at Seminole Valley Farm, where the restored family farm and outbuildings are now home to tours and history exhibits. In nearby Marion, the nineteenth-century Granger House is open for tours of the Victorian home and carriage house.

Festivals and Holidays

A festival, parade, or show is scheduled nearly every weekend of the year in Cedar Rapids. The Cedar Rapids Freedom Festival, a city staple for more than 20 years, is an 11-day festival encompassing more than 75 events for all ages during the month of July. Also in July, nearby Hiawatha hosts its Hog Wild Days, a week-long festival that raises money for community programs. During the spring, the Marion Arts Festival brings together 50 artists from across the country, displaying and selling a wide variety of art. Live music, food vendors, and family-friendly activities are also featured. In January, the Amana Colonies is home to WinterFest, a day of Winter fun including a 5K run/walk, wagon rides, cross-country skiing, ice skating, and winery tours.

Sports for the Spectator

The Cedar Rapids Kernels, a Class A farm club of the National League Anaheim Angels professional baseball club, play a full home schedule in the Midwest League at Veterans Memorial Park, which seats 5,300 people. For automobile-racing enthusiasts, Hawkeye Downs Speedway hosts a number of sanctioned racing events in modern facilities. Visiting regional and national series have included the NASCAR REMAX Series, American IndyCar Series, and the IMCA Summer Series. Hockey enthusiasts are crowding games of the new RoughRiders junior hockey team at the Cedar Rapids Ice Arena. In 2004 Cedar Rapids acquired the Cedar Rapids River Raiders, a member of the United States Basketball League. They play home games at U.S. Cellular Center.

The full range of major college sports is presented at the University of Iowa in nearby Iowa City, where the Hawkeyes engage in Big Ten competition. Coe College, Mount Mercy College, and Kirkwood Community College in Cedar Rapids, and Cornell College in Mount Vernon compete in a number of sports.

Sports for the Participant

Cedar Rapids has the largest park system in Iowa, with more than 75 parks on more than 4,000 acres of land. Recreation facilities include 6 aquatic centers, 50 ball fields, 30 volleyball courts, 3 outdoor ice rinks, 4 cross-country ski trails, 50 tennis courts, and 30 soccer fields. For the golfing enthusiast, the city also has 4 municipal golf courses, 4 privately owned golf courses, and 3 country clubs. At Cheyenne Park, dog

owners can use an 18-acre, fenced, off-leash dog exercise area. The area is also home to many miles of nature trails. The Cedar Valley Nature Trail, once a railroad bed, offers 52 miles of trails for biking, hiking, and skiing through recreation areas, along riverbanks, and through small towns. The Sac and Fox National Recreational Trail follows Indian Creek through wooded areas and is used for hiking, horseback riding, bicycling, skiing, and dog sledding.

Recreation Information: Cedar Rapids Parks Department, telephone (319)286-5080

Shopping and Dining

The Cedar Rapids area offers a wide range of shopping and dining attractions. The city is home to two enclosed malls with a combined total of more than 170 shops. Downtown, more than 103 individual stores are woven through the city streets. In nearby Williamsburg, shoppers can find the Tanger Factory Outlet Center, with more than 70 outlet stores. Additionally, Czech Village and the Amana Colonies offer an assortment of specialty shops. Dining choices consist of a mix of ethnic and traditional cuisines, with an abundance of regional and national chains as well as unique locally owned restaurants. Three farmer's markets operate in the warm-weather months, offering locally grown fruits, vegetables, flowers, and baked goods.

Visitor Information: Cedar Rapids Area Convention and Visitors Bureau, 119 First Avenue SE, Cedar Rapids, IA 52406; toll-free (800)735-5557.

Convention Facilities

Cedar Rapids offers a variety of convention facilities depending on one's needs. The multipurpose Cedar Rapids Education and Conference Center, in downtown Cedar Rapids, houses different sized rooms with up-to-date multimedia equipment. The facility partners with a number of local hotels and restaurants. Coe College, Kirkwood Community College, and Mount Mercy College also offer smaller conference facilities, and for those groups looking for an abundance of space, the Hawkeye Downs Speedway, U.S. Cellular Center, and Veterans Memorial Coliseum have facilities available.

Hotels and motels in metropolitan Cedar Rapids offer accommodations for a range of meeting and convention needs. More than 3,000 rooms are available.

Convention Information: Cedar Rapids Convention and Visitors Bureau, 119 First Avenue SE, Cedar Rapids, IA 52406; telephone (319)398-5009, ext. 126.

Transportation

Approaching the City

The Cedar Rapids Airport, just south of the center of the city off of I-380, handles an average of 80 commercial flights daily. It offers direct service to Minneapolis, Denver, Las Vegas, Dallas, Chicago, Detroit, St. Louis, and Cincinnati. One third of the country's population is within an hour's flight from Cedar Rapids. All passengers have access to the airport's Information Center and Business Center. In 2000, one million passengers were served in one year, marking a milestone in the airport's history.

Cedar Rapids is linked with points throughout the nation by two interstate highways, I-380 (north-south) and I-80 (east-west). Federal highways are 30/218, which runs east to west through the south sector Cedar Rapids, and 151, which intersects the city diagonally northeast to southwest. State routes include 150, running parallel with I-380, and east-west 94. Cedar Rapids is located mid-point on the newly designated ''Avenue of the Saints'' that connects St. Louis, Missouri, and St. Paul, Minnesota. The area is also served by a number of commuter rail lines.

Traveling in the City

The Cedar River divides Cedar Rapids into east and west sectors; for address purposes, streets are designated according to quadrants: northeast, northwest, southeast, and southwest. The City Bus Department and taxis are headquartered in the Ground Transportation Center on Fourth Avenue. Linn County LIFTS provides service to the elderly and handicapped in the metropolitan area with specially-equipped buses.

Communications

Newspapers and Magazines

The major daily newspaper in Cedar Rapids is the *Cedar Rapids Gazette,* a locally owned morning paper. Also pub-lished in the city is *Iowa Farmer Today,* a weekly agricultural newspaper; *Iowa Pork Today,* an agricultural magazine pub-lished monthly; and *Buildings,* a monthly magazine about facilities construction and management. The *Fraternal Her-ald (Bratrsky Vestnik)* is a monthly benefit society magazine.

Television and Radio

NBC, CBS, and ABC television affiliates broadcast from Cedar Rapids, and cable service is available. Eleven AM and FM radio stations schedule musical, special interest, nostal-gia, news, and public affairs programming.

Media Information: *Cedar Rapids Gazette,* 500 Third Ave-nue SE, Cedar Rapids, IA 52406; telephone (319)398-8333

Cedar Rapids Online

Cedar Rapids Community Schools. Available www.cr.k12 .ia.us

Cedar Rapids Downtown District. Available www.down towncr.org

Cedar Rapids Gazette online. Available www.gazetteonline .com

Cedar Rapids Public Library. Available www.crlibrary.org

Chamber of Commerce. Available www.cedarrapids.org

City and area information. Available www.fyiowa.com

Convention and Visitor Information. Available www.cedar-rapids.com

Priority One Economic Development Department. Avail-able www.priority1.com

Selected Bibliography

Engle, Paul. *A Lucky American Childhood (Singular Lives)* (Uni-versity of Iowa Press, 1996)

Davenport

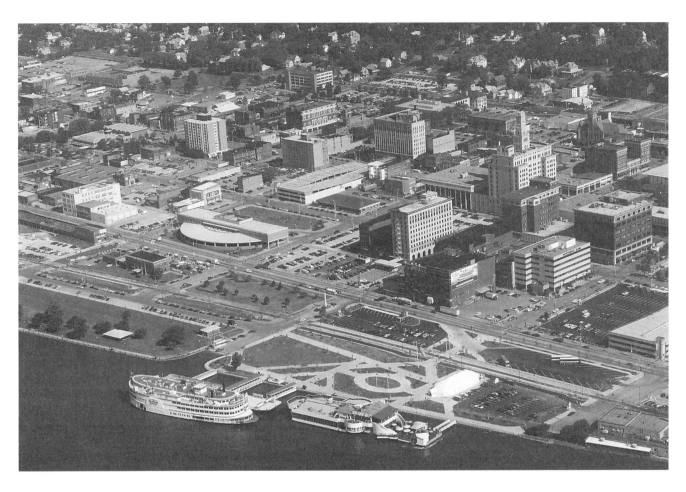

The City in Brief

Founded: 1808 (incorporated, 1836)

Head Official: Mayor Charles W. Brooke (since 2004)

City Population
  1980: 103,264
  1990: 95,333
  2000: 98,359
  2003 estimate: 97,512
  Percent change, 1990–2000: 2.8%
  U.S. rank in 1990: 212th
  U.S. rank in 2000: 267th

Metropolitan Area Population
  1980: 384,000
  1990: 350,855
  2000: 359,062

  Percent change, 1990–2000: 2.3%
  U.S. rank in 1990: Not reported
  U.S. rank in 2000: 114th

Area: 63 square miles (2000)
Elevation: Ranges from 579 to 700 feet above sea level
Average Annual Temperature: 48.1° F
Average Annual Precipitation: 33.7 inches

Major Economic Sectors: Trade, services, manufacturing, government
Unemployment Rate: 5.6% (March 2005)
Per Capita Income: $18,828 (1999)
2004 ACCRA Cost of Living Index: Not reported

2002 FBI Crime Index Total: Not reported

Major Colleges and Universities: St. Ambrose University; Marycrest International University

Daily Newspaper: *Quad-City Times*

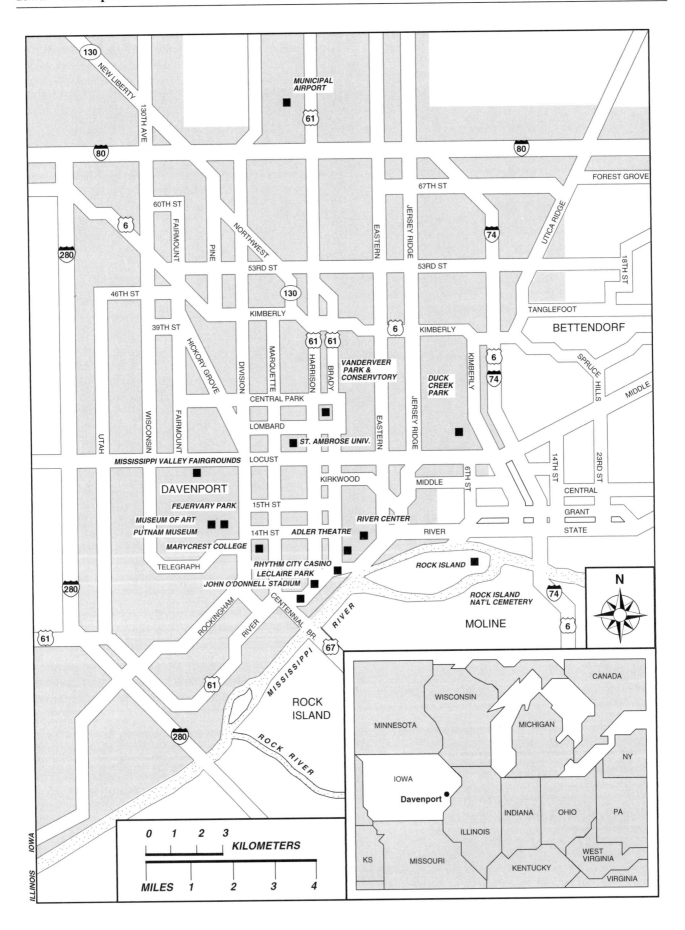

Introduction

Davenport is the seat of Scott County and the largest of four cities in Iowa and Illinois that comprise the Quad Cities metropolitan area; the other three cities are Bettendorf, Iowa, Rock Island, Illinois, and Moline, Illinois. Because of its location on the Mississippi River, Davenport played an important role in western expansion during the nineteenth century; along with the other Quad Cities, Davenport continues to be a world leader in the production of farm equipment. With the introduction of riverboat gambling in the 1990s, Davenport is emerging as a top Midwestern tourist destination. Davenport's economic resurgence, beginning in 2001, has brought millions of dollars of additional development to the city.

Geography and Climate

Davenport is set on a plain on the north bank of the Mississippi River, where the river forms the boundary between Iowa and Illinois. Davenport's section of the generally north-to-south-flowing river flows from east to west. Unlike every other major city bordering the Mississippi, Davenport has no permanent floodwall or levee, as the city prefers to retain open access to the water. Occasionally, flooding occurs and millions of dollars of property damage results. Located in the heart of an agricultural region, the city is within 300 miles of most other major Midwestern cities. Davenport's position near the geographic center of the country produces a temperate, continental climate that is characterized by a wide range in temperatures. Summers are short and hot; winters are usually severe, with an average annual snowfall of just over 30 inches. Although Davenport is located in a tornado zone, no funnel cloud has ever touched down within the city's boundaries.

Area: 63 square miles (2000)

Elevation: 579 feet to 700 feet above sea level

Average Temperatures: January, 21.7° F; July, 76.2° F; annual average, 48.1° F

Average Annual Precipitation: 33.7 inches

History

Westward Expansion Targets Davenport Townsite

In the early 1800s the land now occupied by the city of Davenport was the site of bloody fighting between Native Americans and settlers from the eastern United States. This location was valuable in the westward expansion beyond the Mississippi River, serving as a trading center of the American Fur Company. Early treaties specified that the Sac tribe could remain in their villages until the land was surveyed and sold to settlers; warfare resulted, however, after Chief Black Hawk and his followers refused to leave the land on the order of the United States Government agent at Fort Armstrong. In the fall of 1832, Black Hawk was captured and returned to Fort Armstrong, where he signed a treaty, known as the Black Hawk Purchase, that conveyed to the United States six million acres of land west of the Mississippi River.

Two figures stand out in the period that predates the formation of Davenport. The city was named for Colonel George Davenport, an Englishman who had served in the United States Army and then established a fur trading post in the vicinity. Antoine LeClaire, an interpreter who was fluent in three languages and several Native American dialects, served as interpreter for the Black Hawk Purchase. For his efforts the federal government, at the request of Chief Keokuk, awarded him a section of land opposite Rock Island and another section at the head of the rapids above Rock Island where the treaty was negotiated. In 1833, in a claim dispute over land he owned, LeClaire settled for a quarter-section bounded by Davenport's present-day Harrison Street, Warren Street, and Seventh Street. In 1835 Colonel Davenport and six other men formed a company to survey a townsite; they purchased this section from LeClaire, who succeeded in having the new town named after his good friend Davenport. The town was incorporated in 1836.

The initial sale of lots attracted few buyers and in the first year only a half dozen families relocated to the new town. LeClaire and Davenport erected a hotel on the corner of Ripley and First Streets, naming it the Hotel Davenport. By the spring of 1837, the population was growing; a town retailer, for instance, served customers who traveled hundreds of miles to buy goods from his inventory, valued at $5,000. In December of that year, the Wisconsin Territorial Legislature authorized the creation of Scott County, named after General Winfield Scott. A dispute subsequently broke out between Davenport and neighboring Rockingham for the right to be the county seat. The matter was decided, after three elections, in favor of Davenport; in time, Rockingham was absorbed by the larger city. Davenport received its first city charter in 1839.

Industry and Culture Establish Traditions

During the decade before the Civil War, Davenport increased its population more than fivefold, with an influx of immigrants from Germany that continued unabated into the 1890s. These new residents imported music and other cultural interests to Davenport, creating institutions such as the Davenport Public Museum and the Municipal Art Gallery. The first railroad bridge to span the Mississippi River was completed in 1856 between Davenport and Rock Island, contributing to the development of the western frontier. The Rock Island Arsenal opened in 1861 to help Union war efforts; the arsenal eventually grew to become one of the largest in the world. In the post-Civil War era Davenport prospered as a riverboat town and as a burgeoning industrial center for the manufacture of cement, steel and iron products, and leather goods.

By the turn of the twentieth century, Davenport was considered the ''Washing Machine Capital of the World''—the revolutionary home appliance was invented in the city—and the ''Cigar Making Capital of the Midwest.'' The cigar industry flourished in Davenport until World War II. Davenport counts among its former citizens a number of prominent Americans. B. J. Palmer, the inventor of chiropractics, and his son, D. D. Palmer, were lifelong residents; the younger Palmer used his radio station to introduce Americans to his new medical practice and to Davenport. Buffalo Bill Cody grew up in the rural Davenport area; Dixieland jazz great Bix Beiderbecke was born in the city; and two Pulitzer Prize winners, Charles Edward Russell and Susan Glaspell, once lived there.

Davenport and the Quad Cities region, having invested tens of millions of dollars in the 1990s on lavish riverboat casinos, provide ''Midwest Magic on the Mississippi River.'' In 2001, Scott County voters approved the River Renaissance development program, which commenced a period of downtown revitalization and inspired more than $160 million of investment throughout the region.

Historical Information: Putnam Museum of History and Natural Science Library, 1717 W. 12th Street, Davenport, IA 52804; telephone (319)324-1933

Population Profile

Metropolitan Area Residents
1980: 384,000
1990: 350,855
2000: 359,062
Percent change, 1990–2000: 2.3%
U.S. rank in 1990: Not reported
U.S. rank in 2000: 114th

City Residents
1980: 103,264
1990: 95,333

2000: 98,359
2003 estimate: 97,512
Percent change, 1990–2000: 2.8%
U.S. rank in 1990: 212th
U.S. rank in 2000: 267th

Density: 1,566 people per square mile (2000)

Racial and ethnic characteristics (2000)
White: 82,311
Black or African American: 9,093
American Indian and Alaska Native: 368
Asian: 1,967
Native Hawaiian and Pacific Islander: 24
Hispanic or Latino (may be of any race): 5,268
Other: 2,279

Percent of residents born in state: 61.9% (2000)

Age characteristics (2000)
Population under 5 years old: 7,268
Population 5 to 9 years old: 7,131
Population 10 to 14 years old: 7,100
Population 15 to 19 years old: 7,103
Population 20 to 24 years old: 7,698
Population 25 to 34 years old: 14,894
Population 35 to 44 years old: 14,695
Population 45 to 54 years old: 12,749
Population 55 to 59 years old: 4,282
Population 60 to 64 years old: 3,497
Population 65 to 74 years old: 5,873
Population 75 to 84 years old: 4,406
Population 85 years and over: 1,663
Median age: 33.6 years

Births (2002, Scott County)
Total number: 2,275

Deaths (2002, Scott County)
Total number: 1,318 (of which, 6 were infants under the age of 1 year)

Money income (1999)
Per capita income: $18,828
Median household income: $37,242
Total households: 39,238

Number of households with income of . . .
less than $10,000: 4,056
$10,000 to $14,999: 2,697
$15,000 to $24,999: 5,998
$25,000 to $34,999: 5,756
$35,000 to $49,999: 6,742
$50,000 to $74,999: 7,911
$75,000 to $99,999: 3,565
$100,000 to $149,999: 1,799
$150,000 to $199,999: 350
$200,000 or more: 364

Percent of families below poverty level: 10.5% (61.5% of which were female householder families with related children under 5 years)

2002 FBI Crime Index Total: Not reported

Municipal Government

Davenport, the seat of Scott County, is administered by a council-mayor form of government. Ten aldermen—eight chosen by ward and elected at large—and the mayor serve two-year terms; the mayor appoints a city administrator. Davenport, once the only city in Iowa to hold partisan political elections, has elected its mayor on a non-partisan basis since 1997.

Head Official: Mayor Charles W. Brooke (since 2004; current term expires 2006)

Total Number of City Employees: 900 (2005)

City Information: City Hall, 226 West 4th Street, Davenport, IA telephone (563)326-7701

Economy

Major Industries and Commercial Activity

The Davenport economic base is diversified, with a relatively equal distribution among the manufacturing, wholesale and retail, and services sectors. Manufacturing has traditionally been a principal industry in the city. Davenport is also a primary retail and wholesale trade center, drawing from a market area encompassing a radius of up to 100 miles. Business and industry in Davenport benefit from the Quad City financial community. More than 40 area banks and lending institutions, in conjunction with the state of Iowa, have established a fiscal atmosphere favorable to new business and the expansion of existing firms through progressive and conventional financing procedures. Thirteen industrial islands are located within the Davenport city limits.

Items and goods produced: agricultural implements, construction machinery, military equipment, airplane parts, chemicals, meat and food products, lumber and timber, sheet aluminum, metal products, cement and foundry products, electronic parts, clothing, printing and publishing products

Incentive Programs—New and Existing Companies

Local programs—City programs include loans and tax abatement programs for job creations and investment in real estate. The city of Davenport currently qualifies to offer the advantages of operating in an Enterprise Zone.

State programs—State of Iowa loans/forgivable loans and grants based on payroll and capital investment in plant and equipment. Projects involving larger capital investments and/or higher paying jobs may qualify for property tax exemptions, tax credits and additional training dollars under the New Jobs and Income Program. Additional state funding is also available for infrastructure improvements such as rail spurs, roadways, and others.

Job training programs—Job training programs are available that offset wages and training costs of employees. These programs are paid for through the diversion of payroll and property taxes that would normally accrue to the state/community. They also provide Iowa income tax credits.

Development Projects

A significant development in Davenport and environs was the introduction of riverboat casino gambling in the 1990s. Tens of millions of dollars have been poured into these ventures and tourists have been responding. Other key economic development efforts include the opening of an expanded convention center; a new 220-room hotel; and a 780-car parking garage, surmounted by a $20 million, 10-story building for MidAmerican Energy Company. Just west of these developments are a new Community Health Center, a new Sports Center, and a renovated state-of-the-art educational center for Eastern Iowa Community College District. Davenport's Downtown Partnership has focused on developing the city's central business district by retaining existing businesses, developing opportunities for new businesses, and providing housing for those employed in the urban area. Since 2001, the River Renaissance program has revitalized Davenport's historic downtown through more than $100 million worth of community investment.

Economic Development Information: Quad City Development Group, 1830 Second Avenue, Suite 200, Rock Island, IL 61201; telephone (563)326-1005; toll-free (800)747-7436

Commercial Shipping

Davenport's mid-continent location is favorable to freight distribution, with one-day delivery by highway and rail to points throughout the Midwest. As a U.S. Customs Port of Entry and a Foreign Trade Zone (FTZ), Davenport is also a center for national and international commerce. Its Quad Cities Container Terminal works with the FTZ to permit materials to be shipped around the world without being unpacked or passing through customs until they reach their final destination. The Quad City area comprises the largest market of any major metropolitan region. A regional headquarters of United Parcel Service is located in Davenport; in all, six air freight carriers process cargo through the Quad City Airport. More than 100 motor freight companies maintain warehouses in the Quad Cities. Four rail carriers provide local switching services. Of the regions nearly 50 private and public barge terminals, more than half offer access by rail and/or highway. More than 60 truck terminals and more than 70 motor freight carriers serve the Quad Cities. Bulk commodity shippers find the Quad Cities barge service to be a highly cost-efficient shipping option.

Labor Force and Employment Outlook

Davenport claims a productive, skilled labor force that can be employed at a lower cost than the national average. Because of the area's long history as a manufacturing center, the work force possesses many of the traditional skills associated with equipment manufacturing and metal fabricating. The service sector is the fastest-growing, led by the proliferation of gambling casinos and attendant industries catering to tourists.

The following is a summary of data regarding the Davenport-Rock Island-Moline metropolitan area labor force, 2004 annual averages.

Size of non-agricultural labor force: 182,600

Number of workers employed in . . .
  mining and construction: 8,000
  manufacturing: 24,300
  trade, transportation and utilities: 39,800
  information: 3,200
  financial activities: 8,900
  professional and business services: 22,300
  educational and health services: 22,200
  leisure and hospitality: 18,800
  other services: 7,900
  government: 27,300

Average hourly earnings of production workers employed in manufacturing: $16.17

Unemployment rate: 5.6% (March 2005)

Largest Quad City employers	Number of employees
Deere & Co.	7,750
Aluminum Co. of America (ALCOA)	2,500
IBP Inc. Slaughterhouse	2,200
Rock Island Arsenal	1,814
Oscar Mayer Food Corp.	1,800
Eagle Food Center	1,622

Cost of Living

Davenport offers tax-exempt housing mortgage revenue bonds to prospective homeowners. Health care costs are relatively low.

The following is a summary of data regarding several key cost of living factors in the Davenport area.

2004 (3rd Quarter) ACCRA Average House Price: $241,035 (Quad Cities)

2004 ACCRA Cost of Living Index: Not reported

State income tax rate: Ranges from 0.36% to 8.98%

State sales tax rate: 5.0%

Local income tax rate: None

Local sales tax rate: 2.0%

Property tax rate: $32.49 per $1,000 assessed valuation

Economic Information: Davenport Chamber of Commerce, 102 S. Harrison Street, Davenport, IA 52801; telephone (563)322-1706

Education and Research

Elementary and Secondary Schools

Public elementary and secondary schools in Davenport are part of the Davenport Community School District, which also serves the communities of Buffalo, Blue Grass, and Walcott. Iowa consistently ranks among the top states in the country for average ACT composite scores.

The following is a summary of data regarding the Davenport public schools as of the 2002–2003 school year.

Total enrollment: 16,544

Number of facilities
  preschool center: 1
  elementary schools: 19 (some with preschool)
  middle schools: 6
  high schools: 3
  other: 1 alternative school

Student/teacher ratio: 20:1 K-1st; 21:1 2nd-3rd; 26:1 4th-5th

Teacher salaries
  average: $45,493

Funding per pupil: $8,904 in 2002-2003

Several private and parochial schools offer education alternatives in the Davenport metropolitan region.

Public Schools Information: Davenport Community School District, 1606 Brady Street, Davenport, IA 52803; telephone (563)336-5000

Colleges and Universities

The Quad Cities is home to three private, four-year liberal arts colleges; a state university regional center; two community colleges; a world-famous chiropractic college; and a graduate-level consortium. Among the institutions of higher learning located in Davenport are Marycrest International University and St. Ambrose University, coeducational liberal arts colleges affiliated with the Catholic Church; both grant a masters degree in addition to baccalaureate degrees. The Palmer College of Chiropractic, the country's oldest chiropractic institute, provides a five-year course of study toward the doctor of chiropractic degree, as well as bachelor and master of science degrees. Eastern Iowa Community College, which awards associate degrees, offers continuing education and vocational and technical training. The Quad Cities Graduate Study Center represents a consortium of eight Iowa and Illinois institutions; the center coordinates course offerings and applies credit toward advanced degrees, including more than 80 master's degree programs.

Among colleges and universities within commuting distance of Davenport are Augustana College in Rock Island, Illinois; the University of Iowa in Iowa City; and Knox College in Galesburg, Illinois.

Libraries and Research Centers

The Davenport Public Library operates one branch and a bookmobile in addition to its main facility, which holds more than 294,000 volumes, including periodical subscriptions, CD-ROMs, and audio- and videotapes. Construction began on a second branch in 2005, and planning has begun for a third. Library patrons can also search for materials through the Quad-LINC library catalog, which provides access to more than 30 area libraries. The library, a depository for state and federal documents, maintains special collections on chess and Iowa authors. Also based in Davenport is Southeastern Library Services, which provides libraries in the region with reference back-up, continuing education classes, and library development and support services.

Specialized libraries and research centers in Davenport are affiliated with colleges, museums, corporations, the Scott County Genealogical Society, and the Scott County Bar Association.

Public Library Information: Davenport Public Library, 321 Main Street, Davenport, IA 52801-1490; telephone (563)326-7832; fax (319)326-7809

Health Care

Davenport is a health care center for the Quad City metropolitan area. Genesis Medical Center is a 502-bed facility in two campuses; the West Central Park and East Rusholme Street facilities offer more than 450 physicians and 3,100 staff members. Palmer College operates four chiropractic clinics in the city. Other medical facilities accessible from Davenport include Trinity Medical Center in Rock Island and Moline, Illinois, and Genesis Medical Center Illini Campus in Silvis. Davenport residents have access to the University of Iowa Medical Center, one of the world's largest university-owned research hospitals.

Recreation

Sightseeing

The Village of East Davenport was founded in 1851 and prospered from the logging industry along the Mississippi River, playing a significant role in western migration. Today, the village is 60 square blocks of more than 500 preserved and redeveloped homes and businesses; small shops, new businesses, and one-family residential homes are combined in a variety of historical styles. An elaborate recreation of nineteenth-century America at Christmas time takes place in the village each year on the first Friday and Saturday of December.

Among other historic sites are the Buffalo Bill Cody homestead in nearby McCausland, the Buffalo Bill Museum in LeClaire, and the Rock Island Arsenal, where Colonel George Davenport's home is located. The Davenport House is open for sightseeing from May to October on Thursday through Saturday. Attractions on Arsenal Island include the National Cemetery and the Confederate Cemetery, both dating back to the Civil War. The Vander Veer Botanical Garden, listed on the National Register of Historic Places, is a 33-acre park with annual and perennial beds, a formal rose garden, and a conservatory. The Conservatory is renowned for its floral shows and tropical plants. Another sightseeing attraction near Davenport is located on a 1,000-acre site that overlooks the Rock River Valley in Moline, Illinois, where the Deere & Company Administrative Center—the company's world headquarters—was designed by Eero Saarinen, the celebrated Finnish architect.

Arts and Culture

The Quad City Symphony Orchestra, founded in 1914, is housed in the Adler Theatre, a restored Art Deco movie palace; the orchestra performs a six-concert season with international guest artists. The Adler is also the home of the Broadway Theatre League, which hosts touring shows. Other organizations that sponsor musical events are the Friends of Chamber Music, the Handel Oratorio Society, and the American Guild of Organists. New to Davenport's performing arts scene are the Cassandra Manning Ballet Theatre and Ballet Iowa. Additional restorations to the Adler will be carried out under funding from the River Renaissance initiative.

The Putnam Museum of History and Natural Science, situated on a bluff overlooking the Mississippi River, houses exhibits on natural science, tribal cultures, ancient civilizations, and the Mississippi River valley. The permanent exhibit, ''River, Prairie and People,'' illustrates the history of the Quad Cities from prehistoric times to the present. The museum also houses an IMAX theater and the Heritage Theatre. The Figge Museum, formerly the Davenport Museum of Art, is Iowa's first municipal art museum. It is located next door to the Putnam at the entrance to Fejervary Park and contains more than 13,000 square feet of gallery space, as well as five fully equipped art-making studios and an auditorium. The Winter Garden, a glass-walled structure on the top level of the museum, provides a beautiful view of the Mississippi River. The museum's s Regionalist Collection includes the Grant Wood Display, a permanent collection of the works of Iowas most famous artist. Other collections include European Old Masters, Mexican Colonial Art, and Haitian Art.

The Hauberg Indian Museum, part of Blackhawk State Historic Site in Rock Island, Illinois, preserves the heritage of the Sac and Fox tribes. Local history can be explored at the Family Museum of Arts & Science in Bettendorf. River Music Experience, a museum dedicated to American roots music, opened its doors in 2004. More than a museum, River Music Experience is also an entertainment center, as interactive exhibits expose visitors to the sounds of traditional American music.

Festivals and Holidays

The Mississippi River in the summertime is the focal point for many of Davenport's annual events. The Fourth of July holiday features the Mississippi Valley Blues Festival. The week-long Great Mississippi Valley Fair, featuring a carnival and entertainment, begins in late July. Top Dixieland bands from around the world flock to the Bix Beiderbecke Memorial Jazz Festival in July. During the festival, a nationally known seven-mile race called the Bix Seven is run. On Mother's Day weekend and the weekend after Labor Day, Midwestern artists and craftspeople display their works on the streets of downtown Davenport. Annually in late July or early August the Quad Cities host the Great River Tug Fest, where 10-member teams from Iowa and Illinois play tug-of-war across the Mississippi River.

Sports for the Spectator

The Quad-City Swing, a Midwest League Class A professional baseball affiliate of the Minnesota Twins of the American League, play a home schedule of 70 baseball games at the newly-renovated John O'Donnell Stadium in Davenport. The Quad-City Downs in East Moline sponsors televised harness racing year-round. The *Quad-City Times* Bix 7 Run is held in late July; more than 17,000 runners—including nationally known competitors—challenge the hills of Davenport. The John Deere Classic, a Professional Golfers Association event, is also held locally. Basketball action is provided by the Quad City Thunder, members of the Continental Basketball Association, who play 28 home games from November through March at the Mark of the Quad Cites in Moline. The Quad City Mallards United Hockey League team also plays at the Mark. Cordova Dragway Park offers drag-racing events throughout the summer, and stock car racing is available at several area tracks.

Sports for the Participant

The Davenport Parks and Recreation Department manages 70 sites, on 2,200 acres of parks and public facilities, for golf, tennis, swimming, jogging, and softball. Scott County Park, 6 miles north of Davenport on more than 1,000 acres of land, features picnic grounds, an Olympic-size pool, and an 18-hole golf course. Davenport's proximity to the Mississippi River provides easy access for boating and various other water sports; riverboat casino gambling out of Davenport and Bettendorf is offered November through March. Wacky Waters is a 30-acre amusement park with water rides and a 5-acre swimming lake. Skiing is possible from December to March in Taylor Ridge.

Shopping and Dining

Davenport's Northpark Mall is Iowa's largest mall; anchored by five major stores, it houses more than 165 specialty shops. A variety of specialty and gift shops, clothing stores, restaurants, and taverns are located in the historic Village of East Davenport. American and family dining is the focus of the majority of local restaurants, with a sampling of Chinese cuisine, pubs, and delis also offered.

Visitor Information: Quad Cities Convention and Visitors Bureau, 102 S. Harrison St., Davenport, IA 52801; telephone (563)322-3911; toll-free (800)747-7800; email cvb @quadcities.com

Convention Facilities

The RiverCenter, located in downtown Davenport and accessible to the airport and interstate highways, is a complex consisting of an exhibition hall, a theater, and a luxury hotel. The exhibition hall contains 13,500 square feet of multipurpose space to accommodate up to 1,800 participants in convention, trade show, banquet, and concert settings. Separate meeting rooms, with customizing features, are designed for groups ranging from 20 to 250 people. Attached to RiverCenter are the 2,500-seat Art Deco-style Adler Theatre, President Casino Hotel, and Radisson Quad City Plaza Hotel.

Hotels and motels in Davenport offer meeting facilities; among them is the Davenport Holiday Inn, with six meeting rooms, a ballroom, and two conference halls; 35,228 square feet of space accommodates up to 1,500 participants. Accommodations are available at traditional hotels and motels as well as bed-and-breakfasts located in historic riverfront homes, mansions, and farmhouses.

Convention Information: Quad Cities Convention and Visitors Bureau, 102 S. Harrison St., Davenport, IA 52801; telephone (563)322-3911 or (800)747-7800

Transportation

Approaching the City

The Quad City International Airport, 15 minutes from downtown Davenport in Moline, Illinois, is served by 5 airlines offering 40 daily direct flights to and from Chicago, Detroit, Atlanta, Orlando, Memphis and Minneapolis-Saint Paul. Davenport Municipal Airport handles corporate aircraft and acts as a reliever airport for Quad City International Airport.

Four interstate, four U.S. highways, and five state highways connect Davenport with points throughout the Midwest and across the United States. I-280 is an outerbelt around the Quad City region. I-80 passes through the city from New York to San Francisco; I-74 links Davenport with Indianapolis and Cincinnati to the east. U.S. 61 runs north-south, from Minneapolis-St. Paul; U.S. 67 extends south to St. Louis; and U.S. 6 connects Davenport with the East and West Coasts.

Traveling in the City

Corresponding to a grid pattern, Davenport's north-south streets are named and east-west streets are numbered. River Drive follows the waterfront of the Mississippi River.

Citibus operates regularly scheduled bus routes in Davenport on weekdays and Saturday. Special bus service is available for the elderly and handicapped.

Communications

Newspapers and Magazines

The Davenport daily newspaper is the morning *Quad-City Times*. Weekly newspapers are *The Catholic Messenger* and *The Davenport Leader*. *Operations Research/Management Science* and a journal about quality control and applied statistics are also published in Davenport.

Television and Radio

Nine commercial television stations are based in Davenport; viewers receive broadcasts from several other stations in Rock Island and Moline, Illinois; cable television service is available. Radio listeners can tune to 11 AM and FM stations broadcasting from Davenport that offer sports plus country, light, oldies, classic hits, and rock music.

Media Information: *Quad-City Times,* 500 E. Third St., Davenport IA 52801 telephone (563)383-2200

Davenport Online

City and area information. Available www.fyiowa.com

Quad Cities Convention and Visitors Bureau. Available quadcities.com/cvb

Quad Cities online. Available www.quadcities.com

Quad City Development Group. Available www.quadcities .org

Selected Bibliography

McKusick, Marshall Bassford. *The Davenport Conspiracy Revisted.* Iowa State University Press, 1991.

Renkes, Jim. *The Quad Cities and Their People.* American World Geographic, 1994.

Des Moines

The City in Brief

Founded: 1843 (incorporated, 1851; chartered 1857)

Head Official: Mayor Frank Cownie (since 2004)

City Population
   1980: 191,000
   1990: 193,189
   2000: 198,682
   2003 estimate: 196,093
   Percent change, 1990–2000: 2.8%
   U.S. rank in 1980: 74th
   U.S. rank in 1990: 80th
   U.S. rank in 2000: 106th (State rank: 1st)

Metropolitan Area Population
   1980: 368,000
   1990: 392,928
   2000: 456,022

   Percent change, 1990–2000: 16.1%
   U.S. rank in 1980: 86th
   U.S. rank in 1990: Not reported
   U.S. rank in 2000: 91st

Area: 76 square miles (2000)
Elevation: 838 feet above sea level
Average Annual Temperature: 49.7° F
Average Annual Precipitation: 33.12 inches of rain, 33.3 inches of snow

Major Economic Sectors: Services; trade; finance, insurance, and real estate; government; manufacturing
Unemployment Rate: 5.1% (March 2005)
Per Capita Income: $19,467 (1999)

2002 FBI Crime Index Total: 13,776

Major Colleges and Universities: Drake University, Grand View College, Des Moines University

Daily Newspaper: *The Des Moines Register*

Introduction

Des Moines is the capital of Iowa, the seat of Polk County, and the center of a metropolitan area consisting of West Des Moines, Urbandale, Ankeny, Johnston, Clive, Windsor Heights, Altoona, and Pleasant Hill. Des Moines is fixed in the national consciousness as the place where the Presidential race begins every four years. It is also acquiring a new identity as a "post-industrial urban center," a term used by experts to describe midwestern communities that, like Des Moines, have acquired the characteristics of East and West Coast cities—impressive skylines, bustling commercial centers, suburban growth—but have at the same time retained their rural, agrarian roots.

Geography and Climate

Des Moines is situated on rolling terrain in south-central Iowa along the banks of the Des Moines River, the longest river in the state and an important tributary of the Mississippi River. Good drainage to the southwest produces fertile farmland, which is surrounded by coal fields. Marked seasonal changes occur in both temperature and precipitation. During winter, snowfall averages more than 30 inches; drifting snow often impedes transportation and sub-zero temperatures are common. Des Moines sits in a tornado zone. The growing season extends from early May to early October; approximately 60 percent of the annual precipitation occurs during this time, with maximum rainfall in late May and June. Autumn is generally sunny and dry, producing favorable conditions for drying and harvesting crops.

Area: 76 square miles (2000)

Elevation: 838 feet above sea level

Average Temperatures: January, 19.4° F; July, 76.6° F; annual average, 49.7° F

Average Annual Precipitation: 33.12 inches of rain, 33.3 inches of snow

History

River Fort Becomes State Capital

The city of Des Moines originated with the building of Fort Des Moines in 1843, at the confluence of the Raccoon and Des Moines rivers, as a military garrison to protect the rights of Sak and Fox tribes. Debate surrounds the correct origin of the name of Iowa's largest city. The Moingona, a native group, had located a village on the river and it appeared on the map of Jacques Marquette, the French explorer. The French expression "la riviere des moines" translates to "the river of the monks," but may approximate the name of the Moingona, who inhabited the riverbank. "De Moyen," meaning "middle," was understood as a reference to the Des Moines River being the middle distance between the Mississippi and Missouri rivers.

The Iowa River Valley was opened to new settlers in 1845; a year later, when Iowa gained statehood, the population of Fort Des Moines numbered 127 residents. After the city charter was adopted in 1857, the word Fort was dropped from the name. Des Moines officially became the state capital—and its future growth was guaranteed—in January 1858 when two oxen-driven bobsleds hauled the state's archives into the city from Iowa City.

Des Moines played an active role in the Civil War. In May 1864 Des Moines women signed a petition pledging to replace working men to free them to fight for the Union cause, but enough male recruits were found to fill the quotas. After the Civil War, in 1875, Des Moines was the site of a nationally significant speech by President Ulysses S. Grant to a reunion of the Army of Tennessee, wherein he reiterated a commitment to universal equality.

During the last quarter of the nineteenth century, wood-frame buildings in Des Moines underwent extensive construction and renovation. The impressive state capitol building, situated on an 80-acre park and featuring a gold-gilded central dome of the revived classical Roman style, was completed in 1884. In the 1880s and 1890s, local businessmen built mansions and the city's cultural life continued to flourish.

Hospitality and Development Shape Des Moines

The history of Des Moines is filled with colorful events such as the arrival in the spring of 1894 of Kelly's Army, 1,000 unemployed men on their way to Washington, D.C., and led by Charles T. Kelly, "King of the Commons." Citizens greeted them with hospitality to prevent trouble. When Kelly's Army seemed reluctant to leave, however, the townspeople bought lumber to construct an "industrial fleet" of 150 flatboats, under local union direction, to transport the men out of the city. Each man was issued a small American flag, and the waving of the flags was the last sight of Kelly's Army. Among them was the American writer Jack London.

Des Moines has distinguished itself in various ways throughout its history. The Des Moines Plan, one of the first of its kind in the nation, streamlined municipal government and charted development, taking into consideration the city's natural setting. Fort Des Moines, dedicated as a calvary post in 1903, became the first training center for the Women's Army Corps, which gained national attention. The economic base of Des Moines was substantially expanded when the city became a national insurance and publishing center. In 1949, Des Moines was named an All-America City by the National Municipal League. The honor was repeated in 1971, then again in 1981 after Des Moines had addressed urban renewal issues by committing $313 million to the restoration of the historic districts of Court Avenue and Sherman Hills.

The city of Des Moines was immobilized in the summer of 1993 by flooding of the Des Moines and Raccoon rivers. The state of Iowa was declared a national disaster area, and preliminary estimates indicated the city alone suffered more than $253 million in damages. By the year 2000 Des Moines was humming with construction activity.

At the dawn of the twenty-first century, residents were enjoying a changing landscape in downtown Des Moines as new buildings were erected or underway, including a new science museum, new main library branch, and new conference venues. In 2003 Des Moines was again named an All-America City by the National Municipal League. Residents today appreciate the small-town atmosphere with big-city amenities afforded them in Des Moines in addition to the city's educational and cultural amenities and well-recognized quality of life.

Historical Information: State Historical Society of Iowa, 600 East Locust Street, Des Moines, IA 50319; telephone (515)281-6200. Polk County Historical Society, 317 SW 42nd St. Des Moines, IA 50312; telephone (515)255-6657

Population Profile

Metropolitan Area Residents
1980: 368,000
1990: 392,928
2000: 456,022
Percent change, 1990–2000: 16.1%
U.S. rank in 1980: 86th
U.S. rank in 1990: Not reported
U.S. rank in 2000: 91st

City Residents
1980: 191,000
1990: 193,189
2000: 198,682
2003 estimate: 196,093

Percent change, 1990–2000: 2.8%
U.S. rank in 1980: 74th
U.S. rank in 1990: 80th
U.S. rank in 2000: 106th (State rank: 1st)

Density: 2,621.3 people per square mile (2000)

Racial and ethnic characteristics (2000)
White: 163,494
Black or African American: 16,025
American Indian and Alaska Native: 705
Asian: 6,946
Native Hawaiian and Pacific Islander: 95
Hispanic or Latino (may be of any race): 13,138
Other: 6,987

Percent of residents born in state: 70.7% (2000)

Age characteristics (2000)
Population under 5 years old: 14,893
Population 5 to 9 years old: 13,945
Population 10 to 14 years old: 13,049
Population 15 to 19 years old: 13,314
Population 20 to 24 years old: 15,198
Population 25 to 34 years old: 32,450
Population 35 to 44 years old: 30,760
Population 45 to 54 years old: 25,037
Population 55 to 59 years old: 8,689
Population 60 to 64 years old: 6,788
Population 65 to 74 years old: 11,934
Population 75 to 84 years old: 9,008
Population 85 years and older: 3,617
Median age: 33.8 years

Births (2002)
Total number: 3,446

Deaths (2002)
Total number: 1,904 (of which, 31 were infants under the age of 1 year)

Money income (1999)
Per capita income: $19,467
Median household income: $38,408
Total households: 80,621

Number of households with income of . . .
less than $10,000: 7,298
$10,000 to $14,999: 5,246
$15,000 to $24,999: 11,813
$25,000 to $34,999: 12,177
$35,000 to $49,999: 15,330
$50,000 to $74,999: 16,929
$75,000 to $99,999: 6,728
$100,000 to $149,999: 3,448
$150,000 to $199,999: 729
$200,000 or more: 923

Percent of families below poverty level: 7.9% (44.1% of which were female householder families with related children under 5 years)

2002 FBI Crime Index Total: 13,776

Municipal Government

Des Moines operates under a mayor/council form of government. The seven-member council is comprised of six council persons and a manager, who are elected to staggered terms in non-partisan elections. The manager serves a term of indefinite length at the pleasure of the council.

Head Official: Mayor Frank Cownie (since 2004; current term expires January 1, 2008)

Total Number of City Employees: 1,852 (2005)

City Information: Des Moines City Hall, Mayor and City Council Office, 400 Robert D. Ray Drive, Des Moines, IA 50309; telephone (515)283-4944

Economy

Major Industries and Commercial Activity

The Des Moines economy consists of a balance among the manufacturing, services, government, wholesale and retail trade, medical, insurance and financial services, printing, publishing, and agribusiness sectors. Manufacturing, while comprising a relatively small percentage of the city's total employment base, has a significant impact on the area economy. Manufacturing firms buy many of their supplies locally, generating more secondary jobs than any other industry. In addition, most of the goods produced are shipped outside the metropolitan area, and approximately 10 percent of manufacturing production is exported, thus contributing to the development of the local shipping industry. Some of the area's best-known manufacturers are Pella windows, Maytag and Amana appliances, and Rockwell Collins avionics equipment.

With the headquarters of nearly 70 insurance companies and the regional offices of 100 other firms located in the metropolitan area, Des Moines is a major insurance center. Other service businesses, including the health care industry, employ nearly one fourth of the work force. Many area firms are active in biotechnology, conducting research in such

fields as human, plant, and animal disease cures; safer pesticides and herbicides; and new, higher crop yields.

A statewide employer based in Des Moines is Meredith Corporation, a diversified communications company specializing in printing, publishing, broadcasting, and real estate. An emerging industry in the Greater Des Moines area is fiber optics telecommunications, which is expected to replace conventional communications systems. Government employs a substantial portion of the city's work force, with the state of Iowa being among the largest employers.

Items and goods produced: flour, cosmetics, furnaces, stove and furnace parts, agricultural implements, automotive and creamery equipment, leather products, medicine, brick, food items, paint, electric switches, and elevators

Incentive Programs—New and Existing Businesses

The Greater Des Moines Partnership assists firms with an interest in applying for economic development financial assistance programs. Other public and private sector groups offer a variety of business assistance programs to businesses expanding in or relocating to Des Moines.

Local programs—A corporation intending to create 100 jobs may be eligible to receive a $400,000 low-interest or forgivable loan to help reduce its relocation cost. The City of Des Moines Office of Economic Development assists businesses in a variety of ways, including project management; identification of land, financing and other resources to facilitate projects; liaison with other city departments; referrals for business licenses; job training and recruitment; and redevelopment assistance. Qualifying Des Moines businesses are able to take advantage of several helpful tax policies, including single factor corporate income tax; tax abatement for new construction; and no property tax on machinery and equipment. Several small business loan programs and funds are available to assist qualifying small businesses in building improvements, equipment purchases, and operating costs.

State programs—Two areas within the City of Des Moines are designated as Iowa Enterprise Zones. New commercial and industrial businesses making a capital investment of at least $500,000 and creating 10 new jobs meeting wage and benefit targets within these designated areas may be eligible for a package of tax credits and exemptions. The State of Iowa New Jobs and Income Program provides a package of tax credits and exemptions to businesses making a capital investment of at least $10 million and creating 50 new production jobs meeting wage and benefit targets. The Iowa New Jobs Training Program offers funds for screening and assessment; travel for the purpose of training; on-the-job training; training facilities or supplies costs; and others. Qualifying businesses utilizing the Iowa New Jobs Training Program may take advantage of the New Jobs Tax Credit of

$1,224 per new employee. Iowa's Regulatory Assistance Program offers assistance to businesses in filling out permit applications for Iowa regulatory agencies.

Job training programs—Des Moines Area Community College (DMACC) has provides a variety of business training programs. A portion of the training dollars may be used for salary reimbursement.

Development Projects

Approximately $1.5 billion in construction projects were completed or underway in 2004 and into 2005, marking a renaissance for Des Moines. Among those projects were the new Science Center of Iowa, featuring an IMAX theater; a new riverfront amphiteater; the new downtown library; and the Jordan Creek shopping complex in West Des Moines.

Construction at the Iowa Events Center, a four-venue multiuse complex, has city planners expecting record numbers of both conventions and convention attendees. The new Hy-Vee Hall opened in winter 2004 at the complex, featuring 250,000 square feet of exhibit space 14,000 square feet of meeting room space, and another 23,700 square feet of prefunction space. Hy-Vee also contains the Iowa Hall of Pride, an interactive center that honors the people and places of Iowa's history. The Wells Fargo Arena at the complex is slated for debut in July 2005. The new arena will seat 17,000 for sports and entertainment events and will be home to the Iowa Stars hockey organization.

Economic Development Information: Greater Des Moines Partnership, 700 Locust Street, Suite 100, Des Moines, IA 50309; telephone (515)286-4950; email info@desmoines metro.com. City of Des Moines, Office of Economic Development, 400 E. First Street, Des Moines, IA 50309; telephone (515)283-4004; email oed@ci.des-moines.ia.us

Commercial Shipping

Des Moines is served by four major railroads that provide full-time switching and piggyback ramp service. A host of motor freight carriers provide overnight and one– to five–day shipping to points throughout the United States; more than 50 terminals are maintained in the community. The Des Moines airport serves as a regional hub for UPS' second-day air service. Approximately 100 companies in the Des Moines area engage in export or import activity.

Labor Force and Employment Outlook

Local analysts contend that the best measurement of the quality of the work force is the site location decisions made by businesses. They say the greatest testimony to the quality of the Des Moines work force is that once a company locates in Des Moines, it continues to expand. Beyond a higher-quality work force, a low crime rate, short commute times in

metro Des Moines, affordable housing, a broad array of education options, and attractive quality of life help local businesses recruit employees.

The major employment industries in Des Moines are financial services, insurance, government, manufacturing, trade, and services. Des Moines businesses draw employees from a five-county area consisting of more than 500,000 residents; in addition, Iowa's work force, with an 80 percent high school graduation rate, ranks among the top five states. Wages are somewhat lower than the national average in Des Moines. Vocational and technical skills training programs are widely available.

The following is a summary of data regarding the Des Moines metropolitan area labor force, 2004 annual average:

Size of nonagricultural labor force: 298,900

Number of workers employed in ...
  construction and mining: 16,900
  manufacturing: 19,700
  trade, transportation and utilities: 64,100
  information: 9,200
  financial activities: 46,800
  professional and business services: 30,700
  educational and health services: 34,700
  leisure and hospitality: 26,500
  other services: 12,100
  government: 38,200

Average hourly earnings of production workers employed in manufacturing: $17.47

Unemployment rate: 5.1% (March 2005)

Largest employers	Number of employees
Principal Life Insurance Co.	7,900
Iowa Health–Des Moines	4,750
Mercy Hospital Medical Center	4,500
Hy-Vee Food Stores Inc.	4,475
City of Des Moines	1,852
United Parcel Service	1,800
Nationwide Mutual Insurance Co.	1,675
Pioneer Hi Bred International Inc.	1,450
Wells Fargo Home Mortgage Inc.	1,320

Cost of Living

Des Moines is often ranked in the top metro areas for housing affordability and a favorable cost of living. State and local taxes are lower than the U.S. average.

The following is a summary of data regarding several key cost of living factors in the Des Moines area.

2004 (3rd Quarter) ACCRA Average House Price: $266,690

2004 (3rd Quarter) ACCRA Cost of Living Index: 94.9 (U.S. average = 100.0)

State income tax rate: Ranges from 0.36% to 8.98%

State sales tax rate: 5.0% (2005)

Local income tax rate: None

Local sales tax rate: None

Property tax rate: $17.04857 per 1,000 of assessed valuation (2005)

Economic Information: Greater Des Moines Partnership, 700 Locust Street, Suite 100, Des Moines, IA 50309; telephone (515)286-4950; email info@desmoinesmetro.com

Education and Research

Elementary and Secondary Schools

The Des Moines Independent Community School District, the largest in the state, is governed by a seven-member board of directors who are elected at large to three-year staggered terms. The head administrator is the superintendent of schools.

The Des Moines public schools implement a variety of curriculum options for students at all levels. The district's Central Academy, established in 1985 for gifted students in grades 8 through 12, brings students together for half of the school day to learn among other gifted students; the other half is spent at their home school. At the middle and secondary levels, several school-to-work programs bring students into the real world of health care, agriculture, and business. The unique Downtown School offers small classes (16:1 student/teacher ratio), a year-round calendar with a six-week summer break and week-long breaks throughout the year, in three downtown locations accessible by skywalk to many downtown businesses. The Downtown School utilizes local businesses and the surrounding neighborhood as opportunities for learning; its locations are accessible to parents working downtown as well. Students in the Downtown School program number 160 and are ages 5 to 11. These and other innovative programs are possible because of the cooperative spirit between the school district and business community in the greater Des Moines area.

A "Schools First" plan is underway, utilizing some $317 million in funds to renovate or replace all schools in the district over a period of 10 years. By August of 2004 construction was completed on 14 schools.

The following is a summary of data regarding Des Moines public schools as of the 2003–2004 school year.

Total enrollment: 32,150

Number of facilities
  elementary schools: 40
  middle schools: 10
  senior high schools: 5
  other: 10 special schools and programs

Student/teacher ratio: 13.5:1

Teacher salaries
  minimum: $29,863
  average: $43,174

Funding per pupil: $7,098

Five private and parochial school districts providing the Des Moines metropolitan area with educational alternatives are Des Moines Christian, Diocese of Des Moines Catholic Schools, Des Moines Jewish Academy, Grandview Park Baptist, and Mount Olive Lutheran. These schools educate approximately 5,700 students in the Des Moines area.

Public Schools Information: Des Moines Public Schools, 1801 16th Street, Des Moines, IA 50314; telephone (515)242-7911; fax (515)242-7579

Colleges and Universities

Drake University, a private institution founded in 1881, enrolls about 4,300 students and grants undergraduate and graduate degrees in a range of disciplines through the College of Arts and Sciences, the College of Business Administration, the School of Journalism and Mass Communication, the School of Education, the College of Pharmacy and Health Sciences, and the Law School. Drake operates a work experience program that includes cooperative education and internships.

Grand View College, a private, Lutheran-affiliated liberal arts school, educates approximately 1,750 students and awards associate and baccalaureate degrees in several fields of study; cross-registration with Drake University and Des Moines Area Community College is available. The Des Moines University College of Osteopathic Medicine offers baccalaureate, master's, and first-professional degrees in a variety of health care areas such as osteopathic medicine and surgery, podiatric medicine and surgery, health care administration, and physical therapy.

Vocational, technical, and pre-professional education in Des Moines is provided by Des Moines Area Community College and AIB College of Business. Within commuting distance of the city are Iowa State University, an internationally renowned research university in Ames, Iowa, and Simpson College, a four-year liberal arts college in Indianola, Iowa.

Libraries and Research Centers

The Public Library of Des Moines houses more than 500,000 volumes and about 950 periodical subscriptions in addition to audiotapes, videotapes, audio CDs, and CD-ROMs. The library system includes five branches in addition to its main building. As part of a $48 million renovation, building, and expansion project, construction on the New Central Library began in 2004 and is expected to be completed in 2005. Renovations at other branches were underway at that time as well. The library system is a depository for federal and state documents and government publications. The State Library of Iowa is also located in downtown Des Moines in the State Capitol Building; holdings include more than 453,000 volumes as well as a complete range of audio-visual materials and special collections on state of Iowa publications, law, medicine, public policy, and patents and trademarks. The library is a depository for state and patent documents.

The Iowa Library for the Blind and Physically Handicapped provides Braille books, large print books, and cassettes and disks. The Drake University Library houses extensive holdings in all major department areas; the law library maintains an Iowa legal history collection. The Iowa Genealogical Society Library and the Grand View College Library also serve the community. The State Historical Society of Iowa Library maintains several collections, some of which reside in Des Moines.

A variety of specialized libraries and research centers located in the city are affiliated with hospitals, corporations, government agencies, law firms, the Blank Park Zoo and the Des Moines Art Center.

Public Library Information: Public Library of Des Moines, 100 Locust Street, Des Moines, IA 50309; telephone (515)283-4152

Health Care

Providing all levels of care in more than 50 specialty fields, the health care network in metropolitan Des Moines consists of 8 hospitals with more than 3,000 beds. A regional trauma center and a helicopter ambulance service are also based in Des Moines.

Iowa Health Des Moines, with 3 hospitals and a total of 1,139 beds, is the city's largest medical group. The complex includes Blank Children's Hospital, Iowa Methodist Medical Center, and Iowa Lutheran hospitals. Mercy Medical Center, an acute care, not-for-profit Catholic-affiliated hospital with 917 beds, provides general care through its 3 Des Moines clinic and hospital campuses; the Des Moines Divi-

sion of the Veterans Administration Central Iowa provides care to veterans; Broadlawns Medical Center consists of an acute care hospital; Mercy Capitol offers emergency, diagnostic, and surgical services and is a teaching hospital affiliated with Des Moines University's medical program.

Recreation

Sightseeing

The starting point for a tour of Des Moines is the State Capitol, one of the nation's most beautiful public buildings and one of the largest of its kind. The 275-foot main dome is covered with 23-karat gold leaf and is flanked by four smaller domes. The capitol's interior features more than 10 different wood grains mixed with 29 types of marble in detailed stone and wood carvings, ornately painted ceilings, and mosaics and murals. Another popular site is Terrace Hill, the present residence of Iowa's governor; considered to be one of the finest examples of Second Empire architecture in the country, Terrace Hill was designed by W.W. Boyington, architect of the Chicago Water Tower. Donated to the state by the Frederick M. Hubbell family, the mansion has been refurbished to its original Victorian elegance.

In both the Courthouse and Sherman Hill districts of Des Moines, residential and commercial buildings dating to 1850 reflect changing tastes and styles in architecture; especially interesting are doorway and entrance designs. The Hoyt Sherman Place, home of one of Des Moines' most successful businessmen and an example of ornate Victorian design, is now owned by the city and open for tours. The Iowa State Historical Building, completed in 1987 and housing the State Historical Library, is dedicated to Iowa's past with exhibits on natural history, Indian lore, and pioneer life. A large outdoor neon sculpture named *Plains Aurora* is displayed on top of the building.

The Des Moines Botanical Center cultivates plants and flowers under one of the biggest geodesic domes in the nation. The Center preserves a permanent collection of more than 1,000 different species of tropical and subtropical plants and cultivars, growing in their natural cycle; six thematic displays are presented each year. Living History Farms in nearby Urbandale is a 600-acre agricultural museum focusing on the history and future of farming in the Midwest; buildings, planting methods, and livestock are authentic to the five time periods represented. At Adventureland Park, more than 100 theme park rides and activities combine with permanent exhibits germane to Iowa. Salisbury House, a 42-room country manor, patterns itself after King's House of Salisbury, England, duplicating Renaissance luxury and splendor; it is

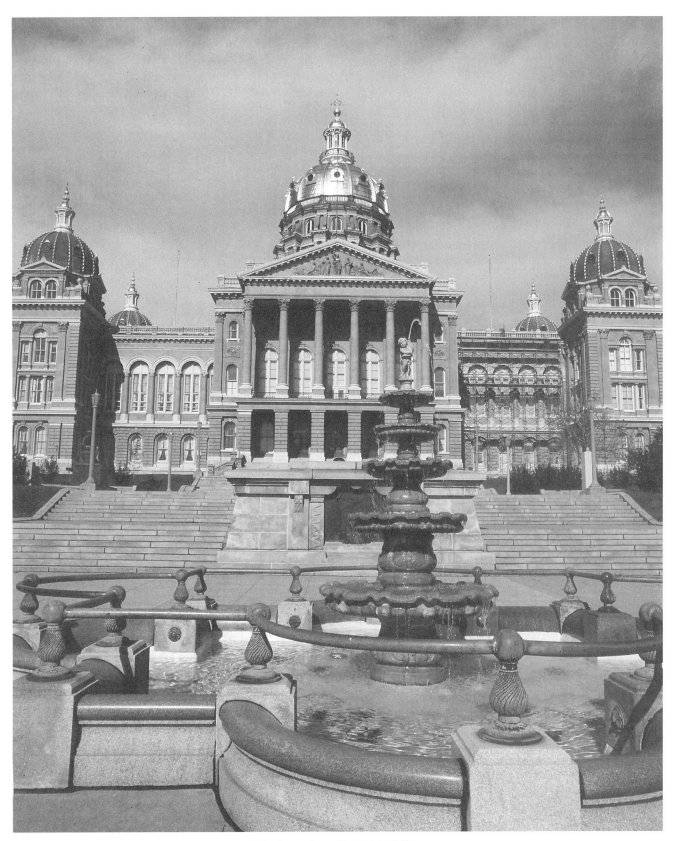

The Iowa State Capitol building.

owned by the Iowa State Education Association, which arranges tours. Temporarily closed in mid-2005 for interior renovations, the home had undergone exterior renovations two years prior. The Science Center of Iowa covers all fields of science; the center's new facility opened to the public in May 2005, featuring a 226-seat IMAX Dome Theater, a 175-seat theater for live performances, and a 50-foot Star Theater, in addition to six "experience platforms" and a changing exhibition platform. At Blank Park Zoo, where more than 1,400 animals from 104 different species inhabit 49 acres, special attractions include the Myron and Jackie Blank Discovery Center, featuring a butterfly garden and a bat cave.

Arts and Culture

One beneficiary of the city's development has been its cultural life. Funds have been invested to house the city's cultural institutions in architecturally significant facilities. The most impressive is the Des Moines Art Center, designed by international architects Eliel Saarinen, I. M. Pei, and Richard Meier. Housing art of the nineteenth and twentieth centuries in a permanent collection, the Center also sponsors international exhibits, educational programs, and film and music series. Nollen Plaza, adjacent to the Civic Center of Greater Des Moines, is a block-square amphitheater and park with a tree-lined "peace garden," a waterfall, and a reflecting pool; Claes Oldenburg's sculpture *The Crusoe Umbrella* is on view in the plaza.

The Des Moines Symphony performs at the Civic Center. The Des Moines Playhouse produces a main stage season of drama, musicals, and light drama as well as Theatre for Young People. The Ingersoll Dinner Theater presents a ten-show season, which features local and guest artists in Broadway musicals and plays, in addition to special attractions.

Festivals and Holidays

In February the downtown skywalk is transformed into a 54-par putt-putt golf course for a tournament with more than 1,300 players competing for prizes. The Drake Relays Downtown Festival, a week-long celebration in April, pits city corporations against one another in the "Fake Relays"; other festival events include a whimsical "most beautiful bulldog" contest, mascot relays, and musical entertainment. The Des Moines Arts Festival features three days of art, entertainment, and children's activities in late June. July's Taste of Des Moines offers visitors a taste of local fare. Summer ends with the Iowa State Fair in August. The Festival of Trees raises money for a local hospital with the decorating of 100 downtown trees in November during Thanksgiving week.

Sports for the Spectator

For nearly 100 years, the Drake Relays hold the distinction of being the country's largest such event, with more than

200 colleges and universities participating from nearly every state and more than 60 countries. The relays, held in Drake Stadium at Drake University the last weekend in April, sell out each year; the competition also includes track and field events. A variety of other events are held throughout the city, making the Relays the focal point for an entire festival.

In addition to the Drake Relays, Drake University offers sporting events, including basketball, football, soccer, tennis, track, crew, softball, and golf.

The Iowa Cubs, the National League Chicago Cubs's top farm team, compete in baseball's Triple A international professional baseball league at Sec Taylor Field at Principal Park. The Des Moines Menace offer soccer action at Waukee Stadium, and the Des Moines Buccaneers, part of the United States Hockey League, play at Buccaneer Arena.

Sports for the Participant

The Des Moines Parks and Recreation Department maintains 62 city parks with a variety of facilities, including softball fields, horseshoe pits, volleyball courts, tennis courts, fitness and bicycle trails, golf courses, trails, soccer fields, play equipment, swimming pools, community centers, gardens, and an amphitheater. The city offers swimming and tennis lessons and arts and crafts programs; softball, volleyball, and tennis leagues are also sponsored by the recreation department. The Des Moines metro area offers nearly 100 public tennis courts, and many golf courses, swimming pools, and country clubs. Both indoor and outdoor sports can be enjoyed during the winter at community center gyms and ice rinks. Swimming, water skiing, fishing, and boating are popular at local rivers and lakes.

Shopping and Dining

The Des Moines downtown shopping district is 20 square blocks connected by a second-level skywalk system that encompasses 150 shops. Altogether, more than 40 shopping squares and plazas serve shoppers throughout the metropolitan area, including five major enclosed malls, one of which is located downtown. The Downtown Farmers Market runs May through October on Saturday mornings and offers shoppers fresh fruits and vegetables, home-baked breads and pastries, hand-made clothing and jewelry, specialty cheeses and wines, and music and entertainment.

Des Moines restaurants offer choices ranging from American and Midwestern fare to ethnic and continental cuisine. Prime rib and steak entrees are specialties at a number of the better restaurants. Chinese cuisine is another local favorite; barbeque, sandwich shops, cafes, vegetarian eateries, and other ethnic restaurants are popular as well. A local seafood restaurant is considered to have one of the largest selections of fresh seafood in the Midwest. Imported Italian pasta is the specialty at one of the city's oldest and most popular eateries.

Visitor Information: Greater Des Moines Convention and Visitors Bureau, 405 Sixth Avenue, Suite 201, Des Moines, IA 50309; toll-free (800)451-2625; email info@desmoines cvb.com

Convention Facilities

Several meeting and convention facilities serve Des Moines. Opened in 1985, the Des Moines Convention Center offers the Polk County Convention Complex and the new Hy-Vee Hall, opened in 2004. Two levels furnish space for trade shows, conventions, meetings, banquets, and other activities at the Polk County Convention Complex, including a 47,000-square-foot exhibit hall with up to 27 meeting rooms. The new Hy-Vee Hall offers 100,000 square feet of expo hall space, up to 150,000 square feet of contiguous expo space, 14,000 square feet of meeting room space, and 23,700 square feet of pre-function space. Also part of the Des Moines Convention Center complex, Veterans Memorial Auditorium provides seating for 7,200 to 14,000 people; a total of 98,000 square feet of space can be used for exhibitions, sporting events, and entertainment. Two other principal meeting places in the city are the Civic Center, located downtown, and the Iowa State Fairgrounds. Area hotels and motels maintain banquet and meeting facilities for large and small groups. Nearly 9,000 rooms (1,500 of them downtown) in 82 hotels and motels are available for lodging in metropolitan Des Moines.

Convention Information: Greater Des Moines Convention and Visitors Bureau, 405 Sixth Avenue, Suite 201, Des Moines, IA 50309; toll-free (800)451-2625; email info @desmoinescvb.com

Transportation

Approaching the City

Des Moines International Airport, 10 minutes from downtown, is served by 12 commercial airlines with daily flights handling nearly two million passengers annually. The airport recently added direct flights to Washington, D.C.

Principal highways that intersect northeast of the city are I-80, running east to west, and I-35, extending north to south. Federal highways include east-west U.S. 6 and north-south U.S. 69.

Traveling in the City

Downtown Des Moines is laid out on a grid pattern; in the northeast sector, streets near the Des Moines River, still conforming to a grid, follow the configuration of the river. North-south streets are numbered and east-west streets are named.

Des Moines is noted for its more than 3.5-mile skywalk system, which makes the city virtually ''weatherproof.'' Forty-four climate-controlled, glass-enclosed bridges provide access to 30 blocks that comprise the downtown core.

Public transportation is provided by the Des Moines Metropolitan Transit Authority, locally known as The Metro; special service for the handicapped is available.

Communications

Newspapers and Magazines

The daily newspaper in Des Moines is the morning *The Des Moines Register,* many time Pulitzer Prizewinner. *Des Moines Business Record,* a weekly newspaper, covers local business news and banking and financial information. *Cityview,* an alternative newspaper featuring investigative journalism, is distributed free throughout the metro area.

Home to the Meredith Corporation and other printing and publishing firms, Des Moines is a major center for the publication of nationally-circulated magazines. Among the popular magazines produced in the city are *Better Homes and Gardens, Ladies' Home Journal, Country Home, Midwest Living,* and *Successful Farming.* A wide range of special-interest publications based in Des Moines are directed toward readers with interests in such subjects as religion, agriculture, hunting, education, and crafts.

Television and Radio

Five commercial television stations are based in Des Moines. Cable service is available. Radio listeners receive programming from 13 AM and FM stations.

Media Information: *The Des Moines Register,* Gannett Co., Inc., PO Box 957, Des Moines, IA 50304; telephone (515)284-8000

Des Moines Online

City of Des Moines home page. Available www.ci.des-moines.ia.us

City of Des Moines Office of Economic Development. Available www.dmoed.org

Des Moines Public Library. Available www.pldminfo.org

Des Moines Public Schools. Available www.dmps.k12.ia.us

The Des Moines Register online. Available www.dmregister.com

Greater Des Moines Convention and Visitors Bureau. Available www.desmoinesia.com

Greater Des Moines Partnership. Available www.desmoines metro.com

Public Library of Des Moines. Available www.pldminfo.org

Selected Bibliography

Friedricks, William B. *Covering Iowa: The History of the Des Moines Register and Tribune Company, 1849-1985.* Iowa State University Press, 2000.

KANSAS

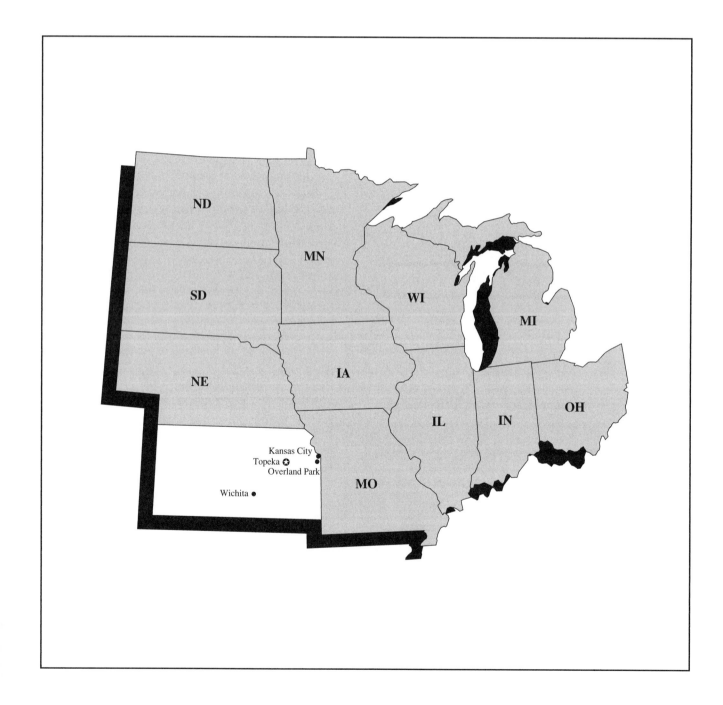

The State in Brief

Nickname: Sunflower State
Motto: *Ad astra per aspera* (To the stars through difficulties)

Flower: Native sunflower
Bird: Western meadowlark

Area: 82,276 square miles (2000; U.S. rank: 15th)
Elevation: Ranges from 680 feet to 4,039 feet above sea level
Climate: Temperate, but with seasonal extremes of temperature as well as blizzards, tornadoes, and severe thunderstorms; semi-arid in the west

Admitted to Union: January 29, 1861
Capital: Topeka
Head Official: Governor Kathleen Sebelius (D) (until 2007)

Population
 1980: 2,364,000
 1990: 2,495,000
 2000: 2,688,824
 2004 estimate: 2,735,502
 Percent change, 1990–2000: 8.5%
 U.S. rank in 2004: 33rd
 Percent of residents born in state: 59.5% (2000)
 Density: 32.9 people per square mile (2000)
 2002 FBI Crime Index Total: 110,997

Racial and Ethnic Characteristics (2000)
 White: 2,313,944
 Black or African American: 154,198
 American Indian and Alaska Native: 24,936
 Asian: 46,806
 Native Hawaiian and Pacific Islander: 1,313
 Hispanic or Latino (may be of any race): 188,252
 Other: 90,725

Age Characteristics (2000)
 Population under 5 years old: 188,708
 Population 5 to 19 years old: 609,710
 Percent of population 65 years and over: 13.3%
 Median age: 35.2 years (2000)

Vital Statistics
 Total number of births (2003): 40,609
 Total number of deaths (2003): 24,840 (infant deaths, 261)
 AIDS cases reported through 2003: 1,123

Economy
 Major industries: Agriculture, oil production, mining, manufacturing
 Unemployment rate: 5.4% (March 2005)
 Per capita income: $29,545 (2003; U.S. rank: 27th)
 Median household income: $43,622 (3-year average, 2001-2003)
 Percentage of persons below poverty level: 10.3% (3-year average, 2001-2003)
 Income tax rate: Ranges from 3.5% to 6.45%
 Sales tax rate: 5.3%

Kansas City

The City in Brief

Founded: 1843 (incorporated, 1859)

Head Official: CEO/Mayor Joe Reardon (since 2005)

City Population
  1980: 161,148
  1990: 151,521
  2000: 146,866
  2003 estimate: 145,757
  Percent change, 1990–2000: −3.0%
  U.S. rank in 1980: 93rd
  U.S. rank in 1990: 115th
  U.S. rank in 2000: 161st

Metropolitan Area Population
  1980: 1,433,000
  1990: 1,582,875

  2000: 1,776,062
  Percent change, 1990–2000: 12.2%
  U.S. rank in 1980: 25th
  U.S. rank in 1990: Not reported
  U.S. rank in 2000: 25th

Area: 124 square miles (2000)
Elevation: 740 feet above sea level
Average Annual Temperature: 54.7° F
Average Annual Precipitation: 37.98 inches

Major Economic Sectors: Services, trade, government, manufacturing
Unemployment Rate: 5.6% (February 2005)
Per Capita Income: $15,737 (1999)

2002 FBI Crime Index Total: 4,087.0

Major Colleges and Universities: Kansas City Kansas Community College; University of Kansas Medical Center

Daily Newspaper: *Kansas City Kansan*

Introduction

Kansas City, Kansas, is part of a metropolitan complex that also includes Kansas City, Missouri. The seat of Wyandotte County, Kansas City is the center of a metropolitan statistical area that covers the counties of Johnson, Leavenworth, Miami, and Wyandotte in Kansas, plus seven Missouri counties. The more industrialized of the two Kansas Cities, it nevertheless is bordered by rich farmland and serves as an agricultural trade center. Established by Wyandot Native Americans, Kansas City was the site of the drafting of the state constitution and played a crucial role in the slavery issue in the Civil War.

Geography and Climate

Gently sloping terrain and forested hills surround Kansas City, which is located on the Kansas-Missouri border at the confluence of the Kansas and Missouri Rivers. The area is laced with lakes, streams, and small rivers. A four-season climate prevails, with a substantial range in temperatures; the average annual snowfall is 20.1 inches.

Area: 124 square miles (2000)

Elevation: 740 feet above sea level

Average Temperatures: January 26.9° F; July, 78.5° F; annual average, 54.7° F

Average Annual Precipitation: 37.98 inches

History

Wyandot Tribe Establishes Townsite

Kansa Native Americans were the first inhabitants to occupy land near both banks of the Kansas (Kaw) River at its confluence with the Missouri River, the site of Kansas City. The explorers Meriwether Lewis and William Clark camped on Kaw Point, the land between the two rivers and now part of Kansas City, in 1804 during their exploration of the Louisiana Purchase. The land became part of the Delaware Indian reservation in 1829, and the Delaware sold the land in 1843 to the Wyandot.

The Wyandot, an integrated tribe of Native Americans and whites from western Lake Erie and the last of the migrating tribes, founded a town called Wyandott in the eastern part of the Wyandott Purchase. An educated and cultured agrarian society, they built the first free school in Kansas and reestablished their Ohio church; they also opened a community-owned store. The Wyandot, knowing their land would be highly prized by white settlers, decided to approach Congress on the issue of establishing a Territory, and elected Abelard Guthrie, a white member of the tribe by marriage, as a delegate to the Thirty-Second Congress. Guthrie was not admitted but Wyandot leaders decided to organize Kansas-Nebraska into a provisional territory on July 26, 1853, thus focusing national attention on their community.

Slavery Issue Dominates Territory

The next year Congress passed the Kansas-Nebraska Act, which inflamed sectional sentiments on the issue of slavery in the territories and helped to contribute to the outbreak of the Civil War. The Wyandot petitioned for and received the rights of citizenship, which enabled them to divide their land among the individual members of the tribe and open the reserve to settlement. The Wyandott City Town Company was formed in 1856 to plan and develop the town, which was incorporated as a town in 1858 and as a city the next year. In July 1859 members of a convention at Wyandott wrote the constitution by which Kansas would enter the Union as a free state; however Senate politics delayed the signing of the bill until January 29, 1861. The state was known as Bleeding Kansas in the decade before the Civil War, as settlers on both sides of the slavery controversy populated the area. Wyandott citizens became active in antislavery efforts and African-Americans began moving to the region after the Civil War, their migration reaching a peak between 1878 and 1882.

Beginning in 1860, when James McGrew opened the first slaughter house, and continuing when eight years later Edward Patterson and J. W. Slavens started a packing house, the city was a meat processing center. This industry received its biggest boost when Charles Francis Adams, descendant of two former presidents, built the first stockyards in the city and convinced Plankington and Armour to relocate their meat packing business from Missouri in 1871.

Stockyards, Consolidation Contribute to Growth

Small towns around Wyandotte such as old Kansas City, Armstrong, and Armourdale sprouted up near the rail lines and packing houses. Through consolidation and legislative annexation, the city of Kansas City was created in 1886 when these towns combined with the larger Wyandotte, which vied for the naming of the new city after itself. The name Kansas City was picked, however, because it would be a more attractive inducement for the selling of municipal bonds. Argentine became part of Kansas City via petition in 1909, and Rosedale followed suit by legislative enactment in 1922. Quindaro Township, once a town named after Guthrie's Wyandot wife, was absorbed through expansion.

Turner was added in 1966, thus continuing the expansion of Kansas City's borders. In 1992, the city annexed part of Wyandotte County.

Kansas City was one of the nation's first cities to locate a model industrial park away from residential areas, the Fairfax Industrial District. The city completed a two-decade urban renewal project in 1980. Still, like many other aging, working- class cities, Kansas City was plagued by a loss of population to the suburbs. Seeking to reverse that trend, a group called the Citizens for Consolidation, backed in part by Kansas City, Missouri, businesses, spearheaded a movement to consolidate city and county governments. In 1997 Kansas City voters overwhelmingly approved the consolidation into a system called the Unified Government of Wyandotte County/Kansas City, Kansas. Former schoolteacher Carol Marinovich was elected the first mayor/CEO of the new government. By 2000, the consolidation had resulted in a considerable increase in government efficiency. With city and county officials on the same team, the city was able to lure the $283 million Kansas International Speedway to Kansas City; the project was completed in 2001.

Today, the Kansas City area is recognized as one of the fastest-growing labor markets in the country. *Entrepreneur* magazine ranks it among top U.S. cities for small business and *Expansion Management* magazine identifies it as one of the best places in the U.S. to locate a company. Kansas City's cultural and recreational attractions also make it a popular Midwest tourist destination.

Historical Information: Wyandotte County Historical Society and Museum, 631 N. 126th St., Bonner Springs, KS 66012; telephone (913)721-1078. Kansas City Kansas Public Library Kansas Collection, 625 Minnesota Avenue, Kansas City, KS 66101; telephone (913)551-3280; fax (913)279-2032

Population Profile

Metropolitan Area Residents
1980: 1,433,000
1990: 1,582,875
2000: 1,776,062
Percent change, 1990–2000: 12.2%
U.S. rank in 1980: 25th
U.S. rank in 1990: Not reported
U.S. rank in 2000: 25th

City Residents
1980: 161,148

1990: 151,521
2000: 146,866
2003 estimate: 145,757
Percent change, 1990–2000: −3.0%
U.S. rank in 1980: 93rd
U.S. rank in 1990: 115th
U.S. rank in 2000: 161st

Density: 1,181.9 people per square mile (2000)

Racial and ethnic characteristics (2000)
  White: 81,910
  Black or African American: 44,240
  American Indian and Alaska Native: 1,103
  Asian: 2,527
  Native Hawaiian and Pacific Islander: 56
  Hispanic or Latino (may be of any race): 24,639
  Other: 12,645

Percent of residents born in state: 55.0% (2000)

Age characteristics (2000)
  Population under 5 years old: 11,953
  Population 5 to 9 years old: 11,868
  Population 10 to 14 years old: 11,388
  Population 15 to 19 years old: 11,314
  Population 20 to 24 years old: 10,975
  Population 25 to 34 years old: 21,341
  Population 35 to 44 years old: 21,946
  Population 45 to 54 years old: 17,717
  Population 55 to 59 years old: 6,253
  Population 60 to 64 years old: 5,072
  Population 65 to 74 years old: 8,973
  Population 75 to 84 years old: 6,056
  Population 85 years and older: 2,010
  Median age: 32.3 years

Births (2003)
  Total number: 2,586

Deaths (2003)
  Total number: 1,383 (of which, 33 were infants under the age of 1 year)

Money income (1999)
  Per capita income: $15,737
  Median household income: $33,011
  Total households: 55,533

Number of households with income of . . .
  less than $10,000: 7,289
  $10,000 to $14,999: 4,310
  $15,000 to $24,999: 8,784
  $25,000 to $34,999: 8,694
  $35,000 to $49,999: 9,962
  $50,000 to $74,999: 9,683
  $75,000 to $99,999: 4,222

$100,000 to $149,999: 2,005
$150,000 to $199,999: 280
$200,000 or more: 304

Percent of families below poverty level: 13.0% (45.7% of which were female householder families with related children under 5 years)

2002 FBI Crime Index Total: 4,087

Municipal Government

The Unified Government of Wyandotte County/Kansas City, Kansas serves as the local government for Kansas City, Kansas, while providing county services for the Cities of Bonner Springs and Edwardsville.

Head Official: CEO/Mayor Joe Reardon (since 2005; current term expires 2009)

Total Number of City Employees: 2,337 (2004)

City Information: Unified Government of Wyandotte County/Kansas City, Kansas, 701 North 7th Street, Kansas City, KS 66101; telephone (913)573-5000

Economy

Major Industries and Commercial Activity

Wyandotte County, which once could claim the second largest meat packing industry in the world, has diversified into a transportation, medical, and manufacturing center. Principal industrial activity involves automobile manufacturing, food production and distribution, railroads, bakery products, and meat processing. Agriculture continues to be important in the rural area west of the city.

Items and goods produced: fiberglass, cement, creamery products, soap, fiber box, brick, tile, automobiles

Incentive Programs—New and Existing Businesses

Local programs—The mission of Wyandotte Development Inc. is to foster, encourage, and assist new and existing businesses in Wyandotte County. Its Economic Development Team consists of the State of Kansas, municipal governments and utilities, and other entities as needed. Its goal is for each member to develop a proposal within 10 days of meeting with a potential business prospect. The Kansas City Kansas Area Chamber of Commerce offers networking opportunities, leg-

islative efforts, community development and business/education partnerships to its 780 member companies.

State programs—The Kansas Department of Commerce is the state's leading economic development agency. It provides incentive programs in the form of tax credits, loans, grants, and services. Its Business Development Division is comprised of five different sections: Business Assistance, Business Finance, National Marketing, Workforce Training, and the Office of Minority and Women-Owned Business Development. The Kansas 1st program links qualified job seekers at post-secondary institutions with employers.

Job training programs—The state of Kansas helps fund the training needs of Kansas businesses through three major workforce training programs: Investments in Major Projects and Comprehensive Training (IMPACT); Kansas Industrial Training (KIT); and Kansas Industrial Retraining (KIR). Qualified businesses include those new to Kansas or existing businesses which are expanding or restructuring. Programs are custom designed to meet a company's specific training needs and can involve pre-employment or on-the-job training.

Development Projects

Adjacent to the Kansas Speedway, the 400-acre Village West project is still under construction. The Legends Shopping Center is scheduled to open in Village West in summer 2005. Kansas City International Airport will finish $218 million worth of terminal renovations in 2005. The University of Kansas Hospital has broken ground for a new state-of-the-art cardiac health facility with completion expected in June 2006. Federal Express has selected the Kansas City area for a new $76 million regional distribution center.

Economic Development Information: Wyandotte Development Inc., 727 Minnesota Avenue, PO Box 171337, Kansas City, Kansas 66117; telephone (913)371-3198; fax (913)371-3732. Kansas Department of Commerce, 1000 S.W. Jackson Street, Suite 100, Topeka Kansas 66612-1354; telephone (785)296-3339; fax (785)296-3490

Commercial Shipping

Kansas City is one of the largest transportation hubs in the nation. Local firms provide a complete range of intermodal services, including rail, air, truck, and water, for the receiving and shipping of goods. The Greater Kansas City area is served by four Class I rail carriers, three regional lines and a local switching carrier.

The Kansas City business community profits from commercial freight activity at Downtown Airport, a general aviation facility in neighboring Kansas City, Missouri. A trans-shipment point for 225 motor freight carriers, Kansas City is part of the Kansas City Commercial Zone, where exemption from Interstate Commerce Commission tariff supervision is granted to shipments originating from and received within this region. Shippers and motor carriers independently negotiate rates. A number of warehouses are maintained in the area.

Seven barge lines offer shipping from the Kansas City area of the Missouri River. There are 41 docks and terminals in the city. The shipping season runs from March through November.

Labor Force and Employment Outlook

The following is a summary of data regarding the Kansas City, Kansas—Kansas City, Missouri metropolitan area labor force, 2004 annual averages.

Size of nonagricultural labor force: 965,900

Number of workers employed in . . .
   construction and mining: 50,800
   manufacturing: 83,700
   trade, transportation and utilities: 202,200
   information: 45,300
   financial activities: 70,900
   professional and business services: 127,700
   educational and health services: 108,900
   leisure and hospitality: 92,300
   other services: 40,400
   government: 143,900

Average hourly earnings of production workers employed in manufacturing: $16.57 (Kansas State)

Unemployment rate: 5.6% (February 2005)

Largest employers	Number of employees
University of Kansas Medical Center	4,900
Kansas City, Kansas Public Schools, USD #500	3,500
General Motors	3,350
Unified Government of Wyandotte County	2,300
Associated Wholesale Grocers	1,300
Burlington Northern-Santa Fe Railroad	1,200
United Parcel Service	907
Teletech	825
Kansas City Kansas Community College	750
U.S. Bulk Mail Center	600
Swift Transportation	600
Keebler Foods	550

Cost of Living

The following is a summary of data regarding several key cost of living factors in the Kansas City area.

2004 (3rd Quarter) ACCRA Average House Price: $228,375 (MSA)

2004 (3rd Quarter) ACCRA Cost of Living Index: 95.5 (MSA) (U.S. average = 100.0)

State income tax rate: Ranges from 3.5% to 6.45%

State sales tax rate: 5.3%

Local income tax rate: None

Local sales tax rate: city, 1.25%; county, 1.0%

Property tax rate: 1.83% per $1,000 assessed value

Economic Information: Kansas City Area Development Council, 2600 Commerce Tower, 911 Main Street, Kansas City, MO 64105-2049; telephone (816)221-2121; fax (816)842-2865; email kcadc@thinkKC.com

Education and Research

Elementary and Secondary Schools

The Kansas City, Kansas Public Schools District is responsible for public education in Kansas City. It recently implemented a Great IDEAS award program to fund innovation in teaching. In 2001, municipal voters approved a $120 million bond issue to fund upgrades to school technology and infrastructure.

The district offers four instructional programs designed to recruit and support aspiring educators.

The following is a summary of data regarding the Kansas City, Kansas Public Schools as of the 2002–2003 school year.

Total enrollment: 20,810

Number of facilities
   elementary schools: 30
   middle schools: 8
   senior high schools: 4
   other: Sumner Academy of Arts and Science (grades 8-12); one alternative school program; one technical school

Student/teacher ratio: 13.1:1

Teacher salaries
   average: $43,511 (Kansas State, 2004)

Funding per pupil: $6,906 (Kansas State, 2004)

Nine accredited private schools provide educational alternatives in Kansas City.

Public Schools Information: Kansas City, Kansas Public Schools, 625 Minnesota Avenue, Kansas City, KS 66101; telephone (913)551-3200; fax (913)551-3217

Colleges and Universities

The University of Kansas Medical Center offers a range of degree programs through its faculties of Allied Health, Medicine, Pharmacy, Nursing, and Graduate Studies. It maintains a prestigious biomedical research facility and provides medical care to the community. Kansas City Kansas Community College provides two-year programs in professional or general studies as well as transfer programs leading to baccalaureate degrees. Donnelly College is a two-year Catholic liberal arts college. The Central Baptist Theological Seminary awards a Master of Divinity degree, a Master of Arts in Religious Studies, and a Diploma in Theological Studies.

Libraries and Research Centers

The main facility of the Kansas City Kansas Public Library is located downtown; three branches and a bookmobile are operated within the system. Holdings total nearly 500,000 items, including books, periodicals and newspapers, microfiche, films, records, tapes, and art reproductions. Special collections include The Kansas Collection, comprised of local historical and genealogical resources, an African American Collection, and a Spanish Language Collection. The Dykes Library, one of the largest health sciences libraries in the Midwest, is open to the public as well as staff and students of the Kansas University Medical Centre. Other specialized libraries and research centers in Kansas City are affiliated with educational institutions, hospitals, and government agencies.

Public Library Information: Kansas City Kansas Public Library, 625 Minnesota Avenue, Kansas City, KS 66101; telephone (913)551-3280; fax (913) 279-2033

Health Care

With two major hospitals and a county health department, Kansas City is a regional leader in health care. The 418-bed University of Kansas Hospital is a teaching hospital for the University of Kansas Medical School. A Carnegie Research I institution, it receives at least $40 million in annual federal research funding. Areas of specialty include cancer treatment and prevention, neurology, kidney disease, liver and kidney transplants, and pain management. A cancer consultation service is available 24 hours a day, 7 days a week.

Providence Medical Center is a 400-bed, not-for-profit community hospital. It offers an extensive array of services including cancer and cardiac care, a Family Care Centre for obstetrical, pediatric and gynecological services, and an outpatient Rehabilitation Center. The Wyandotte County Public Health Department provides clinics for adults and children as well as immunization and family planning information. Most services are available for a nominal or sliding-scale fee.

Recreation

Sightseeing

The National Agricultural Center and Hall of Fame in Bonner Springs was chartered by Congress in 1960 to honor the nation's farmers. Funded by private contributions, the 172-acre facility traces the history of agriculture in the United States with exhibits on rural life, customs, and material culture. Its many attractions include the Museum of Farming, the National Farmer's Memorial, a gallery of rural art, and a restored nineteenth century farming village.

The Huron Indian Cemetery located in the heart of downtown is the burial ground of the Wyandot Nation, founders of the first town in the evolution of Kansas City. Established in 1832, White Church Christian Church is the oldest church in the state that is still in use. The John Brown Statue at 27th Avenue and Sewell pays tribute to the Brown-led antislavery movement from Quindaro, Kansas. In council chambers at City Hall the history of Kansas City is told through stained-glass windows and a large mural. The Rosedale Memorial Arch, dedicated in 1923 as a memorial to World War I soldiers, replicates the Arc de Triomphe in Paris. In 1993 a monument was added underneath the arch in memory of soldiers who served in World War II, Korea and Vietnam. Grinter House, built in 1857 and furnished with authentic period furniture, is the restored home of one of the first white settlers in Kansas City, Moses Grinter, who operated a ferry across the Kaw (Kansas) River.

Children will be interested in the Children's Museum of Kansas City, featuring interactive discovery-based exhibits. Nearby Kansas City, Missouri is home to the Kansas City Zoo; Worlds of Fun, a theme park with more than 50 rides and shows; and Oceans of Fun, a tropical-theme water park.

Arts and Culture

The centerpiece for the performing arts in Kansas City is Memorial Hall, a 3,300-seat venue that hosts cultural, religious, and entertainment events year-round. The Wyandotte Players perform live family-oriented theatre at the Kansas City Kansas Community College Performing Arts Center. Com-media Sans Arte is an improvisational comedy troupe performing at the historic Alcott Arts Center (formerly the Louise May Alcott Grade School). Open-air concerts take place at the Verizon Wireless Amphitheatre in Bonner Springs.

Kansas City, Kansas's Granada Theatre is home to the Grand Barton Theatre pipe organ. One of the most impressive instruments of its kind, it weighs more than 20 tons and rises more than two stories in height. Built in 1928–1929 by Boller Brothers in a Spanish-Mediterranean style, the Granada Theatre was restored in 1986 and operated as a non-profit performing arts center during the 1980s and 1990s. It was under renovation in 2005.

The stone and brick foundations of the Quindaro Ruins and Underground Railroad, called ''the largest known archeological shrine to freedom,'' offer a rare glimpse into Kansas's abolitionist past. The Harry S. Truman Library and Museum in nearby Independence, Missouri contains documents and memorabilia from the Truman presidency, including a popular White House in Miniature exhibit.

The Wyandotte County Historical Museum in Bonner Springs displays local and regional artifacts, including Native American relics and other items from the county's early history. The Strawberry Hill Museum is dedicated to Kansas City's Eastern European heritage. It is located in the former St. John the Baptist Children's Home, an original Queen Anne-style building constructed in 1887. Neighboring Kansas City, Missouri, is the home of the nationally renowned Nelson-Atkins Museum of Art and a number of other museums of note.

Festivals and Holidays

Kansas City is nicknamed the ''City of Festivals.'' The city and Wyandotte County celebrate history, culture, tradition, and ethnic heritage with annual events in which crafts, foods, and music play an important part. Recognized as one of the top 100 attractions in North America, the Renaissance Festival spans six fall weekends beginning on Labor Day weekend. Several ethnic festivals are scheduled throughout the year including Polski Days, the Croatian Festival, the Kansas City Scottish Highland Games, and Oktoberfest. The Wyandotte County Fair takes place the last weekend in July. The Great American Barbecue takes place in May, featuring barbecue contests and a Barbecue Ball. Grinter House is the location of a number of special events, including the Applefest in autumn.

Sports for the Spectator

Greyhound, thoroughbred, and quarter horse racing take place at the dual-track Woodlands complex. The privately funded racetrack includes two separate enclosed spectator facilities, a one-mile horse track with a straightaway for thoroughbreds and quarter horses, and a greyhound track suitable for year-round racing. Lakeside Speedway has a half-mile asphalt oval track and is part of the NASCAR Winston Racing Series. The Speedway hosts many national touring series; racing takes place every Friday night from March through September. The recently completed Kansas Speedway is a state-of-the-art facility featuring a 1.5-mile racing track, 80,000 spectator seats, driving schools, custom car shows and more. In addition to NASCAR, IRL and ARCA races, the Kansas Speedway also hosts community events.

Nearby Kansas City, Missouri has much to offer the sports enthusiast. The American Royal, the world's largest combined livestock show, horse show, and rodeo, takes place in autumn at the American Royal Complex in the stockyard district. The Kansas City Chiefs play in the National Football League at Arrowhead Stadium, part of the Harry S. Truman Sports Complex. Major League Baseball's Kansas City Royals compete in the American League Central Division at Kauffman Stadium. The Kansas City Comets play indoor soccer and the Kansas City Knights play ABA basketball, both at Kemper Arena.

Sports for the Participant

The Unified Government Parks and Recreation Department manages 44 parks and 7 recreational centers with facilities for tennis, golf, swimming and picnicking. Wyandotte County Lake offers a 400-acre lake with marina, 1500 acres of wooded land, a model railroad, picnic shelters and excellent fishing. Private facilities can be reserved for small and large groups. The 360-acre Wyandotte County Park includes lighted softball fields, tennis courts and a soccer pitch. Meeting space is also available.

Wyandotte County has three first-rate golf courses. Painted Hills offers rolling fairways and a panoramic view of the city. Dub's Dread is a challenging 18 hole course. The newly-remodeled Sunflower Hills is considered the premier public course in the metropolitan area, with 18 hole championship design and PGA management staff.

Shopping and Dining

Legends Shopping Center, an open-air shopping and entertainment destination, is expected to open in the Village West district in summer 2005. Village West already offers 400 acres of retail, sports and dining venues. Indian Springs Marketplace is home to the Children's Museum of Kansas City as well as a range of shops and services. Country Club Plaza and Crown Center are located in Kansas City, Missouri. City Market, also in Missouri, is a colorful farmers' market open seven days a week. Union Station is a fully refurbished 1914 landmark, now featuring unique shops and restaurants, an interactive science centre and theatre facilities. Kansas City restaurants are known for their barbecue, steaks, chicken, and ethnic cuisine, including Mexican, Greek, Asian, and Italian.

Visitor Information: Kansas City, Kansas—Wyandotte County Convention and Visitors Bureau, 727 Minnesota Ave., PO Box 171517, Kansas City, KS 66101, telephone (913)321-5800; toll-free (800)264-1563

Convention Facilities

The Jack Reardon Convention Centre in downtown Kansas City is the site of conferences, meetings, banquets, and conventions. The facility contains 20,000 square feet of exhibit space with 12 meeting rooms and 60 booth spaces. Seating is available for up to 1,800 participants. Next door, the Hilton Garden Inn offers 147 rooms and meeting space ranging from 300 to 5,000 square feet. The Best Western Inn and Conference Centre has 113 rooms and meeting space for groups of 15 to 225. Great Wolf Lodge offers 3,000 square feet of meeting space and 281 rooms. Some hotels, motels, and bed-and-breakfasts in the area also maintain meeting and banquet rooms.

Convention Information: Jack Reardon Convention Center, 500 Minnesota, Kansas City, KS 66101; telephone (913)371-1610

Transportation

Approaching the City

Kansas City International Airport is just 16 miles north of downtown in Kansas City, Missouri. Its 15 commercial airlines serve more than 10 million domestic and international travelers each year.

A network of interstate highways links Kansas City with points throughout the nation. I-35 runs from Duluth, Minnesota, southward through Kansas City to Laredo, Texas. I-29, originating in North Dakota, terminates in Kansas City; the Kansas Turnpike, I-70, bisects the city and extends to St. Louis and Denver, Colorado. I-435, an outerbelt, spans western Wyandotte County and connects Kansas City with the airport to the north.

Traveling in the City

North-south streets in Kansas City are numbered and labeled "street;" east-west streets are named and designated "avenue." Public bus transportation is operated by the Kansas City Area Transit Authority and Unified Government Transit. These two bus systems provide integrated service Monday through Saturday. Dial-A-Ride offers public transit

service for persons with disabilities. Senior Group Transportation is also available. Amtrak passenger trains depart from the metro area four times daily.

Communications

Newspapers

The Kansas City, Kansas daily newspaper is the *Kansas City Kansan,* published Tuesday through Saturday. Several neighborhood, ethnic, and suburban newspapers are distributed weekly and monthly, including *Wyandotte West* and the *Kansas City Record. Freethought History* is a quarterly publication that discusses agnosticism, atheism, and free thought. The *Kansas State Globe* serves the African American community. *Dos Mundos* is a bilingual paper aimed at the Hispanic market.

Television and Radio

Kansas City television viewers receive broadcasts from five stations—four commercial network affiliates and one public—based in Kansas City, Missouri, and from one independent channel based in Kansas City, Kansas; cable service is available locally. Seven AM and FM radio stations from Kansas City, Kansas and Kansas City, Missouri provide a complete range of music, news, and special interest programming.

Media Information: Kansas City Kansan, 8200 State Avenue, Kansas City, KS 66112; telephone (913)371-4300; fax (913) 342-8620

Kansas City Online

Kansas City Area Development Council. Available www .smartkc.com

Kansas City Kansas Area Chamber of Commerce. Available www.kckchamber.com

Kansas City Kansas Public Library System. Available www .kckpl.lib.ks.us

Kansas City, Kansas School District. Available www.kckps .k12.ks.us

Kansas City Kansas—Wyandotte County Convention and Visitors Bureau. Available www.kckcvb.org

Kansas Department of Commerce and Housing. Available www.kansascommerce.com

Unified Government of Wyandotte County and Kansas City, Kansas. Available www.wycokck.org

Wyandotte County Historical Society and Museum. Available www.kumc.edu/wcedc/museum/wcmuseum.html

Selected Bibliography

Cutler, William G. *History of the State of Kansas.* Chicago: A.T. Andreas, 1883. Available online at www.ukans.edu/carrie/kancoll/books/cutler/wyandotte/wyandotte-co-p1.html

Hemingway, Ernest, *Ernest Hemingway, Cub Reporter; Kansas City Star Stories* (Pittsburgh: University of Pittsburgh Press, 1970)

Schulz, Constance B., ed., *Bust to Boom: Documentary Photographs of Kansas, 1936–1949* (Univ. Press of Kansas, 1996)

Overland Park

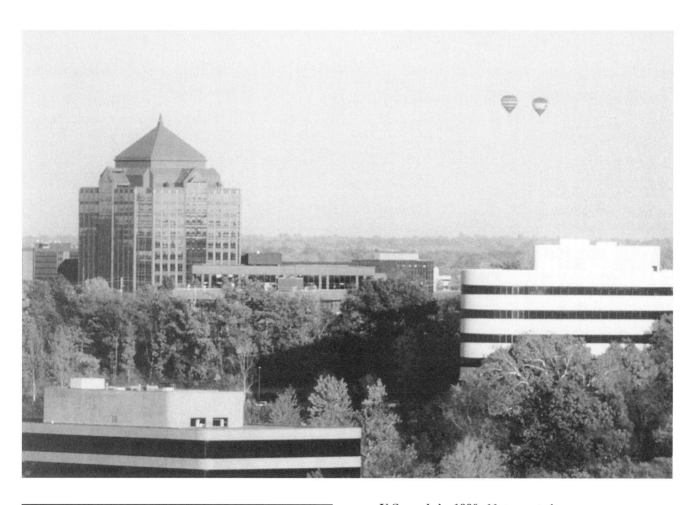

The City in Brief

Founded: 1905 (incorporated 1960)

Head Official: Carl R. Gerlach (R) (since April 2005)

City Population
　1980: 81,784
　1990: 111,790
　2000: 149,080
　2003 estimate: 160,368
　Percent change, 1990–2000: 33.4%
　U.S. rank in 1990: 168th (2nd in state)
　U.S. rank in 2000: 143rd (2nd in state)

Metropolitan Area Population (Kansas City, MO–KS MSA)
　1980: 1,449,374
　1990: 1,582,875
　2000: 1,776,062
　Percent change, 1990–2000: 12.2%

U.S. rank in 1990: Not reported
U.S. rank in 2000: 44th

Area: 56.85 square miles
Elevation: 1,000 feet above sea level
Average Annual Temperature: 56.75° F
Average Annual Precipitation: 40.17 inches of rain; 20 inches of snow

Major Economic Sectors: Professional services, retail trade, manufacturing
Unemployment Rate: 4.4% (February 2005)
Per Capita Income: $32,069 (1999)

2002 FBI Crime Index Total: Not reported

Major Colleges and Universities: University of Kansas–Edwards Campus, Johnson County Community College, Baker University, National American University, Ottawa University–Kansas City Campus, St. Mary College–Kansas City Campus

Daily Newspapers: *The Kansas City Star*

Introduction

Growing up in the shadow of Kansas City, Overland Park has found myriad ways to distinguish itself as an affordable community populated by well-educated professionals. In 2003 Overland Park was ranked 3rd in *Money* magazine's "Hottest Towns" with more than 100,000 people in the central region. The city was also nationally recognized in 2003 as one of "20 Best Places to Live & Work" (*Employment Review* magazine). Other national honors indicate that Overland Park is a community that is child-friendly, welcoming and safe for women, and open for business. Overland Park is an urbane and thriving city in Kansas in the twenty-first century.

Geography and Climate

Located in the sub-basin of the Missouri River, Overland Park exists in the transition area between rolling green hills and the eastern edge of the Great Plains. Ice Age glaciers scoured the land and left silt deposits that have contributed to the rich agricultural history of Kansas. The meandering Missouri further softened the surface of one of the more geologically stable areas in the United States. Overland Park itself is perched on a bluff above Kansas City, protecting it from periodic floods.

Eastern Kansas experiences warm, slightly humid summers that can border on hot; winters can feel quite chilly thanks to the humidity level, but precipitation is relatively moderate. Spring ushers in a season of towering thunderstorms moving across the Plains, along with twisters that frequent the edge of Tornado Alley in which Overland Park resides.

Area: 56.85 square miles

Elevation: 1,000 feet above sea level

Average Temperatures: January, 29.0° F; July, 79.2° F; annual average, 56.75° F

Average Annual Precipitation: 40.17 inches of rain; 20 inches of snow

History

Early Kansas: Lying Low

The Kansas of long ago was wide open—plains scoured by a series of Ice Age glaciers and wandering rivers had become vast, level expanses under a limitless sky. Prior to the 1700s the area was sparsely populated; gradually, a growing number of native tribes discovered the richness of the glacial silt soil and the abundance of bison. The eastern portion of the state was home to many tribes which maintained individual languages and customs: Plains, Wyandotte, Sioux, Osage, Kickapoo, Shawnee, Kanza, Arkansas, Otto, Dahcotah and Ogillahah tribes all called the region home and helped establish the natural passage that would come to be known as the Santa Fe Trail.

A European presence extended into eastern Kansas in the early 1500s with the explorations of Francisco Vasquez de Coronado. The land was first claimed by France, then ceded to Spain as a sop after the country's loss in the French and Indian War. The area was contested until Spain ceded it back to France in 1800; the next year, France sold eastern Kansas to the United States as part of the Louisiana Purchase, and the region was fair game for the Manifest Destiny of the U.S. government.

Born Free: A Matter of Perspective

Kansas didn't have to wait long—in 1802, hunter and trapper James Pursley followed a well-traveled trail to New Mexico to do some trading, following a route that travelers started to call the Santa Fe Trail. As trade heated up between merchants in Missouri and trappers in New Mexico, the trail evolved into the Santa Fe Road. Increased traffic and commerce in the area resulted in friction with native tribes still attempting to live on the land's resources. As a solution, the U.S. government negotiated a treaty in 1825 with the Shawnee Indians in Missouri; in exchange for surrendered land in Missouri, the tribe received an equivalent amount of land on a reservation in what is now Johnson County, Kansas.

A new era began for the formerly nomadic tribe that had up until then lived in eastern woodlands; the move to the plains necessitated much adaptation as the Shawnees became farmers. In 1829 the Rev. Thomas Johnson (for whom the county is named) moved to the reservation, where an Indian Manual Labor School was created. Native American children were tutored in English, manual arts, agriculture, and Christianity.

Kansas Territory became official in 1854, populated by a curious mix of passionate abolitionists and independent pioneers who supported Kansas as a "free state" because it was economically advantageous to keep slave owners out of the territory. On the front edge of the Civil War, Kansas became a state in 1861 and joined the Union. Even prior to the advent of the Civil War, pro-slavery factions warred with abolitionists and free soil advocates in Kansas. Ironically, a number of the free soil advocates were less interested in abolishing slavery and more interested in keeping African Americans out of Kansas altogether. Soon after a "free state'' and Union victory, the U.S. government also recommended getting the Indians out, moving whole tribes south to what was being termed Indian Territory.

Overland Park Takes Shape

Since 1821, a large city just over the Kansas-Missouri state line had begun to evolve into a major stop on the trail, railroad, and road systems. By the early 1900s, Kansas City was a burgeoning metropolitan center and had changed from trading post to destination. In 1905 William B. Strang, Jr., was staying in Kansas City with a relative when he explored the area to the west of the city and recognized its potential as a bedroom community for the metro area. Strang was particularly intrigued by a plot of land owned by several farm families and situated on a bluff; the combination of high ground and proximity to the city led him to purchase the land and start laying out a series of new communities. Thus Overland Park was created—the name is reputed to be a combination of the vision of a ''park-like'' city crossed with the alternate name for the Santa Fe Trail (Overland Trail).

In support of his newly-created bedroom community, Strang went on to develop an interurban train line with trolley service to Kansas City. The Strang Land Company grew busy selling off individual lots of land in business and residential segments of the new town. The city founder also had his hand in the development of Airfield Park in 1909, which combined a landing strip, aviation school, hangars and a grandstand for the locals who were fascinated with flying. Many renowned aviators made Overland Park a stop, including the Wright Brothers; an airplane industry grew up around the airfield that has continued to present day.

Thanks to Strang and other early residents of the area, Overland Park was gradually becoming a viable entity on its own merits. As an attempt to manage the swift growth in Overland Park, Mission, and Prairie Village, these collective communities were organized into an urban township form of government under a law passed by the Kansas legislature in 1940. The reborn entity, Mission Urban Township, was able to form a governmental body but lacked the right to zone or plan independently. In combination with the repercussions of the Dust Bowl days and World War II, Mission Urban Township experienced a time of stasis in the late 1930s and early 1940s, followed by a boom in residential development. In 1951, the Kaw River flooded Kansas City while the community on the bluff stayed nice and dry, and Mission Township began to see an influx of slightly damp folks. The current system of government was insufficient to deal with the resultant growth and development, leading to separation of the township communities into municipalities and the incorporation of Overland Park in 1960.

Out of the Shadow of Kansas City

The 1960s and 1970s ushered in a period of individuation, as Overland Park established its own infrastructure of schools, businesses, and city services. Very early in its formal existence, Overland Park government initiated the practice of citizen surveys to target key concerns of the populace and to measure satisfaction with quality of life. This proactive approach has led to a balanced approach to development and growth, as well as innovative juvenile delinquency and learning disability programs created in the 1970s.

Since the 1980s, Overland Park has experienced a fairly consistent boom pattern, with growth in population, industry and reputation. While continuing to look forward, the city administration has also appreciated its past by supporting extensive renovations of the historic downtown area during the early 1990s. Present day Overland Park has been a regular on national ratings for quality of life, education, affordable housing, appeal to businesses, and population growth. It's a young community in many ways, with a mature approach to living and contributing.

Historical Information: Kansas State Historical Society, 6425 SW Sixth Avenue, Topeka, KS 66615; telephone (785)272-8681

Population Profile

Metropolitan Area Residents (CMSA)
1980: 1,449,374
1990: 1,582,875
2000: 1,776,062
Percent change, 1990–2000: 12.2%
U.S. rank in 1990: Not reported
U.S. rank in 2000: 44th

City Residents
1980: 81,784
1990: 111,790
2000: 149,080
2003 estimate: 160,368
Percent change, 1990–2000: 33.4%
U.S. rank in 1990: 168th (2nd in state)
U.S. rank in 2000: 143rd (2nd in state)

Density: 2,627 people per square mile (2000)

Racial and ethnic characteristics (2000)
White: 135,137

Black or African American: 3,801
American Indian and Alaskan Native: 401
Asian: 5,703
Native Hawaiian and Pacific Islander: 52
Hispanic or Latino (may be of any race): 5,620
Other: 1,852

Percent of residents born in state: 28.9%

Age characteristics (2000)
Population under 5 years old: 10,646
Population 5 to 9 years old: 11,045
Population 10 to 14 years old: 11,027
Population 15 to 19 years old: 9,261
Population 20 to 24 years old: 7,391
Population 25 to 34 years old: 21,695
Population 35 to 44 years old: 26,758
Population 45 to 54 years old: 22,227
Population 55 to 59 years old: 6,825
Population 60 to 64 years old: 5,171
Population 65 to 74 years old: 8,679
Population 75 to 84 years old: 6,057
Population 85 years and over: 2,298
Median age: 36.3

Births (2003; Johnson County)
Total number: 7,475

Deaths (2003; Johnson County)
Total number: 2,847 (of which, 29 were infants under
1 year of age)

Money income (1999)
Per capita income: $32,069
Median household income: $62,116
Total households: 59,703 (2000)

Number of households with income of . . .
less than $10,000: 1,791
$10,000 to $14,999: 1,658
$15,000 to $24,999: 4,175
$25,000 to $34,999: 5,929
$35,000 to $49,999: 9,306
$50,000 to $74,999: 13,257
$75,000 to $99,999: 9,063
$100,000 to $149,999: 8,936
$150,000 to $199,999: 2,959
$200,000 or more: 2,821

Percent of families below poverty level: 2.1% (11.7% of
which were female householder families with related
children under 5 years)

2002 FBI Crime Index Total: Not reported

Municipal Government

Overland Park operates through the Mayor-Council-City
Manager form of government, with the mayor and 12 council
members forming the governing body for the municipality.
The city is divided into six districts, each of which elects two
council members who serve four-year terms with staggered
elections. The mayor is elected by the general populace and
also serves a four-year term in office. In April 2005 the city of
Overland Park elected its first new mayor in 24 years. The
governing body hires a city manager to effect established
policies and to oversee the daily operations of the city.

Head Official: Carl R. Gerlach (R) (since April 2005;
current term expires 2009)

Total Number of City Employees: 1,000 (2005)

City Information: City of Overland Park, 8500 Santa Fe
Drive, Overland Park, KS 66212; telephone (913)895-6000

Economy

Major Industries and Commercial Activity

Overland Park is famous for its high percentage of citizens
with baccalaureate or advanced degrees, making education a
growth industry for the area. Professional service professions, whether in Overland Park or nearby Kansas City,
make up a significant portion of employment in the area.
Retail trade accounts for another large chunk of the local
workforce, and transportation services and products are also
contributors to the Overland Park economy.

Overland Park is the site of Sprint World Headquarters; the
Fortune 100 company is the largest local employer and is a
major supporter of the Overland Park community. Sprint
provides telecommunication services and technology
globally to businesses and the public.

The cattle industry remains powerful and influential in Kansas City, which certainly has an impact on Overland Park
and other surrounding communities.

Items and goods produced: telecommunication technology,
transportation equipment, beef

Incentive Programs—New and Existing Companies

The Chamber of Commerce in Overland Park acts as a
bridge for businesses negotiating the local and state systems
in expanding or creating a new project. Business owners can
tap into the resources of the KSBusinessCenter from the

comfort of their own offices, in order to begin the business and tax registration process.

Local programs—The city of Overland Park encourages new building by allowing for abatement of up to 50 percent of property tax liability for as long as 10 years, dependent upon the size and use of construction projects.

State programs—Kansas offers a wide variety of programs designed to encourage location of new businesses and expansion of existing businesses in the state. The High Performance Incentive Program rewards employers who pay above-average wages by exempting them from sales taxes, and offers tax credits for investment and workforce development. The capital costs of a project's new jobs can be mitigated through Investments in Major Projects and Comprehensive Training (IMPACT), with the state picking up the financing for relocation expenses, recruitment and training costs, building expenditures and cost of equipment.

The State of Kansas additionally has created Enterprise Zones which make manufacturing and non-manufacturing companies eligible for tax credits and sales tax exemptions based on the number of net jobs created. The state can underwrite various business enterprises and expansions through loan programs developed to support the creation of new jobs in Kansas.

Job training programs—The Overland Park Chamber of Commerce schedules two professional development seminars per month and can additionally act as a referral agent for employers looking for advanced training for their employees. The State of Kansas oversees a network of regional and local workforce centers offering seminars and ongoing programs for military veterans, dislocated workers, youth, community members with disabilities, and older employees. Programs such as Trade Adjustment Assistance and the Kansas Industrial Retraining project address the changing face of economic development in the state. The Neighborhood Improvement and Youth Employment Act has provided funding for community enhancement projects for which high school students are hired.

Development Projects

Since opening in the 1970s, the Corporate Woods Business Park has undergone steady expansion and improvement every few years. In the 1990s, the facility added 800,000 square feet, bringing its total capacity to 3,200,000 square feet. New sections were added to the business park in the late 1990s, at the same time a number of older buildings were undergoing a renovation process. In 2004, a putting green was created on the already capacious grounds of Corporate Woods.

Corporate Woods Business Park is now the home of a regional service headquarters branch of QC Holdings, which

operates more than 370 payday loan stores in 22 states. The company leased 38,000 square feet of space beginning in 2004 and will eventually employ 300 people in the facility. ProPharma International Partners, Inc., has also become a recent tenant in Corporate Woods; the company acts as a development consultant for biotechnology and pharmaceutical businesses.

Automatic Data Processing (ADP) brought a number of new jobs to the Overland Park area as it moved into the College Oaks Business Park. The company contracts to handle payroll and other human resource issues for companies around the world.

The City of Overland Park is in the process of designing a new community center as part of its 10-year capital improvement plan. Construction on the center is expected to commence in 2006 and end approximately a year later.

Commercial Shipping

Kansas City International Airport, located 24 miles from the heart of Overland Park, operates an Air Cargo Center complete with extensive cargo-handling capability, an onsite Foreign Trade Zone allowing for storage of imported goods without full U.S. Customs scrutiny, Enterprise Zone tax initiatives, and access to an adjacent interstate highway. The airport's central U.S. location means that most major metropolitan areas in the country are within a one-day shipping radius.

The headquarters for Yellow Roadway Corporation are in Overland Park, allowing easy access to a major cargo shipping and transportation resource. Yellow transports cargo to all 50 states, Canada, the Virgin Islands, and several other international destinations. Butler Transport, Inc. and Core Carrier Corporation are two of the more than 100 trucking companies located in nearby Kansas City, and the region is served by both FedEx and UPS cargo delivery companies. Five railroad companies cross paths in Kansas City as well, increasing shipping options.

Labor Force and Employment Outlook

Overland Park's adult population is one of the most highly educated in the United States, with more than 50 percent of adult residents having earned a baccalaureate degree at minimum. There appears to be a slight shift in philosophy regarding higher education, starting at the K-12 level, with more emphasis on real-world experiences through technical programs and vocational institutions prior to a four-year degree being earned.

It is expected that agricultural employment will continue to decrease in the area, while retail trade and professional services (education and government in particular) are likely to surge. In the past few years, manufacturing has recovered somewhat from a pattern of decreasing productivity and employment; that trend is expected to continue in coming years.

The following is a summary of data regarding the Kansas City, MO-KS, metropolitan statistical area labor force, 2004 annual averages.

Size of nonagricultural labor force: 965,900

Number of workers employed in . . .
   construction and mining: 50,800
   manufacturing: 83,700
   trade, transportation and utilities: 202,200
   information: 45,300
   financial activities: 70,900
   professional and business services: 127,700
   educational and health services: 108,900
   leisure and hospitality: 92,300
   other services: 40,.400
   government: 143,900

Average hourly earnings of production workers employed in manufacturing: $16.92

Unemployment rate: 4.4% (February 2005)

Largest employers	Number of employees (2005)
Sprint Corporation	17,000
Shawnee Mission School District	2,900
Black & Veatch Engineers	2,600
Blue Valley School District	2,525
Internal Revenue Service	1,800
Yellow Roadway Corporation	1,100
City of Overland Park	1,000

Cost of Living

2004 (3rd Quarter) ACCRA Average House Price: $228,375 (MSA)

2004 (3rd Quarter) ACCRA Cost of Living Index: 95.5 (MSA) (U.S. average = 100.0)

State income tax rate: 3.5% to 6.45%

State sales tax rate: 5.3%

Local income tax rate: None

Local sales tax rate: 7.525%

Property tax rate: Annual tax on a $150,000 house is $1,782 (Blue Valley District) or $1,342 (Shawnee Mission District)

Economic information: Overland Park Economic Development Center, 9001 W. 110th Street, Suite 150, Overland Park, KS 66210; telephone (913)491-3600

Education and Research

Elementary and Secondary Schools

In a 2001 report by Population Connection, Overland Park was chosen the number one ''Kid Friendly City'' in the nation, based on factors such as education, health, and public safety, which all impact overall achievement in the K-12 population. Overland Park is served by four public school districts: Blue Valley, Shawnee Mission, Spring Hill, and Olathe.

The Blue Valley School District covers 91 miles in southwestern Johnson County and boasts a growing enrollment that reached 19,104 students in the 2004-2005 academic year. One of its innovative programs is the Wilderness Science Center—this outdoor laboratory encompasses 30 acres of prairie, forest, river, and wetland ecosystems. Students at the WSC put their classroom science theories to work along the trails and learning stations sprinkled throughout the open space.

The Shawnee Mission School District has an enrollment of approximately 29,000 students in suburban Johnson County; each school serves students who live within prescribed attendance areas. Spring Hill School District is comprised of two elementary schools, a middle school, and a high school serving a primarily rural area located just south of Olathe.

The Olathe Unified School District (OUSD) was formerly five separate districts; its enrollment is the third largest in the state of Kansas. Besides its 30 elementary schools, 8 middle schools and 4 high schools, the OUSD provides the Heartland and Prairie Learning Centers for children with special needs and a Head Start program for pre-kindergartners. Approximately 10.5 percent of OUSD students reside in Overland Park, while the majority of the students are from Olathe. The student/teacher ratio in OUSD is 16.5:1, allowing for more individualized attention.

The following is a summary of data regarding Overland Park public schools as of the 2004–2005 school year.

Total enrollment: 73,427

Number of facilities
   elementary schools: 87
   middle schools: 24
   high schools: 14

Student/teacher ratio: Elementary schools, 24:1; high school, 19:1 (Blue Valley School District)

Teacher salaries
   minimum: $30,908
   average: $60,641

Funding per pupil: $6,083 (Blue Valley School District)

Public Schools Information: Blue Valley School District, 15020 Metcalf, PO Box 23901, Overland Park, KS 66283-0901; telephone (913)239-4000. Olathe Unified School District, 14160 Black Bob Road, PO Box 2000, Olathe, KS 66063-2000; telephone (913)780-7000. Shawnee Mission School District, 7235 Antioch Road, Shawnee Mission, KS 66204; telephone (913)993-6200. Spring Hill School District, 101 East South Street, Spring Hill, KS 66083; telephone (913)592-7200

Colleges and Universities

Johnson County Community College (JCCC) offers its students a range of undergraduate courses in a two year post-secondary education program that further develops the local workforce and prepares students for transfer to four-year universities or colleges. JCCC is Kansas' third largest institution of higher learning, with an enrollment of more than 34,000 students in classes for credit or continuing education. The college encourages academic, career, and personal growth through programs such as Student Life and Leadership, the Gallaudet University Regional Center (hearing impairment technical assistance and seminars), International Student Services, the Writing Center, and the Math Resource Center.

Graduate and undergraduate studies in business and management make up the core of Baker University, a private college affiliated with the United Methodist Church. The campus in Overland Park is a branch of the main university and is dedicated to the School of Professional and Graduate Studies. Associate degrees and certifications in management, business, information management, medical assisting, and paralegal studies are available at the National American University.

Overland Park is also home to local branches of St. Mary's College, a Jesuit institution offering liberal arts education; Ottawa University, a small private college with Christian underpinnings offering baccalaureate and masters degrees in the Arts, Education, Human Resources, Professional Counseling and Business Administration; and the University of Kansas Medical Center, located within 15 miles and offering a range of undergraduate and graduate degrees in the health professions.

Vocational training facilities abound in the Overland Park area, as well as in nearby Kansas City.

Libraries and Research Centers

The Johnson County Library system's main location is the Central Resource Library, with 12 branch libraries covering the entire county. Library patrons can access more than one million items in formats such as audio books, video and DVD movies, magazines, newspapers, and hard and soft cover books. Computer services at the library allow visitors to tap into more than 70 databases and online services to search full-text articles and reference books. The Johnson County Library is a repository for federal government documents, available both in hard copy and online. Assistive technology is available for community members with disabilities, and the library serves homebound populations with outreach and delivery programs. Various special events for children and teens are offered throughout the year.

The Billington Library on the campus of Johnson County Community College contains more than 107,000 titles in book or audiovisual form, along with a collection of more than 400,000 microforms and 600 current periodicals.

The Dykes Library, the Clendening History of Medicine Library and the Farha Medical Library, all located at the Medical Center at the University of Kansas in Kansas City, contain a wealth of health-related books, periodicals, digital collections and databases. The Medical Center also houses several research institutes conducting investigations into life processes, function of the human body, disease processes and health care models.

Public Library Information: Johnson County Libraries, 9875 W. 87th Street, Overland Park, KS 66212; telephone (913)495-2400

Health Care

The Overland Park Regional Medical Center is licensed for 244 acute care beds, serving southern Johnson County and surrounding areas with emergency services, a diabetes center, a neonatal intensive care unit, a cardiac rehabilitation program, outpatient pharmacies, and a sleep disorder clinic.

Saint Luke's South Hospital offers emergency services, cardiac diagnostics, surgical intensive care, radiology, pain management, physical and occupational therapies, and the latest in birthing suites. The facility is licensed for 75 beds and is supported by a range of outpatient programs.

The Menorah Medical Center moved to Johnson County in 1996 and now occupies a medical campus that includes an acute care hospital licensed for 158 beds, a doctors' building, and a number of outpatient clinics. Menorah Medical is one of 20 facilities in the country to provide access to cutting edge treatment of previously inoperable tumors and lesions. Other specialties include radiation therapy, audiology services, cancer diagnostics, and a full range of neurological services.

Specialized care is provided at Mid-America Rehabilitation Hospital (physical rehabilitation treatment), Select Specialty Hospital (acute long-term care) and Children's Mercy Hospital (emergency and outpatient pediatric care).

Recreation

Sightseeing

Peace and tranquility are a bargain at the Overland Park Arboretum and Botanical Gardens located on 179th Street about a mile west of U.S. Highway 69. Three hundred acres of land have been dedicated to environmental initiatives that preserve and restore ecosystems while providing educational opportunities for children and adults. Wood chip hiking trails lead through the various gardens, including the Erickson Water Garden, a Xeriscape Garden, a Rotary Children's Garden, a Native American Medicine Wheel, and the Legacy Garden. Concrete paths extending from parking areas allow visitors with physical disabilities to enjoy the rare plant species and varied biodomes that can be viewed on the grounds. An interpretive Environmental Education and Visitors Center at the Gardens offers a peek into the biology of the facility while modeling environmentally-sustainable energy systems in use at the Center.

Families with younger children will enjoy a visit to the Deanna Rose Children's Farmstead located at 13800 Switzer, within the boundaries of the Overland Park Community Park. Named for a local police officer who was killed in the line of duty, the Farmstead is comprised of a petting zoo, farmhouse, a silo with slides, and picture-box gardens. Demonstration gardens depict methods of growing produce such as wheat, corn, and vegetables. The Farmstead is a seasonal operation, opening April 1st and closing for the year at the end of October.

Downtown Overland Park is a great place to wander amid centralized, locally-owned art galleries and interesting shops. The Strang Carriage House in downtown conveys visitors back to the town's beginnings, and the Farmers Market is a feast for the eyes as well as the belly.

Kansas City is just a few minutes away, with attractions as diverse as the Hallmark Visitors Center (the past and present of Hallmark cards), the Harley-Davidson Final Assembly Plant, the Federal Reserve Bank Visitors Center, and the Kansas City Market (an open-air farmers market). The 18th and Vine Historic Jazz District in Kansas City offers a concentrated selection of entertainment venues and museums such as the American Jazz Museum and the Negro Leagues Baseball Museum.

Arts and Culture

The City of Overland Park has created a gallery space at the Overland Park Convention Center; six art exhibitions are presented each year to supplement the permanent displays onsite. Art at the Center focuses on works of local and regional artists. The city also coordinates a new Sculpture Exhibition at the Arboretum and Botanical Gardens; the juried sculpture show features works distributed throughout the natural beauty of the trees and flowers.

The city is committed to an ambitious public art project incorporating sculpture, lighting design, and landform alteration in accessible spots around the community. Projects on deck include landscape art and sculptures at all gateways to Overland Park, beautification projects at parks that are near high-traffic areas, murals and sculpture along a major transport corridor, and landscape sculpture at St. Andrew's Golf Course.

The H&R Block Artspace at the Kansas City Art Institute features permanent and rotating exhibits. The Kemper Museum of Contemporary Art in Kansas City features an international roster of artists who work in all media. A superb Asian collection crowns the exhibits at the Nelson-Atkins Museum of Art in Kansas City, which also boasts nationally-recognized collections of African, American, Native American, European, and ancient art.

Local origins can be plumbed at the Johnson County Museum of History located in Shawnee and housed in a historic school. The museum contains archives documenting the development of Johnson County communities, a research library and an education center. The Arabia Steamboat Museum in Kansas City showcases a cache of well-preserved frontier supplies discovered in the cargo hold of a sunken steamer. The Historic Downtown Airport in Kansas City displays a collection of aeronautical memorabilia and artifacts in Hangar 9, the home of the Airline History Museum.

The greater Kansas City area puts on a great show in the performing arts; Overland Park proper touts its New Theatre Restaurant as one of the best dinner theaters in the country. The cuisine is five-star and the productions frequently feature recognizable stage, film, and television personalities. Martin City Melodrama and Vaudeville Company is a professional theater company in Overland Park, keeping audiences giggling with comedy productions and children's workshops. The Carlsen Center at Johnson County Community College proffers a season that includes 32 special events in six separate series: Center, Celebrity, Vocal Splendor, Dance, Recital, and Family. Internationally-known performers are intermingled with college performing artists in an eclectic mix of opera, jazz, and classical numbers.

Dance and music aficionados can rely on Kansas City to round out the repertoire—the Kansas City Ballet, Kansas

City Symphony, Lyric Opera of Kansas City, Folly Theatre, and the Music Hall host performances all along the spectrum of the arts. Community-based theater productions are held by the Theatre League in Kansas City, and professional theater performances are offered by the Kansas City Repertory Theatre. Outdoor theater can be experienced in Kansas City at the Starlight Theater and in Shawnee at the Theatre in the Park.

Arts and Culture Information: Overland Park Convention and Visitors Bureau, 9001 W. 110 Street, Suite 100, Overland Park, KS 66210; toll-free (800)262-7275

Festivals and Holidays

Comfortable spring temperatures allow for a variety of outdoor celebrations and events, including the farmers market that operates from early April until late September. Vendors of produce, crafts, and art items set up booths near the Clock Tower, attracting hordes of locals and visitors. The Clock Tower is also the scene for a concert series that begins in early April and ends in late September, running in tandem with the farmers market. Spring showers bring more than May flowers at the Arboretum in Overland Park—from mid-May through late October, the botanical gardens and arboretum are the site of a juried Sculpture Exhibition.

''Jazz in the Woods'' is a three-day music festival held in June on the grounds of Corporate Woods office park. Local and national jazz artists perform in Overland Park, with the proceeds going to several charities. The Downtown Overland Park Days and Art Festival in late June revolves around the resumption of an outdoor farmers market. The Fourth of July is celebrated with a bang at SpiritFest, a three-day party featuring local cuisine, three entertainment stages, and a midway.

Cooler fall temperatures bring street fairs and celebrations all around the area. The Kansas City Renaissance Festival in nearby Bonner Springs starts in early September and runs for seven weeks. Overland Park's Annual Fall Festival also occurs in late September and features art and craft booths, food vendors, and street entertainment in downtown Overland Park.

The winter holidays are kicked off in November with the Annual Holiday Market in the Farmer's Pavilion downtown. Vendors offer seasonal arts, crafts, produce, and holiday gifts on Saturdays throughout the month. The Mayor's Lighting Ceremony in mid-November features carolers, cookies, and Santa Claus as the city's communal tree is lit.

Sports for the Spectator

Overland Park's proximity to Kansas City allows sports fans to immerse themselves in professional and amateur sports all year long. The Kansas City Chiefs play in the Western Division of the National Football League American Conference, with home games taking place in the Arrowhead Stadium off I-70. The Kansas City Knights were a founding franchise in the American Basketball Association; home games are played in Kemper Arena from mid-November through mid-April. For the Kansas City Outlaws, the floor of the Kemper Arena is converted to an ice rink to accommodate United League Hockey play. Indoor soccer rounds out the winter season, with the Comets competing in the Major Indoor Soccer League from October through March.

Soccer heads outdoors for the Wizards' season—the team plays home games at Arrowhead Stadium and competes in the Major Soccer League. Summer brings baseball, and Kansas City is home of the Royals. The independent Northern League is also represented by the Kansas City T-Bones.

The newest spectator sport in the area takes place at the Kansas Speedway; completed in 2001, the raceway attracts NASCAR events.

Sports for the Participant

Classes in tai chi, yoga, aerobics, and weight training are offered through the Parks and Recreation department of the City of Overland Park, which also coordinates youth and adult team sports in season. The city maintains the Indian Creek Trail for bikers and hikers, which winds for almost 17 miles along Indian Creek as it passes through Overland Park on its way to a convergence with the Tomahawk Creek Trail system.

The Overland Park Skate Park was created in 1997 through the efforts of an Overland Park Community Resource Officer who saw the need for a safe place for youth to skate. The park challenges users with jumps, ramps, and rails based on the urban landscape often frequented by skaters.

The city operates two public golf courses. St. Andrew's Golf Club is an 18-hole course that underwent a renovation in 1997 that was guided by LPGA player Carol Mann. The front nine holes feature wide fairways with some water hazards, while the back nine are characterized by tighter fairways, doglegs and bunkers. The Overland Park Golf Club offers 27 regulation holes that form three 18-hole courses. Putting greens, chipping greens, a grill and a pro shop round out the amenities at the Overland Park Golf Club. Both public clubs provide adult and youth instruction and leagues.

Johnson County coordinates a wide variety of sports and recreation programs, ranging from nature centers, to golf courses, to stables. The Ernie Miller Park and Nature Center in Olathe contains 114 acres of diverse habitats, trails, a wildlife viewing room, and an aquarium. Outdoor Discovery Camps are offered for younger naturalists. Also located in

Olathe is the TimberRidge Adventure Center—in addition to a professionally-facilitated challenge (ropes) course, the center provides opportunities to hike, fish, and practice archery skills. Anglers can also cast lines at Regency Park Lake in Overland Park; three acres of surface area shelters channel catfish, bluegill, hybrid sunfish, green sunfish, and largemouth bass.

Shopping and Dining

Overland Park is home to two enclosed malls: Metcalf South Shopping Center is anchored by Jones Store Company and Sears, while Oak Park Mall is a 187-store facility anchored by Nordstrom's and Dillard's stores. The Hawthorne Plaza contains a collection of upscale shops, and a walk in downtown Overland Park will take shoppers by unique locally-owned antique stores, art galleries, and specialty stores. Overland Park's proximity to Kansas City means that locals and visitors are within easy reach of more than 90 shopping centers and 38 shopping plazas.

Barbecue figures largely on the menu of local eateries in Overland Park. Approximately 46 restaurants offer barbecue in one form or another. Mexican-American cuisine is also well-represented, with more than 50 establishments. Asian restaurants are almost 80 in number, and Italian food is served at 32 eating places. Other culinary offerings include French, Cajun, Greek, Indian, Irish, and Jewish fare. Coffee houses run the gamut from chain franchises to locally-owned espresso bars.

Convention Facilities

The Overland Park Convention Center hosts trade shows, corporate meetings, conferences, and social events. The facility boasts 60,000 square feet of exhibit space, a 25,000 square foot ballroom, 15,000 square feet for meetings, and a 25,000 square foot outdoor courtyard. Audio-visual connections and high-speed wireless service comprise only a portion of the state-of-the-art technology available to presenters and exhibitors. The Center is decorated with works from local and regional artisans, including a blown-glass chandelier.

Many of the local hotels in Overland Park, Shawnee, Olathe, and Kansas City offer convention areas, banquet halls, meeting rooms, and ballrooms. The Wyandotte County Fairgrounds and Sports Complex in Kansas City can seat 350 in the auditorium and 150 in the banquet hall, while the Community Diversity Center has facilities for meetings, health fairs, seminars and workshops. The Jack Reardon Civic Center at Hilton Garden Inn adds 20,000 square feet of exhibit and conference space; along with its banquet room, the facility can seat up to 2,000 people.

Transportation

Approaching the City

Situated in almost the center of the United States, Kansas City International Airport is a busy transportation hub that serves approximately 10 million passengers every year. The airport was developed with an innovative "drive-to-gate" design that gets passengers to the departure area efficiently and quickly. As part of a 10-year capital improvement plan, the airport is undergoing a variety of runway, equipment, and service upgrades. Travelers can arrive or depart on Air Canada, American Airlines, Delta Continental, America West, United, Southwest, Frontier, and Northwest, among others.

The Johnson County Executive Airport is located between Overland Park and Olathe; originally created as a Naval auxiliary field during the second World War, the airport now provides general aviation services for corporations and other users. Air charters, aircraft sales, and flight instruction are all available onsite.

Ground transportation in the Kansas City area is provided by Amtrak passenger rail service and Greyhound bus company. Greyhound has stops in the Overland Park area and a depot in Kansas City. The north-south Interstate 35 passes along the western edge of Overland Park, and the east-west Interstate 70 runs just to the north. The city is further accessible via a network of bypasses, U.S. highways (56, 69 and 71), and state highways (150 and 350).

Traveling in the City

The major streets in Overland Park are laid out in a grid pattern that is neatly oriented with name streets running due north-south and number streets running east-west. Interstate 35 runs along the western portion of Overland Park, with numerous exits to the community. Metcalf Avenue is a primary artery within Overland Park itself; the street, which runs north and south, makes a handy reference point as it drives right through the heart of the municipality.

Johnson County Transit operates a large number of buses, vans and smaller vehicles to support public transportation in the area. Passengers can take advantage of park-and-ride services, and special programs exist for seniors or disabled riders. Johnson County Transit also organizes shared rides to sporting events and festivals in the Kansas City metro area. A fleet of taxi companies further bolster transportation services within the city and beyond.

Bike commuters into Downtown Overland Park can navigate the street system or utilize the Indian Creek Trail system.

Communications

Newspapers and Magazines

Since 1880, *The Kansas City Star* has been delivering the news to eastern Kansas, with coverage of local, regional, national, and world events. *The Star* publishes three editions daily, including one edition specific to Johnson County. Business news, sports and entertainment are featured daily in the paper.

A number of special interest and religious newspapers are produced in the Overland Park-Kansas City area. Targeted audiences for local magazines include seniors, farmers, alternative health treatment seekers, computer buffs, the business community, and sports coaches.

Television and Radio

Overland Park tends to rely on Kansas City for its radio and television services. The local airwaves carry a variety of news, talk radio, sports and Christian programming on the AM frequency. FM radio locally offers alternative rock, National Public Radio, oldies, classical, country, Christian, and much more. One AM and one FM station broadcast directly from Overland Park.

Television stations broadcast from Kansas City and available in Overland Park include the networks of CBS, NBC and ABC, along with UPN, PAX and the WB. Public television, University of Kansas and Christian channels are also offered.

Media Information: Overland Park Convention and Visitors Bureau, 9001 W. 110 Street, Suite 100, Overland Park, KS 66210; toll-free (800)262-7275

Overland Park Online

City of Overland Park. Available www.opkansas.org

Overland Park Chamber of Commerce. Available www .opks.org

Overland Park Convention and Visitors Bureau. Available www.opcvb.org

Overland Park Economic Development Council. Available www.opedc.org

Johnson County Government. Available www.jocoks.com

Johnson County Library System. Available www.joco library.org

Selected Bibliography

Kansas: A History, New York, NY: Kenneth S. Davis (1984)

Topeka

The City in Brief

Founded: 1854 (incorporated, 1857)

Head Official: Mayor William W. Bunten (since 2005)

City Population
  1980: 118,690
  1990: 119,883
  2000: 122,377
  2003 estimate: 122,008
  Percent change, 1990–2000: 1.3%
  U.S. rank in 1980: 136th
  U.S. rank in 1990: 149th
  U.S. rank in 2000: 197th

Metropolitan Area Population (Shawnee County)
  1980: 154,916

  1990: 160,976
  2000: 169,871
  Percent change, 1990–2000: 5.5%
  U.S. rank in 1990: Not reported
  U.S. rank in 2000: 319th

Area: 56 square miles (2000)
Elevation: Ranges from 876 feet to 971 feet above sea level
Average Annual Temperature: 65.1° F
Average Annual Precipitation: 33 inches of rain, 21 inches of snow

Major Economic Sectors: Services, government, trade, manufacturing
Unemployment Rate: 7.0% (February 2005)

2002 FBI Crime Index Total: 11,294

Major Colleges and Universities: Washburn University

Daily Newspaper: *The Topeka Capital-Journal*

Introduction

Topeka is the seat of Shawnee County, the capital of Kansas, and center of a metropolitan statistical area that includes all of Shawnee County. Throughout its history, Topeka has been at the forefront of progress; created as a principal link in the westward expansion of the railroad and settled by New England antislavery supporters in the nineteenth century, the city was in the twentieth century a world leader in the treatment of mental illness. In the last two decades Topeka has experienced business growth with a number of *Fortune* 500 companies relocating or expanding in the area.

Geography and Climate

Topeka lies on both banks of the Kansas River about 60 miles upriver from the point where the Kansas joins the Missouri River. Two tributaries of the Kansas River, Soldier and Shunganunga Creeks, flow through the city. The valley near Topeka, bordered by rolling prairie uplands of 200 to 300 feet, ranges from 2 to 4 miles in width. Seventy percent of the annual precipitation falls from April through September. Heavy rains pose the threat of flooding, but the construction of dams has reduced the problem. Summers are usually hot, with low humidity and southerly winds; periods of high humidity and oppressively warm temperatures are of short duration. Winter cold spells are seldom prolonged; winter precipitation is often in the form of snow, sleet, or glaze. Severe or disruptive storms occur infrequently.

Area: 56 square miles (2000)

Elevation: Ranges from 876 feet to 971 feet above sea level

Average Temperatures: January, 26.0° F; July, 78.0° F; average, 65.1° F

Average Annual Precipitation: 33 inches of rain, 21 inches of snow

History

Westward Expansion Targets Kaw River Valley

Two historic nineteenth-century movements combined to create the city of Topeka—one was the antislavery issue and the other was the westward expansion made possible by the railroad, which connected the East with the vast unsettled territory in the West. Before the Kansas frontier was opened by the federal government to settlement, the first people of European descent to live on the site of present-day Topeka were the French-Canadian Pappan brothers. They each married a woman from the Kaw tribe in 1842 and opened a ferry service across the Kaw River. The ferry was temporarily replaced in 1857 when bridge builders ignored warnings from the local Native Americans, who insisted that structures built too close to the Kaw would not be secure against flood waters. The bridge was destroyed in a flood the following year.

Colonel Cyrus K. Holliday, a native of Pennsylvania, came to the Kansas Territory in 1854 with funding from Eastern investors to build a railroad. Holliday and a few pioneers had walked 45 miles from Kansas City to Lawrence, where Holliday approached Dr. Charles Robinson, agent of the New England Emigrant Aid Company, an antislavery organization, about his plan. Then Holliday and Robinson traveled 21 miles to Tecumseh, but businessmen there wanted too much money for their land. Holliday located a spot 5 miles from Tecumseh along the river and purchased land from Enoch Chase, who had previously bought it from the Kaws.

Holliday formed a company, naming himself as president and the Lawrence contingent and Chase as stockholders. Holliday wanted to name the town Webster after Daniel Webster, but the others preferred a name whose meaning was local; they chose Topeka, a Native American word meaning ''smokey hill,'' according to one version, or ''a good place to dig potatoes,'' according to another. The City of Topeka was incorporated February 14, 1857 with Holliday as mayor. Dr. Robinson attracted antislavery New Englanders to settle in Topeka, thus counteracting the influence of a proslavery group in Tecumseh. A Free State constitutional convention was held in Topeka but federal troops arrested the new legislators when they tried to meet on July 4, 1855.

Kansas Statehood Brings Capital to Topeka

The Kansas constitution was framed at Wyandotte (later named Kansas City), and Kansas was admitted to the Union in 1861. The constitution specified that the state capital would be selected by election. Dr. Robinson ran for governor, favoring Topeka over Lawrence as the site for the capital; he also supported the Atchison, Topeka & Santa Fe Railway system, which began laying its westward track in 1869. Holliday served as the company's first president, with general offices and machine shops located in Topeka. Topeka's population increased from 700 people in 1862 to 5,000 people in 1870; it then made another dramatic population jump in the late 1880s.

Foundation in Topeka Gains International Fame

During the 20th century Topeka was known internationally as the home of Menninger, a nonprofit organization dedicated to the study of mental illness and founded by Dr. Karl Menninger and his father, Dr. Charles F. Menninger. In 1920 the Menningers opened a group psychiatric practice that they named the Menninger Clinic; they were joined in 1925 by William, Charles's younger son. The Menningers opened the Topeka Institute of Psychoanalysis in 1938 after the brothers had studied formally in Chicago. The family is credited with introducing psychiatry to America. Karl Menninger's *The Human Mind* was the first book on psychiatry to become a bestseller. The Menningers opened the nonprofit Menninger Foundation, the world's largest psychiatric training center, in 1941. The Menninger Clinic moved to Houston, Texas in 2003.

Today, Topeka is recognized for its strong economic development efforts and high quality of life. In 2003 *Business Facilities* magazine wrote, "While the national economy lags, relocations and expansions are happening all over Kansas, with Topeka leading the way."*Expansion Management* magazine gave the city its highest rating in the Annual Quality of Life Quotient survey.

Historical Information: Kansas State Historical Society, 6425 SW Sixth Ave, Topeka, KS 66615; telephone (785)272-8681; fax (785)272-8682

Population Profile

Metropolitan Area Residents
1980: 154,916
1990: 160,976
2000: 169,871
Percent change, 1990–2000: 5.5%
U.S. rank in 1990: Not reported
U.S. rank in 2000: 319th

City Residents
1980: 118,690
1990: 119,883
2000: 122,377
2003 estimate: 122,008
Percent change, 1990–2000: 1.3%
U.S. rank in 1990: 149th
U.S. rank in 2000: 197th

Density: 2,185 people per square mile (2000)

Racial and ethnic characteristics (2000)
White: 96,093
Black or African American: 14,332
American Indian and Alaska Native: 1,603
Asian: 1,340
Native Hawaiian and Pacific Islander: 50
Hispanic or Latino (may be of any race): 10,847
Other: 4,969

Percent of residents born in state: 67.9% (2000)

Age characteristics (2000)
Population under 5 years old: 8,615
Population 5 to 9 years old: 8,224
Population 10 to 14 years old: 7,873
Population 15 to 19 years old: 8,363
Population 20 to 24 years old: 8,710
Population 25 to 34 years old: 17,169
Population 35 to 44 years old: 18,153
Population 45 to 54 years old: 16,553
Population 55 to 59 years old: 5,582
Population 60 to 64 years old: 4,717
Population 65 to 74 years old: 9,031
Population 75 to 84 years old: 6,821
Population 85 years and older: 2,566
Median age: 36.3

Births (2003)
Total number: 2,068

Deaths (2003)
Total number: 1,513 (of which, 18 were infants under the age of 1 year)

Money income (1999)
Per capita income: $19,555
Median household income: $35,928
Total households: 52,143

Number of households with income of . . .
less than $10,000: 5,297
$10,000 to $14,999: 3,929
$15,000 to $24,999: 8,125
$25,000 to $34,999: 8,001
$35,000 to $49,999: 9,675
$50,000 to $74,999: 9,875
$75,000 to $99,999: 3,864
$100,000 to $149,999: 2,413
$150,000 to $199,999: 479
$200,000 or more: 485

Percent of families below poverty level: 8.5% (42.5% of which were female householder families with related children under 5 years)

2002 FBI Crime Index Total: 11,294

Municipal Government

Topeka adopted a City Manager form of government in 2005. Council members from each of nine districts are elected to staggered four-year terms; the mayor is elected at large and sets the council's agenda (but does not vote). A city manager handles daily operations.

Head Official: Mayor William W. Bunten (since 2005; current term expires 2009)

Total Number of City Employees: 1,735 (2005)

City Information: City Hall, 215 SE 7th Street, Topeka, KS 66603-3914; telephone (785)368-3710; fax (785)368-3958

Economy

Major Industries and Commercial Activity

Government and services comprise more than 50 percent of the metropolitan Topeka economy; total state, county, and city government employment accounts for almost one quarter of the work force, and more than 30 percent of area employees are on the service industry payroll. Nearly 15 percent of workers are employed in wholesale or retail trade. The construction and manufacturing industries made modest gains statewide amidst increasing demand for housing and aircraft production.

Fortune 500 companies that have established manufacturing or distribution facilities in Topeka include: Burlington Northern Santa Fe Railway, Frito-Lay, Inc., Goodyear Tire & Rubber, Hill's Pet Nutrition, Payless Shoe Source, and Hallmark Cards, Inc.

Other principal industries located in Topeka include flour mills, printing and publishing companies, iron foundries, and food processing plants.

Items and goods produced: flour, dairy products, meats and poultry, pet foods, tires, tents, awnings, serum, steel fixtures, culverts, tanks, boxes and baskets, medicines, and steel jetties.

Incentive Programs—New and Existing Companies

The state of Kansas and the city of Topeka offer a range of incentives for business expansion, including a state-maintained ''first-stop clearinghouse,'' tax credits and exemptions, utility rate discounts, fee waivers, and loan assistance. Organizations such as Topeka-Shawnee County Development Corporation and Kansas Venture Capital, Inc. promote development in the metropolitan area. *Expansion Management* magazine recently ranked Kansas State's employment training programs among the top ten in the U.S. for ease of access and value to clients.

Local programs—Shawnee County recently implemented a quarter-cent sales tax that will support local economic devel-

opment activities. The anticipated $20 million revenue over the next four years will be earmarked for job creation and investment incentives. The city or county may grant up to 10 years of property tax exemptions to companies that promote employment growth or private investment in the area. GO Topeka offers loans to small businesses and startups owned by women or minorities, as well as job training and counseling. Topeka's One-Stop Business Development Office provides advice, funding and training in affiliation with the Washburn University Small Business Development Center, SCORE, GO Connection Microloan Program, and Wakarusa Certified Development Inc. Downtown Topeka Inc. provides grants to businesses in the downtown area.

State programs—Kansas State offers corporate income tax credits based on job creation and capital investment and sales tax exemptions on equipment purchases or facility construction. The High Performance Incentive Program provides tax exemption, job training credits and matching funds for consulting fees to companies paying above-average wages or investing in workforce training or capital. Tax credits are also available to companies that conduct research, contribute to the community, provide day-care facilities to employees, or invest in accessibility for persons with disabilities.

Job training programs—The Kansas Industrial Training program offers pre-employment training or on-the-job training for new and expanding businesses. The Kansas Industrial Retraining Program is for restructuring companies where existing employees may be displaced due to obsolete skills. The Investments in Major Projects and Comprehensive Training Program (IMPACT) is for companies hiring a large number of employees at higher-than-average wages. Job training programs are available through agencies such as KAW Area Technical School and Topeka Technical College.

Development Projects

The Kansas State Capitol is undergoing a nine-year restoration at a projected cost of $138 million. Components of this massive effort include restoring the historical integrity of the limestone exterior and the marble and wood interior; transforming the virtually unused basement into office space, a cafeteria and a visitor's center; updating mechanical and electrical systems; and conserving murals and decorative painting. Work is likely to continue until 2009.

Target's $80 million distribution centre was recently completed, bringing more than 600 new jobs to the area. A $22 million manufacturing plant expansion is underway at Reser's Fine Foods. Goodyear Tire & Rubber is completing a $100 million plant upgrade. Washburn University will spend $10 million on a Student Recreation and Wellness Center and new student apartments. An $11 million project to restore Monroe School as the Brown v. Topeka Board of

Education National Historic Site was completed in May 2004. Ramada Inn Downtown has been purchased by an investor group and will undergo a $2.5 million renovation. Forbes Field and Philip Billard airports are both in the midst of multi-million-dollar upgrades. Stormont-Vail Health-Care's new $35 million surgery center opened in 2004, replacing surgical facilities from the 1950s.

Economic Development Information: Greater Topeka Chamber of Commerce, 120 SE Sixth Street, Suite 110, Topeka, KS 66603-3515; telephone (785)234-2644; fax (785)234-8656

Commercial Shipping

Topeka is a shipping and distribution hub that links the corn- and wheat-growing region of northeastern Kansas and the cattle-producing states of the Southwest with markets throughout the country via an efficient transportation network. Burlington Northern Santa Fe Railway, Union Pacific, and St. Louis-Southwestern provide commercial rail service to the Topeka area; piggyback service is available within a 60-mile radius. More than 300 motor carriers serve the Topeka region. Two air carriers operate parcel and freight facilities at Forbes Field.

Labor Force and Employment Outlook

According to the Greater Topeka Chamber of Commerce, the entrepreneurial spirit of Topeka residents dates back to 1842 when a group of enterprising settlers founded a ferry service across the Kansas River. Today, Topeka area residents are more educated than the national average; 88 percent have a high school diploma and more than 25 percent have a college degree or higher. Statewide, more than half of Kansas employees have taken advantage of on-the-job training opportunities.

The following is a summary of data regarding the Topeka metropolitan area labor force, 2004 annual averages.

Size of nonagricultural labor force: 111,400

Number of workers employed in . . .
  construction and mining: 6,100
  manufacturing: 8,000
  trade, transportation and utilities: 20,900
  information: 2,900
  financial activities: 6,900
  professional and business services: 8,400
  educational and health services: 16,600
  leisure and hospitality: 9,000
  other services: 5,100
  government: 27,600

Average hourly earnings of production workers employed in manufacturing: $16.57 (Kansas State)

Unemployment rate: 7.0% (February 2005)

Largest employers	Number of employees
State of Kansas	8,612
Stormont-Vail HealthCare	3,100
Unified School District #501	2,270
Blue Cross Blue Shield of Kansas	1,855
St. Francis Hospital & Medical Center	1,837
Payless Shoe Source	1,735
Goodyear Tire & Rubber	1,700
Washburn University	1,455
Burlington Northern Santa Fe Railway	1,100
Jostens Printing and Publishing	1,060

Cost of Living

According to the Greater Topeka Chamber of Commerce, Topeka offers a "quality living experience at a below average cost."

The following is a summary of data regarding several key cost of living factors in the Topeka area.

2004 (3rd Quarter) ACCRA Average House Price: $200,589

2004 (3rd Quarter) ACCRA Cost of Living Index: 92.1 (U.S. average = 100.0)

State income tax rate: Ranges from 3.5% to 6.45%

State sales tax rate: 5.3%

Local income tax rate: None

Local sales tax rate: city, 1.0%; county, 0.50%; Washburn University, 0.65%

Property tax rate: 141.24 mills per $1,000 of assessed value (2004)

Economic Information: Greater Topeka Chamber of Commerce, 120 SE Sixth Street, Suite 110, Topeka, KS 66603-3515; telephone (785)234-2644; fax (785)234-8656. State of Kansas, Department of Human Resources, Labor Market Information Services, 401 SW Topeka Blvd., Topeka, KS 66603; telephone (785)296-5058; fax (785)296-5286

Education and Research

Elementary and Secondary Schools

Public elementary and secondary schools within the Topeka corporation limits are administered by Topeka Public Schools (TPS) United School District #501. The school superintendent is appointed by a nonpartisan, seven-member board of education.

Six elementary schools in the district met the Kansas Standards of Excellence in 2004, a challenging target that no TPS school had attained since 1996. Superintendent W.L. Sawyer credited the hard work of teachers and administrators as well as an increased focus on professional development. Six additional schools posted gains exceeding 15 percent on state reading or math assessments.

The district features two state-of-the-art elementary magnet schools—one emphasizing computer technology and the other with a science and fine arts theme. The district has an extensive special education program, a business partnership program, a school volunteer program, full-day kindergarten in several schools, preschool programs, out-of-district enrollment options, alternative education, and a Kids Voting program.

The following is a summary of data regarding the Topeka public schools as of the 2003–2004 school year.

Total enrollment: 14,058

Number of facilities
   elementary schools: 21
   middle schools: 6
   senior high schools: 4
   other: 4

Student/teacher ratio: 13.1:1 (2002–2003)

Teacher salaries
   minimum: $26,655
   maximum: $45,554

Funding per pupil: $4,946

Educational alternatives are offered by 15 private and parochial private schools in Topeka. Special schools include the Capper Foundation and TARC (the Topeka Association for Retarded Children).

Public Schools Information: Topeka Public Schools, USD 501, 624 W 24th Street, Topeka, KS 66611; telephone (785)575-6100

Colleges and Universities

Washburn University, a public institution enrolling nearly 7,000, offers more than 100 programs in its College of Arts and Sciences and its faculties of Law, Business, Nursing, and Applied and Continuing Education. Washburn's law school counts nationally recognized lawyers, judges and politicians among its alumni. The University of Kansas in Lawrence, Kansas State University in Manhattan and Emporia State University are within 50 miles of Topeka.

Friends University and Baker University offer adult education at campuses in Topeka.

Among the eight occupational/technical schools located in the Topeka area are Kaw Area Technical School and Topeka Technical College.

Libraries and Research Centers

Topeka is home to several major libraries. The Topeka & Shawnee County was reopened in 2002 after a 100,000 square foot expansion designed by renowned architect Michael Graves. The library holds approximately 538,000 items including books, periodicals, microfilms, compact discs, slides, audiotapes and videotapes. Its Alice C. Sabatini Gallery houses the oldest public art collection in the city. The library also offers an outreach program with two Bookmobiles and an Adventure Mobile for children.

The Kansas State Library maintains an extensive collection of books, documents and videos with a focus on government and public affairs. The library also operates a free talking book program for patrons with visual impairments, physical impairments or reading disabilities in Emporia. The Kansas State Historical Society Library contains a state archival collection as well as archaeological and genealogical materials, manuscripts, maps, photographs and federal documents. Washburn University's Mabee Library and Law Library, the Kansas Supreme Court Law Library, the Topeka Genealogical Society Library, and libraries associated with corporations, hospitals, and state agencies are also located in Topeka.

Public Library Information: Topeka & Shawnee County Public Library, 1515 SW Tenth Avenue, Topeka, KS 66604; telephone (785)580-4400

Health Care

The Topeka medical community has expanded with renovation and new construction at the city's major facilities, which include two general and five specialized hospitals. St. Francis Hospital offers 378 patient beds and a premier cancer care centre including the only PET image scanner in the Topeka area. It also specializes in heart disease and rehabilitation. Stormont-Vail Regional Health Center is a 586-bed acute care facility providing a range of inpatient and outpatient services. It operates the only Level III Neonatal Intensive Care Unit in the county and recently completed a new $35 million surgical center. The hospital is part of the Stormont-Vail HealthCare integrated system, which serves 14 counties in northeast Kansas. Both general hospitals maintain emergency departments.

The Colmery-O'Neil Medical Center provides a range of services for veterans, including medical, surgical, psychiatric and nursing home care. The Kansas Neurological Institute is recognized for its programs for persons with developmental disabilities. The Kansas Rehabilitation Hospital provides inpatient and outpatient care in all areas of physical rehabilitation. The Select Specialty Hospital is an acute care facility for patients requiring care for extended periods of time; the average stay is 25 days. Tallgrass Surgical Center provides cost-effective outpatient care.

The nonprofit Capper Foundation provides education and assistive technology for physically handicapped children. It also offers preschool and childcare services.

There are 37 retirement and adult care homes in the Topeka area.

Health Care Information: Ask-A-Nurse referral line, telephone (785)295-8333. Health Connections, telephone (785)354-5225. St. Francis Hospital, telephone (785)295-8000. Stormont-Vail Health Center, telephone (785)354-6000

Recreation

Sightseeing

Historic Ward-Meade Park overlooks the Kansas River valley from its position on a bluff. At the center of the park is the ancestral home of the Anthony Ward family, a Victorian mansion built in 1870. Also on the grounds are the Ward frontier log cabin, a country schoolhouse, botanical gardens, and a restored 1900s Kansas village called Old Prairie Town.

Gage Park includes the 160 acre Topeka Zoo, featuring a gorilla encounter habitat, providing for close observation of great apes through a glass partition; a Lion's Pride exhibit; Black Bear Woods; and a Tropical Rain Forest. Also at Gage Park are the Reinisch Rose Garden and Carousel in the Park.

Topeka's copper-domed state Capitol building is well known for its frescoes and woodworking, but it is the Kansas Murals that give the Capitol its artistic focal point; these murals by John Steuart Curry capture dramatic events in the state's history that proved so controversial at the time they were executed that the project was not finished. The Brown v. Board of Education National Historic Site opened in 2004 at the former Monroe School, marking the 1954 Supreme Court decision that ended segregation in public schools. Topeka High School displays the mast spar from *Old Ironsides* on its lawn.

Great Overland Station is a museum and education center commemorating Topeka's railroad heritage. Future redevel-

opment of the adjacent Kansas Riverfront Park and Historic North Topeka Business District will turn the area into a rich cultural destination for locals and tourists. Potwin Place is an exclusive section of Topeka with Italianate, Victorian, and nineteenth-century farmhouse-style homes. Cedar Crest Governor's Residence, built by Topeka State Journal publisher Frank P. MacLennan in 1928, has been the home of Kansas Governors since 1962. First Presbyterian Church is one of a handful of churches in the nation decorated with Tiffany windows.

Arts and Culture

Musical entertainment in Topeka is provided by the Topeka Symphony Orchestra, the Topeka Community Concert Association, the Topeka Opera Society, the Fine Arts Society, and the Topeka Jazz Workshop. Performances take place at the Kansas Expocentre, the Topeka Performing Arts Center, and elsewhere.

The Topeka Performing Arts Center hosts touring Broadway musicals, dance companies, major symphonies, and other entertainment. The Topeka Civic Theater is one of the nation's oldest and most highly regarded dinner theaters. Other Topeka theater companies include Helen Hocker Theatre in Gage Park and the Washburn University Theatre.

More than 20 art galleries as well as public buildings, businesses, and corporations in Topeka display an array of art. Among the more outstanding pieces are John Steuart Curry's *John Brown* in the State Capitol and Peter Felton's *Amelia Earhart* in the rotunda of the State Capitol. The Mulvane Art Museum on the campus of Washburn University exhibits works by Duerer, Goya, Picasso, and Dali in its permanent collection. The Kansas Museum of History chronicles the history of Kansas from the earliest native cultures to the present, using interactive exhibits, programs and videos. The Combat Air Museum at Forbes Field displays airplanes, missiles, military vehicles and aircraft memorabilia dating back to 1917.

Arts and Culture Information: Topeka Performing Arts Center Box Office, telephone (785)297-9000; Kansas Expocentre Box Office, telephone (785)297-1000; Arts Council of Topeka, telephone (785)234-0378

Festivals and Holidays

Kansas Day Celebration in late January commemorates Kansas's admission into the Union. The featured attraction in March is the St. Patrick's Day Parade and Street Fair. Washburn University hosts the Sunflower Music Festival and the Mountain Plains Art Fair in June. The Spirit of Kansas Celebration, Mexican Fiesta, and Shawnee County Fair make for an active July. The Huff 'N' Puff Balloon Rally is a popular September event, as well as Cider Days and the Kansas River Valley Art Festival. Apple Festival,

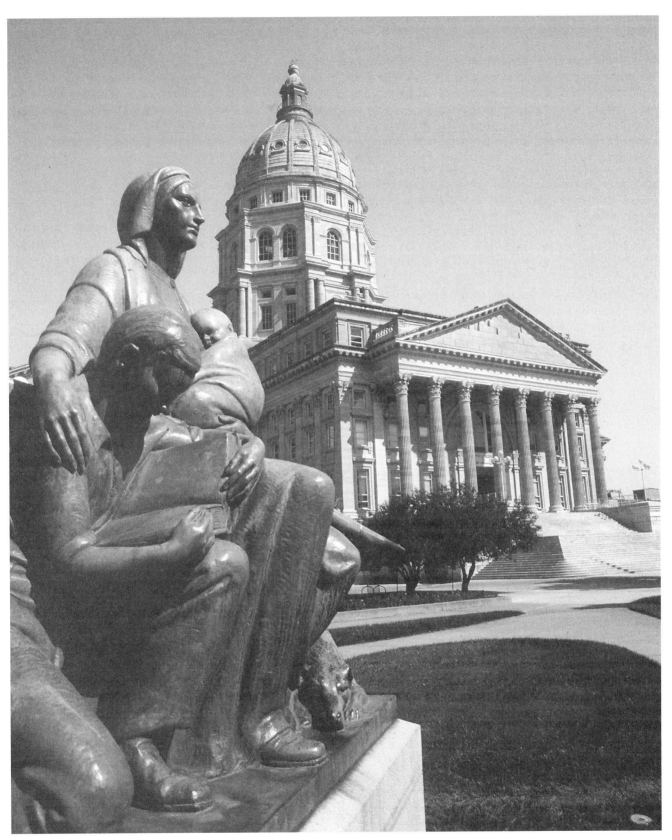

The Kansas Mural, as well as frescoes and woodworking, are popular attractions at Topeka's State Capitol building.

held at Historic Ward-Meade Park in October, celebrates Kansas's folk life. Festival of Trees and Miracle on Kansas Avenue take place during December.

Sports for the Spectator

The Central Hockey League's Topeka Tarantulas play at the Kansas Expocentre. Washburn University fields teams in intercollegiate competition in a number of sports. The Great Plains Rowing Championship takes place in April on Lake Shawnee. The Kansas State High School Rodeo Championships are held at the Kansas Expocentre Livestock Arena in early June. Drag racing action takes place at Heartland Park in Topeka, while sprint car racing happens at Thunder Hill Speedway.

Sports for the Participant

The Topeka Parks and Recreation Department maintains parks with 7 community centers, 69 public tennis courts, 5 public swimming pools, 26 baseball or softball diamonds and a number of playgrounds, picnic facilities and soccer fields. Nine public golf courses are located in the area. East of Topeka is Lake Shawnee, providing opportunities for swimming, fishing, camping, and sailing. Gage Park, in addition to being the home of the Topeka Zoo, features recreational facilities including swimming, volleyball, and tennis. A number of hiking, jogging and nature trails can be found in Topeka. The Topeka Tinman Triathlon takes place at Lake Shawnee in June. Indoor ice skating is offered at the Kansas Expocentre.

Shopping and Dining

The 1.1 million-square-foot West Ridge Mall is Topeka's main shopping venue. More than 30 other shopping areas range from enclosed malls to neighborhood shopping centers.

Steakhouses serving Kansas beef are the main attraction in Topeka. Other dining choices include French, Mexican, Oriental, and Cajun Creole. Topeka's most popular family restaurants specialize in traditional American fare such as Kansas steaks, Southern fried chicken, country fried steaks, barbecued ribs, and homemade pies and pastries. Fine dining is also available.

Visitor Information: Topeka Convention and Visitors Bureau, 1275 SW Topeka Blvd., Topeka, KS 66612-1852; telephone (785)234-1030; toll-free (800)235-1030; fax (785)234-8282

Convention Facilities

The Kansas Expocentre, a multipurpose complex which houses an arena, concert hall, and a convention center ac-

commodates meetings, conventions, trade shows, and entertainment events. The arena seats up to 10,000 people and contains 210,000 square feet of unobstructed space. Parking is provided on-site and catering service is available. The Ramada Inn Downtown is the largest hotel in Topeka with 34,000 square feet of meeting space. Thirty additional hotels and motels, several of which include complete meeting facilities, offer nearly 3,000 rooms for lodgings.

Convention Information: Kansas Expocentre, One Expocentre Drive, Topeka, KS 66612; telephone (785)235-1986; fax (785)235-2967. Topeka Convention and Visitors Bureau, 1275 SW Topeka Blvd., Topeka, KS 66612-1852; telephone (785)234-1030; toll-free (800)235-1030; fax (785)234-8282

Transportation

Approaching the City

Commercial airlines fly into Forbes Field, 7 miles south of downtown Topeka. Daily commuter service is available from Kansas City International Airport, 75 miles from Topeka. The destination for general and business aviation traffic is Phillip Billiard Field, 3 miles northeast of the city. Passenger rail service to Topeka is provided by Amtrak. Greyhound Bus service is also available.

An efficient highway network facilitates access into Topeka. Three interstate and three U.S. highways converge in Topeka: I-70, I-470, and I-335; and U.S. 24, U.S. 40, and U.S. 75.

Traveling in the City

Topeka is laid out on a grid pattern. Streets running east to west are numbered; streets running north to south are named. Topeka Transit schedules 14 public bus routes in the city Monday through Saturday; evening and Sunday service is available by advance reservation. Topeka Transit's Lift Service provides door-to-door service for persons with disabilities. During weekday mornings and afternoons, Topeka Transit operates the Topeka Trolleys, a downtown shuttle and lunchtime circulator service.

Communications

Newspapers and Magazines

Topeka's major daily newspaper is *The Topeka Capital-Journal.* The city is also a center for magazine publishing.

Among the widely circulated periodicals based in Topeka are *Capper's,* a biweekly human interest magazine established in 1879; and *Grit,* a weekly family-oriented tabloid. *Mother Earth News,* a leading environmental magazine, moved from New York City to Topeka in 2001. Other publications pertain to agriculture, commerce and industry, history, food, and rural living.

Television and Radio

Topeka television viewers select programming from two stations based in the city—one commercial network affiliate and one public station. Six AM and FM radio stations schedule a variety of formats such as educational, talk, adult contemporary, and news and sports.

Media Information: Topeka Capital-Journal, 616 SE Jefferson Street, Topeka, KS 66607; telephone (785)295-1111

Topeka Online

City of Topeka home page. Available www.topeka.org

Greater Topeka Chamber of Commerce. Available www.topekachamber.org

The Topeka Capital-Journal online. Available www.cjonline.com

Topeka Public Schools. Available www.topeka.k12.ks.us

Topeka & Shawnee County Public Library. Available www.tscpl.org

Selected Bibliography

Cox, Thomas C. *Blacks in Topeka, Kansas: 1865-1915, a Social History.* Louisiana State University Press, 1982.

Wichita

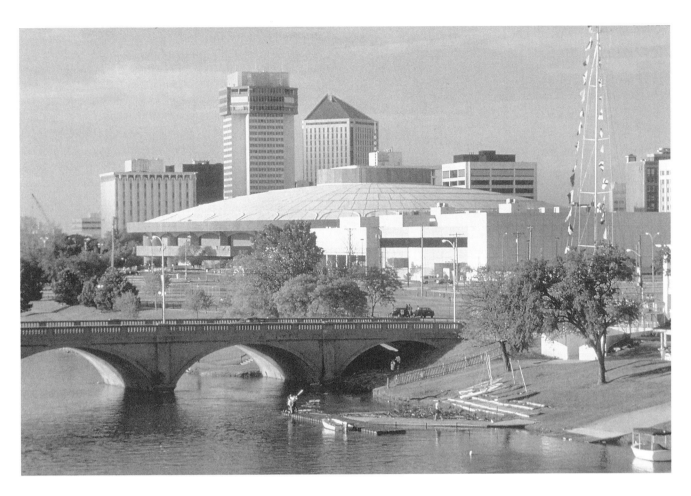

The City in Brief

Founded: 1868 (incorporated, 1871)

Head Official: Mayor Carlos Mayans (since 2003)

City Population
  1980: 279,838
  1990: 304,017
  2000: 344,284
  2003 estimate: 354,617
  Percent change, 1990–2000: 13.2%
  U.S. rank in 1980: 51st
  U.S. rank in 1990: 51st (State rank: 1st)
  U.S. rank in 2000: 59th (State rank: 1st)

Metropolitan Area Population
  1980: 442,000
  1990: 485,270
  2000: 545,220

Percent change, 1990–2000: 12.4%
U.S. rank in 1980: 75th
U.S. rank in 1990: Not reported
U.S. rank in 2000: 77th

Area: 138.93 square miles (2000)
Elevation: 1,300 feet above sea level
Average Annual Temperature: 56.4° F
Average Annual Precipitation: 14.48 inches of rain, 15.9 inches of snow

Major Economic Sectors: Services, manufacturing, trade
Unemployment Rate: 6.3% (February 2005)
Per Capita Income: $20,647 (1999)

2002 FBI Crime Index Total: 24,104

Major Colleges and Universities: Wichita State University; Friends University; Newman University; University of Kansas School of Medicine-Wichita

Daily Newspaper: *Wichita Eagle*

Introduction

Wichita, the largest city in Kansas and the seat of Sedgwick County, is the focus of a metropolitan statistical area that includes Butler and Sedgwick counties. The city's history reflects the major stages of western U.S. development. The primary stop on the Chisholm Trail, Wichita flourished first as a cattle town, then as a rail link and milling center for Kansas grain. Prosperity continued with the discovery of oil near the city limits. Today Wichita, three-time winner of the National Civic League's All-America City Award, is an important technology center, particularly in the aviation industry.

Geography and Climate

Wichita is located on the Arkansas River in the Central Great Plains. The collision of moist air from the Gulf of Mexico with cold air from the Arctic produces a wide range of weather in the Wichita area. Summers, which are generally warm and humid, can often be hot and dry; winters are mild, though cold periods are not infrequent. Temperature variations are extreme, reaching above 110 degrees in the summer and below negative 20 degrees in the winter. Spring and summer thunderstorms can be severe, accompanied by heavy rain, hail, strong winds, and tornadoes. Protection against floods is provided by the Wichita-Valley Center Flood Control Project.

Area: 138.93 square miles (2000)

Elevation: 1,300 feet above sea level

Average Temperatures: January, 30.2° F; July, 81.0° F; annual average, 56.4° F

Average Annual Precipitation: 14.48 inches of rain, 15.9 inches of snow

History

A Cow Capital

The city of Wichita is named after the Wichita tribe, who settled on the site of the present-day city along the banks of the Arkansas River during the U.S. Civil War to avoid conflict with pro-Southern tribes in Oklahoma. James R. Mead and Jesse Chisholm, who was part Cherokee, opened a trading post next to the tribe's village. Chisholm, on a return trip from the Southwest where he had ventured on a trading

expedition, was traveling through a rain storm, and the wheels of his wagon carved deep tracks into the prairie soil. Thus the famous Chisholm Trail was blazed, and the route was used in subsequent years by cattlemen driving cattle to their eventual market destinations.

After the forced relocation of the Wichita tribe to Oklahoma in 1867, the Mead trading post became a center of commerce. As Texas cattlemen drove their longhorn steer up the Chisholm Trail to Abilene, the settlement around the trading post provided a stop on the way. The "first and last chance saloon" was opened there for thirsty cowboys. The settlement, named Wichita, was platted in 1870 and incorporated in 1871. When rail transport reached the town in 1872 and 350,000 cattle were driven in from the grazing ranges, Wichita became the "cow capital" of eastern Kansas. Wichita was a rough place despite signs posted at the corporation limits that warned visitors to check their guns before entering town.

Exit Cattle; Enter Wheat, Oil, and Airplanes

Boom times lasted until 1880, when the Chisholm Trail was blocked by barbed-wire fences protecting land planted with wheat, barring drivers from bringing their cattle to Wichita. Businessmen who made their livelihood from cattle relocated to Dodge City, and Wichita land values temporarily tumbled. But revenues from grain quickly outdistanced cattle when farmers brought their harvest to Wichita, transforming the city into a trading and milling center. Whereas the cattle business had supported dance halls and gambling houses, the wheat industry brought the civilizing forces of churches and schools.

Wichita's population steadily increased in the twentieth century, and new forms of wealth and business opportunity emerged. A major oil deposit discovered in Butler County in 1915 earned the nickname "door-step pool" because of its proximity to the city limits. Wichita's first airplane was manufactured the following year, and during the 1920s the city became known as the "Air Capital of America" in recognition of the number of airplane factories located there. By 1929 Wichita produced a quarter of all commercial aircraft in the United States. The aviation industry played an increased role in the city during World War II, and even more so after the establishment of McConnell Air Force Base in 1951. Beech Aircraft Corp. and Learjet Inc. were founded in Wichita, and such heavy-weights as the Boeing Co., Bombardier Inc., Cessna Aircraft Co., and Raytheon Co. established major facilities in the city. The population explosion that grew from the aviation industry attracted other types of companies. Two big names in the fast-food industry—Pizza Hut Inc. and White Castle System Inc.—were both founded in Wichita. By the turn of the century the city was headquarters for the Coleman Co. and Koch Industries Inc.

An All-American City

Three-time winner (since 1962) of the All American City award, Wichita's residents value the small-town atmosphere with modern-city amenities afforded them. A low crime rate, a nationally-recognized school system, low cost of living, ample opportunities for culture and recreation, and revitalized downtown are part of Wichita's success.

Historical Information: Wichita-Sedgwick County Historical Museum, 204 S. Main, Wichita, KS 67202; telephone (316)265-9314; fax (316)265-9319

Population Profile

Metropolitan Area Residents
1980: 442,000
1990: 485,270
2000: 545,220
Percent change, 1990–2000: 12.4%
U.S. rank in 1980: 75th
U.S. rank in 1990: Not reported
U.S. rank in 2000: 77th

City Residents
1980: 279,838
1990: 304,017
2000: 344,284
2003 estimate: 354,617
Percent change, 1990–2000: 13.2%
U.S. rank in 1980: 51st
U.S. rank in 1990: 51st (State rank: 1st)
U.S. rank in 2000: 59th (State rank: 1st)

Density: 2,536.1 people per square mile (2000)

Racial and ethnic characteristics (2000)
White: 258,900
Black or African American: 39,325
American Indian and Alaska Native: 3,986
Asian: 13,647
Native Hawaiian and Pacific Islander: 198
Hispanic or Latino (may be of any race): 33,112
Other: 17,566

Percent of residents born in state: 59.9% (2000)

Age characteristics (2000)
Population under 5 years old: 27,524
Population 5 to 9 years old: 26,725
Population 10 to 14 years old: 24,688
Population 15 to 19 years old: 23,767
Population 20 to 24 years old: 25,565

Population 25 to 34 years old: 51,619
Population 35 to 44 years old: 53,980
Population 45 to 54 years old: 44,035
Population 55 to 59 years old: 14,377
Population 60 to 64 years old: 11,113
Population 65 to 74 years old: 20,616
Population 75 to 84 years old: 15,297
Population 85 years and older: 4,978
Median age: 33.4 years

Births (Sedgwick County, 2003)
Total number: 7,568

Deaths (Sedgwick County, 2003)
Total number: 3,834 (of which, 46 were infants under the age of 1 year)

Money income (1999)
Per capita income: $20,647
Median household income: $39,939
Total households: 139,127

Number of households with income of . . .
less than $10,000: 12,440
$10,000 to $14,999: 8,713
$15,000 to $24,999: 19,750
$25,000 to $34,999: 20,164
$35,000 to $49,999: 24,812
$50,000 to $74,999: 28,464
$75,000 to $99,999: 13,287
$100,000 to $149,999: 7,887
$150,000 to $199,999: 1,670
$200,000 or more: 1,940

Percent of families below poverty level: 8.4% (46.4% of which were female householder families with related children under 5)

2002 FBI Crime Index Total: 24,104

Municipal Government

The city of Wichita operates under a council-manager form of government, with six council members and a mayor elected to four-year terms.

Head Official: Mayor Carlos Mayans (since 2003; current term expires 2007)

Total Number of City Employees: 3,200 (2004)

City Information: City Hall, 455 N. Main, Wichita, KS 67202; telephone (316)268-4331; fax (316)268-4333; email cshull@wichita.gov.

Economy

Major Industries and Commercial Activity

Wichita's principal industrial sector is manufacturing, which accounted for 21.6 percent of area employment in 2003. Aircraft has long since dominated the industry, and plays such an important role that it has the ability to influence the economic health of the entire region. In the early 2000s a national and international recession combined with the after effects of the terrorist attacks on September 11th to depress the aviation subsector in and around Wichita. Orders for new aircraft plummeted, prompting Wichita's four largest aircraft manufacturers—Boeing Co., Cessna Aircraft Co., Bombardier Learjet Inc., and Raytheon Aircraft Co.—to slash a combined 15,000 jobs between 2001 and 2004. In response, these companies began developing small- and mid-sized airplanes to appeal to business and corporate users.

Healthcare is Wichita's second-largest industry, employing approximately 28,000 people in the local area. Since healthcare needs remain fairly consistent regardless of the economy, this field was not subject to the same pressures that affected other industries in the early 2000s. The Kansas Spine Hospital opened in 2004, as did a critical care tower at Wesley Medical Center.

Several Wichita companies are leaders in their respective fields. Vulcan Chemicals, which operates a manufacturing plant in Wichita, ranks among the country's top producers of chlorinated solvents used to make such products as plastics, film, soft drinks, and electronic circuitry. Cargill Inc., one of the nation's major agribusiness corporations, has made Wichita the corporate headquarters for its Cargill Meat Solution division. The Coleman Company, a pioneer in the production of outdoor recreational gear, was founded in the city in the early twentieth century and remains headquartered there. Other companies based in Wichita include Koch Industries Inc., a diversified company active in chemicals, energy, finance, and paper; Via Christi Health System, a Catholic healthcare system serving Kansas, Oklahoma, and California; and Chance Rides Inc., the nation's largest designer and manufacturer of amusement rides.

Items and goods produced: airplanes, airplane supplies, outdoor recreational equipment and supplies, chemicals, meat products, household appliances, amusement rides

Incentive Programs—New and Existing Companies

Local programs—The City of Wichita offers a number of incentive programs, including Industrial Revenue Bonds and a Neighborhood Revitalization Area Tax Rebate Program, which offers a 75- to 95-percent rebate on increased taxes due to new construction or refurbishment of property in certain areas within the city. The Wichita Business Loan Program has a loan pool of $9 million for existing and new small businesses within Revitalization Strategy Areas. The City of Wichita and the County of Sedgwick may extend tax exemptions for property used for manufacturing, research and development, or storing goods or commodities. Incentives offered by the Wichita Downtown Development Corp. include a Tenant Improvement Grant Fund, Housing and Pilot Landscaping grant programs, Douglas Street Facade Improvement Program, and Historic Preservation Tax Credits.

State programs—Kansas offers Enterprise Zone tax exemptions and credits to manufacturing companies that create at least two new jobs and to non-manufacturing businesses that create at least five new jobs. A Kansas Income Tax Credit may be available to firms that pay above-average wages to employees. The Kansas Existing Industries Expansion Program (KEIEP) and the Kansas Economic Opportunity Initiative Fund (KEOIF) provide loans to existing businesses that invest capital while keeping existing jobs or creating new ones. An income tax credit may be available for research and development expenses. A Kansas constitutional amendment exempts the inventories of merchants and manufacturers from property taxes.

Job training programs—The Investment in Major Projects and Comprehensive Training (IMPACT) program offers assistance in establishing training projects for new employees. The Kansas Industrial Training (KIT) program extends training assistance to new or expanding companies, while the Kansas Industrial Retraining (KIR) program assists companies that are diversifying or restructuring. Training services are also provided by the Wichita Area Technical College, the Kansas Technical Training Institute, and the Greater Wichita Economic Development Coalition, which was founded in 2003.

Development Projects

Downtown Wichita has attracted over $100 million in investment since 2002. In addition to several residential developments, downtown now features the Old Town Square, a $20 million complex encompassing a six-screen movie theater, retail space, and office space. The City Arts buildings opened in 2004, and the Kansas Sports Hall of Fame held its grand opening in April 2005. The largest project in the planning stage is the Wichita Waterwalk. Scheduled for completion in 2007, the $138 million development will house office, retail, and residential space. The River Corridor Improvement Project, which will open in 2006, will enhance public space along the Arkansas River by installing pedestrian bridges, constructing an amphitheater, and erecting the "Keeper of the Plains" statue.

Elsewhere in the city, developments of all sorts are in various stages. VoiceStream Wireless moved into Wichita in 2000, adding 800 new jobs. Other new businesses include Acutel Inc., Advanced Plastic Coating Services Inc., Midwest Technologies Inc., and VeriPrime Inc. The recently renovated Kansas Coliseum opened the Park City Raceway, a dirt racetrack, in May 2003, and the Wichita Art Museum completed a $10 million renovation the following month. The Waterfront shopping district, a 165-acre multi-use complex, and Regency Lakes Shopping Center, a 60-acre retail and restaurant project, were in the works in 2004. The Kansas Spine Hospital opened in Wichita that same year, as did the $70 million critical care tower at Wesley Medical Center.

Economic Development Information: Greater Wichita Economic Development Coalition, 350 W. Douglas, Wichita, KS 67202; telephone (316)268-1133; fax (316)265-7502; email gwedc@wacc.org. Wichita Area Chamber of Commerce, 350 W. Douglas Ave., Wichita, KS 67202; telephone (316)265-7771; fax (306)265-7502; email info@wacc.org

Commercial Shipping

Wichita Mid-Continent Airport is the state's largest commercial and general aviation complex. In addition to transporting passengers, the airport handled 37,000 tons of cargo in 2004. Its major overnight carriers are Airborne Express, DHL, Emery, FedEx, and UPS. Wichita lies on Interstate 35, the only interstate highway that connects the United States with both Canada and Mexico. The city is served by 16 national and regional interstate common carriers. Three major railroads—Union Pacific, Burlington Northern Santa Fe, and Kansas & Oklahoma Railroad—link the city to most major continental markets. Wichita has access to the U.S. Inland Waterway System from two ports located within 200 miles: the Port of Kansas City and the Tulsa Port of Catoosa provide access to the Missouri and Arkansas rivers, respectively. Wichita is home to the Sedgwick County Foreign Trade Zone #161, an area where foreign goods bound for international destinations can be temporarily stored without incurring an import duty.

Labor Force and Employment Outlook

Sedgwick County ranks second in the nation for concentration of manufacturing jobs and skilled labor, and first for employment in aircraft and parts manufacturing. The concentration of manufacturing firms utilizing high technology design is partially responsible for the highly-skilled workforce. Investment in training is also a contributor, as Kansas ranks second in the nation for workforce development spending per capita.

The following is a summary of data regarding the Wichita metropolitan area labor force, 2004 annual average:

Size of nonagricultural labor force: 282,800

Number of workers employed in . . .
  construction and mining: 16,100
  manufacturing: 58,400
  trade, transportation and utilities: 49,500
  information: 6,100
  financial activities: 12,200
  professional and business services: 26,300
  educational and health services: 38,400
  leisure and hospitality: 25,200
  other services: 12,100
  government: 38,500

Average hourly earnings of production workers employed in manufacturing: $19.45 (2004)

Unemployment rate: 6.3% (February 2005)

Largest employers (2004)	Number of Employees
The Boeing Co.	12,300
Cessna Aircraft Co.	8,000
Raytheon Aircraft Co.	7,000
U.S. Government	5,186
Unified School District No. 259	4,955
State of Kansas	4,800
Via Christi Health System	4,795
City of Wichita	3,200
Sedgwick County	2,695
Bombardier Aerospace Learjet	2,500

Cost of Living

The following is a summary of data regarding several key cost of living factors in the Wichita area.

2004 (3rd Quarter) ACCRA Average House Price: $234,693

2004 (3rd Quarter) ACCRA Cost of Living Index: 95.5 (U.S. average = 100.0)

State income tax rate: Ranges from 3.5% to 6.45% (personal); 7.35% (corporate)

State sales tax rate: 5.3%

Local income tax rate: None

Local sales tax rate: 1.0% county tax

Property tax rate: $113.387 per $1,000 assessed valuation (most areas; 2004)

Economic Information: Greater Wichita Economic Development Coalition, 350 W. Douglas, Wichita, KS 67202; telephone (316)268-1133; fax (316)265-7502; email gwedc @wacc.org. Wichita Area Chamber of Commerce, 350 W. Douglas Ave., Wichita, KS 67202; telephone (316)265-7771; fax (306)265-7502; email info@wacc.org

Education and Research

Elementary and Secondary Schools

Unified School District #259, or Wichita Public Schools, is the state's largest elementary and secondary public education system. It is administered by a nonpartisan, seven-member board elected to four-year staggered terms. Board members contract a superintendent.

In 2000 a five-year, $285 million bond issue was implemented to improve all of the district's existing schools and to construct new facilities. Stucky Middle School, the first new middle school in 37 years, opened its doors in 2003, and the Jackson Elementary School opened the following year. All other bond projects are scheduled for completion by the end of 2005.

The following is a summary of data regarding Wichita public schools as of the 2004–2005 school year.

Total enrollment: 48,818

Number of facilities
   elementary schools: 57 (19 are magnet schools)
   middle schools: 17 (5 magnet schools)
   senior high schools: 11 (1 magnet school)
   special schools: 14, including special education centers, early childhood education centers, a boys' ranch, an e-school, and other specialties

Student/teacher ratio: 16:1

Teacher salaries
   minimum: $30,240
   maximum: $46,534

Funding per pupil: $3,863

Wichita offers alternatives to the public school system through a strong parochial school system of approximately three dozen private schools ranging from preschool to high school. The majority of private schools are parochial. Nearly 10,400 students attend facilities of the Catholic Schools of the Diocese of Wichita, which has won numerous national awards from the National Catholic Educational Association. Non-denominational education is offered by Wichita Collegiate School, which offers a college-preparatory curriculum, and the Independent School, which provides the liberal arts education usually reserved for gifted students to average and above-average students.

Public Schools Information: Wichita Public Schools, 201 N. Water, Wichita, KS 67202; telephone (316)973-4000; email info@usd259.net

Colleges and Universities

Wichita State University is a four-year college with about 15,000 students. Six undergraduate colleges (arts and sciences, engineering, fine arts, education, business, and health professions) offer 60 degree programs in more than 200 areas of study. The graduate school offers 44 masters degrees, 10 doctoral programs, and three specialist degree programs in more than 100 areas of study.

Friends University, a liberal arts school founded by Quakers in 1898, is the fastest-growing private university in Kansas. With 3,200 students, it offers an associate degree program, 46 bachelor's degree programs, and nine master's degree programs in the colleges of arts and sciences, business, and continuing education. Newman University, formerly Kansas Newman College, was founded in 1993 as a Catholic two-year teacher's academy. It is now a four-year liberal arts college offering 6 associate's degrees, 27 bachelor's degrees, and 4 master's degree programs.

The University of Kansas School of Medicine-Wichita, at one time affiliated with Wichita State University and now a separate facility, provides medical education in most fields of specialization. The university, which ranks among the top 10 medical schools in the country whose focus is primary care, maintains cooperative programs with area hospitals and operates its own care center on campus and at clinics throughout the city. Other Wichita institutions of higher learning include Southwestern College, Wichita Area Technical College, and Wichita Technical Institute, as well as branches of Baker University, Butler and Cowley county community colleges, and Tabor College of Hillsboro.

Libraries and Research Centers

Nearly two dozen libraries, maintained principally by public institutions and agencies, hospitals, and corporations, are located in Wichita. The Wichita Public Library has 10 branches throughout the city, the newest of which is the Lionel Alford Regional Branch Library, which opened in April 2003. The collection contains more than 900,000 items including books, videos, music CDs, magazines, motor manuals, art prints, CD-ROMs, maps, and books on cassette. Among special collections are the Driscoll Piracy Collection, Kansas and local history, genealogy, motor manuals, music scores, and state documents. The Wichita State University operates a substantial campus library with about one million volumes, more than 4,000 periodical subscriptions, and numerous special collections on a range of subjects pertaining primarily to Kansas and American history. Also based at the university are the Milton Helpern International Center of Forensic Sciences, which specializes in materials relating to crime and forensic problems, and the Institute for Aviation Research.

Among other libraries and research centers in the city are those affiliated with Friends University, the Wichita Art

Museum, the *Wichita Eagle,* the Midwest Historical and Genealogical Society, the Wichita Sedgwick County Historical Society, and the Boeing Co.

The National Institute for Aviation Research, located at Wichita State University (WSU), is home to 15 laboratories for conducting research in such areas as aerodynamics, aging aircraft, crash dynamics, composites and advanced materials, aircraft icing, structural components, virtual reality, and computational mechanics. WSU's College of Engineering is active in a variety of research programs. The Center for the Improvement of Human Functioning conducts research at the far thresholds of disease management, and the John C. Pair Horticulture Research Center conducts turfgrass research.

Public Library Information: Wichita Public Library, 223 S. Main, Wichita, KS 67202; telephone (316)262- 0611; fax (316)262-4540

Health Care

Wichita is a regional center for medical treatment and referral as well as training and research, employing more than 28,000 health care professionals. The region supports 19 acute care and specialty hospitals with approximately 3,000 beds, as well as more than 50 nursing homes and assisted living facilities. Many medical workers and allied staff are educated at the University of Kansas School of Medicine-Wichita, which maintains training programs at three local hospitals. The Kansas Health Foundation, based in Wichita, provides funding in the areas of children's health, leadership, and public health.

Wesley Medical Center, a Level I trauma center and the largest emergency department in the state, provides such services as cancer care, child development, radiosurgery, low vision rehabilitation, senior behavioral health, and treatment of sleep disorders. The Robert J. Dole Department of Veterans Affairs Medical & Regional Office, one of the largest in the nation, treats more than 80,000 outpatients each year. Wesley Medical Center, with 504 beds, provides general medical and surgical care as well as cardiology, neurology, pediatric, and trauma care. Via Christi Health System, a teaching institution affiliated with the University of Kansas School of Medicine-Wichita, provides the largest integrated network of health care providers in Kansas, with such specialized services as gerontology, diabetes, epilepsy, and orthopedics. Other Wichita hospitals include Galichia Heart Hospital, Kansas Heart Hospital, Kansas Surgery & Recovery Center, Select Specialty Hospital of Wichita, Wesley Rehabilitation Hospital, and Kansas Spine Hospital, which opened in 2004.

Health Care Information: Via Christi Regional Medical Center, 929 N. St. Francis St., Wichita, KS 67214; telephone (316)268-5000

Recreation

Sightseeing

Wichita has retained its frontier roots while developing a cosmopolitan ambiance. The Old Cowtown Museum capitalizes on Wichita's past as a stop on the Chisholm Trail with forty-four original, restored, or replica buildings and displays depicting life between 1865 and 1880, along with programs celebrating Wichita's cattle-driving beginnings. Wichita turned the Arkansas River into a cultural asset by redesigning the riverside for public recreation and for popular events such as River Festival. Wichita's sophistication is evident in the city's outdoor sculptures, which number more than 125 and include such works as the large Joan Miro mosaic mural at Wichita State University. Price Woodward Park is located between Century II and the Arkansas River; on the park grounds are several sculptures.

The Botanica, or Wichita Gardens, is located near the banks of the Arkansas River and is the state's only such garden. Lake Afton Public Observatory, with its 16-inch telescope, is open on weekends for astronomy enthusiasts. At the Sedgwick County Zoo, more than 2,500 animals roam an imitation veldt, a tropical rain forest, and a herpetarium that switches night for day. The Great Plains Nature Center features the Koch Habitat Hall, two miles of hiking trails, and the Coleman Auditorium. Tanganyika Wildlife Park, located three miles west of Wichita in Goddard, allows humans to interact with such animals as giraffes, lemurs, and Bengal tigers. Children enjoy the rides and entertainment offered by Joyland, the largest amusement park in Kansas.

Arts and Culture

Wichita supports many organizations in the fine, performing, and visual arts. Century II, the city's center for cultural activities, houses the major performance organizations. The Wichita Symphony Orchestra plays a season of classical, chamber, and pops concerts in Century II's concert hall between September and May; a highlight of the symphony orchestra season is the performance of P.I. Tchaikovsky's *1812 Overture* that concludes the River Festival. The Wichita Pops series features the performances on the "mighty" Wurlitzer organ, which was housed in the New York Paramount Theater. The Metropolitan Ballet's season of concerts always includes a staging of Tchaikovsky's popular *Nutcracker Ballet* during the Christmas season.

The "Keeper of the Plains" statue was donated to the city by its creator, Blackbear Bosin.

Live theater is popular in Wichita. Music Theatre of Wichita features Broadway guest artists performing with a resident company at Century II; the summer season includes five productions in all. The Crown Uptown Dinner Theatre, one of the nation's ten largest dinner theaters, hosts professional performances of Broadway shows. Wichita Children's Theatre & Dance sponsors shows performed by children for children. Wichita Grand Opera offers a professional opera season at Century II, and Wichita Chorus Sweet Adelines International features female barbershop singers.

Museums in the Wichita area are plentiful. The Kansas Sports Hall of Fame opened in Old Town in April 2005 with 126 inductees from Kansas sports. The Wichita Art Museum, the largest museum in Kansas, houses a nationally renowned American Art collection. The Wichita Sedgwick County Historical Museum depicts historical life in the area through unique and informative exhibits. The Museum of World Treasures has an eclectic collection that includes dinosaurs, Egyptian mummies, armor and crown jewels of European royalty, the Hall of American Presidents, and Civil War and World War II artifacts. Exploration Place features interactive exhibits that stimulate curiosity and creativity. The Kansas Underground Salt Museum, located in nearby Hutchinson, will be the Western Hemisphere's only museum to exist in a working salt mine when it opens in late 2005 or early 2006. Other Wichita museums include the Frank Lloyd Wright–Allen Lambe House Museum, the Great Plains Transportation Museum, the Kansas African American Museum, the Kansas Aviation Museum, the Kansas Firefighters Museum, the Lowell D. Holmes Museum of Anthropology, the Mid-America All-Indian Center, the Museum of the Antique Fan Collectors Association, Ulrich Museum of Art at Wichita State University, and Wings Over Wichita.

Festivals and Holidays

The Wichita River Festival, the city's major festival, draws more than 350,000 people for 10 days each May in a celebration centered on the Arkansas River. Held in conjunction with the festival are several other events, including an art and book fair, trolley tours, and a garden party at Botanica. Also held in May is the three-day Kansas Polkatennial. The Old Cowtown Museum presents music and 1870s saloon shows on the weekends from June to Labor Day; the museum also sponsors the Traditional 1870s Independence Days event over the Fourth of July weekend. More than 10,000 people attend the Old Town Concert Series each summer.

Wichita celebrates its jazz heritage with two festivals: the Wichita Jazz Festival in April, and a jazz festival hosted by Friends University in February. The Midwest Winefest is held over three days in April, and the Taste of Wichita takes place in downtown Wichita in early July. The Kansas Flight Festival, founded in 2003 as the Wichita Aviation Festival, features three days of air shows, aircraft displays, and concerts at the Colonel James Jabara Airport in August. September brings the Chili & BBQ Cook-Off. At the Old Cowtown Museum in October the Old-Time County Fair recreates a 1870s Wichita fair.

A number of diversity-based celebrations take place in Wichita throughout the year. Spring brings Multi-Cultural Celebration Week, which features a variety of events celebrating the ethnicity of residents. Traditional Native American dancing is featured at the Intertribal Pow-Wow in July. The Martin Luther King Jr. Celebration is held in January, and an Asian Festival takes place each October. For three days in September, the Wichita Black Arts Festival showcases the artistic heritage of the African American culture. Other multi-cultural events include Cinco de Mayo and the Juneteenth celebration.

Sports for the Spectator

The Wichita Wranglers of the Double-A minor league Texas League play their home baseball games at the Lawrence Dumont Stadium. Each August, this stadium is also the venue for the nation's largest amateur baseball tournament, the National Baseball Congress World Series, which has been held in Wichita since 1931. The Wichita Thunder competes in the Central Hockey League at Kansas Coliseum from October through April.

The Wichita State University baseball team, the Shockers, consistently earns national ranking and holds the record for most victories in a season. Wichita State also fields winning basketball teams in National Collegiate Athletic Association play. Friends University teams, nicknamed the Falcons, play baseball and softball, football, men's golf, women's volleyball, and men's and women's basketball, cross country, soccer, tennis, and track and field. The Jets of Newman University compete in baseball and softball, wrestling, and men's and women's basketball, bowling, cross country, golf, soccer, tennis, and volleyball.

The Wichita International Raceway sponsors drag racing on Saturdays during the summer, while 81 Speedway features dirt track auto races each week between March and October. Parimutuel greyhound racing action takes place year-round at Wichita Greyhound Park.

Sports for the Participant

Wichita maintains 107 municipal parks on nearly 3,000 acres for such activities as volleyball, croquet, softball, and soccer. Eighty-three public tennis courts are augmented by two private clubs; Riverside Tennis Center has been named one of the best public complexes in the country by the U.S.

Tennis Association. For golfers, nine public and nine private courses are located in the area. Fishing and boating are permitted in authorized areas (El Dorado Lake is said to be the spot for prime bass fishing), and water skiing is allowed at Nims Bridge, North Riverside Park. A free fitness trail with 20 exercise stations is maintained in Sim Park. Cycling and rollerskating can be enjoyed in designated areas along the Arkansas River. The Soccer Club operates a regulation size indoor field for practice and league play.

Shopping and Dining

The Wichita area's shopping centers and malls include the state's two largest malls—Towne East and Towne West—with more than 270 stores and restaurants combined. Wichita is an antiques center; a number of antique stores and shops are located in historic houses and in the downtown district. Wichita Old Town, a historic warehouse district, has been restored and offers shops and restaurants. Old Town Underground near the railroad yards has blossomed into an area of unusual shops. Upscale shopping is the attraction on Rock Road, and shoppers also enjoy the Downtown Farm and Art Market. The Newton Factory Outlet Stores lie 20 minutes north of the city.

Wichita restaurants are famous for steaks, prime rib, and barbecue beef, but dining choices also include international cuisine such as Italian, French, Chinese, Mexican, and Indian.

Visitor Information: Greater Wichita Convention & Visitors Bureau, 100 S. Main, Ste. 100, Wichita, KS 67202; telephone (316)265-2800; toll-free (800)288-9424; fax (316)265-0162; email jrolfe@visitwichita.com

Convention Facilities

The principal meeting and convention facility in Wichita is the Century II Performing Arts & Convention Center. With 19 meeting rooms and 3 performance halls, this complex offers 198,000 square feet of exhibit space. The Brown Exposition Center encompasses 93,000 square feet of exhibition space. The Kansas Coliseum, the Cotillion, and the Wichita Scottish Rite Center provide alternatives for corporate events. Many of Wichita's hotels also have meeting space available. The Grand Eagle Ballroom at the Hyatt Regency has 10,164 square feet of meeting space, and the Kansas Grand Ballroom of the Wichita Marriott features more than 7,000 square feet. Two of the exhibit halls at the Radisson Broadview exceed 8,700 square feet of space.

Convention Information: Greater Wichita Convention & Visitors Bureau, 100 S. Main, Ste. 100, Wichita, KS 67202;

telephone (316)265-2800; toll-free (800)288-9424; fax (316)265-0162; email jrolfe@visitwichita.com

Transportation

Approaching the City

Wichita Mid-Continent Airport, a 12-minute drive from downtown, is the destination for most air travelers to Wichita. Thirteen commercial carriers provide 47 daily flights from most cities throughout the United States. In 2004 nearly 1.5 million passengers passed through Mid-Continent, breaking the airport's record. Colonel James Jabara Airport is a general aviation facility accommodating jets and light planes. Amtrak provides passenger rail service 25 miles north of Wichita at Newton, and Greyhound Trailways brings buses into Wichita.

A network of interstate, federal, and state highways links Wichita with the East and West Coasts as well as the Canadian and Mexican borders. Interstates I-35 and I-135 pass directly through metropolitan Wichita, connecting the city with I-40, I-44, and I-70. Major U.S. highways are 54 and 81; state routes include K-42, K-2, K-15, K-254, K-96, and the Kansas Turnpike.

Traveling in the City

Public bus transportation on a fleet of modern, chairlift-equipped buses is operated by Wichita Transit. Nineteenth-century-style streetcars on the Discover Historic Wichita Trolley Tour connect major downtown hotels, Lawrence-Dumont Stadium, Century II Convention Center, and the Old Town area.

Communications

Newspapers and Magazines

Wichita's daily newspaper is the morning *Wichita Eagle*. The *Wichita Business Journal* is the city's weekly business newspaper. Special-interest newspapers and magazines published in Wichita focus on a variety of topics, such as business and economics, aging, antiques and art collectibles, aviation for farmers, shopping news, and community affairs. Feist Publications, publisher of Yellow Book directories, maintains an office in Wichita, and ASR Philanthropic Publishing, producer of books, newsletters, and brochures for fundraising and philanthropic organizations, are headquartered there. Other publications produced in the city include

Wichita Family Magazine, Wichita Kids Newspaper, and *Wichita Register Magazine.*

Television and Radio

Six television stations are based in Wichita; cable service is available. Eleven AM and FM radio stations serve the Wichita metropolitan area with music, news, information, and public interest features.

Media Information: *Wichita Eagle,* 825 E. Douglas, Wichita, KS 67201; telephone (316)268-6000

Wichita Online

City of Wichita home page. Available www.wichitagov.org

Greater Wichita Convention & Visitors Bureau. Available www.visitwichita.com

Greater Wichita Economic Development Coalition. Available www.gwedc.org

Wichita Area Chamber of Commerce. Available www .wichitakansas.org

Wichita Business Journal. Available wichita.bizjournals .com/wichita

Wichita Eagle. Available www.kansas.com/mld/kansas

Wichita Public Library. Available www.wichita.lib.ks.us

Wichita Public Schools. Available www.usd259.com

Selected Bibliography

Beattie, Robert, *Nightmare in Wichita: The Hunt for the BTK Strangler* (New York, NY: New American Library, 2005)

Price, Jay M., *Wichita's Legacy of Flight* (Chicago, IL: Arcadia Publishing, 2003)

Tanner, Beccy, *Bear Grease, Builders and Bandits: The Men and Women of Wichita's Past* (Wichita, KS: Wichita Eagle & Beacon Publishing, 1991)

MICHIGAN

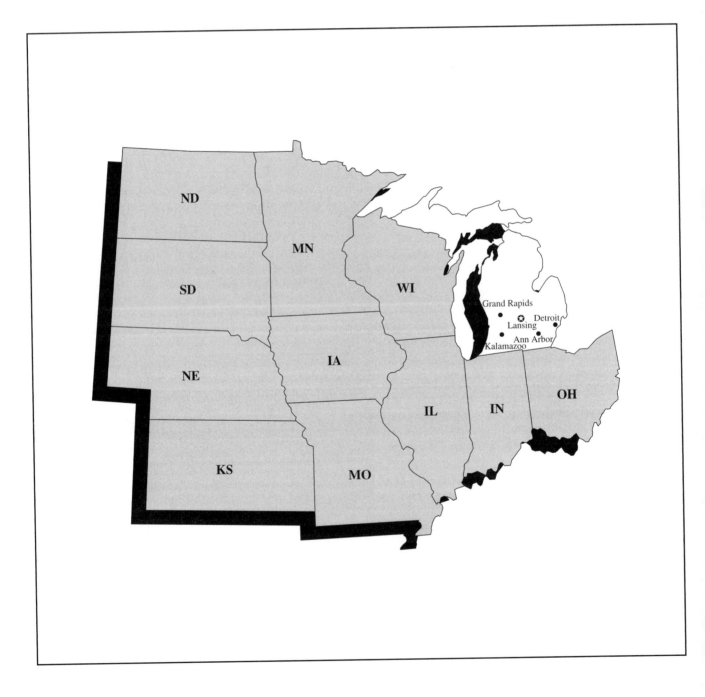

The State in Brief

Nickname: Wolverine State; Great Lakes State
Motto: *Si quaeris peninsulam amoenam circumspice* (If you seek a pleasant peninsula, look about you)

Flower: Apple blossom
Bird: Robin

Area: 96,716 square miles (2000; U.S. rank: 11th)
Elevation: 572 feet to 1,980 feet above sea level
Climate: Temperate with well-defined seasons, tempered by surrounding water; colder in upper peninsula

Admitted to Union: January 26, 1837
Capital: Lansing
Head Official: Governor Jennifer Granholm (D) (until 2007)

Population
  1980: 9,262,000
  1990: 9,368,000
  2000: 9,938,480
  2004 estimate: 10,112,620
  Percent change, 1990–2000: 6.9%
  U.S. rank in 2004: 8th
  Percent of residents born in state: 75.4% (2000)
  Density: 175 people per square mile (2000)
  2002 FBI Crime Index Total: 389,366

Racial and Ethnic Characteristics (2000)
  White: 7,966,053
  Black or African American: 1,412,742
  American Indian and Alaska Native: 58,479
  Asian: 176,510
  Native Hawaiian and Pacific Islander: 2,692
  Hispanic or Latino (may be of any race): 323,877
  Other: 129,552

Age Characteristics (2000)
  Population under 5 years old: 672,005
  Population 5 to 19 years old: 2,212,060
  Percent of population 65 years and over: 12.3%
  Median age: 35.5 years (2000)

Vital Statistics
  Total number of births (2003): 131,024
  Total number of deaths (2003): 86,644 (infant deaths, 1,130)
  AIDS cases reported through 2003: 5,584

Economy
  Major industries: Manufacturing; trade; agriculture; finance, insurance, and real estate; services
  Unemployment rate: 6.9% (March 2005)
  Per capita income: $31,196 (2003; U.S. rank: 20th)
  Median household income: $45,176 (3-year average, 2001-2003)
  Percentage of persons below poverty level: 10.8% (3-year average, 2001-2003)
  Income tax rate: 4.0%
  Sales tax rate: 6.0%

Ann Arbor

The City in Brief

Founded: 1824 (incorporated, 1833)

Head Official: Mayor John Hieftje (D) (since 2000)

City Population
 1980: 107,966
 1990: 109,608
 2000: 114,024
 2003 estimate: 114,498
 Percent change, 1990-2000: 3.5%
 U.S. rank in 1980: 146th
 U.S. rank in 1990: 170th
 U.S. rank in 2000: 195th

Metropolitan Area Population (Washtenaw County)
 1980: 264,740
 1990: 282,937

 2000: 322,895
 Percent change, 1990-2000: 14.1%
 U.S. rank in 1990: 173rd
 U.S. rank in 2000: 179th

Area: 27.0 square miles (2000)
Elevation: 802 feet above sea level
Average Annual Temperature: 49.2° F
Average Annual Precipitation: 30.67 inches

Major Economic Sectors: Government, services, manufacturing, trade, information technology
Unemployment Rate: 4.7% (February 2005)
Per Capita Income: $26,419 (1999)
2004 ACCRA Cost of Living Index: Not reported

2002 FBI Crime Index Total: 3,727

Major Colleges and Universities: University of Michigan; Washtenaw Community College

Daily Newspaper: *The Ann Arbor News*

N

KILOMETERS

0   0.5   1

MILES   0.5   1

NORTH DAKOTA

MINNESOTA

WISCONSIN

SOUTH DAKOTA

MICHIGAN

Ann Arbor

NEBRASKA

IOWA

KANSAS

MISSOURI

ILLINOIS   INDIANA   OHIO

KENTUCKY

HURON RIVER

HISCOCK

FELCH

SPRING

N. MAIN

DEPOT

DETROIT

BEAKES

W. KINGSLEY   E. KINGSLEY

N. FIRST   N. ASHLEY   N. MAIN   N. FOURTH   N. FIFTH   N. DIVISION   N. STATE

E. KINGSLEY

LAWRENCE   INGALLS

MILLER   CATHERINE

CATHERINE

E. ANN

HANDS-ON MUSEUM

E. ANN

W. HURON   E. HURON

E. HURON

E. MEDICAL CENTER

W. WASHINGTON

E. WASHINGTON

FLETCHER

POWER CENTER FOR THE PERFORMING ARTS

WASHINGTON HEIGHTS

S. THAYER

BURTON TOWER

HILL AUDITORIUM

UNIV. OF MICHIGAN NATURAL SCIENCE MUSEUMS

E. LIBERTY

MICHIGAN THEATER

THOMPSON   MAYNARD

N. UNIVERSITY

NATURAL SCIENCE BLDG.

GEDDES

KEMPF HOUSE

PUBLIC LIBRARY

E. WILLIAM

WASHTENAW

GEDDES

W. WILLIAM

HAMILTON

KELSEY MUSEUM OF ARCHAEOLOGY

OBSERVATORY

PACKARD

E. JEFFERSON

UNIVERSITY OF MICHIGAN

W. JEFFERSON

THIRD   SECOND

MUSEUM OF ART

CLEMENTS LIBRARY

S. UNIVERSITY

MICHIGAN UNION

UNIV. OF MICHIGAN FILM & VIDEO LIBRARY

E. UNIVERSITY   CHURCH   S. FOREST

W. MADISON

E. MADISON

S. FIRST   S. ASHLEY   S. MAIN   S. FIFTH   JOHN   S. DIVISION

MONROE

TAPPAN

W. MOSELY

KOCH

HILL

S. STATE

HILL

OLIVIA   LINCOLN

BENJAMIN   MARY

ARBOR

ARCH

OAKLAND

DAVIS

CAMBRIDGE

HOOVER

HOOVER

GREENWOOD

VAUGHN

PAULINE

CIVIC THEATRE

TRACK AND TENNIS BLDG.

PROSPECT

WELLS

MICHIGAN STADIUM

CRISLER ARENA

PACKARD

DEWEY

STADIUM

S. MAIN

STADIUM

Introduction

The seat of Washtenaw County, Ann Arbor is part of a metropolitan statistical area that includes Detroit. Ann Arbor is the home of the University of Michigan, nationally recognized for a tradition of excellence in education. Having gained prominence as a center for high-technology research and development firms, Ann Arbor consistently ranks high on lists of America's best places to live. Frequently noted are its thriving economy, low crime rate, excellent air and water quality, and cultural attractions befitting a much larger city.

Geography and Climate

Ann Arbor is located on the Huron River approximately 40 miles west of Detroit in the heart of southeastern Michigan. It is surrounded by rivers, lakes, forests, and farmland. The continental climate is characterized by four distinct seasons.

Area: 27.0 square miles (2000)

Elevation: 802 feet above sea level

Average Annual Temperature: 49.2° F

Average Annual Precipitation: 30.67 inches

History

Easterners Found Settlement; Industry Attracts Immigrants

By some accounts, Virginians John and Ann Allen and New Yorkers Elisha and Ana Rumsey arrived in the southeastern Michigan Territory in 1824 at a place named Allen's Creek. The men built an arbor for the wild grapevines they found there and named their settlement Anns' Arbor in honor of their wives. According to an unsubstantiated story, however, the settlement was named after a mysterious young woman guide named Ann D'Arbeur who led parties from Detroit westward into the wilderness as early as 1813. Local Native Americans called the settlement ''Kaw-goosh-kaw-nick'' after the sound of John Allen's gristmill. Settlers from Virginia and New York and immigrants from Ireland and Germany soon arrived as other mills, a tannery, and a general store were opened. Ann Arbor was made the seat of Washtenaw County in 1827; it was incorporated as a village in 1833 and chartered as a city in 1851. Ann Arbor's strategic location on the Huron River, the Territorial Road, and the Michigan Central Railroad contributed to its development as a trading center.

City Becomes Site of Major American University

The most significant event in the city's history was the relocation of the University of Michigan from Detroit to Ann Arbor in 1841 by the new state legislature after Ann Arbor citizens effectively lobbied for the move. But it was not until 1852 that the university's first president, Henry Philip Tappan, was appointed. President Tappan broke from academia's traditional classical curriculum and introduced a scientific program and elective courses. Erastus Otis Haven, the university's second president, secured an annual state subsidy to bring the institution's finances under control, and President James Burrill Angell's administration added new buildings and programs during a 38-year tenure. Today the University of Michigan is regarded as one of the nation's top public universities, noted for its undergraduate education, research and graduate programs, and athletic teams that compete in the Big Ten Conference.

The university has been the site of historically significant political announcements. Senator John F. Kennedy introduced his plan for a Peace Corps on the steps of the university's Student Union during his 1960 presidential campaign, and President Lyndon Baines Johnson unveiled his Great Society program at commencement exercises there in 1964. A high proportion of Michigan graduates have become astronauts; in fact, during the *Apollo 15* flight a flag was planted on the moon in recognition of University of Michigan alumni astronauts. The influence of the University of Michigan is such that Ann Arbor is the highest-ranked community in the United States for the educational and medical facilities available to its residents.

High-technology research and development has contributed to the growth in Ann Arbor's population, which also includes an increasing number of residents who commute to work in the Detroit area. Ann Arbor combines big-city amenities with a small-town atmosphere to produce a desirable quality of life. Multi-cultural influences can be seen in the city's shops, restaurants and arts offerings. The arts are a flourishing and integral part of the community, in part fueled by the university.

Historical Information: Kempf House Center for Local History, 312 S. Division, Ann Arbor, MI; telephone (734)994-4898. U of M Bentley Historical Library, 1150 Beal Ave., Ann Arbor, MI; telephone (734)764-3482 (research facility on U of M's North Campus that contains the Michigan Historical Collections)

Population Profile

Metropolitan Area Population (Washtenaw County)
1980: 264,740

1990: 282,937
2000: 322,895
Percent change, 1990-2000: 14.1%
U.S. rank in 1990: 173rd
U.S. rank in 2000: 179th

City Residents

1980: 107,966
1990: 109,608
2000: 114,024
2003 estimate: 114,498
Percent change, 1990-2000: 3.5%
U.S. rank in 1980: 146th
U.S. rank in 1990: 170th
U.S. rank in 2000: 195th

Density: 4,223 people per square mile (2000)

Racial and ethnic characteristics (2000)
  White: 85,151
  Black or African American: 10,070
  American Indian or Alaska Native: 332
  Asian: 13,566
  Native Hawaiian and Pacific Islander: 41
  Hispanic or Latino (may be of any race): 3,814
  Other: 1,384

Age characteristics (2000)
  Population under 5 years old: 5,744
  Population 5 to 9 years old: 5,205
  Population 10 to 14 years old: 5,129
  Population 15 to 19 years old: 12,648
  Population 20 to 24 years old: 20,918
  Population 25 to 34 years old: 20,823
  Population 35 to 44 years old: 14,771
  Population 45 to 54 years old: 12,882
  Population 55 to 59 years old: 4,065
  Population 60 to 64 years old: 2,822
  Population 65 to 74 years old: 4,683
  Population 75 to 84 years old: 3,177
  Population 85 years and over: 1,157
  Median age: 28.1 years

Births (2003, Washtenaw County)
  Total number: 4,210

Deaths (2003, Washtenaw County)
  Total number: 1,924 (of which 27 were infants under the age of 1)

Money income (1999)
  Per capita income: $26,419
  Median household income: $46,299
  Total households: 45,744

Number of households with income of . . .
  less than $10,000: 4,744
  $10,000 to $14,999: 2,543
  $15,000 to $24,999: 5,221
  $25,000 to $34,999: 4,894
  $35,000 to $49,999: 6,873
  $50,000 to $74,999: 8,046
  $75,000 to $99,999: 5,024
  $100,000 to $149,999: 5,129
  $150,000 to $199,999: 1,594
  $200,000 or more: 1,696

Percent of families below poverty level: 4.6% (26.7% of which were female householder families with related children under 5 years)

2002 FBI Crime Index Total: 3,727

Municipal Government

The City of Ann Arbor operates under a mayor-city manager form of government. Half of the ten council members are elected annually by ward (two per ward) to two-year terms. The mayor is elected in a city-wide election to a two-year term every even year.

Head Official: Mayor John Hieftje (D) (since 2000; current term expires 2006)

Total Number of City Employees: 827 permanent employees (2005)

City Information: City Hall, Guy C. Larcom, Jr. Municipal Building, 100 North Fifth Avenue, Ann Arbor, MI 48104; telephone (734)994-2650

Economy

Major Industries and Commercial Activity

The University of Michigan is Ann Arbor's largest employer, accounting for nearly 10 percent of the work force. The majority of remaining jobs are split between manufacturing, health care, automotive, information technology, and biomedical research fields.

Ann Arbor is now the western anchor of high-technology corridors extending from Detroit along I-94 and M-14. Aiding the increase in firms involved in research, development, or testing is the proximity of the University of Michigan and Eastern Michigan University in Ypsilanti, which provide technical resources and an educated workforce. In 2003 the Ann Arbor/Ypsilanti region of Washtenaw County was named a SmartZone by the State of Michigan as one of ten high technology centers with the potential to create jobs of the future. This builds upon the 1999 designation of the Ann Arbor IT Zone. Together these organizations support the area's historically strong industries of information technology, networking and high-speed internet services, life sciences, nanotechnologies, and MEMS. Other high-technology industries include business services, computer and data processing, and instrument development. Ann Arbor's numerous software companies supply a significant amount of the computer programming and devices used in the auto industry.

Trade and information publishing are also strong industries in the region. The Borders Group began as a campus bookstore owned by two University of Michigan graduates and is now a worldwide chain and *Fortune* 500 company with its headquarters in Ann Arbor. The region is also strong in book printing and manufacturing.

Items and goods produced: books, software, computer technology and precision instruments, ball bearings, springs, baling presses, drill heads, tapping and reaming machinery, awnings

Incentive Programs—New and Existing Businesses

Local programs—The Washtenaw Development Council (WDC) is a centralized, free information source for expanding industrial, technological, and major commercial businesses. A public and private partnership, the WDC provides a one-stop source of information and services for new, existing, and relocating businesses in Washtenaw County. Services include company location as well as providing information on location space, financing, and workforce issues. The WDC also works with several industry groups in the county such as the Washtenaw County Manufacturers Council, the Ann Arbor IT Zone, the FastTrack Awards Program, and the Washtenaw Work/Life Consortium. Other areas of service include foreign initiatives, the Business Services Directory and the existing business call program. The WDC also provides community tours and introduction to key business leaders; listing of key resources for start-ups and expanding businesses; tax and financial incentives counseling; access to business, educational and community resources; and provision of business cost, demographic, and other statistical data.

State programs—Incentives on the state level include tax abatements, tax-exempt revenue bonds, public loans, and grants. The Michigan Economic Development Corporation provides a one-stop business assistance resource for any company already in Michigan or considering a location in the state. Professional account managers work with consultants, utilities, associations and local economic development agencies to match businesses with the best opportunities in Michigan. Free services include new business recruitment, business retention, information on the state and its industries, site location and selection, business incentives and financial assistance, employee recruitment and training, permit assistance, and other resources and services.

Job training programs—Michigan offers a coordinated job training system using federal, state, and local resources to provide a highly productive and trained workforce. Grants can provide funding for activities that increase worker productivity. The training itself is done through the institution of the company's choice. Free recruitment and screening services are available for new and expanding employers through the Michigan Employment Security Administration's job service and also through several local school districts. State-sponsored job training programs offered through the Michigan Adult Education Training Initiative include the Job Training Partnership Act, summer youth employment programs, and pre-college programs in engineering and sciences. The Michigan Economic Development Corp. administers a $1.2 million Training Incentive Fund, which provides assistance to employers wishing to upgrade the skills of their current work force. Other programs include Targeted Jobs Tax Credits, and adult and vocational education.

Economic Development Information: Washtenaw Development Council, 3135 South State Street, Suite 205, Ann Arbor, MI 48108; telephone (734)761-9317; fax (734)761-9062

Development Projects

While high-paying automotive manufacturing jobs seem to be disappearing from Ann Arbor as they are throughout the region and, to a lesser extent, from the United States, several automakers continue to invest heavily in new research and development facilities in the area. In 2004 Korean automaker Hyundai broke ground on a new 190,000 square foot Hyundai America Technical Center in nearby Superior Township, a facility that will eventually employ 400. The world's largest pharmaceutical firm, Pfizer, purchased several acres of land in the early 2000s as part of an $800 million expansion and consolidation of its facilities in Ann Arbor. In 2004 Pro Quest, an information publisher, announced plans to sign a 15-year, $35 million lease with a southern Ann Arbor office complex, with plans to build an additional 110,000 square foot facility on the same site. The firm employs 900 workers in the Ann Arbor area.

Commercial Shipping

Air cargo service is available locally at Willow Run Airport, the nation's largest on-demand air charter freight airport. Detroit Metropolitan Airport is a 15-minute drive to the east off I-94. Conrail and three other railroads provide rail freight shipping, and the city is served by six trucking companies. Within a 50-minute drive are the international port facilities of Detroit and Monroe.

Labor Force and Employment Outlook

Ann Arbor employers draw on a pool of well-educated, highly skilled workers. These workers include University of Michigan graduates reluctant to leave the city after graduation and willing to work for less money in exchange for the high quality of life in a small-town setting experienced there.

Still, the number one problem faced by Ann Arbor businesses is the inability to find qualified employees. The city's labor market boasts unemployment rates well below national and state averages, quashing any hopes businesses have of expanding. This problem is coupled with a shortage of land for business. Manufacturing jobs have been on a steady decline that is expected to continue. Additionally, Ann Arbor businesses must increasingly compete with firms located in Detroit and its western suburbs, which have become attractive to Ann Arbor residents willing to commute for higher-paying jobs.

The following is a summary of data regarding the Ann Arbor metropolitan area labor force, 2004 annual average:

Size of non-agricultural labor force: 201,900

Number of workers employed in . . .
   mining and construction: 5,700
   manufacturing: 23,100
   trade, transportation and utilities: 27,400
   information: 3,800
   financial activities: 5,800
   professional and business services: 26,900
   educational and health services: 22,400
   leisure and hospitality: 14,400
   other services: 6,200
   government: 66,000

Average hourly earnings of production workers employed in manufacturing: $25.64 (Detroit metropolitan area)

Unemployment rate: 4.7% (February 2005)

Largest county employers	Number of employees
University of Michigan	30,574
University of Michigan Health Centers	7,645
Visteon	5,581
General Motors Corp./Powertrain Division	4,394
Pfizer Global Research and Development	3,400
St. Joseph Mercy Hospital	3,300

Largest county employers	Number of employees
Eastern Michigan University	2,200
Borders Group	1,295

Cost of Living

Ann Arbor residents enjoy the relative quiet and sophistication of a college town while being afforded tremendous cultural amenities (both in town and within an hour's drive in Detroit)—but all of that does come at a price. A 2004 study placed Ann Arbor housing at $40,000 above the national average. With little available land left within the city limits, homebuyers are increasingly looking to the nearby communities of Chelsea, Dexter, Pinckney, and Superior Township, where construction of new homes boomed throughout the late 1990s and early 2000s. Health care costs in Ann Arbor are above the national norm, a reflection of the high-cost, high-technology care available at the University of Michigan Medical Center.

The following is a summary of data regarding several key cost of living factors in the Ann Arbor area.

2004 (3rd Quarter) ACCRA Average House Price: Not reported

2004 ACCRA Cost of Living Index: Not reported

State income tax rate: 3.9% (2005)

State sales tax rate: 6.0%

Local income tax rate: None

Local sales tax rate: None

Property tax rate: $47.36 per $1,000 of assessed value (2004)

Economic Information: Washtenaw Development Council, 3135 South State Street, Suite 205, Ann Arbor, MI 48108; telephone (734)761-9317; fax (734)761-9062

Education and Research

Elementary and Secondary Schools

The Ann Arbor School District serves the city of Ann Arbor and parts of 8 surrounding townships covering an area of 125 square miles. The district's two conventional high schools, Pioneer and Huron, are among the highest-rated in the state of Michigan. In 2004 the district formulated a plan to build a third high school, an $85 million project to be completed in fall 2007. The alternative high school, Community High near the University of Michigan campus, enjoys tremendous popularity and places students through a lottery program. The Ann Arbor school district is administered by a nine-member non-partisan board that appoints a superintendent. The major emphasis of the system is on early childhood education, mathematics, science, and technology.

The following is a summary of data regarding the Ann Arbor public schools as of the 2003-2004 school year.

Total enrollment: 16,724

Number of facilities
   elementary schools: 20
   junior high schools: 6
   senior high schools: 5 (2 comprehensive and 3 alternative)
   other: 1 preschool

Student/teacher ratio: 16:1

Teacher salaries
   median salary: $48,083

Funding per pupil: $11,125

The Ann Arbor area is also served by several private and religiously affiliated schools.

Public Schools Information: Ann Arbor Public Schools, 2555 South State Street, South, Ann Arbor, MI 48104; telephone (734)994-2200

Colleges and Universities

In Ann Arbor education extends to all facets of life: social, cultural, and economic. The city is home to the University of Michigan, Washtenaw Community College, Concordia College, and Cleary College; located in neighboring Ypsilanti is Eastern Michigan University.

At the heart of the Ann Arbor community is the University of Michigan, recognized as one of the nation's foremost public institutions of higher learning. According to a 2005 survey by *U.S. News & World Report,* the University of Michigan ranked 2nd among U.S. public universities and 22nd among all national universities. The university enrolls about 36,000 students and offers a complete range of programs leading to associate, baccalaureate, master's, and doctorate degrees in 17 schools and colleges. Primary areas of study include liberal arts, architecture and planning, art, business administration, education, engineering, music, natural resources, nursing, pharmacy, dentistry, law, medicine, information and library studies, public health, and social work. Rankings vary from year to year, but several schools, namely law, medicine, business administration, and engineering routinely rank among the top programs in the nation.

Concordia College, affiliated with the Lutheran Church-Missouri Synod, provides associate and undergraduate pro-

grams in such fields as business management, education, and theology. Eastern Michigan University in Ypsilanti is a full-scale state university with an enrollment of 24,000 students. The school is known for its Education program, as well as the colleges of Technology and Business. Washtenaw Community College specializes in vocational and technical training and is the site of a Robotics Repair Program. The school enrolls more than 20,000 annually and has transfer programs with the University of Michigan, Eastern Michigan University, and University of Michigan Dearborn.

Libraries and Research Centers

Approximately 25 libraries and research centers, maintained by a variety of organizations and agencies, are located in Ann Arbor. The Ann Arbor District Library maintains holdings of more than 425,000 materials, including more than 394,000 books and 28,000 CDs, cassette tapes, and books on tapes. There are also more than 315 CD-ROMs for checkout in the collection. In addition to the main Downtown Library, the system operates three branches (Creek, Northeast, and West), with a fourth (Pittsfield) to open soon, plus a bookmobile. In 2005 wireless internet access was added to the Downtown branch, with plans to add it to all branches; all branches currently have wired internet access through a T-1 line.

The Washtenaw County Library is the headquarters of the Huron Valley Library System. The library operates as a traditional public-use facility, and also, through its Library Learning Resource Center, as a center for organizational development to be used for training sessions, meetings, workshops and special events for County government and affiliated organizations. With holdings of more than 40,000 volumes, the library houses a facility for the blind and the physically handicapped; special services include a low-vision center, various aids for the handicapped, homebound service, volunteer taping, and a video library.

The Gerald R. Ford Library contains materials pertaining to the life and career of Gerald R. Ford, former President of the United States. Ford is a University of Michigan alumnus and grew up in Grand Rapids, Michigan, where the library's affiliated Gerald R. Ford Museum is located. The non-circulating collection, which is open to the public, includes 9,000 books, 21 million pages of memos, meeting notes, and other documents, plus papers relating to the war in Vietnam, Cambodia, and Laos, which were released to the public in April 2000.

The University of Michigan library system, consistently ranked among the top 10 research libraries in the country, includes facilities for all colleges within the university as well as for individual academic departments. Holdings of the 19 University Libraries total more than 7 million volumes; nearly 40 special collections include such subjects as American, British, and European literature, radical protest and reform literature, manuscripts, theater materials, and United States and Canadian government documents. In 2005 the library's Shoah Foundation's Visual History Archive was launched, making available 52,000 digitized copies of videotaped testimonies to the persecution of the Nazi regime from nine worldwide Holocaust survivor and Nazi experience groups. The University of Michigan School of Business Administration maintains the Kresge Library; among the nine facilities within the Kresge Library system are the Law Library, the Bentley Historical Library, and the Transportation Institute Library.

Other libraries in Ann Arbor are affiliated with Washtenaw Community College, and corporations, hospitals, and churches.

Research centers are associated primarily with state and federal government agencies. Among the major research centers are the Environmental Research Institute of Michigan, the Institute for Social Research Library, the Michigan Department of Natural Resources Institute for Fisheries Research Library, the National Oceanic and Atmospheric Administration Great Lakes Environmental Research Laboratory, and the Van Oosten Library of the United States Fish and Wildlife Service.

Public Library Information: Ann Arbor Public Library, 343 South Fifth Avenue, Ann Arbor, MI 48104-2293; telephone (734)327-4200; fax (734)327-8309

Health Care

A vital part of the metropolitan Ann Arbor health care community is the University of Michigan Medical Center, ranked in a 2004 *U.S. News & World Report* article as the nation's 11th best hospital. It is a treatment, referral, and teaching complex that houses several facilities: University Hospital, Women's Hospital, Mott Children's Hospital, Holden Perinatal Hospital, Taubman Health Center, and the Medical School as well as emergency services, an adult psychiatric hospital, an anatomical donations program, a burn center, an outpatient psychiatric unit, and an eye care center. The *U.S. News & World Report* also ranked the Medical School 7th among the nation's top research-oriented medical schools; the school graduates about 170 physicians each year. A 2000 theme issue of the *Journal of the American Medical Association,* devoted entirely to the Medical School on its 150th anniversary, described how a university team pioneered extracorporeal membrane oxygenation (ECMO), a device that keeps gravely ill patients alive long enough to allow their bodies to build up their own defenses. ECMO is particularly effective when used on newborns with respiratory failure. The

University of Michigan medical center staff includes more than 800 physicians; about 1,400 more physicians practice within the metropolitan area.

Offering general care are Catherine McAuley Health Center, which operates the Hospice of Washtenaw, home health services, and an Alzheimer's Care and Treatment Center; and St. Joseph Mercy Hospital, which maintains branch clinics in the city and in nearby Saline and the adjacent county of Livingston. Public and private chemical dependency, mental health, urgent care, physical therapy, and fitness programs are also available in Ann Arbor.

Recreation

Sightseeing

A number of museums and buildings of architectural significance are located on the University of Michigan campus. The Rackham Building, which covers two city blocks, is made of Indiana limestone, with bronze window and door frames, a copper-sheathed roof, and Art Deco interior. The University of Michigan Exhibit Museum of Natural History is devoted to Michigan's prehistoric past; it houses the state's largest collection of dinosaur bones, including a 15-foot-tall dinosaur that was the forerunner of the Tyrannosaur, and more than 200 species of birds native to Michigan. There are also exhibits on minerals and biology, Native American life, culture, and artifacts, a planetarium, and a hall of evolution. The most popular exhibit is the Michigan Mastodon, an elephant-like creature that became extinct more than 6,000 years ago.

The Kelsey Museum of Archaeology in Newberry Hall exhibits artifacts, statues, and glass discovered on university excavations in Egypt and Iraq. The Museum of Art in Alumni Memorial Hall is the state's second-largest fine arts collection and exhibits a diverse permanent collection that includes a number of works by James Abbott McNeill Whistler. The Burton Memorial Tower is the world's third-largest carillon and presents weekly concerts during the summer. On the steps of the Michigan Union building, in the heart of the campus, a plaque records the place where in 1962 President John F. Kennedy announced the formation of the Peace Corps.

The Ann Arbor Hands-On Museum displays more than 250 participatory exhibits on the sciences and arts; it is housed in a century-old former fire house. Matthaei Botanical Garden, the university's conservatory and outdoor garden, is a favorite winter oasis.

Domino's Farms is the world headquarters of Domino's Pizza, among several other corporations on a sprawling 217-

acre campus in eastern Ann Arbor. The Prairie House headquarters building was based on a design by architect Frank Lloyd Wright. The site also maintains a petting farm and a herd of American bison. Cobblestone Farm and Kempf House are among the area's other historical tourist attractions. Ann Arbor is rich in architectural history; among some of the city's distinctive buildings are St. Andrew's Church and several homes dating from the early to mid-nineteenth century.

Arts and Culture

The city of Ann Arbor and the University of Michigan offer a broad selection of music, dance, theater, and cinema. The university's Hill Auditorium is considered to rank with the Kennedy Center in Washington, D.C., and Carnegie Hall in New York City as one of the nation's premier performing arts facilities. Built in 1913 and designed by renowned architect Albert Kahn, the venue underwent a massive $40 million renovation before re-opening in 2004. Renovation included interior restorations and improved seating access, but also important infrastructure upgrades to the heating system and the addition, for the first time in its history, of air conditioning. Featuring excellent acoustics, Hill Auditorium houses the Henry Freize Pipe Organ, which was originally unveiled at the 1883 Chicago World's Fair. The University Musical Society, founded in 1879, has hosted virtually all of the world's great performers, conductors, and orchestras throughout its more than 100-year history. The Society schedules dozens of music and dance concerts each year at Hill and other local venues featuring international artists and performing groups.

The Ann Arbor Symphony Orchestra plays a season of concerts at the renovated Michigan Theater, where the Ann Arbor Chamber Orchestra also presents a series of concerts of classical and contemporary music featuring young artists. The Comic Opera Guild is a local amateur company that is the only one of its kind to tour nationally. The university's Gilbert and Sullivan Society presents light opera productions in the spring and winter.

The University's drama and music departments stage several large and smaller productions at campus theaters throughout the year. The Ann Arbor Civic Theater, drawing on experienced local artists, stages 11 dramatic productions a season. The Young People's Theater, recruiting young people from across the country, is an outlet for students to write and perform their own works. Since 1954 the Ann Arbor Civic Ballet has programmed dance performances. The Performance Network is a local studio and theater space for original work by local artists creating theater, film, video, music, and dance. Ann Arbor supports several local art galleries and film theaters, including the Michigan Theater, which shows classic and contemporary films. In addition, several film societies are active in the city—virtually every night of the week there are a variety of classic films

held in small theaters and university lecture halls throughout the city and campus area.

National touring musical acts stage concerts at Hill Auditorium and the University's 13,000-seat Crisler Arena. Smaller acts play any of a number of local clubs, including the Blind Pig and Bird of Paradise for jazz. The Ark is an internationally-recognized venue on the folk music circuit, and also features acoustic blues, rock, and bluegrass.

Festivals and Holidays

The Ann Arbor Folk Festival is one of the largest and most renowned events of its kind, held each January and in 2005 celebrating its 28th year of existence. The Ann Arbor Film Festival (43 years running in 2005) is a week-long event held in March. The juried Spring Art Fair brings together hundreds of artists in all media at the University of Michigan Track and Tennis Building on an early April weekend; a Winter Art Fair is held in October/November. More than 300 dealers gather at the Ann Arbor Antiques Market to sell antiques and collectibles every Sunday from April through November.

''Taste of Ann Arbor'' on Main Street on a Sunday in June offers specialties from participating Ann Arbor restaurants. The Summer Festival, taking place over several weeks in June and July, presents mime, dance, music, and theater. The Ann Arbor Summer Art Fairs, which comprise one of the oldest and largest street art fairs in the country, bring artists from around the country to Ann Arbor to exhibit and sell their work in three separate fairs that spread throughout the entire city and run simultaneously for four days in July; more than a million people attend the Art Fairs. Edgefest, a three-day celebration of jazz and improvised music featuring world-class acts, is held in early October. One hundred fifty artists participate in the Christmas Art Fair at the University of Michigan Coliseum on Thanksgiving weekend.

Sports for the Spectator

The University of Michigan fields some of the country's finest college sports teams, which compete in the Big Ten athletic conference. The Michigan Wolverines football team is among the most storied and recognizable athletic traditions in the nation. Football Saturdays are like a statewide holiday and near-obsession in Ann Arbor during home games; more than 100,000 fans pack Michigan Stadium, the largest college-owned stadium in the country. The Wolverines strongly compete each season for the Big Ten championship and a berth in the Rose Bowl. The Michigan basketball program (home games at Crisler Arena) likewise has a long and celebrated tradition, and the Michigan hockey team (Yost Arena) has won more NCAA championships than any other institution. Other University of Michigan team sports include men's and women's teams competing in gymnastics, wrestling, softball, soccer, baseball, and swimming, golf, and other sports. Professional sporting events in nearby Detroit feature the Tigers (baseball), Pistons (basketball), Lions (football), and Red Wings (hockey).

Sports for the Participant

Among the popular participatory sports that can be enjoyed in Ann Arbor are cycling, running, ice skating, racquetball, paddleball, handball, roller skating, downhill and cross-country skiing, swimming, and tennis. Cycling lanes exist on many of Ann Arbor's main streets; paved paths for walking, running, cycling or skating run along the Huron River. The Ann Arbor Department of Parks and Recreation maintains the city's more than 147 parks and sponsors programs for all age groups. The Nichols Arboretum on the university campus is a 123-acre natural area that serves as a research area for the university and is open to the public for picnicking and hiking. There are more than 50 lakes in Washtenaw County, offering water sports and fishing. The Dexter-Ann Arbor Half-Marathon and 10-K Run is sponsored by the Ann Arbor Track Club and held on a Saturday in May. Ann Arbor is one of the ten best cycling cities in North America, and the Ann Arbor Bicycle Touring Society is the state's largest group for cyclists. The nearby Pinckney-Waterloo Recreation Area has several lakes and miles of trails for hiking and mountain biking. The Huron River can be fished and canoed, and golf is played at city, university-owned, and private courses.

Shopping and Dining

Ann Arbor's Main Street area, consisting of several blocks of specialty shops, brew pubs, nightspots, and restaurants, forms the central commercial district. State Street, the university's major business district, consists of a cluster of retail stores, restaurants, coffee shops, and several record and book shops that include Shaman Drum, one of the nation's best independent book stores, and the original Borders Book Shop. Nickels Arcade, built in 1915 and modeled after a European arcade, houses shops and galleries. South University is a collection of shops and eateries anchoring the other end of central campus. Kerrytown and the Farmers' Market are three restored historic buildings in the Kerrytown district, just east of the Main Street downtown area, that contain more than 30 semi-enclosed shops and other stores offering farm-fresh produce, baked goods, and craft items. Briarwood Mall is anchored by the J.C. Penney and Marshall Field's department stores and has more than 130 stores. Ann Arbor and nearby Saline are considered antiques centers.

The presence of a major state university in Ann Arbor helps explain the city's many fine restaurants and varied cuisines. Hundreds of Ann Arbor restaurants, far more than what is offered in comparably-sized cities, make this a dining destination city. New American cuisine, traditional American fare, Northern Italian, French, Greek, Korean, Ethiopian, Indian,

Japanese, Caribbean, Thai, Turkish, and other cuisines are represented here. A number of restaurants are located in historic or unusual buildings, such as a train depot. Cafe, deli, and pub settings are also popular choices. Zingerman's Delicatessen, near Kerrytown, is an Ann Arbor institution and recognized as one of the top delicatessens in the country. The small shop and its attendant bakery, mail-order business, and catering operations earned it the distinction as *Inc.* magazine's Coolest Small Company in America designation.

Visitor Information: Ann Arbor Convention and Visitors Bureau, 120 West Huron, Ann Arbor, MI 48104; telephone (734)995-7281; toll-free (800)888-9487; email a2info @annarbor.org

Convention Facilities

The major convention and meeting facilities in metropolitan Ann Arbor are situated on the University of Michigan campus. The ballroom of the Michigan Union, containing 6,000 square feet of space, can accommodate 30 exhibit booths and seat 420 people for a banquet and 600 people in a theater setting. The union provides 21 meeting rooms that can be used as break-out rooms. The Rackham Auditorium and Amphitheater seat 1,129 people and 240 people respectively; galleries totaling nearly 4,000 square feet of space hold 25 exhibit booths; and the Assembly Hall hosts receptions for up to 300 participants. The Michigan League offers 5,238 square feet, banquet space for 350, 50 booths, 500 theater seats, and 16 break outs. The Towsley Center for Continuing Medical Education in the medical complex offers two auditoriums, four meeting rooms, a reception area, and a dining room. The Chrysler Center for Continuing Education houses a 225-seat auditorium and four meeting rooms. Among other campus meeting sites for large and small groups are Crisler Arena, Hill Auditorium, Power Center for the Performing Arts, and the Track and Tennis Building.

Washtenaw Community College on Huron River Drive has up to 9,200 feet of space, 8 meeting rooms, and an auditorium. Groups of 30 up to 500 can be accommodated. The Convocation Center at Eastern Michigan University can easily accommodate large groups of up to 9,780 people; floor space in the arena with the seats retracted measures 20,000 square feet or 10,000 with the seats pulled out. The atrium area is 7,000 square feet and is ideal for dinners and receptions; the Convocation Center offers 8 luxury suites and parking for 1,053 cars. Additional meeting facilities are available at the Corporate Training Center on the campus of Eastern Michigan University, Concordia University on Geddes Road, Domino's Farms, the Ypsilanti Marriott (10,000 square feet of function space), the Sheraton (with 2 ballrooms of 6,000 square feet each), Webber's Inn, and the North Campus Holiday Inn. Nearly 3,000 hotel and motel rooms are available.

Convention Information: Ann Arbor Convention and Visitors Bureau, 120 West Huron, Ann Arbor, MI 48104; telephone (734)995-7281; toll-free (800)888-9487; email a2info @annarbor.org

Transportation

Approaching the City

The destination of the air traveler to Ann Arbor is most likely Detroit Metropolitan Airport, which is only 15 minutes east of the city. Served by 14 major commercial airlines, Detroit Metropolitan serviced more than 32 million passengers in 2003, making it the 10th busiest terminal in North America and 17th busiest in the world. 18,000 people are employed at the facility, which also moves more than 500 million pounds of freight each year. Local general aviation facilities include Ann Arbor City Airport and Willow Run Airport. Passenger rail transportation is available from east and Detroit, as well as from the west and Chicago via Amtrak.

Principal highways leading into Ann Arbor are east-west I-94 and M-14 and north-south U.S. 23.

Traveling in the City

Ann Arbor Transit Authority buses link all parts of the city. The University of Michigan also provides free bus service to all campus areas. Downtown, Main Street, and the University of Michigan campus are easily explored on foot.

Communications

Newspapers and Magazines

The Ann Arbor News, which appears evenings Monday through Friday and on Saturday and Sunday mornings, is Ann Arbor's daily newspaper. The student newspaper is *The Michigan Daily,* published daily during the academic year. The *Ann Arbor Observer* is a monthly magazine offering features, profiles, historical articles, business items, restaurant reviews, and a listing of events and exhibits; it also publishes an annual City Guide.

Automobile Magazine, a popular magazine for automobile enthusiasts, is published monthly in Ann Arbor. Other special-interest magazines and scholarly journals cover such subjects as health care, Michigan history, religion, and Asian studies.

Television and Radio

Ann Arbor receives local affiliate television channels, including their national network feeds, broadcasting from surrounding cities such as Lansing and Detroit, plus PBS, and three independents. In addition, local access television is available from CTN on Channels 16-19 via Comcast Cable.

Four AM and FM radio stations based in Ann Arbor furnish diverse programming choices, including jazz, oldies, and middle-of-the-road music; news and information; sports; as well as National Public Radio broadcasting on the Michigan Radio network. Listeners also choose from stations in Detroit; Windsor, Ontario; and other cities.

Media Information: The Ann Arbor News, 340 E. Huron Street, Ann Arbor, MI 48106; telephone (734)994-6989; *Ann Arbor Observer,* 201 Catherine, Ann Arbor, MI 48104; telephone (313)769-3175

Ann Arbor Online

Ann Arbor Area Convention and Visitors Bureau. Available www.annarbor.org

Ann Arbor District Library home page. Available www .annarbor.lib.mi.us

The Ann Arbor News. Available aa.mlive.com

Ann Arbor Public Schools. Available www.aps.k12.mi.us

City of Ann Arbor. Available www.ci.ann-arbor.mi.us

Gerald R. Ford Library. Available redbud.lbjlib.utexas.edu/ ford

Historical Society of Michigan. Available www.atl46.atl .msu.edu/hsm.html

The Michigan Daily. Available www.pub.umich.edu/daily

The University of Michigan home page. Available www .umich.edu

Washtenaw Development Council. Available www.wdc-econdev.com

Selected Bibliography

Along the Huron: The Natural Communities of the Huron River Corridor in Ann Arbor, Michigan (Ann Arbor: University of Michigan Press, 1999)

University of Michigan Museum of Art, et al., *From Ansel Adams to Andy Warhol: Portraits and Self-Portraits from the University of Michigan Museum of Art* (Ann Arbor: University of Michigan Press, 1994)

Detroit

The City in Brief

Founded: 1701 (incorporated, 1815)

Head Official: Mayor Kwame Kilpatrick (D) (since 2001)

City Population
  1980: 1,203,339
  1990: 1,027,974
  2000: 951,270
  2003 estimate: 879,575
  Percent change, 1990–2000: −7.4%
  U.S. rank in 1980: 6th
  U.S. rank in 1990: 7th
  U.S. rank in 2000: 14th

Metropolitan Area Population (CMSA)
  1990: 4,266,654
  2000: 4,456,428

Percent change, 1990-2000: 5.2%
U.S. rank in 1990: Not reported
U.S. rank in 2000: 7th (CMSA)

Area: 138.7 square miles (2000)
Elevation: 581 feet above sea level at Detroit River
Average Annual Temperature: 48.6° F
Average Annual Precipitation: 30.97 inches of rain, 45 inches of snow

Major Economic Sectors: Services; trade; manufacturing; finance, insurance, and real estate
Unemployment Rate: 8.2% (February 2005)
Per Capita Income: $14,717 (1999)

2002 FBI Crime Index Total: 85,035

Major Colleges and Universities: Wayne State University, University of Detroit-Mercy

Daily Newspapers: *Detroit Free Press; Detroit News*

Introduction

Detroit is the seat of Michigan's Wayne County, the center of a consolidated metropolitan statistical area that includes Ann Arbor and Flint, and the center of a metropolitan area that includes Oakland County, third wealthiest in the country. One of the oldest settlements in the Midwest, Detroit played an instrumental role in the development of the Northwest Territory. During the War of 1812 Detroit became the only major American city ever to surrender to a foreign power; in 1847 the city lost its status as state capital when the legislature moved the state headquarters to Lansing. Detroit was a leading regional economic power in the nineteenth century. The invention of the automobile and its mass production in Detroit headed by Henry Ford changed American and world culture. As more and more manufacturing jobs moved to lower-wage areas of the U.S. and increasingly overseas, Detroit's population declined and the economy struggled. In the early 1990s Detroit's position as the automobile capital of the world was being challenged by foreign competition. Throughout, though, the city's metropolitan area has grown and the regional economy diversified, making metropolitan Detroit still one of the largest and most prosperous areas of the country. Detroit has a long history of producing groundbreaking and influential musical talent, such as the Motown greats Iggy Pop, Bob Seger, and the White Stripes, known throughout the world. City sports franchises such as the Detroit Tigers, Red Wings, and Pistons are among the most storied in American history.

Geography and Climate

Detroit is set on the Detroit River; the metropolitan area includes the St. Clair River, Lake St. Clair, and the west end of Lake Erie. The land is nearly flat, rising gently northwestward from the waterways, then becoming rolling terrain. The climate is influenced by the city's location near the Great Lakes and its position in a major storm track; climatic variations also arise from the urban heat island, the effect becoming most apparent at night, when temperatures downtown will remain significantly higher than those in suburban locations. The city enjoys four distinct seasons. Winters are generally long and cold, and storms can bring combinations of rain, snow, freezing rain, and sleet with heavy snowfall possible at times. Annual snowfalls average around 45 inches. During the summer, storms pass to the north, allowing for intervals of warm, humid weather with occasional thunderstorms that are followed by days of mild, dry weather. Autumn colors can be spectacular, particularly to the north of the city. Air pollution coming from heavy

industry in the area is said to have been minimized with state-of-the-art pollution control efforts.

Area: 138.7 square miles (2000)

Elevation: 581 feet above sea level at Detroit River

Average Daily Temperatures: January, 28.1° F; July, 72.3° F; annual average, 48.6° F

Average Annual Precipitation: 30.97 inches of rain, 45 inches of snow

History

Riverside Stronghold Established by French

In July 1701, Antoine de la Mothe Cadillac and his party landed at a riverbank site chosen because the narrow strait there seemed strategically situated for protecting French fur trading interests in the Great Lakes. The river was called d'Etroit, a French word meaning "strait." Cadillac and his men built Fort Pontchartrain on the site, naming the fort after Comte de Pontchartrain, French King Louis XIV's minister of state; soon a palisaded riverfront village developed nearby. Cadillac named the settlement "ville d'etroit," or city of the strait. Eventually the name was simplified to Detroit.

The control of Detroit changed hands three times during the eighteenth century. At the conclusion of the French and Indian War, the resulting treaty specified the surrender of Detroit to Great Britain. Under Henry Hamilton, the settlement's British governor, armies of Native Americans were encouraged to scalp frontier settlers for rewards, earning Hamilton the sobriquet, "Hair Buyer of Detroit." France's tribal allies, led by Ottawa chief Pontiac, plotted to capture Detroit; when the plot failed, they continued their siege of the fort.

At the end of the American Revolution, the United States claimed lands west of the Alleghenies by treaty, but the British refused to leave Detroit and other western forts, encouraging allied tribes to attack settlers. It was not until two years after General Anthony Wayne defeated the Native Americans at the Battle of Fallen Timbers in 1796 that the British finally left Detroit. During the War of 1812, General William Hull turned Detroit's fort over to the British without a fight, thus making Detroit the only major American city ever to be occupied by a foreign power. The United States regained control of the settlement in 1813 following Oliver H. Perry's victory in the Battle of Lake Erie.

Manufacturing Center Becomes Automobile Capital

Detroit was incorporated as a town in 1802 and as a city in 1815. In 1805 Detroit was selected the capital of the newly created Michigan territory. On June 11, 1805, a fire totally destroyed the city, and while all residents survived, 200 wood structures were reduced to ashes. Local Catholic leader Father Gabriel Richard observed at the time, ''Speramus meliora; resurget cineribus (We hope for better things; it will arise from the ashes).'' His statement became the city's motto. Augustus B. Woodward, one of the new territory's judges, awarded a larger piece of land to each citizen who had lost his home. To create a street design for Detroit, Woodward selected Pierre Charles L'Enfant's plan for Washington, D.C.: a hexagon with a park in the middle and wide streets radiating outward in a hub-and-spoke pattern. As Detroit grew, additional hexagons could be added parallel to the original one. This idea was adopted then eventually abandoned and a grid street pattern was superimposed over the hexagonal design. Michigan gained statehood in 1837; ten years later, fearing Detroit's vulnerability to foreign invasion, the young legislature relocated Michigan's capital from Detroit to Lansing.

Detroit's early economic development was spurred by a combination of factors: the opening of the Erie Canal in 1826, the city's Great Lakes location, the increasing use of rail transport, the growing lumber and flour-milling industries, and the availability of a skilled labor force. The Detroit Anti-Slavery Society was organized in 1837 and the city was a station on the Underground Railroad. Abolitionist John Brown brought slaves to Detroit in 1859 and there purportedly planned with Frederick Douglass the notorious raid on Harpers Ferry, Virginia. During the Civil War Detroit provided supplies and provisions to the Union cause. By the end of the century Detroit had emerged as an important industrial and manufacturing center.

In 1896 Charles B. King determined Detroit's destiny when he drove a horseless carriage on the city streets. Soon Henry Ford introduced his own version of the conveyance, and Detroit was on its way to becoming the automobile capital of the world. Along with Ford, such automotive pioneers as W.C. Durant, Walter P. Chrysler, Ransom Olds, Henry Leland, and the Dodge brothers laid the foundation for the companies that emerged as the Big Three auto makers— Ford, General Motors, and Chrysler—by the latter half of the twentieth century.

Development Brings New Challenges

The automotive industry brought thousands of immigrants into Detroit during the 1920s. Then during the Great Depression the industry was severely shaken, leaving one-third of the workforce out of jobs in 1933. The rise of the union movement under the leadership of Walter Reuther led to sit-down strikes in Detroit and Flint in 1937, resulting in anti-union violence. Federal legislation helped the United Automobile Workers win collective bargaining rights with General Motors and Chrysler in 1937 and with Ford Motor

Company in 1941. During World War II, Detroit turned its energies to the war effort as Ford opened a bomber factory and Chrysler a tank plant, leading to a new nickname for Detroit—''the arsenal of democracy.''

Detroit's racial tension, traceable to a race riot in 1863, erupted in 1943 when violence resulted in the deaths of 35 people and injury to more than 1,000 others. Much progress was made in solving Detroit's race problems after the 1943 outbreak. Like many urban areas in the late 1960s, however, the city was forced to confront the issue once again when civil disturbances exploded in July 1967; 43 people were killed, hundreds injured, and entire city blocks burned to the ground. The organization New Detroit was founded as an urban coalition to resolve issues of education, employment, housing, and economic development, which were seen as the root causes of race problems.

A Modern Detroit Emerges

In 1970 a group of business leaders formed Detroit Renaissance to address questions of Detroit's future. The following year the group, restructured under chairman Henry Ford II, announced plans for construction of the Renaissance Center, the world's largest privately financed project, as a symbol of the new Detroit. In 1996 General Motors Corporation purchased the Renaissance Center for its new global headquarters.

In 1974 Detroit elected its first African American mayor, Coleman A. Young. In common with mayors of other large ''rust belt cities,'' Mayor Young oversaw a city in which white residents fled to the suburbs and Detroit went into a severe economic decline. In 1993 Mayor Young announced that he would not seek a sixth term. The following year Dennis W. Archer assumed the mayorship of Detroit. Highly regarded by citizens and business leaders, Archer won national recognition for himself and his city. By the mid-1990s, after many years of headlines that linked the city with words like ''crime,'' ''decay,'' and ''arson,'' Detroit was being described as ''the comeback city,'' where according to the *Chicago Tribune,* ''a new day may be dawning on this most maligned of America's big cities.''

The early years of the twenty-first century saw mixed results in Detroit's resurgence. New Mayor Kwame Kilpatrick, a charismatic, young politician born and bred in the city, took over the reins at City Hall in 2001. While several large-scale development projects, including three new casinos, continued downtown's transformation, the neighborhoods continued to struggle with problems of blight, poor city services, and declining population. The 2005 elections would be a referendum on Mayor Kilpatrick's direction for the city.

Historical Information: Detroit Public Library, Burton Historical Collection, 5201 Woodward Ave., Detroit, MI

48202; telephone (313)833-1480. Detroit Historical Museum, 5401 Woodward Ave., Detroit, MI 48202; telephone (313)833-1805

Population Profile

Metropolitan Area Residents
1990: 4,266,654
2000: 4,456,428
Percent change, 1990–2000: 5.2%
U.S. rank in 1990: Not reported
U.S. rank in 2000: 7th (CMSA)

City Residents
1980: 1,203,339
1990: 1,027,974
2000: 951,270
2003 estimate: 879,575
Percent change, 1990–2000: −7.4%
U.S. rank in 1980: 6th
U.S. rank in 1990: 7th
U.S. rank in 2000: 14th

Density: 6,858 people per square mile (2000)

Racial and ethnic characteristics (2000)
  White: 116,599
  Black or African American: 775,772
  American Indian and Alaskan Native: 3,140
  Asian: 9,268
  Native Hawaiian and Other Pacific Islander: 251
  Hispanic or Latino (may be of any race): 47,167
  Other: 24,199

Percent of residents born in state: 70.6% (2000)

Age characteristics (2000)
  Population under 5 years old: 76,232
  Population 5 to 9 years old: 93,882
  Population 10 to 14 years old: 83,361
  Population 15 to 19 years old: 68,707
  Population 20 to 24 years old: 65,654
  Population 25 to 34 years old: 144,323
  Population 35 to 44 years old: 136,695
  Population 45 to 54 years old: 115,971
  Population 55 to 59 years old: 38,045
  Population 60 to 64 years old: 29,344
  Population 65 to 74 years old: 52,863
  Population 75 to 84 years old: 35,213
  Population 85 years and over: 10,980
  Median age: 30.9 years

Births (1999)
  Total number: 15,800

Deaths (1999)
  Total number: 10,104

Money income (1999)
  Per capita income: $14,717
  Median household income: $29,526
  Total households: 336,482

Number of households with income of . . .
  less than $10,000: 64,304
  $10,000 to $14,999: 27,914
  $15,000 to $24,999: 54,133
  $25,000 to $34,999: 45,063
  $35,000 to $49,999: 49,930
  $50,000 to $74,999: 50,432
  $75,000 to $99,999: 23,430
  $100,000 to $149,999: 15,291
  $150,000 to $199,999: 2,887
  $200,000 or more: 3,098

Percent of families below poverty level: 21.7% (of which, 48.6% were female householder families with related children under 5 years)

2002 FBI Crime Index Total: 85,035

Municipal Government

The government of the city of Detroit is administered by a mayor and a nine-member council. The mayor, who is not a member of council, and councilpersons are elected to four-year terms. Council members are elected in city-wide elections, as opposed to a ward system.

Head Official: Mayor Kwame Kilpatrick (D) (since 2001; current term expires December 31, 2005)

Total Number of City Employees: 13,468 (2004)

City Information: Office of the Mayor, Coleman A. Young Municipal Center, 2 Woodward Ave., Detroit, MI 48226; telephone (313)224-3400

Economy

Major Industries and Commercial Activity

Automobile manufacturing continues to be a primary force in the Detroit economy, and Detroit is the nation's only older city that is home to a state-of-the-art auto assembly plant. In recent years, however, dependence on the auto industry has decreased—the city lost 39 percent of its manufacturing jobs in the 1980s—while the services sector has increased. Still, the automobile rules, and as go auto sales, so goes the Detroit area economy. While manufacturing has globalized, virtually all of the key engineering, administrative, and testing functions of the Big Three take place in the Detroit area, employing thousands of highly-skilled and well-paid workers. Most of the world's suppliers of auto parts, such as Delphi and Guardian Industries are also located in Detroit, and advertising firms such as Campbell-Ewald, BBDO, and McCann-Erickson, do millions of dollars in annual business with the large automakers.

There is also a budding industry growing up around firms researching hydrogen fuel cells and other non-petroleum power generating technologies that may drive the automobiles of the future. More than 75 percent of the labor force is employed in non-manufacturing jobs in such areas as research and development; accounting, law, and financial services; computer services; and personnel and clerical support. The Henry Ford Health System is the sixth largest employer in the state and is a major research center. Detroit ranks among the five major financial centers in the United States; offices of all the ''Big Eight'' accounting firms are also located there.

Metropolitan Detroit is the world headquarters for General Motors Corp., Ford Motor Co., DaimlerChrysler Corp., and Volkswagen of America. Other national and international corporations headquartered there include Kmart (which merged with Chicago-based Sears & Roebuck in 2004), Compuware, The Budd Company, American National Resources, and Federal Mogul. Oakland County, one of the country's wealthiest counties and directly north of the city, promotes its Auburn Hills area as ''Automation Alley'' due to the large number of robotics firms that have located there in recent years.

Items and goods produced: automobiles and automobile products, gray iron, machine tools and fixtures, foundry products, paints, varnishes, lacquers, chemicals, pleasure boats, paper and twine, air conditioning equipment, aircraft bearings and cushions, bolts, screws, nuts, boilers, tanks, ball bearings, tools, steel plates, flues and tubes, rubber goods, non-electrical machinery and automation equipment in pharmaceuticals, rubber products, synthetic resins, computer software, and robotics equipment and technology.

Incentive Programs—New and Existing Companies

Local programs—Revitalization of Detroit's downtown and neighborhoods is a top priority for city leaders. The Mayor's Office of Neighborhood Commercial Revitalization offers help via grants to community organizations operating or opening shops in city neighborhoods.

State and federal programs—Parts of Detroit are designated Michigan Renaissance Zones, which are virtually tax free

for any business or resident presently in or moving there. Detroit is one of only five cities nationwide designated a federal empowerment zone. Businesses in the 18.35-square-mile zone are eligible for federal incentives. Other incentives on the state level include tax abatements, tax-exempt revenue bonds, public loans and grants. The state administers an award-winning brownfield redevelopment program, community development block grants, long-term fixed rated financing for small and medium-sized businesses, and more.

Job training programs—In 2003 new mayor Kwame Kilpatrick created the Detroit Economic Development Organization, which has an Employment and Training Department. Several outstanding nonprofit organizations also maintain job training facilities, including Goodwill Detroit and Focus:HOPE, a now-legendary Detroit organization founded by a Catholic priest and other community leaders in the aftermath of the devastating 1967 riots. The center provides training in everything from basic reading to high-technology machining and computer-aided design.

Michigan offers a coordinated job training system using federal, state, and local resources to provide a highly productive and trained workforce. Grants can provide funding for activities that increase worker productivity. The training itself is done through the institution of the company's choice. Free recruitment and screening services are available for new and expanding employers through the Michigan Employment Security Administration's job service and also through several local school districts. Michigan Economic Development Corp. (MEDC) administers a $30 million job training program, which provides assistance to employers to train or retrain workers to meet marketplace needs. MEDC also administers Michigan Economic Growth Authority grants, which award credits against Michigan's single business tax to new or expanding businesses.

Development Projects

While Detroit continues to experience population loss similar to other large industrial cities, significant incentives such as the availability of inexpensive land and federal empowerment zone money have led to a development boom over the last decade. Since the late 1990s and the administration of former Mayor Dennis W. Archer, business investment in the city of Detroit has surpassed $15 billion. So many projects were announced that in 1999 *Site Selection* magazine named Detroit its number one metropolitan area for business development for the third consecutive year. Detroit attracted 1,133 new or expanded facilities that year, almost double the nearest competitor, Chicago. Among the new projects in Detroit completed in the early 2000s are Campus Martius, a giant office (housing the headquarters of Compuware, one of the world's largest software development companies), retail, and hotel development considered the most important downtown project in decades; two stadiums—the $450-million Ford Field, a domed multi-use stadium built in part from the massive Hudson's warehouse building, and the $285 million Comerica Park, which opened in 2000 as the new home of the Major League Baseball's Detroit Tigers; and three casinos, which generate hundreds of millions of dollars in much-needed tax revenue and provide hundreds of jobs. Further south, Wayne State University broke ground on an expansion of its 200-acre Detroit campus by establishing a research and technology park amid an evolving residential and office district. The Detroit Symphony Orchestra also got into the action, with a privately funded renovation of Orchestra Hall on Woodward, along with construction of the adjacent Max M. Fisher Music Center, a new 450-seat recital hall, and a multi-million dollar, state-of-the-art music education center.

Economic Development Information: Detroit Regional Chamber of Commerce, One Woodward Ave., Suite 1900, PO Box 33840, Detroit, Michigan 48232-0840; telephone (313)964-4000.

Commercial Shipping

Detroit is a major international market. The Greater Detroit Foreign Trade Zone, the largest zone in the country, processes $2 billion in goods annually. The passage in 1989 of the United States/Canada Free Trade Agreement established the largest free trading block in the world, further expanding the parameters of the Detroit market. Detroit is adjacent to Windsor, Ontario, Canada, and more foreign trade passes through the port than any other in the United States.

The Port of Detroit has direct access to world markets via the Great Lakes/St. Lawrence Seaway System. The Port is comprised of seven privately-owned terminals with thirteen berths on the Detroit and Rouge Rivers. All types of cargo can be processed through port facilities; in 2000 cargo volume totaled more than 17 million tons. Service is provided by four tug and barge lines as well as two auxiliary companies, one of which operates a mail boat that is the only boat in the United States with its own zip code.

The tremendous amount of goods produced in Detroit requires a vast distribution system relying not just on the waterways, but also rail and truck carriers. More than 700 motor freight carriers use Greater Detroit's extensive highway system to transport goods to points throughout the United States and Canada. Trucking service is coordinated with that provided by the four rail lines maintaining facilities in Detroit.

Labor Force and Employment Outlook

Despite the efforts of Governor Jennifer Granholm to maintain the state's manufacturing base and recruit new companies to Michigan, Michigan's unemployment rate of 7.2 percent in 2005 was among the highest in the U.S. in the early 2000s. Reflecting a nationwide trend, the biggest loss of jobs was in the generally high-paying manufacturing sector. In addition, the nation's deep recession following the 2001 World Trade Center attack brought deep job cuts and layoffs in the automotive industry; not surprisingly Detroit fared even worse, and in 2005 the jobless rate in the city was at 8.2 percent. Much of an anticipated rebound in the region's economy and job growth the second half of the decade was expected to come in the high-growth regions of Oakland County (to the north of Detroit), Macomb County (northeast), and Washtenaw County and greater Ann Arbor (to the west).

The following is a summary of data regarding the Detroit metropolitan area labor force, 2004 annual average:

Size of non-agricultural labor force: 2,051,000

Number of workers employed in . . .
   construction and mining: 85,800
   manufacturing: 297,800
   trade, transportation and utilities: 383,000
   information: 36,200
   financial activities: 117,000
   professional and business services: 357,700
   educational and health services: 256,200
   leisure and hospitality: 181,600
   other services: 98,500
   government: 237,300

Average hourly earnings of production workers employed in manufacturing: $24.85

Unemployment rate: 8.2% (February 2005)

Largest employers (2002)	Number of employees
Detroit Public Schools	26,000
City of Detroit	20,799
The Detroit Medical Center	11,836
U.S. Government	11,363
Chrysler Group	9,707
Henry Ford Health System	7,337
General Motors Corp.	6,865
U.S. Postal Service	6,157
St. John Health	5,767
State of Michigan	5,637

Cost of Living

A 2004 worldwide survey conducted by Mercer Human Resource Consulting ranked Detroit the 16th costliest American city to live in, and the 101st most expensive worldwide. In 2003 the median home price in the city was $145,000, compared to $163,000 nationally.

The following is a summary of data regarding several key cost of living factors in the Detroit area.

2004 (3rd Quarter) ACCRA Average House Price: $324,420

2004 (3rd Quarter) ACCRA Cost of Living Index: 107.5 (U.S. Average = 100.0)

State income tax rate: 3.9% (2005)

State sales tax rate: 6.0%

Local income tax rate: 3.0% residential; 1.5% non-residential

Local sales tax rate: None

Property tax rate: $67.97 per $1,000 assessed valuation (2003 millage)

Economic Information: Detroit Regional Chamber of Commerce, One Woodward Ave., Suite 1700, PO Box 33840, Detroit, MI 48232-0840; telephone (313)964-4000.

Education and Research

Elementary and Secondary Schools

Like many large urban school districts, the Detroit Public School District has struggled mightily to maintain a quality level of education in the face of such daunting problems as loss of population, budget shortfalls due to a dwindling local tax base and state-supplied resources, political infighting, and the enormous social implications of a largely impoverished city population. In 1999 the Michigan state legislature authorized the Detroit mayor's office to take control of the Detroit Public Schools after years of failed efforts at reform by the school board. The mayor appoints six of seven school board members, but the chief executive of the school district makes all the decisions. By 2005, under new CEO Kenneth C. Burnley, the district was able to report some positive gains in state-mandated test scores, as well as an ongoing school consolidation plan that sought to make the district more financially workable. A large number of state-mandated charter schools also provided some relief to the district, giving parents more options in placing children in smaller schools, many of which stress discipline, fundamental education in reading and mathematics, and even institute a dress code or school uniform policy. In addition, Rogers High School, Renaissance High, and Detroit Cass Technical High School consistently rank among the best schools in the state in the numbers of students that graduate and go on college.

The following is a summary of data regarding the Detroit public schools as of the 2003–2004 school year.

Total enrollment: 173,742

Number of facilities
  elementary schools: 168
  middle schools: 85
  high schools: 40
  other: 12 alternative education; 4 vocational-technical schools

Student/teacher ratio: 30.6:1

Teacher salaries
  average (statewide): $54,020

Funding per pupil: $10,031

Several private and parochial school systems offer educational alternatives at pre-school, elementary, and secondary levels, including at the highly regarded University of Detroit Jesuit High School. In 2004 the Roman Catholic Archdiocese was forced to close several of its schools within the city limits and suburbs due mainly to declining populations in some parishes. Specialized curricula have been designed by the Japanese Society of Detroit Hashuko-Saturday School, Burton International School, Liggett and Waldorf schools, Friends School, and W.E.B. DuBois Preparatory School.

Public Schools Information: Detroit Public Schools, 5057 Woodward Ave., Detroit, MI 48202; telephone (313)494-1010

Colleges and Universities

Wayne State University is Detroit's largest institution of higher learning and Michigan's only urban research university. Approximately 33,000 students are enrolled in 12 schools and colleges, including the colleges of medicine, nursing, and pharmacy and allied health, and the law school. More than 350 major courses of study are offered; particularly strong programs are offered in the college of engineering and the school of fine and performing arts, which includes a nationally recognized drama program. Wayne State is one of 98 universities nationwide to be designated a Carnegie One Research University. The university's 203-acre campus forms part of downtown Detroit's cultural center along the Woodward Avenue corridor; nearby are the Detroit Institute of Arts, the main branch of the Detroit Public Library, and the Museum of African American History.

The University of Detroit-Mercy, a Roman Catholic institution run by the Jesuit order of priests for more than 125 years, enrolls more than 6,000 students in baccalaureate, master's, and doctorate programs in the arts and sciences; the university also administers schools of law and dentistry. Approximately one-third of its students are minorities, and the university has been called one of the most diverse and one of the best educational values in the Midwest by *U.S. News and World Report* magazine. Marygrove College, located adjacent to the University of Detroit campus, is also affiliated with the Catholic Church.

The Center for Creative Studies in Detroit's Cultural Center is a private, four-year college that offers bachelor of fine arts degrees in animation and digital media, crafts, communication design, fine arts, industrial design, interior design, and photography. Colleges located in neighboring suburbs include Detroit College of Business in Dearborn, Lawrence Technological University in Southfield, the Dearborn campus of the University of Michigan, Cranbrook Academy of Art in Bloomfield Hills, and Oakland University in Rochester. Greater Detroit has a wide selection of community colleges. Central Michigan University maintains centers throughout metropolitan Detroit. Additionally, Eastern Michigan University and the University of Michigan are within a 40-minute drive to the west of the city; Michigan State University in East Lansing is about a 90-minute drive northwest.

Libraries and Research Centers

The Detroit Public Library, founded in 1865, is not only the city's largest library, it is the largest municipal library system in the state, maintaining 23 branches. The main facility houses more than 3 million book volumes and bound periodicals in addition to 7,200 periodical subscriptions, more than 738,000 microfiche and microfilms, and recordings and videos. Special collections include materials pertaining to national automotive history, Michigan, the Great Lakes, the Northwest Territory, and African Americans in the performing arts.

The Wayne State University Libraries system ranks among the top 60 libraries in the Association for Research Libraries. It is comprised of a central facility with about 3 million volumes and five departmental libraries with separate holdings, including law and medical libraries. In addition, the university offers a nationally ranked American Library Association-accredited Library and Information Science Program. A United States documents depository, the library has special collections in oral history, children and young people, photography, social studies, chemistry, and women and the law.

The University of Detroit-Mercy Library system maintains four separate libraries—the McNichols Campus Library, the Outer Drive Urban Health Education and Dental Library, the Instructional Design Studio/Outer Drive, and the Kresge Law Library. Together they house more than one-half million volumes, 5,000 leading literary, health, scientific and professional print and electronic journals, 11,000 audiovisual titles, and a collection of over 90,000 U.S. Federal and State government documents.

Research centers affiliated with Wayne State University conduct activity in such fields as labor and urban affairs,

ethnic studies, folklore, bioengineering, human growth and development, automotive research, manufacturing, and technology. At centers affiliated with the University of Detroit-Mercy, research is conducted in aging and polymer technologies. The Budd Company, an engineering and manufacturing resource specializing in automotive design, recently opened four research and development centers in southeastern Michigan.

Public Library Information: Detroit Public Library, 5201 Woodward Ave., Detroit, MI 48202-4007; telephone (313)833-1000; fax (313)832-0877

Health Care

Detroit is the primary medical treatment and referral center for southeastern Michigan. Vital factors in the health care industry are the education, training, and research programs conducted by the city's institutions of higher learning. The Wayne State University and University of Michigan schools of medicine, nursing, and pharmacy and allied health services provide area hospitals and clinics with medical professionals and support staff. The University of Detroit-Mercy offers programs in dentistry, nursing, and medical technology, and Madonna University provides a baccalaureate program in nursing.

The Detroit-area health care network is dominated by six health care providers. Those based in Detroit are the Detroit Medical Center and Henry Ford Health System. The Detroit Medical Center is affiliated with Wayne State University; the complex includes Children's Hospital of Michigan, Detroit Receiving Hospital, Harper Hospital, Hutzel Hospital, Sinai-Grace Hospital, Kresge Eye Institute, Karmanos Cancer Center, and the Rehabilitation Institute. The medical center is also home to the Wayne State University School of Medicine.

Henry Ford Hospital operates 32 centers and clinics, with more than 2,800 physicians serving 2.5 million patients throughout Southeastern Michigan each year. Among them are the Center for Chemical Dependency and the new Hermelin Brain Tumor Center, one of only a handful of such facilities in the country. The flagship 903-bed Henry Ford Hospital near Detroit's New Center is consistently ranked among the nation's best hospitals. The Henry Ford Health System is affiliated with the medical school of Case Western Reserve University of Cleveland. Other large hospitals in the metro region include the Renaissance Hospital and Medical Centers, one of Michigan's few minority-owned health systems; St. John Hospital on the city's east side; William Beaumont Hospital in suburban Royal Oak; and the University of Michigan Medical Center in Ann Arbor.

Health Care Information: Detroit Medical Center Referral Service, telephone (800)666-3466

Recreation

Sightseeing

Signs of Detroit's revitalization are particularly apparent in the downtown district. The People Mover, an elevated computerized rail transit system, features 13 stations with some of the most impressive publicly commissioned works of art in the country, all viewable from the train cars. Hart Plaza, named in honor of the late Senator Philip A. Hart, stands adjacent to Detroit's most visible symbol of renewal—the recently renovated Renaissance Center, headquarters of General Motors. Hart Plaza is the center of many downtown festivals, parades, and the Freedom Festival fireworks, and includes the Dodge Memorial Fountain, designed by sculptor Isamu Noguchi. Nearby, at the foot of Woodward Avenue, sits Robert Graham's sculpture *The Fist,* commemorating fighter Joe Louis and considered the city's most controversial piece of art. Another more conventional statue of Joe Louis stands inside the Cobo Hall Convention Center, where a museum dedicated to the boxer's life is open to the public on weekends.

During its heyday in the post-World War I 1920s, Detroit saw the construction of several high-rises built in ornate Art Deco style. Not all of those buildings are still standing, but those that are include the Penobscot, Guardian, and Buhl buildings downtown, as well as the original General Motors and Fisher buildings further uptown, and several magnificent theaters, including the Fox, the Fisher, the Masonic Temple, and Orchestra Hall. Just west of downtown, the Ambassador Bridge, the world's longest international suspension bridge built in 1929, spans the Detroit River and connects Detroit to Windsor, Ontario, a small Canadian city with a casino and charming Italian and Chinese neighborhoods.

The Detroit Zoo in Royal Oak was the first zoo in the United States to make extensive use of barless exhibits; the zoo is home to more than 1,300 animals representing 286 different species. The new "Arctic Ring of Life" exhibit displays several polar bears, arctic foxes, seals, and sea lions in a massive simulated arctic tundra environment. In 2004 the zoo opened the National Amphibian Conservation Center to educate and provide research facilities on amphibians. The "Chimps of Harambee" exhibit covers four acres of naturalistic habitat. Other popular exhibits are the penguinarium, reptile house, free-flying aviary, butterfly garden, and giraffe house.

Belle Isle, located in the Detroit River two miles from downtown, was purchased from the Chippewa and Ottawa native Americans and was landscaped as a 1,000-acre city park in 1879 by Frederick Law Olmsted. Belle Isle is the home of the Anna Scripps Whitcomb Conservatory, a nature center, the nation's oldest fresh water aquarium, the Dossin Great Lakes Museum, the Scott Fountain, and the Floral Clock.

The Cranbrook Institute of Science is a natural history museum and planetarium located north of the city in Bloomfield Hills.

The Detroit area is graced by a number of mansions built by automobile industrialists that are now open to the public. Meadow Brook Hall, a 100-room mansion on a 1,400-acre estate on the campus of Oakland University in Rochester, was built by auto baron John Dodge in 1926. Henry Ford's final home, the 56-room Fairlane, is located on the University of Michigan's Dearborn campus. The Edsel and Eleanor Ford House, overlooking Lake St. Clair in Grosse Pointe Shores on a 90-acre estate, is built with an authentic Cotswold stone roof and leaded glass windows with heraldic inserts. The Fisher mansion on the Detroit River features original Eastern art works, Italian Renaissance and vintage Hollywood architecture, and more than 200 ounces of pure gold and silver leaf on the ceilings and moldings.

Other historic structures in Detroit include Moross House, Old Mariners Church, Sibley House, and Pewabic Pottery, where ceramic Pewabic tiles were first developed. The International Institute of Metropolitan Detroit is an agency for the foreign-born founded by the Young Women's Christian Association (YWCA) in 1919, with a "gallery of nations" featuring the arts and crafts of 43 nations.

Arts and Culture

The Detroit Symphony, one of the country's few orchestras with international stature, plays a September-to-May season of classical and pops concerts at Orchestra Hall as well as a summer season at Meadow Brook, an outdoor amphitheater in Rochester. While Maestro Neeme Jarvi planned to step down as Conductor in 2005, a worldwide search for his successor was underway; meanwhile, famed violinist Itzhak Perlman continues his tenure as principal guest conductor with the Symphony. Michigan Opera Theatre produces classical grand opera in seasons at the magnificently restored 1922 Detroit Opera House, with two productions each fall and three more each spring. In 2005 the Opera premiered one of the most anticipated new American operas in decades when *Margaret Garner* was performed with a cast of international stars, including Denyce Graves. The opera was based on author Toni Morrison's classic novel *Beloved,* with the author also penning the libretto.

Detroit supports an active theater community; performances are staged in some of the finest restored facilities in the country. The Attic Theatre presents the best of the new and the offbeat. The intimate Gem and Century theaters offer

The décor of the Fox Theater, designed by C. Howard Crane in 1928, boasts Far Eastern, Egyptian, Babylonian, and Indian themes.

Broadway-style shows, comedy acts, and other productions in cabaret style seating. The Fox Theatre, the largest movie theater in the United States, was designed by movie palace architect C. Howard Crane in 1928; it has undergone renovation to preserve its ''Siamese Byzantine'' interior featuring Far Eastern, Egyptian, Babylonian, and Indian themes, and is the site of performing arts events. Another opulent theater facility is the Fisher Theatre, designed by Albert Kahn; it sponsors Broadway shows.

The Music Hall Center for the Performing Arts and Masonic Temple Theatre bring professional touring theater and dance companies to Detroit audiences. Meadow Brook Theatre at Oakland University presents an eight-play season of musicals, classics plays, and new works. Wayne State University's Hilberry Theatre produces classic drama performed by graduate student actors; undergraduate productions are staged at the Bonstelle Theatre. The Cranbrook Performing Arts Theatre in Bloomfield Hills offers orchestra, band, and vocal concerts, in addition to dance and drama, by high school students at the Cranbrook Educational Community. Other venues for the performing arts are the Riverfront Music Theatre in Chene Park, Joe Louis and Cobo arenas, the outdoor amphitheaters DTE Energy Music Theater in Clarkston and Meadow Brook Music Theater in Rochester, and the Palace of Auburn Hills, frequently named Arena of the Year by *Performance Magazine.*

The Detroit Institute of Arts, established in 1885, is the nation's fifth-largest fine arts museum. Art treasures from throughout the world and covering a historical period of 5,000 years are housed in 100 galleries. The museum's collection has literally outgrown its space and many major works had to be warehoused; a major renovation and expansion is set to be completed in 2007, adding 77,000 square feet of additional exhibit space. Among the institute's most prized holdings is the four-wall mural *Detroit Industry* by Diego Rivera. Also known worldwide is the Henry Ford Museum and Greenfield Village in Dearborn, which Henry Ford founded in 1929 to document America's growth from a rural to an industrial society by exhibiting objects from the nation's material culture. Henry Ford Museum is a fourteen-acre complex housing major collections in transportation, industry, agriculture, and the domestic arts; the museum features one of the world's most comprehensive car collections, including the vehicle President John F. Kennedy was traveling in when he was assassinated. A state-of-the-art IMAX Theatre was part of a $125 million makeover that started in 1999. Greenfield Village, a 240-acre outdoor museum, gathers on a single site one of the largest collections of historic American homes, workplaces, and communities; among them are Thomas Edison's Menlo Park laboratory, the Wright brothers' bicycle shop, and Noah Webster's Connecticut home.

The Detroit Historical Museum in the Detroit Cultural Center was founded in 1928 as an archive of the history and customs of Detroiters. The museum's collection of more than 250,000 urban historical artifacts is one of the largest such collections in the country. An educational unit of the Detroit Public Schools, the Children's Museum displays collections that focus on African musical instruments, the Inuit, and American folk crafts and toys. The Charles H. Wright Museum of African American History is dedicated to the contributions of African Americans in the humanities and creative arts. The Motown Historical Museum, a Michigan Historic Site, is quartered in the former home of Berry Gordy, Jr., Motown's founder, and preserves the music studio and recording equipment used in pioneering the Motown Sound. The Graystone International Jazz Museum preserves the city's jazz history. Fort Wayne is home to the National Museum of the Tuskegee Airmen, an all-African American unit of World War II fighter pilots.

Arts and Culture Information: Detroit Department of Culture, Arts & Tourism, 2 Woodward Ave., Detroit, MI 48226; telephone (313)224-3470; fax (313)244-3399.

Festivals and Holidays

From April until Labor Day, Detroit's downtown riverfront is the scene of a program of ethnic festivals (the largest is the African World Festival in August) and the Downtown Hoedown. June events include the Annual Heritage Fair at the Dearborn Historical Museum; Art on the Pointe, a juried art show at the Ford Estate; and the Muzzle Loaders Festival at Greenfield Village. The International Freedom Festival, begun in 1959, is a summer celebration of the friendship between Canada and the United States; it attracts more than 3 million people and culminates in a large fireworks display on the Detroit River.

On the Fourth of July weekend the Colonial Music and Military Muster at Greenfield Village features uniformed American and British troops in simulated encampment activities. Also in July at Greenfield Village is the Fire Engine Muster with hand-pulled rigs and horse-drawn pumpers in a re-creation of early fire-fighting techniques. The Blues Festival of Detroit, the Henry Ford Day at the Fairlane Mansion, and the Wyandotte Street Art Fair conclude July activities. The Michigan State Fair at the State Fairgrounds, the nation's oldest state fair, takes place in August, as does the Spirit of Detroit Car Show and the Swap Meets at Historic Fort Wayne. The Montreux Detroit Jazz Festival over Labor Day weekend brings together over 100 international artists and local jazz musicians in the nation's largest free jazz festival. The Autumn Harvest Festival in Dearborn, the Detroit Festival of the Arts, the Hamtramck Polish Festival, and the Old Car Festival at Greenfield Village are popular activities in September.

A major event in November is America's Thanksgiving Day Parade, which presents 20 floats, 15 helium balloons, 25 marching bands, more than 1,000 costumed marchers, and

Santa Claus in one of the nation's largest Thanksgiving Day parades; televised coverage of the parade is broadcast around the country. Other November events include Detroit Aglow and the Festival of Trees and Christmas Carnival at Cobo Conference Center. Christmas at Greenfield Village in December features Christmas past and present at more than two dozen historic village sites, with yuletide meals cooked at open hearths. Other seasonal shows are Noel Night at the Detroit Cultural Center, the Wassail Feast at the Detroit Institute of Arts, and the Christmas dinner at the Fairlane Manor.

Detroit's automotive era is evoked at numerous local events. The North American International Auto Show is among the most important auto shows in the world and is held each January. Autorama comes to Michigan each March and features classic and custom hot rods. The Concours d'Elegance, an exhibition of the world's finest classic cars, is held at Meadow Brook Hall in the summer. And the Woodward Dream Cruise bills itself as the world's largest one-day celebration of car culture, attracting over 1.7 million visitors from around the U.S. and even foreign countries, and more than 40,000 muscle cars, street rods, custom, collector, and special interest vehicles. Cruisers travel a 16-mile, spectator lined section of Woodward Avenue through nine communities on the third Saturday in August, though cruising often begins several days before the official event.

Sports for the Spectator

A tough, gritty, blue-collar town throughout much of its history, Detroit identifies itself through nothing else—except perhaps its rich musical legacy—as it does its passion for the local sports franchises. Detroit supports professional franchises in all the major sports, and each team has a rich tradition of all-time great players, oddball characters, and world championships. The Detroit Red Wings of the National Hockey League host visiting competitors at Joe Louis Arena, located downtown on the riverfront. The Red Wings have won hockey's fabled Stanley Cup 10 times, including 3 between the years 1997-2002. The Detroit Tigers, the city's oldest team, began play in the American League of Major League Baseball in 1901; a few years later the club acquired Ty Cobb, who played 22 years in a Detroit uniform and became one of the most legendary players in the history of the game. The club has won four World Series titles, the latest in 1984. In 2000 the Tigers moved to the new Comerica Park, across from the Fox Theater. The Detroit Lions compete in the National Football Conference of the National Football League. In 2002 the team moved its home field to downtown Detroit, adjacent to Comerica Park. The $450-million, enclosed Ford Field was privately financed and is set to host the 40th Super Bowl in February 2006. The Detroit Pistons of the National Basketball Association play their home games at the Palace of Auburn Hills, a 22,000-seat arena north of the city. Club attendance has led the NBA from 2003-2005, and the

2004 Pistons defeated the Los Angeles Lakers in five games to win the 2004 World Championship, the third title in club history. The Detroit Shock of the Women's National Basketball Association also plays at the Palace. The University of Detroit Mercy plays NCAA Division I basketball and other sports in the Horizon League. Both the University of Michigan Wolverines and the Michigan State Spartans compete in Big Ten athletics within an hour's drive of the city.

The Spirit of Detroit Thunderfest brings super-power hydroplanes to race on the Detroit River in June. Harness Racing is on view at the Hazel Park Harness Raceway and at Northville Downs.

Sports for the Participant

The Detroit Riverfront Conservancy was formed in 2003 with an initial $50 million grant from the Kresge Foundation, to develop and beautify the land along the city's Detroit River frontage. The group's ultimate goal is to raise $110 million and build a five-mile-long RiverWalk connecting the Belle Isle Bridge (east of downtown) and the Ambassador Bridge to the west. The 62-foot wide pathway, expected to be completed by 2006, will have landscaping, lighting, benches, picnic areas, and paved trails for cyclists, skaters, and walkers, and will provide views of the river, its nonstop boating and freighter traffic, and the city of Windsor, Ontario. In addition to this project, the Detroit Department of Parks and Recreation oversees 6,000 acres of park land. More than 350 city parks contain a total of 318 baseball diamonds, 257 tennis courses, six golf courses, and two marinas. Detroit has developed four smaller downtown riverfront parks, and there are miles of paved walkways for walking, running, and biking on Belle Isle. Outdoor sports such as swimming, boating, hiking, fishing, and skating are available at metropolitan parks. There are 170 public golf courses and six ski resorts in the Detroit region.

Runners of the Detroit International Marathon cross borders twice—taking in stunning views on the Ambassador Bridge on the way to Windsor and then hoofing it through the tunnel on the way back to Detroit—as they tour both Detroit and Windsor's downtowns over 26.2 miles.

Shopping and Dining

Detroit offers unique shopping venues like Eastern Market, the largest flower-bedding market in the world and an outlet for fresh meats and produce from neighboring states and Canada. Adjacent to Eastern Market are specialty stores selling fresh meat, poultry, gourmet foods, and wines. Pewabic Pottery, founded in 1903, continues to produce handcrafted vessels and architectural tiles for public and private installations from its East Jefferson factory and gallery. There are numerous shops and restaurants throughout the sprawling Renaissance Center complex, and at the Millender Center directly across Jefferson.

Greektown and International Center, a popular Detroit tourist spot, features bakeries, restaurants, bars, and coffeehouses. Bricktown, located in a refurbished sector of downtown, is anchored by an art gallery selling Oriental vases, Persian rugs, and antique furniture.

Metropolitan Detroit offers about 150 shopping centers of at least 100,000 square feet. Vibrant downtown shopping areas can be found in communities like Birmingham, Grosse Pointe, and Royal Oak. The Somerset Collection and Somerset Collection North in suburban Troy rival the nation's finest shopping areas; the twin centers are anchored by Neiman Marcus, Saks Fifth Avenue, Nordstrom, and Marshall Field's.

Detroit offers elegant dining experiences downtown at Opus One, the Rattlesnake Club, and Sweet Georgia Brown. The Coach Insignia, situated 70 floors atop the Renaissance Center, has dining and panoramic views of Detroit, the river, the Ambassador and Belle Isle bridges, and Windsor, Ontario. Also in the Renaissance Center, Seldom Blues has fine dining, riverfront views, and a lively late-night club scene with some of the best jazz in the city. At the corner of Michigan and Lafayette, the side-by-side Lafayette Coney Island and American Coney Island have been Detroit legend for decades, especially for late-night after-hours crowds, serving up their unique hot dogs on steamed buns with chili, onions, and mustard, plus chili fries, and even a cold beer. Heading north from downtown diners will find sushi at Oslo, the Whitney in a restored Victorian mansion, Agave, Atlas Bistro, and Union Street. West of downtown, near the Ambassador Bridge, Mexican Village has several Mexican restaurants, as well as Spanish and Guatemalan fare. To the east of the city, Grosse Pointe has several excellent restaurants, including The Hill; in the northern suburbs the Lark in West Bloomfield and Tribute in Farmington Hills are consistently given five-star ratings by international publications. Detroit is home to the largest Arab population outside of the Middle East, and many of those immigrants live in Dearborn where a number of authentic Lebanese and Syrian restaurants thrive. Detroit is home to some outstanding Italian restaurants; Creole, Japanese, Chinese, Ethiopian, Thai, Indian, and Turkish cuisine are included among the other ethnic choices.

Visitor Information: Detroit Metropolitan Convention & Visitors Bureau, 211 W. Fort St., Ste. 1000, Detroit, MI 48226; telephone (313)202-1800; toll-free (800)DETROIT

Convention Facilities

Detroit's principal meeting facilities are clustered in the Detroit Civic Center, which stands at the edge of the Detroit

River on the approximate site where the city's founder landed in 1701. The Civic Center consists of five complexes: Cobo Conference/Exhibition Center, Cobo Arena, Joe Louis Arena, Hart Plaza, and the Veterans Memorial Building.

Cobo Conference/Exhibition Center contains a total of 700,000 square feet of meeting space and 85 meeting rooms in five halls. The hall hosts the North American International Auto Show each January and a huge boat show every March, but by 2004 city officials began discussions to expand the Cobo complex even further so the city could attract even larger conventions. The adjacent Cobo Arena, with a seating capacity of 11,000 people, is used for conventions and shows as well as large functions such as concerts and sports events. Joe Louis Arena, named for the heavyweight boxing champion, was the site of the 1980 Republican National Convention and hosts major events. The Veterans Memorial Building, the original Civic Center structure built in 1950, houses a ballroom and meeting rooms.

Convention and meeting facilities are also available at the Detroit Historical Museum, the Detroit Institute of Arts, the Detroit Fox Theatre, Orchestra Hall, the Michigan Exposition and Fairgrounds, and Ford Field, as well as at Henry Ford Museum, the Detroit Zoo, restored estates and historic sites, suburban civic centers, college and university campuses, and on yachts and riverboats. All major downtown and suburban hotels and motels offer meeting accommodations for both large and small functions.

Convention Information: Detroit Metropolitan Convention & Visitors Bureau, 211 W. Fort St., Ste. 1000, Detroit, MI 48226; telephone (313)202-1800; toll-free (800) DETROIT

Transportation

Approaching the City

Served by 14 major commercial airlines, Detroit Metropolitan Airport serviced more than 32 million passengers in 2003, making it the 10th busiest terminal in North America and 17th busiest in the world. The major hub for Northwest Airlines, Metro has more than 100 national and 20 international nonstop flights daily. Since the opening of the new $1.2 billion midfield McNamara terminal in 2002, with its 97 gates, elevated tram, and new parking facilities and access roads, the airport is now mentioned among the most efficient and highly-rated in the country. In 2004 the airport authority announced plans to replace the old Smith and Davey terminals with a new 29-gate terminal set for complete in 2006. Approximately 18,000 people are employed at the facility, which also moves more than 500 million pounds of freight each year. Destinations for charter and private air traffic are Willow Run Airport and Oakland-Pontiac Airport. Amtrak provides passenger rail transportation to Detroit from Chicago. Detroiters have easy access from Windsor via train to Toronto and virtually all of Canada through that country's excellent Via Rail system.

Detroit was built around the automobile; there is no commuter rail system. Hence, the freeways are many and excellent, as they must be in order to get commuters around the sprawling city. Six interstate highways and several limited-access expressways serve the Greater Detroit area. Interstate-75, with its northern terminus in Michigan's Upper Peninsula, extends through the city from north to southwest; north of downtown it is called the Chrysler Freeway, and southwest of downtown it is the Fisher Freeway. I-75 extends all the way to southern Florida. Interstate-375 connects the Fisher and Chrysler Freeways. East-west I-94, known as the Ford Freeway, is the primary connection from Detroit Metropolitan Airport and heads across southern lower Michigan to Chicago and Minneapolis. West-northwest I-96, the Jeffries Freeway, approaches Detroit from Muskegon, Grand Rapids, and Lansing. Interstate-696, the Walter Reuther Freeway, is the main east-west route across the northern suburbs in Macomb and Oakland counties. Interstate-275 is a north-south bypass on the city's west side, linking I-75 and I-96. Other major routes leading into Detroit are north to west U.S. 10 (Lodge Freeway) and north-south S.R. 39 (Southfield Freeway). Canadian Highway 401 enters Detroit from Windsor via the Detroit/Windsor International Tunnel and the Ambassador Bridge.

Traveling in the City

Most Detroit streets conform to a grid system. East-west streets are labeled "mile road" in ascending order northward. The northern boundary of the city is Eight Mile Road. Superimposed on the downtown grid are hubs and squares, the focal point being Kennedy Square and Cadillac Square in the center of the business district. Radiating from this hub are east-west Michigan Avenue, northeast Monroe Street, and east-west Fort Street. The largest hub is Grand Circus Park, which is bisected by Woodward Avenue, a main north-south thoroughfare. Jefferson Avenue follows the curve of the Detroit River and Lake St. Clair past Belle Isle through the Grosse Pointes into Harrison Township and downriver past Wyandotte to Grosse Ile.

Detroit is served by two public transportation systems: the Detroit Department of Transportation (D-DOT) and the Suburban Mobility Authority for Regional Transport (SMART). The People Mover, a 2.9-mile elevated rail circuit, provides travel to major downtown sites from 13 stations.

Communications

Newspapers and Magazines

The Detroit News and the *Detroit Free Press* are the city's two major daily newspapers; they publish joint editions on Saturday, Sunday, and holidays. *Hour Detroit* is a glossy metropolitan lifestyle and interview magazine that aims "to feature Detroit in its finest hour." *Real Detroit* and *Metro Times* provide weekly entertainment schedules as well as reviews, humor, and commentary. The monthly newspaper *Latino Press* aims to help Detroit's growing Hispanic community. The *Michigan Chronicle* is geared toward African American readers.

A number of nationally circulated periodicals originate in Detroit. Among them are *Solidarity,* a monthly publication of the United Automobile Workers; *Better Investing; Manufacturing Engineering; Autoweek,* a weekly magazine for car enthusiasts; and *Automotive News, Ward's Automotive Report* and *Auto World,* auto industry magazines. *Football News* publishes 20 issues during the football season.

Television and Radio

Detroit television viewers receive broadcasts from eight stations: three national networks affiliates, three independent, one public, and the Canadian Broadcasting Corporation (CBC). Pay and cable television services are available in the Detroit metropolitan area. AM and FM radio stations schedule a full range of formats. The most popular is adult contemporary music; other formats include adult-oriented rock, African American and African American contemporary, Motown, classic rock, easy listening, jazz, middle of the road, modern country, news and news-talk, pop, oldies, solid gold, and urban contemporary rhythm and blues. Two of the AM stations with 50,000-watt capacity enjoy a longstanding popularity throughout the Midwest; one FM station was the first in the country to offer a full-time news-talk format. Detroit's public radio station originates from Wayne State University, but other National Public Radio programming can be picked up from Ypsilanti, Ann Arbor, and Lansing stations.

Media Information: *Detroit News* and *Detroit Free Press,* 321 W. Lafayette Blvd., Detroit, Michigan 48226; telephone (313)222-6400

Detroit Online

City of Detroit home page. Available www.ci.detroit.mi.us

Detroit Free Press. Available www.freep.com

Detroit Institute of Arts. Available www.dia.org

Detroit Metropolitan Convention & Visitors Bureau. Available www.visitdetroit.com

Detroit News. Available www.detnews.com

Detroit Regional Chamber of Commerce. Available www.detroitchamber.com

Detroit Riverfront Conservancy. Available www.detroitriverfront.org

''The Fabulous Ruins of Detroit'' (photographs and descriptions of Detroit's proud, old buildings). Available http://detroityes.com

Greater Downtown Partnership. Available www.downtownpartnership.org

Guide to Detroit from The Mining Company. Available detroit.miningco.com

Wayne County Economic Development. Available www.waynecounty.com

Selected Bibliography

Arnow, Harriette Louisa Simpson, *The Dollmaker* (New York: Avon Books, 1972, 1954)

Avery, Joan, *Angel of Passage* (Harper, 1993)

Bak, Richard *Detroit Across 3 Centuries* (Detroit: Thomson Gale, 2001)

Chafets, Ze'Ev, *Devil's Night And Other True Tales of Detroit* (New York: Random House, 1990)

Georgakas, Dan Georgakas, et al., *Detroit, I Do Mind Dying: A Study in Urban Revolution (Classics Series)* (South End Press, 1998)

Henrickson, Wilma Wood, ed., *Detroit Perspectives: Crossroads and Turning Points* (Detroit: Wayne State University Press, 1991)

Leonard, Elmore *Out of Sight* (New York: Delacorte, 1996)

Lichtenstein, Nelson, *The Most Dangerous Man in Detroit: Walter Reuther and the Fate of American Labor* (New York: Basic Books, 1996)

Lindsay, Paul, *Witness to the Truth: A Novel of the FBI* (New York: Random House, 1992)

Grand Rapids

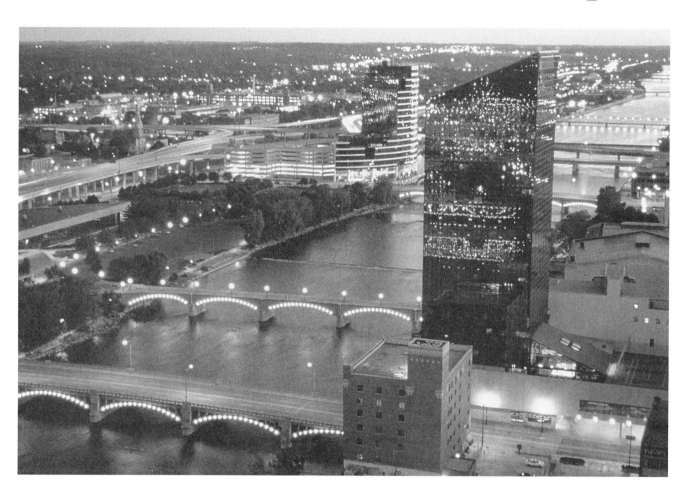

The City in Brief

Founded: 1831 (incorporated, 1850)

Head Official: City Manager Kurt Kimball (since 1987)

City Population
  1980: 181,843
  1990: 189,126
  2000: 197,800
  2003 estimate: 195,601
  Percent change, 1990–2000: 4.3%
  U.S. rank in 1980: 75th
  U.S. rank in 1990: 83rd
  U.S. rank in 2000: 107th (State rank: 2nd)

Metropolitan Area Population
  1980: 602,000
  1990: 937,891
  2000: 1,088,514

Percent change, 1990–2000: 16.1%
U.S. rank in 1980: 56th
U.S. rank in 1990: Not reported
U.S. rank in 2000: 48th

Area: 45 square miles (2000)
Elevation: Ranges from 785 to 1,075 feet above sea level
Average Annual Temperature: 47.4° F
Average Annual Precipitation: 37.13 inches of rain, 71.9 inches of snow

Major Economic Sectors: Manufacturing, services, retail trade
Unemployment Rate: 6.6% (March 2005)
Per Capita Income: $17,661 (1999)

2002 FBI Crime Index Total: 11,292

Major Colleges and Universities: Grand Valley State University

Daily Newspaper: *The Grand Rapids Press*

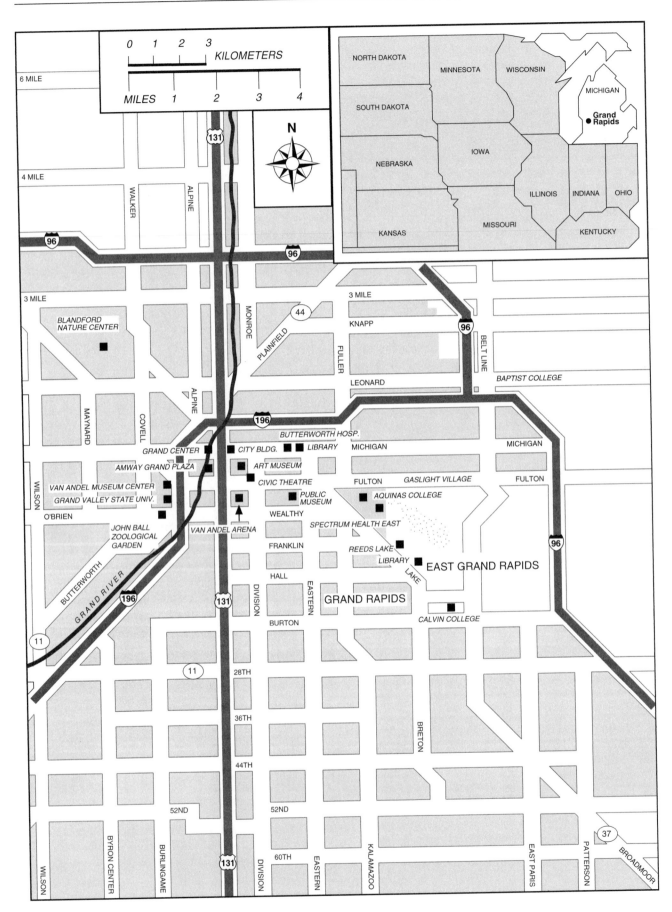

Introduction

The seat of Kent County, Michigan, Grand Rapids is the center of a metropolitan statistical area that includes Kent, Ottawa, Muskegon, and Allegan counties. The Grand River, on which the city is located, shaped the future of Grand Rapids first as a leader in the logging industry, then as one of the world's primary furniture manufacturing centers, and now as the office furniture capital. The city's identity also was determined by thousands of Dutch immigrants who settled in Grand Rapids to work in the furniture factories. Today, the Grand Rapids metropolitan area has more than one million inhabitants, innovative cultural institutions, a revitalized downtown core, a diverse economy, and high marks for quality of life factors.

Geography and Climate

Bisected by the Grand River, Michigan's longest river, Grand Rapids is located in the Grand river valley approximately 30 miles east of Lake Michigan. The region's climate is influenced by the lake, which tempers cold waves from the west and northwest during the winter and produces a regulating effect on both frost and vegetation during the growing season. Consequently, seasonal extremes are infrequent, although hot, humid weather can be expected for about three weeks during the summer and drought occasionally occurs for a short duration; snow cover sometimes remains throughout the winter.

Area: 45 square miles (2000)

Elevation: Ranges from 785 feet to 1,075 feet above sea level

Average Temperatures: January, 21.8° F; July, 71.6° F; annual average, 47.4° F

Average Annual Precipitation: 37.13 inches of rain, 71.9 inches of snow

History

Grand River Valley Site of Land Feud

About 2,000 years ago, the Hopewell Indians planted roots at the rapids near the Grand River. Their presence is still seen in the preserved burial mounds southwest of the city. By the late 17th century, the Ottawa tribe had set up villages on the west bank of the Grand River at the site of present day Grand Rapids. Several Baptist mission buildings were completed in the vicinity in 1826. That same year Louis Campau, a French fur trader, settled in the region, establishing a trading post on the east river bank. Local Native Americans nicknamed him "The Fox" for his shrewd trading skills. Campau purchased 72 acres for $90 in 1831 in what is now the downtown area and named it the Village of Grand Rapids. A land surveyor named Lucius Lyon acquired the platted land to the north and named it the Village of Kent, causing a raging land feud with Campau. By 1838 the Michigan legislature combined both tracts of land to form the Village of Grand Rapids. The area incorporated as a city in 1850.

Inexpensive, fertile land and abundant timber and mineral resources attracted settlers to the area, and by 1860 the population numbered 8,000, more than tripling in 10 years. By then, rail and telegraph had come to Grand Rapids, connecting the community to all parts of the country with travel from the eastern seaboard taking only two days.

Logging Fuels Grand Rapids Development

Grand Rapids began a period of rapid development in the 1850s when logs from Michigan's rich pine and oak forests floated down the Grand River to the city's new mills. After the Civil War, many soldiers found jobs as lumberjacks cutting logs and guiding them down the river with pike poles, peaveys, and cant hooks. The men wore bright red flannel, felt clothes, and spiked boots to hold them onto the floating logs; these boots chewed up the wooden sidewalks and flooring of the local bars, leading one hotel owner to supply carpet slippers to all river drivers who entered his hotel. The "jacks" earned $1 to $3 per day and all the "vittles" they could eat, which was usually a considerable amount.

Upstream mill owners often stole the logs headed for Grand Rapids in a practice called "hogging." To prevent hogging, the mills hired men called river drivers, who rode the logs downstream to their rightful destination. In addition, like cattle, all logs were stamped with the brands of their owners so they could be sorted at the log booms and sent to a specific sawmill. From 1865 to the 1880s the logging industry dominated the local economy. The river also harnessed energy. One of the first hydro-electric plants in the United States was built in Grand Rapids.

River ice and log jams proved to be a continual problem for Grand Rapids. A series of floods and heavy rains that launched runaway logs caused repeated damage to the town, notably in 1838, 1852, and 1883. In 1883, so much rain fell one summer's day that an estimated 80 million board feet of logs broke free and jammed against a railroad bridge, creating what some called the biggest log jam in the nation's history. The bridge swayed, bent, groaned, and finally broke away as part of it was carried steadily down the river. Called the Great Log Jam of 1883, the event was spectacular but also marked the beginning of the end for logging on the Grand River.

Furniture Craftsmanship Gains World Attention

Because of the plentiful supply of fine wood, furniture had been manufactured in Grand Rapids as early as 1838, but it was not until the Philadelphia Centennial Exposition in 1876 that the city gained national recognition for its furniture craftsmanship. Bedroom, dining room, library, and hall furniture made of oak, ash, and maple gained mass popularity. Two years later Grand Rapids held its first furniture mart, attracting buyers worldwide who appreciated the fresh styles and quality work. One of the innovations Grand Rapids manufacturers brought to the furniture industry was catalogs of photographs and color drawings that were distributed throughout the nation.

By 1890, Grand Rapids was home to the nation's largest furniture companies; they set the tone for creative designs, new manufacturing processes and equipment, retailing networks, and inventive marketing schemes. The city ranked third, behind only New York and Chicago, in the amount of furniture its factories produced. Nearly one-third of all city laborers worked in the industry. The high paying and plentiful jobs attracted a large number of immigrants—Dutch, German, Polish, and other northern Europeans. Grand Rapids grew from slightly more than 10,000 residents at the end of the Civil War to nearly 90,000 by 1900. One-third of the city's population had been born in another country by that time.

In Europe, Grand Rapids was best known as the home of Tanglefoot rather than producer of fine furniture. Flies were a nuisance, then as now. An ordinary druggist named Otto Thum developed a sticky paper that not only caught and held flies, but even attracted them. The company is still in existence along with its century old "secret formula."

Another long lived, prosperous Grand Rapids company is Bissell, founded in 1876 and considered the pioneer in the carpet sweeper industry. With the death of company head Melville Bissell in 1889, his wife Anna assumed leadership and became America's first female corporate CEO. She was light-years ahead of her time as an aggressive and innovative manager. Under her guidance, the company developed many new products and expanded the business internationally. Still privately owned, Bissell continues to be an industry pioneer, bringing innovative home- and floor-care products to the international marketplace.

Turn of the Century Brings Changes to Grand Rapids

Depletion of Michigan's forests put an end to the logging industry, requiring furniture companies to import lumber, as they still do today. Due to a nationwide industry slump between 1905 and 1910, furniture workers received only minimal raises or none at all. This, combined with extremely long hours and poor working conditions, led to 3,000 workers striking in 1911 demanding a 9-hour day, a 10 percent wage increase, and the abolition of pay based on piecework. After four months, the strike ended, but later management granted most of the laborer's requests.

The Grand Rapids residential furniture industry never fully recovered after that strike. World War I, the Great Depression, and World War II led to lessening demand for residential furniture and the Grand Rapids furniture companies did not make the transition well during the war economies. Many companies went under or moved south to be closer to a larger lumber supply.

With the end of World War II, a two decades long construction boom began and countless new office buildings were erected throughout the nation and worldwide. Some Grand Rapids companies had begun making fine wood and metal furniture for offices in the early 1900s; they now saw tremendous demand. Steelcase grew from 34 employees in 1912 to become the largest office furniture company worldwide with more than 19,000 people. Because of the many office furniture companies in close proximity, Grand Rapids is now known as the nation's office furniture capital. Experience with wood and metal and a traditional entrepreneurial spirit led to a diversifying economy. No one industry dominates the metropolitan area manufacturers, but furniture, industrial machinery, metals, plastics, food processing, and printing are core industrial clusters.

As with other cities after World War II, many Grand Rapids-based families fled to the suburbs and the city's population began to decline along with the downtown area. In the mid 1990s, Grand Rapids began experiencing a renaissance, with more than $200 million in new cultural, recreational, and sports facilities. Downtown revitalization included the 12,000-seat Van Andel Arena for sports, concerts, and entertainment events; the Van Andel Institute, an independent medical research center; and the refurbishing of many warehouses into retail space and loft apartments. The new millennium has seen even more new projects and expansions. The $210 million De Vos Place project incorporates De Vos Hall and the old Grand Center convention space in a new one-million-square-foot facility, which was completed in 2005. Millennium Park is a 10-year restoration of 1500 acres of industrial land that includes a new beach. New parks, residences, shopping venues, restaurants, and other revitalization projects that mark a new beginning for Grand Rapids abound.

Historical Information: Grand Rapids Public Library, Michigan and Family History Collection, 111 Library St., NE, Grand Rapids, MI 49503; telephone (616)456-3640

Population Profile

Metropolitan Area Residents
1980: 602,000
1990: 937,891
2000: 1,088,514
Percent change, 1990–2000: 16.1%
U.S. rank in 1980: 56th
U.S. rank in 1990: Not reported
U.S. rank in 2000: 48th

City Residents
1980: 181,843
1990: 189,126
2000: 197,800
2003 estimate: 195,601
Percent change, 1990–2000: 4.3%
U.S. rank in 1980: 75th
U.S. rank in 1990: 83rd
U.S. rank in 2000: 107th (State rank: 2nd)

Density: 4,431.2 people per square mile (2000)

Racial and ethnic characteristics (2000)
  White: 133,116
  Black or African American: 40,373
  American Indian and Alaska Native: 1,454
  Asian: 3,195
  Native Hawaiian and Pacific Islander: 238
  Hispanic or Latino (may be of any race): 25,818
  Other: 13,115

Percent of residents born in state: 69.6% (2000)

Age characteristics (2000)
  Population under 5 years old: 16,335
  Population 5 to 9 years old: 15,198
  Population 10 to 14 years old: 13,903
  Population 15 to 19 years old: 15,613
  Population 20 to 24 years old: 18,413
  Population 25 to 34 years old: 33,965
  Population 35 to 44 years old: 28,350
  Population 45 to 54 years old: 21,269
  Population 55 to 59 years old: 6,681
  Population 60 to 64 years old: 5,115
  Population 65 to 74 years old: 10,204
  Population 75 to 84 years old: 8,930
  Population 85 years and older: 3,824
  Median age: 30.4 years

Births (2003)
  Total number: 3,785

Deaths (2003)
  Total number: 1,748 (of which, 46 were infants under
    the age of 1 year)

Money income (1999)
  Per capita income: $17,661
  Median household income: $37,224
  Total households: 73,217

Number of households with income of . . .
  less than $10,000: 3,389
  $10,000 to $14,999: 2,002
  $15,000 to $24,999: 5,633
  $25,000 to $34,999: 5,740
  $35,000 to $49,999: 8,640
  $50,000 to $74,999: 10,439
  $75,000 to $99,999: 5,072
  $100,000 to $149,999: 2,736
  $150,000 to $199,999: 710
  $200,000 or more: 573

Percent of families below poverty level: 11.9% (47.3% of
  which were female householder families with related
  children under 5 years)

2002 FBI Crime Index Total: 11,292

Municipal Government

Grand Rapids operates under a ''weak mayor,'' commission-
manager form of government, in which the seven council
members—one of whom serves as mayor—are elected to
four-year terms. The city manager, who runs the government, is appointed.

The Grand Valley Metro Council, formed in 1990, is a
voluntary coalition of 31 units of government assigned to
coordinate the region's services and investments which have
environmental, economic and social impact.

Head Official: City Manager Kurt Kimball (since 1987)

Total Number of City Employees: 1,800 (2005)

City Information: City Hall, 300 Monroe NW, Grand
Rapids, MI 49503; telephone (616)456-4648

Economy

Major Industries and Commercial Activity

The furniture industry has been a mainstay of the Grand
Rapids economy since the late 1800s. Today the metropolitan area is home to five of the world's leading office furniture companies: Steelcase, Herman Miller, Haworth, Knoll,

and American Seating. Several firms also produce residential furniture. The Grand Rapids metropolitan manufacturing base is among the largest county employers. Steelcase and Amway, manufacturer of home care products, along with Meijer, a supermarket chain, are the largest private companies in the county. In October 2000 Amway became a subsidiary of a newly created company, Alticor.

Grand Rapids has always thrived because of its entrepreneurial, family owned businesses. Among the national firms that began as family operations are Meijer; Bissell, carpet sweeper makers; Wolverine World Wide, makers of Hush Puppies; and Howard Miller, the world's largest manufacturer of grandfather clocks.

Automotive parts, industrial machinery, printing, graphic arts, plastics and chemicals, grocery wholesalers, and food processors comprise a substantial portion of the economic base. International businesses also play an important role, with more than 50 foreign-owned firms in the county and many metropolitan area firms involved in international trade. Tourism is an emerging industry as West Michigan increasingly becomes a popular vacation and convention destination.

Items and goods produced: office furniture and hardware, home furniture, automobile parts, plastics, industrial machinery, tool and dies, home-care products, home appliances, commercial printing, electronic equipment, scientific instruments, food, leather

Incentive Programs—New and Existing Companies

In 2004, the Michigan Economic Development Commission approved a total of more than $10.3 million in Single Business Tax credits for the expansion and consolidation of Steelcase and the redevelopment of two contaminated brownfield sites in the city's downtown. Gaines Township will support the Steelcase expansion with a tax abatement valued at approximately $96,000 over four years.

Local programs—The city of Grand Rapids and its downtown development authority have committed approximately $6.3 million in local incentives toward the brownfield projects through tax abatements and tax increment financing incentives. The Right Place Program (RPP), founded in 1985, is a regional non-profit organization headed by business and government leaders to encourage economic growth through expansion and retention of area businesses and attraction of national and international companies.

State programs—More than 800 properties within 10 areas of the city are designated Renaissance Zones, where Michigan Single Business Tax, the state education tax, Michigan personal and real property taxes, and city income taxes are waived. Tax credits and exemptions are also available in the

city's SmartZone, an area adjacent to downtown where the city is seeking to locate high tech and life sciences companies.

Job training programs—Through the Michigan Economic Development Corporation, employees have the opportunity to improve their skills through three Michigan Technical Education Centers (M-TEC) operated through Grand Rapids Community College.

Development Projects

Rosa Parks Circle, a small, downtown park, opened in 2002. It was designed by architect Maya Lin, who also designed the Vietnam Memorial in Washington, D.C. Millennium Park is a $25 million, 10-year restoration of 1,500 acres of industrial land. A 200-acre section of the park, including Millennium Park Beach, opened in 2003. The $210 million De Vos Place project incorporates De Vos Hall and the old Grand Center convention space in a new one-million-square-foot facility, which was completed in 2005.

Economic Development Information: The Right Place Program, The Waters Building, 111 Pearl Street NW, Grand Rapids, MI 49503; telephone (616)771-0325; fax (616)771-0329

Commercial Shipping

Because of its strategic location, Grand Rapids is no more than two delivery days away from all Midwest, East Coast, mid-south, and eastern Canadian markets. Ground transportation is available through more than 40 motor carriers, several of which operate terminals in Grand Rapids, and three rail freight systems provide a range of services such as piggyback shipments, bulk handling, and refrigeration. The South Beltline Corridor, currently under construction, connects I-96 on the East with I-196 on the West, with U.S. 131 in the center. Portions of this highway opened in 2001 and 2004, with the remainder scheduled to open in 2005. Seven air cargo carriers and a deep-water port on Lake Michigan, 35 miles away in Muskegon, link Grand Rapids with world markets.

Labor Force and Employment Outlook

Employers in the Grand Rapids area have access to a young and growing population with a Midwestern work ethic. Employer relations are said to be excellent and work stoppages rare.

The city and region enjoy a high rate of employment overall. With a designated foreign trade zone, Grand Rapids importers and exporters expect to continue to expand markets internationally.

The following is a summary of data regarding the Grand Rapids metropolitan area labor force, 2004 annual averages.

Size of nonagricultural labor force: 384,100

Number of workers employed in . . .
   construction and mining: 19,300
   manufacturing: 74,100
   trade, transportation and utilities: 73,200
   information: 5,700
   financial activities: 20,900
   professional and business services: 52,900
   educational and health services: 51,400
   leisure and hospitality: 31,700
   other services: 17,100
   government: 37,800

Average hourly earnings of production workers employed in manufacturing: $17.56

Unemployment rate: 6.6% (March 2005)

Largest employers	*Number of employees*
Spectrum Health	14,000
Meijer	9,785
Steelcase	5,400
Johnson Controls	5,000
Herman Miller, Inc.	4,400
Alticor, Inc.	4,000
Farmers Insurance Group	3,500
Grand Rapids Public Schools	3,490

Cost of Living

Grand Rapids is noted for its quality of life and affordable health care costs.

The following is a summary of data regarding several key cost of living factors in the Grand Rapids area.

2004 (3rd Quarter) ACCRA Average House Price: $229,900

2004 (3rd Quarter) ACCRA Cost of Living Index: 97.7 (U.S. Average = 100.0)

State income tax rate: 4.3%

State sales tax rate: 6.0%

Local income tax rate: 1.3% for residents; 0.65% for non-residents

Local sales tax rate: None

Property tax rate average: varies from 22.1515 to 29.0215 mills per $1,000 of assessed home value (2004)

Economic Information: The Right Place Program, The Waters Building, 111 Pearl Street NW, Grand Rapids, MI 49503; telephone (616)771-0325; fax (616)771-0329

Education and Research

Elementary and Secondary Schools

Grand Rapids Public School District is the largest in the area. The distict's goal is that by 2007 all students will be at or above grade level in reading, writing, and math, and that 80 percent of incoming ninth graders will graduate.

The following is a summary of data regarding the City of Grand Rapids public schools as of the 2003–2004 school year.

Total enrollment: 24,219

Number of facilities
   elementary schools: 44
   middle schools: 6
   high schools: 5
   other: 31

Student/teacher ratio: 14.3:1

Teacher salaries
   average: $53,517 (2002)

Funding per pupil: $11,274

At least 122 parochial, private, church-affiliated, alternative, and specialty schools offer educational curricula from preschool through grade 12 in the Grand Rapids area.

Public Schools Information: Grand Rapids Public Schools, 1331 Franklin SE, PO Box 117, Grand Rapids, MI 49501; telephone (616)771-2182. Kent County Intermediate School District, 2930 Knapp NE, Grand Rapids, MI 49525; telephone (616)364-1333

Colleges and Universities

A variety of institutions of higher learning offer undergraduate and graduate degrees in the Kent County; among them are Aquinas College, Calvin College, Central Michigan University, Cornerstone University, Davenport College, Ferris State University, Grand Valley State University, Kendall College of Art and Design (of Ferris State University), Michigan State University, Spring Arbor College, University of Phoenix, and Western Michigan University. Two-year programs are available at Grand Rapids Community College and ITT Technical Institute. Colleges and seminaries providing religious training are Calvin Theological Seminary, Grace Bible College, Grand Rapids Baptist Seminary, and Reformed Bible College.

Libraries and Research Centers

The Grand Rapids Public Library is the second largest public library system in Michigan; it operates seven branches in addition to its main facility, which is a depository for federal and state documents. Library holdings consist of 660,000 books, tapes, films, maps, and compact discs; periodicals; and special collections covering several fields, such as furniture, foundations, and Michigan history.

Kent District Library maintains 19 branches and houses about 774,000 books plus magazines, videos, and compact disks. Lakeland Library Cooperative serves 1 million people in the area. Several libraries have in-depth collections in fields such as law, personal finance, business, art and architecture, antiques and collectibles, and materials for the blind and handicapped.

Research is conducted at Grand Valley State University in water resources, aquatic conservation, land use change, air quality, and waste management. At Steelcase Inc.'s $111 million Pyramid research center, behavioral scientists, designers, and engineers study emerging trends such as ergonomics and translate them into office products. The Van Andel Research Institute (VARI) opened its $60 million, 162,000-square-foot building in May 2000. Its Board of Scientific Advisors includes four Nobel Laureates; cancer research is the primary focus.

Public Library Information: Grand Rapids Public Library, 111 Library St. NE, Grand Rapids, MI 49503-3268; telephone (616)588-5400; fax (616) 588-5420

Health Care

Spectrum Health is ranked as one of the top 100 hospitals in the country, especially in orthopedics and cardiac bypass surgery. The hospital also serves as the western Michigan regional center for cancer, diabetes, poisons, sleep disorders, and burn treatment. It has a nationally recognized children's hospital. The $137 million Fred and Lena Meijer Heart Center opened on the hospital's Butterworth Campus in 2004. In March 2005, the hospital announced it would be upgrading its Blodgett Campus at a cost of $7.5 million.

St. Mary's Health Care is an integrated health care system that has specialists in kidney transplantation, cardiac care, bloodless medicine, psychiatric medicine, neonatology, gastroenterology and endocrinology. St. Mary's opened a $42 million, 180,000-square-foot, five-story Lacks Cancer Center in January 2005. The Wege Institute offers traditional services, such as family practice, internal medicine and general surgery, side by side with complementary therapies, including massage, acupuncture, biofeedback, manipulation, and Feldenkrais.

Recreation

Sightseeing

The Gerald R. Ford Museum in Grand Rapids honors the 38th President of the United States; permanent exhibits, including a replica of the Oval Office, highlight the significant events of the Ford presidency, such as the Bicentennial celebration, President Nixon's resignation, and the Cambodian conflict. The contributions of Betty Ford as First Lady are also represented.

The Public Museum of Grand Rapids concentrates on the furniture industry, Michigan mammals, archeology, costumes, an 1890s gaslight village and Native American artifacts.

Heritage Hill is one of the largest urban historic districts in the country. Located near downtown, it contains more than 1,300 structures built in 60 different architectural styles, including Frank Lloyd Wright's Meyer May house.

A Grand Rapids highlight is Alexander Calder's *La Grande Vitesse* (The Grand Rapids), a large-scale outdoor sculpture located in the center of the city. Another Calder work, an abstract painting, has been installed atop the County Building adjacent to the sculpture. Joseph Kinnebrew's *Fish Ladder* sculpture has been placed on the Sixth Street dam. Noted architect and artist Maya Lin (designer of the Vietnam Memorial in Washington D.C.) designed Rosa Parks Circle, a park and amphitheater located in the downtown Monroe Center.

The 150-passenger sternwheeler Grand Lady offers a narrated river cruise pointing out the river landings and town sites of the 1800s.

The John Ball Zoo features more than 237 species and 1,183 specimens. Recent additions include a komodo dragon and a chimpanzee exhibit.

Arts and Culture

The Arts Council coordinates the Festival of the Arts, the largest volunteer-run festival in the nation and a showcase of the arts. The arts in Grand Rapids are celebrated for three days each June with more than one-half million attendees. During the regular season, the Grand Rapids Symphony, an award-winning orchestra recognized for its innovative programming, presents a program of classical, pops, and family concerts. Opera Grand Rapids is the oldest opera theater in Michigan and stages both classical operas and musical theater productions. The Grand Rapids Ballet presents *The Nutcracker* in December plus several other productions each year. Founded in 1883 and designated as a Landmark of American Music, the St. Cecilia Music Society presents public programs and educational opportunities for youth and

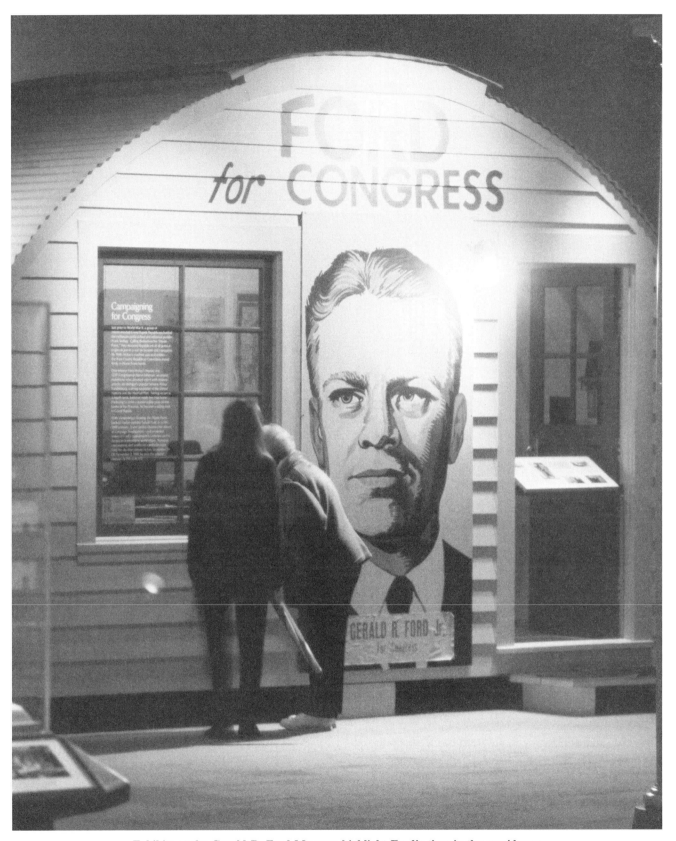

Exhibits at the Gerald R. Ford Museum highlight Ford's time in the presidency.

adults at Royce Auditorium. Other organizations perform at DeVos Hall and the Van Andel Arena.

Grand Rapids Civic Theatre, the second largest community theater in the country and Michigan's oldest community theater, presents six main stage productions and two children's plays annually. Its School of Theater Arts offers a complete range of theatrical training courses as well as one-day workshops and summer programs. Circle Theatre, one of the country's largest summer community theaters, is housed at Aquinas College and features children's theater and a cabaret series in addition to its standard summer offerings. Spectrum Theatre, located downtown at Grand Rapids Community College, features innovative and local plays and is the performance home for Actors' Theatre, GRCC Players, the Jewish Theatre Grand Rapids, and Heritage Theatre Group.

The Grand Rapids Art Museum, opened in 1913 and renovated in 1981, houses a permanent collection of paintings, sculpture, and graphic and decorative arts in ten galleries and hosts traveling art exhibits. The furniture-design wing features period furniture from the Renaissance to the present. The Urban Institute for Contemporary Arts provides exhibition and performance space for concerts, performance art, lectures, and readings. The 125-acre Frederik Meijer Gardens and Sculpture Park hosts the largest tropical conservatory in Michigan, in addition to indoor and outdoor plant and butterfly gardens, nature trails, a boardwalk, three indoor art galleries, and the three-story-tall Leonardo da Vinci's Horse, plus 100 other world-class sculptures from classical and contemporary artists.

Arts and Culture Information: Arts Council of Greater Grand Rapids, 532 Ottawa NW, PO Box 2265, Grand Rapids, MI 49503 telephone: (616)459-2787 fax: (616)459-7160

Festivals and Holidays

The major festival in Grand Rapids is a three-day arts celebration in June that initiates the summer season. Ethnic festivals take place nearly every summer weekend: Irish, Italian, Polish, German, Native American, Mexican, Latino, and African American celebrations of cultural heritage feature song, food, art, and costumes. The Covered Bridge Bike Tour lets cyclists explore Kent County by bicycle in mid-July. The summer season concludes with the Celebration on the Grand during the second weekend in September. Pulaski Days celebrate Polish heritage in October. One of the state's original nighttime parades starts off the Christmas festivities in early December in nearby downtown Coopersville.

Sports for the Spectator

The Grand Rapids Hoops team competes in the semi-professional Continental Basketball League. The Grand Rapids Griffins belong to the International Hockey League, and the Grand Rapids Rampage to the Arena Football League. All three teams play at Van Andel Arena. The West Michigan Whitecaps, a Class A minor affiliate of the Detroit Tigers baseball team, play at Fifth Third Park. Berlin Raceway features stock car racing, and Gratton Raceway presents auto, motorcycle, and go-cart races.

Sports for the Participant

Sports enthusiasts are provided numerous opportunities to enjoy the outdoors in Grand Rapids and the vicinity. Cross-county ski trails wind through scenic apple orchards and across golf courses. The Winter Sports Complex in nearby Muskegon provides the longest lighted ski trail in the Midwest; the center also maintains a 600-meter chute for luge, one of only four in the nation. Three local resorts feature downhill skiing. Year-round fishing is another popular sport, especially trout and perch fishing.

Charter boats on Lake Michigan are available for salmon and lake trout fishing. Swimmers and sunbathers populate the miles of sandy beaches of Lake Michigan and the many inland lakes during the summer. Rowers are often seen on the Grand River, as are salmon fishers in October and November. The Fifth Third River Bank Run, a 25K event attracts runners from around the country. The Gus Macker three-on-three basketball tournament began in Kent County and happens each summer in downtown Grand Rapids.

Recreational facilities within a 60-mile drive include 11 public and several private golf courses, 21 inland lakes, and dozens of tennis courts and baseball fields. Also under development is Millennium Park, a 10-year project launched in 2004, which will return approximately 1,500 acres of industrial land along the Grand River to publicly-owned green space. Once completed, the park will be nearly two and a half times larger than New York's Central Park, making it one of the largest urban parks in the country. Millennium Park currently features a beach house, playground, picnic areas, and fishing ponds. The Grand Rapids recreation department sponsors hundreds of softball teams in league competition, as well as programs in swimming, soccer, baseball, basketball, tennis, golf, scuba diving, and social dancing.

Shopping and Dining

While Grand Rapids doesn't have a true downtown shopping district, it does offer several smaller neighborhood shopping areas in addition to several malls and a strip on 28th Street off of I-96, with many restaurants, larger shops, and strip malls. Woodland Mall offers three major department stores and 120 smaller shops. Breton Village Shopping Center features 40 stores, many locally-owned. RiverTown Crossings contains 120 stores, including six anchor stores, as well as a movie theater. Small shopping districts located throughout the city and surrounding towns include the quaint Squire Street Square in Rockford and the Gaslight Village district in East Grand Rapids, a residential district where fine shops are located in period homes.

The city's best restaurants are clustered downtown. The 1913 Room in the Amway Grand Plaza Hotel is Michigan's only five-diamond restaurant. The award-winning Sierra Room serves Southwestern cuisine in an old warehouse. The B.O.B. features five restaurants, a micro-brewery, night club, comedy club, 2,500 bottle cellar, and billiards.

Visitor Information: Grand Rapids/Kent County Convention and Visitors Bureau, 171 Monroe Ave NW, Suite 700, 49503; telephone (616)459-8287; toll-free (800)678-9859; fax (616)459-7291. Grand Rapids Area Chamber of Commerce, Chamber of Commerce Building, 111 Peal St. NW, Grand Rapids, MI 49503; telephone (616)771-0300; fax (616) 771-0318

Rapids. Eight airlines provide direct service to and from 15 major cities.

A network of interstate, federal, and state highways provides access into Grand Rapids from surrounding communities as well as points throughout the United States and Canada. Interstate highways serving the metropolitan area are I-96, I-196, and I-296. U.S. highways extending through the city are 16 and 131; state routes include 11, 44, 50, 21, and 37. Daily rail passenger transportation from Chicago is provided by Amtrak.

Traveling in the City

Grand Rapids Area Transportation Authority (GRATA) schedules public bus service in the metropolitan area. Go Bus provides door-to-door transportation for the elderly and disabled; the Gus Bus, a commuter shuttle, operates from near-downtown parking lots to the downtown district.

Convention Facilities

Grand Rapids was one of the first cities in the country to build a convention center. The 1933 Art Deco-style Civic Auditorium, renamed Welsh Auditorium, was demolished in 2003 to make way for expansion around De Vos Hall, a performing arts venue, which reopened as part of De Vos Place in 2003. De Vos Place features one million square feet of new and renovated space, including a 160,000-square-foot exhibit hall and 21 meeting rooms. Additional convention facilities include the Amway Grand Plaza Hotel, the Courtyard by Marriott Downtown, and Van Andel Arena. The convention centers are all located within a five block area and are connected by a skyway.

Kent County offers 6,600 hotel rooms, with 1,071 of those in Grand Rapids; many hotels also provide meeting and convention accommodations.

Convention Information: De Vos Place, 303 Monroe St., Grand Rapids, MI 49503 telephone: (616)742-6500; fax: (616)742-6590

Transportation

Approaching the City

Michigan's second-largest airport, Gerald R. Ford International Airport is located 30 minutes from downtown Grand

Communications

Newspapers and Magazines

The Grand Rapids Press is the city's daily newspaper, appearing in the evening. Other newspapers circulating in the community include *The Grand Rapids Times,* targeted to African American community interests, and *Grand Rapids Business Journal. Grand Rapids Magazine* is a monthly publication that features articles of regional interest. Several special-interest magazines are also published in Grand Rapids; a number of them focus on religious topics.

Television and Radio

Six television stations broadcast in Grand Rapids—affiliates of PBS, NBC, ABC, Fox, UPN, and PAX. Twenty-three AM and FM radio stations are based in the city; several of them broadcast Christian inspirational programming, others broadcast sports, music, news, and information.

Media Information: The Grand Rapids Press, Booth Newspapers, Inc., 155 Michigan Street NW, Grand Rapids, MI 49503; telephone (616)459-1567. *Grand Rapids Magazine,* Gemini Publications, 549 Ottawa Ave. NW, Ste. 201, Grand Rapids, MI 49503; telephone (616)459-4545

Grand Rapids Online

De Vos Place. Available www.devosplace.org

Grand Rapids Area Chamber of Commerce. Available www .grandrapids.org

Grand Rapids/Kent County Convention and Visitors Bureau. Available www.grcvb.org

Grand Rapids Press. Available gr.mlive.com/grpress

Grand Rapids Public Library. Available at www.grpl.org

Selected Bibliography

Bratt, James D., et al. *Gathered at the River: Grand Rapids, Michigan, and Its People of Faith* (Wm. B. Eerdmans Publishing Co, 1993)

Ford, Gerald R., et al. *Greater Grand Rapids: City that Works* (Towery Publishing, 1998)

Kalamazoo

The City in Brief

Founded: 1829 (incorporated, 1883)

Head Official: Mayor Robert B. Jones (since 1998)

City Population
  1980: 79,722
  1990: 80,277
  2000: 77,145
  2003 estimate: 75,312
  Percent change, 1990–2000: −3.9%
  U.S. rank in 1980: 271st
  U.S. rank in 1990: 322nd
  U.S. rank in 2000: 390th

Metropolitan Area Population (MSA)
  1980: 279,192 (SMSA)
  1990: 429,453 (MSA)
  2000: 452,851 (MSA)
  Percent change, 1990–2000: 5.4%

  U.S. rank in 1990: 82nd (MSA)
  U.S. rank in 2000: 91st (MSA)

Area: 25.18 square miles (2000)
Elevation: Ranges from 700 to 1,000 feet above sea level
Average Temperatures: January, 24.7° F; July, 72.9 ° F
Average Annual Precipitation: 36.4 inches of rain, 70 inches of snow

Major Economic Sectors: Services, manufacturing, trade, government
Unemployment Rate: 6.5% (February 2005)
Per Capita Income: $16,897 (1999)
2004 ACCRA Average House Price: Not reported
2004 ACCRA Cost of Living Index: Not reported

2002 FBI Crime Index Total: 6,315

Major Colleges and Universities: Western Michigan University, Kalamazoo College, Davenport University, Kalamazoo Valley Community College

Daily Newspaper: *Kalamazoo Gazette*

To Gilmore Classic Car Museum

N

| 0 | 0.25 | 0.5 |
KILOMETERS

MILES   0.25   0.5

To Kalamazoo College, Western Michigan University

NORTH DAKOTA
MINNESOTA
WISCONSIN
SOUTH DAKOTA
MICHIGAN
Kalamazoo
NEBRASKA
IOWA
ILLINOIS
INDIANA
OHIO
KANSAS
MISSOURI
KENTUCKY

Introduction

Kalamazoo, whose name has inspired songs and poems by Carl Sandburg, Glenn Miller, and others, is a small Midwestern town whose several colleges, symphony orchestra, and arts institute lend it a sophistication not usually found in a town its size. The seat of Kalamazoo County, Kalamazoo is an industrial and commercial center in a fertile farm area that produces fruit, celery, and peppermint. The addition of a substantial research and development park along with community leaders willing to collaborate to overcome economic challenges has created a positive business climate; the area's 83 lakes offer fantastic tourist appeal especially for water sports enthusiasts.

Geography and Climate

Kalamazoo lies on the lower reaches of the Kalamazoo River at its confluence with Portage Creek, 35 miles east of Lake Michigan, 107 miles west of Ann Arbor, and 70 miles west of Lansing. The city also represents the halfway point between Chicago and Detroit. The mucky marshland between the river and the creek once supported vast celery fields; today the fertile soil supports large bedding-plant fields.

Nearby Lake Michigan and the prevailing westerly winds produce a lake effect, which increases cloudiness and snowfall during the fall and winter months. Kalamazoo rarely experiences prolonged periods of hot, humid weather in summer or extreme cold during the winter. Precipitation is generally well distributed throughout the year, and the wettest month is usually June. Average seasonal snowfall is nearly 70 inches annually.

Area: 25.18 square miles (2000)

Elevation: Ranges from 700 to 1,000 feet above sea level

Average Temperatures: January, 24.7° F; July, 72.9° F

Average Annual Precipitation: 36.4 inches of rain, 70 inches of snow

History

Early Days as "Celery City"

Sometime before the early seventeenth century, the Potawatomi Indians moved from the east coast of the United States and established settlements in southern Michigan, where they fished and hunted for wild game. They called the river that flows through present-day Kalamazoo "Kikalamazoo," which means "boiling water" because of the hundreds of bubbling springs in it. In 1823, a trading post called Kikalamazoo was established on the banks of the river.

In 1827 the Potawatomi ceded their Michigan lands to the United States, and permanent settlers began to arrive in 1829. They were led by Titus Bronson, who called the town Bronson. But Titus Bronson was an outspoken man who voiced strong political opinions, and some critics say he was overly fond of alcohol. Historians say his crankiness and restless, erratic behavior, symptomatic of what is today called Tourette's syndrome, did not endear him to settlers who came after.

In 1833, with a population of about 100 people, Kalamazoo demonstrated its commitment to higher education by establishing Kalamazoo College. During the winter of 1835, a movement began to officially change the name of the town from Bronson back to its Indian name in the shortened form Kalamazoo. This was finalized before the state of Michigan was entered into the Union in January 1837.

The years 1834 to 1837 were a time of prosperity in the United States and the greatest land sales in American history took place. In 1835, the land office at Kalamazoo sold more acres than any other land office in the history of the country. More than 1.6 million acres were sold, accounting for more than $2 million in receipts. According to the *Detroit Democratic Free Press* newspaper: "We are informed that the village of Kalamazoo is literally thronged with purchasers. The public and private houses are full and . . . in some instances, they are compelled to retire to the barns for . . . lodging."

In 1847, a group of religious refugees from The Netherlands settled in Kalamazoo at the same time a Scotsman named James Taylor was experimenting with celery seeds imported from England. Taylor could not convince the townsfolk of the joys of eating celery (they thought it was poisonous). His experiment languished for 10 years until a Dutchman named Cornelius De Bruin began to cultivate celery in the rich black muck along the Kalamazoo River. The De Bruin children sold the celery door to door. Before long, the celery fields of "Celery City" were flourishing and it was not uncommon to see Kalamazoo peddlers selling celery on the streets of the little town.

Transition to "Paper and Rice City"

With their marshes proving so profitable, civic leaders turned their attention to advertising the city's water resources to potential investors in a paper mill. In 1874, Kalamazoo Paper was established, just the first of many companies that would make Kalamazoo a paper mill center.

Soon other industries were attracted to the town, which was strategically located between Detroit and Chicago.

One early entrepreneur was William Erastus Upjohn, who graduated from the University of Michigan Medical School in 1875 and opened up a private practice and a pharmaceutical laboratory in Kalamazoo. He developed a process for making pills and granules that resulted in 1885 in the Upjohn Pill and Granule Company. Upjohn's experiment became Pharmacia & Upjohn Company then Pharmacia Corp. More industries followed at the end of the nineteenth century, and Kalamazoo was turning out stoves, essential oils, and iron and allied products.

Growth as Educational Center

Kalamazoo was incorporated as a city in 1883 and began a rapid modernization, installing a horse-car line that year and following two years later with an electric light and power plant. The city's educational system also experienced steady growth with the opening of the all-women's Nazareth College in 1871 then Western Michigan University's founding in 1903.

In 1918, Kalamazoo was one of the first cities in Michigan to adopt the commission-manager form of government, led by Dr. Upjohn as the inaugural mayor. Many fine buildings were constructed, including city hall in 1931, the five-story county building in 1937, and fine homes representing several architectural styles, including a number of Frank Lloyd Wright's "Usonian" homes constructed during the 1940s.

By 1937, Kalamazoo boasted 151 industrial establishments manufacturing goods valued at more than $70 million. Thirteen paper mills dominated the industrial scene; other industries included cultivated peppermint and the manufacture of taxicabs, furnaces, auto bodies, transmissions, caskets, clothing, fishing rods and reels, playing cards, and musical instruments. Kalamazoo has nurtured cultural activities as well as industry. The Kalamazoo Symphony Orchestra was established in 1921; the city also boasts the Kalamazoo Institute of Arts, founded in 1924, and numerous performing arts groups.

Kalamazoo opened the country's first permanent outdoor pedestrian shopping mall in 1959. Despite economic turbulence in the early 2000s, the city remains a prosperous center of diverse industries and agricultural products. City planners have worked actively to overcome the loss of major area businesses. One such example is the flourishing of the Business Technology and Research Park at Western Michigan University to compensate for job losses tied to Pfizer's acquisition of Kalamazoo's largest employer, Pharmacia & Upjohn Company. In July 2002 the multimillion-dollar producer of pharmaceuticals and agricultural seeds was bought out for $60 billion in stock by New York City-based Pfizer,

but retains the Kalamazoo laboratories. The area appeals to workers for its small-town charm coupled with a wide variety of cultural activities. A variety of tax incentives make it enticing to high-growth businesses as well.

Historical Information: Western Michigan University Archives & Regional History Collection, Rm. 111, East Hall, Western Michigan University, Kalamazoo, MI 49008; telephone (269)387-8490; fax (269)387-8484; email arch_collect@wmich.edu

Population Profile

Metropolitan Area Residents
1980: 279,192 (SMSA)
1990: 429,453 (MSA)
2000: 452,851 (MSA)
Percent change, 1990–2000: 5.4%
U.S. rank in 1990: 82nd (MSA)
U.S. rank in 2000: 91st (MSA)

City Residents
1980: 79,722
1990: 80,277
2000: 77,145
2003 estimate: 75,312
Percent change, 1990–2000: −3.9%
U.S. rank in 1990: 322nd
U.S. rank in 2000: 390th

Density: 3,125.4 people per square mile (2000)

Racial and ethnic characteristics (2000)
  White: 54,593
  Black or African American: 15,924
  American Indian and Alaska Native: 445
  Asian: 1,847
  Native Hawaiian and Pacific Islander: 50
  Hispanic or Latino (may be of any race): 3,304
  Other: 1,836

Percent of residents born in state: 69.2% (2000)

Age characteristics (2000)
  Population under 5 years old: 4,786
  Population 5 to 9 years old: 4,530
  Population 10 to 14 years old: 4,121
  Population 15 to 19 years old: 9,315
  Population 20 to 24 years old: 14,179
  Population 25 to 34 years old: 11,585
  Population 35 to 44 years old: 9,095
  Population 45 to 54 years old: 7,434
  Population 55 to 59 years old: 2,458

Population 60 to 64 years old: 1,845
Population 65 to 74 years old: 3,505
Population 75 to 84 years old: 2,919
Population 85 years and over: 1,373
Median age: 26.1 years (2000)

Births (2003)
Total number: 1,411

Deaths (2003)
Total number: 640 (of which, 15 were infants under the age of 1 year)

Money income (1999)
Per capita income: $16,897
Median household income: $31,189 (1999)
Total households: 29,415

Number of households with income of . . .
less than $10,000: 4,527
$10,000 to $14,999: 2,757
$15,000 to $24,999: 4,932
$25,000 to $34,999: 3,790
$35,000 to $49,999: 4,801
$50,000 to $74,999: 4,733
$75,000 to $99,999: 1,880
$100,000 to $149,999: 1,305
$150,000 to $199,999: 316
$200,000 or more: 374

Percent of families below poverty level: 13.6% (46.9% of which were female householder families with related children under 5 years)

2002 FBI Crime Index Total: 6,315

Municipal Government

Kalamazoo, seat of Kalamazoo County, has a commission/manager form of government. The city commissioners are elected on an at-large basis during odd-numbered calendar years. The mayor is the commissioner who received the largest number of votes at the preceding election, and is responsible for representing the city at ceremonial functions and signing contracts; the city manager transacts the city's daily business affairs.

Head Official: Mayor Robert B, Jones (since 1998; current term expires 2005)

Total Number of City Employees: 915 (2005)

City Information: Mayor's Office, City of Kalamazoo, 241 W. South St., Kalamazoo, MI 49007-4796; telephone (269)337-8046; fax (269)337-8182; email jonesr@kalamazoocity.com

Economy

Major Industries and Commercial Activity

Kalamazoo is located close to the automobile manufacturing center of Detroit, Michigan, and the Kalamazoo area has automotive components companies and plastics firms that make automotive testing equipment and hydraulic systems. Eaton Corporation's North American truck component headquarters and Checker Motors are also based in the city.

Kalamazoo's diversified economic base also includes the production of pharmaceutical and medical products, cereals, and paper products, as well as financial services.

Downtown Kalamazoo remains the site of Pfizer's offices, manufacturing facilities, and research labs following its buyout of the homegrown Pharmacia & Upjohn Company (whose presence in the community dated back more than a century) which has helped to keep the local economy somewhat stable. Once a giant paper production area, Kalamazoo's importance in this field has greatly diminished. However, several paper manufacturing firms, such as the James River Corporation, continue to manufacture paper items locally.

Western Michigan University, which employs nearly 2,900 people, also makes a significant contribution to the local economy. One of Kalamazoo County's fastest growing employers is National City Bank. Farms near the city produce hay and corn, as well as fruit.

Items and goods produced: fruit, flowering plants, peppermint, and other agricultural products; pharmaceuticals; paper and paper products; metal products; machinery; guitars

Incentive Programs—New and Existing Companies

Local programs—Kalamazoo's Community Planning and Development Department assists local businesses and industries by providing technical assistance with site selection for expansion or relocation, through tax abatements, and by providing help with permits and other paperwork. The Brownfield Redevelopment Financing Act is operated by the city and provides many tax relief benefits to redevelopers. Southwest Michigan First is an organization dedicated to developing and implementing a successful long-term economic strategy for the area. Kalamazoo College's Stryker Center provides small businesses with information in obtaining commercial loans. The Small Business Revolving Fund can supply up to $40,000 in funding.

State programs—The Michigan Economic Growth Authority (MEGA) was created to further the formation of new jobs that feed into a prosperous economy. Small Business Tax (SBT) credits are available for fiscally-responsible companies in the fields of manufacturing, research and development, wholesale trade, or office operations. Michigan communities can abate up to 50 percent of local property taxes for up to 12 years. Since 2001 the Kalamazoo area has six designated Renaissance Zones that, if a business locates inside the zone, allows for waiving a variety of taxes such as the single business tax, local real property tax, and utility users tax. State law also exempts inventory, pollution control equipment, and certain tools, dies, jigs, and fixtures from local property taxes.

Job training programs—Michigan offers a coordinated job training system called "Michigan Works!" using federal, state, and local resources to provide a highly productive and trained workforce. The federal Workforce Investment Act (WIA) and state Michigan Department of Labor and Economic Growth (MDLEG) provide funding for the grants that assist in increasing worker productivity. The training itself is done through the institution of the company's choice. Free recruitment and screening services are available for new and expanding employers through the Michigan Employment Security Administration's job service and also through several local school districts. However, all hiring decisions belong to the company.

Development Projects

Kalamazoo's Neighborhood and Economic Development office helps in identifying and promoting properties that are prime for building. A $2.83 million grant from the Clean Michigan Initiative Waterfront Redevelopment is playing a part in the "Riverfront Redevelopment Plan" that strives to utilize the land for a mix of business and residential purposes.

Western Michigan University's Business Technology and Research Park continued expansion of its Southwest Michigan Innovation Center (SMIC) and ability to draw advanced engineering, life sciences, and information technology companies has proved to be a major economic catalyst for the area. When Pfizer acquired Pharmacia & Upjohn Company in 2002, the Southwest Michigan First organization played a vital role in retaining scientists with its "Stick Around" campaign. This effort has allowed for nearly two dozen companies to move into the research park including VDDI Pharmaceuticals in 2003 and TEKNA Solutions Inc., who announced in March 2005 that it will build a 24,000-square-foot facility.

In a continued effort for a new justice center in the downtown area to centralize Kalamazoo's public safety and court

facilities, a bond proposal was put into action in April 2005 by the Kalamazoo County Board of Commissioners. A new $32 million wing terminal was to begin construction in the summer of 2005 that will increase the Kalamazoo/Battle Creek International Airport to 93,000 square feet.

In 2005 a groundbreaking was planned for a new Michigan Space & Science Center at the Air Zoo. It will host a $30 million space artifact collection acquired from the previous facility at Jackson Community College and be located on 30,000 square feet of land that will include a 120-seat theater. Nearby Gilmore Car Museum expanded their facilities by 50 percent with the addition of three exhibit buildings in 2004.

Economic Development Information: Southwest Michigan First, 346 W. Michigan Ave., Kalamazoo, MI 49007; telephone (269)553-9588; fax (269)553-6897; email info @southwestmichiganfirst.com

Commercial Shipping

Kalamazoo County has 26 motor carriers; ConRail and Grand Trunk Western railways provide freight rail service.

Labor Force and Employment Outlook

Kalamazoo is said to have a diverse labor force with a wide range of skills. Local colleges assist job seekers via training and placement programs in conjunction with area businesses. The economic recession in the early 2000s took a toll on area employment opportunities, though, with dramatic declines in the manufacturing sector. According to the W. E. Upjohn Institute, as of March 2005 the manufacturing industry failed to progress at a similar rate to national levels resulting in the loss of several hundred potential positions. Private education and healthcare were great performers for Kalamazoo, both exceeding national growth. Overall, the Institute does project modest gains in total employment, particularly in the service industry, with manufacturing looking toward slight improvement.

The following is a summary of data regarding the Kalamazoo-Portage metropolitan area labor force, 2004 annual average.

Size of nonagricultural labor force: 144,300

Number of workers employed in . . .
   construction and mining: 6,500
   manufacturing: 24,500
   trade, transportation, and utilities: 25,500
   information: 1,500
   financial activities: 7,600
   professional and business services: 14,100
   educational and health services: 19,800
   leisure and hospitality: 14,900

other services: 6,700
government: 23,300

Average hourly earnings of production workers employed in manufacturing: $15.90

Unemployment rate: 6.5% (February 2005)

Largest employers
(*Kalamazoo-Portage area*)	*Number of employees*
Pfizer	6,100
Bronson Hospital	3,000
National City Bank	2,922
Western Michigan University	2,887
Borgess Health Alliance	2,410
Meijer, Inc.	2,400
Kalamazoo Public Schools	2,300
Portage Public Schools	2,300
Stryker Corporation (hospital equipment)	1,400
Kalamazoo Valley Community College	1,100

Cost of Living

The following is a summary of data regarding several key cost of living factors for the Kalamazoo area.

2004 ACCRA Cost of Living Index: Not reported

2004 ACCRA Average House Price: Not reported

State income tax rate: 3.9%

State sales tax rate: 6.0%

Local income tax rate: None

Local sales tax rate: None

Property tax rate: up to 25 mills per $1,000 (2005)

Economic Information: Kalamazoo Regional Chamber of Commerce, 346 W. Michigan Ave., Kalamazoo, MI 49007; telephone (269)381-4000; fax (269)343-0430; email editor @kazoochamber.com

Education and Research

Elementary and Secondary Schools

The students in Kalamazoo's schools have access to the Education for Employment (EFE) program, which helps them in planning for their future careers, as well as the Education for the Arts (EFA) program, which enhances their art education with dance, literary arts, media arts, music,

theater, and visual arts classes. The Kalamazoo Area Mathematics & Science Center offers accelerated programs in math, science, and technology to public and private high school students.

The following is a summary of data regarding the Kalamazoo public school system as of the 2004–2005 school year.

Total enrollment: 10,500

Number of facilities
  elementary schools: 16
  middle schools: 3
  senior high schools: 2
  other: 8

Student/teacher ratio: 17:1

Teacher salaries
  average: $54,020

Funding per pupil: $9,304 (2002-2003)

Approximately 1,500 Kalamazoo students attend local Christian schools, more than 1,700 attend Catholic schools, and about 500 attend other non-public schools.

Public Schools Information: Kalamazoo Public Schools, 1220 Howard St., Kalamazoo, MI 49008; telephone (269)337-0100

Colleges and Universities

Kalamazoo is the site of two universities and two colleges. Western Michigan University (WMU), one of the top public research universities in the country, offers 254 degree and certificate programs to its nearly 28,000 students. Its wide array of centers and institutes conduct research and share knowledge gained with business, government, and other organizations. *U.S. News and World Report* magazine has consistently ranked WMU as a leading national university throughout the 1990s and 2000s.

Kalamazoo College, Michigan's oldest (founded in 1833), is located in Kalamazoo's historic district and offers its 1,234 students bachelor of arts degree programs in 25 majors and 9 areas of concentration, such as international and area studies, environmental studies, public policy and urban affairs, and others. Among its 19 buildings and facilities are the Dow Science Center, and the Stryker Center, which offers seminars in business and management.

Davenport University, the largest independent university system in the state, is based in Grand Rapids but has more than 1,000 students on its Kalamazoo campus. The Kalamazoo campus offers bachelor of science, bachelor of applied science, associate of science, and associate of applied science degrees, as well as certificate programs, in a variety of areas in business, health care, and legal studies. Kalamazoo Valley Community College offers its 9,300 students associate in arts, associate in science, and associate in applied science degrees, as well as certificates. It prides itself on its flexible scheduling and provides areas of study that include liberal arts, health and sciences, business, and the technologies.

Libraries and Research Centers

With a stunning granite and limestone exterior, the Kalamazoo Public Library has a four-level rotunda that admits natural light through a skylight via a 79-foot dome. The library's five buildings feature holographic materials and light sculptures that result in an ever-changing rainbow of colors. In addition to the main branch the library maintains four branches and one bookmobile, contains roughly 436,000 volumes and has special collections in history, culture, African American studies, and Kalamazoo history.

Davenport University, Kalamazoo College, Kalamazoo Valley Community College, and Western Michigan University all have libraries. The W. E. Upjohn Institute Library has titles focusing on labor market issues, and state and local economic development, among other topics. Borgess Health Information Library has a special community health information section, and Bronson Methodist Hospital Library focuses on allied and consumer health issues.

Two research centers in Kalamazoo are the Kalamazoo Nature Center and the W. E. Upjohn Institute for Employment Research. Western Michigan University is the site of several research and technology centers and also has centers focusing on computer graphics, design excellence, environmental signal transduction, and biological imaging, Black Americana studies, business, women's studies, and ethics.

Public Library Information: Kalamazoo Public Library, 315 S. Rose St., Kalamazoo, MI 49007; telephone (269)342-9837

Health Care

Kalamazoo is home to three major health care facilities. Borgess Medical Center, with 426 beds, has special units in coronary, cardiac surgery, intensive, and neuro-intensive care and offers a wide range of diagnostic and therapeutic facilities. Bronson Methodist Hospital, with 343 beds, is a Level 1 Trauma Center, designated Children's Hospital, and Level 3 Perinatal Center. The hospital has special care units that treat patients for burns and for cardiac and coronary problems. It also offers intensive care, neonatal intensive care, pediatric intensive care, trauma care, and a hyperbaric unit.

Kalamazoo Regional Psychiatric Hospital, established in 1859, provides inpatient service for up to 173 adults throughout the southwestern Michigan region.

Recreation

Sightseeing

Kalamazoo's Bronson Park is the centerpiece of the city's downtown and features sculptures, war monuments, and historical markers and hosts various festivals and cultural events. Maps for self-directed walking/driving tours of three historic districts throughout Kalamazoo are available from the Convention Bureau and at City Hall. The Village of Schoolcraft offers tours by appointment of the 1835 Underground Railroad Home where a local physician once hid escaped slaves.

Kalamazoo Valley Museum, in the city's downtown, features a Digistar theater and planetarium, a creative preschool activity area, and the Challenger Learning Center, in which children can take off on a simulated space mission. It also houses a 2,300-year-old mummy and hands-on science and history exhibits. The Kalamazoo Institute of Arts includes an interactive gallery called ARTworks, a new community auditorium, and a museum store.

The Kalamazoo Nature Center has an exhibit hall where visitors can perform experiments, learn about plants and animals, and view natural objects magnified 10-fold. Its Parfet Butterfly House provides an indoor tropical sun-rain room, an outdoor garden, and a barn which houses farm animals. Also on site are an 11-acre arboretum and nature trails that are wheelchair and stroller accessible. In nearby Augusta is the Kellogg Bird Sanctuary where year-round visitors can walk a self-guided trail and observe the native waterfowl and birds of prey along Wintergreen Lake. Also in Augusta is the Fort Custer National Cemetery, an official burial ground for U.S. veterans, which contains the graves of 26 German soldiers held as American prisoners during World War II.

The Kalamazoo Air Zoo presents a display of over 60 vintage aircraft and an area that allows visitors to climb into mock cockpits and pretend to fly. Rides include a virtual reality simulator and a four-dimensional theater that puts visitors in the middle of a World War II bombing mission. In nearby Hickory Corners, auto buffs can visit Gilmore Car Museum, rated one of the ten best in the country. The museum outlines the development of the American car in a six-barn, 90-acred, landscaped setting and features almost 200 vehicles from the past century.

Visitors to what was once known as "Celery City" can experience what life was like during the city's past in nearby

Portage, were the Celery Flats Interpretive Center features exhibits of the age of celery production. Music lovers can visit the Gibson/Heritage Guitar building, a factory where Gibson Guitars were built in the early 1900s.

The Wolf Lake State Fish Hatchery, eight miles west of Kalamazoo, has hourly tours, a slide show, and a display pond. The Kellogg Dairy Center in Hickory Corners provides various tours where visitors can learn about the dairy cycle and observe a computerized milking parlor.

Arts and Culture

Miller Auditorium at the Western Michigan University campus made its debut in 1968 and now is the site of touring Broadway shows, conventions, and jazz, rock, and symphonic concerts. Wings Stadium hosts arena-style concerts of popular music acts for audiences of about 8,000. The 1,569-seat State Theatre, built in 1927, features music and comedy performers under a star-spangled sky projected on the ceiling. Chenery Auditorium hosts concerts and travel-film series at this handsome 1,900-seat public facility. The intimate 200-seat Suzanne D. Parish Theatre carries several plays throughout the year while the Carver Center hosts the Civic Arena Theatre, Civic Black Theatre, and Kalamazoo Civic Youth Theatre, among others.

Western Michigan University's Miller Auditorium is also the home of the Kalamazoo Symphony Orchestra (KSO) that presents a full concert series, as well as chamber and family concerts year-round. KSO also offers free summer concerts at local parks. Fontana Chamber Arts presents chamber music concerts at various sites throughout the city. The Kalamazoo Concert Band, made up of adult musicians and founded in 1961, presents a series of concerts at several local venues. An array of dance performances, from ballet and folk to highland flings are presented by the Kalamazoo Ballet Company at the Comstock Community Auditorium and other sites throughout the city.

Several area theaters offer a variety of performances such as WMU's Irving S. Gilmore Theatre Complex, the Actors & Playwrights' Initiative (API) Theatre, and the Whole Art Theater Company. The New Vic Theatre presents both experimental and traditional fare, including an annual holiday schedule of *A Christmas Carol*. During its 16-week summer-stock season, the Barn Theatre in nearby Augusta draws about 50,000 patrons.

Festivals and Holidays

Autumn in Kalamazoo offers the National Street Rod Association race at the Kalamazoo County while the annual Festival of Trees takes place at the Radisson Plaza Hotel in November. December brings the New Year's Fest at Bronson Park and surrounding buildings.

The cold winter weather is perfect for January's Great Winter Adventure featuring ice sculpting, and at nearby Timber Ridge visitors can enjoy a variety of snow-related activities at the Winter Fest Fun event. March turns downtown green for the St. Patrick's Day parade; the Kalamazoo Nature Center is sticky sweet with the Maple Sugar Festival.

The Annual Spring Conference on Wind and Percussion takes place at WMU/Miller Auditorium in early April and proud canines are the focus of the West Michigan Apple Blossom Cluster A.K.C. Dog Show at the Kalamazoo County Fairgrounds in May.

Among June's activities are the Mayfair celebration at Bronson Park, the Dionysos Greekfest, and the Island Fest at Arcadia Festival Site. Also in June are the Kalamazoo Institute of Arts's Art Fair at Bronson Park, the Do-Dah Parade downtown, and the Parade of Homes, which takes place throughout the Kalamazoo area. The actors of the Michigan Shakespeare Festival take the stage at the Celery Flats Amphitheater at the end of the month.

In July, the Great Lakes Folk Festival is at Celery Flats and the Team U.S. National Hot-Air Balloon championship takes flight at Kellogg Airfield in Battle Creek. Other July events include the Blues Festival, a Taste of Kalamazoo at the Arcadia Festival Place, Warbirds Over Kalamazoo at the Kalamazoo Aviation History Museum, and the Silver Leaf Renaissance Faire, which is presented on certain weekends at the River Oaks County Park.

The Kalamazoo County Fair at the Fairgrounds brings food and fun to the citizenry in August, which is also the month for the Ribfest at the Arcadia Festival Site, the weeklong Black Arts Festival that can be seen at various downtown locations, the two-day Red Barns Spectacular at the Gilmore Car Museum, and the Scottish Fest at the Kalamazoo County Fairgrounds.

Arcadia Creek in downtown Kalamazoo is a popular festival area that features a natural river encased underground and surrounded by a park. Every other spring, Kalamazoo is the site of the Gilmore International Keyboard Festival, which involves more than 100 keyboard-related events that take place throughout western Michigan.

Sports for the Spectator

Kalamazoo's professional hockey team, the Michigan K-Wings, is in the United Hockey League (UHL) and plays at Wings Stadium. The Kalamazoo area is also home to the men's Kalamazoo Kingdom and women's Kalamazoo Quest of the United Soccer Leagues. Stowe Stadium at Kalamazoo College hosts the U.S. Tennis Association Boys' 18–16 National Championships every year. Since 1980 the Little League Girls' Softball Senior and Big League World Series is held at Vanderberg Park. NASCAR racing has a weekly series at the Kalamazoo Speedway.

Fans of college sports have many events from which to choose. Western Michigan University has men's baseball, basketball, football, ice hockey, soccer, tennis, and track/cross country, while women compete in basketball, gymnastics, indoor and outdoor track, soccer, softball, tennis, volleyball, golf, precision ice skating, and track/cross country. Many of the competitions are open to spectators.

Kalamazoo College has varsity men's teams competing in baseball, basketball, cross-country, football, golf, soccer, swimming, and tennis. Women's teams compete in basketball, cross country, softball, soccer, swimming, tennis, volleyball, and golf. The Cougars of Kalamazoo Valley Community College have intercollegiate competitions in volleyball, basketball, softball, and tennis for women, and basketball, baseball, tennis, and golf for men.

Sports for the Participant

The city of Kalamazoo has 55 parks that cover nearly 1,300 acres. The city has three golf courses and many more are nearby. Kalamazoo County offers more than 100 public outdoor tennis courts including Kalamazoo College's Stowe Stadium and boating opportunities on nearby Gull Lake and Lake Michigan. The Kal-Haven Trail, which runs from the city to South Haven, Michigan, is a biking/hiking/snowmobile/cross country skiing trail that runs for 34 miles. Water sports are readily accessed via the area's 83 public-access lakes.

Shopping and Dining

Kalamazoo has four major shopping malls. Kalamazoo Mall, once famous as the first outdoor pedestrian shopping mall in the country, is now open to traffic and features a variety of shops, galleries, and dining establishments. Four large department stores anchor the Crossroads regional shopping mall, which has more than 100 specialty stores and restaurants. Maple Hill Mall, home to a major office store and discount and specialty stores, underwent renovations in 2001, expanding to 642,000 square feet. Southland Mall features office, book, and clothing shops, as well as other retail stores.

Southwestern Michigan is known for its wineries and microbreweries, whose products can be enjoyed at the wide selection of restaurants in Kalamazoo. Dining choices run from ethnic restaurants featuring Mexican, Italian, Greek, Australian, and Chinese to local and chain establishments that serve hearty American fare, such as St. Louis-style ribs, seafood, fresh fish, prime rib, and other favorites. The Black Swan provides gourmet continental cuisine with choices like leg of lamb or beef Wellington for two in its attractive

location on Willow Lake. Webster's Restaurant at the Radisson Plaza hotel is western Michigan's only AAA Four Diamond Award-winning restaurant, and features seafood, chops, pasta, and fresh desserts.

Visitor Information: Kalamazoo County Convention & Visitors Bureau, The Chamber Building, 346 W. Michigan Ave., Kalamazoo, MI 49007-3783; telephone (269)381-4003; toll-free (800)530-9192

Convention Facilities

Among Kalamazoo's major conference facilities are Bernhard Center at Western Michigan University, which has 25 meeting rooms with a maximum capacity of 1,700 people in meeting-style and 1,250 in banquet-style rooms. The John E. Fetzer Center on the Western Michigan University campus has 13 meeting rooms that can handle 280 banquet-style, 90-seat lecture hall, and a 250-seat auditorium.

The Clarion Hotel offers 13 meeting rooms and features a 400-seat ballroom along with several banquet-style and classroom-style options in 5,000 square feet of meeting space. The Radisson Plaza Hotel & Suites has 44,000 square feet of meeting space including 21 meeting rooms with a capacity of 1,000 people, 850 for a banquet, or 544 in classrooms. Holiday Inn West has six meeting rooms including a 400-seat ballroom for receptions.

The County Center Building furnishes five meeting rooms that can accommodate 2,000 banquet-style; the largest exhibit space is 20,000 square feet. The James W. Miller Auditorium, on Western Michigan University's campus, has two meeting rooms that support 3,485 meeting-style or classroom-style. The Wings Stadium Complex has three meeting rooms that seats 8,032 in the stadium, 2,850 in "The Annex," and 250 in "The Cube." The largest exhibit space is 17,000 square feet and seats 5,113 arena-style.

Dr. William E. Upjohn's former home, Brook Lodge, provides 12,000 square feet of meeting space on an exquisite 637-acre estate. The Yarrow Golf & Conference Center has 12 meeting rooms for up to 300 guests with an 18-hole championship course as the backdrop.

Convention Information: Kalamazoo County Convention & Visitors Bureau, The Chamber Building, 346 W. Michigan Ave., Kalamazoo, MI 49007-3783; telephone (269)381-4003; toll-free (800)530-9192

Transportation

Approaching the City

Kalamazoo/Battle Creek International Airport is located on Portage Road in Kalamazoo, just south of Interstate 94. The airport serves about 500,000 passengers annually on American Eagle, ComAir, Continental Express, Northwest Airlines, and United Express. Major highways leading to Kalamazoo include Interstate-94 (running east-west) and U.S. highway 131 (running north-south).

With more than 75,000 riders in 2004, Amtrak provides daily rail service including Chicago and Detroit. In 2002 part of Michigan's Detroit-to-Chicago line, the 30-mile stretch between Kalamazoo and Niles, became the nation's first high-speed rail service outside the northeast. B & W Charters and Indian Trails Motorcoach offer bus transportation to other areas of the state and beyond.

Traveling in the City

Local bus service is provided by Kalamazoo Metro Transit, which also operates Metro Van service, a demand-response service for people with disabilities. Two charter bus lines along with several cab services are available.

Communications

Newspapers and Magazines

Kalamazoo's daily paper is the *Kalamazoo Gazette.* Western Michigan University's *The Western Herald* student newspaper is published Monday-Thursday throughout the academic year. *Flashes Shopping Guide* appears weekly.

Local magazines include *Bloodlines,* featuring various breeds of dogs; *Coonhound Bloodlines*; *Hunting Retriever*; *Business Outlook for West Michigan*; and *Third Coast,* a magazine by the Western Michigan University English Department.

A number of journals are associated with WMU that cover business, accounting, drama, Medieval studies, and socio-logy. Fetzer Institute publishes *Advances,* a journal on mind-body health.

Television and Radio

Kalamazoo has one network, one independent, and one cable television station. The city has four AM radio stations, two with news formats, one with a sports format, and one with a music format. Two of the seven local FM-radio stations have adult contemporary music formats, while the formats of the other five include Top 40, classic rock, alternative music, classical music, and an independent format.

Media Information: *The Kalamazoo Gazette,* 401 S. Burdick St., Kalamazoo, MI 49007; telephone (269)345-3511

Kalamazoo Online

City of Kalamazoo home page. Available www.ci.kalamazoo.mi.us

Kalamazoo County community profile. Available www.multi mag.com/county/mi/kalamazoo/demo.html

Kalamazoo County Convention & Visitors Bureau. Available www.kazoofun.com

Kalamazoo Gazette. Available www.mlive.com/kzgazette

Kalamazoo Public Library. Available www.kpl.gov

Kalamazoo Public Schools. Available www.kalamazoopublicschools.com

Kalamazoo Regional County Chamber of Commerce. Available www.kazoochamber.com

Selected Bibliography

Connable, Al (Alfred Barnes) as told to Tom Thinnes, *Michigan Man: The Life and Times of Kalamazoo's Al Connable* (Allegan Forest, MI: Priscilla Press, 2000)

Durant, Samuel W., and Ruth Marian Robbins Monteith, *History of Kalamazoo County, Michigan: with illustrations and biographical sketches of its prominent men and pioneers* (Evansville, IN: Unigraphic, 1976)

Lane, Kit, *Built on the Banks of the Kalamazoo* (Douglas, MI: Pavilion Press, 1993)

Massie, Larry B. and Peter J. Schmitt, *Kalamazoo: The Place Behind the Products* (Sun Valley, CA: American Historical Press, 1998)

Lansing

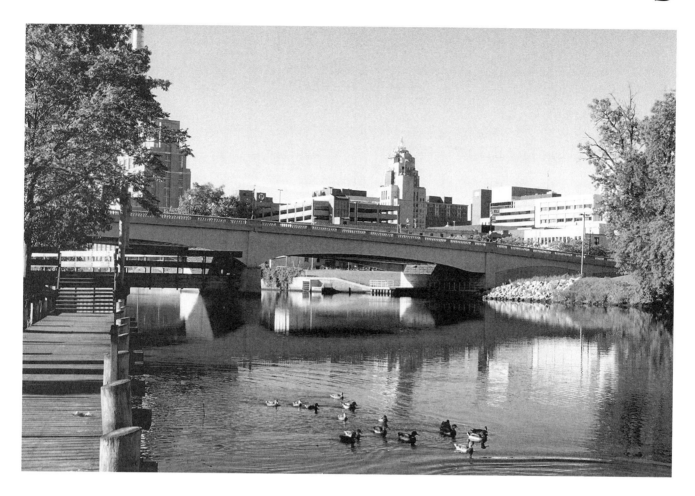

The City in Brief

Founded: 1837 (incorporated, 1849)

Head Official: Mayor Tony Benavides (NP) (since 2003)

City Population
  1980: 130,414
  1990: 127,321
  2000: 119,128
  2003 estimate: 118,379
  Percent change, 1990–2000: −6.4%
  U.S. rank in 1980: 122nd
  U.S. rank in 1990: 142nd
  U.S. rank in 2000: 204th

Metropolitan Area Population
  1980: 420,000
  1990: 432,684
  2000: 447,728
  Percent change, 1990–2000: 3.5%

  U.S. rank in 1980: 81st
  U.S. rank in 1990: Not reported
  U.S. rank in 2000: 92nd

Area: 35.24 square miles (2000)
Elevation: 880 feet above sea level
Average Annual Temperature: 48° F
Average Annual Precipitation: 30.8 inches of rain, 48.9 inches of snow

Major Economic Sectors: Government, trade, services, manufacturing
Unemployment Rate: 6.4% (February 2005)
Per Capita Income: $17,924 (1999)
2004 ACCRA Average House Price: Not reported
2004 ACCRA Cost of Living Index: Not reported

2002 FBI Crime Index Total: 6,601

Major Colleges and Universities: Michigan State University (in East Lansing), Lansing Community College

Daily Newspaper: *Lansing State Journal*

Introduction

Lansing is the capital of Michigan and the focus of a metropolitan statistical area that includes the city of East Lansing and Clinton, Eaton, and Ingham counties. Virtually a wilderness when the site was designated for the building of the state capital, Lansing was slow to develop until the arrival of the railroad. The nation's first land grant college was founded in Lansing, and the city became a world leader in the automotive industry through the pioneering work of the Olds Motor Vehicle Company. Today Lansing's status as the state capital, its industrial base including General Motors, a stable economy, and the presence of Michigan State University in East Lansing contribute to the city's overall strength. These attributes also led *Expansion Management* magazine to name Lansing as Michigan's only "Five Star" city for "Quality of Life Quotient" in 2003 and 2004.

Geography and Climate

Lansing is located on the Grand River at its junction with the Red Cedar. The area climate alternates between continental and semi-marine. When little or no wind is present, the weather becomes continental, producing pronounced fluctuations in temperature. The weather turns semi-marine with a strong wind from the Great Lakes. Snowfall averages about 49 inches annually. Tornadoes occur occasionally, as do thunder and wind storms. Flooding is likely one year out of three; floods cause extensive damage one year out of ten.

Area: 35.24 square miles (2000)

Elevation: 880 feet above sea level

Average Temperatures: January, 22° F; July, 71° F; annual average, 48° F

Average Annual Precipitation: 30.8 inches of rain, 48.9 inches of snow

History

Wilderness Site Chosen for State Capital

The original settlers of Lansing arrived at the junction of the Grand and Red Cedar rivers expecting to find New Settlement, a city that turned out to exist only on paper. Most of the pioneers were from the village of Lansing, New York,

and some decided to settle the area, deciding to call it Lansing Township in honor of their former home. James Seymour, another resident of New York State, migrated to Detroit in the mid-1830s and acquired land holdings in the Michigan interior for purposes of speculation. Seymour was aware that the Michigan constitution of 1835 specified that a permanent site be found by 1847 for the state capital, which was then temporarily located in Detroit. The legislators feared Detroit's proximity to Canada would make it susceptible to foreign invasion, as had been the case in the War of 1812 when it fell under British rule. Since no mutually agreed-upon township could be found, Seymour pressed the idea of Lansing as the site, but his suggestion initially evoked laughter from the legislators. Seymour's persistence finally prevailed and Lansing, a wilderness spot with one log house and a sawmill, became the new center of Michigan's government.

By December 1847, a frame capitol building had been built, and the creation of a business district had begun at the point where Main Street and Washington Avenue now meet. Lansing was incorporated with a population of 1,500 inhabitants in 1849. Five years later a new brick capitol was constructed. Small agricultural implement industries began to introduce mechanical farming techniques to combat the manpower shortage caused by the Civil War. Development, however, was slowed by lack of transportation and the uncertainty of retaining the state capital at Lansing. But the arrival of the railroad boosted the economy by linking Lansing with the rest of the state. The legislature appropriated funding for a new capitol, which was completed in 1878 on a 10-acre park near the Grand River in the center of the city at a cost of more than $1.4 million.

Industry and Education Join Government

Automotive innovator Ransom E. Olds, who used gasoline power instead of steam, founded the Olds Motor Vehicle Company in 1897. Olds is credited with building the first practical automobile, and by the turn of the century his company was the world's largest car manufacturer and had earned a reputation for high quality. Olds's company lived on as the Oldsmobile Division of General Motors until its discontinuation in 2004. By 1904 Lansing was the base of more than 200 manufacturing businesses and a world leader in the production of agricultural implements, automobiles, and gasoline engines.

Farmers had created the Michigan Agricultural Society in 1850 as a means to be heard in the state legislature. Many of the settlers from the East placed high value on education and culture; they petitioned the state legislature through the Agricultural Society for a college of agriculture to be founded separately from the University of Michigan in Ann Arbor. The nation's oldest land-grant institution, created as part of Michigan's state constitution of 1850, was thus granted authorization in 1855. The Michigan Agricultural College was founded on 676 acres in the woods three miles east of Lansing in present-day East Lansing, which was granted a city charter in 1907. The name of the college was changed to Michigan State College of Agriculture and Applied Sciences in 1923, and became a university upon its centennial celebration in 1955. Finally, in 1964, the name was shortened to Michigan State University.

Today, Lansing is a community where government, industry, education, and culture thrive. Although the city itself has witnessed a population decrease of 6.4 percent, the metropolitan area has increased by 3.5 percent. Residents enjoy the area for its economic stability and variety of activities. The business climate is active and was recognized by *Entrepreneur* magazine in 2003 as number seven on its list of ''Best Cities for Entrepreneurs: Top Midsize Cities in the Midwest.'' The nearby residence of Michigan State University fosters an academia-minded atmosphere that contributed to the area's seventh place ranking in Richard Florida's bestselling book ''Rise of the Creative Class'' in 2002 as one of the ''Top Ten Most Creative Small Cities.''

Historical Information: Library of Michigan, 702 W. Kalamazoo St., Lansing, MI 48909-7507; telephone (517)373-1580; fax (517)373-4480

Population Profile

Metropolitan Area Residents
1980: 420,000
1990: 432,684
2000: 447,728
Percent change, 1990–2000: 3.5%
U.S. rank in 1980: 81st
U.S. rank in 1990: Not reported
U.S. rank in 2000: 92nd

City Residents
1980: 130,414
1990: 127,321
2000: 119,128
2003 estimate: 118,379
Percent change, 1990–2000: −6.4%
U.S. rank in 1980: 122nd
U.S. rank in 1990: 142nd
U.S. rank in 2000: 204th (State rank: 6th)

Density: 3,399.0 people per square mile (2000)

Racial and ethnic characteristics (2000)
White: 77,766

Black or African American: 26,095
American Indian and Alaska Native: 953
Asian: 3,367
Native Hawaiian and Pacific Islander: 62
Hispanic or Latino (may be of any race): 11,886
Other: 5,410

Percent of residents born in state: 72.8% (2000)

Age characteristics (2000)
Population under 5 years old: 9,725
Population 5 to 9 years old: 9,247
Population 10 to 14 years old: 8,235
Population 15 to 19 years old: 7,828
Population 20 to 24 years old: 10,492
Population 25 to 34 years old: 20,931
Population 35 to 44 years old: 18,055
Population 45 to 54 years old: 14,772
Population 55 to 59 years old: 4,770
Population 60 to 64 years old: 3,468
Population 65 to 74 years old: 6,210
Population 75 to 84 years old: 4,121
Population 85 years and over: 1,274
Median age: 31.4 years

Births (2003)
Total number: 2,365

Deaths (2003)
Total number: 947 (of which, 18 were infants under the age of 1 year)

Money income (1999)
Per capita income: $17,924
Median household income: $34,833
Total households: 49,458

Number of households with income of . . .
less than $10,000: 2,240
$10,000 to $14,999: 1,620
$15,000 to $24,999: 3,766
$25,000 to $34,999: 4,322
$35,000 to $49,999: 5,287
$50,000 to $74,999: 6,552
$75,000 to $99,999: 2,983
$100,000 to $149,999: 1,366
$150,000 to $199,999: 220
$200,000 or more: 194

Percent of families below poverty level: 13.2% (48.4% of which were female householder families with related children under 5 years)

2002 FBI Crime Index Total: 6,601

Municipal Government

Lansing city government is administered by an eight-member council and a mayor, who does not serve as a member of council; all are elected to a four-year term.

Head Official: Mayor Tony Benavides (NP) (since 2003; current term expires 2007)

Total Number of City Employees: 1,292 (2005)

City Information: City Hall, 124 W. Michigan Ave., Lansing, MI 48933; telephone (517)483-4000

Economy

Major Industries and Commercial Activity

The state government is naturally the most significant employer within the city. Services, wholesale and retail trade, education, and manufacturing (primarily of transportation products) comprise the economic base of the Lansing metropolitan area. Health care accounts for the largest share of the services sector, followed by business services and trade associations. Many insurance companies have corporate or regional offices in Lansing; several are headquartered there. Other important sectors are education—with nearby Michigan State University having annual revenues of about $1.6 billion—along with transportation and public utilities.

The Lansing region is an important notch in the Midwest manufacturing belt. Despite the 2004 departure of the historic Oldsmobile plant, the city received a huge boost by the 2001 opening of the new General Motors (GM) plant. Industrial leaders such as GM adapt progressive manufacturing processes and new technology. Many firms are following GM's lead to institute advanced materials-handling techniques and to encourage participatory management, with the goal of improving product quality and increasing competitiveness. A variety of high-technology firms spawned at Michigan State University has pushed for rapid growth in that industry.

Incentive Programs—New and Existing Companies

Local programs—Promoting the local economy and providing assistance to businesses is the Lansing Economic Development Corporation. The Lansing Brownfield Redevelopment Authority (LBRA) is operated by the city and provides many tax relief benefits to redevelopers. Partnering with the Michigan Economic Development Corporation (MEDC), the LBRA assists in finding sites for businesses to

locate and has also received two grants from the U.S. Environmental Protection Agency that it awards. Technology-based business growth in the area is encouraged by the MEDC and the Lansing Regional SmartZone program.

State programs—The creation of new jobs that feed into a prosperous economy is the purpose behind the Michigan Economic Growth Authority. Fiscally-responsible companies in the fields of manufacturing, research and development, wholesale trade, or office operations can make use of Small Business Tax credits. The Lansing area has two designated Renaissance Zones that, if a business locates inside the zone, allows for waiving a variety of taxes such as the single business tax, local real property tax, and utility users tax.

Michigan communities can abate up to 50 percent of local property taxes for up to 12 years. State law also exempts inventory, pollution control equipment, and certain tools, dies, jigs, and fixtures from local property taxes. State law also allows the city of Lansing to abate all new personal property taxes in certain geographic areas to spur economic development. Abatements include all millage, state and local. Eligible projects include manufacturing, mining, research and development, wholesale and trade, and office operations, but not retail businesses.

Michigan has created a system of financial institutions called BIDCOs (Business and Industrial Development Corporations). These semiprivate, independent operations are chartered and partially capitalized by the state and are designed to provide mezzanine-level financing. This is for capital of higher risk than traditional banks will consider and of lower return than venture-capital companies demand.

Job training programs—Michigan offers a coordinated job training system called "Michigan Works!" using federal, state, and local resources to provide a highly productive and trained workforce. The federal Workforce Investment Act and the Michigan Department of Labor and Economic Growth provide funding for the grants that assist in increasing worker productivity. The training itself is done through the institution of the company's choice. Free recruitment and screening services are available for new and expanding employers through the Michigan Employment Security Administration's job service and also through several local school districts.

Development Projects

Lansing's downtown area continues to undergo a facelift that began in the late 1990s. Loft development is bolstered by grant monies if certain criteria are met. One such project that is scheduled for completion in late 2006 is the $7 million conversion of the downtown Plaza One building into offices, retail stores, and about 50 apartments.

In 2001 General Motors (GM) built its first new assembly plant in the United States since 1986, an innovative 1.9 million-square-foot, $585 million Lansing factory whose 11,000 workers produce three different types of Cadillac automobiles. Nearby Delta Township witnessed the opening of a GM stamping plant in 2003 and another new assembly plant is expected to start operations in 2006.

A $67.5 million bond approved in 2003 has allowed for the building of a 175,000-square-foot middle school that represents the first new school in the Lansing School District in 30 years.

Economic Development Information: Lansing Regional Chamber of Commerce, 300 E. Michigan Ave., Ste. 300, PO Box 14030, Lansing, MI 48901; telephone (517)487-6340; fax (517)484-6910

Commercial Shipping

The CN North America, CSX, and Norfolk Southern rail freight lines serve Lansing. More than 30 motor freight carriers transport goods from the city to markets throughout the country. About 24 million pounds of air cargo is handled by several companies at Capital City Airport. Four interstate highways connect the area to all major North American markets, including Canada.

Labor Force and Employment Outlook

Lansing area employers draw from a large, stable pool of highly skilled, educated, professional workers. Michigan State University's thousands of graduates add to the pool; 31 percent of the labor force that is 25 years old and older has at least an undergraduate degree; 39 percent has a graduate or professional degree.

The forecast for occupational categories in the Lansing/East Lansing area by the Michigan Department of Labor & Economic Growth projects a 10 percent increase in all occupations by 2012. Professions such as healthcare, computer and mathematical, and personal care and service lead with gains of at least 20 percent.

The following is a summary of data regarding the Lansing-East Lansing metropolitan area labor force, 2004 annual average:

Size of non-agricultural labor force: 230,500

Number of workers employed in . . .
  construction and mining: 9,300
  manufacturing: 22,600
  trade, transportation, and utilities: 37,000
  information: 3,200
  financial activities: 15,600
  professional and business services: 21,100

  educational and health services: 25,800
  leisure and hospitality: 19,800
  other services: 10,900
  government: 65,400

Average hourly earnings of production workers employed in manufacturing: $25.03

Unemployment rate: 6.4% (February 2005)

Largest employers	Number of employees
State of Michigan	14,041
General Motors	11,000
Michigan State University	10,000
Sparrow Health System	8,000
Lansing School District	3,500
Ingham Regional Medical Center	2,450
Lansing Community College	2,200
Meijer Inc.	2,175
Jackson National Life	1,385
City of Lansing	1,292

Cost of Living

The following is a summary of data regarding several key cost of living factors in the Lansing area.

2004 ACCRA Average House Price: Not reported

2004 ACCRA Cost of Living Index: Not reported

State income tax rate: 3.9%

State sales tax rate: 6.0%

Local income tax rate: 1.0% resident, 0.5% non-resident

Local sales tax rate: None

Property tax rate: Varies widely from 34.7 to 52.7 mills per $1,000 assessed value

Economic Information: Lansing Regional Chamber of Commerce, 300 E. Michigan Ave., Ste. 300, PO Box 14030, Lansing, MI 48901; telephone (517)487-6340; fax (517)484-6910

Education and Research

Elementary and Secondary Schools

The Lansing School District, one of the largest in the state of Michigan, is administered by an elected nine-member, non-partisan board of education that appoints a superintendent. Board members serve six-year terms and receive no salary for their positions. In 2002, Superintendent Dr. E. Sharon Banks was recognized by the Michigan Association of School Administrators as ''Superintendent of the Year.'' The district has witnessed steady improvements in the students' standardized test scores since Banks assumed office in 2000.

The following is a summary of data regarding the Lansing public schools as of the 2003–2004 school year.

Total enrollment: 16,939

Number of facilities
  elementary schools: 29
  middle schools: 6
  senior high schools: 3
  other: 4

Teacher salaries
  average: $54,020 (state)

Funding per pupil: $5,887

In addition to the public system, church-affiliated schools provide K-12 education, and independent private schools and charter schools offer elementary education. Ingham, Eaton, and Clinton counties have 25 private and parochial schools with an enrollment of approximately 3,500 students; denominations include Roman Catholic, Lutheran, Baptist, and Seventh Day Adventist. There are also five non-religious private schools, and charter schools enroll about 1,700 students.

Public Schools Information: Lansing School District, 519 W. Kalamazoo St., Lansing, MI 48933; telephone (517)325-6200

Colleges and Universities

Michigan State University (MSU) in East Lansing is the largest institution of higher learning in the area, with an enrollment of 44,836 students as of the fall of 2004. It maintains 660 buildings on about 5,200 acres of land for its diverse curriculum of more than 200 programs. According to a 2005 survey by *U.S. News & World Report,* MSU ranks 71st among the nation's top schools. The university has gained an international reputation for research and its sponsored funding topped $300 million in the 2003–2004 school year.

Cooley Law School in Lansing serves working professionals with a program leading to a Juris Law degree. Great Lakes Christian College offers undergraduate programs in theology, fine arts, and interdisciplinary studies. Lansing Community College in downtown Lansing provides vocational and technical curricula as well as training programs in more than 300 areas of study for its 40,000 annual students. Other schools in the three-county region are Olivet College, Dav-

enport University, Capital Area Career Center, and Harry Hill Vocational Center.

Libraries and Research Centers

About 25 libraries located in Lansing are maintained by educational institutions, government agencies, and hospitals. The Lansing Library and Information Center is part of the Capital Area District Library. The Lansing branch houses about 400,000 items for patron usage including books, periodical titles, microfilm, audio and video tapes, maps, and art reproductions. Materials pertaining to local history are among the special collections; the district library operates 13 branches and a bookmobile. Michigan State University maintains a main library and nine branches on campus with a collection of 28,000 periodicals, 200,000 maps, and 40,000 sound recordings.

Established in 1928, the Library of Michigan maintains holdings of well over five million volumes and special collections in such fields as Michigan local and family history and eighteenth- and nineteenth-century periodicals. The library also provides Braille and large-type books and serves as a depository for federal and state documents. Thomas M. Cooley Law School, Lansing Community College, and Great Lakes Christian College also maintain campus libraries.

World-class research is conducted at Michigan State University (MSU) in diverse disciplines related to communications, packaging, food science, and environmental engineering. MSU is home to the National Superconducting Cyclotron Laboratory (NSCL), the Composite Materials and Structures Center, the Crop and Food Bioprocessing Center, the Digital Learning Center for Microbial Ecology, and WKAR, a top public broadcasting center. Adjacent to MSU, the University Corporate Research Park is comprised of building sites on four to 40 acres. Resident companies, including Montell's Research Headquarters for North America, enjoy access to MSU's scientific and technical facilities (laboratories, libraries, computerized data and research networks, closed circuit TV, and satellite systems).

The Composite Materials and Structure Center is a research partner with the Michigan Molecular Institute, the National Science Foundation, the Ford Motor Company, and the U.S. Department of Defense. The Pesticide Research Center works with pesticides and pest control. The Michigan Biotechnology Institute, a non-profit corporation, applies recombinant deoxyribonucleic acid, plant tissue culture, and immobilized enzymes to the commercialization of biotechnology in the state of Michigan.

Public Library Information: Lansing Library and Information Center, 401 S. Capitol Ave., PO Box 40719, Lansing, MI 48901-7919; telephone (517)367-7919; fax (517)367-6363

Health Care

Six hospitals, with a total of about 1,500 beds, serve metropolitan Lansing. Ingham Regional Medical Center (formerly the Michigan Capital Medical Center) is a general acute care, nonprofit hospital with 338 beds. Sparrow Health System, with 710 beds, maintains a wound center, a dialysis unit, and a family practice center. The 257-bed St. Lawrence Hospital, part of the Sparrow Health System, operates a poison control center, a health service for persons without physicians, and an alcohol detoxification and counseling unit. All major facilities in the city offer 24-hour emergency care and maintain maternity units. Michigan State University provides medical education and training through the College of Human Medicine and the College of Osteopathic Medicine; it also operates an outpatient clinic open to the public.

Recreation

Sightseeing

Completed in 1879, Lansing's Capitol was one of the first state edifices built to emulate the nation's Capitol, and this National Historic Landmark is the center of attraction in Lansing's downtown sector. Two blocks southwest of the Capitol is the Michigan Library and Historical Center, a modern facility with an outdoor courtyard. The museum traces the history of Michigan from its remote past to the twenty-first century, including the evolution of the state's economy in agriculture, timber, mining, and manufacturing to the rise and dominance of the automobile. Impression 5 Science Museum stimulates the senses with interactive displays including a "Bubble Room" that was remodeled in 2005. Next to Impression 5 is the R. E. Olds Transportation Museum, a major transportation museum recognizing the contribution of Ransom E. Olds to the automotive industry and the evolution of transportation in Lansing.

Michigan State University (MSU) in neighboring East Lansing provides many sightseeing opportunities beginning with the W.J. Beal Botanical Gardens, the oldest, continuously operated garden of its type in the country, with 5,000 different types of plants. The university's horticultural demonstration gardens cover seven-and-a-half acres. Abrams Planetarium presents programs on space science topics in the 150-seat Digistar sky theater along with an exhibition area and the astronomy-related paintings at the "Blacklight Gallery." The MSU Museum houses displays on cultural and scientific development, and the MSU Dairy Plant and Dairy Store offers daily tours at milking time.

Potter Park Zoo places its 100 species of animals in natural settings, with a special display on Michigan animals. The zoo has been actively expanding to include an Education Center, an Animal Clinic with the zoo's first full-time veterinarian, and the planned construction of a new pool for the otter exhibit in 2005.

At the Rose Lake Wildlife Research Station, 3,000 acres of woods and marsh are accessible via hiking trails; Woldumar Nature Center stresses environmental education and its five miles of trails are open to the public for hiking or cross country skiing. Fenner Arboretum maintains self-guided trails leading to a prairie scene with live bison. Nature trails Red Cedar, Sanford Natural Area, and Baker Woodlot are islands of wilderness on the Michigan State University campus. The Ledges in Grand Ledge, 10 miles west of Lansing, is named for its rock formations, which rise along the Grand River and are over 300 million years old.

Arts and Culture

Many of Lansing's cultural events take place at the Wharton Center for Performing Arts' two theaters on the campus of Michigan State University. Cobb Great Hall seats 2,500 guests and hosts Broadway and variety shows, while the Pasant Theatre has 600 seats for family presentations. Founded in 1929, the Greater Lansing Symphony Orchestra presents a season of classical and pops concerts with an annual attendance of 15,000 for about one dozen performances. Stage and concert operas are put on by the Lansing Lyric Opera. Volunteer singers selected via auditions make up the Greater Lansing Arts Chorale, which presents three concerts per year.

Lansing is particularly strong in theater. The nationally known BoarsHead Theater, a residential professional company based at the Wharton Center, presents a season of modern and classical drama and comedy. Community theater companies are: the Lansing Civic Players Guild, the oldest group in the area, dating back to 1929; Lansing Community College's LCC Theater Program at Dart Auditorium; MSU's Department of Theatre, which features student productions; Riverwalk Theatre, the home to the Community Circle Players; and Spotlight Theatre in nearby Grand Ledge, with several American dramas running from May through early September.

The Greater Lansing Ballet Company is a semi-professional organization that presents classical and contemporary ballets and offers two international exchange programs with companies in Poland and Russia. The Children's Ballet Theatre of Michigan at the Wharton Center puts on holiday and spring shows.

The Lansing Arts Gallery, established in 1964, has two exhibition spaces with different exhibitions every month. At

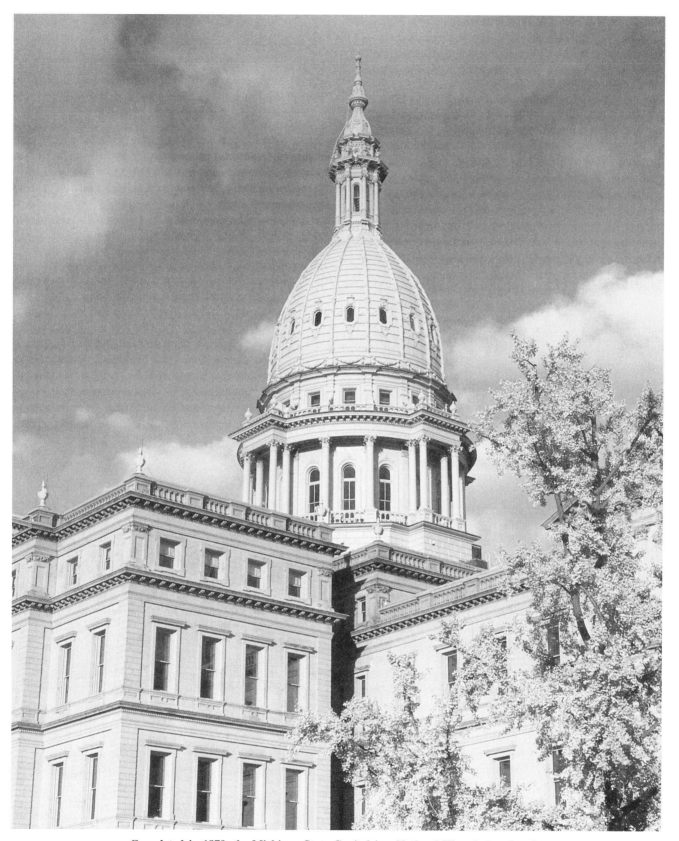

Completed in 1879, the Michigan State Capitol is a National Historic Landmark.

Michigan State University, the Department of Art and Art History displays student art throughout the year at the Kresge Art Museum.

Arts and Culture Information: Arts Council of Greater Lansing, 425 S. Grand Ave., Lansing, MI 48933; telephone (517)372-4636; fax (517)484-2564; email info@lansingarts .org

Festivals and Holidays

Greater Lansing hosts dozens of festivals and special events year-round. In late winter and early spring, the East Lansing Film Festival previews over 30 independently-made films worldwide but also challenges local talent (Michigan, Illinois, and Wisconsin) to a competition. The East Lansing Art Fair is held the third weekend in May, followed by the Lansing Festival of Art in the Park the last weekend in June at Ferris Park. Also in May, the Fiesta celebrates the Hispanic community with music, folklore performances, and a ''Mexican Marketplace.'' The Lansing Concert Band gives a performance in Riverfront Park for the Fourth of July holiday with fireworks at dusk. Early August brings the Lansing Jazz Fest for two days of live jazz and music clinics; later in the month, the Great Lakes Folk Festival is three days of various activities including music, dance, and storytelling along with ethnic foods. The holiday season is celebrated in three major events: the MSU (Michigan State University) Holiday Arts & Crafts Show, held at the MSU Union for two days to present the works of about 200 regional artisans and crafters; Silver Bells in the City, which draws 80,000 to its parade and fireworks celebrating the lighting of Michigan's official holiday tree; and Wonderland of Lights at Potter Park, with thousands of lights adorning holiday displays along with carolers and other musical performances.

Sports for the Spectator

The Michigan State Spartans compete in the Big Ten athletic conference and field nationally competitive teams. The football team plays its home games in the 76,000-seat Spartan Stadium that was expanded in 2005 to accommodate 24 new suites and 862 club seats with access to an 18,500-square-foot club. Munn Ice Arena seats 6,470 fans and is the home of the Spartan hockey team. The Jack Breslin Student Events Center has been the home of the MSU basketball program since 1989; it seats 15,085 people.

Lansing's professional minor-league baseball team, the Lugnuts, play an April through September season at Oldsmobile Park. Playing in the western division of the Midwest League, the Lugnuts were previously affiliated with major league's Chicago Cubs but the 2005 season brought a switch to the Toronto Blue Jays. The Spartan Speedway attracts super and hobby stock car racing on Friday nights from mid-

May through mid-September. Jackson Harness Raceway features seasonal parimutuel racing at night in nearby Jackson.

Sports for the Participant

Golf is particularly popular at about three dozen public and private courses of varying difficulty in the area, and many golf tournaments are held in the summer. East Lansing's Timber Ridge was rated one of the top 50 courses in America by *Golf Digest* magazine.

Nearly 200 city, county, and state parks, campgrounds, and recreation areas offer several thousand acres of green space and leisure opportunities in the Lansing region. River Trail features a canoeing route that follows the banks of the Grand and Red Cedar rivers through urban and natural environments and the campus of Michigan State University. The Brenke Fish Ladder is stocked with salmon and steelhead for urban fishing. Well supplied with bowling centers and ball fields, the Lansing area also has riding stables, about 300 indoor and outdoor tennis courts, and seven public access sites for boating.

The Summit at The Capital Centre is a modern, 180,000-square-foot facility that offers a wide array of sporting activities including ice hockey, soccer, dodge ball, and lacrosse. It also hosts one of the region's top gymnastics clubs, Geddert's Twisters. Other public ice skating facilities are available at Washington Park and Munn Arena at Michigan State University.

The region is noted for the variety of fish in rivers and lakes full of largemouth bass, northern pike, muskie, bluegill, crappie, and perch. Streams contain smallmouth bass, northern pike, walleye, and panfish. In addition, there are spawning runs of steelhead and Chinook salmon in several locations. Throughout the vicinity, state game lands and wooded areas offer rabbit, squirrel, pheasant, deer, and other game.

Shopping and Dining

The largest shopping center in the region is the Lansing Mall, with over 125 stores and restaurants. An antiques and collectibles store called Pennyless in Paradise opened in 2004. However, one of the state's biggest antiques shops is The Mega Mall with over 300 booths on 40,000 square feet of space. In East Lansing, near the Michigan State University campus, specialty shops that cater to students are clustered among small restaurants, bookstores, and record shops.

The Lansing City Market, at the corner of Cedar Street and Shiawassee since 1909, offers a large selection of fresh fruits and vegetables. The Nokomis Learning Center, next door to Meridian Historic Village, sells beaded jewelry and other items handcrafted by local Native American Artists. Several upscale restaurants are located near the university.

Visitor Information: Greater Lansing Convention and Visitors Bureau, 1223 Turner St., Ste. 100, Lansing, MI 48906; telephone (517)487-6800 or (800)252-6746

Convention Facilities

Meeting and convention planners can choose among several facilities in the Lansing area. The Lansing Center is situated downtown on the Grand River and Riverwalk near the Capitol Complex. It adjoins the Radisson Hotel and a 1,600-car parking area via an enclosed walkway. Accommodating up to 5,600 people and 71,000 square feet of exhibition space, the exhibit halls and meeting rooms function as separate units or in multiple combinations. In downtown Lansing, the Center for the Arts adjoins an art gallery and provides barrier-free space for functions with up to 240 participants.

The Breslin Center on the campus of Michigan State University (MSU) is a 254,000-square-foot facility offering 17,500 square feet of exhibition space, 30,000 maximum square feet of concourse area for product display, and state-of-the-art sound and lighting systems. MSU's Pavilion Agriculture and Livestock Education Center offers over 77,000 square feet in its facilities for trade shows, exhibitions, demonstrations, and livestock auctions.

Lansing-area hotels and motels, containing about 4,000 rooms for lodgings, also offer banquet and meeting rooms. One example is the Sheraton Lansing Hotel, with seven ballrooms and several rooms and suites that can handle from 10 to 1,500 guests in spaces varying from 480 to 8,600 square feet.

Convention Information: Greater Lansing Convention and Visitors Bureau, 1223 Turner St., Ste. 100, Lansing, MI 48906; telephone (517)487-6800 or (800)252-6746

Transportation

Approaching the City

Seven commercial airlines schedule regular daily flights into Capital City Airport, located 15 minutes from downtown Lansing. The airport has experienced increasing passenger numbers since 2003; in March 2005 more than 54,000 traveled on its airlines. Daily rail service to East Lansing from Chicago and Toronto is provided by Amtrak; Greyhound Bus Lines has terminals in Lansing and East Lansing.

An efficient highway system facilitates access to Lansing and its environs. Part of a beltway circling the southern half of the city, I-96 is intersected by several major and secondary routes; east-west I-69 completes the beltway around the northern sector. I-496 bisects the downtown area westward from north-south U.S. 127 in East Lansing. Other principal highways are U.S. 27 and M 99, both running north-south, and east-west M 43.

Traveling in the City

Downtown Lansing streets are laid out on a strict grid system with the Capitol Complex as the center of orientation; the web of one-way streets can be confusing. Public bus transportation is provided by Capital Area Transportation Authority (CATA), which operates seven days a week in Lansing and East Lansing as well as to points throughout the metropolitan region. CATA's shuttle service to downtown Lansing and the Capital Loop reduces rush-hour traffic and parking congestion in central city areas. Special service for elderly, handicapped, commuting, and rural patrons is available.

Communications

Newspapers and Magazines

The major daily newspaper in Lansing is the morning *Lansing State Journal.* A number of trade publications originate in Lansing, aimed at farmers, florists, grocers, and small business owners. Other Lansing publications include *Michigan History Magazine* and *The State News,* a daily published by Michigan State University.

Television and Radio

Two commercial television stations are based in Lansing, where cable television service is also available. Lansing radio listeners receive broadcasts from eight AM and FM radio stations in the city and several additional stations in neighboring communities. Musical programming includes country, classical, rock and roll, religious, top 40, and easy listening.

Media Information: Lansing State Journal, 120 E. Lenawee, Lansing, MI 48919; telephone (517)377-1000

Lansing Online

Arts Council of Greater Lansing. Available www.lansing arts.org

City of Lansing home page. Available www.cityoflansingmi .com

Greater Lansing Convention & Visitors Bureau. Available www.lansing.org

Lansing Regional Chamber of Commerce. Available www.lansingchamber.org

Lansing School District. Available www.lansingschools.net

Lansing State Journal. Available www.lansingstatejournal.com

Library of Michigan. Available www.michigan.gov/hal

Michigan Historical Center. Available www.michigan.gov/hal

Selected Bibliography

Celizic, Mike, *The Biggest Game of Them All: Notre Dame, Michigan State, and the Fall of '66* (New York: Simon & Schuster, 1992)

Lansing State Journal, *One Shining Season: The Amazing Story of Michigan State University's 1998–99 Men's Basketball Team* (Sports Publishing, Inc., 1999)

Seale, William, *Michigan's Capitol: Construction & Restoration* (University of Michigan Press, 1995)

MINNESOTA

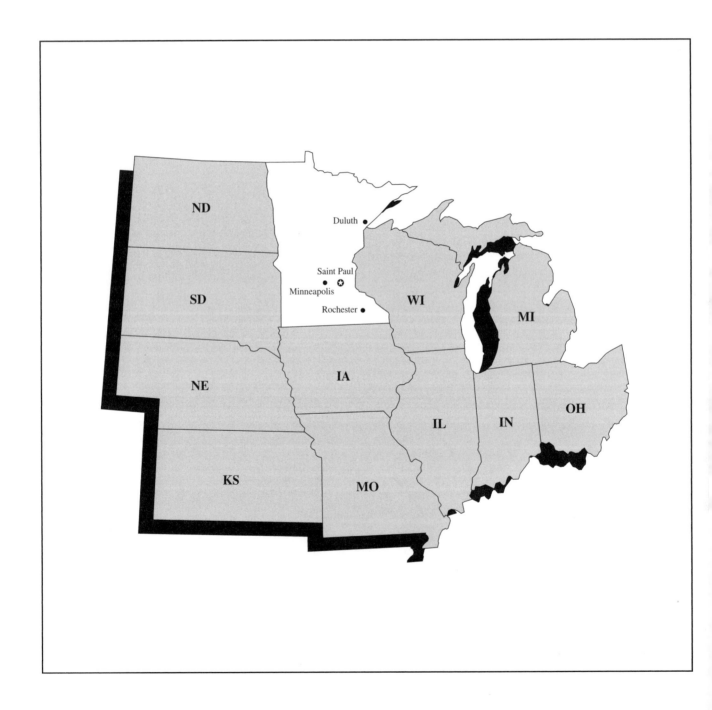

The State in Brief

Nickname: North Star State
Motto: *L'etoile du nord* (Star of the north)

Flower: Pink and white lady's slipper
Bird: Common loon

Area: 86,938 square miles (2000; U.S. rank: 12th)
Elevation: Ranges from 600 feet to 2,301 feet above sea level
Climate: North part of state lies in the moist Great Lakes storm belt; western border is at the edge of the semi-arid Great Plains; spring is brief; summer is short, hot, and humid; winter is long and severe with heavy snowfall.

Admitted to Union: May 11, 1858
Capital: Saint Paul
Head Official: Governor Tim Pawlenty (R) (until 2007)

Population
  1980: 4,076,000
  1990: 4,432,000
  2000: 4,919,492
  2004 estimate: 5,100,958
  Percent change, 1990–2000: 12.4%
  U.S. rank in 2004: 21st
  Percent of residents born in state: 70.2% (2000)
  Density: 61.8 people per square mile (2000)
  2002 FBI Crime Index Total: 177,454

Racial and Ethnic Characteristics (2000)
  White: 4,400,282
  Black or African American: 171,731
  American Indian and Alaska Native: 54,967
  Asian: 141,968
  Native Hawaiian and Pacific Islander: 1,979
  Hispanic or Latino (may be of any race): 143,382
  Other: 65,810

Age Characteristics (2000)
  Population under 5 years old: 329,594
  Population 5 to 19 years old: 1,105,251
  Percent of population 65 years and over: 12.1%
  Median age: 35.4 years (2000)

Vital Statistics
  Total number of births (2003): 70,248
  Total number of deaths (2003): 37,558 (infant deaths, 325)
  AIDS cases reported through 2003: 1,900

Economy
  Major industries: Manufacturing; trade; finance, insurance, and real estate; agriculture; services
  Unemployment rate: 4.4% (March 2005)
  Per capita income: $34,039 (2003; U.S. rank: 9th)
  Median household income: $54,480 (3-year average, 2001-2003)
  Percentage of persons below poverty level: 7.1% (3-year average, 2001-2003)
  Income tax rate: 3.0%
  Sales tax rate: 6.25%

Duluth

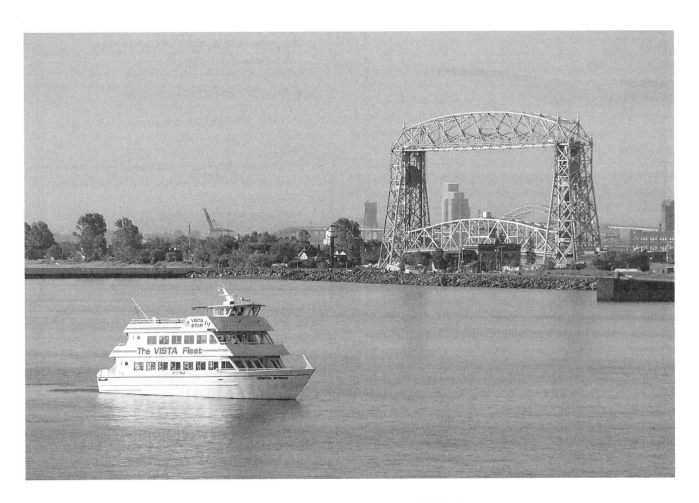

The City in Brief

Founded: 1852 (chartered, 1870)

Head Official: Mayor Herb W. Bergson, Jr. (NP) (since 2003)

City Population
  1980: 92,811
  1990: 85,493
  2000: 86,918
  2003 estimate: 85,734
  Percent change, 1990–2000: 1.01%
  U.S. rank in 1980: 184th
  U.S. rank in 1990: 243rd
  U.S. rank in 2000: 321st (State rank: 4th)

Metropolitan Area Population
  1980: 266,650
  1990: 239,971

  2000: 243,815
  Percent change, 1990–2000: 1.02%
  U.S. rank in 1990: Not reported
  U.S. rank in 2000: 146th

Area: 87.32 square miles (2000)
Elevation: Ranges from 605 to 1,485 feet above sea level
Average Annual Temperature: 39.8° F
Average Annual Precipitation: 30 inches of rain, 80.7 inches of snow

Major Economic Sectors: Services, trade, government
Unemployment Rate: 6.1% (February 2005)
Per Capita Income: $18,969 (1999)
2004 ACCRA Average House Price: Not reported
2004 ACCRA Cost of Living Index: Not reported

2002 FBI Crime Index Total: 5,340

Major Colleges and Universities: University of Minnesota–Duluth; College of St. Scholastica

Daily Newspaper: *Duluth News-Tribune*

Introduction

The seat of St. Louis County in Minnesota, Duluth is the focus of a metropolitan statistical area comprising both St. Louis County and Wisconsin's Douglas County. The city has developed into the second-largest port on the Great Lakes and is the commercial, industrial, and cultural center of northern Minnesota. Duluth is noted for its dramatic geographic setting. Steep inclines, dotted with buildings that seem to pop out of hillsides, provide the backdrop for Duluth's famous 30-mile-long Skyline Parkway, which winds above the city.

Geography and Climate

Duluth is located on a natural harbor at the western tip of Lake Superior and at the base of a range of hills overlooking the St. Louis River. This position below high terrain and along the lake permits easterly winds to cool the area automatically, thus earning Duluth the nickname of the ''Air-Conditioned City.'' During the summer a westerly wind flow abates at night, and the cool lake air moves back in toward the city. High and low pressure systems and proximity to Lake Superior, the coldest of the Great Lakes, have an important influence on the climate, which is predominantly continental. Summer temperatures are thus cooler and winter temperatures warmer; the frequency of severe storms—wind, hail, tornadoes, freezing rain, and blizzards—is also low in comparison to other areas at a distance from the lake. Fall is an especially pleasant season in Duluth, as the changing leaves produce a striking combination of reds, yellows, and browns.

Area: 87.32 square miles (2000)

Elevation: Ranges from 605 to 1,485 feet above sea level

Average Temperatures: January, 10.3° F; July, 65.8° F; annual average, 39.8° F

Average Annual Precipitation: 30 inches of rain, 80.7 inches of snow

History

Harbor, Timber, and Ore Attract Development

The western Lake Superior area was originally occupied by members of the Sioux and Chippewa tribes. One of the first explorers of European descent to arrive in the area now occupied by Duluth was Frenchman Pierre Esprit Radisson, who explored the region in the 1650s or 1660s. The city was ultimately named, however, for Daniel Greysolon, Sieur du Lhut (variously spelled Dulhut, Derhaut, and du Luth), who visited the southern shore of Lake Superior in 1679 in an attempt to make peace between the Ojibway and Sioux tribes and to secure trading and trapping rights. A fur trading outlet remained in the area until 1847. The site's first permanent resident was George P. Stuntz, who was attracted by the beautiful wilderness landscape surrounding Lake Superior and settled there in 1852.

In 1854 and 1855 settlers flocked to the unnamed town hoping to discover copper deposits, although the Grand Portage and Fon du Lac people had not yet signed the Treaty of La Pointe that relinquished their mineral rights. In 1856 the village was named Duluth and designated the seat of St. Louis County. Almost immediately Duluth was beset by troubles. The panic of 1857 devastated the economy, and in 1859 a scarlet fever epidemic caused a further setback to the community. By the end of the Civil War, only two houses remained occupied in Duluth.

The town's fortunes were quickly reversed when geologists found iron ore and gold-bearing quartz at nearby Lake Vermillion. Then the Eastern financier Jay Cooke selected Duluth as the northern terminus of the Lake Superior & Mississippi Railroad. Adding to the boom, Maine woodsmen relocated to the region to establish a lumber industry. By 1869 the population of Duluth had grown to 3,500 residents, and the city received its first charter a year later.

Growth Includes New Immigrants

The new prosperity was short-lived, however, as bank and real estate failures hurt the economy and plunged the city government into debt. Duluth was forced to revert to village status. The city's topsy-turvy early history reversed itself once again, however, when the lumbering industry was revitalized and grain business fueled the economy. By 1887 Duluth's population reached 26,000 residents, and the state legislature granted permission for reclassification as a city. Six lakeshore communities were absorbed into the city by the end of the nineteenth century.

Among the settlers who had made Duluth home were immigrants from the Scandinavian countries and Finland, who settled in the city's West End. These people possessed a commitment to cooperative undertakings, a strong sense of individualism, and a respect for organizational arrangements—qualities that have shaped the city's character. In addition to its residents, Duluth is defined by its topography. The natural harbor is the base of the economy and the source of the city's scenic beauty. Duluth, home to institutions of higher learning, a symphony orchestra, a community theater, ballet, and museums, is highly rated among small Midwestern cities for its livability. In 2002 the American Lung Association State of the Air report ranked Duluth number 11 among cities with the cleanest air.

Historical Information: Northeast Minnesota Historical Center Archives, University of Minnesota, 10 University Dr., Duluth, MN 55812; telephone (218)726-8526. Minnesota Historical Society, 345 Kellogg Blvd. W., Saint Paul, MN 55102-1906; telephone (651)296-6126

Population Profile

Metropolitan Area Residents
1980: 266,650
1990: 239,971
2000: 243,815
Percent change, 1990–2000: 1.02%
U.S. rank in 1990: Not reported
U.S. rank in 2000: 146th

City Residents
1980: 92,811
1990: 85,493
2000: 86,918
2003 estimate: 85,734
Percent change, 1990–2000: 1.01%
U.S. rank in 1980: 184th
U.S. rank in 1990: 243rd
U.S. rank in 2000: 321st (State rank: 4th)

Density: 1,278.1.6 people per square mile (2000)

Racial and ethnic characteristics (2000)
  White: 80,532
  Black or African American: 1,415
  American Indian and Alaska Native: 2,122
  Asian: 993
  Native Hawaiian and Pacific Islander: 25
  Hispanic or Latino (may be of any race): 921
  Other: 251

Percent of residents born in state: 75.1% (2000)

Age characteristics (2000)
  Population under 5 years old: 4,695
  Population 5 to 9 years old: 4,924
  Population 10 to 14 years old: 5,505
  Population 15 to 19 years old: 7,886
  Population 20 to 24 years old: 9,549
  Population 25 to 34 years old: 10,484
  Population 35 to 44 years old: 12,222

  Population 45 to 54 years old: 11,615
  Population 55 to 59 years old: 3,913
  Population 60 to 64 years old: 2,978
  Population 65 to 74 years old: 5,684
  Population 75 to 84 years old: 5,116
  Population 85 years and over: 2,347
  Median age: 35.4 years

Births (2003)
  Total number: 1,054

Deaths (2003)
  Total number: 2,182 (of which, 10 were infants under the age of 1 year) (St. Louis County data)

Money income (1999)
  Per capita income: $18,969
  Median household income: $33,766
  Total households: 35,547

Number of households with income of . . .
  less than $10,000: 4,398
  $10,000 to $14,999: 3,338
  $15,000 to $24,999: 5,465
  $25,000 to $34,999: 5,061
  $35,000 to $49,999: 5,826
  $50,000 to $74,999: 6,334
  $75,000 to $99,999: 2,752
  $100,000 to $149,999: 1,579
  $150,000 to $199,999: 366
  $200,000 or more: 428

Percent of families below poverty level: 8.6% (48.3% of which were female householder families with related children under 5 years)

2002 FBI Crime Index Total: 5,340

Municipal Government

The city of Duluth operates under a mayor-council form of government. The mayor and nine council members are elected to a four-year term. The city's mandatory arrest in domestic violence cases program is a national model.

Head Official: Mayor Herb W. Bergson, Jr. (NP) (since 2003; current term expires January 2008)

Total Number of City Employees: 1,258 permanent and approximately 160 seasonal workers (2002)

City Information: City Hall, Mayor's Office, 411 W. 1st St., Ste. 403, Duluth, MN 55802; telephone (218)730-5230

Economy

Major Industries and Commercial Activity

Principal manufacturing firms in Duluth include heavy and light manufacturing plants, food processing plants, woolen mills, lumber and paper mills, cold storage plants, fisheries, grain elevators, and oil refineries. The city is also a regional center for banking, retailing, and medical care for northern Minnesota, northern Wisconsin, northern Michigan, and northwestern Ontario, Canada. More than 8,000 jobs in Duluth are directly related to the hospital industry. Arts and entertainment offerings as well as year-round recreation in a natural environment have contributed to expansion of the tourist industry in Duluth. Some 3.5 million visitors each year contribute $400 million to the local economy.

Items and goods produced: steel, cement, metal and wood products, electrical equipment, textiles, prepared foods.

Incentive Programs—New and Existing Companies

Local programs—The Duluth Department of Planning and Development is responsible for overseeing Duluth's growth. Its Business Development Division is the focus of the city's efforts to attract new businesses to Duluth and retain existing firms. It promotes overall development in Duluth through agencies such as the Duluth Economic Development Authority, The 1200 Fund, Inc., the Duluth Airport Authority, The Seaway Port Authority of Duluth, Team Duluth, and others. It also coordinates economic development with the State of Minnesota and the U.S. Department of Commerce.

State programs—The Tax Increment Financing Program, a state authorized financing mechanism, is offered to assist basic businesses in financing their local expansion or location. Funds may be used to purchase land and make public improvements that support business development projects. Minnesota also offers programs to provide a mechanism for businesses to sell bonds at tax-exempt interest rates, allowing firms to receive long-term, low interest financing for fixed assets.

Job training programs—The Minnesota Department of Employment and Economic Development operates a network of workforce centers throughout the state. This WorkForce Center System, which has an office in Duluth, partners with local businesses to provide customized job training and other workforce development services. Additionally, the University of Minnesota–Duluth houses a College of Engineering and the Natural Resources Research Institute, while both the College of St. Scholastica and Lake Superior College provide customized training.

Development Projects

As the new century gets underway, expansion and retention of existing business continues to be Duluth's major focus. In recent years, more than $2 billion in private and public money has been invested in Duluth's projects. Among these over the past decade are a $20 million Duluth Entertainment Convention Center facility expansion, a $30 million University of Minnesota–Duluth library construction and Weber Music Center project, a $15 million United Health Care Claims processing center, a $26 million Air National Guard aircraft maintenance facility, a $34 million airport improvement program, a $11 million Airpark development project, a $10 million Port Terminal development plan, a $90 million St. Mary's/Duluth Clinic expansion, and a $10 million East First Street parking ramp.

Economic Development Information: Duluth Area Chamber of Commerce, 5 W. 1st St., Ste. 101, Duluth, MN 55802; telephone (218)722-5501; fax (218)722-3223; email commerce@chamber.duluth.mn.us. Duluth Office of Business Development, City Hall, Ste. 400, Duluth, MN 55802; telephone (218)723-3556

Commercial Shipping

A vital part of the Duluth economy is the Port of Duluth-Superior, which is designated a Foreign Trade Zone and ranks among the top ports in the country in total volume of international and domestic cargo shipped in a 10-month season. An average of 40 million tons of cargo is handled at Duluth-Superior each year. The impact on the local economy is $200 million annually, and some 2,000 jobs are dependent on the port. Duluth-Superior operates one of the largest grain-handling facilities in the world. Grain is the primary export product; domestic shipments consist mainly of iron ore and taconite, in addition to metal products, twine, machinery, coal, cement, salt, newsprint, lumber, and general cargo.

Connecting the port and the city of Duluth with inland markets are five railroads and 26 common motor freight carriers. Air cargo carriers serving Duluth International Airport with daily flights are Federal Express, United Parcel Service, and Northwest Airlines.

Labor Force and Employment Outlook

Duluth boasts an abundant, quality workforce, as well as a commitment to bringing new and expanded job opportunities into the community. Minnesota has the highest high school graduation rate in the nation; more than 70 percent of Duluth students go on to college or post-secondary education.

The following is a summary of data regarding the Duluth metropolitan area labor force, 2004 annual averages.

Size of nonagricultural labor force: 127,800

Number of workers employed in . . .
 construction and mining: 8,300
 trade, transportation, and utilities: 25,800
 information: 2,500
 financial activities: 5,800
 professional and business services: 7,100
 educational and health services: 24,400
 leisure and hospitality: 13,300
 other services: 5,900
 government: 27,200

Average hourly earnings of production workers employed in manufacturing: $12.73

Unemployment rate: 6.1% (February 2005)

Largest employers	Number of employees
St. Mary's/Duluth Clinic	3,800
Duluth Public Schools-ISD #709	1,700
St. Louis County	1,640
University of Minnesota-Duluth	1,571
City of Duluth	1,060
St. Luke's Hospital	1,143

Cost of Living

The median sale price of a home in Duluth during the first quarter of 2004 was $125,000, up from $116,900 in the first quarter of 2003.

The following is a summary of data regarding several key cost of living factors in the Duluth area.

2004 ACCRA Cost of Living Index: Not reported

2004 ACCRA Average House Price: Not reported

State income tax rate: Ranges from 5.85% to 7.85%

State sales tax: 6.5%

Local income tax rate: None

Local sales tax rate: 1.0% (food, clothing, and prescription drugs exempt)

Property tax rate: Single family homestead property—1.0% times the first $72,000 of estimated market value (EMV) plus 2.0% times the excess over $72,000

Economic Information: Duluth Area Chamber of Commerce, 5 W. 1st St., Ste. 101, Duluth, MN 55802; telephone (218)722-5501; fax (218)722-3223; email commerce @chamber.duluth.mn.us. Minnesota Department of Employment and Economic Development, 332 Minnesota St., Ste. E200, St. Paul, MN 55101; telephone (612)297-1291; toll-free 800-657-3858

Education and Research

Elementary and Secondary Schools

The Duluth School District (ISD #709) covers 337 square miles, including Duluth. It offers K-12 education, special services for students with handicaps and special needs, an Early Childhood Family Education program, Head Start, alternative schools, and community education.

The following is a summary of data regarding Duluth public schools as of the 2003–2004 school year.

Total enrollment: 10,824

Number of facilities
 elementary schools: 13
 middle schools: 4
 high schools: 3
 other: 5 (including magnet, academy, and adult education programs)

Student/teacher ratio: 22.1:1

Teacher salaries
 minimum: $32,517
 maximum: $54,323

Funding per pupil: $7,736 (2002 state figure)

The Marshall School, an independent, coeducational day school, offers college preparatory classes for students in grades 5–12. Holy Rosary offers Catholic education for grades K–8. Lakeview Christian Academy, an interdenominational, Christian school, serves students from preschool through grade 12 with a Bible-centered curriculum. Summit School is an independent school for children from kindergarten through grade four.

Public Schools Information: Independent School District #709, 215 N. 1st Ave. E., Duluth, MN 55802; telephone (218)723-4150

Colleges and Universities

The University of Minnesota–Duluth enrolls 10,300 students and offers a dozen bachelor's degrees in 75 majors, graduate programs in 19 fields, and the first two years of a medical program. The College of St. Scholastica, a private four-year institution enrolling about 3,000 students, has gained recognition in the areas of nursing, management, exercise physiology, health information management, occupational therapy, physical therapy, and education. Lake Superior College offers more than 70 majors to its 8,500 students and operates an Aircraft Rescue and Fire Fighting Center and a Computer Flex Lab. Business and medical training and college-level general education is available at Duluth Business University. Fond du Lac Tribal and Community College in Cloquet is a joint effort between the Fond du Lac Reservation and the state of Minnesota.

Libraries and Research Centers

The Duluth Public Library houses more than 360,000 volumes, magazines, maps, charts, video and audio recordings, and framed prints; special collections relate to Duluth, the Great Lakes region, and Minnesota. The library, a depository for federal documents, operates two branches. The University of Minnesota–Duluth and the College of St. Scholastica maintain substantial campus libraries. Duluth is home to the Saint Louis County Health Department Library, the Saint Louis County Law Library, the Environmental Protection Agency library, the Karpeles Manuscript Library, and the Northeast Minnesota Historical Center Archives, in addition to the libraries of health service and religious organizations.

The Natural Resources Research Institute, affiliated with UMD and staffed by scientists, engineers, and business consultants, conducts research and development projects in fields such as forest products and the environment.

Public Library Information: Duluth Public Library, 520 W. Superior St., Duluth, MN 55802; telephone (218)723-3800

Health Care

Duluth is a regional health care center for the northern sections of Minnesota, Wisconsin, and Michigan and for northwestern Ontario, Canada. The St. Mary's/Duluth Clinic (SMDC) Health System was initially comprised of St. Mary's Medical Center and the Duluth Clinic, and in 2001 absorbed Miller-Dwan, further enhancing the services available to patients. These three hospitals, with a bed capacity of more than 600, provide complete medical services.

St. Mary's offers 24-hour emergency treatment and maintains trauma and poison information units in addition to outpatient services, home care, and community education programs. It also operates the Regional Heart Center and Regional Neuroscience Center, which and provides cardiac surgery, cancer care, orthopedic surgery, intensive care, and level three prenatal care.

Miller-Dwan administers the largest mental health program in the region and operates a burn clinic along with hemodialysis, medical rehabilitation, rheumatic disease, and radiation therapy units.

St. Luke's Hospital, which was the first hospital in Duluth, has been federally designated as a Level II Regional Trauma Center; it houses the Regional Vascular Institute, Poison Control Center, and Mental Health Services and has more than 400 physicians on its staff. A full range of general services is supplemented by such specialties as psychiatry, oncology, physical medicine, hospice care, high cholesterol treatment, occupational health services, lithotripsy, and magnetic resonance imaging.

Recreation

Sightseeing

The St. Louis County Heritage and Arts Center is housed in the 1892 Union Depot, a renovated railroad depot with four levels of history and arts exhibits. On display are antique doll and toy collections, a Victorian parlor, Indian crafts, and Depot Square, a recreation of 1910 Duluth that contains 24 old-time stores, a silent movie theater, and an ice-cream parlor. The old immigration room that once processed newcomers to the United States is preserved in its original condition. Railroad cars and locomotives, including the first locomotive in Minnesota and one of the largest steam locomotives ever built, are on exhibit.

The Canal Park Marine Museum houses exhibits on the history of Lake Superior Shipping, while the Lake Superior Museum of Transportation maintains one of the nation's finest collections of historical railroad equipment. At Lake Superior Zoological Gardens, animals from around the world can be viewed in facilities that include a nocturnal house and a children's zoo. Located on the shore of Lake Superior, Glensheen is a Jacobean-style mansion featuring original furnishings and a collection of carriages and sleighs.

The Skyline Parkway, a 30-mile boulevard above Duluth, provides a dramatic view of the city, the harbor, and Lake Superior. Lake Shore Drive parallels Lake Superior from Duluth to Thunder Bay and is considered one of the most scenic coastal highways in the nation. The Aerial Lift Bridge, which connects Minnesota Point with the mainland and spans Duluth harbor, is one of Duluth's most popular tourist attractions. The present bridge, built in 1930, is the world's largest and fastest lift bridge.

Arts and Culture

The Depot houses eight of Duluth's major arts and cultural institutions. The Duluth Art Institute sponsors major exhibitions in addition to its instructional programs. Rooted in classical ballet with contemporary dance influences, Minnesota Ballet stages three major performance series annually. The Duluth Playhouse, founded in 1914 and one of the nation's oldest community theaters, produces a variety of theatrical

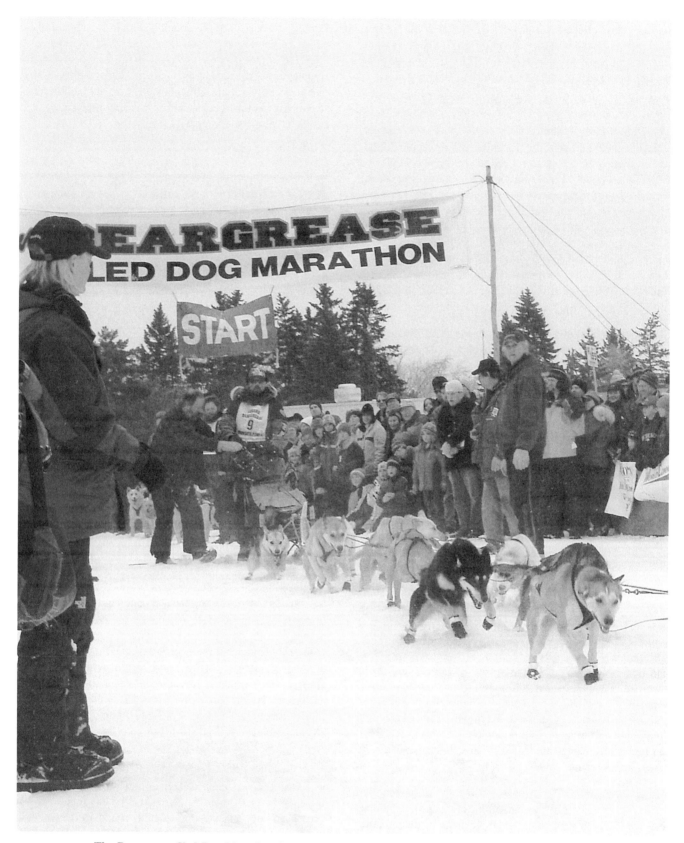

The Beargrease Sled Dog Marathon is an annual event to honor the memory of John Beargrease.

presentations. Organized in 1932, the Duluth-Superior Symphony Orchestra presents seven concerts each season, as well as three Pops performances and an annual holiday concert. The Matinee Musicale, Duluth's oldest cultural organization, promotes promising young musicians. The Tweed Museum of Art at the University of Minnesota–Duluth presents historical and contemporary exhibitions in nine galleries and is home to the Sax Sculpture Conservatory.

Festivals and Holidays

The summer season in Duluth features Grandma's Marathon, a run along Lake Superior, and the Park Point Art Fair in June, the Fourth Fest in July, and Bayfront Blues Festival in August. The International Folk Festival presents music, ethnic foods, and dance at Leif Erikson Park in August.

Sports for the Spectator

The University of Minnesota–Duluth competes nationally in Division I hockey, playing a 20-home-game schedule at the Duluth Entertainment Convention Center (DECC). The Beargrease Sled Dog Marathon, the premier dog race of the lower 48 states, is a 400-mile wilderness race held every winter. The race's route, from Duluth to Grand Portage and back, includes 14 checkpoints along Lake Superior's North Shore.

The Duluth Winter Festival begins at the same time as the Beargrease and runs until the end of January. The Duluth Yacht Club sailboat races from Duluth and Port Wing take place on Labor Day weekend.

Sports for the Participant

Spirit Mountain Recreation Area offers downhill skiing, cross-country trails, tennis, camping, and hiking. Duluth maintains, on 11,000 acres of land, 105 municipal parks and playgrounds, two 27-hole golf courses, 41 tennis courts, 20 baseball and softball fields, and 22 community recreation centers. Athletic leagues are available for softball, basketball, no-check hockey, volleyball, touch football, broomball, and bocce. In addition are 45 miles of snowmobile trails, seven hiking trails, and 44 kilometers of groomed cross-country ski trails maintained by the city. Residents and visitors can compete in Grandma's Marathon, which is run along the North Shore the third weekend in June. The Fond-Du-Luth Gaming Casino, located in downtown Duluth, is another popular attraction.

Shopping and Dining

The development of Duluth's historic waterfront downtown and the conversion of a local brewery into a hotel, restaurant, and shopping complex on the shore of Lake Superior have modernized Duluth's shopping milieu. The three-mile-long downtown Skywalk system offers protected access to area shops and restaurants. Duluth restaurants offer freshwater fish from Lake Superior. Ethnic cuisine consists principally of Greek, Italian, and Chinese dishes.

Visitor Information: Duluth Convention and Visitors Bureau, 21 W. Superior St., Ste. 100, Duluth, MN 55802; telephone (218)722-4011; toll-free (800)4-DULUTH; email cvb@visitduluth.com

Convention Facilities

The Duluth Entertainment Convention Center is the principal site for conventions and a wide range of other functions. Attracting more than one million visitors each year, the complex houses 200,000 square feet of meeting and exhibit space along with an 8,000-seat arena and a 2,400-seat auditorium. The facility also includes a 26,000-square-foot ballroom, 15 meeting rooms, and exhibit space. Numerous hotels and motels, several of them with meeting facilities, provide more than 4,200 rooms for lodgings in the Duluth area.

Convention Information: Duluth Convention and Visitors Bureau, 21 W. Superior St., Ste. 100, Duluth, MN 55802; telephone (218)722-4011; toll-free (800)4-DULUTH; email cvb@visitduluth.com

Transportation

Approaching the City

The Duluth International Airport, located six miles from downtown, is the destination for most air traffic into the city. Domestic and international commercial carriers schedule daily flights into the passenger terminal.

Duluth is the terminus point for Interstate 35, which extends from the United States-Mexico border into northern Minnesota; federal highways providing easy access into the city include U.S. 53, 61, and 2. State routes running through Duluth are 23, 39, and 194.

Traveling in the City

Duluth Transit Authority (DTA) provides public bus transportation throughout the metropolitan area with a fleet of 65 modern transit buses. Among the DTA's special services are A Special Transit Ride (STRIDE) for handicapped passengers and carpool and rideshare programs. The DTA operates the Port Town Trolley, a downtown circulator, during the summer months. Visitors may also explore the city on horse-drawn carriages or via the Canal Park waterfront tram.

Communications

Newspapers and Magazines

Duluth's major daily newspaper is the morning *Duluth News-Tribune.* Several suburban newspapers and shopping guides circulate weekly. *Labor World,* a labor newspaper established in 1895, appears biweekly on Wednesdays. *The Duluthian,* a bimonthly, is published by the Chamber of Commerce with a business and community orientation. *Lake Superior Magazine,* also published bimonthly, features articles and photography about the region. A number of special-interest magazines are published in the city on such subjects as mining and mineral processing, the restaurant industry, and the dental profession.

Television and Radio

More than a dozen television stations, representing the major networks and PBS, broadcast in Duluth, which also receives programming from Hibbing; cable programming is available by subscription. Some 30 AM and FM radio stations offer a variety of formats, including classical, contemporary, and country music, religious programming, news, and public interest features.

Media Information: *Duluth News-Tribune,* 424 W. 1st St., Duluth, MN 55802; telephone (218)723-5313. *The Duluthian,* Duluth Area Chamber of Commerce, 5 W. 1st St., Ste. 101, Duluth, MN 55802; telephone (218)722-5501

Duluth Online

City of Duluth home page. Available www.ci.duluth.mn.us

Duluth Area Chamber of Commerce. Available www.duluthchamber.com

Duluth Convention & Visitors Bureau. Available www.visitduluth.com

Duluth Entertainment Convention Center. Available www.duluthconventioncenter.com or www.decc.org

Duluth News-Tribune. Available www.duluthsuperior.com

Duluth Public Library. Available www.duluth.lib.mn.us

Duluth Public Schools. Available www.duluth.k12.mn.us

Minnesota Historical Society. Available www.mnhs.org

Northeast Minnesota Historical Society Archives. Available www.d.umn.edu/lib/collections

Selected Bibliography

Hertzel, Laurie (ed.), *Boomtown Landmarks* (Pfeifer-Hamilton Publishing, 1993)

Sutter, Barton, *Cold Comfort: Life at the Top of the Map* (University of Minnesota Press, 1998)

Minneapolis

The City in Brief

Founded: 1849 (incorporated, 1866)

Head Official: Mayor R. T. Rybak (D) (since 2002)

City Population
  1980: 370,951
  1990: 368,383
  2000: 382,618
  2003 estimate: 373,188
  Percent change, 1990–2000: 3.9%
  U.S. rank in 1980: 34th
  U.S. rank in 1990: 42nd
  U.S. rank in 2000: 45th

Metropolitan Area Population
  1980: 2,137,133
  1990: 2,538,776

  2000: 2,968,806
  Percent change, 1990–2000: 19.6%
  U.S. rank in 1990: 17th
  U.S. rank in 2000: 16th

Area: 54.9 square miles (2000)
Elevation: Ranges from 687 feet to 1,060 feet above sea level
Average Annual Temperature: 44.7° F
Average Annual Precipitation: 26.36 inches

Major Economic Sectors: Services, trade, manufacturing, government
Unemployment Rate: 4.2% (February 2005)
Per Capita Income: $22,685 (1999)

2002 FBI Crime Index Total: 26,630

Major Colleges and Universities: University of Minnesota–Twin Cities; University of St. Thomas-Minneapolis

Daily Newspaper: *Star Tribune*

Introduction

The largest city in Minnesota, Minneapolis is the seat of Hennepin County and the sister city of Saint Paul, with which it forms the 15-county Minneapolis-Saint Paul metropolitan statistical area. Strategically located on the navigable head of the Mississippi River, Minneapolis traces its history to the early exploration of the Northwest Territory. The city encompasses within its boundaries 16 lakes (said to have been formed by Paul Bunyan's footprints) and is noted for its natural beauty and parklands. First a milling and lumbering center, Minneapolis today has one of the largest concentrations of high-technology firms in the nation. The combined cities of Minneapolis and Saint Paul are highly rated for their livability and rank among the country's best places for growing a business.

Geography and Climate

Minneapolis is part of a 15-county metropolitan statistical area. (In addition to Hennepin, Ramsey, Anoka, Washington, Dakota, Scott, Carver, Wright, Sheburne, Chisago, and Isanti counties in Minnesota, and Pierce and St. Croix counties in Wisconsin, two counties in St. Cloud were added in 1993; they were Stearns and Benton.) Minneapolis, which shares geographic and climatic characteristics with Saint Paul, is situated at the point where the Minnesota River joins the Mississippi River on flat or gently rolling terrain. Sixteen lakes are located within the city limits. Most of the lakes are small and shallow, covered by ice in the winter. The city's climate is continental, with large seasonal temperature variations and a favorable growing season of 166 days. Severe weather conditions, such as blizzards, freezing rain, tornadoes, and wind and hail storms are fairly common; winter recreational weather is excellent, however, because of the dry snow, which reaches average depths of 6 to 10 inches.

Area: 54.9 square miles (1999)

Elevation: Ranges from 687 feet to 1,060 feet above sea level

Average Temperatures: January, 11.2° F; August, 70.6° F; annual average, 44.7° F

Average Annual Precipitation: 26.36 inches

History

Falls Provide Townsite and Waterpower

The area where Minneapolis is now located was farmed and hunted by the Sioux tribe before the arrival of Father Louis Hennepin, a French Franciscan missionary who explored the Mississippi River in 1680. Father Hennepin discovered the future site of Minneapolis at a waterfall on the navigable head of the Mississippi River; the falls, which he named after St. Anthony, have since played a crucial role in the city's development. Permanent settlement came in 1820, when Federal troops under the command of Colonel Josiah Snelling built Fort St. Anthony on a bluff overlooking the confluence of the Minnesota and Mississippi Rivers. Renamed Fort Snelling in 1825, it safeguarded fur traders from the warring Sioux and Chippewa and served as a trading center and outpost to the Upper Midwest.

The St. Anthony Falls provided the source of power for lumber and flour milling, the two industries that fueled the city's rapid growth. Soldiers built the first flour mill in 1823 and the first commercial sawmill was in operation in 1841. Attracting settlers from New England, particularly lumbermen from Maine, the rich land was ready for settlement. A geographical fault discovered at the falls in 1869 nearly led to economic disaster and the demise of these industries, but an apron built with federal funding secured the source of waterpower and helped the city to grow in wealth and prosperity.

In 1849 the village of All Saints was founded on the west side of the falls and nine years later settlers who squatted on U.S. military reservation land were awarded land rights. Also in 1855, the village of St. Anthony on the east side of the falls was incorporated. In 1856 the name of All Saints was changed to Minneapolis, which was derived from the Sioux "minne" for water and the Greek "polis" for city. St. Anthony was chartered as a city in 1860 and Minneapolis six years later. Then in 1872 the two cities become one, spanning both sides of the Mississippi River, with the name of the larger being retained.

Flour, Lumber Industries Attract New Residents

Immigrants from Northern Europe, particularly Sweden but also Norway, Denmark, and Finland, flocked to Minneapolis to work in the new industries. A shoemaker named Nils Nyberg is credited as being the first Swede to settle, having arrived in St. Anthony in 1851. The wave of Scandinavian immigration after the Civil War was felt in every aspect of life in Minneapolis.

In one short generation Minneapolis emerged as a great American city. The original New England settlers platted the streets to reflect order and prosperity, with the boulevards lined with oak and elm trees. The Mississippi River divided the city and served as the focal point of the street grid. The city's rapid population growth and booming economy were attributable in part to the perfection of the Purifer, a flour-sifting device, that made possible the production of high-quality flour from inexpensive spring wheat and led to the construction of large flour mills.

A mill explosion in 1878 that destroyed half the flour mill district prompted residents to research methods to reduce mill dust. Minnesota emerged as the world's leading flour-milling center by 1882. Steam-powered machinery propelled the lumber industry and during the period 1899 to 1905 Minneapolis was the world's foremost producer of lumber. Production was so high that logs actually jammed the river from the timberlands of the north in 1899. Minneapolis became a rail transportation center during this period, further contributing to economic prosperity.

Progressive Programs Revitalize City

The lumber industry in Minneapolis declined once the great forest lands of the north were exhausted, and the large milling companies were forced to relocate some of their plants in other cities to combat the high cost of transportation, which further hurt the economy. After World War II Minneapolis rebounded and became a national leader in the manufacture of computers, electronic equipment, and farm machinery. It established a reputation as a progressive city, undertaking an ambitious urban development project that improved the downtown core and revitalized the economic base. The innovative Nicollet Mall, with a skywalk system, was one of the first of its kind in a major city. Minneapolis and its twin city, Saint Paul, emerged as one of the nation's fastest-growing metropolitan areas in the 1960s and 1970s. By the end of the century, the area continued its growth, ranking as the eighth fastest growing in the country.

Minneapolis embraces continued growth and beautification in the twenty-first century. Leveraging its early roots in the flour milling and lumber industry the city has become the home of such major corporations as General Mills, International MultiFoods, and Anderson Windows as well as attracting growth in the technology and healthcare services fields. Development of sporting venues and cleanup of the city's brownfields add to the appeal of living in the Twin Cities area; Minneapolis's successful transformation has inspired other cities to find solutions to the problems of urban decay.

Historical Information: Hennepin History Museum Library, 2303 Third Avenue, South, Minneapolis, MN 55404; telephone (612)870-1329. Minnesota Historical Society, 345 Kellogg Blvd. West, Saint Paul, MN 55102-1906; telephone (651)296-6126

Population Profile

Metropolitan Area Residents

1980: 2,137,133
1990: 2,538,776
2000: 2,968,806
Percent change, 1990–2000: 19.6%
U.S. rank in 1980: 17th
U.S. rank in 2000: 16th

City Residents

1980: 370,951
1990: 368,383
2000: 382,618
2003 estimate: 373,188
Percent change, 1990–2000: 3.9%
U.S. rank in 1980: 34th
U.S. rank in 1990: 47th
U.S. rank in 2000: 45th

Density: 6,970.3 people per square mile (2000)

Racial and ethnic characteristics (2000)
   White: 365,924
   Black or African American: 68,818
   American Indian and Alaska Native: 8,378
   Asian: 23,455
   Native Hawaiian and other Pacific Islander: 289
   Hispanic (may be of any race): 29,175
   Other: 15,789

Percent of residents born in state: 52% (2000)

Age characteristics (2000)
   Population under 5 years old: 25,187
   Population 5 to 9 years old: 23,960
   Population 10 to 14 years old: 22,291
   Population 15 to 19 years old: 26,866
   Population 20 to 24 years old: 40,953
   Population 25 to 34 years old: 78,978
   Population 35 to 44 years old: 60,904
   Population 45 to 54 years old: 45,961
   Population 55 to 59 years old: 13,199
   Population 60 to 64 years old: 9,441
   Population 65 to 74 years old: 15,332
   Population 75 to 84 years old: 13,172
   Population 85 years and over: 6,374
   Median age: 31.2 years

Births (2003)
   Total number (Hennepin County): 16,440

Deaths (2003)
Total number (Hennepin County): 7,752 (of which, 65 were infants under the age of 1 year)

Money income (1999)
Per capita income: $22,685
Median household income: $37,974
Total households: 162,382

Number of households with income of . . .
less than $10,000: 17,543
$10,000 to $14,999: 11,031
$15,000 to $24,999: 23,063
$25,000 to $34,999: 22,957
$35,000 to $49,999: 27,374
$50,000 to $74,999: 28,990
$75,000 to $99,999: 14,607
$100,000 to $149,999: 10,528
$150,000 to $199,999: 2,821
$200,000 or more: 3,468

Percent of families below poverty level: 11.9% (44.2% of which were female householder families with related children under 5 years)

2002 FBI Crime Index Total: 26,630

Municipal Government

Minneapolis, the seat of Hennepin County, is governed by a mayor and a 13-member council, all of whom are elected to four-year terms. The mayor, who is not a member of council, shares equally-distributed powers with council members.

Head Official: Mayor R.T. Rybak (since 2002; current term expires January 2006)

Total Number of City Employees: 7,000 (2005)

City Information: City Hall, 350 South Fifth Street, Minneapolis, MN 55415; telephone (612)673-3000

Economy

Major Industries and Commercial Activity

Manufacturing is the primary industry in Minneapolis's diversified economic base. Principal manufacturing areas are electronics, milling, machinery, medical products, food processing, and graphic arts. Sixteen of the *Fortune* 500 largest U.S. corporations are headquartered in the Twin Cities,

which is among the largest commercial centers between Chicago and the West Coast. The area is also home to 30 *Fortune* 1000 companies and several of the world's largest private companies.

Also integral to the local economy are high-technology industries. With the University of Minnesota and other colleges and technical schools providing applied research and well-trained scientists and engineers, one of the largest concentrations of high-technology firms in the nation—more than 1,300—developed in metropolitan Minneapolis-Saint Paul.

Among the banks and other financial institutions that make the Twin Cities the financial center of the upper Midwest, seven of the largest are based in Minneapolis. In addition, the headquarters of the Ninth Federal Reserve District Bank is located in the city. Local banks, savings and loan companies, venture capital concerns, and insurance companies play a major role in the economic development of the region.

Items and goods produced: electronics, food and dairy products, super computers, structural steel, thermostatic controls, conveyor systems, medical electronics equipment, farm machinery, ball bearings, tools, construction machinery, boilers, tanks, burglar alarms, underwear and hosiery, packaging, garden tools, lawn mowers, sprinklers

Incentive Programs—New and Existing Companies

The Twin Cities area offers a variety of programs for new and expanding businesses.

Local programs—The Minneapolis Community Development Agency (MCDA), the development arm of the City of Minneapolis, provides a host of affordable financing packages and site-search assistance for businesses expanding in or relocating to Minneapolis. As an authorized agent for the federal Small Business Administration, the MCDA can combine federal small business financing with Minneapolis' own unique finance tools to help companies grow. MCDA business experts help businesses realize their goals from preliminary negotiations to closing. BusinessLink is a one-stop business service center located at the MCDA.

State programs—State business tax incentives include research and development credits, foreign income deductions, and sales tax exemptions and reductions. In addition the state of Minnesota offers, through a network of five job-training programs, assistance to businesses in locating and training employees.

Job training programs—The Minneapolis Employment and Training Program (METP), a service of the City of Minneapolis, offers a variety of training and job placement services for youth, adult, and mature workers as well as dislocated and welfare workers.

Development Projects

Fueling the local economy is the redevelopment of downtown Minneapolis. Since the expansion of the now-famous Nicollet Mall in the 1980s and the initiation of the innovative skyway system, billions of dollars have been invested in construction projects. The Franklin-Portland Gateway is a phased multi-use development; the first phase was completed in April 2004 and included rental and ownership residential units as well as the four-story community and education Children's Village Center. Future phases will add an additional 65 rental units, 13 ownership units, and 14,000 square feet of commercial-use space. Nearly $10 million of city-assisted financing have made the Augustana Chapel View Homes a reality; Minneapolis seniors are welcomed home in this rental and nursing facility. The Boulevard is a mixed-use affordable living center with more than 60,000 square feet of community space. In 2006 a new Central Minneapolis Public Library will open in downtown Minneapolis. Voters approved spending $110 million to build the main library; an additional $30 million will aid community improvements at the library's 14 branches.

Economic expansion and construction activity have placed a strain on the city's transportation infrastructure; to address that issue, more than $1 billion in road improvement projects will take place over several years. The Hiawatha Light Rail opened to travelers in 2004; future expansion will make it into a 13-mile line that will connect downtown Minneapolis with Minneapolis-Saint Paul International Airport and the Mall of America in Bloomington. Planning is complete for a regional rail route, the Northstar Corridor, which will connect St. Cloud with Minneapolis using an existing 40-mile freight corridor. The $265 million project is projected to be in service in late 2008.

The city completed a $175 million expansion of the Minneapolis Convention Center in 2002. The expansion added 600,000 square feet of exhibit space, making the center one of the 20 largest in the country. The new section includes 190,000 square feet of exhibition space, with 60,000 square feet of that space divisible into 44 individual meeting rooms, and a 3,400 seat auditorium.

Economic Development Information: Minneapolis Regional Chamber of Commerce, Chamber of Commerce Building, Young Quinlan Building, 81 South Ninth Street, Suite 200, Minneapolis, MN 55402; telephone (612)370-9100; fax (612)370-9195; email info@minneapolischamber.org.

Commercial Shipping

An important factor in the Minneapolis economy is the Minneapolis-Saint Paul International Airport, which is served by 16 cargo carriers and air-freight forwarders. The airport handles more than 170,000 tons of freight yearly. The Twin Cities area is also linked with major United States and Canadian markets via a network of four railroad companies.

Considered one of the largest trucking centers in the nation, Minneapolis-Saint Paul is served by 150 motor freight companies that provide overnight and four- to five-day delivery in the Midwest and major markets in the continental United States. Vital to the Twin Cities' role as a primary transportation hub is the port of Minneapolis, which together with the port of Saint Paul processes annually more than 11 million tons of cargo to and from domestic and foreign markets.

Labor Force and Employment Outlook

The Twin Cities boasts an educated work force; 24.3 percent of people 25 years old or older have four or more years of college. Unemployment in the Twin Cities remained low in the early 2000s. Companies are expanding rapidly and there is considerable competition for skilled workers especially in the areas of healthcare and technical positions, social services, personal care, construction, and computer professions.

The suburban Mall of America, one of the most popular tourist destinations in the United States, has a significant economic impact. The Twin Cities' economy is keeping pace with, and in some cases surging ahead of the national economy. Some of the leading industries are medical instrument and supplies manufacturing, printing and publishing, transportation equipment, computer and data processing services, finance, and engineering and management services. In 2005, BestJobsUSA.com selected Minneapolis one of the Top 20 Best Places to Live & Work in America.

The following is a summary of data regarding the Minneapolis-Saint Paul metropolitan area, 2004 annual average:

Size of non-agricultural labor force: 1,738,000

Number of workers employed in . . .
  mining and construction: 82,800
  manufacturing: 202,700
  transportation and utilities: 335,900
  information: 43,000
  financial activities: 140,500
  professional and business services: 245,900
  educational and health services: 216,100
  leisure and hospitality: 154,500
  other services: 75,800
  government: 240,300

Average hourly earnings of production workers employed in manufacturing: $17.59

Unemployment rate: 4.2% (February 2005)

Largest employers

(Twin Cities area)	Number of employees
State of Minnesota	55,294
U.S. Government	35,047
Target Corp.	35,047
University of Minnesota	29,498
Mayo Clinic	23,378
Allina Health	22,454
Northwest Airlines	21,301
Fairview Health Services	18,700
3M Corporation	18,179
Wells Fargo	13,938

Cost of Living

The Twin Cities region has one of the lowest costs of living among the 25 largest cities in the United States.

The following is a summary of data regarding several key cost of living factors in the Minneapolis area.

2004 (3rd Quarter) ACCRA Average House Price: $296,846

2004 (3rd Quarter) ACCRA Cost of Living Index: 109.3 (Minneapolis/St. Paul) (U.S. average = 100.0)

State income tax rate: Ranges from 5.35% to 7.85%

State sales tax rate: 6.5%

Local income tax rate: None

Local sales tax rate: 0.5%

Property tax rate: $118.42 per $1,000 assessed value (2005)

Economic Information: Minneapolis Regional Chamber of Commerce, Young Quinlan Building, 81 South Ninth Street, Suite 200, Minneapolis, MN 55402; telephone (612)370-9100

Education and Research

Elementary and Secondary Schools

The Minneapolis Public Schools, the largest school district in Minnesota, provides students with a truly international education that will better prepare them for life in a global community. Students in the districts who are currently learning English also speak one of 90 other languages in their home. Families may choose community or magnet schools, with at least 10 school options available for kindergarten families and more than 15 programs available for high school students. Ninety-eight percent of incoming kindergarten families receive their first choice. The district introduced all-day kindergarten in 2001.

While many districts are cutting funding for arts programs, 35 Minneapolis Public Schools have received a $10 million Annenberg Challenge Grant to integrate the arts throughout the curriculum, a strategy that has been shown to improve academic achievement. Middle school students benefit from a $650,000 grant from the Medtronic Foundation that is revitalizing the kindergarten through fifth grade science program. Nearly $10 million from the Walling family makes college scholarships available for Minneapolis Public School seniors to further their education in college.

The following is a summary of data regarding the Minneapolis public schools as of the 2002–2003 school year.

Total enrollment: 43,429 (excludes charter schools)

Number of facilities
  elementary schools: 63
  middle schools: 8
  senior high schools: 7
  other: 6 special education schools; 31 alternative schools

Student/teacher ratio: 18.4:1

Teacher salaries
  minimum: $31,549
  maximum: $73,143

Funding per pupil: $10,226 (actual expenditures, 2003)

Hennepin County is served by 45 private schools offering alternative educational curricula.

Public Schools Information: Minneapolis Public Schools, 807 Northeast Broadway, Minneapolis, MN 55413-2398; telephone (612)668-0000.

Colleges and Universities

The University of Minnesota—Twin Cities, a state institution with an enrollment of more than 45,000 full-time students, is located in Minneapolis. The university ranks among the nation's top 20 universities. Five degree levels—baccalaureate, first-professional, master's, intermediate, and doctorate—are available in 250 fields, including architecture, medicine, engineering, journalism, management, teacher education, public health, and music. Former students and faculty members have been awarded 12 Nobel Prizes in physics, medicine, chemistry, economics, and peace.

Augsburg College and North Central Bible College, private religious institutions, award associate, baccalaureate, and master's degrees. The Minneapolis College of Art and Design offers four-year programs in fine and applied arts. Community and technical colleges in the metropolitan area include Minneapolis Community College, Minneapolis Technical College, and Hennepin Technical College.

Libraries and Research Centers

The Minneapolis Public Library operates a Central Library and 14 branches. The Central Library has the largest collection of any public library in Minnesota. In 2000 a $140 million referendum was passed for the building of a new Central Library and improvements to all 14 branches over a 10-year period. In 2002 the Central Library collection was moved to a branch location for the rebuilding of the new Central Library, opening spring 2006. The new, $110 million, five-story facility will house more books and computers, community spaces, a gallery, a proposed planetarium, and other features.

The University of Minnesota Libraries—Twin Cities, also located in Minneapolis, have total holdings of more than 6 million volumes in major academic departments and more than 36,000 periodical subscriptions. Special collections include literature on ballooning, the Hess Dime Novel Collection, the Charles Babbage Institute, and the Performing Arts Archives. The library is a depository for federal and state documents. The Immigration History Research Center at the university houses one of the nation's most comprehensive collections of the immigrant past.

More than 70 special libraries and research centers serve the city. Most are affiliated with state and county government agencies, businesses and corporations, hospitals, churches and synagogues, and arts organizations.

Public Library Information: Minneapolis Public Library, 250 Marquette Ave, Minneapolis, MN 55401; telephone (612)630-6000; fax (612)630-6210

Health Care

A vital force in the Minneapolis medical community is the University of Minnesota Medical Center, where the first open heart surgery was performed in 1954. The hospital is also known as a leading organ transplant center. Among the other major hospitals in Minneapolis are the University of Minnesota Children's Hospital, Shriner's Hospital, the Veteran's Administration Medical Center, the Hennepin County Medical Center, and the Sister Kenny Rehabilitation Institute. The Mayo Clinic is located 75 miles southeast of Minneapolis, in Rochester.

Recreation

Sightseeing

Sightseeing in Minneapolis might begin with the Chain of Lakes—Lake of the Isles, Lake Calhoun, and Lake Harriet—

just a few miles west of downtown; in all, 16 lakes are located within the city limits and more than 1,000 are in close proximity. Minnehaha Falls, the point at which Minnehaha Creek plunges into the Mississippi River, was made famous by Henry Wadsworth Longfellow in his poem *The Song of Hiawatha*. A life-size statue of Hiawatha holding his wife Minnehaha is located on an island just above the falls.

For those with an interest in Minneapolis's historical roots, the American Swedish Institute maintains a turn-of-the-century 33-room mansion that displays Swedish immigrant artifacts as well as traveling exhibits. The Ard Godrey House, built in 1849 and the oldest existing frame house in the city, features authentic period furnishings. Minneapolis's early history and development are captured at the Hennepin History Museum.

Fort Snelling, a historic landmark dating from 1820 overlooking Fort Snelling State Park, has been restored to its frontier-era appearance and is open six months a year. At the Minnesota Zoo, seven trails lead to exhibits in natural settings. The Minneapolis Planetarium, with a 40-foot dome, projects over 2,000 stars. More than 1,000 acres cultivated with numerous varieties of trees, flowers, and shrubs make up the Minnesota Landscape Arboretum.

Arts and Culture

In both Minneapolis and Saint Paul, business and the arts go hand-in-hand. The Five Percent Club consists of local businesses and corporations that donate five percent of their pre-tax earnings to the arts, education, or human services. This investment results in such high-quality institutions as the Guthrie Theater, named for Sir Tyrone Guthrie, which ranks as one of the best regional and repertory theater companies in the United States. The Walker Art Center exhibits progressive modern art in an award-winning building designed by Edward Larrabee Barnes, which has been judged among the best art exhibition facilities in the world. The center, housing a permanent collection that represents major twentieth-century movements, also sponsors a program of music, dance, film, theater, and educational activities.

The Minnesota Orchestra, performing at Orchestra Hall on Nicollet Mall and at Ordway Music Theater in Saint Paul, presents a season of concerts that includes a great performers series, the weekender series, a pop series, and a summer festival. Family holiday concerts are performed at Christmas time. The Minnesota Opera performs traditional and new works at the Ordway theater in Saint Paul. Touring Broadway musicals and musical stars perform at the restored Orpheum Theater. The Children's Theater Company offers a world-class theater education program for young people. International theater professionals work with student actors and technicians to present productions of the highest quality.

The Minneapolis Sculpture Garden, adjacent to the Walker Art Center, was designed by landscape architect Peter Rothschild; it consists of four symmetrical square plazas that display more than 55 works by Henry Moore, George Segal, and Deborah Butterfield, among others. The Minneapolis Institute of Arts showcases world art in a collection of more than 100,000 objects from every period and culture.

Festivals and Holidays

Minneapolis celebrates March with a St. Patrick's Day Parade and a Spring Flower Show. The Minneapolis Aquatennial, established in 1940, is a 10-day extravaganza held in late July with a special theme each year; the Aquatennial Association programs over 250 free events that focus on the city's proximity to water. Many Minneapolis festivals honor the city's Scandinavian heritage. Other festivals celebrate ethnic cultures with music, dance, food, arts, and crafts. Uptown Art Fair, one of the largest such events in the country, is held on a weekend in early August.

Sports for the Spectator

The Hubert H. Humphrey Metrodome is home to two of the city's major sports franchises; the Minnesota Twins of the Central Division of baseball's American League and the Minnesota Vikings of the Central Division of the National Football League play their home games in this domed stadium, conveniently located downtown. The National Basketball Association's Timberwolves play at the Target Center. Women's National Basketball Association team the Minnesota Lynx came to the Twin Cities in 2000. Sports fans can also attend major and minor sporting events at the University of Minnesota–Twin Cities, which fields Big Ten teams like the Gophers, who play to sellout crowds.

Sports for the Participant

Minneapolis is one of the country's most naturally beautiful cities, enhanced by 107 playgrounds, 8 community centers, 7 municipal golf links, and 16 lakes within the city limits. The abundance of easily accessible water makes possible a full range of water sports and activities in both summer and winter. Four thousand acres of city park land are available for swimming, canoeing, sailing, windsurfing, waterskiing, roller-skating, and biking along with softball, tennis, and golf; about 136,900 acres of land are set aside in the Twin Cities region for parks, trails, and wildlife management areas. Winter sports include skating, skiing, snowshoeing, and ice fishing.

Shopping and Dining

Minneapolis is the originator on a grand scale of the "second floor city" concept, integrating essentially two downtowns—a sidewalk-level traditional downtown and a second city joined by an elaborate skywalk system. Nicollet

Mall, completed in 1967, redefined the urban downtown and eliminated the element of weather as a deterrent to the shopper. This all-weather skywalk system connects an indoor shopping center whose four major department stores and hundreds of specialty shops cover 34 city blocks. Shopping activity is also a part of the City Center mall, undergoing renovations in 2005. St. Anthony Main, along the historic Mississippi riverfront, consists of old warehouses and office buildings converted to a shopping center. Suburban Bloomington is home to the largest mall in North America, the Mall of America.

Elegant dining is possible at The 510 Restaurant, Goodfellow's, and Rosewood Room, named by *Food and Wine* magazine as Distinguished Restaurants of North America. Dinner cruises on the Mississippi River are offered during the summer.

Visitor Information: The Greater Minneapolis Convention & Visitors Center, 250 Marquette South, Ste 1300, Minneapolis, MN 55402; telephone (612)335-5827 or (800)445-7412

Convention Facilities

The primary meeting and convention site in Minneapolis is the Minneapolis Convention Center, which opened in 1990 and underwent major renovations in 2002. More than 5,000 guest rooms are located downtown, nearly 3,000 of which are connected to the Minneapolis Convention Center via the skyway system.

Convention Information: Minneapolis Convention Center, telephone (612)661-4700

Transportation

Approaching the City

Located southeast of downtown Minneapolis, the Minneapolis-Saint Paul International Airport is in the midst of a three-phase, $860 million expansion in 2005. In 2004, Minneapolis-St. Paul International Airport was named Best Airport in the Americas and Best Domestic Airport by the International Air Transport Association and Airports Council International. The airport is served by ten major domestic carriers. Six reliever airports are also located in the metropolitan area. Amtrak runs a major east-west line from Chicago and the East into Saint Paul.

Two major interstate highways serve Minneapolis: I-94 (east-west) and I-35W (north-south). Two belt-line freeways, I-494 and I-694, facilitate travel around the Twin-City suburbs. Seven federal and 13 state highways link the city with points throughout the United States and Canada.

Traveling in the City

Minneapolis is laid out on a grid pattern, with streets south of Grant Street intersecting on a north-south axis and those north of Grant running diagonally northeast-southwest. Residents think of their hometown as made up of five major parts: North Side, South Side, Northeast, Southeast, and downtown, each with its own distinct character and attractions. The Minneapolis Skywalk System connects major downtown public buildings and retail establishments with elevated, covered walkways. There are also smaller communities such as Uptown on the South Side and Dinkytown on the edge of the University of Minnesota's Minneapolis campus.

Serving Minneapolis, Saint Paul, and the surrounding suburbs is the Metropolitan Council Transit Operations (MCTO), the second-largest bus system in the United States. Additional bus service is provided by five private operators, including Gray Line, which conducts sightseeing tours, stopping at Nicollet Mall and at various hotels in Minneapolis and Saint Paul. The city is noted for efficiency of commuting time: the freeway system, moderate population density, and two central business districts contribute to high levels of mobility during peak and non-peak hours.

In 2004 the first route of the Hiawatha Light Rail Transit (LRT) was opened to the public; the light rail will be developed to include 13 miles or rail along Hiawatha Avenue taking passengers into downtown Minneapolis, the airport, and the Mall of America.

Communications

Newspapers and Magazines

The major daily newspaper in Minneapolis is the *Star Tribune.* Several neighborhood and suburban newspapers are distributed weekly in the city.

Mpls. St.Paul is a magazine focusing on metropolitan life in the Twin Cites. A popular publication with a national distribution is *The Utne Reader.* Other special interest magazines based in Minneapolis pertain to such subjects as religion,

aviation, business, entertainment, hunting and conservation, minority issues, medicine, politics, and computers.

Television and Radio

Four television stations broadcast out of Minneapolis, as do two cable stations. Radio listeners can choose from 17 AM and FM stations. Programming includes ethnic music, jazz, gospel, classical music, easy listening, and news and public affairs.

Media Information: *Star Tribune,* 425 Portland Avenue, Minneapolis, MN 55415; telephone (612)673-4000; toll-free (800)827-8742

Minneapolis Online

BusinessLink, Minneapolis Community Development Agency home page. Available www.mcda.org

City of Minneapolis home page. Available www.ci .minneapolis.mn.us

Greater Minneapolis Chamber of Commerce home page. Available www.minneapolischamber.org

Greater Minneapolis Convention and Visitors Association home page. Available www.minneapolis.org/gmcva

Hennepin History Museum home page. Available www .hhmuseum.org/index.htm

Mall of America home page. Available www.mallofamerica .com

Minneapolis Public Library home page. Available www .mpls.lib.mn.us

Minneapolis Public Schools home page. Available www .mpls.k12.mn.us

Minnesota Historical Society home page. Available www .mnhs.org

Star Tribune home page. Available www.startribune.com

Selected Bibliography

Carlson, Peggie, *The Girls Are Coming (Midwest Reflections)* (Minnesota Historical Society)

Millett, Larry, *Lost Twin Cities* (Minnesota Historical Society)

Weiner, Jay, *Stadium Games: Fifty Years of Big League Greed and Bush League Boondoggles* (University of Minnesota Press, 2000)

Rochester

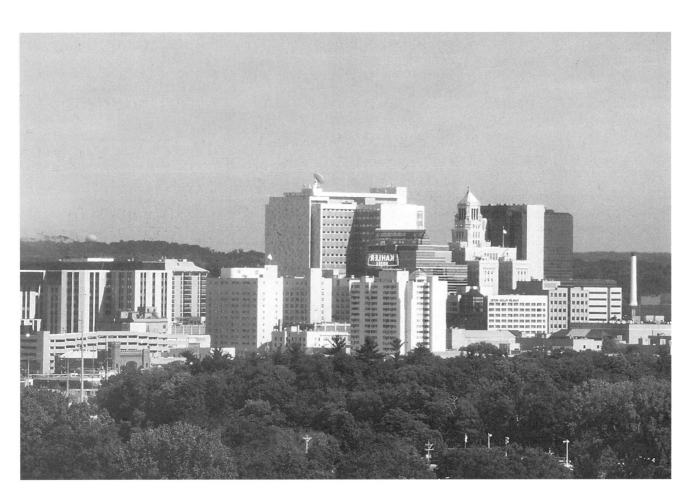

The City in Brief

Founded: 1854, incorporated 1858

Head Official: Mayor Ardell F. Brede (NP) (since 2002)

City Population
  1980: 57,906
  1990: 70,729
  2000: 85,806
  2003 estimate: 92,507
  Percent change, 1990–2000: 12.9%
  U.S. rank in 1980: 349th
  U.S. rank in 1990: 319th (State rank: 5th)
  U.S. rank in 2000: 329th (State rank: 3rd)

Metropolitan Area Population
  1980: 92,006
  1990: 106,470
  2000: 124,277
  Percent change, 1990–2000: 11.7%

U.S. rank in 1980: 292nd
U.S. rank in 1990: 238th
U.S. rank in 2000: 231st

Area: 39.61 square miles (2000)
Elevation: 1,320 feet above sea level
Average Annual Temperature: 43.4° F
Average Annual Precipitation: 32.3 inches of rain, 48.8 inches of snow

Major Economic Sectors: services, trade, manufacturing
Unemployment Rate: 4.2% (February 2005)
Per Capita Income: $24,811 (1999)

2002 FBI Crime Index Total: 3,003

Major Colleges and Universities: Mayo Foundation, Minnesota Bible College, Rochester Community and Technical College, Saint Mary's University of Minnesota–Rochester, Winona State University–Rochester Center

Daily Newspaper: *Post-Bulletin*

Introduction

Rochester, the seat of Olmsted County, is known worldwide as the home of the famed Mayo Clinic. The city is the business and cultural hub for southeastern Minnesota, and its local health care facilities are among the finest in the world. Clean air, low crime, and a strong sense of community, as well as attractive offerings in the arts and recreational areas, contribute to the city's appeal as a place to settle. Rochester was rated the nation's best small city to live in 2000 by *Money* magazine. In its review, *Money* praised Rochester's good schools, high-tech job growth, easy commuting, and the Mayo Clinic.

Geography and Climate

Rochester is located 76 miles southeast of Minneapolis/Saint Paul, 41 miles north of the Iowa border, and 36 miles west of the Wisconsin border. The Zumbro River flows through the city, which is set on rolling farmland. There are also three creeks within the city limits.

Rochester enjoys a four-season climate. Spring is usually brief, and summer is pleasant and occasionally very hot, with approximately seven days exceeding 90 degrees. In July the relative humidity ranges between a high of 90 percent and a low of 62 percent. Summer brings prevailing winds from the south and southwest, and the winds shift during the winter months to come from the northwest. Autumn offers beautiful sunny days. Winter is cold, with snowfall averaging 48.8 inches annually. Severe storms, including blizzards, freezing rain, and tornadoes are not uncommon. There are occasional flash floods of the Zumbro River.

Area: 39.61 square miles (2000)

Elevation: 1,320 feet above sea level

Average Temperatures: January, 11.8° F; July, 70.2° F

Average Annual Precipitation: 32.3 inches of rain, 48.8 inches of snow

History

Long before the coming of Europeans, members of the Chippewa and Sioux nations lived in the area of the Minnesota Territory. Rochester was founded in 1854 when a group of U.S. surveyors staked claims on the banks of the Zumbro River. George Head began a pioneer settlement there, and by 1888, the settlement, which Head named in honor of his hometown in New York, had grown to 1,500 people. Many of those drawn to the area came because of the fertile farmland. In 1863 William Worall Mayo, examining surgeon for the Union Army Enrollment Board, settled in the town and, along with his sons, founded a medical practice. The Mayo Medical Center, which started out in a five-story brick building, now occupies about 10 million square feet.

The coming of the east-west railroad in the 1880s, which provided an excellent distribution system for the local farmers' products, added to the growth of the community, and agriculture has continued to be an important part of the local economy. A terrible tornado struck the city in 1883, and doctors were forced to treat its many victims under inadequate, makeshift conditions. Mother Alfred Moes, founder of the Sisters of St. Francis, proposed the building and staffing of a hospital, in which W.W. Mayo would provide the care. In 1889 St. Mary's Hospital opened with 27 beds.

Beginning in 1892, new staff members were added to the Mayo Clinic team. Dr. Henry Plummer, from a nearby small town, joined the Mayos in 1892, and designed many group practice systems that are the basis for those used today. They include the use of a common medical record, X-rays, conveyors for moving records, a registration system, and one of the first telephone paging systems. In 1907 the first patient registration number was assigned.

As physicians from around the world came to observe how the Mayo Clinic was operated, the clinic in 1915 initiated one of the world's first graduate training programs for doctors, called the Mayo Graduate School of Medicine. In 1919 the Mayos turned over all their profits and established the nonprofit Mayo Properties Association. Both of the Mayo brothers died within months of one another in 1939, but their work continued.

The local economy developed in a new direction with the establishment of an International Business Machines (IBM) plant in the 1950s. In 1990 that plant earned the prestigious Malcolm Baldrige National Quality Award.

The Mayo Medical School opened in 1972. The integration of Mayo Clinic Rochester, Saint Mary's Hospital, and Rochester Methodist Hospital took place in 1986, and that same year the clinic expanded with the opening of Mayo Clinic Jacksonville (Florida). In 1987 Mayo Clinic Scottsdale (Arizona) opened, and St. Luke's Hospital in Jacksonville became part of Mayo.

In 1992 a merger took place between Mayo Clinic and Luther Hospital and Midelfort Clinic in Eau Claire, Wisconsin. That same year Mayo affiliated with Decorah Medical Associates in Decorah, Iowa, and Community Clinics in

Wabasha, Minnesota. Today, the Mayo Clinic along with a symphony orchestra, museums, and other amenities contribute to Rochester's livability. Since the turn of the century, Rochester has become the new home for more than 2,000 citizens each year. As a result, the city's mayor adopted a "smart growth" program to accommodate these newcomers into Rochester's existing population.

Historical Information: History Center of Olmstead County, 1195 W. Circle Dr. SW, Rochester, MN 55902; telephone (507)282-9447

Population Profile

Metropolitan Area Residents

1980: 92,006
1990: 106,470
2000: 124,277
Percent change, 1990–2000: 11.7%
U.S. rank in 1980: 292nd
U.S. rank in 1990: 238th
U.S. rank in 1990: 231st

City Residents

1980: 57,906
1990: 70,729
2000: 85,806
2003 estimate: 92,507
Percent change, 1990–2000: 12.9%
U.S. rank in 1980: 349th
U.S. rank in 1990: 319th
U.S. rank in 2000: 329th

Density: 2,166.3 people per square mile (2000)

Racial and ethnic characteristics (2000)
　White: 75,088
　Black or African American: 3,064
　American Indian and Alaska Native: 258
　Asian: 4,830
　Native Hawaiian and Pacific Islander: 33
　Hispanic or Latino (may be of any race): 2,565
　Other: 996

Percent of residents born in state: 55.4% (2000)

Age characteristics (2000)
　Population under 5 years old: 6,401
　Population 5 to 9 years old: 5,939
　Population 10 to 14 years old: 6,195
　Population 15 to 19 years old: 5,642
　Population 20 to 24 years old: 5,765
　Population 25 to 34 years old: 13,891

Population 35 to 44 years old: 14,734
Population 45 to 54 years old: 10,754
Population 55 to 59 years old: 3,675
Population 60 to 64 years old: 2,959
Population 65 to 74 years old: 4,686
Population 75 to 84 years old: 3,543
Population 85 years and over: 1,622
Median age: 34.3 years

Births (2003)
　Total number: 1,593

Deaths (2003)
　Total number: 729 (of which, 9 were infants under the age of 1 year)

Money income (1999)
　Per capita income: $24,811
　Median household income: $49,090
　Total households: 34,009

Number of households with income of . . .
　less than $10,000: 652
　$10,000 to $14,999: 550
　$15,000 to $24,999: 1,352
　$25,000 to $34,999: 1,996
　$35,000 to $49,999: 3,453
　$50,000 to $74,999: 5,954
　$75,000 to $99,999: 3,381
　$100,000 to $149,999: 2,691
　$150,000 to $199,999: 838
　$200,000 or more: 745

Percent of families below poverty level: 4.7% (26.7% of which were female householder families with related children under 5 years)

2002 FBI Crime Index Total: 3,003

Municipal Government

Rochester has a strong council/weak mayor form of government with an executive city administrator. The city council is comprised of seven council persons, the mayor, and the city administrator, each of which serve a four-year term.

Head Official: Mayor Ardell F. Brede (NP) (since 2002; current term expires 2006)

Total Number of City Employees: 800 (2005)

City Information: Rochester City Hall, 201 4th St. SE, Rochester, MN 55904; telephone (507)285-8086

Economy

Major Industries and Commercial Activity

The health care industry dominates Rochester's economy, with more than 2 million people coming to the Mayo Clinic each year to seek treatment. The clinic admitted 127,300 patients in 2003. Mayo Medical Ventures licenses medical products and treatments worldwide that are developed at Mayo.

Wholesale and retail trade is the second-largest employment sector in the county. Many local industries sell their goods to the local International Business Machines (IBM) plant and to Mayo Medical Center.

Rochester has been rated by *Inc.* magazine as one of the top entrepreneurial cities in the country. The manufacturing industry employs almost 15 percent of the work force. Production includes food and dairy processing, computer and computer components, electronics, and precision machining. Strong areas of growth in the economy are agricultural, metal fabrication, and distribution companies. Other businesses having a major impact on the local economy are construction, printing, packaging, hotels, restaurants, communications, and entertainment facilities. The continuing growth of the economy is evidenced by the addition of some 20 firms over the past several years.

Agriculture still plays an important role in Rochester's economy, along with food processing and dairy production. Area farms produce annual crops of soybeans, corn, and a variety of fruits and vegetables, and dairy farms generate more than 2 million pounds of milk each year. Rochester is the home of Marigold Foods, which produces the well-known Kemps brand of ice cream.

Items and goods produced: hospital/surgical equipment, electronics, metal fabrication, food processing, agricultural-related products, home pasteurizers, silos, beverages, toilet preparations, computer equipment, grain, poultry

Incentive Programs—New and Existing Companies

Local programs—It is the mission of the Rochester Area Economic Development, Inc. (RAEDI) to assist new and existing companies with expansion, location, or research efforts. RAEDI has a corporation to provide better access to the U.S. Small Business Administration's 504 Loan Program, which finances long-term assets for 10- or 20-year terms. The program normally leverages a bank loan with a 504 loan to finance up to 90 percent of the project costs. RAEDI also administers the MicroEnterprise Loan Fund, which aids eligible businesses that are located in the city, five or fewer employees, a written business plan, and an owner or 51 percent of the employees who are at low or moderate income levels. The maximum loan amount is $7,500.

State programs—The Tax Increment Financing Program, a state authorized financing mechanism, is offered by the city to assist basic businesses in financing their local expansion or location. Funds may be used to purchase land and make public improvements that support business development projects. Minnesota offers programs to provide a mechanism for businesses to sell bonds at tax-exempt interest rates, allowing firms to receive long-term, low interest financing for fixed assets.

Job training programs—The Minnesota Department of Employment and Economic Development operates a network of workforce centers throughout the state. This WorkForce Center System, which has an office in Rochester, partners with local businesses to provide customized job training and other workforce development services.

Development Projects

The Mayo Foundation is currently undergoing major expansion and renovation. A series of projects, which began in 1997, are integrating patient care facilities on Mayo's downtown campus, from Rochester Methodist Hospital on the north to the Mayo Building on the south, into an interconnected facility. The projects involve adding about 850,000 square feet of new space as well as renovation of existing space. When completed, costs will reach well over $125 million.

The new Rochester Art Center opened in May 2004 and is the most recent addition to the downtown Rochester Cultural Campus. The creation of Cascade Lake Park will support a lake with the best possible water quality and will provide residents and visitors with a variety of recreational and educational opportunities. The refurbishment of Highway 52 has been recently completed.

Rochester Area Economic Development, Inc. (RAEDI), Rochester's one-stop shop for businesses seeking economic assistance, has as its goal the development of a varied economy. It reports that Rochester and environs have the highest concentration of high-tech industries among all U.S. metropolitan areas. Rochester' technology base has continued to grow over the past decade with the addition of more than 20 new technology firms.

Economic Development Information: Rochester Area Economic Development, 220 S. Broadway, Ste. 100, Rochester, MN 55904; telephone (507)288-0208

Commercial Shipping

Daily freight rail service is offered by the Dakota Minnesota & Eastern Railroad. Rochester has more than 20 motor freight carriers.

Labor Force and Employment Outlook

The following is a summary of data regarding the Rochester metropolitan area labor force, 2004 annual average:

Size of nonagricultural labor force: 101,900

Number of workers employed in . . .
    construction and mining: 4,700
    manufacturing: 13,200
    trade, transportation, and utilities: 15,600
    information: 1,500
    financial activities: 2,700
    professional and business services: 5,300
    educational and health services: 35,900
    leisure and hospitality: 8,500
    other services: 3,700
    government: 10,400

Average hourly wage of production workers employed in manufacturing: $13.56 (statewide)

Unemployment rate: 4.2% (February 2005)

Largest employers	Number of employees
Mayo Clinic	28,000
International Business Machines (IBM)	4,400
Rochester School District 535	2,120
Olmstead County	1,182
Hyvee	771
Olmsted Medical Center	974

Cost of Living

The cost of living in the Rochester area is slightly below the national average, except for housing prices, which tend to be slightly above the median. Nevertheless, Rochester residents can be assured that real estate is a good investment; Rochester's home appreciation rate is in the top quarter of all metropolitan areas.

The following is a summary of data regarding several key cost of living factors for the Rochester metropolitan area.

2004 (3rd Quarter) ACCRA Average House Price: $234,900

2004 (3rd Quarter) ACCRA Cost of Living Index: 95.8 (U.S. average = 100.0)

State income tax rate: Ranges from 5.85% to 7.85%

State sales tax rate: 6.5%

Local income tax rate: 1.0% of first $72,000; 2.0% over $72,000

Local sales tax rate: 0.5%

Property tax rate: tax capacity (1.0 to 1.25%) multiplied by 118.794%

Economic Information: Rochester Area Chamber of Commerce, 220 S. Broadway, Ste. 100, Rochester, MN 55904; telephone (507)288-1122; fax (507)282-8960

Education and Research

Elementary and Secondary Schools

Independent School District #535 covers 205 square miles and has the sixth-largest enrollment in the state. Rochester students consistently rank higher than average on standardized test scores.

The following is a summary of data regarding the Rochester School District as of the 2003–2004 school year.

Total enrollment: 16,013

Number of facilities
    elementary schools: 16
    junior high/middle schools: 4
    senior high schools: 3

Student/teacher ratio: elementary, 17:1; middle school, 26:1; high school, 27:1

Teacher salaries
    average: $44,872

Funding per pupil: $7,772 (2003–2004)

Public Schools Information: Rochester Public Schools, 615 7th St. SW, Rochester, MN 55902; telephone (507)285-8551

Colleges and Universities

Rochester is the home of an impressive number of quality educational institutions. The Mayo Foundation conducts formal education in five areas: Mayo Graduate School of Medicine, Mayo Graduate School, Mayo Medical School, Mayo School of Health-Related Sciences, and Mayo Section of Continuing Medical Education. In 2003, well over 1,000 residents and students were enrolled full-time.

The University of Minnesota–Rochester offers more than a dozen graduate degrees in a variety of programs, as well as several post-baccalaureate licensure and certificate programs. This school draws on the faculty of University of Minnesota–Twin Cities, and enrolls more than 1,500 students. Winona State University–Rochester Center, with 8,236 students in 2003, offers a variety of undergraduate programs, and participates in the "2 plus 2" program, whereby students can complete an undergraduate degree in Rochester by transferring credits from other institutions. Rochester Community and Technical College provides its 3,300 students with technical and transfer programs in a wide variety of majors, including business, trade/industry, allied health, human services, science, and social science.

Other colleges are the Minnesota Bible College, which enrolls nearly 100 students in courses that fulfill associate of art, bachelor of art, and bachelor of science degree requirements for the professional ministry and related areas, and Saint Mary's College Rochester Center.

Libraries and Research Centers

The Rochester Public Library houses a material collection of 370,183. These include films, multimedia resources, and in-house CD-ROMs, and magazines. The library is a document depository for the City of Rochester.

Special libraries are maintained by the Mayo Foundation, Mayo Clinic, Minnesota Bible College, the History Center of Olmsted County, the *Post Bulletin,* and International Business Machines (IBM).

The Mayo Clinic research budget exceeds $300 million annually. Research is performed at several institutes associated with the Mayo Clinic, including the Mayo Biomedical Imaging Resource, Mayo Cancer Center, a $15-million broad-based cancer research institute, and Mayo Clinic and Foundation, which studies allergic diseases. Other research institutes in Rochester are the Center for Basic Research in Digestive Diseases and the North Central Cancer Treatment Group.

Public Library Information: Rochester Public Library, 101 2nd St. SE, Rochester, MN 55904; telephone (507)285-8011; fax (507)287-1910

Health Care

The world famous Mayo Clinic is a one-stop shop for the diagnosis and treatment of just about any medical problem. The clinic admitted 127,300 patients in 2003, who were served by a staff of more than 40,000 physicians, scientists, and administrative and support staff. The clinic has the largest association of physicians in the private practice of medicine in the world.

Staffed by Mayo Clinic physicians, Rochester Methodist and Saint Mary's Hospital are also world-renowned. Rochester Methodist is a 794-bed acute-care facility that began renovations in May 2005. The hospital provides care in such

areas as organ transplantation, human fertility, oncology/hematology, and bone marrow transplantation. Its nursing units have been uniquely designed to allow research personnel to study the methods that serve patients most efficiently.

Saint Mary's Hospital, one of the largest private not-for-profit hospitals in the world, implements some of the most current advances in medical science. These include computer-assisted laser neurosurgery, kidney stone and gallstone dissolution without surgery, and magnetic resonance imaging. The hospital has 1,157 beds, 53 operating rooms, and eight intensive care units. The buildings that make up Saint Mary's Hospital are named in honor of Saint Marys' foundress, Mother Alfred, and its administrators—Sisters Joseph, Domitilla, Mary Brigh, and Generose. Mayo Eugenio Litta Children' Hospital is an 85-bed hospital within Saint Marys.

The Federal Medical Center, a federal correctional facility, has an 850-bed hospital that provides medical, psychiatry, and chemical dependency services for more than 800 inmates.

Recreation

Sightseeing

Mayo Clinic, Rochester's most famous institution, offers general tours Monday through Friday. Self-guided tours of St. Mary's Hospital and Rochester Methodist Hospital are also available. Mayowood Mansion is the former home of Doctors Charles H. and Charles W. Mayo. The 50-room mansion is full of many beautiful objects collected by the Mayos throughout their lifetime. It is open for viewing throughout the year, and is especially popular during the holiday season, when Christmas at Historic Mayowood is presented. Two local residences, the 1856 Heritage House in Town Square and the Plummer House of the Arts, are open to the public. The 49-room Tudor-style Plummer House is set on an 11-acre site with beautiful gardens.

Arts and Culture

The major setting for arts activities in Rochester is the Mayo Civic Center, with its 7,200-seat arena. Throughout the year the center presents artistic performances of all sorts, as well as sports, exhibitions, and conventions. Rochester Civic Theater offers nine performances yearly, including comedies, dramas, and musicals. The Rochester Repertory Theatre presents contemporary and classic productions. Hill Theatre, at the University Center Rochester, offers theatrical programs and productions in conjunction with classes. Children's plays are the focus of the Masque Youth Theatre.

The Plummer House.

Music thrives in Rochester, and the Rochester Civic Music–Riverside Concerts presents live concerts, featuring local, national, and international acts in rock, pop, R&B, and many other genres. Riverside Live! is a series of outdoor concerts held from May to September in the Mayo Civic Center. Talented young musicians participate in the Southern Minnesota Youth Orchestra. Recently privatized, the Rochester Orchestra and Chorale offers six concerts of chamber, symphonic, and pops programs featuring local talent.

The Mayo Clinic Collection displays throughout its facilities works of art that were donated by benefactors and former patients. Traveling exhibits of arts and crafts are on view at the Rochester Art Center, which opened a new facility in May 2004. The center also offers classes for adults and children, as well as films and other special events. Famed Rochester sculptor Charles Eugene Gagnon has more than 40 bronze sculptures on display at his studio and galleries. The Southeastern Minnesota Visual Artists Gallery presents a rotating display of works by more than 80 artists, including basketry, paintings, sculpture, pottery, wearable art, and jewelry. The Museum of the History Center of Olmstead contains more than 600,000 items, including photos, books, and maps related to Rochester and the county.

Festivals and Holidays

Rochester salutes spring with its annual Daffodil Days, sponsored by the American Cancer Society, and the Rochester World Fest, a celebration of the cultures of the world. April brings the Arts and Craft Show at Graham Arena, and the Gingerbread Craft show at Mayo Civic Center. The Rochester Art Fair in Central Park, the Covered Bridge Festival, and Rochesterfest, with its food, street dances, parade, music, and crafts displays enliven the summer.

July brings the Independence Day celebration at Silver Lake; the two-day threshing show, with hayrides, food, and demonstrations of early crafts; and the Olmsted County Fair at Rochester Fairgrounds, which continues into August and features a midway, grandstand shows, livestock competitions, and the largest county draft horse show in the country.

The Fall Festival is held at Mayowood, and features an open-air market of Minnesota produce, a flower show, and woodworking exhibits and demonstrations. During Thanksgiving weekend the Festival of Trees spotlights special displays and holiday foods.

Sports for the Spectator

The Minnesota Ice Hawks Junior B U.S. Hockey league plays its games at the Rochester–Olmstead Recreation Center from November through May. Rochester Honkers collegiate baseball league takes place at Mayo Field downtown from June through August. The Rochester Giants semi-professional football team plays at Soldiers Field.

Sports for the Participant

Rochester has approximately 100 parks on more than 3,200 acres, 11 golf courses, four swimming pools, seven tennis courts, and a state-of-the-art Recreation Center and Athletic Club. The Quarry Hill Nature Center offers hiking and biking trails on more than 270 acres of parkland, including a pond, stream, quarry, cave and restored prairies, as well as deciduous pine forests. Every year, more than 30,000 Canadian geese make their home at Silver Lake Park, which is the summertime site of canoeing and paddle boat rentals, walking paths, and picnicking. Whitewater State Park offers camping, trout fishing, picnic grounds, and hiking trails.

The Rochester Amateur Sports Commission spotlights the many amateur sporting events that take place in the area throughout the year. From May through September patrons enjoy activities at the Skyline Raceway & Waterslide, while bowling is offered year-round at Colonial Lanes and Recreation Lanes.

Shopping and Dining

Apache Mall, with 100 specialty shops, is the city's premier shopping site. The Kahler Plaza, located beneath the Kahler Grand and Marriott hotels, offers 60 shops and businesses, as well as eight restaurants. Small, unique shops are the focus of Rochester's Historic Mercantile District, and the Centerplace Galleria Mall is at the center of the skyway system. Other popular shopping centers include Crossroads, King's Row, Maplewood, Miracle Mile, and Silver Lake. Contemporary fine art is offered at Callaway Galleries, and Wild Wings Gallery features the work of local wildlife artists.

Rochester has restaurants to appeal to every taste—from informal bar and grills to more formal dining rooms. Ethnic cuisine runs the gamut from American barbecue to Greek and Mexican, and just about everything in between. At the Lord Essex in the Kahler Hotel, patrons can enjoy fine dining in a pub atmosphere. The Henry Wellington is another popular restaurant.

Visitor Information: Rochester Convention and Visitors Bureau, 150 S. Broadway, Ste. A, Rochester, MN 55904; telephone (507)288-4331; toll-free 800-634-8277; fax (507)288-9144

Convention Facilities

Rochester's primary meeting place is the Mayo Civic Center, which houses the 11,000-square-foot Grand Lobby and the

25,000-square-foot Taylor Arena, accommodating 4,500 theater-style and 1,000 classroom style. The civic center's 15,700-square-foot auditorium can seat 1,700 theater-style and 600 classroom-style, while its theater can handle 1,340 theater-style and provides up to 17 breakout rooms. The facility also has many patios and a 3,000-square-foot outdoor stage. Graham Arena and Graham Arena East are at the Olmsted County Fairgrounds. Graham Arena provides a total exhibit area of 28,000 square feet with seating for 2,500. Graham Arena East has 22,000 square feet of exhibit space.

Rochester has about 4,600 hotel rooms, with more than 1,500 of them linked by climate-controlled skyways and subways to dining, shopping, services, the Mayo Clinic, and the Mayo Civic Center. There are 52 hotels and motels in the Rochester area.

Convention Information: Rochester Convention and Visitors Bureau, 150 S. Broadway, Ste. A, Rochester, MN 55904; telephone (507)288-4331; toll-free 800-634-8277; fax (507)288-9144

Transportation

Approaching the City

U.S. Highway 14 and State Highway 30 run east and west through Rochester, while U.S. Highway 52 and U.S. Highway 63 run north and south. Interstate 35 is 35 miles west of the city. Rochester International Airport, located south of the city just off U.S. Highway 63, handled 277,504 passengers in 2004. The airport is served by American Airlines, which has daily flights to Chicago, and Northwest Airlines, with daily flights to Minneapolis. Local van service is also available to Minneapolis Airport. Plans for expansion are currently underway to increase its capacity by extending the primary runway. Intercity bus lines include Greyhound and Rochester. Daily bus service is offered to Winona, Minnesota, 45 miles east, where the closest Amtrak depot is located.

Traveling in the City

In Rochester, streets generally run east and west, and avenues run north and south. The city is divided into quadrants designated NW, NE, SW and SE. Broadway is the east/west divider street, and Center Street is the north/south divider street. Local bus service is provided by Rochester City Lines.

Communications

Newspapers and Magazines

The *Post-Bulletin,* Rochester's daily, is an evening newspaper. The *Agri-News* is a farm newspaper that appears weekly. Monthly journals published in Rochester are *Fertility and Sterility,* a journal on reproductive medicine, and the *Mayo Clinic Proceedings.* The *Journal of Andrology* is a bi-monthly featuring articles on the male reproductive system.

Television and Radio

Rochester has nine television stations broadcasting in the area. The city is served by almost 30 AM and FM stations with diverse formats, including news/talk, country, and public radio.

Media Information: Post-Bulletin, 18 1st Ave. SE, PO Box 6118, Rochester, MN 55903; telephone (507)285-7600

Rochester Online

City of Rochester home page. Available www.ci.rochester .mn.us

Mayo Clinic Health Oasis (information on cancer, Alzheimer's, heart disease, and more). Available www.mayo clinic.com

Mayo Clinic Rochester. Available www.mayo.edu

Minnesota Historical Society. Available www.mnhs.org

Rochester Convention & Visitors Bureau. Available www .rochestercvb.org

Rochester *Post-Bulletin.* Available www.postbulletin.com

Rochester Public Library. Available www.rochesterpublic library.org

Rochester Public Schools. Available www.rochester.k12 .mn.us

Selected Bibliography

Hodgson, Harriet, W., *Rochester: City of the Prairies* (Northridge, CA: Windsor Publications, 1989)

Leonard, Joseph A., *History of Olmsted County Minnesota* (Chicago: Goodspeed History Association, 1910)

Severson, Harold R., *Rochester: Mecca for Millions* (Rochester: Marquette Bank & Trust, 1979)

Saint Paul

The City in Brief

Founded: 1846 (incorporated, 1849)

Head Official: Mayor Randy Kelly (since 2002)

City Population
   1980: 270,230
   1990: 272,235
   2000: 287,151
   2003 estimate: 280,404
   Percent change, 1990–2000: 5.5%
   U.S. rank in 1980: 54th
   U.S. rank in 1990: 57th (State rank: 2nd)
   U.S. rank in 2000: 59th (State rank: 2nd)

Metropolitan Area Population
   1980: 2,137,133
   1990: 2,538,776
   2000: 2,968,806
   Percent change, 1990–2000: 19.6%

U.S. rank in 1980: 17th
U.S. rank in 1990: Not reported
U.S. rank in 2000: 16th

Area: 53 square miles (2000)
Elevation: 834 feet above sea level
Average Annual Temperature: 44.7° F
Average Annual Precipitation: 26.36 inches

Major Economic Sectors: Services, trade, manufacturing, government
Unemployment Rate: 4.2% (February 2005)
Per Capita Income: $20,216 (1999)

2002 FBI Crime Index Total: 17,308

Major Colleges and Universities: University of Minnesota–Twin Cities, Metropolitan State University, Macalester College, University of St. Thomas, College of St. Catherine, Hamline University, William Mitchell College of Law

Daily Newspaper: *Saint Paul Pioneer Press*

Introduction

Saint Paul is the capital of Minnesota and the seat of Ramsey County. Along with Minneapolis, it occupies the center of the fifteen-county Twin Cities metropolitan statistical area. The city developed in the late nineteenth century through the efforts of railroad baron James Hill and religious leader Archbishop John Ireland. In addition to being a primary transportation and distribution hub, Saint Paul has gained a national reputation for its effective local government, attractive architecture, rich cultural environment, and quality of life. The combined cities of Minneapolis and Saint Paul are highly rated for their livability and rank among the country's best places for growing a business.

Geography and Climate

Saint Paul occupies with Minneapolis the center of the 15-county Twin Cities metropolitan statistical area. (In addition to Hennepin, Ramsey, Anoka, Washington, Dakota, Scott, Carver, Wright, Sheburne, Chisago, and Isanti counties in Minnesota, and Pierce and St. Croix counties in Wisconsin, two counties in St. Cloud were added in 1993; they were Stearns and Benton.) Saint Paul is located with Minneapolis at the confluence of the Mississippi and Minnesota Rivers over the heart of an artesian water basin. The surrounding terrain is flat or rolling and dotted with lakes. The climate is predominantly continental with wide seasonal temperature variations, ranging from minus 30 degrees to 100 degrees and above.

Area: 53 square miles (2000)

Elevation: 834 feet above sea level

Average Temperatures: January, 11.2° F; July, 70.6° F; annual average, 44.7° F

Annual Average Precipitation: 26.36 inches

History

River Fort Draws Traders, Settlers

Jonathan Carver, a New Englander, was attempting to find a northwest passage to the Pacific Ocean in the winter of 1766 when he stopped near the future site of Saint Paul, where he discovered a Native American burial ground (now known as Indian Mound Park). When the Louisiana Purchase became part of United States territory in 1803, federally-financed expeditions explored the new territory,

which included present-day Saint Paul. In 1805 Lieutenant Zebulon M. Pike camped on an island later named Pike Island and entered into an unofficial agreement with the Sioux tribe for land at the confluence of the Mississippi and Minnesota rivers; also included in the pact was land that became the site of Fort Snelling.

In 1819, Colonel Henry Leavenworth built an army post on the Minnesota River on a spot named Mendota south of present-day Saint Paul; the next year the fortress was moved across the river where Colonel Josiah Snelling constructed Fort Anthony, which was later renamed Fort Snelling. The presence of the fort allowed an Indian agency, fur trading post, missionaries, and white settlers to gain a foothold there. Settlers living on federal land were eventually expelled, and Pierre "Pig's Eye" Parrant, a French Canadian, joined others in building a settlement named after Parrant's colorful nickname near Fort Snelling. In 1841, Father Lucian Galtier named a log chapel in Pig's Eye after his patron saint, Saint Paul, and persuaded others to accept the name for their emerging community, as well.

Saint Paul was platted in 1847; two years later it was named the capital of the Minnesota Territory and incorporated as a town. Saint Paul received its city charter in 1854 and when Minnesota became a state in 1858, the city retained its status as state capital. By the start of the Civil War, 10,000 people lived in Saint Paul.

Rail Transport and New Residents Shape City

Two men had major roles in the development of Saint Paul in the post-Civil War period. The railroad magnate James J. Hill used the city and the Great Northern Railroad to accumulate great individual wealth and to wield immense political power. Hill envisioned his adopted city of Saint Paul as the base for an empire in the northwest, built on his railroad holdings. The other major influence on Saint Paul's development was Catholic Archbishop John Ireland, a native of Ireland who settled in Saint Paul at the age of fourteen and, as an adult, established a religious base for community endeavors. He brought thousands of destitute Irish families to Saint Paul, where they relocated in colonies and started a new life. The Catholic influence in the shaping of Saint Paul can be traced to the pioneering efforts of Archbishop Ireland. Another notable figure who called Saint Paul home is F. Scott Fitzgerald.

In the nineteenth century a number of distinct population groups contributed to the character of Saint Paul. One was from the New England states and New York; these transplanted Easterners brought their educational values and business experiences to the prairie community. Another consisted of immigrants from Germany and Ireland who flocked to the United States by the tens of thousands. Among the professional groups were German physicians and Irish politicians and lawyers. German musical traditions and beer-making practices found a new home in Saint Paul. Scandinavians also immigrated to the city, but in fewer numbers than those who settled in neighboring Minneapolis.

In the twentieth century, Saint Paul erected fine buildings like the state capitol and developed many cultural institutions, including theaters; a notable peace monument in the concourse of the city hall; the state historical society building, containing a museum and library; and the Saint Paul Arts and Science Center. Saint Paul is also home to many educational institutions. Although its Twin City, Minneapolis, surpassed Saint Paul shortly before the turn of the twentieth century as the larger, wealthier, industrially more powerful of the two cities, Saint Paulites believe their city possesses more character and charm. Contributing to that charm are a good symphony orchestra and the stately mansions of former railroad and timber barons along Summit Avenue.

Historical Information: Minnesota History Center, 345 Kellogg Blvd W., Saint Paul, MN 55102; telephone (651)296-6126

Population Profile

Metropolitan Area Residents
1980: 2,137,133
1990: 2,538,776
2000: 2,968,806
Percent change, 1990–2000: 19.6%
U.S. rank in 1980: 17th
U.S. rank in 1990: Not reported
U.S. rank in 2000: 16th

City Residents
1980: 270,230
1990: 272,235
2000: 287,151
2003 estimate: 280,404
Percent change, 1990–2000: 5.5%
U.S. rank in 1980: 54th
U.S. rank in 1990: 57th (State rank: 2nd)
U.S. rank in 2000: 59th

Density: 5,441.7 people per square mile (1999)

Racial and ethnic characteristics (2000)
  White: 192,444
  Black or African American: 33,637
  American Indian and Alaskan Native: 3,259
  Asian: 35,488
  Native Hawaiian or Pacific Islander: 203
  Hispanic (may be of any race): 22,715
  Other: 11,021

Percent of residents born in state: 59.6% (2000)

Age characteristics (2000)
  Population under 5 years old: 21,747
  Population 5 to 9 years old: 22,273
  Population 10 to 14 years old: 21,572
  Population 15 to 19 years old: 22,233
  Population 20 to 24 years old: 25,947
  Population 25 to 34 years old: 48,210
  Population 35 to 44 years old: 43,792
  Population 45 to 54 years old: 34,035
  Population 55 to 59 years old: 9,974
  Population 60 to 64 years old: 7,721
  Population 65 to 74 years old: 13,292
  Population 75 to 84 years old: 11,180
  Population 85 years and over: 5,175
  Median age: 31.0 years

Births (2001, Ramsey County)
  Total number: 7,414

Deaths (2001, Ramsey County)
  Total number: 4,144 (of which, 34 were infants under the age of 1 year)

Money income (1999)
  Per capita income: $20,216
  Median household income: $38,774
  Total households: 112,128

Number of households with income of . . .
  less than $10,000: 11,221
  $10,000 to $14,999: 7,608
  $15,000 to $24,999: 15,289
  $25,000 to $34,999: 16,535
  $35,000 to $49,999: 18,932
  $50,000 to $74,999: 21,911
  $75,000 to $99,999: 10,200
  $100,000 to $149,999: 6,957
  $150,000 to $199,999: 1,807
  $200,000 or more: 1,668

Percent of families below poverty level: 11.7% (43.3% of which were female householder families with related children under 5 years)

2002 FBI Crime Index Total: 17,308

Municipal Government

Saint Paul, the seat of Ramsey County, operates under a mayor-council form of government, with strong power being delegated to the mayor, who serves for four years. The seven council members are elected by ward to two-year terms.

Head Official: Mayor Randy Kelly (since 2002; current term expires January 2006)

Total Number of City Employees: 3,000 (2005)

City Information: City Hall, 400 City Hall Annex Saint Paul, MN 55102; telephone (651)266-8510

Economy

Major Industries and Commercial Activity

The principal economic sectors in Saint Paul are services, wholesale and retail trade, manufacturing, and government. Along with Minneapolis, Saint Paul is the site of one of the largest concentrations of high-technology firms in the United States and ranks among the major commercial centers between Chicago and the West Coast. The city is also among the two or three largest livestock and meatpacking centers in the nation. Sixteen of the *Fortune* 500 largest U.S. corporations are headquartered in the Twin Cities. The area is also home to 30 *Fortune* 1000 companies and several of the world's largest private companies. Local companies are involved in the manufacture of super computers, electronics, medical instruments, milling, machine production, food processing, and graphic arts.

Items and goods produced: hoists and derricks, rugs, computers, food products, medical products, machinery, electronic materials, automobiles, appliances, chemicals, abrasives, beer, printed products

Incentive Programs—New and Existing Companies

Various programs are available for small business incentive and expansion; among them are the Small Business Development Loan Program, offering fixed-rate low-interest direct loans, and tax credits for corporations that assist small businesses.

Local programs—The City of Saint Paul's Department of Planning and Economic Development offers a variety of services to assist new or expanding businesses; services include small business financing and loan guarantees/direct loans.

State programs—State business tax incentives include research and development credits, foreign income deductions, and sales tax exemptions and reductions. In addition, the state of Minnesota offers, through a network of five job-training programs, assistance to businesses in locating and training employees.

Job training programs—The City of Saint Paul's Business Resource Center offers a variety of services including infor-

mation, technical assistance, financing, site searches, and job training. Other programs are available through area colleges and universities.

Development Projects

Downtown Saint Paul has undergone extensive revitalization, with investment in development projects exceeding $1 billion.

Saint Paul continues to profit from the Neighborhood Development Program, a unique redevelopment initiative that has gained the city national recognition. Since 1997, the Saint Paul Port Authority has partnered with neighborhood organizations to select brownfield sites for redevelopment. Through creative use of public and private funding, it has completed several projects, replacing brownfields with light industrial manufacturing facilities and donating land for designated open spaces. Saint Paul funds its brownfield projects with a combination of general obligation bonds, tax increment financing, local sales tax revenues, municipal grants, loan guarantees, Economic Development Administration grants, Community Development Block Grants, Enterprise Community grants, and EPA Brownfields Pilot grants.

The Saint Paul Port Authority has several projects underway. The Great Northern project will clean up and develop 13 acres of brownfield formerly owned by the Great Northern Railroad Shops and the Saint Paul Foundry. Twenty-two acres are already completed; the resulting business center is expected to create more than 500 new jobs. Another twenty-two acres along the Mississippi River are part of the River Bend project; 10 acres of land have been cleaned up, and 120,000 square feet of space has been completed as of early 2005. The $120 million Westminster Junction project is focused on health care; facilities include a new home for Regions Hospital outpatient clinic.

The Phalen Corridor Initiative will bring jobs, housing, transit, workforce, and prosperity to Saint Paul's east side; investors have already invested $570 million in the greenspace multi-use creation.

Economic Development Information: Saint Paul Port Authority, Suite 1900 Landmark Towers, 345 St. Peter St., Saint Paul, MN 55102

Commercial Shipping

Saint Paul is a Foreign Trade Zone with duty free facilities. The ports of Saint Paul and Minneapolis are served by nine barge lines operating on the Mississippi, Minnesota, and St. Croix rivers; together the ports handle more than 11 million tons of cargo annually. Considered one of the largest trucking centers in the United States, the Twin Cities are a hub for over 150 motor freight companies that provide overnight and four- to five-day delivery throughout the country. Six rail lines are integrated with both the United States and Canadian railway systems. Air transportation is available at Minneapolis-Saint Paul International Airport from 16 air cargo carriers and 37 air freight forwarders.

Labor Force and Employment Outlook

Local educational institutions assure employers of well-trained workers, particularly in high-technology areas, where engineers, scientists, researchers, and technicians are in demand. The highest growth is expected in the areas of healthcare, technical and social services, personal care, construction, and computer professional occupations. Current projections indicate that workforce participation in the Twin Cities areas should expand faster than population growth.

The following is a summary of data regarding the Minneapolis-Saint Paul metropolitan area labor, 2004 annual average:

Size of non-agricultural labor force: 1,738,000

Number of workers employed in . . .
   mining and construction: 82,800
   manufacturing: 202,700
   transportation and utilities: 335,900
   information: 43,000
   financial activities: 140,500
   professional and business services: 245,900
   educational and health services: 216,100
   leisure and hospitality: 154,500
   other services: 75,800
   government: 240,300

Average hourly earnings of production workers employed in manufacturing: $17.59

Unemployment rate: 4.2% (February 2005)

Largest employers (Twin Cities area)	Number of employees
State of Minnesota	55,294
U.S. Government	35,047
Target Corp	35,047
University of Minnesota	29,498
Mayo Clinic	23,378
Allina Health	22,454
Northwest Airlines	21,301
Fairview Health Services	18,700
3M Corporation	18,179
Wells Fargo	13,938

Cost of Living

The Twin Cities' region has one of the lowest costs of living among the 25 largest cities in the United States. The cost of living is reported as being near the national average; the cost of housing and food is below the national average.

The following is a summary of data regarding several key cost of living factors in the Saint Paul area.

2004 (3rd Quarter) ACCRA Average House Price: $296,846 (Minneapolis)

2004 (3rd Quarter) ACCRA Cost of Living Index: 109.3 (Minneapolis/St. Paul) (U.S. average = 100.0)

State income tax rate: Ranges from 5.35% to 7.85%

State sales tax rate: 6.5%

Local income tax rate: None

Local sales tax rate: None

Property tax rate: 17.0% of first $68,000 of market value; 27.0% over $68,000

Economic Information: Saint Paul Area Chamber of Commerce, 401 North Robert Street, Suite 150, Saint Paul, Minnesota 55101; telephone (651)223-5000; fax (651)223-5119

Education and Research

Elementary and Secondary Schools

Public schools in Saint Paul are administered by Independent School District 625, the second-largest school system in Minnesota. A superintendent is chosen by a seven-member, nonpartisan board of education.

The following is a summary of data regarding the Saint Paul public schools as of the 2004–2005 school year.

Total enrollment: 42,000

Number of facilities
   elementary schools: 50
   middle schools: 9
   senior high schools: 8
   other: 1 open school; 1 special education school; 87 other programs including a creative arts high school, area learning center, and adult education center

Student/teacher ratio: not available

Teacher salaries
   average: $44,745 (Minnesota, 2002-2003)

Funding per pupil: $8,644

A variety of private schools in Saint Paul enroll more than 12,000 students.

Public Schools Information: Saint Paul Public Schools, 360 Colborne Street, Saint Paul, MN 55102; telephone (651)293-5100

Colleges and Universities

Saint Paul is home to several colleges and universities. The University of Minnesota–Twin Cities operates a main campus in Saint Paul as well as in Minneapolis. An important research institution with a total enrollment of more than 45,000 full-time students, the university awards a full range of undergraduate and graduate degrees in 250 fields of study, including first-professional degrees in dentistry, law, medicine, pharmacy, and veterinary medicine. University of Minnesota faculty and graduates have been awarded 12 Nobel Prizes for physics, medicine, chemistry, economics, and peace.

Metropolitan State University, part of the Minnesota State University system, offers undergraduate and graduate programs in liberal arts, nursing, and management; the administrative offices of Minnesota State University are located in Saint Paul. The William Mitchell College of Law is a privately operated professional school devoted solely to the study of law. A fine arts curriculum leading to a baccalaureate degree is offered by the School of the Associated Arts.

Hamline University, affiliated with the United Methodist Church, provides undergraduate and graduate programs in such areas as chemistry, law, music, and teacher education. Bethel University is a four-year institution associated with the Baptist General Conference. The four-year Concordia College is operated by the Lutheran Church-Missouri Synod. Lutheran Northwestern Seminary is the divinity school for the American Lutheran Church and the Lutheran Church in America. Other church-related colleges include Northwestern College and Macalester College, which is associated with the Presbyterian Church. The College of St. Catherine, the College of St. Thomas, and the Saint Paul Seminary School of Divinity are Roman Catholic institutions.

Vocational and technical training is available at community colleges and specialized schools in Saint Paul and Minneapolis; among them is Saint Paul Technical Vocational Institute. In all, the Twin Cities support 13 colleges and universities, 6 state-supported comprehensive community colleges, and 9 publicly supported technical institutions.

Libraries and Research Centers

Nearly 70 public and private libraries are based in Saint Paul. The Saint Paul Public Library system includes a main facility, 12 branches, and a bookmobile. The library, which is a depository for federal and city documents, houses more than 1 million volumes as well as 2,000 periodicals, and CDs, maps, and other items. Special collections include oral history and the history of the city of Saint Paul. Adjacent to the Saint Paul Public Library is the James J. Hill Reference Library; its business and economic collection is open to the public. The Minnesota Historical Society maintains an extensive reference library with subject interests in genealogy,

Minnesota history, and Scandinavians in the United States among other areas. Most colleges and universities in Saint Paul operate campus libraries, the largest being the University of Minnesota system, which consists of a main facility and four department libraries; its collection numbers more than four million catalogued volumes.

Among the larger state agency libraries in the city are the Minnesota State Law Library and the Minnesota Legislative Reference Library. Other specialized libraries are associated primarily with corporations, churches, and hospitals.

Research centers in the Twin Cities affiliated with the University of Minnesota include the Center for Urban Design; the Hubert H. Humphrey Institute of Public Affairs; the Industrial Relations Center; the Metropolitan Design Center; the Northern Tier Technology Corridor; the Underground Space Center; the Immigration History Research Center; and the Minnesota Center for Twin and Adoption Research.

Public Library Information: Saint Paul Public Library, 90 West Fourth Street, Saint Paul, MN 55102-1668; telephone (651)266-7000; fax (651)292-6660

Health Care

Minneapolis-Saint Paul is a regional health care center. Six hospitals are based in Saint Paul. The largest facility is Regions Medical Center, a teaching and research hospital that specializes in heart care, women's services, cancer, digestive care, seniors' services, burns, emergency, and trauma. Regions also houses an ambulatory care clinic and provides general medical, surgical, pediatric, psychiatric, and chemical dependency services. Gillette Children's Specialty Healthcare is a center specializing in children's health issues; it is located in Regions Hospital.

Children's Hospital, a teaching and referral center for infants and children with pediatric disorders, includes among its specialties open heart surgery and cardiac catheterization, and infant apnea diagnosis. Other hospitals in Saint Paul include St. John's, St. Joseph's, United Hospital, and Bethesda Healtheast.

Recreation

Sightseeing

Landmark architectural structures provide unique space for Saint Paul's arts institutions. The state Capitol was designed by

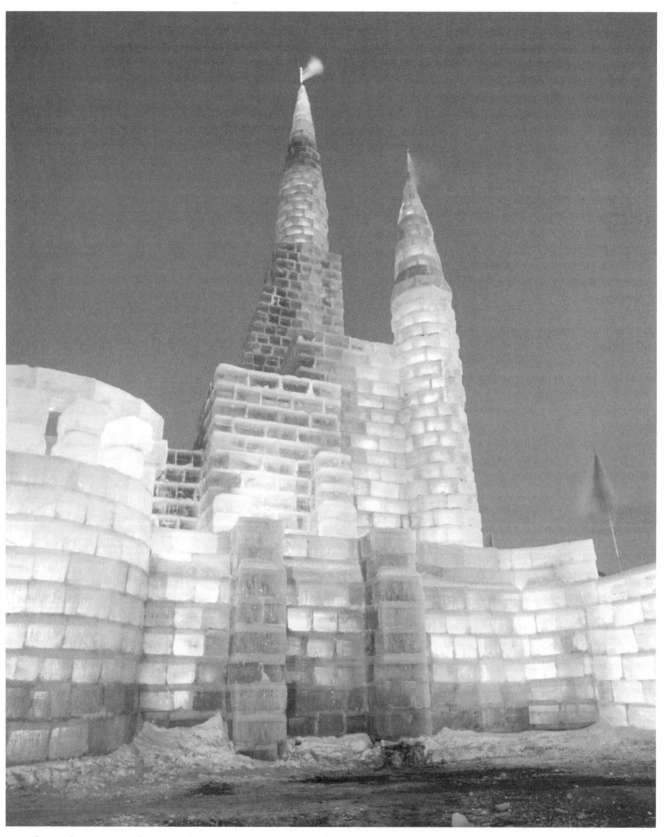

Ice sculptures, parades, and winter sporting events are a few of the activities revolving around the Winter Carnival.

Cass Gilbert in 1904 and blends Minnesota stones with imported marble; paintings, murals, and sculptures represent the state's history. A trip to Saint Paul might include a visit to Saint Paul Cathedral, which is modeled after St. Peter's in Rome. Landmark Center, once a Federal Courts Building, is now the city's arts center and winner of a national restoration award.

Historic Fort Snelling has been restored to its original state; costumed guides tell about the fort's early history as the first non-Native American settlement in the Saint Paul area. The Alexander Ramsey House was the home of Minnesota's first territorial governor; tours of the home are available year round. Reflecting the opulence of Saint Paul's most famous nineteenth-century railroad baron, the 32-room James J. Hill House was at one time the largest home in the Midwest. A 5-mile stretch of Summit Avenue is lined with Victorian homes. A few blocks away, at 481 Laurel, is writer F. Scott Fitzgerald's birthplace (not open to the public).

Como Park, Zoo, and Conservatory features a children's zoo, a large cats house, an aquatic house, and a new visitor's center. Town Square Park in Saint Paul Center, the largest indoor public park in the world, cultivates more than 1,000 plants and trees. The Children's Museum features hands-on exhibits.

Arts and Culture

Like Minneapolis, Saint Paul enjoys a national reputation in the performing arts. The Ordway Center for the Performing Arts is the home of the Saint Paul Chamber Orchestra and the Minnesota Opera Company. The Landmark Center is a Romanesque Revival building whose south tower is modeled after Boston's Trinity Church. The Schubert Piano Club and Keyboard Instruments Museum is located in the center. The American Museum of Art recently opened its Riverfront Gallery on Kellogg Boulevard; the museum houses contemporary and Asian art as well as sculpture, paintings, photography, and drawings.

The Science Museum of Minnesota features the Dinosaurs and Fossils Gallery, Omnitheater and a 3D cinema representing the latest in high-tech entertainment. At the Mississipi River Gallery, visitors can unlock the secrets of locks and dams, explore an authentic Mississippi River towboat, and view the river from the museum's balcony. At the Human Body Gallery, visitors can view their own cells through a microscope; in the Experiment Gallery, visitors can make a tornado and create waves in the wave tank. The Minnesota History Center presents interpretations of the state's history through exhibits and material objects.

Saint Paul's theater companies include the Park Square Theater, which concentrates on classic plays; the Great North American History Theater, which presents local historical drama; and Penumbra Theater, a professional African American theater company.

Arts and Culture Information: Metropolitan Regional Arts Council, 2324 University Ave. W., Saint Paul, MN 55114; telephone (651)645-0402

Festivals and Holidays

The Saint Paul Winter Carnival is the largest winter celebration in the nation. This annual festival, held the last weekend in January through the first weekend in February, features parades, ice and snow sculpture, fine arts performances, a ball, unusual winter sporting events, and a re-enactment of the legend of King Boreas. Saint Paul hosts the largest celebration of St. Patrick's Day outside of New York City. The Festival of Nations in late April celebrates the food and cultures of more than 50 countries. Grand Old Day on an early June Sunday begins with a parade on a one-mile stretch of Grand Avenue and includes entertainment, food, and crafts; the celebration is the largest one-day street fair in the Midwest. Taste of Minnesota on the Fourth of July weekend is held on the Minnesota State Capitol Mall and concludes with a fireworks display on Independence Day. The Minnesota State Fair, one of the largest state fairs in the country, runs for 10 days ending on Labor Day at the Minnesota State Fairgrounds.

Sports for the Spectator

The Twin Cities are home to five professional sports teams. The Minnesota Vikings compete in the National Football Conference in the Central Division. The Minnesota Twins are in the Central Division of baseball's American League. The Minnesota Timberwolves are in the National Basketball Association. The baseball and football teams play home games in the Hubert H. Humphrey Metrodome in downtown Minneapolis. The Timberwolves compete at the Target Center in downtown Minneapolis. The Minnesota Wild of the National Hockey League play in the new 650,000 square foot Xcel Energy Center. Women's National Basketball Association team the Minnesota Lynx came to the Twin Cities in 2000.

University of Minnesota teams compete in the Big Ten in football, baseball, hockey, and basketball. Thoroughbred horses run at Canterbury Downs Racetrack in Shakopee in a mid-May to mid-August season.

Sports for the Participant

The Rice & Arlington Sports Dome hosts softball, soccer, and baseball leagues. In addition, the dome is used for private lessons, clinics, parties, and batting practice. The playing area of the dome features a full-size softball field with a 330-foot, straight-away center and two soccer fields that are 50 yards wide by 60 yards long. The soccer fields can also be played on lengthwise, creating a field 100 yards long by 60 yards wide.

Outdoor sports in the Saint Paul area include fishing, swimming, boating, and water skiing in the summer and ice fishing, ice skating, cross-country skiing, and hockey in the winter. The Twin Cities Marathon is an annual event that attracts as many as 10,000 runners and is usually held the first or second Sunday in October.

Shopping and Dining

Saint Paul boasts the world's longest public skyway system; it consists of 5 miles of second-level walkways that link downtown hotels, restaurants, stores, and businesses. The Saint Paul World Trade Center is four square blocks of more than 100 retail and dining establishments; at the center is the Town Square Park, which is an enclosed, year-round park. The Farmers Market is an old-world open market selling home-grown foods and crafts on weekends. Historic Grand Avenue is lined with private homes, retail shops, boutiques, and antique stores. A local shopping square is housed in a turn-of-the-century railroad building. There are antique stores as well as specialty stores promoting Minnesota goods located throughout the Twin Cities.

Saint Paul restaurants stress American home cooking and Midwest cuisine; ethnic choices range from Afghan and Vietnamese menus to continental and French restaurants. Fresh fish, prime rib, and 16-ounce steaks are local favorites. Dinner cruises on the Mississippi River are offered. The quaint river town of Stillwater, 25 miles east of Saint Paul, also offers dining and shopping opportunities.

Visitor Information: Saint Paul Convention and Visitors Bureau, 175 West Kellogg Boulevard, Suite 502, Saint Paul, MN 55102; telephone (651)265-4900; toll-free (800)627-6101. Explore Minnesota Tourism, 100 Metro Square, 121 7th Place East, Saint Paul, MN 55101-2112; telephone (651)296-5029; toll-free (800)657-3700

Convention Facilities

River Centre Convention and Entertainment facility, providing a total of 68,000 square feet of exhibit space and 15 meeting rooms, accommodates events such as seminars, banquets, and conventions. Saint Paul's skyway system connects the facility to more than 700 downtown hotel rooms. The Radison Riverfront Hotel offers 55,000 square feet of flexible meeting space, 25 meeting rooms, and a glass ballroom overlooking the Mississippi River and Kellogg Square Park. The Arena adjacent to Saint Paul/NHL Arena seats 18,000 people and the Roy Wilkins Auditorium offers space for up to 5,500 people. The Fitzgerald Theatre, the city's oldest standing theater, provides seating for more than 900 people for meetings and various kinds of presentations in a two-balcony hall.

The Minnesota State Fair Grounds maintains 13 indoor facilities, ranging from 2,000 to 100,000 square feet, for use outside fair season. Four conference sites, accommodating from 100 to 4,000 people, and lodging rooms for 1,000 people are available on the Macalester College campus.

Several hotels and motels offering meeting and banquet facilities for both large and small groups. Nearly 5,000 lodging rooms can be found in Saint Paul.

Convention Information: Saint Paul Convention and Visitors Bureau, 175 West Kellogg Boulevard, Suite 502, Saint Paul, MN 55102; telephone (651)265-4900 or 1-800-627-6101

Transportation

Approaching the City

The principal destination of most air travelers to Saint Paul is the Minneapolis-Saint Paul International Airport, 15 minutes from downtown Saint Paul. It is the hub of locally headquartered Northwest Airlines and is the ninth largest airport in America. Eleven commercial airlines and seven regional carriers schedule daily flights to 104 United States cities; direct international flights area also available. There are six reliever airports in the Saint Paul area.

An efficient highway system permits easy access into Saint Paul. Interstate-94 intersects the city from east to west and I-35E from north to south. I-494 and I-694 form a beltway circling the north, south, east, and west perimeters. Serving metropolitan Minneapolis-Saint Paul are seven federal and 13 state routes.

Passenger rail service to Saint Paul from Chicago and Seattle is provided by Amtrak. Bus service is by Greyhound.

Traveling in the City

Saint Paul proper has an East Side roughly east of downtown, but its West Side actually lies south of the central business district. The West Side should not be confused with West Saint Paul, which is a suburb on the south edge of town (on the west edge of South Saint Paul, another suburb). Other Saint Paul communities include Frogtown, the Historic Hill District, the Midway, Macalester-Groveland, and Highland Park.

Saint Paul's freeway system, moderate population density, and two business districts facilitate high levels of traffic mobility throughout Minneapolis-Saint Paul during both peak and non-peak hours. The average commuting time from home to workplace is twenty-one minutes. The Twin

Cities' Metropolitan Council Transit Operations (MCTO), one of the largest bus transportation systems in the country, operates regularly scheduled routes in Saint Paul as well as Minneapolis and the surrounding suburbs.

Communications

Newspapers and Magazines

Saint Paul's major daily newspaper is the *Saint Paul Pioneer Press.* Other newspapers appearing daily in the Twin Cities area are the *Minneapolis Star Tribune, Minnesota Daily,* and *Finance and Commerce. Minnesota Monthly* is a magazine focusing on topics of state and regional interest.

Approximately 60 magazines, journals, and newsletters originate in the metropolitan area, covering topics such as law, furniture, religion, feminist issues, and agriculture. Member or special interest publications for professional associations, religious organizations, trade groups, and fraternal societies are also based in the city.

Television and Radio

Two commercial and two public television stations broadcast from Saint Paul; cable service is also available. Four FM and two AM radio stations furnish music, news, and information programming. The headquarters of the Minnesota Public Radio Network, an affiliate of National Public Radio, is located in Saint Paul. American Public Media produces ''Saint Paul Sunday,'' a popular program that is broadcast live nationally from Saint Paul.

Media Information: Saint Paul Pioneer Press, 345 Cedar Street, Saint Paul, MN 55101; telephone (651)222-1111.*Minnesota Monthly,* Minnesota Monthly Publications, Inc., 730 Second Ave., Minneapolis, MN 55402; telephone (612)371-5800

Saint Paul Online

City of Saint Paul home page. Available www.ci.stpaul.mn.us

Mall of America home page. Available www.mallofamerica.com

Minnesota Department of Trade and Economic Development home page. Available www.deed.state.mn.us

Minnesota Historical Society home page. Available www.mnhs.org

Saint Paul Area Chamber of Commerce home page. Available www.saintpaulchamber.com

Saint Paul city guide online. Available www.saint-paul.com

Saint Paul Convention and Visitors Bureau home page. Available www.stpaulcvb.org

Saint Paul Pioneer Press home page. Available www.twincities.com

Saint Paul Public Library home page. Available www.st.paul.lib.mn.us

Selected Bibliography

Brin, Ruth F., *Bittersweet Berries: Growing Up Jewish in Minnesota* (Holy Cow Press, 1998)

Cleary, Edward J., Robin Desser (ed.), *Beyond the Burning Cross: A Landmark Case of Race, Censorship and the First Amendment* (Vintage Books, 1995)

Fitzgerald, F. Scott, *Taps at Reveille* (New York: C. Scribner's Sons, 1935)

MacCabee, Paul, *John Dillinger Slept Here: A Crooks' Tour of Crime and Corruption in St. Paul, 1920-1926* (Minnesota Historical Society)

Millett, Larry, *Lost Twin Cities* (Minnesota Historical Society)

Valdes, Dionicio Nodin, *Barrios Nortenos: St. Paul and Midwestern Mexican Communities in the Twentieth Century* (University of Texas Press, 2000)

MISSOURI

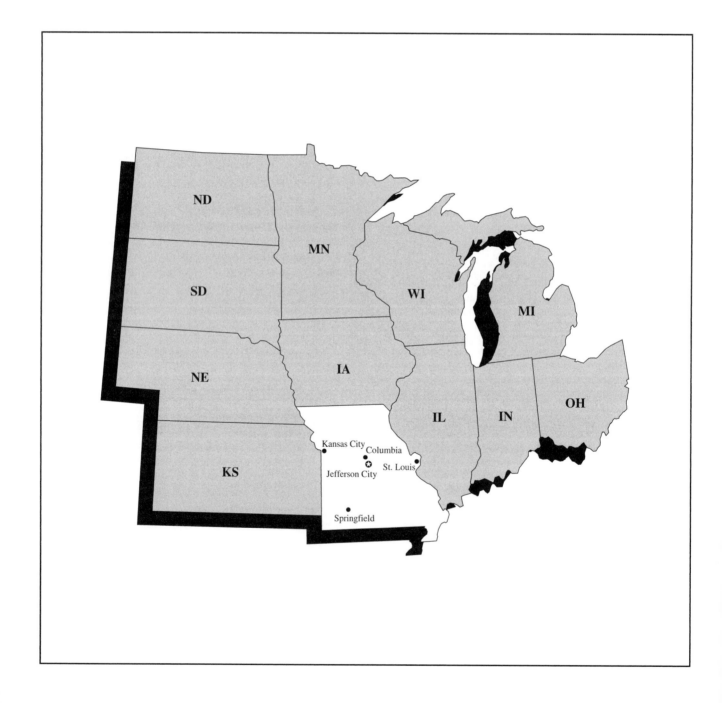

The State in Brief

Nickname: Show Me State
Motto: *Salus populi suprema lex esto* (The welfare of the people shall be the supreme law)

Flower: Hawthorn
Bird: Bluebird

Area: 69,704 square miles (2000; U.S. rank: 21st)
Elevation: Ranges from 230 feet to 1,772 feet above sea level
Climate: Continental, with seasonal extremes; affected by cold air from Canada, warm moist air from the Gulf of Mexico, and dry air from the Southwest

Admitted to Union: August 10, 1821
Capital: Jefferson City
Head Official: Governor Matt Blunt (R) (until 2009)

Population
1980: 4,917,000
1990: 5,117,073
2000: 5,595,211
2004 estimate: 5,754,618
Percent change, 1990–2000: 9.3%
U.S. rank in 2004: 17th
Percent of residents born in state: 67.8% (2000)
Density: 81.2 people per square mile (2000)
2002 FBI Crime Index Total: 261,077

Racial and Ethnic Characteristics (2000)
White: 4,748,083
Black or African American: 629,391
American Indian and Alaska Native: 25,076
Asian: 61,595
Native Hawaiian and Pacific Islander: 3,178
Hispanic or Latino (may be of any race): 118,592
Other: 45,827

Age Characteristics (2000)
Population under 5 years old: 369,898
Population 5 to 19 years old: 1,224,274
Percent of population 65 years and over: 13.5%
Median age: 36.1 years (2000)

Vital Statistics
Total number of births (2003): 76,097
Total number of deaths (2003): 55,318 (infant deaths, 587)
AIDS cases reported through 2003: 5,060

Economy
Major industries: Manufacturing; trade; finance, insurance, and real estate; retail trade; services
Unemployment rate: 5.6% (April 2005)
Per capita income: $29,094 (2003; U.S. rank: 29)
Median household income: $43,492 (3-year average, 2001-2003)
Percentage of persons below poverty level: 8.8% (3-year average, 2001-2003)
Income tax rate: Graduated from 1.5% to 6.0%
Sales tax rate: 4.225%

Columbia

The City in Brief

Founded: 1819 (incorporated 1826)

Head Official: Mayor Darwin Hindman (NP) (since 1995)

City Population
1980: 62,061
1990: 69,101
2000: 84,531
2003 estimate: 90,947
Percent change,1990–2000: 18.25%
U.S. rank in 1980: 324th
U.S. rank in 1990: 331st (state rank: 6th)
U.S. rank in 2000: 339th (state rank: 6th)

Metropolitan Area Population
1980: 100,376
1990: 112,379
2000: 135,454

Percent change, 1990–2000: 20.5%
U.S. rank in 1980: 282nd
U.S. rank in 1990: 288th
U.S. rank in 2000: 221st

Area: 58 square miles (2005)
Elevation: 889 feet above sea level
Average Annual Temperature: 53° F
Average Annual Precipitation: 39.43 inches of rain; 20.7 inches of snow

Major Economic Sectors: education, government, insurance, trade, services
Unemployment Rate: 3.6% (May 2005)
Per Capita Income: $27,991 (2003)
2002 Total FBI Crime Index: 3,837

Major Colleges and Universities: University of Missouri-Columbia, Stephens College, Columbia College

Daily Newspaper: *Columbia Daily Tribune, Columbia Missourian*

Introduction

Known as ''College Town U.S.A.,'' Columbia is the seat of Boone County in central Missouri, about midway between Kansas City and St. Louis. This fast-growing city offers a top rated school system, fine health care facilities, cultural opportunities, a low cost of living, and a clean environment. Columbia, with its highly educated populace, consistently ranks among the best places to live in the United States.

Geography and Climate

Columbia is located halfway between St. Louis to the east and Kansas City to the west, with the state capital, Jefferson City, about 25 miles directly south. It is also halfway between Des Moines and Memphis. The city is set on gently rolling terrain where prairie meets forest. It has cold winters and warm, often humid summers. In winter the cold periods are often interrupted by a warm spell, and the temperature only drops below zero for a few days. Snows rarely last longer than a week, most commonly appearing in March. Freezing temperatures usually end after April first, and the first frost is generally in late October. Late spring and early summer are the rainiest seasons, and summertime temperatures sometimes reach above 100° F.

Area: 58 square miles (2000)

Elevation: 889 feet above sea level

Average Temperatures: January, 25.5° F; July, 79.1° F; annual average, 53°F

Annual Average Precipitation: 39.43 inches of rain; 20.7 inches of snow

History

Before the coming of Europeans, Osage and Missouri tribes roamed the area of Columbia and Boone County. The ''Missouri,'' meaning ''people with dugout canoes,'' were originally from the Ohio River Valley, prehistoric evidence shows. The fierce and fierce-looking Osage were the predominant tribe of the area. They were a pierced and tattooed, jewelry bedecked, tall, robust, warlike people who dominated other tribes in the region. The men shaved their heads but for a strip at the crown, and wore loincloths and buckskin leggings; the women wore deerskin dresses, and leggings and moccasins as well. They were primarily migrating hunters and gatherers, although they also farmed corn, beans, and pumpkins. The Osage are considered a fringe Plains tribe even though they dwelled mostly in forested areas, because they spoke a Sioux branch of language and went on buffalo hunting excursions on the Great Plains twice annually.

The first Europeans to encounter the Osage were the French, led by Marquette's exploration down the Mississippi for New France in the 1670s. The French and the Osage soon became partners in the fur trade, and with guns and horses gained from this union, the Osage dominated other tribes even more than before. They helped the French defeat the British in 1755, but stayed out of the colonial war. More Europeans came to the area; the Spanish influence grew as that of the French waned. The Osage were pushed to reservations in Kansas and finally what is now Oklahoma by a series of ''treaties'' made through the 1800s.

The United States gained the Missouri Territory from France in 1803. The Lewis and Clark expedition passed nearby in that same year, and Daniel Boone and his sons started a settlement in 1806. They also established the Booneslick Trail which led all the way from Kentucky to the Columbia area. In 1818 the town of Smithton, named for its purchaser, the Smithton Land Company, was established. However, in need of a better water supply, the entire town of 20 residents was moved to its present site in 1821. The settlement of mud-daubed log huts, which was surrounded by wilderness, was renamed Columbia, a popular name at the time, and became the seat of Boone County. Although Columbia is in the Midwest it had a very Southern feel in the early days, as many of its settlers were from below the Mason-Dixon line.

From its beginnings, the economy of Columbia has rested on education. It also benefited from being a stagecoach stop of the Santa Fe and Oregon trails, and later from the Missouri Kansas Texas Railroad (nicknamed Katy). Columbia was incorporated in 1826, five years after Missouri became the 24th state. The city's progress can be traced through the development of its institutions. In 1824 Columbia was the site of a new courthouse; in 1830 its first newspaper began; in 1832 the first theater in the state was opened; and in 1834 a school system began to serve its by then 700 citizens. The state's first agricultural fair was held in Columbia in 1835. A school for girls was opened in 1833, and an institution called Columbia College (unrelated to the present school) was opened in 1834. Also in 1834, one of the country's finest portrait artists, George Caleb Bingham, opened a studio in Columbia. In 1841, the University of Missouri was built in Columbia after Boone County won out over several competing counties in raising money and setting aside land. In 1851, Christian Female College was established; it went coed in the 1970s and changed its name to Columbia College. In 1855, Baptist Female College was established; still a women's-only school, it is now known as Stephens College. By 1839, the population and wealth of Boone County, with 13,000 citizens, was exceeded only by that of St. Louis County.

Slavery was a largely accepted practice in Columbia in its early days, and the slave population had reached more than 5,000 by the beginning of the Civil War. In fact, the sale of slaves continued until 1864. Before the Civil War many Columbians were very nationalistic and supported the Missouri Compromise, which would admit Missouri into the Union as a slave state, but would placate northerners with the admission of Maine as a free state and the establishment of the rest of the Louisiana Purchase, north and west of Missouri's southern border, as free territory. Early in the Civil War, Union forces secured the area and enforced mandatory draft into the local militia; however, although the state was officially Union, people were in reality sharply divided, and supported both sides with supplies and men.

Since the turmoil of the Civil War and Reconstruction, Columbia's history is marked by steady and quiet growth and prosperity, based on its roots in education, as well as health care and insurance. The health care business can be said to have started in 1822 when Dr. William Jewell set up a hospital in his own home; today Columbia is among the top in the nation for medical facilities per capita. The insurance business has its roots in Columbia's early days as well, when pragmatic local businessmen started a fund to aid one another in case of fire.

Historical Information: State Historical Society of Missouri, Lowry Mall, University of Missouri, Columbia campus; telephone (573)882-7083. Boone County Historical Society, 3801 Ponderosa Street, Columbia, MO; telephone (573)443-8936

Population Profile

Metropolitan Area Residents

1980: 100,376
1990: 112,379
2000: 135,454
Percent change, 1990–2000: 20.5%
U.S. rank in 1980: 282nd
U.S. rank in 1990: 288th
U.S. rank in 2000: 221st

City Residents

1980: 62,061
1990: 69,101
2000: 84,531
2003 estimate: 90,947

Percent change, 1990–2000: 18.25%
U.S. rank in 1980: 324th
U.S. rank in 1990: 331st
U.S. rank in 2000: 339th (state rank: 6th)

Density: 1,592.8 people per square mile (2000)

Racial and ethnic characteristics (2000)
White: 68,923
Black or African American: 9,173
American Indian and Alaska Native: 331
Asian: 3,636
Native Hawaiian and Pacific Islander: 30
Hispanic or Latino (may be of any race): 1,733
Other: 684

Percent of residents born in state: 62.5% (2000)

Age characteristics (2000)
Population under 5 years old: 4,884
Population 5 to 9 years old: 4,706
Population 10 to 14 years old: 4,537
Population 15 to 19 years old: 9,275
Population 20 to 24 years old: 15,885
Population 25 to 34 years old: 13,420
Population 35 to 44 years old: 10,817
Population 45 to 54 years old: 8,865
Population 55 to 59 years old: 2,729
Population 60 to 64 years old: 2,133
Population 65 to 74 years old: 3,440
Population 75 to 84 years old: 2,678
Population 85 years and older: 1,162
Median Age: 26.8 years

Births (2003)
Total number: 1,875

Deaths (2003)
Total number: 902 (of which, 12 were infants under the age of 1 year)

Money Income (1999)
Per capita income: $27,991
Median household income: $33,729
Total households: 33,819

Number of households with income of . . .
less than $10,000: 5,007
$10,000 to $14,999: 2,705
$15,000 to $24,999: 5,208
$25,000 to $34,999: 4,436
$35,000 to $49,999: 4,870
$50,000 to $74,999: 5,347
$75,000 to $99,999: 3,072
$100,000 to $149,999: 2,125
$150,000 to $199,999: 509
$200,000 or more: 540

Percent of families below poverty level: 9.4% (29.1% of which were female householder families with related children under 5 years)

2002 FBI Crime Index Total: 3,837

Municipal Government

Columbia has a council-manager form of government, with a mayor and six council members elected by ward, who serve three-year terms. The mayor is also elected every three years as a council member at-large. This unpaid elected body directly supervises a city manager, city clerk, and three municipal judges.

Head Official: Mayor Darwin Hindman (NP) (since 1995; current term expires 2007)

Total Number of City Employees: 1,168 (2005)

City Information: City of Columbia, Daniel Boone Building, 701 East Broadway, Columbia, MO 65201; telephone (573)874-7111

Economy

Major Industries and Commercial Activities

Columbia, whose thriving economy has always been based on the education, health care, and insurance industries, is known as a recession-resistant community. Columbia has 13 banks and saving and loans with assets totaling more than $1.6 billion. The city is consistently named as a top place in the nation to live, retire, and do business, in publications such as *Money, Entrepreneur, Kiplinger's Personal Finance* and *Expansion Management. Forbes* listed Columbia as a ''Best Small Place to do Business'' in May 2004. The city is home to Shelter Insurance Company, MFA Incorporated, and is a regional center for State Farm Insurance.

Columbia's manufacturers make and sell a wide variety of products. 3M is a major employer, producing projection lenses, optical equipment, electronic products, and interconnect systems. MBS is a textbook distribution center. There are three different factories making various automotive parts. Columbia Foods, a division of Oscar Mayer, employs about 700 workers at its food processing plant. Watlow-Columbia, Inc. manufactures electrical heating elements; the Square D Corporation makes circuit breakers; and Hubbell/Chance produces electric utility equipment.

Items and goods produced: all manner of electronic parts and equipment, air filters, optic lenses, plastic pipe, custom foam rubber products, automobile parts, coal, stone quarry products, corn, wheat, and oats

Incentive Programs—New and Existing Companies

*Local programs—*The Columbia and Boone County area's main economic development contact is the Regional Economic Development, Inc. (REDI). REDI is a public/private entity created to promote economic expansion while maintaining a great quality of life. REDI provides services, financing, tax credits and exemptions, job training, and other local perks for businesses such as no local income tax, moderate property taxes and low sales tax that barely effect business, and Community Development Block Grants available outside the city limits for public infrastructure. Financing takes the form of Industrial Revenue Bonds for qualifying projects, and other low interest loans and incentive financing for large development projects. Tax exemptions include no sales taxes on manufacturing equipment nor on materials used to install such equipment, no sales taxes on air or water pollution control devices, and finally a property tax exemption on business and industrial inventories. The State of Missouri reimburses employers for both onsite and classroom job training, designs programs tailor made to specific tasks, and in turn will help screen and test potential new hires.

*State programs—*The Missouri Small Business Development Center has a branch in Columbia which offers technical and management assistance for small businesses in service, retail, construction, and manufacturing. Other incentive programs are available at the state level. The Missouri Business Expansion and Attraction Group (BEA) is responsible for working with businesses and communities in Missouri to assist in the retention and expansion of existing businesses and the attraction of new businesses. Incentives include business financing and tax credits. Twenty-four programs or services are offered by the Missouri Department of Economic Development, including the Welfare-to-Work Grant program and the Welfare-to-Work Tax Credit program, which encourages employers to hire certain groups, such as ex-felons, who have a harder time finding jobs. There are programs for youths and adults, for workers affected by downsizing or other types of displacement such as that caused by NAFTA, for women, for seasonal or migrant farm workers, veterans' services, and apprenticeship information.

*Job Training—*The Missouri Department of Economic Development's Division of Workforce Development offers training or retraining of employees, in a classroom setting, in cooperation with the public schools systems. To be eligible for funding, employers must increase employment above the previous year's level, and must retrain existing employees due to substantial capital investment in the state. Fourteen of the Division of Workforce Development's 24 services offered involve job training or retraining, targeted at various groups.

Development Projects

Growing somewhat naturally out of Columbia's strength in the education and health care industries is the biological sciences research business. There are three organizations in the area that promote expansion into this growing field: the Life Sciences Business Coalition, Mid-MO BIO, and Scientific Partnership and Resource Connection, or SPARC. SPARC works with Regional Economic Development, Inc. (REDI) and University of Missouri's College of Agriculture, Food, and Natural Resources to procure funding for research and the building of facilities necessary to research. So far this has resulted in a new $60 million Life Sciences Center which opened in 2004 on the University of Missouri-Columbia's campus, and a proposed $175 million Human Health Research Center.

REDI was also involved in the $5.5 million project to purchase and renovate Boone County Fairgrounds, completed in 2003, and is now working with the Columbia Chamber of Commerce and the Columbia Convention and Visitors Bureau (CVB) on annexing an 80 acre field adjacent to the 134 acre Fairgrounds, and adding an ice skating rink, several playing fields, a dog park, community gardens, and walking trails. The Flat Branch Park beautification project was completed in 2004, with funds contributed by corporate sponsors of REDI, as well as the Chamber of Commerce and CVB, which own the adjacent Walton Building of which REDI is a tenant. Downtown renovation projects have been ongoing for over a decade, and central Columbia today sports widened streets, benches and trees, new street lights and decorative trash can lids, all with an eye to both retail and residential use. The latest is the Eighth Street Beautification Project. In 2002 REDI unveiled its "Incentives White Paper," which proposed more ways to expand established businesses and bring in new ones. It focused on using Chapter 100 bonds but had other ideas such as a "microloan" program to help businesses which didn't fit the criteria for the many other incentive programs offered by REDI. Two other projects are focused on improving traffic flow. One is a new interchange at Highway 63 and Gans Road, which will improve the infrastructure and perhaps pave the way for future development near the intersection, besides allaying traffic woes. The second is a $1.3 million railroad terminal and warehouse made possible through cooperation between REDI and Columbia Terminal Railroad (nicknamed COLT). The terminal itself is expected to cut down traffic on I-70 by giving businesses the option to ship by rail, and the warehouse allows companies that don't have locations near the terminal to nevertheless use the rail option.

Economic Development Information: Regional Economic Development, Inc., 300 South Providence Road, Columbia,

MO 65203; telephone (573)442-8303; fax (573)443-3986. Missouri Department of Economic Development, 301 West High Street, PO box 118, Jefferson City, MO 65101, telephone (573)751-4962, fax (573)526-7700

Commercial Shipping

Boone County has 20 Interstate motor freight lines serving it, with 14 terminals in Columbia. Railroads serving the area are COLT (Columbia Terminal), Amtrak, Norfolk Southern, and Gateway Western. Seven air freight carriers serve the area, and Trans World Express offers nine flights daily to St. Louis.

Labor Force and Employment Outlook

Boone County's main area of job growth is in the service industry, although most of these jobs are lower-paying. One recent study found that approximately 33,000 of the area's more than 240,000 civilian labor force was underemployed, meaning they possessed skills, training, or degrees beyond what their jobs required.

The following is a summary of data regarding the Boone County labor force, 2004 annual averages.

Size of nonagricultural labor force: 86,600

Number of workers employed in . . .
   trade, transportation and utilities: 14,400
   government: 29,200

Average hourly wage of production workers employed in manufacturing: $12.74

Unemployment rate: 3.6% (May 2005)

Largest county employers	Number of employees
University of Missouri	11,868
University hospital and clinics	4,320
Columbia Public Schools	3,000
Boone Hospital Center	2,028
City of Columbia	1,168
State of Missouri, (excludes UMC)	1,071
MBS Textbook Exchange, Inc.	1,006
Harry S. Truman Veteran's Hospital	1,000
Shelter Insurance	991
State Farm Insurance	952
U.S. Government (excludes VA hospital)	926
Hubbell/Chance Company	908

Cost of Living

Columbia consistently ranks below the national average for cost of living. The following is a summary of data regarding several key cost of living factors for the Columbia metropolitan area.

2005 (1st Quarter) ACCRA Average House Price: $234,580

2005 (1st Quarter) ACCRA Cost of Living Index: 90.8 (U.S. average = 100.0)

State income tax rate: Ranges from 1.5% to 6.0%

State sales tax rate: 4.225%

Local income tax rate: none

Local sales tax rate: 3.125%

Property tax rate: $6.32 per $100 of assessed value (2004)

Economic Information: Missouri Department of Economic Development, PO Box 118, Jefferson City, MO 65102-0118; telephone (573)751-4241; toll-free (800)523-1434

Education and Research

Elementary and Secondary Schools

The Columbia Public School District is the seventh largest in the state of Missouri. Local students rank in the 80th to 95th percentile on the Missouri Mastery and Achievement Tests for elementary schools. Over a four year period, Columbia students taking the national Scholastic Aptitude Tests averaged more than a hundred points higher than national average on both the verbal and math portions of the test. The district is among only a few in the nation that have graduated more than a half dozen Presidential Scholars since the honor was first established in 1964. The National Governor's Association has named the district one of only 16 model districts in the country.

In response to the No Child Left Behind Act, superintendent Phyllis Chase, new to the district in 2003 and the first African American to hold the position, has made impressive progress in closing the achievement gap between economically advantaged and disadvantaged students, as well as between African American and white students. Chase has chosen an elementary school—with a majority of African American students and more than 70 percent from lower income levels—to transform into a model school, lengthening the school year and considering a substantial raise in teacher pay. The community has voted to support this by approving a $22.5 million bond issue, even amidst a budget crunch. More than 60 percent of all teachers hold a master's degree. Special assessment efforts, reading intensive activities, and summer school programs are directed at students at risk of dropping out. At the other end of the achievement spectrum is the A+ program in which students with superior attendance, grades, and citizenship records can earn free

tuition to a two-year community college, vocational-technical schools, or the Columbia Area Career Center (run by the public school district). The free Summer Enrichment program offers core academic studies in the morning and enrichment activities in the afternoon. There is a Parents As Teachers program, a family literacy program in which adults can work on GED certification or other educational goals such as learning English, while their children attend pre-school, and other volunteer programs which encourage adult volunteers from the community to join in a partnership for mentoring or service skills education.

The following is a summary of data regarding the Columbia Public Schools System as of the 2003–2004 school year.

Total enrollment: 16,240

Number of facilities
   elementary schools: 20
   junior high/middle schools: 6
   high schools: 4
   other: 2 vocational centers

Student/teacher ratio: 22.5:1

Teacher salaries
   minimum: $26,700
   maximum: $47,229

Funding per pupil: $6,117

Columbia also has 11 private schools, mostly maintained by religious organizations, with enrollments totaling about 1,100.

Public Schools Information: Columbia Public Schools, 1818 W. Worley St., Columbia, MO 65203; telephone (573)886-2100

Colleges and Universities

The University of Missouri-Columbia (MU), with more than 27,000 students, offers 286 degree programs, including 95 bachelor degrees. MU was founded in 1839 and was the first public university west of the Mississippi. Columbia College, a private, coeducational institution, was originally called Christian Female College when it was founded in 1851. It was the first women's college west of the Mississippi to be chartered by a state legislature. It changed its name in 1970 when it went coed and offered bachelor's and post-graduate degrees in addition to associate's degrees. Columbia College now has almost 1,000 students at its day campus, and over 3,000 working adults at its evening campus, 30 extended campuses around the nation, including Guantanamo Bay, and an impressive online college. Stephens College, founded in 1833, is the nation's second oldest women's college. Stephens offers a liberal arts curriculum and pre-professional programs, with 23 majors and 20 minors in three schools of study. Stephens is the only four year women's college in Missouri and remains dedicated to women's education in the new millennium.

Libraries and Research

The Columbia Public Library is the newest addition to Daniel Boone Regional Libraries, which more than doubled its size. The $22 million project was completed in 2002 and boasts 110,000 square feet of space, 444,897 volumes, and 50 computer terminals. The design of the new building features curves and cylindrical shapes and a carefully planned system of signs that allow patrons to find things easily. Ellis Library at the University of Missouri-Columbia, with holdings of 10.2 million items including 3.2 million volumes, is one of the largest libraries in the Midwest. MU also has the Law Library, and six other specific branches for veterinary medicine, geological sciences, health sciences, engineering, journalism, and mathematical sciences. Its on-line catalog of resources, called MERLIN for Missouri Education and Research Libraries Information Network, makes materials available from the University of Missouri's four campuses and St. Louis University. MU's Special collections include an extensive historical and contemporary collection of government documents, Microform Collection, Rare Book Collection, Newspaper Collections, and the Comic Art Collection with original and reprints of classic comic strips, underground comics, and graphic novels. The State Historical Society of Missouri Library has special collections on church histories, literature, Midwestern history, and Missouri newspapers. Columbia College's Stafford Library has special collections in biography, history, American civilization, and costume. The Midwest Science Center Library features a collection on wildlife research. Stephens College has special libraries which encompass women's studies, educational resources, and children's literature.

A number of institutions have research facilities in Columbia. These include the Ellis Fischel Cancer Research Center at University of Missouri; the Center for National Food and Agricultural Policy (also at MU); the Mid-Missouri Mental Health Center, which does research along with providing psychiatric inpatient treatment; the Missouri Coop Fish and Wildlife Research Unit; a division of the U.S. Geological Survey of the Department of the Interior; Missouri Lions Eye Research Foundation, which holds an eye tissue bank and does research into glaucoma treatment and all things involving preserving and restoring eyesight; the Rehabilitation Research Foundation, part of MU's Health Psychology Department; and the U.S.D.A. Biological Control of Insects Research Laboratory.

The University of Missouri at Columbia has a budget of $141 million for research with an additional $161 million that is externally funded. Research topics include computer assisted reporting, agriculture and agronomy, animal sciences, arthri-

tis, business and public administration, social sciences including studies on aging, spectrometry (analytical tools to identify chemical compounds and structures of molecules) diseases such as diabetes, cardiological disorders, and cystic fibrosis, exercise physiology, engineering, water resources, magnetic imaging technology, and nuclear engineering.

Public Library Information: Daniel Boone Regional Library, PO Box 1267, Columbia, MO 65205; telephone (573)443-3161; fax (573)499-0191

Health Care

Columbia's hospitals provide the best health care for Central Missourians, comparable to that of cities many times its size. Nine major hospitals serve the area, with specializations such as a children's hospital, a Ronald McDonald house (hospices for families of children undergoing long hospital stays), residential schools for the mentally handicapped, rehabilitation services, many full service nursing homes or assisted living facilities, and a large corps of visiting nurses. Columbia has the only Level I trauma unit between St. Louis and Kansas City. In addition there are facilities for organ transplantation, cancer treatment, and centers for people with spinal cord injuries and birth defects, notably the Howard A. Rusk Rehabilitation Center. The 344-bed Boone Hospital specializes in surgery, oncology, cardiology, neurology, and obstetrics. Columbia Regional Hospital, with 265 beds, excels at sports medicine, opthamology, and outpatient surgery, among others. The 96-bed Charter Behavioral Health System of Columbia treats emotional and mental disorders of patients of all ages, while the Mid-Missouri Mental Health Center offers short term intensive psychiatric help for children and adults. Eligible veterans are served by the 54-bed Harry S. Truman Memorial Veteran's Hospital. Columbia Regional, Ellis Fischel Cancer Center, and Children's Hospital are under the umbrella of University of Missouri Health Sciences Center as well as University Hospitals and Clinics and its School of Medicine, Nursing, and Health Related Professions. Family Health Center provides comprehensive care for uninsured and underinsured people, and for Medicare and Medicaid recipients.

Recreation

Sightseeing

Downtown Columbia itself is a stunning sight to see, where four massive columns stand in front of the stately Boone

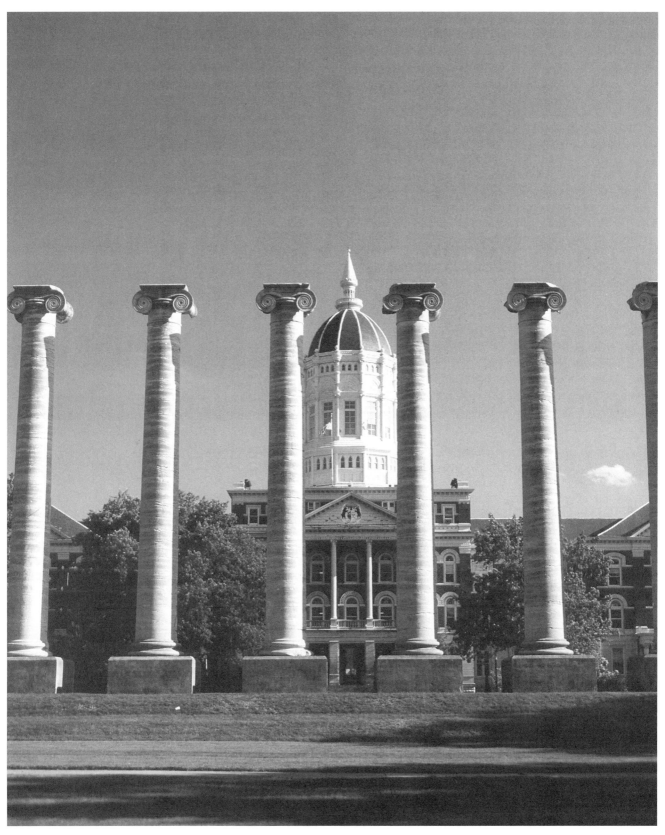

The University of Missouri-Columbia, founded in 1839, was the first public university west of the Mississippi River.

County Courthouse. The Firestone Baars Chapel, which was designed by architect Eero Saarinen of the St. Louis Arch fame, is also in the heart of downtown Columbia. Tours of the Victorian-era Maplewood Home, built in 1877 and beautifully restored, are available to give the public a glimpse into 19th century country estate life. The Columbia Audubon Trailside Museum has exhibits on birds and other creatures and offers workshops on nature. A genealogy center, a photo collection, an art collection and works of local artists are among many historical artifacts on display at the State Historical Society Housed in the Ellis Library on the MU campus. More than 1,500 types of flowers and 300 trees can be seen at Shelter Insurance Gardens, which also features a one-room red brick school house, a "sensory garden" designed for the visually impaired, many other attractions such as a giant sundial, and free summer concerts on its five acres. The writings of Dr. Martin Luther King, Jr., as part of a sculptured amphitheater at King Memorial Gardens, is another must-see in Columbia, where its landscaping with benches and walkways provides a placid setting for cultural events.

Historic Rocheport, just 12 miles west of the city, began as an early trading post on the Missouri River in 1825 and prospered due to the building of the railroad. Now on the National Register of Historic Places, this charming town offers top-rate antique and craft shops, excellent restaurants, a local winery, and an annual RiverFest in early June.

Arts and Culture

The Missouri Theatre is central Missouri's only pre-Depression-era movie palace and vaudeville stage. It presents a variety of programs throughout the year. The Rhynsberger Theater, on the University of Missouri's campus, is the site for dramatic performances by visiting actors as well as faculty and students. The Repertory Theatre performs there in the summertime. Both professional and student productions can be enjoyed at Stephens College's Macklanburg Playhouse and Warehouse Theatre. Columbia's primary community theater group is the Maplewood Barn Theater, part of the historic Maplewood Home in Rocheport, which performs outdoors in summer months. The Columbia Entertainment Company is a dynamic theatrical troupe that gives rousing musical and dramatic performances throughout the year, as well as offering a drama school for adults and children. Columbia can also boast of Arrow Rock Lyceum Theater and two acting groups that focus on children, PACE or Performing Arts in Children's Education, and TRYPS, acronym for Theater Reaching Yong People and Schools.

The Missouri Symphony makes its home in the historic Missouri Theatre and holds its summer festival every June and July. The University Concert Series brings opera, ballet, orchestra, chamber music, jazz, dance, and theatrical performances. Other musical groups in the city are the Columbia Community Choir and the Columbia Chorale Ensemble.

Columbia's museums offer a variety of lectures, classes, and exhibits. More than 13,000 artifacts and works of art from prehistoric times to the present are housed at the University of Missouri-Columbia's Museum of Art and Archeology. Also on campus, the Museum of Anthropology displays Native American materials and archeology from the Midwest, and the Rogers Gallery highlights exhibits on architecture and interior design, as well as student art works. Rotating exhibits of professional and amateur artists are showcased at the Columbia Art League Gallery, while the work of students and faculty is shown at the Columbia College Art Gallery.

African American intellectual culture is the focus of the Black Culture Center, which offers various programs and conducts research. The story of Boone County over the decades is the subject of the Walters-Boone County Historical Museum and Visitor's Center, set in a wood-hewn family farmhouse with weathered boards and wide porches. This 16,000-square-foot house features exhibits on westward expansion along the Booneslick Trail, and portrays the pioneers who settled in the region.

Festivals and Holidays

Columbia ushers in spring in April with the annual Earth Day celebration. With May comes the Salute to Veterans Air Show and Parade, the largest free air show in the United States. June is the time for the annual Art in the Park Fair and the weekly Twilight Festivals. June also features the J.W. Boone Ragtime Festival, where folks can enjoy the sounds of early jazz and ragtime of the Roaring '20s. The Fourth of July celebration, called Fire in the Sky, kicks off the month, and the Boone County Fair and Horse Show keeps the excitement going. The International Buckskin Horse World Championship and the Lion's Antique show are held in August. In September the Twilight Festivals restart, but the highlight of the month must be the Heritage Festival. October sees the annual Missouri Fall Festival, in which the courthouse Square is transformed into a showcase of regional arts and crafts. November events include the Annual Fall Craft Show and the Downtown Holiday Parade. The downtown Holiday Festival and the Christmas Past 1865 at the Maplewood Home celebrate the December holiday season, which is capped by the First Night Celebration and Midway Invitational Rodeo and Dance on December 31st and January 1st.

Sports for the Spectator

Big 12 conference basketball, football, NCI Division baseball, wrestling, volleyball, softball, gymnastics, and track and field are all available for sports fan to watch. The city is close enough to both St. Louis and Kansas City to enjoy their major league baseball, football, and basketball teams.

Sports for the Participant

Columbia enjoys 58 parks stretching over 2,400 acres of land, with such facilities as swimming pools, tennis courts, softball fields, volleyball courts, fishing lakes, hiking and wheelchair accessible trails, golf courses, and even horseshoe pits. The Show-Me State Games, an annual Olympic style athletic competition, welcomes amateur competitors. Bikers and runners enjoy the MKT Nature & Fitness Trail, an 8.9 mile path that connects with the 225 mile Katy Trail, the nation's longest rails-to-trails conversion.

Shopping and Dining

Columbia provides a variety of shopping experiences with 16 shopping centers in addition to its major downtown shopping district. The largest mall is the 140 store Columbia Mall, which features major national chain stores. Forum Shopping Center has a big indoor entertainment center for children. The city's downtown, bordered on three sides by college campuses, features specialty shops and retail stores, and especially an abundance of antique shops, such as the 6,000 square foot Grandma's Treasures, which features antique jewelry, glass collectibles, and furniture.

Dining establishments come in all forms in the city; more than 300 restaurants, from American bistros, haute cuisine, ethnic eateries, and one of central Missouri's only brewpubs, the Flat Branch Pub & Brewery, located near the courthouse. Les Bourgeois Vineyard in Rocheport offers an elegant menu and variety of award-winning wines.

Convention Facilities

There are 34 hotels and motels in and around Columbia with more than 3,500 rooms. The largest facilities for conventions and exhibitions are at Boone County Fairgrounds with 107,300 square feet, the Hearnes Center with 70,000 square feet, the Midway Expo Center with 66,000 square feet, and the Holiday Inn Executive Center with 20,000 feet.

Transportation

Approaching the City

Columbia is located on Interstate 70, which runs east and west, and U. S. Highway 63, which runs north and south. It is twenty minutes away from U.S. 54 to the east, and the Missouri River to the west. Columbia Regional Airport offers four daily flights to St. Louis. Amtrak rail service is available to nearby Jefferson City, and Greyhound has daily bus service to St. Louis and Kansas City, all with connections to many other places.

Traveling in the City

Columbia's relatively flat streets are arranged in an easy grid pattern, with numbered streets running north and south. Columbia Area Transit (CAT) provides bus service in the city and the University of Missouri has its own shuttle, as does Columbia Regional Airport. Greyhound provides charter service and regularly scheduled trips out of the city.

Communications

Newspapers and Magazines

Columbia's two daily newspapers are the *Columbia Daily Tribune,* which appears every weekday evening and Saturday and Sunday evening, and the *Columbia Missourian,* which is the morning paper. The weekly *Missourian Weekend* is a general interest newspaper. People in the area also read the *Boone County Journal, Columbia Business Times, Columbia Senior Times,* and the *Centralia Fireside Guard.*

Publications affiliated with the University of Missouri include the monthly *Journal of Chemical Crystallography,* semi-annuals *Journal of Dispute Resolution* and *Theatre Topics,* and the quarterlies *Missouri Historical Review* and *Missouri Law Review.* Other publications coming out of Columbia are the *Missouri Free Press* and *Sheep Breeder and Sheepman,* the quarterlies *Voice of the Diabetic, Monthly Realtor, Ruralist, MIZZOU Magazine,* an MU alumni quarterly, and *School and Community,* a journal of the Missouri State Teacher's Association. *Today's Farmer* appears ten times a year.

Television and Radio

The city has four television network affiliates and one cable television network. The formats of the 20 FM and 8 AM radio stations available to Columbia listeners cover the gamut of musical tastes along with news, talk, and public broadcasting

Media Information: Columbia Daily Tribune, 101 N. Fourth St., PO Box 798, Columbia, MO 65205; telephone (573)815-1500.*Columbia Missourian,* 221 S 8th St., PO Box 917, Columbia, MO 65202; telephone (573)882-5700

Columbia Online

City of Columbia, Missouri. Available www.gocolumbiamo .com

Columbia Chamber of Commerce. Available www.chamber.columbia.mo.us

Columbia Convention and Visitors Bureau. Available www.visitcolumbiamo.com

Columbia Daily Tribune. Available www.showmenews.com

Columbia, Missouri Economic Development. Available www.columbiaredi.com

Columbia Public Schools. Available www.columbia.k12.mo.us

State Historical Society of Missouri. Available www.system.missouri.edu/shs

Selected Bibliography

Batterson, Paulina Ann, *The First Fifty Years* (Columbia Public Relations Committee, Columbia Chamber of Commerce, 1965)

Havig, Alan, *Columbia, An Illustrated History*

Jefferson City

The City in Brief

Founded: 1823 (incorporated 1825)

Head Official: Mayor John Landwehr (since 2003)

City Population
  1980: 33,619
  1990: 35,481
  2000: 39,636
  2003 estimate: 37,550
  Percent change, 1990–2000: 10.8%
  U.S. rank in 1990: Not reported
  U.S. rank in 2000: (State rank: 15th)

County Population (Cole County)
  1980: 56,663
  1990: 63,579
  2000: 71,397

Percent change, 1990–2000: 12.3%
U.S. rank in 1990: Not reported
U.S. rank in 2000: 693rd

Area: 27.3 square miles (2000)
Elevation: 702 feet above sea level
Average Annual Temperature: 54.4° F
Average Annual Precipitation: 38.43 inches of rain; 23.5 inches of snow

Major Economic Sectors: Government, trade, services
Unemployment Rate: 5.1% (February 2005)
Per Capita Income: $21,268 (1999)

2002 FBI Crime Index Total: Not reported

Major Colleges and Universities: Lincoln University, Columbia College-Jefferson City

Daily Newspaper: *Daily Capital News, Jefferson City Post Tribune*

Introduction

Jefferson City, the seat of Cole County, is named after the esteemed third president of the United States. It is a genteel, conservative city full of charming and refurbished old homes. The Missouri State Capitol building, reminiscent of the U.S. Capitol, stands grandly at the center of this planned city, which serves as a center for midwestern trade. Visitors view its many historic structures while enjoying the friendly, easygoing family atmosphere the city offers.

Geography and Climate

Jefferson City lies in the geographical center of Missouri, extending east, south, and westward from a bluff on the Missouri River. The city spreads inland across finger-like ridges and valleys paralleling the river.

Like the rest of the state, Jefferson City is affected by cold air blowing down from Canada, warm, moist air from the Gulf of Mexico, and dry southwestern air. Spring is the rainy season. Snowfall averages 23.5 inches per year and snow is most prevalent from December through February. Like all of Missouri, Jefferson City lies in a region where tornadoes are a danger. Summers can be hot with temperatures sometimes reaching more than 100° F.

Area: 27.3 square miles (2000)

Elevation: 702 feet above sea level

Average Temperatures: January, 28.7° F; July, 77.9° F; annual average, 54.4° F

Average Annual Precipitation: 38.43 inches of rain; 23.5 inches of snow

History

Missouri's Early Development

Before the coming of white settlers, the region surrounding Jefferson City was home to an ancient group known as the Mound People. In fact, America's largest prehistoric city was located only 160 miles away at what is now Cahokia, Illinois. Why this civilization disappeared remains a mystery.

At the time Europeans arrived in the area in the seventeenth century, the Osage Indians inhabited the region. In 1673, the French explorers Joliet and Marquette explored the region. In 1682, the explorer LaSalle sailed down the Mississippi River and claimed the area of Jefferson City for France. In 1715, Antoine de la Mothe Cadillac opened a lead mine nearby, where until 1744 white men used slaves to work the mines. During the mid-1700s, settlements were begun at Ste. Genevieve and at St. Louis. Soon many new settlers began arriving from Kentucky and Tennessee by way of the Ohio River and its tributaries.

In the 1780s, the Spanish built a road northward from New Madrid, Missouri to St. Louis, which today is known as U.S. Route 51. The area was explored by members of the Lewis and Clark expedition in 1804. In the early 1800s, frontiersman Daniel Boone carved out the Boone's Lick Trail, which is now Interstate Highway 70. It ran westward from St. Charles to the Missouri River at Franklin. In time the Santa Fe Trail was developed, running from Franklin westward to Independence, then southward. The Oregon Trail branched westward from Independence.

Created to Serve as Capital

Jefferson City holds the distinction of having been created specifically to serve as the state capital by a commission appointed by the Missouri state legislature in 1821. But until government buildings could be constructed, the town of St. Charles served as the capital.

Jefferson City was laid out by Daniel Morgan Boone, the son of the frontiersman. It was named for U.S. President Thomas Jefferson, who served from 1801-1809. The town was incorporated in 1825, and the general assembly moved there in 1826. At that time, the town had thirty-one families, a general store, a hotel, and a few other buildings.

For several years, other towns attempted to have the capital city changed, and in 1832 Governor John Miller suggested that a state penitentiary be built in Jefferson City to strengthen the town's position as capital. The prison was completed in 1836.

The next year, the Capitol burned and all the state records went up in flames. Five years later, a new statehouse was completed at the site of the present Capitol building. At that time, although pigs still wandered in the streets, modern steamboats regularly visited the city and stage coach routes brought travelers. These facilities encouraged the growth of local industries, including grist mills, flour mills, tanneries, and distilleries. The 1830s saw the influx of German immigrants, who were mostly farmers.

Civil War Brings Strife and Division

In 1839, Jefferson City was incorporated as a city, and in 1840 the population stood at 1,174 people, including 262 slaves. A frightening incident took place in 1849, when a ship carrying Mormon church members, some of whom had cholera, landed at the city dock. For two years, the plague infected residents in the area, paralyzing the local trade.

In 1855, the Pacific Railroad line was completed between St. Louis and Jefferson City. However, the first trip between the two cities was a disaster. As residents waited for the president of the railroad and other dignitaries to arrive, a pier collapsed on a bridge that crossed the Gasconade River, and the resulting train accident killed 28 people and injured 30 others. Regular train service did not begin until the next year.

The coming of the Civil War (1860–1865) brought to a head the question of whether slavery would continue in Missouri. While President Abraham Lincoln encouraged an end to slavery, Missouri Governor Claiborne F. Jackson favored the retention of slavery and the secession of the southern states, including Missouri.

Decades Pass Before Wounds Heal

Soon after, a convention was held in Missouri to decide which position the state assembly would embrace. The convention voted to remain in the Union. But Governor Jackson refused to recognize federal authority and also refused to send troops to fight for the Union Army.

Instead, he rallied 50,000 volunteers for the state militia and marched from the capital to join Confederate forces at Booneville. But two days later, Union troops overran Jefferson City and pitched camp on Capitol Hill. In 1864, Confederate General and former Missouri Governor Sterling Price and his men marched to within four miles of the city and announced they would attack. Troops exchanged fire, but in the end Price withdrew and fled westward toward Kansas City, and Jefferson City remained in Union hands.

Decades passed before the city recovered from the rifts occasioned by the Civil War. But the Missouri constitution of 1875 restored peace of mind to the citizens and a period of expansion began. Such industries as printing and shoe manufacturing developed in the city, and within ten years a bridge was built across the Missouri River, uniting the pro-South Jefferson City with its pro-North neighbors in Kansas. In 1896, the town of Sedalia tried to wrest the capital from Jefferson City, but the attempt failed when Jefferson City triumphed in a popular vote among Missouri citizens.

The City in the Twentieth Century

After 1900, the local economy began to grow again with the expansion of the state government. In 1904, The Supreme Court Building was constructed with funds from the St. Louis World's Fair. The next year St. Mary's Hospital was built. In 1911, street car service began in the city, and a dramatic fire brought the destruction of the old State House.

A new one was completed in 1917 and the present Capitol building was dedicated in 1924.

For the next forty years, the business of state government business continued to dominate the local scene, throughout the periods of two world wars and the Great Depression. The city slowly continued to grow, as more people left the local farms and gravitated to the city.

In 1951, Still Hospital was built, and in 1954 a major prison riot took place at the state prison in Jefferson City. The 1960s saw the construction of Memorial Hospital, the opening of Rex M. Whitten Expressway, and Jefferson City's development as a manufacturing center. In 1983, the John G. Christy Municipal Building opened. A major flood in 1993 caused extensive damage, but by the end of the 1990s the city had fully recovered. Jefferson City, notable for its liveability, and relatively low cost of living and high per capita income, has entered the 2000s with vitality.

Historical Information: Cole County Historical Society, 109 Madison St., Jefferson City, MO, 65101; telephone (573)635-1850

Population Profile

Cole County Population
1980: 56,663
1990: 63,579
2000: 71,397
Percent change, 1990–2000: 12.3%
U.S. rank in 1990: Not reported
U.S. rank in 2000: 693rd

City Residents
1980: 33,619
1990: 35,481
2000: 39,636
2003 estimate: 37,550
Percent change, 1990–2000: 10.8%
U.S. rank in 1990: Not reported
U.S. rank in 2000: (State rank: 15th)

Density: 1,454.4 people per square mile (2000)

Racial and ethnic characteristics (2000)
   White: 32,303
   Black or African American: 5,828
   American Indian and Alaska Native: 150
   Asian: 488
   Native Hawaiian and Pacific Islander: 20
   Hispanic or Latino (may be of any race): 616
   Other: 847

Percent of residents born in state: 71.7%

Age characteristics (2000)
Population under 5 years old: 2,314
Population 5 to 9 years old: 2,210
Population 10 to 14 years old: 2,295
Population 15 to 19 years old: 2,705
Population 20 to 24 years old: 3,133
Population 25 to 34 years old: 6,202
Population 35 to 44 years old: 6,518
Population 45 to 54 years old: 5,613
Population 55 to 59 years old: 1,766
Population 60 to 64 years old: 1,337
Population 65 to 74 years old: 2,646
Population 75 to 84 years old: 2,023
Population 85 years and older: 874
Median age: 36.5 years (2000)

Births (2003, Cole County)
Total number: 963

Deaths (2003, Cole County)
Total number: 584 (of which, 2 were infants under the age of 1 year)

Money income (1999)
Per capita income: $21,268
Median household income: $39,628
Total households: 15,870

Number of households with income of . . .
less than $10,000: 1,488
$10,000 to $14,999: 1,034
$15,000 to $24,999: 2,329
$25,000 to $34,999: 2,189
$35,000 to $49,999: 2,628
$50,000 to $74,999: 3,212
$75,000 to $99,999: 1,725
$100,000 to $149,999: 839
$150,000 to $99,999: 142
$200,000 or more: 284

Percent of families below poverty level: 7.2% (30.6% of which were female householder families with related children under 5 years)

2002 FBI Crime Index Total: Not reported

Municipal Government

Jefferson City is the capital of Missouri and the seat of Cole County. The city itself has a mayor-council form of government; there are ten councilmen, each of whom serves a two-year term and may be elected to serve a total of up to eight years. The mayor serves for four years and may be re-elected for a second term.

Head Official: Mayor John Landwehr (since 2003; current term expires 2007)

Total Number of City Employees: 387 (2005)

City Information: Mayor's Office, City of Jefferson City, 231 Madison Street, Jefferson City, MO 65101; telephone (573)634-6304

Economy

Major Industries and Commercial Activity

The major business in Jefferson City is government, which provides more than 28,000 local jobs; nearly 17,000 of these jobs are for the Missouri state government. Much of the state government business is carried on in the city, home of the Missouri Legislature, Missouri Supreme Court, and many offices that house the different state departments.

Jefferson City also serves as a trading center for the agricultural produce grown in the area. The main cash crops raised are corn, wheat, and soybeans. Between 1997 and 2002, the number of farms in the county decreased by 6 percent, from 1,162 farms to 1,098; however, the size of farms increased by 4 percent, from 162 acres to 169 acres.

More than 20 different industries make up the economic base of Jefferson City, including the manufacture of electric appliances, book binding, shoemaking, and steel fabrication. Per capita personal income in the county increased by 51.7 percent from 1991 to 2001, and the city has one of the lowest costs of living in the state; these factors, plus an increase in visitors to Jefferson City, have boosted local retail in recent years.

Items and goods produced: structural steel products, heat transfer equipment, books, cosmetics, automotive seating, radiators, washer parts

Incentive Programs—New and Existing Companies

Business incentive and economic programs are administered at the state level to Jefferson City businesses.

State programs—The state of Missouri offers numerous major tax exemptions, abatements, and credits for qualifying businesses. They include exemptions involving the purchase of new machinery and equipment; tax credits to small businesses; property tax abatement and state tax credit for property in a "blighted area"; and tax credits for vineyards and wine producers, and for film production companies. The

Missouri Department of Economic Development and other agencies offer business finance programs.

Job training programs—The Missouri Training and Employment Council, a division of the state of Missouri, works with local, regional, and state businesses to create programs that help hire and train employees, such as career centers and educational systems. The Jefferson/Franklin Consortium Career Center acts as a "one-stop shop" for both employers and prospective employees. The Missouri Community College New Jobs Training Program offers assistance to companies expanding or relocating to Missouri and creating substantial new jobs; the program assists with employee training costs.

Economic Development Information: Jefferson City Chamber of Commerce, 213 Adams St., Jefferson City, MO 65101; telephone (573)634-3616; fax (573)634-3805. Missouri Department of Economic Development, 301 W. High Street, Jefferson City, MO 65102; telephone: (573)751-4962; fax (573)526-7700; email ecodev@ded.mo.gov.

Commercial Shipping

The Union Pacific Railroad provides rail freight service. Several motor freight carriers serve the city. Barge lines ship cargo through Jefferson City via the Missouri River.

Labor Force and Employment Outlook

The labor force of Jefferson City is technologically competent. That, combined with the cooperation among city, state, and county governmental offices, the school district, chamber of commerce, public utilities, and industries, has helped to make this small metropolitan area among the fastest growing in the state. The city continues to attract new businesses and new jobs are being created. A 2004 study shows that job prospects in Cole County and surrounding counties are the best in the state; prospects are especially strong in the categories of durable goods manufacturing, transportation/public utilities and services.

The following is a summary of data regarding the Jefferson City labor force, 2004 annual averages.

Size of nonagricultural labor force: 78,400

Number of workers employed in . . .
  trade, transportation and utilities: 13,800
  government: 28,800

Average hourly earnings of production workers employed in manufacturing: Not reported

Unemployment rate: 5.1% (February 2005)

Largest employers	*Number of employees*
Missouri State Government	16,864
Scholastic, Inc.	more than 1,000
Capital Region Medical Center	more than 1,000
St. Mary's Health Center	more than 1,000
Jefferson City Public Schools	more than 1,000
ABB Power T&C Company	500 to 999
Von Hoffman Press	500 to 999
UNILEVER Home & Personal Care, USA	500 to 999
Wal-Mart Super Center	500 to 999

Cost of Living

The following is a summary of data regarding several key cost of living factors for the Jefferson City area.

2004 (3rd Quarter) ACCRA Average House Price: $207,800

2004 (3rd Quarter) ACCRA Cost of Living Index: 91.7 (U.S. average = 100.0)

State income tax rate: 1.5% to 6.0%

State sales tax rate: 4.225%

Local income tax rate: None

Local sales tax rate: 2.0% (1.5% city; 0.5% county)

Property tax rate: $.72 per $100 assessed valuation

Economic Information: Jefferson City Chamber of Commerce, 213 Adams St., Jefferson City, MO 65101; telephone (573)634-3616

Education and Research

Elementary and Secondary Schools

Jefferson City School District elementary schools offer instruction in language arts, social studies, science, math, fine arts, and physical education. Two middle schools, identical in physical design, feature innovative curriculums for grades 6-8. All ninth graders attend the Simonsen Center; in tenth grade, the students transfer to Jefferson City High School. High school students may also opt to enroll in classes offered by Nichols Career Center, which offers classes in a variety of vocational areas.

The following is a summary of data regarding the Jefferson City public school system as of the 2002–2003 school year.

Total enrollment: 8,338

Number of facilities
  elementary schools: 11
  junior high/middle schools: 2
  senior high schools: 1

Student/teacher ratio: 14.5:1

Teacher salaries
   average: $41,062

Funding per pupil: $6,095

Jefferson City is home to 10 private schools. The largest of these is Helias Interparish High School, which enrolls about 900 students from three local Catholic parishes. Emphasis at Helias is placed on a four-year program in math, science, English, social studies, and foreign language. Courses are taught in computer applications with computer assisted instruction in other courses.

Public Schools Information: Jefferson City Public Schools, 315 E. Dunklin St., Jefferson City, MO 65101; telephone (573)659-3000

Colleges and Universities

Lincoln University, founded in 1866 by African American Civil War veterans, has changed over time from an African American university to a major coeducational state university with a multi-ethnic student body. The university offers undergraduate degrees in arts and sciences, as well as accounting, business administration, public administration, marketing, business education, economics, computer science, technology, military science, and agribusiness. Graduate programs are available in business, education, and social science.

Libraries and Research Centers

Jefferson City is served by the Missouri River Regional Library, which has nearly 200,000 volumes and approximately 400 periodical subscriptions. The library has special collections on local and state history. The system has one branch and two bookmobiles.

The Missouri State Library has special collections on health and education policy issues, human service, legislative reference, public finance, and state government. The Wolfner Library for the Blind and Physically Handicapped, featuring braille and large-type books, has holdings of 321,832 volumes and 70 periodical subscriptions. Other state libraries located in the city are the Missouri Committee on Legislative Research, with 5,200 volumes and 125 periodical subscriptions; the Missouri Department of Corrections Libraries, with more than 100,000 book titles; the Missouri Supreme Court Library, which has more than 110,000 volumes; and the Office of the Secretary of State, Missouri State Archives, which has 12,500 volumes.

Other local libraries include Lincoln University's Inman E. Page Library, which has nearly 180,000 volumes, and special collections on ethnic studies, and the library of the Cole County Historical Society, which has special collections on oral history.

Lincoln University's Cooperative Research Program conducts studies in agricultural science, nutrition, and environmental science.

Public Library Information: Missouri River Regional Library, 214 Adams St., Jefferson City, MO 65102; telephone (573)634-2464; fax (573)634-7028

Health Care

Capital Region Medical Center is a 100-bed facility affiliated with the University of Missouri Health Sciences System. The affiliation combines the strengths of an academic medical center with the strengths of a community-based hospital. Capital Region offers prenatal and maternity services, an inpatient rehabilitation center, advanced cardiac and oncology services, and ambulance service. An expansion of the hospital is slated for completion by the end of 2005; its major component will be the addition of 44 private in-patient rooms. In addition to being a full-service hospital, the center operates an extensive clinic system from urgent care centers to specialty physician practices. St. Mary's Health Center is a faith-based, full-service hospital, with 167 beds, extensive cardiology and open-heart surgery, a maternal and child care center, an oncology center, and a network of primary care clinics. Also at St. Mary's is Villa Marie Skilled Nursing Facility, a 120-bed facility offering intermediary and skilled nursing care as well as a complete rehabilitation program.

Health Care Information: Capital Region Medical Center, 1125 Madison Street, Jefferson City, MO 65101; telephone (573)632-5000

Recreation

Sightseeing

The State Capitol, which houses the Missouri State Museum, is the third state Capitol building, the first two having been destroyed by fires in 1837 and 1911. The stone building, built between 1913-1917, sits on a limestone bluff on the south bank of the Missouri River. A 1936 mural within the capitol building's House Lounge, painted by Missouri artist Thomas Hart Benton, is entitled *A Social History of the State of Missouri*. The mural, which depicts average citizens involved in their daily activities, was at first criticized for showing a lack of refinement, but has since become a beloved visual record. Free guided tours of the building are

Construction began on the Missouri State Capitol building in 1913.

available daily. Located adjacent to the Capitol Rotunda, the Missouri State Museum houses a History Hall and a Resource Hall. The latter tells the story of Missouri from its earliest history to modern times. Located on the Capitol grounds is the large Fountain of Centaurs that was designed by sculptor Adolph A. Weinman.

The Missouri Governor's Mansion is perched on a bluff within walking distance of the State Capitol. An outstanding example of Renaissance Revival style architecture, the mansion has been beautifully restored. The three-story red brick building is trimmed in stone and has an imposing portico with four stately pink granite columns, and its mansard roof is crowned by iron grillwork. The work of Missouri painters Thomas Hart Benton and George Caleb Bingham adorns the walls. The mansion is decked out as a haunted house at Halloween, and is ornately decorated at holiday time.

The Jefferson Landing State Historic Site is a complex of three historic buildings—the Christopher Maus House, the Lohman Building, and the Union Hotel—located just one block from the Capitol. They form the state's oldest remaining Missouri River commercial district. The buildings were restored in 1976 and serve as the Capitol complex's visitors center. The 1854 Christopher Maus House typifies the small, red brick residences of its time; the Union Hotel, built in 1865, houses a gallery with historical exhibits; and the Lohman Building, which serves as the visitor center for the Missouri State Museum, was once a store that supplied boat merchandise and general items to the local citizenry. Across the street, the Cole County Historical Society displays artifacts of the city's earlier days, including a collection of inaugural ball gowns of former Missouri first ladies.

The Runge Conservation Nature Center has a 3,000-square-foot exhibit hall that provides hands-on exhibits of Missouri wildlife habitats, and features a 2,400-gallon fish aquarium holding indigenous fish. Adjacent to the Runge conservation Nature Center are five hiking trails with self-guided exhibits. More than 3,500 veterinary artifacts and instruments, some more than a century old, can be viewed at the Missouri Veterinary Medical Foundation Museum, along with old diaries and sample drug cases.

The Missouri State Information Center, which houses the State Records and Archives Division of the Secretary of State's office, is a must for genealogy buffs. Visitors to the Missouri State Highway Patrol Safety Education Center and Law Enforcement Museum can view old patrol cars, gun, drug, alcohol, and seat belt displays, and various law enforcement antiques.

Arts and Culture

The Little Theatre of Jefferson City, based at Lincoln University's Richardson Auditorium, stages musicals, drama, and comedy. Four major productions are presented annually. The Stained Glass Theatre Mid-Missouri, a non-denominational Christian theatre, stages seven shows per year. The Capitol City Players presents dinner theater entertainment ranging from traditional Broadway musicals to more contemporary fare.

The Jefferson City Symphony offers three annual concerts at Richardson Auditorium, in cooperation with the Community Concert Association. In addition, Lincoln University's University Vocal Ensemble, Dance Group, and "Share in the Arts" series invites members of the community the enjoy its theatre, music, dance, and poetry events.

Festivals and Holidays

Jefferson City keeps things lively with a number of annual events. January is highlighted by a bridal show and a boat show. In mid-March the Annual Ice Show provides a colorful extravaganza at the covered Washington Park Ice Arena. May brings the Collectibles and Antique Show and Antique Fair. The city welcomes Independence Day with the Salute to America, featuring musical entertainment, a parade, historical reenactments, arts and crafts, and fireworks. In September, the town celebrates the colors of fall with the Cole County Fall Festival, an arts and crafts fair; the Jefferson City Multicultural Fall Festival, focusing on the city's diversity; Art inside the Park, where contemporary artists create installations in Memorial Park; and the Annual JazzFest on the Capitol grounds. Oktoberfest celebrates resident's German heritage with a festival featuring a beer garden, wine, carriage rides, food, and home tours.

December is filled with holiday activities that begin during the first weekend with the Living Christmas Showcase downtown. It features music, carriage rides, hayrides, tours of historic buildings, and living window displays. Candlelight tours of the Governor's Mansion, decorated for the holiday season, are available. The Annual Christmas Parade takes place on the first Saturday of the month.

Sports for the Spectator

Both students and community members like to watch the Blue Devils in action during athletic activities that take place at Lincoln University. These events include women's basketball, softball, cross-country/track and field, and tennis, as well as men's basketball, baseball, cross-country/track and field, soccer, and golf. In 2005 the women's cross-country/track and field team won their third straight NCAA Division II Track and Field Championship.

Sports for the Participant

Ellis Porter Riverside Park offers 60 acres on a bluff overlooking the Missouri river. The park includes a 9,500 square-foot swimming pool, ball playing areas including a basketball court and three lighted handball/racquetball courts, trails, and an outdoor amphitheater. Binder Park, with 644 acres, is the city's largest park. It provides a 155-acre lake for fishing, a boat launch ramp, a campground, lighted softball fields, and two sand volleyball courts. Oak Hills Golf Center/Hough Park complex has an 8-acre lake with a boat launching area and an 18-hole golf course. Other parks in the city offer a variety of facilities including trails, horseshoe pits, ball fields, and an ice arena. Public and private golf courses in the area include Eagle Knoll, Railwood Golf Club, Turkey Creek Golf Center (public); and Jefferson City Country Club and Meadow Lake Acres Country Club (private).

South of Jefferson City, the Lake of the Ozarks State park offers more than 17,000 acres of camping, hiking, swimming, and boating facilities.

Shopping and Dining

High Street is the focal point of downtown shopping, with restaurants and galleries tucked among the brick-fronted shops. Shoppers may also browse at the Capital Mall, which offers dozens of stores, three department stores—Dillard's, Sears, and JCPenney—and a multiscreen cinema. Other local shopping areas include the Southside area, the Eastend with its many quaint shops, and the Westend area, which has more than 30 restaurants concentrated along Missouri Boulevard.

Local restaurants offer many opportunities to sample the cuisines of various cultures. Menus feature big Midwestern steaks and local catfish, as well as Greek, Asian, Mexican, Italian, and German offerings.

Visitor Information: Jefferson City Convention & Visitors Bureau, 213 Adams St., Jefferson City, MO 65102; telephone (573)632-2820; fax (573)638-4892

Transportation

Approaching the City

Jefferson City is located at the crossroads of U.S. Highways 54 and 63, which run north and south, and U.S. Highway 50, which runs east and west. Columbia Regional Airport, about twelve miles north of downtown, has commuter air carrier service. The airport shuttle offers trips downtown, and taxi service is also available. Amtrak offers train transportation to the city and bus service is provided by Sho-Me Coach Lines.

Traveling in the City

Highway 50/63 runs east and west through the city just two blocks south of the State Capitol Building; in town it is known as the Whitton Expressway. Highway 54, known as

Christy Lane, runs north to Fulton and south to the Lake of the Ozarks State Park. Downtown, West Main Street and East Capitol Avenue run directly to the Missouri Capitol Building. Jefferson City is served by Jefferson City Transit's JEFFTRAN bus line.

Communications

Newspapers and Magazines

The *Jefferson City Post Tribune* is published weekday afternoons; the *Daily Capital News* is published Tuesday through Saturday mornings, and the *Sunday News Tribune* is a combination of both publications.

The Catholic Missourian is the official newspaper of the Diocese of Jefferson City, while *Word and Way* is a religious tabloid published by the Missouri Baptist Convention.

Local magazines include the *Journal of the Missouri Bar, Rural Missouri, Missouri Municipal Review, Missouri Conservationist, The Missouri Engineer, The Missouri Nurse, Missouri Pharmacist, Missouri Wildlife,* and *Show Me Missouri Farm Bureau News.* Also published in Jefferson City are *Something Better,* an education magazine, and *MLPGA News,* a magazine for the gas industry. Locally produced journals include *Focus MDA,* a dental journal, and *Missouri Medicine,* a journal reporting on the interests of medical and public health professionals.

Television and Radio

Local radio stations include an FM oldies station, an FM jazz and urban contemporary station, an FM top 40 station, an FM country station, and an AM news and talk station. There are ABC, CBS and NBC-affiliated television stations in the city.

Media Information: *Jefferson City News & Tribune,* PO Box 420, Jefferson City, MO 65102; telephone (573)636-3131

Jefferson City Online

City of Jefferson City home page. Available www.jeffcity .com/cityclerk

Jefferson City Chamber of Commerce. Available www .jcchamber.org

Jefferson City Convention & Visitors Bureau. Available www.visitjeffersoncity.com/default.htm

Jefferson City Public Schools. Available www.jcps.k12.mo .us

Missouri River Regional Library. Available www.mrrl.org

News Tribune. Available www.newstribune.com

Selected Bibliography

Digges, Deborah, *Fugitive Spring: A Memoir* (New York: Vintage Books, 1993)

Ford, James E., *History of Jefferson City, Missouri's State Capital and of Cole County* (Salem, MA: Higginson Book Company, 1994)

Young, Robert Emmett, *Pioneers of High, Water, and Main: Reflections of Jefferson City* (Jefferson City, MO: Twelfth State, 1997)

Kansas City

The City in Brief

Founded: 1821 (incorporated 1853)

Head Official: Mayor Kay Barnes (since 1999)

City Population
  1980: 448,028
  1990: 431,236
  2000: 441,545
  2003 estimate: 442,768
  Percent change, 1990–2000: 1.5%
  U.S. rank in 1980: 27th
  U.S. rank in 1990: 31st
  U.S. rank in 2000: 45th

Metropolitan Area Population
  1980: 1,433,000
  1990: 1,582,875
  2000: 1,776,062

Percent change, 1990–2000: 12.2%
U.S. rank in 1980: 25th
U.S. rank in 1990: Not reported
U.S. rank in 2000: 26th

Area: 314 square miles (2000)
Elevation: 742 feet above sea level
Average Annual Temperature: 54.6° F
Average Annual Precipitation: 38.21 inches; 20 inches of snow

Major Economic Sectors: Trade, transportation, and utilities; government; professional and business services; educational and health services
Unemployment Rate: 5.7% (February 2005)
Per Capita Income: $20,753 (1999)

2002 FBI Crime Index Total: 42,100

Major Colleges and Universities: University of Missouri at Kansas City

Daily Newspaper: *The Kansas City Star*

Introduction

Kansas City is a thriving cultural and economic center at the heart of the United States. The largest city in Missouri, Kansas City is the center of a bi-state Metropolitan Statistical Area composed of 15 counties: Platte, Clinton, Caldwell, Clay, Ray, Jackson, Lafayette, Cass, and Bates counties in Missouri and Leavenworth, Wyandotte, Johnson, Franklin, Miami, and Linn counties in Kansas. First a trading post and river port settlement, the city developed after the Civil War as a link in the intercontinental railroad network, which led to prosperous grain, livestock, and meat-packing industries. During the twentieth century Kansas City garnered a national reputation for its distinctive architecture, boulevard system, and innovations in urban redevelopment. This redevelopment has continued into the twenty-first century, prompting *Expansion Management* magazine to name Kansas City the third "hottest city" in the United States for business expansion (2005).

Geography and Climate

Surrounded by gently rolling terrain, Kansas City is located near the geographical center of the United States. It is situated on the south bank of the Missouri River at the Missouri-Kansas state line. The climate is modified continental, with frequent and rapid fluctuations in weather during early spring. Summer is characterized by warm days and mild nights; fall days are mild and the nights cool. Winter is cold with the heaviest snowfall coming late in the season.

Area: 314 square miles (2000)

Elevation: 742 feet above sea level

Average Temperatures: January, 29° F; July, 78° F; annual average, 54.6° F

Average Annual Precipitation: 38.21 inches; 20 inches of snow

History

River Site Aids Westward Expansion

The area along the Missouri River now occupied by Kansas City was originally territory within the domain of the Kansa (Kaw) Native Americans. The first persons of European descent to enter the region were Meriwether Lewis and William Clark, who camped at the confluence of the Kansas and Missouri rivers in 1804 during their Louisiana Purchase expedition. Several years later, in 1821, Francois Chouteau opened a depot for the American Fur Company on the site; after a flood destroyed his warehouse in 1826, he relocated to the site of a ferry boat service, where the town of Kansas soon developed.

In 1832 John Calvin McCoy settled nearby and built a store; the following year he platted the town of Westport in Missouri, offering lots for new business development. Westport was soon competing with neighboring Independence, the seat of Jackson County, to be chosen as the eastern terminus of the Santa Fe Trail. Meanwhile Chouteau's settlement, Kansas, developed more slowly; in 1838 the Kansas Town Company was formed to sell property near Chouteau's warehouse. Both Westport and Kansas Town prospered under westward migration until the height of the Gold Rush in 1849, when an epidemic of Asiatic cholera reduced the local population by one-half and drove business elsewhere.

The Kansas Town settlement remained substantial enough, however, to be incorporated in 1850 as the Town of Kansas and then as the City of Kansas in 1853. By 1855 overland trade had returned and the city began to prosper once again, just in time to be disrupted by the nation's conflict over the issue of slavery, during which Southern and Northern forces vied for dominance in the Kansas Territory. Kansas border ruffians invaded Wyandotte County, Kansas, creating havoc in the City of Kansas, which fell into disrepair and economic difficulty with the outbreak of the Civil War. In a pivotal conflict, the Union Army resisted a Confederate Army attack at the Battle of Westport (Missouri) in October of 1864.

Rail Center Develops Architectural Refinement

When the Missouri Pacific Railroad arrived in 1865, the City of Kansas at the confluence of the Kansas and Missouri rivers was found to be the perfect location for a railroad distributing center. The first stockyards opened in 1870 and, after weathering the grasshopper plagues of 1874, the City of Kansas emerged as a wheat and grain exchange center. The economy was further stimulated when the Kansas River was bridged in 1866, followed by the construction of the Hannibal Bridge across the Missouri River in 1869. Kansas City adopted its current name in 1889 and annexed Westport in 1897.

The figure who exercised the greatest impact in transforming Kansas City into a beautiful metropolis was William Rockhill Nelson, an Indiana native who settled in Kansas City in 1880 to become owner and editor of the *Kansas City Star*. Nelson persuaded the community's elite to commit themselves to civic betterment. Through Nelson's constant nudging, a residential development project was begun, turning a rundown neighborhood into the exclusive Country Club district that contained the internationally acclaimed business section, Country Club Plaza. Carefully landscaped with parks, fountains, and European statuary, this enclave remains Kansas City's most popular tourist attraction. At Nelson's encouragement, George E. Kessler planned Kansas City's much-admired boulevard system, which helps define its distinctive character. The city still contains a number of architecturally significant buildings, especially in the Art Deco style, which credit their existence to Nelson's ability to convince people to express their civic pride through architecture, landscaping, and city planning.

In the 1920s Democrat Thomas J. Pendergast introduced machine politics to Kansas City, with mixed blessings. Although civic improvements were initiated, Kansas City developed a reputation for a corrupt government that functioned under "boss rule," a reputation that continued until 1940 when reformers were voted into office. Since then, Kansas City has prospered through urban redevelopment projects. Crown Center, Hallmark Cards' "city within a city," is credited by some with halting the drain of business into the suburbs. As of 2005, $4 billion in major infrastructure improvements are planned or in progress. The development touches nearly all areas of Kansas City life—business, entertainment, arts and culture, residential housing, and transportation. The local life sciences industry is also growing and garnering Kansas City international respect.

Kansas City is a sophisticated community offering many attractions, from a lyric opera company to five professional sports teams, and from world-class shopping to its famous Kansas City barbeque. Famous natives include pioneering pilot Amelia Earhart; director Robert Altman; actors Edward Asner, Noah and Wallace Beery, and Jean Harlow; composers Virgil Thompson and Burt Bacharach; rocker Melissa Etheridge; professional golfer Tom Watson; and baseball player Casey Stengel.

Historical Information: Kansas City Museum, 3218 Gladstone Boulevard, Kansas City, MO 64123; telephone (816)483-8300. University of Missouri, Western Historical Manuscript Collection, 302 Newcomb Hall, 5100 Rockhill Road, Kansas City, MO 64110; telephone (816)235-1543

Population Profile

Metropolitan Area Residents
1980: 1,433,000
1990: 1,587,875
2000: 1,776,062
Percent change, 1990–2000: 12.2%
U.S. rank in 1980: 25th
U.S. rank in 1990: Not reported
U.S. rank in 2000: 26th

City Residents
1980: 448,028
1990: 431,236
2000: 441,545
2003 estimate: 452,768
Percent change, 1990–2000: 1.5%
U.S. rank in 1980: 27th
U.S. rank in 1990: 31st (State rank: 1st)
U.S. rank in 2000: 45th (State rank: 1st)

Density: 1,408.2 persons per square mile (2000)

Racial and ethnic characteristics (1990)
White: 267,931
Black or African American: 137,879
American Indian and Alaska Native: 2,122
Asian: 8,182
Native Hawaiian and Pacific Islander: 493
Hispanic or Latino (may be of any race): 30,604
Other: 14,158

Percent of residents born in state: 57% (2000)

Age characteristics (2000)
Population under 5 years old: 31,755
Population 5 to 9 years old: 31,829
Population 10 to 14 years old: 30,770
Population 15 to 19 years old: 29,053
Population 20 to 24 years old: 31,590
Population 25 to 34 years old: 72,393
Population 35 to 44 years old: 71,309
Population 45 to 54 years old: 56,492
Population 55 to 59 years old: 19,544
Population 60 to 64 years old: 15,118
Population 65 to 74 years old: 27,163
Population 75 to 84 years old: 18,263
Population 85 years and older: 6,266
Median age: 34.0 years

Births (2003)
Total number: 7,345

Deaths (2003)
Total number: 3,742 (of which, 30 were infants under the age of 1 year)

Money income (1999)
Per capita income: $20,753
Median household income: $37,198
Total households: 184,028

Number of households with income of . . .
less than $10,000: 21,385
$10,000 to $14,999: 11,745
$15,000 to $24,999: 26,325
$25,000 to $34,999: 27,110
$35,000 to $49,999: 31,731

$50,000 to $74,999: 34,354
$75,000 to $99,999: 16,037
$100,000 to $149,999: 10,330
$150,000 to $199,999: 2,213
$200,000 or more: 2,798

Percent of families below poverty level: 11.1% (30.1% of which were female householder families with related children under 5 years)

2002 FBI Crime Index Total: 42,100

Municipal Government

Kansas City operates under a council-manager form of government, with the mayor and 12 council members all elected to four-year terms. The city manager serves and advises the mayor and council.

Head Official: Mayor Kay Barnes (D) (since 1999; current term expires in 2007)

Total Number of City Employees: approximately 4,500 (May 2005)

City Information: City Hall, 414 East Twelfth St, Kansas City, MO 64106; telephone (816)513-3500 (Mayor's office); fax (816)513-3518; email mayor@kcmo.org

Economy

Major Industries and Commercial Activity

Both the geographic and population centers of the United States lie within 250 miles of Kansas City, making the metropolitan area a natural hub for intermodal transportation, warehousing, manufacturing, and distribution. The Kansas City area economy is a diverse one. The trade, transportation, and utilities category is the region's largest employer; government is second, followed by professional and business services, then educational and health services. Major manufacturing employers are Hallmark Cards (founded in Kansas City in 1910); Harmon Industries, Inc. (founded in Kansas City in 1946), manufacturers of railroad signal and communication equipment, traffic control systems, rail/highway grade crossing hardware and allied components; and American Italian Pasta, the largest producer of pasta in North America.

In addition to the federal and state governments, local employers with more than 5,000 workers include Sprint, Ford Motor Company, Kansas City School District, and the University of Kansas. A number of companies have made recent announcements to relocate significant operations or expand existing operations to the Kansas City metropolitan area. These include Federal Express, Wausau Supply, Procter & Gamble, and H&R Block.

Items and goods produced: grain mill products, roasted coffee, chips and similar snacks, meat products, bakery products, apparel, millwork and plywood, furniture, paperboard containers and boxes, converted paper products, commercial printing and publishing, drugs, soaps and detergents, agricultural chemicals, plastics, concrete, mineral wool, fabricated structural metal products, ordnance and accessories, industrial machinery and equipment, electronic/electrical equipment, motorvehicles, search and navigation equipment

Incentive Programs—New and Existing Companies

Local programs—The Kansas City Area Development Council is a bi-state, regional coalition of business, government, economic development, and chambers of commerce leaders. The council works with community partners to attract business and industry to the bi-state metropolitan area. Businesses locating within the Kansas City area are eligible for several incentive programs that, at the time of initial investment, offer direct cost reductions. Some of the programs also reduce annual operating costs. Businesses and individuals located in the metropolitan area are also affected by a tax structure that is quite favorable when compared to most regions of the United States. The Greater Kansas City Chamber of Commerce's Business Resource Center provides information for the research and business planning stage.

State programs—Businesses relocating to or expanding in the Kansas City area can take advantage of a wide range of financial incentives provided by state and local government agencies. These include state income tax credits, real and personal property tax exemptions, sales tax exemptions, financing programs, workforce training, and a number of other programs.

Job training programs—The New Jobs Training Program (NJTP) provides education and training to workers employed in newly created jobs in Missouri. The new jobs may result from a new industry locating in Missouri or an existing industry expanding its workforce in the state. In greater Kansas City, NJTP services are provided by the Metropolitan Community Colleges system. The program provides assistance in reducing the cost associated with expanding a workforce or locating a new facility through several training services, including customized training designed for the specific needs of the industry, adult basic education, general occupational skill training, and on-the-job training. The Missouri Customized Training Program (MCTP) helps Missouri employers with funding to offset the costs of employee training and retraining. It assists new and expanding businesses in recruiting, screening, and training workers, and it helps existing employers retain their current workforce when faced with needed upgrading and retraining.

Kansas City's Center for Workforce and Diversity Development, the hub of workforce development initiatives designed to seek solutions by building coalitions and collaborations to overcome workforce barriers. Initiatives include centralizing and supplying information about legislation and activities relating to the Welfare-to-Work program, child care and school-to-career initiatives; promoting diversity programs in the workplace; facilitating the metropolitan-wide Workforce Industry Consortia, where workforce issues are discussed and solutions created. Through the Workforce Industry Consortia, area businesses identify specific industry skill standards, gaps, and required training needs.

Development Projects

In 2004 Mayor Kay Barnes envisioned a "New Kansas City," driven primarily by development projects in the metropolitan area's urban core. More than $4 billion in major infrastructure improvements are planned, with work currently progressing on a $200 million expansion of the Nelson-Atkins Museum of Art, a $157 million Convention Center renovation and expansion project, and a $330 million entertainment district. Future projects include the new H&R Block headquarters, a Metropolitan Performing Arts Center, a Collegiate Basketball Hall of Fame, and Sprint Center, a $250 million sports arena slated for completion in 2007. Beginning in summer 2005, a new bus rapid transit system, the Metro Area Express (MAX), connects many of these destinations.

Since 2000, more than $500 million has been invested in new downtown residences, and another Sewer and Water Bond is being proposed to update the city's aging infrastructure and promote even more residential development.

Jim and Virginia Stowers have committed $300 million to build a second facility for the existing Stowers Institute for Medical Research; each facility will employ 500 people when staffed to capacity.

Economic Development Information: Greater Kansas City Chamber of Commerce, 2600 Commerce Tower, 911 Main St., Kansas City, MO 64105-2049; telephone (816)221-2424; fax (816)221-7440; email info@kcchamber.com. Kansas City Area Development Council, 2600 Commerce Tower, 911 Main St., Kansas City, MO 64105-2049; telephone (816)221-2121; toll-free (888)99KCADC; fax (816)842-2865; email kcadc@thinkKC.com. Economic Development Corporation of Kansas City, Missouri, 10 Petticoat Lane, Ste. 250, Kansas City, MO 64106; telephone (816)221-0636; toll-free (800)889-0636; fax (816)221-0189

Commercial Shipping

Located at the juncture of three interstate highways, four interstate linkages, and 10 federal highways, Kansas City is served by more than 300 motor freight carriers, including Yellow Corp., the nation's largest less-than-truckload carrier, which is headquartered in Kansas City. Kansas City is the third largest truck terminal in the United States. The second-largest rail center in the United States, Greater Kansas City is served by four of the country's eight Class I rail carriers, as well as three regional lines and one local switching carrier (Kansas City Terminal). Kansas City is connected via the Kansas and Missouri rivers to the nation's inland water system and is served by seven barge lines; 41 docks and terminal facilities exist in the metropolitan area. As an important inland port, Kansas City ranks first in the country in Foreign Trade Zones space. Kansas City International Airport (KCI) and four other airports in the metropolitan area are capable of supporting large cargo aircraft.

Labor Force and Employment Outlook

Employment in the Kansas City area economy increased by 20 percent during the 1990s, which ranked Kansas City among the fastest growing major Midwest labor markets. Unemployment, however, has risen steadily from 3.1 percent in 1999 to 6.2 percent in 2004. The Kansas City area labor force is said to be well-educated, motivated, and highly productive. Production workers in Kansas City take fewer sick days than workers in 33 major metros. Like the rest of the country, Kansas City has experienced a labor shortage; in the late 1990s this resulted in the loss of potential major employers to other parts of the country.

The local economy has managed to remain remarkably steady, largely due to its diversity; because it is not tied too closely to one particular industry, it is not subject to rapid economic peaks and valleys.

The following is a summary of data regarding the Kansas City metropolitan area labor force, 2004 annual averages.

Size of nonagricultural labor force: 965,900

Number of workers employed in . . .
   construction and mining: 50,800
   manufacturing: 83,700
   trade, transportation and utilities: 202,200
   information: 45,300
   financial activities: 70,900
   professional and business services: 127,700
   educational and health services: 108,900
   leisure and hospitality: 92,300
   other services: 40,400
   government: 143,900

Average hourly earnings of production workers employed in manufacturing: $20.65

Unemployment rate: 5.7% (February 2005)

Largest employers	Number of employees
Federal government	29,452
Sprint Corporation	9,300
State of Missouri	8,987
Hallmark Cards, Inc.	6,900
A T & T	6,200

Cost of Living

Kansas City's cost of living has consistently been at or below the national average. A major component of the overall low cost of living is the affordability of housing in the area. In the first quarter of 2005, Kansas City was the second most affordable market among metropolitan areas with populations exceeding one million.

The following is a summary of data regarding several key cost of living factors in the Kansas City area.

2004 (3rd Quarter) ACCRA Average House Price: $228,375

2004 (3rd Quarter) ACCRA Cost of Living Index: 95.5 (U.S. average = 100.0)

State income tax rate: graduated from 1.5% to 6.0%

State sales tax rate: 4.225%

Local income tax rate: 1.0% of earnings

Local sales tax rate: 1.5%

Property tax rate: 1.32 per $100 of assessed value of improved and unimproved land, personal property, and footage on or abutting boulevards, parkways, and trafficways

Economic Information: Greater Kansas City Chamber of Commerce, 2600 Commerce Tower, 911 Main St., Kansas City, MO 64105-2049; telephone (816)221-2424; fax (816)221-7440; email info@kcchamber.com. Kansas City Area Development Council, 2600 Commerce Tower, 911 Main St., Kansas City, MO 64105-2049; telephone (816)221-2121; toll-free (888)99KCADC; fax (816)842-2865; email kcadc@thinkKC.com. State of Missouri, Department of Economic Development, 301 W. High St., PO Box 157, Jefferson City, MO 65102; telephone (573)751-4962; fax (573)526-7700; email ecodev@ded.mo.gov

Education and Research

Elementary and Secondary Schools

Kansas City 33 School District is a major provider of public elementary and secondary education in Kansas City. It is also one of the most comprehensive magnet school systems in the country.

The following is a summary of data regarding the Kansas City 33 School District as of the 2003–2004 school year.

Total enrollment: 35,964

Number of facilities
  elementary schools: 61
  middle schools: 9
  senior high schools: 18
  other: 23 magnet schools; 6 alternative schools

Student/teacher ratio: 12:1

Teacher salaries
  average: $41,356 (2004)

  Funding per pupil: $9,813

More than 150 private and parochial schools operate in the metropolitan area.

Public Schools Information: Kansas City School District 33, 1211 McGee, Kansas City, MO 64106; telephone (816)418-7000

Colleges and Universities

Kansas City is home to several colleges and universities. The largest institution is the University of Missouri at Kansas City, with an enrollment of about 15,000 students. Granting baccalaureate, first-professional, master's, and doctorate degrees, the university operates a College of Arts and Sciences, a conservatory of music, and schools of business and public administration, computing and engineering, education, law, pharmacy, dentistry, nursing, medicine, and biological sciences.

Undergraduate and graduate degrees are awarded in specialized and professional areas by a number of the area's colleges. The Kansas City Art Institute, which began as a sketch club in 1885, offers a four-year fine and applied arts curriculum. Church-related institutions in the city include Avila College, which serves 1,800 undergraduate and graduate students in average class sizes of 18; MidAmerica Nazarene University, which offers bachelor's and master's degrees, as well as a Play Therapy Certificate Program and an adult-friendly Accelerated Associate of Arts; and Rockhurst University, a Jesuit institution that awards bachelor's and master's degrees in several programs and also awards nursing degrees to students at the Research College of Nursing. An extended campus of Central Missouri University offers courses and Internet classes in Kansas City.

Libraries and Research Centers

Approximately 60 libraries are maintained in Kansas City by public agencies, educational institutions, private corporations, cultural organizations, hospitals, and churches and synagogues. The Kansas City Public Library, with holdings of over 2 million volumes and more than 34,000 periodical subscriptions, operates 10 branches, including the new $50 million Central Library Branch unveiled in 2004 and the Plaza Branch opened in April 2005. Special collections include African American history, Missouri Valley history and genealogy, oral history, and federal and state government documents.

The Linda Hall Library of Science, Engineering & Technology is one of the largest privately endowed libraries of its kind in the country, holding more than 1 million volumes and more than 15,000 periodicals. Special collections include National Aeronautics and Space Administration (NASA) and Department of Energy technical reports, Soviet and European scientific and technical publications, and United States patent specifications. The Kansas City Branch of the National Archives and Records Administration holds records of various federal government agencies. The University of Missouri–Kansas City operates four facilities, specializing in law, dentistry, health sciences, and the humanities.

The 600,000-square-foot Stowers Institute for Medical Research boasts one of the nation's finest laboratory complexes dedicated to conducting basic research into complex genetic systems to unlock the mysteries of disease and find the key to their causes, treatment, and prevention. Jim and Virginia Stowers have committed $300 to build a second facility as large as the first, which already enjoys a nearly $2 billion endowment.

Public Library Information: Kansas City Public Library, 14 West 10th St., Kansas City, MO 64105; telephone (816)701-3400; fax (816)701-3401

Health Care

Among the primary health care facilities in Kansas City are more than 20 hospitals providing over 5,000 beds. The 508-bed Research Medical Center, founded in 1896, offers general and specialized care in such areas as arthritis, cardiac, and pulmonary rehabilitation, pain management, and speech and hearing disorders. In 2005 the Research Cancer Center unveiled a new genetic counseling/screening program. The Research Psychiatric Center provides a complete range of psychiatric treatment for adults and adolescents. St. Luke's Hospital, a 629-bed tertiary care institution, operates the Mid America Heart Institute and Mid America Brain and

Stroke Institute, as well as a school of nursing. Truman Medical Center is the primary teaching hospital for the University of Missouri—Kansas City schools of medicine, dentistry, pharmacy, and nursing. Other major health care facilities located in the city include Menorah Medical Center, Trinity Lutheran, and the Children's Mercy Hospital. A number of public and private special clinics, chemical dependency centers, mental health centers, and fitness centers also serve Kansas City.

Health Care Information: Research Medical Center, 2316 E. Meyer Blvd., Kansas City, MO 64132; telephone (816)276-4000. Research Psychiatric Center hotline, telephone (816)444-8161. Saint Luke's NurseLine, telephone (816)932-6220; toll-free (800)932-6220.

Recreation

Sightseeing

Kansas City is regarded as one of the most cosmopolitan cities of its size in the United States. Second only to Rome, Italy, in the number of its fountains (more than 200), Kansas City also has more miles of boulevards than Paris, France. Country Club Plaza, the nation's first planned community, boasts Spanish-style architecture, beautiful landscaping, and a plethora of shops, restaurants, hotels, and apartments. More than 1,000 of the city's structures are included on the National Register of Historic Places; among them are the Scarritt Building and Arcade, the *Kansas City Star* Building, Union Station, and the Kansas City Power and Light Building. The Mutual Musicians Foundation, a hot-pink bungalow acquired by the Black Musicians Union Local 627 in 1928, received a National Historic Landmark designation.

A unique feature of the city is a system of underground limestone caves that were formerly quarries. This 20-million-square-foot ''subtropolis'' is now a commercial complex used for offices and warehouses. The Hallmark Visitors Center showcases the history and most recent developments of the Hallmark Greeting Card Company. The Harry S. Truman Library and Museum in Independence, Missouri, captures Truman's political career and years as 33rd President of the United States. The nation's second largest urban park, Swope Park, includes the Kansas City Zoo and a braille trail.

One of the city's most popular attractions is Worlds of Fun, a 175-acre theme park featuring MAMBA, one of the tallest, longest, fastest steel coasters in the world. Also extremely popular are the Sprint IMAX Theatre in Swope Park and Oceans of Fun, a tropically-themed water park featuring a million-gallon wave pool and giant water slides.

The history of black baseball prior to 1947 is documented in the Negro Leagues Baseball Museum.

The towns around Kansas City are full of historic homes and sites, including the home and presidential library of Harry S. Truman in Independence. One of the more unusual sites is the Jesse JamesBank Museum in Liberty, the site of the first daylight bank robbery in the United States. History aficionados can still see ruts created by covered wagons along the Santa Fe Trail, established in 1821, and the Quindaro Ruins in Kansas City, Kansas, represent the largest underground-railroad archeological site in the nation.

The Negro Leagues Baseball Museum in Kansas City's 18th and Vine District honors the history of African American baseball before 1947, when Kansas City Monarchs shortstop Jackie Robinson broke the color barrier by joining major league baseball. Sports fans will also enjoy a tour of the National Collegiate Athletic Association Hall of Champions in Overland Park, Kansas, to commemorate great moments in intercollegiate athletics through multi-image and video presentations, displays, and exhibits.

Arts and Culture

Kansas City's Nelson-Atkins Museum of Art, one of the largest museums in the United States and ranked in the top 15, maintains a permanent collection that represents art from all civilizations and periods, from Sumeria to the present. Opened in 1933, the museum covers 20 landscaped acres and is home to the only Henry Moore Sculpture Garden outside the artist's native England. A new 165,000-square-foot expansion designed by internationally acclaimed architect Steven Holl is slated to open in 2007.

The Kemper Museum of Contemporary Art, built in 1994, presents rotating contemporary exhibits free of charge to the public. The Liberty Memorial Museum, conceived as a "monument to peace," is the nation's only public museum devoted solely to World War I and America's involvement in that conflict. Its dedication in 1921 brought together five Allied commanders who met for the first and only time in their lives. The Toy and Miniature Museum of Kansas City is one of only three museums of its kind in the country. The Kansas City Museum features hands-on science and history exhibits; its "If I Had a Hammer" program gives fourth through twelfth graders hands-on experience assembling a house. The museum's Science City at Union Station, a $234 million project that opened in 1999, combines the best of a museum, science center, theme park, and theater. Other museums in the city include the Black Archives of Mid-America, the Federal Reserve Bank Visitors Center, and the home and studio of the late painter, Thomas Hart Benton.

Kansas City, "the mother of swing and the nurturer of bebop," is noted for a distinctive jazz musical style, which consists of a two-four beat, predominance of saxophones, and background riffs. It has been played by musicians in local clubs since the early 1900s. The late Count Basie and Charlie "Bird" Parker, regarded as two of the greatest practitioners of the genre, began their careers in Kansas City. The Museums at 18th and Vine celebrate this heritage. The American Jazz Museum section is the first museum in the country devoted exclusively to this art form. The museum's interactive exhibits tell the story of "America's classical music" in an entertaining and educational format. In addition to in-depth exhibits on such greats as Count Basie, Ella Fitzgerald, and Charlie Parker, the museum includes artifacts such as a Charlie Parker saxophone and a discovery room where visitors can listen to jazz performances. In the evenings, visitors can swing into the Blue Room, a jazz club recognized by *Downbeat Magazine* in 2004 as one of the 100 greatest jazz clubs in the world.

Kansas City ranks third in the nation for professional theaters per capita, boasting more than 20 equity and community theater companies. The Gem Theater Cultural and Performing Arts Center, one of the Museums at 18th and Vine, is a historic structure. With its neon marquee, it has been transformed into a 500-seat state-of-the-art facility for musical and theatrical performances. The center also hosts dance theaters and multimedia events for the public.

The Missouri Repertory Theatre performs a seven-show season, hosting nationally known actors and performing a stage adaptation of Charles Dickens's *A Christmas Carol* each holiday season. Among the other theater companies in Kansas City are the Coterie Family Theatre, American Heartland Theatre, Quality Hill Playhouse, Unicorn Theatre, and Kansas City Repertory Theatre.

Folly Theatre, a former burlesque house refurbished in 1981, is the first theater to appear on the National Historic Register; it hosts professional theater productions. The Midland Center for the Performing Arts, also on the National Historic Register, is a 1920s movie palace that was refurbished and reopened in 1981. Touring Broadway shows are presented in this ornate structure, which is decorated with gold leaf overlays, Tiffany glass, and bronze chandeliers.

The Lyric Theater is the home of the Kansas City Symphony and Lyric Opera, which presents all of its performances in English, as well as the headquarters of the State Ballet of Missouri. The Heart of America Shakespeare Festival presents professional productions of Shakespeare's plays in Southmoreland Park in June and July. One of the nation's largest outdoor amphitheaters, the 7,795-seat Starlight Theatre is located in Swope Park and presents musicals and concerts in the summer.

Festivals and Holidays

Kansas City offers entertaining, educational, and flavorful festivals and events year-round. The culture and unique foods of many different countries are celebrated at the

Northland Ethnic Festival (April), Taiwanese Festival (May), Annual Greek Festival (June), Sugar Creek Slavic Festival (June), and Ethnic Enrichment Festival (August), and Kansas City Irish Festival (September). The "Rhythm&Ribs" Jazz Festival in June combines two of Kansas City's favorite things—barbeque and jazz. Food is also the theme of the Platte City BBQ Fest (June) and a festival introduced in 2005 that is sure to become a favorite: the Kansas City Chocolate Festival on October 1.

Other events celebrate Kansas City's Midwestern heritage: notably the Prairie Village Art Show (June), Heart of America Quilt Festival (October), and Missouri Town 1855 Festival of Arts, Crafts, and Music (October). There are fairs aplenty, including the Platte County Fair (July), the oldest continuously running fair west of the Mississippi. The more arts-minded visitor will appreciate the Women' Playwriting Festival and the Kansas City Comedy Arts Fest in March, the Filmmakers Jubilee Film Festival in April, and the variety of music and theater festivals throughout the summer.

Autumn brings a full calendar of harvest festivals and horse racing. In November the 100-foot-tall Mayor's Christmas Tree is illuminated by 7,200 white lights, with 47,500 more strung throughout Crown Center Square. After Christmas the tree is made into ornaments for the next year, which are sold with proceeds going to the Mayor's Christmas Tree Fund. Christmas in Kansas City would not be the same without the annual production of "A Christmas Carol" by the Kansas City Repertory Theatre or the "Festival of Lights" at Country Club Plaza.

Sports for the Spectator

Kansas City athletes compete in three of the most modern sports facilities in the United States. The Truman Sports Complex consists of 40,000-seat Kauffman Stadium and 79,000-seat Arrowhead Stadium. Arrowhead is the home of the Kansas City Chiefs in the Western Division of the American Conference of the National Football League, and of the Major League Soccer team the Kansas City Wizards, MLS Cup Champions in 2000. Kauffman Stadium is the home of the Kansas City Royals of the Central Division of baseball's American League. Kemper Arena, close to downtown Kansas City, features an award-winning circular and pillarless structure that allows unobstructed and intimate viewing from all locations. The Kansas City Blades of the International Hockey League play home games at Kemper Arena. Professional golfer Tom Watson, a Kansas City native, is affectionately known as the city's "fourth sports franchise."

Sprint Center, the 20,000-seat arena scheduled to open in 2007, will house the National Collegiate Basketball Hall of Fame. Kansas City is also headquarters of the National Association of Intercollegiate Athletics (NAIA) and the Fel-

lowship of Christian Athletes (FCA). Since the Kansas City Speedway was inaugurated in 2001, racing fans have enjoyed NASCAR, Indy Racing, and Truck series events at the 1.5 mile tri-oval track.

Sports for the Participant

The beautiful and popular Kansas City parks offer an outlet for sports enthusiasts who enjoy fishing, golf, hiking, jogging, swimming, boating, ice skating, or tennis. Swope Park, the second largest city park in the nation, provides two 18-hole golf courses, a swimming pool, and a braille trail. The 250-acre Shawnee Mission Park is one of the best spots for sailing and canoeing. Fishing and sailing are available at nine public access lakes within an hour's drive. The area has facilities for amateur auto racing as well as horse- and dog-race tracks.

Those who enjoy gambling spend time on the Missouri River just north of downtown, where four riverboats offer a number of opportunities to court Lady Luck. There is no admission charge to board the boats, most of which have cruise times every two hours from 8 a.m. to 3 a.m. and offer numerous dining choices and virtually nonstop entertainment.

Shopping and Dining

The City Market, at the north end of Main Street, offers shopping in a bazaar-like atmosphere. A Saturday morning trip to City Market for produce is a local tradition. Further south on Main Street, the Country Club Plaza, developed by Jessie Clyde Nichols in 1922, enjoys the distinctions of being "America's Original Shopping Center" and Kansas City's most popular tourist attraction, welcoming 10 million visitors each year. Located five miles south of downtown, the Plaza covers 55 acres and contains almost 200 retail and service businesses, including 40 restaurants. The Plaza, with its tile-roofed, pastel-colored buildings and imported filigree ironwork, borrows heavily from Hispanic architecture in honor of Seville, Spain, Kansas City's sister city. The European ambiance is enhanced with a number of towers, fountains, and horse-drawn carriages. The Plaza inaugurated America's outdoor Christmas lighting tradition in 1926.

Hallmark Cards's Crown Center, described as a city within a city, is a one-half billion-dollar downtown complex of shops, restaurants, hotels, offices, apartments, and condominiums over 85 acres. The Crown Center Shops occupy three levels topped by Halls Crown Center, a 100,000-square-foot specialty store. Crown Center revitalized the inner city by creating a downtown suburb where families can live and work. Town Pavilion, a tri-level shopping complex at the base of a major office building downtown, is connected by walkways to other office complexes. Just a couple miles from downtown lies Westport, Kansas City's historic district, featuring boutiques, restaurants, and nightly entertainment. In nearby

Olathe, Kansas, shoppers converge at the 130 outlet stores of the Olathe Great Mall of the Great Plains.

Kansas City barbecue is one of America's most savory contributions to world cuisine. Since 1908, when Henry Perry first started selling 25-cent slabs of barbecued meat cooked on an outdoor pit and wrapped in newspaper, Kansas City barbecue has held its own alongside traditional Texas and Carolina versions. The process requires that the meat be dry rubspiced, cooked slowly over wood—preferably hickory—for as long as 18 hours, and slathered with rich, sweet-tangy sauce. More than 90 Kansas City barbecue establishments serve ribs, pork, ham, mutton, sausage, and even fish. Each establishment prides itself on its own unique recipe for sauce; the most famous sauce, KC Masterpiece, was developed in the 1980s by Rich Davis. The barbecue restaurant owned by the legendary Arthur Bryant has been described by food critic Calvin Trillin as "the single, best restaurant in the world."

Kansas City ranks number three in the United States for sheer number of restaurants. Elegant dining is possible at establishments like the Savoy Grill, Le Fou Frog, Fedora Café & Bar, and the Peppercorn Duck Club, famous for its rotisserie duck and ultra chocolatta bar.

Visitor Information: Kansas City Convention and Visitors Association, 1100 Main St., Ste. 2200, Kansas City, MO 64105; telephone (816)221-5242; toll-free (800)767-7700

Convention Facilities

Kansas City is a popular convention destination, ranking among the top meeting centers in the nation. The Kansas City Convention and Entertainment Centers, site of most major functions in the city, consist of H. Roe Bartle Hall and Municipal Auditorium and covers a four-block downtown area. The two buildings are linked by an underground walkway that is also connected to a parking garage and three hotels. A renovation project that ended in January 2005 reconfigured more than half the facility into 26 meeting rooms, offering more than 67,704 square feet of meeting space. An additional expansion project will spend $135 million by 2007 to add 135,000 square feet, including a 46,450-square-foot grand ballroom/multipurpose space and 35,000 square feet of pre-function space. A previous expansion of Bartle Hall made it the largest contiguous column-free exhibit space in the nation.

Located near the convention center is the American Royal Center, a 14-acre complex that includes Kemper Arena, the American Royal Arena, Hale Arena, and American Royal Museum. The newly expanded Kemper Arena is the site of large functions such as political conventions.

Additional convention facilities for both large and small groups can be found at metropolitan area hotels and motels, where more than 17,000 rooms are available.

Convention Information: Kansas City Convention and Visitors Association, 1100 Main St., Ste. 2200, Kansas City, MO 64105; telephone (816)221-5242; toll-free (800)767-7700

Transportation

Approaching the City

Kansas City International Airport, 17 miles northwest of downtown, is served by 15 commercial carriers with daily direct and connecting flights from all major United States cities and from points abroad. In 2005 Kansas City International is currently undergoing a 10-year, $1.2 billion improvement program.

Primary highway routes into Kansas City are north-south I-35 and I-29, which join U.S. 71 leading into the city. The I-435 bypass links with east-west I-70 from the south.

At 2200 Main Street, Amtrak provides passenger rail service to two stops in the metropolitan area. Greyhound and Jefferson bus lines, headquartered at 1101 Troost Avenue, serve destinations around the country.

Traveling in the City

Kansas City's streets are laid out in a basic grid pattern except in areas contiguous with the Kansas and Missouri rivers, where one-way streets predominate. The principal downtown thoroughfare is Main Street, which runs north to south. Beginning at the Missouri River, east-west streets are numbered in ascending order southward through the city. State Line Road separates Kansas City, Missouri, from Kansas City, Kansas; the two cities are connected via I-70.

The Kansas City Area Transportation Authority operates the Metro, a public bus system that serves most metropolitan area cities. The new MAX, Metro Area Express, connects the River Market, downtown Kansas City, Crown Center, and Country Club Plaza, carrying travelers along exclusive lanes through coordinated traffic signals.

Communications

Newspapers and Magazines

The major daily newspaper in Kansas City is the morning *The Kansas City Star.* Several community newspapers also circulate weekly and monthly, including *Dos Mundos* bilingual newspaper. *Ingram's* is a monthly business and lifestyle magazine.

A number of magazines and journals are published in Kansas City. Among them are the nationally distributed *Flower and Garden Magazine* (the magazine's demonstration garden is also located in Kansas City) and *Fishing World*.

Television and Radio

Five television stations—major network affiliates and one PBS—are based in Kansas City. Broadcasts are also received from stations in neighboring Fairway, Kansas, and Shawnee Mission, Kansas. Five AM and FM radio stations in Kansas City broadcast a range of program formats, including music, news, and information; many more are available from nearby cities.

Media Information: Kansas City Star, 1729 Grand Blvd., Kansas City, MO 64108; telephone (816)234-4636

Kansas City Online

City of Kansas City home page. Available www.kcmo.org

Economic Development Corporation of Kansas City, Missouri. Available www.edckc.com

Experience Kansas City. Available www.experiencekc.com

Greater Kansas City Chamber of Commerce. Available www.kcchamber.com

Kansas City Area Development Council. Available www.smartkc.com

Kansas City Convention and Visitors Association. Available www.visitkc.com

Kansas City Star. Available www.kansascity.com

Missouri Department of Economic Development. Available www.ecodev.state.mo.us

Missouri Department of Elementary and Secondary Education. Available www.dese.mo.gov

Selected Bibliography

Christo, Wrapped Walk Ways, Loose Park, Kansas City, Missouri, 1977-78: Essay by Ellen R. Goheen; photos by Wolfgang Volz (New York: H.N. Abrams, 1978)

DeAngelo, Dory, *Kansas City, A Historical Handbook* (Kansas City, MO: Two Lane Press, 1995)

Fleisher, Mark S., *Dead End Kids: Gang Girls and the Boys They Know* (University of Wisconsin Press, 1998)

Hemingway, Ernest, *Ernest Hemingway, Cub Reporter; Kansas City Star Stories* (Pittsburgh: University of Pittsburgh Press, 1970)

Kansas City: A Celebration of the Heartland, (Kansas City: Hallmark Cards, Inc., 1991)

Pearson, Nathan W., Jr., *Goin' to Kansas City (Music in American Life)* (University of Illinois Press, 1988)

St. Louis

The City in Brief

Founded: 1763 (incorporated 1822)

Head Official: Mayor Francis G. Slay (D) (since 2001)

City Population
  1980: 453,085
  1990: 396,685
  2000: 348,189
  2003 estimate: 332,223
  Percent change, 1990–2000: − 12.2%
  U.S. rank in 1980: 26th
  U.S. rank in 1990: 34th
  U.S. rank in 2000: 53rd

Metropolitan Area Population
  1980: 2,377,000
  1990: 2,492,348
  2000: 2,698,687

Percent change, 1990–2000: 4.6%
U.S. rank in 1980: 14th
U.S. rank in 1990: Not reported
U.S. rank in 2000: 18th

Area: 62 square miles (2000)
Elevation: 535 feet above sea level
Average Annual Temperature: 55.4° F
Average Annual Precipitation: 46.06 inches of rain; 23.5 inches snow

Major Economic Sectors: Services, wholesale and retail trade, manufacturing, government
Unemployment Rate: 6.3% (February 2005)
Per Capita Income: $16,108 (1999)

2002 FBI Crime Index Total: Not reported

Major Colleges and Universities: Washington University; Saint Louis University

Daily Newspaper: *St. Louis Post-Dispatch*

Introduction

St. Louis, the second largest city in Missouri, is the center of the metropolitan statistical area comprised of Franklin, Jefferson, Lincoln, St. Charles, St. Louis, and Warren counties in Missouri and Bond, Calhoun, Clinton, Jersey, Macoupin, Madison, Monroe, St. Clair, and Washington counties in Illinois. Since its founding St. Louis has undergone several significant stages of development, which parallel the nation's westward expansion, symbolized by the city's famous Gateway Arch. St. Louis enjoys a rich and culturally diverse life and a revitalized downtown commercial district. As one of the first regions in the country to confront defense cutbacks in the 1990s and develop plans for dealing with them, the St. Louis area has emerged as a national laboratory for the post-Cold-War economy.

Geography and Climate

Located at the confluence of the Mississippi and Missouri rivers, St. Louis is near the geographic center of the United States. Its modified continental climate is characterized by four seasons without prolonged periods of extreme heat or high humidity. Alternate invasions of moist air from the Gulf of Mexico and cold air masses from Canada produce a variety of weather conditions. Winters are brisk and seldom severe; annual snowfall averages about eighteen inches. Hot days with temperatures of 100 degrees or higher occur on the average of five days per year. Severe storms are often accompanied by hail and damaging winds, and tornadoes have caused destruction and loss of life.

Area: 62 square miles (2000)

Elevation: 535 feet above sea level

Average Temperatures: January, 29.5° F; July, 80.5° F; annual average, 55.4° F

Average Annual Precipitation: 46.06 inches of rain; 23.5 inches of snow

History

Fur Trade Establishes St. Louis Townsite

The first known attempted settlement near present-day St. Louis was the Jesuit Mission of St. Francis Xavier, established in 1700 at the mouth of the Riviere des Peres (River of the Fathers). Two Native American bands settled at the site with the Jesuit party, but within three years the mission was abandoned and no permanent settlement was attempted again in that area for more than 60 years.

Around 1760 the New Orleans firm of Maxent, Laclede & Company secured exclusive rights from France to trade with Native Americans in the Missouri River Valley and the territory west of the Mississippi River as far north as the St. Peter River. Pierre Laclede Liguest selected the present site of St. Louis for a trading post in December 1763. Laclede said his intent was to establish ''one of the finest cities in America.'' The village was named for the patron saint of France's King Louis XV. North of the village were Native American ceremonial mounds; these mounds stood outside the original village boundary but were eventually leveled as the city expanded. The largest, known as Big Mound, was located at the present-day St. Louis intersection of Mound and Broadway streets.

In its early years St. Louis was nicknamed *Pain Court* (short of bread) because of the absence of local agriculture to supply such staples as bread flour. Laclede's fur business prospered but in time France lost control of the territory and the ruling Hispanic government withdrew Laclede's exclusive fur-trading rights. This opened the city to new settlers and new businesses. During the American Revolutionary War, the Mississippi-Ohio River route was protected when soldiers and townsmen successfully rebuffed an attack by British General Haldimand's troops; this victory secured the strategic importance of St. Louis. After the Revolution Mississippi River pirates disrupted trade on the river but in 1788 boats carrying fighting crews from New Orleans defeated the pirates. St. Louis quickly emerged as a trading center as the village grew into an oasis of wealth, culture, and privilege.

American Influence Brings Westward Expeditions

This early period of splendor ended in 1803 when France, which had regained control of the surrounding territory, sold the vast tract of land to the new government of the United States in a land deal known as the Louisiana Purchase. American migrants soon brought gambling, violence, and mayhem into the community. Nearby Bloody Island gained a national reputation as a place of infamous duels, such as the one in 1817 when Thomas Hart Benton shot and killed a man. The rough-and-tumble village life eventually stabilized itself; the *Missouri Gazette,* St. Louis's first newspaper, and the opening of the first English school helped to improve the local environs.

St. Louis-based fur trappers and traders were the source of great local wealth; the Missouri Fur Company was founded in 1809 and dominated the Missouri Valley for the next 40 years. The city became a logical point of departure for explorers setting off on westward journeys. The most famous of these undertakings is the Lewis and Clark expedition of 1804 to 1806. Eventually as many as 50 wagons a day crossed the Mississippi River at St. Louis on the trek westward, and the arrival of the first steamboat from New Orleans in 1817 was the first sign of the city's importance as a river trading center.

St. Louis was incorporated as a village in 1808 and as a city in 1822. The city asserted its political dominance early in Missouri's public life, but tension between businessmen and farmers in outlying areas resulted in the election of Alexander McNair as the state's first governor and the eventual establishment of the state government in Jefferson City.

Industry and Immigration Prompt Development

St. Louis's first manufacturing enterprises were operated by craftsmen in small shops, but by mid-century the city was an industrial center as the development of flour mills, ironworks, and factories for the production of foodstuffs and manufactured goods fueled the economy. Between 1832 and 1850 more than 30,000 German immigrants started new lives in St. Louis. As industry brought another wave of new wealth, many of the city's existing civic, educational, and cultural institutions were established. During this period, credit for introduction of the highball, Southern Comfort, and Planter's Punch was attributed to local bartenders.

Serious damage to the city's downtown resulted when a fire on the steamboat *White Cloud* in 1849 spread to the wharf district and destroyed 15 blocks in the commercial district; estimates of property damage ran as high as $6 million. St. Louis rebuilt by replacing log and wood buildings with masonry; public health issues such as sewage disposal and contaminated water were also addressed.

At the outset of the Civil War St. Louis was divided in its sympathies. The city's role was decided when General Nathaniel Lyon led the Union Army action, surrounding Missouri state troops at Camp Jackson. St. Louis became a base of Federal operations, and the city benefited from the purchase of manufactured goods by the Chief Quartermaster that totaled $180 million. St. Louis's industrial capability increased by almost 300 percent in the decade between 1860 and 1870.

Prosperity, Culture Draw World Notice

In the post-Civil War period railroads replaced steamboats as the primary transportation mode, and a new route to the east was opened. The Eads Bridge, the world's first arched steel truss bridge, was completed in 1874 and the city's first Union Station was built in 1878. The new prosperity was diverted in part to cultural enrichments such as the Missouri Botanical Gardens and Tower Grove Park. The St. Louis Symphony Orchestra, the nation's second oldest, was founded in 1880.

The Mercantile Library Association, which opened in 1846, began purchasing and commissioning original art works. Joseph Pulitzer's *Globe-Democrat* and Carl Schurz's *Westliche Post* were two of many newspapers that reported on the political and social issues of the day. St. Louis was, in 1876, the first city west of the Mississippi River to host a national political convention. In 1877 St. Louis's city charter separated it from the county and freed the city from state government control except for general laws.

By the turn of the century St. Louis had a population of 575,000 residents. In 1904 the city hosted the Louisiana Purchase Exposition, which focused national and world attention on St. Louis. Many European nations were represented in yearlong festivities that were considered a success. The first Olympiad to be held in the United States took place in St. Louis in 1904. The ice cream cone, the hot dog, and iced tea mark their beginnings at this world's fair. In 1926 an $87 million bond issue improved the city's infrastructure and financed the construction of new public buildings. A second bond issue in 1934 continued the improvements. New industrial initiatives in the late 1930s helped St. Louis pull out of the Great Depression.

In 1965 the Gateway Arch became a part of the St. Louis skyline, marking the spot where Laclede first established St. Louis. After failing to solve public housing problems in the 1950s, 1960s, and 1970s, the city emerged in the 1980s as a model for urban housing renewal, with stable neighborhoods of rehabilitated structures. A renovated warehouse district near the Gateway Arch called Laclede's Landing attracts tourists to the historic roots of modern St. Louis.

St. Louis Approaches the Millennium

In the summer of 1993 St. Louis suffered extensive damage from flooding when the Missouri and Mississippi rivers joined forces just north of the city and swept down over its protective levees in some of the worst flooding in the country's history. Damage in the flood region was estimated at more than $10 billion.

Also in 1993, Democrat Freeman Bosley, Jr. was elected St. Louis's first African American mayor. Four years later African American police chief Clarence Harmon became mayor after an acrimonious campaign in which the vast majority of white voters preferred Mr. Harmon, while Mr. Bosley claimed the support of African American ministers and civil-rights activists. Race relations remain a thorny issue in St. Louis, but city leaders continue to address the problem.

St. Louis in the New Millennium

St. Louis entered the twenty-first century recognizing itself as a big city without some of the major big city problems. Looking past a downturn in population and instead focusing on a vibrant future, St. Louis has attracted major companies, revitalized the downtown area, and improved the educational system. Renovations, remodels, and additions to St. Louis arts and history establishments, parks, buildings, infrastructure, and athletic venues have modernized the city, while traditional values continue to reign supreme in this mid-America city. Mayor Francis Slay, in one of his Neighborhood Newsletters, stated it well, "... the people of St. Louis embody the values that make America a great country. We applaud hard work, dedication and effort. We judge players by their performance on the field—not where they came from. We demand integrity, selflessness, and teamwork. We never give up, no matter how hard the task."

Historical Information: Missouri Historical Society, PO Box 11940, St. Louis, MO 63112-0040; telephone (314)454-3150; fax (314) 454-3162; email info@hohistory .org. City of St. Louis, 1200 Market St., St. Louis, MO 63103; telephone (314)622-4000

Population Profile

Metropolitan Area Residents
1980: 2,377,000
1990: 2,492,348
2000: 2,698,687
Percent change, 1990–2000: 4.6%
U.S. rank in 1980: 14th
U.S. rank in 1990: Not reported
U.S. rank in 2000: 18th

City Residents
1980: 453,085
1990: 396,685
2000: 348,189
2003 estimate: 332,223
Percent change, 1990–2000: 12.2%
U.S. rank in 1980: 26th
U.S. rank in 1990: 34th (State rank: 2nd)
U.S. rank in 2000: 53rd (State rank: 2nd)

Density: 5,622.9 people per square mile (2000)

Racial and ethnic characteristics (2000)
   White: 152,666
   Black or African American: 178,266
   American Indian and Alaska Native: 950
   Asian: 6,891
   Native Hawaiian and Pacific Islander: 94
   Hispanic (may be of any race): 7,022
   Other: 2,783

Percent of residents born in state: 70.3% (2000)

Age characteristics (2000)
   Population under 5 years old: 23,477
   Population 5 to 9 years old: 26,709
   Population 10 to 14 years old: 25,014
   Population 15 to 19 years old: 24,729
   Population 20 to 24 years old: 26,541
   Population 25 to 34 years old: 54,395
   Population 35 to 44 years old: 53,144
   Population 45 to 54 years old: 41,260
   Population 55 to 59 years old: 13,466
   Population 60 to 64 years old: 11,612
   Population 65 to 74 years old: 23,047
   Population 75 to 84 years old: 17,482
   Population 85 years and over: 7,313
   Median age: 33.7 years

Births (2002)
   Total number: 5,145

Deaths (2002)
   Total number: 4,104 (of which, 71 were infants under
      the age of 1 year)

Money income (1999)
   Per capita income: $16,108 (1999)
   Median household income: $27,156
   Total households: 147,076

Number of households with income of . . .
   less than $10,000: 28,384
   $10,000 to $14,999: 13,927
   $15,000 to $24,999: 26,238
   $25,000 to $34,999: 21,352
   $35,000 to $49,999: 22,803
   $50,000 to $74,999: 19,692
   $75,000 to $99,999: 8,130
   $100,000 to $149,999: 4,406
   $150,000 to $199,999: 1,120
   $200,000 or more: 1,234

Percent of families below poverty level: 9.2% (56.2% of
   which were female householder families with related
   children under 5 years)

2002 FBI Crime Index Total: Not reported

Municipal Government

St. Louis functions with a mayor-council form of government; the mayor and 29 aldermen are elected to four-year terms. Voters choose a mayor in April of odd-numbered years; half the number of aldermen, each from a single ward, are selected every two years. Established as both a city and a county, the city of St. Louis operates under home rule, but St. Louis County, without home rule, conforms to Missouri's state requirements for county government.

Head Official: Mayor Francis G. Slay (D) (since 2001; current term expires April 2009)

Total Number of City Employees: 7,076 (2005)

City Information: City of St. Louis, Office of the Mayor, 200 City Hall, 1200 Market Streets, St. Louis, MO 63103; telephone (314)622-3201

Economy

Major Industries and Commercial Activity

St. Louis is the world headquarters of 19 *Fortune* 1000 companies, including Anheuser-Busch Companies, Inc., Emerson Electric, May Department Stores, Graybor Electric, and Monsanto Company. Greater St. Louis ranks thirteenth in the United States as a headquarters location for *Fortune* 500 companies. The city boasts three of the nation's 100 fastest-growing companies; Talx, Panera Bread, and Engineered Support Systems. St. Louis supports a strong manufacturing sector; the three major American automakers—General Motors, Chrysler, and Ford—operate assembly plants in the area. St. Louis is also the base for the Eighth Federal Reserve District Bank and several national insurance and brokerage firms.

In March 2002 *Fortune* magazine recognized St. Louis as "among the regional hubs in the United States for both agricultural and health care biotechnology"; the city is emerging as a center for major new economy industries. World class research and development in plant and life sciences is conducted by industry giants such as Pfizer and Centocor; St. Louis is becoming known as the heart of the bio-belt for progress in this arena. The city boasts of a high concentration of information technology jobs. With an already-strong manufacturing base, St. Louis is a center for advanced manufacturing; the area boasts of 190,000 jobs and 4,000 establishments applying advanced technology innovations.

Items and goods produced: meat, bread, beer, flour, granary products, malt, liquors, chemicals, drugs, paints and varnish, machinery, refrigerators, clothing, iron and steel, street and railroad cars, shoes, paper products, hardware, millinery, trucks, automotive parts, petroleum and coal, non-ferrous metals, stone, clay and glass, furniture, aircraft, aerospace equipment

Incentive Programs—New and Existing Companies

Local programs—The St. Louis Regional Chamber and Growth Association (RCGA) is the economic development organization for the Greater St. Louis region. Developers may receive assistance with renovations and new construction projects through the St. Louis Real Estate Tax Abatement program.

State programs—The State of Missouri offers a variety of incentives to assist new and existing businesses. Financing, taxation, and incentive programs available through the state of Missouri include the Missouri Build-Incentive Program, by which the state provides state income-tax credits to businesses locating to Missouri or expanding their business. Eligible businesses include manufacturing-type companies that invest a minimum of $15 million and create at least 100 new jobs within 3 years, and office projects that invest a minimum of $10 million and create at least 500 new jobs within 3 years. The Missouri Small Business Development Center and the University of Missouri provide business counseling, new and ongoing employee training, and online resources for small businesses. Missouri offers a variety of programs that grant tax credits based upon factors such as job creation and/or capital investment. Examples include enterprise zones, and Missouri New and Expanding Business Facility Tax Credits. Tax increment financing is also available.

Job training programs—Several programs are designed to improve worker productivity, such as grants to businesses that provide training to employees. Comprehensive training and employment services are offered by the Missouri Career Centers. Federal programs such as the Job Training Partnership Act are also available. The Missouri Customized Job Training Program is designed to assist new and expanding businesses in recruiting, screening, testing and training workers, and to help existing employers retain their current workforce when faced with needed upgrading and re-training. On-the-job-training is also available, with up to 50 percent of trainee wages being reimbursable. The Ozarks Technical College New Jobs Training Program provides training funding for new and expanding companies that create new jobs. Services include customized training, adult basic education, on-the-job training, and general occupational skill training. Funding is based on the number of new jobs created and the average annual salary of the new jobs.

Development Projects

St. Louis has a variety of development projects underway or recently completed to restore the city's history and revitalize it for the future. In 2005, ongoing and proposed development investments totaled more than $4.5 billion dollars. Rehabilitation and new development projects include construction of commercial and office buildings, hotels and entertainment centers, residential facilities, education centers, industrial manufacturing sites, institutional and health care centers, parks and recreation, and community and government facilities.

The massive Forest Park, site of the 1904 World's Fair and the home to St. Louis' main cultural institutions, has undergone a $100 million transformation. Once stagnant ponds and lakes are now connected by a river that greatly improves park aesthetics. More than 7,500 new trees were planted, historic areas and buildings were preserved, and recreational facilities and park facilities were upgraded.

The St. Louis Commerce Center was recently completed. GPX, Inc is the main tenant of the $15 million center, occupying 180,000 of the center's 486,000 square feet.

The home of the Cardinals will be destroyed and completely rebuilt. The new Busch Stadium will offer seating for 46,000 fans when the facility opens for the 2006 baseball season. Adjacent to the new Busch Stadium and in the footprint of the old stadium will be BallPark Village, a $300 million mixed use development that will include residential and office space, an aquarium, and a Cardinals museum.

The Lambert-St. Louis International Airport is expanding. The first of three phases in the expansion plan includes a new 9,000 foot taxiway. The $10 million project is expected to be complete in November 2005 and will allow the airport to manage simultaneous landings even in inclement weather.

Economic Development Information: St. Louis Regional Chamber and Growth Association, One Metropolitan Square, Suite 1300, St. Louis, MO 63102; telephone (314)231-5555; fax (314)206-3277; email RCGAInfo @stlrcga.org

Commercial Shipping

St. Louis is a primary national center for air, land, and water transportation networks. Among the commodities shipped through the city are coal, grain, cement, petroleum products, and chemicals. One of the nation's leading rail centers, St. Louis is served by six Class I, two regional, and three switching railroad lines. Four interstate highways converge in St. Louis, affording trucking companies overnight to third-morning access to markets throughout the country. Many of these firms maintain terminals within the Commercial Truck Zone, which covers all or portions of a seven-county area. St. Louis is the nation's third-largest inland port, as well as the country's northernmost port with ice-free access year round; the port connects St. Louis via the Mississippi, Illinois, and Missouri river system with New Orleans and international waterways. St. Louis waterways offer more than 100 docks and terminal facilities; 32 million tons of freight are handled annually.

Air freight service is available at Lambert-St. Louis International Airport. MidAmerica Airport in St. Clair County in Illinois provides state-of-the-art facilities for cargo.

Labor Force and Employment Outlook

Experienced workers are available in St. Louis. During the 1990s thousands of jobs were lost as major employers downsized, moved out, or merged. In response to the state and nation-wide economic downturn of the early 2000s, the Missouri state legislature has passed several legislative bills to stimulate economic growth and decrease unemployment. The state as a whole continues to experience stability and growth, recognizing four times the national growth rate in the manufacturing sector. In the northern metro St. Louis region, several areas show strong momentum with St. Charles, Warren, and Franklin counties ranked as top performers. According to a Missouri Department of Economic Development news release in April 2005, St. Louis also continues to experience decreasing unemployment and increasing employment growth. In November 2004, it was reported that the city experienced the second fastest job growth year-to-year for the nation. Main industries in the St. Louis area include: aviation, biotechnology, chemicals, electrical utilities, food and beverage manufacturing, refining, research, telecommunications, and transportation.

The following is a summary of data regarding the St. Louis metropolitan area labor force, 2004 annual averages.

Size of non-agricultural labor force: 1,322,800

Number of workers employed in . . .
    natural resources and mining: 80,500
    manufacturing: 144,700
    trade, transportation and public utilities: 253,200
    information: 29,600
    financial accounting: 77,600
    professional and business services: 179,800
    educational and health services: 195,700
    leisure and hospitality services: 136,900
    other services: 58,000
    government: 167,000

Average hourly earnings of production workers employed in manufacturing: $21.90

Unemployment rate: 6.3% (February 2005)

Largest employers	Number of employees
BJC Health Systems	21,468
Boeing International Defense Systems	15,500
Scott Air Force Base	12,600
Washington University in St. Louis	12,324
Wal-Mart Stores	12,250
SSM Health Care	11,951

Largest employers	Number of employees
U.S. Postal Service	11,447
Schnuck Markets, Inc.	10,800
SBC Communications.	9,250

Cost of Living

Among the nation's top 20 metro areas, St. Louis boasts the second most affordable housing market and one of the lowest costs of living in the country. A typical management transferee home—a 2,200 sq. ft. home with four bedrooms, 2.5 baths, a family room, and two-car garage— could be purchased at an average price of $229,325.

The following is a summary of data regarding several key cost of living factors in the St. Louis area.

2004 (3rd Quarter) ACCRA Average House Price: $241,522

2004 (3rd Quarter) ACCRA Cost of Living Index: 100.7 (U.S. average = 100.0)

State income tax rate: graduated from 1.5% to 6.0%

State sales tax rate: 4.225%

Local income tax rate: 1.0%

Local sales tax rate: 1.375%

Property tax rate: personal property is assessed at 33-1/3%. Rates vary by tax jurisdiction

Economic Information: St. Louis Regional Commerce and Growth Association, One Metropolitan Square, Suite 1300, St. Louis, MO 63102; telephone (314)231-5555; fax (314)206-3277. State of Missouri, Department of Economic Development, P.O. Box 1157, Jefferson City, MO 65102-0118. Missouri Department of Labor and Industrial Relations, 3315 W. Truman Blvd., PO Box 504, Jefferson City, MO 65102; telephone (573)751-4091; fax (573) 751-4135

Education and Research

Elementary and Secondary Schools

Education in the St. Louis area was ranked fourth by *Forbes* magazine in its list of 'Best Places With the Best Education' in February 2003. The St. Louis Public Schools are administered by a seven-member, nonpartisan, elected board of education that appoints a superintendent and serves a six-year term without compensation. The district received an $8.4 million federal grant for elementary school programs. The

Clyde C. Miller Academy, which teaches technical and career training to 800 students, opened in 2003.

The following is a summary of data regarding St. Louis public schools as of the 2003–2004 school year.

Total enrollment: 37,563

Number of facilities
  elementary schools: 59
  middle schools: 21
  senior high schools: 10
  other: 5

Student/teacher ratio: elementary, 23:1; middle school 27:1; high school 33:1

Teacher salaries
  average: $41,388

Funding per pupil: $9,995

The St. Louis area has 115 public school districts offering everything from innovative urban magnet to excellent suburban school programs. More than 300 private schools are available in the St. Louis area.

Colleges and Universities

St. Louis is home to 12 universities, 8 professional schools, 9 graduate schools, 8 two-year colleges and 89 vocational schools. Washington University, a private independent institution, offers 90 programs and 1,500 courses in such fields as business, architecture, engineering, social work, and teacher education; the university operates schools of medicine, dentistry, and law. More than 6,500 undergraduates and 5,000 graduates attend this research university. Saint Louis University, established in 1818 and affiliated with the Roman Catholic Church, also operates schools of medicine and law and offers 50 graduate and 86 undergraduate programs in its 13 colleges/schools. Sixteen NCAA Division I athletics teams including baseball, basketball, swimming, and cross country compete for the University. Webster University, located in suburban Webster Groves, awards baccalaureate and master's degrees in 13 bachelors and 9 graduate programs. The University of Missouri at Saint Louis is both a graduate and undergraduate institution and part of the state university system. More than 16,000 students attend classes on the 300-acre campus; The University of Missouri at St. Louis is the third largest university in Missouri. Southern Illinois University at Edwardsville, also a state university, is in neighboring Edwardsville, Illinois.

Fontbonne College, Harris-Stowe State College, Maryville University, Missouri Baptist University, and Saint Louis Christian College are four-year institutions located in the St. Louis area; the St. Louis Conservatory of Music offers both graduate and undergraduate programs. Theological schools in the city include Covenant Theological Seminary, Concordia Seminary and Eden Theological Seminary. St. Louis Community College is the largest community college in Missouri and one of the largest in the United States; the college's three campuses offer college transfers, career and developmental programs, and non-credit courses. There are several large technical and vocational schools in the region.

Libraries and Research Centers

A variety of public and private libraries are maintained in St. Louis by various organizations and institutions. The Saint Louis Public Library operates a main facility, a bookmobile, and 15 branches with holdings of 2.8 million book volumes and bound periodicals, periodical titles, and CDs, microfiches, films, audio- and videotapes, slides, maps, and art reproductions. Special collections include African American history, genealogy, architecture, and federal and state documents. The Saint Louis County Library, with 19 branches and 9 bookmobiles, maintains a primary facility housing more than 2.3 million books and federal, state, and county documents; the library also offers a special collection in genealogy. The Missouri Historical Society holds a reference collection on topics pertaining to regional and state history.

Most area colleges and universities maintain substantial campus libraries; among the most extensive is the Washington University Libraries system.

The city is fast becoming a center for the bio-tech industry; the industry is supported by several research facilities in this area. Monsanto's multimillion-dollar agricultural headquarters and Life Science Research Center are both based in St. Louis, comprising one of the world's largest and most sophisticated facilities searching for ways to improve agriculture through biotechnology and genetic engineering. The Donald Danforth Plant Science Center is another major component in the area's biotech development, along with the 40,000 square foot plant and life sciences incubator, the Nidus Center.

The Sigma-Aldrich Corp Life Science Technology Center is a $57 million, four-story research and technology center near its headquarters in mid-town St. Louis. The center is home to 220 life science chemists and also serves as a corporate learning center. The 150,000-square-foot building makes possible continuing technical discovery that builds on Sigma-Aldrich's half-century of success in advancing life through science through development of life science and high-tech products.

Public Library Information: Saint Louis Public Library, 1301 Olive Street, St. Louis, MO 63103; telephone (314)241-2288; fax (314)539-0393. Saint Louis County Library, 1640 S. Lindbergh Blvd., St. Louis, MO 63131; telephone (314)994-3300; fax (314)997-7602

Health Care

As one of the country's leading medical care centers, St. Louis is served by more than 50 hospitals, two of which—the Washington University Medical Center and the St. Louis University Hospital—are top-rated teaching facilities. Providing a range of general and specialized services is Barnes-Jewish Hospital; the hospital was ranked 8th among the nation's best hospitals by *U.S. News and World Report*. St. Louis Children's Hospital was ranked as the 10th best children's hospital in the nation in *Child* magazine's 2005 rankings.

Recreation

Sightseeing

The Gateway Arch, which rises 630 feet above the banks of the Mississippi River, is the starting point of a tour of St. Louis. Designed by Eero Saarinen and commemorating the nineteenth-century westward movement and St. Louis's role in settling the frontier, the Gateway Arch is the nation's tallest memorial. Beneath the Arch is the Old Courthouse, where the Dred Scott case was heard. A proud Greek revival structure, its dome was a forerunner of the style in public architecture that would sweep the country. The building holds displays relating to the Scott case and is home to the Museum of Westward Expansion, which documents the westward movement and life in St. Louis in the 1800s.

An attraction popular with kids of all ages, Six Flags St. Louis is an amusement park offering thrilling rides and attractions. The St. Louis Zoo in Forest Park houses more than 11,400 animals in naturalistic settings. New in 2005 is the Fragile Forest, which features chimpanzees, orangutans and lowland gorillas in an outdoor habitat. The zoo also features an insectarium, Children's Zoo, and Big Cat Country, a habitat for feline predators. Opposite from the zoo is the newly expanded Missouri History Museum. The Museum's featured exhibit celebrates St. Louis' history-making 1904 World's Fair with documents, sights and sounds that bring the century-old event alive. Also featured are exhibits on slave trade and the American presidency.

A Digistar computerized planetarium projector, OMNI-MAX Theater, hands-on science and computer exhibits, and outdoor science exhibits are featured at the St. Louis Science Center in Forest Park. The center's Discovery Room is currently under renovation; when complete, children will enjoy dressing as a surgeon, exploring fossils, and playing with robots as well as other participative activities. The 79-

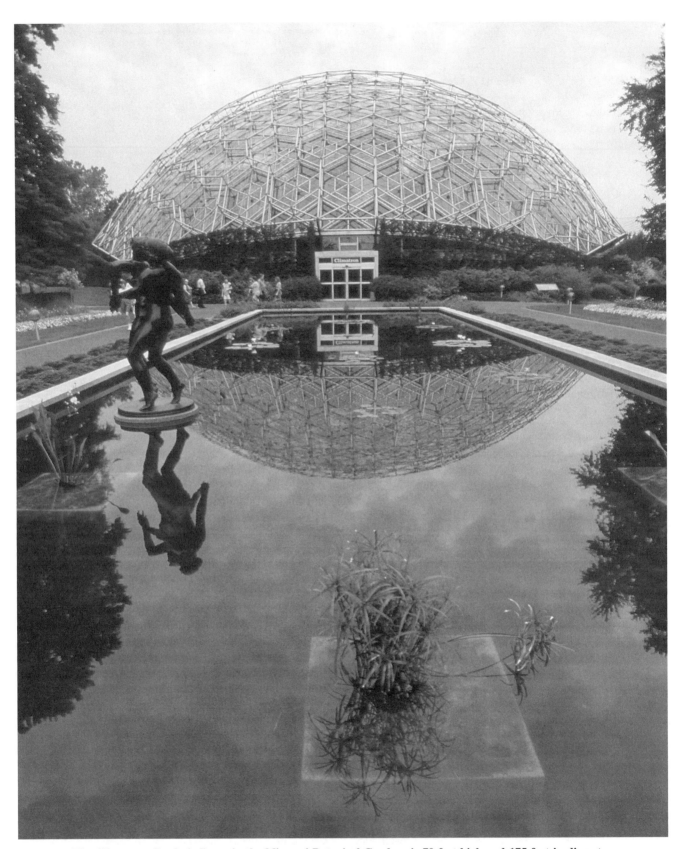

The Climatron Geodesic Dome in the Missouri Botanical Gardens is 70 feet high and 175 feet in diameter.

acre Missouri Botanical Garden, founded in 1859, is one of the oldest botanical gardens in the country and is considered one of the most beautiful; unique features include a 14-acre Japanese strolling garden and the Climatron conservatory, a domed greenhouse featuring tropical plants and birds. Sightseers can view one of the nation's few contemporary sculpture parks at the Laumeier Sculpture Park. The St. Louis Carousel provides a rare opportunity to ride an authentic carousel at its Faust County Park location. Operated by Anheuser-Busch and ranked seventh best family attraction in the nation by U.S. Family Travel Guide, Grant's Farm features a cabin built by General Grant in 1856; the farm's miniature zoo features a Clydesdale stallion barn and bird and elephant shows. Jefferson Barracks Historical Park combines military history and recreation with two museums and a number of sports fields; Robert E. Lee and Ulysses S. Grant are two of the many famous American military leaders whose service included a stay at Jefferson Barracks.

St. Louis museums include the National Museum of Transport, which highlights rail, road, air, and water modes of transportation; the AKC Museum of the Dog, which presents exhibits on the dog through history; the recently expanded Magic House—St. Louis Children's Museum; and the Soldiers' Memorial Military Museum.

The Missouri Chapter of the American Institute of Architects is located in St. Louis and provides complete information about this architecturally rich city. Among some of the significant structures are the Cathedral of St. Louis (New Cathedral), which houses 41.5 million pieces of glass tessarae, one of the largest collections of mosaic art in the West; Christ Church Cathedral, the first Episcopal church west of the Mississippi; and Old Cathedral, the city's first church.

Arts and Culture

St. Louis is a major cultural center for the Midwest. The award-winning St. Louis Symphony Orchestra, winner of six Grammies and 36 nominations, presents a season of classical music concerts with internationally known guest artists at Powell Symphony Hall. In the summer the orchestra plays a series of pops concerts at Greensfelder Recreation Center. Theater is presented year round in St. Louis by a diverse range of organizations. The Repertory Theatre of St. Louis performs a season of plays on two stages, including modern drama, musicals, and comedies at the recently-expanded Loretto Hilton Center. The Opera Theatre of St. Louis performs its four dramatic productions of classical and new opera in English during a month-long season beginning in late May. The Fox Theatre was restored in 1982 and now sponsors a Broadway series, ballet, and pop music concerts as well pre-event buffet dining. The Muny in Forest Park is a 12,000-seat outdoor amphitheater that stages Broadway musical theater during the summer. History is re-lived in words

and music in four shows per year by the Historyonics Theatre Company.

The Black Repertory Company performs at the 450-seat Grandel Square Theater, a handsome 1883 structure that was once a church and has undergone extensive renovation. Other theater companies and organizations in St. Louis include the TheatrGROUP and Stages St. Louis, a musical theater group.

Dance St. Louis sponsors performances with local, national, and international companies, and offers a dance education program. The First Street Forum is a multipurpose arts center that sponsors exhibitions, performances, lectures, and symposia.

The St. Louis Art Museum in Forest Park was the Fine Arts Palace of the 1904 World's Fair and today offers contemporary and audio/video art in additional to traditional pieces. Washington University's Gallery of Art was the first museum west of the Mississippi River. At the Missouri Historical Society Museum, the major events and individuals in St. Louis history from the first settlers to Charles Lindbergh are recaptured. The Concordia Historical Institute maintains an authentic collection of American Lutheran historical documents as well as Protestant Reformation artifacts. Among St. Louis's other museums are the newly restored Campbell House Museum, which features a Victorian era home and furnishings; the Holocaust Museum and Learning Center, which is dedicated to educating and preserving the Holocaust's history and consequences; and the Eugene Field House and Toy Museum, which presents an extensive collection of antique toys and dolls.

Festivals and Holidays

Major venues for celebrations in St. Louis are the Missouri Botanical Gardens and Jefferson Barracks Historical Park. At the Botanical Gardens, an orchid show in January features more than 800 plants. The Spring Floral Display begins in March. November brings the St. Louis International Film Festival, the African Arts Festival, and a Festival of Trees. The city rings in the new year with a community celebration called First Night Saint Louis & Riverfront Fireworks festival.

Jefferson Barracks Historical Park presents a World War II Reenactment in April and American Indian Days in May. May is also the month for arts and crafts displays at Laumeier Sculpture Park and Tilles County Park. Parades and other events at various locales mark St. Patrick's Day, Independence Day, Veterans' Day, and Christmas.

Sports for the Spectator

The St. Louis Cardinals compete in the Central Division of Major League Baseball's National League and play their home games in Busch Stadium; a new Busch Stadium is scheduled to open in 2006. The St. Louis Cardinals Hall of Fame, which is located inside the International Bowling Museum and Hall of Fame, houses displays and movies on baseball, football, basketball, hockey, golf, bowling, and soccer. The St. Louis Rams play home games at the Dome at America's Center downtown. The International Bowling Museum and Hall of Fame recently received a $50,000 grant from the Reichert Foundation which allows underprivileged kids to take advantage of the museum's programs.

The St. Louis Blues compete in the National Hockey League and play home games in Savvis Center, also home to the professional roller-hockey team, the St. Louis Vipers. The St. Louis Aces play professional tennis at the Dwight Davis Tennis Center. The River City Rage of the National Indoor Professional Football League, the St. Louis Streamers of the World Indoor Soccer League; and the River Otters minor league hockey team play at the Family Arena.

Balloonists compete in the Great Forest Park Balloon Race scheduled in September; the balloon race is one of the largest sporting events in Missouri with 70 balloons and 130,000 spectators. For two weeks in September horse owners and trainers from around the country participate in the St. Louis National Charity Horse Show at Queen County Park.

Sports for the Participant

A city of parks and sports enthusiasts, St. Louis offers attractive outdoor facilities and a selection of major and minor sports for the individual, including golf, tennis, bicycling, and softball, and water sports such as swimming, water skiing, and boating. Forest Park, the recipient of a recent $100 million facelift, offers recreational opportunities, including skating, jogging, and tennis, on nearly 1,300 acres; the park is 500 acres larger than New York City's Central Park. Michelob Ultra sponsors a St. Patrick's Day Parade costumed run in St. Louis.

Riverboat gambling on the Mississippi River is a popular activity, with boats departing from East St. Louis and St. Charles.

Shopping and Dining

Downtown St. Louis offers boutique shopping in the Union Station complex, the city's major train terminal and inspiration for the classic "Meet Me in St. Louis." Featuring vaulted ceilings and stained glass windows, Union Station is an historical, architectural, shopping, and dining landmark. St. Louis Centre is anchored by Famous-Barr department store and is located near Metro Link, the Arch, and the Edward Jones Dome. Plaza Frontenac is anchored by Missouri's only Neiman-Marcus and Saks Fifth Avenue. Crestwood Plaza offers more than 100 upscale stores and

restaurants. Cherokee Street Antique Row offers restaurants, cafes, antiques, collectibles, and specialty shops in a six-block historic area.

The Saint Louis Galleria in Richmond Heights consists of three levels, 165 stores, an Italian marble interior, and a 100-foot-high atrium; Lord & Taylor, Mark Shale, Dillard's and famous Barr anchor the Galleria.

Diners in St. Louis can choose from among hundreds of fine restaurants, including Cafe de France, Giovanni's, and Tony's. The city boasts an Italian district, known as "the Hill," which offers a number of fine moderately priced Italian eateries; a popular appetizer is fried ravioli. Chinese, German, and other ethnic restaurants are located throughout the city. Regional specialties available in St. Louis include barbecued lamb, ribs, pork, ham, and sausage; pecan pie; and sweet potato pie.

Visitor Information: St. Louis Convention and Visitors Commission, One Metropolitan Square, Suite 1100, St. Louis, MO 63102; telephone (314)421-1023; toll-free (800)916-8938; fax (314)421-0394; email visinfo@explorestlouis .com

Convention Facilities

The major convention facility is the America's Center convention complex. The America's Center offers 502,000 square feet of contiguous, one-level exhibit space that can be broken down into six separate exhibition halls, including the 162,000-square-foot domed stadium/exhibit hall, the Edward Jones Dome. Other amenities offered by America's Center are 83 flexible meeting rooms, a 28,000-square-foot grand ballroom, a 1,411 fixed-seat lecture hall, and the St. Louis Executive Conference Center.

Ample hotel space is available in the metropolitan area. More than 35,000 hotel rooms are available area-wide; several luxury hotels have been built in recent years, and thousands of first-class hotel rooms are located near America's Center.

Convention Information: St. Louis Convention and Visitors Commission, One Metropolitan Square, Suite 1100, St. Louis, MO 63102; telephone (314)421-1023; toll-free (800)916-8938; fax (314)421-0394; email visinfo@explorestlouis.com

Transportation

Approaching the City

One of the busiest airports in the country, Lambert-St. Louis International Airport, provides non-stop service to 81 cities and is the 23rd largest airport in the country. Daily, more than 889 flights arrive and depart Lambert for destinations in North America and Europe. In 2005 the first of a three-phase expansion project was underway; the $10 million taxiway reconstruction is projected to be complete in November 2005. The project will construct a new, 9,000-foot runway that will allow for simultaneous landings and fewer flight delays in inclement weather. Rail transportation to St. Louis is provided by Amtrak and bus transportation is by Greyhound.

St. Louis, with a geographically central location, is easily accessible from points throughout the United States via four interstate highways that converge in the city: I-44, I-55, I-64, and I-70.

Traveling in the City

St. Louis's public bus system is operated by Metro St. Louis system, which offers service free in some downtown areas; 53 routes are available. Market Street downtown is the dividing point for north and south addresses. The city's 22-mile light rail MetroLink system offers shuttle service from the airport to America's Center as well as to other area attractions. Approximately 38 miles and 28 stations of existing rail will be expanded in future years to include at least 8 more miles and 9 additional stations.

Communications

Newspapers and Magazines

The city's major daily newspaper is the morning *St. Louis Post Dispatch*. The *St. Louis Business Journal* is a business weekly. A variety of other newspapers, including the *St Louis Small Business Monthly* and *Call* neighborhood newspapers circulate in the area. The Associated Press and United Press International operate offices in St. Louis.

Several specialized magazines and journals are based in St. Louis; the majority are journals published for medical professionals by the Elsevier Health Sciences Publishing Com-

pany and other firms. In addition to health care, subjects include religion, agriculture, engineering, environmental issues, business, insurance, and construction trades.

Television and Radio

Television viewers in metropolitan St. Louis tune in broadcasts from six stations, and cable is available. A complete range of radio programming—including classical, jazz, classic rock, "oldies," Christian, and gospel music, as well as news and public interest features—is offered by 23 AM and FM radio stations.

Media Information: St. Louis Post-Dispatch, 900 North Tucker Boulevard, St. Louis, MO 63101-9990; telephone (314)340-8000; toll-free (800)365-0820.

St. Louis Online

City of St. Louis home page. Available www.stlouis .missouri.org

Missouri Department of Economic Development home page. Available www.ecodev.state.mo.us

St. Louis Commerce magazine home page. Available www .stlcommercemagazine.com

St. Louis Convention & Visitors Commission home page. Available www.explorestlouis.com

St. Louis Front Page (development news) home page. Available www.slfp.com

St. Louis Post-Dispatch home page. Available www .stltoday.com

St. Louis Public Library home page. Available www.slpl.lib .mo.us

St. Louis Regional Chamber and Growth Association home page. Available www.stlrcga.org

Selected Bibliography

Clamorgan, Cyprian, *The Colored Aristocracy of St. Louis* (University of Missouri Press, 1999)

Peters, Frank, et al., *A Guide to the Architecture of St. Louis* (University of Missouri Press, 1990)

Twain, Mark, *The Adventures of Huckleberry Finn* (New York: Puffin, 1988, 1953)

Twain, Mark, *The Adventures of Tom Sawyer* (Hartford, Conn.: The American Publishing Co., 1876)

Springfield

The City in Brief

Founded: 1830 (incorporated 1838)

Head Official: City Manager Tom Finnie (since 1990)

City Population
  1980: 133,116
  1990: 140,494
  2000: 151,580
  Percent change, 1990–2000: 7.4%
  U.S. rank in 1980: 118th
  U.S. rank in 1990: 126th
  U.S. rank in 2000: 151st

Metropolitan Area Population
  1980: 207,704
  1990: 264,346
  2000: 325,721

Percent change, 1990–2000: 23%
U.S. rank in 1990: Not reported
U.S. rank in 2000: 122nd

Area: 73.16 square miles (2000)
Elevation: 1,268 feet above sea level
Average Annual Temperature: 56.2° F
Average Annual Precipitation: 41 inches of rain; 15 inches of snow

Major Economic Sectors: Services, wholesale and retail trade, manufacturing, government
Unemployment Rate: 5.1% (February 2005)
Per Capita Income: $17,711 (1999)

2002 FBI Crime Index Total: 12,066

Major Colleges and Universities: Southwest Missouri State University, Drury University

Daily Newspaper: *The News-Leader*

0   1   2
KILOMETERS

MILES   0.5   1   1.5   2

N

TO SNOW BLUFF
SKI RESORT

13

FANTASTIC
CAVERNS

NORTH DAKOTA

MINNESOTA   WISCONSIN

MICHIGAN

SOUTH DAKOTA

IOWA

NEBRASKA

ILLINOIS   INDIANA   OHIO

KANSAS   MISSOURI

Springfield   KENTUCKY

DICKERSON
PARK ZOO

SPRINGFIELD
REGIONAL
AIRPORT

FAIRGROUNDS

44

60

65   44

KEARNEY

KANSAS EXPRESSWAY

DIVISION

HISTORY MUSEUM OF SPRINGFIELD

BROADWAY

GRANT

CAMPBELL

BENTON

DOWNTOWN
AIRPORT

DRURY COLLEGE

EXPRESSWAY

CHESTNUT

CITY HALL

NATIONAL

SCENIC

COLLEGE

WEST BY-PASS

CHERRY

S.M.S.U.

GRAND

ART MUSEUM

FORT

GRANT

CAMPBELL

KIMBROUGH

NATIONAL

BENNETT

GLENSTONE

SUNSHINE

SCHOOLCRAFT FREEWAY

TO EXOTIC ANIMAL PARADISE

U.S. MEDICAL CENTER

KANSAS EXPRESSWAY

NATHANAEL
GREEN PARK

BASS
PRO SHOPS

SEMINOLE

ST. JOHN HOSPITAL

NATIONAL CEMETERY

DURST PARK

MEADOR PARK

JAMES
RIVER

BATTLEFIELD

MEDICAL MILE

60

SEQUIOTA
PARK

65

SCENIC

REPUBLIC

WILSON CREEK
NATIONAL BATTLEFIELD

NATURE CENTER

TO WILDER MUSEUM

LAKE
SPRINGFIELD

Introduction

Springfield is the seat of Missouri's Greene County and the center of a metropolitan statistical area that includes Christian and Greene counties. Called the Gateway to the Ozark Mountains, Springfield is part of a resort area whose primary attractions are the largest cave in North America, an outdoor exotic animal park, and Bass Pro Shops Outdoor World, one of the most-visited tourist attraction in the state. The Battle of Wilson's Creek was fought in the first year of the American Civil War near Springfield and the site is now a national battlefield monument. Today the city is a regional agribusiness center and a dairy-product shipping center. In 2004 *Expansion Management* magazine ranked Springfield 6th out of 331 U.S. metro areas for business expansion, citing its excellent public schools, low health care costs, and high quality of life.

Geography and Climate

Surrounded by flat or gently rolling tableland, Springfield is set atop the crest of the Missouri Ozark Mountain plateau. The climate is characterized as a plateau climate, with a milder winter and a cooler summer than in the upland plain or prairie. Springfield occupies a unique location for natural water drainage: the line separating two major water sheds crosses the north-central part of the city, causing drainage north of this line to flow into the Gasconade and Missouri Rivers; drainage to the south flows into the White and Mississippi Rivers. The average annual temperature range is over 140 degrees with lowest temperatures below minus 25 degrees and highest temperatures above 115 degrees.

Area: 73.16 square miles (2000)

Elevation: 1,268 feet above sea level

Average Temperatures: January, 32.5° F; July, 78.6° F; annual average, 56.2° F

Average Annual Precipitation: 41 inches of rain; 15 inches of snow

History

Removal of Delaware Tribe Opens Farmland

Pioneer Thomas Patterson attempted, in 1821, to make the first permanent settlement on the site of present-day Springfield; however, the Delaware people arrived the following year to claim the land as a federal Indian reservation. James Wilson was the lone settler to remain, and after the further relocation of the Delaware in 1830 he farmed land in the area. New settlers followed immediately. Among them was John Polk Campbell, who staked a claim in 1829 on a site that was then called Kickapoo Prairie; he carved his initials in an ash tree where four springs unite to form Wilson's Creek. This location was well situated, and a settlement soon grew up around the Campbell homestead.

Campbell was made county clerk when Missouri's Greene County was organized in 1833, and two years later he and his wife deeded land for a townsite. Springfield's name comes from a spring that creates Jordan Valley Creek downtown. Springfield was incorporated in 1838 and chartered in 1847.

Springfield's location and commercial base made it a military target during the Civil War. Sentiments regarding the war were split in the town, with the professional classes descended from Tennessee slaveholders supporting the Southern cause and rural settlers favoring the North. The Battle of Wilson's Creek was fought on August 10, 1861, resulting in a victory for the Confederate army; Union forces won the next battle in February, 1862, however, and held the area until the end of the war. Among the soldiers based at the Union Army's Springfield headquarters was James Butler Hickok, nicknamed Wild Bill, who served as a scout and spy. During a gun fight in July 1865 on the city square with his former friend, gambler Dave Tutt, Hickok shot Tutt through the heart. Hickok was acquitted in a trial in which he was defended by John S. Phelps, a future Missouri governor.

Railroad Brings Expansion, New Business

In 1870 land speculators persuaded the Atlantic & Pacific Railroad to build a railroad through a new town north of Springfield despite the protests of Springfield citizens, who claimed that the new route violated the original charter. Nonetheless, the Ozark Land Company was organized and the new town was deeded to the company. As both communities grew, they were consolidated in 1887.

During the first half of the twentieth century, Springfield became an agricultural and distribution center; after World War II, the population grew rapidly as the result of the expansion of Eastern manufacturing companies into the West. The city's proximity to the Ozark Mountains makes it a popular tourist destination.

A vital economy, low cost of living, commitment to education, scenic location, and commitment to downtown revitalization are ensuring the city's steady growth in population.

Historical Information: Springfield-Greene County Public Libraries, 4653 South Campbell, Springfield, MO 65810; telephone (417)874-8110

Population Profile

Metropolitan Area Residents
1980: 207,704
1990: 264,346
2000: 325,721
Percent change, 1990–2000: 23%
U.S. rank in 1990: Not reported
U.S. rank in 2000: 122nd

City Residents
1980: 133,116
1990: 140,494
2000: 151,580
Percent change, 1990–2000: 7.4%
U.S. rank in 1980: 118th
U.S. rank in 1990: 126th (State rank: 3rd)
U.S. rank in 2000: 151st (State rank: 3rd)

Density: 2,072 people per square mile (2000)

Racial and ethnic characteristics (2000)
White: 138,987
Black or African American: 4,961
American Indian and Alaska Native: 1,142
Asian: 2,060
Native Hawaiian and Pacific Islander: 136
Hispanic (may be of any race): 3,501
Other: 1,332

Percent of residents born in state: 60.1% (2000)

Age characteristics (2000)
Population under 5 years old: 8,635
Population 5 to 9 years old: 8,439
Population 10 to 14 years old: 7,987
Population 15 to 19 years old: 12,155
Population 20 to 24 years old: 19,064
Population 25 to 34 years old: 22,032
Population 35 to 44 years old: 20,438
Population 45 to 54 years old: 17,912
Population 55 to 59 years old: 6,563
Population 60 to 64 years old: 5,469
Population 65 to 74 years old: 10,572
Population 75 to 84 years old: 8,545
Population 85 years and over: 3,469
Median age: 33.5 years

Births (2003, Greene County)
Total number: 11,785

Deaths (2003, Greene County)
Total number: 18,054 (of which, 54 were infants under
the age of 1 year)

Money income (1999)
Per capita income: $17,711
Median household income: $29,563
Total households: 64,779

Number of households with income of . . .
less than $10,000: 2,267
$10,000 to $14,999: 2,105
$15,000 to $24,999: 5,499
$25,000 to $34,999: 6,199
$35,000 to $49,999: 7,882
$50,000 to $74,999: 6,411
$75,000 to $99,999: 2,681
$100,000 to $149,999: 1,739
$150,000 to $199,999: 468
$200,000 or more: 680

Percent of families below poverty level: 9.9% (48.5% of
which were female householder families with related
children under 5 years)

2002 FBI Crime Index Total: 12,066

Municipal Government

The city of Springfield, which is also the seat of Greene
County, is administered by a council-manager form of
government. Eight council members are elected for a four-
year term on a non-partisan basis, and a mayor is elected for
a two-year term. The city manager is appointed by the
council to be the chief executive and administrative officer
of the city.

Head Official: City Manager Tom Finnie (since 1990)

Total Number of City Employees: 1,565 (2004)

City Information: City of Springfield, 840 Boonville Avenue, PO Box 8368, Springfield, MO 65801-8368; telephone:
(417)864-1000; fax (417)864-1114; email city@ci.spring
field.mo.us

Economy

Major Industries and Commercial Activity

Principal industries in Springfield include agriculture and
dairy farming; trade, transportation, and utilities; educational and health services; government; and manufacturing.
The Springfield area is rich in natural resources such as
stone, lime, zinc, barium, coal, marble, sand, gravel, and

lead. Abundant hardwood forests yield white oak, post oak, black oak, scarlet oak, hickory, maple, and black walnut. Indigenous wildlife include deer, furbearing animals, quail, rabbits, squirrels, doves, and waterfowl.

As an agribusiness center, the city is home to Springfield Regional Stockyards, one of the nation's largest stockyards and feeder cattle facilities. Other agriculture-related firms are creameries, meatpacking plants, and flour mills. Springfield is also a shipping center for poultry, eggs, and milk. Diversified manufacturing comprises nearly one-fourth of the metropolitan area employment base; major manufacturers include Willow Brook Foods, Aarons Automotive Products, Kraft Foods, FASCO Industries (electric motors), Sweetheart Cup Co., and General Electric.

Springfield is a regional hub for retailing and financial services, and is a popular tourist destination. The health care industry employs 25,000 people, or 15 percent of the Springfield area's total workforce, and has an economic impact of more $3 billion. The third-largest retail market in Missouri—sales total more than $3 billion annually—Springfield ranks in the top 170 markets in the nation. Two medical centers, which are among Springfield's top employers, form the basis of the major health care system in the area. As the gateway to the Ozark Mountain country, the city receives millions of visitors each year.

Items and goods produced: flour, dairy products, clothing, paper cups and containers, furniture, plastics, trucks and trailers, iron and steel, concrete products, feed, fertilizers

Incentive Programs—New and Existing Businesses

Local programs—The Springfield Business Development Corporation is the economic development subsidiary of the Springfield Area Chamber of Commerce. It offers competitive rates and reliable service through City Utilities of Springfield, and administers enterprise zone tax credits and abatements through the Missouri Department of Economic Development. The Partnership Industrial Center, which broke ground in 1993, is part of the economic development public/private partnership between the City of Springfield, city utilities, the Springfield Area Chamber of Commerce, and the Springfield Business and Development Corporation. The partnership was formed in 1991 to promote and encourage the retention and creation of quality manufacturing and industrial jobs in the Springfield area. There are 20 companies located in the industrial park, which has currently reached 95 percent completion.

State programs—Programs offered by the state of Missouri that are available to Springfield businesses include enterprise zones, tax-exempt industrial revenue bonds, Small Business Administration programs, state financing incentive programs, and others.

Job training programs—The Springfield Business Development Corporation coordinates customized training programs through Ozarks Technical Community College.

Development Projects

According to the Chamber of Commerce, Springfield is known as Missouri's "economic engine" because in 2004, 25 percent of all new jobs in Missouri were created in Springfield even though the city represents only 3 percent of the state's workforce. Recent development projects include the Jordan Valley Park, which consists of a greenway, a public ice arena, and $1 million waterway, as well as a new expo center. The new expo facility, connected to the renovated Trade Center, results in about 110,000 square feet of contiguous convention and exhibition space. The building can accommodate 280 booths and about 4,400 people, with seating available for 3,000, and 950 spaces available for parking. A former creamery and tobacco warehouse is being converted into teaching, exhibition, and office space for arts groups in the city. This $3 million project is being funded partially through private donations. The new Hammons Field, home to the minor league baseball team the Springfield Cardinals, opened in spring 2004.

Downtown Springfield continues to be a focus for developers. Plans were announced in 2005 for a retail, entertainment, and parking complex for the Market Avenue Redevelopment Area in downtown Springfield. Developers have presented plans for College Station, which would include a six-screen movie theater within an urban entertainment destination complex that would also house restaurants and retail space. The city also plans to build a 450-space, three-story parking deck above 43,000 square feet of first-floor commercial space designed for smaller retailers.

Recent expansion projects at the airport included tripling the size of the baggage claim area, roadway realignment, an expanded long-term parking lot, and construction of an intermodal facility. The intermodal terminal, next to the existing terminal, is reserved for all passengers intending to board motorcoaches, vans, and taxis or planning to rent cars.

Economic Development Information: Springfield Area Chamber of Commerce, 202 S. John Q. Hammons Parkway, Springfield, MO 65801-1687; telephone (417)862-5567; fax (417)862-1611; email spfdcham@springfieldchamber.com

Commercial Shipping

Springfield is linked with national and international markets by a network of air, rail, and motor freight carriers. Exporting has become an integral part of the local economy; because Springfield is the site of a Port of Entry operated by the United States Customs Service, national companies can provide customs house and freight forwarding services. Air cargo services are available at Springfield-Branson Regional Airport. Rail transportation is provided by Missouri-North Arkansas and Burlington Northern and Santa Fe Railway, which maintains an intermodal hub for piggyback trailer shipping in the city. More than 40 trucking companies, many with terminals in Springfield, offer express delivery.

Labor Force and Employment Outlook

Springfield's population is growing at an annual rate of 2.2 percent. The labor force is described as productive and possessing a Midwestern work ethic, and there is ample access to training and retraining facilities. The metro area's workforce has grown more than 16 percent in the past decade and accounted for more than one-third of Missouri's total job growth in 2004. In addition, Springfield's economic output has doubled in the past 10 years, which makes it the fastest-growing output in the entire state of Missouri.

The following is a summary of data regarding the Springfield metropolitan area labor force, 2004 annual averages.

Size of nonagricultural labor force: 183,400

Number of workers employed in . . .
   construction and mining: 8,800
   manufacturing: 18,400
   trade, transportation, and utilities: 44,400
   information: 4,600
   financial activities: 11,400
   professional and business services: 14,400
   educational and health services: 32,200
   leisure and hospitality: 17,400
   other services: 8,500
   government: 23,300

Average hourly earnings of production workers employed in manufacturing: $11.87

Unemployment rate: 5.1% (February 2005)

Largest employers	Number of employees
CoxHealth	9,100
St. John's Health System	7,900
Wal-Mart Stores	4,300
Springfield Public Schools	3,000
Southwest Missouri State University	2,665
Bass Pro Shops/Tracker Marine	2,640

Cost of Living

Salaries are low in Springfield, but so is the cost of living. The American Chamber of Commerce Research Association Cost of Living Index has rated Springfield 8 to 10 percent below the national cost of living average. Housing costs have indexed at nearly 10 percent below the national average and utility rates rank in the bottom 25 percent of those

charged in the United States. According to the Greater Springfield Board of Realtors, the average sales price for a home was $135,600 in 2004. Average rent for a single family was around $745 per month.

The following is a summary of data regarding several key cost of living factors in the Springfield area.

2004 (3rd Quarter) ACCRA Average House Price: $195,000

2004 (3rd Quarter) ACCRA Cost of Living Index: 88.8 (U.S. average = 100.0)

State income tax rate: graduated from 1.5% to 6%

State sales tax rate: 4.225%

Local sales tax rate: city, 1.375%; county, 0.875%

Property tax rate: $4.5262 per $100 assessed valuation. Assessed valuation is 33 1/3%

Economic Information: Springfield Area Chamber of Commerce, 202 S. John Q. Hammons Parkway, Springfield, MO 65801-1687; telephone (417)862-5567; fax (417)862-1611; email spfdcham@springfieldchamber.com. Missouri Division of Community and Economic Development, PO Box 118, Jefferson City, MO 65102

Education and Research

Elementary and Secondary Schools

Public school education began in Springfield in 1867; today, Central High and Lincoln School are on the National Register of Historic Places. Public elementary and secondary schools in Springfield are part of the School District of Springfield R-XII, the third-largest public school system in Missouri. An elected seven-member, nonpartisan board of education selects the superintendent. Special courses for high school students are available through Ozarks Technical Community College.

The following is a summary of data regarding the Springfield public schools as of the 2003–2004 school year.

Total enrollment: 24,119

Number of facilities
   elementary schools: 37
   middle schools: 9
   senior high schools: 5
   other: 2 (including one alternative education center and one gifted center)

Student/teacher ratio: 22:1

*Teacher salaries
    average:* $38,065

Funding per pupil: $6,000 to $7,000 average (varies per school)

Private schools are Assemblies of God Christian School, Christian Schools of Springfield, New Covenant Academy, Springfield Catholic School System, Seventh-Day Adventist School, and Springfield Lutheran School.

Public Schools Information: Springfield Public Schools, 940 N. Jefferson Ave., Springfield, MO 65802; telephone (417)523-0000.

Colleges and Universities

Southwest Missouri State University is Springfield's largest institution of higher learning and the second-largest university in the state. It enrolls nearly 20,000 students and awards associate, baccalaureate, and master's degrees in more than 80 disciplines in its 7 colleges, which include the colleges of business administration, education, natural and applied sciences, health and human services, arts and letters, and humanities and public affairs. The first doctoral program to be offered by the university was recently initiated in audiology. Private, church-related colleges are Assemblies of God Theological Seminary, Baptist Bible College, Baptist Bible Graduate School of Theology, Central Bible College, Drury University, and Evangel University; all offer a predominantly liberal arts curriculum at the undergraduate level, while Assemblies of God and Drury University grant graduate degrees. Ozarks Technical Community College, St. John's School of Nursing, Bryan Career College, Springfield College, Lester L. Cox College of Nursing and Health Sciences, and Vatterott College provide vocational and technical education. Also in Springfield is the Forest Institute of Psychology.

Libraries and Research Centers

The Springfield-Greene County Library District's main library is a newer facility that occupies an 82,000-square-foot former home improvement store and features a café, gift shop, and other amenities. The former Main Library was recently renovated to make it a cozier neighborhood library where patrons are welcomed with more reading chairs. With eight branches and a state-of-the-art bookmobile, the system has holdings of well over half a million volumes in addition to periodicals and special collections in such areas as genealogy and Missouri history, and Ozarks folklore. Southwest Missouri State University maintains the Duane G. Meyer Library, which houses a collection of more than 835,000 volumes and current subscriptions to 3,600 periodicals and newspapers, as well as the Greenwood Laboratory School Library, a music department library, and a campus library in

West Plains. Assemblies of God Graduate School, Baptist Bible College, Central Bible College, Drury University, and Evangel University house holdings ranging from approximately 60,000 to more than 175,000 volumes. Specialized libraries located in the city are operated by the Missouri State Court of Appeals and the Springfield Art Museum among other organizations.

Public Library Information: Springfield-Greene County Public Libraries, 4653 South Campbell, Springfield, MO 65810; telephone (417)874-8110; fax (417)874-8121

Health Care

Springfield's health care community serves the area with more than 1,000 medical doctors practicing in all fields of specialization. The city's major hospitals are St. John's Regional Health Center, Cox Medical Center South/Cox Walnut Lawn, Cox Medical Center North, Lakeland Regional Hospital, and Doctors Hospital of Springfield. St. John's, the state's second-largest private health care facility, maintains centers specializing in the heart, cancer, sports medicine and rehabilitation, fitness, emergency trauma, and burn care. The many health care facilities located on South National Avenue have given rise to the nickname Medical Mile, where more than $200 million has been invested.

Recreation

Sightseeing

One of Springfield's major sightseeing attractions is Wilson's Creek National Civil War Battlefield, the site of the first battle between Union and Confederate armies in Missouri and west of the Mississippi. An automobile tour of nearly five miles encompasses all the major points with historic markers and exhibits. Springfield National Cemetery is the only cemetery where soldiers from both the North and South are buried side by side. The Wonders of Wildlife American National Fish and Wildlife Museum entertains and educates visitors about the need to preserve the environment and protect fish and wildlife. This new museum facility is adjacent to the Bass Pro Shops Outdoor World.

Fantastic Caverns, a natural wonder, is the only cave in North America and one of three in the world that is so large visitors must tour it in motorized vehicles. Exotic Animal Paradise, 12 miles east of Springfield in Stratford, is a 400-acre park that is home to more than 3,000 wild and exotic

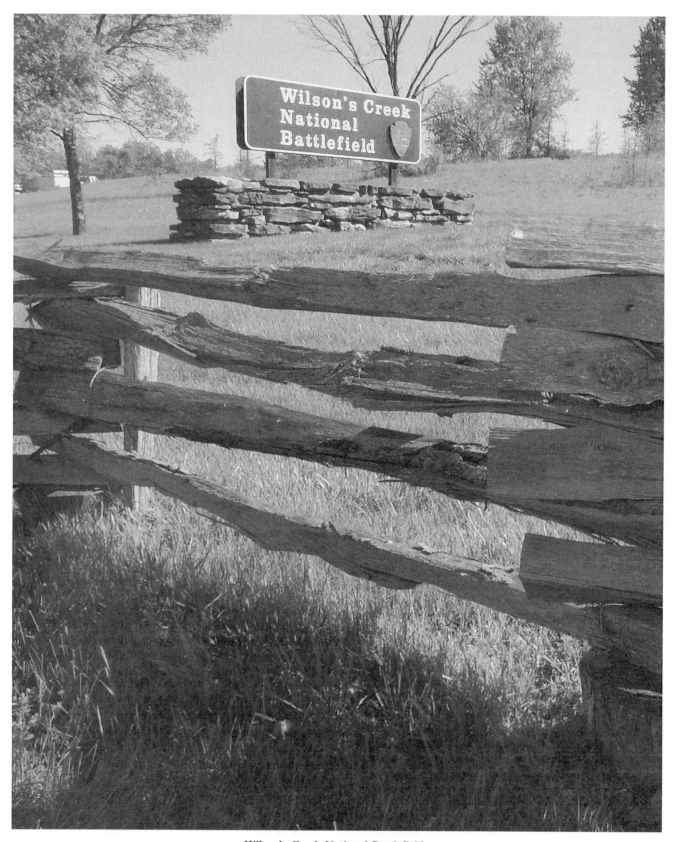

Wilson's Creek National Battlefield.

animals and birds. Springfield's Dickerson Park Zoo, nationally known for its elephant herd, offers elephant rides to children. The zoo also breeds cheetahs and bald eagles.

Arts and Culture

A principal venue for the performing arts in Springfield is the Juanita K. Hammons Hall for the Performing Arts. A variety of cultural events are staged there, including touring Broadway productions and performances by the symphony.

The Springfield Symphony Orchestra and the Little Theater are the city's two oldest cultural organizations, with beginnings in 1934. Among the city's other performance arts institutions are the Springfield Regional Opera (performing at the 1909 Landers Theater, a historic landmark) and the Springfield Ballet. Southwest Missouri State University offers a summer series at its Tent Theater. Within the area, more than 20 music theaters like the Roy Clark Celebrity Theater and the Ray Price Show entertain country-music lovers. The Shepherd of the Hills is an outdoor theater in Branson that attracts a large audience each season with its stories on Ozark mountain families. Numerous local museums and other historic points of interest increase cultural awareness in the Springfield area. The Air and Military Museum of the Ozarks houses more than 5,000 pieces of military history. Nearby Mansfield is home to the Laura Ingalls Wilder Museum.

Festivals and Holidays

Bass Pro Shops, "the world's greatest sporting goods store," presents a Spring Fishing Classic in Springfield in March. Historic Walnut Street is the site of a May Artsfest. A balloon race and Firefall—a fireworks display accompanied by the Springfield Symphony—are popular Fourth of July events. The Ozark Empire Fair in August also attracts large crowds. The Springfield Art Museum hosts a national "Watercolor USA" show each summer. In nearby Silver Dollar City, the Mountain Folks Music Festival is held the third week of June. Ozark Empire Fair, Missouri's second largest and one of the top rated fairs in the country, is held in late July. Wilson's Creek National Battlefield sponsors special programs each year on Memorial Day, Independence Day, August 10, and Labor Day. The Ozark Auto Show, a collector car auction, draws vintage automobile buffs to nearby Branson on the last weekend of October.

Arts and Culture Information: Springfield Regional Arts Council, 411 N. Sherman Parkway, Springfield, MO 65802; telephone (417)862-2787

Sports for the Spectator

The minor league baseball team the Springfield Cardinals play in Hammons Field, a multimillion baseball park that opened in 2004. Six local colleges and universities field a variety of teams in intercollegiate sports competition. The Drury Panthers and the Southwest Missouri State University Bears basketball teams frequently compete in national tournament play, as do the Lady Bears. The Springfield Lasers, a professional team, compete at the Cooper Tennis Complex.

Sports for the Participant

Some 50 city parks are located throughout Springfield. Nearby is the Mark Twain National Forest and Mincy Wildlife area. A number of freshwater lakes close to Springfield provide opportunities for fishing, swimming, boating, and water skiing. For the golfer Springfield offers three municipal courses. The city maintains more than 50 tennis courts and 6 city pools. A variety of sports programs are sponsored by the city. Skiing in the Ozark Mountains is possible year-round.

Recreation Information: Parks Department, telephone (417)864-1049. For hunting and fishing information, Missouri Department of Conservation, 2901 West Truman Boulevard, Jefferson City, MO 65102; telephone (573)751-4115

Shopping and Dining

Battlefield Mall, one of the state's largest shopping malls, with 170 shops and 4 anchor department stores, is located in Springfield. A popular shopping district is a nineteenth-century village consisting of renovated buildings with shops offering quilts, crafts, and folk art. An antique mall and flea market houses more than 70 dealers in a three-story building, the largest such enterprise in the Ozarks. This antique mart sells everything from comic books and baseball cards to antique coins, dolls, toys, jewelry, furniture, and furnishings. A large reproduction shop is also on the premises. Nearby Silver Dollar City features products made by resident craftsmen using nineteenth-century skills. Bass Pro Shops, billing itself as the world's largest sporting goods store, is located in Springfield and specializes in equipment for anglers, hunters, and others. This unusual shop sports a two-story log cabin with water wheel, a four-story waterfall, fresh water and salt water aquariums, and daily fish feedings by divers, as well as a 300,000-square-foot showroom and a NASCAR shop.

The more than 600 restaurants in Springfield specialize in a variety of cuisines that include authentic ethnic foods and Southern cooking. One of the more popular dining establishments serves fish one night and prime rib the next, in addition to an eclectic menu that offers Ozark dishes.

Visitor Information: Springfield Convention and Visitors Bureau, 3315 East Battlefield Road, Springfield, MO 65804; telephone (417)881-5300; toll-free (800)678-8767; fax (417)881-2231

Convention Facilities

Several meeting sites in Springfield cater to a full range of meeting needs, from small parties to merchandise shows. A new expo center at Jordan Valley Park and improvements to an existing trade center were completed in September 2003, and include 40,000 square feet of exhibition space and 13,000 square feet of pre-function space. The expo facility connected to the renovated Trade Center results in about 110,000 square feet of contiguous convention and exhibition space. The building can accommodate 280 booths and about 4,400 people, and has a seating capacity of 3,000. There is also a 950-space parking garage.

The Shrine Mosque features a 19,600-square-foot auditorium with variable capacity that includes up to 60 exhibit booths and seating for 3,355 people in a theater setting and 900 people for banquets. A lower-level, 15,000-square-foot exhibit area can contain as many as 96 additional booths and accommodate up to 2,500 people for a reception.

Centrally located near the Southwest Missouri State University (SMSU) campus is the University Plaza Trade Center, a two-level complex that provides a combined total of more than 66,000 square feet of multipurpose space. The facility's meetings rooms host functions for 30 to 180 participants; banquet capacity for the first level is 1,824 people and 1,248 people for the second level. A parking garage for 550 vehicles is attached.

Hammons Student Center and McDonald Arena on the SMSU campus, designed principally for university use, are also available for special events. The Ozark Empire Fairgrounds can be rented April 1 through November 15 for meetings and conventions. Several Springfield area hotels and motels offer meeting accommodations; more than 5,000 lodging rooms are available in metropolitan Springfield.

Convention Information: Springfield Convention and Visitors Bureau, 3315 East Battlefield Road, Springfield, MO 65804; telephone (417)881-5300; toll-free (800)678-8767; fax (417)881-2231

Transportation

Approaching the City

Several commercial airlines schedule regular daily flights into Springfield-Branson Regional Airport. Principal highway routes into Springfield are I-44, U.S. 60, 65, 66, 160, and 266, and Missouri 13. Greyhound Trailways provides bus transportation.

Traveling in the City

Ground transportation is provided by Fisk Transportation and Tours, City Bus Service, Gray Line, Ozarks Shuttle, Springfield City Cab, Yellow Cab, and Medi Transit Wheelchair Service.

Communications

Newspapers and Magazines

Springfield's daily newspaper is *The News-Leader,* which appears in daily and Sunday morning editions. The *Springfield Business Journal* is a weekly publication. The monthly *Springfield! Magazine* features articles on topics of local and community interest; *417 Magazine* caters to the area's upscale residents with lifestyle, decorating, travel, and entertainment articles.

The General Council of the Assemblies of God Gospel Publishing House, which produces a variety of religious magazines and journals for church leaders and members, is based in Springfield.

Television and Radio

Five television stations, including four major network affiliates and one public network outlet, plus cable, broadcast in Springfield. Twenty AM and FM radio stations schedule music, religious, and news and information programming.

Media Information: The News-Leader, 651 N. Boonville Ave., Springfield, MO 65806; telephone (417)836-1100. *Springfield! Magazine,* PO Box 4749, Springfield, MO 65808; telephone (417)831-1640

Springfield Online

City of Springfield home page. Available www.springfield .missouri.org

The News-Leader. Available www.springfieldnews-leader .com

Southwest Missouri State University. Available www.smsu .edu

Springfield Business Development Corporation. Available www.business4springfield.com

Springfield Convention and Visitors Bureau. Available www.springfieldmo.org

Springfield Museum. Available www.wondersofwildlife
.org

Springfield Public Schools. Available sps.k12.mo.us

Springfield Regional Arts Council. Available www.spring
fieldarts.org

Selected Bibliography

Boyle, Shanna, et al., eds. *Crossroads at the Spring: A Pictorial History of Springfield, Missouri* (Donning Marketing Company, 1997)

NEBRASKA

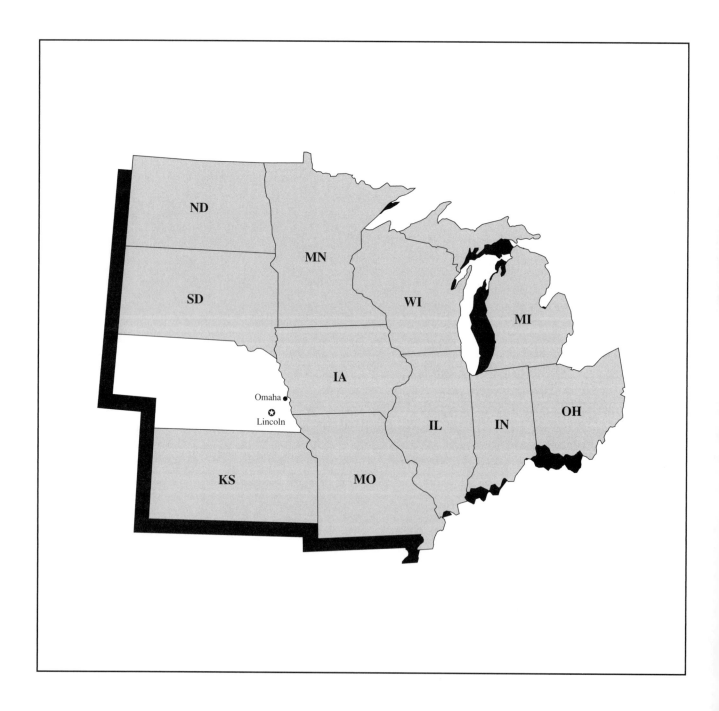

The State in Brief

Nickname: Cornhusker State
Motto: Equality before the law

Flower: Goldenrod
Bird: Western meadowlark

Area: 77,353 square miles (2000; U.S. rank: 16th)
Elevation: Ranges from 840 feet to 5,426 feet above sea level
Climate: Continental, with wide variations of temperature: intensely hot summers, and severely cold winters. Rainfall twice as heavy in east as in west

Admitted to Union: March 1, 1867
Capital: Lincoln
Head Official: Governor David Heineman (R) (until 2007)

Population

1980: 1,570,000
1990: 1,578,385
2000: 1,711,263
2004 estimate: 1,747,214
Percent change, 1990–2000: 8.4%
U.S. rank in 2004: 38th
Percent of residents born in state: 67.1% (2000)
Density: 22.3 people per square mile (2000)
2002 FBI Crime Index Total: 73,606

Racial and Ethnic Characteristics (2000)

White: 1,533,261
Black or African American: 68,541
American Indian and Alaska Native: 14,896
Asian: 21,931
Native Hawaiian and Pacific Islander: 836
Hispanic or Latino (may be of any race): 94,425
Other: 47,845

Age Characteristics (2000)

Population under 5 years old: 117,048
Population 5 to 19 years old: 387,288
Percent of population 65 years and over: 13.6%
Median age: 35.3 years (2000)

Vital Statistics

Total number of births (2003): 25,760
Total number of deaths (2003): 15,444 (infant deaths, 145)
AIDS cases reported through 2003: 598

Economy

Major industries: Finance, insurance, and real estate; trade; agriculture; manufacturing; services
Unemployment rate: 3.9% (April 2005)
Per capita income: $30,331 (2003; U.S. rank: 24)
Median household income: $44,357 (3-year average, 2001-2003)
Percentage of persons below poverty level: 9.9% (3-year average, 2001-2003)
Income tax rate: Graduated from 2.56% to 6.84% (2000; rate set yearly by state legislature)
Sales tax rate: 5.5%

Lincoln

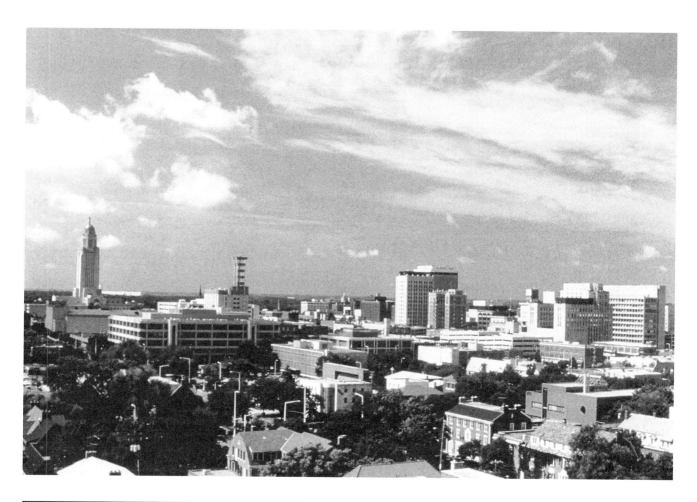

The City in Brief

Founded: 1864 (incorporated 1869)

Head Official: Mayor Coleen J. Seng (D) (since 2003)

City Population
  1980: 171,932
  1990: 191,972
  2000: 225,581
  2003 estimate: 235,594
  Percent change, 1990–2000: 11.7%
  U.S. rank in 1980: 81st
  U.S. rank in 1990: 81st
  U.S. rank in 2000: 87th

Metropolitan Area Population
  1980: 192,864
  1990: 213,641
  2000: 250,291
  Percent change, 1990–2000: 17.2%
  U.S. rank in 1990: Not reported
  U.S. rank in 2000: 144th

Area: 75.38 square miles (2000)
Elevation: 1,167 feet above sea level
Average Annual Temperature: 51° F
Average Annual Precipitation: 28.3 inches of rain; 26 inches of snow

Major Economic Sectors: Government, services, wholesale and retail trade, manufacturing
Unemployment Rate: 3.9% (February 2005)
Per Capita Income: $20,984 (1999)

2002 FBI Crime Index Total: 15,005

Major Colleges and Universities: University of Nebraska–Lincoln, Nebraska Wesleyan University, Union College

Daily Newspaper: *Lincoln Journal Star*

Introduction

Lincoln is the capital of Nebraska and the seat of Lancaster County. Lincoln and Lancaster County form a metropolitan statistical area, which serves as a commercial, educational, and government center for a grain and livestock producing region. Named after President Abraham Lincoln, the city was an important railroad junction for major western routes during the nineteenth century. William Jennings Bryan dominated the political life of Lincoln when he ran for president three times. The Nebraska state Capitol building, completed in 1932, rises 400 feet above the prairie and was designed to symbolize the spirit of the Plains. Voted by *Expansion Management* magazine in 2003 as a ''Five Star Community,'' Lincoln is appealing for its small-town feel yet offers a wide array of cultural attractions and business development opportunities.

Geography and Climate

Set near the center of Lancaster County in southeastern Nebraska, Lincoln is surrounded by gently rolling prairie. The western edge of the city lies in the valley of Salt Creek, which flows northeastward to the lower Platte River. The upward slope of the terrain to the west causes instability in moist easterly winds. Humidity remains at moderate to low levels except during short summer periods when moist tropical air reaches the area. The summer sun shines an average of two-thirds of possible duration; high winds combined with hot temperatures occasionally cause crop damage. A chinook or foehn effect often produces rapid temperature rises in the winter. Although annual snowfall is approximately 26 inches, it has sometimes exceeded 59 inches.

Area: 75.38 square miles (2000)

Elevation: 1,167 feet above sea level

Average Temperatures: January, 20° F; July, 77° F; annual average, 51° F

Average Annual Precipitation: 28.3 inches of rain; 26 inches of snow

History

Saline Deposits Attract First Settlers

As early as 1853, salt companies were sending men to study the possibility of salt manufacture in the salt flats northwest of the present city of Lincoln. Actual processing by any salt company did not start until the early 1860s, but it was never commercially successful, and efforts to manufacture salt were abandoned around 1887. However, Captain W. T. Donovan, representing the Crescent Salt Company, settled on the west bank of Salt Creek near the intersection of Oak Creek in 1856. He named his claim Lancaster. By 1859 the area had sufficient population to be considered for organization of a county. Donovan participated in the committee that was to determine the site and name of the county seat. It was named after Donovan's home town of Lancaster, Pennsylvania.

Lancaster was a compromise choice between North Platters—who favored Omaha, the territorial capital since 1854—and South Platters—who vied for a capital site south of the Platte River. Ultimately Lancaster was chosen and a new name proposed: ''Capital City.'' Lancaster was finally renamed Lincoln, after President Abraham Lincoln. August F. Harvey, a state surveyor, replatted Lincoln in 1867, setting up a grid system of streets lettered from A to Z, with O as the division point, and north and south blocks numbered. In the heart of downtown were four square blocks for the state Capitol and a proposed university. The city plan also called for the planting of more than two million trees, mostly oak, which would line boulevards and parks. The attention to the natural landscaping of the city is a civic responsibility each generation of Lincolnites since has taken seriously.

In December 1868, the state government moved its property in covered wagons to hide the transfer of power from armed Omahans upset with the relocation. Local investors feared that Lincoln would not remain the state capital long since it numbered just 30 inhabitants in 1867, but within a year 500 people lived there, and new businesses started to develop. One event in Lincoln's history at this time symbolized the early difficulties. A herd of 1,000 Texas longhorns collapsed the wooden bridge over Salt Creek at O Street, but the wild herd blocked local officials from locating the cattle's owner and monetary restitution for the bridge's reconstruction was never obtained.

State Capital Weathers Troubled Times

At the first meeting of the Nebraska legislature in Lincoln in 1869, immediate action was taken to authorize land grants for railroad construction and a bill was passed to establish the University of Nebraska. The Burlington & Missouri River railroad line reached Lincoln in 1870, the same year the population reached 2,500 people. One popular rumor of the time was that Lincoln was built over an underground ocean that would provide a source of saline springs with commercial potential, but nothing of this sort materialized.

In the 1870s Lincoln suffered a difficult period. The state's first governor was impeached, a depression hit the local economy, and the legality of transferring the capital was questioned. Grasshoppers infested the area for more than three years. Saloons, gambling, and prostitution flourished, prompting the formation of the Women's Christian Temperance Union, which set a moral tone that dominated local politics until Prohibition. Lincoln reversed its fortunes in the 1880s, as public services were introduced, businesses prospered, and a reform party was victorious in 1887. But as the new mayor and city council began cleaning up the local government, a crooked judge had them arrested and convicted in a circuit court case that was eventually reversed by the U.S. Supreme Court.

Twentieth Century Brings New Challenges

At the turn of the century William Jennings Bryan dominated the political life of Lincoln, running unsuccessfully for president as the Democratic candidate in 1896, 1900, and 1908. Bryan published *The Commoner,* a weekly newspaper with a circulation of more than 100,000 after his defeat in 1900. Bryan was an oddity—a radical Democrat in conservative Lincoln. During World War I, segments of Lincoln's German population openly supported the Central Powers. A misplaced sense of American patriotism gripped the Lincoln populace and local German culture was shunned. The University Board of Regents conducted a hearing in which 80 professors faced charges of "lack of aggressive loyalty" and three were asked to resign.

The Capitol structure built in Lincoln in the 1880s began to settle into the ground, and one corner had sunk eight inches by 1908. Serious concern for the condition of the Capitol prompted a contest to select the best new cost-effective design. All the entries except two involved the traditional federal dome style. The winning design featured a 400-foot tower that could be built around the old Capitol, saving Nebraska nearly $1 million in office rental and making it possible to defray the costs of construction by the time the new capitol was completed in 1932. Its design revolutionized public and government buildings by ushering in a modernist style.

Lincoln today is a typical "All-American" city, boasting clean, healthy air and safe streets. Answering a question about where he sees Lincoln by the year 2006, former Mayor Mike Johanns (now the state governor) declared: "Lincoln will continue to be a vibrant and healthy community with a unique sense of place. Growth will continue to occur at locations carefully chosen in the 1990s, maintaining Lincoln's interface with its agricultural hinterland. Lincoln in 2006 will still be one of the best cities in which to live in the United States."

Planning for Lincoln's Future

Current community planners have continued this vision by actively working to develop the downtown area. In 2004, a comprehensive plan was drafted by the Downtown Lincoln Association that included a civic center, hotels, and additional parking. Residents enjoy cultural amenities along with outdoor and professional sports. Meanwhile, Lincoln has been cited by Population Connection's *Kid-Friendly Cities Report Card* as number 17 of 80 on "Kid-Friendly Cities" 2004 list and *Child* magazine's "Best Cities for Families" in the twentieth position. Further, it has been featured as an economical travel destination by AAA in 2005. And with a diversified business climate, population growth, and increase in the area's workforce, it follows that Lincoln would be tenth on a *Expansion Management* list of "Best Places in the U.S. to Locate a Company."

Historical Information: Nebraska State Historical Society, 1500 R St., PO Box 82554, Lincoln NE 68501; telephone (402)471-3270. American Historical Society of Germans from Russia (AHSGR), 631 D St., Lincoln, NE 68502-1199; telephone (402)474-3363; fax (402)474-7229; email ahsgr @ahsgr.com

Population Profile

Metropolitan Area Residents
1980: 192,864
1990: 213,641
2000: 250,291
Percent change, 1990–2000: 17.2%
U.S. rank in 1990: Not reported
U.S. rank in 2000: 144th

City Residents
1980: 171,932
1990: 191,972
2000: 225,581
2003 estimate: 235,594
Percent change, 1990–2000: 17.5%
U.S. rank in 1980: 81st
U.S. rank in 1990: 81st
U.S. rank in 2000: 87th (State rank: 2nd)

Density: 3,370.7 people per square mile (2000)

Racial and ethnic characteristics (2000)
    White: 201,322
    Black or African American: 6,960
    American Indian and Alaska Native: 1,537
    Asian: 7,048
    Native Hawaiian and Pacific Islander: 141
    Hispanic or Latino (may be of any race): 8,154
    Other: 4,081

Percent of residents born in state: 66.6% (2000)

Age characteristics (2000)
   Population under 5 years old: 15,199
   Population 5 to 9 years old: 14,272
   Population 10 to 14 years old: 13,840
   Population 15 to 19 years old: 18,472
   Population 20 to 24 years old: 27,110
   Population 25 to 34 years old: 35,820
   Population 35 to 44 years old: 33,481
   Population 45 to 54 years old: 28,430
   Population 55 to 59 years old: 8,832
   Population 60 to 64 years old: 6,624
   Population 65 to 74 years old: 11,794
   Population 75 to 84 years old: 8,490
   Population 85 years and over: 3,217
   Median age: 31.3 years

Births (2003)
   Total number: 3,793

Deaths (2003)
   Total number: 1,591 (of which, 21 were infants under
      the age of 1 year)

Money income (1999)
   Per capita income: $20,984
   Median household income: $40,605
   Total households: 90,560

Number of households with income of . . .
   less than $10,000: 6,934
   $10,000 to $14,999: 5,801
   $15,000 to $24,999: 12,987
   $25,000 to $34,999: 13,028
   $35,000 to $49,999: 16,261
   $50,000 to $74,999: 19,185
   $75,000 to $99,999: 8,344
   $100,000 to $149,999: 5,493
   $150,000 to $199,999: 1,289
   $200,000 or more: 1,238

Percent of families below poverty level: 5.8% (40.9% of
   which were female householder families with related
   children under 5 years)

2002 FBI Crime Index Total: 15,005

Municipal Government

The city of Lincoln is governed by a mayor and seven-
member council, all of whom are elected to four-year terms
on a nonpartisan ballot.

Head Official: Mayor Coleen J. Seng (D) (since 2003;
current term expires 2007)

Total Number of City Employees: 2,746 (2003)

City Information: City of Lincoln, 555 S 10th St., Lincoln,
NE 68508; telephone (402)441-7511; fax (402)441-7120

Economy

Major Industries and Commercial Activity

In May 2005, *Forbes* chose Lincoln as the seventh ''Best
Smaller Metro'' area for business and careers with a third
place ranking for income growth. Located in a grain and
livestock producing region, Lincoln has since its founding
been a communications, distribution, and wholesaling hub.
Important industries are the manufacture and repair of locomotives, flour and feed milling, grain storage, and diversified
manufacturing. State government and the University of Nebraska constitute approximately a quarter of the city's economy, but about 90 percent of Lincoln's some 8,000 employers
are companies with 20 or fewer employees. Lincoln is also the
corporate headquarters of several insurance companies.

During the 1980s and 1990s Lincoln experienced sustained
growth that brought economic expansion, with the employment base increasing 2.5 percent annually. Despite the recession in the early 2000s, retail trade, for example, continued to
grow at a higher rate than other metropolitan areas in the state.
Although the manufacturing industry has typically shown
growth above the state average, the overall employment figures have declined with the economic downturn.

A number of Lincoln's local companies conduct business
throughout the United States and in foreign countries.
Among them are Ameritas Financial Services, Selection
Research Inc./Gallup Poll, Lester Electrical, and Cook Family Foods. Sandhills Publishing (formerly Peed Corporation), publishers of national trade magazines, has maintained
its facilities in Lincoln since 1985. MDS Harris Laboratories, a pharmaceutical testing and research firm that serves
all 50 states and dozens of nations abroad has an office in
Beijing, China, and has expanded its medical testing business into the development of a biological warfare vaccine
for the U.S. Army, which was the first such test conducted
under Food and Drug Administration standards. In addition
to its traditional strength of testing medicines on ''well
normal'' people to confirm safety standards, the company
tests how people with illnesses react to new medicines.
Pfizer Laboratories supplies veterinary products in the
United States and dozens of foreign countries.

Items and goods produced: creamery products, farm machinery, farm belts, veterinary supplies, radiator hoses, telephone equipment, biological products, pharmaceutical supplies, plumbing supplies, pumps, motors, motor scooters, wax, filing equipment and office supplies, and printing, lithographic, engraving, metal, stone, and concrete products

Incentive Programs—New and Existing Businesses

Local programs—The Lincoln Independent Business Association, the Chamber of Commerce, Southeast Community College, the University of Nebraska-Lincoln, and the city of Lincoln operate a small business resource center that helps businesses secure financing, permits, and information about other resources. Several major established industrial parks cover more than 1,000 acres and are designed for both heavy industry and multiple use. The City of Lincoln Research and Development Department, with assistance from the Nebraska Research and Development Authority, provides block grant funds to aid startup businesses. The Lincoln Partnership for Economic Development (LPED) began formal operations in 1996. LPED is a community-based, public-private, permanent venture to provide strategic, focused direction for Lincoln's economic development activities. The Community Development Resources (CDR) provides loans and capital with a focus on assisting low-income, minority groups, and women.

State programs—Qualified Omaha businesses can take advantage of state and local programs such as the Nebraska Business and Development Center and the Procurement Technical Assistance Center, which provide technical and research assistance. Invest Nebraska partners with the state of Nebraska along with other donations to introduce entrepreneurs to individual investors and venture capital firms. Federal and state programs include the Minority Enterprise Small Business Investment Corporation, the Nebraska Investment Finance Authority (NIFA), various Small Business Administration loans, the Nebraska Research and Development Authority, the Small Business Innovation Research Program (SBIR), and the Urban Development Action Grant.

The state of Nebraska has emphasized its commitment to revitalized economic growth in all parts of the state with a series of laws designed to make the state an even better place to do business. Firms can now earn a series of tax credits and refunds for investment and new job creation through the provisions of the Employment and Investment Growth Act (LB 775), as well as the Employment Expansion and Investment Incentive Act (LB 270), the Enterprise Zone Act (LB 725), Quality Jobs Act (LB 829), Incentive Electric Rates (LB 828), and Nebraska Redevelopment Act (LB 830).

Job Training—The Community Development Resources (CDR) offers a variety of training and workshops for both profit and nonprofit businesses, such as writing a business plan. For manufacturing firms, the Nebraska Department of Economic Development facilitates a Customized Job Training Program for eligible companies and disperses job training grants. The Nebraska Worker Training Program works to update the skills of existing employees and awards grants quarterly.

Development Projects

Lincoln's downtown business district continues to thrive and its growth is a critical focus for city planners who implemented a "Downtown Master Plan" beginning in 2004 that works to ensure new construction and renovation along with maintaining the natural beauty of the area. Proposals include a civic square with 100,000 square feet of office space and 5,000 square feet of retail space along with new hotels, conversion of a power station to condominiums, and additional parking structures. Several projects have already been completed including a new movie theater and renovation of the Cornhusker Hotel.

The Lincoln Public Schools system expanded with the opening of two new high schools, Lincoln North Star in 2003 and Lincoln Southwest in 2002, with monies from a $100 million school bond.

Economic Development Information: Lincoln Partnership for Economic Development, 1135 M St., Ste. 200, Lincoln, NE 68508; telephone (402)436-2350; Fax (402)436-2360

Commercial Shipping

Lincoln is connected with national and world markets via 2 major railroads—Burlington Northern/Santa Fe and Union Pacific—that provide piggyback transportation; 22 interstate and 9 intrastate motor freight companies; and 6 national and several local air express and freight carriers. Next to the Lincoln Municipal Airport lies a 372-acre Foreign Trade Zone (FTZ) that helps in facilitating imported goods. The city is also conveniently situated within 50 miles of water transportation atMississippi River terminals.

Labor Force and Employment Outlook

Lincoln's labor force is described as dependable, productive, and highly skilled and educated. Employers may draw from a large student population. Work stoppages are rare, with unionization estimated around 25 percent. As agriculture declines, more rural laborers are seeking jobs in the city.

A diversified economy has enabled employment in Lincoln to remain resilient since the nationwide recession during the early 2000s. Among non-manufacturing categories, Lincoln has been strong in construction, wholesale and retail trade, and services. Lincoln has a large number of information systems jobs with small companies that continues to grow at a rate of nearly eight percent.

The following is a summary of data regarding the Lincoln metropolitan area labor force, 2004 annual average:

Size of non-agricultural labor force: 168,000

Number of workers employed in . . .
  construction and mining: 8,800
  manufacturing: 15,500
  trade, transportation, and utilities: 28,600
  information: 3,900
  financial activities: 11,600
  professional and business services: 16,900
  educational and health services: 23,400
  leisure and hospitality: 15,700
  other services: 6,900
  government: 36,700

Average hourly earnings of production workers employed in manufacturing: $15.95

Unemployment rate: 3.9% (February 2005)

Largest employers	Number of employees
State of Nebraska	18,653
Lincoln Public Schools	5,900
University of Nebraska	5,534
BryanLGH Medical Center	4,200
City of Lincoln	2,746
B&R Stores, Inc.	1,814
Alltel Communications	1,000 to 2,499
Ameritas Life Insurance Corp.	1,000 to 2,499
Burlington Northern/Santa Fe	1,000 to 2,499
Duncan Aviation, Inc.	1,000 to 2,499

Cost of Living

The city of Lincoln boasts a low tax burden with a high quality of services. The following is a summary of data regarding several key cost of living factors in the Lincoln area.

2004 (3rd Quarter) ACCRA Average House Price: $271,419

2004 (3rd Quarter) ACCRA Cost of Living Index: 95.9 (U.S. average = 100.0)

State income tax rate: Graduated from 2.56% to 6.84% (2004; rate set yearly by state legislature)

State sales tax rate: 5.5%

Local income tax rate: None

Local sales tax rate: 1.5%

Property tax rate: $2.051 per $100 of actual value (consolidated, 2004)

Economic Information: Lincoln Partnership for Economic Development, 1135 M St., Ste. 200, Lincoln, NE 68508; telephone (402)436-2350; Fax (402)436-2360

Education and Research

Elementary and Secondary Schools

The Lincoln Public Schools system is the second largest district in the state of Nebraska. A seven-member, non-partisan board of education selects a superintendent. Lincoln's students consistently score above the national average on standardized tests, and the system's high school graduation rate is one of the highest in the country at about 82 percent. *Expansion Management* magazine has ranked public education in Lincoln in the top five nationwide for quality. The first new schools to open in 35 years were two high schools, Lincoln Southwest (in 2002) and Lincoln North Star (in 2003).

The following is a summary of data regarding the Lincoln public schools as of the 2003–2004 school year.

Total enrollment: 32,120

Number of facilities
  elementary schools: 36
  junior high schools: 11
  senior high schools: 6
  other: 1

Student/teacher ratio: 13.5:1

Teacher salaries
  minimum: $28,512
  maximum: $60,584

Funding per pupil: $7,568

The city is served by 30 private and parochial schools.

Public Schools Information: Lincoln Public Schools, 5901 O St., Lincoln, NE 68510; telephone (402)436-1000

Colleges and Universities

The University of Nebraska–Lincoln (UNL), with an enrollment of 22,569 students in 2004, maintains two campuses in Lincoln. Selected as fourth place overall by *The Scientist* on its ''2004 Best Places to Work in Academia,'' UNL offers 140 undergraduate (with 275 programs of study) and 112 graduate programs along with operating a law school and a dental college. Two liberal arts colleges, Nebraska Wesleyan University and Union College, schedule courses leading to the baccalaureate degree. Union, which is affiliated with the

Seventh-day Adventist church, enrolls more than 900 students from 42 states and 26 countries; the functioning one-room George Stone School on campus permits education majors to acquire small-class teaching experience. Founded in 1887 by Nebraskan Methodists, Wesleyan is comprised of 1,500 students and was chosen by *U.S. News and World Report* as the leading liberal arts college in the state of Nebraska.

Technical and vocational schools located in the Lincoln area include Southeast Community College–Lincoln Campus, and The Lincoln School of Commerce. Of historical interest, Charles Lindbergh learned to fly at the Lincoln Airplane and Flying School, though it is no longer in business.

Libraries and Research Centers

The Lincoln City Libraries system, headquartered downtown, operates seven branches and a bookmobile; it maintains holdings of about 800,000 volumes, more than 2,000 periodical titles, plus microfiche, books on tape, videos, CDs, DVDs, and CD-ROMs. Special collections feature Nebraska authors and sheet music; the library is a depository for state documents. Free Internet access is available.

Union College, Nebraska Wesleyan University, and Southeast Community College–Lincoln Campus operate campus libraries. Several federal and state agencies maintain libraries in Lincoln; among them are the National Park Service, the Nebraska Game and Parks Commission, the Nebraska Legislative Council, the Nebraska Library Commission, and the Nebraska State Historical Society. The American Historical Society of Germans from Russia, as well as hospitals, churches and synagogues, and corporations, also operate libraries in the city.

The University of Nebraska–Lincoln maintains extensive holdings in several academic libraries, including a collection of Great Plains art. It is also a center for specialized research; facilities include the Barkley Memorial Center for speech therapy and hearing impaired study, the Engine Technology Center, the Food Processing Center, and the UNL Center for Mass Spectrometry. The Nebraska Technology Development Corporation and the Nebraska Research and Development Authority provide links between research and commercial product development.

Public Library Information: Lincoln City Libraries, 136 S 14th St., Lincoln, NE 68508; telephone (402)441-8500

Health Care

In 2001 Lincoln was declared a "Well City USA" by the Wellness Councils of America along with receiving an "A"

for air quality from the American Lung Association in 2004. BryanLGH Medical Center, with 583 beds, specializes in cardiac and pulmonary care and rheumatology, oncology, dialysis, and ophthalmology services and operates the BryanLGH College of Health Sciences. Saint Elizabeth Regional Medical Center operates a regional burn care unit and a neonatal care center. Lincoln is also home to a Veterans Administration Medical Center, Madonna Rehabilitation Hospital, eight nursing homes, nationally recognized substance-abuse services, and several in-home care agencies.

Recreation

Sightseeing

The Nebraska State Capitol Building was designed to reflect the spirit of the state of Nebraska; its large square base represents the Plains and its 400-foot tower is meant to convey the dreams of the pioneers. Described as the nation's first state Capitol to be designed to depict the state's cultural heritage and development, the building features an interior enhanced with mosaics, paintings, and murals portraying the history of Nebraska. On the Capitol grounds is Daniel Chester French's sculpture of the seated Abraham Lincoln.

Folsom Children's Zoo and Botanical Gardens presents more than 300 exotic animals from around the world on 19 acres that are lined with 7,000 annual flowers and more than 30 varieties of trees. Antelope Park stretches throughout the city and contains the Sunken Gardens with thousands of flowers, lily pools, and a waterfall. Pioneers Park Nature Center focuses on animals and prairie grasses native to 1850s Nebraska; animal exhibits include deer, elk, red foxes, wild turkeys, and wild buffalo.

Historic houses on view in Lincoln include Kennard House, home of Nebraska's first U.S. secretary of state Thomas P. Kennard; Fairview, residence of William Jennings Bryan; and the governor's mansion, which features a collection of dolls depicting Nebraska's first ladies in their inaugural gowns.

Arts and Culture

Lincoln is highly rated for the quality of the cultural activities in a city its size. The Lincoln Symphony opens its season with a pops concert followed by a subscription series of classical music at Lied Center for Performing Arts, which also hosts performances by Lincoln Midwest Ballet Company. Other local music offerings include the Nebraska Symphony Chamber Orchestra, Abendmusik, and the Kimball Series at the University of Nebraska. Lincoln's Zoo Bar is one of the nation's oldest blues clubs booking touring blues bands and rock artists.

The Nebraska State Capitol was constructed from 1922 to 1932 out of Indiana limestone.

Designed by Phillip Johnson, the Sheldon Memorial Art Gallery is located on the campus of the University of Nebraska and exhibits American art from the eighteenth through the twentieth centuries with an emphasis on the realist tradition and abstract expressionism.

The Museum of Nebraska History exhibits depict Nebraska from prehistoric times through the days of the Native American tribes of the Great Plains and on to pioneer days. The world's largest articulated fossil elephant is on display at the University of Nebraska State Museum's Elephant Hall, which is also home to Mueller Planetarium that offers laser shows. The American Historical Society of Germans from Russia Museum traces the history and culture of this ethnic group that settled in Lincoln in the nineteenth century. Lincoln is also home to the National Museum of Roller Skating, Great Plains Art Collection, and the Lincoln Children's Museum.

Arts and Culture Information: Lincoln Arts Council, 920 O St., Lincoln, NE 68508; telephone (402)434-2787; fax (402)434-2788; email info@artscene.org

Festivals and Holidays

Held the third weekend in June is Haymarket Heydays, a celebration of the state's railroad heritage that features a street fair, Farmers Market Craft Fair, musical events, and activities for children. July starts off with the bang of Independence Day fireworks at Oak Lake Park after a day of food and fun; later in the month, the July Jamm brings jazz, fine artists, and restaurateurs from around the state for a three-day event. In August, the largest downtown event is the RibFest, sponsored by the Nebraska Pork Producers, which features four days of barbequing and live music. The Nebraska State Fair draws about 600,000 visitors for 10 days, ending on Labor Day; the fair features national performers of country and rock music, midway rides, livestock shows, and agricultural and industrial exhibits. The Christmas season begins with the parade of the Star City Holiday Festival, a colorful event with floats, giant balloon characters, and costumed participants, held on the first Saturday in December; meanwhile the downtown area is aglow in holiday lights and decorations.

Sports for the Spectator

When the University of Nebraska Cornhuskers football team plays home games at Lincoln's Memorial Stadium on fall Saturday afternoons, the crowd of nearly 74,000 fans becomes the state's third-largest "city." Nicknamed Big Red because of their bright red uniforms, the team competes in the Big Twelve conference and had won nine or more games each season and played in a bowl game each season since 1972 until the streak ended with the 2004 season. The University of Nebraska also fields competitive teams in

wrestling, volleyball, track and field, and men's and women's basketball.

The Lincoln Capitols of the National Indoor Football League is a minor league team in the Pacific Conference. Playing 13 regular-season games from March through July with home games at the Pershing Center, the team fields players from most of the state colleges and draws talent from across the country. Lincoln is also home to the Lincoln Stars in the western division of the United States Hockey League (USHL) who play at the State Fair Park Coliseum (the "Ice Box"). After winning the championship in the debut season in 1996–1997, they remained one of the league's top teams despite not capturing the Clark Cup again until 2002–2003.

Lincoln is the site of the high school state championships in basketball, wrestling, volleyball, gymnastics, and swimming and diving. Thoroughbred horse racing with parimutuel betting permitted takes place at the State Fair Park.

Sports for the Participant

For sports enthusiasts in Lincoln there are 106 parks on about 6,000 acres, more than 80 miles of bike paths and trails (most are paved), 11 golf courses, 11 outdoor pools, 8 recreation centers, about 65 tennis courts, and surrounding recreation areas totaling 15,000 acres with 10 lakes. Team and league sports for all age levels are also available. The Lincoln Track Club sponsors the Lincoln Marathon and Half Marathon each May. The Cornhusker State Games, attracting nearly 10,000 competitors, features sports such as badminton, biathlon, fencing, tae kwon do, archery, and wrestling. Wilderness Park, Lincoln's largest park, maintains bridle trails, jogging and exercise trails, and cross country ski trails. Holmes Lake and Park is available for non-motorized boating on its large lake; it also features the Hyde Memorial Observatory. The Pioneers Park Nature Center includes five miles of trails. Lincoln is surrounded by the seven Salt Valley Lakes with recreational areas providing opportunities for such pursuits as fishing, camping, and boating.

Shopping and Dining

The nation's longest straight main street is Lincoln's O Street, which runs all the way through the city; a number of retail centers are located along the route. Antiques, art galleries, and specialty shops are the focus in the Central Business District and Historic Haymarket District, which features more than 100 restaurants and clubs. Westfield Shoppingtown Gateway Mall is the area's largest enclosed shopping center with five department stores and a children's "Playtown." SouthPointe Pavilions claims 50 stores in its outdoor mall and presents free concerts on Friday nights throughout the summer. Local dining specialties include succulent Nebraska beef, barbecue ribs, and chicken, served at Skeeter Barnes among others, as well as other traditional American fare and ethnic favorites. Many of the national chain restaurants are represented, such as Olive Garden and Red Lobster.

Visitor Information: Lincoln Convention & Visitors Bureau, 1135 M St., Ste. 300, Lincoln, NE 68501; telephone (402)434-5335; toll-free (800)423-8212; fax (402)436-2360; email info@lincoln.org

Convention Facilities

Meeting and convention planners may choose from several major facilities that accommodate a full range of group functions. Pershing Center, located downtown on Centennial Mall, houses an arena with more than 28,000 square feet of exhibit space and a capacity for 200 booths. The arena has eight different floor arrangements with a seating capacity of up to 7,500 guests. Other amenities include concession facilities, catering services, and sound and lighting systems. Devaney Sports Center and Nebraska State Fair Park host trade shows, exhibitions, and athletic events as well as banquets and meetings; ample parking is provided at both sites.

The Cornhusker Hotel's Burnham Yates Conference Center in Lincoln offers 46,000-plus square feet of meeting room space, and reception, exhibit, and banquet space designed to accommodate up to 1,500 people. It features the latest in meeting space design and a state-of-the-art acoustic system. The center is decorated in the grand style and tradition of The Cornhusker, a Marriott hotel with one of the only AAA, Four-Diamond ratings in the state.

Lodging for meeting-goers is available at downtown and metropolitan area hotels and motels offering a total of about 3,000 rooms; several also provide meeting facilities.

Convention Information: Lincoln Convention & Visitors Bureau, 1135 M St., Ste. 300, Lincoln, NE 68501; telephone (402)434-5335; toll-free (800)423-8212; fax (402)436-2360; email info@lincoln.org

Transportation

Approaching the City

Lincoln Municipal Airport is served by three commercial air carriers with regularly scheduled daily direct and connecting flights from major United States cities as well as points throughout the world. Commuter service is also provided

from cities in central and western Nebraska. Amtrak provides railway transportation into Lincoln, and Greyhound provides bus transportation.

An efficient highway system permits easy access into Lincoln. I-80 approaches from the northeast and exits due west; U.S. 6 also bisects the city from northeast to west. U.S. 34 runs northwest to south, in the center of downtown joining U.S. 77, which extends from the south, and joining Nebraska Highway 2, which approaches from the southeast.

Traveling in the City

Lincoln's streets are laid out on a grid pattern, with lettered streets running east and west and numbered streets running north and south. The main east-west thoroughfare is O Street. Public bus service is provided by StarTran with 60 full-size coaches and 9 vans.

Communications

Newspapers and Magazines

Lincoln's daily newspaper is the *Lincoln Journal Star*. Several neighborhood newspapers and shopping guides are distributed weekly.

A number of special-interest magazines are based in Lincoln. The Sandhills Publishing Company publishes four national trade magazines plus *Smart Computing*. The Christian Record Services publishes magazines for blind adults and children and has a lending library as well. *Letras Femeninas* is a journal of contemporary Hispanic literature by women published two times a year in Lincoln; *Prairie Schooner* is a quarterly literary magazine published by the University of Nebraska. Other publications pertain to such subjects as agriculture, medicine, education, college engineering students, outdoor recreation and conservation, Nebraska history, and literature.

Television and Radio

Four television channels, including a PBS affiliate, a CBS affiliate, and an ABC affiliate, broadcast in the city, which also has cable and receives channels from nearby communities. Fourteen Lincoln AM and FM radio stations schedule a complete range of musical programming such as rock and roll, classical, country, big band, jazz, blues, and gospel. Lincoln radio listeners can also tune into a several Omaha stations.

Media Information: Lincoln Journal Star, 926 P St., Lincoln, NE 68508; telephone (402)475-4200; email feedback @journalstar.com

Lincoln Online

American Historical Society of Germans from Russia. Available www.ahsgr.org

City of Lincoln Home Page. Available www.ci.lincoln.ne.us

Lincoln Arts Council. Available www.artscene.org

Lincoln Chamber of Commerce. Available lcoc.com

Lincoln City Libraries. Available www.lcl.lib.ne.us

Lincoln Convention and Visitors Bureau. Available www.lincoln.org

Lincoln Journal Star. Available www.journalstar.com

Lincoln Partnership for Economic Development. Available www.lincolnecdev.com

Lincoln Specialty Care Home Page. Available lincoln.specialtycare.org

Nebraska Economic Development Information. Available sites.nppd.com

Nebraska State Historical Society. Available www.nebraskahistory.org

State of Nebraska. Available www.nebraska.gov

Selected Bibliography

Cather, Willa, *O Pioneers!* (Boston, New York, Houghton Mifflin, 1913)

Cather, Willa, *The Song of the Lark* (Boston, New York, Houghton Mifflin, 1915)

Keteyian, Armen, *Big Red Confidential: Inside Nebraska Football* (Chicago: Contemporary Books, 1989)

Lincoln Star Journal, *A Salute to Nebraska's Tom Osborne: A 25-Year History* (Sports Publishing Inc., 1998)

Neihardt, John Gneisenau, *The End of the Dream and Other Stories* (Lincoln: University of Nebraska Press, 1991)

Osborne, Tom, *More Than Winning* (Nashville: T. Nelson, 1985)

Omaha

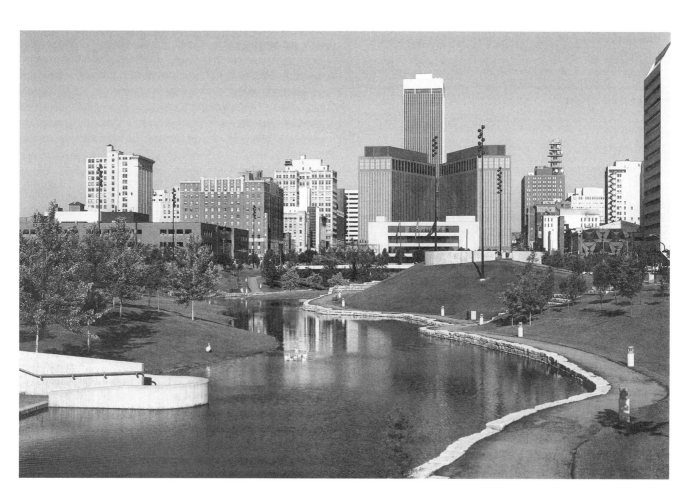

The City in Brief

Founded: 1854 (incorporated 1857)

Head Official: Mayor Mike Fahey (D) (since 2001)

City Population
　1980: 314,255
　1990: 344,463
　2000: 390,007
　2003 estimate: 404,267
　Percent change, 1990–2000: 13.2%
　U.S. rank in 1980: 48th
　U.S. rank in 1990: 48th
　U.S. rank in 2000: 53rd

Metropolitan Area Population
　1980: 585,122
　1990: 618,262
　2000: 716,998

Percent change, 1990–2000: 16.0%
U.S. rank in 1980: 57th
U.S. rank in 1990: Not reported
U.S. rank in 2000: 60th

Area: 118.88 square miles (2000)
Elevation: ranges from 965 to 1,300 feet above sea level
Average Annual Temperature: 52° F
Average Annual Precipitation: 30 inches of rain; 32 inches of snow

Major Economic Sectors: Services, wholesale and retail trade, government, manufacturing
Unemployment Rate: 5.0% (February 2005)
Per Capita Income: $21,756 (1999)

2002 FBI Crime Index Total: 28,781

Major Colleges and Universities: University of Nebraska at Omaha, Creighton University, University of Nebraska Medical Center

Daily Newspaper: *The Omaha World-Herald*

Introduction

Omaha, the seat of Douglas County, is the focus of a metropolitan statistical area that includes Douglas, Sarpy, Cass, and Washington counties in Nebraska and Pottawattamie County in Iowa. The city's development as a railroad center was augmented by the Union Stockyards and the meat-packing industry. Throughout its history Omaha has benefited from the civic commitment of its citizens. Father Edward J. Flanagan's establishment of Boys Town in the Omaha area brought national recognition to the plight of homeless children. Today, Omaha is an insurance and telecommunications center, home to the U.S. Air Force Strategic Command, and notable for its inexpensive housing, good schools, and relatively few social and environmental problems. The downtown is vibrant and growing and the business climate is thriving as recognized by *Forbes* magazine's 11th-place ranking in its "Best City for Business and Careers" list in 2004.

Geography and Climate

Omaha is located on the bank of the Missouri River and is surrounded by rolling hills. The area's continental climate, which produces warm summers and cold, dry winters, is influenced by its position between two zones: the humid east and the dry west. Low pressure systems crossing the country also affect the weather in Omaha, causing periodic and rapid changes, especially in the winter. An annual average of 32 inches of snow falls during Omaha's winters, which are relatively cold. Sunshine occurs 50 percent of the possible time in the winter and 75 percent in the summer.

Area: 118.88 square miles (2000)

Elevation: Ranges from 965 to 1,300 feet above sea level

Average Temperatures: January, 21° F; July, 76° F; annual average, 52° F

Average Annual Precipitation: 30 inches of rain; 32 inches of snow

History

Omaha Furthers Westward Expansion

The first people to live in the area surrounding present-day Omaha were the Otoe, Missouri, and Omaha tribes, who roamed and hunted along the Missouri River, which divides Iowa and Nebraska. The Mahas, a Nebraska plains tribe, lived where Omaha now stands. Meriwether Lewis and William Clark, on their mission to chart the Louisiana Purchase, reached the future site of Omaha in the summer of 1804, and held council with Otoe and Missouri Native Americans. As early as the War of 1812, Manuel Lisa established a fur-trading post in the area.

Mormon pioneers set up camp in Florence, a small settlement north of Omaha, in the winter of 1846 to 1847. Six hundred residents died during that harsh winter, and the Mormon Pioneer Cemetery today contains a monument by sculptor Avard Fairbanks that marks the tragedy. Florence, later annexed by Omaha, served for years as a Mormon way station in the westward journey to Utah. Omaha served as the eastern terminus and outfitting center for pioneers headed to the west to find their fortune in the California gold fields or to settle available inexpensive land.

A rush for land officially began in the area on June 24, 1854, when a treaty with the Omaha Native Americans was concluded. The Council Bluffs & Nebraska Ferry Company, the town's founders, named the new town Omaha, from the Maha word meaning "above all others upon a stream" or "up-river people." When it seemed likely that a Pacific Railroad line was to be constructed out of Omaha, the new town was proposed as the site of the future state capital. The first territorial legislature did meet in Omaha on January 16, 1855. Omaha was incorporated in 1857, but Lincoln was designated the capital when Nebraska was admitted to the Union in 1867.

Rail Transport Establishes Omaha's Future

The city's early years were full of incidents that prompted the administering of so-called frontier justice, including lynchings, fist and gun fights, and an arbitration body calling itself the Claim Club. Ignoring Federal land laws in favor of local interpretations, the Claim Club even went so far as to construct a house on wheels that could be used to protect the claims of people in need of a home to retain possession of the land. The U.S. Supreme Court in later rulings decided not to go against land title disputes made during this colorful but lawless time.

The fortunes of Omaha took a positive turn when President Abraham Lincoln selected Council Bluffs, Iowa, for the terminus of the Pacific Railroad, which was subsequently relocated on Omaha's side of the Missouri River. Actual construction began in 1863, the first step in Omaha's development into one of the nation's largest railroad centers.

The historic trial that gave Native Americans their citizenship took place in Omaha and was decided by Judge Elmer Dundy of the U.S. District Court for Nebraska on May 12,

1879; the case is known as *Standing Bear* v. *Crook.* The Poncas, after accepting a reservation in southeastern South Dakota, decided to return to their homeland. Led by Chief Standing Bear, they were arrested by a detachment of guards sent by Brigadier General George Crook, commander of the Department of the Platte, who was based at Ft. Omaha. General Crook, a veteran fighter in the Indian campaigns, was nonetheless an advocate of fair treatment of Indians. He cooperated fully in the trial, and some evidence indicates he even instigated the suit. Thomas Henry Tibbles, an editor of the *Omaha Daily Herald,* publicized the case nationwide, focusing attention on Omaha and on the humanitarian sentiments of General Crook and Tibbles, who was an abolitionist-turned-journalist.

Meatpacking Industry Spurs New Growth

The establishment of the Union Stockyards and the great packing houses in the 1880s invigorated the Omaha economy and drew to the city immigrants from Southern Europe and an assortment of colorful individuals who figured prominently in the city's growth. After a flood in 1881, residents relocated to the other side of the Missouri River, triggering another real estate boom. Fifty-two brickyards were by that time in operation, producing more than 150 million bricks each year. Omaha's first skyscraper, the New York Life Insurance Building (renamed the Omaha Building in 1909), dates from this era.

The Knights of Ak-Sar-Ben (Nebraska spelled backwards), Omaha's leading civic organization, was created in 1895 to promote the city; they organized the Trans-Mississippi and International Exposition in 1898, bringing more than one million people to a city of less than 100,000 in a year-long event. The Omaha Grain Exchange was established at the turn of the century, helping the city develop as a grain market. Agriculture has proved to be the city's economic base, augmented by insurance.

The Father Edward J. Flanagan founded Boys Town in the Omaha area in 1917 with 90 dollars he borrowed and with the philosophy that "there is no such thing as a bad boy." This internationally famous boys' home, which was incorporated as a village in 1936, is located west of the city and now provides a home for boys and girls alike. After World War II, Omaha native and aviation pioneer Arthur C. Storz, son of brewing giant Gottlieb Storz, lobbied to have Omaha designated the headquarters of the U.S. Air Force. Today, Omaha's Offutt Air Force Base serves as headquarters of the Strategic Command, or USSTRATCOM.

Telecommunications Replaces Meatpacking

During the 1980s, while other cities were trying to attract industries, Omaha began a highly successful campaign to attract telecommunications companies. Promoting advantages like cheap real estate, comparatively low wage and cost of living, and its educated and reliable work force, Omaha succeeded to the point that by 1991 its telecommunications jobs were more than twice the number of meatpacking jobs. Omaha is also home to several of the nation's largest telemarketers.

Downtown Growth in the 2000s

Omaha's community leaders have addressed the need for growth within the city by implementing a $2 billion downtown development plan including condominiums and townhouses along with considerable business growth. A new Hilton Hotel accompanies the expansive Qwest Center Omaha that opened in 2003. The commitment to Omaha's healthy business environment is reflected in several recognitions such as *Expansion Management* magazine's third-place ranking for "Best Place to Locate Your Company" in 2003 and its inclusion on *Entrepreneur* magazine's 20 best cities for small business.

Historical Information: Douglas County Historical Society Library/Archives Center, 5730 N. 30 St., #11B, Omaha, NE 68111-1657; telephone (402)451-1013; fax (402)453-9448; email archivist@omahahistory.org. Great Plains Black History Museum Library, 2213 Lake St., Omaha, NE 68111; telephone (402)345-2212

Population Profile

Metropolitan Area Residents
1980: 585,122
1990: 618,262
2000: 716,998
Percent change, 1990–2000: 16.0%
U.S. rank in 1980: 57th
U.S. rank in 1990: Not reported
U.S. rank in 2000: 60th

City Residents
1980: 314,255
1990: 344,463
2000: 390,007
2003 estimate: 404,267
Percent change, 1990–2000: 13.2%
U.S. rank in 1980: 48th
U.S. rank in 1990: 48th
U.S. rank in 2000: 53rd (State rank: 1st)

Density: 3,370.7 people per square mile (2000)

Racial and ethnic characteristics (2000)
   White: 305,745

Black or African American: 51,917
American Indian or Alaska Native: 2,616
Asian: 6,773
Native Hawaiian and Pacific Islander: 228
Hispanic or Latino (may be of any race): 29,397
Other: 15,250

Percent of residents born in state: 60.1% (2000)

Age characteristics (2000)
Population under 5 years old: 28,249
Population 5 to 9 years old: 27,721
Population 10 to 14 years old: 27,420
Population 15 to 19 years old: 28,359
Population 20 to 24 years old: 31,178
Population 25 to 34 years old: 60,292
Population 35 to 44 years old: 59,917
Population 45 to 54 years old: 50,496
Population 55 to 59 years old: 16,839
Population 60 to 64 years old: 13,514
Population 65 to 74 years old: 23,832
Population 75 to 84 years old: 16,286
Population 85 years and over: 5,904
Median age: 33.5 years

Births (2003)
Total number: 6,933

Deaths (2003)
Total number: 3,320 (of which, 51 were infants under the age of 1 year)

Money income (1999)
Per capita income: $21,756
Median household income: $40,006
Total households: 157,034

Number of households with income of . . .
less than $10,000: 13,842
$10,000 to $14,999: 9,203
$15,000 to $24,999: 22,319
$25,000 to $34,999: 23,026
$35,000 to $49,999: 27,310
$50,000 to $74,999: 30,643
$75,000 to $99,999: 14,953
$100,000 to $149,999: 10,128
$150,000 to $199,999: 2,471
$200,000 or more: 3,139

Percent of families below poverty level: 7.8% (45.6% of which were female householder families with related children under 5 years)

2002 FBI Crime Index Total: 28,781

Municipal Government

The city of Omaha operates under a mayor-council form of government. The mayor, who does not serve on the council, and seven council members are all elected to four-year terms.

Head Official: Mayor Mike Fahey (D) (since 2001; current term expires 2009)

Total Number of City Employees: 2,800 (2003)

City Information: Mayor's Office, 1819 Farnam St., Ste. 300, Omaha, NE 68183; telephone (402)444-5000; email mfahey@ci.omaha.ne.us

Economy

Major Industries and Commercial Activity

There are more than 20,400 businesses located in the metropolitan statistical area, with total employment approaching 375,000. The city is home to five *Fortune* 500 companies: ConAgra, Peter Kiewit Sons, Berkshire Hathaway, Union Pacific, and Mutual of Omaha. More than 30 other *Fortune* 500 companies have manufacturing plants in the metropolitan area.

The headquarters of about 30 insurance companies call Omaha home. More than half of the two dozen telemarketing/direct response/reservation centers operating in Omaha also have their corporate headquarters located in the metropolitan area. Many other large firms have their headquarters in Omaha, including Lozier Corporation, First Data Corp, ITI Marketing Services, Omaha Steaks International, Pamida, Oriental Trading Company, Valmont Industries, Inc., and Godfather's Pizza, Inc.

The Omaha economy is well diversified, with no industry sector accounting for more than a third of total employment. Omaha's highest concentration of employment is in trade, transportation, and utilities with strong showings in education and health services as well as professional and business services. This is offset by a relatively smaller share of total employment in the manufacturing, construction and mining, and information sectors.

Items and goods produced: a variety of food items from raw products like meat and flour to finished consumer goods like frozen dinners and cereal; irrigation equipment; phone apparatus; store fixtures; hydraulic motors and pumps; paper boxes and packaging materials; furniture; computer components

Incentive Programs—New and Existing Companies

Local programs—Assisting in the expansion of new and existing business at the local level are the Small Business Council, the Omaha Small Business Network, Inc., and the Omaha Regional Minority Purchasing Council. Among other finance programs are community development block grants, improvement financing, industrial development revenue bonds, and a range of local and state tax credits.

State programs—In addition to receiving conventional financing from banks and other lending institutions, qualified Omaha businesses can take advantage of state and local programs. Among them are the Nebraska Business and Development Center and the Procurement Technical Assistance Center, which provide technical and research assistance. Invest Nebraska partners with the state of Nebraska along with other donations to introduce entrepreneurs to individual investors and venture capital firms. Federal and state programs include the Minority Enterprise Small Business Investment Corporation, the Nebraska Investment Finance Authority (NIFA), various Small Business Administration loans, the Nebraska Research and Development Authority, the Small Business Innovation Research Program (SBIR), and the Urban Development Action Grant.

The state of Nebraska has emphasized its commitment to revitalized economic growth in all parts of the state with a series of laws designed to make the state an even better place to do business. Firms can earn a series of tax credits and refunds for investment and new job creation through the provisions of the Employment and Investment Growth Act (LB 775), as well as the Employment Expansion and Investment Incentive Act (LB 270), the Enterprise Zone Act (LB 725), Quality Jobs Act (LB 829), Incentive Electric Rates (LB 828), and Nebraska Redevelopment Act (LB 830).

Development Projects

During the past decade, many development projects were successfully completed in Omaha. Work began in 1999 on a 33-block redevelopment area in downtown with a total investment of $2 billion. In 2003 the $291 million Qwest Center Omaha was constructed on the northeast edge of downtown Omaha that includes a 17,000-seat arena and a convention center highlighted by 194,000 square feet of exhibition space. In 2003 the Gallup Organization opened a $75 million campus for executive and management training. The spring of 2004 saw the debut of the $66 million, 450-room Hilton Hotel that is attached to the Qwest Center Omaha by an elevated walkway.

Economic Development Information: Economic Development Council, Greater Omaha Chamber of Commerce, 1301 Harney St., Omaha, NE 68102; telephone (402)346-5905; toll-free (800)852-2622

Commercial Shipping

More than 144 million pounds of cargo passed through Eppley Airfield in 2004. An international point of entry with access to a Foreign Trade Zone, it is served by eight air freight carriers. The Union Pacific and several other major railroads provide freight service that is coordinated with many of the trucking companies serving the metropolitan area.

Labor Force and Employment Outlook

The Omaha labor force is described as highly productive, possessing an old-fashioned work ethic, and lacking a regional accent, so workers are considered excellent for the phone operations and high-technology jobs proliferating there. While unemployment has increased since 2000, there has been consistent growth in the overall labor force. However, the workforce does suffer from wage rates that are approximately 14 percent below the national average.

The following is a summary of data regarding the Omaha, Nebraska-Council Bluffs, Iowa metropolitan area labor force, 2004 annual averages.

Size of non-agricultural labor force: 446,500

Number of workers employed in . . .
   construction and mining: 25,500
   manufacturing: 32,900
   trade, transportation, and utilities: 98,100
   information: 13,500
   financial activities: 37,200
   professional and business services: 60,800
   educational and health services: 62,300
   leisure and hospitality: 40,500
   other services: 16,300
   government: 58,900

Average hourly earnings of production workers employed in manufacturing: $17.93

Unemployment rate: 5.0% (February 2005)

Largest employers	Number of employees
Offutt Air Force Base	10,500
Alegent Health	7,500
Omaha Public Schools	7,040
First Data Corp.	7,000
Methodist Health System	6,200
Nebraska Medical Center	5,300
Mutual of Omaha Insurance	4,600
Union Pacific Corporation	4,500
First National Bank	4,300
West Corporation	4,000

Cost of Living

The following is a summary of data regarding several key cost of living factors in the Omaha area.

2004 (3rd Quarter) ACCRA Average House Price: $224,312

2004 (3rd Quarter) ACCRA Cost of Living Index: 92.0 (U.S. average = 100.0)

State income tax rate: Graduated from 2.56% to 6.84% (2004; rate set yearly by state legislature)

State sales tax rate: 5.5%

Local income tax rate: None

Local sales tax rate: 1.5%

Property tax rate: $1.85460 to $2.39067 per $100 of assessed valuation (2004)

Economic Information: Greater Omaha Chamber of Commerce, 1301 Harney St., Omaha, NE 68102; telephone (402)346-5000; fax (402)346-7050; email info@omahachamber.org

Education and Research

Elementary and Secondary Schools

Omaha Public Schools is the largest elementary and secondary public education system in Nebraska. A nonpartisan, twelve-member board of education appoints a superintendent.

The following is a summary of data regarding the Omaha public schools as of the 2003–2004 school year.

Total enrollment: 46,035

Number of facilities
  elementary schools: 63
  middle schools: 11
  high schools: 8
  other: 5

Student/teacher ratio: 16:1

Teacher salaries
  average: $46,666

Funding per pupil: $7,293

An extensive parochial school system as well as a number of private schools provides complete curricula, including religious instruction, for students in kindergarten through twelfth grade. The most notable private institution is Boys Town, a residential facility founded in 1917 as the "city of little men" by Father Edward J. Flanagan.

Public Schools Information: Omaha Public Schools, 3215 Cuming St., Omaha, NE 68131-2024; telephone (402)557-2222

Colleges and Universities

The University of Nebraska at Omaha, with an enrollment of 14,000 students, awards graduate and undergraduate degrees in such fields as business, chemistry, engineering, social work, criminal justice, elementary education, and fine and dramatic arts. Affiliated with the university is the University of Nebraska Medical Center, which offers programs at all degree levels from associate to doctorate in areas that include dental hygiene, dentistry, medical technology, medicine, nuclear medicine technology, nursing, pharmacy, physical therapy, physician's assistant, radiation technology, and radiological technology.

Awarding associate through doctorate degrees, Creighton University is a private institution with colleges of arts and sciences and business administration and schools of law, nursing, pharmacy and allied health, dentistry, medicine, and graduate study and an annual enrollment of more than 6,500 students. Opened in 1943, Grace University is a private school with some 500 enrollees. Among the colleges located in the Omaha area are the College of Saint Mary (more than 900 attendees) and Metropolitan Community College (nearly 13,000 students). Area vocational schools offer specialized and technical training.

Libraries and Research Centers

The Omaha Public Library operates a main downtown facility, the W. Dale Clark Library (built in 1976), and nine branches while also providing services for the hearing- and visually-impaired. With holdings of nearly 800,000 volumes, plus videos, music cassette tapes, and compact discs, the library is also a depository for federal and state documents. Extensive main and departmental libraries are located on the campuses of all colleges and universities in the city. The University Library at the University of Nebraska consists of more than 750,000 volumes including 3,000 newspaper and journal subscriptions plus about two million microforms. Other libraries in Omaha are associated with government agencies, corporations, hospitals, religious groups, arts organizations, and the local newspaper.

Research centers affiliated with Omaha-area colleges and universities conduct studies in such fields as cancer, allergies, gerontology, human genetics, and neonatology. Founded in 1960, the Eppley Institute for Research in Cancer and Allied Diseases, is funded by the National Cancer Institute and housed at the University of Nebraska Medical

Center, conducts research programs in biochemistry, biology, chemistry, immunology, nutrition, pathology, pharmacology, and virology.

Public Library Information: Omaha Public Library, 215 S 15th St., Omaha, NE 68102; telephone (402)444-4800; email webdesk@omaha.lib.ne.us

Health Care

The health care industry, which consists of nine hospitals, several clinics, and a number of other medical facilities, is one of Omaha's largest employers. The city is a center for medical education and research, with medical schools at Creighton University and the University of Nebraska Medical Center, a dental school, and a number of schools of nursing.

St. Joseph Hospital is the teaching hospital for the Creighton University School of Medicine, specializing in renal dialysis, metabolic research, cardiac diagnosis and treatment, and cancer care. Adjacent to St. Joseph is the Boys Town National Research Hospital, a national diagnostic, treatment, and research facility for children with hearing, speech, or learning disorders. The University of Nebraska Medical Center, the teaching hospital for the University of Nebraska School of Medicine, operates units for pediatric cardiology, cancer therapy, and high-risk newborn care, and a pain rehabilitation institute.

Recreation

Sightseeing

Omaha received national attention when the Hollywood movie *Boys Town,* starring Spencer Tracy and Mickey Rooney, was released in 1938. Today Tracy's Academy Award Oscar is on display in the Hall of History Museum on the Boys Town campus. The Hall traces the history of the country's most famous institution for the care of homeless children, presenting exhibits on the history of juvenile delinquency and of social programs designed to address it.

The PhilaMatic Museum exhibits stamp, coin, and currency collections for the hobbyist. General Crook House, a restored Victorian house on the grounds of Ft. Omaha, was the home of General George Crook, head of the Army of the Platte, who gained fame for his testimony in the trial of Chief Standing Bear. The Gerald Ford Birthplace, an outdoor park and rose garden, contains a replica of the home where former President Ford was born as well as memorabilia from his White House years and is often used for weddings.

The U.S. Air Force Strategic Air Command Museum, located in nearby Mahoney State Park, charts the history of the United States Air Force in indoor and outdoor exhibits; the $29.5 million museum displays 31 vintage and modern airplanes year round. The Henry Doorly Zoo has been ranked the country's number one zoo by *Family* magazine and attracts about 1.6 million visitors annually. Species include rare white Siberian tigers. The zoo's aviary is the second largest in the world with 500 exotic species, and its indoor rain forest is the world's largest. The Lied Jungle at the zoo, winner of *Time* magazine's 1992 design award, was described by the magazine as "architecturally stupendous . . . and zoologically thrilling." It features a half-mile maze of trails offering views of exotica such as Malayan tapirs and pygmy hippos in an authentic rain forest atmosphere. In 2002 an indoor desert, the world's largest, was constructed and features plant and animal life from deserts in Africa, Australia, and the United States. The Mutual of Omaha Wild Kingdom wildlife pavilion presents the theme of animal adaptation for survival. Ak-Sar-Ben Aquarium, the only aquarium between Chicago and the West Coast, is open year-round and exhibits 50 species of fresh-water fish.

The Mutual of Omaha Dome exhibits memorabilia from the Mutual of Omaha's "Wild Kingdom" television program; the Dome is an underground facility topped by a large glass dome. Completely redesigned, the Union Pacific Historical Museum at the Union Pacific Railroad's headquarters building traces the history of the company's railroad.

Twenty-five miles north of Omaha, the 7,800-acre DeSoto Bend National Wildlife Refuge offers opportunities in the spring and fall to view thousands of migrating birds that use the Missouri Valley flyway for their seasonal migration. Fontenelle Forest in North Bellevue is a 1,300-acre sylvan area within the city. Peony Park, Nebraska's largest amusement park, combines amusement park rides, shows in an outdoor amphitheater, and the state's largest swimming pool.

Arts and Culture

Omaha Community Playhouse, founded in 1924, is one of the nation's largest and most recognized community theaters—whose alumni include Henry Fonda and Dorothy McGuire—and schedules year-round productions. Main-stage productions as well as studio and experimental theater are presented in what is physically the largest amateur theater facility in the country. Omaha Theater Company for Young People is a professional company offering original adaptations of classic children's literature. At Diner Theater, original drama written by an Omaha native is produced in a real diner.

The Omaha Symphony plays a season of classical, pop, and chamber music; and Opera Omaha sponsors three produc-

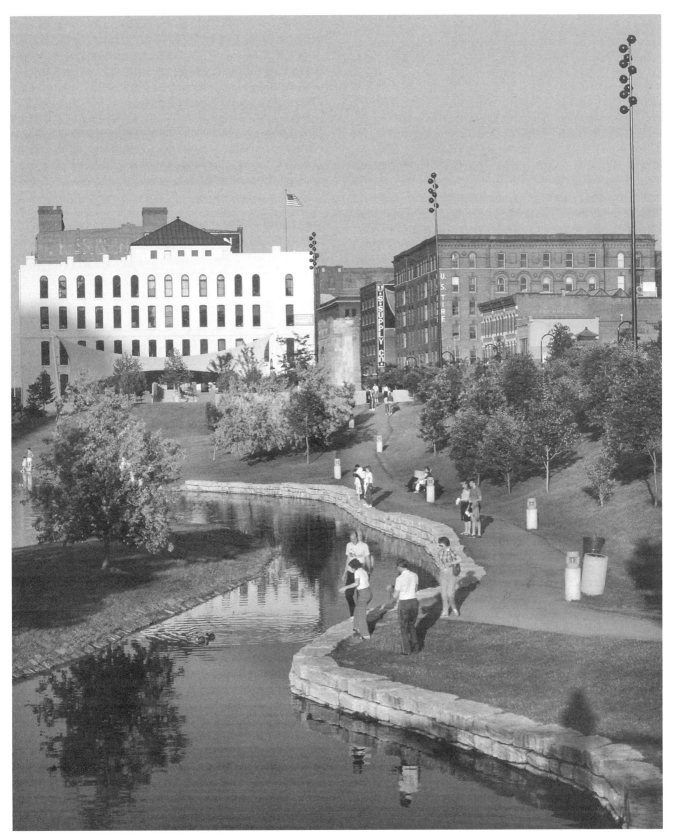

Omaha's Old Market began as a warehouse district selling goods to pioneers for their journey West and is now a contemporary shopping district.

tions annually. Incorporated in 2000, the Omaha Chamber Music Society performs a summer concert series along with monthly "Music at Midday" concerts. The Tuesday Musical Concert Series brings internationally-known classical musicians to the Holland Performing Arts Center.

The Joslyn Art Museum, built in 1931 in honor of business leader George Joslyn, is an Art Deco facility on three levels that houses a permanent collection emphasizing European, American, and Western art. The Durham Western Heritage Museum is housed in the restored Union Station depot. The museum charts the city's history from pioneer days to the 1950s and features a vintage soda fountain manned by volunteer soda jerks. The Great Plains Black History Museum chronicles the contributions and achievements of African Americans in the Midwest. Designed for children to interact with the exhibits, the Omaha Children's Museum features art projects that complement the displays. John Raimondi's *Dance of the Cranes* at Eppley Airfield, the largest bronze sculpture in North America, is a five-story, 15-ton sculpture depicting sandhill cranes in a ritual dance.

Festivals and Holidays

Omaha sponsors festivals and special indoor and outdoor events year round. The major cultural institutions of the city host many of these festivals in honor of the city's heritage. During the second weekend in February a softball tournament held throughout the city raises money for the March of Dimes. In mid-March Triumph of Agriculture Exposition, one of the largest farm equipment shows in the world, draws participants to the Qwest Convention Center.

Nearly 200 artists and crafters are featured at the Summer Arts Festival, held at the Gene Leahy Mall for three days in late June. The Nebraska Shakespeare Festival is presented outdoors in Elmwood Park on weekends through June and July. In August the Offutt Air Force Base open house and air show enjoys the participation of the 55th Strategic Reconnaissance Wing. The Omaha Federation of Labor sponsors Septemberfest in honor of Omaha's working men and women over Labor Day weekend at the Qwest Center. This is also when La Festa Italiana brings music, dance, and food to a celebration at Roncalli High School.

Ak-Sar-Ben Rodeo and Livestock Exposition in October is the world's largest 4-H livestock show; the rodeo attracts the nation's top rodeo competitors. Dickens in the Market takes place the first weekend in December at Old Market and features costumed entertainers performing holiday music and vignettes of Charles Dickens' novels.

Sports for the Spectator

Omaha hosts the National Collegiate Athletic Association (NCAA) College baseball World Series each June at Rosenblatt Stadium. The Omaha Golden Spikes, the Triple-A farm team of professional baseball's American League Kansas City Royals, compete in the International League and play their home season at Rosenblatt Stadium. Bluffs Run in Council Bluffs offers greyhound dog racing with individual televisions in the clubhouse for viewing each race.

Late-model stock car racing takes place at Little Sunset Speedway at the I-80 Speedway from May through October. College sports are played by the Creighton Bluejays and the University of Nebraska at Omaha Mavericks; the Mavericks rank high among the nation's most competitive wrestling teams.

Sports for the Participant

The Omaha Parks and Recreation Department administers more than 200 city parks on 8,300 acres of land, 14 neighborhood recreation centers, and various recreational leagues. The most popular is the summer softball program; Omaha claims the title of "Softball Capital of the World" with 2,500 teams and 60 fields. The metropolitan area boasts 50 golf courses, 19 public pools along with several private pools, outdoor and indoor tennis courts, and facilities for hockey and ice skating. Three figure-skating clubs offer instruction. One downhill skiing facility operates in nearby Crescent, Iowa though the area's relative flatness lends well to cross-country skiing trails at Elmwood Park and N.P. Dodge Park.

Shopping and Dining

Omaha's Old Market in its earliest days was a warehouse district where pioneers purchased the goods they needed for the journey to the West. In 1968 Old Market began renovation, first converting to an artists colony; today it is a thriving shopping and restaurant district as well as a fruit and vegetable marketplace. A number of downtown locations have been renovated into malls as part of the revitalization of Omaha's downtown commercial district. The Crossroads Mall and Oak View Mall both house around 100 stores on about 875,000 square feet of shopping space. Omaha claims the largest retail jewelry store in the United States. Possibly the city's most visited store is the Nebraska Furniture Mart, which records the nation's largest volume of furniture sales.

Some of the best beefsteaks in the world are served in Omaha restaurants; the city is also noted for catfish caught in the Missouri River, and for Continental, French, East Indian, and Creole cuisine. *Food and Wine* magazine named Omaha's Le Cafe de Paris a "Distinguished Restaurant of North America." A local Chinese restaurant replicates Beijing's imperial palace. "Runza," a dough pocket filled with ground beef and cabbage, is a local specialty served at Runza Hut. Godfather's Pizza, one of the largest pizza chains in the country, originated in Omaha.

Visitor Information: Greater Omaha Convention & Visitors Bureau, 1001 Farnam St., Ste. 200, Omaha, NE 68102;

telephone (402)444-4660; toll-free (866)937-6624; fax (402)444-4511

Convention Facilities

Centrally located downtown, within easy access of sightseeing, entertainment, shopping, dining, and lodging, the Omaha Civic Auditorium is a popular site for regional events as well as national conventions, trade shows, and meetings and has 122,000 square feet of floor space. The main exhibition hall, with more than 67,800 square feet of space, accommodates up to 300 booths and can be partitioned into separate meeting rooms. The multipurpose, 25,000-square-foot convention hall, providing space for 176 booths, hosts banquets and large meetings.

In 2003 the newly constructed Qwest Center Omaha and Arena debuted with its 194,000 square foot exhibition hall (that can be divided into three separate spaces) and 17,000-seat arena. Highlighted by a 31,000-square-foot ballroom, the center also has 12 meeting rooms with seating ranging from 71 to 503 guests.

The Peter Kiewit Conference Center, located in the new mall area, is operated by the College of Continuing Studies of the University of Nebraska at Omaha. Accommodations include an auditorium with a seating capacity of more than 500 people, 18 meeting rooms for groups of five to 500 people, dining and catering service, and teleconferencing and computer access. Additional convention and meeting facilities are available at two clusters of hotels at 72nd and Grover Streets and 108th and L Streets; some of these offer a selection of meeting rooms for functions involving from 35 to 1,800 participants. One example is the Holiday Inn Convention Center with 61,000 square feet of meeting space featuring the 23,000 square foot "Palace Ballroom" that can seat 4,000 for receptions or 2,800 theater-style.

Convention Information: Greater Omaha Convention & Visitors Bureau, 1001 Farnam St., Ste. 200, Omaha, NE 68102; telephone (402)444-4660; toll-free (866)937-6624; fax (402)444-4511

Transportation

Approaching the City

The terminal at Eppley Airfield, four miles northeast of downtown Omaha, is served by nine national air carriers and three regional airlines with direct flights to most major

United States cities and connecting flights to points throughout the world. Located on 2,650 square feet of land, it served nearly four million passengers in 2004. Four general aviation airports in the metropolitan area are open to the public.

Principal highway routes providing access to the Omaha metropolitan area are I-80 and I-29; U.S. 6, 30, 75, and 275; and Nebraska 36, 38, 50, 64, 85, 92, 131, 133, and 370.

Traveling in the City

Omaha's streets are arranged in a grid pattern, with Dodge Street dividing the city into north and south sectors. Streets running north-south are numbered; east-west streets are named. Public bus transportation is provided by Metro Area Transit (MAT), which operates routes in Omaha, Council Bluffs, Bellevue, Papillion, Ralston, Boys Town, Carter Lake, La Vista, and Northeast Sarpy County. MAT schedules morning and evening express service; reduced fares for students and senior and handicapped passengers are available.

Communications

Newspapers and Magazines

Omaha's daily newspaper is *The Omaha World-Herald,* published daily in the morning and evening and on Saturday and Sunday mornings. Several special-interest newspapers and magazines are also published in Omaha. Among them are *The Catholic Voice* and *Jewish Press.* The weekly *Midlands Business Journal* presents local business information on a weekly basis.

Television and Radio

Five television stations, affiliated with CBS, Fox, PBS, ABC, and NBC, broadcast from Omaha; two additional channels are received from Lincoln. Several companies supply cable television service to the metropolitan area. Radio programming that includes a range of musical formats such as rock, classical, jazz, and religious, as well as educational, information, and news features, is provided by 17 AM and FM stations based in Omaha.

Media Information: Omaha World-Herald, 1334 Dodge St., Omaha, NE 68102; telephone (402)444-1000

Omaha Online

City of Omaha Home Page. Available www.ci.omaha.ne.us

Greater Omaha Chamber of Commerce. Available www.accessomaha.com

Omaha Convention and Visitors Bureau. Available www
.visitomaha.com

Omaha by Design community development home page.
Available www.livelyomaha.org

Omaha Public Library. Available www.omaha.lib.ne.us

Omaha Public Schools. Available www.ops.org

Omaha World-Herald. Available www.omaha.com

Selected Bibliography

Crary, Margaret, *Susette La Flesche: Voice of the Omaha Indians*
(New York: Hawthorn Books, 1973)

Larsen, Lawrence H., and Barbara J. Cottrell, *The Gate City: A
History of Omaha* (University of Nebraska Press, 1997)

Menard, Orville D., *Political Bossism in Mid America: Tom Denni-
son's Omaha, 1900–1933* (University Press of America, 1989)

Oursler, Fulton, *Father Flanagan of Boys Town, by Fulton Oursler
and Will Oursler* (New York: Doubleday, 1949)

NORTH DAKOTA

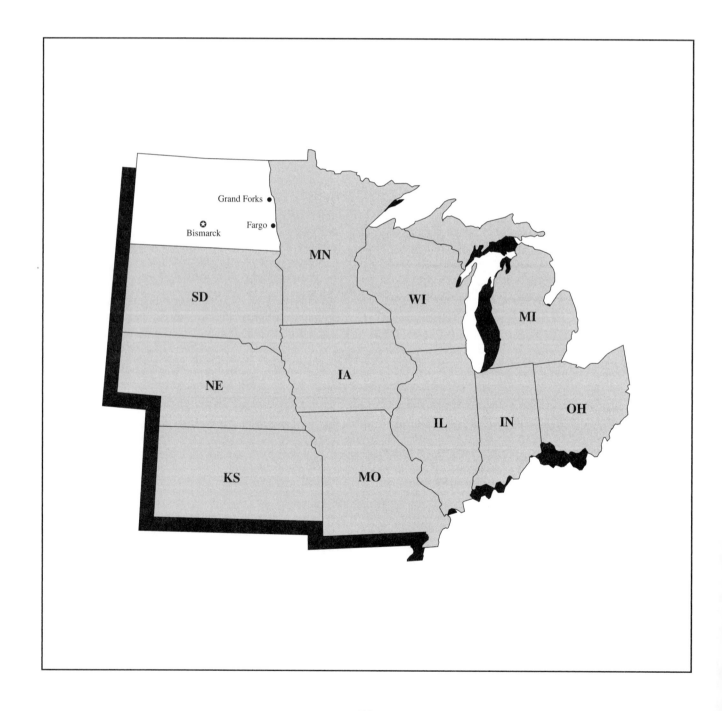

The State in Brief

Nickname: Flickertail State; Sioux State; Peace Garden State

Motto: Liberty and Union, now and forever, one and inseparable

Flower: Wild prairie rose
Bird: Western meadowlark

Area: 70,699 square miles (2000; U.S. rank: 19th)
Elevation: Ranges from 750 feet to 3,506 feet above sea level
Climate: Continental, with a wide variety of temperatures; brief, hot summers; winter blizzards; semi-arid in the west and 22 inches average rainfall in the east

Admitted to Union: November 2, 1889
Capital: Bismarck
Head Official: Governor John Hoeven (R) (until 2008)

Population
   1980: 653,000
   1990: 638,800
   2000: 642,200
   2004 estimate: 634,366
   Percent change, 1990–2000: 0.5%
   U.S. rank in 2004: 48th
   Percent of residents born in state: 72.5% (2000)
   Density: 9.3 people per square mile (2000)
   2002 FBI Crime Index Total: 15,258

Racial and Ethnic Characteristics (2000)
   White: 593,181
   Black or African American: 3,916
   American Indian and Alaska Native: 31,329
   Asian: 3,606
   Native Hawaiian and Pacific Islander: 230
   Hispanic or Latino (may be of any race): 7,786
   Other: 2,540

Age Characteristics (2000)
   Population under 5 years old: 39,400
   Population 5 to 19 years old: 144,064
   Percent of population 65 years and over: 14.7%
   Median age: 36.2 years (2000)

Vital Statistics
   Total number of births (2003): 7,938
   Total number of deaths (2003): 6,090 (infant deaths, 57)
   AIDS cases reported through 2003: 57

Economy
   Major industries: Agriculture, manufacturing, mining
   Unemployment rate: 3.2% (April 2005)
   Per capita income: $28,521 (2003; U.S. rank: 35)
   Median household income: $38,212 (3-year average, 2001-2003)
   Percentage of persons below poverty level: 11.7% (3-year average, 2001-2003)
   Income tax rate: Ranges from 2.1% to 5.54%
   Sales tax rate: 5.0% (food and prescription drugs are exempt)

Bismarck

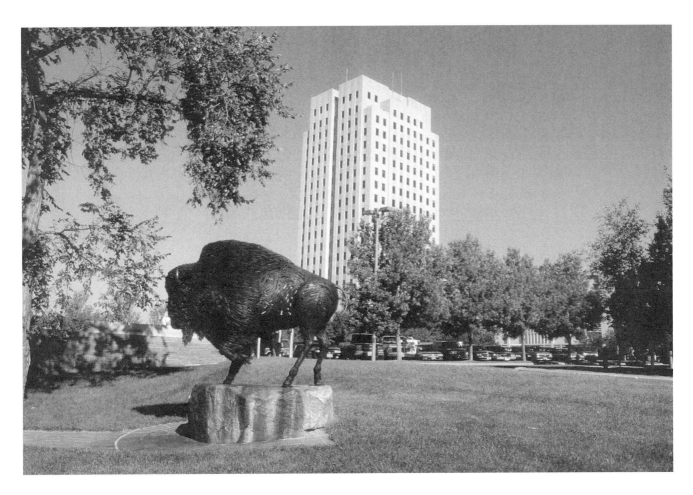

The City in Brief

Founded: 1871 (incorporated 1875)

Head Official: Mayor John Warford (since 2002)

City Population
 1980: 44,485
 1990: 49,256
 2000: 55,532
 2003 estimate: 56,344
 Percent change, 1990–2000: 11.1%
 U.S. rank in 1990: 527th
 U.S. rank in 2000: 620th

Metropolitan Area Population
 1980: 54,811 (Burleigh County)
 1990: 83,831 (MSA)
 2000: 94,719 (MSA)

Percent change, 1990–2000: 13.0%
U.S. rank in 1990: Not reported
U.S. rank in 2000: 260th

Area: 27.0 square miles (2000)
Elevation: 1,700 feet above sea level
Average Annual Temperature: 53.8° F
Average Annual Precipitation: 15.47 inches of rain; 44 inches of snow

Major Economic Sectors: Services, trade, transportation, energy, government
Unemployment Rate: 3.9% (February 2005)
Per Capita Income: $20,789

2002 FBI Crime Index Total: 1,698

Major Colleges and Universities: Bismarck State College, University of Mary, University of North Dakota School of Medicine, United Tribes Training College

Daily Newspaper: *The Bismarck Tribune*

Introduction

Bismarck, the capital of North Dakota, seat of Burleigh County, and part of the metropolitan statistical area that also includes Mandan, is known as the hub city for the Lewis and Clark Trail. Since the time that Meriwether Lewis and William Clark explored the region's rolling plains in 1804-05, the Bismarck region has remained a center for outdoor adventures, from hiking and canoeing to mountain biking and boating, offering some of the finest fishing and hunting opportunities in the country. It is also recognized as the region's business, cultural, and financial center.

Geography and Climate

Bismarck is located on the east bank of the Missouri River in south-central North Dakota. It is situated on butte-like hills overlooking the river, and lies within one of the country's leading wheat-producing areas. North Dakota's climate is continental and fairly uniform throughout; the Bismarck region is temperate with moderate rainfall. Winters are long and severe; summers are short but favorable for agriculture because of the long hours of sunshine.

Area: 27.0 square miles (2000)

Elevation: 1,700 feet above sea level

Average Temperatures: January, 20.0° F; July, 84.4° F; annual average, 53.8° F

Average Annual Precipitation: 15.47 inches of rain; 44 inches of snow

History

Crossing on the Missouri Exploited by Indians, Whites

Long before white settlement of the Northern Plains began, a natural ford on the site of present-day Bismarck was known to Plains Indian tribes as one of the narrowest and least dangerous crossings on the Missouri River. Stone tools and weapons found in the vicinity indicate that the area was used thousands of years ago by prehistoric big-game hunting tribes. By the time white explorers arrived in the 1700s, those tribes had been displaced by the Mandan and Hidatsa peoples. Unlike nomadic Plains tribes, the Mandan and Hidatsa built fortified towns, raised cultivated plants in

settled communities in and around present-day Bismarck, and developed a thriving Northern Plains trading hub.

The Mandan were among the first people on the Plains to be contacted by whites, and relations between them were generally friendly. The first recorded visitor was French explorer Pierre Gaultier de Varennes, Lord de La Verendrye, who discovered Mandan earthen lodges in present-day Bismarck in 1738 while searching for a water route to the Pacific Ocean. Most subsequent contact was with Canadian fur traders, until Lewis and Clark camped with the Mandan in 1804-1805. In the 1820s and 1830s, American traders out of St. Louis, Missouri, began to ply the Missouri River in steamboats and an outpost of the American Fur Company was established near Bismarck. Contact with white traders and white diseases proved nearly fatal to the Mandan; in 1837, the tribe was virtually destroyed by smallpox. By that time, a small white settlement had been established at present-day Bismarck called Crossing on the Missouri, and it thrived in a small way as a port for steamboats carrying military troops and supplies to forts and Indian agencies in the Missouri River basin.

Dakota Territory Opened; Railroad and Gold Spur Settlement

The U.S. Congress organized the Dakota Territory in 1861 (originally consisting of the two present-day Dakotas plus parts of Montana and Wyoming), but white settlement did not begin in earnest until the indigenous tribes had been expelled. In 1871-1872, squatters who anticipated the arrival of Northern Pacific Railway tracks settled at the Crossing on the Missouri. In 1872, Camp Greeley (later Camp Hancock), a military post, was established nearby to protect the railroad crews, and in June 1873, the railroad reached the crossing. It carried printing presses for the *Bismarck Tribune,* which published its first edition in July 1873; today it is North Dakota's oldest newspaper still publishing. The paper scored its greatest scoop when it was first to publish the story of Custer's last stand at the Little Big Horn in Montana in 1876. Bismarck mourned the loss of Custer and his men, who often left their post at nearby Fort Abraham Lincoln to join in the social life of the town. (In 1881 Mandan, Bismarck's sister city, was established across the Missouri River just north of Fort Lincoln.)

In 1873, the settlement was renamed Bismarck in honor of the first chancellor of the German Empire. Germans had previously invested in American railroads, and it was hoped that Germany would invest in the financially ailing Northern Pacific. Bismarck's first church service was organized in 1873 by distinguished citizen, author, and suffragette Mrs. Linda Warfel Slaughter, who also started the first school, became the first county school superintendent, and organized the Ladies Historical Society. In her book *The New*

Northwest, Mrs. Slaughter estimated the 1874 population of Bismarck at 1,200 people. Bismarck was incorporated in 1875 and began to grow as a steamboat port and, until 1879, as the western terminus of the Northern Pacific Railway. The town attracted rivermen and wood choppers, who supplied personnel and fuel needs for riverboats.

Life in the little town was rugged. River traffic closed in the winter because of low water, and the railroad discontinued operating out of Fargo, North Dakota, into Bismarck until spring, when Bismarck residents might look forward to the flooding of the river. Fires were frequent, thanks to poorly constructed, flimsy homes, tents, and rough wooden buildings lit by kerosene lamps.

In 1874, gold was discovered in the Black Hills of South Dakota. Bismarck experienced its first boom as gold seekers poured in to outfit themselves for the 200-mile trip to Deadwood, South Dakota. Some stayed to take advantage of new business opportunities.

As railroad tracks were laid across America, word spread to the East and to Europe of the rich land of the Plains, suitable for growing wheat and grazing livestock. Men and women came to break the virgin soil and to build sod houses, barns, frame houses, and windmills. Those who settled around Bismarck suffered considerably when the Missouri River flooded in 1881; livestock drowned, homes were destroyed, and wildlife were carried down the river on ice floes. Bismarck residents who lived on higher ground were more fortunate. In 1882, Northern Pacific built a bridge across the Missouri River at Bismarck. While the trains would no longer have to cross the river on barges in the summer and on tracks laid over the ice in the winter, the event marked the end of Bismarck's prominent position as a center for railroad freight transfers.

City Becomes Center for Dakota Government

In 1882 Bismarck replaced Yankton, South Dakota, as the capital of the Dakota Territory, and a second boom began. The price of land skyrocketed, and everyone believed that Bismarck was on its way to becoming a major population center. It was with high hopes that the cornerstone of the capitol building was laid in 1883 in a gala ceremony that included many prominent figures of the day. Some, such as ex-President U.S. Grant, were members of the Golden Spike Excursion, on their way west to mark the completion of the Northern Pacific Railway. Others present at the ceremony included U.S. congressmen, foreign noblemen, and the Sioux chief Sitting Bull. The high hopes did not pan out; Bismarck grew steadily but slowly as federal and state government offices located there and it became a center for shipping wheat to Minneapolis. Other businesses flourished, including flour mills, creameries, grain elevators, and the innovative Oscar H. Will Company, specialists in seed corn

like that used by the Mandan Indians, as well as several varieties of hardy, drought-resistant plants.

When the Dakota Territory was divided and North and South Dakota entered the Union in 1889, Bismarck became the capitol of North Dakota. As the town developed politically, new buildings went up, including schools, churches, and frame houses to replace sod shanties. By 1890, 43 percent of the population was foreign-born, and mostly comprised of Russians, Germans, Norwegians, Canadians, English, Irish, and Swedes. In 1898 the Northern Pacific freight depot caught fire; the fire spread and destroyed most of downtown Bismarck. However, citizens rallied and the town was quickly rebuilt.

The population around Bismarck swelled in 1903 when thousands of German farmers moved from Wisconsin and began producing dairy products, wool, honey, and corn, all of which were shipped out of Bismarck. In 1909 the Bureau of Indian Affairs opened an Indian boarding school in Bismarck. By 1910 the population had risen to 4,913 people; by 1920 the population was 7,122; and by 1930 it reached 11,090. The population increase was mostly due to farmers moving into town to retire or because they were looking for an education for their children. A drought and an invasion of hordes of grasshoppers in the 1930s destroyed wheat crops and brought home the need to diversify farming in the region.

In December 1930, with the Great Depression and the drought under way, the old capitol building burned down and talk turned to moving the capitol elsewhere. By a popular statewide vote in 1932, it was decided to keep Bismarck as the capitol. On October 8, 1932, the cornerstone was laid for a new statehouse.

Manmade Changes Usher in the Modern Era

Bismarck farmers and ranchers benefited from the 1947 construction of the Garrison Dam, 75 miles up the Missouri River, as spring flood danger was lessened, but the project remains controversial. Local Indian tribes claim that land was taken from them for the massive project, and environmentalists decry the loss of the natural shortgrass land and the flooding of countless acres of bottomland. The project was headquartered at Fort Lincoln, and attracted new residents to Bismarck. Sister projects the Heart Butte Dam and the Dickinson Dam opened up new recreational opportunities to Bismarckers. By 1950, 18,541 people called Bismarck home.

In 1951, oil was discovered near Tioga, North Dakota. Although it was flowing from wells 200 miles away, it led to the formation of state agencies and oil company offices in Bismarck, and the city became a center for oil leasing activities. Bismarck continued to cope with floods and droughts, but farms thrived because of improved farming methods. Bismarck's population soared to 27,670 people in 1960. During that decade, attention turned to soil and wildlife preservation and water conservation, and new office buildings, a junior college, a conservatory of music, and highways were constructed. Construction continued into the 1970s, when shopping centers and homes were built, and prospects for Bismarck's growth and prosperity looked bright.

Today Bismarck is the center of North Dakota state government and home to an impressive historical museum as well as several colleges, including a unique intertribal college owned and operated by five Native American tribes. A thriving medical, transportation and trade center, Bismarck boasts amenities typically found in much larger cities.

Famous or notorious former residents of Bismarck include poet James W. Foley, author of the official state song and several books including *Prairie Breezes*; Alexander McKenzie, politician, friend of the railroads, and the man credited with moving the Dakota Territory capital to Bismarck; the French-born Marquis de Mores, who hoped to establish a huge meat packing industry in the Badlands, was tried three times in a sensational murder case and found not guilty, and who founded the town of Medora, North Dakota, named in honor of his wife; former President Theodore Roosevelt, who owned a cabin in town from 1883 to 1885 when he was a rancher in the Badlands; and General E.A. Williams, first representative from Burleigh County to the Territorial Assembly.

Historical Information: State Historical Society of North Dakota, State Archives & Historical Research Library, Heritage Center, Capitol Grounds, 612 East Boulevard Avenue, Bismarck, ND, 58505-0830; telephone(701)328-2666, fax (701)328-3710

Population Profile

Metropolitan Area Residents
1980: 54,811 (Burleigh County)
1990: 83,831 (MSA)
2000: 94,719 (MSA)
Percent change, 1990–2000: 13.0%
U.S. rank in 1990: Not reported
U.S. rank in 2000: 260th

City Residents
1980: 44,485
1990: 49,256
2000: 55,532
2003 estimate: 56,344
Percent change, 1990–2000: 11.1%
U.S. rank in 1990: 527th
U.S. rank in 2000: 620th

Density: 2,065.2 people per square mile (2000)

Racial and ethnic characteristics (2000)
White: 52,634
Black or African American: 156
American Indian and Alaska Native: 1,884
Asian: 251
Native Hawaiian and Pacific Islander: 15
Hispanic or Latino (may be of any race): 415
Other: 95

Percent of residents born in state: 77.4% (2000)

Age characteristics (2000)
Population under 5 years old: 3,356
Population 5 to 9 years old: 3,431
Population 10 to 14 years old: 3,790
Population 15 to 19 years old: 4,308
Population 20 to 24 years old: 4,380
Population 25 to 34 years old: 7,339
Population 35 to 44 years old: 8,842
Population 45 to 54 years old: 7,815
Population 55 to 59 years old: 2,545
Population 60 to 64 years old: 2,084
Population 65 to 74 years old: 3,888
Population 75 to 84 years old: 2,631
Population 85 years and older: 1,123
Median age: 36.5 years

Births (2001)
Total number: 865 (Burleigh County)

Deaths (2001)
Total number: 481 (Burleigh County; the infant death rate was 7.8 per 1,000 live births)

Money income (1999)
Per capita income: $20,789
Median household income: $39,422
Total households: 23,163

Number of households with income of . . .
less than $10,000: 2,065
$10,000 to $14,999: 1,682
$15,000 to $24,999: 3,255
$25,000 to $34,999: 3,337
$35,000 to $49,999: 4,102
$50,000 to $74,999: 4,910
$75,000 to $99,999: 2,129
$100,000 to $149,999: 1,102
$150,000 to $199,999: 286
$200,000 or more: 295

Percent of families below poverty level: 5.7% (59.1% of which were female householder families with related children under 5 years)

2002 FBI Crime Index Total: 1,698

Municipal Government

The city of Bismarck operates under the commission form of government. Four commissioners and a president (who also serves as mayor) are elected at large to four-year terms. The commission meets regularly on the second and fourth Tuesday of each month.

Head Official: Mayor John Warford (since 2002; current term expires 2006)

Total Number of City Employees: 471 (full-time; 2003)

City Information: City/County Office Building, 221 N 5th Street, PO Box 5503, Bismarck, ND 58506-5503; telephone (701)222-6471; fax (701)222-6470

Economy

Major Industries and Commercial Activity

Bismarck has a strong, diversified economy that has been continually expanding since the 1980s. As the capital city of North Dakota, it serves as a major hub for government, business and finance; it is also a major distribution center for the agricultural industry. Services and retail trade continue to dominate the local market, together employing more than 50 percent of the non-agricultural workforce.

The state government is Bismarck's largest employer with more than 4,300 workers. The health care industry is second; MedCenter One and St. Alexius hospitals and their related clinics employ more than 4,100. Bismarck Public Schools and the federal government each employ more than 1,000 people.

Items and goods produced: energy (coal, natural gas), food and food products, heavy equipment

Incentive Programs—New and Existing Companies

Local programs—Interest buydowns, reduced interest loans, grants, exemptions, and other financial incentives are available through the Bismarck Vision Fund. Other local sources of funding include micro-loan programs that provide short-term loans of $15,000 to $25,000 with a bank turndown at standard bank rates; the Bismarck Loan Pool, a group of local lending institutions and utilities; Bismarck Industries, Inc., which offers supporting participation in construction or leasing of buildings and equipment purchase; and the Small Business Investment Company, a private investment firm that uses its own funds plus money backed by federal Small Business Administration guaran-

tees to make capital investments in small businesses. The Bismarck-Mandan Development Association can help new and expanding companies negotiate preferred terms or grants from local service providers.

State programs—North Dakota is the only state in the nation to control its own development bank. The Bank of North Dakota (BND) arranges financing for the MATCH program, aimed at attracting financially strong companies to North Dakota via loans and low interest rates. The BND also administers the Business Development Loan Program, for new and existing business with higher risk levels; and the PACE fund, which targets community job development. The North Dakota Development Fund provides ''gap financing'' to primary sector businesses. The SBA 504 Loan Program offers long-term, fixed asset financing in partnership with private lenders; the borrower provides 10 percent in cash equity. The SBA 7(a) Loan Program is available to small businesses unable to obtain financing in the private credit marketplace.

Job training programs—Job Service North Dakota administers state- and federally-funded workforce training programs including customized training, on-the-job training, occupational upgrading and Workforce 2000 employee training. The North Dakota New Jobs Training Program provides incentives to businesses that create new employment opportunities in the state. Bismarck State College and the University of Mary are both recognized for meeting the needs of Bismarck-area business and industry; both institutions also offer scholarships and grants for expanding businesses requiring employee training.

Development Projects

The new $25 million Bismarck Airport Terminal opened as scheduled in May 2005; the state-of-the-art facility incorporates high ceilings and glass walls in an ''open spaces'' concept designed to complement its prairie setting. Gateway to Science recently moved to a new location in the High Prairie Arts and Science Complex, the first phase of a planned expansion project that will include a larger gallery, laboratory, classrooms, exhibit space and a community meeting facility. The Capital Area Transit fixed-route public bus system was launched in May 2004.

Economic Development Information: Bismarck/Mandan Chamber of Commerce, 2000 Schafer Street, Bismarck, ND, 58501; telephone (701)223-5660; fax (701)255-6125

Commercial Shipping

The city of Bismarck lies at the intersection of Interstate 94 and U.S. Highway 83. Bismarck is served by Burlington Northern Santa Fe Railroad Company and Dakota, Missouri Valley, and Western Rail. Air freight service is available at the Bismarck Airport.

Labor Force and Employment Outlook

Employment in Bismarck is provided by state and federal government, energy companies, trade, transportation, and health services. Growing fields include data processing and customer service. Statewide, agriculture and tourism are top industries.

The 2003 Bismarck-Mandan Labor Study reports high workforce productivity and credits a well-educated population combined with a Midwest work ethic. The local workforce is also considered loyal and dependable; 85.2 percent of employers report daily absenteeism below 6 percent and the average length of employment at the current job is more than 8 years.

The following is a summary of data regarding the Bismarck metropolitan area labor force, 2004 annual averages.

Size of nonagricultural labor force: 55,200

Number of workers employed in . . .
  construction and mining: 3,100
  manufacturing: 2,900
  trade, transportation and utilities: 11,400
  information: 1,500
  financial activities: 3,000
  professional and business services: 4,700
  educational and health services: 9,400
  leisure and hospitality: 5,000
  other services: 2,900
  government: 2,700

Average hourly earnings of production workers employed in manufacturing: $14.35 (statewide average)

Unemployment rate: 3.9% (February 2005)

Largest employers	Number of employees
State of North Dakota	4,309
MedCenter One Health Systems	2,250
St. Alexius Medical Center	1,900
Bismarck Public Schools	1,506
Federal Government	1,198
Bobcat/Ingersoll Rand	867
City of Bismarck	444
University of Mary	400
Basin Electric Power Cooperative	399
Wal Mart	380

Cost of Living

Bismarck-Mandan ranks consistently high in quality of life surveys. In 2003 *Expansion Management* magazine listed the Bismarck MSA among its "Five Star Communities;" Bismarck also ranked second in a Harvard University study of "community attitudes and civic engagement." North Da-

kota was recognized as the safest state in the nation in seven of the past eight years.

The following is a summary of data regarding several key cost of living factors for the Bismarck area.

2004 (3rd Quarter) ACCRA Average House Price: $220,000

2004 (3rd Quarter) ACCRA Cost of Living Index: 93.1 (U.S. average = 100.0)

State income tax rate: Ranges from 2.1% to 5.54%

State sales tax rate: 5%

Local income tax rate: None

Local sales tax rate: 1%

Property tax rate: 483.72 mills per $1,000 (2003)

Economic Information: Bismarck-Mandan Chamber of Commerce, 2000 Schafer Street, PO Box 1675, Bismarck, ND, 58502-1675; telephone (701)223-5660; fax (701)255-6125

Education and Research

Elementary and Secondary Schools

The Bismarck Public School system is the second-largest school district in the state. The drop-out rate in 2002-2003 was only 1.5 percent. Special education and early learning opportunities are offered in both private and public schools. Several local schools have earned the national honor of being designated "Blue Ribbon Schools.". Bismarck Public School District has been recognized year after year for meeting the needs of families in a national "What Parents Want" competition; the annual survey honored just 16 percent of public school districts in the country in 2005.

The following is a summary of data regarding the Bismarck public school system as of the 2002–2003 school year.

Total enrollment: 10,400

Number of facilities
  elementary schools: 15
  junior high/middle schools: 3
  senior high schools: 2
  other: 3

Student/teacher ratio: 13.35:1

Teacher salaries
  minimum: $26,000
  maximum: $53,964

Funding per pupil: $7,034 (State of North Dakota)

In 2002, Bismarck/Mandan had 1,789 students in 9 private elementary schools, 9 private middle schools, and 2 private high schools.

Public Schools Information: Bismarck Public Schools, 806 North Washington, Bismarck, ND 58501; telephone (701)355-3000; fax (701)355-3001

Colleges and Universities

Bismarck State College (BSC) is a two-year college offering more than 30 vocational and technical programs. BSC students may also take their first two years towards a bachelor's degree in arts or sciences. Medcenter One College of Nursing accepts students in their junior year for a two-year bachelor's degree focusing on general nursing science, clinical practice and research. Minot State University offers four-year degree programs in criminal justice, social work, management, and psychology; it also offers nine online degrees. The University of North Dakota (UND) Graduate Center offers master's programs in such fields as education, business administration, social work, and public administration; students can enroll in online, evening, and weekend classes. The UND School of Medicine offers a four-year doctor of medicine degree.

The University of Mary is a private Christian school offering four-year degrees in 34 programs, as well as graduate degrees in nursing, management, education, and physical therapy. St. Alexius Medical Center is home of the North Dakota School of Respiratory Care and St. Alexius School of Radiologic Technology. The United Tribes Training College is a unique intertribal college, owned and operated by five Native American tribes. The college offers 10 associate degree programs and certificates in 10 other areas, as well as adult education and on-site daycare.

Libraries and Research Centers

The Bismarck Veterans Memorial Public Library has more than 169,000 book titles, 553 magazine subscriptions, 4,320 audiotapes and compact discs, 4,338 videotapes and DVDs, and 945 miscellaneous items ranging from artwork to fishing poles. Its bookmobile collection includes 21,274 items. A U.S. government document depository, the library has special collections on Northern Missouri River history and the Lewis and Clark Expedition.

The North Dakota State Library on the Capitol grounds specializes in state government publications. Holdings include more than 132,000 books, nearly 15,000 tape cassettes, more than 111,000 state documents dating from 1889 to the present, and nearly 25,000 federal documents. The State Historical Society of North Dakota Library houses the official state archives. It has special collections on anthro-pology and the history of the Northern Great Plains, as well as archaeological artifacts.

Other major libraries in Bismarck are the Bismarck State College Library, which has 55,000 book titles and specializes in North Dakota history; the University of Mary's Welder Library, which holds 65,000 volumes; and the Q&R MedCenter One Health Sciences Library, which specializes in clinical medicine and nursing.

Public Library Information: Bismarck Public Library, 515 N. Fifth St., Bismarck, ND 58501; telephone (701)222-6410

Health Care

St. Alexius Medical Center was opened in 1885 by a group of Benedictine Sisters and was the first hospital in Dakota Territory. The 285-bed facility serves the Bismarck area as well as central and western North Dakota, northern South Dakota and eastern Montana. Medcenter One Health Systems offers a range of services, including nine primary care clinics, a home health agency, three long-term care facilities and a 238-bed hospital. The two institutions have combined resources to offer state-of-the-art cancer care at the Bismarck Cancer Center.

Recreation

Sightseeing

Visitors to the grounds of the North Dakota State Capitol, also known as the ''Skyscraper on the Prairie,'' can tour the building and also enjoy the arboretum trail that winds among various state buildings, and features 75 species of trees, shrubs, and blooming flowers. Also on site is a statue of Sacajawea, the Indian woman who accompanied Lewis and Clark on their expedition through Bismarck. The statue of the guide was erected by the North Dakota Federation of Women's Clubs in 1910. Nearby, the North Dakota Heritage Center, the most comprehensive of the state's museums, houses one of the largest collections of Plains Indian artifacts in the United States. Also open for tours is the Historic Governor's Mansion that served as the governor's residence from 1893 to 1960.

Docked at the historic Port of Bismarck, the *Lewis & Clark* riverboat offers paddlewheel cruises of the Missouri River. Open daily from April through September (and only weekends in the winter season), the Dakota Zoo is home to more than 125 species of birds, reptiles, and mammals. Camp

From the Port of Bismarck the *Lewis & Clark* riverboat provides paddlewheeler cruises along the Missouri River.

Hancock State Historic Site includes an interpretive museum of military life and local history in its original log building, an early Northern Pacific Railroad locomotive, and Bismarck's first Episcopal church. Double Ditch Indian Village State Historic Site displays the ruins of a Mandan Indian earthlodge village inhabited from years A.D. 1500-1781. The restored Fort Lincoln Trolley offers a unique scenic rail trip from Bismarck to Fort Abraham Lincoln State Park.

Fort Abraham Lincoln houses the reconstructed home of General George Custer. Visitors can view a staff performance set in Custer's time, visit the soldiers' central barracks, and shop at the commissary store. The hill above the fort provides panoramic views of the Missouri Valley. On-a-Slant Indian Village displays replicas of Indian earth lodges on the site of an ancient Mandan village. An on-site museum contains Native American and military artifacts. Visitors to Fort Abraham Lincoln State Park can experience the Custer Trail Ride and explore the panoramic views from bluffs overlooking the Missouri River.

The Lewis & Clark Interpretive Center, 35 miles north of Bismarck in Washburn, provides a view of what life was like on the trail for the explorers, and features the world-famous artwork of Karl Bodmer, who chronicled Plains Indian life and local river landscapes.

North Bismarck's Gateway to Science offers hands-on exhibits that provide learning opportunities for visitors of all ages. The Railroad Museum, north of nearby Mandan, has on view handmade models, photographs, and uniforms, and offers miniature train rides. Located just a few miles east of Bismarck, Buckstop Junction contains reconstructed buildings that date back to the 1800s and early 1990s. Visitors can tour a mining camp complete with a coal mine, gas shovel, scale house, and mine buildings.

Bismarck is about 130 miles east of the South Unit of Theodore Roosevelt National Park and is a stopping-off point for visitors to that monument to the 26th President of the United States.

Arts and Culture

A primary venue for the performing arts in Bismarck is the Belle Mehus Auditorium, which is on the National Register of Historic Places. Built in 1914, the auditorium hosts performances of the Bismarck-Mandan Symphony Orchestra and the Northern Plains Ballet, one of the state's newest and fastest growing performing arts organizations.

Sleepy Hollow Summer Theatre offers live performances and classes. The Shade Tree Players is a children's theater group offering summer productions. The Bismarck/Mandan area is also home to the North Dakota Association of Dance and Drill and to the Dakota West Arts Council, the area's arts umbrella agency.

Arts and Culture Information: Bismarck-Mandan Symphony Orchestra, PO Box 2031, Bismarck, ND 58502; telephone (701)258-8345

Festivals and Holidays

September is a festive month in Bismarck. The city hosts one of the nation's largest Native American cultural events—the annual United Tribes International Pow Wow. More than 70 tribes are represented at this award-winning festival, which features 1,500 dancers and drummers and draws 30,000 spectators. Also in September is the Annual International Indian Art Expo, which highlights Native American artists and provides traditional song, music, dance, and storytelling. The Folkfest Celebration takes place over four days in September, with a parade, carnival, street fair, book festival, tractor pull, walking and running events, and plenty of food. Bismarck Marathon, North Dakota's only major marathon, is also held in September and attracts runners from around North America.

The highlight of October is the Edge of the West PRCA Rodeo, featuring the nation's toughest rough stock and champion cowboys. Month's end brings the Children's All-City Halloween Party. December begins with the annual Fantasy of Lights Parade, featuring lighted holiday floats. Sertoma Park is the site of the Christmas In The Park display of lighted trees. Fort Abraham Lincoln State Park hosts *Custer Christmas;* guests can tour General Custer's home decorated for the holidays and celebrate the season with sleigh rides and a buffalo burger buffet.

July events include Frontier Army Days at Fort Abraham Lincoln State Park, featuring a look at the lives of the ladies of the frontier army, as re-enactors cook and launder and hold cavalry and artillery drills. The annual Mandan Rodeo Days celebration also takes place in July, with more than 100 artist booths, ethnic food, music, a carnival, and a petting zoo.

August is the month for the Bismarck Art & Galleries Association annual art fair on the State Capitol Grounds. Also in August, the Fur Trader Rendezvous at Fort Abraham Lincoln features demonstrations of fire starting, toolmaking, rifle marksmanship, and dancing.

The Bismarck Civic Center hosts a number of annual events, including the Bismarck Tribune Sport Show in February, the Spring Blossoms Craft Fair in May, the Missouri River Festival in June, and the Monaco International Motorcoach Event in August.

The Bismarck-Mandan Symphony League, a volunteer organization, schedules festive fundraisers throughout the year, such as a Holiday Home Walk and a spring Wild n' Wooly Wing Ding. This fun activity has received two national awards from the American Symphony Orchestra League as one of the six most unique and effective fundraisers in the nation.

Sports for the Spectator

The Bismarck Bobcats bring exciting North American Hockey League action to the VFW Sports Center. The Dakota Wizards play professional basketball at the Bismarck Civic Center.

Sports for the Participant

Bismarck has an outstanding parks and recreations system that includes bicycle and skate parks, an archery range, baseball diamonds, boat ramps, jogging and exercise tracks, hockey and figure skating rinks, all-season arenas, racquetball courts, swimming pools, tennis courts, and soccer fields. There are seven golf courses in the area; Bismarck's Hawk Tree Golf Course placed second on Golf Digest's 2000 list of the top new courses in the United States.

With its location on the Missouri River in the North Central Flyway, the Bismarck-Mandan area offers some of the best fishing and hunting opportunities available in North America. Nineteen of North Dakota's 23 game fish species are found in the Missouri River. Some of the best natural areas of the relatively unaltered habitat left on the Missouri River system are just upstream and downstream from Bismarck-Mandan. The habitat is home to abundant upland and big game. Pheasant, grouse, partridge, dove white-tailed deer and many other non-game species of birds and animals are available for picture taking, observing, and hunting. Other activities enjoyed in the Bismarck area include camping, curling, gymnastics, horseshoes, cross-country skiing, go-cart racing, and downhill skiing.

Shopping and Dining

Bismarck-Mandan is the retail hub for south-central North Dakota, a retail trade area that includes nearly 170,000 people. Downtown Bismarck offers more than 70 stores of all sorts, as well as art galleries and antique shops. Kirkwood Mall features more than 100 specialty stores and five major department stores. Other malls include Arrowhead Plaza, Northbrook Shopping Center, Gateway Mall, and Upfront Plaza.

The historic Burlington Northern Railroad Depot on Main Street in Mandan is home to Native American arts and crafts. Works of more than 200 North Dakota American Indian artists are available for purchase.

A variety of dining establishments can be found in Bismarck, from the Captains Table Restaurant, boasting one of the largest menus in the upper Midwest, to Space Aliens restaurant, which promises ''out of this world food,'' to the Fiesta Villa, where south-of-the-border food is served in

Bismarck's historic Spanish mission-style depot. Other restaurants feature hot buffets, Italian food, regional beef and prime rib, and seafood.

Visitor Information: Bismarck-Mandan Convention and Visitors Bureau, 1600 Burnt Boat Drive, Bismarck, ND, 58503; toll-free (800)767-3555

Convention Facilities

The Bismarck Civic Center features 16 meeting rooms, 84,000 square feet of exhibit space and arena seating for 10,000 in two separate but connected buildings. The Pavilion at Prairie Knights Casino and Resort seats 2,000 and offers 34,000 square feet of meeting and exhibit space. The Mandan Community Center is a full-service recreation and convention center. Bismarck-Mandan also has more than 2,600 rooms in 30 hotels and motels.

Convention Information: Bismarck-Mandan Convention and Visitors Bureau, 1600 Burnt Boat Drive, Bismarck, ND, 58503; telephone (800)767-3555

Transportation

Approaching the City

The Bismarck Airport has daily commercial service via Northwest, United Express, Big Sky, and Allegiant airlines to Minneapolis, Denver, and Las Vegas. The airport is served by three major national auto rental chains. Rimrock Stages provides bus service in the area.

Traveling in the City

The Capital Area Transit System, known as the CAT, serves the Bismarck-Mandan area. The Bis-Man Transit Board offers Greyhound bus service, a Taxi 9000 on-demand service, and an elderly and handicapped transit system. A restored trolley car that once ran in Bismarck now offers a unique trip to Fort Abraham Lincoln State Park.

Communications

Newspapers and Magazines

The Bismarck Tribune, North Dakota's oldest newspaper still publishing, appears every morning. Other newspapers published in Bismarck are the biweekly *Farm and Ranch Guide,* and the monthly *Dakota Catholic Action.*

Magazines published in Bismarck include the monthlies *Enterprise Connection,* a business publication; *Dakota Country,* which promotes hunting and fishing; *North Dakota Stockman;* and *Vintage Guitar,* which focuses on the hobby of guitar playing. *North Dakota Outdoors,* a natural resources magazine, is issued ten times per year. *The Sunflower,* a magazine for sunflower producers, is issued six times per year. Locally published quarterlies include *North Dakota Horizons,* a consumer magazine of North Dakota lifestyles and *North Dakota History,* which focuses on the history and culture of North Dakota and the Great Plains.

Television and Radio

Bismarck has six television stations—four network stations, one public station, and one community access station. The city is also served by three AM radio stations and six FM stations.

Media Information: *Bismarck Tribune,* PO Box 5516, Bismarck, ND 58506; telephone (701)223-2500; fax (701) 223-2063

Bismarck Online

Bismarck-Mandan Chamber of Commerce. Available www .chmbr.org

Bismarck-Mandan Convention & Visitors Bureau. Available www.bismarckmandancvb.com

Bismarck-Mandan Development Association. Available www.bmda.org

Bismarck Public Schools. Available www.bismarck.k12.nd .us

The Bismarck Tribune. Available www.bismarcktribune .com

City of Bismarck Home Page. Available www.bismarck.org

North Dakota State Library. Available ndsl.lib.state.nd.us

State Historical Society of North Dakota. Available www .state.nd.us/hist

Theodore Roosevelt National Park. Available www.nps .gov/thro

Selected Bibliography

Bird, George F., and Edwin J. Taylor, Jr., *History of the City of Bismarck North Dakota: The First 100 Years 1872-1972,* (Bismarck: Bismarck Centennial Association, 1972)

Rogers, Ken, Allison Hawes Bundy, Laura Seibel, eds., *Bismarck by the River* (Bismarck, North Dakota: The *Bismarck Tribune,* 1997)

Remele, Larry, ed., *The North Dakota State Capitol: Architecture and History* (Bismarck, ND: the state Historical Society of North Dakota, 1989)

Fargo

The City in Brief

Founded: 1871 (incorporated, 1875)

Head Official: Mayor Bruce Furness (D) (since 1994)

City Population
1980: 61,383
1990: 74,084
2000: 90,599
2003 estimate: 91,484
Percent change, 1990–2000: 22.3%
U.S. rank in 1980: 329th
U.S. rank in 1990: 297th
U.S. rank in 2000: 302nd

Metropolitan Area Population
1980: 137,574
1990: 153,296

2000: 174,367
Percent change, 1990–2000: 13.7%
U.S. rank in 1990: Not reported
U.S. rank in 2000: 179th

Area: 38 square miles (2000)
Elevation: 900 feet above sea level
Average Annual Temperature: 41° F
Average Annual Precipitation: 19.6 inches of rain; 35 inches of snow

Major Economic Sectors: Wholesale and retail trade, services, government
Unemployment Rate: 3.8% (February 2005)
Per Capita Income: $21,101 (1999)

2002 FBI Crime Index Total: 3,266

Major Colleges and Universities: North Dakota State University

Daily Newspaper: *The Forum*

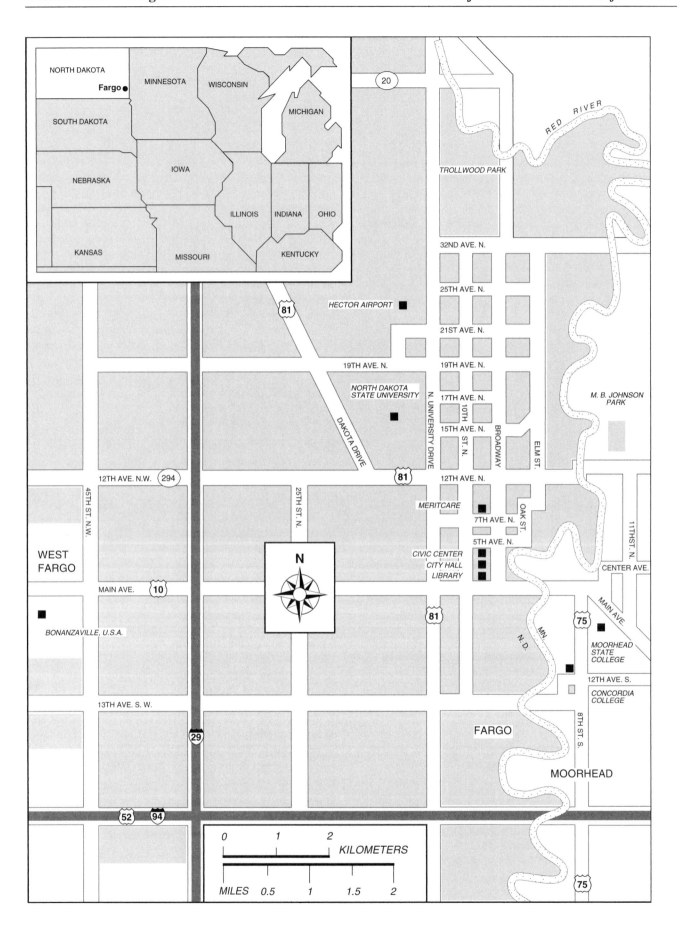

NORTH DAKOTA

Fargo

MINNESOTA

WISCONSIN

MICHIGAN

SOUTH DAKOTA

IOWA

NEBRASKA

ILLINOIS INDIANA OHIO

KANSAS

MISSOURI

KENTUCKY

RED RIVER

20

TROLLWOOD PARK

32ND AVE. N.

25TH AVE. N.

HECTOR AIRPORT

81

21ST AVE. N.

19TH AVE. N.

19TH AVE. N.

NORTH DAKOTA
STATE UNIVERSITY

17TH AVE. N.

M. B. JOHNSON
PARK

DAKOTA DRIVE

N. UNIVERSITY DRIVE

10TH ST. N.

15TH AVE. N.

BROADWAY

ELM ST.

12TH AVE. N.W. 294

45TH ST. N.W.

25TH ST. N.

81

12TH AVE. N.

MERITCARE

OAK ST.

7TH AVE. N.

11TH ST. N.

5TH AVE. N.

WEST
FARGO

CIVIC CENTER
CITY HALL
LIBRARY

CENTER AVE.

MAIN AVE. 10

N

81

75

MAIN AVE.

BONANZAVILLE, U.S.A.

N.D.

MN.

MOORHEAD
STATE
COLLEGE

12TH AVE. S.

CONCORDIA
COLLEGE

13TH AVE. S. W.

29

FARGO

8TH ST. S.

MOORHEAD

52 94

0	1	2

KILOMETERS

75

MILES 0.5 1 1.5 2

Introduction

Fargo is the largest city in North Dakota and the seat of Cass County. It is the focus of a metropolitan statistical area that extends over Cass County, North Dakota, and Clay County, Minnesota, where Fargo's sister city, Moorhead, is located. Founded by the Northern Pacific Railway, the city was an important transportation and marketing point for the surrounding fertile wheat-growing region. Today it is an agribusiness and agricultural research center. *Money Magazine* consistently ranks Fargo among the nation's most livable small cities, noting that it is a safe city and a "booming regional center for health care and financial services." The city has been declared a "Great Plains success story, with locally grown high-tech firms and a state university" by *Kiplinger's Personal Finance Magazine.*

Geography and Climate

Flat and open terrain surrounds Fargo, which is situated on the eastern boundary of North Dakota opposite Moorhead, Minnesota, in the Red River Valley of the North. The Red River, part of the Hudson Bay drainage area, flows north between the two cities.

Precipitation is generally Fargo's most significant climatic feature. The Red River Valley lies in an area where lighter amounts of precipitation fall to the west and heavier amounts to the east. Seventy-five percent of the precipitation, accompanied by electrical storms and heavy rainfall in a short period of time, occurs during the growing season, April to September.

Summers are comfortable, with low humidity, warm days, and cool nights. Winters are cold and dry, the temperatures remaining at zero or below approximately half of the time; snowfall is generally light. The legendary Dakota blizzards result from drifting of even minimal snowfall, caused by strong winds that blow unimpeded across the flat terrain.

Area: 38 square miles (2000)

Elevation: 900 feet above sea level

Average Temperatures: January, 6° F; July, 71° F; annual average, 41° F

Average Annual Precipitation: 19.6 inches of rain; 35 inches of snow

History

Railroad Route Creates Townsite

The city of Fargo was founded by the Northern Pacific Railway in 1871 in expectation of the railroad track to be built across the Red River of the North. This particular location was selected as a safeguard against flooding because it represented the highest point on the river. The city was named for William G. Fargo, founder of the Wells-Fargo Express Company and a director of the Northern Pacific Railway. When the railroad announced in 1871 that a track would be laid from Lake Superior to the Pacific Ocean, land speculators sought to capitalize on the opportunity. Thus ensued attempts on the part of both the railroad and the speculators to outwit one another and to gain first possession of the land. For a time the railroad staked a claim but after much litigation decided to withdraw.

During the winter of 1871 to 1872, the settlement was divided into two distinct communities. One of them, "Fargo on the Prairie," became headquarters of the Northern Pacific engineers and their families. Although they lived in tents, the accommodations were the best available given the conditions. The other, "Fargo in the Timber," was much cruder and more primitive, consisting of huts, log houses, dugouts, and riverbank caves. The Timber community became known for its hard-drinking, gun-carrying men who had a rough sense of humor and enjoyed practical jokes. A delivery of potatoes to the Prairie community was once sabotaged by the Timber men, who loosened the wagon endgates and shot their guns to scare the horses. The potatoes that spilled onto the ground turned out to be the only supply available for the winter.

Fargo was located in what was still legally Native American territory, and the railroad company claimed the Timber residents were illegal squatters on Native American land and were selling illegal liquor. In February of 1872, federal troops surrounded the Timber settlement, issuing warrants for the arrest of those accused of selling liquor and ordering the others to leave under threat of destruction of their crude homes. The settlers appealed to the government, claiming their land rights had been violated. A treaty was negotiated with the native tribes that opened the land to settlement and those who had not broken the law were able to retain their land.

Agricultural Prosperity Survives Disasters

Law and order followed with the arrival of new settlers on the first train of the Northern Pacific to cross the Red River on June of 1872. Soon residents were surprised to learn that Fargo was situated on rich wheat land. With the reduction of freight rates in 1873, farming became economically profitable and the town prospered. Two decades later Fargo suffered a severe fire, which began on one of the main streets and consumed the entire business district as well as the northwestern sector. This tragedy led to many civic improvements and put an end to wood construction.

Near disaster struck again four years later, when the Red River, dammed by ice north of Fargo, began rising. It continued to rise for a week; in order to save the railroad bridges, locomotive and threshing machines were placed on them. Citizens were forced to evacuate through second-story windows, and the flood carried away 18 blocks of sidewalk and 20 blocks of wooden street paving.

During the first 30 years of the twentieth century, Fargo prospered from an influx of Norwegian immigrants who were attracted by the promise of a better life and a free farm. Fleeing economic depression in their own country, they introduced their customs to the upper Red River Valley, thus helping to shape the character of present-day Fargo. The city remains an important agricultural center as well as a regional distribution and transportation hub.

Due to its affordable housing, workforce availability, high standards of living and education, and low unemployment rate, in 2004 *Expansion Management* magazine awarded Fargo a "Five Star Community" rating in its annual "Quality of Life Quotient."

Historical Information: North Dakota State University Library, North Dakota Historical Manuscript, Photograph, and Book Collection, 1301 12th Ave. N., PO Box 5599, Fargo, ND 58105; telephone (710)231-8886

Population Profile

Metropolitan Area Residents
1980: 137,574
1990: 153,296
2000: 174,367
Percent change, 1990–2000: 13.7%
U.S. rank in 1990: Not reported
U.S. rank in 2000: 179th

City Residents
1980: 61,383
1990: 74,084
2000: 90,599
2003 estimate: 91,484
Percent change, 1990–2000: 22.3%

U.S. rank in 1980: 329th
U.S. rank in 1990: 297th (State rank: 1st)
U.S. rank in 2000: 302nd (State rank: 1st)

Density: 2,388.2 people per square mile (2000)

Racial and ethnic characteristics (2000)
White: 85,321
Black or African American: 922
American Indian and Alaska Native: 1,119
Asian: 1,482
Native Hawaiian and Pacific Islander: 40
Hispanic or Latino (may be of any race): 1,167
Other: 400

Percent of residents born in state: 59%

Age characteristics (2000)
Population under 5 years old: 5,763
Population 5 to 9 years old: 5,263
Population 10 to 14 years old: 5,008
Population 15 to 19 years old: 7,012
Population 20 to 24 years old: 13,477
Population 25 to 34 years old: 15,144
Population 35 to 44 years old: 13,051
Population 45 to 54 years old: 11,054
Population 55 to 59 years old: 3,157
Population 60 to 64 years old: 2,550
Population 65 to 74 years old: 4,532
Population 75 to 84 years old: 3,171
Population 85 years and older: 1,417
Median age: 30.1 years

Births (2001, Cass County)
Total number: 1,727

Deaths (2001, Cass County)
Total number: 747

Money income (1999)
Per capita income: $21,101
Median household income: $35,510
Total households: 39,354

Number of households with income of . . .
less than $10,000: 3,888
$10,000 to $14,999: 3,022
$15,000 to $24,999: 6,384
$25,000 to $34,999: 6,085
$35,000 to $49,999: 6,861
$50,000 to $74,999: 7,010
$75,000 to $99,999: 2,898
$100,000 to $149,999: 2,095
$150,000 to $199,999: 454
$200,000 or more: 657

Percent of families below poverty level: 6.6% (45% of which were female householder families with related children under 5 years)

2002 FBI Crime Index Total: 3,266

Municipal Government

Fargo, the seat of Cass County, is governed by a city commission comprised of five at-large members, one of whom serves as mayor. Commissioners are elected to a four-year term. All commissioners, including the mayor, are subject to a limit of three consecutive terms.

Head Official: Mayor Bruce Furness (D) (since 1994; current term expires June 2006)

Total Number of City Employees: 750 (2005)

City Information: City Commission, 200 North Third Street, Fargo, ND 58102; telephone (701)241-1310

Economy

Major Industries and Commercial Activity

The Fargo economy is based on education, the medical industry, agricultural equipment manufacturing, retailing, and services. The city is a retail magnet for the entire Upper Plains; its per capita retail spending is usually among the nation's highest because so many people from the region go to Fargo to do their shopping. Because of its central location, the city is a transportation hub for the northern Midwest region. Agriculture has long been of primary importance to Fargo, as the Red River Valley area contains some of the richest farmland in the world; related industries include agribusiness and agricultural research. However, in recent years, software companies have brought a touch of Silicon Valley to the area.

The principal manufacturing employer is Case I H, makers of heavy-duty tractors. Terminals for two oil pipeline systems—Standard Oil Company of Indiana and Great Lakes Pipeline Company of Oklahoma—are located in Fargo-Moorhead. The Standard Oil pipeline is connected with the company's refinery in Whiting, Indiana, which produces more than 30,000 barrels of oil a day.

Fargo has received many accolades for its economy and pro-business environment. In 2004, *Business Development Outlook* magazine ranked the Fargo-Moorhead area fifth on its

list of "Best Places for a Thriving Economy." Also in 2004, *Expansion Management* magazine rated the area as one of the top places to locate a company, and *Forbes* magazine ranked it the second-best small city in the country for business and careers.

Items and goods produced: food, concrete, dairy and meat products, fur coats, jewelry, luggage, neon signs, electrical apparatus, sweet clover and sunflower seeds

Incentive Programs—New and Existing Companies

Local programs—Several incentive programs are available to businesses that locate or expand in Cass County; among them are property tax and income tax exemptions, an interest rate subsidy program, and loans of up to $8,000 at U.S. treasury rates. The Chamber of Commerce of Fargo Moorhead offers business services to its members, including an employee assistance program, group medical insurance, and seminars.

State programs—North Dakota's Economic Development & Finance Division assists businesses with start-up, expansion, and recruitment. Dakota Certified Development Company (CDC) administers the Small Business Administration 504 program in North Dakota. The program creates and retains jobs via the financing of real estate and equipment. The North Dakota Development fund provides secondary sources of funding to businesses through loans and equity investments.

Job training programs—Several state and federal programs assist in training or retraining workers. Workforce 2000 aids North Dakota employers in implementing new technologies and work methods. Under the Workforce 2000 program, the cost of employee training may be reimbursed. New Jobs Training provides financial assistance to businesses filling hourly job positions.

Economic Development Information: Fargo-Cass County Economic Development Corporation, 51 Broadway, Suite 500, Fargo, ND 58102; telephone (701)364-1900

Development Projects

In 1999, the North Dakota legislature established the Renaissance Zone program to encourage private sector investment in neglected areas. Approved projects are eligible for tax exemptions and credits. Fargo's Renaissance Zone, which encompasses 35 blocks of the downtown area, saw more than $200 million worth of development projects each year between 1999 and 2004. The downtown revitalization has included storefront rehabilitation, beautification and the conversion of unused buildings into commercial and residential space.

In 2002, MeritCare Health System began a five-year, $55 million renovation to the downtown MeritCare Medical Center campus. The first major renovation to the facility since the 1970s will see the expansion and renovation of the children's hospital, the conversion of most patient hospital rooms into private rooms, an addition to house the Heart Services department, and the construction of a two-tier parking facility.

Commercial Shipping

Fargo is served by the Burlington Northern/Santa Fe Railroad, which has its Dakota Division headquarters in Fargo; the average daily number of trains is 60. More than 120 regional, national, and international truck lines serve Cass County, transport products, machinery, and bulk commodities to and from Fargo.

Labor Force and Employment Outlook

Fargo has become a resettling point for Bosnians, Somalis, Sudanese, and others who have joined Fargo's labor force. Fargo boasts a well-educated labor force that has been shown to be 20 percent more productive than the national average. A strong Midwestern work ethic contributes to a low absentee rate, and over half of Cass County businesses have a turnover rate of 5 percent or less. In 2003, more than 80 percent of Fargo's workforce held high school diplomas. North Dakota is a right to work state. In February of 2005 Fargo's unemployment rate was just under 4 percent; an unemployment rate of 3 percent or less is considered full employment.

The following is a summary of data regarding the Fargo-Moorhead metropolitan area labor force, 2004 annual average.

Size of non-agricultural labor force: 109,600

Number of workers employed in . . .
   construction and mining: 6,500
   manufacturing: 8,900
   trade, transportation, and utilities: 24,900
   information: 3,200
   financial activities: 8,100
   professional and business services: 10,300
   educational and health services: 15,600
   leisure and hospitality: 11,100
   other services: 4,900
   government: 16,100

Average hourly earnings of production workers employed in manufacturing: $13.90

Unemployment rate: 3.8% (February 2005)

Largest employers	*Number of employees*
MeritCare Health System	6,100
North Dakota State University	3,391
Fargo Public School District Number One	1,320
Dakota Clinic, Ltd.	1,200
Microsoft	960
US Bank Service Center	925

Largest employers	*Number of employees*
City of Fargo	750
Innovis Health	740

Cost of Living

The cost of living in Fargo is well below the national average.

The following is a summary of data regarding several key cost of living factors in the Fargo area.

2004 (3rd Quarter) ACCRA Average House Price: $228,990

2004 (3rd Quarter) ACCRA Cost of Living Index: 90.4 (U.S. average = 100.0)

State income tax rate: Ranges from 2.67% to 12.0%

State sales tax rate: 5.0% (food and prescription drugs are exempt)

Local income tax rate: None

Local sales tax rate: 1.5%

Property tax rate: 484.06 mills for School District #1; 418.53 mills for School District #6 (2004). An individual property's annual property tax is determined by multiplying the taxable value by that year's mill levy. An assessment ratio of 50% is multiplied by the Assessor's appraisal to get assessed value. Then, the assessed value is multiplied by 9% for residential and 10% for all other property classes to get taxable value. Therefore, the taxable value of residential property is 4.5% of the Assessor's estimate of value and 5% of the Assessor's value for commercial and agricultural property.

Economic Information: Fargo-Cass County Economic Development Corporation, 51 Broadway, Suite 500, Fargo, ND 58102; telephone (701)364-1900

Education and Research

Elementary and Secondary Schools

Public elementary and secondary schools in Fargo are part of Fargo Public School District #1. A superintendent is appointed by a nine-member, nonpartisan school board. The district offers special education classes to students with special needs. Advanced placement classes are available to high-performing high school students. Career and technical education classes at the high school level allow students to receive instruction in fields that pertain to specific careers or interests.

The following is a summary of data regarding Fargo public schools as of the 2002–2003 school year.

Total enrollment: 11,095

Number of facilities
elementary schools: 14
middle schools: 3
senior high schools: 3

Student/teacher ratio: 21.6:1

Teacher salaries
average: $39,029

Funding per pupil: $6,795

Six parochial schools are operated by the Catholic and Lutheran churches in Fargo.

Public Schools Information: Fargo Public Schools, 415 4th Street North, Fargo, ND 58102; telephone (701)446-1000

Colleges and Universities

The Fargo-Moorhead community is served by three universities as well as several vocational schools. North Dakota State University in Fargo, with an enrollment of nearly 12,000 students, awards baccalaureate, master's, and doctorate degrees in a wide range of disciplines; colleges within the university are humanities and social sciences, agriculture, engineering and architecture, home economics, pharmacy, science and mathematics, and teacher education. Located on the university campus is Tri-College University, a consortium of area colleges and universities that allows students to take classes at Concordia College and Minnesota State University Moorhead at no extra charge. Cardinal Meunch Seminary trains young men for the priesthood. Aakers College is a private, two-year degree granting institution. Concordia College, Moorhead State University, and Moorhead Technical College are located in Moorhead.

Libraries and Research Centers

The Fargo Public Library maintains holdings of more than 133,000 volumes, more than 250 magazine and newspaper subscriptions, and compact discs, films, DVDs, and audio- and videotapes. The library maintains computers with Internet access and various software applications that are available to the public. Children's services include story time and a summer reading program. The library operates one branch library and a bookmobile in addition to the main branch. Online research databases may be accessed through the library's Internet website. The North Dakota State University Library houses about 402,807 books, 5,090 periodical and subscription titles, and CD-ROMs, audio- and video-tapes, and maps. Special collections include bonanza farming, the North Dakota Biography Index, North Dakota

Pioneer Reminiscences, and the North Dakota Historical Manuscript, Photograph and Book Collection; the library is also a depository for federal and state documents. Specialized libraries in the city are affiliated with hospitals, fraternal societies, and religious organizations.

The Northern Crop Science Laboratory on the North Dakota State University campus is a division of the Agricultural Research Service of the U.S. Department of Agriculture. Government and university scientists conduct cooperative research on barley, hard red spring wheat, durum wheat, flax, sunflowers, and sugar beets; the goal is to expand and retain profitable production of these crops through the use of the most advanced equipment and research techniques.

Public Library Information: Fargo Public Library, 102 North Third Street, Fargo, ND 58102; telephone (701) 241-1472

Health Care

Fargo is the primary health care center for the region between Minnesota and the West Coast. The major health system is MeritCare Health System, which is the largest group practice and largest hospital in the state. Nearly 400 physicians specialize in 74 areas of medicine, including internal medicine, prenatal care, cancer care, and eating disorders. Three hospital locations, including the new Children's Hospital, provide 583 patient beds. In 2004, MeritCare was rated one of the nation's top 100 hospitals in a *Modern Healthcare* report.

Recreation

Sightseeing

A visit to Fargo might begin with a stop at the Fargo-Moorhead Convention & Visitors Bureau's Visitors Center, where the Walk of Fame has been providing a little bit of Hollywood in the Midwest since 1989 with hand prints or footprints of more than 80 musicians, athletes, movie stars and dignitaries, including Neil Diamond, Bob Costas, Garth Brooks, President George W. Bush, and the Eagles.

One of downtown Fargo's more recent attractions is the Plains Art Museum; it offers regional art, guided tours, and facilities for receptions. Included in the museum's permanent collection are pieces by Mary Cassatt, Luis Jimenez, and William Wegman. Bonanzaville USA is a recreated pioneer village of 40 restored buildings on a 15-acre site; the

The Plains Art Museum covers 9,000 square feet on three floors, and houses a collection totaling more than 2,400 pieces.

structures were relocated from a number of small North Dakota towns and represent various types of architecture. Included among them are a drugstore, general store, sod and farm houses, district courtroom, and barber shop. Vintage automobiles, farm machinery, and airplanes are also on exhibit. The main attraction at Moorhead's Heritage Hjemkomst Interpretive Center is the sailing ship the late Robert Asp of Moorhead modeled after ancient Viking vessels. Housed in an architecturally distinctive building that also includes the Clay County Historical Museum, the ship made a journey from Duluth, Minnesota, to Bergen, Norway, in 1982.

The Solomon G. Comstock Historic House in Moorhead is the former home of this prominent Fargo-Moorhead figure who was a financier and political and cultural force in the community. The authentically restored Victorian house contains its original furnishings. The Roger Maris Museum in the West Acres Shopping Center pays tribute to the city's most famous athlete, who broke Babe Ruth's single-season home run record in 1961 when he hit 61 home runs. Maris donated all of his trophies and sports memorabilia to the museum as a tribute to the city in which he grew up. The Children's Museum at Yunker Farm, a century-old farm house, presents participatory learning exhibits in the physical, natural, and social sciences.

Arts and Culture

The Fargo Theatre, a landmark movie theater built in 1926, has been fully restored and is the site of film showings as well as live theater, music, and dance performances. On weekends, the Mighty Wurlitzer organ performs intermission music during each show at the theater. The Fargo-Moorhead Community Theater group stages 12 annual productions at the Fargo-Moorhead Community Theatre. Other local performing groups are the Fargo-Moorhead Symphony Orchestra, the Fargo-Moorhead Opera, and the Red River Dance and Performing Company. The Trollwood Performing Arts School provides arts education, entertainment, and activities for children.

Festivals and Holidays

The Fargo Film Festival, in March, screens the best in independent filmmaking at the Fargo Theatre and other downtown locations. In July, the Downtown Street Fair features craft booths, food, and entertainment. Bonanzaville USA holds Pioneer Days in August, when more than 100 demonstrators revive the skills and crafts of the past. The Fargo Blues Festival, in August, is a two-day event that features world class bands; more than 20 Grammy winners or nominees have performed at the event, which has been called one of "America's Best" by actor Dan Aykroyd. A Winter Blues Fest is held in February. The Big Iron Farm Show fills the Red River Valley Fairgrounds on the second

weekend in September, bringing the latest farm products and services from 400 agribusiness exhibitors. The holiday season brings Christmas on the Prairie at Bonanzaville USA and the annual Santa Village at Rheault Farm, with opportunities to feed deer, meet Santa, and enjoy a sleigh ride.

Sports for the Spectator

Although Fargo does not field any major league sports teams, it is home to other professional and collegiate teams. The Fargo-Moorhead Redhawks of the Northern League play baseball at Newman Outdoor Field. The Fargo-Moorhead Jets are a Junior A developmental league hockey team for 17- to 20-year-olds making the transition from high school to college; they play a 54-game season from September through March at the John E. Carson Coliseum.

The North Dakota State University Bison have won 20 National Collegiate Athletic Association (NCAA) Division II national championships, including the 2002 women's indoor track and field championship. The university fields men's and women's teams in 10 sports, including football, basketball, baseball, and softball. The Moorhead State University Dragons, and the Concordia College Cobbers also present a complete schedule of men's and women's major and minor sports. The Red River Valley Speedway presents stock car racing.

Sports for the Participant

The Fargo Park District sponsors an extensive program of sports for all age groups. Recreational facilities include 73 public parks, 12 public golf courses, 38 public tennis courts, and 4 public swimming pools. Winter sports are particularly popular with ice skating, figure skating, and youth and adult hockey available at both indoor and outdoor facilities; outdoor rinks are equipped with warming houses. Other recreational pursuits include volleyball, basketball, track, soccer, walking, cross-country skiing, ballroom dancing, table tennis, and broom ball. The Scheels Fargo Marathon is held in May.

Charitable and cultural organizations sponsor gaming operations at 39 casinos in Fargo-Moorhead's public establishments. Profits benefit the programs of the sponsoring organizations, and fraternal groups allocate profits to public causes. Games include blackjack, paper slot machines, bingo, and tri-wheel.

Shopping and Dining

The Fargo shopping scene is a mix of unique local establishments and national retailers. The Crafters Mall, open year round, has more than 250 display areas featuring crafts from around the country. The Fargo Antique Mall is one of the largest in the state, with more than 7,000 square feet of antiques, books, and collectibles. Gordmans is a local department store selling name brand clothing and shoes, fragrances, furniture, and home accessories. West Acres Shopping Center, the largest mall in the region with more than 120 stores and restaurants, is anchored by Marshall Field's, JC Penney, Sears, and Herberger's.

Fargo restaurants offer a range of choices. Ethnic options include Asian, Indian, Italian, Mediterranean, and Mexican. Dining in historic settings is offered at Runck Chateau Ranch, a working cattle ranch, and at The White House, District 31—Victoria's, and The Conservatory.

Visitor Information: Fargo-Moorhead Convention & Visitors Bureau, 2001 44th Street SW, Fargo, ND 58103; telephone (701)282-3653; toll-free (800)235-7654

Convention Facilities

Fargo's main convention/multipurpose facility, the $48 million FARGODOME, opened in 1992. It is the largest multipurpose facility of its kind between Minneapolis and Spokane. FARGODOME's seven meeting rooms total more than 13,500 square feet; the 80,000 square foot arena seats more than 26,000 guests. Eighteen luxury suites each accommodate up to 16 guests.

Constructed in 1960, the Fargo Civic Center hosts a variety of events, including state political conventions, concerts, trade exhibitions, sporting events, and business gatherings. The 11,000-square-foot arena accommodates up to 3,333 persons for sports events and concerts and 1,200 people in a banquet setting. The exhibition hall, measuring 40 feet by 150 feet, seats 600 people for both theater-style and banquet functions; the hall can be divided into four rooms for private meetings.

The Red River Valley Fairgrounds offers facilities for agricultural expositions, trade shows, conventions, and entertainment.

Convention Information: Fargo-Moorhead Convention & Visitors Bureau, 2001 44th Street SW, Fargo, ND 58103; telephone (701)235-7654; toll-free (800)235-7654. FARGODOME, 1800 North University Drive, Fargo, ND 58102; telephone (701)241-9100

Transportation

Approaching the City

Hector International Airport is situated 10 minutes northwest of downtown Fargo. United Express and Northwest Airlines offer daily flights to Minneapolis, Chicago, and Denver. Amtrak provides two daily trains, one eastbound and one westbound. Bus service by Greyhound is available.

Highways serving metropolitan Fargo include I-94, extending east to west through the south sector of the city, and I-29, which runs north to south and provides links to I-70, I-80, and I-90, all east-west connections. U.S. 10 and 52 are east-west routes, and U.S. 81 extends through the city from north to south. State routes serving Fargo are 20 and 294, both running east to west.

Traveling in the City

Except for streets following the configuration of the Red River, Fargo is laid out on a grid pattern. The city is divided into quadrants; roadways running north to south are designated "street," while those running east to west are labeled "avenue." First Avenue and Main Avenue are major thoroughfares crossing the river to connect Fargo with Moorhead, Minnesota.

Public bus transportation in Fargo is provided by Fargo Metropolitan Area Transit (MAT). MAT operates 10 bus routes in Fargo and one in West Fargo; the system is coordinated with the Moorhead Transit System for a combined total of 18 bus routes. Passengers with disabilities who are unable to ride without assistance may use the MAT Paratransit service.

Communications

Newspapers and Magazines

Fargo's daily newspaper is *The Forum.* The paper's Internet website also provides daily coverage as well as archives of previous stories. Other newspapers include *New Earth,* a Catholic Diocese publication, and *Spectrum,* the bi-weekly North Dakota State University student newspaper. *The Area Woman* is a free quarterly magazine. *The Fargo-Moorhead Magazine* is a free local-interest magazine published every-other month. *Prairie Business,* a regional business magazine targeted toward readers in North Dakota, South Dakota, and western Minnesota, is published monthly.

Television and Radio

Six television stations—five commercial and one public—broadcast in Fargo; cable service is available. Sixteen AM and FM radio stations schedule a variety of programming.

Media Information: The Forum, 105 5th Street North, Fargo, ND 58102-4826; telephone (701)235-7311

Fargo Online

City of Fargo home page. Available www.ci.fargo.nd.us

Fargo-Cass County Economic Development Corporation. Available www.fedc.com

Fargo-Moorhead Chamber of Commerce. Available www .fmchamber.com

Fargo-Moorhead Convention & Visitors Bureau. Available www.fargomoorhead.org

Fargo Public Library. Available www.ci.fargo.nd.us/library

The Forum. Available www.in-forum.com

North Dakota State University. Available www.ndsu.nodak .edu

Selected Bibliography

Gudmundson, Wayne, *Crossings: a photographic document of Fargo, North Dakota* (North Dakota Institute)

Grand Forks

The City in Brief

Founded: 1875

Head Official: Mayor Michael R. Brown (since 2000)

City Population
 1980: 43,765
 1990: 49,417
 2000: 49,321
 2003 estimate: 48,618
 Percent change, 1990–2000: −0.2%
 U.S. rank in 1990: 511th (State rank: 2nd)
 U.S. rank in 2000: 404th (Grand Forks, ND and East
 Grand Forks, MN combined; State rank: 2nd)

Metropolitan Area Population
 1980: 66,100
 1990: 103,272

 2000: 97,478
 Percent change, 1990–2000: −5.6%
 U.S. rank in 1980: 280th
 U.S. rank in 1990: Not reported
 U.S. rank in 2000: 258th

Area: 19.2 square miles (2000)
Elevation: 834 feet above sea level
Average Annual Temperature: 40.3° F
Average Annual Precipitation: 19.3 inches of rain; 41
 inches of snow

Major Economic Sectors: Trade, government, services
Unemployment Rate: 4.1% (February 2005)
Per Capita Income: $18,395 (1999)

2002 FBI Crime Index Total: 2,442

Major Colleges and Universities: University of North Dakota

Daily Newspaper: *Grand Forks Herald*

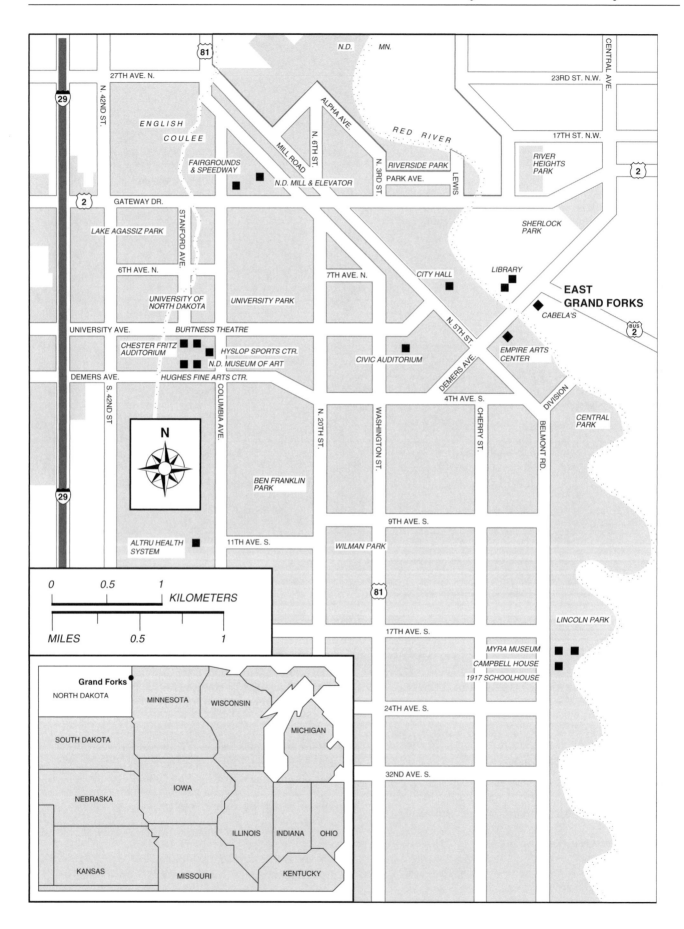

Introduction

Since the 1870s when the juncture of the Red River of the North and the Red Lake River became a crossroads for people and their river-oriented business, the cities of Grand Forks and East Grand Forks have been a focal point of trade and services between the plains of North Dakota and the pine forests of northern Minnesota. Located 75 miles south of the Canadian border, the city is centered in one of the world's richest agricultural regions. The business community is deeply rooted in agriculture and its related enterprises. Today more than 300,000 people in an 18-county area come to Greater Grand Forks for the commercial, recreational, and cultural services it has to offer, which include nearly 40 arts organizations. The city is headquarters for a major university and boasts a key military installation that has an important economic impact on the local economy.

Geography and Climate

Flat and open terrain surrounds Grand Forks, which is just 75 miles south of the Canadian border, and situated on the western boundary of the Red River Valley of the North. Seventy-five percent of precipitation accompanied by electrical storms and heavy rainfall in a short period of time occurs during the growing season, April through September. Summers are comfortable with low humidity, warm days and cool nights. Winters are cold and dry with temperatures remaining at zero or below approximately half the time. Snowfall is generally light. The legendary Dakota blizzards result from drifting of even minimal snowfall caused by strong winds that blow unimpeded across the flat terrain.

Area: 19.2 square miles (2000)

Elevation: 834 feet above sea level

Average Temperatures: January, 5.3° F; July, 69.2° F; annual average, 40.3° F

Average Annual Precipitation: 19.3 inches of rain; 41 inches of snow

History

Railroads Stimulate Growth of City

Located at the junction of the Red Lake River and the Red River of the North, the area of Grand Forks served as a camping and trading site for Native Americans for centuries.

French, British, and American fur traders peddled their wares in and around "La Grand Fourches," as the French named it, meaning "the great forks."

In the 1850s, furs and trade goods passed through the Forks on oxcarts enroute between Winnipeg, Canada, and St. Paul, Minnesota. Steamboats replaced oxcarts in 1859. The shallow-draft steamboats could operate in less than three feet of water as they negotiated the Red River from Fargo to Winnipeg. Alexander Griggs, an experienced Mississippi River steamboat captain, established the town site of Grand Forks in 1870. Griggs teamed up with James J. Hill in the Red River Transportation Line of steamboats in the 1870s.

Grand Forks really began to grow after James J. Hill's Great Northern Railroad came to town in 1880. The Northern Pacific Railroad also built tracks to the city in 1882 and business boomed. Early arrivals who stayed in the region were mostly of northern European background including Scandinavian, German, and Polish immigrants.

Wheat and Lumber Anchor Economy

Wheat farming served as the basis of the Red River Valley prosperity. In 1893 Frank Amidon, chief miller at the Diamond Mills in Grand Forks, invented "Cream of Wheat." George Clifford, George Bull, and Emery Mapes financed the new breakfast porridge venture, and the city became a part of a national breakfast legend.

From the 1880s to 1910, pine logs were floated down the Red River or brought in by rail to sawmills in the city. Many houses in Grand Forks were built of the majestic white pines from the vast forests of northern Minnesota. The University of North Dakota, founded in 1883, became the premier liberal arts institution in the state. The city grew from the river toward the college campus to the west. The Metropolitan Theatre opened in 1890 and for the next 25 years it presented quality productions of music and drama. During the period of the "Gilded Age" at the end of the last century, spacious and elegant houses were built along historic Reeves Drive and South Sixth Street for the local elite.

By 1900, Grand Forks had a population of almost 10,000 people. The wealth from the lumber companies, wheat farms, and railroads enabled the community to take its place as a leading city of the "Great Northwest." After his arrival in the early 1880s, local architect Jon W. Ross designed many of the area's most beautiful buildings. In 1902, Joseph Bell Deremer, trained at Columbia University, began to make his mark upon the community through the new buildings he designed.

The North Dakota Mill and Elevator, the only state-owned flour mill in the country, opened in 1923. The mill allowed North Dakota farmers to bypass Minneapolis-based railroads and milling monopolies. The mill distributed free flour to needy people during the Great Depression of the 1930s. Even today, the mill sends its trademark flour "Dakota Maid" around the world.

Twentieth Century Ends in Disaster; City Rebuilds

Grand Forks grew as a regional trade center in the twentieth century. In recent times Grand Forks residents have endured several hardships. The winter of 1995–1996 brought record snowfall (more than 100 inches in many areas) and eight blizzards. In April 1997, Grand Forks was devastated by a flood that saw the Red River rise to more than 53 feet; flood stage is 28 feet. With 60 percent of the city covered with water, most residents were forced to abandon the city, and the state was declared a disaster area. Damage from the flood was about $1.3 billion. Many residents pledged to return and rebuild, although Mayor Patricia Owens acknowledged that some residents would probably never return. She declared: "The lesson we've learned is that material things don't mean a thing. . . . Pretty soon we'll be back, bigger and better."

Analysts estimated that Grand Forks lost about 2,000 residents, nearly 4 percent of its population, because of destroyed homes and lost job opportunities from the great flood. But, with the initiative of then-Mayor Patricia Owens, the city began to rebuild. She secured $171.6 million in Community Development Block Grant money to help Grand Forks rebuild. She also got the federal government to earmark more than $1 billion for buyouts and relocations of homes, businesses, and schools; money for farmers who lost livestock; and money for infrastructure repair (including the town's sewer system, which was particularly hard-hit). Today, under the leadership of Mayor Brown, the city continues to grow. In 2004 the city was on a record pace for building and expansion, with a total construction value of $106 million. Less than a decade after the flood, Grand Forks has become known as a "Destination City" for its pro-business practices, affordable housing, and community events.

Historical Information: University of North Dakota, Elwyn B. Robinson Department of Special Collections, Chester Fritz Library, Box 9000, Grand Forks, ND 58202-9000; telephone (701)777-2617

Population Profile

Metropolitan Area Residents
1980: 66,100
1990: 103,272
2000: 97,478
Percent change, 1990–2000: −5.6%

U.S. rank in 1980: 280th
U.S. rank in 1990: Not reported
U.S. rank in 2000: 258th

City Residents
1980: 43,765
1990: 49,417
2000: 49,321
2003 estimate: 48,618
Percent change, 1990–2000: −0.2%
U.S. rank in 1990: 511th (State rank: 2nd)
U.S. rank in 2000: 404th (Grand Forks, ND and East Grand Forks, MN combined; State rank: 2nd)

Density: 2,563 people per square mile (2000)

Racial and ethnic characteristics (2000)
White: 46,040
Black or African American: 426
American Indian and Alaska Native: 1,357
Asian: 472
Native Hawaiian and Pacific Islander: 28
Hispanic or Latino (may be of any race): 921
Other: 288

Percent of residents born in state: 63% (2000)

Age characteristics (2000)
Population under 5 years old: 2,910
Population 5 to 9 years old: 2,819
Population 10 to 14 years old: 2,924
Population 15 to 19 years old: 5,012
Population 20 to 24 years old: 8,174
Population 25 to 34 years old: 6,981
Population 35 to 44 years old: 6,657
Population 45 to 54 years old: 5,867
Population 55 to 59 years old: 1,747
Population 60 to 64 years old: 1,394
Population 65 to 74 years old: 2,317
Population 75 to 84 years old: 1,768
Population 85 years and older: 751
Median age: 28.3 years

Births (2001, Grand Forks County)
Total number: 788

Deaths (2001, Grand Forks County)
Total number: 454

Money income (1999)
Per capita income: $18,395
Median household income: $34,194
Total households: 19,658

Number of households with income of . . .
less than $10,000: 2,390
$10,000 to $14,999: 1,438

$15,000 to $24,999: 3,055
$25,000 to $34,999: 3,153
$35,000 to $49,999: 3,436
$50,000 to $74,999: 3,463
$75,000 to $99,999: 1,564
$100,000 to $149,999: 706
$150,000 to $199,999: 230
$200,000 or more: 223

Percent of families below poverty level: 9.3% (64.1% of which were female householder families with related children under 5 years)

2002 FBI Crime Index Total: 2,442

Municipal Government

Grand Forks has been a home rule city since 1970; it was the first city in the state to adopt home rule. Home rule means that cities may act on local matters without going to the state legislature for specific authority.

Grand Forks has a mayor-council form of government. The mayor and 14 councilpersons representing 7 wards or districts in the city are elected to four-year terms. The formal powers of the mayor of Grand Forks are limited. The mayor presides over city council meetings but can vote only if there is a tie. The mayor can veto actions of the council.

Head Official: Mayor Michael R. Brown (since 2000; current term expires June 2008)

Total Number of City Employees: 517 (2004)

City Information: City Hall, 255 North 4th St. PO Box 5200, Grand Forks, ND 58206-5200; telephone (701)746-2607; fax (701)787-3773

Economy

Major Industries and Commercial Activity

Grand Forks has a stable, agriculturally-based economy that has been expanding and diversifying since the early 1980s. Abundant moisture assists the growth of the hard spring wheat, corn, oats, sunflowers, durum, barley, potatoes, sugar beets, dry edible beans, soybeans, and flax that represent its major crops. Cattle, sheep and hogs also contribute to the local farm economy. Plants operate for the processing of potatoes, for the conversion of locally grown mustard seed for table and commercial use, for the refining of beets into

sugar, and for the pearling of barley. Much of the area's durum wheat is marketed through the North Dakota State Mill and Elevator.

While in the early 1980s almost all businesses were agriculturally based, other enterprises such as high-technology firms, a wood products company, and concrete firms now play an important role in the local economy. Some important local firms include: J. R. Simplot, which processes potatoes and other foods; American Woods, a relatively new company that produces outdoor lawn furniture; Strata Corporation, which produces ready-mix concrete and handles asphalt and masonry; the American Crystal Sugar refinery; Young Manufacturing, which custom designs, engineers, and manufactures metal products; Energy Research Center, which conducts research on energy-related products; and R. D. O., which deals in processed foods. In 2001 and 2002, after its 1999 acquisition of Acme Tool Crib of the North, Internet retailer Amazon.com expanded and located a portion of its customer service operations in Grand Forks. Amazon.com is now one of the region's top employers.

The University of North Dakota (UND) is a major contributor to the city's economic life as well as its cultural and entertainment life. UND is the second largest employer in the state.

Grand Forks U.S. Air Force Base is one of the bases in the Air Mobility Command, headquartered at Scott AFB, Illinois. The base is home to the 319th Air Refueling Wing. Announcements in early 2005 about military base closings and realignments may bring changes to Grand Forks AFB, affecting jobs in the community.

Items and goods produced: farm crops, fertilizer, chemicals, seeds, wood products, metal products, concrete, computer software

Incentive Programs—New and Existing Companies

Local programs—The Office of Urban Development (OUD) is responsible for the administration and management of a variety of economic development programs. These activities are performed under the guidance and supervision of the Grand Forks City Council, Growth Fund Board of Directors, Grand Forks Housing Authority, and miscellaneous advisory bodies. For example, the OUD works with the Grand Forks Region Economic Development Corporation to assist businesses and industries wishing to expand or locate in Grand Forks by helping secure funding through various local, state, and federal resources. With the grantsmanship available through the OUD, the city has been successful in securing grants and loans to update the Grand Forks Industrial Park.

State programs—North Dakota's Economic Development & Finance Division assists businesses with start-up, expansion, and recruitment. Dakota Certified Development Company (CDC) administers the Small Business Administration 504 program in North Dakota. The program creates and retains jobs via the financing of real estate and equipment. The North Dakota Development fund provides secondary sources of funding to businesses through loans and equity investments.

Job training programs—The North Dakota New Jobs Training Program offers incentives to businesses creating new job opportunities that are expanding or relocating to the state. Job Service North Dakota works with businesses to develop training programs, and administers state and federal training programs including the Workforce Investment Act, New Jobs Training program, and Workforce 2000.

Development Projects

Slowly but surely downtown Grand Forks has rebuilt itself. To prevent another flood disaster, the city, along with East Grand Forks, Minnesota and the St. Paul District of the U.S. Army Corps of Engineers, has begun an estimated $386 million flood protection project. The city recently secured $40 million of the U.S. President's 2006 budget to assist with construction, which includes a 100,000 gallon per minute pump station to divert runoff that would otherwise flow into the community. Other major features include 12.3 miles of levees and 1.1 miles of floodwall. Completion of the five-year project is scheduled for 2005.

With a scheduled completion date of 2006, the Wellness Center at the University of North Dakota will provide for the wellness needs of the university community. The $19.3 million building will offer fitness oriented programs such as group exercise and personal training, fitness assessments, weight and cardio machines, and massage therapy.

Economic Development Information: Office of Urban Development, 1405 1st Ave. N., Grand Forks, ND 58203; telephone (701)746-2545. Grand Forks Region Economic Development Corp., 600 DeMers Avenue, Suite 501, Grand Forks, ND 58201; telephone (701)746-2720.

Commercial Shipping

Burlington Northern-Santa Fe schedules 200 freight trains peer week through the region. Seventy motor carriers and several package service carriers are located in the city.

Labor Force and Employment Outlook

Post-flood, Grand Forks civic leaders are looking for ways to make Grand Forks more appealing to professionals and young people.

The following is a summary of data regarding the Grand Forks metropolitan area labor force, 2004 annual averages.

Size of civilian non-agricultural labor force: 50,800

Number of workers employed in . . .
  construction and mining: 2,800
  manufacturing: 3,500
  trade, transportation and utilities: 10,900
  information: 700
  financial activities: 1,600
  professional and business services: 3,000
  educational and health services: 8,300
  leisure and hospitality: 5,300
  other services: 1,900
  government: 12,800

Average hourly earnings of production workers employed in manufacturing: $14.35 (North Dakota average)

Unemployment rate: 4.1% (February 2005)

Largest employers	Number of employees
University of North Dakota	4,945
Grand Forks Air Force Base	4,265
Altru Health System	3,550
Grand Forks Public Schools	1,310
Hugo's Stores	775
Simplot	539
City of Grand Forks	517
Valley Memorial Homes	500
Amazon.com	400

Cost of Living

The following is a summary of data regarding several key cost of living factors in the Grand Forks area.

2004 (3rd Quarter) ACCRA Average House Price: $243,600

2004 (3rd Quarter) ACCRA Cost of Living Index: 96.0 (U.S. average = 100.0)

State income tax rate: Ranges from 2.67% to 12%

State sales tax rate: 5.0% (food and prescription drugs are exempt)

Local income tax rate: None

Local sales tax rate: 1.75%

Property tax rate: 2.25% of appraised value (2005)

Economic Information: Grand Forks Chamber of Commerce, 203 Third Street North, Grand Forks, ND 58203; telephone (701)772-7271

Education and Research

Elementary and Secondary Schools

The Grand Forks Public School District is a progressive school district, with both standard and non-traditional subjects covered in the curriculum. Students routinely use computers and other technologies in the classroom, and all students receive some foreign language instruction prior to high school. The district's special education department is recognized as one of the best in the state; it provides services to disabled persons ages 3 through 21. Gifted students are provided with enrichment opportunities, including Advanced Placement courses at the high school level. Extracurricular opportunities in sports and the arts are offered to students in all grades. The Grand Forks Foundation for Education is a private organization that provides private donations, scholarships, and endowments to the district's schools and its students.

The following is a summary of data regarding Grand Forks's public schools as of the 2003–2004 school year.

Total enrollment: 8,008

Number of facilities
   elementary schools: 12
   middle schools: 4
   senior high schools: 2
   alternative schools: 1

Student/teacher ratio: 18.5:1

Teacher salaries
   average: $39,007

Funding per pupil: $6,663

Five parochial and private schools provide an alternative to the public school curriculum. Two schools at Grand Forks Air Force Base provide education for students in grades kindergarten through eighth grades; high school students on the base are bused to Central High School.

Public Schools Information: Grand Forks Public Schools, 2400 47th Avenue South, Grand Forks, ND 58201; telephone (701)746-2200

Colleges and Universities

The University of North Dakota (UND), with more than 13,000 students, is one of the largest institutions of higher learning in the Upper Midwest. Founded in 1883, the university has a strong liberal arts course and a constellation of 10 professional and specialized colleges and schools. Academic programs are offered in 188 fields, and the curriculum spans arts and sciences, aviation, business, fine arts, engineering, human resources, education, nursing, law, medicine, and graduate studies. UND's school of medicine is recognized as a national leader in training rural health care providers.

Libraries and Research Centers

The Grand Forks City-County Library houses more than 300,000 volumes and subscribes to nearly 400 periodicals. Its Grand Forks Collection includes books, pictures, and oral history of the local area. The library hosts story hours for young children, and has meeting facilities available to the public for a small fee. The library's computer facilities offer free word processing and Internet access. Patrons can access the library's catalog via its Internet website. Within Greater Grand Forks's libraries are more than 3 million volumes as well as periodicals, reports, microfilms, and documents.

The University of North Dakota has an international reputation for research. Among its research centers and service units are the Energy and Environmental Research Center, the Bureau of Governmental Affairs, the Bureau of Educational Services and Applied Research, the Center for Rural Health, and the Upper Midwest Aerospace Consortium.

The Research Center at Altru Hospital participates in research and clinical trials in specialties that include cardiology, oncology, infectious diseases, pain management, and surgery. The Center collaborates with other healthcare providers and academic institutions in a 17 county region of northeastern North Dakota and northwestern Minnesota.

Public Library Information: Grand Forks City-County Library, 2110 Library Circle, Grand Forks, ND 58201; telephone (701)772-8116

Health Care

Altru Health System of Grand Forks serves the more than 200,000 residents of northeast North Dakota and northwest Minnesota. Altru is an integrated health system with headquarters on a 90-acre medical campus. It was created July 1, 1997 when the Grand Forks Clinic and United Health Services integrated following the Red River Flood. Facilities include a 277-bed acute care hospital, a 34-bed rehabilitation center, a 156-physician medical group, and an assisted living community. Specialized services include a surgical center; women's services; heart services; and cancer, diabetes, rehabilitation, and vascular centers. Altru provides care from 7 locations in Grand Forks and 13 regional clinics in northeast North Dakota and northwest Minnesota.

Recreation

Sightseeing

The Grand Forks County Historical Society grounds feature the Myra Museum, which displays the heritage of the Grand Forks area. Exhibits and displays include the Quiet Room, which contains furnishings from the 1700s; the Chapel, with its stained glass windows and objects from historic local churches; and the Lake Agasssiz display, which offers a history lesson in the ancient lake that produced the rich Red River Valley soil. The 1879 Campbell House displays furnishings of family life including a working loom, toys, and a summer kitchen. A 1917 school house, and the 1870s post office are some of the first buildings constructed in the town. The grounds are open for tours May 15 through September 15, with guided tours available every day of the week.

Arts and Culture

Grand Forks has a thriving cultural scene, with performing arts venues that include the Fire Hall Theatre, which offers a season of musicals, dramas, classics, and comedies in an intimate 114-seat setting, and the restored 1919 Empire Arts Center. The Chester Fritz Auditorium on the University of North Dakota (UND) campus presents a diversity of national, regional, and local theatrical productions and is home of the Greater Grand Forks Symphony Orchestra. The campus's Burtness Theatre is the site of excellent college dramatic productions. Community performing arts groups include the Greater Grand Forks Symphony and Youth Symphony, Grand Forks Master Chorale, Grand Forks City Band, and North Dakota Ballet Company.

The North Dakota Museum of Art, located on the UND campus, is the state's official art gallery and serves as the center of cultural life for a five-state region. The museum exhibits national and international contemporary art with shows changing every six to eight weeks. During the winter, the Museum Concert Series presents classical music concerts. The Hughes Fine Arts Center Gallery on the UND campus exhibits the works of national and regional artists as well as students. The UND Witmer Art Center displays quality works by professional artists.

Festivals and Holidays

February's Winterthing is a two-day indoor art festival with demonstrations and music. Guest writers and poets from across the nation come to the city in March for the Writer's Conference. April's Time Out/WACIPI, sponsored by the Native American Studies Department at UND, offers a variety of activities and entertainment focused on Native American life. During three weekends in June, July, and August, Summerthing in the Park presents Music in the Park, Kids Days, and Artfest. In June, the Greater Grand Forks Fair and Exhibition offers carnival rides, concerts, 4-H entries, and races. From June through September, an outdoor farmers market with free entertainment and concessions is held on the town square. August's Catfish Days is an event for those who love to catch or eat fish or even just enjoy watching the entertainment in the evenings. A popular summer Grand Forks U.S. Air Force Base event, Friends and Neighbors Day, brings thousands of people to watch aerial demonstrations and to peer into cockpits. Crazy Days offers bargain shopping at many local marketplaces in August, and later in the month the two-day Heritage Days Festival includes old time threshing demonstrations and antique machinery. The Potato Bowl in September features football games, a queen pageant, and a golf tournament, among other activities. Christmas in the Park, held from late November through early January, is a driving tour of holiday light displays.

Sports for the Spectator

The University of North Dakota is the home of the Fighting Sioux, with nationally ranked NCAA Division I ice hockey and Division II men's and women's basketball, football, and swimming programs.

Sports for the Participant

The Grand Forks Park District maintains 43 parks and facilities on more than 850 acres of land. Facilities include biking and jogging lanes and paths, two golf courses (including an Arnold Palmer signature golf course), one public swimming pool, eleven outdoor skating rinks, four indoor ice arenas, and tennis and racquetball courts. The Park District's Center Court Fitness Club houses indoor tennis courts, aerobics studios, and a weight room. Two rivers provide outstanding fishing opportunities; the Red River is internationally known for its trophy-sized channel catfish. Winter offers opportunities for snowmobiling, ice fishing, and cross-country skiing.

Shopping and Dining

The largest indoor mall in the region is Columbia Mall, whose stores are anchored by JCPenney, Marshall Field's, and Sears. The Grand Cities Mall, anchored by Big K-Mart, includes stores such as Grand Cities Antiques and Collectibles and Zimmerman's Furniture. The Grand Forks Marketplace, located off of Interstate 29, is home to national retailers such as Target and Lowe's. The Riverwalk Centre, in East Grand Forks, offers unique shopping opportunities in a scenic setting along the Red River. Barnes and Noble University Bookstore is the anchor for a planned ''University Village'' on the UND campus.

East Grand Forks, Minnesota, is home to Cabela's, featuring an extensive collection of hunting, fishing, and outdoor gear in a five-story-high store with a 35-foot high mountain with game mounts, a gigantic aquarium, and indoor firearm testing areas.

The Grand Forks area has more than 85 restaurants serving fast food to gourmet meals, including Chinese, Mexican, Bavarian, and Italian fare as well as the Midwest staple steak-and-potatoes dinner.

Visitor Information: Greater Grand Forks Convention & Visitors Bureau, 4251 Gateway Drive, Grand Forks, ND 58203; telephone (701)746-0444; toll-free (800)866-4566. Grand Forks Parks District, 1210 7th Avenue South, Grand Forks, ND 58208; telephone (701)746-2750

Convention Facilities

Grand Forks is the largest sports, convention, and entertainment center between Minneapolis and Seattle. Its Alerus Center is the largest sports, entertainment, and convention facility in the upper Midwest. The facility includes more than 145,000 square feet of banquet, meeting, and exhibit space; adjustable concert seating for up to 22,000 people; 12 conference rooms; and a 26,000 square foot ballroom. Several local banquet halls, hotels, and restaurants also provide meeting facilities.

Convention Information: Alerus Center, 1200 42nd Street South, Grand Forks, ND 58203; telephone (701)792-1200. Greater Grand Forks Convention & Visitors Bureau, 4251 Gateway Drive, Grand Forks, ND 58203; telephone (701)746-0444; toll-free (800)866-4566

Transportation

Approaching the City

Grand Forks is accessible by two major highways, Interstate 29, which runs north and south, and U.S. Highway 2, which runs east and west. Grand Forks International Airport, located 4.5 miles west of the city, is North Dakota's busiest commercial airport. Northwest Airlines operates daily flights that connect travelers to more than 750 cities worldwide. Amtrak operates daily passenger trains. Interstate bus service is provided by Greyhound and Triangle bus lines.

Traveling in the City

The Cities Area Transit (CAT) provides bus service to both Grand Forks and East Grand Forks Monday through Satur-

day. CAT offers a door-to-door senior ride service for adults 55 and older. Dial-a-Ride service is available for the physically handicapped.

Communications

Newspapers and Magazines

The city's daily newspaper is the *Grand Forks Herald*; although its building burned to the ground in April 1997 during the great flood, the newspaper managed to win a Pulitzer Prize for its coverage of the flood. The paper maintains an Internet website with daily news, a week's worth of archived news, local classified ads, and "online extras." The *Dakota Student,* the student-published campus newspaper of UND, is published twice weekly during the fall and spring semesters. The paper is free to students and community members. The University of North Dakota publishes scholarly journals, including *North Dakota Quarterly,* a literary review.

Television and Radio

Residents of Grand Forks receive programming from one public and one commercial television station and from nine AM and FM radio stations. Grand Forks also receives programming from Fargo. Cable service is available.

Media Information: *Grand Forks Herald,* Knight-Ridder, Inc., 375 2nd Ave. N., PO Box 6008, Grand Forks, ND 58206-6008; telephone (701)780-1100; toll-free (800)477-6572

Grand Forks Online

City of Grand Forks Home Page. Available www .grandforksgov.com

Grand Forks Air Force Base home page. Available www .public.grandforks.amc.af.mil

Grand Forks Chamber of Commerce. Available www .gfchamber.com

Grand Forks Convention and Visitors Bureau. Available www.grandforkscvb.org

Grand Forks County Historical Society. Available www .grandforkshistory.com

Grand Forks Herald. Available www.grandforksherals.com

Grand Forks Park District. Available www.gfparks.org

Grand Forks Public Library. Available www.grandforksgov .com/library

Grand Forks Public Schools. Available www.gfschools.org

Grand Forks Region Economic Development Corporation. Available www.grandforks.org

Office of Urban Development. Available www.grandforks gov.com/gfgov/home.nsf/Pages/Urban + Development

University of North Dakota home page. Available www.und .edu

OHIO

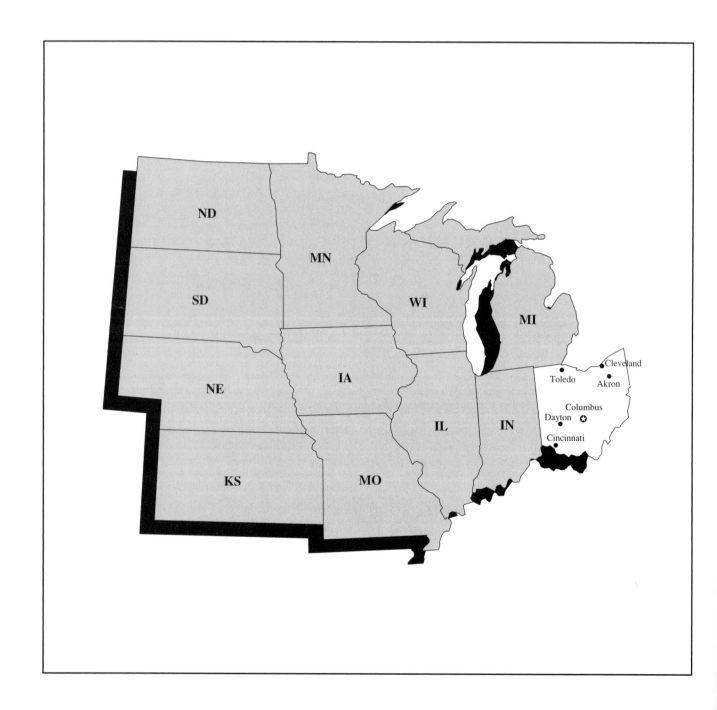

The State in Brief

Nickname: Buckeye State
Motto: With God, all things are possible

Flower: Scarlet carnation
Bird: Cardinal

Area: 44,825 square miles (2000; U.S. rank: 35th)
Elevation: Ranges from 455 feet to 1,550 feet above sea level
Climate: Temperate and continental; humid with wide seasonal variation

Admitted to Union: March, 1, 1803
Capital: Columbus
Head Official: Governor Bob Taft (until 2007)

Population
    1980: 10,798,000
    1990: 10,847,115
    2000: 11,353,140
    2004 estimate: 11,459,011
    Percent change, 1990–2000: 4.7%
    U.S. rank in 2004: 7th
    Percent of residents born in state: 74.7% (2000)
    Density: 277.3 people per square mile (2000)
    2002 FBI Crime Index Total: 469,104

Racial and Ethnic Characteristics (2000)
    White: 9,645,453
    Black or African American: 1,301,307
    American Indian and Alaska Native: 24,486
    Asian: 132,633
    Native Hawaiian and Pacific Islander: 2,749
    Hispanic or Latino (may be of any race): 217,123
    Other: 88,627

Age Characteristics (2000)
    Population under 5 years old: 754,930
    Population 5 to 19 years old: 1,633,214
    Percent of population 65 years and over: 5.4%
    Median age: 36.2 years (2000)

Vital Statistics
    Total number of births (2003): 149,412
    Total number of deaths (2003): 109,700 (infant deaths, 1,162)
    AIDS cases reported through 2003: 6,583

Economy
    Major industries: Trade; finance, insurance, and real estate; manufacturing; agriculture; tourism; services
    Unemployment rate: 6.1% (April 2005)
    Per capita income: $29,953 (2003; U.S. rank: 26)
    Median household income: $43,535 (3-year average, 2001-2003)
    Percentage of persons below poverty level: 10.4% (3-year average, 2001-2003)
    Income tax rate: Ranges from 0.743% to 7.5%
    Sales tax rate: 6.0% (food and prescription drugs are exempt)

Akron

The City in Brief

Founded: 1825 (incorporated 1836)

Head Official: Mayor Donald L. Plusquellic (D) (since 1987)

City Population
  1980: 237,177
  1990: 223,019
  2000: 217,074
  2003 estimate: 212,215
  Percent change, 1990–2000: −2.7%
  U.S. rank in 1990: 71st (State rank: 5th)
  U.S. rank in 2000: 82nd (State rank: 5th)

Metropolitan Area Population (Cleveland–Akron CMSA)
  1980: 2,938,277

  1990: 2,859,644
  2000: 2,945,831
  Percent change, 1990–2000: 3.0%
  U.S. rank in 1990: Not reported
  U.S. rank in 2000: 16th

Area: 62.41 square miles
Elevation: 1,050 feet above sea level
Average Annual Temperature: 49.2° F
Average Annual Precipitation: 35 inches of rain; 48 inches of snow

Major Economic Sectors: research and development, manufacturing, healthcare, education
Unemployment Rate: 7.1% (February 2005)
Per Capita Income: $17,596 (1999)

2002 FBI Crime Index Total: Not reported

Major Colleges and Universities: University of Akron

Daily Newspapers: *The Akron Beacon Journal*

Introduction

Akron is the cradle of the rubber industry in the United States, home of the National Inventors Hall of Fame, birthplace of Alcoholics Anonymous and current site of the leading edge of polymer engineering and research. Akron's history has been one of adaptation, of seeing opportunity and developing a response, all of which has led to the community becoming an industrial power. The city balances a long tradition of manufacturing and transportation businesses with fine cultural tastes. Akron has given the U.S. a century of automotive tires, plastics, oatmeal, roundballer LeBron James, rocker Chrissie Hynde of the Pretenders, New Wave band Devo, and the All–American Soap Box Derby—a true show of the city's diversity.

Geography and Climate

Akron's natural surroundings provide a little of everything—to the south and east lie the gently rolling Appalachian Foothills, to the north is the glacial legacy of Lake Erie, and Akron itself sits on the Cuyahoga River in the Great Lakes Plains region. The Plains are renowned for their fertility, while the Appalachian Plateau is not only beautiful but a concentrated repository of minerals.

Akron experiences four distinct seasons throughout the year. A consistently high level of humidity makes for cold winters and hot summers. The winter season can be quite snowy, although Akron's relative distance from Lake Erie protects it from the full barrage of lake effect precipitation experienced by Cleveland. Year-round moisture generates an excellent growing climate.

Area: 62.41 square miles

Elevation: 1,050 feet above sea level

Average Temperatures: January, 24.8° F; July, 71.5° F; annual average, 49.2° F

Average Annual Precipitation: 35 inches of rain; 48 inches of snow

History

Great Lake, Good Spot to Settle

The last Ice Age left northern Ohio a priceless gift—a mammoth body of water to support fish, game and agriculture, along with rich soil and mineral deposits. Lake Erie was named for a tribe of native people who lived on its shores; other early inhabitants attracted by the bountiful flora and fauna included Iroquois, Miami, Shawnee, Wyandot, Delaware, and Ottawa Indian tribes. The first residents left little mark on the land, aside from a well-worn trail that became known as the Portage Path used to transport canoes between large bodies of water. The native tribes also left a linguistic heads-up— their words for the concepts of ''hunger'' and ''cold'' were soon understood by subsequent European explorers.

Northern Ohio's riches of fish and furs couldn't be ignored by adventurers from across the pond; French trappers set up outposts to protect their fur trade and subsequently fought the British for the area in what came to be known as the French and Indian War. As part of a treaty, France ceded Ohio and the Great Lakes to Great Britain, which forbade U.S. settlers to occupy the area. Not known for obedience to the Queen, pioneers from the eastern U.S. colonies continued to traverse the area; following the American Revolution, Great Britain ceded Ohio and the Northwest Territories to the U.S. However, the British continued to occupy fortifications that they had agreed to leave. Tensions had continued to run high between the U.S. and Great Britain after the war of American independence, and a new generation of ''warhawks'' on the east coast fed the unrest with reports that the Brits were inciting native tribes to perpetrate violence on U.S. pioneers and explorers along the Great Lakes. War was declared in 1812, with British and Canadian troops taking on an under-prepared U.S. military. Native American tribes picked a side and fought for reasons ranging from survival to revenge, although the tribes's alliance with the British was effectively ended when the Shawnee Chief Tecumseh was killed shortly after the Battle of Lake Erie.

The War of 1812 ultimately ended in a stalemate but with lasting effects on both Canada and the U.S.—national identity was cemented in both countries, and a firm border was established along the Great Lakes. Ohio had been a state since 1803, and the U.S. had just spent a great deal of effort to ensure that the productive, fertile area remained part of the Union. But how to bring those riches to the rest of the country?

The Ohio-Erie Canal

Ever since humans first cast eyes on the ocean-like expanse of Lake Erie, the creation of a navigable route between the lake and other major water systems nearby was a primary objective. The Appalachian and Adirondack Mountains created obstacles to ground transportation methods of the time, and water was viewed as an easy route. Plans for a canal system had been percolating for decades before the War of 1812; after the war, construction commenced on the Erie Canal that would connect the northeast end of the lake with the Hudson River, allowing for transportation of goods and people on to the Atlantic Ocean. A parallel canal was begun from the south shore of Lake Erie with a plan to join the Ohio River at Portsmouth, then proceed east through Pennsylvania to the wealthy eastern communities hungry for Ohio wheat, furs, and minerals.

Communities sprang up along the canal construction route and its attendant industries. An hour south of Lake Erie, at the high point of the Ohio-Erie canal, the town of Akron (Greek for "high") was platted in 1811 and founded in 1825. The canal required 17 locks to be passed in the vicinity of Akron, necessitating that passengers spend a number of hours in the burgeoning town. Businesses were developed to meet the needs and desires of the pass-through traffic as well as to facilitate the freight trade—barrels and pottery containers were manufactured in Akron amid taverns, general stores and boat building enterprises. Hard-working immigrants came to Akron to labor on the canal and stayed to prosper in canal-related businesses after the waterway was completed. Akron was established as a true crossroads, and then found itself at the figurative crossroads of the U.S. Civil War.

"Farmers of Rich and Joyous Ohio . . ."

In the mid-1800s, Ohio was a microcosm of the nation. The northern counties, including Summit, were home to some of the most passionate abolitionists in the country. The southern counties, abutting pro-slavery states Kentucky and Virginia, were equally passionate in support of states' rights. In this atmosphere of division, the pro-abolition family of John Brown moved to northern Ohio in search of a politically supportive community. Brown and his family lived a somewhat chaotic existence, as he struggled to provide for his wife and children as a tanner, sheep farmer and wool merchant. In 1844, Brown moved to Akron and partnered with city founder Simon Perkins in a wool business; the partnership was dissolved in 1851 for financial reasons and Brown moved his family out of Ohio as he became increasingly troubled by slavery in the U.S. Events in "bleeding Kansas" inspired Brown and several of his sons to travel to the free state to take part in raids on pro-slavery factions. Brown gained a national platform for his views and actions, which culminated in his band's raid on Harper's Ferry, Virginia (now West Virginia). Brown was apprehended by Robert E. Lee and was hanged in 1859—arguably, the raid on Harper's Ferry pushed the country into Civil War and ultimately gained Brown's goal of ending slavery in the U.S.

With Brown's fierce beliefs in its memory and Sojourner Truth's Akron speech ringing in its ears, Ohio joined the Union and contributed more than its conscripted quota of volunteers to the army during the Civil War. During and after the war, life in Akron and northern Ohio underwent a shift from the agrarian to the industrial, as entrepreneurs

adapted to meet the demands of a nation doing battle. Railroads began to crisscross the country, and Akron was not immune—train transport of goods eventually led to the demise of the Ohio-Erie Canal in 1913. However, in the late 1800s, Akron needed all the freight transport systems available: B.F. Goodrich had come to town.

Akron's Beginnings in Rubber

Dr. Benjamin Franklin Goodrich grew up on the east coast and received his medical education in Cleveland, Ohio. After serving as a surgeon during the Civil War, Goodrich could see the potential in vulcanized rubber products as developed by Charles Goodyear and decided in 1870 to locate a company in Akron. A couple of decades later, the Goodyear Tire and Rubber Company, named in honor of Charles Goodyear, based its headquarters in Akron and provided competition for Goodrich. Firestone Rubber followed in 1900 and General Tire in 1915, establishing Akron as the "Rubber Capital of the World." Rubber production at that time consisted mainly of bicycle and carriage tires and rubber pads for horseshoes. The industry pulled in workers not only from other states but from other countries, making for a motivated and diverse population.

Akron's fortunes were boosted by rubber demand during World War I; the ensuing Great Depression had an economic impact on the industry and the city as a whole, but the American love affair with the automobile came to the rescue. In the early 1900s, the Model T had been outfitted with Goodyear tires; by 1926, Goodyear had become the world's largest rubber company as it sprinted to keep ahead of its competitors in Akron. World War II again increased the need for fighter plane tires and other equipment, bringing more growth and wealth to the Rubber Capital. With many men serving in the military, women entered the industrial workforce in droves; the local rubber manufacturers used women in advertising to both promote the war effort and their products.

After the war, change was in the air. In the 1950s and 1960s, radial tires became the industry standard and Akron's factories weren't equipped for the switch. Some companies attempted a hybrid tire with poor results, and B.F. Goodrich converted its machinery over to radial production equipment at great expense to the company. These costs, coupled with industry strikes and factory shutdowns in the 1970s and 1980s, decimated the rubber business in Akron. Today, Firestone maintains a technical research center in Akron and Goodyear continues to produce racing tires while researching new tire technology, but most of the other rubber companies have left.

Post-Rubber Akron

Akron has rebounded from the tough days in the rubber industry, again demonstrating its ingenuity and resourcefulness in the field of polymer research and engineering. More than 400 polymer-related companies operate in the area, and the University of Akron has created both a degree program in polymer engineering and a research facility that supports local efforts. In addition, aerospace design is taking flight in local industry.

The city of Akron is redefining itself and rediscovering itself as it celebrates its contributions to American inventiveness, music, and sports. The downtown area is undergoing a renaissance, and the Ohio & Erie Canal National Heritage Corridor has been preserved in recognition of the history of the waterway. Akron is facing forward, but it remembers how it got where it is today.

Historical Information: Summit County Historical Society, 550 Copley Road, Akron, OH 44320; telephone (330) 535-1120; email schs@summithistory.org

Population Profile

Metropolitan Area Residents (Cleveland-Akron CMSA)
1980: 2,938,277
1990: 2,859,644
2000: 2,945,831
Percent change, 1990–2000: 3.0%
U.S. rank in 1990: Not reported
U.S. rank in 2000: 16th

City Residents
1980: 237,177
1990: 223,019
2000: 217,074
2003 estimate: 212,215
Percent change, 1990–2000: −2.7%
U.S. rank in 1990: 71st (5th in state)
U.S. rank in 2000: 82nd (5th in state)

Density: 3,497.3 people per square mile (2000)

Racial and ethnic characteristics (2000)
  White: 145,924
  Black or African American: 61,827
  American Indian and Alaskan Native: 575
  Asian: 3,257
  Native Hawaiian and Pacific Islander: 48
  Hispanic or Latino (may be of any race): 2,513
  Other: 940

Percent of residents born in state: 75.6%

Age characteristics: (2000)
  Population under 5 years old: 15,661
  Population 5 to 9 years old: 16,309

Population 10 to 14 years old: 14,809
Population 15 to 19 years old: 14,591
Population 20 to 24 years old: 16,464
Population 25 to 34 years old: 33,234
Population 35 to 44 years old: 32,546
Population 45 to 54 years old: 27,565
Population 55 to 59 years old: 9,003
Population 60 to 64 years old: 7,567
Population 65 to 74 years old: 14,631
Population 75 to 84 years old: 11,321
Population 85 years and over: 3,373
Median age: 34.2

Births (2002, Summit County)
  Total number: 7,015

Deaths (2002, Summit County)
  Total number: 5,352

Money income (1999)
  Per capita income: $17,596
  Median household income: $31,835
  Total households: 90,143

Number of households with income of . . .
  less than $10,000: 5,259
  $10,000 to $14,999: 3,070
  $15,000 to $24,999: 7,703
  $25,000 to $34,999: 7,856
  $35,000 to $49,999: 10,251
  $50,000 to $74,999: 11,648
  $75,000 to $99,999: 4,654
  $100,000 to $149,999: 2,485
  $150,000 to $199,999: 558
  $200,000 or more: 620

Percent of families below poverty level: 14% (36% of which were female householder families with related children under 5 years)

2002 FBI Crime Index Total: Not reported

Municipal Government

The City of Akron operates under the council-mayor form of government, with the 13-member council and the mayor working together to establish administrative departments and to oversee the city finances. The city is divided into 10 wards, each of which elect a council member for a two-year term of service. The other three council members are elected by the city populace at-large and serve four-year terms in office. The mayor is also elected by the general populace of Akron and serves a four-year term. The mayor selects a cabinet composed of the Deputy Mayors of Economic Development, Planning, Public Service, Safety, Labor Relations, Intergovernmental Relations, Finance, and Law.

Head Official: Mayor Donald L. Plusquellic (D) (since 1987; current term expires 2008)

Total Number of City Employees: 3,000 (2005)

City Information: City of Akron, 102 Municipal Building, 166 South High Street, Akron, OH 44308; telephone (330)875-2320

Economy

Major Industries and Commercial Activity

From its former honor as the "Rubber Capital of the World," Akron has moved forward into the world of liquid crystal and polymer research, development, and technology. More than 400 companies in the area are at work on one aspect or another of polymers, creating what is now referred to as "The Polymer Valley." The University of Akron supports the industry with both a College of Polymer Engineering and a specialized laboratory and research facility accessible by Akron area business partners.

As a transportation hub between the east coast of the U.S. and parts west, Akron has built an industry around motor vehicle production, movement of freight, and aeronautics. In 2003 the local branch of Lockheed-Martin was awarded a $2 million Department of Defense contract to develop a new high altitude airship capable of carrying a variety of payloads. Local researchers in the aeronautics field have been studying "lighter than air" technology for aircraft since the days of the Goodyear Blimp being docked in Akron.

Items and goods produced: plastic products, polymers, chemicals, metals, motor vehicles and related equipment, biomedical products, aeronautical instruments, and controls

Incentive Programs—New and Existing Companies

Local programs—Through Tax Increment Financing, the City of Akron offers businesses the opportunity to apply real property taxes to a public infrastructure improvement that will directly benefit the business. In addition, businesses that locate or expand into an Akron Enterprise Zone are eligible for a tax abatement program that allows for up to 100 percent of tangible personal property taxes to be in abatement for up to 10 years.

State programs—The State of Ohio encourages new businesses, expansion of existing businesses, export of Ohio-produced goods, and flexibility of production via a variety of incentive programs. The Machinery and Equipment Tax Credit is based on the amount of a company's investment in machinery purchase or retooling in an Ohio county over the three years preceding claim of the tax credit and is divided evenly over seven years. A Research and Development Tax Credit is available for machinery and equipment purchased for pure and directed research activities. Those manufacturers who get their goods into international circulation may be able to capitalize on the Export Tax Credit, which is based on the average increase in export sales over the two years prior to the tax credit claim. The Brownfields Tax Credit provides a break for private sector businesses that rehabilitate and reuse properties once considered environmentally contaminated.

A refundable Job Creation Tax Credit is available to businesses that locate or expand in Ohio; the tax credit may be as much as 75 percent for up to 10 years. The Working Opportunity and Welfare to Work tax credit programs encourage employers to hire individuals from seven targeted groups of potential employees, including food stamp recipients, vocational rehab referrals from the Department of Veteran Affairs, Supplemental Security Income recipients, participants in Temporary Assistance for Needy Families, and 18-24 year olds. Employers may also receive tax breaks to offset costs of training current employees via the Ohio Training Tax Credit Program.

Job training programs—The state of Ohio has created the Enterprise Ohio Network of public community colleges and universities that work with businesses and organizations to provide continuing education for employees. The Ohio Investment in Training Program offers reduced-cost training and materials to new or expanding businesses, with an emphasis on employment sectors in which training costs are comparatively high.

Summit County's Employment Resource Center assists employers with recruitment and skills testing for prospective employees, customizes on-the-job training for new or reallocated workers, and can advise employers and employees during layoff situations.

Development Projects

In an effort to counter the outflow of businesses and residents to malls and suburbs, downtown Akron became a Special Improvement District in the mid-1990s. This designation as a private nonprofit entity has allowed the city to enhance parking and transit services, marketing of the downtown area, business recruitment and retention, and the physical presentation and security of the area. The restoration project has included adaptive reuse of large, unoccupied businesses in the district; examples include the Roetzel & Andress Office Center (bringing 85,000 square feet of retail space and 100,000 square feet of office space to the downtown area) and Advanced Elastomer Systems (now located in buildings 40 and 41 of the B.F. Goodrich complex and continuing the trend of innovation in a most appropriate setting).

The City of Akron has a number of business and industrial parks under development or open for new enterprises. The Ascot Business Park is being cultivated for light industrial and manufacturing businesses, with 85 of 228 total acres complete in 2005. Current tenants include companies that produce plastics, chemicals, aluminum, glass, and graphic art rubber products. The Airport Development Area encourages location of businesses that fit within the existing aviation, commercial, and industrial themes. Current tenants include a bottling company, flight schools, and plastic producers. The University Technology Park is located near the University of Akron Polymer Science Center and is dedicated to industrial research and technology businesses specializing in polymers. Nine acres are available for development.

New businesses established in the Akron area include the headquarters of both Newell Rubbermaid and Neighborhood Development Corporation, L'Oreal Cosmetics, Feature Foods, Lockheed-Martin, RJS Manufacturing, 24 Brown Street Corporation, Spectrum Brands, and Includis Manufacturing Software.

In 2005 the Akron-Canton Airport completed a $7 million renovation of its terminal building, with improvements made to the food court, baggage claim wing, entrances, parking lots and Internet access at the airport. Runway improvements are anticipated in the near future.

Commercial Shipping

Akron businesses have a variety of choices when it comes to shipping, considering the city's proximity to major waterways, airports, roadways, and rail systems. The Akron Fulton Airport, located in the southeast corner of the municipality, was home to the original Goodyear Airdock and site of the first lighter-than-air craft. The airport has four paved runways and can accommodate all types of private, single- and multi-engine aircraft. The Akron-Canton Airport offers a range of commercial flight and cargo shipping options. Carriers include AirTran, Delta, Frontier, Northwest, United and US Airways Express. Further air cargo options are available up the road 40 miles in Cleveland, where Cleveland Hopkins International Airport hosts a number of carriers that include UPS, FedEx and the United States Postal Service.

A multitude of interstate, U.S. and state highways intersect in Akron, providing ready access to and from all points in the country. Interstates 71, 76 and 77 all pass through the city; bypasses have been created to encourage smooth traffic flow. Local trucking and transport firm Roadway Express, a subsidiary of Yellow Roadway Corporation, leads the ground transport field with a network of shipping options extending to Canada, Alaska, Hawaii, Puerto Rico and across the globe. Akron's industrial history has made the city a magnet for many other companies that specialize in handling and transport of a range of freight. Several rail systems pass through Akron as well, including CSX and Norfolk Southern Railroads.

The Great Lakes Seaway from the Port of Cleveland and the St. Lawrence Seaway link the Akron area to the Atlantic Ocean, providing access to Europe, Africa, South America, Australia and Asia.

Labor Force and Employment Outlook

Developments in the early 2000s portend that the manufacturing sector is likely to see more layoffs and lost jobs in the future. The manufacture of durables may rebound somewhat, but the employment sectors expected to demonstrate significant growth are projected to be health care and social assistance, science and technology professions, administration and support services, leisure and hospitality, wholesale trade, transportation and warehousing, construction, retail trade, services, and recreation, arts and entertainment. Adaptation and retraining will be critical for workers to make the shift from production to a more service oriented job market.

The following is a summary of data regarding the Cleveland-Akron metropolitan statistical area labor force, 2004 annual averages.

Size of nonagricultural labor force: 328,500

Number of workers employed in . . .
   construction and mining: 13,900
   manufacturing: 49,300
   trade, transportation and utilities: 65,700
   information: 4,700
   financial activities: 14,600
   professional and business services: 43,600
   educational and health services: 42,800
   leisure and hospitality: 30,300
   other services: 13,600
   government: 50,000

Average hourly earnings of production workers employed in manufacturing: $15.25

Unemployment rate: 7.1% (February 2005)

Largest employers	*Number of employees (2005)*
Goodyear Tire and Rubber Co.	4,700
Summa Health System	3,650

Largest employers   *Number of employees (2005)*

Akron Public Schools	3,000
City of Akron	3,000
Akron General Medical Center	2,794
Fred Albrecht Grocery Co.	2,000
Children's Hospital Medical Center	1,543
Roadway Express	1,500
FirstMerit Corp.	1,475
FirstEnergy	1,400
Sterling Inc.	1,313

Cost of Living

The following is a summary of data regarding several key cost of living factors in the Akron area.

2004 (3rd Quarter) ACCRA Average House Price: $205,000

2004 (3rd Quarter) ACCRA Cost of Living Index: 91.5 (U.S. average = 100.0)

State income tax rate: Ranges from .0743% to 7.5% maximum

State sales tax rate: 6%

Local income tax rate: 2.25% (Akron)

Local sales tax rate: 0.75% (Summit County)

Property tax rate: $89.270 per $1,000 assessed value

Economic Information: Greater Akron Chamber, One Cascade Plaza, 17th Floor, Akron, OH 44308-1192; telephone (303)376-5550; toll-free (800)621-8001.

Education and Research

Elementary and Secondary Schools

In 2001 Akron Public Schools committed to a 10-point contract with the community, vowing to heighten academic standards, raise test scores and graduation rates, keep schools safe, cut costs and limit growth, execute and enforce contracts with parents of students, move students into alternative school programs as necessary, provide continuing education for teachers and administrators, work closely with community partners, monitor the budget closely, and delay requests for more operational monies until the 10 points of the contract were met (which happened as of the 2004-2005 school year). Akron Public Schools is a large district that boasts a student body that is approximately half African American and half Anglo-American, along with representation from Asian, Pacific Islander, Latino, and American

Indian cultural and ethnic groups. The district's diverse language program is a source of pride.

A plethora of specialized programs and studies are offered in classes that meet all state standards for education. Team and individual sports, music, and art offerings have been supported in Akron Public Schools, demonstrating the district's commitment to individualized learning. The district has incorporated alternative school facilities that serve students who are at risk of dropping out of the general school population or who pose a discipline problem.

In 2003 the district embarked on an ambitious 15-year plan to renovate existing school structures into state-of-the-art community learning centers. The updated facilities will serve as modern school buildings for Akron Public School students during the day, and in the evening will be available for community programs, adult education, recreation, and after-school enrichment activities.

The following is a summary of data regarding Akron public schools as of the 2004–2005 school year.

Total enrollment: 27,595

Number of facilities
  elementary schools: 39
  middle schools: 10
  high schools: 8

Student teacher ratio: 15.2:1

Teacher salaries
  minimum: $31,769
  maximum: $69,753

Funding per pupil: $9,360

The city of Akron is also home to a number of private middle and high school programs, most of which are operated under the auspices of religious institutions. A Waldorf school is located in nearby Copley, Ohio, and several Montessori schools are located in Akron and surrounding communities.

Public Schools Information: Akron Public Schools, Administration Building, 70 N. Broadway, Akron, OH 44308-1911; telephone (330)761-1661

Colleges and Universities

With the unlikeliest of mascots (Zippy the Kangaroo), the University of Akron has a student body of 24,129. The university functions on the semester system and offers more than 200 undergraduate majors, more than 100 master's degrees, 17 doctoral degrees and 4 law degrees. The university has adapted to economic trends in the Akron area by instituting a College of Polymer Science and Engineering; other degree programs prepare students for careers in nursing, education, the fine arts, the social sciences and more.

Adult vocational education is available at several institutions in the Akron area, including the Ohio College of Massotherapy (OCM). Enrolling approximately 250 full-time students, OCM combines classroom and experiential work in pursuit of an associates degree in Applied Science or a diploma in Massage Therapy. Specialized healthcare programs in x-ray technology or nursing can be studied through the local hospitals organized under the Summa Health System, including St. Thomas Medical Center and Akron City Hospital.

Other institutions for post-secondary education include Southern Ohio University's northeast campus, the Academy of Court Reporting, Wooster Business College, Akron Barber College, Stafford Flight Academy, Advanced Career College, and the Akron Machining Institute.

Akron is a mere hour south of Cleveland and within easy reach of the main campuses and branches of several post-secondary education programs. Kent State University is located about 24 miles to the northeast of Akron.

Libraries and Research Centers

Akron and its surrounding communities are served by the Akron-Summit County Public Library system, which is comprised of a main library facility in Akron, 17 branch libraries, and a bookmobile. The library system provides access to more than 1.2 million books, approximately 250,000 audio-visual materials, and 1,800 periodicals. The main library houses a number of special collections centered around local history; one of the newer collections has preserved musical contributions of local Summit County performers from the past to present day. Photographs, books, articles, and other materials chronicle the history of the rubber industry, the World Series of Golf, and the Soap Box Derby in Akron. Each branch of the library system offers a variety of reading and education programs for children, teens, and adults throughout the year. Book delivery is available for homebound readers.

Located on the fourth floor of the Summit County Courthouse, the Akron Law Library promotes "the study and investigation of law and legal research . . . " to its membership of attorneys, judges, magistrates, and other court personnel. More than 81,500 volumes are on hand for browsing, along with an increasing number of audio-visual formats. Library members can also utilize online legal research resources, and three professional law librarians are onsite to assist with research questions and access to materials.

Future legal eagles conduct research in the Law Library associated with the law school at the University of Akron. The library maintains a comprehensive selection of books, audio-visual materials and periodicals related to the legal profession, supporting the academic work of students and the pedagogical efforts of faculty members. The university also provides a general library service for students in other degree programs, with materials including electronic books, government documents, maps, periodicals, and printed books.

The University of Akron is the site of breakthrough research efforts such as an examination of the D.A.R.E. (Drug Abuse Resistance Education) program, with procedural revisions expected as an outcome, and applied polymer research taking place in the Institute of Polymer Engineering. The institute works with a variety of businesses in the polymer industry, providing lab equipment and personnel trained in research and testing techniques. The Polymer Engineering program has gone so far as to convince nationally-recognized glass artist Dale Chihuly to create a large-scale polymer sculpture for the campus, with installation expected during the summer of 2005.

Public Library Information: Akron-Summit County Public Library, 60 South High Street, Akron, OH 44326; telephone (330)643-9000

Health Care

One of the Akron area's largest employers, Summa Health System operates two medical facilities for a total of 694 licensed beds in the city. Akron City Hospital specializes in diagnosis, treatment and ongoing care in the areas of orthopedics, oncology, cardiovascular issues, geriatrics, and obesity. St. Thomas Hospital offers wound care, eye surgery, orthopedics and behavioral health treatment. Both Summa hospitals provide emergent and acute care.

Akron General Medical Center was founded in 1914 and has evolved into a tertiary care, nonprofit teaching hospital with 537 licensed beds. The facility provides emergency and trauma care, critical care, and services in a wide variety of specialties such as sleep disorder diagnosis and treatment, pain management, heart and vascular treatment, endocrinology and diabetes care. Akron General is equipped to respond to many conditions, disorders and diseases; as a full-service medical facility, it provides its students with opportunities to research, observe and intervene with a broad spectrum of health concerns.

The Children's Hospital Medical Center of Akron is licensed for 253 beds and is the largest pediatric care provider in northeast Ohio. The design of the structure and the approach of the staff are intended to promote calm and healing in the hospital's young patients, who visit the hospital for treatment of conditions such as trauma, cystic fibrosis, speech and hearing issues, and cancer. The hospital houses a regional burn trauma center for the treatment of both adults and children, and a Ronald McDonald House is located across from the facility for the convenience and comfort of families whose children have been admitted.

Edwin Shaw Rehabilitation Hospital provides therapeutic treatment for patients recovering from disorders that have disrupted physical or mental function. The hospital employs traditional methods along with fun and innovative approaches such as the Challenge Golf Course designed to improve the skills of players with identified disabilities.

Private practices in general and specialized medicine are available in Akron, as are walk-in and urgent care clinics. Practitioners of massage therapy, chiropractic care, acupuncture and hypnotherapy also exist in the metro area.

Recreation

Sightseeing

Sightseeing in Akron might start where the city itself started—with the Ohio & Erie Canal. The original canal route has been transformed into a recreational and historical education zone called the CanalWay, which was designated as a National Heritage site in 1996. The 110-mile area can be explored by biking or walking all or part of the 60 miles of Towpath Trail along the route where mules once towed barges, or by driving the CanalWay Ohio National Scenic Byway that stretches from Canton to Cleveland, or by riding the Cuyahoga Valley Scenic Railroad. Both the Byway and the Railroad pass near destinations such as Inventure Place, Akron's Northside, the Visitors Center for the Canal, Rockside Road, and Quaker Square. The original Quaker Oats Company building has been converted into a unique center for entertainment, shopping, and dining; the silos of the old factory can be rented as lodging in one of Akron's most memorable hotels.

The CanalWay transports visitors to downtown Akron by way of the Northside District, a collection of restored buildings, outdoor sculptures, unique cafés, galleries, and restaurants in the city's reborn city center. Northside makes a good jumping-off point for a tour of Akron history; just north of the train station in Northside are the nine locks that allowed barges to climb the canal from Little Cuyahoga River to the Portage Summit. The restored Mustill Store reflects the 19th century canal-era design and houses a visitors center with exhibits on local industry related to the canal.

The Glendale Cemetery was established in 1839 and reveals much of the history of Akron in its engravings and epitaphs. A restored 1876 Gothic chapel remains on the grounds, and

mausoleums exhibiting Egyptian, Greek, Roman, Gothic, and Art Moderne influences line Cypress Avenue as it runs through the grounds.

At the Goodyear World of Rubber Museum on East Market Street, visitors can retrace the beginnings of vulcanization, observe modern rubber production processes, and check out an Indy 500 race car with Goodyear tires.

Heading south and east through downtown, visitors will come upon the National Inventors Hall of Fame, which honors the creative and brave individuals who have advanced technology and the sciences over the course of the country's existence. The Inventors Workshop onsite stimulates innovation and problem-solving in visitors who participate in interactive and fun exhibits, demonstrations, and experiments. Camp Invention provides a week-long immersion experience during the summer for children in grades two through six, and older students can compete in the Collegiate Inventors Competition sponsored by the museum.

The Akron Zoological Park is home to more than 400 animals in exhibits such as the Tiger Valley habitat, the Bald Eagle Exhibit, the Otter Exhibit, and the Penguin Point Exhibit. The aviary and Lemur Island are perennially popular attractions. As an accredited world conservation zoo, the Akron Zoo coordinates breeding programs to conserve endangered species. The zoo offers seasonal and special events throughout the year, including Spring Surprise, Senior Safari, Boo at the Zoo, and Snack with Santa.

The home of Dr. Bob, co-founder of Alcoholics Anonymous back in 1935, is open to tourists. It all started in a tidy house on Ardmore Avenue when Bill Wilson helped Dr. Robert Smith kick his alcohol addiction. The two opened the house to other alcoholics, creating a grassroots addiction treatment program that is thriving today.

Other must-see attractions include Stan Hywet Hall and Gardens (former home of Goodyear co-founder Frank Seiberling), St. Bernard Church, the American Marble and Toy Museum, and the Pan African Culture and Research Center on the grounds of the University of Akron.

Arts and Culture

The Akron Art Museum is undergoing extensive renovations that are expected to be unveiled in 2006; in the interim, temporary exhibits are scattered throughout the city to keep the taste for art alive. When reopened, the museum will be expanded to 65,000 square feet of soaring architecture with tripled gallery space and increased outdoor exhibit areas. The museum's collections include works of Warhol, Stella, Bourke-White, and Callahan.

The Akron Symphony is the headliner for local performing arts; comprised of a symphony orchestra, a youth symphony

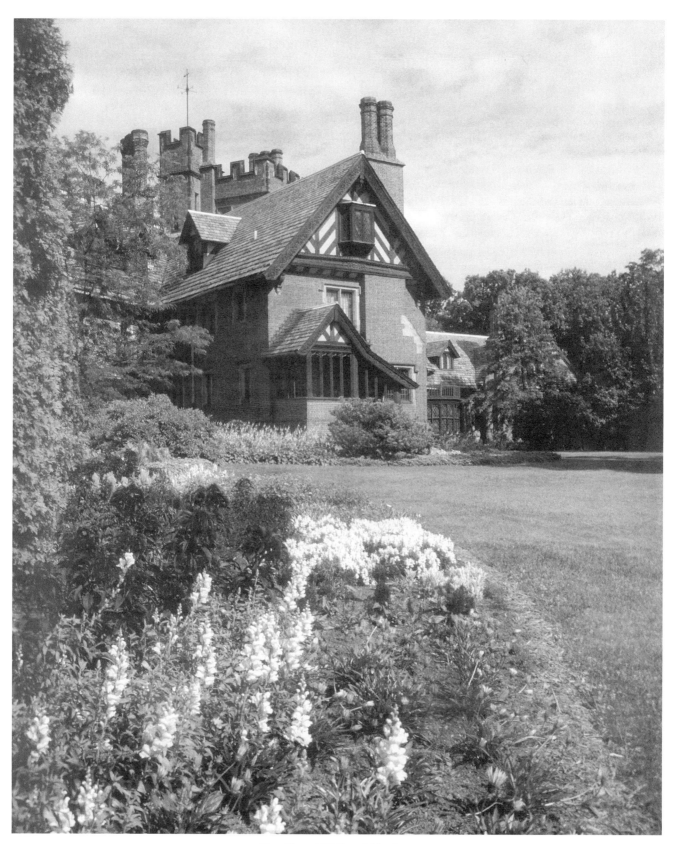

Stan Hywet Hall and Gardens.

and a symphony chorus. The professional orchestra offers free Picnic Pops concerts in local parks, chamber music during Sundays at the Elms, three Family Series concerts, seven Classic Series concerts, a Gospel Meets Symphony performance, and educational outreach programs and concerts for the public schools.

The E.J. Thomas Performing Arts Hall at the University of Akron hosts musical performances (both national and local), plays and musicals. The performance hall has joined forces with Broadway Across America, one of the largest live theater production companies in the U.S., and now offers a Broadway in Akron series. The Civic Theatre in Akron participates in the Broadway in Akron series production and provides an elegant venue for musical, dramatic and comedic performances. Nationally-recognized musical performers are often booked at the Blossom Music Center in Cuyahoga Falls.

The Ohio Ballet, a professional company in residence at the University of Akron, performs classical and more contemporary ballet pieces. The Children's Ballet Theatre in Akron was founded in 1993 to provide a pre-professional performance opportunity for select young dancers from 10 to 18 years of age. The Children's Ballet Theatre annually performs "The Nutcracker" and has become recognized for productions of "Coppelia" and "Cinderella."

The Weathervane Playhouse is a community theater that produces a year-round schedule of family theater, musicals, and contemporary comedies and dramas. The 2004-2005 season offered an eclectic mix, ranging from "Winnie the Pooh" and "Forever Plaid" to "The Rocky Horror Picture Show." The Playhouse holds classes in Hands-On Theater, audition tactics, and musical theater techniques in addition to summer camps for younger performers.

Akron is home to the largest professional dinner theater in the world—in its 51,000 square feet of space, the Carousel Dinner Theatre can entertain up to 1,000 guests with dinner and a show.

Arts and Culture Information: Akron-Summit Convention and Visitors Bureau, 77 E. Mill Street, Akron, OH 44308; telephone (330)374-7560; toll-free (800)245-4254

Festivals and Holidays

The cold of the Ohio winter means festivities are either inside or on the ski slopes in January—early in the month, the One Act Play Festival takes place at the Miller South School for the Visual and Performing Arts, while a number of races and demo events are occurring at nearby Boston Mills and Brandywine ski resorts. Ski and snowboard events continue throughout February, and the heart can be warmed by the Valentine Exhibit held each year at Hower House Victorian mansion. The Akron/Canton Home and Flower Show in Feb-

ruary awakens thoughts of spring, with gardening seminars held in the John S. Knight Center. March is a month of festival as well as weather extremes, with the Annual Spring Needlework Show and the Fists Against Hunger Martial Arts Tournament. March also brings an Akron tradition of wintry night hikes in anticipation of spring.

Earth Day activities and resumption of baseball season herald the arrival of spring in April. Akron's newest extravaganza is the National Hamburger Festival, to be held each Memorial Day weekend in celebration of an all-American culinary creation. The first festival is expected to take place in May of 2006 in downtown Akron.

Fathers Day in Akron is observed with the high-flying antics of the Aero Expo air show at the Akron Fulton Airport. Throughout the weekend, aerobatic performances are staged by modern military aircraft and the Tuskegee Airmen. The AA Founders Day Celebration in mid-June coincides with the Riverfest Irish Festival in Cuyahoga Falls. Toward the end of June, Boston Mills Ski Resort hosts its annual Artfest, with juried fine arts and crafts shows featuring more than 160 artists.

The Fourth of July weekend sets off musical and culinary fireworks with the Akron Family Barbecue at Lock 3 on the Canal. Rib vendors, carnival rides and games, street entertainers, and children's activities light up the July nights. At the end of the month, the annual Akron Arts Expo coordinates a juried art show with more than 165 exhibitors, plus food and live entertainment. July winds up with the All-American Soap Box Derby World Championships at Derby Downs. In the heat of August, folks from around the region dress up in Civil War garb for the Annual Civil War Encampment and Reenactment held at Hale Farm and Village.

During the entire month of September, locals take advantage of cooler temperatures by indulging in Metro Parks' Fall Hiking Spree, following any of the 13 trails that wander through prime fall foliage. Two festivals at the end of the month say goodbye to summer (the Annual Mum Fest at Lake Anna Park) and hello to fall (the Annual Loyal Oak Cider Fest at Crawford Knecht Cider Mill). In October, the Annual Wonderful World of Ohio Mart is held at Stan Hywet Hall and Gardens, while the Akron Zoo celebrates Halloween with Boo at the Zoo. The month of November ushers in the Annual Holiday Mart at the Summit County Fairgrounds Arena, followed by the Holiday Tree Festival at the John S. Knight Center later in the month. The annual Christmas Music Spectacular in mid-December has become a beloved tradition, and FirstNight Akron is catching on as a family-friendly, alcohol-free way to see in the New Year.

Sports for the Spectator

The big event in Akron is the All-American Soap Box Derby World Championship Finals, held each August at Derby

Downs. Since 1934, the Soap Box Derby has been encouraging youth to build and race their own non-motorized vehicles. The race has become increasingly sophisticated and now has three divisions ranging from beginners in the Derby to more advanced participants to a Masters Division. The festivities last for a week and are attended by locals, celebrities, and sports personalities from across the country.

From April to September, hardball fans enjoy Akron Aeros games at beautiful Canal Park Stadium. The Aeros are the AA farm team affiliate of the Cleveland Indians, drawing half a million fans each season. The Akron Racers are one of six national pro fast-pitch women's softball teams; games are played at Firestone Stadium.

The University of Akron Zips play a number of sports in Division I of the National Collegiate Athletic Association, providing college sports fans with football, baseball, basketball, softball, volleyball, and track events. Cleveland is also home to several professional teams, including the Indians baseball franchise, the Browns football team, the Cavaliers basketball organization, and the Barons hockey club.

Sports for the Participant

The City of Akron organizes year-round individual and team sports through its recreation bureau, including basketball, wrestling, baseball, softball, volleyball, and weight training at local community centers operated by the city. Akron also maintains a championship golf course; Good Park Golf Course is located on the west side of the city and offers watered tees, greens, and fairways during golf season. A snack bar and pro shop are onsite as well. Riverwoods Golf Course provides nine holes for public use, and Turkeyfoot Lake Golf Links has an 18-hole course located in the Portage Lakes area. Valley View Golf Club has 27 holes. Mud Run has a nine-hole course and a driving range.

The Metro Parks system, which serves Akron and the greater Summit County community, maintains more than 8,700 acres of recreational and educational space. A 33-mile Bike and Hike Trail provides safe workout areas for cyclists and walkers, and the extensive trail systems throughout Metro Parks are appropriate for light hiking and mountain biking in the warmer seasons and cross-country skiing in the winter.

Camping, boating, swimming, and fishing can be enjoyed within the bounds of Portage Lakes State Park in Akron. The Portage Lakes formed when chunks of glacier settled in depressions in the ground; the resulting plants in the area are unique and consist of tamarack trees, skunk cabbage, and cranberry. A wide variety of animals and birds can be observed near the lakes, and anglers can fish for largemouth bass, walleye, bullhead, carp, pickerel, pan fish, and channel catfish.

Great fishing can also be experienced on Lake Erie, otherwise known as the "Walleye Capital of the World." Besides walleye, anglers can hook smallmouth bass, yellow perch, salmon, and silver bullet steelhead. For a fish-eye view of the lake, it's possible to scuba dive into the depths of Lake Erie to explore a number of shipwreck sites.

Cuyahoga Valley National Park contains more than 125 miles of hiking trails that cross a variety of habitats and ecosystems. Some trails are accessible to all visitors; others are more challenging, though elevation change on the trails is relatively minimal. When winter hits, sledding and cross-country skiing fun can be had at the Kendall Lake Winter Sports Center in the Park. All trails can be accessed by snowshoe, and Kendall Lake often reaches sufficient thickness for ice skating.

The Road Runner Akron Marathon has gained a reputation as one of 50 great marathons in the U.S., based on the organization of the race and the quality of the course. Participants can choose to run the full marathon or be part of a marathon relay team. The event kicks off with inspirational speakers and a pasta party, followed by a celebration at Canal Park Stadium after the race has ended. A Kids Fun Run is also available.

In the winter months, the Brandywine and Boston Mills Ski Resorts are the scene of downhill skiing, snowboarding, and sledding galore.

Shopping and Dining

The former Quaker Oats Factory has been given new life as the Quaker Square Complex, home of unique specialty stores, galleries, and restaurants. The Trackside Grille in Quaker Square serves up food and displays of authentic railroad artifacts. The shopping experience continues in local shops throughout the downtown area. The Summit Mall on West Market Street is anchored by Dillard's and Kaufmann's stores and houses more than 120 vendors beneath its roof. The Plaza at Chapel Hill incorporates a collection of 45 stores and an 8-screen theater. Don Drumm Studios and Gallery in Akron features works by more than 500 artists in a gallery that spans two buildings. Foodies will appreciate the West Point Market, a 25,000 square foot buffet of gourmet foods such as Belgian chocolates, premium wines, imported caviar, homemade breads and a convenient café.

Akron's dining scene is continental, in reflection of its immigrant past; Italian and Chinese eateries abound, as do Mexican restaurants. Many culinary tastes are represented, however, including Cajun, Thai, Korean, Indian, French, Greek, Japanese, and Irish. Establishments range from homey cafés to fine dining bistros. The Menches Brothers Restaurant experience commemorates the invention of two American favorites by the local Menches Brothers of Akron: hamburgers, and the cornucopia ice cream cone. After-dinner coffee can be found at a small selection of local coffee houses.

Convention Facilities

The John S. Knight Center has served downtown Akron since 1994, greeting conventioneers and meeting participants with its dramatic glass rotunda and spiral staircase in the 22,000 square foot lobby. The facility offers a 30,000 square foot exhibition hall, 12,000 square feet of banquet space, and another 12,600 square feet for meetings. Meeting areas are flexible and can be customized in a variety of configurations; all spaces meet specifications of the Americans with Disabilities Act.

The Akron Complex at the Summit County Fairgrounds contributes 68,000 square feet of exhibition space capable of accommodating 296 booths and seating for up to 2,500 people. The complex adds 3,000 square feet of meeting space and 2,500 square feet for banquet functions.

Greystone Hall and Theater in Akron contains 10,000 square feet of exhibition space, with seating for 400; 120 square feet of meeting space and 400 square feet of banquet area are also available. Two local theaters can also be utilized for meetings and conventions: the Carousel Dinner Theatre can be converted into 14,000 square feet of exhibition area with seating for 1,000, and the Akron Civic Theatre has seating for 2,700 in the performance hall.

Transportation

Approaching the City

The Akron-Canton Airport is located just south of Akron proper and is accessed by Interstate 77. The airport offers a range of commercial flight options, with carriers such as AirTran, Delta, Frontier, Northwest, United, and US Airways Express. The Cleveland Hopkins International Airport 40 miles north of Akron provides another air option, with flights serving all regions of the U.S. and the globe. Amtrak supplies passenger train service to the area.

A number of interstate, U.S. and state highways intersect in Akron, making the city easily accessible by road. Interstates 71, 76, and 77 all pass near or through the city, and U.S. highway 224 cuts a north-south swath through its heart. State highways 18, 21, and 8 aid travelers in entering Akron. Greyhound bus service provides ground transportation to supplement personal vehicle travel.

Traveling in the City

Market Street runs from the northwest to the southeast through the center of Akron, where it is intersected at almost a 90-degree angle by Main Street as it runs from the northeast to the southwest edge of the city. These streets make good navigational reference points in a city where several of the arterials are not constructed on a grid but rather radiate out from the city center like spokes in a wheel. Interstate 76 and state highway 8 also can guide travelers within Akron.

Bus service within the city is provided by the Metro Transit Authority, with an extensive route system and customized transportation options for senior or disabled riders. Taxi companies supplement the mass transit services. The CanalWay offers safe bike passage to portions of Akron, and the city is in the process of implementing a 20-year strategic plan that will allow for creation of more bike lanes and increased options for alternative transportation.

Communications

Newspapers and Magazines

The mainstream daily paper in the area is the *Akron Beacon Journal,* which is available in both home delivery and digital versions. The newspaper covers international, national, and local news, along with sports, entertainment and business happenings. Special sections are published periodically to address seasonal interests in gardening, sports, and travel. Community news is the focus of Akron's *West Side Leader* periodical. Several other local newspapers address specific groups or interest areas, including the legal community, seniors, the rubber and plastics industry, and women's issues.

The City of Akron has recently begun publication of *Akron City Magazine* to keep the community abreast of developments and events. Several industry-specific publications are produced locally and distributed nationally.

Television and Radio

No television stations broadcast from Akron; most programming is relayed from the Cleveland area. A governmental channel for City of Akron issues exists, and the region receives network channels ABC, CBS and NBC in addition to the WB, PBS and PAX. Cable service is available.

Akron's three AM and 6 FM radio stations offer oldies, adult contemporary, talk, news, and alternative programming. Other radio station options are received via Cleveland and other nearby cities..

Media Information: Akron-Summit Convention and Visitors Bureau, 77 E. Mill Street, Akron, OH 44308; telephone (330)374-7560; toll-free (800)245-4254

Akron Online

Akron Public Schools. Available www.akronschools.com

Akron-Summit Convention & Visitors Bureau. Available www.visitakron-summit.org

Akron-Summit County Public Library. Available www .akronlibrary.org

City of Akron. Available www.ci.akron.oh.us

Greater Akron Chamber. Available www.greaterakron chamber.org

Summit County Historical Society. Available summithistory .org

Selected Bibliography

Endres, Kathleen L., *Rosie the Rubber Worker: Women Workers in Akron's Rubber Factories During World War II* Kent, OH: Kent State University Press (2000)

Havighurst, Walter, *Ohio: A History* New York: Norton (1976)

Cincinnati

The City in Brief

Founded: 1789 (incorporated 1819)

Head Official: Mayor Charlie Luken (since 1999)

City Population
 1980: 385,457
 1990: 364,040
 2000: 331,285
 2003 estimate: 317,361
 Percent change, 1990–2000: −9.1%
 U.S. rank in 1980: 32nd
 U.S. rank in 1990: 45th
 U.S. rank in 2000: 63rd

Metropolitan Area Population (PMSA)
 1980: 1,660,000
 1990: 1,525,090
 2000: 1,646,395

Percent change, 1990–2000: 8.9%
U.S. rank in 1980: 20th
U.S. rank in 1998: 23rd
U.S. rank in 2000: 23rd

Area: 78 square miles (2000)
Elevation: 869 feet above sea level
Average Annual Temperature: 53.3° F
Average Annual Precipitation: 40.14 inches (23.9 inches of snow)

Major Economic Sectors: Services, wholesale and retail trade, manufacturing, government
Unemployment Rate: 6.2% (February 2005)
Per Capita Income: $19,962 (1999)

2002 FBI Crime Index Total: 29,205

Major Colleges and Universities: University of Cincinnati, Xavier University

Daily Newspapers: *The Cincinnati Enquirer, The Cincinnati Post*

Introduction

Cincinnati, the seat of Hamilton County, is Ohio's third largest city and the center of a metropolitan statistical area comprised of Clermont, Hamilton, and Warren counties in Ohio, Kenton County in Kentucky, and Dearborn County in Indiana. Praised by Charles Dickens and Winston Churchill among others, Cincinnati is noted for its attractive hillside setting overlooking the Ohio River. The city enjoys a rich cultural history, particularly in choral and orchestral music, dating from German settlement in the nineteenth century. Once the nation's pork capital and the country's largest city, Cincinnati today is home to several leading national corporations.

Geography and Climate

Cincinnati is set on the north bank of the Ohio River in a narrow, steep-sided valley on the Ohio-Kentucky border in southwestern Ohio. The city is spread out on hills that afford beautiful vistas of downtown and give the city a picturesque landscape. The area's continental climate produces a wide range of temperatures from winter to summer. Winters are moderately cold with frequent periods of extensive cloudiness; summers are warm and humid with temperatures reaching 90 degrees about 19 days each year.

Area: 78 square miles (2000)

Elevation: 869 feet above sea level

Average Temperatures: January, 28.9° F; July, 75.3° F; annual average, 53.3° F

Average Annual Precipitation: 40.14 inches (23.9 inches of snow)

History

Ohio River Crossing Part of Northwest Territory

The Ohio River basin first served as a crossing point for Native Americans traveling south. It is believed that Robert Cavelier, sieur de La Salle, was the first explorer to reach this spot on the Ohio River as early as 1669. Part of the Northwest Territory that the newly formed United States government received from England at the conclusion of the Revolutionary War, Cincinnati became a strategic debarkation point for settlers forging a new life in the wilderness.

Congressman John Cleves Symmes of New Jersey purchased from the Continental Congress one million acres of land between the two Miami rivers, and three settlements were platted. In February 1789, John Filson named one of the settlements Losantiville, meaning "the place opposite the Licking [River]." The next year, General Arthur St. Clair, governor of the Northwest Territory, renamed the village Cincinnati in honor of the Roman citizen-soldier Lucius Quinctius Cincinnatus and after the Society of the Cincinnati, an organization of American Revolutionary army officers. He made Cincinnati the seat of Hamilton County, which he named after Alexander Hamilton, then president general of the Society of Cincinnati.

River Traffic Swells City's Population

Fort Washington was built in the area in 1789 as a fortification from which action was mounted against warriors of the Ohio tribe, but the military efforts proved unsuccessful until General Anthony Wayne trained an army that defeated the Ohio at Fallen Timbers in 1794, securing the area for settlement. Cincinnati was chartered as a town in 1802 and as a city in 1819. The introduction of the river paddle-wheeler on the Ohio River after the War of 1812 turned Cincinnati into a center of river commerce and trade. The opening of the Miami Canal in 1827 added to the town's economic growth. William Holmes McGuffey published his Eclectic Readers in Cincinnati in 1836, and eventually 122 million copies were sold. The first mass migration of Germans in 1830 and Irish a decade later swelled Cincinnati's population to 46,338 people.

The economy continued to boom as the South paid cash for foodstuffs produced in the city, and by 1850 Cincinnati was the pork-packing capital of the world. More than 8,000 steamboats docked at Cincinnati in 1852. Cincinnati merchants protested the cutoff of Southern trade at the outbreak of the Civil War, but federal government contracts and the city's role as a recruiting and outfitting center for Union soldiers righted the economy. Cincinnati was a major stop on the Underground Railroad, a secret network of cooperation aiding fugitive slaves in reaching sanctuary in the free states or Canada prior to 1861. Cincinnati also served as a center of Copperhead political activity during the Civil War; Copperheads were Northerners sympathetic to the Southern cause. The city's proximity to the South spread fear of invasion by the Confederate Army, and martial law was decreed in 1862 when raiders led by Edmund Kirby-Smith, a Confederate commander, threatened invasion.

Cincinnati residents played an important role in the Abolitionist cause. James G. Birney, who published the abolitionist newspaper *The Philanthropist,* and Dr. Lyman Beecher of the Lane Theological Seminary were leading Northern antislavery activists. Dr. Beecher's daughter, Harriet Beecher Stowe, lived in Cincinnati from 1832 to 1850 and wrote much of her best seller, *Uncle Tom's Cabin,* there. African Americans have in fact been prominent in Cincinnati's history since its founding. The city's first African American church was built in 1809 and the first school in 1825. African Americans voted locally in 1852, 18 years before the passage of the Fifteenth Amendment. The first African American to serve on city council was elected in 1931, and two African Americans have served as mayor.

Prosperity Follows End of Civil War

A suspension bridge designed by John R. Roebling connected Ohio and Kentucky upon its completion in 1867. Cincinnati prospered after the Civil War, and, with a population that grew to 200,000 people became the country's largest city before annexing land to develop communities outside the basin. Cincinnati's most revered public monument, the Tyler Davidson Fountain, was unveiled in 1871 in the heart of downtown. During this period Cincinnati's major cultural institutions were founded, including the art museum and art academy, the conservatory of music, the public library, the zoo, and Music Hall. Two of the city's most cherished traditions also date from this time: the May Festival of choral music at Music Hall and the first professional baseball team, the Cincinnati Red Stockings.

In reaction to the decline of riverboat trade in the 1870s, the city of Cincinnati built its own southern rail line—it was the first and only city to do so—at a cost of $20 million, rushing to complete the project in 1880. The era of boss-rule in the municipal government was introduced in 1884 when newly elected Governor Joseph B. Foraker appointed George Barnsdale Cox, a tavern keeper, to head the Board of Public Affairs. With control of more than 2,000 jobs, Cox and his machine ruled Cincinnati through a bleak period of graft and corruption, which finally came to an end with a nonpartisan reform movement that won election in 1924. The city's new charter corrected the abuses of the Cox regime.

On the national scene, a political dynasty was established when Cincinnatian William Howard Taft was elected President and then became the only President to be appointed Chief Justice of the U.S. Supreme Court. Taft's son, Robert A. Taft, was elected to three Senate terms; and his grandson, Robert Taft, Jr., was elected to the U.S. House of Representatives.

City Retains Vitality in Twentieth Century

Cincinnati weathered the Great Depression better than most American cities of its size, largely because of a resurgence of inexpensive river trade. The rejuvenation of downtown began in the 1920s and continued into the next decade with the construction of Union Terminal, the post office, and a large Bell Telephone building. The flood of 1937 was one of the worst in the nation's history, resulting in the building of protective flood walls. After World War II, Cincinnati

unveiled a master plan for urban renewal that resulted in modernization of the inner city. Riverfront Stadium and the Coliseum were completed in the 1970s, as the Cincinnati Reds baseball team emerged as one of the dominant teams of the decade. Tragedy struck the Coliseum in December 1981 when eleven people were killed in a mass panic prior to The Who rock and roll concert. In 1989, the two-hundredth anniversary of the city's founding, much attention was focused on the city's Year 2000 plan, which involved further revitalization.

The completion of several major new development projects enhance the city as it enters the early years of the new millennium. Cincinnati's beloved Bengals and Reds teams both have new, state-of-the-art homes: Paul Brown Stadium, opened in 2000, and the Great American Ball Park, opened in 2003, respectively. Two new museums have opened: the Rosenthal Center for Contemporary Art in 2003, and the National Underground Railroad Freedom Center in 2004. The Banks is a new, developing 24-hour urban neighborhood of restaurants, clubs, offices, and homes with sweeping skyline views, along the city's riverfront. Cincinnati has received such accolades as "Most Liveable City," Partners for Livable Communities, April 2004; number five U.S. arts destination, *American Style Magazine,* Summer 2004; and inclusion in the top 10 "Cities that Rock," *Esquire Magazine,* April 2004.

Historical Information: Cincinnati Historical Society, Museum Center, Cincinnati Union Terminal, 1301 Western Avenue, Cincinnati, OH 45203; telephone (513)287-7030

Population Profile

Metropolitan Area Residents (PMSA)
 1980: 1,660,000
 1990: 1,525,090
 2000: 1,646,395
 Percent change, 1990–2000: 8.9%
 U.S. rank in 1980: 20th
 U.S. rank in 1998: 23rd
 U.S. rank in 2000: 23rd

City Residents
 1980: 385,457
 1990: 364,040
 2000: 331,285
 2003 estimate: 317,361
 Percent change, 1990–2000: −9.1%
 U.S. rank in 1980: 32nd
 U.S. rank in 1990: 45th (State rank: 3rd)
 U.S. rank in 2000: 63rd

Density: 4,249.0 people per square mile (2000)

Racial and ethnic characteristics (2000)
White: 175,492
Black or African American: 142,176
American Indian and Alaska Native: 709
Asian: 5,132
Native Hawaiian and Pacific Islander: 130
Hispanic or Latino (may be of any race): 4,230
Other: 7,646

Percent of residents born in state: 71.6%

Age characteristics (2000)
Population under 5 years old: 23,862
Population 5 to 9 years old: 22,810
Population 10 to 14 years old: 22,109
Population 15 to 19 years old: 23,805
Population 20 to 24 years old: 31,327
Population 25 to 34 years old: 56,094
Population 35 to 44 years old: 48,757
Population 45 to 54 years old: 38,757
Population 55 to 59 years old: 12,777
Population 60 to 64 years old: 10,333
Population 65 to 74 years old: 19,761
Population 75 to 84 years old: 14,645
Population 85 years and older: 6,248
Median age: 32.1 years

Births (2002, Hamilton County)
Total number: 11,031

Deaths (2002, Hamilton County)
Total number: 8,461 (of which, 114 were infants under the age of 1 year)

Money income (1999)
Per capita income: $19,962
Median household income: $29,493
Total households: 147,979

Number of households with income of . . .
less than $10,000: 26,690
$10,000 to $14,999: 12,786
$15,000 to $24,999: 24,409
$25,000 to $34,999: 21,197
$35,000 to $49,999: 22,172
$50,000 to $74,999: 20,451
$75,000 to $99,999: 9,282
$100,000 to $149,999: 6,301
$150,000 to $199,999: 2,025
$200,000 or more: 2,666

Percent of families below poverty level: 18.2% (37.6% of which were female householder families with related children under 5 years)

2002 FBI Crime Index Total: 29,205

Municipal Government

Since 1926, the top vote-getter of city council had automatically become mayor, but as of 2001, the mayor is elected independently. A city manager is appointed by the mayor and the city's nine-member council. Council members are elected to two-year terms; the city manager serves for an indefinite period.

Head Official: Mayor Charlie Luken (since 1999; current term expires 2005)

Total Number of City Employees: 7,223 (2004)

City Information: City Hall, 801 Plum Street, Cincinnati, OH 45202; telephone (513)591-6000

Economy

Major Industries and Commercial Activity

Cincinnati's diversified economic base includes manufacturing, wholesale and retail trade, insurance and finance, education and health services, government, and transportation. Known worldwide for Procter & Gamble soap products and U.S. Playing Cards, the city ranks high nationally in the value of manufacturing shipments. Ten *Fortune* 500 companies have established headquarters in Cincinnati: AK Steel (steel manufacturer), American Financial (financial services), Ashland Inc. (chemicals), Cinergy Corp. (public utilities), Federated Department Stores (retail stores), Fifth Third Bancorp (financial services), The Kroger Co. (grocery stores), Omnicare (pharmacy services), Procter & Gamble Co. (consumer goods), and Western & Southern Financial (financial services). More than 360 other *Fortune* 500 companies maintain operations in Cincinnati. Retail sales in the metropolitan Cincinnati area average $2.8 billion annually.

More than one thousand area firms have contributed to Cincinnati's position as an international trade center, generating approximately $6.7 billion in sales to markets outside the United States each year. Foreign investment in the local economy is substantial; more than 300 Cincinnati-area firms are presently owned by companies in Asia (especially Japan), Europe (especially France, Germany, and the United Kingdom), Canada, South America, and Africa. Among these companies are: AEG, Bayer, Faurecia, Krupp-Hoesch, Mitsubishi Electric, Siemens, Snecma, Sumitomo Electric, Toyota Motor Mfg.-North American Headquarters, and Valeo. Toyota, one of Cincinnati's largest employers, chose the greater Cincinnati area for its North American manufacturing plant because, in the words of its Senior Vice President of Corporate Affairs, Dennis C. Cuneo, ''The area has an excellent transportation system, a world-class airport, an excellent quality of life and a positive business climate.'' In 2003, *Expansion Management* magazine ranked Cincinnati 11th for European investment.

Federal agencies with regional centers located in the city are the United States Postal Service, the U.S. Internal Revenue Service, the U.S. Environmental Protection Agency, and the National Institute for Occupational Safety and Health.

The University of Cincinnati, the city's largest employer, has an economic impact of more than $3 billion.

Items and goods produced: aircraft engines, auto parts, motor vehicles, chemicals, valves, alcoholic beverages and soft drinks, food and kindred products, playing cards, drugs, cosmetics, toiletries, detergents, building materials, cans, metalworking and general industrial machinery, toys, apparel, mattresses, electric motors, robotics, electronic equipment, housewares, shoes, printing and publishing

Incentive Programs—New and Existing Companies

Greater Cincinnati offers a wide range of economic development assistance programs to businesses planning to expand or locate new operations within the 13-county region.

Local programs—Local organizations offer assistance for small businesses, women, and minority business owners. One such organization, the Cincinnati Business Incubator (CBI), specializes in assisting woman- and minority-owned small businesses operating—or seeking to start a business—in designated Empowerment Zones. CBI offers training and workshops that focus on business skills and profit building.

State programs—In Ohio, incentive programs are administered by the Ohio Department of Development, which operates a system of regional development offices. Incentive programs in Ohio include enterprise zones, Community Reinvestment Areas, job creation and training tax credit programs, and a variety of loan programs, as well as machinery and equipment tax credits; research and development, warehouse, and manufacturing equipment sales tax exemption; storage-only warehouse property tax exemption; and tax increment financing.

Job training programs—The City of Cincinnati Employment and Training Division oversees vocational, life, and pre-employment skills training and job placement employment initiatives. Cincinnati Works focuses on four service areas: job readiness, job search, retention, and advancement. Great Oaks Center for Employment Resources offers customized training and services to meet the needs of companies. Services and programs include: Comprehensive vocational assess-

ment, employee assessment, employment services, professional development, job profiling, return to work services, workplace programs, and customized training. TechSolve, a non-profit organization for manufacturers, offers help with change in manufacturing operations; its training programs aim to maintain a high performance workforce.

Development Projects

The Dr. Albert B. Sabin Cincinnati Convention Center expansion, scheduled for completion in 2006, is projected to have an economic impact of $417 million. The expanded 750,000 square foot center will feature nearly 200,000 square feet of exhibition space. Major developments completed in Cincinnati in recent years include the new home of the Bengals, state-of-the-art Paul Brown Stadium, opened in 2000; and the new home of the Reds, the Great American Ball Park, opened in 2003. Hallmarks of a rebirth of the city's riverfront, the Stadium forms the western anchor of this revitalized area, while the Ball Park forms the eastern anchor. Development of The Banks, a 15-acre, 24-hour urban neighborhood of restaurants, clubs, offices, apartments and homes with sweeping skyline views, has begun to unfold near the Stadium. The Banks is projected to have an economic impact of $1.9 billion. Other developments include the opening of the National Underground Railroad Freedom Center in 2004. This new museum offers lessons on the struggle for freedom, and celebrates Cincinnati's role as a transit point for runaway slaves in the mid-1800s. Another museum, the Rosenthal Center for Contemporary Art, opened in 2003.

Economic Development Information: Ohio Department of Development, PO Box 1001, Columbus, OH 43216; telephone (800)848-1300

Commercial Shipping

The Greater Cincinnati Airport pumps approximately $4 billion into the local economy; contributing significantly to the region's transportation system, it is considered a major inducement in attracting new industry. The airport is the primary U.S. hub for DHL Worldwide Express, which ships one million pounds of cargo from the airport daily. The area has two foreign trade zones, one in Hamilton County and the other in Boone County, Kentucky near the international airport. Greater Cincinnati has the fifth largest inland U.S. port for domestic loads, with approximately 52.3 million tons of cargo transported annually through Cincinnati on the Ohio River system.

All major markets are easily reached from Greater Cincinnati via interstate. Three interstates (I-71, I-74 and I-75) link Cincinnati with the nation, while I-70, 55 miles to the north, links the east and west coasts. Twenty major metropolitan areas are served by one day's trucking service and another

30 metropolitan areas are within two days. Three major railroad systems—CSX Transportation, Norfolk Southern Corp., and Conrail—serve the region.

Labor Force and Employment Outlook

More than 1.56 million workers live within 50 miles of downtown Cincinnati. Graduates from the colleges and universities within a 200-mile radius add more than 100,000 young professionals to the workforce each year. The region is noted for its strong work ethic, which translates into a workforce that is productive, responsible, and dedicated. The city has been successful in attracting new business including company headquarters in recent years, and considers itself well positioned for further economic growth, citing its outstanding airport service, high worker productivity, and quality of life among other positive factors. Among the rapidly growing sectors of the area's economy are high-tech manufacturing, aerospace (in 2003, the Cincinnati-Dayton corridor was awarded $2.5 billion in defense spending and $1.4 billion in U.S. defense projects), automotive manufacturing, and life sciences. Long-term labor market projections are available at the Chamber's web site for industry employment, occupational employment, and labor force size. Projected annual job openings by occupation, reflecting employment growth, and replacement needs are included.

The following is a summary of data regarding the Cincinnati-Middletown metropolitan area labor force (2004 annual averages):

Size of non-agricultural labor force: 1,021,800

Number of workers employed in . . .
　construction and mining: 52,700
　manufacturing: 125,700
　trade, transportation and utilities: 208,100
　information: 16,300
　financial activities: 65,000
　professional and business services: 144,700
　educational and health services: 130,300
　leisure and hospitality: 102,700
　other services: 42,500
　government: 133,900

Average hourly earnings of production workers employed in manufacturing: $15.94

Unemployment rate: 6.2% (February 2005)

Largest employers	*Number of employees*
University of Cincinnati	15,400
Kroger Company	13,000
The Procter & Gamble Company	13,000
Toyota Motor Manufacturing North America Inc.	8,360
Fifth Third Bank	7,800
Cincinnati Public Schools	7,335
City of Cincinnati	7,223
Trihealth, Inc.	7,055
Cincinnati Children's Hospital Medical Center	7,029
Mercy Health Partners	6,785

Cost of Living

The following is a summary of data regarding several key cost of living factors in the Cincinnati area.

2004 (3rd Quarter) ACCRA Average House Price: $210,949

2004 (3rd Quarter) ACCRA Cost of Living Index: 93.8 (U.S. average = 100.0)

State income tax rate: Ranges from 0.742% to 7.5%

State sales tax rate: 5.0%

Local income tax rate: 2.1%

Local sales tax rate: 1.0%

Property tax rate: ranges from $61.66 to $133.45 per $1,000 of assessed valuation; assessed at 35% of market value (Hamilton County)

Economic Information: Greater Cincinnati Chamber of Commerce, 441 Vine Street, Suite 300, Cincinnati, OH 45202; telephone (513)579-3100; fax (513)579-3101

Education and Research

Elementary and Secondary Schools

The Cincinnati Public School (CPS) district is spread across the city plus Amberley Village, Cheviot, Golf Manor, most of the city of Silverton, parts of Fairfax and Wyoming, and parts of Anderson, Columbia, Delhi, Green, and Springfield townships, with a total area of about 90 square miles. It is the third-largest public school district in the state. CPS opened the first public Montessori elementary school in the country in 1975. The district now offers 21 high schools with specific focuses, and 22 elementary magnet schools offering nine programs such as the arts, foreign language, and Montessori and Paideia teaching styles. The district's $985 million Facilities Master Plan, launched in 2002, is financing the building or renovation of more than a dozen schools; the first new school resulting from this plan—Rockdale Academy—was completed in January 2005.

The following is a summary of data regarding the CPS district as of the 2003–2004 school year.

Total enrollment: 38,779

Number of facilities
    elementary schools: 58 (consisting of both K-6 and K-8 schools)
    high schools: 21

Student/teacher ratio: 13.2:1

Teacher salaries
    minimum: $34,888
    maximum: $69,609

Funding per pupil: $9,749 (2001-2002)

A parochial school system operated by the Catholic Diocese as well as a variety of private schools throughout the area provide instruction from kindergarten through twelfth grade. Cincinnati is home to more than 130 private schools. Its Catholic school system is the ninth largest in the nation.

Public Schools Information: Cincinnati Public Schools, PO Box 5381, Cincinnati, OH 45201; telephone (513)363-0000

Colleges and Universities

The University of Cincinnati (UC), part of Ohio's state higher education system, was founded in 1819. The university has an enrollment of more than 34,000 students and grants degrees at all levels, from associate through doctorate, in a complete range of fields. The university includes a main academic campus, a medical campus, a branch campus in suburban Blue Ash, and a rural branch campus in Clermont County, east of Cincinnati. The university is a nationally recognized research institution known for its professional schools, notably the colleges of medicine, engineering, law, business, applied science, and design, architecture, art, and planning. Cooperative education originated at the University of Cincinnati, in 1906; other UC firsts include the development of the oral polio vaccine and the first antihistamine.

Cincinnati is also home to Xavier University, a Jesuit institution founded in 1831, which offers undergraduate and graduate programs in such areas as theology, criminal justice, psychology, business, education, English, health services administration, nursing, and occupational therapy.

Hebrew Union College-Jewish Institute of Religion, a graduate rabbinical seminary, was founded in 1875 and is the nation's oldest institution of higher Jewish education. In addition to its Rabbinical School, the College-Institute includes Schools of Graduate Studies, Education, Jewish Communal Service, Sacred Music, and Biblical Archaeology. Branch campuses are located in Los Angeles, New York, and Jerusalem.

The Athenaeum of Ohio is an accredited center of ministry education and formation within the Roman Catholic tradition. Other colleges in Cincinnati are the Art Academy of Cincinnati, a small independent college of art and design; The Union Institute, designed for adults who have the desire to assume a significant measure of personal responsibility for planning and executing their degree programs; and Cincinnati Bible College and Seminary.

Colleges and universities in the metropolitan area include Miami University in Oxford, offering specialized studies in more than 100 academic majors and pre-professional programs, and particularly known for its business school; Northern Kentucky University; Thomas More College; St. Thomas Institute; and College of Mount St. Joseph.

Vocational and technical education is available at a variety of institutions such as Cincinnati State Technical and Community College, and Gateway Community and Technical College.

Libraries and Research Centers

The Public Library of Cincinnati and Hamilton County is the third-oldest library in the nation, with holdings totaling 9.6 million items. The library system is comprised of a downtown facility and 57 branches. The 542,527 square-foot main library has 15 departments, among them a library for the blind. Special collections cover a range of topics, among them inland rivers, sacred music, patents from 1790 to the present, nineteenth and twentieth century illustrators, and Bibles and English language dictionaries; the library is also a depository for federal documents.

Cincinnati-area colleges and universities also maintain campus libraries. The largest is the University of Cincinnati Libraries, which include a central facility with more than 2.1 million volumes and nearly 20,000 periodical subscriptions; the law school and the University of Cincinnati Medical Center operate separate library systems. The Hebrew Union College-Jewish Institute of Religion Klau Library, with holdings of 425,000 volumes and 2,340 periodical subscriptions, is an important center for such subject interests as Hebraica, Judaica, ancient and near-Eastern studies, and rabbinical studies. Several cultural and scientific organizations operate libraries, including the Art Museum, the Cincinnati Museum Center, the Taft Museum, and the Zoological Society. The Cincinnati Historical Society Library holds 90,000 books relating to the history of the United States, Ohio, and the Old Northwest Territory, especially metropolitan Cincinnati.

The U.S. Department of Health and Human Services has a library in Cincinnati that is open to the public. Collections of approximately 200,000 volumes are maintained by the Cincinnati Law Library Association and the Young Men's Mercantile Library Association. Among corporations housing libraries for their own personnel and researchers are General

Electric and the Andrew Jergens Co. Other specialized libraries are affiliated with hospitals, churches, and synagogues.

The University of Cincinnati (UC) is a major research center, and its research funding continues to increase steadily. In 2003, UC earned more than $300 million in research grants and contracts, an 18 percent increase over the previous year. In addition to the funding increase, the university's Intellectual Property Office reported 86 invention disclosures, 25 U.S. patents filed, and 9 U.S. patents issued during fiscal year 2003. Research is conducted in a wide variety of fields, including sociology, biology, aeronautics, health, psychology, and archaeology. The university's Medical Center campus features such research facilities as the Genome Research Institute, and is home to BIO/START, a biomedical business incubator.

Public Library Information: Public Library of Cincinnati and Hamilton County, 800 Vine Street, Cincinnati, OH 45202-2009; telephone (513)369-6900

Health Care

The Cincinnati medical community, a regional health care center, has gained prominence for education, treatment, and research. The University of Cincinnati maintains the oldest teaching hospital/medical center in the country and is the place where Albert Sabin developed the first polio vaccine and Leon Goldman performed the first laser surgery for the removal of cataracts. In 1994, University Hospital joined with The Christ Hospital to form the Health Alliance, which consists of six hospitals—University Hospital; Christ Hospital; Jewish Hospital, where Henry Heimlich, when he was chief of surgery there, developed his famous maneuver; Fort Hamilton Hospital; and St. Luke Hospitals East and West—in Cincinnati and northern Kentucky. Children's Hospital Medical Center, one of the nation's largest and most respected pediatric hospitals, also operates the largest pediatric residency program and developed the first heart-lung machine.

More than 30 hospitals serve the Cincinnati area. Among the general care and specialized facilities are the Shriners Burns Institute, St. Elizabeth Medical Center, Good Samaritan, Bethesda, Deaconess, Providence, and St. Francis-St. George hospitals.

Recreation

Sightseeing

A tour of Cincinnati can begin downtown at Fountain Square, the site of the Tyler Davidson Fountain, one of the city's most revered landmarks, which was made in Munich, Germany, and erected in 1871. Several historic monuments, including statues in honor of three United States presidents—James A. Garfield, William Henry Harrison, and Abraham Lincoln—are also located in the downtown area.

Eden Park in Mt. Adams, one of Cincinnati's oldest hillside neighborhoods and named after President John Quincy Adams, provides a panoramic view of the city and of northern Kentucky across the Ohio River. In Eden Park the Irwin M. Krohn Conservatory maintains several large public greenhouses showcasing more than 3,500 plant species: the Palm House features palm, rubber, and banana trees in a rainforest setting with a 20-foot waterfall; the Tropical House has ferns, bromeliads, begonias, chocolate and papaya trees, and vanilla vine; the Floral House has seasonal floral displays among its permanent collection of orange, kumquat, lemon, and grapefruit trees; the Desert Garden is home to yuccas, agaves, cacti, and aloes; and the Orchid House displays 17 genera of orchids.

The Cincinnati Zoo, opened in 1872, is the second oldest zoo in the United States. Set on 75 acres, the zoo is home to 510 animal species as well as 3,000 plant varieties. The zoo is recognized worldwide for the breeding of animals in captivity; the zoo park introduced the nation's first insect world exhibit. The zoo features such rare animals as the white Bengal tiger, Sumatran rhinoceros, and lowland gorilla, as well as manatees, alligators and crocodiles, orangutans, elephants, giraffes, and polar bears. The zoo's newest permanent exhibit, Wolf Woods, opened in May 2005. Here, visitors can view the rare Mexican gray wolf and other North American animals, including river otters, gray fox, wild turkey, striped skunk, and thickbilled parrots.

Historic houses open for public viewing include the former homes of Harriet Beecher Stowe, author of *Uncle Tom's Cabin;* and William Howard Taft, 27th President of the United States. The Harriet Beecher Stowe House displays artifacts of African American history, featuring documents from the Beecher family. The William Howard Taft National Historic Site was Taft's birthplace and boyhood home; several rooms have been restored to reflect Taft's family life. Dayton Street on Cincinnati's West End features restored nineteenth-century architecture. The Spring Grove Cemetery and Arboretum, a national historic landmark, contains 1,000 labeled trees on 733 landscaped acres lined with statuary and sculpture.

Paramount's Kings Island Theme Park, 20 minutes north of Cincinnati, features more than 80 amusement attractions and is known nationally for its daring rollercoasters and water rides, among them The Beast, the world's longest wooden rollercoaster. The nearby Beach Waterpark has nearly 50 waterslides and rides. Sharon Woods Village, in nearby Sharonville, is an outdoor museum of restored nineteenth-

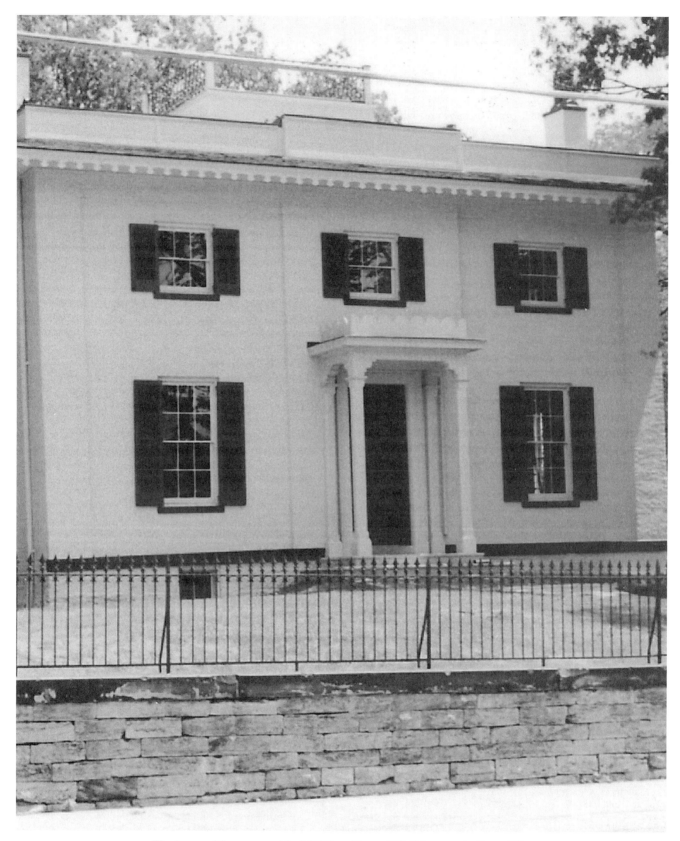

The home of former president William Howard Taft is open to the public.

century southwestern Ohio buildings. Meier's Wine Cellar, Ohio's oldest and largest winery, offers tours.

Arts and Culture

Many of Cincinnati's cultural institutions date from the mid-nineteenth century, and the city takes particular pride in their longevity and quality. The primary venues for the performing arts are Music Hall which, built in 1878, retains its nineteenth-century elegance and is affectionately known as the city's Grand Dame; and the Aronoff Center for the Arts, opened in 1995, which features three performance spaces as well as the Weston Art Gallery, and presents thousands of exhibits and performances each year. Cincinnati is home to the Cincinnati Symphony Orchestra, Cincinnati Ballet, and Cincinnati Opera. The symphony, established in 1895, performs classical and pops concert series. The ballet company, based at the Aronoff Center, offers more than 30 performances annually, presenting both classical and contemporary dance. The opera company, the second oldest in the United States, presents four productions during a summer season. Based at Music Hall, a new four-story opera headquarters is being built in the hall's underutilized north wing, scheduled for completion in October 2005.

Riverbend Music Center, an open-air amphitheater designed by noted architect Michael Graves, is the summer performance quarters for the Cincinnati Pops Orchestra and Symphony Orchestra, as well as the site for concerts by visiting artists. Popular music traditions in Cincinnati include the Matinee Musicale, founded in 1911, the Cincinnati Chamber Music Series, and the Taft Chamber Concerts.

Music in Cincinnati is not limited to the classical tradition. Cincinnati and nearby Covington, Kentucky, support an active jazz club scene. The Blue Wisp Jazz Club features local and national talent.

Cincinnati Playhouse in the Park, a professional regional theater, is housed in a modern facility in Eden Park. Recipient of the 2004 Regional Theatre Tony Award, the Playhouse presents a September-June season of comedies, dramas, classics, and musicals on a main stage and in a smaller theater. The University of Cincinnati's College—Conservatory of Music presents nearly 1,000 events per year and is most noted for its philharmonic orchestra concerts, operas, and musical theater productions; many performances are free. The Showboat Majestic, a restored nineteenth-century showboat on the Ohio River Public Landing, is one of the last original floating theaters still in operation. Performances on the showboat include dramas, comedies, old-fashioned melodramas, and musicals. The Ensemble Theatre of Cincinnati presents regional, world, and off-Broadway premiere productions at its theater downtown.

In addition to music and performing arts, the visual arts are an integral part of the city's cultural heritage. The Woman's Art Museum Association was responsible for the construction of the Cincinnati Art Museum in 1871; the museum, which has undergone an extensive renovation, houses nearly 100 galleries. Its permanent collection features an outstanding collection of Asian art and musical instruments, and a Cincinnati Wing with local artworks dating from 1788 through the present. Downtown's Taft Museum, housed in an 1820 mansion and formerly the home of art patrons Charles and Anna Taft, was presented as a gift to the city in 1932. The museum holds paintings, decorative arts, sculpture, furniture, and more. The Rosenthal Center for Contemporary Art, also located downtown, opened in 2003 and presents changing exhibitions of modernist art in a variety of forms; its "UnMuseum" is designed for children. A number of art galleries occupy converted warehouses near the shopping district.

Union Terminal, a former train station declared a masterpiece of Art Deco construction when it opened in 1933, has been restored and is home to the Cincinnati Museum Center at Union Terminal. The center includes the Cincinnati History Museum, featuring recreations of historical settings showcasing the city's past; the Museum of Natural History and Science, where visitors can walk through glaciers, explore caves, and learn about the human body; the Cinergy Children's Museum, where kids can climb, crawl, explore, and learn about the world in educational exhibits; and an Omnimax theater. The National Underground Railroad Freedom Center, opened in 2004, is a 158,000 square-foot facility tracing the 300-year history of slavery in America and highlighting the role of the Underground Railroad. The Cincinnati Fire Museum, located in a 1907 firehouse, exhibits the history of fire fighting in Cincinnati.

Festivals and Holidays

Each year Cincinnati presents a number of festivals that celebrate the city's heritage and institutions. The Celtic Lands Culture Fest in March includes storytelling, dancing, food, music and crafts. The nation's professional baseball season opens in April with the Cincinnati Reds game at Riverfront Stadium. Preceding the game is an Opening Day Parade originating at historic Findlay Market. The Appalachian Festival, held in May, has mountain crafts, live music, dancing, and storytellers; it is said to be the largest craft show in the country. May Festival, a tradition begun in 1873, is the oldest continuing festival of choral and orchestral music in the country. The Taste of Cincinnati celebration held over Memorial Day weekend downtown affords the city's best restaurants an opportunity to feature some of their favorite menu items. Summerfair brings an arts and crafts show to the city's riverfront the second weekend in June. Juneteenth Festival is a celebration of African-American freedom, featuring diverse music and food. The day-long Riverfest celebration on Labor Day honors the area's river heritage and is the city's largest celebration. The festival features water skiing, sky diving and air shows, and riverboat cruises, and is capped by a spectacular fireworks display. The Harvest Home Fair, held the following weekend in nearby Cheviot, features horse, art, and flower shows, a parade, 4-H auction, petting zoo, and more. The Valley Vineyards Wine Festival, also in September, features wine, tours, food, music, camping, arts, crafts and activities. Oktoberfest Zinzinnati features German food, customs, dancing, and beer; downtown streets are blocked off for the festivities. Early December brings Balluminaria at Eden Park, where hot air balloons are lit up at dusk near Mirror Lake.

Popular Christmas-holiday events in Cincinnati include the annual tree-lighting on Fountain Square, the Festival of Lights at the Cincinnati Zoo, and the Boar's Head and Yule Log Festival at Christ Church Cathedral downtown, a Cincinnati tradition since 1940.

Events are held throughout the year in nearby Sharon Woods Village and in the MainStrasse Village in Covington, Kentucky, across the Ohio River.

Sports for the Spectator

The Cincinnati Reds, World Series winners in 1975, 1976, and 1990, is America's oldest professional baseball team; they play their home games at the new Great American Ball Park. Opened in 2003, the park has a seating capacity of 42,059 and is praised for its innovative features, breathtaking views, and tributes to the Reds' rich history. The Cincinnati Bengals, who captured the American Football Championship in 1981 and 1988, play home games at Paul Brown Stadium, opened in 2000. The stadium has a seating capacity of 65,535, on three levels; its open-ended design allows for stunning views of the downtown skyline and the riverfront.

The Cincinnati Mighty Ducks of the American Hockey League play at the Cincinnati Gardens. The Cincinnati Cyclones are in the International Hockey League and play at the Crown. The University of Cincinnati and Xavier University provide a schedule of college sports teams and crosstown rivalry in basketball, in which both schools enjoy strong traditions and some national prominence.

Thoroughbred racing takes place at River Downs Racetrack in late April through Labor Day, and at Turfway Park in Florence, Kentucky, from September through mid-October, and Thanksgiving through mid-April. The Association of Tennis Professionals compete in tournament play each August in nearby Mason.

Sports for the Participant

Cincinnati maintains more than 5,000 acres of park land in attractive urban settings. Alms Park and Eden Park offer dramatic views of the Ohio River and northern Kentucky, and these parks, as well as others, attract joggers because of their natural beauty and challenge for runners. The Cincin-

nati Nature Center—Rowe Woods is comprised of 1,025 acres with nature trails covering more than 17 miles, and a nature center featuring a bird-viewing area, library, and displays. The 1,466 acres of Mount Airy Forest feature hiking and picnic areas. The city's recreation department sponsors an array of sports from softball to soccer for all age groups and manages neighborhood swimming pools and tennis courts throughout the summer. Sawyer Point on the Ohio River provides facilities for pier fishing, rowboating, skating, tennis, and volleyball.

Shopping and Dining

Cincinnati consists of distinct neighborhoods where shopping districts provide an atmosphere not found in many cities today. The city's revitalization is most evident downtown in the area known as Over-the-Rhine, the old German neighborhood around Vine and Main Streets. There, art galleries, restaurants, and breweries flourish in restored nineteenth-century buildings. Cincinnati's skywalk system connects downtown stores, hotels, and restaurants, allowing visitors to explore the shopping district free of traffic and weather concerns. The downtown Tower Place mixes local and nationally known stores with specialty shops in a compact area. Other downtown Cincinnati shopping highlights include a Lazarus-Macy's and Saks Fifth Avenue department stores. Neighborhood and suburban shopping districts and malls abound on both sides of the river, and the region offers endless antique shops, boutiques, arts and crafts shops, and ethnic and fashion collections. Other shopping opportunities include large regional malls, factory outlets, discount houses, and museum stores. The Findlay Market, an open-air marketplace that has been in operation since 1852, offers ethnic foods in an old-world atmosphere.

Cincinnati restaurants have been rated highly by critics and travel guides. The city is home to several restaurants that have received critical acclaim nationally, including Maisonette, a French restaurant that has received Five Stars from Mobil for 40 consecutive years. Both the number and variety of first-rate restaurants are impressive. One of Cincinnati's specialties is moderately priced German cuisine. Cincinnati restaurateurs have been successful in opening establishments in architecturally interesting buildings, such as firehouses, police precincts, or riverboat paddle-wheelers. A locally made ice cream, Graeter's, is widely popular, as is a downtown New York-style deli, Izzy's, known for its corned beef. The city's oldest tavern, opened in 1861, is still in business as a bar and grill. Cincinnati chili, Greek in origin, is flavored with cinnamon and chocolate as the ''secret'' ingredients and served over spaghetti; 3-way, 4-way, or 5-way chili choices consist of various combinations of grated cheese, onions, beans, and oyster crackers.

Visitor Information: Greater Cincinnati Convention and Visitors Bureau, 300 West Sixth Street, Cincinnati, OH 45202; telephone (513)621-2142

Convention Facilities

The Dr. Albert B. Sabin Cincinnati Convention Center is conveniently situated downtown and connected via the 20-block Skywalk system with shops and stores, restaurants, entertainment and cultural activities, and hotels. The architecturally interesting entrance to the post-modern style Convention Center features the preserved facade of the historic Albee Theatre, which once stood near Fountain Square and was demolished several years ago. The center is undergoing a $160 million renovation and expansion, scheduled for completion in 2006.

The complex consists of three levels: the exhibit level contains three halls with 162,000 square feet of combined space that will accommodate up to 15,000 meeting participants; on the second level 41 separate rooms provide banquet and meeting capacities ranging from 30 to 2,300 people; the third level is comprised of three ballrooms that combine to offer 30,000 square feet of space. Convention center amenities include a banquet kitchen, teleconferencing facilities, handicapped access, and adjacent parking for 5,000 vehicles. When expanded in 2006, the 750,000 square foot center will feature nearly 200,000 square feet of exhibition space, and $4.5 million in technology upgrades.

Meeting and convention accommodations can also be found at several luxury hotels clustered downtown near the Convention Center and at other hotels and motels throughout the Greater Cincinnati area. More than 22,500 lodging rooms are available citywide.

Convention Information: Greater Cincinnati Convention and Visitors Bureau, 300 West Sixth Street, Cincinnati, OH 45202; telephone (513)621-2142

Transportation

Approaching the City

Nearly 1,200 flights depart and arrive and depart daily at Cincinnati/Northern Kentucky International Airport. Located only 15 minutes from downtown Cincinnati, it is one of the fastest growing airports in the world. It is the second largest hub for Delta Air Lines. The airport offers non-stop air service from the region to 130 cities, including international service to Frankfurt, London, Paris, Rome, Amsterdam, Montreal and Toronto.

Metropolitan Cincinnati is linked to other areas via I-75, a major north/south route running between the Canadian border through Florida; I-71, running between Louisville and northeast Ohio; and I-74, the area's principal link from the west. I-70, a major transcontinental route, runs east/west approximately 55 miles north of the city. Other highways providing access to downtown and the metropolitan region are: Interstates 275, which circles the metropolitan area, and 471, which runs in to downtown; U.S. 50 and 52; and several state and county routes.

Passenger rail service into renovated Union Terminal is available by Amtrak. Bus transportation is provided by Greyhound.

Traveling in the City

Downtown streets are in a grid pattern, making travel within the city relatively easy. Streets running east/west are numbered, beginning with 2nd Street near the Ohio River. The public transit bus system is operated by Metro, which schedules regular routes in the city and the suburbs.

Communications

Newspapers and Magazines

Cincinnati's major daily newspapers are *The Cincinnati Enquirer,* circulated every morning, and the evening *The Cincinnati Post.* The *Cincinnati Herald,* an African American oriented newspaper, appears weekly. Both the Associated Press and United Press International maintain offices in Cincinnati. *Cincinnati Magazine* is a monthly publication focusing on topics of community interest.

A number of nationally circulated magazines are published in Cincinnati; among them are *Writer's Digest,* a professional magazine for writers; *Dramatics Magazine,* for students interested in theatre as a career; and *St. Anthony Messenger,* a family-oriented Catholic magazine. Cincinnati-based Standard Publishing Company produces religious magazines like *Weekly Bible Reader,* for children, and *Seek,* for young adults and adults. Specialized publications originating in the city are directed toward readers with interests in business, medicine, pharmacy, engineering, the arts, crafts, and other fields.

Television and Radio

Cincinnati is the broadcast media center for southwestern Ohio, northern Kentucky, and southeastern Indiana. Eight commercial, public, and independent television stations are received in the city; cable service is available. Thirty-five AM and FM radio stations broadcast educational, cultural, and religious programming as well as rock and roll, contemporary, classical, gospel, blues, jazz, and country music.

Media Information: *The Cincinnati Enquirer,* Gannet Co., 312 Elm Street, Cincinnati, OH; telephone (513)721-2700; and, *The Cincinnati Post*, E.W. Scripps Co., 125 E. Court, Cincinnati, OH 45202; telephone (513)352-2000

Cincinnati Online

The Cincinnati Enquirer. Available enquirer.com/today

Cincinnati Museum Center. Available www.cincymuseum .org

Cincinnati Public Schools. Available www.cpsboe.k12.oh .us

Cincinnati Regional Links. Available www.rcc.org/reglinks .html

City of Cincinnati home page. Available www.ci.cincinnati .oh.us

Greater Cincinnati Chamber of Commerce. Available www .cincinnatichamber.com/home.htm

Greater Cincinnati Convention and Visitors Bureau. Available www.cincyusa.com

Public Library of Cincinnati and Hamilton County. Available www.cincinnatilibrary.org

University of Cincinnati Medical Center. Available medcenter.uc.edu

Selected Bibliography

Chambrun, Clara Longworth, Comtesse de, *Cincinnati: Story of the Queen City* (New York, London: Scribner, 1939)

Fuller, John Grant, *Are the Kids All Right?: The Rock Generation and Its Hidden Death Wish* (New York: Times Books, 1981)

Howells, William Dean, *A Boy's Town: Described for ''Harper's Young People''* (New York: Harper & Brothers, Franklin Square, 1890)

Howells, William Dean, *My Year in a Log Cabin* (New York, Harper & Brothers, 1893)

Lewis, Sinclair, *Babbitt* (New York: Harcourt, Brace, 1922)

Miller, Zane L., and Bruce Tucker, *Changing Plans for America's Inner Cities: Cincinnati's Over-The-Rhine and Twentieth-Century Urbanism (Urban Life and Urban Landscape Series)* (Ohio State University Press, 1998)

Walker, Robert Harris, *Cincinnati and the Big Red Machine* (Indiana University Press, 1988)

Cleveland

The City in Brief

Founded: 1796 (incorporated 1836)

Head Official: Mayor Jane Campbell (D) (since 2001)

City Population
   1980: 573,822
   1990: 505,616
   2000: 478,403
   2003 estimate: 461,324
   Percent change, 1990–2000: −5.4%
   U.S. rank in 1980: 18th
   U.S. rank in 1990: 23rd
   U.S. rank in 2000: 40th (State rank: 2nd)

Metropolitan Area Population
   1990: 2,202,069
   2000: 2,250,871
   Percent change, 1990–2000: 0.2%

U.S. rank in 1980: 11th
U.S. rank in 1990: Not reported
U.S. rank in 2000: 16th (PMSA)

Area: 82.42 square miles (2000)
Elevation: most of the city is on a level plain 60 to 80 feet above Lake Erie
Average Annual Temperature: 49.6° F
Average Annual Precipitation: 38.71 inches of rain; 55.8 inches of snow

Major Economic Sectors: Services, wholesale and retail trade, manufacturing, government
Unemployment Rate: 6.3% (March 2005)
Per Capita Income: $14,291 (1999)

2002 FBI Crime Index Total: 33,209

Major Colleges and Universities: Case Western Reserve University; Cleveland State University

Daily Newspaper: *Plain Dealer*

Introduction

The seat of Cuyahoga County, Cleveland is Ohio's second largest city and is at the center of a metropolitan statistical area that encompasses Cuyahoga, Geauga, Lake, and Medina counties. The city's location on Lake Erie accounts for its success as a transportation, industrial, and commercial center. Cleveland contributed a number of industrial discoveries that benefited national growth and prosperity in the nineteenth century. In the early twentieth century, the local political system set a standard for reform that contributed to the general welfare of its citizens. Today Cleveland's revitalized central business and commercial districts complement its cultural institutions and major professional sports teams.

Geography and Climate

Extending 31 miles along the south shore of Lake Erie, Cleveland is surrounded by generally level terrain except for an abrupt ridge that rises 500 feet above the shore on the eastern edge of the city. Cleveland is bisected from north to south by the Cuyahoga River. The continental climate is modified by west to northerly winds off Lake Erie, which lower summer temperatures and raise winter temperatures. Summers are moderately warm and humid, winters relatively cold and cloudy. Snowfall fluctuates widely, ranging from 45 inches in west Cuyahoga County to 90 inches in the east. Thunderstorms often bring damaging winds of 50 miles per hour or greater; tornadoes occur frequently.

Area: 82.42 square miles (2000)

Elevation: most of the city is on a level plain 60 to 80 feet above Lake Erie

Average Temperatures: January, 25.7° F; July, 71.9° F; annual average, 49.6° F

Average Annual Precipitation: 38.71 inches of rain; 55.8 inches of snow

History

Lake Erie Port Attracts Development

U.S. General Moses Cleaveland was sent in 1796 by the Connecticut Land Company to survey the Western Reserve, a one-half million acre tract of land in northeastern Ohio, which was at that time called "New Connecticut." General

Cleaveland platted a townsite on Lake Erie at the mouth of the Cuyahoga River, named from a Native American term for crooked river because of the unusual U shape that causes it to flow both north and south. Cleaveland copied the New England style of town square layout. The settlement was abandoned, however, when dysentery and insects drove Cleaveland and his company back to New England. The eventual taming of the Western Reserve wilderness has been credited to Lorenzo Carter, who arrived at General Cleaveland's original townsite in 1799. Carter, a man of impressive ability and stature, brought stability to the primitive setting and established friendly relations with the Native Americans in the area. The revived settlement was named for its initial founder; the current spelling of the name can be traced to a newspaper compositor who dropped the first "a" from Cleaveland in order to fit the name on the newspaper masthead. Cleveland's geographic position as a Lake Erie port made it ideally situated for development in transportation, industry, and commerce.

By 1813 the port was receiving shipments from the cities in the East. Cleveland was chosen as the northern terminus of a canal system connecting the Ohio River and Lake Erie; it was completed in 1832. Cleveland was incorporated in 1836 as its population increased dramatically. Telegraph lines were installed in 1847, and shortly thereafter Western Union telegraph service was founded in Cleveland by Jeptha H. Wade. The opening of the Soo Canal in 1855 and the arrival of the railroad soon thereafter strengthened Cleveland's position as a transportation center.

The city played a significant role in the Civil War. Clevelanders generally opposed slavery, and a prominent local lawyer defended abolitionist John Brown. As a principal stop along the Oberlin-Wellington Trail, Cleveland was active in the Underground Railroad. While the city sent its share of volunteers to fight for the Union cause, during the Civil War the ironworks industry grew, aided by the discovery of soft coal in canal beds. After the war the iron industry continued to expand in Cleveland, and local fortunes were made in steel and shipping; those who benefited created the Cleveland residential district known as "Millionaires Row."

Industry and Reform Spell Progress

John D. Rockefeller's Standard Oil Company, organized in 1870, put Cleveland on the map as the nation's first oil capital. A rise in trade unionism paralleled Cleveland's industrialization. The Brotherhood of Locomotive Engineers established headquarters in the city, which was the site of national labor meetings that eventually led to walkouts and brought about better conditions for workers. Inventors found a hospitable environment in Cleveland. Charles F. Brush, originator of the carbon arc lamp, founded the Brush Electric Light and Power Company and installed arc lamps throughout the city. He also invented and manufactured the first practical storage battery. Worcester R. Warner and Ambrose Swasey perfected automotive gear improvements and designed astronomy instruments, bringing about innovations in both industries.

Cleveland gained a reputation as a reform city during the five-term administration of Thomas Loftin Johnson, a captain of the steel and transportation industries. Johnson was influenced by the American social philosopher Henry George, and his administration won high praise from muckraking journalist Lincoln Steffens, who called Johnson the nation's "best mayor" and Cleveland "the best governed city in the United States." First elected to office on the "three-cent fare program," Johnson fought to overcome the entrenched political interests of his nemesis, Mark Hanna, who used his power to work against Johnson's reforms. Johnson, a mentor to a generation of young politicians, improved life in Cleveland by building new streets and parks, creating a municipal electric company to curb the abuses of private utilities, and introducing city-owned garbage and refuse collection. He also set standards for meat and dairy products, and even took down "keep off the grass" signs in city parks.

Like other Rust Belt cities, Cleveland suffered in the 1950s and 1960s, becoming the subject of national attention and ridicule when the polluted Cuyahoga River burst into flames in 1969. The event, a low point in Cleveland history, became a rallying point in the passage of the Clean Water Act of 1972.

Cleveland's renaissance began in the early 1980s. From grass roots efforts initiated by neighborhood groups, to the city's top brass—business, civic, and political leaders—citizens have worked hard to mold Cleveland into a model city for America. The result—$7 billion in capital investment, including new hotels and world-class attractions. The city has also gained international and national attention as a model city for urban progress. Cleveland has been awarded the coveted "All America City" distinction five times.

The sheen from that title was growing tarnished by the mid-2000s, however. With a high school graduation rate among the lowest in the nation, along with taxes among the highest, Cleveland faced challenges in many arenas. Community leaders and businesses united to tackle these problems by stimulating innovation and entrepreneurship, attracting new businesses while retaining existing ones, and encouraging education and workforce development.

Historical Information: Western Reserve Historical Society, 10825 East Blvd., Cleveland, OH 44106; telephone (216)721-5722; email webmaster@wrhs.org. Great Lakes Historical Society, Clarence Metcalf Research Library, 480 Main St., PO Box 435, Vermillion, OH 44089; telephone (216)967-3467; email glhs1@inlandseas.org.

Population Profile

Metropolitan Area Residents
1990: 2,202,069
2000: 2,250,871
Percent change, 1990–2000: 0.2%
U.S. rank in 1980: 11th
U.S. rank in 1990: Not reported
U.S. rank in 2000: 16th (PMSA)

City Residents
1980: 573,822
1990: 505,616
2000: 478,403
2003 estimate: 461,324
Percent change, 1990–2000: −5.4%
U.S. rank in 1980: 18th
U.S. rank in 1990: 23rd
U.S. rank in 2000: 40th (State rank: 2nd)

Density: 6,166.5 people per square mile (2000)

Racial and ethnic characteristics (2000)
   White: 198,510
   Black or African American: 243,939
   American Indian and Alaska Native: 1,458
   Asian: 6,444
   Native Hawaiian and Pacific Islander: 178
   Hispanic or Latino (may be of any race): 34,728
   Other: 17,173

Percent of residents born in state: 71.2% (2000)

Age characteristics (2000)
   Population under 5 years old: 38,594
   Population 5 to 9 years old: 41,708
   Population 10 to 14 years old: 36,799
   Population 15 to 19 years old: 32,495
   Population 20 to 24 years old: 32,061
   Population 25 to 34 years old: 71,847
   Population 35 to 44 years old: 73,822
   Population 45 to 54 years old: 55,111
   Population 55 to 59 years old: 18,857
   Population 60 to 64 years old: 17,130
   Population 65 to 74 years old: 31,573
   Population 75 to 84 years old: 21,266
   Population 85 years and older: 7,140
   Median age: 33.0 years

Births (2002, Cuyahoga County)
   Total number: 17,375

Deaths (2002, Cuyahoga County)
   Total number: 15,177 (of which, 180 were infants under the age of 1 year)

Money income (1999)
    Per capita income: $14,291
    Median household income: $25,928
    Total households: 190,725

Number of households with income of . . .
    less than $10,000: 40,118
    $10,000 to $14,999: 18,446
    $15,000 to $24,999: 33,725
    $25,000 to $34,999: 28,228
    $35,000 to $49,999: 28,814
    $50,000 to $74,999: 25,592
    $75,000 to $99,999: 9,328
    $100,000 to $149,999: 4,336
    $150,000 to $199,999: 820
    $200,000 or more: 1,318

Percent of families below poverty level: 22.9% (59.4% of which were female householder families with related children under 5 years)

2002 FBI Crime Index Total: 33,209

Municipal Government

Cleveland city government is administered by a mayor and a 21-member council. Councilpersons and the mayor, who is not a member of council, are elected to four-year terms.

Head Official: Mayor Jane Campbell (D) (since 2001; current term expires November 2005)

Total Number of City Employees: 8,743 (2003)

City Information: Cleveland City Hall, 601 Lakeside Ave., Cleveland, OH 44114; telephone (216)664-2000

Economy

Major Industries and Commercial Activity

Diversified manufacturing is a primary economic sector, resting on a traditional base of heavy industry in particular. Consistent with a nationwide trend, the services industry—transportation, health, insurance, retailing, utilities, commercial banking, and finance—is emerging as a dominant sector. Cleveland serves as headquarters to 11 companies on the *Fortune* 500 list, both industrial and non-industrial. These firms are, in order of their *Fortune* 500 rank: National City Corp., Eaton Corp., Parker Hannifin Corp., Sherwin-Williams Co., KeyCorp, Nacco Industries, American Greet-

ings Corp., Ferro Corp., Medical Mutual of Ohio, Applied Industries Technologies, and Lincoln Electric Holdings. Cleveland is also home to nearly 150 international companies from 25 different countries.

Manufacturing has traditionally been the primary industry of northeast Ohio. It remains so today, although the local economy has suffered along with the rest of the nation during the recession of the late 1990s and early 2000s. Dubbed "Polymer Valley," the metropolitan Cleveland area has the largest concentration of polymer companies in the United States; for example, Goodyear Tire & Rubber Co., the world's largest tire company, is headquartered in nearby Akron. The area's other manufacturing companies are engaged in such areas as the automotive industry, fabricated metals, electrical/electronic equipment, and instruments and controls.

Supported by the manufacturing industry is the science and engineering field. More than 168 engineering companies are located in the Cleveland metro area. These firms engage in civil engineering, construction, and the burgeoning field of information technology, which employs approximately 73,500 area workers. Among the local institutions of science and engineering are the Cleveland Engineering Society, the Cleveland Society of Professional Engineers, the Great Lakes Science Center, the NASA John H. Glenn Research Center, ASM (American Society for Metals) International, and the engineering schools of Case Western Reserve University, Cleveland State University, and the University of Akron.

Cleveland's research base for the biotechnology and biomedical industry has tripled in recent years, from $50 million to $150 million. More than 100 biotechnology firms are located in northeast Ohio, along with more than 100 research laboratories. The Cleveland Clinic Foundation has the nation's largest hospital-based department of biomedical engineering. Area colleges offer training in biomedical or bioscience technology; among them are Case Western Reserve University, Cleveland State University, Kent State University, Lakeland Community College, and the University of Akron.

Items and goods produced: automobile parts, bolts and nuts, machine tools, paints and lacquers, rubber and oil products, chemicals, rayon, foundry and machine shop products, electrical machinery and appliances, men's and women's clothing, iron and steel

Incentive Programs—New and Existing Businesses

Local programs—The Greater Cleveland Partnership (GCP) was formed in 2003 through the merger of the Greater Cleveland Roundtable, the Greater Cleveland Growth Association, and Cleveland Tomorrow. GCP provides access to local and state business incentives and job training programs. It can link businesses with a variety of assistance including international trade, business financing, tax credits and abatement programs, technology transfer, labor force recruitment, and training and market data. GCP is also affiliated with Growth Capital Corp., which provides financing assistance to businesses in northeast Ohio to facilitate business expansion, new facility construction, and equipment purchases. Neighborhood Progress Inc. is a non-profit organization that offers up to $5 million per year in low-interest funds to develop Cleveland's neighborhoods.

State programs—The state of Ohio offers a number of incentives designed to encourage new companies and retain existing businesses. Tax credit programs include those for job creation, machinery and equipment investment, export, research and development franchise, and technology investment. Ohio also offers a property tax abatement for areas identified as enterprise zones, and sales tax exemptions for research and development.

Job training programs—Ohio Industrial Training Program (OITP) is a state program that can provide assistance to a business through a competitive grant award. Funds are used to reimburse the incurred eligible training costs. OITP may assist a company up to a maximum of one-half of the project's total eligible training costs. The Ohio Job Training Tax Credit is offered to businesses engaged in manufacturing and other specified service industries. Career Service Centers offer customized training programs designed to meet the needs of a specific business, as well as other ongoing skill training for current or new employees; these Career Service Centers are operated by Case Western Reserve University, Cleveland Institute of Art, Cleveland State University, Cuyahoga Community College, and David N. Myers College.

Development Projects

In March 2004 *Site Selection* magazine ranked the Cleveland area, with 96 projects, the 10th in the nation for number of new and expanded corporate facility projects. Among these corporate projects were the expansion of Minolta's Cleveland facility, which added 25,000 square feet; the $4.5 million expansion of U.S. Cotton's facility; and a new, 5,000-square-foot distribution center for Netflix Inc.

The Milton & Tamar Maltz Jewish Heritage Museum is scheduled to open in the fall of 2005. The $13.5 million, 24,000-square-foot facility will house displays, interactive exhibits, and a 60-seat theater. Groundbreaking will begin in September 2005 on a six-year, $258-million expansion and renovation of the Cleveland Museum of Art. The Western Reserve Historical Society will spend $30 million to create an additional 100,000 square feet of space to house its car and plane collection. Euclid Avenue is undergoing a $168 million renovation between the downtown Public Square and the Playhouse Square Center; construction is scheduled for completion in 2007.

Economic Development Information: Greater Cleveland Partnership, Tower City Center, Ste. 200, 50 Public Sq., Cleveland, OH 44113; telephone (216)621-3300; toll-free (888)304-GROW; fax (216)621-4617; email customer service@clevegrowth.com

Commercial Shipping

Cleveland is at the center of the nation's largest concentration of industrial and consumer markets. The city of Cleveland is home to more than 100 offices of motor freight carrier companies and there are many others located throughout the metropolitan area. Three railroads—Norfolk Southern, CSX Transportation, Wheeling & Lake Erie Railroad—serve the region. More than 1,200 miles of highways connect the region with other U.S. markets, and the World Trade Center Cleveland assists companies with international business ventures. Cleveland-Hopkins International Airport is served by 11 cargo-only carriers.

The Port of Cleveland, the largest overseas general cargo port on Lake Erie and third largest port on the Great Lakes, serves more than 50 countries, shipping cargo to and receiving cargo from 120 ports around the world. The Port is also the site of Foreign Trade Zone #40, an area where foreign goods bound for international destinations can be temporarily stored without incurring an import duty. Every service for shippers—banking, insurance, customs, stevedoring, and storage—is available from experienced firms. Each year the port handles 13 to 15 million tons of cargo, primarily semi-finished products, machinery, and such bulk cargo as iron ore, stone, cement, and salt. The port was visited by 898 ships in 2003.

Labor Force and Employment Outlook

The following is a summary of data regarding the Cleveland metropolitan area labor force, 2004 annual average.

Size of nonagricultural labor force: 1,073,400

Number of workers employed in . . .
  construction and mining: 44,600
  manufacturing: 151,900
  trade, transportation and utilities: 200,100
  information: 20,200
  financial activities: 81,100
  professional and business services: 132,800
  educational and health services: 164,700
  leisure and hospitality: 92,400
  other services: 44,200
  government: 141,600

Average hourly earnings of production workers employed in manufacturing: $18.64

Unemployment rate: 6.3% (March 2005)

Largest metropolitan
area employers　　　　　　　　　*Number of employees*

Federal Government	18,728
Ford Motor Co.	11,800
Catholic Diocese of Cleveland	10,000
Board of County Commissioners	9,963
Cleveland Clinic Foundation	9,445
Cleveland Municipal School District	8,520
Charter One Bank	7,057
Invacare Corp.	5,630
The MetroHealth System	5,300
Cole Vision Corp.	5,168

Cost of Living

Cleveland's taxes are moderately high. According to the strategic plan presented by the Greater Cleveland Partnership in September 2004, "we are strangling ourselves with high taxes both on individuals and businesses." The report goes on to say that "local and state tax rates place many Cleveland suburbs among the highest-taxed communities in the country."

The following is a summary of data regarding several key cost of living factors in the Cleveland area.

2004 (3rd Quarter) ACCRA Average House Price: $253,363

2004 (3rd Quarter) ACCRA Cost of Living Index: 103.4 (U.S. average = 100.0)

State income tax rate: Ranges from 0.691% to 6.980%

State sales tax rate: 7.0% (food and prescription drugs are exempt)

Local income tax rate: 2.0%

Local sales tax rate: 7.5%

Property tax rate: basic rate ranges from 96.5 to 183.40 mills per $1,000 of assessed value

Economic Information: Greater Cleveland Partnership, Tower City Center, Ste. 200, 50 Public Sq., Cleveland, OH 44113; telephone (216)621-3300; toll-free (888)304-GROW; fax (216)621-4617; email customerservice@cleve growth.com

Education and Research

Elementary and Secondary Schools

The Cleveland Municipal School District, administered by a seven-member nonpartisan board that appoints a superinten-

dent, enrolls the largest student population of any Ohio school system. It is one of 31 districts in Cuyahoga County. More than 300 businesses and other organizations have joined in a partnership with the city's 121 schools; one of these is NASA John H. Glenn Research Center.

Cleveland's schools experienced academic, financial, and structural crises in the mid-2000s. In 2004 the high school graduation rate was only 40.8 percent, while only 11.3 percent of residents achieved a college degree. Worsening the situation, the Cleveland Municipal School District had a $36 million operating deficit; in order to rectify the shortfall, the board of education planned to close a number of schools and lay-off part of the workforce for the 2005–2006 school year. In June 2002, prompted by the collapse of a school gym roof, a $1.5 billion Facilities Plan was approved to replace or renovate each school in the district within 10-12 years.

The following is a summary of data regarding Cleveland public schools as of the 2004–2005 school year.

Total enrollment: 73,943

Number of facilities
　elementary schools: 59
　K–8 schools: 31
　middle schools: 13
　senior high schools: 19
　other: 2

Student/teacher ratio: 16.5:1

Teacher salaries
　average: $45,156

Funding per pupil: $8,950

More than 30 parochial and private schools offer a range of educational alternatives at the pre-school, kindergarten, elementary, and secondary levels in the Cleveland metropolitan area. Among them is the University School, a more than 100-year-old kindergarten-through twelfth-grade independent day school for boys.

Public Schools Information: Cleveland Municipal School District, 1380 E. 6th St., Cleveland, OH 44114; telephone (216)574-8000; email info@cmsdnet.net

Colleges and Universities

Cleveland State University (CSU), predominantly a commuter institution, enrolls more than 16,500 students. The university grants undergraduate and graduate degrees in 60 fields, including doctoral programs in regulatory biology, chemistry, engineering, urban studies, and urban education. CSU's Cleveland-Marshall College of Law is the largest law school in Ohio. Case Western Reserve University offers undergraduate, graduate, and professional education in 60 areas of study such as medicine, dentistry, nursing, law, management, and applied social sciences; it is a major research institution ranking among the best in undergraduate engineering and business programs. Cleveland College of Jewish Studies is one of only five colleges in North America to be accredited as an institution of higher Jewish learning.

The Cleveland Institute of Art offers a five-year bachelor of fine arts program. The Cleveland Institute of Music grants baccalaureate, master's, and doctoral degrees in various music fields in conjunction with Case Western Reserve University, which provides the academic curriculum. Other colleges in Cleveland include David N. Myers University, formerly known as Dyke College, and Cuyahoga Community College (CCC), which is the city's largest college and the fourth largest in the state. Offering career education leading to an associate degree and enrolling more than 22,000 students at its Metropolitan, Eastern, and Western campuses, CCC's programs include allied health, business technologies, engineering technologies, early childhood education, law enforcement, and mental health.

Among the colleges and universities enrolling more than 1,000 students and located in the surrounding area or within commuting distance of Cleveland are Baldwin-Wallace College, John Carroll University, Kent State University, Lakeland Community College, Lorain County Community College, Oberlin College, University of Akron, and Ursuline College, which is the oldest Catholic women's college in the nation.

Libraries and Research Centers

Approximately 90 libraries are operated in Cleveland by a diverse range of public agencies, private corporations, and other organizations. The Cleveland Public Library maintains a main facility (recently restored), 28 branches, a Library for the Blind and Physically Handicapped, and a Public Administration Library in City Hall. The Cleveland Public Library, said to be the nation's second largest municipal library, has more than 9 million items that include more than 3 million volumes, more than 6,000 current periodical titles, 4 million microforms, 1 million photographs, 137,000 sound recordings, 173,000 maps, 97,000 videos and DVDs, as well as computer software and CD-ROMS. The library is a depository for federal, state, international, local, and United Nations documents. The Library for the Blind and Physically Handicapped offers 11,000 Braille titles, 150,000 cassettes, and 48,000 discs; the library also includes material on visual and physical disabilities in their collection.

In 2003 the Ohio Center for the Book was dedicated at the main Cleveland Public Library, enabling it to serve the entire state. That year the library system became the first in the nation to offer eBooks to patrons. The Langston Hughes branch was the recipient of an Ohio Historical Marker in

December 2003 in honor of its namesake, the Cleveland poet James Mercer Langston Hughes.

The Cuyahoga County Public Library, which houses nearly 3 million books, operates four large regional libraries, 22 branch libraries, and two mini libraries in communities throughout the county. The Western Reserve Historical Society, the Cleveland Museum of Art, and the Cleveland Museum of Natural History maintain reference libraries. As a major research institution, Case Western Reserve University maintains holdings of more than 1.5 million books, nearly 14,000 periodical subscriptions, and approximately 35 special collections in such fields as literature, history, philosophy, urban studies, psychology, and the sciences; six departmental libraries are also located on campus. The Cleveland Health Sciences Library is operated by Case Western Reserve University and the Cleveland Medical Library Association. Other colleges and universities, as well as several corporations, hospitals, and religious organizations, maintain libraries in the city.

More than 400 public and private research centers are based in the Cleveland metropolitan area. Among them are the John H. Glenn Research Center of the National Aeronautics and Space Administration (NASA), the Cleveland Clinic Educational Foundation, and the Cleveland Psychoanalytic Institute. In 2003 Case Western Reserve University was awarded an $18 million grant to create the Wright Center of Innovation to focus on fuel cell research. University Hospitals represents the largest concentration of biomedical research in Ohio. Greater Cleveland's medical community as a whole receives more than $100 million in research dollars from the National Institutes of Health each year, making Cleveland a leading center nationwide for biomedical research and spending.

Public Library Information: Cleveland Public Library, 325 Superior Ave. NE, Cleveland, OH 44114-1271; telephone (216)623-2800; fax (216)623-7015; email info@library.cpl.org

Health Care

Cleveland is home to a number of the nation's top institutions providing health care, medical education, and medical research and technology. The Cleveland metropolitan area is served by 50 hospitals; 23 are affiliated with medical schools, including Case Western Reserve University School of Medicine. The region employs more than 9,000 physicians and 23,000 health care professionals.

Cleveland Clinic and University Hospital Health Systems control 90-plus percent of the area's hospital beds. The Cleveland Clinic Foundation, which pioneered kidney transplants and open-heart surgery, is a 945-bed treatment and referral center for patients throughout the United States and the world. It consistently ranks among the best hospitals in the country in *U.S. News & World Report* surveys. Cleveland Clinic rates highly for care in cardiology, gastroenterology, neurology, orthopedics, and urology. Rainbow Babies and Childrens Hospital is one of the country's best for pediatric and neonatal intensive care. University Hospitals, nationally recognized for cancer research and treatment, receives excellent rankings in three specialties. Among other Cleveland facilities in the medical forefront is St. Vincent Charity Hospital, which participated in the development of the first heart-lung machines.

Health Care Information: Cleveland Health Education Museum, 8911 Euclid Ave.; Cleveland, OH; telephone (216)231-5010

Recreation

Sightseeing

One of Cleveland's most popular attractions is the Rock and Roll Hall of Fame and Museum, the world's only facility dedicated to the living heritage of rock and roll music. Situated on the shores of Lake Erie, the museum houses six floors of costumes, interactive exhibits, and original films, along with the most extensive collection of rock and roll artifacts and memorabilia in the world. Adjacent to the Rock and Roll Hall on North Coast Harbor is the Great Lakes Science Center. Visitors can explore the wonders of science, the environment, and technology via more than 400 interactive exhibits. Located inside the center is the six-story OMNI-MAX theater, with supersized images and digital sound that allows viewers to feel as though they were actually in the film.

North America's largest collection of primate species is housed at the Cleveland Metroparks Zoo and RainForest, located five miles south of downtown. The zoo has more than 3,300 animals from around the world, including 84 endangered species, and occupies 168 rolling, wooded acres. The two-acre RainForest is home to more than 600 animals and 10,000 plants from the jungles of the world, and features a 25-foot waterfall and simulated tropical storm.

The NASA John H. Glenn Research Center is the only NASA facility north of the Mason-Dixon line. Named after the Ohio astronaut, it presents programs on space exploration, aircraft propulsion, satellites, and alternative energy sources. Two of Cleveland's best-known monuments are the Garfield Monument in Lakeview Cemetery and the National Shrine of Our Lady of Lourdes, which resembles the original shrine in France and is located 10 miles east of the city.

Seasonal amusement parks located in Greater Cleveland Geauga Lake and Cedar Point, known for its world-record-breaking collection of roller coasters and rides, (located 63 miles from Cleveland, in Sandusky, Ohio). Sandusky is also home to Kalahari Resort, the largest indoor waterpark in Ohio.

Arts and Culture

University Circle, located four miles east of downtown, boasts the largest concentration of cultural institutions and museums in the country. Within one square mile, visitors will find more than 40 non-profit institutions including the Cleveland Museum of Art, Cleveland Museum of Natural History, Cleveland Botanical Garden, Children's Museum of Cleveland, HealthSpace Cleveland, Crawford Auto-Aviation Museum, and Museum of Contemporary Art Cleveland (MOCA), which, in honor of its 35th anniversary, changed its name from the Cleveland Center for Contemporary Art in 2003.

Museums located outside of University Circle include the Hungarian Heritage Society, the Shaker Historical Society and Museum, the Steamship William G. *Mather* Museum, and the Dunham Tavern Museum, the oldest Cleveland museum building on its original site. The Milton & Tamar Maltz Museum of Jewish Heritage is scheduled to open in the fall of 2005.

The Cleveland Orchestra, considered one of the nation's top orchestras, plays a season of concerts at Severance Hall from September to May; the summer season is scheduled at the open-air Blossom Music Center from June to August. Blossom also hosts opera, classical, pop, jazz, rock, and folk concerts during the summer months. The Cleveland Chamber Music Society and the Cleveland Chamber Symphony offer a schedule of chamber music each year. The Cleveland Institute of Music presents hundreds of concerts by faculty, students, and visiting artists, and the Cleveland Pops Orchestra performs music from motion pictures and Broadway shows. The internationally acclaimed Cleveland Quartet gives performances throughout the world. The nation added its eighth House of Blues with the 2004 opening of Cleveland's concert club.

Two dance companies perform in Cleveland: Dance Cleveland and North Coast Ballet Theatre. Cleveland's three opera companies, Opera Cleveland at the State Theater, Lyric Opera, and Cleveland Institute of Music's Opera Theater, stage operatic presentations.

Cleveland supports a number of theater companies. Cleveland Play House, the country's first professional resident company, presents a season of classical drama and new works. Playhouse Square Center, with its five beautifully restored circa 1920 theaters, is the nation's second largest performing arts center. The Ohio Theatre is home to the Great Lakes Theater Festival; the others host touring Broad-

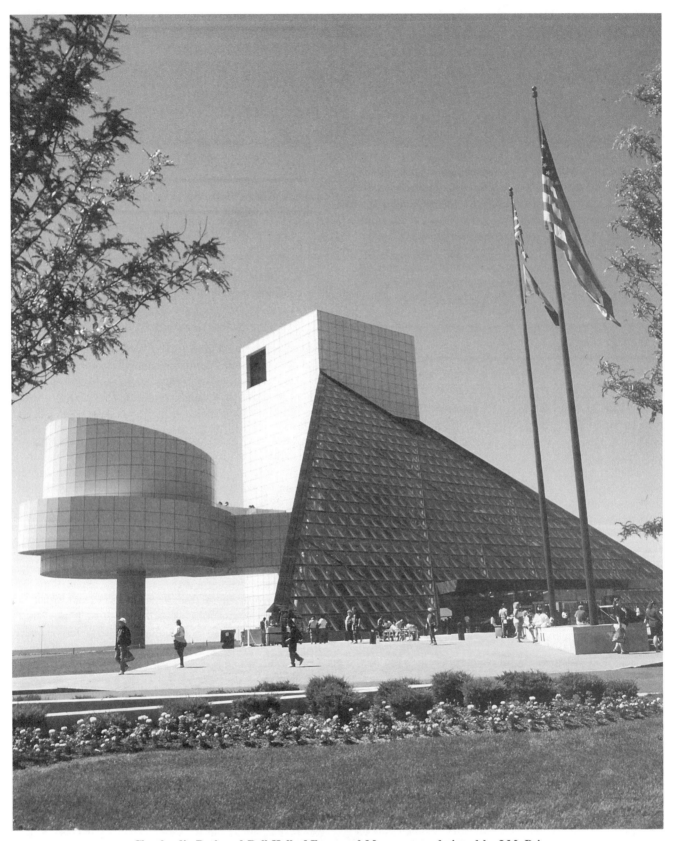

Cleveland's Rock and Roll Hall of Fame and Museum was designed by I.M. Pei.

way shows, musicals, concerts, opera, and ballets. Karamu House, from the Swahili for "a center of enjoyment, a place to be entertained," has earned a national reputation as a center of African American culture.

Festivals and Holidays

Cleveland schedules a full calendar of annual events. Each January, Cleveland organizes a Martin Luther King Jr. celebration, followed two months later by a festive St. Patrick's Day Parade through downtown. The Cleveland International Film Festival also takes place in March with nearly than 200 film screenings. The state's largest environmental event is EarthFest, held in April at the Cleveland Metroparks Zoo. The Cleveland Botanical Garden Flower Show, the largest outdoor flower show in North America, takes place in May at the Cleveland Botanical Gardens.

June brings the Parade the Circle Celebration, featuring an art parade and free admission to University Circle facilities. Visitors can join in Cleveland's annual July birthday bash in the Flats with riverfront festivities and performances as well as an amazing fireworks and laser light show. Samples of savory ribs, live entertainment, and family fun are on the menu at the New Cleveland Rib Burnoff in July. Cleveland showcases its diversity at summer festivities such as the Irish Cultural Festival, Puerto Rican Friendly Days, the Annual Polish Heritage Festival, and the Cleveland Pride Parade & Festival, celebrating the lesbian-gay-bi-transsexual community.

The week-long Cuyoga County Fair in August features rides, exhibits, and shows. An unforgettable Labor Day weekend event is the Cleveland National Air Show at Burke Lakefront Airport. Art meets technology at the Ingenuity Festival, taking place at various downtown locations in early September; running nearly simultaneously with this event is Taste of Cleveland, at which food from more than 30 local restaurants can be sampled. The Johnny Appleseed Festival at Mapleside Farms, and the Midwest Oktoberfest are among the area's many fall festivals. The Christmas season marks its start with the annual Holiday Lighting ceremony on downtown's Public Square the day after Thanksgiving.

Sports for the Spectator

Cleveland is a major-league sports city with major-league sports facilities. Gund Arena hosts NBA Cleveland Cavaliers basketball, the WNBA Cleveland Rockers basketball, and the American Hockey League's Cleveland Barons, as well as more than 200 family events and concerts each year. State-of-the-art Jacobs Field is home to Major League Baseball's Cleveland Indians. The Cleveland Browns professional football team, named for their first coach, the legendary Paul Brown, is part of the National Football League's American Conference and play home games at the lakefront Cleveland Browns Stadium. Indoor soccer action is brought to fans by the Cleveland Force at the Cleveland State University Convocation Center. The Cleveland Junior Lumberjacks play youth hockey at the Metroplex. The Champ Car Grand Prix of Cleveland is held over three June days at the Burke Lakefront Airport. Thistledown Race Track offers thoroughbred racing and Northfield Park schedules harness races.

Sports for the Participant

Cleveland's Metroparks system, consisting of 20,000 acres in 15 parks that surround the city's core, represents one of the nation's largest concentrations of park land per capita. Facilities are available for hiking, cycling, tennis, swimming, golf, boating, and horseback riding. Winter activities include cross-country skiing, tobogganing, ice skating, and ice fishing. Downhill skiing is available at three nearby resorts. Greater Cleveland encompasses more than 70 public and private golf courses. One hundred miles of Lake Erie shoreline, as well as inland lakes, reservoirs, rivers, and streams, make fishing a favorite pastime; the annual catch in Lake Erie equals that of the other four Great Lakes combined. Cuyahoga Valley National Park, Cleveland Lakefront State Park, Huntington Beach, and Mentor Headlands State Park are popular summer spots for water sports enthusiasts. The Cleveland Marathon and 10K is held downtown in May.

Shopping and Dining

More than 600 retail businesses are located in downtown Cleveland. The elegant Tower City Center offers shopping and dining at more than 100 establishments. ETON, situated on Chagrin Boulevard, houses retail and dining establishments amid fountains, gardens, and sculptures, and recently underwent a $50 million expansion and renovation. Just west of downtown Cleveland is the new Crocker Park, a $450 million shopping center that encompasses 12 city blocks in Westlake. Unique shopping opportunities can be found throughout the city, such as: Antique Row on Lorain Avenue which attracts antique buyers; the Arcade, a nineteenth-century marketplace containing more than 100 shops and restaurants; and West Side Market in nearby Ohio City which sells fresh fish and meats, vegetables and fruits, baked goods, cheeses, and ethnic foods.

Visitor Information: Convention & Visitors Bureau of Greater Cleveland, 3100 Terminal Tower, 50 Public Sq., Cleveland, OH 44113; telephone (216)621-4110; toll-free 800-321-1001; fax (216)623-4499; email cvb@travel cleveland.com

Convention Facilities

The *Tradeshow Week Major Exhibit Hall Directory* ranks the International Exposition & Conference Center ninth in the nation for exhibition space. Situated on a 175-acre site next to Cleveland-Hopkins International Airport, the center contains 902,000 square feet of exhibit space, 800,000 of which is contained in a single room. The Cleveland Convention Center, located downtown, contains 375,000 square feet of flexible exhibit space that can be divided into four separate meeting halls; 37 meetings rooms are available to accommodate up to 10,000 attendees. The largest room in the Cleveland Masonic Temple & Auditorium is 15,000 square feet, and the largest in the Cleveland State University Convocation Center is 23,520 square feet.

Other convention and meeting facilities are located throughout the Greater Cleveland area; among them are the Forum, Grays Armory, Play House Square Center, and the Spitzer Conference Center, located in Elyria approximately 20 minutes from the Cleveland-Hopkins International Airport.

Convention Information: Convention & Visitors Bureau of Greater Cleveland, 3100 Terminal Tower, 50 Public Sq., Cleveland, OH 44113; telephone (216)621-4110; toll-free 800-321-1001; fax (216)623-4499; email cvb@travel cleveland.com

Transportation

Approaching the City

Cleveland-Hopkins International Airport, the Midwestern hub for Continental Airlines, is served by 12 national, two international, and 11 commuter carriers that schedule direct and connecting flights throughout the United States and to major foreign cities. A rapid transit system connects the airport to downtown. Commuter air service to regional cities is available at Burke Lakefront Airport; business and general aviation traffic is handled at Cuyahoga County Airport. Twenty-one other general aviation facilities are located in the metropolitan area.

Three major interstates intersect downtown Cleveland: I-77 and I-71, which run north and south, and I-90, which runs east and west. In addition, I-480 connects the eastern and western Cleveland suburbs and runs south of the city, bypassing the downtown area; I-490 does the same by connecting I-90 and I-71 to I-77. Amtrak provides rail transportation service into Cleveland.

Traveling in the City

The Regional Transit Authority (RTA) operates Cleveland's extensive rapid transit system. RTA has a direct link from downtown Public Square to Hopkins International Airport. The Waterfront Line, a light rail transportation system, connects Cleveland's downtown attractions. Visitors can conveniently and economically travel from Public Square and Tower City Center's hotels and shopping venues to the Flats Entertainment District and North Coast Harbor attractions like the Rock and Roll Hall of Fame, Great Lakes Science Center, and Cleveland Browns Stadium. Trolley tours and riverboat cruises offer unique and informative views of the city. Average intracity commuting time is under 24 minutes.

Communications

Newspapers and Magazines

Cleveland's major daily newspaper is the *Plain Dealer,* which is also Ohio's largest daily newspaper. Numerous community newspapers, including the *Call & Post,* an African American community newspaper, also circulate in the city. *Cleveland Magazine,* for readers in the Cleveland metropolitan area, features articles on politics and urban and suburban contemporary living and events. *Northern Ohio LIVE,* a monthly magazine describing entertainment opportunities, and *Crain's Cleveland Business* are also published there. The award-winning *Cleveland Scene* is an alternative magazine published weekly.

About 80 specialized magazines and trade, professional, and scholarly journals are published in Cleveland on such subjects as explosives engineering, local history, fraternal organizations, lawn care, ethnic culture, business and economics, religion, medicine, welding and metal production, food service, and building trades.

Television and Radio

Cleveland is the broadcast media center for northeastern Ohio. Greater Cleveland television viewers tune into programming scheduled by five stations based there. A dozen AM and FM radio stations broadcast a wide range of listening choices, from religious and inspirational features to news and talk shows to all major musical genres.

Media Information: Plain Dealer, 1801 Superior Ave., Cleveland, OH 44114; telephone (216)999-6000. *Cleveland Magazine,* 1422 Euclid Ave., Ste. 730, Cleveland, OH 44115; telephone (216)771-2833; fax (216)781-6318. *Northern Ohio LIVE,* 11320 Juniper Rd., Cleveland, OH 44106; telephone (216)721-1800; email info@livepub.com

Cleveland Online

City of Cleveland Home Page. Available www.city .cleveland.oh.us

Cleveland Municipal School District. Available www .cmsdnet.net

Cleveland Public Library. Available www.cpl.org

Convention & Visitors Bureau of Greater Cleveland. Available www.travelcleveland.com

Greater Cleveland Partnership. Available www.cleveland growth.com

Plain Dealer. Available www.plaindealer.com

Rock and Roll Hall of Fame. Available www.rockhall.com

Selected Bibliography

Chapman, Edmund H., *Cleveland, Village to Metropolis: A Case Study of Problems of Urban Development in Nineteenth-* *Century America* (Cleveland, Ohio: Western Reserve Historical Society, 1964)

Grubb, Davis, *The Night of the Hunter* (New York: Harper & Row, 1953)

Grubb, Davis, *Oh Beulah Land: A Novel* (New York: Viking, 1956)

Jones, Jennie, *Cleveland: A Celebration in Color* (2nd ed., Cleveland, OH: Cleveland Stock Images, 1987)

Miller, Carl H., *Breweries of Cleveland* (Schnitzelbank Press, 1998)

Phillips, Kimberley L., *Alabama North: African-American Migrants, Community, and Working-Class Activism in Cleveland, 1915-45 (The Working Class in American History)* (University of Illinois Press, 2000)

Schneider, Russell, *The Boys of the Summer of '48* (Sports Publishing Inc., 1998)

Columbus

The City in Brief

Founded: 1797 (incorporated 1834)

Head Official: Mayor Michael B. Coleman (D) (since 2003)

City Population
  1980: 564,871
  1990: 632,945
  2000: 711,470
  2003 estimate: 728,432
  Percent change, 1990–2000: 12.4%
  U.S. rank in 1980: 19th
  U.S. rank in 1990: 16th
  U.S. rank in 2000: 15th

Metropolitan Area Population
  1980: 1,244,000
  1990: 1,345,450

  2000: 1,540,157
  Percent change, 1990–2000: 14.5%
  U.S. rank in 1980: 28th
  U.S. rank in 1990: Not reported
  U.S. rank in 2000: 32nd

Area: 225.9 square miles (2000)
Elevation: Ranges from 685 to 893 feet above sea level
Average Annual Temperature: 52.8° F
Average Annual Precipitation: 39.4 inches of rain; 27.7 inches of snow

Major Economic Sectors: Services, wholesale and retail trade, government, manufacturing, education
Unemployment Rate: 6.3% (February 2005)
Per Capita Income: $20,450 (1999)
2003 FBI Crime Index Total: 94,326

Major Colleges and Universities: The Ohio State University, Capital University, Ohio Dominican University

Daily Newspaper: *The Columbus Dispatch*

0 1 2 3
KILOMETERS

MILES 1 2 3 4

N

OLENTANGY RIVER

RIVERSIDE HOSPITAL

BROADWAY

315

HUDSON

UNIVERSITY HOSPITAL

OHIO VILLAGE

STATE FAIRGROUNDS

TO ST. ANN'S HOSPITAL

STADIUM

SEVENTEENTH AVE.

OHIO STATE UNIVERSITY

SUMMIT

ELEVENTH AVE.

CLEVELAND

WOODLAND

COLUMBUS-MILLERSBURG

STELZER

71

BATELLE MEMORIAL INST.

FIFTH AVE.

HIGH

THIRD ST.

FOURTH ST.

FIFTH AVE.

LEONARD

NELSON

PORT COLUMBUS INT'L AIRPORT

FIFTH AVE.

FIFTH AVE.

VICTORIAN VILLAGE

GOODALE PARK

ITALIAN VILLAGE

670

33

NORTH MARKET

COLUMBUS STATE COMMUNITY COLLEGE

BROAD

SPRING

C.O.S.I.

COLLEGE OF ART & DESIGN

THURBER HOUSE

FRANKLIN PARK CONSERVATORY

DREXEL

LONG

MUSEUM OF ART

CITY HALL

70

BROAD

LIBRARY

CAPITAL UNIVERSITY

JAMES

STATE CAPITOL

TOWN

FRANKLIN UNIVERSITY

CITY CENTER

MAIN

MAIN

COLLEGE

LIVINGSTON

LIVINGSTON

BROAD

40

CENTRAL

PARSONS

CHAMPION

LOCKBOURNE

FAIRWOOD

33

COOPER STADIUM

GREENLAWN

SCIOTO RIVER

FREBIS

70

JENKINS

HIGH

REFUGEE

104

3

62

WILLIAMS

270

PARSONS

LOCKBOURNE

GROVEPORT

ALUM CREEK

CANADA

WISCONSIN

MINNESOTA

MICHIGAN

NY

IOWA

ILLINOIS

INDIANA

Columbus

PA

OHIO

KS

MISSOURI

KENTUCKY

WEST VIRGINIA

VIRGINIA

Introduction

Columbus, the capital of Ohio and the state's largest city, is the seat of Franklin County. The focus of an urban complex comprised of Grandview Heights, Upper Arlington, Worthington, Bexley, and Whitehall, Columbus is the center of the metropolitan statistical area that includes Delaware, Fairfield, Franklin, Licking, Madison, Pickaway, and Union counties. Chosen by the Ohio General Assembly as the state capital because of its central location, Columbus developed in the nineteenth century as an important stop on the National Highway and as a link in the nation's canal system. Today, the city is a leader in research, education, technology, and insurance. *Inc.* magazine describes Columbus as "clean, with good schools, reasonably priced housing, and a college-town atmosphere that helps attract and retain young people."

Geography and Climate

Situated in central Ohio in the drainage area of the Ohio River, Columbus is located on the Scioto and Olentangy rivers; two minor streams running through the city are Alum Creek and Big Walnut Creek. Columbus's weather is changeable, influenced by air masses from central and southwest Canada; air from the Gulf of Mexico reaches the region during the summer and to a lesser extent in the fall and winter. The moderate climate is characterized by four distinct seasons. Snowfall averages around 27 inches annually.

Area: 225.9 square miles (2000)

Elevation: Ranges from 685 to 893 feet above sea level; average elevation is 777 feet

Average Temperatures: January, 28.3° F; July, 75.1° F; annual average, 52.8° F

Average Annual Precipitation: 39.4 inches of rain; 27.7 inches of snow

History

Central Location Makes Columbus Ohio's Capital

After Ohio gained statehood in 1803, the General Assembly set out to find a geographically centralized location for the capital. Congress had enacted the Ordinance for the Northwest Territory in 1787 to settle claims from the American Revolution and a grant was given to Virginia for lands west of the Scioto River. Lucas Sullivant, a Virginia surveyor, established in 1797 the village of Franklinton, which quickly turned into a profitable trading center. In 1812 plans for a state Capitol building and a penitentiary at Franklinton were drawn up and approved by the legislature, which also agreed to rename the settlement Columbus. Construction of the state buildings was delayed for four years by the War of 1812.

During its early history the major threat to Columbus was a series of fever and cholera epidemics that did not subside until swamps close to the center of town were drained. With the opening in 1831 of the Ohio & Erie Canal, which was connected to Columbus by a smaller canal, and then the National Highway in 1833, Columbus was in a position to emerge as a trade and transportation center. Then, on February 22, 1850, a steam engine pulling flat cars made its maiden run from Columbus to Xenia, 54 miles away, and Columbus entered the railroad age. Five locally financed railroads were in operation by 1872.

Columbus, with a population of 20,000 people in 1860, became a military center during the Civil War. Camp Jackson was an assembly center for recruits and Columbus Barracks—renamed Fort Hayes in 1922—served as an arsenal. Camp Chase, also in the area, was the Union's largest facility for Confederate prisoners, and the Federal Government maintained a cemetery for the more than 2,000 soldiers who died there.

Academic Prominence Precedes High-Technology Growth

Columbus prospered economically after the Civil War, as new banks and railroad lines opened and horse-and-buggy companies manufactured 20,000 carriages and wagons a year. The city's first waterworks system and an extended streetcar service were built during this period. In 1870 the Ohio General Assembly created, through the Morrill Land Grant Act, the Ohio Agricultural and Mechanical College, which became a vital part of the city's life and identity. This coeducational institution, renamed The Ohio State University in 1878, is now one of the country's major state universities. The Columbus campus consists of nearly 400 permanent buildings on 1,644 acres of land. Today, the university's technological research facilities, coupled with the Battelle Memorial Institute, comprise one of the largest private research organizations of its kind in the world.

Two events prior to World War I shook Columbus's stability. The streetcar strike of 1910 lasted through the summer and into the fall, resulting in riots and destruction of street cars and even one death. The National Guard was called out to maintain order, and when the strike finally ended, few concessions were made by the railway company. Three years later, the Scioto River flood killed 100 people and left 20,000 people homeless; property damages totaled $9 million.

Traditionally a center for political, economic, and cultural activity as the state capital, Columbus is today one of the fastest-growing cities in the east central United States. The downtown area underwent a complete transformation in the 1990s, and the economy surged as high-technology development and research companies moved into the metropolitan area. Franklin County saw its population top 1,000,000 for the first time in the 2000 census and celebrated its bicentennial in 2003.

Historical Information: Ohio Historical Society, 1985 Velma Avenue, Columbus, OH 43211; telephone (614)297-2510

Population Profile

Metropolitan Area Residents
1980: 1,244,000
1990: 1,345,450
2000: 1,540,157
Percent change, 1990–2000: 14.5%
U.S. rank in 1980: 28th
U.S. rank in 1990: Not reported
U.S. rank in 2000: 32nd

City Residents
1980: 564,871
1990: 632,945
2000: 711,470
2003 estimate: 728,432
Percent change, 1990–2000: 12.4%
U.S. rank in 1980: 19th
U.S. rank in 1990: 16th
U.S. rank in 2000: 15th

Density: 3,225 people per square mile (2000)

Racial and ethnic characteristics (2000)
White: 483,332
Black or African American: 174,065
American Indian and Alaska Native: 2,090
Asian: 24,495
Native Hawaiian and Pacific Islander: 367
Hispanic (may be of any race): 17,471
Other: 8,292

Percent of residents born in state: 67.8%

Age characteristics (2000)
Population under 5 years old: 53,347
Population 5 to 9 years old: 50,119
Population 10 to 14 years old: 44,291
Population 15 to 19 years old: 48,663
Population 20 to 24 years old: 74,938
Population 25 to 34 years old: 139,434
Population 35 to 44 years old: 110,351
Population 45 to 54 years old: 81,256
Population 55 to 59 years old: 25,724
Population 60 to 64 years old: 20,316
Population 65 to 74 years old: 33,793
Population 75 to 84 years old: 21,705
Population 85 years and over: 7,533
Median age: 30.6 years

Births (2002, Franklin County)
Total number: 17,013

Deaths (2002, Franklin County)
Total number: 8,351

Money income (1999)
Per capita income: $20,450
Median household income: $37,897
Total households: 301,800

Number of households with income of . . .
less than $10,000: 32,322
$10,000 to $14,999: 19,282
$15,000 to $24,999: 41,998
$25,000 to $34,999: 44,296
$35,000 to $49,999: 53,290
$50,000 to $74,999: 60,876
$75,000 to $99,999: 27,505
$100,000 to $149,999: 15,584
$150,000 to $199,999: 3,516
$200,000 or more: 3,131

Percent of families below poverty level: 10.8% (19% of which were female householder families with related children under 5 years)

2002 FBI Crime Index Total: 94,326

Municipal Government

The city of Columbus is governed by a mayor and a council comprised of seven members who are elected at large to a four-year term.

Head Official: Mayor Michael B. Coleman (D) (since 2003; current term expires 2007)

Total Number of City Employees: 7,724 (2004)

City Information: City Hall, 90 W. Broad St., Rm. 247 Columbus, Ohio 43215. Mayor's Action Center, telephone

(614)645-CITY (2489); Information (city operator), telephone (614)645-8100

Economy

Major Industries and Commercial Activity

Columbus's diversified economy is balanced among the services, trade, government, and manufacturing sectors. State government, education, banking, research, insurance, and data processing in particular have helped the city to resist recession. Telecommunications, retailing, health care, and the military are other strong employment areas. Home to more than 70 insurance companies, Columbus ranks among the insurance capitals of the United States. The city is the corporate headquarters for nationwide firms such as Nationwide Insurance Enterprise, Banc One Corporation, The Limited, Inc., American Electric Power, Wendy's International, Huntington Bancshares, Inc., Consolidated Stores Corporation, Borden Inc., Ashland Chemical, Battelle Memorial Institute, and Bob Evans Foods Inc. Twenty of Columbus's largest financial institutions operate more than 400 offices throughout the metropolitan region.

The U.S. government is the city's third largest employer; it operates the Defense Supply Center, whose 3,000 employees operate a massive central storehouse that ships up to 10,000 items a day to military posts around the world. Manufacturing comprises about 10 percent of the metropolitan Columbus economic base; the main production categories being machinery, fabricated metal, printing and publishing, and food processing. Local industry profits from proximity to coal and natural gas resources. Limestone and sandstone quarries operate in the area.

Items and goods produced: airplanes, auto parts, appliances, telephone components, computer equipment, glass, coated fabrics, shoes, food products

Incentive Programs—New and Existing Companies

Several city and state programs are available to assist existing companies and proposed startups in the Columbus metro area.

Local programs—The Columbus Development Department incentive programs focus on small business lending and inner-city revitalization, including the Office of Business Assistance and Office of Financial Assistance to help create and sustain jobs and companies; among their specialties are infrastructure assistance and urban brownfields redevelopment. The Greater Columbus Chamber of Commerce oversees very successful public and private partnerships and small business programs to ensure the success of the region's businesses. Training programs are available through the Small Business Administration and the Central Ohio Industrial Training Program.

State programs—State of Ohio incentive programs include loans, loan guarantees, and industrial revenue bonds.

Job training programs—Ohio's Adult Vocational Education Full-Service Centers offer customized training programs designed to meet the needs of a specific business, as well as other ongoing skill training for current or new employees.

Development Projects

Columbus is one of the nation's fastest-growing cities. The city's focus is on downtown development; in 2001 the city commenced a Strategic Business Plan to revitalize downtown Columbus and bring jobs and investment to the city center. The city sought input from businesses and from the community with a "Tell Us Your Great Idea" campaign, and the Columbus Downtown Development Corporation was formed to bring the ideas to fruition. Public and private entities invested $1.72 billion in the downtown area between 2001 and 2004.

In 2000 the new $150 million, 800,000 square foot Nationwide Arena opened and is home to the NHL's Columbus Blue Jackets. In 2001 the Greater Columbus Convention Center celebrated the completion of an $85 million expansion and renovation, which increased the center's size from 1.4 million to 1.7 million square feet. The renovations include an additional 120,000 square feet of exhibit space, a 15,000 square foot ballroom, and 11 new meeting rooms (for a total of 426,000 square feet of exhibit space, 2 ballrooms, and 61 meeting rooms). An additional 1,100 parking spaces and new shops and restaurants round out the improvements.

Economic Development Information: Greater Columbus Chamber of Commerce, telephone (614)221-1321

Commercial Shipping

Strategically located between the Northeast and Midwest regions and served by an excellent transportation system, Columbus is a marketing, distribution, and warehouse center. An important link in the import/export shipping network is Rickenbacker Air/Industrial Park, which has been designated a free trade zone. Twenty-one passenger and freight air carriers serve Port Columbus International Airport, two passenger carriers and a number of freight carriers fly out of Rickenbacker, and Bolton Field provides runway space and amenities for charter air services. Three major railroads operate routes through Columbus; all provide piggyback and rail car shipping and two have export-import containerization facilities. Completing the ground transportation system are more than 100 motor freight companies. One of three inland ports in the United States, Columbus receives and ships U.S. Customs-sealed containers to the Pacific Rim.

Labor Force and Employment Outlook

Among Ohio's 10 largest cities, Columbus is the only one whose population increased in the 1990s, and this trend continues in the 2000s. Eighty-three percent of the population over age 25 are high school graduates and 29 percent have college degrees; 71 percent of the population over the age of 16 is in the labor force. While the region has a more desirable workforce than most of the nation, the increase in average age is causing some concern. The Chamber of Commerce has launched several projects to give businesses the tools to compete in such a market.

Traditional economic mainstays such as government, the Ohio State University, corporate headquarters, and large financial institutions continue to lend stability to the local economy. The Columbus area has lost manufacturing jobs in the last decade but has added positions in services to create a net gain in jobs overall.

The following is a summary of data regarding the Columbus metropolitan area labor force, 2004 annual averages.

Size of non-agricultural labor force: 922,616

Number of workers employed in . . .
   construction and mining: 40,900
   manufacturing: 82,000
   trade, transportation, and utilities: 183,900
   information: 19,700
   financial activities: 74,500
   professional and business services: 132,800
   educational and health services: 100,700
   leisure, hospitality, and other services: 125,400
   government: 153,400

Average hourly earnings of production workers employed in manufacturing: $18.80

Unemployment rate: 6.3% (February 2005)

Largest employers	*Number of employees*
State of Ohio	28,015
The Ohio State University	22,100
The United States Federal Government	17,000
Banc One Corporation	15,500
Limited Brands	15,250
Ohio Health	15,000
Nationwide Insurance	12,520

Cost of Living

The following is a summary of data regarding several key cost of living factors in the Columbus area.

2004 (3rd Quarter) ACCRA Average House Price: $257,430

2004 (3rd Quarter) ACCRA Cost of Living Index: 101.7 (U.S. average = 100.0)

State income tax rate: Ranges from 0.743% to 7.5%

State sales tax rate: 5.0% (food and prescription drugs are exempt)

Local income tax rate: 2%

Local sales tax rate: 6.75% (total)

Property tax rate: Taxes on real property are assessed on 35 percent of the property's total market value. Businesses with personal property valued at $10,001 or more must also pay personal property tax in the state of Ohio.

Economic Information: Greater Columbus Chamber of Commerce, telephone (614)221-1321

Education and Research

Elementary and Secondary Schools

The Columbus Public Schools (CPS) are administered by a seven-member board of education that supports a superintendent. The system's Alexander Graham Bell Elementary School for the hearing impaired is considered one of the nation's finest. Alternative/magnet schools; a high school for the performing arts; a virtual high school; and the International Baccalaureate diploma program, giving qualified graduates access to the world's leading universities, are also among the system's offerings.

According to the 2004 report by the superintendent of schools, in 2003–2004 the CPS graduation rate rose to 59.9 percent, a 0.6 percent increase over the previous year and a 3.9 percent increase over the year 2000. In 2002–2003 CPS met 5 of 18 state standards on proficiency tests and graduation and attendance rates; by 2003–2004 the rate remained at 5 of 18 standards, and the district maintained or improved performance in 16 of 18 standards. In 2004, CPS had more teachers achieve National Board Certified Status than any other school district in Ohio.

The following is a summary of data regarding the Columbus public schools as of the 2003–2004 school year.

Total enrollment: 62,201

Number of facilities
   elementary schools: 90
   middle schools: 26

senior high schools: 18, plus 4 career centers and 4 special schools

Student/teacher ratio: 18.6:1

Teacher salaries
  minimum: $35,089
  maximum: $76,302

Funding per pupil: $10,757

Columbus is also served by more than 13 charter schools and 12 private and parochial schools that offer a range of curricula, including special education programs.

Colleges and Universities

The Ohio State University, a major institution of higher learning at both the state and national levels, with an enrollment of more 58,000 students as of April 2005, awards undergraduate through doctorate degrees. In addition to its Columbus campus, the university maintains four regional campuses and a two-year branch facility. The Ohio State system includes eight schools and 18 colleges that administer 12,000 courses, 174 undergraduate majors, and 204 graduate programs.

Capital University schedules courses leading to undergraduate and graduate degrees in such fields as arts and sciences, music, nursing, business administration, and law; the university also operates an adult education division. Other four-year institutions located in the Columbus area include the Columbus College of Art and Design and Franklin University. Columbus State Community College, enrolling more than 11,000 students, grants two-year associate degrees in business, health, public service, and engineering technologies.

Libraries and Research Centers

Columbus is home to more than 60 libraries that are maintained by a range of institutions, corporations, government agencies, and organizations. The Columbus Metropolitan Library (CML) operates 21 branches in Columbus and throughout Franklin County in addition to the Main Library. CML also jointly operates the Northwest Library with the Worthington Public Library. The collections of several Central Ohio library systems, including CML, are linked electronically in the Discovery Place Libraries consortium, offering customers access to a total of over 3 million items. CML's collection contains more than 2.4 million items, including books, periodicals, videotapes, DVDs, CD-ROMs, films, audiocassettes, compact discs, circulating visuals, maps, charts, microfilm/microfiche, sheet music, and photos. In addition, the Library maintains special collections on local and state history and federal and state documents. CML is also part of the Ohio Public Library Information Network (OHIOLINK), a statewide on-line resource. OHIOLINK was created to help

guarantee that all Ohio citizens continue to have access to information regardless of location or format.

The Ohio State University Libraries hold about 5.7 million book volumes and operate numerous department libraries and five campus facilities. Included in the more than 25 special collections are the American Association of Editorial Cartoonist Archives, including a long term loan of more than 3,000 original "Calvin and Hobbes" cartoons by Bill Watterson; American playwrights' theater records; film scripts; Ohio News Photographers Association Archives; and various author collections featuring the works of such writers as Miguel de Cervantes, Emily Dickinson, Nathaniel Hawthorne, Edith Wharton, James Thurber, and Samuel Beckett. The library is a depository for federal, state, and European Economic Community documents.

As the state capital, Columbus is the site of libraries associated with state governmental divisions, including the Supreme Court of Ohio, the Ohio Department of Transportation, the Ohio Environmental Protection Agency, the Ohio Legislative Service Commission, and the Public Utilities Commission of Ohio. The *Columbus Dispatch,* all local colleges and universities, most major hospitals, several churches and synagogues, and cultural organizations maintain libraries in the city. Private corporations and law firms provide library facilities for both employee and public use. Among the research institutions that house libraries are Battelle Columbus Laboratories, Chemical Abstracts Service, National Center for Research in Vocational Education, and the Institute of Polar Studies at Ohio State University, housing the Byrd Polar Collection.

Columbus is home to the headquarters of Battelle Memorial Institute, considered the world's largest independent research organization, which conducts research, analysis, testing, design, and consultation in fields that include energy, environmental quality, health sciences, engineering and manufacturing technology, and national security. The American Ceramic Society performs educational, technical, scientific, and information services for the international ceramic community. The Online Computer Library Center (OCLC) maintains an automated information and cataloging system for more than 6,000 libraries in the United States.

More than 60 research centers at The Ohio State University provide research, testing, analysis, design, and consultation services. Other research facilities located in Columbus are Chemical Abstracts Service of the American Chemical Society, The Applied Information Technologies Research Center, Edison Welding Institute, Honda of America Transportation Research Center, and several engineering, pharmaceutical, and chemical firms.

Public Library Information: Columbus Metropolitan Library, 96 South Grant Avenue, Columbus, OH 43215; telephone (614)645-2800; fax (614)645-2050

Health Care

The Columbus and Franklin County metropolitan region is served by 15 hospitals and three nationally recognized medical research facilities including The Ohio State University's Arthur G. James Cancer Hospital and Research Institute.

Children's Hospital, one of the country's largest children's health care institutions, conducts research on childhood illnesses and specializes in burn treatment. Among the other hospitals in Columbus are Columbus Community Hospital, Riverside Methodist Hospital, Grant Medical Center, and Doctors Hospital, the largest osteopathic teaching facility in the nation.

Recreation

Sightseeing

At the center of Columbus's downtown is the State Capitol Building, an example of Greek Doric architecture. Several blocks south of the Capitol, German Village, one of the city's major attractions, is a restored community in a 230-acre area settled by German immigrants in the mid-1800s. The largest privately funded restoration in the United States, the district features German bakeries, outdoor beer gardens, restaurants, and homes.

The Center of Science and Industry (COSI) maintains hands-on exhibits in health, history, science, and technology for all ages. COSI's 300,000 square foot building consists of a modern style element joined to the existing historic building. The facility features a curved facade, a large atrium, a host of Learning Worlds, and two unique theaters, the Space Theater, and the IWERKS Theater. The Space Theater boasts all new DIGISTAR 3-D technology; the IWERKS Theater, a six-story plus, multimillion-dollar theater, seats 400 people and presents nationally known films.

The Columbus Zoo displays animals in natural habitats and has gained a reputation for successfully breeding endangered species, including gorillas, cheetahs, snow leopards, polar bears, and eagles. The zoo houses the world's largest reptile collection and is the home of four generations of gorillas. The first phase of the zoo specializes in North American wildlife and features the Manatee Coast Exhibit; this is modeled after the 10,000 Island wildlife area in southwestern Florida, one of the few remaining untouched natural places in the United States. The zoo's second phase, the African Forest project, opened in June 2000. The African Forest outdoor gorilla exhibit features two large glass view-

ing areas and landscaping. Creative exhibits and a holding building reflect simple African forest architecture and offer indoor viewing of colobus monkeys and Congo gray parrots, as well as a mixed species aviary. The next phase, Gateway to Asia, began construction in March 2005 and is scheduled to open in the fall of 2006.

Franklin Park Conservatory and Garden Center cultivates tropical, subtropical, and desert plants. Columbus's Park of Roses, the world's largest municipal rose garden, displays 450 varieties of roses. Located seven minutes from downtown, the Ohio Historical Center and Ohio Village recreate a nineteenth-century Ohio town, where period dishes are served at the Colonel Crawford Inn. Costumed craftspeople add to the authenticity of the exhibits. The Mid-Ohio Historical Museum displays antique dolls and toys. Hanby House, a station on the Underground Railroad, is now a memorial to Ben Hanby, who composed "Darling Nelly Gray."

Arts and Culture

Columbus is a national leader in local government support of the arts. The Greater Columbus Arts Council distributes $2 million annually to support a more than $52 million cultural industry. One focus of cultural activities is the Martin Luther King, Jr. Complex, which showcases African American cultural events, while the Cultural Arts Center, located in a renovated arsenal, hosts visual and performing arts events classes.

Three elegant theaters are also the scene of cultural activity in Columbus. The Palace Theatre, opened in 1926, has been completely renovated and now houses Opera Columbus and presents Broadway touring musicals and plays, concerts, and films. The Ohio Theatre, a restored 1928 movie palace and the official theater for the state of Ohio, is the home of the Columbus Symphony Orchestra, BalletMet, the new Broadway series, and presentations sponsored by the Columbus Association for Performing Arts. The 102-year-old Southern Theatre closed between 1979 and 1998 and then reopened after a $10 million restoration project.

The Reality Theatre, Contemporary American Theatre Company, Gallery Players, and the theater department at The Ohio State University stage live theater performances ranging from world premieres to revivals of classic plays.

The Columbus Museum of Art houses a sculpture garden and a permanent collection of European and American art works. The restored Thurber House, the home of James Thurber during his years as a student at Ohio State, is now a writers' center that displays Thurber memorabilia.

Festivals and Holidays

The first weekend of March marks the annual Arnold Fitness Weekend, a health and fitness convention headed by

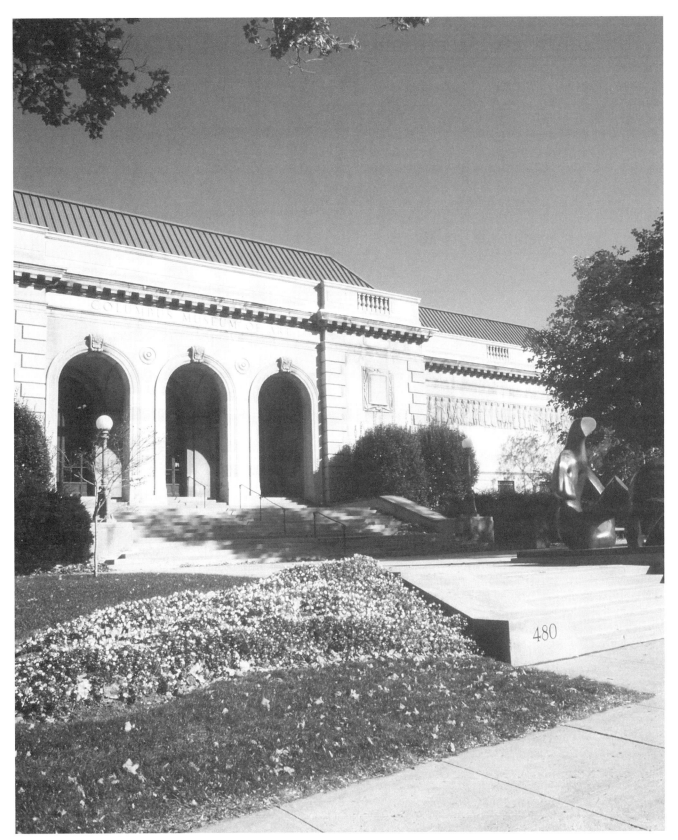

The Columbus Museum of Art has a permanent collection of European and American art.

actor Arnold Schwarzenegger at which bodybuilders and other athletes come together to socialize and compete. The Open Garden Tour, featuring both parks and private homes, is held in April. Music in the Air, sponsored by the city Recreation and Parks Department, is the country's largest free outdoor concert series; 200 concerts are presented at Columbus parks beginning in late May and concluding on Labor Day weekend. The Columbus Arts Festival, which draws 500,000 people to the city, begins the summer festival season in early June. The city's Red, White & Boom! Parade in early July is followed by one of the largest fireworks displays in the Midwest. The Columbus Jazz and Rib Fest draws participants to downtown locations the last weekend in July. A major event in Columbus is the Ohio State Fair; held in August, the fair features livestock shows, agricultural and arts exhibitions, horse shows, rides, and concessions. Columbus observes First Night Columbus on December 31 to bring family-friendly New Year's celebrations to the area.

Sports for the Spectator

Columbus is home to a Major League Soccer team, the Columbus Crew, who play in Columbus Crew Stadium. The stadium, opened in 1999, is the first specifically built for professional soccer in the United States and combines European soccer atmosphere with traditional American amenities to make it one of the premier soccer venues in the country. The Columbus Blue Jackets, a National Hockey League team, first played in 2000 at Nationwide Arena, a 20,000-seat, 685,000-square-foot, $150 million venue.

The Big Ten conference Ohio State Buckeyes, one of the nation's top college football teams, play a home schedule to sold-out crowds on fall Saturday afternoons in the 90,000-seat Ohio Stadium. The Buckeyes also field men's and women's basketball teams that play home games at Jerome Schottenstein Center, a 20,000-seat arena that opened in October 1998. The Columbus Clippers, a Triple-A affiliate of baseball's professional New York Yankees, play a 70-game home schedule at 15,000-seat Cooper Stadium, and the city is finalizing funding to build a larger, newer stadium near the Nationwide Arena to replace the 1932 Cooper Stadium.

The Columbus Marathon, held each October, attracted 4,500 finishers in 2004, and the Capital City Half Marathon, first run in April 2004, is planned to be an annual event. Harness racing is on view at Scioto Downs, where more than a dozen world records have been set in a season that runs from early May to mid-September. The Little Brown Jug, the year's biggest harness race, is held at the Delaware County Fairgrounds. Columbus's most important golf event, Jack Memorial Tournament, is sometimes referred to as the "fifth major"; competitors tee-off in nearby Dublin at the Muirfield Village course that Jack Nicklaus designed.

Sports for the Participant

Columbus city parks number more than 165 on 5,400 acres; 10 metroparks cover an additional 9,400 acres. Water sports can be enjoyed on two major rivers and three lakes in the city; among the area's popular activities are fishing, boating, sailing, water skiing, and paddleboating. The city maintains municipal tennis courts; indoor tennis and racquetball courts are available at private clubs. The city's scenic commuter routes are popular among joggers and cyclists. Year-round recreational programs for all age groups are available at the city parks.

Shopping and Dining

One of the largest shopping showcases in Columbus is the innovative outdoor shopping and entertainment district called Easton, said to be a larger complex than Minnesota's Mall of America. Easton features nearly 120 shops, a luxury Hilton Hotel and Easton Town Center, anchored by the world's first Planet Movies by AMC, a 6,200 seat, and a 30-screen megaplex movie theater. In addition, Easton includes a mall with a Nordstrom's and other national retailers.

Columbus City Center downtown offers 130 upscale stores and restaurants. Among the distinctive shopping districts in Columbus is German Village, where small shops and stores offer specialty items. Short North exhibits and sells the works of Columbus and national artists as well as clothing and home furnishings. High Street, the Main Street of the university district, offers eclectic shopping and dining options.

Diners in Columbus can choose from among a number of restaurants serving contemporary American, European, and ethnic cuisine. In 2005 *Food and Wine* magazine named Kahiki one of the world's five coolest bars. Several restaurants are housed in architecturally interesting buildings such as churches and firehouses. The renovated North Market features local produce and German, Middle Eastern, Indian, and Italian delicatessens. Columbus is also home base to both Wendy's and Bob Evans national restaurant chains.

Visitor Information: Greater Columbus Convention and Visitors Bureau, telephone (614)221-6623; toll-free (800)354-2657

Convention Facilities

Convention and meeting planners are offered a wide range of facilities in the metropolitan Columbus area. The Greater Columbus Convention Center, which opened in 1993 and underwent expansion in 2001, hosting more than 2,500,000 attendees and delegates that year. The Convention Center features 1.7 million square feet of exhibition space and

100,000 square feet of retail space. The nearby Ohio Center Mall is an added attraction to the convention center. Other meeting facilities include Franklin County Veterans Memorial, Ohio Expo Center (site of the Ohio State Fair), and the Palace and Ohio theaters.

First-class downtown hotels, including the Hyatt Regency, the Westin, the Courtyard by Marriott, and the Doubletree Guest Suites, maintain a complete range of meeting and banquet facilities. There are more than 3,000 hotel rooms within walking distance of the Convention Center.

Convention Information: Greater Columbus Convention Center; telephone (614) 827-2500; toll-free (800)626-0241

Transportation

Approaching the City

Twenty-one commercial domestic and international airlines schedule daily flights into Port Columbus International Airport, which recently underwent a $92 million improvement to celebrate its 75th anniversary in 2005. Port Columbus, just eight minutes from downtown, is serviced by 21 airlines and has more than 350 arrivals and departures daily. Rickenbacker International Airport also services the Columbus area. General aviation facilities are provided at Bolton Field.

Two interstate highways—north-south I-71 and east-west I-70—intersect in the city; I-270 serves as a bypass, and I-670 is a downtown innerbelt. Several other major highways provide convenient access into and out of Columbus.

Traveling in the City

Columbus streets conform to a grid pattern, the principal thoroughfares being Broad Street (U.S. 40/62) and High Street (U.S. 23 south of I-70), which form the main downtown intersection and divide north-south streets and east-west avenues. Efficient traffic flow into the center city permits commuting time of no more than 45 minutes from outlying areas.

The public bus system is operated by Central Ohio Transit Authority (COTA).

Communications

Newspapers and Magazines

The principal daily newspaper in Columbus is *The Columbus Dispatch* (morning). *Business First,* a business weekly, presents current news as well as analyses of local commerce. Several suburban newspapers also have a wide circulation in the metropolitan area.

Columbus is the publishing base for magazines and journals with extensive state and national distribution. Especially popular with Ohio readers is *Ohio Magazine,* which contains articles on local and state topics. A number of professional organizations publish their official journals in the city; among them are the Ohio Academy of Science, the Ohio State Bar Association, the Ohio Historical Society, and the Ohio Education Association. Other specialized publications are directed toward Ohio readers with interests in such fields as agriculture, religion, education, library science and communications, banking, business and industry, and sports.

Columbus is also home to membership publications of several national organizations, including Business Professionals of America and the American Society for Nondestructive Testing. The Ohio State University Press publishes several scholarly journals in such fields as theoretical geography, higher education, banking, and urban planning; several academic departments and colleges also issue publications.

Television and Radio

Columbus is the broadcast media center for central Ohio. Three commercial network affiliates and one public station—all locally based—provide television programming for viewers in the city and surrounding communities. Cable service is also available. Radio listeners tune in to music, news, special features, and public-interest programs scheduled by 13 locally-based AM and FM radio stations.

Media Information: The Columbus Dispatch, 34 South Third Street, Columbus, OH 43215; telephone (614)461-5000. *Columbus Monthly,* PO Box 29913, Columbus, OH 43229; telephone (614)888-4567

Columbus Online

City of Columbus home page. Available ci.columbus.oh.us

The Columbus Dispatch. Available www.dispatch.com (subscription based)

Columbus Metropolitan Library. Available www.cml.lib.oh.us

Columbus Public Schools. Available www.columbus.k12.oh.us/schools.html

The Greater Columbus Convention & Visitors Bureau. Available www.columbuscvb.org

Greater Columbus Super Site. Available www.columbus
.org

Ohio Historical Society Archives/Library. Available www
.ohiohistory.org/resource/archlib

Ohio State University Extension Data Center. Available
www.osuedc.org/current

Selected Bibliography

Conway, W. Fred, *The Most Incredible Prison Escape of the Civil War* (Fire Buff House, 1991)

Howells, William Dean, *Years of My Youth* (New York and London: Harper & Brothers, 1916)

Jacobs, Gregory S., *Getting Around Brown: Desegregation, Development, and the Columbus Public Schools (Urban Life and Urban Landscape)* (Ohio State University Press, 1998)

Dayton

The City in Brief

Founded: 1795 (incorporated, 1805)

Head Official: Mayor Rhine D. McLin (since 2002)

City Population
  1980: 203,371
  1990: 182,011
  2000: 166,179
  2003 estimate: 161,696
  Percent change, 1990–2000: −8.7%
  U.S. rank in 1980: 70th
  U.S. rank in 1990: 89th
  U.S. rank in 2000: 141st

Metropolitan Area Population
  1980: 942,000
  1990: 951,270
  2000: 950,558
  Percent change, 1990–2000: −0.1%
  U.S. rank in 1980: 39th
  U.S. rank in 1990: 51st
  U.S. rank in 2000: 52nd

Area: 56.63 square miles (2000)
Elevation: 750 feet above sea level
Average Annual Temperature: 51.7° F
Average Annual Precipitation: 36.6 inches

Major Economic Sectors: Wholesale and retail trade, manufacturing, services, government, transportation
Unemployment Rate: 7.1% (March 2005)
Per Capita Income: $15, 547 (2000)

2002 FBI Crime Index Total: 15,932

Major Colleges and Universities: University of Dayton; Wright State University

Daily Newspaper: *Dayton Daily News*

Introduction

Dayton, the seat of Ohio's Montgomery County, is the focus of a four-county metropolitan statistical area that includes Montgomery, Miami, Clark, and Greene counties and the cities of Kettering, Miamisburg, Xenia, Fairborn, Oakwood, and Vandalia. World-famous through the pioneering efforts of the Wright brothers, today Dayton is an aviation center and home of Wright-Patterson Air Force Base, headquarters of the United States Air Force bomber program. Dayton, once vulnerable to severe flooding, was the site of the first comprehensive flood control project of its kind. Today the city is at the center of industrial and high-technology development, serving traditional and new markets.

Geography and Climate

Surrounded by a nearly flat plain that is 50 to 100 feet below the elevation of the adjacent rolling countryside Dayton is situated near the center of the Miami River Valley. The Mad River, the Stillwater River, and Wolf Creek, all tributaries of the Miami River, join the master stream within the city limits. The Miami Valley is a fertile agricultural region because of evenly distributed precipitation and moderate temperatures. High relative humidity throughout the year can cause discomfort to people with allergies. Winter temperatures are moderated by the downward slope of the Miami River; cold polar air from the Great Lakes produces extensive cloudiness and frequent snow flurries, but snow accumulation averages only nine inches annually.

Area: 56.63 square miles (2000)

Elevation: 750 feet above sea level

Average Temperatures: January, 26.6° F; July, 74.7° F; annual average, 51.7° F

Average Annual Precipitation: 36.6 inches

History

Town Planned Despite Flood Danger

The point where the Mad River flows into the Great Miami was a thoroughfare for native tribes on their way from Lake Erie to Kentucky and for frontier heroes such as George Rogers Clark, Simon Kenton, Daniel Boone, and Anthony Wayne. Revolutionary War veterans General Arthur St. Clair, General James Wilkinson, Colonel Israel Ludlow, and

Jonathan Dayton of New Jersey, for whom Dayton is named, purchased 60,000 acres in the area from John Cleves Symmes. Ludlow surveyed the town plot in the fall of 1795, and the first settlers arrived on April 1, 1796. In spite of well-founded Native American warnings against the danger of floods, settlers occupied the area where Dayton now stands at the confluence of four rivers and creeks.

Ohio gained statehood in 1803, and two years later Dayton was incorporated as a town and became the seat of Montgomery County. The opening of the Miami & Erie Canal in 1828 brought booming cannons and cheering crowds in celebration of future economic prosperity. That year 100,000 people descended upon Dayton, whose population then numbered 6,000 people, to hear William Henry Harrison, Whig presidential candidate. A year later Dayton was incorporated as a city. In 1851 the Mad River & Lake Erie Railroad reached Dayton, motivating Daytonians to establish new industries that were expanded during the Civil War boom years. Local Congressman Clement L. Vallandigham was head of the anti-Lincoln Copperhead faction in the North, which brought riots, murder, and the destruction of the Republican *Dayton Journal* newspaper office. Vallandigham was banished from the Union for treason.

Industrial Innovation Characterizes Dayton

Dayton entered its golden age of invention and business acumen when John Patterson bought James Ritty's cash register company and his "mechanical money drawer" in 1884. Two years later, Patterson introduced the "daylight factory," a new work environment in which 80 percent of the walls were glass. National Cash Register soon set the standard for this indispensable business device. Dayton-based inventors Wilbur and Orville Wright taught themselves aerodynamics by reading every book on the subject in the Dayton public library. They experimented with kites and gliders and built the world's first wind tunnel to test their ideas. Then on December 17, 1903, the Wright brothers made aviation history at Kitty Hawk, North Carolina, when their flying machine made its first successful flight. The Wrights' commonsensical approach to solving the centuries-old problem of heavier-than-air flight is considered one of the great engineering achievements in history.

The next inventor and engineer to make his mark in Dayton was Charles "Boss" Kettering, who began his career at National Cash Register by inventing an electric cash register. Kettering and a partner founded the Dayton Engineering Laboratories Company (Delco), which became a subsidiary of General Motors in 1920 when Kettering was appointed a vice president and director of research at General Motors. Kettering repeatedly revolutionized the automobile industry; he designed the motor for the first practical electric starter, developed tetraethyl lead that eliminated engine knock and led to ethyl gasoline, and, with chemists, discovered quick-drying lacquer finishes for automobile bodies. Kettering is considered to have demonstrated the value of industrial research and development.

Reform, Cooperation Meet City's Challenges

Newspaper publisher James Cox bought the *Dayton News* in 1898 and then purchased other newspapers in Ohio, Florida, and Atlanta, Georgia. Cox turned to politics in 1909, serving as Dayton's congressman, then as Ohio governor, and running for the presidency in 1920 on the Democratic ticket but losing to Warren G. Harding. As governor, Cox initiated a number of reforms, including the initiative and referendum, minimum wage, and worker's compensation.

Destructive floods had frequently plagued Dayton during the city's first 100 years. Total devastation came on March 25, 1913, when the Great Miami River, swollen by a five-day downpour that brought ten inches of rain, burst through protective levees and flooded the city. So powerful was the flood that houses were literally wrenched from their foundations and sent down the Great Miami. The water level did not recede until March 28, by which time 361 people had died and property damage had reached $100 million.

The flood forced citizens to find a solution to this perennial threat; they responded by raising $2 million in 60 days. Arthur E. Morgan, a self-taught engineer who was then head of the Tennessee Valley Authority—and later became the president of Antioch College in nearby Yellow Springs—was charged with the responsibility of finding solutions. A systematic plan of flood protection consisting of five huge dams and retaining basins was proposed. The Miami Conservancy District, the first comprehensive flood-control project of its kind in the United States, was established by the state legislature on June 18, 1915. Construction was completed in 1922. In another response to the flood crisis, Dayton turned to the nonpartisan, democratically controlled commission-manager form of government, becoming the first major American city to do so and inspiring other cities to follow suit.

During both World Wars, Dayton's manufacturing facilities produced planes, tanks, guns, and other war materials that were vital to successful military efforts. In the post-war years, the focus of Dayton's industry shifted to consumer products. Household appliances, automobiles, and early components of the computer industry were manufactured in Dayton from mid-century on.

In 2005 the city celebrated its bicentennial anniversary of incorporation. Today, Dayton is home to fine educational institutions, an art institute, a symphony orchestra, a natural history museum, and Wright-Patterson Air Force Base. Dayton blends metropolitan amenities with the feel of an All-American city.

Population Profile

Metropolitan Area Residents
1980: 942,000
1990: 951,270
2000: 950,558
Percent change, 1990–2000: −0.1%
U.S. rank in 1980: 39th
U.S. rank in 1990: 51th
U.S. rank in 2000: 52nd

City Residents
1980: 203,371
1990: 182,011
2000: 166,179
2003 estimate: 161,696
Percent change, 1990–2000: −8.7%
U.S. rank in 1980: 70th
U.S. rank in 1990: 89th
U.S. rank in 2000: 141st (State rank: 6th)

Density: 2,979.4 people per square mile (2000)

Racial and ethnic characteristics (2000)
White: 88,676
Black or African American: 71,668
American Indian and Alaska Native: 500
Asian: 1,075
Native Hawaiian and Pacific Islander: 63
Hispanic (of any race): 2,626
Other: 1,160

Percent of residents born in state: 70.6%

Age characteristics (2000)
Population under 5 years old: 11,786
Population 5 to 9 years old: 12,065
Population 10 to 14 years old: 11,350
Population 15 to 19 years old: 13,287
Population 20 to 24 years old: 16,868
Population 25 to 34 years old: 23,490
Population 35 to 44 years old: 24,738
Population 45 to 54 years old: 20,051
Population 55 to 59 years old: 6,773
Population 60 to 64 years old: 5,811
Population 65 to 74 years old: 10,589
Population 75 to 84 years old: 7,340
Population 85 years and over: 2,031
Median age: 32.4

Births (2002, Montgomery County)
Total number: 7,235

Deaths (2002, Montgomery County)
Total number: 5,641 (of which, 60 were infants under the age of 1 year)

Money income (1999)
Per capita income: $15,547
Median household income: $27,423
Total households: 67,476

Number of households with income of . . .
Less than $10,000: 12,622
$10,000 to $14,999: 6,419
$15,000 to $24,999: 11,951
$25,000 to $34,999: 9,818
$35,000 to $49,999: 10,416
$50,000 to $74,999: 9,746
$75,000 to $99,999: 3,815
$100,000 to $149,999: 2,044
$150,000 to $199,999: 255
$200,000 or more: 390

2002 FBI Crime Index Total: 15,932

Municipal Government

The Dayton City Commission is comprised of the mayor and four commissioners, who serve part-time. They are elected at large on a non-partisan basis for four-year overlapping terms. Each member of the commission has equal voting power.

Head Official: Mayor Rhine D. McLin (since 2002; current term expires January 2006)

Total Number of City Employees: 2,944 (2000)

City Information: City of Dayton, 101 W. Third St., Dayton, OH 45402; telephone (937)333-3333

Economy

Major Industries and Commercial Activity

Dayton's balanced economy is supported principally by manufacturing, wholesale and retail trade, and services. In recent years, Dayton has suffered from many of the ills plaguing the national economy. Most major industries have charted reductions in jobs in the past three to five years, and those industries related to the automotive industry have been the hardest hit. Dayton businesses are working towards a resurgence by focusing on increased business investment and diversifying into the manufacturing of technical products and services. Dayton

employers are also concerned about the constraints of a stagnant and aging population; employers are working to recruit highly skilled employees to the region, particularly in the high-tech fields. The most important factor in determining Dayton's economic future, however, is the fate of the area's major manufacturing employers such as Delphi Automotive, General Motors, and Behr, whose presence is so vital to the area's continued prosperity.

In the past ten years, employment in education and health services has grown steadily in Dayton. More than 35 institutions of higher learning in the metropolitan area provide a significant number of jobs. Area health care facilities have been steadily expanding both their physical facilities and the services offered. Technological advances in health care have been readily adopted in Dayton area hospitals, making this economic sector one of the most promising for the region.

More than 1,500 other firms in the Dayton area manufacture accounting systems, bicycles, castings and forgings, compressors, concrete products, washing machines, generators, hoists and jacks, industrial belts, machine tools, name plates, paints and varnishes, paper and paper-making machinery, plastics, precision gauges, tools and dies, and meat products.

Wright-Patterson Air Force Base, the research and development arm of the U.S. Air Force, is the fifth largest employer in the state of Ohio and the largest employer at a single location. Wright-Patterson employs almost one of every twelve people working in the greater Dayton area. Approximately 10,000 of its more than 20,000 employees are civilians; though, as part of announcements of major base consolidations and closings throughout the U.S., Wright-Patterson was slated to gain nearly 600 more military personnel and lose just under 200 of its civilian population. Wright-Patterson is the headquarters of the Air Force Logistics Command, Air Force Material Command, and the Aeronautical Systems Division (ASD), in addition to more than 100 other Department of Defense divisions. The U.S. Defense Department Joint Logistics Systems Center, affiliated with Wright-Patterson, oversees the installation of new computer systems for all military services; the center generates many private sector jobs. The ASD at Wright-Patterson manages the U.S. Air Force bomber program; also housed at the base is the Center for Artificial Intelligence Applications (CAIA). Wright-Patterson also houses the Air Force Institute for Technology, which trains thousands of students each year. In addition, Wright-Patterson is credited with bringing to Dayton one of the highest concentrations of aerospace/high-technology firms in the nation. These firms employ scientists, engineers, technicians, and specialists actively involved in development and application in both the private and public sectors.

Another vital factor in the metropolitan area economy is the Miami Valley Research Park, supported by the Miami Valley Research Foundation, a private, nonprofit corporation; the 1,500-acre park is a university-related research facility that is the site of corporate and government research firms. The Research Park's goal is to promote research, technology, and science in the region, while helping to create and preserve employment opportunities.

Incentive Programs—New and Existing Companies

Local programs—The CityWide Direct Loan program offers assistance for the acquisition of real estate, facility renovation and construction, and equipment purchasing.

State programs—The State of Ohio grants direct low interest loans, industrial revenue bonds, and financial assistance for research and development to companies creating or retaining jobs in Ohio. Additionally, the Ohio Job Creation Tax Credit provides tax credits for Ohio companies that expand as well as companies relocating to Ohio. Enterprise zones provide significant tax reductions on property investments made by businesses expanding in or relocating to specific areas of Ohio.

Job training programs—The Ohio Investment in Training program provides financial assistance and technical resources for assisting Ohio businesses in the training of employees. Additionally, area colleges and universities offer many options for training.

Development Projects

The Dayton Downtown Partnership has been committed to the development of Dayton's urban space for more than a decade. Ongoing development is occurring at RiverScape, a riverside park and event venue that has attracted nighttime crowds of up to 50,000. The second phase of the project, completed in 2003, added improvements and extensions to RiverScape's pathways, bridges, gardens, and fountains. Discussions are currently underway for a potential third phase, which will include a whitewater park and an entertainment venue. The Schuster Performing Arts Center, another product of the Dayton Downtown Partnership, opened in 2003 to immediate success. The Center includes two theatres as well as office and residential space, and has greatly contributed to Dayton's effort to become a regional center for the arts.

Economic Development Information: Dayton Area Chamber of Commerce, 1 Chamber Plaza, Dayton, OH 45402-2400; telephone (937)226-1444

Commercial Shipping

Dayton International Airport, ranking among the nation's busiest air-freight facilities, is the midwestern hub for Emery Worldwide, a CF company. Dayton's central location means that the Dayton International Airport is within 90 minutes by air from 55 percent of the nation's population.

Passengers can find nonstop flights from Dayton International to 19 major cities, including Detroit, Chicago, New York, Atlanta, and Houston. Ten airlines fly approximately 80 daily flights in and out of Dayton International. Thirty trucking companies maintain terminals in the metropolitan area. Just north of the city, the intersection of interstates 70 and 75 creates a hub that is a focal point of the nation's transportation network and has lured transportation companies to the Dayton area.

Three Class I rail systems furnish rail cargo transportation, including trailer on flat car service; both CSX and Conrail operate switching yards in the city. Because of its transportation system, which affords direct access to major markets, Dayton has become an important warehouse and distribution center.

Labor Force and Employment Outlook

Dayton educational institutions provide employers with skilled workers. In particular, the region abounds with employees highly educated in the fields of science and engineering. Dayton area businesses have increasingly been attempting to retain area-educated employees to their workforces. Recently, jobs have been lost in Dayton's traditional manufacturing sectors, which are highly dependent on the fortunes of the automobile industry.

The following is a summary of data regarding the Dayton-Springfield metropolitan area labor force, 2004 annual averages.

Size of non-agricultural labor force: 412,300

Number of workers employed in . . .
construction and mining: 15,700
manufacturing: 59,300
transportation, trade, and utilities: 71,400
information: 11,100
financial activities: 18,700
professional and business services: 53,200
educational and health services: 62,300
leisure and hospitality: 38,200
other services: 17,000
government: 65,400

Average hourly earnings of production workers employed in manufacturing: $20.97

Unemployment rate: 7.1% (March 2005)

Largest employers	Number of employees
Wright-Patterson Air Force Base	22,000
Premier Health Partners	9,000
Delphi Automotive Systems	8,700
AK Steel Corp.	3,800
Good Samaritan Hospital	3,000

Cost of Living

The following is a summary of data regarding several key cost of living factors in the Dayton area.

2004 (3rd Quarter) ACCRA Average House Price: $210,857

2004 (3rd Quarter) ACCRA Cost of Living Index: 93.5 (U.S. average = 100.0)

State income tax rate: Ranges from 0.743% to 7.5%

State sales tax rate: 5.0% (food and prescription drugs are exempt)

Local income tax rate: 2.25%

Local sales tax rate: 1.5%

Property tax rate: $61.55 per $1,000 assessed valuation (2005)

Economic Information: Dayton Area Chamber of Commerce, 1 Chamber Plaza, Dayton, OH 45402-2400; telephone (937)226-1444

Education and Research

Elementary and Secondary Schools

The Dayton City Schools system, the sixth largest district in the state of Ohio, is administered by a seven-member, nonpartisan board of education that appoints a superintendent. The system supports magnet schools, a Partners in Education program, and a Challenger Learning Center. The aerospace industry supports a District Space Symposium.

The following is a summary of data regarding the Dayton public schools as of the 2001–2002 school year.

Total enrollment: 19,813

Number of facilities
  elementary schools: 25
  junior high schools: 4
  senior high schools: 6

Student/teacher ratio: 13.6:1

Teacher salaries
  average: $39,912 (1999-2000)

Funding per pupil: $10,123

Catholic, Jewish, Baptist, Seventh Day Adventist, Church of God, and nondenominational groups also operate schools in the region.

Colleges and Universities

A wide range of higher learning resources are available within driving distance of Dayton. Located in the area are 26 colleges and universities, and 10 vocational and technical schools that offer curricula for traditional as well as nontraditional students. The largest state-funded institution is Wright State University, with an enrollment of more than 16,000 students in 100 undergraduate and 50 Ph.D., graduate, and professional degree programs; Wright State operates schools of law, medicine, pharmacy, and nursing.

The University of Dayton, founded in 1850, is the state's largest independent university and grants associate, baccalaureate, master's, and doctorate degrees in 120 fields of study. The university operates professional schools in education, business administration, engineering, and law. The United Theological Seminary, affiliated with the United Methodist Church, offers graduate programs in theology. Based near Dayton in Yellow Springs is Antioch University; founded by Horace Mann in 1852, Antioch has long been respected for its innovative role in alternative and cooperative education. Central State University, in neighboring Wilberforce, is Ohio's only public university with a traditionally African American student enrollment.

Sinclair Community College, located in downtown Dayton, awards two-year associate degrees in such areas as allied health, business, engineering technologies, and fine and applied arts. With an enrollment of 24,000 students, Sinclair is one of the largest community colleges in the nation. The school is known for its robotics program, operated in association with General Motors Fanacu. The Air Force Institute of Technology (AFIT) at Wright-Patterson Air Force Base is operated by the Air Force for military personnel. Designed primarily as a graduate school, AFIT also offers upper-level baccalaureate study as well as continuing education for civilians. Included among AFIT graduates are 25 U.S. astronauts.

Libraries and Research Centers

Dayton is home to approximately 30 libraries operated by a variety of institutions, businesses, and organizations. The Dayton and Montgomery County Library is the largest facility in the Miami Valley. Containing about 1.7 million books, more than 1,100 periodicals, and compact discs, microfiche, audio- and videotapes, and films, the library operates a main library and 21 branches; special collections include local history and federal and state documents. All of the colleges and universities in the area maintain substantial campus libraries with holdings in a wide range of fields. Most specialized libraries are affiliated with hospitals, law firms, major corporations, and government agencies.

Dayton's higher education community is involved in technological research of national scope. The University of Dayton

Research Institute works in association with Wright-Patterson Air Force Base, the foremost aeronautical research and development center in the Air Force; about 10,000 scientists and engineers are employed at the base. Human-computer interaction is studied at the university's Information System Laboratory. The engineering department at Central State University conducts projects for the National Aeronautics and Space Administration and for high-technology firms. Wright State University School of Medicine's Cox Heart Institute has received recognition for the development of diagnostic and surgical treatment of heart disease. Also located in Dayton is the Hipple Cancer Research Center, one of several independent cancer research facilities in the country.

Public Library Information: Dayton and Montgomery County Public Library, 215 East Third Street, Dayton, OH 45402-2103; telephone (937)227-9500; fax (937)227-9524

Health Care

Eighteen hospitals, four of which are teaching hospitals, and a medical community that comprises the third-largest employment sector in the Miami Valley combine to make Dayton a primary health care center for southwestern Ohio. Miami Valley Hospital, providing 827 beds, is the city's largest medical facility; Miami Valley operates an air ambulance service and maintains a Level 1 regional trauma center as well as units specializing in kidney dialysis, burn treatment, maternity services, and women's health programs.

In addition to furnishing in-patient and out-patient care, 560-bed Good Samaritan Hospital houses the Family Birthing Center, the Marie-Joseph Living Care Center, and a substance abuse treatment center. St. Elizabeth Medical Center, founded in 1878 near downtown Dayton, provides 631 beds and specializes in family medicine, physical therapy, sports medicine, women's health programs, and senior health care. In suburban Kettering, the Kettering Memorial Hospital/Sycamore Hospital provides 630 beds. Among other medical facilities in Dayton are Children's Medical Center, Grandview Hospital, Dartmouth Hospital, and Veterans Affairs Medical Center.

Recreation

Sightseeing

The Dayton Museum of Natural History maintains a planetarium and observatory, and operates SunWatch, a twelfth-century Native American village restoration south of the city, which is considered the most complete prehistoric settlement of any culture east of the Mississippi. The United States Air Force Museum is the world's largest military aviation museum. Historic Dayton buildings and collections of artifacts from the city's golden age of invention are presented at the Kettering Moraine Museum. The Oregon Historic District, Dayton's oldest neighborhood, is a center of shopping, dining, and nightlife amidst nearly 200-year-old architecture. In downtown Dayton on Thursdays, Fridays, and Saturdays, the new "market district," centered around the National City 2nd Street Public Market and the Webster Street Market, showcases home-baked bread, fresh produce, and other foods and crafts. The National Afro-American Museum and Cultural Center, located in Wilberforce, a stop on the Underground Railroad, consists of the museum and renovated Carnegie Library.

At Carillon Historical Park, on 65 acres next to the Great Miami River, the carillon bells that are a Dayton landmark are among the featured displays, which also include the Wright Flyer III and the Barney & Smith railroad car. RiverScape provides facilities for paddleboating on the river and a venue for live music as well as serving as the setting for displays relating to Dayton's history and the many inventions born in the city. Festival Plaza, the focal point of Riverscape, features gardens, fountains, and pools in the summer and a skating rink during winter months. The Cox Arboretum is a 160-acre public garden set in native woodlands. Five miles of trails wind through woods and meadows containing more than 150 indigenous Ohio plant species at Aullwood Audubon Center, a 200-acre nature sanctuary. Other nature preserves in the Dayton area include Wegerzyn Horticultural Center and Bergamo/Mt. St. John.

The Paul Laurence Dunbar House, the restored home of one of the country's great African American poets, is open to the public. The Wright Memorial commemorates the spot where the Wright brothers tested their airplane during its invention; the Wright Brothers Bicycle Shop is a National Historic Landmark. At the center of Dayton's downtown district, the Montgomery County Historical Society is housed in the Old Courthouse, which was built in 1850 and is considered one of the nation's finest examples of Greek Revival architecture.

Arts and Culture

Dayton supports an active cultural community. The Arts Center Foundation was created in 1986 to plan and fund new facilities to house Dayton's major arts institutions. The restoration and renovation of Victoria Theatre, listed on the National Register of Historic Places, transformed the theatre into a modern performing arts complex. The Victoria Theatre is home to the Fifth Third Bank Broadway Series, a summer film series, the Victoria Children's Theatre Festival, the Dayton Ballet, and the Dayton Contemporary Dance Company. The Dayton Art Institute, founded in 1919, sponsors exhibition programs, Sunday afternoon musicales, twilight concerts, gallery talks, and studio classes. Artworks by the members of the Dayton Society of Painters and Sculptors, Inc., are exhibited in two galleries at the society's Victorian mansion quarters in the historic St. Anne's Hill district. Permanent collections include Oceanic, Native American, and African art, as well as a sizeable glass collection.

The Dayton Philharmonic Orchestra, founded as a chamber orchestra in 1933, is now an 85-member orchestra performing classical, pops, chamber, and a summer band concert series at Memorial Hall and other Dayton locations. Dayton Opera, founded in 1960, presents four fully staged operas at the new Benjamin and Marian Schuster Performing Arts Center. The Center, which opened in 2003, includes a 2,300-seat performance hall as well as a rehearsal hall, a Wintergarden and glass atrium, and an 18-story tower with first-class office and condominium space. Dayton Ballet's season of four productions includes traditional and new ballet works. Dayton Contemporary Dance Company, nationally acclaimed for innovative work, presents three performances a year in addition to national tours.

The Dayton Music Club celebrated its centennial in 1988; it sponsors free music programs at various city locations with performances by local and national artists. Other regularly scheduled musical events include the chamber concert Vanguard Series, the Soirees Musical piano performances, the Bach Society choral productions, the CityFolk ethnic and folk music series, and concerts at area churches.

Theater companies offering full seasons of traditional and experimental works include the Dayton Playhouse, the Human Race, and the Dayton Theatre Guild. The Victoria Theatre, which opened in 1865 as Dayton's first theatrical house for live entertainment, sponsors touring companies' productions as well as a season of children's drama. Wright State University, the University of Dayton, Sinclair Community College, and Antioch College stage theater performances for the general public. The Muse Machine, a Dayton organization designed to inform young people about the arts and culture, each year stages a theatrical production showcasing student performers. *Blue Jacket,* an outdoor drama about the white Shawnee war chief, is presented each summer at a facility 6 miles southeast of neighboring Xenia.

Festivals and Holidays

Art in the Park in May attracts artists from around the nation for an outdoor fine arts and crafts show. At A World A'Fair, held in May at the Convention Center, 35 countries share their native culture, cuisine, and costumes. Dave Hall Plaza Park hosts music festivals in the summer.

The Vectren Dayton Air Show, one of the largest of its kind in the world, draws more than 200,000 spectators to the Dayton International Airport in July. Aerobatic displays, military jet demonstrations, and entertainment for the whole family make the Air Show one of the most important events on Dayton's calendar. Arts and crafts, ethnic foods, music and dancing, and special children's activities are featured at Oktoberfest, held in early October on the grounds of the Dayton Art Institute. Each year the Dayton Holiday Festival begins the day after Thanksgiving with a tree-lighting ceremony at Courthouse Square. Ohio Renaissance Festival is held on weekends in August and September near Waynesville. In May, the Dayton Amateur Radio Association hosts Hamvention, a convention that draws ham radio enthusiasts from across the country.

Sports for the Spectator

Dayton is home to the Dayton Dragons, a Midwest League baseball Class A club in the Cincinnati Reds' farm system; they play at Fifth Third Field. Dayton also boasts a class AA ECHL ice hockey team, the Dayton Bombers. The Bombers play at the Nutter Center, which also hosts Wright State University athletic events and various regional and state high school tournaments. Dayton sports fans support both the Cincinnati Reds baseball team and the Cincinnati Bengals football team. The University of Dayton Flyers field a football team in National Collegiate Athletic Association (NCAA) Division III, as does Wittenberg University in nearby Springfield. The Flyers' basketball team has a record of successful competition on the national level and is now in the Midwestern Collegiate Conference.

Sports for the Participant

The Dayton Recreation and Parks Department sponsors sports programs for preschoolers to senior citizens at 78 parks and 10 recreation centers. Programs include soccer and tennis camps, summer-day camps for children, and softball leagues. Swimming, canoeing, golf, tennis, basketball, volleyball, boating, sailing, fishing, and winter sports are also available. Among the facilities managed by the department are the Jack Nicklaus Sports Center, the Wesleyan Nature Center, and the Horace M. Huffman River Corridor Bikeway, a 24-mile path along the Great Miami River. Golfing opportunities in Dayton include Kittyhawk Golf Center, the largest public golf facility in Ohio, and the Madden Golf Center, designed by notable course architect Alex Campbell. The Urban Krag Climbing Center features an 8,000 square foot vertical climbing wall in a beautifully restored church.

Shopping and Dining

Downtown, the Merchants Row District offers jewelry, antiques, books, and more. The Oregon Historic District is a

12-block area near downtown that features shops, restaurants, and clubs among restored turn-of-the-century homes. The National City Second Street Public Market features the wares of local farmers and food and gift vendors, including fresh flowers and produce, gourmet coffee, and homemade baked goods. The Webster Street Market, housed in a restored nineteenth-century railroad freight depot, also provides a unique market-style shopping experience. The public markets are open Thursday through Sunday. There are nearly 30 shopping centers in the region, the largest being Dayton Mall and Fairfield Commons Mall.

Dining choices in Dayton include Japanese, Chinese, Mexican, Italian, Indian, and American cuisine. One critically acclaimed restaurant, which specializes in French and continental cuisine, is known for its rack of lamb, duck, and fresh seafood. Another serves authentic German dishes. One of the city's most popular eateries is a traditional steak and chop house that does not take reservations or serve desserts.

Visitor Information: Dayton/Montgomery County Convention and Visitors Bureau, 1 Chamber Plaza, Suite A, Dayton, OH 45402; toll-free (800)221-8235

Convention Facilities

Situated in the central business district, the Dayton Convention Center is within walking distance of hotels, restaurants, shopping, and entertainment. The Convention Center offers two exhibit halls, with capacities of 47,000 square feet and 21,300 square feet, which can be combined to accommodate from 3,600 to 9,970 people in a variety of settings. Also part of the complex are 22 meeting rooms, a 674-seat theater, a fully equipped kitchen, and teleconferencing, sound, and lighting systems. Hara Arena Conference and Exhibition Center, the second-largest facility of it kind in the state of Ohio, contains a total of 165,575 square feet of space, which includes an 8,000-seat arena. On the Wright State University campus is the multipurpose Ervin J. Nutter Center, which seats up to 300 people in 5,500 square feet of space.

Dayton-area hotels and motels offer meeting and banquet accommodations for large and small groups; more than 7,500 lodging rooms can be found in the Dayton-Montgomery County area.

Convention Information: Dayton/Montgomery County Convention and Visitors Bureau, 1 Chamber Plaza, Suite A, Dayton, OH 45402; telephone (800)221-8235. Dayton Convention Center, telephone (937)333-4707

Transportation

Approaching the City

The destination for the majority of air traffic into Dayton is the Dayton International Airport, near the junction of I-70 and I-75 north of the city. Dayton International is served by nine airlines. In 2004 more than 1.4 million passengers were enplaned at Dayton. Seven general aviation airports are located throughout the Miami Valley.

Highways into metropolitan Dayton include two major interstate freeways, east-west I-70 and north-south I-75; I-675, a bypass connects these highways and provides direct access to the city from Columbus and Cincinnati. U.S. 35 extends from east to west through the southern sector of Dayton. State routes leading into Dayton from points throughout the state and the immediate vicinity are 4, 202, 48, 49—all with a general north-south orientation.

Traveling in the City

Regional Transit Authority (RTA) provides regularly scheduled mass transit bus service throughout Montgomery County and in parts of Greene County; RTA operates special routes to Wright-Patterson Air Force Base and Wright State and Central State Universities. Dayton is one of the few U.S. cities to have retained an electric trolleybus system.

Communications

Newspapers and Magazines

Established in 1808 and merged with the *Journal Herald* in 1988, the *Dayton Daily News* is the city's daily morning newspaper. More than 20 suburban newspapers plus local college and university publications circulate weekly. Special-interest magazines published in Dayton cover such subjects as religion, African American culture, and management.

Television and Radio

Dayton is the primary center for television and radio north of Cincinnati in southwestern Ohio. Six television stations—four commercial affiliates and two public—broadcast from Dayton; cable service is available. Sixteen AM and FM radio stations schedule a variety of programs such as jazz, gospel, Celtic and folk, African American, contemporary, and classical music, educational features, and news.

Media Information: Dayton Daily News, Dayton Newspapers Inc., 45 South Ludlow Street, Dayton, OH 45402; telephone (937)222-5700

Dayton Online

City of Dayton Home Page. Available www.ci.dayton.oh.us

Dayton Area Chamber of Commerce. Available www
.daytonchamber.org

Dayton/Montgomery County Convention & Visitors Bureau. Available daytoncvb.com/index.php

Dayton Public Schools. Available www.dps.k12.oh.us

Dayton Public Schools, school district report card. Available www.ode.state.oh.us/reportcard/archives

Wright-Patterson Air Force Base. Available www.wpafb.af
.mil/index.html

Selected Bibliography

Bernstein, Mark, *Grand Eccentrics: Turning the Century: Dayton and the Inventing of America* (Orange Frazer Press, 1996)

Huffman, Dale, Andy Snow, et al. *Dayton: The Cradle of Creativity (Urban Tapestry Series)* (Towery, 1998)

Wright, Wilbur, and Orville Wright, *Miracle at Kitty Hawk: The Letters of Wilbur and Orville Wright,* Fred C. Kelly, ed. (Da Capo, 1996)

Toledo

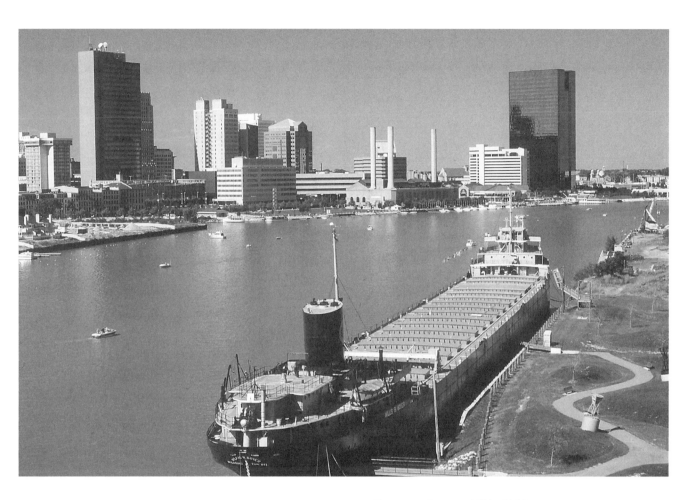

The City in Brief

Founded: 1817 (incorporated 1837)

Head Official: Mayor Jack Ford (since 2001)

City Population
  1980: 354,635
  1990: 332,943
  2000: 313,619
  2003 estimate: 298,242
  Percent change, 1990–2000: −5.8%
  U.S. rank in 1980: 40th
  U.S. rank in 1990: Not reported
  U.S. rank in 2000: 66th

Metropolitan Area Population
  1980: 617,000
  1990: 614,128
  2000: 618,203
  Percent change, 1990–2000: −0.7%
  U.S. rank in 1980: 55th
  U.S. rank in 1990: Not reported
  U.S. rank in 2000: 69th

Area: 81 square miles (2000)
Elevation: 615 feet above sea level
Average Annual Temperature: 48.5° F
Average Annual Precipitation: 33 inches

Major Economic Sectors: Services, wholesale and retail trade, manufacturing, government
Unemployment Rate: 7.4% (March 2005)
Per Capita Income: $17,388 (1999)

2002 FBI Crime Index Total: 26,717

Major Colleges and Universities: University of Toledo; Davis College; Stautzenberger College; Medical College of Ohio; Owens Community College

Daily Newspaper: *The Toledo Blade*

Introduction

Toledo, the seat of Ohio's Lucas County, is the focus of a metropolitan complex comprised of Ottawa Hills Maumee, Oregon, Sylvania, Perrysburg, and Rossford. The city played a strategic role in the War of 1812, after which the victorious Americans enjoyed unimpeded settlement of the Northwest Territory. The site of pioneer advancements in the glass-making industry, today Toledo continues to be headquarters of international glass companies. The Port of Toledo is a major Great Lakes shipping point. Toledo's commitment to arts, culture, education, and citywide revitalization has residents and city leaders looking toward a bright future.

Geography and Climate

Toledo is located on the western end of Lake Erie at the mouth of the Maumee River, surrounded by generally level terrain. The soil is quite fertile, particularly along the Maumee Valley toward the Indiana state line. The proximity of Lake Erie moderates temperatures. Snowfall in Toledo is normally light.

Area: 81 square miles (2000)

Elevation: 615 feet above sea level

Average Temperatures: January, 22.5° F; July, 72.1° F; annual average, 48.5° F

Average Annual Precipitation: 33 inches

History

French, British Settle Maumee Valley

As early as 1615 Etienne Brule, Samuel de Champlain's French-Canadian scout, discovered the Erie tribe of Native Americans living at the mouth of the Maumee River, the largest river that flows into the Great Lakes. Robert Cavelier, sieur de La Salle, claimed the territory in the name of France's King Louis XIV in 1689, and French trading posts were subsequently established in the Maumee Valley. A century later the British built Fort Miami there. Following the French and Indian War in 1763, France ceded all claims in the territory to Britain, who annexed the region to the Canadian Province of Quebec in 1774. At the end of the American Revolution, the region became part of the United States and was designated as part of the Northwest Territory

in 1787. Renegade agents incited Native American warriors to attack settlers in the area; when American military forces were sent there in 1790, the native tribes prevailed. Four years later, General Anthony Wayne defeated 2,000 Native Americans at the Battle of Fallen Timbers southwest of present-day Toledo. General Wayne then directed the building of several forts, of which one was Fort Industry, constructed at the present site of Toledo.

At the outbreak of the War of 1812 the few settlers in the vicinity fled. In January, 1813, General William Henry Harrison, later President of the United States, erected Fort Meigs, a massive fortification enclosing 9 acres, which became known as the "Gibraltar of the Northwest." In the Battle of Lake Erie, off Put-In-Bay, the U. S. Navy's young Commodore Perry defeated the British naval force, followed by Harrison's defeat of General Proctor at the Battle of the Thames. These victories re-secured the Northwest Territory for the United States. After the war, a permanent settlement was formed on the northwest side of the Maumee River near the mouth of Swan Creek. In 1817 an Indian treaty conveyed most of the remaining land in the area to the federal government. The village of Port Lawrence near Fort Industry was formed by a Cincinnati syndicate in 1817, but it failed in 1820 and was then revived. Port Lawrence voted in 1835 to consolidate with the settlement of Vistula, one mile away, and the two were incorporated as Toledo in 1837.

The choice of the name of Toledo for the new city is shrouded in local legend. Popular versions give credit to a merchant who suggested Toledo because it "is easy to pronounce, is pleasant in sound, and there is no other city of that name on the American continent." Whatever the source, friendly relations with the city of Toledo, Spain, have resulted. The Hispanic government awarded *The Blade,* the city's oldest newspaper, the royal coat of arms, and the University of Toledo has permission to use the arms of Spain's Ferdinand and Isabella as its motif.

Border Dispute Precedes Industrial Growth

The "Toledo War" of 1835-36 between Ohio and Michigan over their common boundary did not involve bloodshed but it did result in federal intervention to resolve the dispute. Governor Robert Lucas of Ohio led a force of 1,000 soldiers to Perrysburg in March 1835, with the intent of driving Michigan militia from Toledo, but emissaries sent by President Andrew Jackson arranged a truce. Governor Lucas held a special session of the legislature in June, creating Lucas County out of the land in Wood County involved in the dispute. The new county held court in Toledo on the first Monday of September, which proved it had exercised jurisdiction over the disputed territory by holding a Court of Common Pleas in due form of law. Finally, Congress settled the issue by stipulating that the condition of Michigan's entrance into the Union would award Ohio the contested land and Michigan, in compensation, would receive what is now the state's Upper Peninsula.

Toledo in the mid-nineteenth century benefitted from the opening of new canals, the establishment of businesses along the river bank to accommodate trade and new shipping industries, and the arrival of the railroad. Prosperity continued during the Civil War, and by the end of the century the city became a major rail center in the United States. During the 1880s Toledo's industrial base, spurred by the discovery of inexpensive fuel, attracted glass-making entrepreneurs. Edward Libbey established a glassworks in Toledo, and then hired Michael Owens to supervise the new plant. The two pioneers revolutionized the glass business with inventions that eliminated child labor and streamlined production. Edward Ford arrived in the Toledo region in 1896 to found the model industrial town of Rossford and one of the largest plate-glass operations of its time.

Two politicians stand out in the history of Toledo. Samuel M. "Gold Rule" Jones was elected mayor on a nonpartisan ticket and emerged as a national figure. His reform efforts in city government introduced one of the first municipal utilities, the eight-hour workday for city employees, and the first free kindergartens, public playgrounds, and band concerts. Mayor Brand Whitlock continued Jones's reforms by securing a state law for the nonpartisan election of judges and Ohio's initiative and referendum law in 1912.

John Willys moved his Overland automobile factory from Indianapolis to Toledo in 1908, and, in time, automotive-parts manufacture flourished in the area; the industry was firmly established by such firms as Champion Spark Plug and Warner Manufacturing Company, maker of automobile gears. A strike by Auto-Lite workers in 1934 was marred by violence and prompted the intervention of U.S. troops and the Federal Department of Labor; the resolution of this strike, which received national attention, helped contribute to the unionization of the automotive industries. The Toledo Industrial Peace Board, set up in 1935 to resolve labor disputes by round-table discussion, served as a model for similar entities in other cities.

An All-American City

Toledo today boasts amenities and points of interest including the University of Toledo, the Medical College of Ohio at Toledo, a symphony, ballet and opera company, the Toledo Museum of Art, the Toledo Zoo, and the Anthony Wayne suspension bridge (1931). The site of the battle of Fallen Timbers, a national historic landmark, is in a nearby state park. Toledo's commitment to arts and culture is evident, as is its focus on neighborhood revitalization. A renewed vitality, even in the face of diminishing central-city residents, has city planners looking toward the future.

Historical Information: Toledo-Lucas County Public Library, History-Travel-Biography Department, 325 Michigan Street, Toledo, OH 43624; telephone (419)259-5207

Population Profile

Metropolitan Area Residents
1980: 617,000
1990: 614,128
2000: 618,203
Percent change, 1990–2000: −0.7%
U.S. rank in 1980: 55th
U.S. rank in 1990: Not reported
U.S. rank in 2000: 69th

City Residents
1980: 354,635
1990: 332,943
2000: 313,619
2003 estimate: 298,242
Percent change, 1990–2000: −5.8%
U.S. rank in 1980: 40th
U.S. rank in 1990: Not reported
U.S. rank in 2000: 66th

Density: 3,890 people per square mile (2000)

Racial and ethnic characteristics (2000)
   White: 220,261
   Black or African American: 73,854
   American Indian and Alaska Native: 970
   Asian: 3,233
   Native Hawaiian and Pacific Islander: 76
   Hispanic or Latino (may be of any race): 313,619
   Other: 7,166

Percent of residents born in state: 77.4 % (2000)

Age characteristics (2000)
   Population under 5 years old: 22,849
   Population 5 to 9 years old: 23,879
   Population 10 to 14 years old: 22,737
   Population 15 to 19 years old: 22,343
   Population 20 to 24 years old: 24,977
   Population 25 to 34 years old: 47,580
   Population 35 to 44 years old: 45,816
   Population 45 to 54 years old: 38,256
   Population 55 to 59 years old: 12,993
   Population 60 to 64 years old: 10,989
   Population 65 to 74 years old: 20,799
   Population 75 to 84 years old: 15,374

Population 85 years and older: 5,027
Median age: 33.2 years

Births (2003)
Total number: 6,075

Deaths (2003)
Total number: 4,601

Money income (1999)
Per capita income: $17,388
Median household income: $32,546
Total households: 128,925

Number of households with income of . . .
less than $10,000: 18,198
$10,000 to $14,999: 11,090
$15,000 to $24,999: 20,117
$25,000 to $34,999: 18,859
$35,000 to $49,999: 20,942
$50,000 to $74,999: 23,201
$75,000 to $99,999: 9,798
$100,000 to $149,999: 5,035
$150,000 to $199,999: 908
$200,000 or more: 694

Percent of families below poverty level: 14.2% (58.1% of which were female householder families with related children under 5 years)

2002 FBI Crime Index Total: 26,717

Municipal Government

The city of Toledo is administered by a strong-mayor form of government. The mayor and 12 council members are elected to four-year terms.

Head Official: Mayor Jack Ford (since 2001; current term expires 2005)

Total Number of City Employees: about 2,950 (2005)

City Information: City Hall, telephone (419)936-2020

Economy

Major Industries and Commercial Activity

Manufacturing comprises about one-fifth of Toledo's economic base. Nearly 1,000 manufacturing facilities are located in the metropolitan area. Such manufacturing facilities include automotive assembly and parts production, glass, plastic, and metal parts. Toledo is home to the headquarters of such corporations as The Andersons, Dana Corporation, Libbey, Inc., Libbey-Owens-Ford Company, Owens Corning, Owens-Illinois, and Seaway Food Town. Major employers include DaimlerChrysler, General Motors/Powertrain, ProMedica Health Systems, and Toledo Public Schools. With 10 major financial institutions, Toledo is also a banking and finance center for northwestern Ohio.

Medical and technologically-oriented businesses are a major force in the local economy; Lucas County ranks among the 50 counties in the United States that account for 50 percent of medical industry production. Several private testing laboratories and manufacturers of medical instruments and allied products are located in the Toledo area. In addition, more than 400 plastics, metalworking, and electronics companies adapt engineering and production capabilities to the medical device and instrument industries. With its many nearby universities and large public school system, education is also an economic pillar. The Medical College of Ohio is the eighth largest employer in Toledo, and contributes nearly $500 million to the economy per year.

Items and goods produced: automotive and truck components, health care products, glass products, fiberglass, packaged foods, plastic and paper products, building materials, furniture, metal products

Incentive Programs—New and Existing Companies

The Regional Growth Partnership, Inc. (RGP) is the principal agency for facilitating business expansion and location in the Toledo metropolitan area. Created as a non-profit public/private partnership, the RGP is charged with the mission of creating employment and capital investment needed to generate economic growth in greater Toledo and northwest Ohio. The RGP works closely with all public and private economic development organizations. The RGP provides customized services to fit the individual needs of each business client. Services include customized location proposals and sales presentations, comprehensive site and facility searches, project financial and incentive packaging, labor market information, other market and community data, regional evaluation tours, and leadership networking. A number of tax incentives, technology, and training assistance programs are available at the state and local level.

Economic Development Information: Regional Growth Partnership, 300 Madison Avenue, Suite 270, Toledo, OH 43604; telephone (419)252-2700; fax (419)252-2724

Development Projects

The economy continues to thrive in Toledo. Production of Jeep Liberty began in April of 2001 at the new Jeep assembly plant. Major university projects include the Toledo Science and Technology Center, a program to stimulate economic development by creating jobs and assisting local businesses. Downtown Toledo, Inc. is an ongoing public-private partnership made up of local business leaders, property owners, and citizens. It was created to enhance the quality of life and economy of the downtown Toledo area.

Significant investment has been made at the University of Toledo and Owens Community College. The Medical College of Ohio Cancer Center Institute opened in January of 2000.

Commercial Shipping

Toledo is situated at the center of a major market area; located within 500 miles of the city are 43 percent and 47 percent, respectively, of U.S. and Canadian industrial markets. A commercial transportation network, consisting of a Great Lakes port, railroads, interstate highways, and two international airports, provides access to this market area as well as points throughout the nation and the world.

Toledo is served by both Toledo Express in Toledo and Detroit Metropolitan Airport in nearby Detroit, Michigan. Toledo Express, served by seven airlines, carries passengers and is a major air freight center. Named one of the five best small airports in the Midwest, Toledo Express is the international hub for Burlington Air Express. It has recently begun a 4-year, $22 million renovation project. Detroit Metropolitan Airport is within a 50-minute drive.

The Port of Toledo, on the Maumee River, is a 150-acre domestic and international shipping facility that includes a general cargo center, mobile cargo handling gear, and covered storage space. In 2004 the port handled 122,514 tons of cargo. Designated as a Foreign Trade Zone, the complex affords shippers deferred duty payments and tax savings on foreign goods.

Toledo is served by four railroad systems, which provide direct and interline shipping; Norfolk/Southern maintains piggyback terminal facilities in the city. More than 90 truck firms link Toledo with all major metropolitan areas in the United States and points throughout Canada.

Labor Force and Employment Outlook

Farming, industrial production, and agriculture contribute to the area's growing economy. Manufacturing accounts for about 18 percent of the jobs in metropolitan Toledo. The Toledo area has a strong automotive industry base and is one of the top three machine tooling centers in the United States. The area has experienced strong growth in the steel, metals, and plastic industries. Retail and service businesses continue to expand.

Businesses in Toledo have access to graduates from at least 20 higher educational institutions within a one-hour drive of the city.

The following is a summary of data regarding the Toledo metropolitan area labor force, 2004 annual averages:

Size of nonagricultural labor force: 329,600

Number of workers employed in . . .
  construction and mining: 15,800
  manufacturing: 51,300
  trade, transportation and utilities: 64,800
  information: 4,700
  financial activities: 13,200
  professional and business services: 34,600
  educational and health services: 46,700
  leisure and hospitality: 32,900
  other services: 15,400
  government: 50,200

Average hourly earnings of production workers employed in manufacturing: $21.87

Unemployment rate: 7.4% (March 2005)

Largest manufacturing/ utility employers	Number of employees
DaimlerChrysler Corp./Toledo	5,583
GM Corp./Powertrain Div. Corp.	3,860
Libbey, Inc.	1,329
Dana Corporation.	1,225
Owens-Illinois, Inc.	1,200

Cost of Living

The following is a summary of data regarding several key cost of living factors in the Toledo area.

2004 (3rd Quarter) ACCRA Average House Price: $212,283

2004 (3rd Quarter) ACCRA Cost of Living Index: 95.4 (U.S. average = 100.0)

State income tax rate: 2.25%

State sales tax rate: 6.0% (food and prescription drugs are exempt)

Local income tax rate: 2.25%

Local sales tax rate: 1.25% (county)

Property tax rate: 60.65 mills (2002)

Economic Information: Regional Growth Partnership, 300 Madison Avenue, Suite 270, Toledo, OH 43604; telephone (419)252-2700

Education and Research

Elementary and Secondary Schools

Public elementary and secondary schools in Toledo are administered by the Toledo Public Schools system, the fourth largest public school system in the state of Ohio, with just over 35,000 students. Five partisan board of education members select a superintendent. Washington Local Schools serve much of the northwest area of the city.

The following is a summary of data regarding Toledo public schools as of the 2002–2003 school year.

Total enrollment: 35,533

Number of facilities
  elementary schools: 47
  junior high schools: 7
  senior high schools: 8

Student/teacher ratio: 23–25:1

Teacher salaries
  minimum: $32,697
  maximum: $65,520

Funding per pupil: $7,838

The Catholic Diocese of Toledo operates an extensive parochial school system in the city and surrounding area. Other private and church-related schools also offer educational alternatives.

Public Schools Information: Toledo Public Schools, 420 East Manhattan, Toledo, OH 43608; telephone (419)729-8200

Colleges and Universities

The University of Toledo's eight colleges enroll nearly 21,000 students and offer degrees in undergraduate and graduate fields, including engineering and pharmacy. The Medical College of Ohio (MCO) grants a medical degree as well as graduate degrees in medical science and industrial hygiene; MCO conducts joint educational programs and collaborative research with area businesses and educational institutions. Owens Community College offers two-year programs in biomedical equipment, computer-integrated manufacturing, and glass engineering, among others.

Within commuting distance of Toledo are Bowling Green State University and the University of Michigan.

Libraries and Research Centers

Toledo is home to about two dozen libraries operated by public agencies, private organizations, and corporations. The Toledo—Lucas County Public Library houses about 2.3 million books and has an annual circulation of over 6 million; the library system includes 18 branches and two bookmobiles located throughout the city and the county. The University of Toledo, the Medical College of Ohio at Toledo, and Owens Community College maintain campus libraries. Other libraries are associated with the Toledo Museum of Art, companies such as Libbey-Owens-Ford, law firms, hospitals, and churches and synagogues.

The Medical College of Ohio (MCO) in Toledo is active in medical research and development. MCO has created the Health Technology Park to house college facilities and the Northwest Ohio Health Technology Center (NOHTC), which serves as a research and development incubator for private companies and academic institutions.

Research and development is also conducted at the University of Toledo's Polymer and Thin Films Institute and Eitel Institute for Silicate Research as well as at Edison Industrial Systems Center. The federally-funded National Center for Tooling and Precision Products research is housed at the University of Toledo. The National Drosophilia Species Resource Center, affiliated with nearby Bowling Green State University, is internationally known for fruit-fly research.

Public Library Information: Toledo-Lucas County Public Library, 325 Michigan Street, Toledo, OH 43624-1332; telephone (419)259-5207; fax (419)255-1332

Health Care

Eight hospitals serve the metropolitan Toledo area with complete general, specialized, and surgical care. The largest facilities are Toledo Hospital, with 620 beds, and St. Vincent Mercy Medical Center, with 576 beds and Life Flight operations. Other hospitals include St. Anne Mercy Hospital, Flower Hospital, St. Charles Mercy Hospital, Riverside Medical College, Wood County, and St. Luke's. A valuable resource in the community is the Medical College of Ohio, which operates three hospitals and provides training for health care professionals. In 2000 the Medical College of Ohio Cancer Institute opened to provide patients with cutting-edge treatment while conducting cancer research at the molecular, cellular, and physiological levels. The Center also offers a specialty center for the treatment of breast cancer.

Recreation

Sightseeing

Fort Meigs, located near Toledo along the southern bank of the Maumee River west of Perrysburg, was the largest walled fortification in North America. Built in 1813 under the direction of General William Henry Harrison (who later became president of the United States), Fort Meigs is an impressive structure of earthworks and timber. Toledo's Old West End, covering 25 blocks, is one of the largest collections of late-Victorian architecture in the country; Frank Lloyd Wright studied the Old West End in preparing his plans for Oak Park, Illinois.

The freighter SS *Willis* was first launched in 1911 and served for many years on the Great Lakes as the largest ship of its type. Now restored, it is docked at International Park and open for tours. The Sauder Farm and Craft Village, a living-history museum in nearby Archbold, recaptures life in northwest Ohio in the 1830s. Wolcott House Museum in Maumee depicts life in the Maumee Valley from 1840 to 1860.

The Toledo Zoo, one of the nation's highest rated zoological parks, offers state-of-the-art exhibits, together with historical architecture, fully integrated to provide more than 4,000 animals with the best possible environment and offer visitors an exciting experience. An innovative exhibition called Africa! opened in May of 2004.

Toledo Center of Science & Industry (COSI) is located at the corner of Summit and Adams streets on the riverfront. With eight Exhibition Learning Worlds, a restaurant, and a retail store, COSI also offers exciting firsthand science learning and fun for visitors of all ages. There are opportunities to ride the high wire cycle, play virtual volleyball, or experience the full-motion simulator theater.

Located in a firehouse that dates from around 1920, the Toledo Firefighters Museum preserves 150 years of fire fighting in the city. Thousands of items are on exhibit, including many of large pieces of vintage fire fighting equipment. The Toledo Botanical Garden cultivates herbs, roses, azalea, rhododendron, and wildflowers; artists' studios and galleries are maintained on the grounds.

Toledo boasts 144 parks covering 2,367 acres. The Metroparks of the Toledo Area preserves 8,000 acres of parks in Lucas County. The nine metroparks of the Toledo area preserve sand dunes, tall grass prairies, upland woody swamp forests, and oak savannahs. The parks offer elevated views of the Maumee River Valley. From May through October, the Miami and Erie Canal Restoration at Providence Metropark features a mule-drawn canal boat that carries passengers along a one and one-fourth mile stretch of the original canal, through a working canal lock, and past the Isaac Ludwig Mill, which features heritage crafts and water-powered milling demonstrations. Oak Openings Preserve protects threatened and endangered plant species, while Pearson Preserve protects one of the few remnants of the Great Black Swamp. The metroparks present many free nature and history programs and capture a sense of the natural beauty of the area at the time it was first settled.

Arts and Culture

The Toledo Museum of Art was founded in 1912 when Edward Libbey made a contribution of money and land to help initiate the museum's first stage of construction. Today the museum's permanent collection represents holdings from diverse cultures and periods, including ancient Egyptian tombs, a medieval cloister, a French chateau, glass, furniture, silver, tapestries, and paintings by world masters.

Without a doubt, the cultural highlight of Toledo's downtown revitalization efforts is the Valentine Theatre. When it originally opened in 1895, the Valentine was the finest theatrical venue between New York and Chicago. The Valentine Theatre is also home of the Toledo Symphony and the Toledo Ballet. The intimate and acoustically superior 901-seat, $28 million theater allows for excellent viewing of the stage and projected English titles when necessary.

The Toledo Symphony Orchestra presents a full season of concerts in Peristyle Hall at the Toledo Museum of Art. Stranahan Theater hosts performances by the Toledo Opera Association and touring Broadway shows. Two community theater groups, Toledo Repertoire Theatre and the Village Players, stage several productions annually, while Junior Theatre Guild stages four annual professional family-oriented shows. The Toledo Ballet Association presents local and guest performers, sometimes in collaboration with the opera and symphony. Both the University of Toledo and Bowling Green State University schedule plays and other cultural events, many featuring well-known performing artists and speakers.

Festivals and Holidays

Many festivals celebrate Toledo's history and its ethnic diversity. The festival season starts Memorial Day weekend with the Rock, Rhythm 'n Blues Festival in downtown Toledo. Through the summer, Rallies by the River offer music and refreshments at Promenade Park on Friday evenings. In June, the Old West End Festival opens restored Victorian homes to the public. The Crosby Festival of the Arts is held in late June at the Toledo Botanical Garden. The annual fireworks display takes place downtown on the river. Also in July, the Lucas County Fair is held at the fairgrounds. The Northwest Ohio Rib-Off takes place in August at Promenade Park.

Sports for the Spectator

The Toledo Mud Hens, the Triple A farm team for professional baseball's Detroit Tigers, compete in the International League with home games at Fifth Third Field. The Toledo Storm, East Coast Hockey League affiliates for the National Hockey League's Detroit Red Wings, entertain fans at Toledo Sports Arena. Raceway Park presents harness racing on a spiral-banked five-eighths mile track from March to December. Stock car racing is on view at Toledo Speedway. The University of Toledo Rockets and the Bowling Green State University Falcons field teams in Mid-American Conference sports.

Sports for the Participant

Toledo, the largest port on Lake Erie, offers some of the best fishing in the world. Walleye season runs from May to August, followed by perch in the fall; white and smallmouth bass are other popular catches. Ice fishing is available in January and February. Toledo maintains one of Ohio's best park systems, with more than 140 areas for sports and relaxation. The Lucas County Recreation Department provides facilities for swimming, tennis, track, handball, and softball. Toledo Area Metroparks offer boating, cycling, hiking, jogging, water and field sports, and fitness trails on over 6,600 acres. Toledo boasts some of the finest golf courses in the country. The Toledo Roadrunners Club has been holding the Glass City Marathon for more than 29 years; runners race along country roads and through neighboring communities and downtown Toledo. The race pays tribute to the memory of Sy Mah, a Toledo runner who once held the Guinness World Book record for running 524 marathons in his lifetime.

Shopping and Dining

Unique shopping opportunities in Toledo and environs include glass factory outlet stores, featuring all types and styles of glassware; flea markets; the Erie Street Market; and art galleries. Four major shopping centers are located in the area.

Among Toledo's hundreds of restaurants is Tony Packo's Cafe, celebrated by Corporal Klinger, a character on the television program ''M*A*S*H.'' Featuring an extensive Tiffany lamp collection, the restaurant serves a distinctive hot dog, Hungarian hamburgers, and a vegetable soup with Hungarian dumplings. The Docks on the Maumee River offer a variety of interesting restaurants; these include Gumbo's, Real Seafood Co., Zia's Italian, Tango's Mexican Cantina, and Cousino's Navy Bistro.

Visitor Information: The Greater Toledo Convention and Visitors Bureau, 401 Jefferson Avenue, Toledo, OH 43604; telephone (419)321-6404; toll-free (800)243-4667

Convention Facilities

The principal meeting and convention site in Toledo is the SeaGate Convention Centre, situated downtown one block from the Maumee River; connected to the convention center is the University of Toledo at SeaGate Center facility. When combined, the three-level complex features 75,000 square feet of multipurpose space, which can be divided into three separate halls, and 25 meeting rooms. Hotels and motels provide additional meeting space, accommodating groups ranging from 12 to 800 participants; more than 7,000 guest rooms are available in the greater Toledo area.

Convention Information: The Greater Toledo Convention and Visitors Bureau, 401 Jefferson Avenue, Toledo, OH 43604; telephone (419)321-6404; toll-free (800)243-4667. SeaGate Convention Center, 401 Jefferson Avenue, Toledo, OH 43604; telephone (419)255-3300

Transportation

Approaching the City

Toledo Express Airport is served by five commercial airlines providing direct and connecting flights to major cities throughout the United States. The airport also handles corporate and private aircraft. Additional general aviation services are available at Metcalf Field, operated by the Port Authority and located south of the city. Detroit Metropolitan Airport, less than an hour's drive from Toledo, is served by international as well as domestic flights.

A network of interstate, federal, and state highways facilitates access into and around the city and links Toledo to points in all sectors of the nation. Interstate 75 extends north through Michigan and south through Florida; the Ohio Turnpike (I-80 and I-90) connects Toledo with the East and West Coasts. Other highways include U.S. 24, 25, 20, and 23.

Amtrak provides east-west rail service to Toledo plus daily service from Detroit. Greyhound and Trailways buses travel into the city.

Traveling in the City

Streets in the city of Toledo are laid out on a grid pattern; downtown streets are tilted on a northwest-southeast axis to conform to the Maumee River. Toledo's bus-based public transportation system, TARTA, schedules routes throughout the city and suburban areas. Boat, train, trolley, and horse-drawn carriage tours are available.

Communications

Newspapers and Magazines

The major daily newspaper in Toledo is *The Blade. The Toledo Journal* is a weekly African American newspaper. Several neighborhood newspapers, as well as scholarly, academic, and religious journals, and special-interest tabloids and magazines are also published in the city, including the *Toledo Union Journal,* a bimonthly labor newspaper.

Television and Radio

Toledo is the broadcast media center for northwestern Ohio and parts of southeastern Michigan. Television viewers receive programs from six stations—one public and five commercial—based in the city. Twelve AM and FM radio stations schedule a complete range of music, news, information, and public interest features; one broadcasts performances by local cultural groups.

Media Information: The Toledo Blade Company, 541 N. Superior Street, Toledo, OH 43660; telephone 1-800-724-6000

Toledo Online

The Blade. Available www.toledoblade.com

City of Toledo Home Page. Available www.ci.toledo.oh.us/Homepage.html

Greater Toledo Convention and Visitors Bureau. Available www.toledocvb.com

Regional Growth Partnership. Available www.rgp.org

Toledo Area Chamber of Commerce. Available www.toledochamber.com

Toledo-Lucas County Public Library. Available www.library.toledo.oh.us

Selected Bibliography

Geha, Joseph, *Through and Through: Toledo Stories* (Saint Paul: Graywolf Press, 1990)

Jones, Marnie, *Holy Toledo: Religion and Politics in the Life of 'Golden Rule' Jones* (University Press of Kentucky, 1998)

Toledo Museum of Art et al. *Toledo Treasures: Selections from the Toledo Museum of Art* (Hudson Hills Press, 1995)

SOUTH DAKOTA

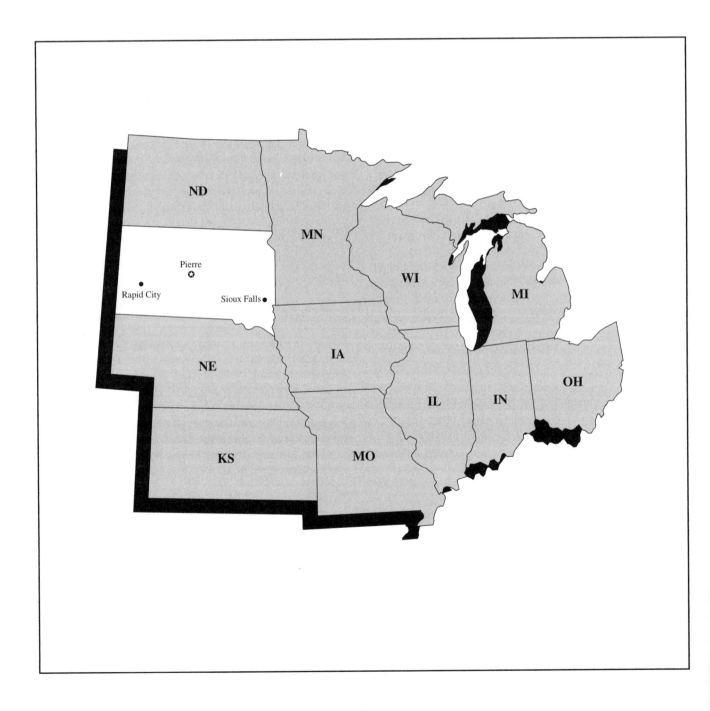

The State in Brief

Nickname: Coyote State; Mount Rushmore State
Motto: Under God the people rule

Flower: Pasque flower
Bird: Ringnecked pheasant

Area: 77,116 square miles (2000; U.S. rank: 17th)
Elevation: 966 feet to 7,242 feet above sea level
Climate: Continental, characterized by seasonal extremes of temperature as well as persistent winds, low humidity, and scant rainfall

Admitted to Union: November 2, 1889
Capital: Pierre
Head Official: Governor Mike Rounds (R) (until 2007)

Population
  1980: 691,000
  1990: 696,004
  2000: 754,844
  2004 estimate: 770,883
  Percent change, 1990–2000: 8.5%
  U.S. rank in 2004: 46th
  Percent of residents born in state: 68.1% (2000)
  Density: 9.9 people per square mile (2000)
  2002 FBI Crime Index Total: 17,342

Racial and Ethnic Characteristics (2000)
  White: 669,404

Black or African American: 4,685
American Indian and Alaska Native: 62,283
Asian: 4,378
Native Hawaiian and Pacific Islander: 261
Hispanic or Latino (may be of any race): 10,903
Other: 3,677

Age Characteristics (2000)
  Population under 5 years old: 51,069
  Population 5 to 19 years old: 176,412
  Percent of population 65 years and over: 14.3%
  Median age: 35.6 years (2000)

Vital Statistics
  Total number of births (2003): 11,254
  Total number of deaths (2003): 7,142 (infant deaths, 80)
  AIDS cases reported through 2003: 105

Economy
  Major industries: Finance, insurance, and real estate; agriculture; tourism; wholesale and retail trade; services
  Unemployment rate: 3.7% (April 2005)
  Per capita income: $28,299 (2003; U.S. rank: 38)
  Median household income: $39,829 (3-year average, 2001-2003)
  Percentage of persons below poverty level: 10.9% (3-year average, 2001-2003)
  Income tax rate: None
  Sales tax rate: 4.0%

Pierre

The City in Brief

Founded: 1880 (incorporated 1883)

Head Official: Mayor Dennis Eisnach (since 2002)

City Population
  1980: 11,973
  1990: 12,906
  2000: 13,267
  2003 estimate: 13,939
  Percent change, 1990–2000: 2.7%
  U.S. rank in 1990: 1,963rd
  U.S. rank in 2000: Not reported (State rank: 7th)

Hughes County Population

  1980: 14,244
  1990: 14,814
  2000: 16,416
  Percent change, 1990–2000: 9%

U.S. rank in 1990: Not reported
U.S. rank in 2000: Not reported

Area: 13.01 square miles (2000)
Elevation: 1,484 feet above sea level
Average Temperatures: Annual average 44° F
Average Annual Precipitation: 16.8 inches of rain; 40 inches of snow

Major Economic Sectors: Finance, insurance, real estate, trade
Unemployment Rate: 3.7% (March 2005, state of South Dakota)
Per Capita Income: $20,462 (1999)
2004 ACCRA Average House Price: Not reported
2004 ACCRA Cost of Living Index: Not reported

2002 FBI Crime Index Total: Not reported

Major Colleges and Universities: Capital University Center

Daily Newspaper: *Capital Journal*

Introduction

Pierre (pronounced peer) is the seat of Hughes County and the second smallest capital city in the United States. Pierre is located on the east bank of the Missouri River in central South Dakota. Pierre is the administrative center of South Dakota and a major distribution point for the area's agricultural concerns. Except for the winter months each year, when the legislature is in session, Pierre remains a sleepy small town with a beautifully restored state capitol building.

Geography and Climate

Pierre is located in the center of South Dakota on the Missouri River, 105 miles west of Huron, South Dakota, and 2 miles from the geographical center of the United States.

Seventy percent of the time, the skies over Pierre are clear and visibility is more than forty-five miles. Like the rest of the state, Pierre has cold winters, warm to hot summers, light moisture in the winter, and moderate moisture in the summer.

Area: 13.01 square miles (2000)

Elevation: 1,484 feet above sea level

Average Temperatures: January, 7.8° F; July, 77.1° F; annual average 44° F

Average Annual Precipitation: 16.8 inches of rain; 40 inches of snow

History

Early History and Exploration by Whites

The first white men to see the Pierre area were the two LaVerendrye brothers. They were the sons of the French explorer who first claimed the region for France in 1743, Pierre Gaultier de Varennes. At the site above present-day Fort Pierre, South Dakota, at one of the bluffs above the Missouri River, the brothers left an inscribed lead plate, which thereafter lay covered until found by a group of children in 1913. The plate is now on display at the South Dakota Cultural Heritage Center in Pierre.

In the mid-eighteenth century, the Sioux Indians, who had been pushed out of Minnesota by the Chippewa, arrived at the Missouri River. Their arrival challenged the claim of the Arikara, the native people who lived in palisaded forts around present-day Pierre. In 1794, the battle for control of central South Dakota finally came to an end when the Sioux drove the Arikara from the area.

In 1803, the United States completed the Louisiana Purchase from France, which included the area that would later be named South Dakota. In September 1804, Meriwether Lewis and William Clark anchored their canoe at the site of present-day Pierre. During that time, Lewis and Clark met with 50 or more chiefs and warriors, including the Teton Sioux. They named the nearby river Teton, in honor of the tribe, but it is now called the Bad River.

The meeting started out badly but negotiations soon improved when the explorers and the Indians shared a feast of buffalo meat, corn, pemmican, and a potato dish. After all present smoked a peace pipe, the explorers continued their journey upriver. During their visit to the Pierre area, Lewis and Clark raised the United States flag there.

City Is Established

When the explorers returned to St. Louis in 1806, they described the streams full of beaver and grasslands full of buffalo, and they noted the lack of trading forts in the Pierre area. Their report soon attracted people interested in exploiting the riches of the region.

In 1817, Joseph LaFramboise built a fur trading post across the river from where Pierre now sits. In 1831, a representative of the American Fur Company, Pierre Chouteau, Jr., built Fort Pierre to replace the old LaFramboise trading post. In 1855, the U.S. Army bought Fort Pierre for use as a military post, but abandoned it two years later in favor of nearby Fort Randall. Even after the army departed, people continued to live at the site of Fort Pierre.

In 1861, the Dakota Territory was formally established. Once the railroad line made South Dakota more accessible, settlers began to pour in, causing the Great Dakota Boom of 1878-1887. During that period, in 1880, the new town of Pierre began as a ferry landing at the site of a railroad terminal, across the river from Fort Pierre on what was formerly Arikara Indian tribal grounds. Rapid growth ceased when droughts struck throughout South Dakota, bringing the period of prosperity to a quick end. On February 22, 1889, South Dakota entered the union as the 40th state.

Pierre Chosen as Capital

The period from 1889 to 1897 saw development slowed by a depressed national economy, a time known in South Dakota as the Great Dakota Bust The number of new settlers greatly declined and some who had moved to Pierre and the rest of the state departed. But by the late 1890s, the state and the nation began to recover.

In 1890 Pierre was made the capitol of South Dakota after a drawn-out political battle between its supporters and supporters of the town of Mitchell, which was situated further east and nearer to the bulk of the state's population. In the end, however, Pierre won a statewide vote by a large margin.

In 1908 the cornerstone for the new capitol was set down, and the Capitol Building in Pierre opened its doors in 1910. As state government grew, the building expanded and separate office buildings were constructed. The original structure still stands today as part of the capitol complex.

Pierre in the Twentieth Century

During the 1930s, South Dakotans faced not only the Great Depression but severe problems caused by drought and dust. Many jobs were created for Pierre citizens by the Civilian Conservation Corps and other government agencies.

In 1944, the U.S. Congress passed legislation that resulted in the construction of the Oahe Dam near Pierre, which still serves the region. In 1949 a terrible blizzard struck the area, and the railroad line from Pierre to Rapid City, South Dakota, was blocked for weeks. A 1952 flood of the Missouri River caused severe damage to the town of Pierre but it was not destroyed, making clear to the citizens of Pierre the wisdom of the Oahe Dam building project. The project remains controversial among the Cheyenne River Sioux, who believe land was taken from them illegally for the dam construction.

The dam, the largest of six Missouri River dams and one of the largest dams in the world, has a generating capacity of 700,000 kilowatts. Along with the other dams on the Missouri River in South Dakota, it generates more than 2 million kilowatts of electricity. Other benefits of the dam include expanded recreation areas, irrigation, increased public water supplies, and fish and wildlife development.

During the wintertime, Pierre is abuzz with activity, as legislators from various parts of the state meet for three months to decide issues of state government. The rest of the year, Pierre is a quiet tourist town and farming center. In recent years, Pierre has invested millions of dollars in projects that benefit businesses and the community.

Historical Information: The South Dakota State Historical Society, 900 Governors Drive, Pierre, SD 57501; telephone (605)773-3458

Population Profile

Hughes County Residents
1980: 14,244
1990: 14,814
2000: 16,416

Percent change, 1990–2000: 9%
U.S. rank in 1990: Not reported
U.S. rank in 2000: Not reported

City Residents
1980: 11,973
1990: 12,906
2000: 13,876
2003 estimate: 13,939
Percent change, 1990–1999: 2.7%
U.S. rank in 1990: 1,963rd
U.S. rank in 2000: Not given (State rank: 7th)

Density: 9.9 people per square mile (2000, South Dakota state figure)

Racial and ethnic characteristics (2000)
White: 12,337
Black or African American: 28
American Indian or Alaska Native: 1,188
Asian: 64
Native Hawaiian and Pacific Islander: 3
Hispanic (may be of any race): 173
Other: 40

Percent of residents born in state: 74.8% (2000)

Age characteristics (2000)
Population under 5 years old: 909
Population 5 to 9 years old: 954
Population 10 to 14 years old: 1,208
Population 15 to 19 years old: 1,023
Population 20 to 24 years old: 583
Population 25 to 34 years old: 1,716
Population 34 to 44 years old: 2,248
Population 45 to 54 years old: 2,076
Population 55 to 59 years old: 699
Population 60 to 64 years old: 505
Population 65 to 74 years old: 913
Population 75 to 84 years old: 680
Population 85 years and over: 362
Median age: 37.6 years

Births (2003, Hughes County)
Total number: 213

Deaths (2003, Hughes County)
Total number: 150

Money income (1999)
Per capita income: $20,462
Median household income: $42,962

Number of households with income of . . .
less than $10,000: 431
$10,000 to $14,999: 301
$15,000 to $24,999: 745
$25,000 to $34,999: 835

$35,000 to $49,999: 1,070
$50,000 to $74,999: 1,276
$75,000 to $99,999: 522
$100,000 to $149,999: 249
$150,000 to $199,999: 96
$200,000 or more: 79

Percent of families below poverty level: 5.5% (37.9% of which were female householder families with related children under 5 years)

2002 FBI Crime Index Total: Not reported

Municipal Government

Pierre is the seat of Hughes County and the state capital of South Dakota. The city has a mayor-commission form of government. Its five commissioners, including the mayor, each serve three-year terms.

Head Official: Mayor Dennis Eisnach (since 2002; current term expires June 2005)

Total Number of City Employees: 123 (2005)

City Information: Mayor's Office, 222 E. Dakota, Pierre, SD 57501; telephone (605)773-7407

Economy

Major Industries and Commercial Activity

Pierre serves as the major trading center for central South Dakota. Its economy is supported by government, agriculture, and recreational activities tied in with the Missouri River reservoirs. Pierre's retail area has a radius of 100 miles and comprises approximately 100,000 people. Nearby lakes Oahe and Sharpe, both reservoirs on the Missouri River, make it possible for Pierre businesses to enjoy low electric rates and abundant water for production processes.

Pierre's economy depends largely on the state government, which has its operations in the city and is the largest local employer. The largest private employer is St. Mary's Hospital, with 485 employees. Small businesses and tourism are the remaining sources of jobs and income. Tourism was spurred by the lakes created by the Missouri Basin Development Plan.

Agriculture remains an important part of the economy of Hughes County, home to about 380 farms. The principal crops in the area are wheat, rye, oats, wild hay, flax, corn, barley, mint, soy beans, and alfalfa. Farmers raise cattle, chickens, hogs, buffalo, and horses, and produce eggs and milk.

Items and goods produced: assembly metal works, water conditioners, helicopters, dairy products, bottled beverages, wheat, corn, barley, processed furs

Incentive Programs—New and Existing Companies

Local programs—Development assistance and financing programs are offered by the Pierre Economic Development Corporation (PEDCO) and the Economic Development Administration. Free business consultation and a local revolving loan fund have helped dozens of new businesses get started and older ones to expand. PEDCO also works with business owners contemplating selling their businesses, and offers a free office and manufacturing space database to help in finding locations for businesses. E-commerce is well supported through seminars and other programs. The Small Business Administration Development Center helps with business plan development, market surveys, cash flow projections, and financing options.

State programs—The South Dakota MicroLOAN program offers funds of up to $20,000 to qualifying businesses for working capital, equipment, real estate, or other fixed costs. The USDA Business & Industry Guaranteed Loans make funds available for working capital, equipment, buildings, and debt refinancing.

Job training programs—The Work Force Development Program provides companies with the money needed to train new and existing employees. Job Service of South Dakota and Capital University Center provide training in leadership, customer service, and business. The Capital University Center offers short-term training and certificate programs to meet the needs of businesses in central South Dakota. The Right Turn, a career learning center, offers programs to help individuals train for employment; programs include GED preparation and testing, the Alternative High School program, medical transcription, clerical/computer skills, and other short term training programs, a basic skills brush-up class, career/education counseling, and job search assistance.

Development Projects

Building projects that have been completed since the beginning of the new century include dedication of the $3.9 million Aquatic Center, the opening of a 72,000-square-foot distribution center for Running Supply Inc., and a $2 million city golf course renovation. On top of the recent $11 million addition to St. Mary's Healthcare Center, another $12 million expansion is underway there, and will include a new area for transitional care, kidney dialysis and rehabilitation. A ribbon cutting was held for the expanded, four-lane Pierre-to-Interstate connection. A brand new soccer complex also held its first statewide tournaments.

Economic Development Information: Pierre Economic Development Corporation (PEDCO), Business Expansion Office; telephone (605)224-6610; toll-free (800)962-2034

Commercial Shipping

In addition to the Pierre Municipal Airport, the city is served by numerous trucking companies, and package service is provided by Federal Express, United Parcel Service, DHL, and Airborne Express. The Dakota, Minnesota & Eastern Railroad also serves the city.

Labor Force and Employment Outlook

Well-known for its superb labor force, the Greater Pierre area has a labor force of approximately 14,000 people, and they have among the highest educational level in the state. The area has a good balance of skilled, semi-skilled, technical, and entry-level workers.

According to the Pierre Area Chamber of Commerce, the total number of employed residents was 13,480 out of a labor force figure for the entire area of 14,055. The South Dakota Department of Labor affirms that the fastest growing industries in the state are health care and social assistance, followed by accommodation and food services, finance and insurance, and construction. Industries that are declining on a statewide basis include local government positions, manufacturing, agriculture, forestry, fishing and hunting.

The following is a summary of data regarding the Pierre labor force as of April 2005.

Size of civilian labor force: 13,430

Number of workers employed in . . .
   natural resources/mining/construction: 750
   manufacturing: 100
   trade, transportation, and utilities: 2,575
   information: 185
   financial activities: 680
   professional and business services: 535
   educational and health services: 1,360
   leisure and hospitality: 1,590
   other services: 725
   government: 4,930

Average hourly earnings of production workers employed in manufacturing: Not reported

Unemployment rate: 3.7% (March 2005, South Dakota)

Largest employers	*Number of employees*
South Dakota State Government	2,140
St. Mary's Healthcare Center	485
Pierre School District	350
Federal government	240
Dakotamart	200
Morris, Inc.	150
Pierre Indian Learning Center	150

Cost of Living

The following is a summary of data regarding several key cost of living factors for the Pierre area.

2004 ACCRA Average House Price: Not reported

2004 ACCRA Cost of Living Index: Not reported

State income tax rate: None

State sales tax rate: 4.0%

Local income tax rate: None

Local sales tax rate: 2.0% (plus 1.0% on hotel/motel, restaurant, and liquor establishments. Food and drugs are exempt)

Property tax rate: $3.71 per $1,000 of assessed valuation, city of Pierre, plus $23.53 per $1,000, Hughes County and schools (2001)

Economic Information: Pierre Area Chamber of Commerce, PO Box 548, Pierre, SD 57501; telephone (605)224-7361

Education and Research

Elementary and Secondary Schools

The Pierre School District has always held itself to high academic standards and the community has long been a source of support for its schools. Increased communication through the use of the Oahe Cable Channel by airing drama, chorus, band performances, and activities and lessons is a current focus of the district. Riggs High School hosts adult education classes, and is home to the Community Concert Series and the Short Grass Arts Council. Pierre Public Schools currently partners with the Capital University Center providing classrooms and technology. The Pierre Education Foundation provides financial support via grants for innovative Pierre educators. A cooperative spirit with the community of Pierre flourishes through several programs including: Right Turn, Advanced High, Character Education, Youth to Youth, Junior Achievement, Reading Buddies, the Mentorship Program for Students at Risk, Fine Arts and Athletic Booster Clubs, and Native American Liaison.

The following is a summary of data regarding the Pierre public school system as of the 2004–2005 school year.

Total enrollment: 2,624

Number of facilities
    elementary schools: 4
    junior high/middle schools: 1
    senior high schools: 1

Student/teacher ratio: elementary, 20.7:1, junior high, 17.2:1, senior high, 20:1

Teacher salaries
    average: $32,414 (2002–2003)

Funding per pupil: $5,607 (2002–2003)

Pierre also has a Catholic elementary school, an Indian Learning Center, and an alternative education program operated in conjunction with The Right Turn, a career learning center.

Public Schools Information: Pierre Public Schools, 302 E. Dakota, Pierre, SD 57501; telephone (605)773-7300

Colleges and Universities

While Pierre is not the site of any colleges or universities, it does boast the Capital University Center. This non-profit institution helps students earn university degrees through Northern State University, South Dakota State University, the University of South Dakota, and South Dakota School of Mines & Technology. The center offers courses that enable students to obtain associate degrees in business, and master's degrees in business administration, industrial management, and technology management.

Libraries and Research Centers

Rawlins Municipal Library, which celebrated 100 years in 2003, contains nearly 50,000 books and has special collections on the history of South Dakota. The South Dakota State Library houses more than 180,000 volumes, with special collections on Native American and South Dakota history.

Other libraries in the city include those of the South Dakota State Historical Society, the South Dakota Supreme Court, St. Mary's Healthcare Center, the South Dakota Braille & Talking Book Library, and the South Dakota Department of Game, Fish & Parks Wildlife Division Library.

Public Library Information: Rawlins Municipal Library, 1000 E. Church St., Pierre, SD 57501; telephone (605)773-7421; fax (605)773-7423

Health Care

Pierre is served by St. Mary's Healthcare Center, an 86-bed acute care facility. The center's north building facility includes a laboratory, expanded radiology lab, and an obstetrics unit with home-like labor, delivery, and recovery rooms. Services at St. Mary's include medical, surgical, pediatrics, obstetrics, ambulatory care, home health care, and Countryside Hospice, as well as a variety of specialties.

Health Care Information: St Mary's Health Care Center, 801 E Sioux Ave, Pierre, SD 57501; telephone (605)224-3100

Recreation

Sightseeing

A must-see for Pierre visitors is the beautiful 1910 state capitol, one of the most fully restored in the nation. Its rotunda reaches 96 feet and features a brightly colored Victorian glass top. Pillars flank the marble staircase, and the terrazzo tile floor includes 66 blue tiles, each representing one of the artisans who worked on laying it by hand. Finishing touches are provided by marble water fountains and brass door fixtures, art murals and sculptures. Out on the capitol grounds is a fountain fed by an artesian well with a natural gas content so high it can be lit. The glowing fountain serves as a memorial to war veterans.

At the Cultural Heritage Center, South Dakota history is brought to life through museum exhibits and publications, educational programming and research services. High-tech exhibits feature early Native American cultures, an early history of white settlement, the river boat era, and the railroad period. Among the Native American exhibits are a teepee visitors can walk through, a rare Sioux horse effigy, and a full headdress. The Verendrye Museum in Fort Pierre, across the river from the city, provides an eclectic display of exhibits and items of historical interest.

The Discovery Center and Aquarium is a hands-on display of 50 self-guided science activities in the areas of sound, vision, light, electricity, and motion. Its Aquatic Education wing has three aquariums featuring Missouri River fish. The planetarium provides a look at the skies overhead.

The South Dakota National Guard Museum displays a wide range of military weapons and other items such as an A-7D jet fighter plane, a Sherman tank and several artillery pieces, military uniforms, small arms, and helicopter and jet engines.

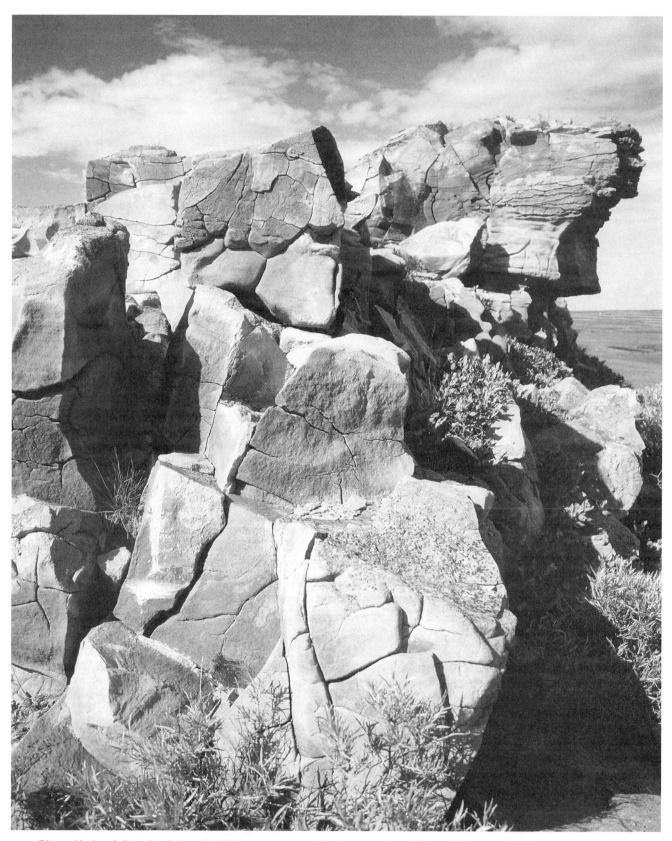

Pierre National Grasslands is a 116,000-acre preserve allowing camping, hiking, fishing, and other outdoor activities.

Six miles north of Pierre, tours of the Oahe Dam are available. The dam is the second largest rolled-earth dam in the world. A visit to the Oahe Dam and Powerhouse and Oahe Visitor Center, dedicated in 1962, tells the story of the dam and has displays on such topics as the Lewis and Clark Expedition and the dam itself. On site is the Oahe Chapel, removed from its original site at the old Arikara Indian Village, which was flooded when the dam was built.

Arts and Culture

Pierre Players, the longest running community theater group in South Dakota, offers productions throughout the year. The Pierre Concert Series presents a variety of musical and dance productions by professional touring troupes.

Festivals and Holidays

September activities in Pierre center on statewide softball tournaments held in the city and Goosefest, an outdoor festival that features a South Dakota Arts Showcase, craft and Native American pottery and food booths, and Lewis and Clark reenactments. October brings the Native American Day festival and the Annual Governor's Hunt. The holidays are heralded by the Pierre Players' Christmas Pageant and the Capitol Christmas Tree display. June's many events include softball tournaments, band concerts, and concerts in the parks. July is highlighted by the Independence Day celebration, including a rodeo and parade, baseball and softball tournaments, concerts, summer theater, and the governor's Cup Walleye Tournament. August is enlivened by the 4-H Rodeo and the three-day Riverfest Festival, which features music; water ski, car, and air shows; water events; and a kids' carnival.

Sports for the Spectator

Pierre's Expo Center features indoor hockey and skating events. In nearby Fort Pierre, pari-mutuel horse racing is offered in the springtime; rodeos and stock shows are also held there.

Sports for the Participant

Farm Island and the La Framboise Island offer such activities as biking, hiking, camping, and wildlife observation. Pierre's city parks system boasts 11 parks, 11 tennis courts, a beach volleyball court, a Frisbee course, basketball courts, horseshoe pits, two swimming beaches, indoor and outdoor swimming pools, a band concert shell, an assortment of playground equipment, fishing piers, seven little league baseball fields, baseball diamond, pony league field, eight softball fields, eight soccer fields, an outdoor skate park, and 3.5 miles of bike path. Griffin Park, the major park area, is located in a riverside setting and has a swimming pool and newly renovated camping facilities.

Five miles upstream from Pierre, Lake Oahe's 2,250-mile shoreline offers swimming, boating, water skiing, scuba diving, snorkeling, camping and picnicking. Anglers come to Lake Oahe in search of a variety of sport fish, including walleye, northern pike, Chinook salmon, channel catfish, small mouth bass, white bass, sauger, bluegill, and crappies. Public hunting grounds offer excellent waterfowl and upland game hunting, featuring Canada geese, mallards, pheasants, and grouse. Whitetail and mule deer and antelope also abound, offering challenges to the big game hunter. Knowledgeable guides and game lodges are available to provide enjoyable and successful hunting experiences.

Shopping and Dining

The city's main shopping center is the 34-store Pierre Mall, which is anchored by JCPenney, Sears, and Kmart. There is also a Wal-Mart in the city.

Pierre's variety of restaurants primarily offer American cuisine and include Smokees BBQ, Classy's, Outpost Lodge, and Jake's Good Times Place.

Visitor Information: Pierre Convention & Visitors Bureau, 800 West Dakota Ave., Pierre, SD 57501; telephone (605)224-7361

Convention Facilities

Pierre is the meeting headquarters for many South Dakota organizations. The King's Inn Hotel and Conference Center, located downtown, provides meeting and banquet space for up to 750 people. The Rivercenter Best Western Ramkota Convention Center has 16 different rooms that can accommodate groups of 15 to 15,000. Guests are served by a dozen hotels and motels throughout Pierre.

Convention Information: Pierre Convention & Visitors Bureau, 800 West Dakota Ave., Pierre, SD 57501;telephone (605)224-7361

Transportation

Approaching the City

The Pierre Regional Airport, located three miles from central Pierre, includes offices, and boarding and baggage terminals. It is served by Mesaba (a Northwest Airlink) and Great Lakes Aviation. Greyhound and Jack Rabbit offer bus transportation.

Traveling in the City

U.S. highway 148 runs north and south through Pierre, connecting State Highway 34 that runs east and west and U.S. Highway 14/83 that extends eastward to Pierre from Ft. Pierre and turns north, then northeast as it runs through the city of Pierre. Other main streets are Missouri, Dakota, and Sioux avenues, which run east and west, and Capitol, Nicolett, and Broadway avenues, which surround the State Capitol Building.

Communications

Newspapers and Magazines

The *Capital Journal* is Pierre's daily paper; *The Times* appears weekly, and there are two weekly trade papers: *The Farmer & Rancher Exchange* and the *Reminder Plus.* Local magazines include *Dakota Outdoors* and the *South Dakota High Liner.* The journal *South Dakota History* covers the history of the Northern Great Plains.

Television and Radio

Pierre is served by some 20 radio station. There are two local television channels.

Media Information: *The Capital Journal,* 333 W. Dakota, PO Box 669, Pierre, SD 57501-0669, telephone (605)224-7301

Pierre Online

Pierre Area Chamber of Commerce. Available www.pierre .org

Pierre *Capitol Journal.* Available www.capjournal.com

Pierre Convention & Visitors Bureau (includes fishing report and hunting information). Available www.pierre chamber.com

Pierre School District. Available pierre.k12.sd.us

Rawlins Municipal Library. Available rpllib.sdln.net

Selected Bibliography

Hoover, Herbert T., and Larry J. Zimmerman, *South Dakota Leaders: From Pierre Choteau, Jr. to Oscar Howe* (Vermillion, SD: University of South Dakota Press: 1989)

Jensen, Delwin, *Fort Pierre-Deadwood Trail* (Pierre, SD: State Publishing Company, 1989)

Rapid City

The City in Brief

Founded: 1876 (incorporated 1882)

Head Official: Mayor Jim Shaw (R) (since 1999)

City Population
   1980: 46,492
   1990: 54,523
   2000: 59,607
   2003 estimate: 60,876
   Percent change, 1990–2000: 8.1%
   U.S. rank in 1990: 445th
   U.S. rank in 2000: 472nd

Metropolitan Area Population
   1980: 70,361
   1990: 81,343
   2000: 88,565
   Percent change, 1990–2000: 8.9%
   U.S. rank in 1980: 276th

U.S. rank in 1990: Not reported
U.S. rank in 2000: 327th

Area: 45 square miles (2000)
Elevation: 3,200 feet above sea level
Average Annual Temperature: 46.6° F
Average Annual Precipitation: 16.7 inches of rain; 39.1 inches of snow

Major Economic Sectors: Agriculture, wholesale and retail trade, services, government
Unemployment Rate: 4.0% (February 2005)
Per Capita Income: $19,445 (1999)
2004 ACCRA Average House Price: Not reported
2004 ACCRA Cost of Living Index: Not reported

2002 FBI Crime Index Total: 2,930

Major Colleges and Universities: South Dakota School of Mines and Technology, Western Dakota Technical Institute, National American University

Daily Newspaper: *Rapid City Journal*

Introduction

Rapid City, the seat of Pennington County, is a diverse and thriving small Midwestern city that refers to itself as "The Star of the West." Tourists are drawn to the area, which was celebrated in the 1990 award-winning film *Dances With Wolves,* to see the presidents' busts carved into Mount Rushmore and to visit the Black Hills. The city enjoys a thriving economy based on the farmers who have been raising beans, wheat, and alfalfa since the turn of the last century. A regional center for retail shopping and medical facilities, the city is home to the South Dakota School of Mines and Technology as well as Ellsworth Air Force Base. Seven percent of Rapid City's population is made up of Native Americans whose arts and crafts abound in the city's shops. Locals like to say that the city has the quality of life of a small town with the business and cultural benefits of a city.

Geography and Climate

Rapid City, the natural eastern gateway to the great growing empire known as the West River Region, is surrounded by contrasting land forms. The forested Black Hills rise immediately west of the city, while the other three edges of the city look out on the prairie. Protected by the 6,000- to 7,000-foot peaks of the Black Hills, Rapid City enjoys an enviable climate, free of the icy blizzards and scorching summers typical of much of the rest of the Dakotas. Summers are warm but dry and autumn is noted for its delightful "Indian summer" weather. Mild, sunny days are common throughout the winter and occasional "chinook" or warm winds frequently follow a stint of snowy weather. Snowfall is normally light with the greatest monthly average less than eight inches. Spring is characterized by wide variations in temperature and occasionally some wet snowfall. Low humidity levels, infrequent precipitation, and northwesterly winds prevail in the city.

Area: 45 square miles (2000)

Elevation: 3,200 feet above sea level

Average Temperatures: January, 21.9° F; July, 72.6° F; annual average, 46.6° F

Average Annual Precipitation: 16.7 inches of rain; 39.1 inches of snow

History

New City Becomes Regional Trade Center

The discovery of gold in 1874 brought an influx of settlers into the Black Hills region of South Dakota. Rapid City was founded in 1876 by a group of disappointed miners, who promoted their new city as the "Gateway to the Black Hills." John Brennan and Samuel Scott, with a small group of men, laid out the site of the present Rapid City, which was named for the spring-fed Rapid Creek that flows through it. A square mile was measured off and the six blocks in the center were designated as a business section. Committees were appointed to bring in prospective merchants and their families to locate in the new settlement. Although it began as a hay camp, the city soon began selling supplies to miners and pioneers. By 1900 Rapid City had survived a boom and bust and was establishing itself as an important regional trade center.

Tourism and the Military Spur Economy

The invention of the automobile brought tourists to the Black Hills. Gutzon Borglum, the famous sculptor, began work on Mount Rushmore in 1927, and his son, Lincoln Borglum continued the carving of the presidents' faces in rock following his father's death. The massive sculpture was completed in 1938. Although tourism sustained the city throughout the Great Depression of the 1930s, the gas rationing of World War II had a devastating effect on the tourist industry in the town.

The city benefited greatly from the opening of Ellsworth Air Force Base, an Army Air Corps base. As a result, the population of the area nearly doubled between 1940 and 1948, from almost 14,000 to nearly 27,000 people. Military families and civilian personnel soon took every available living space in town, and mobile parks proliferated. Rapid City businesses profited from the military payroll.

Rapid City Since Mid-Century

In 1949 city officials envisioned the city as a retail and wholesale trade center for the region and designed a plan for growth that focused on a civic center, more downtown parking places, new schools, and paved streets. A construction boom continued into the 1950s. Growth slowed in the 1960s, but the worst natural disaster in Rapid City's history led to another building boom a decade later. On June 9, 1972, heavy rains caused massive flooding of the Rapid Creek. More than 200 people lost their lives and more than $100 million in property was destroyed.

The devastation of the flood and the outpouring of private donations and millions of dollars in federal aid led to the completion of one big part of the 1949 plan—clearing the area along the Rapid Creek and making it a public park. New homes and businesses were constructed to replace those that had been destroyed. Rushmore Plaza Civic Center and a new Central High School were built in part of the area that had been cleared. In 1978, Rushmore Mall was built, adding to the city's position as a retail shopping center.

In recent times, Rapid City has been highly rated for its manufacturing climate. A hardworking labor force and a governmental structure deeply rooted in the concept of being a partner in the success of its business community remain major assets. The city offers an extraordinary quality of life with abundant recreational activities, culture, and short workplace commutes. Recent city development efforts show a continued vision for improvement and growth in the area.

Population Profile

Metropolitan Area Residents
1980: 70,361
1990: 81,343
2000: 88,565
Percent change, 1990–2000: 8.9%
U.S. rank in 1980: 276th
U.S. rank in 1990: Not reported
U.S. rank in 2000: 222nd

City Residents
1980: 46,492
1990: 54,523
2000: 59,607
2003: 60,876
Percent change, 1990–2000: 8.1%
U.S. rank in 1990: 445th
U.S. rank in 2000: 472nd

Density: 1,336.7 people per square mile (2000)

Racial and ethnic characteristics (2000)
White: 50,266
Black or African American: 579
American Indian and Alaska Native: 6,046
Asian: 594
Native Hawaiian and Pacific Islander: 35
Hispanic (may be of any race): 1,650
Other: 434

Percent of residents born in state: 58% (2000)

Age characteristics (2000)
Population under 5 years old: 4,169
Population 5 to 9 years old: 3,973
Population 10 to 14 years old: 4,309

Population 15 to 19 years old: 4,654
Population 22 to 24 years old: 5,009
Population 25 to 34 years old: 7,866
Population 35 to 44 years old: 9,259
Population 45 to 54 years old: 7,768
Population 55 to 59 years old: 2,533
Population 60 to 64 years old: 2,179
Population 65 to 74 years old: 4,017
Population 75 to 84 years old: 2,781
Population 85 years and older: 1090
Median age: 34.8 years

Births (2003, Pennington County)
Total number: 1,424

Deaths (2003, Pennington County)
Total number: 810 (of which, 5 were infants under the age of 1 year)

Money income (1999)
Per capita income: $19,445
Median household income: $35,978
Total households: 23,969

Number of households with income of . . .
less than $10,000: 2,291
$10,000 to $14,999: 1,625
$15,000 to $24,999: 4,080
$25,000 to $34,999: 3,765
$35,000 to $49,999: 4,537
$50,000 to $74,999: 4,263
$75,000 to $99,999: 1,782
$100,000 to $149,999: 1,057
$150,000 to $199,999: 266
$200,000 or more: 366

Percent of families below poverty level: 9.4% (53% of which were female householder families with related children under 5 years)

2002 FBI Crime Index Total: 2,930

Municipal Government

Rapid City has a mayor-council form of government with an elected, full-time mayor and two part-time council members from each of the city's five wards, who are elected to staggered two-year terms. All positions are non-partisan.

Head Official: Mayor Jim Shaw (R) (since 1999; current term expires May 2007)

Total Number of City Employees: 675 (2005)

City Information: City of Rapid City, 300 Sixth Street, Rapid City, SD 57701; telephone (605)394-4136

Economy

Major Industries and Commercial Activity

Agriculture, tourism, mining, logging, professional services/
retail, and Ellsworth Air Force Base are the major factors in
Rapid City's economy. The area is also known for the
manufacture of high-value, low-bulk items that can be
swiftly shipped to market or assembly centers in other parts
of the nation.

Agriculture is a major industry in South Dakota, and Rapid
City is the regional trade center for farm-ranch activity in the
southwest part of the state and neighboring counties in Montana, Wyoming, and Nebraska. Cattle and sheep production
dominate the agricultural scene, as well as processing and
packing of meat and meat byproducts, but the cultivation of
small grains is also important. Services offered to area
farmers and ranchers include selling of new and used farm
equipment, spare parts and repairs, and flour milling.

The health care sector is strong, employing more than 8,000
people in the Black Hills region at major health care organizations such as Rapid City Regional Hospital. Other important industrial and employment institutions include several
large construction companies, rock quarries, steel fabrication firms, and trucking firms. Several light industries and
services located in the city include manufacturing of computer parts, printing, Native American crafts, and headquarters for insurance companies and other businesses. Regional
or headquarters facilities of many state and federal offices
also operate in the city.

Centrally located in the beautiful Black Hills region, Rapid
City benefits from a large annual tourist trade. Within half a
day's drive of Rapid City are five of the country's most
famous national park areas: Mount Rushmore National Memorial, Devil's Tower National Monument, Badlands National Park, Jewel Cave National Monument, and Wind Cave
National Park. The area further boasts of a variety of restaurants, several large annual events and attractions, more than
4,400 hotel/motel rooms and many modern campgrounds.

Each year the multimillion-dollar payroll for workers at
Ellsworth Air Force Base, the largest employer in the state,
boosts the local economy. Ellsworth was slated for closure
as part of a proposal in mid-2005 to close 33 large bases and
150 smaller ones, which would have a devastating effect on
the Rapid City economy; an Air Force study in 2004 estimated the base's economic impact on the state at $278
million annually.

Items and goods produced: computer components, jewelry,
   cement, processed foods, steel products, printing, wood
   products

Incentive Programs—New and Existing Companies

The city of Rapid City, along with Pennington County and
the Governor's Office of Economic Development, offers a
number of financial incentives to aid industry looking to
establish operations in the area.

Local programs—Black Hills Vision is a regional economic
development initiative that encourages tech-based employment and seeks to develop a high-tech corridor in the Rapid
City area. A small business incubator, which is to be called
The Black Hills Business Development Center, is a cornerstone of the Black Hills Vision; it will offer technical
support and collaboration opportunities for emerging businesses. Projected to open in late 2005, the center will be
located on the South Dakota School of Mines & Technology
Campus. The Rapid City Economic Development Partnership oversees the incubator jointly with West River Foundation. Rapid City rebates the tax increment created by
investments in real property for up to 15 years. The Rapid
City Economic Development Loan Fund (dba Rapid Fund)
is a low-interest loan program that is focused on the development of primary jobs in the manufacturing sector. A portfo-
lio of 14 different loans are available for business expansion,
relocation, or start-up. Pennington County has a real estate
tax incentive offered to new industrial or commercial structures, or new non-residential agricultural structures.

State programs—The South Dakota REDI Fund lends
money at three percent interest to companies creating new
jobs in the state. Designed and administered by a board of 13
business leaders, the program is known to be efficient,
flexible, and responsible. The money can be used for almost
any capital purchase or operating financing for which a
company qualifies under standard banking guidelines. The
state offers a variety of other loans, subfunds and training
assistance. Federal Small Business Administration (SBA)
participation loans and SBA Direct loans are also available.

Job training programs—Career counseling and customized
job training are offered at the Career Learning Center. The
South Dakota Workforce Development Program extends
training opportunities in conjunction with approved educational institutions; new employee skills, retraining, and ad-
vancement/promotion assistance is offered.

Development Projects

In 1992, gathering energy and tax dollars after redevelopment efforts following the 1972 flood, Rapid City formed
Vision 2012, a program of long-term planning for the community. More than $65 million has been spent from the fund
on improvements already; projects include the Meadow-
brook Golf Course, Canyon Lake Restoration, the Journey
Museum, and the Rapid City Boys Club.

In April 2005, 49 new projects were recommended for
funding by the city council; projects include a variety of

civic improvement, municipal infrastructure and economic development projects. Among the projects is the $10.8 million Dahl Arts Center building which is to include a 457-seat theater, 3 multi-purpose spaces, 3 gallery spaces, 3 art education classrooms, a gift shop, kitchen, administration wing, and art reference library; groundbreaking for the center is scheduled in September 2005. Other important proposed projects include a Children's Care Rehab and Development Center, which would service youth on an outpatient basis; Rushmore Civic Plaza Addition, a $14.5 million project that would add seating for sporting events; and an emergency Response Training Center. The Rapid City Regional Airport is undergoing facilities renovations and repairs in 2004/2005.

Economic Development Information: Rapid City Area Economic Development Partnership, 444 Mt. Rushmore Road N., PO Box 747, Rapid City, SD 57701; telephone (605)343-1880; toll free (800)956-0377; fax (605)343-1916; email info@rapiddevelopment.com

Commercial Shipping

Rapid City is served by the Dakota, Minnesota, & Eastern Railroad and offers piggyback service with daily switching service. Nearly 30 motor freight carriers, as well as terminals, are located in Rapid City. Parcel service is provided by United Parcel Service.

Labor Force and Employment Outlook

Rapid City boasts of a young and eager workforce that is well educated. Ninety-six percent of residents have a high school diploma; 20 percent have a bachelors degree.

The following is a summary of data regarding the Rapid City metropolitan area labor force, 2004 annual averages.

Size of non-agricultural labor force: 58,800

Number of workers employed in . . .
  mining and construction: 4,600
  manufacturing: 3,900
  trades, transportation and utilities: 12,400
  information: 1,100
  financial activities: 3,200
  professional and business services: 4,100
  educational and health services: 9,000
  leisure and hospitality: 8,000
  other services: 2,700
  government: 9,700

Average hourly earnings of production workers employed in manufacturing: $13.36

Unemployment rate: 4% (February 2005)

Largest employers	*Number of employees*
Ellsworth Air Force Base	3,943
Rapid City Regional Hospital	3,000
Rapid City School District	1,593
Federal Government	1,435
City of Rapid City (includes seasonal workers)	1,375
State of South Dakota	1,049
Walmart/Sams Club	965

Cost of Living

Low utility costs and no personal income taxes are factors that help Rapid City offer a reasonable cost of living. The 2003 average sales price for a single family home was $136,707; the average rental for a two-bedroom apartment was $639.

The following is a summary of data regarding several key cost of living factors in the Rapid City area.

2004 ACCRA Average House Price: Not reported

2004 ACCRA Cost of Living Index: Not reported

State income tax rate: None

State sales tax rate: 4.0%

Local income tax rate: None

Local sales tax rate: 2.0%

Property tax rate: $30.1323 per $1,000; assessed at 85 percent (2000)

Economic Information: Rapid City Area Economic Development Partnership, 444 Mt. Rushmore Road N., PO Box 747, Rapid City, SD 57701; telephone (605)343-1880; toll free (800)956-0377; fax (605)343-1916; email info @rapiddevelopment.com

Education and Research

Elementary and Secondary Schools

The Rapid City School District, second largest in the state, covers 419 square miles. The district offers services to special education and academically gifted children as well as technology staff development and Indian education programs. Serving Ellsworth Air Force Base and surrounding area, the Douglas School District has 2,400 students, one preschool, three elementary schools, one middle school, and one high school.

The following is a summary of data regarding Rapid City's public schools as of the 2003–2004 school year.

Total enrollment: 12,914

Number of facilities
   elementary schools: 16
   middle schools: 5
   high schools: 3

Student/teacher ratio: 16.5:1

Teacher salaries
   minimum: $25,006
   maximum: $53,601

Funding per pupil: $5,648 (2001-2002)

Rapid City also has several private and parochial schools.

Colleges and Universities

South Dakota School of Mines and Technology (SDSM&T) has long been recognized as one of the best science and engineering colleges in the county. SDSM&T, which enrolls about 2,400 students, is known for its technological expertise and innovation, as well as for its world-famous Museum of Geology. The school offers 16 bachelors, 12 masters, 3 doctoral and several co-curricular degrees. Western Dakota Technical Institute provides diplomas and Associate in Applied Science degrees in 25 career fields to more than 4,000 students; fields of study include business and construction trades, agricultural, electronics, human services, computer aided drafting, and mechanical career fields. Western Dakota Tech works closely with the local business community to provide student training programs. National American University offers a wide variety of bachelor and associate degrees in business.

Libraries and Research Centers

The Rapid City Public Library, with more than 147,000 volumes, has strong collections in business and audio-visual materials, and operates one bookmobile, a homebound service and homework help. Its South Dakota collection includes many items for historical research. The library subscribes to several hundred magazines and newspapers and houses the collection of the Rapid City Society for Genealogical Research Inc. South Dakota School of Mines and Technology (SDSM&T), National American University, and Rapid City Regional Hospital also have libraries.

SDSM&T has been involved in providing research services for government, industry, and business for at least a century, with a primary emphasis on energy, the environment, and mineral development. They are also a regional Patent and Trademark Depository and house a 15-seat computer lab.

Public Library Information: Rapid City Public Library, 610 Quincy Street, Rapid City, SD 57701; telephone (605)394-4171; fax (605)394-6626

Health Care

Rapid City Regional Hospital provides comprehensive acute care services to South Dakota and portions of North Dakota, Nebraska, Wyoming, and Montana. The hospital is the main health care center between Minneapolis and Denver with 42 specialties including radiation, cardiology, and emerging medicine. Employing more than 3,000 people, the hospital system offers care at Black Hills Rehabilitation Hospital, the John T. Vucurevich Cancer Care Center and the Regional West Center for Behavioral Health as well as clinics and out-patient care.

The Black Hills Regional Eye Institute is a not-for-profit corporation dedicated to providing the most modern and complex eye care for children and adults of the region. More than 2,000 eye surgeries are performed each year in one of the four surgical rooms at the Eye Surgery Center. The Institute physicians and staff travel to 12 satellite clinics throughout the 5-state area served to provide treatment of eye problems within the local communities.

Health care is also available at Rapid City Community Health Center, Sioux San Hospital, and the Black Hills Surgery Center.

Recreation

Sightseeing

The Black Hills Visitor Information Center has maps and brochures and is a good first stop on a trip to Rapid City. Visitors may wish to begin with a trip to Storybook Island, an 11-acre park with free attractions for youngsters. It is filled with dozens of larger-than-life sets that depict children's nursery rhymes and tales, including Yogi Bear's picnic basket and the Crooked Man's house. The unique Stavkirk Chapel, an exact replica of the famous 830-year-old Borgund Church in Norway, features intricate woodcarvings, strange dragon heads, and ingenious pegged construction. Fossil skeletons of giant, prehistoric marine reptiles command attention at the Museum of Geology at the South Dakota Schools of Mines and Technology. The museum also houses the world's finest exhibits of Badlands fossils and an extensive collection of rare and beautiful rocks, gems, and minerals from the Black

The Indian Museum of North America celebrates North American Indian life and history, operating as part of the Crazy Horse Memorial in Rapid City.

Hills; more than 250,000 vertebrate fossils and 6,000 minerals are housed at the museum. Seven life-size concrete replicas of monstrous prehistoric reptiles are located in the outdoor park-like setting at Dinosaur Park.

With four different major collections, the Journey Museum tells the story of the Great Plains. Displays of rock formations, fossilized remains and documentation of significant scientific discoveries are found at The Museum of Geology. Collections from thousands of archeological sites can be examined at the Archeological Research Center. The Black Hills region's frontier past can be relived at the Minnilusa Pioneer Museum, which focuses on historic events and people. The Sioux Indian Museum celebrates Native Americans of the present and past through their artistry and achievements.

Discovered in 1900, Jewel Cave, a national monument, contains more than 132 miles of surveyed passageways in an underground labyrinth that offers rare and unusual calcite crystal formations. Wind Cave, the first cave designated as part of the National Parks system, provides more than 116 miles of mapped corridors and halls, making it the fifth-longest cave in the world. With its jagged cliffs, deep canyons, flat-topped buttes, and rich fossils, Badlands National Park is one of the most stunning geological displays on earth. Crazy Horse Memorial, a still-in-progress mountain carving of the great Indian hero, is open for visitors. Reptile Gardens, founded in 1937, gives spectators the opportunity to observe colorful birds and reptiles surrounded by thousands of orchids and other tropical and desert plants in its Skydome. The gardens also feature miniature horses and donkeys; the Bird Program featuring hawks, owls, eagles, parrots, and other birds; an alligator and crocodile show; Bewitched Village featuring trained animals; and the Snake Program. Bear Country U.S.A., a 250-acre drive-through wildlife park, features the world's largest collection of black bears plus a large and varied collection of North American wildlife including grizzly bears, timber wolves, mountain lions, buffalo, moose, elk, and more. Visitors are treated to the recently expanded visitor center, which allows visitors to step out of their vehicles and see young and smaller animals up close. The Air and Space Museum at the entrance of Ellsworth Air Force Base features 25 vintage aircraft. Several tour companies offer guided tours to some of the memorable sites featured in the award-winning film *Dances With Wolves.*

Arts and Culture

Dahl Fine Arts Center features exhibits of paintings and sculptures by local artists, especially local Native American artists. A 180-foot-long oil-on-canvas mural depicts 200 years of American History. The museum, which will move into a new facility in 2007, offers tours and family events. The Black Hills Community Theatre, Inc., the city's only community theater, is based in the Dahl Center's 170-seat auditorium. The nearby Black Hills Playhouse at Custer State Park is a professional theater and training center. Two puppet theaters entertain the community. Black Hills Dance Theatre, Inc. engages a variety of regionally and nationally recognized dance companies. The Black Hills Symphony Orchestra's 80 members offer educational outreach programs in the community as well as perform a variety of concerts. Other community arts attractions include the Blacks Hills Chamber Music Society, Rapid City Municipal band, the Dakota Voices, and other musical groups.

Festivals and Holidays

More than 25 years of music and family entertainment is the focus of The Black Hills Bluegrass Music Festival, which is held in June. July's Black Hills Heritage celebrates the cultural heritage of the Black Hills. The Sturgis Motorcycle Rally in nearby Sturgis attracts more than 500,000 visitors each August for concerts, food, vendors and demo and scenic motorcycle rides. The Central States Fair, a week-long extravaganza that entertains crowds from all over the region, also occurs in August. September brings fall color to the hills and a treat to the tastebuds at the nearby Taste of Spearfish celebration. October's Buffalo Roundup, where the visitor is invited to 'feel the thunder' of 1,500 herded buffalo, is held annually at nearby Custer State Park. Rodeo fun is the attraction at January's Black Hills Stock Show and Rodeo. In addition, Indian pow wows are scheduled at various times throughout the state.

Sports for the Spectator

The Rushmore Plaza Civic Center Arena plays host to the Indoor Football League's Black Hills Red Dogs. Rapid City's Annual Black Hills Stock Show & Rodeo in late January-early February, draws large crowds.

Sports for the Participant

Rapid City has 26 parks, playgrounds and special outdoor public facilities spanning 1,500 acres of park land inside the city limits. The largest, Sioux Park, offers 210 acres. A 13.5-mile bicycle path spans the town, which boasts 17 golf courses, 36 tennis courts, 16 horseshoe courts, 10 racquet-ball courts, 3 outdoor swimming pools, an indoor aquatic facility, 9 ball field complexes, 8 soccer facilities, an ice arena, 1 hockey rink, and 2 frisbee golf courses.

Outdoor lovers enjoy two ski areas, 400 miles of trails and nature walks, 14 mountain lakes and 300 miles of streams and reservoirs; blue ribbon trout fishing and many types of hunting are also available.

Shopping and Dining

Since its inception, Rapid City has been a commercial center for miners, ranchers, the military, and tourists. Downtown

Rapid City, with more than 400 businesses, is a diverse mix of retail stores, financial institutions, service businesses, and lodging. Anchored by JCPenney, Sears, Herbergers and Target, the Rushmore Mall has a total of 120 retail stores. Other local shopping areas include Baken Park, the city's first shopping center; Eastside Family Thrift Shopping Center; Northgate Shopping Center; Haines Station; and the Sturgis Road shopping area. A number of Rapid City shops specialize in fine hand-crafted paintings, pottery, jewelry, and museum quality reproductions created by the Sioux who live in the region. Manufacturers and retailers of the areas famous Black Hills Gold abound; many offer tours as well as retail stores.

Many fine restaurants are located throughout the city, featuring sizzling steaks cut from prime South Dakota beef.

Visitor Information: Rapid City Convention and Visitors Bureau, PO Box 747, Rapid City, SD 57709; telephone (605)718-8484; toll-free (800)487-3223; fax (605)348-9217; email tourist@rapidcitycvb.com. South Dakota Department of Tourism, 711 Wells Avenue, Pierre, SD 57501; toll-free (800)773-3301; email sdinfo@state.sd.us.

Convention Facilities

The Rushmore Plaza Civic Center, located near the heart of downtown Rapid City, provides an 11,500-seat arena, 120,000 square feet of exhibit space, a luxurious 1,774-seat theater, meeting rooms, and catering facilities. Seventy-five motels/hotels provide 4,400 rooms. Alongside a flowing creek, greenway, and bike path is the Central States Fairgrounds convention facilities, which can accommodate groups of 25 to 6,000 and offers services such as a 224-unit campground, 6,000 seat grandstand, 8,000 vehicle parking spaces, 8 acres of asphalt display area and food service locations.

Convention Information: Rapid City Convention and Visitors Bureau, PO Box 747, Rapid City, SD 57709; toll-free (800)487-3223; email tourist@rapidcitycvb.com

Transportation

Approaching the City

The Rapid City Regional Airport, 9 miles east of the city, is the third most active airport in the Northern Rockies. It offers flights to and from Las Vegas, Minneapolis, Salt Lake City, Chicago, and Denver via four carriers. Two fixed-base operators provide charter service. Charter bus service is provided by Rapid City Charter Bus, Deadwood Express, Jack Rabbit Lines, Stagecoach West, and Gray Line of the Black Hills. Dakota Minnesota and Eastern Railroad offers transport to the east, south and west.

Several wide, modern highways intersect in the city including Interstate 90, which runs east and west; State Highway 79, which runs north and south is being expanded to a four-lane highway; U.S. Highway 14, which cuts through the city on an angle running northwest to southeast; and U.S. Highway 16, which approaches the city center from the south. Six highways lead from the north, west, and south into the canyons and mountains.

Traveling in the City

The city is divided into three main areas named by locals according to compass direction: South Robbinsdale, North Rapid City, and West Rapid. Two inter-city bus lines serve Rapid City. City bus service is offered by the Rapid Transit System; Dial A Ride offers curb to curb service for transport of ADA certified passengers; Rapid Ride, a fixed-route bus system takes passengers to more than 200 stops along five city and two connector routes.

Communications

Newspapers and Magazines

The city's daily newspaper is the *Rapid City Journal*. Other local newspapers include the weeklies *The Plainsman* and *Indian Country Today*. *The Visitor* is a quarterly magazine; *Investment Report* is a monthly magazine published in Rapid City.

Television and Radio

Rapid City is served by four network television stations and two cable companies. The city has 11 AM and FM radio stations.

Media Information: *Rapid City Journal,* 507 Main Street, PO Box 450, Rapid City, SD 57701; telephone (605)394-8400

Rapid City Online

City of Rapid City home page. Available www.rcgov.org

Ellsworth Air Force Base home page. Available www.ellsworth.af.mil

Rapid City Area Economic Development Partnership home page. Available www.rapiddevelopment.com

Rapid City Convention & Visitors Bureau home page. Available www.rapidcitycvb.com

Rapid City Public Library home page. Available www.rapidcitylibrary.org

South Dakota Arts Council home page (directory of arts festivals and pow wows). Available www.sdarts.org

Selected Bibliography

Riney, Scott, *The Rapid City Indian School, 1898-1933* (University of Oklahoma Press, 1999)

Sioux Falls

The City in Brief

Founded: 1870 (incorporated, 1889)

Head Official: Mayor Dave Munson (since 2002)

City Population
 1990: 100,836
 2000: 123,975
 2003 estimate: 133,834
 Percent change, 1990–2000: 22.9%
 U.S. rank in 1980: 223rd
 U.S. rank in 1990: 194th
 U.S. rank in 2000: 195th

Metropolitan Area Population
 1980: 109,435
 1990: 139,236
 2000: 172,412

 Percent change, 1990–2000: 23.8%
 U.S. rank in 1980: 270th
 U.S. rank in 1990: Not reported
 U.S. rank in 2000: 180th

Area: 56.34 square miles (2000)
Elevation: 1,421 feet above sea level
Annual Average Temperature: 45.1° F
Average Annual Precipitation: 24.69 inches of rain, 38.1 inches of snow

Major Economic Sectors: Wholesale and retail trade, services, manufacturing
Unemployment Rate: 3.5% (February 2005)
Per Capita Income: $21,374 (1999)

2002 FBI Crime Index Total: 4,189

Major Colleges and Universities: Augustana College; University of Sioux Falls

Daily Newspaper: *Argus Leader*

Introduction

Sioux Falls, seat of South Dakota's Minnehaha County, is the largest city in the state and the center of the metropolitan statistical area that includes Sioux Falls as well as Lincoln and Minnehaha counties. The city first grew during the Dakota boom years of the late nineteenth century as the arrival of the railroad made possible the nationwide transportation of granite quarried in Sioux Falls. Sioux Falls has grown in many ways since then, and consistently tops the rankings by *Forbes* and *Inc.* magazines of top cities for business.

Geography and Climate

Located in the Big Sioux River Valley in southeast South Dakota, Sioux Falls is surrounded by gently rolling terrain that slopes to higher elevations approximately 100 miles to the north-northeast and to the south. The city's climate is continental, exhibiting frequent weather changes from day to day and from week to week as differing air masses move into the area. During the late fall and winter, strong winds cause abrupt drops in temperature, but cold spells are usually of short duration. Snowfall and sleet average 38.1 inches yearly, and one or two heavy snows fall each winter, with blizzard conditions sometimes resulting. Thunderstorms are common in late spring and summer; tornadoes can occur from spring through summer. Flooding from melting snow runoff in the spring along the Big Sioux River and Skunk Creek is reduced by a diversion canal around the city.

Area: 56.34 square miles (2000)

Elevation: 1,421 feet above sea level

Average Temperatures: January, 14.0° F; July, 73.0° F; annual average, 45.1° F

Average Annual Precipitation: 24.69 inches of rain, 38.1 inches of snow

History

Falls on Big Sioux River Attract Settlers

Attracted by the economic potential of the Sioux Falls on the Big Sioux River, Dr. George M. Staples of Dubuque, Iowa, organized Western Town near the falls in 1856. Staples and his group hoped that the settlement would become the capital of the Territory of Dakota, but it was not chosen. Instead, in the winter of 1856, the Legislature of Minnesota Territory chartered the Dakota Land Company and established the town of Sioux Falls.

In August 1862 the settlers, fearing violence from the local Native Americans, abandoned the village. Raiders did burn the buildings and destroy everything, including an old Smith printing press used by the *Sioux Falls Democrat* that was dumped in the Big Sioux River after it was stripped of decorative items. Fort Dakota, a military post, was established in the area in May 1865, to help assure the resettlement of Sioux Falls. Another incentive came when the water power of the falls was harnessed in 1873. A scourge of grasshoppers in 1874 hurt resettlement, but by 1876 Sioux Falls claimed a population of 600 people. Sioux Falls was incorporated as a town in 1877 and as a city in 1889.

In the last decades of the nineteenth century, Northern European immigrants were attracted to the Territory of Dakota, which resembled their homeland. The establishment of rail transport in the area in 1878 enabled locals to begin shipping ''Sioux Falls granite,'' a pink quartzite bedrock second only to diamond in hardness. The city's two church-affiliated private schools date to this period; Augustana College, a Lutheran school, was founded in 1860, and the University of Sioux Falls, a Baptist school, opened in 1883.

Agriculture Provides Economic Base

Life on the Plains was a test of endurance. Snow began falling in October 1880 and continued until the following spring, isolating residents and forcing them to burn corn, wheat, hay, and railroad ties for heat sources. In spite of hardship, Sioux Falls gained in economic importance. South Dakota's lenient divorce law brought outsiders into Sioux Falls until the law was changed in 1908. One memorable case unfolded when the wife of heavyweight boxing champion Bob Fitzsimmons sought a divorce in Sioux Falls. Her distraught husband followed her and managed to change her mind. To celebrate their reunion, Fitzsimmons forged horseshoes and passed them out to admirers; in the process, the local blacksmith shop's floor gave way, injuring a young boy. Fitzsimmons then organized a benefit performance and gave the proceeds to the boy's family.

In 1942 the U.S. War Department leased Sioux Falls land for the construction of the Air Force Technical Radio School, invigorating the local economy and social life. Sioux Falls native Joe Foss won the Congressional Medal of Honor for shooting down 31 enemy airplanes in the Pacific campaign of World War II; after the war, Foss returned to Sioux Falls to become a successful businessman and commander of the South Dakota Air National Guard.

A Leader in Financial Services and Retail

Today Sioux Falls, through the processing of agricultural products, serves as a distribution center for farms in Iowa, Minnesota, and South Dakota. Ushered in by Citicorp, financial services has emerged as a primary industry, with healthcare close behind. The city is also a retail hot spot—the largest retail center between Denver and Minneapolis-St. Paul, Sioux Falls attracts more than 14 million shoppers each year. Spurred in part by a statewide initiative, the city is focusing on becoming a driving force in research and technology. Sioux Falls offers amenities and points of interest including the University of Sioux Falls and Augustana College, a Baptist seminary, a school for the deaf, and its namesake, the Falls of the Big Sioux River.

Historical Information: Pettigrew Home & Museum, 200 W. 6th St., Sioux Falls, SD 57102; telephone (605)367-7097

Population Profile

Metropolitan Area Residents
1980: 109,435
1990: 139,236
2000: 172,412
Percent change, 1990–2000: 23.8%
U.S. rank in 1980: 270th
U.S. rank in 1990: Not reported
U.S. rank in 2000: 180th

City Residents
1990: 100,836
2000: 123,975
2003 estimate: 133,834
Percent change, 1990–2000: 22.9%
U.S. rank in 1980: 223rd
U.S. rank in 1990: 194th
U.S. rank in 2000: 195th (State rank: 1st)

Density: 2,201.4 people per square mile (in 2000)

Racial and ethnic characteristics (2000)
  White: 113,938
  Black or African American: 2,226
  American Indian and Alaska Native: 2,627
  Asian: 1,479
  Native Hawaiian and Pacific Islander: 68
  Hispanic or Latino (may be of any race): 3,087
  Other: 1,521

Percent of residents born in state: 60.2%

Age characteristics (2000)
  Population under 5 years old: 9,072
  Population 5 to 9 years old: 8,619
  Population 10 to 14 years old: 8,461
  Population 15 to 19 years old: 9,073
  Population 20 to 24 years old: 10,601
  Population 25 to 34 years old: 19,853
  Population 35 to 44 years old: 20,257
  Population 45 to 54 years old: 15,513
  Population 55 to 59 years old: 4,915
  Population 60 to 64 years old: 3,879
  Population 65 to 74 years old: 6,908
  Population 75 to 84 years old: 4,908
  Population 85 years and older: 1,916
  Median age: 33.0 years

Births (2003, Minnehaha County)
  Total number: 2,485

Deaths (2003, Minnehaha County)
  Total number: 1,156 (of which, 11 were infants under the age of 1 year)

Money income (1999)
  Per capita income: $21,374
  Median household income: $41,221
  Total households: 49,740

Number of households with income of . . .
  less than $10,000: 3,367
  $10,000 to $14,999: 2,827
  $15,000 to $24,999: 7,146
  $25,000 to $34,999: 7,133
  $35,000 to $49,999: 9,740
  $50,000 to $74,999: 10,468
  $75,000 to $99,999: 4,526
  $100,000 to $149,999: 3,056
  $150,000 to $199,999: 799
  $200,000 or more: 678

Percent of families below poverty level: 5.6% (40.4% of which were female householder families with related children under 5 years)

2002 FBI Crime Index Total: 4,189

Municipal Government

Sioux Falls is governed by a full-time mayor and eight part-time council persons. Voters elect the mayor and council persons to staggered four-year terms.

Head Official: Mayor Dave Munson (since 2002; current term expires 2006)

Total Number of City Employees: 944 (2003)

City Information: City of Sioux Falls, 224 W. 9th St., Sioux Falls, SD 57104-6407; telephone (605)367-8000

Economy

Major Industries and Commercial Activity

In May 2005, for the third consecutive year, *Forbes* magazine named Sioux Falls the best small city for business and careers, a ranking based on employment, job and income growth, cost of doing business, labor pool, crime rate, housing costs, and net migration. The Sioux Falls economy is comprised of a diversity of sectors, including finance, healthcare, retailing, agriculture, tourism, and distribution and trade.

Set in a fertile agricultural region and the site of one of the world's largest stockyards, Sioux Falls has traditionally been a center for the agricultural industry. John Morrell & Company, a meat packer, is the city's third largest employer. Among other agriculture-related activities are meat processing, the production of dairy and bakery items, livestock feed milling, and the manufacture of farm implements and equipment.

When Citicorp moved its credit card operations to Sioux Falls in 1980, it launched the city to new heights in financial services. In the two decades since that time, other financial companies followed, as did those in such related sectors as insurance and real estate. The main offices of state and regional banks, as well as brokerage and insurance firms with nationwide connections, are based in the downtown financial district.

The healthcare industry figures significantly in the city's economic stability. Sioux Falls has emerged as a regional health care center, with the two major hospitals ranking as the top employers in the city, employing roughly 9,000 combined. Private physician clinics employ more than 1,000 workers.

Sioux Falls is the largest retail center between Denver and Minneapolis-St. Paul. As such, it attracts more than 14 million shoppers annually from throughout the state as well as from Iowa, Minnesota, and Nebraska. Approximately 3,228 retail outlets employ 20 percent of Sioux Falls' labor force.

Other economic sectors important to the city are tourism, which is South Dakota's second largest industry, and distribution and trade, which take advantage of the interstate highway network and the Sioux Falls Regional Airport.

Items and goods produced: meat and meat products, fabricated steel, concrete blocks and prestressed concrete, millwork, sewn items, electronic test equipment, corrugated boxes, computer components

Incentive Programs—New and Existing Companies

Local programs—To encourage economic expansion, the Sioux Falls Development Foundation and the Chamber of Commerce jointly undertook a long-range marketing program titled "Forward Sioux Falls." The program goals include diversification of the local and state economies, creation of new enterprises, expansion of existing businesses, growth of the tax base through capital investment, and continued development of medical services, food processing, and retailing.

The Sioux Falls Development Foundation offers a number of incentives to attract new companies and retain existing businesses. The Property Tax Abatement allows new structures to be taxed at a lower rate. The Rural Electric Economic Development Fund, available in the eastern part of the state, offers financing for business development. The Minnehaha County Economic Development Association offers a Revolving Loan Fund for projects that result in significant capital investment and/or the creation of quality jobs.

State programs—The business climate of South Dakota is the first big plus for new and expanding businesses. Company owners pay no corporate or personal state income tax, no business inventory tax, and very low workers compensation rates. Additionally, the MicroLOAN South Dakota Program offers loans to small businesses in amounts up to $50,000 for use as working capital or for equipment, real estate, or other project costs. The state also offers the Revolving Economic Development & Initiative Fund to provide financing for new or existing businesses, and Economic Development Finance Authority Bonds to finance up to 80 percent of new construction and 75 percent of new equipment expenditures.

Job training programs—The state's Workforce Development Program provides businesses with partial funding to train new employees, retrain existing workers, or upgrade the training of current employees. Kilian Community College meets the educational demands of the local labor force by providing continuing education and customized training programs.

Development Projects

By the early 2000s, the population of Sioux Falls was growing at a rate of more than 3,000 residents each year, putting a strain on indoor public facilities. In response, the city established the Public Facilities Task Force in early 2004 to examine alternatives for accommodating this growth while still attracting visitors and new residents. One problem in particular needed to be addressed- the 40-year-old Sioux Falls Arena was typically booked with sporting events, rendering it unavailable for conventions and meetings. The task force arrived at a three-pronged solution. An Event Center would be constructed to accommodate stage productions and professional, college, and high school sports, as well as such events as rodeos, circuses, and rallies. A Recreation Center would offer indoor features including swimming pools, hockey rinks, soccer fields, a walking/jogging track, adventure gym, playground area, and conditioning area. Finally, the existing Sioux Falls Arena would be redesigned as a convention center complex. The Event Center would be located downtown, and the Recreation Center would be built at Nelson Park; construction on both is scheduled to begin in 2006 and end in 2008. Remodeling of the Sioux Falls Arena will begin in 2008 and be completed in one year.

The ''Phillips to the Falls'' project was underway in the mid-2000s. This expansion project will connect Falls Park, the city's natural beauty centerpiece, to downtown via Phillips Avenue, enabling people to walk from the park through the city's showcase of restored twentieth-century commercial architecture. By acquiring additional land, the city was also pursuing expansion of Falls Park to the north.

South Dakota has adopted the ''2010 Initiative,'' a state-wide program to increase economic growth and visitor spending by the year 2010. Among the goals of the initiative are to double visitor spending from $600 million to $1.2 billion; to increase the gross state product by $10 billion; and become a recognized leader in research and technology. By 2005 Sioux Falls was already experiencing success in these areas, especially in the third goal. In 2003 Hematech LLC, a biotechnology firm, announced plans to construct a $15 million headquarters and plant in the city. ''This is exactly the type of economic development we are looking for,'' said Governor Mike Rounds in the *Argus Leader,* continuing, ''It promises to bring together the academic research and corporate worlds.''

Economic Development Information: Sioux Falls Development Foundation, 200 N. Phillips Ave., Ste. 101, Sioux Falls, SD 57104; telephone (605)339-0103; toll-free (800)658-3373; fax (605)339-0055; email sfdev@siouxfalls .com

Commercial Shipping

Sioux Falls, known as one of the ''Crossroads of the Nation,'' is situated at the intersection of I-90, an east-west highway connecting Boston, MA, with Seattle, WA, and I-29, which runs north-south between Kansas City, Kansas, and Winnipeg, Manitoba, Canada. So situated, the city has long been a hub for the distribution of automobiles, trucks, food, fuel, oil, gasoline, machinery, plastics, and paper products. More than 50 truck lines provide over-the-road trans-

portation through Sioux Falls to markets throughout the nation. Rail service is provided by Burlington Northern Santa Fe and the Ellis & Eastern railroads. Air cargo services at Joe Foss Field, the largest regional airport in South Dakota, are provided by FedEx, United Parcel Service, and DHL Worldwide. Additionally, the airport serves as the state's only Foreign Trade Zone, an area where foreign goods bound for international destinations can be temporarily stored without incurring an import duty.

Labor Force and Employment Outlook

Sioux Falls is consistently listed among the top metropolitan areas for economic strength and an expanding business community. Companies moving to Sioux Falls routinely report an increase in productivity and a decrease in overhead costs. In 2003 the total available labor supply was approximately 11,986, drawn from 12 counties in three states.

The following is a summary of data regarding the Sioux Falls metropolitan area labor force, 2004 annual average.

Size of nonagricultural labor force: 122,900

Number of workers employed in . . .
construction and mining: 6,800
manufacturing: 12,400
trade, transportation and utilities: 26,700
information: 2,700
financial activities: 15,300
professional and business services: 8,200
educational and health services: 22,400
leisure and hospitality: 12,000
other services: 5,100
government: 11,400

Average hourly earnings of production workers employed in manufacturing: $13.36 (2004; statewide figure)

Unemployment rate: 3.5% (February 2005)

Largest non-government employers	Number of employees
Sioux Valley Hospital and University of South Dakota Medical Center	5,379
Avera McKennan Hospital and University Medical Center	3,449
John Morrell & Company	3,301
Citigroup Inc.	3,200
Sioux Falls School District	3,000
Wells Fargo Bank Operations Center	2,316
Hy-Vee Food Stores	1,676
Midwest Coast Transport	1,290
Evangelical Lutheran Good Samaritan Society	1,200
WalMart/Sam's Club	1,152

Cost of Living

The following is a summary of data regarding several key cost of living factors in the Sioux Falls area.

2004 (3rd Quarter) ACCRA Average House Price: $211,250

2004 (3rd Quarter) ACCRA Cost of Living Index: 95.2 (U.S. average = 100.0)

State income tax rate: None

State sales tax rate: 4.0%

Local income tax rate: None

Local sales tax rate: 1.92%

Property tax rate: $24.546 per $1,000 of assessed valuation (2003)

Economic Information: Sioux Falls Development Foundation, 200 N. Phillips Ave., Ste. 101, Sioux Falls, SD 57104; telephone (605)339-0103; toll-free (800)658-3373; fax (605)339-0055; email sfdev@siouxfalls.com

Education and Research

Elementary and Secondary Schools

South Dakota boasts one of the highest graduation rates in the country. Public elementary and secondary schools in Sioux Falls are in Sioux Falls School District 49-5, which enrolls the highest number of students in the state. A five-member, nonpartisan school board appoints a superintendent. Teachers in the district have an average of 15.6 years of experience, and 45.5 percent hold advanced degrees.

The following is a summary of data regarding Sioux Falls public schools as of the 2003–2004 school year.

Total enrollment: 20,337

Number of facilities
  elementary schools: 23
  middle schools: 5
  senior high schools: 4
  other: 4

Student/teacher ratio: 16:1

Teacher salaries
  average: $37,728

Funding per pupil: $5,071

Fifteen parochial and private elementary and secondary schools provide alternative educational curricula to about 3,700 students. Special schools in the city include a vocational school for the handicapped, a school and hospital for disabled children, and a school for the deaf.

Public Schools Information: Sioux Falls School District, 201 E. 38th St., Sioux Falls, SD 57105; telephone (605)367-7900

Colleges and Universities

Sioux Falls is home to Augustana College, the largest private college in the state. Affiliated with the Evangelical Lutheran Church and enrolling 1,800 students each year, the college awards Bachelor of Arts degrees in more than 40 areas of study and Masters of Arts in nursing and secondary/special education. The University of Sioux Falls, affiliated with the American Baptist Churches USA, enrolls nearly 1,500 students pursuing degrees in such areas as business administration, elementary education, exercise science, biology, and theology/philosophy. USDSU Sioux Falls is a partnership of three universities—the University of South Dakota, South Dakota State University, and Dakota State University. USDSU Sioux Falls caters to adult students by offering evening and once-per-week classes; each year more than 1,900 students pursue degrees at the certificate, associate, bachelors, masters, and doctoral levels.

In 2001 the Southeast Technical Institute, which serves 3,500 full- and part-time students, opened the newest building on its 168-acre campus. The Sioux Falls campus of Colorado Technical University offers associate, bachelors, and masters degrees in such areas as technology, business, criminal justice, and health sciences. Sioux Falls serves as the primary clinical campus of the University of South Dakota School of Medicine, as well as site for the nurse anesthesia graduate program of Mount Marty College. Kilian Community College, located in downtown Sioux Falls, offers studies in such areas as accounting, business management, computers, chemical dependency, medical office professional, and word processing. Other institutions of higher learning include National American University, North American Baptist Seminary, and Sioux Valley Hospital's School of Medical and Radiologic Technology.

Libraries and Research Centers

The Siouxland Libraries System maintains holdings of about 387,000 items including periodical titles, tapes, videos, and art prints. It consists of the main library, two city branches, eight county branches, a bookmobile, and an outreach service van. The library, a depository for federal and state documents, houses special collections in South Dakota history and oral history. A new, 14,900-square-foot Oak View city branch will open its doors in the spring of 2005.

The Mikkelsen Library and Learning Resources Center at Augustana College holds more than 200,000 volumes; the Center for Western Studies, a special collection within the library system, brings together 30,000 volumes pertaining to the Upper Great Plains and oral history.

A dozen or so other libraries and research centers are operated by colleges, hospitals, Siouxland Heritage Museums, and such government agencies as the Sioux Falls Police Department, the South Dakota State Penitentiary, and the United States Geological Survey.

Public Library Information: Siouxland Libraries, 201 N. Main Ave., Sioux Falls, SD 57104-6002; telephone (605)367-8720; fax (605)367-4312

Health Care

Sioux Falls has emerged as a major center for health care in a four-state region of the Upper Midwest. Central to the health care community is the University of South Dakota School of Medicine; several of the city's practicing physicians serve on the faculty of the School of Medicine, which maintains an association with five hospitals in the area. The Sioux Valley Hospitals and Health System is a network of more than 150 healthcare facilities with 537 beds. The largest hospital in the system in Sioux Valley Hospital USD Medical Center, and the Sioux Valley Clinic is the largest and most comprehensive in the region. In 2002 Sioux Valley opened the NORTH Center, specializing in orthopedic and neurosciences. The Heart Hospital of South Dakota is the area's only hospital specializing in cardiovascular disease, and the 429-bed Avera McKennan Hospital offers the region's only burn unit, bone marrow transplant program, and kidney transport program. Other facilities include the Sioux Falls Department of Veterans Affairs Medical and Regional Office Center, the Children's Care Hospital and School, and Select Specialty Hospital, providing long-term acute care to patients with such health problems as traumatic brain injuries, ventilator dependence, and postsurgical complications.

Recreation

Sightseeing

Local sightseeing revolves around the natural beauty and history of Sioux Falls. A good place to begin a sightseeing tour is at the Visitor Information Center and 50-foot observation tower at Falls Park. This park is located where the Big Sioux River forms the Falls, a natural phenomenon from which the city takes its name. Falls Park is home to two buildings listed on the National Register of Historic Places—the 1907 Sioux Falls Light & Power Hydroelectric Plant, known as the "NSP Building," and the Queen Bee Mill, a flour mill built in the nineteenth century that proved to be too large for the river's typical water flow. The Memorial to the Pioneers at the junction of North Drive and North Cliff Avenue marks the spot where pioneers from Iowa first saw the Falls of the Sioux. The Monarch of the Plains Sculpture is a 12-ton piece of mahogany granite, and the Horse Barn Arts Center features the works of local artists. Falls Park also offers Sound and Light shows, self-guided historic walking tours, and a farmers market.

The 45-acre Great Plains Zoo is home to more than 100 species represented by more than 400 live reptiles, birds, and mammals from around the world. The adjoining Delbridge Museum of Natural History features an extensive display of mounted animals. Sertoma Park, situated aside the Big Sioux River, features picnic shelters, the Outdoor Campus park, and the Sertoma Butterfly House, a facility housing nearly 1,000 butterflies that opened in 2002. Created between 1928 and 1936, the Shoto-teien Japanese Gardens near Covell Lake have been restored. The Pettigrew Home and Museum is the renovated home of one of South Dakota's first two United States Senators. The USS *South Dakota* Battleship Memorial honors the most decorated battleship of World War II. At EROS Data Center, a United States Department of Interior research and development facility near Sioux Falls, millions of satellite and aircraft photos of the earth are on display together with a pictorial history of Sioux Falls from 1937 to the present. Located five miles west of Sioux Falls is Buffalo Ridge, a cowboy ghost town featuring more than 50 exhibits, a buffalo herd, and the region's largest souvenir and fireworks store.

Arts and Culture

The Sioux Falls Community Playhouse stages a season of theater productions at the Orpheum Theatre; these range from drama to musicals and children's shows and draw casts from local performers. The Olde Towne Dinner Theatre in Worthing presents live theater and dinner. The drama departments at Augustana College and Sioux Falls College mount productions during the school year. Local cultural groups sponsor touring dance, musical, and Broadway performances at Sioux Falls College's Jeschke Fine Arts Center.

The Washington Pavilion of Arts & Science is the region's leading entertainment, cultural, and educational facility, comprised of several distinct components. The Husby Performing Arts Center is home to the South Dakota Symphony, which presents classical and pops concerts featuring guest artists and soloists during a September-through-May

The Old Courthouse Museum.

season. The Kirby Science Discovery Center features inter-active exhibits, and the Wells Fargo CineDome Theater presents IMAX motion pictures in a 60-foot domed theater. Six art galleries comprise the Visual Arts Center. The Washington Pavilion also houses an educational and gift shop, as well as a café.

Exhibits at the Siouxland Heritage Museums and Center for Western Studies capture the culture of the area's Plains tribes and the city's early settlers. The Old Courthouse Museum features a restored 1890s courtroom and law library. Art from the nation's top western artists, including work by the late Jim Savage, and Sioux culture items are on display at the Center for Western Studies. Minnehaha County's historic rural churches offer a chance to examine nineteenth-century church architecture and religious customs imported to the western frontier from Norway, Sweden, and other Scandinavian countries.

Festivals and Holidays

More than 30,000 visitors attend the Sioux Falls and Sioux Empire farm shows at the W.H. Lyon Fairgrounds over four days in January. St. Patrick's Day is celebrated with a parade downtown. A major spring event is the Festival of Choirs at Augustana College. June brings RibFest, known as "South Dakota's Biggest Backyard BBQ." Also taking place that month are the Siouxland Renaissance Festival, the Sioux Falls Festival of Cultures, Artfalls Fine Arts Festival, and Nordland Fest, Augustana College's tribute to Scandinavia. Free jazz and blues music can be heard for two days in July at JazzFest. Hot Harley Nights, which includes a motorcycle parade through downtown, and Hot Summer Nites, offering rock and roll music and a display of hundreds of Corvettes and Harleys, both take place in July as well.

The Sidewalk Arts Festival, the region's largest one-day outdoor festival, draws 50,000 people each September with 350 fine art, folk art, craft, and food booths. German Fest, the Downtown Harvest Festival, and Spirit of the West, a tribute to the area's western heritage, are also held in September. High school marching bands participate in competitions and a parade in October's Festival of Bands. The holiday season begins in November with the Parade of Lights, Festival of Trees, and Winter Wonderland at Falls Park. The year comes to a close with First Night, an alcohol-free family celebration taking place throughout Sioux Falls during the day and evening of December 31st.

Sports for the Spectator

The Sioux Falls Arena hosts home games of the Continental Basketball Association's Sioux Falls Skyforce, the U.S. Hockey League's Sioux Falls Stampede, and the Indoor Football League's Sioux Falls Storm, which had its inaugural season in 2001. The Sioux Falls Canaries play baseball at Sioux Falls Stadium. O'Gorman High School hosts the soccer games of the Sioux Falls Spitfire and the minor league football competitions of the Dakota Lawdawgs.

Augustana College and the University of Sioux Falls both have successful football college teams that compete in most collegiate sports. State high school basketball tournament competition takes place at Sioux Falls Arena in March. Sioux Falls softball and baseball fields and the Sioux Falls Stadium host local, regional, and national competition throughout the season. The acclaimed Howard Wood Field hosts track and football events.

Sports for the Participant

Golf magazine has raved about Sioux Falls's golf courses and the opportunities they offer for "prairie golf." The magazine praised the area's "gently rolling topography with an ambiance close to the links courses of Scotland, minus the heather and ocean spray." The city of Sioux Falls maintains 67 parks and outdoor recreation centers totaling more than 2,800 acres. In addition to the usual park facilities there can be found swimming pools, soccer fields, lighted skating areas, sand volleyball courts, a disc golf course, and cross-country ski trails. The 16-mile Greenway system of bicycle and hiking trails is a popular attraction. The city is the gateway to the glacial lakes region and the Missouri River, where the walleye fishing is said to be the best in the country. Hundreds of thousands of hunters come to South Dakota each fall for ring-neck pheasant and waterfowl hunting. Winter sports enthusiasts gather at Great Bear Ski Resort for downhill skiing, snowboarding, and tubing.

Shopping and Dining

Shopping malls and a redeveloped downtown retail district in Sioux Falls offer shoppers more than 3,200 options ranging from small specialty shops to major retail outlets. The Empire and Empire East Mall contain 180 retail establishments. Park Ridge Galleria, the oldest enclosed shopping center in Sioux Falls, is an upscale specialty mall located downtown. Sioux Falls is a central trading center for Native American crafts. Buyers travel to state reservations, including Rosebud and Pine Ridge, to supply local outlets such as Prairie Star Gallery with star quilts, painted hides, sculpture, and jewelry, designed and made by tribal crafters. Shopping is also available at the Old Courthouse Museum downtown.

More than 500 restaurants present menu choices that include Japanese, Chinese, French, Mexican, and Greek dishes. The local specialty is beefsteak; venison is also popular.

Visitor Information: Sioux Falls Convention & Visitors Bureau, 200 N. Phillips Ave., Ste. 102, Sioux Falls, SD 57104; telephone (605)336-1620; toll-free 800-333-2072; fax (605)336-6499; email sfcvb@siouxfalls.com

Convention Facilities

With more than 50,000 square feet of column-free exhibit space on the main floor and an additional 11,000 square feet in meeting rooms, the Sioux Falls Convention Center is the largest in the state. It hosts major national and regional conventions, meetings, and trade shows. The convention center is physically attached to the Sioux Falls Arena, which adds seating for 8,000 people and brings the total amount of exhibit space to more than 100,000 square feet; the Sioux Falls Arena will undergo a transformation into an exclusive convention and meeting facility in 2008. Meeting facilities are also offered by hotels and motels that provide more than 3,800 guest rooms in metropolitan Sioux Falls.

Convention Information: Sioux Falls Convention & Visitors Bureau, 200 N. Phillips Ave., Ste. 102, Sioux Falls, SD 57104; telephone (605)336-1620; toll-free 800-333-2072; fax (605)336-6499; email sfcvb@siouxfalls.com

Transportation

Approaching the City

The largest air facility in South Dakota, Sioux Falls Regional Airport at Joe Foss Field is the destination for air traffic into Sioux Falls. The airport reported 92,482 landings and takeoffs in 2003, serving more than 300,000 passengers. Eight commercial carriers schedule daily flights, providing direct or connecting service to most major cities in the country.

East-west I-90, joining Boston and Seattle, and north-south I-29, connecting metropolitan Kansas City with Winnipeg, Canada, intersect northwest of Sioux Falls. I-229, a beltway around the eastern sector of the city, links I-90 and I-29. U.S. highways 18 and 81 also serve the area.

Traveling in the City

Sioux Falls Transit provides bus transportation and a trolley available for special tours, and Sioux Falls Paratransit provides service to the elderly and disabled. The Sioux Falls Trolley offers free transport to Falls Park and downtown attractions on weekdays and Saturdays throughout the summer.

Communications

Newspapers and Magazines

The Sioux Falls daily newspaper is the *Argus Leader*, which is distributed every morning. Other newspapers, including a farm tabloid and college publications, appear weekly and bimonthly. Several magazines are published in Sioux Falls on such subjects as education, wool growing, trucking, knitting and weaving, and poetry.

Television and Radio

Five television stations are received in Sioux Falls; cable channels are available by subscription. Radio listeners tune in programs on nearly two dozen AM and FM radio stations in the city, which also receives radio broadcasts from Florence and Reliance, South Dakota.

Media Information: Argus Leader, 200 S. Minnesota Ave., PO Box 5034, Sioux Falls, SD 57117-5034; telephone (605)331-2205; toll-free (800)222-5207

Sioux Falls Online

Argus Leader. Available www.argusleader.com

City of Sioux Falls home page. Available www.siouxfalls.org

Sioux Falls Chamber of Commerce. Available www.siouxfallschamber.com

Sioux Falls Convention & Visitors Bureau. Available www.siouxfallscvb.com

Sioux Falls Development Foundation. Available www.siouxfallsdevelopment.com

Sioux Falls School District. Available www.sf.k12.sd.us

Siouxland Libraries. Available www.siouxland.lib.sd.us

Selected Bibliography

Brown, Dee Alexander, *Bury My Heart at Wounded Knee: An Indian History of the American West* (New York: Holt, Rinehart & Winston, 1971, 1970)

Christopherson, Marie, *Driftwood in a Time of War (Prairie Plains, No 4)* (Center for Western Studies, 1995)

Cook-Lynn, Elizabeth, *The Power of Horses and Other Stories* (New York: Arcade Pub., 1990)

Landau, Elaine, *The Sioux* (New York: F. Watts, 1989)

LaPointe, Frank, *The Sioux Today* (New York: Crowell-Collier Press, 1972)

Turner, Ann Warren, *Grasshopper Summer* (New York: Mac-Millan, 1989)

Wilder, Laura Ingalls, *By the Shores of Silver Lake* (New York: Harper & Row, 1971)

Wood, Ted, *A Boy Becomes a Man at Wounded Knee: Ted Wood with Wanbli Numpa Afraid of Hawk* (New York: Walker, 1992)

Woster, Terry, Stephen Thurman, and Catherine Thurman, *The Spirit of Sioux Falls* (Towery Publ., 1992)

WISCONSIN

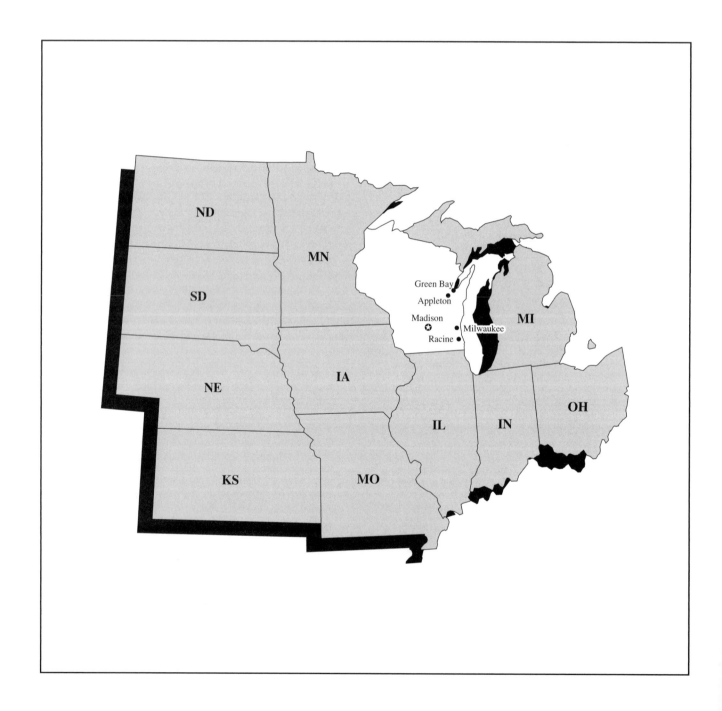

The State in Brief

Nickname: Badger State
Motto: Forward

Flower: Wood violet
Bird: Robin

Area: 65,498 square miles (2000; U.S. rank: 23rd)
Elevation: Ranges from 579 feet to 1,951 feet above sea level
Climate: Tempered by the Great Lakes, with winters more severe in the north and summers warmer in the south

Admitted to Union: May 29, 1848
Capital: Madison
Head Official: Governor Jim Doyle (D) (until 2007)

Population
  1980: 4,706,000
  1990: 4,891,769
  2000: 5,363,675
  2004 estimate: 5,509,026
  Percent change, 1990–2000: 9.6%
  U.S. rank in 2004: 20th
  Percent of residents born in state: 73.4% (2000)
  Density: 98.8 people per square mile (2000)
  2002 FBI Crime Index Total: 176,987

Racial and Ethnic Characteristics (2000)
  White: 4,769,857

Black or African American: 304,460
American Indian and Alaska Native: 47,228
Asian: 88,763
Native Hawaiian and Pacific Islander: 1,630
Hispanic or Latino (may be of any race): 192,921
Other: 84,842

Age Characteristics (2000)
  Population under 5 years old: 342,340
  Population 5 to 19 years old: 1,189,753
  Percent of population 65 years and over: 13.1%
  Median age: 36 years (2000)

Vital Statistics
  Total number of births (2003): 69,963
  Total number of deaths (2003): 46,194 (infant deaths, 451)
  AIDS cases reported through 2003: 1,848

Economy
  Major industries: Manufacturing; agriculture; finance, insurance, and real estate; wholesale and retail trade; services
  Unemployment rate: 4.5% (April 2005)
  Per capita income: $30,723 (2003; U.S. rank: 21)
  Median household income: $46,782 (3-year average, 2001-2003)
  Percentage of persons below poverty level: 8.8% (3-year average, 2001-2003)
  Income tax rate: Ranges from 4.6% to 6.75% (tax year 2000)
  Sales tax rate: 5.0%

Appleton

The City in Brief

Founded: 1835 (incorporated 1853)

Head Official: Mayor Timothy Hanna (NP) (since 1996; current term expires 2008)

City Population
   1980: 58,913
   1990: 65,695
   2000: 70,087
   2003 estimate: 70,354
   Percent change, 1990–2000: 6.6%
   U.S. rank in 1980: 340th
   U.S. rank in 1990: 352nd
   U.S. rank in 2000: 435th

Metropolitan Area Population (Appleton-Oshkosh-Neenah, WI MSA)
   1980: 291,369
   1990: 315,121
   2000: 358,365
   Percent change, 1990–2000: 13.7%
   U.S. rank in 1980: 131st
   U.S. rank in 1990: Not reported
   U.S. rank in 2000: 115th

Area: 20.88 square miles (2000)
Elevation: 780 feet above sea level
Average Annual Temperature: 43.6° F
Average Annual Precipitation: 30 inches of rain; 47 inches of snow

Major Economic Sectors: Manufacturing, services, trade
Unemployment Rate: 5.2% (February 2005)
Per Capita Income: $22,478 (1999)

2002 FBI Crime Index Total: 1,967

Major Colleges and Universities: Lawrence University, Fox Valley Technical College

Daily Newspaper: *The Post-Crescent*

Introduction

Appleton, once known as the "woodland city" and later "the Lowell of the West" (after the city in Massachusetts) grew up along the Fox River, which provided water power and transportation for the paper manufacturing industry that still dominates the area. Today, fourteen Wisconsin communities including Appleton refer to themselves as Fox Cities. Appleton's history is strongly tied to that of Lawrence University, which grew up with the town after it was chartered in 1847. Lawrence University's 84 acre campus, 32 instructional, recreational and administrative buildings, 1,200 students, and a faculty of more than 100 men and women, lies east of the city's downtown. Students and faculty members supply the community with a variety of music, drama, and sports activities.

Appleton is the seat of Outagamie County, but parts of Appleton are also located in Calumet and Winnebago counties. The many trees, city parks, a river lined with old mansions, and interesting shops provide the community with a lively downtown. The once-polluted river, unique in that it is one of the few American rivers flowing northward for its entire course, has been largely restored and is a popular site for swimming, fishing, and boating. Appleton consistently scores high on lists of the best places to live in the United States; it is safe, affordable, and offers a variety of cultural and artistic events.

Geography and Climate

Appleton is located on rolling terrain that was carved out by glaciers. The city has a continental climate and experiences four distinct seasons, with cold winters and warm summers. It has an average annual snowfall of 47 inches. The ground usually remains snow-covered from late November through late March. April is the most common time for flooding to occur.

Area: 20.88 square miles (2000)

Elevation: 780 feet above sea level

Average Temperatures: January, 15.3° F; July, 71.4° F; annual average is 43.6° F

Average Annual Precipitation: 30 inches of rain; 47 inches of snow

History

Long before the coming of the Europeans, the area that is now Appleton was inhabited by the Menominee Indians. The Outagamie Indians, also known as the Fox, lived nearby, as did the Winnebago. Early French explorers such as Duluth, Hennepin, and LaSalle floated up the northerly-flowing Fox River into the Indian lands. In the mid-1600s French trappers and traders traveled the waterway of the Fox River in search of furs, particularly beaver pelts. They were followed by Catholic missionaries, including Pere Marquette and Louis Joliet, who passed by in 1673 on their search for the Mississippi River. Later, soldiers crossed the area as they made their way to the three forts that were built on the Fox-Wisconsin waterway, and settlers followed in 1835. That year, Hyppolyte Grignon and his family opened the White Heron trading post just above the Grand Chute. They were followed soon after by John and Jeanette Johnson, whose house became the first hotel, trading post, church, and hospital.

After the building of a canal around the river rapids, steamboats bearing travelers and cargo became a common sight. Wheat farming in the surrounding area gave way to the dairy farms, for which the region is now famous.

However, Appleton itself was first established as the site for a university. At that time it was one of three villages clustered together, the others being Grand Chute (site of the treacherous river rapids) and White Heron. When Amos Lawrence, a Boston Methodist, donated money for a "university in the wilderness" to be constructed in 1847, he decided to honor his wife's family, the Appletons, in naming the new site.

Outagamie County was founded in 1851, and Grand Chute was named the county seat. As neighboring settlements developed, they decided to incorporate under the single name Appleton in 1853. By the next year the new village included a paper mill, two sawmills, several flour mills, and a newspaper. As the center grew, it was incorporated as a city on May 2, 1857.

The power of the Fox River was harnessed in 1882 with the establishment of the world's first hydro-electric plant. The paper mills that developed along the river, and the support industries that grew along with them, played a major role in the economy of the "Paper Valley" that continues into the present day.

New Englanders were the first settlers of the region, but Dutch, German, and Polish settlers had become part of the city by the early twentieth century. More recent immigrants, the Hmong-Laotian refugees from the period of the Viet

Nam War, have made their mark on the area's culture since the late 1970s.

Appleton today is a prosperous community founded in an appreciation for education, maintaining a certain "small-town charm" in the midst of economic prosperity and downtown revitalization.

Historical Information: Outagamie County Historical Society and Museum, 330 E. College Avenue, Appleton, WI 54911; telephone (920)735-9370

Population Profile

Metropolitan Area Residents
1980: 291,369
1990: 315,121 (MSA)
2000: 358,365
Percent change, 1990–2000: 13.7%
U.S. rank in 1980: 131st
U.S. rank in 1990: Not reported
U.S. rank in 2000: 115th

City Residents
1980: 58,913
1990: 65,695
2000: 70,087
2003 estimate: 70,354
Percent change, 1990–2000: 6.6%
U.S. rank in 1980: 340th
U.S. rank in 1990: 352nd
U.S. rank in 2000: 435th

Density: 3,356 people per square mile (2000)

Racial and ethnic characteristics (2000)
   White: 64,116
   Black or African American: 695
   American Indian and Alaska Native: 401
   Asian: 3,231
   Native Hawaiian and Pacific Islander: 21
   Hispanic or Latino (may be of any race): 1,775
   Other: 733

Percent of residents born in state: 73.3% (2000)

Age characteristics (2000)
   Population under 5 years old: 4,834
   Population 5 to 9 years old: 5,401
   Population 9 to 14 years old: 5,631
   Population 15 to 19 years old: 5,481
   Population 20 to 24 years old: 4,667
   Population 25 to 34 years old: 10,333
   Population 35 to 44 years old: 11,979
   Population 45 to 54 years old: 9,009
   Population 55 to 59 years old: 2,795
   Population 60 to 64 years old: 2,033
   Population 65 to 74 years old: 3,877
   Population 75 to 84 years old: 2,835
   Population 85 years and over: 1,212
   Median age: 33.8 years

Births (2004, Outagamie County)
   Total number: 2,286

Deaths (2003, Outagamie County)
   Total number: 1,147

Money income (1999)
   Per capita income: $22,478
   Median household income: $47,285
   Total households: 26,899

Number of households with income of . . .
   less than $10,000: 1,343
   $10,000 to $14,999: 1,317
   $15,000 to $24,999: 3,246
   $25,000 to $34,999: 3,265
   $35,000 to $49,999: 5,046
   $50,000 to $74,999: 6,701
   $75,000 to $99,999: 3,216
   $100,000 to $149,999: 1,755
   $150,000 to $199,999: 430
   $200,000 or more: 580

Percent of families below poverty level: 3.3% (36.2% of which were female householder families with related children under 5 years)

2002 FBI Crime Index Total: 1,967

Municipal Government

Appleton has a mayor-council form of government, made up of 16 city council members plus the mayor. Each term, council members elect a Council President. Council members serve two-year terms, and the mayor serves for four years.

Head Official: Mayor Timothy M. Hanna (NP) (since 1996; current term expires 2008)

Total Number of City Employees: 2,500 (2004)

City Information: City of Appleton, 100 N. Appleton St., 54911; telephone (920)832-5599

Economy

Major Industries and Commercial Activity

Since the mid-nineteenth century the paper industry and its allied industries have been the foundation for Appleton's economy. In fact, the Fox River Valley is home to the highest concentration of paper-making facilities in the world, and accounts for more than 10 percent of the area's total employment and one-third of all manufacturing employment. With 80 paper manufacturing facilities and 90 publishing companies, the Fox Cities (a cluster of 16 small cities along the region's Fox River) has the highest concentration of paper-related companies in the world. Of nearly as great importance is the metals-machinery industry, which produces welders, fire and utility trucks, crushing and screening equipment, farm machinery, and iron and brass castings. The local economy is also diversifying; six insurance companies are headquartered in the Fox Valley, as well as a growing network of thriving financial institutions. The Fox Cities region is also an important center for regional trade and services. The Wisconsin Department of Revenue predicts a 5.1 percent increase in employment in the Appleton area between 2003 and 2007, with most of that growth coming in the service, finance, insurance, and real estate sectors.

Items and goods produced: paper; paper products; books; metals and machine products; farm machinery; knit; wire; canned goods

Incentive Programs—New and Existing Companies

Local programs—The city of Appleton has four tax incremental financing programs, which it uses to finance public costs like infrastructure and land assembly and sometimes to assist in development costs of a project. The city also has a gap financing program—a community development loan pool resulting from a partnership between the city and seven of Appleton's financial institutions. It provides funds to fill the gap between what a bank will lend and the full cost of a project, and can be used for capital expansion, procuring new business locations, and capital equipment.

State programs—Wisconsin corporate taxes remain among the lowest in the nation due to property tax exemptions on manufacturing machinery and equipment, inventory exemptions, and lack of franchise and unitary taxes, according to a study done by the Federal Reserve Bank of Boston.

The Wisconsin Economic Development Association (WEDA) and the Wisconsin Economic Development Institute (WEDI) are two nonprofit agencies that provide information and financial services, legal and legislative assistance, and networking opportunities for their member businesses. On the government side, the Division of Busi-

ness Development of the Wisconsin Department of Commerce provides technical assistance and financial incentives to businesses in the areas of business planning, site selection, capitalization, permits, training and recruitment, and research and development. On April 28, 2000, Governor Tommy G. Thompson signed into law a bill that created the Wisconsin Technology Council, a nonprofit, nonpartisan board that serves to create, develop and retain science and technology-based business in Wisconsin, and to serve as an advisor to the Governor and the Legislature. The Council also serves as the key link between the state's colleges and universities and the business expertise and capital offered by the financial service industry. Recently the firm published its "Vision 2020: A Model Wisconsin Economy" as a blueprint for its efforts over the next two decades.

Job training programs—Wisconsin ranks in the top 10 states for high school graduation rate, educational expenditures, income distribution and voting rate. A local Chamber of Commerce study found that partnerships between social service providers and employers in the Fox Cities have led to successful workforce development, particularly in creating entry-level employment. The State of Wisconsin has programs available to provide grants to businesses training workers in new technologies. The Fox Valley Technical College is an award-winning vocational and technical training institute that has formed long-standing relationships with several area companies to provide top-quality customized training programs.

Development Projects

Since its inception in 1996, Appleton's Neighborhood Revitalization Program has won national awards, by 2005 having helped four neighborhoods improve both residentially and commercially, with a fifth well underway. In addition, residents have access to the HOME Rental Rehabilitation Loan Program and the Housing Rehabilitation Loan Program for access to low-interest loans for improving their homes or rental units.

Major advancements in the manufacturing sector included the one made by Thomson Newspapers Inc., the parent company of *The Post-Crescent,* which completed a $35 million printing and distribution facility in Appleton's Northeast Industrial Park in 2001; in 2002 the local design, construction, and engineering firm Hoffman Corporation moved into its own new 40,000 square foot office building.

Also in 2002 the city opened its Fox Cities Performing Arts Center, a $45 million facility that includes a 2,100-seat theater for concerts and theater events, and a 4,000 square foot multi-use hall that can host banquets, meetings, and conventions.

The city also has four designated business parks, the latest opening in 2003 as the Southpoint Commerce Park near

State Highway 441. The city also has several redevelopment sites, including Fox River waterfront property, available for residential, commercial, and office development.

Economic Development Information: Fox Cities Chamber of Commerce & Industry, 227 S. Walnut Street, PO Box 1855, Appleton, WI 54913-1855; telephone (920)734-7101. City of Appleton Department of Development, Jim Van Dyke, Development Specialist, 100 North Appleton Street, Appleton, WI 54911; telephone (920)832-6468; fax (920)832-5994; email jim.vandyke@appleton.org

Commercial Shipping

Outagamie County Regional Airport is served by Federal Express and Airborne Express. Rail freight is provided by Canadian National, while more than 60 trucking and warehouse firms service the greater Fox Cities area. The Port of Green Bay, 30 miles north of Appleton, and the Port of Milwaukee, 100 miles south, provide access to the Great Lakes shipping corridor.

Labor Force and Employment Outlook

Of some 202,000 workers in the Fox Cities area, 87 percent declared themselves satisfied with the local job market according to a Chamber of Commerce study. The Wisconsin Department of Revenue predicts 5.1 percent employment growth in the Fox Cities region between 2003 and 2007, with the greatest increase in services, finance, insurance, and real estate. The Fox Valley Technical College is an award-winning vocational and technical training institute that has formed long-standing relationships with several area companies to provide top-quality customized training programs.

The following is a summary of data regarding the Appleton labor force, 2004 annual average.

Size of nonagricultural labor force: 118,000

Number of workers employed in . . .
 construction and mining: 8,600
 manufacturing: 24,400
 trade, transportation and utilities: 23,200
 information: 2,100
 financial activities: 6,700
 professional and business services: 11,300
 educational and health services: 11,700
 leisure and hospitality: 10,500
 other services: 5,900
 government: 11,300

Average hourly earnings of production workers employed in manufacturing: $16.19 (Wisconsin statewide)

Unemployment rate: 5.2% (February 2005)

Largest employers
(2003, Fox Cities region)	*Number of employees*
Kimberly-Clark Corporation	5,782
Theda Care Health System	5,000
Affinity Health System	4,300
City of Appleton	2,500
Plexus Corp. & Affiliates (electronic design)	2,200
Banta Corp. & Affiliates (book and periodicals printing)	1,850
Appleton Area School District	1,724

Cost of Living

The Fox Valley offers a very affordable cost of living, typically two percent below the national average, according to a national research study. With a Median Household Effective Buying Income of more than $40,000 in 2003, the Appleton MSA ranked 87th of 323 in buying income nationally.

The following is a summary of data regarding several key cost of living factors for the Appleton metropolitan area.

2004 (3rd Quarter) ACCRA Average House Price: $214,900

2004 (3rd Quarter) ACCRA Cost of Living Index: 92.2 (U.S. average = 100.0)

State income tax rate: Ranges from 4.6% to 6.75% (tax year 2005)

State sales tax rate: 5%

Local income tax rate: None

Local sales tax rate: None

Property tax rate: $23.56 per $1,000 of full market value (2003, Outagamie County assessment)

Economic Information: Fox Cities Chamber of Commerce and Industry, 227 South Walnut Street, P.O. Box 1855, Appleton, WI 54912-1855; telephone (920)734-7101; toll-free (800)999-3224; email econ@foxcitieschamber.com

Education and Research

Elementary and Secondary Schools

The Appleton Area School District (AASD) is Wisconsin's sixth largest school district and is one of its fastest growing. The district encompasses the city of Appleton, and the towns of Grand Chute, Buchanan, Harrison, and a small part of Menasha. Wisconsin traditionally leads the nation in test scores, and Appleton area students consistently exceed state and national test score averages. Since 1997 the Appleton Education Foundation, an independent organization of concerned citizens and business leaders, has awarded grants to Appleton schools totaling more than $800,000 to fund educational programs not funded by public sources. The Fox Cities Alliance for Education helps 13 local school districts collaborate with area businesses on school-to-work initiatives.

The following is a summary of data regarding the Appleton Area School District as of the 2002–2003 school year.

Total enrollment: 14,948

Number of facilities
  elementary schools: 16
  junior high/middle schools: 4
  senior high schools: 3
  other: 1 pre-elementary school; 12 charter schools covering all grades K-12

Student/teacher ratio: 15.3:1

Teacher salaries (2005)
  average: $41,892

Funding per pupil: $8,953

The Appleton Catholic Education System (ACES) consists of four elementary schools, and a middle school. The city's ACES schools strive to foster higher level thinking skills. There is also a Catholic High School, Xavier. Appleton has a non-denominational school and seven Lutheran schools.

Colleges and Universities

Lawrence University has been a coeducational institution since its founding in 1847 and is the second oldest co-ed college in the country. In 1964 the college merged with Milwaukee's Downer College, a well regarded women's college. Lawrence, ranked among the nation's top 50 liberal arts colleges in 2003 by *U.S. News & World Report* enrolls 1,200 full-time students. B.A. programs are offered in more than 30 areas. The Fox Valley Technical College offers a diverse curriculum and is regarded as one of the most progressive technical institutions in the country. The college has more than 70 associate degree programs, apprenticeship training, continuing education, and customized training. Also located in the Fox Cities are the University of Wisconsin-Oshkosh, the University of Wisconsin-Fox Valley, and a branch of the Milwaukee School of Engineering (Appleton).

Libraries

Appleton Public Library has 300,000 volumes and 500 periodical subscriptions as well as a CD collection and audio- and videotapes. The library is a state document depository and has a special area on local history. An expansion in the late 1990s resulted in more space for children's programs and added shelf space for books. More than 1,500 people visit the 85,000 square foot facility daily, and the library website is accessed 75,000 times per month. The special subject interests of the Fox Valley Technical College, which has more than 61,000 volumes, include agriculture, business and management, environmental studies, medicine, and science and technology. Lawrence University Library, with holdings of nearly 337,000 volumes, is also a state document depository.

Public Library Information: Appleton Public Library, 225 N. Oneida St., Appleton, WI 54911-4780; telephone (920)832-6170; fax (920)832-6182

Health Care

The city of Appleton is served by two hospitals with a total of 700 beds—St. Elizabeth Hospital and the Appleton Medical Center (which, along with its regional partner Theda Clark Medical Center, was named one of the nation's top 100 hospitals in 2003 by HCIA-Sachs). There are two walk-in emergency clinics. The Fox Cities rank among the least expensive regions in the United States for hospital and physician care. In 2004 St. Elizabeth Hospital embarked on an ambitious three-phase renovation and expansion plan. St. Elizabeth offers specialized services in cardiac care, behavioral medicine, a center for women and families, extensive rehabilitation facilities, and the Comprehensive Cancer Center. Appleton Medical Center supports the Warner Wellness and Rehabilitation Center, which brings together therapies, cardiac rehabilitation, sports medicine, occupational health, and nutritional services. The hospital also offers magnetic resonance imaging and a linear accelerator. Theda Clark Medical Center in Neenah is also home to Children's Hospital of Wisconsin.

Recreation

Sightseeing

Visitors learn about the life of what may be Appleton's most famous citizen, Harry Houdini, by taking the Houdini Walking Tour of the city, and observing the collection of his many magic feats. From mid-May through mid-September tours are available to the grand log home of James Doty, Wisconsin's second territorial governor. In nearby Kaukauna, guides dressed in circa-1830s garb escort visitors through the Greek revival mansion of prominent fur trader

Hearthstone Mansion, owned by Henry J. Rodgers, was the first residence in the world lighted with a hydroelectric system designed by Thomas A. Edison.

Charles Grignon, which captures the flavor of the fur trading era. The Children's Farm at Plamann Park gives kids the chance to observe young farm animals in a lovely park setting, and the Memorial Park Arboretum & Gardens displays a variety of native Wisconsin trees and plants. The Paper Discovery Museum has exhibits which educate about one of the region's most important industries. The Fox Cities Children's Museum has hands-on activities for kids. At the Hearthstone Historic House Museum, visitors can observe the world's first home lit by a central hydro-electric power plant, and can try generating hydro-power at the new Hydro Adventure Center. More than 1,000 dolls dating from 1850 to the present are on display at the Amelia Bubolz Doll Collection. The Gordon Bubolz Nature Preserve is an 862-acre park with eight miles of hiking trails. The Tayco Street Bridge Tower Museum, in nearby Menasha, has exhibits concerning the bygone era of river navigation during the time when the Fox River was the main highway for commerce and travel in the area. Menasha's University of Wisconsin Center Fox Valley Planetarium presents various shows explaining the wonders of the stars.

Arts and Culture

The major performing arts facilities in Appleton are the new Fox Cities Performing Arts Center, which has Broadway shows, concerts by the Fox Valley Symphony and national acts, and other events in its 2,100 seat theater; the 1883 Grand Opera House, which presents more than 200 events annually; the Performing Arts at Lawrence University, which offers an artists series, a jazz series and a variety of concerts; and the Lawrence Conservatory of Music, which schedules more than 130 classical performances each year.

The semi-professional Little Sandwich Theatre in the Mall presents live dinner theater productions of musicals, dramas, and children's plays at the Avenue Mall. Community theater for the Fox Valley is provided by the Attic Theatre, which produces four summer shows and a holiday production. The Children's Ballet Theatre provides training for young dancers and performs for schools, clubs, festivals, and conventions.

The Fox Valley Symphony has a more than 30-year history, and presents five subscription concerts each year, plus a holiday concert and two concert chamber series. Appleton's citizens enjoy music making and some of the more prominent musical groups include the Appleton MacDowell Male Chorus, the Chaminade Women's Chorus, the Fox Cities Handbells, the Green Apple Folk Music Society, and the White Heron Chorale.

The Bergstrom-Mahler Museum displays the world's foremost collection of glass paperweights and an exhibit of Germanic glass dating back to the 1500s, as well as a variety of traveling exhibits. The Outagamie Museum/(Harry) Houdini Historical Center features Houdini memorabilia,

including a fascinating handcuff display, and magic shows in the summer. The museum also has paper-making exhibits, and exhibits on subjects of local interest. Works of fine art and student exhibits are on display at the architecturally whimsical Wriston Art Center on the Lawrence University Campus, with its glass walls and turrets, fanciful curves, and recessed amphitheater.

The Fox Cities Children's Museum provides youngsters with 27,000 square feet of opportunities for hands-on exploration. The museum features a giant human heart kids can climb onto and slide out of, and interactive displays on electricity, wildlife, rocks, bubbles, fire trucks, other cultures, music and machines, as well as the Science Spectrum, a trip through the world of science.

The city also has some impressive public artworks, including the Appleton Aurora, a unique 10 by 60 foot sculpture atop the Appleton Center, and the Fox River Oracle, a massive sculpture at the north end of Appleton's Skyline Bridge.

Arts and Culture Information: Fox Valley Arts Alliance; telephone (920)734-4860

Festivals and Holidays

Spring events include the Nature's Image Spring Fair at the 1,000 Islands Environmental Center in Kaukauna; the Antiques Showcase & Sale in April; the Memorial Garden Festival, which takes place at Memorial Park Arboretum & Gardens in May; and the grand finale of the month of May, the Memorial Day Parade downtown. June brings the Flag Day Parade in downtown Appleton, and the Great Wisconsin Cheese Festival in Little Chute. Independence Day is saluted at the Civic Celebration held at Memorial Park; also in July is the annual Paperfest in Kimberly. The Fox Cities Marathon is held in September. The enjoyment of German food and culture, including a variety of beer, is the focus of Oktoberfest, one of the highlights each year in Appleton and held in September. The Harvest Song Fall Festival at Bubolz Nature Preserve, the Crop Walk, and the Romp in the Swamp are the city's highlights for October. Christmas is celebrated with Holiday Candlelight Tours followed by January's Victorian Christmas.

Sports for the Spectator

The Timber Rattlers, the Class A affiliate of the Seattle Mariners, play baseball in the 3,400-seat Fox Cities Stadium. World class runners congregate in the area each October to trek over seven bridges through seven cities, part of the 26.2-mile route of the Fox Cities Marathon. The thrills and spills of stock-car racing can be enjoyed at nearby Kaukauna's Wisconsin International Raceway. Sports enthusiasts have easy access to the excitement of the Green Bay Packers, the Milwaukee Bucks, and the Milwaukee

Brewers; the University of Wisconsin Badgers compete collegiately in the Big Ten conference in Madison, just a 90 minute drive away.

Sports for the Participant

The Gordon Bubolz Nature Preserve offers 762 acres of wildlife habitat. Hikers and skiers enjoy eight miles of trails along a trout pond and through a white cedar forest. The 1,140 acres of Highcliffs State Park rest on limestone cliffs overlooking Lake Winnebago. The park offers swimming, camping, marina facilities, and an adjacent golf course. The city of Appleton's Parks and Recreation System consists of 600 acres and 26 parks, plus an ice arena. Appleton's Talulah and Memorial parks feature bike paths, and Lutz Park has a boat landing. Golfers enjoy the Chaska and Reid public golf courses, and the city has five parks with lighted tennis courts. The USA Youth Sports Complex has 12 soccer fields and 7 baseball diamonds. The Appleton Rugby Club holds a spring and a fall season of games, and the Appleton Soccer Club offers both adult and youth leagues. Erb and Meade Parks have public swimming pools and Plamann Park offers snowmobile trails and access to the state trail system.

Shopping and Dining

Appleton's Fox River Mall, with 165 retail shops, is one of the largest in Wisconsin. The mall is anchored by large department stores such as Marshall Fields, JC Penney, Sears, and Target, as well as Scheels All Sports. Other major malls include the Avenue Mall, featuring specialty shops and Herberger's Department Store; the Valley Fair Mall, and the Jansport Outlet. Lamers Dairy in Appleton has tours of its milk-bottling plant as well as a country gift store. Simons Specialty Cheese in Little Chute has 100 varieties of cheese and Wisconsin-themed gifts. The Country Squire Christmas Shoppe in Neenah is locally famous for ornaments and Christmas decorations from around the world. The Frame Workshop in Appleton is an award-winning frame shop and art gallery that also has hand-blown glass ornaments from Germany. Vande Walle's Candy Shop offers self-tours of candy-making and pastry-making. The Abracadabra Magic Shop, owned by a local magician, offers magic trick materials and books. More than 60,000 titles, a coffee bar, and a fine selection of gifts is available at Conkey's Book Store, a 100-year old landmark that was recently expanded.

The city offers a variety of restaurants featuring the cuisines of Greece, Italy, Japan, Mexico, Thailand, China, and France, as well as casual American fare or upscale continental dining. For fine dining try Peggy's Café on College Avenue downtown, The Seasons on Nicolet, or George's Steak House, a family-owned institution for more than 50 years. Mark's East Side and Old Bavarian celebrate the area's strong German influences.

Visitor Information: Fox Cities Convention & Visitors Bureau, 110 Fox River Drive, Appleton, WI 54915-9108; telephone (920)734-3358; fax (920)734-1080

Convention Facilities

The Radisson Paper Valley Hotel and Conference Center has 390 guest rooms and 25 meeting rooms. Overall the Fox Cities region has more than 80 meeting rooms, a 2,000 person capacity theater style room, a 1,000 person capacity banquet style room, more than 30 hotels and motels, and nearly 3,000 hotel rooms. The renovated Tri-County Arena and Expo Center in nearby Neenah offers more than 35,000 square feet of floor space, plus special use rooms. The facility is available for trade shows and exhibitions from April through September; in the winter months it serves as an ice rink. The Fox Cities Convention and Visitors Bureau offers a variety of site selection and planning services.

Convention Information: Fox Cities Convention & Visitors Bureau, 110 Fox River Drive, Appleton, WI 54915-9108; telephone (920)734-3358; toll-free (800)236-4114

Transportation

Approaching the City

Located two miles west of the city, Outagamie County Airport, one of the fastest-growing airports in Wisconsin, offers service by United Express, Comair/Delta Connection, Northwest Airlink, and Midwest/Express/Skyway Airlines. The airport has nonstop flights to Milwaukee, Atlanta, Cincinnati, and Chicago. In 2000 Northwest upgraded to nonstop service between Appleton and Midwest hubs in Detroit and Minneapolis/Saint Paul; now both turboprop and jet service is available. Additional flights can be taken from Green Bay's Austin Straubel Field just 30 minutes away. Inter-regional bus service is provided by Greyhound Bus Lines, with daily trips to Milwaukee, Green Bay and Stevens Point. Lamers Bus Lines offers one daily departure to the Amtrak station in Milwaukee.

Traveling in the City

Appleton's main thoroughfares include U.S. Highways 10, 41, and 45. Secondary passages are State Highways 47, 55, 76, 96, 114, 150, and 441. Valley Transit offers local bus service.

Communications

Newspapers and Magazines

The Post-Crescent, Appleton's daily paper, appears in the evenings. The *Milwaukee Journal & Sentinel* also covers news in the city. Magazines published in Appleton include *The New American,* a conservative magazine covering international affairs, and *Marketplace Magazine,* a business magazine covering northeastern Wisconsin. *Fox Cities Magazine, Fox Life,* and *The Scene* focus on what's happening in the Fox Cities.

Television and Radio

Time Warner Cable offers both digital cable and Roadrunner high-speed internet. Appleton television viewers have broadcast access to network programming from ABC, CBS, NBC, PBS, and UPN. Approximately 25 radio stations broadcast to the Appleton area, with programming ranging from adult contemporary, to news/talk, public radio, big band, and classic rock.

Media Information: The Post-Crescent, 306 West Washington Street, PO Box 59, Appleton, WI 54912-0059; telephone (800)236-6397

Appleton Online

Appleton Public Library. Available www.apl.org/index .html

City of Appleton home page. Available www.appleton.org

Fox Cities Chamber of Commerce and Industry. Available www.foxcitieschamber.com

Fox Cities Convention and Visitors Bureau. Available www .foxcities.org

The Heart of the Valley Chamber of Commerce. Available www.heartofthevalleychamber.com

Selected Bibliography

Bubolz, Gordon, ed., *Land of the Fox, Saga of Outagamie County* (Outagamie County State Centennial Committee, 1949)

Kort, Ellen, *The Fox Heritage* (Woodland Hills, CA: Windsor Publications, 1984)

Ryan, Thomas Henry, *History of Outagamie County, Wisconsin: Being a General Survey Including a History of the Cities, Towns, and Villages* (Chicago: Goodspeed Historical Association, 1911)

Green Bay

The City in Brief

Founded: 1701 (incorporated, 1854)

Head Official: Mayor James J. Schmitt (since 2003)

City Population
  1980: 87,899
  1990: 96,466
  2000: 102,213
  2003 estimate: 101,467
  Percent change, 1990–2000: 5.9%
  U.S. rank in 1980: 200th
  U.S. rank in 1990: 205th
  U.S. rank in 2000: 240th

Metropolitan Area Population
  1980: 175,280
  1990: 194,594
  2000: 226,178

Percent change, 1990–2000: 16.2%
U.S. rank in 1990: Not reported
U.S. rank in 2000: 153rd

Area: 43.8 square miles (2000)
Elevation: 582 feet above sea level
Average Annual Temperature: 43.6° F
Average Annual Precipitation: 28.83 inches of rain, 46.3 inches of snow

Major Economic Sectors: Wholesale and retail trade, services, manufacturing
Unemployment Rate: 5.6% (February 2005)
Per Capita Income: $19,269 (1999)

2002 FBI Crime Index Total: 3,762

Major Colleges and Universities: University of Wisconsin–Green Bay, St. Norbert College, Northeast Wisconsin Technical College

Daily Newspapers: *Green Bay Press-Gazette, Green Bay News-Chronicle*

Introduction

Green Bay, named for the green-tinted streaks that stripe its bay in springtime, is the seat of Wisconsin's Brown County and the center of a metropolitan statistical area that includes the entire county. The oldest permanent settlement in Wisconsin, Green Bay began as a French fur-trading post and mission that was important to the exploration of the Upper Midwest in the early seventeenth century. Since the nineteenth century the local economy has been based on the lumbering, meat packing, and paper making industries, with a currently expanding service sector. Today Green Bay is known as ''the tissue paper capital of America'' and is home to the famous Green Bay Packers professional football team. Green Bay was recently named an All-America city and consistently ranks high on ''best-places'' lists and is noted for being child-friendly and safe.

Geography and Climate

Green Bay is located at the mouth of the Fox River, one of the largest northward-flowing rivers in the United States, which empties into the south end of Lake Michigan's Green Bay. The surrounding topography—the bay, Lakes Michigan and Superior, and to a lesser extent the slightly higher terrain terminating in the Fox River Valley—modifies the continental climate. The lake effects and the limited hours of sunshine, caused by cloudiness, produce a narrow temperature range. Three-fifths of the total annual rainfall occurs during the growing season, May through September; the high degree of precipitation, combined with the low temperature range, is conducive to the development of the dairy industry. Long winters with snowstorms are common, though winter extremes are not so severe as would be indicated by Green Bay's northern latitude location. Snowfall averages 46.3 inches each year.

Area: 43.8 square miles (2000)

Elevation: 582 feet above sea level

Average Temperatures: January, 13.9° F; July, 69.5° F; annual average, 43.6° F

Average Annual Precipitation: 28.83 inches of rain, 46.3 inches of snow

History

Great Lakes-Mississippi Water Link Sought

On a mission for Samuel de Champlain, the governor of New France, Jean Nicolet was charged with finding a route from the Great Lakes to the Mississippi River. In 1634 he arrived at La Baye des Puans, where the Fox River empties into Lake Michigan, and claimed the region for France. But La Baye did not gain importance until 1669 when Jesuit missionary Father Claude Allouez, who established a mission there, traveled the length of the Fox River and discovered a waterway to the Mississippi River, indirectly linking the St. Lawrence and the Gulf of Mexico.

La Baye became a fur-trading center and its future importance was secured when Nicolas Perrot was made commandant of La Baye. Perrot was an effective diplomat who made alliances and trade agreements with Native Americans. The lands of the upper Mississippi became the possession of the French Empire when a formal agreement was signed at Fort St. Antoine in 1689, turning a lucrative fur trading region over to the French. But when Perrot was recalled to France in 1716, his diplomatic policy was replaced by a military regime. The resulting tensions developed into warfare with the Fox Indians that continued until 1740, when fur trading again prospered and permanent housing was constructed.

In 1745 Augustin de Langlade established a trading center on the bank of the Fox River; his relations with Native Americans were built on trust and respect. Langlade's large family controlled the region's trade, owned large parcels of land, married Menominee tribe women, and lived independent of French rule. During the French and Indian War, the Langlades left La Baye to fight against the British in Ohio and Canada. The British gained control of what was known as the Northwest Territory and captured Fort La Baye, which they rebuilt and renamed Fort Edward August. The British also renamed the area Green Bay, after the green-tinted streaks that stripe the bay in springtime. Trade flourished for both French and English settlers during the period of British rule and continued to prosper after the Northwest Territory was transferred to the U.S. government after the Revolutionary War.

City Develops With Lumber, Professional Sports

It was not until after the War of 1812 that financier John Jacob Astor's American Fur Company secured control of the fur trade. Fort Howard at Green Bay and Fort Crawford at Prairie du Chine were built to protect U.S. commercial interests. The opening of the Erie Canal, linking the Great Lakes to New England, further advanced Green Bay as a trading center. Daniel Whitney platted one part of present-day Green Bay in 1829 and named it Navarino while Astor platted an opposite section and built the Astor Hotel to attract settlers. Astor priced his land too high and when the hotel burned down in 1857 his company relinquished claims on the land. Farming was soon replaced by lumber as the dominant economic activity in Green Bay and in 1853, the year the city was incorporated, 80 million feet of pine lumber were milled.

Today, Green Bay is known as the smallest city in the United States to sponsor a professional football team. The Green Bay Packers were founded in 1919 by "Curly" Lambeau and George Calhoun, sports editor of the *Green Bay Press-Gazette,* and the team takes its name from the Indian Packing Corporation, which purchased the team's first uniforms. The Packers joined the National Football League in 1919 and have had a distinctive history. Under coach Vince Lombardi in the 1960s the Packers set a standard of team performance and dedication that other teams in the league have come to emulate in the modern football era. The Packers won the first two Super Bowl games in 1967 and 1968, and Lombardi and his players became national heroes. Thirty years later, the team won Super Bowl XXXI, beginning a new era under coach Mike Holmgren and general manager Ron Wolf. In addition to championship sports teams, Green Bay supports colleges, a symphony, community chorus, community theater, and several museums. And unlike many Midwestern cities with lagging economic growth, Green Bay has enjoyed a diverse and growing local economy. Using job growth and economic balance as its measures, in 2004 *Inc.* magazine ranked Green Bay as the country's top medium-sized metropolitan area for doing business.

Historical Information: University of Wisconsin-Green Bay-Area Research Center, 2420 Nicolet Drive, Green Bay, WI 54311-7001; telephone (920)465-2539

Population Profile

Metropolitan Area Residents
1980: 175,280
1990: 194,594
2000: 226,178
Percent change, 1990–2000: 16.2%
U.S. rank in 1990: Not reported
U.S. rank in 2000: 153rd

City Residents
1980: 87,899
1990: 96,466
2000: 102,213
2003 estimate: 101,467
Percent change, 1990–2000: 5.9%
U.S. rank in 1980: 200th

U.S. rank in 1990: 205th
U.S. rank in 2000: 240th

Density: 2,333.6 people per square mile (2000)

Racial and ethnic characteristics (2000)
White: 87,841
Black or African American: 1,407
American Indian or Alaska Native: 3,355
Asian: 3,845
Hawaiian and Other Pacific Islander: 36
Hispanic or Latino (may be of any race): 7,294
Other: 3,809

Percent of residents born in state: 74.4% (2000)

Age characteristics (2000)
Population under 5 years old: 7,359
Population 5 to 9 years old: 7,254
Population 10 to 14 years old: 7,168
Population 15 to 19 years old: 7,492
Population 20 to 24 years old: 8,632
Population 25 to 34 years old: 16,074
Population 35 to 44 years old: 16,349
Population 45 to 54 years old: 12,766
Population 55 to 59 years old: 3,985
Population 60 to 64 years old: 3,192
Population 65 to 74 years old: 5,783
Population 75 to 84 years old: 4,535
Population 85 years and over: 1,724
Median age: 33.2 years

Births (2004, Brown County)
Total number: 3,200

Deaths (2003, Brown County)
Total number: 1,565

Money income (1999)
Per capita income: $19,269
Median household income: $38,820
Total households: 41,656

Number of households with income of . . .
less than $10,000: 1,091
$10,000 to $14,999: 1,049
$15,000 to $24,999: 2,594
$25,000 to $34,999: 3,072
$35,000 to $49,999: 5,045
$50,000 to $74,999: 7,052
$75,000 to $99,999: 2,614
$100,000 to $149,999: 1,648
$150,000 to 199,999: 418
$200,000 or more: 276

Percent of families below poverty level: 7.4% (42.7% of which were female householder families with related children under 5 years)

2002 FBI Crime Index Total: 3,762

Municipal Government

The Green Bay city government is administered by a mayor and 12 alderpersons. The mayor is elected to a four-year term; the alderpersons are elected for two years.

Head Official: Mayor James J. Schmitt (since 2003; current term expires in 2007)

Total Number of City Employees: 1,010 (2005)

City Information: City of Green Bay, 100 N. Jefferson St., Green Bay, WI 54301; telephone (920)448-3010

Economy

Major Industries and Commercial Activity

Green Bay's economy is highly diversified. The majority of jobs in the area are service providing—following sectors are goods producing; trade, transportation, and utilities; manufacturing; and government. One of every five jobs in the county is in manufacturing, many of which are within or directly related to the paper industry. Growing industries in Green Bay are healthcare, insurance, and transportation. Tourism is growing, as well. A study in the late 1990s found that the Green Bay Packers generated $144 million in total annual spending in Brown County, 1,620 full- and part-time jobs, and $9.6 million in annual tax revenue to local and state government.

Brown County is among the top four jobbing, wholesale, and distribution points in Wisconsin. Green Bay is the site of a petroleum storage terminal. The city ranks as a major retailing center for northeastern Wisconsin and Upper Michigan.

Items and goods produced: tissue paper and paper products, cheese, food products, lumber, woodwork, paper mill machinery, paper boxes, clothing, steel furniture, auto parts, dairy products, gloves, fertilizers, foundry products, brick tile, sheet metal, awnings

Incentive Programs—New and Existing Businesses

Local programs—The principal economic development organization in Green Bay is Advance, a publicly and privately supported branch of the Green Bay Area Chamber of Commerce. Advance uses its online database to inform interested business about available sites and buildings. The Business Retention committee assists companies in troubleshooting municipal service problems, job training needs, and other issues. The Chamber's Small Business Council assists and meets regularly to promote the interests of businesses with

up to 300 employees. The Advance Business Development Center is one of the most successful incubators in Wisconsin, having graduated more than 100 start-up firms by allowing them to lease increasingly larger amounts of shared light industrial and office space as their firms grow.

State programs—The Wisconsin Economic Development Association (WEDA) and the Wisconsin Economic Development Institute (WEDI) are two nonprofit agencies that provide information and financial services, legal and legislative assistance, and networking opportunities for their member businesses. On the government side, the Division of Business Development of the Wisconsin Department of Commerce provides technical assistance and financial incentives to businesses in the areas of business planning, site selection, capitalization, permits, training and recruitment, and research and development. On April 28, 2000, Governor Tommy G. Thompson signed into law a bill that created the Wisconsin Technology Council, a nonprofit, nonpartisan board that serves to create, develop and retain science and technology-based business in Wisconsin, and to serve as an advisor to the Governor and the Legislature. The Council also serves as the key link between the state's colleges and universities and the business expertise and capital offered by the financial service industry. Recently the firm published its "Vision 2020: A Model Wisconsin Economy" as a blueprint for its efforts over the next two decades.

Job training programs—Partners in Education (PIE), coordinated by the Green Bay Area Chamber of Commerce, works with businesses, educators, and community organizations to provide skills that help students transitioning from school to work.

Development Projects

Downtown Green Bay, Inc. brings together people, organizations, and funds to implement and facilitate downtown development projects. As of 2005 the organization had assisted with Baylake Bank's restoration of the old Boston Store property; a $4.5 million, 26,000 square-foot addition to the YWCA; construction of a $16 million, four-story building for the Nicolet National Bank at the corner of Cherry and Washington; and won approval from the Common Council on a riverfront redevelopment plan that will include an urban beach and boardwalk. Other projects in the works were a major hotel/condominium project for the old Younkers Building site on Washington, and a proposed $10 million riverfront loft development. Additionally, the Green Bay Packers completed a $295 million renovation of historic Lambeau Field in 2003, adding 11,625 seats, 166 private boxes, twice as many concession stands, 500 restrooms, and a new concourse.

Economic Development Information: Green Bay Area Chamber of Commerce, 400 S. Washington St., PO Box

1660, Green Bay, WI 54305-1660; telephone (920)437-8704; fax (920)437-1024

Commercial Shipping

The Port of Green Bay is an international and domestic port with a navigation season extending from April through December. More than 200 commercial vessels transport cargo through the channel each year; port tonnage averages more than 2.4 million metric tons annually. Linking the port with inland markets are an interstate highway, air cargo service, 40 motor freight carriers and the Green Bay & Western, Soo Line, Chicago & Northwestern, and Escanaba & Lake Superior railroads.

Labor Force and Employment Outlook

A relatively diverse economy and an attractive small-town lifestyle have kept Green Bay's job outlook ahead of the curve in the early 2000s, despite a nationwide rise in unemployment in recent years. The local education prospects are excellent on both a secondary and university/technical level, providing a pool of well-trained workers. During years of strong economic growth, however, firms have often found a shortage of qualified workers and recruitment and retention become issues of concern. Partners in Education (PIE), coordinated by the Green Bay Area Chamber of Commerce, provides a link between businesses, educators, and community organizations with an objective to assist students in developing the skills necessary for successful transition from school to an eventual career involving lifelong learning.

The following is a summary of data regarding the Green Bay metropolitan area labor force, 2004 annual averages.

Size of non-agricultural labor force: 167,900

Number of workers employed in . . .
  mining and construction: 9,100
  manufacturing: 31,200
  trade, transportation and public utilities: 36,000
  information: 2,500
  financial activities: 11,000
  professional and business services: 14,700
  educational and health services: 20,500
  leisure and hospitality: 15,100
  other services: 7,100
  government: 20,800

Average hourly earnings of production workers employed in manufacturing: $16.19 (statewide figure)

Unemployment rate: 5.6% (February 2005)

Largest employers	Number of employees
Schneider National, Inc.	3,599
Georgia-Pacific Corp.	3,590

Largest employers	Number of employees
Humana	2,700
Green Bay Public Schools	2,655
Bellin Health	1,863
St. Vincent Hospital	1,853
Shopko Stores, Inc.	1,753
WPS Resources	1,545
Packerland Packing Co. Inc.	1,500
Brown County	1,424
American Medical Security	1,378
American Foods Group	1,377
Aurora Health Care	1,272

Cost of Living

The cost of living in Green Bay ranks consistently below the national average in health care, utilities, housing, food, and miscellaneous goods and services.

The following is a summary of data regarding several key cost of living factors in the Green Bay area.

2004 (3rd Quarter) ACCRA Average House Price: $277,172

2004 (3rd Quarter) ACCRA Cost of Living Index: 96.7 (U.S. average = 100.0)

State income tax rate: Ranges from 4.6% to 6.75% (tax year 2005)

State sales tax rate: 5.0%

Local income tax rate: None

Local sales tax rate: None

Property tax rate: $25.75 per $1,000 of assessed value

Economic Information: Advance, Green Bay Area Economic Development, PO Box 1660, Green Bay, WI 54305-1660; telephone (920)437-8704.

Education and Research

Elementary and Secondary Schools

The Green Bay Area Public School District, the fourth largest school system in the state of Wisconsin, includes, in addition to the city of Green Bay, the towns of Allouez and Scott and parts of the towns of Bellevue, DePere, Eaton, and Humboldt. A seven-member nonpartisan board hires a superintendent.

The following is a summary of data regarding the Green Bay public schools as of the 2002–2003 school year.

Total enrollment: 19,789 (2005)

Number of facilities
  elementary schools: 25 (K-5); 2 (K-8)
  middle schools: 4
  senior high schools: 4
  other: Elective academies in all district high schools;
  Fine Arts Academy

Student/teacher ratio: 14.3:1

Teacher salaries
  average: $47,000

Funding per pupil: $9,506

Nearly 30 parochial schools, including Catholic and Lutheran, enroll students in kindergarten through twelfth grade curricula.

Public Schools Information: Green Bay Area Public Schools, PO Box 23387, Green Bay, WI 54305; telephone (920)448-2000

Colleges and Universities

Part of the statewide university system, the University of Wisconsin-Green Bay grants associate, undergraduate, and graduate degrees in such areas as arts and sciences, business, and natural and biological sciences. Of 5,500 students in 2005, nearly 2,000 lived on campus. Top fields of study are business administration, psychology, and human development. St. Norbert College is a four-year liberal arts institution operated by the Norbertine Fathers. Vocational, technical, and adult education is provided by the Northeast Wisconsin Technical College as well as trade schools specializing in particular skills.

Libraries and Research Centers

The largest library in Green Bay is the award-winning Brown County Library, with a circulation of over 2.3 million materials annually. These resources are available through a central library, a bookmobile, and eight branch libraries. Special collections pertain to Brown County history, genealogy, Wisconsin history, and oral history; the library is a depository for state documents. The Nicolet Federated Library is a regional library, serving a population of more than 330,000. The University of Wisconsin-Green Bay Cofrin Library serves the University of Wisconsin system as well as the northeast Wisconsin community. Libraries are also maintained by Northern Wisconsin Technical College, county agencies, health care organizations, churches, and corporations.

Public Library Information: Brown County Library, 515 Pine Street, Green Bay, WI 54301; telephone (920)448-4400; fax (920)448-4364

Health Care

Green Bay is served by three major hospitals providing more than 1,200 beds, several clinics and health care agencies, and 20 nursing homes. St. Vincent Hospital, with 542 beds, is the city's largest hospital and a regional center for cancer treatment, neuroscience, pediatrics, trauma, rehabilitation, perinatal care, and poison information. Operated by Bellin Health, Bellin Memorial Hospital is a 167-bed general care facility that specializes in the treatment of heart disease, mental health and addictive services, obstetrics, and orthopedics. Employing more than 2,300 people, Bellin Health also operates the four-year Bellin School College of Nursing. St. Mary's Hospital, with 158 private rooms, houses one of the state's largest 24-hour emergency-wards; other services include an alcohol and drug abuse program and a sick child day care program. The Prevea Clinic has more than 100 physicians trained in 21 specialty care areas who treat patients from throughout northeastern Wisconsin.

Recreation

Sightseeing

The recently expanded, 25,000 square-foot Green Bay Packer Hall of Fame was moved to the Lambeau Field atrium as part of the newly renovated stadium project. One of Green Bay's most popular attractions, the museum has trophies, memorabilia, and mementos of the Green Bay Packers, including the Vince Lombardi collection and displays on the club's league championships and Super Bowl victories; tours of Lambeau Field are also available. The 40-acre Heritage Hill State Historical Park features furnished historical buildings grouped according to four heritage themes: pioneer, small town, military, and agricultural. Among them are a 1762 fur trader's cabin, a reproduction of Wisconsin's first courthouse, Wisconsin's oldest standing house, Fort Howard buildings dating from the 1830s, and a Belgian farmhouse.

Hazelwood, a home built by Morgan L. Martin, president of the second Wisconsin Constitutional Convention, dates from 1837 and contains the table on which Wisconsin's constitution was drafted. The National Railroad Museum is a locomotive museum that exhibits locomotives and cars from the steam and diesel eras, including "Big Boy," one of the world's largest locomotives. Special attractions are U.S. Army General Dwight D. Eisenhower's World War II staff train and British Prime Minister Winston Churchill's travel-

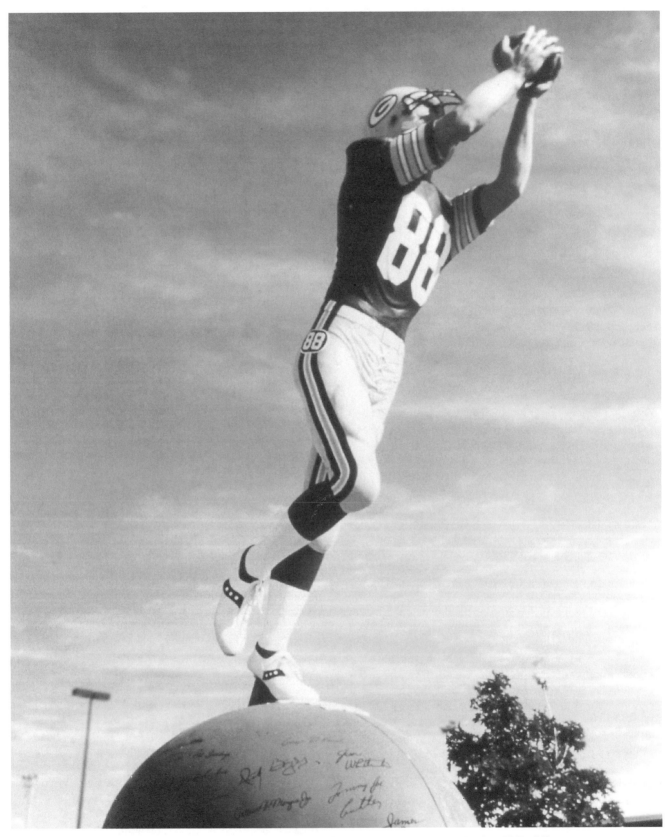

A statue entitled *The Receiver* stands at the entrance to the Green Bay Packer Hall of Fame.

ing car. Other popular attractions are Oneida Bingo and the NEW Zoo, a life science institute that seeks to enhance visitors' understanding of animal life and its relationship to ecological systems.

Many visitors to Green Bay like to take a side trip to Door County, 90 minutes north; it offers miles of shoreline, state parts, and lighthouses, and is home to many artists and craftspersons.

Arts and Culture

The Green Bay Symphony performs a six-concert season at the new Edward W. Weidner Center for the Performing Arts at the University of Wisconsin-Green Bay. Both classic and modern plays, ballet, musical events, and nationally touring musical acts are featured at the beautifully-restored Meyer Theater, a 1,000-seat member of the League of Historic American Theaters. The Civic Music Association sponsors visiting artists. St. Norbert College hosts a performing Arts Series and college theater productions, and the Weidner Center also hosts a variety of entertainments, including ballet performances and Broadway musicals. Concerts and ice shows take place at the Resch Center and Brown County Veterans Memorial Complex.

Brown County's Neville Public Museum houses six galleries of art, natural history, and science exhibits; the ''On the Edge of the Inland Sea'' exhibit traces 13,000 years of northeast Wisconsin history. The Oneida Nation Museum captures the history of the Oneida Utopian community's life after it moved from New York to Wisconsin.

Festivals and Holidays

Artstreet is Green Bay's annual celebration of the performing and visual arts, held in the downtown district. Other annual celebrations include Arti Gras, Bayfest, Celebrate Americafest, the Oneida Indian Pow Wow, Brown County Fair, the Wet Whistle Wine Festival and Ethnic Festival in September, the Terror on the Fox Haunted House and Train Ride in October, and the Holiday Parade.

Sports for the Spectator

The Green Bay Packers, the oldest modern professional football team, enjoy one of the most heralded histories in professional sports; the team plays in the National Football Conference of the National Football League. They compete at home at Lambeau Field against perennial rivals—the Detroit Lions, Chicago Bears, and Minnesota Vikings. Playing in by far the smallest city in the entire NFL, the Packers are the local passion and enjoy a national following; despite the town's size, Packers games are always sold out. In fact, football Sundays in the autumn in Green Bay are treated as community holidays, with tailgate parties, bratwurst on the grill, plenty of beer drinking, and of course, the game. In

college athletics, St. Norbert College provides small-college football and baseball in nearby DePere. The University of Wisconsin-Green Bay supports a successful soccer program and competes in Division I basketball, making the NCAA basketball tournament, and even winning one game in 2005. The national champion Green Bay Gamblers play in the Junior A U.S. Hockey League.

Sports for the Participant

The Green Bay parks and recreation department oversees numerous city parks large and small, including the Bay Beach Amusement Park and Wildlife Sanctuary, the Metro Boat Launch at the mouth of the Fox River, the SK8 Park for skateboarders and inline skaters, and the Triangle Recreation Area. The department also sponsors sports leagues for all age groups. Facilities include courts for indoor tennis and racquetball, indoor and outdoor public swimming pools, ice skating and hockey rinks, outdoor tennis courts, ski and toboggan hills, and cross-country ski trails. Soccer and rugby teams compete in leagues. Several more boating facilities are available along Green Bay. Green Bay, Fox River, and Lake Michigan provide fishermen with pike, bass, salmon, trout, muskie, and panfish. Hunters can obtain licenses to bag duck, deer, and small game. Children enjoy rides and other activities at Bay Beach Amusement Park. Across the street from the amusement park at Wildlife Sanctuary, a 700-acre urban wildlife refuge, visitors can observe native fauna and hike the nature trails.

Shopping and Dining

The Green Bay area is the regional shopping center for northeastern Wisconsin. Shoppers may choose from among three major shopping malls with nearly 200 stores, mini-malls, and craft stores. There are quaint shopping districts with unique shops in the Historic Broadway District of Green Bay on Broadway, and on Main Street in nearby DePere. The Flying Pig gallery and greenspace in Algoma is a local attraction. Of unique interest is the Green Bay Packer Hall of Fame Store, offering Packer treasures, at the Lambeau Field Atrium.

Green Bay's more than 100 restaurants offer options ranging from gourmet cuisine to ethnic menus, sports bars, and casual dining establishments, and the options continue to expand. A more recent addition to the menu, diners can enjoy a sunset dinner boat that cruises the Green Bay waterways. Patrick's on the Bay offers beautiful waterside views and what many consider to be the best dining in the area.

Visitor Information: Green Bay Area Visitor and Convention Bureau, 1901 S. Oneida St., PO Box 10596, Green Bay, WI 54307; telephone (920)494-9507; toll-free (888)867-3342; email tourism@dct.com

Convention Facilities

With the recent opening of the KI Convention Center, Green Bay has established itself as a leading regional meeting and convention destination. Offering more than 46,000 square feet of flexible meeting and convention space, the KI is connected to the Regency Suites hotel and is within walking distance of the downtown business and shopping district. A popular meeting site in Green Bay is the Brown County Expo Centre Complex, which includes the Brown County Veterans Memorial Arena and Exposition Hall—offering a combined total of 60,680 square feet of exhibition space. Providing modern equipment and facilities, the complex accommodates a variety of functions such as trade and consumer shows, conventions, and banquets, in addition to sports events. Brown County Veterans Memorial Arena features a number of floor layout options, ranging from 185 exhibit booths to portable seating for nearly 3,000 people. The Exposition Hall also offers multiple layouts, with a maximum of 255 exhibit booths and a seating capacity of 2,500 people for dining and 3,000 people in a theater setting. The Green Bay Packer Hall of Fame at the new Lambeau Field Atrium hosts breakfast meetings, cocktail receptions, and banquets for groups of 50 to 500 people. Parking for 7,000 automobiles is available on the grounds. Alternative sites for small to mid-sized meetings can be found at the Neville Public Museum, St. Norbert College, and the Weidner Center for the Performing Arts.

About 74 downtown and suburban hotels and motels provide lodging for visitors and many have complete meeting accommodations, including the Radisson Inn and Conference Center and Kress Inn on the St. Norbert College campus; more than 3,000 guest rooms are available in the Green Bay metropolitan area.

Convention Information: Green Bay Area Visitor and Convention Bureau, 1901 S. Oneida St., PO Box 10596, Green Bay, WI 54307; telephone (920)494-9507; toll-free (888)867-3342; email tourism@dct.com

Transportation

Approaching the City

Three commercial airlines schedule daily flights into Austin Straubel Airfield, operated by Brown County and located in Ashwaubenon on the outskirts of the city.

As the transportation hub for northeastern Wisconsin, Green Bay is served by motor routes linked by the state's only complete beltline. Interstate 43, connecting Green Bay with Milwaukee, circles the east side of the city from northwest to southeast and is linked with the north-south U.S. 41 on the west side by Highway 172. Other principal highways are U.S. 141 and state 29, 32, 54, and 57.

Traveling in the City

Intracity public bus transportation on Green Bay Metro Transit is available Monday through Saturday on regularly scheduled routes throughout Green Bay and the nearby towns of Allouez, Ashwaubenon, Bellevue, De Pere, and the Oneida Casino. The Titletown Trolley offers rides to and from several local attractions (no service on Mondays).

Communications

Newspapers and Magazines

The major daily newspapers in Green Bay are the *Green Bay Press-Gazette,* published evenings and Saturday and Sunday mornings, and the *Green Bay News-Chronicle,* published every morning except Sunday. Several neighborhood and regional newspapers appear weekly. *Musky Hunter,* a magazine for anglers, is published six times a year.

Television and Radio

There are local network affiliates in Green Bay for ABC, CBS, NBC, Fox, PBS, WB, and UPN; subscription cable service is available. Six FM and AM radio stations broadcast out of Green Bay; from nearby cities, more than 30 FM and 9 AM radio stations are available to Green Bay listeners. Most stations schedule music programming, with an emphasis on country, oldies, and light rock; there are several news/talk stations, sports talk, and two public radio outlets.

Media Information: Green Bay News-Chronicle, PO Box 2467, Green Bay, WI 54306; telephone (920)432-2941. *Green Bay Press-Gazette,* 435 East Walnut, PO Box 19430, Green Bay, WI 54307-9430; telephone (920)435-4411

Green Bay Online

Brown County Library. Available www.co.brown.wi.us/library

City of Green Bay home page. Available www.ci.green-bay.wi.us

Green Bay Area Public Schools. Available www.greenbay.k12.wi.us

Green Bay Area Visitors & Convention Bureau. Available www.greenbay.com

Green Bay Packers team website. Available www.packers .com

Selected Bibliography

Carlson, Chuck, *Tales from the Packers Sidelines: A Collection of the Greatest Stories Ever Told* (Sports Publishing, 2003)

The Door County Peninsula (Marina del Rey, CA: Bennett Marine Video, 1991. Videorecording)

Madison

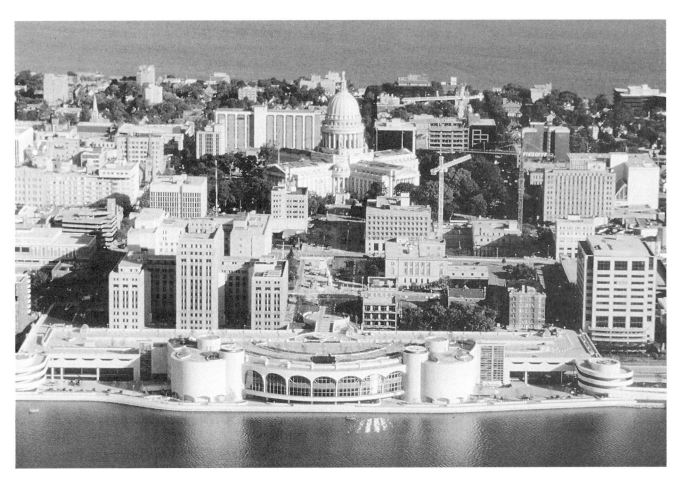

The City in Brief

Founded: 1836 (incorporated 1856)

Head Official: Mayor Dave Cieslewicz (since 2003)

City Population
1980: 170,616
1990: 190,766
2000: 208,054
2003 estimate: 218,432
Percent change, 1990–2000: 8.9%
U.S. rank in 1980: 84th
U.S. rank in 1990: 82nd
U.S. rank in 2000: 81st

Metropolitan Area Population
1980: 324,000
1990: 367,085
2000: 426,526
Percent change, 1990–2000: 16.2%

U.S. rank in 1980: 100th
U.S. rank in 1990: Not reported
U.S. rank in 2000: 97th

Area: 68.7 square miles (2000)
Elevation: 845.6 feet above sea level (average)
Average Annual Temperature: 45.2° F
Average Annual Precipitation: 30.16 inches of rain; 37 inches of snow

Major Economic Sectors: Government, services, wholesale and retail trade
Unemployment Rate: 3.9% (February 2005)
Per Capita Income: $23,498 (1999)
2004 ACCRA Average House Price: Not reported
2004 ACCRA Cost of Living Index: Not reported

2002 FBI Crime Index Total: 8,847

Major Colleges and Universities: University of Wisconsin–Madison

Daily Newspapers: *Wisconsin State Journal; The Capital Times*

Introduction

The capital of Wisconsin, Madison is also the seat of Dane County and the focus of a metropolitan statistical area that includes the entire county. The city was founded as the state capital, where no other permanent settlement had previously existed, on a unique geographic site, a narrow isthmus of land called Four Lakes Isthmus between two lakes. Since Madison was founded, the natural beauty of its setting has been enhanced by parks and boulevards with an impressive State Capitol Building and plaza at the center of the city. Madison is the base of the University of Wisconsin, a nationally respected research institution known for a tradition of academic excellence.

Geography and Climate

Set on a narrow isthmus of land between Lake Mendota and Lake Monona, Madison is surrounded by a network of lakes and rivers. The topography is rolling. The continental climate is consistent with the city's location in interior North America; the temperature range is wide, with an extreme winter low of minus 40 degrees and an extreme summer high of 110 degrees. Tornadoes can be prevalent during spring, summer, and fall; moderate temperatures and humidity prevail during a generally pleasant summer. Annual average snowfall is 37 inches; the growing season is approximately 175 days.

Area: 68.7 square miles (2000)

Elevation: 845.6 feet above sea level (average)

Average Temperatures: January, 19.4° F; July, 68.6° F; annual average, 45.2° F

Average Annual Precipitation: 30.16 inches of rain; 37 inches of snow

History

Land Speculator Prevails in State Capital Bid

The Winnebago tribe were the first inhabitants of the area where the city of Madison now stands; these Native Americans lived off the land's bounty and camped alongside Lake Monona and Lake Mendota. Madison owes its founding to James Doty, a native New Yorker who served as circuit judge of the Western Michigan Territory, which included Wisconsin and points as far west as the Dakotas and Iowa.

Doty became a land agent for fur trader and financier John Jacob Astor and in August 1835, he started buying land around the site that was to become Madison; soon he owned more than 1,200 acres on the Four Lakes isthmus.

When the Wisconsin Territorial legislature convened for the first time in October 1836, with the task of selecting the site for the capital, land speculators flocked to the village with "paper" towns for the legislators to consider. In all, 18 townsites were considered, but Doty's vision proved to be the most persuasive. Doty had selected the name Madison in honor of James Madison, the former United States President, for the state capital. The recently deceased Madison had been the last surviving signer of the U.S. Constitution. Doty's design of Madison, with a square in the middle housing the Capitol and streets radiating diagonally from it like spokes in a wheel, was the same as Pierre Charles L'Enfant's street plat of Washington, D.C. The widest street was to be named Washington, and the other streets named after the other signers of the Constitution. When the legislators complained of being cold during their meetings, Doty dispatched a man to Dubuque, Iowa, to purchase Buffalo robes to warm the freezing public officials.

Eben and Rosaline Peck and their son Victor were the first non-Native American family to settle in Madison, arriving in the spring of 1837. They built a crude log inn and named it Madison House, which became the center of early activity and boarded the workmen who had arrived to begin work on the new capitol. Augustus A. Bird supervised a crew of workmen who first built a steam-driven sawmill and then proceeded to try to complete the capitol building before the first legislative session. In November 1838, the legislators arrived to find the statehouse incomplete; when they finally moved into the new statehouse, the conditions were terrible: inkwells were frozen, ice coated the interiors, and hogs squealed in the basement. Legislators threatened to move the capital to Milwaukee but better accommodations could not be guaranteed. The statehouse was not completed until 1848.

Growth and Development Preserve Natural Setting

Improvements were slow to come to Madison and the living conditions remained crude until the arrival of Leonard J. Farwell in 1849. Farwell, a successful Milwaukee businessman, began developing the land by channeling a canal between Lakes Mendota and Monona, damming one end of Lake Mendota, building a grist and flour mill, and opening streets and laying sidewalks. But even as late as 1850, when Madison's population numbered more than 1,600 people, the isthmus thickets were still dense and impenetrable.

The University of Wisconsin was founded in 1848, the year Wisconsin was admitted to the Union. The first graduating class, in 1854, numbered two men. That year the first railroad service arrived in Madison and during the decade before the

Civil War, Madison's business economy began to grow. The Madison Institute sponsored a successful literary lyceum and boasted 1,300 volumes in its library. Streets were gas-illuminated by 1855, when three daily and five weekly newspapers were published in the new capital and the population had increased to more than 6,800 people. The city was incorporated in 1856. The following year Madison's citizens voted to donate $50,000 in city bonds to enable the legislature to enlarge and improve the Capitol building.

The Madison Park and Pleasure Drive Association was organized in 1894 and citizens donated lakeshore and forest-bluff tracts as well as money to create scenic drives, parks, and playgrounds in the city. Four years later, the city council started annual contributions to the park association. By 1916, the park association had spent more than $300,000 on improvements to the shoreline and parks. In February 1904, a fire destroyed much of the Capitol's interior. A new Capitol was constructed in stages between 1906 and 1917 on the site of the old one, featuring the only granite state Capitol dome in the United States. As both a state capital and home to a major state university, Madison has experienced a stable economic and educational base.

In rankings of U.S. cities, Madison consistently scores very high on seemingly every form of criteria. In recent years Madison has appeared several times on *Money* magazine's list of the best places to live. It has been cited by *Zero Population Growth* as the "#1 healthiest city in the nation to raise children." *Outside* magazine calls Madison a "Dream Town"; *The Utne Reader* calls it one of America's "10 Most Enlightened Towns" and "The Heartland's Progressive Hotbed." In addition, *Sports Illustrated* called Madison America's #1 College Sports Town, while *Prevention* magazine labeled it one of its "12 Best Walking Towns."

Historical Information: State Historical Society of Wisconsin, 816 State Street, Madison, WI 53706; telephone (608)264-6534

Population Profile

Metropolitan Area Residents
1980: 324,000
1990: 367,085
2000: 426,526
Percent change, 1990–2000: 16.2%
U.S. rank in 1980: 100th
U.S. rank in 1990: Not reported
U.S. rank in 2000: 97thth

City Residents
1980: 170,616
1990: 190,766
2000: 208,054
2003 estimate: 218,432
Percent change, 1990–2000: 8.9%
U.S. rank in 1980: 84th
U.S. rank in 1990: 82nd
U.S. rank in 2000: 81st

Density: 3,028.4 people per square mile (2000)

Racial and ethnic characteristics (2000)
   White: 174,689
   Black or African American: 12,155
   American Indian and Alaska Native: 759
   Asian: 12,065
   Native Hawaiian and Pacific Islander: 77
   Hispanic or Latino (may be of any race): 8,512
   Other: 3,474

Percent of residents born in state: 58.2%

Age characteristics (2000)
   Population under 5 years old: 10,815
   Population 5 to 9 years old: 10,016
   Population 10 to 14 years old: 10,332
   Population 15 to 19 years old: 18,192
   Population 20 to 24 years old: 32,394
   Population 25 to 34 years old: 37,054
   Population 35 to 44 years old: 29,925
   Population 45 to 54 years old: 26,553
   Population 55 to 59 years old: 7,941
   Population 60 to 64 years old: 5,648
   Population 65 to 74 years old: 9,508
   Population 75 to 84 years old: 7,025
   Population 85 years and over: 2,651
   Median age: 30.6 years

Births (2003)
   Total number: 3,097

Deaths (2003)
   Total number: 2,657 (of which, 12 were infants under the age of 1 year)

Money income (1999)
   Per capita income: $23,498
   Median household income: $41,941
   Total households: 89,267

Number of households with income of . . .
   less than $10,000: 8,645
   $10,000 to $14,999: 5,285
   $15,000 to $24,999: 10,696
   $25,000 to $34,999: 11,561
   $35,000 to $49,999: 15,934

$50,000 to $74,999: 18,338
$75,000 to $99,999: 9,271
$100,000 to $149,999: 6,542
$150,000 to $199,999: 1,631
$200,000 or more: 1,364

Percent of families below poverty level: 5.8% (39.3% of which were female householder families with related children under 5 years)

2002 FBI Crime Index Total: 8,847

Municipal Government

The city of Madison operates under a mayor-alderperson form of government; 20 alders, representing 20 city districts, are chosen for a two-year term in a nonpartisan election. The mayor, who is not a member of council, is chosen for a four-year term in a non-partisan election.

Head Official: Mayor Dave Cieslewicz (since 2003; current term expires 2007)

Total Number of City Employees: 2,741 (2005)

City Information: City Hall, 210 Martin Luther King Jr. Boulevard, Madison, WI 53710; telephone (608)266-4611

Economy

Major Industries and Commercial Activity

The principal economic sectors in Madison are manufacturing, services, and government. Meat packing and the production of agriculture and dairy equipment have long been established industries in the city; among other items produced by area manufacturing firms are hospital equipment, advanced instrumentation, storage batteries, and air circulating fixtures. Diversified farming contributes significantly to the Madison economy; nearly one-sixth of all Wisconsin farms are located within the Greater Madison market region. Dane County ranks among the top ten counties in the nation for agricultural production, the primary products being corn, alfalfa, tobacco, oats, eggs, cattle, hogs, and dairy foods.

The home offices of more than 30 insurance companies are located in Madison; included among them are American Family, CUNA Mutual Insurance Group, and General Casualty. The city is also the world headquarters of Rayovac Corporation, Promega Corporation, and Oscar Mayer. Government and education are major economic sectors; about

one third of the area work force is employed in federal, state, and local government jobs, and the University of Wisconsin employs more than 36,000 workers. Madison is a banking and finance center, serving the metropolitan region with more than 120 banks, credit unions, and savings and loan institutions. Other service areas important to the local economy are health care and research and development.

Items and goods produced: agricultural products, food packaging products, dry cell batteries, farm machinery, hospital equipment, optical instruments, lenses, fabricated structural steel

Incentive Programs—New and Existing Businesses

Local programs—The city of Madison Office of Business Resources leads start-up, relocating, and expanding businesses through the range of available financial and consultative benefits the local government has to offer. The Small Business Development Center (SBDC) at the University of Wisconsin is an award-winning community resource that aids small businesses by providing practical, customer-focused management education, training, counseling and networking. In addition to counseling, the SBDC conducts workshops and seminars. The city provides below market-rate interest loans for real estate projects in the Downtown Isthmus area and selected other areas of the city. Madison Development Corporation (MDC) provides loans of up to $200,000 to businesses in the City of Madison that show continued job growth.

State programs—The Wisconsin Economic Development Association (WEDA) and the Wisconsin Economic Development Institute (WEDI) are two nonprofit agencies that provide information and financial services, legal and legislative assistance, and networking opportunities for their member businesses. On the government side, the Division of Business Development of the Wisconsin Department of Commerce provides technical assistance and financial incentives to businesses in the areas of business planning, site selection, capitalization, permits, training and recruitment, and research and development. On April 28, 2000, then Governor Tommy G. Thompson signed into law a bill that created the Wisconsin Technology Council, a nonprofit, nonpartisan board that serves to create, develop and retain science and technology-based business in Wisconsin, and to serve as an advisor to the Governor and the Legislature. The Council also serves as the key link between the state's colleges and universities and the business expertise and capital offered by the financial service industry. Recently the firm published its "Vision 2020: A Model Wisconsin Economy" as a blueprint for its efforts over the next two decades.

Job training programs—The area's universities and technical colleges offer ample education and training programs.

Development Projects

In July 1998, Madison businessman W. Jerome Frautschi announced a major civic gift to improve the cultural arts facilities in downtown Madison. Called the Overture Center for the Arts, it is a privately funded initiative to promote excellence in the arts and stimulate a downtown Madison renaissance. The Overture Project will transform the current Civic Center block, remodeling and expanding the existing facilities and adding new ones. Phase One of the project, including the brand new, state-of-the-art Overture Hall, a 2,250-seat theater which houses the Madison Symphony, Madison Opera, and the Madison Ballet, was completed in 2004, and by 2005 construction had begun on Phase Two, which includes a renovation of the old Capitol Theater and a new Madison Museum of Contemporary Art. All design comes under the guise of internationally known architect Cesar Pelli and as plans have expanded development costs have surpassed $205 million, all of which was being funded by Mr. Frautschi. In 2005 the Overture Foundation acquired the old Capital Square Building as the new home for the Madison Children's Museum.

Economic Development Information: Greater Madison Chamber of Commerce, 615 E. Washington Ave., PO Box 71, Madison, WI 53701-0071; telephone (608)256-8348. City of Madison Department of Planning and Development, 215 Martin Luther King, Jr. Blvd., Madison, WI 53710; telephone (608)266-4635; fax (608)267-8739.

Commercial Shipping

Madison is served by the Chicago & Northwestern, Soo/Milwaukee, and Wisconsin & Calumet railroads. More than 40 motor freight carriers link the city with markets throughout the nation via an extensive interstate highway system. Air cargo is shipped through Dane County Regional Airport by two companies.

Labor Force and Employment Outlook

Madison enjoys relatively low unemployment and a high percentage of high-paying jobs in the growing high-technology sector of the economy, all of which provides a strong boost to the local economy in many ways. *Forbes* magazine has called Madison a hotbed of biocapitalism and *Entrepreneur* ranks Madison as one of the top five cities in which to start a business. Many of these new businesses are in the high-tech sector of the local economy. In 2005 more than 450 firms in the Madison area were identified as high-tech. Madison Schools are consistently ranked among the best in the nation, and the University of Wisconsin is regarded as one of the nation's finest public universities, turning out thousands of graduates each year and providing a high number of jobs in research and development.

The following is a summary of data regarding the Madison metropolitan area labor force, 2004 annual averages.

Size of non-agricultural labor force: 343,100

Number of workers employed in . . .
  mining and construction: 16,700
  manufacturing: 31,900
  trade, transportation and utilities: 60,400
  information: 8,000
  financial activities: 27,500
  professional and business services: 32,000
  educational and health services: 33,800
  leisure and hospitality: 28,700
  other services: 17,000
  government: 79,700

Average hourly earnings of production workers employed in manufacturing: $16.19

Unemployment rate: 3.9% (February 2005)

Largest employers	*Number of employees*
University of Wisconsin—Madison	25,614
State of Wisconsin	22,186
U.S. Government	3,900
American Family Insurance	3,570
Madison Metropolitan School District	3,462
WPS Insurance	2,789
UW Health Hospitals/Clinics	2,729
CUNA Mutual Group	2,600

Cost of Living

The following is a summary of data regarding several key cost of living factors in the Madison area.

2004 ACCRA Average House Price: Not reported

2004 ACCRA Cost of Living Index: Not reported

State income tax rate: Ranges from 4.6% to 6.75%

State sales tax rate: 5.0%

Local income tax rate: None

Local sales tax rate: 0.5% (Dane County)

Property tax rate: Effective tax rate $23.46 per $1,000 of assessed valuation (2004)

Economic Information: Greater Madison Chamber of Commerce, 615 E. Washington Ave., PO Box 71, Madison, WI 53701-0071; telephone (608)256-8348.

Education and Research

Elementary and Secondary Schools

Madison was recently singled out by *Money* magazine as the country's "best place for education." Public, elementary, and secondary schools in Madison are part of the Madison Metropolitan School District, the third-largest system in the state of Wisconsin. The Madison Metropolitan School District serves about 25,000 students in 46 schools, including 30 elementary schools (grades K-5), 11 middle schools (6-8), four comprehensive high schools and one alternative high school. The district also has early childhood programs and alternative programs at the secondary level (6-12). The district covers approximately 65 square miles, including all or part of the cities of Madison and Fitchburg, the villages of Maple Bluff and Shorewood Hills, and the towns of Blooming Grove, Burke and Madison. A superintendent is appointed by a seven-member, nonpartisan board of education.

The following is a summary of data regarding Madison public schools as of the 2004–2005 school year.

Total enrollment: 25,000

Number of facilities
   elementary schools: 30
   middle schools: 11
   high schools: 4
   other: 1 alternative

Student/teacher ratio: 12.3:1 (2002–03)

Teacher salaries
   average: $37,701 (2002–2003)

Funding per pupil: $11,118 (2002–2003)

Parochial elementary and secondary school systems are operated by the Roman Catholic and Lutheran churches; three private schools in Dane County provide a kindergarten through grade eight curriculum; and four interdenominational schools offer instruction at all grade levels. There are also services for those with special mental and physical needs.

Public Schools Information: Madison Metropolitan School District, 545 West Dayton Street, Madison, WI 53703-1967; telephone (608)266-6270

Colleges and Universities

The University of Wisconsin—Madison, chartered in 1848, is one of the country's top 10 public universities. It enrolls more than 41,000 students and grants undergraduate and graduate degrees in more than 100 disciplines, including agriculture, allied health professions, education, environmental studies, law, pharmacy, medicine, veterinary medicine, and nursing. As a major research institution, the university is known for work in a variety of fields such as agriculture, bacteriology, chemistry, engineering, forest products, genetics, land use, medicine, nuclear energy, and physics. Edgewood College is a private liberal arts college awarding associate and baccalaureate degrees; a cooperative program in medical technology with area schools and limited cross-registration with the University of Wisconsin—Madison are available. Vocational training and/or bachelors degrees are offered by Madison Area Technical College (which enrolls more than 50,000), Herzing College of Technology, and Madison Media Institute; areas of specialization include aviation, computers, cosmetology, dance, electronics, music, nursing, recreation, and television.

Libraries and Research Centers

Madison is home to 180 public, governmental, special, and academic libraries. The Madison Public Library, with a centrally located main facility, operates nine branches throughout the city. Holdings include about 1.2 million volumes, including periodicals, and compact discs, DVD and video recordings, books on tape, maps, charts, and art reproductions; the library is a partial depository for federal and city documents. In 2004 the Library had 2.2 million visitors, another 2 million hits on its online databases, and circulated 4.3 million volumes. The University of Wisconsin-Madison Memorial Library is a major research facility, housing more than 5.5 million volumes, with more than 80 special collections in a wide range of scholarly fields. The State Historical Society library specializes in Wisconsin lore and has a special African American History Collection.

As the state capital, Madison is the site for libraries affiliated with governmental agencies; among them are the Wisconsin Department of Justice Law Library, the Wisconsin Legislative Reference Bureau, the Wisconsin Department of Public Instruction, the Public Service Commission of Wisconsin, the Wisconsin Department of Transportation Library, and the Wisconsin State Law Library. Several county agencies also maintain libraries in the city. Other specialized libraries are operated by colleges, public interest groups, labor organizations, churches, hospitals, corporations, museums, and newspapers.

The University of Wisconsin-Madison ranks among the top American research universities. UW-Madison annually receives total research funding exceeding $360 million. According to recent figures available from the National Science Foundation, this makes the University of Wisconsin-Madison the third largest funded research university in the country. U.S. government research laboratories located in Madison include the U.S. Forest Products Lab, the U.S. Fish and Wildlife Laboratory, the Space Science and Engineering

Center, the Waisman Center on Mental Retardation and Human Development, the Enzyme Institute, the Sea Grant Institute, Air Pollution Lab, and the U.S. Department of Agriculture Research Service. A number of private research and testing centers, such as Hazelton Laboratories America, Inc., are also based in Madison.

Public Library Information: Madison Public Library, 201 West Mifflin Street, Madison, WI 53703; telephone (608)266-6300

Health Care

Madison, home to the University of Wisconsin Medical School, is a major center for medical research and testing. The University of Wisconsin Hospital and Clinics is comprised of 60 clinics throughout the state, with 44 in Dane County alone, including the UW Comprehensive Cancer Center, which has a national reputation for excellence in cancer care and research. As of 2005 the UW Children's Hospital was 75 percent toward its goal of raising $80 million for a new facility in Madison. Additional medical service for the region is provided by 6 Dane County general hospitals and 92 general and urgent-care clinics. Among the principal facilities are Meriter Hospital and St. Mary's Hospital.

Recreation

Sightseeing

The starting point for sightseeing in Madison is the State Capitol building, located between lakes Mendota and Monona. The dome is topped with Daniel Chester French's gilded bronze statue, *Wisconsin.* The Capitol's interior features 43 varieties of stone and murals, glass mosaics, and hand-carved wood furniture. The State Historical Society on the Capitol Square recaptures the history of Wisconsin with exhibits on Native American tribal life from prehistoric times to the present, pioneer days, paintings and statues. Adjacent is the Wisconsin Veterans Museum, which honors Wisconsin's citizen-soldiers through large-scale exhibits, displays, and presentations.

The architect Frank Lloyd Wright, who resided in nearby Spring Green, designed two buildings that are open to the public in Madison. In 1997, the Monona Terrace Community and Convention Center opened its doors some 60 years after Wright first proposed the project, which marries the

capitol with Lake Monona. The Unitarian Meeting House, opened in 1951, still serves as a venue for Unitarian Universalist services. About 45 minutes away is Taliesin, Wright's home and architectural school in Spring Green.

To the north of town visitors will find the Circus World Museum, the Wollersheim Winery in Prairie du Sac (which holds a Grape Stomp Festival each fall at harvest time), and the Wisconsin Dells, a favorite family vacation destination with natural beauty, lakes and rivers, shopping, and ''the waterpark capital of the world''.

The University of Wisconsin Arboretum, maintained for research and instruction by the institution, consists of 1,200 acres of natural forests, prairie, and orchards inside the city; 250 varieties of lilacs and a number of effigy mounds highlight the Arboretum's park trails. Olbrich Botanical Gardens, a 52-acre park and conservatory, displays gorgeous annuals, perennials, and shrubs outside and a lush tropical paradise inside the 50-foot glass pyramid. The Tenney Park Locks and Dam connect Lakes Mendota and Monona, providing passageway for nearly 20,000 watercraft each season and a popular spot for fishing or feeding ducks. On the other end of Lake Mendota is the University of Wisconsin campus with its rich architectural history and scenic beauty. Along Observatory Drive is the Carillon Tower and Bells, the only carillon to be supported at a university by gifts of senior classes.

The Henry Vilas Park Zoo, bordering the shore of Lake Wingra, is home to hundreds of species of exotic animals.

Arts and Culture

The new jewel in downtown Madison's restoration and the city's arts scene is the Overture Center for the Arts, anchored by Overture Hall, new home of the Madison Symphony, the Madison Opera, and national touring productions. The Madison Art Center maintains six galleries and concentrates on modern and contemporary visual art by local, regional, and national artists; the intimate Isthmus Playhouse provides the stage for the Madison Repertory Theatre. Summer performances of Shakespeare and other classics by the American Players Theater are held in Spring Green.

Music is a popular pastime too, as evidenced by the free concerts throughout the year at Monona Terrace Community and Convention Center and the summertime Wisconsin Chamber Orchestra Concerts on the Square. The University of Wisconsin Elvehjem Museum of Art maintains an eclectic permanent collection ranging from Native American miniatures, Japanese prints, and European medals to Soviet paintings and European and American art. The university's other museums concentrate in the fields of geology and zoology. Exhibits at the Madison Children's Museum involve children in learning about science, culture, and art.

Festivals and Holidays

USA Today said about Madison: "There's always something to do. . . . an almost constant parade of free events." The Capitol Square is the center of many of Madison's special events and activities. In June "Cows on the Concourse" celebrates dairy month. The Badger States Games are held in June, attracting from throughout the state thousands of amateur athletes who participate in 18 different sports. Rhythm and Booms is Madison's Independence Day Celebration; it sets spectacular fireworks to music over Lake Mendota. Art Fair on the Square, held the second weekend in July, brings nearly 500 artists to the Capitol Square to exhibit their works. It is accompanied by Art Fair off the Square, highlighting Wisconsin artists. The Maxwell Street Days, a bazaar of bargains along Madison's famous State Street, is another popular event, as is the Paddle 'N Portage Canoe Race and Taste of Madison, held on Labor Day weekend, when area restaurants serve their most exotic and popular dishes. From May to October, the Dane County Farmers' Markets is held on Wednesday and Saturday mornings around the picturesque Capitol. Autumn features the Thirsty Troll Brewfest and the Annual Mount Horeb Fall Heritage Festival. The grey days of winter are brightened by the Madison Auto Show, a Travel & Vacation Show, and Kites on Ice, a two-day kite-flying event that attracts participants from around the world to Lake Monona in February. There is an annual St. Patrick's Day Parade on Capitol Square.

Sports for the Spectator

The University of Wisconsin Badgers compete in the Big Ten athletic conference in 12 sports; the football, basketball, and hockey teams consistently draw large crowds. Home football Saturdays in Madison are like a community holiday, with tailgate parties beginning early in the morning and parties lasting well into the night, regardless of how the team fared on the field that day. In 2004 *Sports Illustrated* magazine named Madison "Best College Sports Town" in America for its spirited support of the Badgers. The Madison Mallards is a collection of promising collegiate baseball players that play summer ball in the Northwoods League. The Green Bay Packers of the National Football League are adopted by the entire state of Wisconsin, and in nearby Milwaukee, professional baseball (the Brewers) and basketball (the Bucks) are closely followed by Madison fans.

Sports for the Participant

Water sports are particularly attractive in Greater Madison, where five lakes provide ideal conditions for swimming, fishing, boating, canoeing, windsurfing, and ice skating in winter. Year-round fishing is popular, with typical catches including muskie, northern pike, walleye, bass, panfish, and cisco. The Madison Parks Department maintains 7,213 acres of park land. Forty parks maintain ice skating ponds, the majority of which are lighted for evening skating; many provide warming houses. Cross country ski trails line city parks. Many of the parks are equipped with outdoor tennis courts. The Dane County Park System offers a spectacular array of scenery and recreational opportunities at more than 30 area metroparks.

In a city where bicycles may outnumber automobiles, 100 miles of bicycle paths are provided for cycling enthusiasts. Favorite routes circle Lake Monona and the University of Wisconsin Arboretum, cutting through Madison's historic residential district, the zoo, and alongside Lake Wingra. Public golf courses, of varying lengths and difficulties for golfers of all ability levels, are located in Madison. The Springs Golf Course and University Ridge are a highly rated 18-hole courses designed by Robert Trent Jones. In 2004 nearby Whistling Straits Golf Course in Kohler hosted the PGA Championship; the public course was designed by legendary golf course architect Pete Dye. The Mad City Marathon in late May brings thousands of runners to test their mettle against 26.2 miles through some of the most scenic spots in town.

Shopping and Dining

The major shopping malls—East Towne, Hilldale, West Towne, and Westgate—offer comprehensive selection and competitive prices. The Johnson Creek Outlet Center just 30 miles east of Madison has more than 60 brand name stores. The State Capitol district offers a selection of restaurants and stores in a park setting. The pedestrians-only State Street Mall connects the Capitol Square with the University of Wisconsin; the lower section of the Mall is populated by street vendors selling crafts and food. Madison boasts that it has more restaurants per capita than any city in America, with cuisine from around the world appealing to the eclectic tastes of the city's progressive population. Specialty shops and some of the city's finest restaurants are located on State Street. Monroe Street on Madison's near west side also offers charm and unique restaurants and shops. Friday night fish fries are a local custom, and one restaurant caters to specialties native to Wisconsin. The Farmers' Market comes highly recommended for purchasing fresh produce from local growers.

Visitor Information: Greater Madison Convention & Visitors Bureau, 615 East Washington Avenue, Madison, WI 53703; telephone (608)255-2537; toll-free (800)373-6376

Convention Facilities

In all, the Madison area has more than 8,000 hotel rooms and 400,000 square feet of meeting space, which makes it an annual gathering place for such conventions as the World Dairy Expo. Located on the shore of Lake Monona and inspired by a design created by Frank Lloyd Wright in 1938, Monona Terrace is two blocks from Capitol Square, to which it is linked by a pedestrian promenade. In 2001 the facility added the 250-room Hilton Madison Monona Terrace with direct access to the convention facility by enclosed walkway. The facility offers 250,000 square feet of convention and meeting space including a ballroom, an exhibit hall, a multimedia auditorium, gift shop, prefunction areas, and a 90-foot extension over the water. The roof features a park and bandshell, and there is parking for about 550 cars.

The Dane County Expo Center is a 160-acre multibuilding complex including 100,000 square feet of column-free exhibition space and a 9,500-seat arena. The brand new Overture Center for the Arts has unique meeting space for smaller groups in several spectacular settings. Three downtown hotels providing meeting and convention facilities are The Concourse, with three ballrooms and several meeting rooms; the Best Western Inn on the Park, with a variety of meeting room styles; and The Edgewater, with five meeting rooms.

Additional meeting accommodations are available on the campus of the University of Wisconsin—Madison, as well as at numerous hotels and motels throughout metropolitan Madison.

Convention Information: Greater Madison Convention & Visitors Bureau, 615 East Washington Avenue, Madison, WI 53703; telephone (608)255-2537; toll-free (800)373-63763

Transportation

Approaching the City

The Dane County Regional Airport, east of the city, is an international airport served by 11 commercial airlines with 75 regularly scheduled daily flights. Renovations and expansions to be completed in 2005 are to double the airport's square footage.

I-90 and I-94, two of Wisconsin's interstate highways, pass through Madison, connecting the city with Chicago (2.5 hours), Minneapolis (4.5 hours), and Milwaukee (1.5 hours). The highway system also includes U.S. routes 12, 14, 18, 51, and 151 and state roads 30 and 113. The West Beltline, formed by U.S. 18, 151, 12, and 14, bypasses the city. Three companies provide inter-city bus service.

Traveling in the City

Madison is long and narrow, following a northeast-southwest orientation along the shores of Lakes Mendota and Monona. Within this configuration, downtown streets radiate from the Capitol hub; principal thoroughfares are Washington, Johnson, and Williamson, which run northeast and southwest, and State Street and University Avenue, which extend due east.

Madison is one of the most bicycle-friendly cities in America, with miles of paved bike paths and an extensive map system to help bikers get around. Intracity public bus transportation is operated by Madison Metro Bus Company, which provides Metro Plus service for elderly and handicapped patrons. Unlimited access to the bus system comes for just $3 per day.

Communications

Newspapers and Magazines

Daily newspapers in Madison are the morning and Sunday *Wisconsin State Journal* and the evening (Monday through Friday; mornings on Saturday) *The Capital Times.* Several other newspapers also circulate in the city; among them are the alternative weekly *Isthmus,* and University of Wisconsin student dailies.

Madison is the center of extensive magazine and journal publishing activity, including *Madison Magazine* and *In Business.* Magazines with wide circulation focus on such subjects as agriculture, athletics, money management, economic justice, and Wisconsin recreation. Several academic journals are based at the University of Wisconsin, and numerous specialized magazines and journals, many affiliated with government agencies, are printed in Madison.

Television and Radio

Six television channels—four commercial and two public—broadcast from Madison, which also receives programming from Green Bay and Wausau. Cable service is available. Several television production firms are located in the city.

Thirteen AM and FM radio stations serve Greater Madison with a variety of programming that includes classical music, jazz, easy listening, farm news, and topics of public interest.

Media Information: The Capital Times, 1901 Fish Hatchery Road, PO Box 8060, Madison, WI 53708; telephone (608)252-6363; and, *Wisconsin State Journal,* 1901 Fish Hatchery Road, PO Box 8058, Madison, WI 53708; telephone (608)252-6363

Madison Online

City of Madison Home Page. Available www.ci.madison.wi.us

Greater Madison Chamber of Commerce. Available www.greatermadisonchamber.com

Greater Madison Convention and Visitors Bureau. Available www.visitmadison.com

Madison Metropolitan School District. Available www.madison.k12.wi.us

Madison Public Library. Available www.madisonpublic library.org

University of Wisconsin-Madison. Available www.wisc.edu

Selected Bibliography

Brown, Harriet, *Madison Walks* (Madison, WI: Jones Books, 2003)

Guide to Archives and Manuscripts in the University of Wisconsin, Green Bay Area Research Center/State Historical Society of Wisconsin (Madison, WI: State Historical Society of Wisconsin. University of Wisconsin–Green Bay, 1982)

Milwaukee

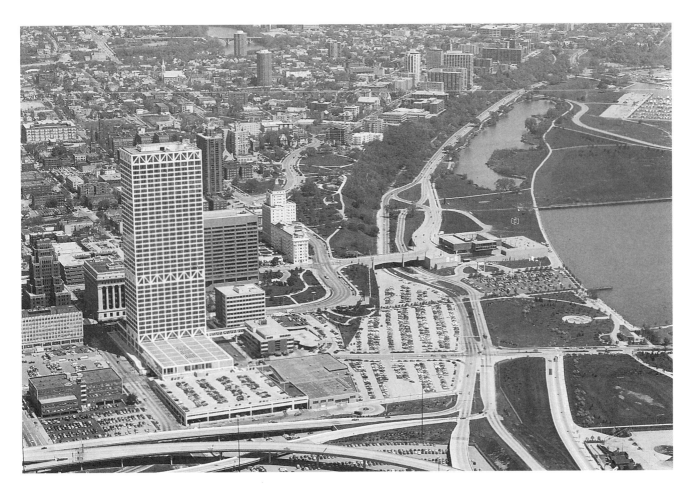

The City in Brief

Founded: 1839 (incorporated 1846)

Head Official: Mayor Tom Barrett (since 2004)

City Population
  1980: 636,212
  1990: 628,088
  2000: 596,974
  2003 estimate: 559,843
  Percent change, 1990–2000: −5.0%
  U.S. rank in 1980: 16th
  U.S. rank in 1990: 17th
  U.S. rank in 2000: 25th (State rank: 1st)

Metropolitan Area Population
  1990: 1,607,183
  2000: 1,689,572

Percent change, 1990–2000: 5.1%
U.S. rank in 1990: Not reported
U.S. rank in 2000: 64th (CMSA)

Area: 96.1 square miles (2000)
Elevation: 581.2 feet above sea level
Average Annual Temperature: 46.8° F
Average Annual Precipitation: 32 inches of rain; 45 inches of snow

Major Economic Sectors: Services, wholesale and retail trade, manufacturing
Unemployment Rate: 5.6% (February 2005)
Per Capita Income: $16,181 (1999)
2001 FBI Crime Index Total: 76,100

Major Colleges and Universities: University of Wisconsin-Milwaukee; Marquette University

Daily Newspapers: *Milwaukee Journal Sentinel*

WALNUT

GALENA

GOLDA MEIR SCHOOL

CHERRY

VLIET

KING PARK

MCKINLEY

JUNEAU

HIGHLAND

STATE

AURORA SINAI MEDICAL CENTER

KILBOURNE

WELLS

WISCONSIN

MARQUETTE UNIVERSITY

HAGGERTY MUSEUM

CLYBOURN

MENOMONEE RIVER

NATIONAL

PABST BREWERY

BRADLEY CTR.

MILWAUKEE AREA TECH.

U. OF W.

AUDITORIUM

BRADLEY CENTER ARENA

PUBLIC MUSEUM

LIBRARY

CONVENTION HALL

MICHIGAN

FOND DU LAC

COMMERCE

WATER

MARKET

BROADWAY

MILWAUKEE

JEFFERSON

MARTIN LUTHER KING JR.

3RD ST

HIGHLAND

PERFORMING ARTS CTR.

PABST THEATER

EDISON

WATER

MARKET

KILBOURNE

MILWAUKEE

BROADWAY

JEFFERSON

JACKSON

VAN BUREN

CASS

MARSHALL

ASTOR

CITY HALL

MUNICIPAL BLDG

MASON

WISCONSIN

MICHIGAN

CLYBOURN

PLANKINTON

2ND

MILWAUKEE INSTITUTE OF ART & DESIGN

TO MITCHELL INT'L AIRPORT

AMTRAK STATION

MILWAUKEE RIVER

JACKSON

VAN BUREN

CASS

MARSHALL

PLEASANT

LYON

WARREN

OGDEN

WI CONSERVATORY OF MUSIC

KNAPP

LINCOLN CTR.

JUNEAU

STATE

JUNEAU PARK

WAR MEMORIAL & ART MUSEUM

LINCOLN

HENRY MAIER FESTIVAL GROUNDS

LAKE MICHIGAN

FARWELL

PROSPECT

N

0   0.5   1

KILOMETERS

MILES   0.5   1

CANADA

WISCONSIN

MINNESOTA

MICHIGAN

Milwaukee

NY

IOWA

ILLINOIS   INDIANA   OHIO   PA

KS   MISSOURI   KENTUCKY   WEST VIRGINIA   VIRGINIA

Introduction

Milwaukee, the seat of Milwaukee County, is the largest city in Wisconsin and the center of a metropolitan statistical area comprised of Milwaukee, Ozaukee, Washington, and Waukesha counties. Mid-nineteenth century German immigration laid the foundation for Milwaukee's "golden age," when cultural and political life flourished, culminating in the election of the country's first socialist mayor in 1912. The city is a major Great Lakes port, traditionally known for manufacturing and breweries. Milwaukee has in recent years reemerged as a primary cultural and entertainment center for the Upper Midwest.

Geography and Climate

Situated on the western shore of Lake Michigan at the confluence of the Milwaukee, Menomonee, and Kinnickinnic rivers, Milwaukee experiences a continental climate characterized by a wide range of temperatures. The frequently changeable weather is influenced by eastward-moving storms that cross the middle section of the nation. Severe winter storms often produce ten inches of snow, and incursions of arctic air result in several days of bitterly cold weather. The Great Lakes influence the local climate during all seasons, modifying air masses before they reach the city; Lake Michigan, in particular, causes dramatic shifts in temperature. Summer temperatures seldom exceed 100 degrees, although a combination of high temperatures and humidity occasionally develops.

Area: 96.1 square miles (2000)

Elevation: 581.2 feet above sea level

Average Temperatures: January, 29.4° F; July, 77.7° F; annual average, 46.8° F

Average Annual Precipitation: 32 inches of rain; 45 inches of snow

History

Tribal Meeting Place Draws Permanent Settlement

Mahn-a-waukee Seepe, a Native American word meaning "gathering place by the river," was the name given to the land next to the natural bay where the Milwaukee, Menomonee, and Kinnickinnic rivers flow into Lake Michigan and where a number of tribes met to hold counsel. The Potawatomi was the largest of the local tribes and they, along with the Menominee, were under French control in the seventeenth century. As white traders moved into the territory, the Native Americans withdrew into the wilderness. The Menominee gave up land east and north of the Milwaukee River in 1831, and the United Nation of Chippewa, Ottawa, and Potawatomi signed a treaty in Chicago in 1833 that relinquished a large section of land south and west of the Milwaukee River.

In 1835 three men bought the first land holdings in Milwaukee at a land auction in Green Bay. French trader Solomon Juneau had operated a trading post near the Milwaukee River since 1818, and he purchased the land between the Milwaukee River and Lake Michigan that he named Juneautown. Byron Kilbourn named his western tract Kilbourntown, and George H. Walker claimed a southern section. Juneau accrued great wealth through his trading business; he also served as an interpreter and peacemaker between the Native Americans and white settlers. Juneau sold some of his land, and he and the new investors established a village that they named Milwaukee. The first population wave took place when Irish and New England settlers and German immigrants arrived. In 1838 the Potawatomi were relocated to Kansas.

A feud called the Bridge War, notorious in Milwaukee history, began in 1840 when the villages of Juneautown and Kilbourntown, which were consolidated in 1839, disputed payments for river bridges required by the legislature. This feuding continued for five years and in 1845 erupted in violence. The Bridge War was finally resolved when the legislature ordered that costs be shared equally between the two founding communities. The next year the city charter was ratified, and Solomon Juneau was elected the first mayor of Milwaukee.

By that time the city's population numbered 10,000 people, half of them German and a higher percentage Catholic. John Martin Henni was appointed bishop of the new diocese, becoming the first German Catholic bishop in America. In 1848 the arrival of the "forty-eighters," German intellectuals forced to flee their homeland after their rebellion failed, helped to influence the direction of Milwaukee history. These men wanted to establish a free German republic but settled for improving the cultural and political life of the city by creating theaters and musical societies, and generally upgrading Milwaukee's intellectual life. Between 1850 and 1851 Milwaukee's population more than doubled to 46,000 people. The economy prospered during the Civil War as local industries grew rapidly and filled in the gaps created by the closing of southern markets.

Progress Continues Despite Setbacks

Several disasters threatened Milwaukee's progress. In 1867, the city's first major labor union, the Knights of St. Crispin, was formed in the shoe industry. As the economy expanded so did the labor movement, which received a setback when state troops fired on labor demonstrators in 1886, killing five. Almost 300 people drowned in 1859 when the *Lady Elgin* collided with the *Augusta*; Milwaukee again mourned when a fire at the Newhall House in 1883 took at least sixty-four lives. Both events were commemorated in popular ballads. In 1892 sixteen residential and business blocks between the Milwaukee River and Lake Michigan were destroyed by fire. Despite this tragedy, the decade of the 1890s in Milwaukee was described as the "golden age," marked by the flourishing of German theater and musical societies.

The rise of Milwaukee's brand of socialism dates from this period, when Socialist leader Victor L. Berger forged an alliance with labor, bringing the Social Democratic party into existence. Emil Seidel was elected the first Socialist mayor in 1910 and Berger became the first Socialist in the U.S. House of Representatives. The "bundle brigade" delivered campaign pamphlets in twelve languages to rally votes. In addition to Seidel, Daniel W. Hoan and Frank P. Zeidler later also served as Socialist mayors. In keeping with anti-German sentiments during World War I, the statue of *Germania* was removed from the Brumder Building and Berger was convicted of conspiracy to violate the Espionage Act. This decision was, however, reversed by the U.S. Supreme Court in 1921.

Milwaukee has been a shipping center and industrial giant in the Midwest, noted in the nineteenth century for wheat and then in the twentieth century for manufacturing, primarily the metal trades, meat packing, tanning and leather goods, brewing, and durable goods. Milwaukee industry has contributed to national and international progress with steam shovels to dig the Panama Canal, turbines to harness Niagara Falls, and agricultural equipment to farm the world's land. Today Milwaukee maintains its status as a leader in manufacturing technology and practice while it makes the transition to a service-based economy. Milwaukee boasts good schools, a diverse economy, a strong work ethic, a high quality of life, and a beautiful location on the western edge of Lake Michigan in the rolling hills of the Kettle Moraine. The city has also become a cultural leader, with a world-class symphony orchestra, 20 performing arts groups, a ballet, two opera companies, a zoo, six professional sports teams, several major universities, and Summerfest, the world's largest music festival.

Historical Information: Milwaukee County Historical Society, 910 N. Old World 3rd St., Milwaukee, WI 53203; telephone (414)273-8288

Population Profile

Metropolitan Area Residents
1990: 1,607,183
2000: 1,689,572
Percent change, 1990–2000: 5.1%
U.S. rank in 1990: Not reported
U.S. rank in 2000: 64th (CMSA)

City Residents
1980: 636,212
1990: 628,088
2000: 596,974
2003 estimate: 559,843
Percent change, 1990–2000: −5.0%
U.S. rank in 1980: 16th
U.S. rank in 1990: 17th (State rank: 1st)
U.S. rank in 2000: 25th (State rank: 1st)

Density: 6,214.3 people per square mile (2000)

Racial and ethnic characteristics (2000)
White: 310,734
Black or African American: 230,503
American Indian and Alaska Native: 9,116
Asian: 20,166
Native Hawaiian and Pacific Islander: 809
Hispanic or Latino (may be of any race): 71,646
Other: 43,201

Percent of residents born in state: 65.2% (2000)

Age characteristics (2000)
Population under 5 years old: 47,545
Population 5 to 9 years old: 50,555
Population 10 to 14 years old: 46,688
Population 15 to 19 years old: 47,231
Population 20 to 24 years old: 51,814
Population 25 to 34 years old: 94,451
Population 35 to 44 years old: 85,792
Population 45 to 54 years old: 68,351
Population 55 to 59 years old: 21,586
Population 60 to 64 years old: 17,838
Population 65 to 74 years old: 33,015
Population 75 to 84 years old: 23,727
Population 85 years and over: 8,381
Median age: 30.6 years

Births (2002, Milwaukee County)
Total number: 14,332

Deaths (2002, Milwaukee County)
Total number: 9,022 (of which, 155 were infants under the age of 1 year)

Money income (1999)
    Per capita income: $16,181
    Median household income: $37,879
    Total households: 232,312

Number of households with income of . . .
    less than $10,000: 32,701
    $10,000 to $14,999: 18,446
    $15,000 to $24,999: 37,867
    $25,000 to $34,999: 35,509
    $35,000 to $49,999: 40,961
    $50,000 to $74,999: 39,490
    $75,000 to $99,999: 16,387
    $100,000 to $149,999: 7,778
    $150,000 to $199,999: 1,599
    $200,000 or more: 1,574

Percent of families below poverty level: 17.4% (53.2% of
    which were female householder families with related
    children under 5 years)

2001 FBI Crime Index Total: 76,100

Municipal Government

Milwaukee is governed by a 15-member council and a
mayor, who is not a member of council; all are elected to a
four-year term. The council holds all policy-making and
legislative powers of the city, including the adoption of
ordinances and resolutions, the approval of the city's annual
budget, and the enactment of appropriation and tax levy
ordinances. In addition to their powers as legislators, council
members serve as district administrators, responsible to the
citizens in their districts for city services.

Head Official: Mayor Tom Barrett (since April 2004; current term expires March 2008)

Total Number of City Employees: 8,907 (2004)

City Information: City Hall, 200 E. Wells St., Milwaukee,
WI 53202; telephone (414)286-2200

Economy

Major Industries and Commercial Activity

Milwaukee, a commercial and industrial hub for the Great
Lakes region, is home to six *Fortune* 1000 manufacturers
(including Harley-Davidson Inc., Rockwell Automation,
and Johnson Controls), banks, and diversified service companies as well as one of the nation's ten largest insurance

firms. The metropolitan area places among the top manufacturing centers in the United States, ranking second among
major metropolitan areas in the percentage of its workforce
in manufacturing. The economy is dominated by small- to
medium-size firms with representatives in nearly every industrial classification.

Metropolitan area firms are engaged primarily in the manufacture of machinery; contrary to Milwaukee's reputation as
a brewery capital, less than one percent of the city's industrial output is related to brewing. In recent years, the metro
region has earned a reputation as a center for precision
manufacturing. It leads the nation in the production of industrial controls, X-ray equipment, steel foundry parts, and
mining machinery. The area is also considered a printing and
publishing center, housing more than 11 percent of the top
70 printing companies in North America. Publishers and
printers combined employ more than 21,000 people, about
2.5 percent of the workforce.

Professional and managerial positions are the fastest-
growing occupations in Milwaukee, accounting for almost
27 percent of the workforce. Service businesses constitute
the largest sector of the local economy, and health care
positions account for about 27 percent of service sector jobs.
The area is home to four major multi-hospital health systems. Other major areas of service employment include
business services (27 percent), educational services (7 percent) and social services (10 percent).

Nearly a quarter of the state's high-tech firms, employing
more than one-third of Wisconsin's technology industry
staff, are located in Milwaukee County. Between 1990 and
1999, Milwaukee led Wisconsin in the creation of high-tech
jobs, adding 10,000 positions.

Tourism is also a major contributor to the local economy.
Milwaukee hosts many festivals and parades throughout the
year, and is home to nationally recognized museums, a zoo,
professional sports teams, and entertainment venues. Altogether these attractions bring more than 5 million tourists
and generate $1.9 billion annually.

Items and goods produced: automobile frames and parts,
    heavy pumping machinery, gas engines, heavy lubricating
    and agricultural equipment, large mining shovels, dredges,
    saw mill and cement machinery, malt drinks and products,
    packaged meat, boots, shoes, leather products, knit goods,
    women's sportswear, gloves, children's clothes, diesel en-
    gines, motorcycles, outboard motors, electrical equipment,
    products of iron and steel foundries, metal fabricators

Incentive Programs—New and Existing Businesses

Milwaukee is known for its harmonious working relationship with the business community throughout the entire

area. Its Milwaukee Economic Development Corporation (MEDC) is a nonprofit corporation offering financial resources to aid in the city's economic growth. Its staff provides financial, technical, training, and ombudsman services to Milwaukee businesses and also assists in securing state of Wisconsin business development funds for Milwaukee firms. MEDC is very supportive of minority-owned businesses. Additionally, the city of Milwaukee's Emerging Business Enterprise Program helps emerging and small businesses with support services, contract opportunities, and financial resources, and helps establish mentor relationships between emerging and established businesses.

Local programs—The city's Community Block Grant Administration oversees the use of approximately $30 million of federal funds or programs in targeted central city neighborhoods. The funding is used for housing rehab programs, special job and business development, and public service programs such as crime prevention, job training, housing for homeless, youth recreation programs and community organization programs.

State programs—Wisconsin's Department of Commerce was created in 1996; it offers a variety of loan and grant programs for both businesses and communities. The department's Disadvantaged Business Enterprise Program was created to increase participation of firms owned by disadvantaged individuals in all federal aid and state transportation facility contracts. The department's Minority Business Development loan program provides financial assistance for the creation and expansion of minority-owned businesses in Wisconsin through low interest loans. The Employee Ownership Assistance Loan Program helps groups of employees purchase businesses that would otherwise close by providing individual awards up to $15,000 for feasibility studies or professional assistance.

Job training programs—The Milwaukee industrial and business community profits from area educational institutions, which provide technology transfer, research services, and training programs. The state's Customized Labor Training program assists companies that are investing in new technologies or manufacturing processes by providing a grant of up to 50 percent of the cost of training employees on the new technologies. Also available in Milwaukee is the "Small Business School" television program, a series that highlights some of America's most successful small businesses and their owners.

Development Projects

In 2005, the city of Milwaukee received $20.2 million in federal assistance for continued economic development. This assistance took the form of an $18 million New Market Tax Credit allocation and $2.2 million in brownfield grants from the U.S. Environmental Protection agency. The New

Market Tax Credit will be used to offer low-interest loans to businesses in low-income areas of the city. The brownfield grants will be used to clean up properties contaminated from previous uses, such as former gas station sites. In 2004, Real Estate Recycling spent $10 million to renovate a former foundry plant, creating the 200,000 square foot Stadium Business Park. The area will be used for light industrial businesses.

Economic Development Information: Metro Milwaukee Association of Commerce, 756 N. Milwaukee St., Ste. 400, Milwaukee, WI 53202; telephone (414)287-4100. Milwaukee Economic Development Corporation, 809 N. Broadway, PO Box 324, Milwaukee, WI 53201; telephone (414)286-5840

Commercial Shipping

Because of its location near the nation's population center—nearly 66 million people and one-third of U.S. manufacturing output is within 600 miles of the city—Milwaukee is a major commercial shipping hub. Of vital importance to both the local and state economies is the Port of Milwaukee, a shipping and receiving point for international trade as well as the primary heavy-lift facility on the Great Lakes. A protected harbor permits year-round navigation through the port from three rivers in addition to Lake Michigan. With access to the eastern seaboard via the St. Lawrence Seaway and to the Gulf of Mexico through the Mississippi River, the Port of Milwaukee processes three million tons of cargo annually and has helped the state maintain an export growth rate twice the national average. Principal inbound commodities include cement, coal, machinery, steel, salt, limestone, asphalt, and crushed rock.

More than 500 multiservice motor freight carriers are engaged in shipping goods from Milwaukee to markets throughout the country. Two major rail lines serve the greater Milwaukee area; altogether, Wisconsin has 4,500 miles of track and 12 freight railroads handling 94 million tons of cargo. More than 200 million pounds of cargo and mail are handled annually by air freight carriers at General Mitchell International Airport, Wisconsin's primary terminal for commercial air travel and freight shipments.

Labor Force and Employment Outlook

Milwaukee is noted for a well educated workforce with a strong work ethic. Employees call in sick less frequently than those in other major urban areas, and children consistently rank near the top in scholastic achievement tests. Private business drives the city's economy, with less than 11 percent of area employees working in the public sector. Just under 22 percent of Milwaukee's workers are in manufacturing jobs, the second-highest percentage among U.S. metropolitan areas. While manufacturing is a strong component of the city's economy, service jobs have shown the most growth in recent years.

The city's diverse economy and strong work ethic has helped keep area unemployment under the national average in each of the last 30 years. Milwaukee ranks slightly below the national average in pay levels for most occupations.

The following is a summary of data regarding the Milwaukee metropolitan area labor force, 2004 annual average.

Size of non-agricultural labor force: 832,300

Number of workers employed in . . .
   manufacturing: 134,200
   trade, transportation and utilities: 152,500
   information: 18,400
   financial activities: 57,400
   professional and business services: 106,800
   educational and health services: 131,400
   leisure and hospitality: 65,200
   other services: 41,500
   government: 91,500

Average hourly earnings of production workers employed in manufacturing: $17.22

Unemployment rate: 5.6% (February 2005)

Largest employers (2004)	Number of employees
Aurora Health Care	15,500
Covenant Healthcare System Inc.	9,520
Roundy's	7,400
Marshall & Ilsley Corp.	6,800
Wisconsin Energy	6,000
GE Healthcare	5,800
Quad/Graphics	5,300
Kohl's	5,500
Northwestern Mutual	4,600

Cost of Living

Metropolitan Milwaukee's cost of living ranks below other major metropolitan areas. The area offers a wide array of homes in a variety of price ranges.

The following is a summary of data regarding several key cost of living factors in the Milwaukee area.

2004 (3rd Quarter) ACCRA Average House Price: $296,114

2004 (3rd Quarter) ACCRA Cost of Living Index: 101.7 (U.S. average = 100.0)

State income tax rate: Ranges from 4.90% to 6.93%

State sales tax rate: 5.0%

Local income tax rate: None

Local sales tax rate: 0.6%

Property tax rate: Range from $14.79 to $39.45 per $1,000 assessed valuation (2004)

Economic Information: Metro Milwaukee Association of Commerce, 756 N. Milwaukee St., Ste. 400l, Milwaukee, WI 53202; telephone (414)287-4100

Education and Research

Elementary and Secondary Schools

The Milwaukee Public Schools system, serving almost 100,000 students, is administered by a nine-member, nonpartisan board of school directors that appoints a superintendent. The system employs more than 6,700 full-time, part-time, and substitute teachers. In 2003, Milwaukee Public Schools had a 60 percent graduation rate; more than 50 percent of graduating students planned on attending some sort of college or university. Overall, students maintained an 89.9 percent attendance rate. Milwaukee public school-teachers are well-educated; in 2004, 46 percent of teachers held a master's degree or higher.

The following is a summary of data regarding the Milwaukee public schools as of the 2004–2005 school year.

Total enrollment: 105,000

Number of facilities
   elementary schools: 125
   middle schools: 16
   high schools: 18 (plus 23 middle/high combined)
   other: 72 (including alternative, partnership, and charter schools; and other programs)

Student/teacher ratio: 15:1

Teacher salaries
   minimum: $29,224
   maximum: $62,368

Funding per pupil: $11,219

More than 100 private elementary and secondary schools serve metropolitan Milwaukee. Choices include 7 Montessori schools, 21 charter schools, and 11 year-around schools as well as a number of parochial schools.

Public Schools Information: Milwaukee Public Schools, Administration Building, 5225 W. Vliet St., Milwaukee, WI 53208; telephone (414)475-8393

Colleges and Universities

Milwaukee is home to many higher education institutions. A 2000 study by McGill University in Montreal ranked Milwaukee 5th in a list of U.S. and Canadian cities with the highest number of college students per 100 residents. One of the largest schools in the area is the University of Wisconsin-Milwaukee. It is one of two doctoral universities in the University of Wisconsin system, and has an enrollment of 23,000. The school offers more than 120 undergraduate majors, 47 master's degrees, and 17 doctorate degrees. It is also one of the top research institutions in the country, ranking in the top 3.5 percent of national universities.

Marquette University is a Catholic, Jesuit school composed of 6 colleges with 60 undergraduate majors. Still, it keeps class sizes small, with an average freshman class size of 32. It was recently named one of the nation's 50 best college values by *U.S. News and World Report* magazine. The Medical College of Wisconsin is part of the Milwaukee Regional Medical Center. It is a private, academic institution that emphasizes education, research, patient care, and local partnerships. Other schools in the area include Alverno College, Cardinal Stritch University, Carroll College, Carthage College, Concordia University Wisconsin, the Milwaukee Institute of Art and Design, Mount Mary College, and Wisconsin Lutheran College.

The area also boasts a number of technical colleges. Milwaukee Area Technical College offers more than 150 associate degrees, technical diplomas, and short-term certificates. At nearby Gateway Technical College, the school has more than 70 career options. Waukesha County Technical College focuses on technical education, occupational training, and enrichment programs.

Libraries and Research Centers

In addition to its main facility, the Milwaukee Public Library operates 12 branches throughout the city and a bookmobile. Total library holdings include about 2.7 million books, and other materials such as periodicals, films, CDs, records, art reproductions, sheet music, and art objects, in addition to more than 1.5 million government documents. Special collections are maintained on a wide range of subjects, and computer resources are also available. The library was a recipient of the University of Wisconsin-Milwaukee School of Education 2004 Promoting Educational Achievement for Kids Award for its many literacy and education programs. The Golda Meir Library at the University of Wisconsin-Milwaukee maintains holdings of 1.3 million books as well as special collections in many scholarly fields. The library's largest and most distinguished research collection is the American Geographical Society Library. It holds more than one million items dating from 1452 to the present, with items ranging from rare old manuscripts to early printed books of satellite data. Additional resources are found in such specialized collections as the Hebraica and Judaica Collection, the Slichter and Hohlweck Civil War Collections, and the Harry and Dorothy Jagodzinski Franklin Delano Roosevelt Collection.

The James J. Flannery Map Library is another University of Wisconsin-Milwaukee collection that includes U.S. Geological Survey topographical maps, wall maps, air photos, and various other maps; the Map Library is a government depository library for maps and is open to the public. The Medical College of Wisconsin Libraries have three facilities housing 76,000 books and 130,000 bound periodical volumes pertaining to basic sciences, clinical medicine, and nursing; the main library is a depository for World Health Organization publications. The Medical College is recognized as a leading center for research in such fields as interferon, obesity, allergies, eye disorders, arthritis, heart disease, childhood cancer, and diagnostic imaging.

The University of Wisconsin-Milwaukee maintains the Office of Industrial Research and Technology Transfer, the International Business Center, and the Femtosecond Laser Laboratory. Marquette University conducts in-house training programs in management development, computer technology, and industrial technology. The Biological and Biomedical Research Institute at Marquette University stimulates collaborative research by scientists in the life sciences. The Milwaukee School of Engineering houses the Applied Technology Center, the nationally known Fluid Power Institute, and the Biomedical Research Institute.

Public Library Information: Milwaukee Public Library, 814 W. Wisconsin Ave., Milwaukee, WI 53233; telephone (414)286-3000

Health Care

The metropolitan Milwaukee area has been a leader in developing managed care programs to control health care costs while providing quality care. Forty percent of residents belong to a health maintenance organization or point of service plan, more than double the national average. One of the city's largest facilities is the Milwaukee Regional Medical Center, a sprawling campus of hospitals, outpatient clinics, health-related educational facilities, and research centers. The center is home to Children's Hospital of Wisconsin, a 222-bed pediatric facility; the Curative Rehabilitation Center, with 40 specialty clinics; Froedtert Memorial Lutheran Hospital, which operates a Level One Trauma Center; the Blood Center of Southeastern Wisconsin; and the Medical College of Wisconsin. Almost 1,400 students are enrolled at the school, including 800 medical students and 554 graduate students, and physicians enrolled in the masters of public health degree program. Medical College faculty supervise 700 physicians in residency training and provide continuing medical education to more than 12,000 health professionals annually.

Milwaukee residents also have access to three multi-hospital healthcare delivery systems in a four-county area: Aurora Health Care, Covenant Healthcare, and Horizon Healthcare. Aurora Health Care operates 13 hospitals, 140 pharmacies, and more than 100 clinics. The organization employs 620 physicians; its Milwaukee hospitals are St. Luke's and Aurora Sinai Medical Center. Covenant Healthcare operates four major acute-care hospitals and a joint venture affiliation with the Wisconsin Hearth Hospital. It also oversees three extended care facilities, a hospice agency, and a full-service medical laboratory. The network is affiliated with more than 1,500 physicians in the metropolitan area. Horizon Healthcare operates 8 hospitals and nearly 30 clinics.

Recreation

Sightseeing

Milwaukee successfully mixes old and new architectural styles that tell the history of the city from its beginning to the present. Kilbourntown House, the 1844 home of one of the city's founding fathers, was built by Benjamin Church and is an example of temple-type Greek Revival architecture. It is open to the public and furnished with mid-nineteenth century furniture and decorative arts. The Jeremiah Curtin House, built in 1846, is an example of Irish cottage architecture, and was the first stone house to be built in the town of Greenfield. Built about the same time, the Lowell Damon House exemplifies the colonial style and is furnished with nineteenth century furniture, décor, and art. Milwaukee's City Hall, completed in 1894, was designed by Henry C. Koch and Company, and cost more than $1 million to build. The building stands more than 350 feet tall and is in Flemish Renaissance style, featuring carved woodwork, black granite, leaded glass, stenciled ceilings, and stained-glass windows. The Pabst Mansion, another example of Flemish Renaissance architecture, was built in 1892 and contains decorative woodwork and ironwork.

Milwaukee is also noted for its church architecture. The St. Joan of Arc Chapel at Marquette University is a fifteenth-century French chapel moved from France to Milwaukee in 1965. Under its dome, modeled after St. Peter's in Rome, the Basilica of St. Josaphat displays stained glass, murals, and a collection of relics and portraits. Designed during a time of revival fantasy architecture, the Tripoli Shrine Temple is one

of a few examples of the Indian Saracenic architectural style in the U.S. It was modeled after the Taj Mahal in India, and features three domes, two recumbent camel sculptures, ceramic tile, plaster lattice work, and decorative floral designs. The Holy Hill National Shrine of Mary looks out onto one of Wisconsin's national parks, and features spires, mosaics, stained glass windows, and a nineteenth-century statue of Mary and Jesus. St. Stephen's Catholic Church is the last remnant of the 1840 German settlement of New Coeln, and the church's wood carvings are said to be world famous.

The Milwaukee County Zoo is home to more than 2,000 mammals, birds, fish, amphibians, and reptiles, representing more than 350 species; the zoo also features workshops, holiday celebrations, concerts, and food festivals. The Mitchell Park Horticultural Conservatory, also known as "the Domes," cultivates tropical, arid, and seasonal plant displays in three beehive-shaped domes. The Boerner Botanical Gardens at Whitnall Park displays perennials, wildflowers, annuals, and herbs, and features a highly praised rose garden. The Wehr Nature Center, also in Whitnall Park, offers self-guided tours, nature programs, live animals, and three formal gardens. The Center also features 200 acres of land with 5 miles of hiking trails.

Arts and Culture

Milwaukee's cultural heritage dates to the nineteenth century when German immigrants established the city's first music societies and theater groups. Today the Milwaukee Symphony Orchestra—the state's only professional orchestra—performs more than 150 classical and pop concerts each season, with 88 full-time musicians. The Orchestra is attended by more than 300,000 people annually, and runs one of the largest state touring programs of any U.S. orchestra. At home, the Orchestra plays at the Marcus Center for the Performing Arts, which is also the home of the Milwaukee Ballet Company, the Milwaukee Youth Symphony, and the Florentine Opera Company. The Skylight Opera Theatre, founded in 1959, presents a season of more than 80 productions ranging from Mozart to Gilbert and Sullivan. The Theatre is located in the Broadway Theatre Center in the city's historic Third Ward.

For more than 50 years, the Milwaukee Repertory Theater's multi-play season is produced in the Patty and Jay Baker Theater Complex, which includes a Mainstage theater seating 720 patrons, the Stiemke Theatre featuring flexible seating, and the Stackner Cabaret where patrons take advantage of the full-service bar and restaurant. Riverside Theater presents theatrical shows and musical performances. The Milwaukee Chamber Theater has been producing first-class live theater for more than 30 years.

Milwaukee's museums present a variety of choices for the art enthusiast. The Milwaukee Art Museum on Lake Michi-

The Pabst Mansion.

gan is housed in the War Memorial Center designed by Finnish architect Eero Saarinen, who also designed the St. Louis Arch. The Museum's permanent collection consists of nineteenth- and twentieth-century painting and sculpture, extensive Haitian art holdings, and the Bradley gift of modern art displayed in a wing built in 1975. In 2001, the Museum unveiled its newest addition—the Quadracci Pavilion, designed by Santiago Calatrava. The Charles Allis Art Museum houses its collection of nineteenth-century French and American paintings in a 1911 Edwardian mansion. The collection spans 2,000 years and includes original and antique furnishings. The American Geographical Society Collection at the University of Wisconsin-Milwaukee exhibits material related to geography, exploration, cartography, and the earth and social sciences.

Other Milwaukee museums include the Discovery World Museum with 150 hands-on exhibits and live theater shows; Thomas A. Greene Memorial Museum with minerals, crystals, and fossils; the Haggerty Museum of Art at Marquette University with a wide range of art forms; the Milwaukee County Historical Center; and America's Black Holocaust Museum. With more than 150,000 square feet of exhibit space, the Milwaukee Public Museum features a Costa Rican rainforest, archeological exhibits, and a live butterfly house. The Villa Terrace Decorative Arts Museum, overlooking Lake Michigan, displays its collections in an Italian Renaissance-style villa.

Festivals and Holidays

Milwaukee, dubbed the ''City of Festivals,'' is the site of a wide variety of ethnic and cultural festivals, many of them held along the city's lakefront. Most events are scheduled in the summer, beginning with RiverSplash in June, which hosts a paddleboat race, canoe rides, fireworks, street vendors, food booths, and live music. In July, Bastille Days celebrates all things French with French cuisine, live entertainment, and a 5K run. Summerfest, billed as the world's largest music festival, attracts national headliners for a week-plus celebration. Set on the shore of Lake Michigan, Summerfest takes place in a 23,000-seat amphitheater and offers unique attractions and food from more than 50 restaurants in addition to live music.

For parade fans, Milwaukee hosts a St. Patrick's Day Parade every March, complete with bagpipes, clowns, local politicians and celebrities, floats, and marching bands. The annual Great Circus Parade in July, presented by Baraboo's Circus World Museum, attracts hundreds of thousands of spectators. The event features 75 historical circus wagons, clowns, 750 horses, and elephants, camels, and zebras. On parade day, circus performers and animals follow a three-mile route for an authentic recreation of a turn-of the century circus parade. Another popular event close to Milwaukee is the

Wisconsin State Fair in August; the Fair runs 11 days and features agriculture, food, shopping, and 28 stages of local and national entertainment.

Sports for the Spectator

Major league baseball's Milwaukee Brewers compete in the National League and play their home games at Miller Park. The Milwaukee Bucks of the National Basketball Association are based at the Bradley Center, a privately funded $94 million sports and concert facility that provides the city with one of the nation's most architecturally significant and functional sports facilities. Bradley Center is also home to the Marquette University Golden Eagles NCAA basketball team and the Milwaukee Admirals of the American Hockey League. From its home at the U.S. Cellular Arena, the Milwaukee Wave became the 2005 Major Indoor Soccer League Champions.

Marquette University and the University of Wisconsin-Milwaukee Panthers field teams in most collegiate sports. Jetrockets, wheelstanders, and funny cars are featured in a season of competition at the Great Lakes Dragway from April through November. The Milwaukee Mile, the oldest operating motor speedway in the world, attracts nationally known drivers for Indy car, Stock Car, and NASCAR events.

Sports for the Participant

The Milwaukee County Park System maintains more than 140 parks on nearly 15,000 acres. Indoor and outdoor recreational activities offered year-round include rugby, soccer, softball, baseball, swimming, tennis, golf, ice skating, tobogganing, and boating. Public skating is available at the Pettit National Ice Center, which contains the country's first U.S. indoor 400-meter racing oval, one of only five worldwide. The center was the first facility to house speed skating, hockey, and figure skating under one roof, and has hosted events such as the World Sprint Speed Skating Championships and the U.S. Olympic Speed Skating Time Trials. Milwaukee's location on Lake Michigan offers a myriad of water-related recreational opportunities.

Shopping and Dining

Milwaukee is one of a few Midwestern cities with a skywalk system connecting the downtown commercial district; one section, called Riverspan, bridges the Milwaukee River. The Riverwalk walkway along the Milwaukee River is lined with shops and restaurants. Downtown, the Shops of Grand Avenue is an enclosed multilevel four-block marketplace of 150 shops and restaurants and five historic buildings forming the core of the glass skywalk system. The Historic Third Ward is a restored warehouse district featuring art galleries, restaurants, antiques, and the Milwaukee Institute of Art and Design. Old World Third Street gives visitors a taste of Old Milwaukee with cobblestone intersections and ethnic markets and restaurants. Brady Street serves as Milwaukee's Italian neighborhood with authentic restaurants, markets, bakeries, and an artistic, student-oriented crowd. Several neighborhood and regional shopping malls also serve the metropolitan area. Fondy Farmers' Market, the city's largest farmers' market, is open six days a week in season and specializes in locally grown and produced fruits, vegetables, and food products.

Some of the best German restaurants in the country are located in Milwaukee, such as Karl Ratzsch's, Restaurant, Mader's Restaurant, and the Bavarian Wurst Haus. Dining in Milwaukee is not limited to award-winning German cuisine, however; besides Continental, Italian, Mexican, and Chinese restaurants, Milwaukee offers a surprising mix of other ethnic choices, such as African, Irish, Cajun, Polish, Serbian, and Thai. One of the city's most popular food specialties is the fish fry, which can be found at Buck Bradley's, Harry's Bar and Grill, Red Rock Café, and the Potawatomi Bingo Casino.

Visitor Information: Greater Milwaukee Convention and Visitors Bureau, Inc., 648 Plankinton Ave., Ste. 425, Milwaukee, WI 53203; telephone (800)554-1448

Convention Facilities

The Midwest Airlines Center opened in 1998; the $170 million, 667,475-square-foot center is located in the heart of Milwaukee and features 188,695 square feet of exhibit space, a 37,506-square-foot grand ballroom, and 28 meeting rooms, as well as cutting-edge technology and $1.2 million in public artwork. More than 3,000 hotel rooms, a theater, shopping, nightlife, the RiverWalk, restaurants, and museums are within walking distance of the Midwest Airlines Center. The city has a number of other convention and meeting facilities for groups of any size. Recent area hotel renovations have included an $8 million renovation of the Hyatt Regency Milwaukee and a nearly $4 million renovation at the Wyndham Milwaukee Center.

Convention Information: Greater Milwaukee Convention and Visitors Bureau, Inc., 648 Plankinton Ave., Ste. 425, Milwaukee, WI 53203; toll-free (800)554-1448

Transportation

Approaching the City

General Mitchell International Airport is the destination for most air traffic into Milwaukee. Situated adjacent to I-94, 8

miles south of downtown, Mitchell Airport is served by 14 commercial airlines and is the largest airport in Wisconsin. Mitchell offers approximately 196 daily departures and 220 daily arrivals, serving 90 cities nonstop. The terminal accommodates more than 4 million passengers each year and is highly regarded by frequent travelers. Based at General Mitchell International Airport is Midwest Airlines; in 2000 readers of *Conde Nast Traveler* magazine ranked the airline as the #1 U.S. airline for the sixth year in a row. The principal general aviation facility for Milwaukee is Timmerman Field.

A 160-mile freeway system permits direct access to central Milwaukee within 20 minutes from points throughout a 10-mile radius, except during the peak rush-hour period. Milwaukee's average commute time of 20 minutes is the shortest among the nation's 36 largest metro areas.

Amtrak and Greyhound provide passenger rail and bus services into Milwaukee.

Traveling in the City

The city of Milwaukee lies along the shore of Lake Michigan and is intersected from north to south by the Milwaukee River. Streets are laid out on a grid pattern; Lincoln Memorial Drive runs along the lake shore downtown. North-south streets are numbered and east-west streets are named.

The Milwaukee County Transit System, which ranks among the nation's largest all-bus transportation systems, operates bus routes in Milwaukee County. The System has 480 air-conditioned buses that operate frequently from 5 a.m. until after midnight. Additional services include express routes from park-ride lots and special routes to the university area and the stadium. Taxi and limousine services are also available.

Communications

Newspapers and Magazines

The major daily newspaper of the Greater Milwaukee area is the morning *Milwaukee Journal Sentinel,* with a daily circulation of 258,000. Several other newspapers, including the *Business Journal of Milwaukee,* circulate biweekly or weekly.

At least 35 trade and special-interest magazines and journals are published in Milwaukee; they cover such subjects as personal improvement, religion, hobbies, the social sciences, business and finance, computers, railroads, construction and building trades, and archaeology.

Television and Radio

Seven commercial, two public, and one Christian television stations broadcast in Milwaukee. More than forty AM and FM radio stations play a wide range of music, news, and talk radio in the county. The Milwaukee Symphony Orchestra produces national radio broadcasts.

Media Information: *Milwaukee Journal Sentinel,* P.O. Box 661, Milwaukee, WI 53201; telephone (414)224-2000.

Milwaukee Online

City of Milwaukee home page. Available www.ci.mil.wi.us

Greater Milwaukee Convention and Visitors Bureau. Available www.milwaukee.org

Historic Milwaukee Inc. Available www.historicmilwaukee .org

James J. Flannery Map Library. Available www.uwm.edu/ Dept/GML

Metro Milwaukee Association of Commerce. Available www.mmac.org

Metro Milwaukee Guide to Relocation. Available metro milwaukee.org

Milwaukee Department of City Development. Available www.milwaukeebiz.com

Milwaukee Economic Development Corporation. Available www.medconline.com

Milwaukee Journal Sentinel. Available www.jsonline.com

Milwaukee Public Library. Available www.mpl.org

Wisconsin Department of Commerce. Available www .commerce.state.wi.us

Selected Bibliography

Buck, Diane M. and Virginia A. Palmer, *Outdoor Sculpture in Milwaukee: A Cultural and Historical Guidebook* (State Historical Society of Wisconsin, 1994)

Derleth, August William, *The Wind Leans West* (New York: Candlelight Press, 1969)

Leavitt, Judith Walzer, *The Healthiest City: Milwaukee and the Politics of Health Reform* (University of Wisconsin Press, 1996)

Racine

The City in Brief

Founded: 1834 (incorporated 1848)

Head Official: Mayor Gary Becker (since April 2003)

City Population
  1980: 85,725
  1990: 84,298
  2000: 81,855
  2003 estimate: 80,266
  Percent change, 1990–2000: −3.0%
  U.S. rank in 1990: 248th
  U.S. rank in 2000: 356th (State rank: 5th)

Metropolitan Area Population
  1990: 175,034
  2000: 188,831
  Percent change, 1990–2000: 7.9%

U.S. rank in 1980: 23rd
U.S. rank in 1990: Not reported
U.S. rank in 2000: 26th (CMSA)

Area: 16 square miles (2000)
Elevation: 620 feet above sea level
Average Annual Temperature: 47.2° F
Average Annual Precipitation: 35.3 inches

Major Economic Sectors: Manufacturing, services, trade
Unemployment Rate: 6.6% (March 2005)
Per Capita Income: $17,705 (2000)
2004 ACCRA Average House Price: Not reported
2004 ACCRA Cost of Living Index: Not reported

2002 FBI Crime Index Total: 3,736.2
Major Colleges and University University of Wisconsin-Parkside, Gateway Technical College

Daily Newspaper: *Journal Times*

Introduction

Located on Lake Michigan in the corridor between Milwaukee and Chicago, the lakeside city of Racine has been primarily manufacturing-oriented for at least a century. With the construction in the 1980s of the largest recreational boat harbor on Lake Michigan, Racine diversified its economy from one based on durable goods to one that embraces tourism. The marina and its restaurants, the development of bed and breakfast inns, a charming lakefront zoo, and one of the largest and most prestigious furniture galleries in the Midwest add to the city's attractions. Racine County hosts more than a hundred festivals, concerts, carnivals, fairs, parades, sporting events, picnics and celebrations annually, which also boosts tourism to the "Belle City of the Lakes."

Geography and Climate

Racine is located on the western shore of Lake Michigan in southeastern Wisconsin about 75 miles north of Chicago and 30 miles south of Milwaukee. Racine's weather is influenced to a considerable extent by Lake Michigan, especially when the temperature of the lake differs markedly from the air temperature. During spring and early summer a wind shift from westerly to easterly can cause a 10 to 15 degree drop in temperature. In autumn and winter the relatively warm water of Lake Michigan prevents nighttime temperatures from falling as low as they do a few miles inland from shore.

Area: 16 square miles (2000)

Elevation: 620 feet above sea level

Average Temperatures: January, 20.5° F; July, 71.5° F; annual average, 47.2° F

Average Annual Precipitation: 35.3 inches

History

City Settled by Yankees

The first known visit by white men to the Root River area, the site of present-day Racine, occurred in 1679 when explorers LaSalle and Tonti stopped there on their search for a route to the Mississippi River. Prior to the 1830s, the area of southeastern Wisconsin was inhabited by the Potawatomi tribe, whose rights to the lands were recognized by the federal government. By 1833 the U.S. government made an

agreement with the Potawatomi to purchase five million acres of land, including the area where Racine is located. Soon after, the Potawatomi were moved by the government to areas in the western United States. The first settlers arrived in what came to be Racine County about 1820 and established trading posts along the Root River in the present day cities of Racine and Caledonia.

In 1834 Gilbert Knapp settled at the mouth of the Root River and blazed out a 160-acre claim. From 1834 to 1836 the community was named Root for the river on which the city was settled (Root being the English translation for the name the Potawatomi called the river). After 1836 the name was changed to Racine, the French word for root, but the English word was retained for the name of the river. From the spot at the mouth of the river and spreading westward across the entire county, commercial and industrial enterprises sprang up. In 1834 and 1835 hundreds of settlers migrated west to the newly open lands. Northern Europeans settled along waterways throughout Racine County, utilizing them for transportation and power.

Shortly after Racine's founding, a saw mill was constructed, which proved to be a real convenience to the settlers. By 1840, 337 settlers lived in the area and by 1844 the city had 1,100 people. The government built a lighthouse in 1839, a $10,000 courthouse in 1840, and several bridges and a major hotel. Between 1844 and 1860 the government assisted in the completion of the harbor. A large elevator was built in 1867 to load the ships with wheat that was brought to Racine and stored in dozens of grain warehouses. The elevator was destroyed by a fire in 1882.

Manufacturing Anchors Local Economy

The young city was supported by a large farming community that came to town for manufactured goods. The city's growth coincided with the invention and development of agriculture machinery and other labor-saving devices. A flour and feed business was Racine's first. Other early industries were boots and shoes, tanneries, clothing, wagons and carriages, soap and candles, saddles, trucks, harnesses, and blacksmithing. By 1860 boat building and brick making were added.

Racine's first school was built in 1836. During the Civil War, the Camp Utley federal war camp was built in Racine. In 1884 the first ship entered the newly built harbor. That same year, upon the city's fiftieth birthday, a monument that still stands in Monument Square was erected to honor the city's Civil War soldiers.

Over the years, as waterways declined in importance, railroads became the major transport for freight. The first railroad to reach Racine arrived in 1853 and the first steam engine came into use in 1867.

A number of local industries have had a vital relation to the growth and prosperity of the city itself. The J. I. Case Plow Threshing Machine Works was established in 1844. In 1886 S.C. Johnson began a parquet flooring manufacturing operation, which diversified over the years and is now one of the city's largest employers. Gold Metal Camp Furniture was started in 1892, the Racine Rubber Company in 1910, Mitchell Motor Car Company in 1903, and Western Publishing in 1908.

The Great Depression of the 1930s was especially severe in the agricultural sector and the sale of farm machinery drastically declined. By 1937 recovery had begun, and World War II accelerated that recovery. However, from 1945 through 1960 the business community, always sensitive to national business cycles, experienced slow post-war growth. In the 1960s, the voluntary desegregation of the schools became a national model. During the 1960s and 1970s Racine manufacturing entered a growth cycle, and printing, publishing, and chemical production became more predominant.

During the 1970s there was an increased movement of industry from central Racine to the outlying areas. In 1971 the University of Wisconsin-Parkside was founded in a rural setting between Racine and the nearby city of Kenosha.

The construction of the multimillion-dollar Racine On The Lake Festival Park marina complex in the 1980s spurred the growth of tourist visits to the city, particularly from the Chicago and Milwaukee areas. Today, Racine's waterfront community thrives with cultural attractions, sporting activities, festivals, and other tourist attractions. This influx of tourism has boosted many areas of Racine's economy.

Historical Information: Racine County Historical Society and Museum, 701 S. Main St., PO Box 1527, Racine, WI 53401; telephone (414)637-8585

Population Profile

Metropolitan Area Residents
1990: 175,034
2000: 188,831
2003 estimate: 192,284
Percent change, 1990–2000: 7.9%
U.S. rank in 1980: 23rd
U.S. rank in 1990: Not reported
U.S. rank in 2000: 26th (CMSA)

City Residents
1980: 85,725
1990: 84,298
2000: 81,855

2003 estimate: 80,266
Percent change, 1990–2000: −3.0%
U.S. rank in 1990: 248th (State rank: 4th)
U.S. rank in 2000: 356th (State rank: 5th)

Density: 5,267.6 people per square mile (2000)

Racial and ethnic characteristics (2000)
White: 58,214
Black or African American: 17,692
American Indian or Alaska Native: 736
Asian: 669
Native Hawaiian and Pacific Islander: 74
Hispanic or Latino (may be of any race): 11,422
Other: 6,714

Percent of residents born in state: 70.2% (2000)

Age characteristics (2000)
Population under 5 years old: 6,565
Population 5 to 9 years old: 6,594
Population 10 to 14 years old: 6,500
Population 15 to 19 years old: 6,390
Population 20 to 24 years old: 5,544
Population 25 to 34 years old: 11,682
Population 35 to 44 years old: 12,837
Population 45 to 54 years old: 9,840
Population 55 to 59 years old: 3,255
Population 60 to 64 years old: 2,623
Population 65 to 74 years old: 4,906
Population 75 to 84 years old: 3,776
Population 85 years and older: 1,343
Median age: 33.1 years

Births (2003, Racine County)
Total number: 2,539

Deaths (2003, Racine County)
Total number: 1,492

Money income (1999)
Per capita income: $17,705
Median household income: $37,164
Total households: 31,358

Number of households with income of . . .
less than $10,000: 3,036
$10,000 to $14,999: 2,271
$15,000 to $24,999: 4,885
$25,000 to $34,999: 4,592
$35,000 to $49,999: 5,514
$50,000 to $74,999: 6,647
$75,000 to $99,999: 2,793
$100,000 to $149,999: 1,209
$150,000 to $199,999: 191
$200,000 or more: 220

Percent of families below poverty level: 10.8% (47.1% of which were female householder families with related children under 5 years)

2002 FBI Crime Index Total: 3,736.2

Municipal Government

The city of Racine has a mayor-council form of government.

Head Official: Mayor Gary Becker (since April 2003; current term expires March 30, 2007)

Total Number of City Employees: 1,038 (2004)

City Information: City of Racine, 730 Washington Ave., Racine, WI 53403; telephone (262)636-9111

Economy

Major Industries and Commercial Activity

The recent history of the city of Racine is a story of downtown revitalization. During the 1980s Racine County lost an average of 1,000 jobs per year and many downtown retailers closed or moved to new outlying malls or elsewhere. A group of local business leaders marshaled private, county, and city support in their efforts to turn a declining downtown area with a failing commercial harbor into a vital, attractive harbor complex that would attract tourism and convention activity. The project includes a 110-acre 921-slip luxury harbor/marina; a 16-acre county park; and a 6-acre city-owned festival park that contains both indoor and outdoor facilities designed for year-round use. The city, county, and private sector have pumped more than $25 million into the projects. By the early 1990s, 50 new retailers had moved to the central city and more than 100,000 square feet of first-class office space was added to the downtown. In addition, the revitalized lakefront has spurred more than $30 million in private investment, including a 76-unit lakefront condominium.

Racine's small-business, industrial base is an important part of the region's economy. There are more than 300 established manufacturing firms across Racine County, employing 25,000 people; a number of the firms are based in the city of Racine. The 10 largest manufacturers employ about 60 percent of the workers, with the remaining 40 percent working for small companies. Racine is world headquarters of S.C. Johnson Wax, one of the world's leading manufacturers of chemical specialty products for home care, insect control, and personal care. One of the largest privately-held family controlled businesses in the United States, it is the city's major

employer. Another important local firm is In-Sink-Erator, the world's largest manufacturer of food waste disposers and hot water dispensers. The first food disposer was created in 1927 in Racine by John W. Hammes, founder of the company that began operations in 1937. Today the company also markets water heaters, dishwashers, and trash compactors.

In 1842 Jerome Increase Case began a threshing machine works in Racine, and today CNH (formerly J.I. Case) is known worldwide for its quality agricultural and construction equipment. With origins in the city dating back more than 40 years, Master Appliance Corporation has become one of the world's leading designers, manufacturers and marketers of heat tools for industry. Golden Books (formerly Western Publishing Company), the nation's largest publisher and producer of children's storybooks, was founded in Racine in 1907 as a small printing company. The company is also a major producer of puzzles and youth electronic books and products, and ranks among the largest commercial printers in the United States. Founded in Racine more than 70 years ago, Jacobsen, a Textron company, has built a worldwide reputation for delivering the finest in turf maintenance equipment, from precision greenmowers to giant 16-foot rotary mowers.

Items and goods produced: paper products, electric and electronic products, rubber and plastic products, fabricated metal products, wood products, apparel, transportation equipment, printing and publishing

Incentive Programs—New and Existing Companies

Local programs—The Racine County Economic Development Corporation (RCEDC) offers a number of different loans for purposes such as purchase of land, buildings, machinery and equipment, new construction or relocation, working capital, inventory, and fixed assets; some are specific to companies in Racine county, others to companies in the city of Racine. With the Racine Development Group loan fund, businesses and developers that are interested in working in low or moderate income Racine neighborhoods are eligible to apply. Other RCEDC loans benefit businesses that are women- or minority-owned. The Racine Area Manufacturers and Commerce (RAMAC) organizes a number of projects and programs to assist area businesses. RAMAC's Golden Key Awards recognize outstanding businesses in the Racine area; the Business After 5 program offers local networking opportunities; RAMAC's Speakers Bureau provides knowledgeable speakers on a variety of subjects; and the International Outreach Office assists local businesses in accessing world markets.

State programs—Wisconsin's Department of Commerce was created in 1996; it offers a variety of loan and grant programs for both businesses and communities. The department's Disadvantaged Business Enterprise Program was created to increase participation of firms owned by disadvantaged individuals in all federal aid and state transportation facility contracts. The department's Minority Business Development loan program provides financial assistance for the creation and expansion of minority-owned businesses in Wisconsin through low interest loans. The Employee Ownership Assistance Loan Program helps groups of employees purchase businesses that would otherwise close by providing individual awards up to $15,000 for feasibility studies or professional assistance. The state of Wisconsin extends tax exemptions for manufacturing machinery and equipment, inventories, and pollution control equipment; tax credits for research and development and energy conservation; and a 60 percent exclusion of state capital gains held for twelve months. The state provides labor training, infrastructure, asset-based lending, and high-technology awards.

Job training programs—Gateway Technical College, in addition to offering both associate and technical degrees in 77 different fields, can create customized training programs offered either on campus or at employer sites. The school also provides one-on-one technical assistance in areas such as production and marketing. Gateway's staff consults with local businesses to determine employee retraining needs, and can also give technical assistance to those companies seeking to develop grants for other local, state, or federal training programs. The Wisconsin Department of Development offers Customized Labor Training grants for training or retraining of in-state workers, providing an economic contribution to the area. Through the Job Training Partnership Act, the Southeastern Wisconsin Private Industry Council provides trained employees and customized training to unskilled adults and youths for entry into the labor force and offers on-the-job training with 50 percent wage reimbursement offered to employers along with summer youth programs.

Development Projects

In 2004, the city of Racine was awarded $550,000 from the Wisconsin Department of Commerce to clean up a contaminated brownfield site and develop an industrial park, where up to 200 people would be employed. Plans continue to move forward with the Kenosha-Racine-Milwaukee (KRM) commuter rail Metra extension. Wisconsin government and business community officials plan to advance development plans that would add a 33-mile extension of the Chicago Metra service that currently ends in Kenosha. The expansion would use existing upgraded rail right-of-way, and provide seven round-trip trains per day between Chicago and Milwaukee, with stops planned in Milwaukee, Cudahy-St. Francis, South Milwaukee, Oak Creek, Caledonia, Racine, and Somers.

Economic Development Information: Racine County Economic Development Corporation, 2320 Renaissance Blvd., Sturtevant, WI 53177; telephone (262)898-7400; email rcedc@racinecountyedc.org

Commercial Shipping

Rail freight service is provided by the Union Pacific Railroad, the Wisconsin Central Ltd., and the CP Rail System. There are 95 widely distributed trucking and warehousing establishments in Racine County; the area has direct access to Interstate Highway 94 via state trunk highways. The city is located 30 miles south of the Port of Milwaukee, which provides Great Lakes Seaway access and a Foreign Trade Zone. Three Racine County aviation facilities accommodate all business aircraft, with Chicago's O'Hare International Airport and Milwaukee's Mitchell International Airport both less than 60 miles away.

Labor Force and Employment Outlook

The Racine County labor force is just under 100,000 people; together with the labor force from surrounding communities, Racine has an abundant supply of workers. In Wisconsin, absenteeism is below the national average, and the state has the lowest national percentage of employees who leave jobs because they choose to. Wisconsin's labor hours lost due to work stoppages were only one-fifth that of the nation, which contributed to businesses' increased productivity and reduced manufacturing costs.

Industry Week Magazine named the Racine metropolitan area one of 50 world class manufacturing centers in 2000, indicating the strength of the city's manufacturing sector.

The following is a summary of data regarding the Racine metropolitan area labor force, 2004 annual averages.

Size of non-agricultural labor force: 79,600

Number of workers employed in . . .
   construction and mining: 4,000
   manufacturing: 19,000
   trade, transportation, and utilities: 15,200
   information: 600
   financial activities: 2,600
   professional and business services: 6,400
   educational and health services: 10,400
   leisure and hospitality: 6,600
   other services: 4,700
   government: 10,200

Average hourly earnings of production workers employed in manufacturing: $16.19 (statewide)

Unemployment rate: 6.6% (March 2005)

Largest employers
(Racine County)	*Number of employees*
All Saints Medical Center Inc.	(No figures
Racine Unified School District	available)
S.C. Johnson and Son, Inc.	

Largest employers
(Racine County)   *Number of employees*
  CNH America LLC   (No figures
  County of Racine   available)
  City of Racine
  Emerson Electric Co.
  Wal-Mart Associates, Inc.
  Adecco USA Inc.
  Department of Corrections
  Modine Manufacturing Co.
  JohnsonDiversey Inc.
  Department of Health and Family
  Bombardier Motor Corp.
  Aurora Health Care of Southern Lake

Cost of Living

The following is a summary of data regarding several key cost of living factors in the Racine area.

2004 ACCRA Average House Price: Not reported

2004 ACCRA Cost of Living Index: Not reported

State income tax rate: Ranges from 4.6% to 6.75% (tax year 2004)

State sales tax rate: 5.0%

Local income tax rate: None

Local sales tax rate: 0.1%

Property tax rate: $27.97 per $1,000 of equalized valuation

Economic Information: Wisconsin Department of Commerce, 201 W. Washington Ave., Madison, WI 53708; telephone (608)266-1018

Education and Research

Elementary and Secondary Schools

The Racine Unified School District is a composite of city, suburban, and rural areas contained in a 100-square-mile area. Racine County is known for having outstanding schools, and many innovative, state-wide models have been developed in the school districts. The district achieves above national test score averages on standardized tests and on both SAT and ACT tests. More than 70 percent of district high school graduates indicate attending a post-secondary institution. The district's 2003 graduation rate was 75.7 percent; 48 percent of the district's teachers hold a master's degree or higher.

The following is a summary of data regarding Racine's public schools as of the 2003–2004 school year.

Total enrollment: 21,500

Number of facilities
  elementary schools: 21
  middle schools: 6
  senior high schools: 4
  other: 2 charter schools

Student/teacher ratio: 14:1

Teacher salaries
  minimum: $28,318
  maximum: $58,716

Funding per pupil: $10,048

There are dozens of private schools in Racine, including the Prairie School, an independent college preparatory school that teaches nursery through twelfth grade and emphasizes arts education. Racine has thirty parochial schools in the area, accommodating approximately 6,400 students.

Public Schools Information: Racine Unified School District, 2220 Northwestern Ave., Racine, WI 53404; telephone (262)635-5600

Colleges and Universities

The University of Wisconsin-Parkside, part of the University of Wisconsin system, serves more than 4,700 undergraduate and graduate students on its 700-acre campus located between the cities of Racine and Kenosha. The university has schools of liberal arts and science and technology, and offers undergraduate course work in 24 major fields of study. In addition, the school offers a master's degree in business administration and a master's degree in applied molecular biology, the only one of its kind in Wisconsin. Gateway Technical College offers associate degree, diploma, and certificate programs, as well as educational classes offered to specifically meet area employment needs. The school works with more than 20,000 enrollees annually, and offers programs in more than 77 fields. Its facilities include three full-service campuses.

In nearby Kenosha County, Carthage College offers liberal arts degrees in 33 major fields and enrolls approximately 1,500 students. The short commute to Milwaukee allows Racine residents to attend classes at dozens of colleges and universities, including Marquette University, Milwaukee School of Engineering, and the University of Wisconsin-Milwaukee.

Libraries and Research Centers

The Racine Public Library contains more than a quarter of a million volumes, subscribes to nearly 650 publications, and has more than 5,000 microfilms and films. The library's special collections include works on Racine history and the Early Childhood Resource Collection. In addition to the spacious main library that offers views of Lake Michigan, the library operates a bookmobile and has a number of return box locations. Programs for teens, children, adults, and families are also available.

At the University of Wisconsin-Parkside Center for Survey and Marketing Research, studies on travel and tourism and product and market feasibility are conducted. The university's Industrial Automation Research Center researches real time computer application with an emphasis on automation systems, and the Bio Medical Institute conducts applied and fundamental research in drug design, evaluation, and electromagnetic field application.

Public Library Information: Racine Public Library, 75 Seventh St., Racine, WI 53403; telephone (262)636-9252; email ref_rac@racinelib.lib.wi.us

Health Care

Racine's two hospitals are St. Luke's Memorial Hospital and Saint Mary's Medical Center, which are part of the All Saints Healthcare System, Inc. and are affiliated with Wheaton Franciscan Services, Inc. Founded in 1872, St. Luke's Memorial Hospital has more than 160 available beds and includes the All Saints Center for Women and Children; All Saints Mental Health and Addiction Services (both inpatient and outpatient); Clinical Dietetics; Women's Imaging Center; Pediatric Rehabilitation; Emergency; Diabetes Management Program; and St. Catherine's Infirmary, a long-term care facility.

Founded in 1882, Saint Mary's Medical Center has more than 225 available beds and includes the All Saints Cardiovascular Institute (including open heart surgery); the Comprehensive Headache Center; Center for Inpatient Rehabilitation; Center for Inpatient Rehabilitation; Pediatrics; Emergency Department; All Saints Cancer Center; All Saints Center for Plastic and Reconstructive Surgery; and Sports Medicine. Both hospitals offer community education programming and older adult services.

Altogether, All Saints Healthcare System employs more than 3,000 workers, making it one of the largest employers in the area. Its organization includes All Saints Medical Group, which consists of more than 100 primary and specialty care physicians who practice at nine locations, All Saints Visiting Nurse Association and Hospice, and All Saints Healthcare Foundation.

Recreation

Sightseeing

Racine's Southside Historic District has an impressive collection of more than 14 blocks of homes and buildings on the National Register of Historic Places. The district contains many architectural styles, including Tudor, Victorian, Federal, Italianate, and Queen Anne. Of special interest are the English Gothic-style buildings at the DeKoven Center Retreat/Conference Center. The Henrietta Benstead Hall, built in the Colonial Revival style, incorporates the classical details of the Queen Anne style, and features Tiffany windows and quality furnishings. Across the street is the Italianate style Masonic Temple, built circa 1856. The mansion contains two operable theaters and features a unique Egyptian motif in the style of the 1920s. Both structures are lavishly lighted and decorated during the Christmas season and are open for tours.

A favorite local site for picnic outings and observation of more than 200 resident animals is the 32-acre Racine Zoological Society, located on the shores of Lake Michigan. One of the few free zoos in the country, it is home to popular exhibits such as the recently remodeled primate and large cat building. Each summer, the zoo's amphitheater hosts nationally known jazz musicians and weekly concerts by the Racine Concert Band. The Firehouse 3 Museum, in an authentic fire house, features antique fire fighting equipment including an 1882 steamer, a 1930 pumper, a working Gamewell Telegraphic Alarm System, and a hand-drawn hose cart. A theater shows films and videos on fire prevention. The Modine-Benstead Observatory is open to the public to examine the skies when visibility allows; its facilities include two dome observatories and a main building that houses a telescope, an observation deck, library, and meeting room.

The beautiful grounds of the S.C. Johnson Wax Company, one of the city's largest employers, house the Golden Rondelle Theater, the center for the company's guest relations and public tour program. Originally designed by Lippincott and Margulies as the S.C. Johnson Pavilion at the 1964 World's Fair, it featured the film *To be Alive!,* which summarized the joys of living through sight and sound. After the fair, the theater was relocated to Racine, where the structure was redesigned to complement the Frank Lloyd Wright-designed Administration Building and Research Tower, which is open for tours. The theater, which is also open to the public, features films on flight, ecology, and U.S. history.

West of Racine are rural communities, including Union Grove, Wind Lake, Caledonia, Burlington, and Waterford. These western Racine County towns and cities offer a wide

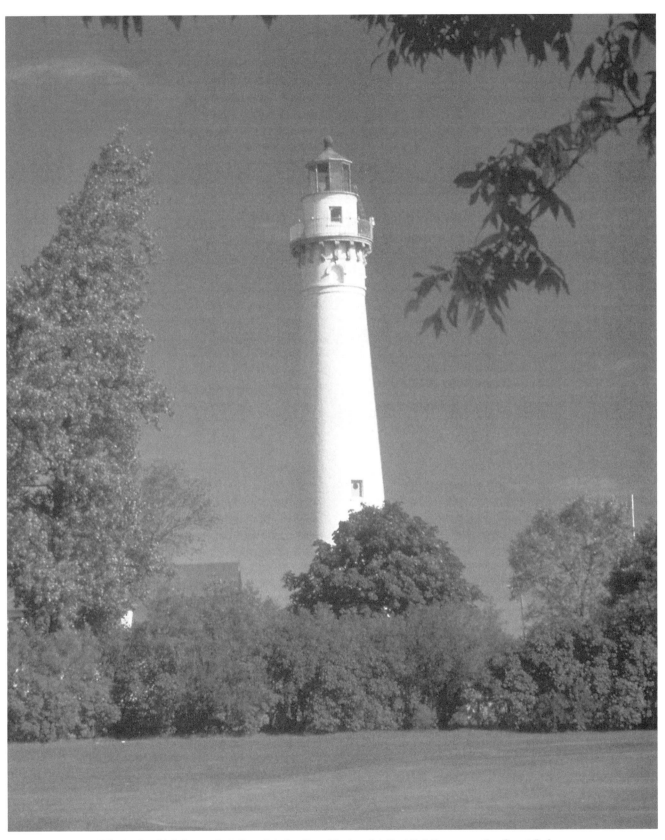

Windpoint Lighthouse is believed to be the oldest and tallest lighthouse on the Great Lakes.

variety of interests including antique shops, plenty of parks for picnicking, plenty of lakes and rivers for watersports, and farmers markets.

Arts and Culture

For more than 60 years, the Racine Theatre Guild has produced comedies, suspense thrillers, musicals, and dramas in an 8-play season. The Malt House Theater, in nearby Burlington, is home of the Haylofters, Wisconsin's oldest community theater group. The group presents three productions and a children's play each year in the renovated malt house.

Founded in 1932, the Racine Symphony Orchestra is the only orchestra in the state to perform year-round. The Orchestra performs three distinct concert series annually in addition to a summer Lakeside Pops series. The Racine Choral Arts Society, founded in 1987, performs a varied repertoire ranging from medieval chant to African American gospel. The Chorus schedules solo performances and performs with the Racine and Milwaukee symphony orchestras.

Racine's Charles A. Wustum Museum of Fine Arts has, for more than 60 years, provided changing exhibits, classes, tours, and lectures. It features one of the top-10 craft collections in the country and houses a shop with artist-made gifts. The museum is located in a historic Italianate mansion on 13 acres of land, complete with a formal garden. The Racine County Historical Museum, a registered historic landmark, is devoted to the preservation of county artifacts and archives through its exhibits, events, and other educational programs.

Festivals and Holidays

May's Lakefront Artist Fair features original art and handicrafts by more than 100 artists, and is the Racine Montessori School's major fundraiser. In September the Racine Antiques Fair at the County Fairgrounds offers one of the Midwest's finest collections of antiques, while later that month Preservation Racine's annual Tour of Historic Homes features tours of houses of historical interest. For more than 16 years, November's Festival of Trees at the Racine on the Lake Festival Hall displays more than 100 professionally decorated Christmas trees, wreaths, and gingerbread houses. Thousands are drawn to May's two-day Chocolate City Festival in nearby Burlington, which features outdoor music, a city bike ride, parade, and many chocolate exhibits—with tasting encouraged.

One of Racine's most popular events is Harbor Fest, held at the Lake Festival Park every June. The festival hosts more than 25 live musical performances on 3 stages, 12 regional restaurants, a children's area, and numerous special events and displays. In July, also along the lakefront, Racine's Salmon-A-Rama is considered the world's largest freshwater fishing event. The nine-day fishing contest, with prizes totaling $100,000, is accompanied by a festival featuring live music, food vendors, and commercial exhibits.

Sports for the Spectator

Professional baseball, hockey, soccer, basketball, and football sporting events can be found in Racine and in nearby Kenosha, Milwaukee, and Chicago. The Racine Raiders, part of the Mid-Continental Football League, stir up semi-pro football excitement at historic Horlick Field.

Sports for the Participant

The YWCA Riverbend Nature Center, an 80-acre year-round nature and recreation center, offers hiking, bird watching, demonstrations, nature studies, and canoe rental along Racine's Root River. Quarry Lake Park, a former limestone quarry, is a mecca for scuba divers and a great place for swimmers looking for spring-fed waters. The 40-acre park has an 18-acre lake that varies in depth up to 100 feet and an expansive sandy beach. North Beach provides more than a mile of clean, white sandy beach with lifeguards and picnic areas. Sixteen-acre Racine County Harbor Park, which extends out into Lake Michigan, offers fishing, a modern fish-cleaning station, and an observation deck with spectacular views. Visitors can enjoy a peaceful stroll around the Reefpoint Marina. Racine is host to the world's biggest freshwater fishing contest, Salmon-a-Rama, an annual event that attracts thousands of fishermen to take their shot at landing "the big one."

Racine County is home to a number of 18-hole golf courses and one 27-hole golf course located on rolling green hills. The City of Racine maintains the grounds of more than 85 parks that feature baseball diamonds, boat launches, soccer fields, fishing facilities, picnic areas, and tennis courts. Racine County also offers one of the most complete and varied bicycle trail networks, with a signed 100-mile bicycle route that circles the entire county. Off-road bicycle trails, surfaced with either crushed limestone or blacktop, total 17 miles. Lake Michigan provides opportunities for both boating and game fishing.

Shopping and Dining

The city and county of Racine offer many shops filled with antiques, resale items, and collectibles. A waterfront showplace, downtown Racine, which is linked with the Racine Civic Centre complex and the nearly 1,000-slip Reefpoint Marina, has many beautifully renovated buildings housing fine jewelry shops and unique collections of sportswear, quality clothing, fine furniture, and specialty shops. Porter's of Racine, an 80,000 square-foot fine furniture store, is recognized throughout the region and may be the oldest retail establishment in the Midwest. Milaeger's offers a wide variety of flowering plants in 71 greenhouses; the company specializes in perennials, and has merchandize pertaining to all facets of gardening and outdoor living. The county is also home to The Seven Mile Fair, Wisconsin's largest flea market. Open every weekend, the market features hundreds of vendors selling clothes, toys, tools, jewelry, electronics, luggage, and more. During the summer months a farmers market is also in operation.

No visit to Racine would be complete without sampling the local delicacy, Danish Kringle, a flaky, oval-shaped coffee cake made of traditional Danish pastry and filled with a variety of fruits or nuts. O&H Danish Bakery, founded in 1949, makes them daily using all-natural ingredients. Kewpee Sandwich Shop, known throughout the Midwest, is one of the oldest hamburger restaurants in the area. Mid-priced family restaurants share the local spotlight with ethnic eateries, including Italian and Chinese, as well as places offering meat and potatoes or the catch of day from the Great Lakes.

Visitor Information: Racine County Convention and Visitors Bureau, 14015 Washington Ave., Sturtevant, WI 53177; toll-free (800)C-RACINE

Convention Facilities

Situated on five acres along the shores of Lake Michigan, Racine On The Lake Festival Park is the city's newest multiuse facility. Opened in 1987, Festival Park can accommodate conventions, trade shows, meetings, art exhibits, and concerts. Facilities include Festival Hall, a 15,700-square-foot area with a theater that can seat 1,500 people, a classroom that can accommodate 1,000, and banquet space for 1,200 people; the Green Room, designed for private gatherings, a 1,050-square-foot space that can handle 75 people in theater-style seating, 50 people classroom-style, and 60 people for banquets; the Colonnade, a free-standing covered structure measuring nearly 9,000 square feet under its canopy; and a 40-by-80-foot outdoor stage with a 43,000-square-foot concert area.

Overlooking Lake Michigan, Memorial Hall is the location for many concerts, crafts, and various local functions. It features an 8,400 square-foot main auditorium and the 2,400 square-foot East Hall. Built in 1938 by Frank Lloyd Wright as a private residence, Wingspread, a National Historic Landmark, is a private international conference facility operated by the Johnson Foundation.

Convention and Meeting Information: Racine County Convention and Visitors Bureau, 14015 Washington Ave., Sturtevant, WI 53177; toll-free (800)C-RACINE

Transportation

Approaching the City

General Mitchell International Airport, located seven miles north of the city in Milwaukee, is the nearest commercial airport. Chicago's O'Hare International Airport is 60 miles to the south. Three Racine County general aviation facilities can accommodate all types of business aircraft.

Interstate 94, situated eight miles west of the city, links Racine County with Milwaukee and Chicago. State highways 11, 20, 31, 32, and 38 also serve the city. Passenger service is provided by Amtrak and by Wisconsin Coach Lines, Inc., which provides intercity bus service between Kenosha, Racine, and Milwaukee every day.

Traveling in the City

The city of Racine owns and operates the Belle Urban System. Downtown Racine Lakefront Trolleys, with clanging bells, shuttle visitors to shops and sites along the lakefront.

Communications

Newspapers and Magazines

The daily paper is the morning *Journal Times.* The *Milwaukee Journal Sentinel* publishes a multi-page tabloid Racine section that is inserted into the Sunday paper. The city is also served by *Racine Labor,* a biweekly newsletter, and the *Communicator News,* which publishes weekly.

Television and Radio

Racine receives 12 network, independent, and public television stations from Milwaukee, as well as several Chicago stations. The city has three FM stations and two AM stations and receives many stations from Milwaukee and Chicago.

Media Information: Journal Times, 212 Fourth St., Racine, WI 53403; telephone (262)634-3322

Racine Online

City of Racine Home Page. Available www.cityofracine.org

Community Point, the Racine area comprehensive community web site directory. Available www.visitracine.org/point/main.html

Downtown Racine. Available www.downtownracine.com

The Journal Times online. Available www.journaltimes.com

Racine Area Manufacturers and Commerce. Available www.racinechamber.com

Racine County Convention and Visitors Bureau. Available www.visitracine.org

Racine County Economic Development Corporation. Available www.racinecountyedc.org

Racine Public Library. Available www.racinelib.lib.wi.us

Wisconsin Department of Commerce. Available www.commerce.state.wi.us

Selected Bibliography

Kherdian, David, *I Called It Home* (Blue Crane Books, 1997)

Cumulative Index

The one hundred eighty-nine cities featured in *Cities of the United States*, Volume 1: *The South*, Volume 2: *The West*, Volume 3: *The Midwest*, and Volume 4: *The Northeast*, along with names of individuals, organizations, historical events, etc., are designated in this Cumulative Index by name of the appropriate regional volume, or volumes, followed by the page number(s) on which the term appears in that volume.

University of North Dakota **Midwest:** 437; 439; 441; 443; 444

University of Notre Dame **Midwest:** 107; 110; 111; 113; 114

University of Pittsburgh **Northeast:** 451; 461

University of Rochester **Northeast:** 367; 373; 374; 376

University of South Alabama **South:** 19; 26; 28

University of South Carolina **South:** 451; 453; 455; 458; 459; 461

University of South Florida **South:** 151; 158; 177; 184; 186; 187; 188

University of Southern Maine **Northeast:** 107; 111; 117

University of Tampa **South:** 177; 184; 186; 187

University of Tennessee at Chattanooga **South:** 467; 474; 477

University of Tennessee at Knoxville **South:** 481; 483; 485; 486; 488; 489; 490; 491

University of Texas at Austin **South:** 527; 529; 531; 532; 533; 534; 536; 537; 538

University of Texas at El Paso **South:** 553; 557; 559; 560; 561; 563; 564; 565

University of Texas Southwestern Medical Center **South:** 545

University of Toledo **Midwest:** 521; 525; 526; 527

University of Vermont **Northeast:** 523; 529; 530; 532; 533

Upjohn, William Erastus **Midwest:** 250

Upper Arlington, OH **Midwest:** 497

Urbandale, IA **Midwest:** 143

Valencia, CA **West:** 135

Valmont, CO **West:** 245

Van der Rohe, Ludwig Mies **Midwest:** 25

Vance, AL **South:** 10

Vandalia, OH **Midwest:** 509

Vanderbilt University **South:** 509; 512; 516; 517; 518; 520; 522

Vanderbilt University Medical Center **South:** 517

Varennes, Pierre Gaultier de **Midwest:** 535

Venice Beach, CA **West:** 135

Verrazzano, Giovani **Northeast:** 349; 485; 509

Virginia Beach, VA **South:** 641–652

Virginia City, NV **West:** 384

Virginia Commonwealth University **South:** 625; 632; 633; 636; 637

Wallace, George Corley **South:** 34

Walt Disney World **South:** 139; 140; 141; 144; 145; 184

Wang Laboratories Inc. **Northeast:** 146

War of 1812 **Midwest:** 453

Warhol, Andy **South:** 329

Warwick, RI **Northeast:** 490; 494; 495; 505; 507–521

Washington University **Midwest:** 364; 365; 367

Washington, Booker T. **South:** 676

Washington, D.C. **South:** 653–667; **West:** 323

Washington, George **South:** 446; 453; 655; 656; **Midwest:** 69; **Northeast:** 29; 157; 161; 163; 251; 257; 271; 283; 297; 303; 350; 453; 504; 510

Waterbury, CT **Northeast:** 67–79

Waterbury, VT **Northeast:** 541

Waterford, NY **Northeast:** 313

Watertown, CT **Northeast:** 69

Watkins Glen, NY **Northeast:** 388

Wayne State University **Midwest:** 226; 227

Wayne, Anthony **Midwest:** 221; 469; 509; 521; 69; **Northeast:** 405; 410

Wayne, Anthony, General **Midwest:** 69

Waynesville, OH **Midwest:** 515

Weiser, ID **West:** 323

Welty, Eudora **South:** 355

West Branch, IA **Midwest:** 126

West Des Moines, IA **Midwest:** 143

West Hartford, CT **Northeast:** 34; 75

West Memphis, AR **South:** 505

West Springfield, MA **Northeast:** 163; 164; 165

Western Connecticut State University **Northeast:** 17; 21; 23; 25

Western Dakota Technical Institute **Midwest:** 543; 549

Western Michigan University **Midwest:** 247; 253

Westminster, MD **South:** 326

Wethersfield, CT **Northeast:** 11; 14; 57

Whistler, James Abbott McNeill **Midwest:** 214

Whitehall, OH **Midwest:** 497

Whitney, Eli **South:** 221

Wichita, KS **Midwest:** 191–202

Wilberforce, OH **Midwest:** 513; 514

Wilkes-Barre, PA **Northeast:** 471; 476; 478

William J. Clinton Presidential Center **South:** 71

Williams, William Carlos **Northeast:** 285, 292

Williamsburg, IA **Midwest:** 128

Williamsburg, VA **South:** 643; 650

Wilmington, DE **South:** 79; 87; 89–102

Wilson, Woodrow **South:** 459

Windsor Heights, IA **Midwest:** 143

Windsor Locks, CT **Northeast:** 26; 38; 75

Windsor, Ontario **Midwest:** 225

Winston-Salem, NC **South:** 377; 380

Winter Park, FL **South:** 139; 144; 147

Winthrop, MA **Northeast:** 132

Wolfsonian Museum **South:** 129

Wood, Grant **Midwest:** 121; 126; 138

Woodstock, VT **Northeast:** 547

Worcester, MA **Northeast:** 167–179

Works Progress Administration **South:** 8

Worthing, SD **Midwest:** 562

Worthington, OH **Midwest:** 497

Wright Brothers **Midwest:** 170